# Teaching Techniques and Insights
## for
# Instrumental Music Educators

G-3723R

# Teaching Techniques and Insights
# for
# Instrumental Music
# Educators

### Revised Edition

## Joseph L. Casey

**GIA Publications, Inc.**
**Chicago**

**Teaching Techniques and Insights for Instrumental Music Educators**
by Joseph L. Casey, Ph.D.
Copyright © 1991, 1993 by G.I.A. Publications, Inc.
7404 S. Mason Avenue, Chicago, Illinois 60638
International Copyright Secured

Library of Congress Catalog Card Number: 91-76805
ISBN: 941050-28-9
Printed and bound in the United States of America

# table of contents

# *acknowledgments*

No one associated with this book has been more helpful than the contributors and they deserve my utmost appreciation. Everyone took time to look over the materials, to prepare for the phone interviews, and to offer their ideas and teaching techniques. Without exception the contributors exhibited a positive attitude about music and music education, and they willingly gave their ideas and teaching techniques so other music educators could use and build upon them.

One intent in this research was to gather from the contributors the ideas and ways to teach that they felt were their most effective. The book, however, has been ultimately formed by the thoughts of the author and his awareness of the underlying relationships among learning, psychology, music, and the purposes for education. But the comments themselves remain those of the contributors and therefore their names are placed with their comments.

H. Robert Reynolds provided valuable assistance and support. He gave excellent suggestions for this research project and I am pleased he also was willing to write the foreword to the book. He has my most sincere appreciation and thanks.

Margaret Merrion, Steven Brown, and Steven J. Paul have been successive chairpersons of Instructional Strategies, a sub-group of the Research Council of the Music Educators National Conference. They were enthusiastic and encouraging from the beginning of the project.

Delphine Casey has made vital suggestions about the essay-introductions that open each topic. Her knowledge and skill with writing and organization, and her astute insights, helped me make significant changes.

William Hughes edited, designed, proofread, and typeset the first edition of this book. His contributions have gone beyond this, however, since his own musical background as a composer enhances and underlies his curiosity, interest, and understanding of the book's substance. Jean Harrison and Wesley Vos proofread the revised edition and have my thanks and appreciation for their valuable contributions.

Wesley Vos also has my utmost appreciation for many things, and he has believed in and supported this endeavor from its inception through the completion of both manuscripts. He also read the manuscript under less than perfect times and conditions, which warrants special thanks.

There have been many music educators who have convinced me that this project would be worthwhile. The first supportive persons were Roman Palmer of Indian Trail Junior High School and Richard Kennell of Bowling Green State University of Ohio. There are others whose support also has been of great benefit. These are Richard F. Grunow of the Eastman School of Music, James O. Froseth of the University of Michigan, Edward S. Lisk of Oswego, New York and the President of the National Band Association, Pamela Gearhart who conducts the orchestra at Ithaca College, John Williamson of Central Michigan University, John Kinnison who is the Executive Director of the Illinois Music Educators Association, John Pingel and Michael George of the Wisconsin School Music Conference, Michael Hiatt President of Minnesota Music Educators, Gordon Childs President of Wyoming Music Educators, Donald

Casey of Northwestern University, Alfred Reed of the University of Miami, Gerald Olson of the University of Wisconsin, Frank Bencriscutto of the University of Minnesota, Walter Rodby who is a former President of Illinois Music Educators, Dominic Spera of Indiana University, Daniel L. Kohut of the University of Illinois, and Richard Rosewall formerly of Evanston Township High School. There have been many other teachers and supervisors in schools, and professors in colleges and universities, who have conveyed their interest and enthusiasm for this material. Their encouragement has helped me realize that the task was worth pursuing, and the time and expense it entailed would be worthwhile.

The DePaul University Research Council approved two grants for this project that helped with expenses. Marjorie P. Piechowski, Director of Sponsored Programs and Research, was particularly helpful with preparing the grant proposals. I also thank those colleagues at the School of Music of DePaul University, Chicago, Illinois who were helpful and encouraging throughout this endeavor.

Daniel L. Kohut of the University of Illinois offered material from his two books, *Instrumental Music Pedagogy: Teaching Techniques for School Band and Orchestra Directors* (Prentice-Hall, Inc. 1973) and *Musical Performance: Learning Theory and Pedagogy* (Prentice-Hall, Inc. 1985). Since this book grew to such length and his published books contain the materials he offered, I decided not to include what he and Prentice-Hall so generously offered. The contributions of Sherman Hong of the University of Southern Mississippi were lost because of a technical error and I ask him to understand.

I appreciate and thank my own teachers, and former colleagues, whose influence can be seen in this book. They are H. D. Harmon and Arthur J. Nix of Moorhead State University, and James D. Ployhar. From the University of Northern Colorado, I thank William T. Gower, Jr., Dale Dykins, Donald Garlick, and Douglas McEwen. At the University of Wisconsin—Eau Claire, Leon Fosha, Walter May, James Stivers, David Kuehn, and Peter Tanner were stimulating colleagues. I also want to thank Himie Voxman and Edwin E. Gordon, and especially Neal Glenn, for their influence and support during my graduate work at the University of Iowa.

There are several people who did important and tedious clerical and transcription work. They were Diane Hull, Cynthia Serrano, Anthony Dolezal, Melanie Michalak, Robert Vos, Barbara Ferrier, Janet Prybil, and Anthony Salvaggione. Had they not been able to do such work, the date of publication would have been considerably delayed.

I also want to thank T-Maker Company of 1390 Villa Street, Mountain View, California 94041 for allowing the book to contain the french horn graphic taken from their *Click-Art* series of computer graphics. I also thank Star Piping and Heating of Lyons, Illinois for their generous use of a fax machine.

# *foreword*

This is a book that had to be written. My only regret is that is was compiled decades after I began teaching and conducting. In my early years I had so many basic questions, and I remember asking myself, "How would the experts answer this, and what approach would they take with this issue?" I would make believe that I was asking one of my heroes his opinion and then would try to imagine his response and perceive what might be in his mind. Well now we don't have to imagine it anymore. In fact, we don't even have to ask the right questions. Dr. Joseph Casey has done it all for us and gone beyond our wildest dreams by organizing it all into a variety of sections related to focused topics.

This is not just a book of helpful suggestions by the most highly respected people in the profession, this is the life experiences, perceptions, and examples gained by careful planning as well as trial and error of the leaders to whom we all look for guidance. Imagine being able to ask Frederick Fennell how to conduct, or Mark Hindsley how to rehearse, or Frank Battisti about his philosophy of music education and so much more. It is all here.

We owe a great debt to Dr. Casey for his planning and keen insight, along with his ability to pull together the ramblings of those he so painstakingly interviewed. It is not just anyone who could have done such a service for the profession. It took a person of rare gifts, himself a highly successful band conductor and music educator, to understand the task at hand and its importance to the present and the future. It took someone who had the instinct to pursue a line of questioning with each contributor that would elicit not only their insightful suggestions, but lead each to reveal those special secrets that are rarely told to others.

In addition, he wrote introductions for each of the more than fifty topics in the book. His discussions convey astute and thought-provoking musical and educational insights, and as such, provide a counterpoint for the comments of the contributors. Many of the discussions are complete, fully-realized essays in their own right.

We come away from this book with so much more than *tricks that click* in each situation. Yes, this is a book on how to do it, but more importantly the real message is the imagination and creativity that is behind the suggestions. The reader will be able to climb into the head and heart of those quoted and gain understanding of the larger issues. If you read the words only in order to find those aspects that will contribute to the success of your next rehearsal, you will find them. You must not, however, miss the food for the future, the basis or philosophy upon which these wonderful suggestions are made. The magic is not in the words of Craig Kirchhoff, Donald Hunsberger, John Paynter, James Croft, Larry Rachleff, Allan McMurray, or Eugene Corporon, it is in the thoughts, feelings, and philosophies that lead to these words.

No more will we have to wonder what each one believes and thinks; we can find it written here for ourselves and we can learn from the best. I can hardly wait to get at it.

H. Robert Reynolds
Ann Arbor, Michigan

# *preface*

The term *teaching technique* refers to what a teacher does or says, and what a teacher asks students to do that might help them learn. The teacher may conduct, describe, demonstrate, or draw pictures to teach dynamics. He can ask students to make a dynamic change two different ways and then invite them to judge which was the more appropriate musically. Both are examples of teaching techniques; the first represents what the teacher said or did, and the second shows what he asked students to do for them to learn.

There also are ideas and insights in this book. Here are three examples of insights into the process of music instruction and learning, each followed by a teaching technique based upon its idea: (1) if the teacher sees that singing is a way to develop instrumental students' aural skills, that is an insight about instruction. If he asks students to sing the tuning note before they perform it, that is a teaching technique based upon the insight; (2) if the teacher understands the Pestalozzi idea of "sound before sign," he can use it as a teaching technique by having the students sing, hear, or play a crescendo before he shows them the sign or notation for the crescendo; and, (3) if a teacher believes that students become more involved in the learning process if their efforts are reinforced, that is an insight. If a student or the group makes an advance in a skill or in grasping an idea, the teacher can reward the student's or group's learning by positive comments or in other ways. When that occurs, the teaching technique includes reinforcement.

There are different ways to use this book.

1. Instrumental music teachers can look over the ideas and insights in this book, increase their repertoire of teaching techniques, and refine the purposes for the use of teaching techniques. A teacher will see that the techniques and insights are of several different and specific types. The techniques might:

   a. be new to teachers.
   b. be variations of familiar teaching techniques and ideas.
   c. be techniques that teachers have forgotten they used before.
   d. be techniques the teacher set aside for whatever reason that ought to be tried again.
   e. stimulate teachers to think of new techniques.
   f. stimulate teachers to find new applications for familiar techniques.

2. Instrumental music teachers can find many comments about the values, beliefs, and philosophies of instrumental music educators. The ideas can help them:

   a. express certain viewpoints about teaching and keep these insights at the forefront of their minds.
   b. see a contributor's way of articulating ideas that can help a teacher's phraseology and improve his communication about music and the arts.
   c. modify thinking or form conclusions about the purposes and practices

of instrumental music education so the teacher can change or apply them if they choose.

    d. realize how their beliefs, approaches, and techniques parallel those of other teachers. Through dialogue and exchange, and agreement or disagreement, they can build upon their identification with other music educators. Through these endeavors they can experience an increase in the feeling of oneness with others in the music education profession.

    e. create a basis to examine and inventory their own teaching techniques and insights for instrumental music education.

3. College and university professors of music pedagogy and music education can use the material for a variety of educational purposes. In undergraduate or graduate classes, they can extract specific techniques and ideas:

    a. to illustrate ways to teach.

    b. to discuss the practical application of the purposes of music education.

    c. to introduce specific educational issues that are implied by the teaching techniques.

    d. to consider suggestions for administration and organization of music programs.

    e. to define the responsibilities and roles of the music educator.

    f. to emphasize the musical, organizational, interpersonal, communication, conducting, and performance skills needed by music teachers.

    g. to review the priorities teachers place upon aesthetic experience, skill training, musical understanding, public relations, pre-professional or career preparation, educational psychology, administrative expertise, curriculum, multi-cultural education, recreation, etc. in light of primary and secondary values in music education and the arts.

    h. to stimulate potential ideas for research efforts that can spring from the teaching techniques or discussions of them.

    i. to discuss and research ways to assess the effectiveness of different teaching techniques and determine the choice of teaching techniques. Therefore, these insights and teaching techniques can foster thought about many issues in music education as well as describe ways to instruct.

4. Department chairpersons, cooperating teachers, and supervisors of teachers or student teachers can offer this book as a resource when a teacher is seeking a solution to a musical problem, and ways to understand and teach a class.

## The Rationale for this Publication

There are a number of reasons and assumptions which formed the basis for researching and writing the material about *Teaching Techniques and Insights for Instrumental Music Educators*.

1. Nearly every teacher is interested in learning how another teacher instructs his students. They often talk with each other about teaching and they attend workshops, observations, concerts, and clinics. They seek ideas that will provide them with solutions to problems and ways to attain objectives they need to address. Teachers also seek new and unfamiliar ideas, familiar ideas that support their own thoughts and teaching techniques, or ideas that show them how to vary and apply the teaching techniques they already are using.

2. All music educators, whether they are undergraduates, experienced, or inexperienced, learn from concrete examples of ways to teach instrumental music. Many can incorporate an example into their teaching quicker than they can incorporate a teaching principle that does not include a concrete illustration.

3. Many teachers also find that learning is easier when they see multiple examples of a variety of teaching techniques. This gives teachers several chances to absorb and understand the ideas, and to consider how the technique will be adapted to fit their class and their own style of teaching.

4. The more examples teachers see, the easier it is for them to see the relationship to an underlying principle, a theory, or an explanation of instruction. While they are learning to understand the relationships of the idea to a teaching technique, they can try techniques immediately that might prove to be practical and effective ways to instruct their students. The immediate and repeated use of an idea helps a teacher verify what the principle or theory suggests is true.

5. College texts and other books provide some teaching techniques but their authors often face certain limitations. For example, the material in these books must address many different subjects. The typical textbook about instrumental music education includes topics such as administration, uniforms, instrumental techniques, care of instruments, history of instrumental music education, organization of classes, budgets, recruiting beginners, scheduling, jazz education, marching bands, public relations, and the like. When teaching principles and theoretical explanations are found in textbooks, often the ideas are illustrated with only a few examples. With few exceptions, the primary purpose of this type of textbook is not to convey teaching techniques; it is to survey a variety of important topics. To cover such a range of topics, the author must limit the discussion of one topic in order to talk about many topics.

6. Young music educators usually have considerable enthusiasm and a strong desire to teach well; because of their age, they have minimal experience. They are very interested in ideas about teaching but they have just begun to think about what to teach and a way to teach it. They have not had enough time to develop their own teaching techniques both in number and variety. Their growth in expertise can be slowed since few sources give them numerous examples to try in the classroom, and they have little opportunity to observe more experienced teachers from whom they could take ideas that increase their repertoire.

7. Out of necessity, and because it is natural, novice teachers use teaching techniques that their own teachers used in high school and college. To these techniques they add others used by their student teaching supervisors. As indispensable and appropriate as these techniques may be, they represent the

thinking and experience of a small number of teachers and a small number of ideas in proportion to what teachers need and what other teachers could offer.

8. There is a final assumption that completes the rationale for this book. There are many books about the teaching of instruments and the organization and administration of music programs. They are indispensable for band and orchestra teachers who intend to be knowledgeable music educators. However, the unintended consequence of these books is that they can influence music teachers to assume that the teaching of instruments and technical facility represent the end goals of instrumental music education.

This assumption about the primacy of instrumental skills has also been reinforced throughout the music teacher's own school experiences. In every ensemble, in which he was a member, the conductor was likely stressing a concern for accuracy, and performance skill and facility. It should not be a surprise, therefore, if new teachers also expect that instrumental performance skills should be the preferred result if they teach their classes successfully.

This is not to say that the teaching of instrumental technique and facility is unimportant. Teaching these skills and such others as reading, listening, analysis, and performance in an ensemble is *essential*; but educators must keep the ends and means in an appropriate balance. Skills are essential, but they are the *means* that music educators develop in students so they can interact with music and experience the ultimate ends. Even when skill acquisition is pursued with intensity, both momentarily and continually as it should be, acquiring these skills is not the ultimate value of a musical education. If *all* of the student's time is spent developing the means of musical expression, the student will have little time for the real musical experience itself before completing his education. The real *point* of a musical education will have been missed.

Therefore, one value of this publication is that it complements other books about the techniques of instruments, and about the administration and organization of music programs. The materials in this book stress a different aspect of music education; the book contains insights and teaching techniques that emphasize the musical aspects of instrumental music education. The ideas and discussions can help the music educator decide the balance of ends to means; they can encourage him to think about curriculum, invite him to plan, and suggest how he might teach classes and rehearsals so the teaching reflects these decisions.

It is imperative to teach to the end goals while one is teaching to the objectives that provide the means. Only thus can we provide real musical experiences through performance and literature, and through that real experience develop the student's understanding, judgment, values, and thinking in relation to the substance of music. We need not wait until all of the means have been acquired by students; they can learn and experience some of each end goal during the process of acquiring the technical facility to command their instrument and play, not only skillfully, but poetically.

9. With these assumptions and observations in mind, the project resulting in this book was initiated to collect teaching techniques and insights for class lessons,

sectionals, and rehearsals. The overall intent of this research was to provide a source for music educators in an area where material is lacking and that addresses the musical and practical concerns music educators face.

The teaching ideas were gathered from among the most effective college and pre-college teachers. The initial group was college band conductors. They were asked to contribute what they believe were their own most effective teaching ideas and techniques. They also were asked to recommend the two or three most effective teachers they had ever seen. They recommended teachers from every level, from fourth and fifth grade through college teachers of instrumental music education and ensembles. Those recommended were also invited to participate in the project. (See Appendix I and II)

## The Features of This Book

One great value of this book is that more than 2,500 ideas are under one cover; the nature of the book enables readers to learn what teachers believe, think, feel, and do. To observe and talk with that many teachers would be too expensive and too time consuming since one would have to travel all over the country to observe each of the teachers at work.

Another strength is the variety of contributions. They come from band and orchestra directors who teach beginners in the fourth and fifth grade through those who teach and conduct professional musicians and graduate students. Unlike many books written by one author only, this publication contains substantive and interesting material from over one hundred and thirty music educators.

The plan of the document allows the material to be grouped into seven sections and more than fifty sub-sections that have several sub-parts each. The comments themselves are often detailed. The detail requires less inference on the part of the reader and enables the reader to develop a clearer picture of a specific teaching and learning event; as a result, the reader can use or adapt the material quickly for his own use.

Each sub-section opens with an essay by the author of this book. This is a discussion of ideas that stresses important points in relation to each topic. The essay also serves as a reference point to which individual comments within each topic can be compared and contrasted.

There is a further comment about the premise of this book and the relationship of an objective being learned to the way it is being taught. Every teaching technique in this book and many of the insights can be looked at from two points of view: one view is that any objective can be attained using teaching techniques of many different types; the other view is that a single type of teaching technique can be used to teach students many different objectives.

For example, if one decides to teach dynamics one can use many different types of teaching techniques such as drawings, imagery, symbols, spoken descriptions, contrasts and comparisons, gestures, modeling, planning, evaluation, reinforcement, feedback, literature, drill, repetition, imitation, questioning, movement, listening, improvisation, and games. This long list emphasizes that there are many ways to teach dynamics, even if some ways are more effective at some times and with some students.

Conversely, since nearly every type of teaching technique can be used for a variety of objectives, one could imagine that gestures can be used to teach intonation, blend, facility, phrasing, balance, style, articulations, breathing, meter, relaxation, rhythm, dynamics, and enharmonic tones.

As a result of looking at teaching techniques from these two vantages, the reader can gain a broader view of teaching techniques. He can observe there are at least two ways to view the technique: by its type and by its objective. In other words, by how something is being taught and by what is being taught. From that point on, the reader can appreciate that to gain a full understanding of teaching techniques the reader must look beyond the obvious and below what is on the surface.

Music teachers can draw several assumptions about learning and teaching from this material: students are more apt to learn if music teachers use a way to teach that is effective for the learning style of a particular student, age, or group; often different students learn more from one way of instruction than another; and teaching an objective in different ways can increase understanding and achievement.

This suggests that a student will be more successful if the teacher's awareness and skill helps him fit teaching techniques with objectives properly; fit both to the way he comes to know students learn more effectively; and choose techniques to help students increase their motivations, become part of the class, and attain the objectives.

## The Organization of the Book

The purpose for the topic placed first in the book (Part I) is to present what instrumental music educators believe and value. This body of ideas gives focus to the book in the same way the ideas can give focus to one's approach to teaching so it is positive, musical, and educational.

The five sub-sections—instruction, teaching, music making, literature, and preparing for performance—can be seen as commenting about a progression that moves from knowing what one believes through retaining and applying one's values from the outset of teaching in classes and rehearsals through the end of each year and each performance.

The statements address a wide range of ideas, but what most comments have in common is that they convey a belief or a value that is one corner stone of the contributor's reason for his actions as a professional music educator.

The contributions in Part II expand upon the purposes of music education by addressing ideas about helping students toward maturity. The comments often convey the teacher's intentions and techniques to help students learn to make judgments and act independently. Crucial to this purpose is to channel students' motivations toward making musical judgments and reinforcing their efforts as they do so.

Teachers also want students to recognize and accept that they should raise and seek higher standards, and to practice and learn successfully. An important step in their growth is when they learn how to be their own teachers through the use of feedback, from seeing their teachers' examples of practice procedures and decision making, and from experience.

The focus in Part III moves from concerns about the guiding principles of music education and students' growth to the issue of planning in music education. Comments that describe broad examples of planning appear first. Next come comments that are more specific, such as ideas how to sequence instruction, suggestions about planning the learning process in class and group lessons, and the use of repetition and drill. Finally, there are comments that show what and how some teachers evaluate the instruction they have planned and carried out.

Comments in Part IV show ideas that enable music educators to look at the process of learning from a different perspective. They suggest how to communicate with and involve music students. One of the powerful and appropriate ways to communicate is to do so through conducting and gestures. Furthermore, the involvement and concentration of students also helps make communication successful. A student's identification with the group and its purposes improves when students experience rapport and camaraderie with each other and their teachers. There also are other engaging teaching techniques and one is music related games. These are especially attractive to young students during their first few years of instruction.

The material in Part V invites teachers to look at music teaching in an entirely different way. Instead of addressing objectives such as intonation, phrasing, blend, and dynamics as can be done in Part VI, the purpose in Part V is to emphasize the different learning styles of students.

The concept that embraces different ways to learn is commonly called input modes or learning styles. The assumption is that different students learn in different ways; there are different ways through which all students can learn; and, all students can learn more successfully if they are taught in a variety of ways. For example, we can learn to phrase musically by hearing, seeing, feeling, and hearing spoken descriptions, Students could also learn by noticing relationships, thinking abstractly, and manipulating symbols.

Hearing can be a natural input mode in music education because students can learn from the examples to which teachers have them listen. The input mode of seeing is engaged when students learn by what is shown through drawings and gestures, or when they see others perform and learn, and; input through feeling can occur when students change musical dynamics, phrasing, accents, etc. Such events can cause students to experience different intensities during physical and musical events, which might lead them to experience affective responses. Input modes less rooted in direct experience, for example, are those that occur when students hear a description of how they should play a phrase or when they read music notation.

We can further refine how to phrase through different types of learning experiences; that is, we learn through different input modes. The student can learn by comparing different examples of phrasing, by hearing a statement of well-chosen words, or by hearing an interestingly worded image that shows how to phrase, by answering questions, by seeing an association to another experience, by isolating this element of performance, by noticing similarities and differences in the performance of the same and different phrases, or by trying different versions of a phrase. The last way essentially is improvisation.

Part VI contains material that is organized in a way familiar to readers. These teaching techniques address twelve basic and common objectives for instrumental music performance. This part is the longest major section in the book. What can often be seen among these teaching techniques and the objectives they address is the theme that music making is the purpose for acquiring technical and ensemble skills.

The title for Part VII could have been the title for this book because most of the content could be used in rehearsals. For example, the section on planning could have been placed in Part VII. It is also true that communication, organization, and rehearsal techniques could have been placed under the title of rehearsal techniques and ideas. The decision, therefore, to have a large section devoted to rehearsal techniques is based upon practicality from the teacher's point of view. The idea of rehearsal techniques is not esoteric; rehearsal techniques are used daily and teachers see immediate application and practical value in this material.

## THE KEY TO USING TEACHING TECHNIQUES EFFECTIVELY

Many music educators believe that among the most powerful teaching skills of all is the ability to convey and to transfer insight. When a teacher has education, wisdom, and knowledge, however and wherever acquired, and approaches his responsibility with determination, the teacher can improve and he will find a way to plan and teach effectively. If these critical skills are not possessed by a music teacher, all the techniques in the world will be ineffective. The teacher will not know the ultimate purpose for using them and his success in teaching music will be uneven.

There is another way to say this. If an architect does not have the aesthetic judgment to know what a well-designed and beautiful house is, all the training, plans, tools, materials, construction and administrative skills, and measuring devices are ultimately useless. Likewise, only when keeping his musical instincts and judgment at the forefront will the music educator understand what music's substance is, recognize how and when music learning occurs, and know what a truly musical performance is. Then, with his musical and teaching judgments as a guide, he can search the wealth of ideas and techniques in this book to find those that he can use effectively, and adapt them to his own teaching style, students, and musical intentions.

## SELECTED SOURCES FOR INSTRUMENTAL MUSIC EDUCATION

There are books and sources of different types that have value for instrumental music educators. For example, there are a number of books about string, brass, woodwind, and percussion instruments and many books about the craft of conducting. Periodically new books are published about each of these topics: coaching the jazz ensemble and teaching jazz improvisation; solo, small ensemble and large ensemble literature; teaching the high school band and orchestra; directing the marching band; band and orchestra arranging; and studying the conductor's score.

There is another type of source in instrumental music. The focal point of these books is more broad than teaching techniques used to teach students to phrase, play in tune, or balance and blend within the ensemble. One such publication is *MMCP Synthesis*, which is one of the products from the Manhattanville Music Curriculum Project, commonly known as MMCP. This was published by Media Materials, Inc. Box 533, Bardonia, New York 10954; it is out of print, but still available in many libraries and from many teachers. It is an excellent source of ideas for teaching music through compositional experiences and has been used by many general music teachers. Unfortunately this source is not widely known or used by instrumental teachers. One leading advocate of this approach for instrumental music instruction is John McManus at the University of Oregon.

Stanley L. Schleuter wrote *A Sound Approach to Teaching Instrumentalists: An Application of Content and Learning Experiences,* which was published by Kent State University Press in 1984. The discussions explain how to plan instruction in instrumental music classes so they include the singing of and listening to rhythm and tonal content. The discussions show ways to relate and integrate the listening and singing of this content with the instrumental skills.

There are several sources that discuss instrumental music education from the viewpoint of comprehensive musicianship. These are *Teaching Musicianship in the High School Band* by Joseph Labuta (Parker) and *Blueprint for Band,* by Robert Garofalo (Meredith Music Publications). Several volumes from the *Hawaii Curriculum Project* address band and orchestra instruction. The editors are Leon Burton and William Thompson, and the publisher is Addison-Wesley Publishing Company.

There are other important, recent publications that band and orchestra teachers should study because they contain thought-provoking and innovative ideas. Edward S. Lisk has written *The Creative Director: Alternative Rehearsal Techniques* published by Meredith Music Publications. This book presents a holistic approach to teaching many aspects of musicianship and performance skills. The approach utilizes the Circle of Fourths to organize material and is an effective way to foster the musical development of students. The book contains teaching techniques but also presents an overall approach to developing musical and skilled instrumentalists and ensembles.

Richard F. Grunow and Edwin E. Gordon have written new method books for band and orchestra. This series, entitled *Jump Right In: The Instrumental Series,* follows the tradition of innovation begun by James O. Froseth through publication of his own two method books, *The Individualized Instructor* and *Listen, Move, Sing, and Play,* and through other curricular materials for instrumental and general music education.

A main feature of Froseth's materials are recordings that provide a musical context for students as they practice and a more detailed sequencing of content and learning than is usually found in traditionally organized method books. Over time and with the advent of additional practical and experimental research in instrumental music teaching, the *Jump Right In: The Instrumental Series* comprises a more complete application of music learning theory to beginning instrumental instruction. These books are published by G.I.A. Publications.

James O. Froseth and Richard F. Grunow share authorship of a score reading program for instrumental music teachers. Its title is *MLR Instrumental Score Reading Program*; later Richard F. Grunow and Milford H. Fargo wrote and produced *The Choral Score Reading Program* that is similar. The purpose of these programs is to improve the college student's and music teacher's skills when reading the score. The books build these skills by asking the listener to compare recorded performances of scores to the notated score. The listener is to find when and where there are discrepancies between the performance and the score. The listener then corrects the score so it accurately represents the performance on the recording.

For a number of years, instrumental music educators have found value in three books. Two were written by Daniel L. Kohut. The titles are *Instrumental Music Pedagogy: Teaching Techniques for School Band and Orchestra Directors* (Prentice-Hall, Inc. 1973) and *Musical Performance: Learning Theory and Pedagogy* (Prentice-Hall, Inc. 1985). The third book is *How to Design and Teach a Successful School String and Orchestra Program* by Dillon and Kriechbaum (Kjos, 1978).

Music educators should notice two recent publications. One book contains material about managing the music program and another describes research in music education. Darwin E. Walker wrote *Teaching Music: Managing the Successful Music Program* (Schirmer Books, 1989), which meets a need for fresh ideas related to music administration. Richard Colwell edited a book entitled *Handbook of Research on Music Teaching and Learning* (Schirmer, 1992). This contains explanations of important concepts in music education and discussions of research studies. Its contents can help music educators benefit from the results of pertinent research in music education.

Special attention should be given five MENC publications: *Instrumental Music* by George L. Duerksen (Music Educators National Conference), *WHAT WORKS: Instructional Strategies for Music Education* edited by Margaret Merrion (Music Educators National Conference, 1989), *Guide to Evaluating Teachers of Music Performance Groups* by David P. Doerksen (Music Educators National Conference, 1990), *Dimensions of Musical Thinking* edited by Eunice Boardman (Music Educators National Conference, 1989), and *Musicianship in the Beginning Instrumental Class* by Merry Texter (Music Educator's National Conference, 1979).

The Boardman book contains twelve essays on music thinking. One essay by Richard Kennell addresses instrumental music in particular and is entitled "Musical Thinking in the Instrumental Rehearsal." The David P. Doerksen book can be helpful to school principals, music supervisors, parents as well as teachers of performance groups. George L. Duerksen wrote a valuable pamphlet that presented only those ideas about instrumental music instruction that were based in research. *WHAT WORKS* is more recent and extensive than Duerksen, and is valuable because of its many contributions based upon research findings. The book includes descriptions of a wide variety of teaching approaches for general, choral, and instrumental music along with bibliographies of research studies. The Texter book contains ideas that show how to enrich the beginning instrument class musically.

Frank Bencriscutto wrote instructional materials called *Total Musicianship* (Kjos). The material represents his beliefs that students will become more interested in music learning if they learn additional content and skills such as music theory and improvisation, and have the opportunity and guidance needed to practice being inventive and creative. There are tapes included that help a student work with the material.

A recent book about score study entitled *Guide to Score Study: For the Wind Band Conductor* by Frank Battisti and Robert Garofalo (Meredith Music Publications, 1990) contains valuable suggestions. This book also contains a selected bibliography of related books in such areas as score reading, score analysis, orchestration and arranging, Twentieth-Century composition, interpretation, and literature lists.

Thomas L. Dvorak wrote two books, *Best Music for Young Bands* and *Best Music for High School Band-Wind Ensemble* both published by Manhattan Beach. The latter is to be released in 1992. Cynthia Crumps Taggert, now at Case Western Reserve University, and Peter Schmalz from Oshkosh West High School shared authorship on the first book; Robert Grechesky, of Butler University, and Gary Ciepluch, of Case Western Reserve University, were co-authors of the second book with Thomas L. Dvorak. A third volume, likely to be available in 1993, will be called *Best Music for Beginning Band.* Linda Dvorak is the co-author of this publication.

*Wind Ensemble/Band Repertoire* is published by the University of Northern Colorado, Greeley, Colorado and its authors are David Wallace and Eugene Corporon. The literature (Grade V-VI) is most suitable for high school bands and wind ensembles who can perform literature of those levels; and for college wind ensemble-symphonic bands.

Many states have literature lists for solo, small, and large ensemble music, but the leading state lists for music are Wisconsin (especially the solo-small ensemble portion), a newly revised and excellent list from Texas (1992), and a list from New York that is not as large as the Texas list. In the opinion of many, the leading list of the three is the Texas list. Anyone can purchase these lists from the respective state music associations. These three states are the basis for most contest lists throughout the country.

Two periodicals, the *BDGuide* and the *Instrumentalist*, have published recent articles that suggest a basic repertoire for band. The *Band Music Notes: Composer Information and Program Notes for over 600 Band Favorites* is compiled and written by Norman Smith and Albert Stoutamire; a revised edition was published in 1979 by Kjos. Norman Smith also wrote *March Music Notes*, which was published by Program Notes Press in 1986. The *Band Music Guide* is published by the *Instrumentalist* and the National Band Association publishes the *Selected Music List for Band.*

There is a recent publication (1991) from Integrity Press, 61 Massey, Westerville, Ohio. The title is *Heritage Encyclopedia of Band Music*; the author is William Rehrig and the editor is Paul Bierley. This publication is in two volumes and includes about 54,000 titles of music written for or adapted for band, over 3,600 biographical sketches, and lists 8,953 composers and arrangers. This publication's valuable literature lists complement the other books, articles, and state literature lists mentioned above.

Two books in choral and vocal music should be mentioned because their intent and methodology are similar to this publication. The most recent is *In Quest of Answers: Interviews with American Choral Conductors* edited by Carol Glenn (Hinshaw Music, Inc. 1991) and *Training the Singing Voice: An Analysis of the Working Concepts Contained in Recent Contributions to Vocal Pedagogy* by Victor Alexander Fields (Da Capo 1979).

There are a few sources that discuss teaching techniques that can be used in rehearsals and class lessons. The sources are: *Efficient Rehearsal Procedures for School Bands* by Nilo Hovey (The Selmer Company, 1976) and *Expression in Music* by H. A. Vandercook (Rubank Publications). The latter was published originally in 1926 and revised in 1942, and is still available. Other sources are: *The Teaching Skills Workbook* by James Froseth and Judy Delzell (G.I.A. Publications, 1976), and *Playing the String Game* by Phyllis Young (University of Texas Press, 1978).

# *Beliefs and Values of Instrumental Music Educators*

# BELIEFS AND VALUES

When a teacher guides an instrumental music program, he is responsible for a myriad of processes: planning, recruiting, teaching, conducting, performing, testing, communicating, and evaluating. The impetus for completing these comes from his own personal, musical, and educational experiences; we assume that the teacher fulfills these processes based upon personal values.

We can make only two broad assumptions about the teacher's awareness of his values: he is aware why he does things or he is not. To be fair, no one can totally know why things are being done; but, a teacher *should* consciously and actively be aware of the values, principles, and purposes of music education—it is the teacher's professional responsibility.

It is generally held that a teacher has a philosophy whether or not he knows it and can articulate it. Most educators contend, though, that a teacher can be more effective if he brings these ideas into his consciousness and examines them. Only when the teacher discovers and articulates his values, can he consciously consider the significance of what has been done and knowingly implement ideas which strengthen his program, curriculum, or teaching. This process must be continuous, and through the process the teacher must decide which values should be retained and which should be changed or clarified; this is essential for the professional music educator.

This chapter contains many excellent ideas, from some of our finest music educators, that can help teachers guide their programs to more effective musical and educational ends. These ideas are especially critical at this time in music education. While there have often been intense pressures upon music education, pressures are more intense in the 1990's than at any other time: public attitudes are more indifferent to arts education than before; the financial support for music education and other arts has been reduced in many schools and is threatened in others; the student's academic requirements and expectations are increasing, which complicates scheduling, threatens music enrollment, and demands more time of students; some

families need additional financial support which means some students must choose part-time jobs instead of extra-curricular experiences, and these are added to the number of students that choose part-time jobs just to increase their spending money; and some students who do choose to study music must reject highly appealing alternatives—some have little substance and long-term value while others can lead to important professions and careers, some potentially more lucrative than music.

Student participation in the school music curriculum and their preparedness for music classes cannot be taken for granted—and never should have been. Not the least or the last, the purpose for music education reflects an alarming drift toward an emphasis upon entertainment and public relations, and upon performing music that students and the public will immediately like—rather than educating and cultivating expanded, mature tastes.

This is neither encouraging nor positive; but there still are many programs of significance with remarkable participation, instruction, and achievement. One reason for excellent programs may be the teacher's, school's and community's commitment and clear vision about the value, place, and process of music education.

In every school, it is the music teacher's responsibility to develop a recognition of and an appreciation for the arts among every segment of the community: the school administration, teachers, staff, parents, community members, and students. The music teacher must disseminate and cultivate these values and insights; no teacher can presume that the community and school possesses these values inherently and that an enthusiasm for a quality arts program is always present. The teacher must do more than merely arrive at the school expecting that the attitudes, enrollment, values, and curricula will be in place.

The comments in this section are intended to cause the reader to *think* about music education, and they show ways that excellent instrumental music educators articulate their beliefs. Their comments about what they believe, and why they do things will help the readers examine their own philosophy and communicate their own ideas to others at a time when strong leadership in the profession is vital to its survival and to its growth.

# CHAPTER ONE

# INSTRUCTION

Music teachers have many opinions, beliefs, and values. Some teachers do not think such ideas constitute a philosophy, but often they do. At a minimum the ideas represent the teacher's conscious or unconscious ideas and attitudes about music education. The inevitable effect of these ideas is to provide a stance that gives impetus for what a teacher does.

Deciding the extent to which these ideas are philosophical statements is not of prime importance here, but the ideas are worth thinking about for the guidance one can take from them. They can give the reader food for thought about such questions as what should be the substance we are teaching? What makes effective teaching? What should we know about the teaching process? And why should we teach what we do?

Clifford K. Madsen contributed a very important and interesting article entitled *Intensity as an Attribute of Effective Teaching*. In the article there is a detailed discussion about effective teaching. Effective teaching appears to include two important and basic elements: (1) knowledge of the subject matter and precisely what it is students should learn; and (2) effective delivery and sequencing of the subject matter. Both elements seem to have an inextricable interaction with each other, especially in relationship to long-term learning effects.

If a teacher has limited or inaccurate knowledge or objectives, even highly enthusiastic delivery can only maintain short-term attention and inadequate learning. Alternately and regardless of subject-matter knowledge, low-intensity teacher delivery will not often maintain enough student attentiveness for the subject matter to be learned.

The article includes discussion of many research studies that address a number of issues of teaching and instruction, including initiating and maintaining student attention; teacher behaviors that can be observed accurately, and which can be taught to teachers in training; student selection for teacher training experiments; intensity levels between student and subject matter; and intensity levels found in social interaction. To extract parts of the article could make its contents less useful to the reader; thus the complete article and bibliography are included in Appendix IV.

## INSTRUCTION

### Retention in instrumental music

If students are learning something *each day* of *each* music class or ensemble rehearsal, if they see and hear progress being made, and if they receive a musical, aesthetic experience at some time during the week—even if it is only from a simple folk song in a beginning class—they will stay in the program. Attrition rates, which deplete the group, cannot be blamed solely on counselors or college preparatory requirements.

*(Gordon Childs)*

### Fundamentals of good teaching

Planning, defining objectives and purposes for students, structuring a lesson, evaluating their progress, and developing a summation of the lesson are fundamental to good teaching.

Choosing techniques, no matter what type they are, is a means to complete this process effectively. I am not as concerned with how they do something as long as they thoroughly know why they were doing it and how they are going to produce the desired result.

There are multiple ways to do things—but, if you do not know what you are doing, the entire thing could fall apart. Once the process is in place, the techniques are absolutely necessary and essential then. I feel that the process problem is where many problems are in music education. Process problems happen ninety-eight percent of the time.

*(George R. Bedell)*

### Make a decision

Settle on your philosophy: are you in this to teach and to make a name for yourself; or are you in this to teach music, teach students, and enrich their lives?

*(Ed Schaefle)*

## The main issue

In spite of what I believe and what I have said about conducting and rehearsing, *making music* is the main issue. Conducting just helps you do it better. Many people get seduced into feeling that if they look good as a conductor, it's musical. They don't need to think that way; there are so many conducting classes going on now that could help them reexamine their thoughts. In some ways, conducting workshops do a great service—but they sometimes can be focused on the language rather than the idea.

*(H. Robert Reynolds)*

## Expectations

Teachers underestimate what their students can accomplish and their limited expectations result in less achievement for students. Remember and accept that some students will be more apt musically and academically than the teacher. We must recognize that the relationship between general intelligence and musical aptitude is not strong. This means that mentally retarded students might perform well musically and that geniuses might be musically retarded. Good teachers must work with the entire spectrum of learners.

*(Stanley L. Schleuter)*

Our priorities become the students' priorities.
*(Patricia Brumbaugh)*

Often teachers tend to believe that they can reach *every* student, "if only we can find the 'right' approach." This brings to mind several short anecdotes. A well-known, successful piano teacher was listening to an audition by a prospective student. Upon hearing the student play, she said to herself, "Wonderful talent . . . poor teaching." She accepted the student and one year later she was listening to her student in the Annual Recital. She listened carefully to this particular student and said to herself, "Wonderful talent . . . poor teaching!"

*(Pamela Gearhart)*

## Reviewing and showing relationships

Teachers must review ideas taught in prior lessons. We also show students the relationship of a new idea to the ideas that a student already knows. Teachers must never underestimate this. Students seldom think in such a way as to make connections and see relationships on their own. The teacher, therefore, needs to guide this kind of thinking process.

*(Sharon Rasor)*

## The teacher and the student must have a focus

We should be able to ask a student at most anytime in a lesson, "What is your teacher trying to teach you now?"

*(James Froseth)*

Some teachers believe that simply saying, "Play letter B again," is enough for students to understand why. If you ask students in rehearsal why they stopped, they cannot tell you why the teacher asked them to play that section again.

Here is an example that helps students know the reason for rehearsing a certain section. In *Variations on America* by Charles Ives, there is a busy passage of sixteenth notes in three-note groups. Each group is repeated twice and is in a sequence. To make the students understand that this is not a maze but an organized passage, I may explain to them how it is put together. This makes the indecipherable clear to the students. Knowing this, allows them to approach it with a greater chance of success, because they know what we are working on and how it might be approached.

We play the first three sixteenth notes and I say, "Look to see that the next three are the same, then the sixteenth-note groups are played together." We may slow the pulse down, but we drill this to place all the notes into one group—a group of at least six notes. Then, we go to the next pattern to execute that correctly. I refer to the measure number in the music, to the instruments, and I also name what it is we will be trying to accomplish.

A detailed explanation of this passage helps the success of the instruction. Sometimes I ask them to determine if there is a pattern, or I ask them in another way to figure out how to approach the performance of a passage. In small groups, I give them chances to offer an analysis. In a large group, I save time by giving the information myself. I can check their understanding by listening to their performance, which should show comprehension.

Some students who do not have this part, can do silent practice on another tune or specific spots I specify. Some sections have the same material, but at a different spot. These students can relate the instruction for that problem to a different spot in the music.

*(George R. Bedell)*

## Teacher skills

The ideal, even the requirement, is that the teacher can demonstrate everything that he is trying to teach; there may be exceptions, but that is the ideal. Teachers also must have a thorough understanding of how they are doing what they are demonstrating for students. For example, if a teacher can produce a beautiful tone, that is not enough; he also must know how he does it. This is necessary for truly effective instruction to take place. When we look for the missing ingredient in those teachers who are not effective, it is either the process of instruction or the understanding of how to do what is being taught. A teacher is not effective if the student is not focused upon what is to be learned. Someone must instruct teachers how to teach.

The lack of focus by the teacher and student is one of the biggest problems in music education. Both the teacher and student need to know what they are trying to do. Different teachers and students teach and learn in different ways. We are arriving at the point in public education where we are more aware of the process of teaching and learning.

*(George R. Bedell)*

### Teaching students

Teach the heck out of the kids, then get out of their way and let them play.

*(Stanley Cate)*

Without listening, instruction is just an activity.

*(Frank Battisti)*

Teaching without talking solves most of the problems, because teaching can then be modeling and non-verbal instruction. Less talking means that we can teach, which in the dictionary means "to show."

*(James Froseth)*

With a professional group one can give them the downbeat and they will play: but with students we have an obligation as teachers to develop some musicality and musical instincts in our students. If we demand that they sit being neutral, waiting for us to tell them how to play, they will be passive. They will not be making any musical gestures, not learning how to be musically independent. Conductors who control all the musical nuances are teaching them to be musically dependent—a musical marionette.

By emphasizing sound and phrasing, most intonation problems are solved by students on their own. I do not want to sacrifice the musical result to achieve technical cleanliness.

*(Robert Grechesky)*

### Teaching tone

You must begin treating them like musicians from the very beginning, teaching them immediately what to listen to and how to discriminate. We must teach them the idea of good tonal quality; we can point to a professional sound as the proper example to emulate.

*(Barbara Buehlman)*

### Ensemble and individual tone

I think that characteristic tone is very important. Especially with the concert band, I stress tone quality, phrasing, intonation, and musicianship more than virtually anything.

*(Phillip A. Weinberg)*

### The center of music teaching is the music

I have believed that everything musical that one wants to teach, can be taught through a piece of music. We do not have to prepare them to play the music. I do not like the idea of a formal warm up, nor do I teach that way. If everyone is warmed up and tuned up, then we are ready to perform. I do not get everyone ready in a warm up and therefore solved everything that was to come up, and then play. I do not prefer going through a long training session during warm up. Then, after the warm up, one must start on a piece of music and begin all over again. I would prefer going through the music to meet those objectives. I would not categorically disagree with those using a warm up teaching component in a rehearsal, if they are successful. A warm up may be needed; it may maintain integrity in their teaching. If it is simply time-filling, it is not justifiable.

*(Barbara Buehlman)*

### Musical or technical development

Technical skills must be related to musical expression and vise versa. Science and Art can not be separated. Technical problems often are solved when playing is merged with expressive attempts. I often can get a problem solved by asking students to play musically, getting them involved—much more than by always trying to solve separate technical issues in isolation.

*(Frank Bencriscutto)*

### Answering questions about teaching

I needed to think through many issues by and for myself; there were people who helped with certain challenges, but the aesthetic questions were those that were the most difficult to answer. For example, "Why am I doing what I am doing?" "What is the purpose for all this?" I had to answer those questions for myself. Now many people are asking and answering these questions; there are interesting and musical band directors out there who have ideas about this.

*(H. Robert Reynolds)*

### What we should teach students

Learning, improvisation, and composition are more interesting than just playing music. These can invigorate our band programs considerable by introducing some creativity. This can happen because we have introduced a musical vocabulary that they can use, be creative with, and apply it right then to music. Vocabulary in English deals with the words and in music we deal with the sounds, which are the components of music.

*(Frank Bencriscutto)*

I firmly believe, since I also teach theory, that I should teach students in rehearsals something of the form of the piece. In the Mendelssohn *Overture for Band* they all knew where the exposition, development, recapitulation, etc. occurred.

*(Kjellrun K. Hestekin)*

For the artistic experience with music to be meaningful to students, they must understand that there is a form, there is such a thing as a chord, and there is the third or the fifth of the chord. In my materials, *Total Musicianship*, we try to bring this out, for example, by playing and singing the notes of the chord—the fifth, seventh, polychords, etc.

We can achieve a higher level of experience and more clearly maintain the meaning in their experience and indelibly mark the student, if they learn and know something about the music. We may be missing an ingredient. Developing technical skills and growth in the area of facility alone is not enough to reach this higher level.

*(Frank Bencriscutto)*

The proper perspective for any music teacher is to realize that the most powerful educational experiences that go on in the classroom are those when the students are dealing with a whole musical object, not just a note, bar, or figure. I hope students are dealing with something that is at least a phrase, probably even more than that. The analogy I use is the difference between a word or a letter in the English language. Words and letters have meaning and are useful to help one understand the alphabet, for example, but it is below the level of literature or poetry. Something small, like a note or one chord, is devoid of the kind of meaning we expect in an art form. When we get to a sentence, a verse, a stanza, or paragraph then we can carry some real meaning, which can be of the level that is art music.

The best teaching, therefore, happens when we are dealing with a whole musical object. Teachers ought to be thinking in student centered terms. They should think of what the students are going through, not just what has to be done to prepare the next concert. Teachers ought to take every opportunity to deal with the whole musical object, instead of just a little part of it—such as the attack, the clarinet chord, or the rhythmic background figure. We ought to recognize that students probably are not as facile or adept at responding to artistic ideas as we are. So, if we listen to a little phrase and say, "That is lovely"—meaning we were touched by the way the phrase was shaped—most students are not able to respond that quickly. So when we try to put the music together and really have a musical experience with a capital M, it may have to be a minute long, or four minutes long before we can expect that students will be touched in special ways by the music.

All music teachers must return to the practice of listening to a big chunk of music, or rehearsing a big chunk of music as often as possible. I recognize that we need to say sometimes, ". . . wait a minute, the horn part is not working out three measures after letter C, we better go over that again." We then go into an analytical mode and say, "Let's go over that again to clean up the articulation." But, during the whole time I am in the analytical mode, I am sorry I am and I am looking for the opportunity to return to the musical mode.

A good musical class then is, I think, in constant alternation between what we call a synthesis of all the musical elements—a whole object, and then going into an analytical mode where we try to understand how some small musical elements interact—how they can be refined, what makes them performed better or function better. But, always with the idea that we should take the new information or understanding and plug it back into the musical whole.

Many famous directors never or rarely, until the concert, put together big chunks of music. Instead, they rehearse this six or that twelve measures. Students may have become technically able to rehearse and perfect the elements of the music, the right dynamics, notes, rhythms, tone quality, etc. But, not until the concert was the music ever put together in such a fashion as to make artistic sense: the art object was never placed before the students so they could respond. Therefore, their artistic training was badly inhibited.

It might be that nothing below the length of a phrase can be considered a musical object. True or not, this might be a guideline in rehearsals. Then, one uses entities of sufficient size so the entities are musical objects as often as possible during rehearsals and classes.

*(Donald Casey)*

### With what and how should we be teaching

We first must decide the music through which we want them to learn. (I don't mean the beginning method books.) In a group rehearsal at any level, most of the music must be well within the technical capabilities of the players, but there should be a piece or two that stretches them technically.

The most fun I have is rehearsing and performing pieces that are technically very simple for that group. With excellent players, I can play with it and have *them* play with it. The interaction and concentration they can give to each other, to their own playing, and to watching the conductor while listening to everyone else—three ears on the tubas, two ears on the percussion—can give them a level of concentration and objects for their attention that are more varied, enriching, and encompassing. The performance then can be staggering in terms of sensitivity; and the interactive qualities among the players, between the players and the conductor, the conductor and the players, and the players and each other are very rewarding.

Though the best of the directors in the preceding era were also concerned with musical values, most focused primarily on the band's performance polish and upon the elimination of audible errors. These directors developed players who could play better and they stressed that students should *constantly* be trying to play better. However, *before* the students were ready for musical independence and judgment or before they were ready to do much musically and expressively, we felt compelled to *develop the students' technique to the maximum degree.*

Achieving performance polish is a necessity, but it is not the reason for rehearsal; making music is the reason for rehearsal. The acquisition of skill allows the music to be interpreted and to become fully alive. Students need to experience music as fully alive or we have not achieved the purpose of their music education. Without attaining ensemble polish and individual skill, the music cannot be made alive for the student or by the conductor.

It also takes imagination and creativity to do this, and their emergence helps us experience something more substantive than satisfaction with the level of virtuosity we have reached. When imagination and creativity emerge, we see other values; they help us see a direction during music making, they transform skills from ends to means, and we then see the musical purpose for acquiring and using skills.

In no way am I implying that imagination and creativity can be substituted for performance skill. The lack of performance polish can only inhibit the ultimate musical expression. The performer's efforts inhibit musical expression when he lacks performance skill, just as the efforts of a reader of poetry are inhibited when he cannot pronounce the words and inflections properly. The lack of instrumental skill and instances of mispronunciations both interfere with what the performer is saying and what the audience is hearing.

I think, when we select pieces that are technically less demanding relative to the student's ability, we can develop their sensitivity. When the technical demands are immense, such as in *Music for Prague*, this is harder to do. During rehearsals of *Music for Prague* one is much less able to develop sensitivity, because their concentration must be focused much more on technique, that is to get the part played, so one doesn't have the mental or emotional energy to be attentive to all those other things and other people. It can be imperative to think, "Don't bother me, I have too many problems of my own right now." The unfortunate result of playing difficult pieces is that it can force us to avoid or forego the issue of musical expression. That is why we must select literature that is both easier and harder than students' instrumental proficiency.

*(H. Robert Reynolds)*

## A musical way to develop technique

Scales are the result of pieces. That is, of music compositional choices, procedures, practices, and results. But, pieces themselves are not the result of scales. My intent is to develop ways to build technique or skills in a way that is more musical, develop more sound and sound relationships than can be done through scales.

*(Richard Grunow)*

## The nature of music and instruction

The greatest idea we can contribute, is that music is an aural phenomenon. The games and clever ways to teach are often left brain intellectual ideas, instead of right brain experiences. Counting games, for example, fall into the "left-brain" area. High level music learning and performance is a non-discursive, non-cognitive mindless experience that is all imagery, feelings, sounds, and emotions involving the right brain. Wouldn't it be a great idea to make music a true alternative to academic subjects, but not making it mathematics—not making it intellectual in the customary way intellectual is understood.

The art of teaching would be advanced by a gigantic, *humongous* step, if the distinction were made between teaching music and teaching about music. Let us think of language for a moment and compare it to music. If one is not familiar with a word, one is illiterate. If one is not familiar with a tonal or rhythmic pattern, one is illiterate in the musical sense; looking up new words refers one to known words!

We must consider the student's musical dictionary. If we ask them to compute a rhythm pattern that is new, they must have known things with which to compare. Taking this idea to music, means that if one were to compute an unfamiliar rhythmic pattern by breaking it down into mathematical relations, they would not be consulting their musical dictionary. Figuring it out mathematically is non-musical and would require some masterful association to produce a musically correct rhythm. Musical rhythm is not the mathematical relationship between notes. This is so since mathematical relationships are not analogous to musical experience.

One's musical dictionary, on the other hand, is compiled from the literature that one learns aurally. The idea is to provide these musical dictionaries that will lead students to have material where they can look up rhythmic and melodic patterns in their aural dictionary. A musical dictionary is a memory bank of many many patterns, songs, movements, etc. In the kids, there should be a mental bank or dictionary that is activated by singing, playing and moving, and remembering. This should happen when they are confronted with reading music notation. To some extent, these dictionaries exist through folk songs, pop songs, advertisements on television, and other musical repertoire from our culture.

One unfortunate thing occurs when educators use "Twinkle Twinkle," and "Jingle Bells" in instructional literature. They are included in versions that remove the rhythmic character that students already know. The writers simplify the tunes tonally or rhythmically, or ask the student to play them in half-fast or at some unacceptable tempo. This is done by reducing the experience in consideration of musical notation and technical demands. The altering of these tunes does not preserve the integrity of the literature in their dictionary. We have taken music notation out of musical context. If we don't preserve their music dictionary, the literature, students have very many difficulties figuring out rhythmic and tonal notation.

We do this in service to the perceived demands of the instruments or certain traditions. In fact, *the* tradition is not a musical one it is instrumental. We are changing the music dictionary to meet the alleged difficulties found in learning the instrument.

*( James Froseth)*

### Mnemonic reminders

The reason why teachers use mnemonic reminders such as "one-e-and-ah," "one-ta-ne-ta," "du du-de du," and "January-February" is not that the reminders are the music, instead they can be steps somewhere along the way toward understanding music. Later, when such steps are no longer needed and when results are obtained, we wean ourselves from them.

*(Gerald Olson)*

### The content of music

Music is an aural phenomenon and people could teach music that way. Then, students would have aural musicianship and aural skills. Not enough teachers now possess the skills to teach the music this way. The situation is that we are strapped into the repertoire—the book first, instead of the ears. Addressing the book should not be done until the kids have had sufficient aural and rhythmic experiences to prepare them. Words should be used to name, to communicate, to instruct, etc. The words are not the content or the skill; words are not what music is. They only can tell us about music.

*(James Froseth)*

### Teacher training

It has taken me fifteen years to define the task of teacher training. My observation is, "We can give people a lot of information and if we observe them, we see that they do little with the information." In the dictionary, teach means "to show," it is not defined as "to tell." Therefore, we need to build teaching skills so teachers can show things. Skill training seems to make a greater difference in the success of teachers than giving them information. We have a lot of new ideas, but they usually are not that new. The problem is the implementation of the ideas.

*(James Froseth)*

Most of the musical things that first-year conductors think they need to know are going to be learned, not from their music education techniques class, but from their private teaching. Much of what they use in their day-to-day teaching during rehearsal is from their private teacher. In these issues, the private teacher is of benefit. I believe that to be a good conductor, they first must be a good musician. Often I find myself feeling like rehearsal is mass private lesson. Right now, what I'm doing with my students is what I got as a private student. In music education classes, you're going to learn all the fingerings on the clarinet that you have to teach also. To balance the two is hard.

*(Michael Kaufman)*

Explanations of learning and approaches to learning need to be understood and explained in more simple terms.

*(James Froseth)*

### The musical context in teaching

Music context is the most important element that we can provide for our students. If students are going to sing, listen, move, or play, they should be doing this in a rhythmic and harmonic context. Street musicians certainly do not make music without a context; they won't even have a session without a drummer, a bass player: *some* other element.

The music elements should be presented in context. The context provides a structure that includes rhythm and harmony. All the basic elements are in it: timbre, form, pitch, harmony, dynamics, etc. When the context—a musical environment—is provided for students, a lot of learning can take place despite the wealth of information presented to them. This learning will be more significant than anyone can write in a lesson plan.

*(James Froseth)*

### Practicing

It is not true that the more a student practices the more he learns. This idea is incorrect and it has little validity. On the other hand, if he practices in a musical context, he will learn because he hears himself and also hears himself immersed in music.

*(James Froseth)*

### The way we teach and express our musicianship

In music teaching, we express what we understand about what music is and what music isn't. We express this spontaneously as modelers and performers. This requires high level skill, awareness, sensitivity, and visual and aural discrimination. Teachers must be aware and skilled enough to monitor all this in students and in themselves. Then, they must apply the entire array of methodology, pedagogy, and psychology—the challenge and responsibility is awesome!

*(James Froseth)*

### Teaching is the process of engineering instruction

Teaching is a scientific process of planning instruction. This means that if a problem is seen, one engineers a solution. Since we need to be very observant to gain the information we need for planning, I try to raise the awareness of what students see and do not see.

*(James Froseth)*

### Trends in teaching

Analogy relates previous life experiences to music, which requires an additional thought process by the students. This approach enriches teaching. Only using clinical descriptions such as "play louder or softer" is limiting.

*(James Arrowood)*

## Learning styles

There is research on learning styles of minority students. Some research suggests that some minorities think more holistically and view things as function oriented. If we diagnose well, we notice the response of kids. Then, teachers can develop or choose the more effective teaching strategy.

*(James Froseth)*

## Goals

If one wants to balance numbers with quality and if one considers all the competing activities, one must have realistic goals for a program. If the students can practice, keep prepared for lessons, and play individually, they usually are motivated and will work. They are motivated by the basics required, and solos and ensembles are a chance for enrichment.

*(R. G. Conlee)*

## Educational and musical issues

Teachers are increasingly more concerned about the musical aspects; that is what some people are telling me. Students often are well trained, but they can't make musical judgments. Trainers get instant gratification since their kids place well in auditions, in festivals, or in contests. None of that is necessarily related to musical learning. There are also "fix-it bands." This means if you fix this and fix that, you will have a good result—if you can fix enough things!

I also am very concerned about the bands that use competition mainly or exclusively to motivate their group. If it isn't competition for chairs, it is for awards, contest ratings, or trips. The result is, the kids do not know how or why to prepare unless competition is part of it of the performance. Also, they cannot decide if what they did was important, unless a rating or chair advancement tells them so.

*(Richard Floyd)*

## Training versus teaching

We can train someone to follow the metronome and play the right rhythm, but I am not sure that is teaching students to be pulse conscious. Many outstanding bands are not well taught—they are well trained! I would prefer to develop the students' ability to internalize rhythm and pulse, so they do not have to be dependent on the metronome. Furthermore, when I transfer the responsibility for pulse to the students, I can concern myself with the music and quit being a human metronome that mainly provides time.

*(Richard Floyd)*

## Enthusiasm

There are people who have a gift with the technology of the instrument. Bill Gower, Jr. was one of the best ever, at any time, on any instrument, or no instrument. Number one was his enthusiasm for the instruments. He had the smarts to go with it and everything else to go with it but, it was Bill's enthusiasm's for playing the instruments that was critical.

*(Frederick Fennell)*

In making music with any players, regardless of age, the number one thing is enthusiasm. You cannot do a damn thing without enthusiasm. There are all kinds of enthusiasms, there are my kind, there are Lennie Bernstein's kind and we are very much the same. There are other people quiet in enthusiasm. A quiet enthusiasm *is* enthusiasm and it should not be misconceived to be reticence; it is enthusiasm of a different kind. There are other men who are quiet, meticulous, very persistent, and their voice barely goes above quiet speech. But, there is a great enthusiasm and a marvelous communication there if you can see it, feel it or hear it.

I remember hearing Eleanor Roosevelt on a radio interview as she came off a boat. She was explaining all the things she did on a trip . She was asked, "How can you be so enthusiastic at this late hour of the night, after so long a transatlantic trip?" She said, "My dear man it is enthusiasm, you can't do anything without enthusiasm." Something about the way she said it was so striking to me that it burned itself right into my head. I knew that and I have always lived that way, but it was the way she expressed it. That is what we conductors must do.

The number one thing for me in all these years of teaching, of conducting, is enthusiasm. This goes to all the great orchestras of the world—don't think they cannot relate to it. Maybe not in the first couple of seconds when someone looks up and says, "Oh there's that Yank from Ohio." But, after the first fifteen minutes of a recording session, everyone is really at it. For me, enthusiasm is number one, but it comes from the music, not from me, I am only the agent. You cannot really do anything without enthusiasm!

*(Frederick Fennell)*

## After enthusiasm

If enthusiasm is job one, then making a constant adjustment of priorities during rehearsals is job two. Don't go in with a pre-arranged idea of what is going to happen. I have seen people go in with a list of what is going to go wrong and it doesn't go wrong. They still stand there with item no. 4!

You must be like a good chamber music player or a good tennis partner. You must read what is happening musically, technically, and psychologically, and adjust to it quickly. In the midst of making this kind of adjustment, this is the golden time to reward with the fewest words like, "Hey, that was terrific." That is a golden time when they zing and really come together. Every now and then a group experiences that four minutes out of the two-hour rehearsal.

One should reinforce student's performance, especially when things are hot. That is a critical point of the observation of others. We are like the traffic controllers with lots of radar scopes and a lot of planes out there, and we have a schedule—we are observers—we are the guys in the tower. The job of the conductor is to manipulate creatively the events so there is something to reward.

*(Frederick Fennell)*

## Significant learning

Anything that is truly significant, cannot be done in thirty seconds. If you want to get through the next hour, that is okay—but it is superficial. Young kids will do what you ask because they have the human trait of belief. This belief must be kept alive. With this, you can have him do things that take longer than thirty seconds. When you can no longer command that kind of experience, you will have to organize learning into thirty-second packages.

*(Frank Battisti)*

## Inviting students to interpret music

One of the things I do in conducting workshops and with my own group is talk about interpretation: I might say, "We have these decisions to make—we can go any one of these three ways—let's talk about it. What are we going to do?" In a sense, this is like exposing what you should be doing with a Mozart concerto when you are working with your private teacher. You don't go in the teacher and wait for the teacher to say, "Put in a ritard here." You go in there thinking, "I believe there should be a ritard here; what do you think?"

*(H. Robert Reynolds)*

## Employing formulas

I know some teachers who apply formulas to music. An example is the pyramid idea of balance to create a band sound, which can clarify an insight. If applied as a formula across the board, though, then all pieces will sound exactly the same! A formula approach applied excessively makes a recreative art into a science. This minimizes responses to the intangible, to the individual differences in music— it makes the response a preconceived notion. That "bugs" me! That is what I try to get students not to do!

I say to aspiring teachers there aren't that many "givens" and you can't fall into the trap of "formalized instruction." There are things you believe in and methods you can use. But, you should be willing to take on more ideas and bend any ideas. Particularly, you should always be willing to listen to what you are actually hearing.

*(Michael Haithcock)*

## Two phases of one's teaching career

During my first year of instrumental music teaching, a more experienced member of the department offered his "secret formula for success" as a teacher. He said, "All teachers have two phases to their teaching career. In the

first phase, you teach exactly as your teachers taught you. In the second phase, you are more eclectic—borrowing the best ideas from many experienced teachers. My advisor continued, "Some teachers teach in the first stage their entire life. Others are able to shift into the second phase in a matter of hours!"

*(Richard Kennell)*

## Use time wisely

On a day to day basis, a teacher can let students abuse them. I can remember when students descended upon me or other conductors just before a rehearsal to buy reeds, to get an extra part, to sell candy, or to repair an instrument. Sometimes five or six kids are gathered around the conductor when he is trying to begin the rehearsal. Teachers also try to squeeze in the extra lesson at every possible opportunity. This also stresses and burns out teachers who do not have extra time. They do not take care of their own need to think straight, to plan, to relax, or to recover from busy days.

A teacher also needs enough time to have an effective first lesson for beginners. Without time for lessons, the teacher faces pressure from the clock. The teacher will feel pressed when trying to teach something thoroughly. If a teacher continues with such a pace, it is possible he will suffer burn-out and the students will experience less than thorough instruction. All such distractions and stresses eventually affect the students' achievement, their sense of progress and accomplishment—not to mention the toll it can take upon the teachers' morale and well being.

*(Richard K. Hansen)*

## A challenge for instrumental music education

Learning to perform music without the instrument being a barrier is a real problem. If they can get over the mechanical interference between themselves and the music, there is a big improvement in the quality of the students' performance. The great artists really aren't playing the instrument, they are playing the music. The instrument is merely singing the music they are playing. This is one reason why I like Jim Froseth's approach, because immediately one is teaching phrasing, style, etc. It is a mistake to wait to teach these things until later—after students learn technical skills.

*(Gary Hill)*

Good bands are built with good *individual* players. Even the very best directors will see only limited success unless they place importance on the development of the *individual*.

*(David Deitemyer)*

## The mind has a marvelous power to discriminate

Without a doubt, unconsciously or subconsciously, everything that you are doing is constantly being referred to this background by the brain—the mind itself. We have seen again and again and again that our sensory organs are marvelously attuned to comparing things. In this process, they are not coming up with an absolute quantification.

If you play two different tones as close together as possible, maybe a few vibrations apart, the ear is sensitive enough in most people to tell which tone is higher or lower than the other. But, if you ask someone to sing a note that vibrates at exactly four hundred and seventeen times per second, you're not going to get it. Thus, our sensory organs are comparative in nature. The organ can perceive this is bigger than, this is smaller than, this is sweeter than, this is more sour than: this is higher or lower, louder or softer. We believe this is the way our sensory organs receive information—at least the people who have researched into the matter believe this. I agree with this view because of my own experience. We believe that the mind itself works totally on a comparative basis. When we hear two notes, we may not know how many vibrations per second each of these two notes is, but we can tell which is higher or lower!

*(Alfred Reed)*

### Intuition and understanding

There's an intuitive assessment, an intuitive grasp, an intuitive comprehension, and an intuitive putting of all the little pieces of music that we hear sequentially—one after the other—that we hear together to form a meaningful pattern. Once that pattern has been formed and recognized, then some other part of the brain, God only knows which, triggers off all the usual physical responses; the changes in blood pressure, the changes in respiration, the change in the heartbeat, and all these things. But, the hell of it is, we don't know. And, we the teachers are the ones who need to know to do the job. So, you've got to take this lightly, because otherwise, you're going to take your head by the hair and bang it against the wall. You've got to be humble in the face of the nature of things.

*(Alfred Reed)*

### Literature, performance, and culture

The ability to do something, either to play or to sing, or to write, or to conduct, or a little bit of all is what we are after. Listening and appreciation require literature and literature provides the background for everything. This is why we have literature courses in every language, in every country on the face of the globe, including the Aborigines or Western Australia, a retelling of the myths and the common heritage of an entire society.

I believe that culture in general, that overworked misused word, is one of these ideas that most people don't really see clearly. Because, when I attempt to get a definition of culture, I really can't get one. I get a lot of examples and I get a lot of "well, you know . . . you know . . . ," but I don't know and I want to find out. I'm interested in what the word culture really means.

Now to me, culture is not what you know, but what you are. What you are at any one moment of your life, is

the summation of everything that you do—the way you eat, the way you sleep, the way you dress, the way you walk, the way you talk, what you have heard, what you have seen—it's constantly being amalgamated.

At first, music, learning, and whatever are being received by the human mind. The mind is that super-computer up there and what it is receiving is constantly being worked over. Now, this obviously means that you can only go as far as you are permitted to go on the basis of what you know, what you've been taught, and what you've experienced.

Therefore, literature is really experience to me. I use that word to sum up everything that you have heard. In music, it is the works themselves and everything that you have learned about the works. We learn this by talking to people, by reading about it, etc. Everything you think about the works that you have heard, and all of this makes the background against which you consciously practice your art at any given moment on any given day.

To me, that is the basis for music education. To me, what we are really after in music education isn't so much to teach little Suzy or Tommy how to play a flutaphone, recorder, or a pre-band instrument; and later on, he or she or they will move over to legitimate instruments. Far more important than that, is to begin to inculcate this cultural background. Then, what they see, hear, and experience today is referred to this aural frame of reference. In other words, what you hear today compared to what you have heard in the past.

*(Alfred Reed)*

### Using singing in instruction

I think singing works; I've used it probably more in the last two years than I ever used it before. I've finally learned that it pays off. I think that singing works not because it develops better singers, but because it develops better listeners—that's the whole key right there. Too many instrumentalists are like the piano player who never has to listen to that pitch; they often are more typewriter-like players. (Some in undergraduate school were terrible in sight singing class!) I think that singing helps to develop the ear and it also helps to develop their sensitivity to everything—ensemble—everything! It's a quieter approach that makes the difference when they pick up the horns. It's very easy to teach kids to play loudly and with a bad sound. It's difficult to first convince kids, to make them believe, and then to have it actually happen physically so they play softly, sensitively, and in legato style.

*(Michael Kaufman)*

### Singing is important in tuning

A group that plays well in tune does so primarily because the individuals have anticipated the pitch of the next note before they play it. Anticipating the pitch center is more important than adjusting the pitch after it has been sounded. I think singing for the band and the conductor is extraordinarily important and it can develop this important skill.

I find, if you want a simple thing to improve intonation immediately, just sing the note. "This E flat is out of tune; okay, everybody just sing that note." Then play it again and it's immediately a lot better. What happens is that the pitch is internalized; when they play against an external pitch they're not nearly as aware of it as when they're playing against a pitch that's inside them—inside their body. So singing puts that pitch inside their body in the tuning up process—what little I do of the tuning-up process.

Very often I have the principal players play and everybody else sing. Those principal players can lock into each other very quickly because they're more adept; then everybody else in the ensemble has a sound that is familiar to them. We don't have tuba players tuning to a clarinetist's B flat. We have tuba players tuning to tuba players. But, the first chair tuba is tuning to the first chair clarinet, trumpet, and trombone so they can all kind of "home-in" on the sound that's familiar to them. In the meantime, they're singing what they are hearing from the first chair players. Everybody's involved; I've isolated the issue.

*(H. Robert Reynolds)*

### Empathize with students

There are still kids out there playing the trumpet—no matter how much you think otherwise, no matter how great the teachers are or think they are—there are kids in those excellent bands for totally negative reasons and not for the reasons teachers want. They may be in band because Mom and Dad said, "You're going to be in it." We can never save them all, and you've got to satisfy that kid, too.

*(William Long)*

### Priorities

Number one, school is for kids, not for bus, cafeteria or room schedules, or the teacher. Number two, music is an academic discipline, it has content. I would not take kids out of class, this puts band and keeps it on an equal basis. Thus, teachers don't ask to take kids from band.

*(Robert Allan)*

### My job is to teach music performance

In my planning and what I teach, I believe I am hired to teach them to perform the music musically. Almost any student can learn all of their own notes. I rarely drill notes in rehearsal, except when I am cranky and upset with a section. When I do this for a minute or so, I teach them how to practice that spot so they will know it better next time.

*(Terry A. Oxley)*

### Two ways to learn

One way to learn is through imitation. With imitation, a teacher knows a student can do something but you're not sure the kid understands it. (It may be possible to test them in some way other than observation, to see if he understands the principles behind what he can do.) The second way to learn is to understand the rules and schemes. Then, the student applies the rules to execute a performance based on those rules. Thus, there are really two learning systems. I think behaviorism tries to explain the one—trying to determine how we imitate. The cognitive approaches the other—how we know and apply the principles. Actually the learner and the teacher use both.

With some teaching, the kid can play something and the teacher will say, "That's good, let's move on." Then, the next week the student can't play the same exercise, nor can they generalize what they learned to unfamiliar music. This may occur because they learned it in the wrong mode. That also happens if there's no content to go with the methodology.

*(Richard Kennell)*

Einstein (if I recall correctly) was asked if example is the best way to teach; he answered, "No, it's the only way to teach."

*(H. Robert Reynolds)*

### Rote is the only way to teach some things

To know anything, you have to experience it, and that experience has to come first. You can use "advance organizers." This means you say to a student, "Remember last week how we did this and we did that? Well, we're going to do something like it today." This statement can relate the unknown to the previously known and this is called an "advance organizer."

The idea is you don't learn anything new; you must anchor new knowledge on something you've already learned. For example, if you're going to talk to students about fractions, you start with things that are like fractions that you are certain the students have already learned. For example, a student may already have divided an apple into parts and shared it.

*(Richard Kennell)*

### Thinking about curriculum

In curriculum development we decided that a music class, in some respects, was no different from a math class. Music education, historically, has been an infinite kind of process. There have been few guidelines other than a kid may finish a book now and then, or they never finish a book. We decided, "What the heck? Why should a kid choose his development, why can't we choose it instead? The math teachers do it."

So we developed a curriculum and we related it in the Junior High schools to the Rubank Series or its equivalent for what a seventh grader should complete by the end of the seventh grade. If I recall correctly, it was a simple standard using the Rubank Series as a point of reference. The seventh graders were expected to finish Rubank

Elementary, eighth grade was Rubank Intermediate and ninth grade was Rubank Advanced. To our surprise, eighth graders were finishing Advanced Volume I, a year ahead of our expectation because they just worked their "buns" off. At least, for the teachers who planned and used that system, it worked great. What I realized was that when a teacher sets a reasonable standard, many students surpass it. If there is no standard, then students achieve much less.

With a tenth grader, we felt that a kid who has acquired his basic technique, scales, arpeggios, and basic rhythms he had gone far enough. From there on, we decided that we couldn't pick an equivalent because there are so many individual differences.

At this point, the nurturing process begins to take an effect and we also felt that was a good time to develop solo skills. With the tenth, eleventh, and twelfth graders, we developed selected lists of solo material with six solos for each level.

In this respect, a contest judge related an experience he had. He had just heard a band that was the poorest he had even heard. The band did so many things wrong, he was unsure what comments to make. Finally, he figured it out and said, "This band certainly lives up to the director's expectations."

*(Kenneth M. Larsen)*

### The development of the individual

What made my band program work over the years, is that I have advocated and I have taught according to a principle. This principle is to consider the importance of the development of the individual.

*(Kenneth M. Larsen)*

### Helping students know what to expect

A student must know what to expect, where you want him to be in a certain amount of time. You can say, "Here's a solo, go home and learn it," and by Easter it isn't done because the teacher did not give a target date. It might be better to say, "Here's a solo, I want this completed and ready for performance by the end of the quarter." With this, the student always has an idea of what is expected of him. Maybe that isn't all good either. This could cause the preparation to be like the Canadian Piano Competition. The pianists can play the heck out of solo number ten, but that doesn't mean they can play diddly if asked to play a solo not on that list of ten approved pieces.

*(Kenneth M. Larsen)*

### This is a hard piece

I do not know their limits and neither do they, thus I do not say, "This is hard." I don't want to set limits for them. We therefore do rather difficult pieces that they do not know are difficult.

*(John W. LaCava)*

If you tell the kids it is going to be difficult, then they give it more of their attention and effort. This also can prevent them from being frustrated and demoralized if at first they face difficulty in learning a piece.

*(Melanie Michalak)*

### Slow motion rehearsal

I compare taking a passage slowly while practicing to what a coach does when he studies film in slow motion—they can see more. When we play in slow motion, we can hear more also. We can fix and improve more of our own mistakes and play better at a less than full tempo. With a slow tempo, students can hear pitch easier, correct or prevent mistakes, correct a missed rhythm, and time is saved because everything is cleaned up faster.

*(John W. LaCava)*

### Band can be a microcosm of life

They must learn to work, handle and cope with stress, be responsible and use their ability. With a good attitude, they can do most anything.

*(John W. LaCava)*

One day in a high school band rehearsal shortly after I had completed my Master's degree something memorable happened. I was committed to the ideals of comprehensive musicianship, as every Northwestern graduate should be, and had selected some Renaissance music to rehearse, striving to bring enlightenment to my band members about the music of this more obscure period. I'd chosen the *William Byrd Suite*, which was about the only piece available then that sounded well. This suite is a set of arrangements of tunes from the *Fitzwilliam Virginal Book* by Byrd. In trying to explore the origins of the music, I asked my band members if anyone knew what kind of instrument a virginal was. Quick as a flash my bass clarinetist answered, "That's one that hasn't been played before."

*(Donald Casey)*

### Memorizing

It is terrible that kids don't memorize solos anymore. This has changed because it is the easier way out. Bloom's list of skills says that *memorization* is the lowest level of learning there is! I tell them, "A duck can memorize." *Knowledge* and *comprehension* also are lower levels of learning. In the classroom, ninety percent of what is done is at those lower levels. The third level is *application*, the fourth is *analysis*, the fifth is *synthesis* and the sixth level is *evaluation*.

While the typical classroom is doing lower level learning ninety percent of the time, band is already at the third level of application at the down-beat. We are constantly analyzing and we are constantly synthesizing. The evaluation process is never ending. Music education, then is quite defensible for these reasons. I write notes to parents several times a year and this is one of the points I try to make.

*(Ross A. Leeper)*

### The importance of music education
Many teachers are using the jazz band and marching band to entertain the populace of the school district, as opposed to giving students a decent music education.

*(Lewis Larson)*

### Teaching and television
To get through to the students, we need to use the idea of the greatest teacher ever—and that is television. If we are not going to use television's little tricks in our teaching, then we are not using things that can be to our advantage. Think about what Sesame Street has done and how long they stay with an idea.

*(Robert Morsch)*

### Approach to classes
We need to change how we approach the classroom. We should use the rehearsal hall as a classroom—not as some place to train notes. We get so concerned about making a perfect performance and getting that one or two rating in state contests. We spend six or seven months of every year, not only the school year but also before the year starts, putting that marching band on the field. We still haven't become wise to the facts about the marching band. While it gets people involved in the program, marching band should only be used for what it is most suited—that is public relations and attention getting.

When marching is over, one must get them sitting behind music stands as soon as you can. Then, take some of the excitement that you have built up and turn it into real teaching. If you have been teaching as well as drilling the marching band, then it would be easier to transfer them to musical issues inside the building.

Some bands use music of the classic composers, such as Saint-Saens or Carl Orff. Teachers use this music for the big numbers because it transcribes and transfers well to marching band. If you don't teach about Carl Orff, Verdi, or Bernstein, whose music is being used for the opener, then you are not being of service to the students: you are not providing education.

You don't have to teach the history of football to have a winning football team, but you can certainly draw upon Knute Rockne and Vince Lombardi to help students out. If students, though, don't know Knute Rockne and Lombardi won most of their games, then why are you using them as examples? When you use Carl Orff's *Carmina Burana* for your marching band opening and if you don't talk about what this piece is, or never take time to play a recording of its performance, then you are also doing students a disservice. Teachers must take those twenty minutes or the two hours of time in a week to teach the kids something. If teachers do that, then maybe they

will get a little more support from the administration and other musicians.

*(Robert Morsch)*

### Teaching music through band
Now, more than ever, we are forgetting about teaching. We do teach them to play an instrument, but we are not teaching music through the band experience. Teaching music is easy to do and we should pull back and reevaluate our goals about what the band is supposed to do. We should reconsider our concern for how many trophies we win and what is good for public relations. The question should be, "What are you going to do to change their lives musically?"

This doesn't mean changing their life as a player. This means being concerned about what they are going to do with that music knowledge. Are they going to pass it on to other people willingly and because they feel comfortable with it? If students cannot or do not feel comfortable talking about the music they play when they are in high school, in college as a music major, or as a non-music major, then how in the world are we going to cause a change in people's ideas? How are we going to make them think about what good music is and the good music that is available?

*(Robert Morsch)*

### The philosophy of the preceding era
Everything was built upon the idea that *the band* was the product. When a band played well, people often said, "You cannot argue with results." Such statements implied, since performance polish and results were excellent, we could assume that the process and the literature being played were also of value to the student. Teachers of the preceding era valued literature and the individual's growth, but they stressed the quality of *the band's* performance more. Now, the product is *the individual's* growth in understanding and their awareness of music, and in the increase in their ability to intuit music. The substance of students' experiences still comes from the literature and the quality of the performance, but we emphasize the growth of the individual.

There is another difference one can see when comparing prior conductors' approaches to current conductors' approaches. Prior conductors often told students what the musical feeling should be and the students performed technically as asked by the conductor, so the conductor's musical vision of the piece was realized. In contrast to this, the conductor now transmits the feeling of the music through mostly non-verbal means, instead of demanding that the students' feelings be identical to his.

There is another comparison: previous student performers probably did not convey their musical insights and interpretations to directors as much as they do now. By comparison, current students now manifest their music feelings and responses through the way they play in response to the conductor's non-verbal messages. Currently, the concern for students' growth dominates; but, we still believe the band is a valuable performance vehicle. Most people learn through performance experiences and we know that performing is a major way to experience music.

*(H. Robert Reynolds)*

## Making music come alive

Teachers should be talking about the composers as people, not just as names that wrote music. Usually, teachers only talk about the piece of music, those black marks on a white page that students put on the stand. We say, "Nothing happens until somebody makes it come alive, until they take it off the page and put it out there for people to hear and understand. You have to make the music come alive through being soft or loud and fast or slow."

The other way to make music come alive is to know things about the composer. Use the popular movies such as Amadeus as an example. Tell them a little about Mozart, but not everything about Mozart. Tell them something that shows that Mozart was a real person, who was just brilliant from the very beginning of his life. Tell them that Mozart died very early, and this and that was behind this music.

The movie *Around Midnight* with Dexter Gordon was released recently. The audience never knew that it was about the life of the pianist Bud Powell, not the saxophone player. Bud Powell was the man who was befriended by that Frenchman. There is another movie about Charlie Parker produced by Clint Eastwood that is interesting. Evidently Eastwood is a big jazz lover.

There is a man who performs a live portrayal of Chopin who plays piano very well. He is dressed as Chopin and talks about his friend George Sand. Then, you find out that George was really a woman. I have seen that performance and thought, "What a great way to understand more about a composer!"

*(Robert Morsch)*

## The nature of music learning

I believe it is very important to use the ear, to go beyond reading, to think, to invent, and to play—not just finger the instrument. This helps us go below the surface.

*(Anthony J. Maiello)*

## Teaching techniques and the Hawthorne Effect

In general, all teaching techniques come from the physiological effect called the Hawthorne effect. Any amount of change produces better results. When a kid is in a group, he is sitting in the same chair for four years or one year—I mean, what kind of newness is that?

For example, to change balance sometimes it's fun to rehearse the music with kids sitting in different chairs. Change their seating so like-instrument timbres are sitting

together. *Ye Bonnie Banks and Braes* or something of Grainger has paired a third clarinet, second flute, and muted third alto sax, but they are seated all over the band. Why not sit them together in rehearsal and possibly in performance? I think the gains from it are clear. First, they begin to realize they are playing something with someone else and they are playing the same or different instrument; they realize that there's a timbre issue here.

They also are sitting in a different seat and that alone is a neat and an exciting change for them, because the routine is altered. Having something new is the Hawthorne idea and this change produces some natural listening. When they return to their original seat, their listening increases and they now are listening across the group. You can see they are beginning to play as though band were chamber music.

*(Larry Rachleff)*

## The ensemble should know the work

They should understand the piece and I constantly emphasize that. I do a lot of analysis, not over-analysis, but I want that group to know the form of the work as well as I do. If they do, then we really have something together; that's teaching again.

*(Richard J. Suddendorf)*

## Competition

We're in the arts and what bothers me are competitions. I'm not a competition person at all and I'm very upset with the marching bands who prepare and perform one show for months and months. They are not really in music education. Instead, we should be dealing with the artistic aspects in rehearsals all the time; that will keep music in schools.

*(Richard J. Suddendorf)*

## The demands upon a musician

Music makers must have the ability to make the horns work—to make the horns go—so the instruments can be an accurate voices for them. I think that the demands of the music are multi-faceted. Music demands many technical skills, demands certain control skills, and demands certain colors and abilities. The performer, then, must have at his command a level of flexibility and mastery with the instrument to meet music's demands.

The technique necessary to play instruments is also at several different levels. There has to be the purely physical, the intellectual, the technical problem solving, and the creative problem solving. So, when one thinks, "How can I make this result happen?" There has to be the idea, there has to be the ability to hear what is supposed to happen. This must be in their mind before it happens through the horn. Those are all technical things that one can teach at various levels to people with various abilities to respond.

*(Charles Olson)*

### Ideas that guide the instructor

I always spend time conquering certain things that deal with mastering the instrument technically. This determines how well the student can play on the horn. These include scales, finger patterns, articulation patterns, repeated interval studies, chromatic studies, tone development, range development, facility—all those things are put together. The intention is to get the students to understand that they must have technical mastery of the instrument. There should be nothing in the music that can stump them, as far as playing the notes in the right place, at the right tempo with accuracy, and with good sound. That's purely a mechanical idea. There's no expression necessarily involved with this aspect of playing an instrument.

*(Charles Olson)*

### Rehearsal behavior

Do not assume students will teach themselves how to act in rehearsal. They do not know how to apply the proper disciplines. Many teachers assume they do not need to teach this, but teachers must teach them everything. For example, they should stop playing when you stop rehearsing to make a comment. You may need to practice these kinds of things.

Learning rehearsal behavior is a positive activity when we do it that way. It acknowledges that we need to work on it. We don't criticize someone because they aren't doing it right. We just acknowledge this as we would something as simple as this: "Look, this is the way you release the ball in the bowling alley. I know that you are not doing it right, so here is the way to do it."

*(Charles Olson)*

### Training them to do, or training them to react artistically

There is always the question if rehearsal time is being wasted when, for example, one tries different versions of a phrase. But, if you train them to respond in one particular way, you will have to train them again and again and again, each time they encounter a new phrase. When you do it this way, you're not training them to think or to react artistically. You are telling them what to do and they're doing what you say. In other words, you are training them as you would a dog. With the dog, we say "Sit, sit . . . !" until the dog gets it right. Then, we think, "I'm a great trainer."

There is a difference between enlightening (educating) and training. I think training is a part of what we need to do for our players. I think if that's all that they get, if they're trained meticulously to react like the dog or a machine, then there is a basic question to ask. "Is that music? Is that the way to make music?"

If preparing concerts are more important than the students' growth, then maybe you have scheduled too many concerts. There are times when we all get under pressure, where we have to say, "For the sake of saving time, we are going to do the passage this way." But, if you have so many concerts scheduled that you must approach the band and the music that way from the beginning through the end of your teaching year, there's never time to teach. Then you should examine your philosophy to look at what you're doing. Look at whether you're overcommitted. If you're committed to a schedule that doesn't allow any learning, then maybe something is wrong with that schedule.

*(Eugene Corporon)*

### Varying the rehearsal

The varying of rehearsal has an enormous amount to do with the attitude of the person in the rehearsal. The attitude in the rehearsal is as important as getting the musical things done because you'll get them done better with a commitment from the players; that is why varying is so important.

You need to look for things in the rehearsal that will break away from a highly concentrated nature—if you have a highly concentrated nature in rehearsal. If someone bought a new instrument or somebody has this or whatever, make mention of it; this also personalizes it for people in the ensemble. I also think just the simple thing of knowing everybody's name and calling them by name in rehearsal instead of saying "2nd oboe" adds to the personalization of everyone.

*(H. Robert Reynolds)*

### The type of rehearsal

For the student, there's a difference between being involved in a process of discovery during rehearsal and being involved in a "do-this-or-do-that rehearsal." A do-this-or-do-that rehearsal style seldom involves students in the process of discovering what is wrong, and how they think they can fix it.

Most people I have watched are very good at saying, "That's out of tune," or "That's a wrong note or a wrong rhythm." Finding the problem is the first thing in the teacher's mind, they feel compelled to find that problem. Secondly, a lot of people are good at giving the solution. They say, "Now, to play in tune you always roll out, or you do this, or you always do that, etc."

Many teachers stop at that point. They don't take it to the next step where the player experiences the solution. If students do not experience the solution, the teacher will need to make a long list of corrections. The players will never hear them and never experience them either.

This reminds me of a great Far Side cartoon. It shows this man talking to a dog. The cartoon says, "What people say to their dogs." They say " . . . Ginger sit, Ginger roll over, Ginger heel, etc." Then the next panel says, "What dogs hear." "Ginger, blah, blah, blah . . . Ginger, blah, blah, blah, Ginger, etc." This is the same thing musicians hear when their conductors talk. They hear, "Trumpets, blah, blah, blah; Horns, blah, blah, blah."

The musicians don't hear anything past the first word unless the rehearsal is done differently than through the "do-this, do-that" approach. With the other approach, We could say "Horns let's play at letter B. Tell me, are you ahead or behind the beat?" Sometimes just asking that question solves the problem—no further work is needed. You don't have to say, "Third horn you're ahead, second horn you're behind, etc." You only have to say, "Notice whether you're ahead or behind the beat," or "Notice whether you're sharp or flat."

You also could explore the possibilities. "Let's play that chord out of tune everybody, now let's play it in tune. How does playing in tune feel versus playing out of tune feel?" I'll ask junior high kids, "Does out of tune playing feel good?" and they'll look at you and say, "Oh no!" They'll make these faces and they tighten their face muscles. They understand the minute it is out of tune and you'd be amazed at how quickly it changes.

On the other hand, if the teacher uses the "do-this or do that" approach and explains, that teacher may think the students understand because he has explained something clearly. They don't understand: they repeat the mistake over and over again! Then that teacher says, "I've told you a million times over and over and over—can't you remember to play short!"

The problem is the students have never cataloged the feeling of short at that moment in that piece, because the teacher has never led them to that. Therefore, they are not going to remember because they have not experienced the change vividly enough to remember it. If that is not happening, then we will hear teachers say many times, "What does piano mean?" They say, "Oh, it means soft."

I think the skills in a rehearsal that increase awareness in a rehearsal are really obvious. I've never been in a rehearsal where these skills haven't been used. They are: what you see, what you feel, what you hear, and what you already know, which is the buried knowledge. There is another point that many people leave out; and the point is, what can you imagine? How does your imagination interact with that rehearsal? How can you create in an involvement of the students with the solution?

We are pretty skilled at finding the errors, but we are not as skilled at leading people to a solution that sticks. We do the first part well, which is giving information and making a diagnosis. That is important, because you've got to be able to know whether it's sharp or flat. However, the implementing is what's so tough.

At first it seems efficient to give them the answer. Then we begin to realize that this approach is really inefficient. Let's face it though, there are times when it's much more efficient to say, "Please, you are out of tune, work on it" when they seem to be totally lost. When they are sharp or flat, or the pulse is rushing, sometimes it's more efficient to just solve it. There are times, though, if you stop and you say "Why did I stop?" They all say that

they are rushing, because they all feel it too. They adjust and solve it on their own.

*(Eugene Corporon)*

### The importance of reading

Sight reading ability is the most accurate measure of a musician. I have been hearing bands for years and it is apparent to me that little is done in this respect. Teachers who avoid the teaching of sight reading are short sighted. Amateurs and professionals are different in two respects: their consistency as a player and their ability to read. An amateur reads well below his performance level, a professional reads nearly or at his performance level. We read everyday because it does so much for the group. Not only will they read well, it reduces rehearsal time considerably. Daily sight reading also increases the musical discrimination opportunities for the conductor and the students because they can experience a vast amount of literature.

*(Butler R. Eitel)*

### The core of music experience

Though my approach changes with the age group, the common goal for all ages is an aesthetic and emotional experience through their participation in music. Their aptitudes and their expectations change for their certain experiences. I feel very strongly that music comes alive when people are involved. Music is of little value resting in a file drawer. Even studying a score is not complete without some kind of release through human contact. In this respect, the response of younger students is much the same as older students.

*(William W. Wiedrich)*

### Making music making meaningful

The first stage is preparation and the second stage is trying to relate something of the music to their experience in real life. I try to make some relationship between what they are doing in their musical experience and what they have experienced in their real life. With this connection, you can give them more of an aesthetic experience to enhance that connection.

The concert or the performance is but the result. The actual process occurs in the rehearsals and in the sensitization processes that occur during rehearsals. The concert is just kind of a finality, the by-product of what has been happening in rehearsals. Good feelings in a situation of learning or in a situation of aesthetic learning will reflect in a concert. The concert brings all of this to closure.

*(William W. Wiedrich)*

### Considering where the student comes from

Teachers have thought about many things and we have an idea of what something is. However, the kids necessarily haven't. Teachers can't just throw things at students and expect them to have the understanding of what they are trying to accomplish.

Because of their real life situation—meaning their experiences, age, background, aptitude, motivation, education, or environment—everyone looks at their musical experience in a different way. Trained musicians have a certain expectation from a performance either as a player or as a listener. It also changes depending on the good or bad experiences they have had. Music can mean something to everyone. It's the teachers' responsibility not only to broaden their scope, but also make sure that people understand that it does apply to them where they are at the moment.

If I'm teaching a junior high group, I am not going to relate the musical concepts and the teaching as I would do with a thirty year old. If you work at the Oldsmobile factory in Lansing, you're not going to get the same thing out of a Bruckner symphony that Bob Reynolds from Michigan will get with graduate students.

On the other hand I feel a responsibility to expose music to people who may not have the educational depth of a graduate student. There are many different aspects of music and I can try to let them appreciate some of them. In a junior high clinic situation one will try to relate things to what they listen to, which is absolutely on the mark. However, if you relate everything to Michael Jackson, Prince, Sting, or whoever the currently hot popular performer is, then you are doing just as much damage as if you left these stars totally out of the picture. We need to use the stars when appropriate because we aren't living in the 1890's, we are living in the 1990's. When students grow up, they aren't expected to go to chamber music concerts for their Saturday night fun. This is not their way of thinking.

There is so much in common among all music. I always remember Leonard Bernstein's comment at the Grammys. He said, "The best artists through the years were so and so, so and so, and Tina Turner." To me that was a real neat thing to say. It took everybody aback, because with his musical background he knows where to put her in the line of things. To relate to their real life situation, you want the people in that group—with the help of your efforts—to find something in that music to be interesting and be meaningful to them.

Then, you want to broaden and build upon what they know at that point. Find new ways for them to understand and relate to the music. Their age, experience, or background is a backdrop that helps the teacher decide how he is going to involve the students. This helps you relate to them and relate them to the music. Then, after I can relate to their experience, I try to broaden their experience and their idea.

*(William W. Wiedrich)*

### How and what we teach

If students have limited technical ability, this can limit their aesthetic experiences. A teacher, then, has a responsibility to achieve a balance of technical and musi-

cal issues. Goals such as intonation, fingering, sight reading, listening, articulation, embouchure, posture, breathing, and all of that has a very, very important place in everyone's learning from the beginning, all the way up to the college level. These must, though, be balanced with the aesthetic experiences.

You can't have one or the other. I can't go into rehearsal and just drill, drill, drill. On the other hand, I can't go into an experience with a younger group, just wave the stick and expect something musical to come rushing out. Their technical abilities are limited; I can only teach through the skills they have. I try to relate those technical needs and teaching to music as an aesthetic medium. Instead of saying, "Johnny and Bonnie, please listen to each other. You have to make that E flat in tune." We try to relate the skill learning to the piece, to the tendency of their instruments, to what is necessary for the phrase or the line, to why that should be in tune, and that this sensitivity applies not only to Johnny and Bonnie but to everybody in the ensemble.

I can give an alternate B flat fingering, tell them to take more reed in their mouth, say their reed's too soft or too hard, or the trumpet needs a cleaning or a third valve adjustment, or the flutes shouldn't rest their elbows on their hips. You can do that, but the teacher also can say, "Now listen, listen to how, at this point in the music we need a velvety, gorgeous warm tone. Now, what do you think we mean by gorgeous, velvety, warm tone?" Then they look at you. Then you say, "Will everybody put your elbows down on your hips; okay, now blow." The teacher can look at the clarinets and say, "Does that sound velvety to you? Now everybody, be relaxed but lift up your right hand. Let's go over the same line and put as much intensity as you can in that air flow." Then, this different sound comes out and you look over to the clarinets and say, "Does that sound more velvety to you?" They will say, "Yeah." I'll say, "See, if you can keep that right elbow up you're going to get a lot more velvety tone. Here, the music demands this because we are in the lower register or you're blending with such and such and you need to play into the sound of others."

There are also time constraints. If you're in a dress rehearsal and you have an alto saxophone duet that's terribly out of tune you're going to say, "Hey, you're flat, your sharp, fix it," and go on. In the teaching experience, the concert is a result and it's a goal: but, it's a result of a learning process. The concert is a chance to show what you've done, not the final evaluation.

*(William W. Wiedrich)*

### The magic of sound

We would like people to become more aware of the magic of sound; this is what the expressive part of music is. We become more and more aware of how these sounds are organized: and the more aware we become of them, the more attractive the sounds become. The more we manipulate them, the more we create things that are interesting. The people who do this well rise to the top like cream and become the Frederick Fennells.

*(James Croft)*

### The individual and the ensemble

Each player must be well grounded in fundamentals through their prior training. When they become a member of a concert band, their individual training should continue. But, as a band member, their instruments are now parts among many players and instruments. These players and instruments must now form a unified group so the band itself is then a single instrument. Their instruments now must contribute to a new sound. All the fundamentals they are learning must be reconsidered in relation to the new environment: the new environment is their section, their instrument family, and the ensemble as a whole.

*(Mark H. Hindsley)*

# CHAPTER TWO

# TEACHING

The comments in this section address several important issues about teaching. The ideas concern the effects of the teacher's personality, and his attitudes, skills, and responsibilities. The comments also reflect important influences and concerns of the teacher, such as the necessity of enthusiasm, the continuance of the teacher's own growth, the effect of the teacher as a role model, and speculations about the future direction of bands and orchestras.

## Characteristics of a teacher

I look for these characteristics in teachers: (1) A secure person who has excellent musical skills, and is a well-trained and good musician. Without this you will not be able to convince the people you are working with that you know what you are doing. The untrained can tell if you know something. The concept "if you can't do, then teach" is the source of one of our problems. (2) I look for someone to take positive control of the situation. Having lots of musical skill or knowledge does not make one able to do this. Students must feel you are in charge and capable. It is important that you are a good subject-matter role model. The chance for personal identification by the students is important. (3) I want them to have a system of rhythmic instruction that is well planned and technically well supported so it can be thoroughly taught.

*(George R. Bedell)*

The personality of the teacher, makes a strong stamp on the way the band sounds and the way someone teaches. In my case, John Whitwell had the biggest impact upon me. He influenced me about what was most important in music and in life. He conveyed the way he believed and how I now believe. His personality, values and beliefs showed a way to treat people.

My desire to do this came from his impact upon me during seven years from junior high through high school. My musical values were formed in this period; I know that I have inherited his musical values. He believed that the important aspect of playing musically, even if there were imperfections in the performance, was to feel, after playing, that it was a moving and musical experience.

*(Patricia Brumbaugh)*

## The director as a role model

The director can help students learn many important behaviors simply by being a good role model. The director can motivate the students, teach them promptness, work ethics, punctuality, efficiency, responsibility, and respect through his actions. Here are some examples of behaviors that I try to show daily so I can consistently be a role model for my students through my non-musical and musical behavior: (1) I am at the door to greet the students as they come into the rehearsal or lesson room. I make comments to them, if possible, that show I am interested in them, what they are doing, or what is happening in the school. (2) I never start late. (3) I have my music ready and in order. (4) I have lesson plans and objectives. (5) I work hard and efficiently at every rehearsal or lesson. (6) I respect the students' problems and provide them with suggestions that might help them find solutions. (7) I keep my promises. (8) I keep the band and lesson rooms clean and neat. (9) I do not make fun of students when they have problems, though I do use humor where appropriate. (10) I am always at the door as the students are leaving the room. (11) I take time to say hello when I see the students away from the rehearsal or lesson room. (12) I never give up on my students. (13) I keep trying to solve problems. (14) I exhibit patience and self-control. (15) I remain a student myself, and keep working on my performance skills and my teaching skills.

*(Roman Palmer)*

## Be professional

Be professional and attend workshops, conventions, in-service meetings, etc. to learn new techniques and ideas from your colleagues. Belong and contribute to the related organizations such as MENC, ASTA, NSOA, and SSA.

*(Dale Kempter)*

## Teachers need to know

We *all* need to know more about literature and musical style, and have a good sense of musical taste.

*(Carl A. Bly)*

None of us has the education or the talent to develop an aural image of how a piece should sound as much as we would like to have. How much one has varies so much in its amount; and some teachers hardly have this at all. But, it is like any technique, one can develop it with study over time. Even though the inner ear has to be very strong at the outset for it to be developed—one can get better at using it. Hearing is a technique; like doing cross-word puzzles, one does them and one learns vocabulary. One can learn— if one uses his inner ear, the inner ear gets better.

*(H. Robert Reynolds)*

## Teaching style

My teaching style is one of giving suggestions and information. I give these to students so they learn how to play the music and their instruments, and how to think for themselves. I am interested in teaching and if I would receive a comment, I would prefer it to be that I am seen as a good teacher.

*(Stanley Cate)*

## Thoughts about teaching

A good deal of what my thinking is, what I am about, is in the book and teacher's manual for *Total Musicianship*. The book starts with some thoughts about making music meaningful.

*(Frank Bencriscutto)*

## Views of teaching and conducting change

The band director's profession is even younger than the music education profession. Our models such as Revelli or Hindsley often were not trained as educators. Their model was of an autocratic conductor and they had only a loose belief, though strong, that contact with music was beneficial. They knew it had enriched their own lives and they concluded that making music was enough, without a realization that much of the work they were doing in their rehearsals to refine performance was what we would now call sub-musical.

This model of teacher has had a tremendous limiting influence on our field. We had these people who were revered as band directors before we, as students, could understand much about what was important in the musical experience and before we knew what the implications were for structuring rehearsals and classes in music education. Now the tragedy is, that our best music educators find difficulty using new ideas, because they fall back on an older model of music instruction. They are not apt to think of us who promote a newer, or different approach. Instead, they imitate the teaching they experienced as students.

*(Donald Casey)*

## A trend toward music making

In the United States and the world, people who teach band are getting more in tune with what real music is. I do not know if the larger proportion of them are any different or are changing in this way, but there are more people who

are climbing on the "we are in the profession of music-making," band wagon.

*(H. Robert Reynolds)*

## Excellent teachers

These teachers are very curious, interested and challenged as they seek the answer to the questions. One question is, "How do we teach what?" Earning degrees mean that the teacher is musically knowledgeable, but not skilled as a teacher of music. Degrees also do not mean they have operant musical skills. They are knowledgeable in the realms such as information, scores, or composers. However, there have no or little training in the ability to teach.

*(James Froseth)*

## Training the teacher to evaluate

While we can say that we know a good teacher when we see one, good teaching is made up of many little parts. It is complex and yet it isn't so complex. Engineering a program to train people to have all these little parts, or even some of them, is an interesting problem. It is a challenge to decide what makes a good teacher and to develop a program to do this.

One view is that of the medical schools, who say, "You have to *know* and you have to *do*." We don't have the "doing" as a training experience in music education, or teacher training in any field. Medical schools say, even if you know, if you cannot diagnose, you are a poor doctor. Teachers also must diagnose well. As complex as diagnosis is, if the program is structured so students both know and do, we would be on the right track—that is the simple explanation.

*(James Froseth)*

## Quality teaching

It all boils down to musicianship, and that is not a new idea.

*(James Froseth)*

## What is crucial for the conductor

There are four important points:
   a. enthusiasm for one's work and responsibility.
   b. ability to adjust priorities in a rehearsal.
   c. consistency in manner, emotional character, and purpose.
   d. mental, musical, and physical preparation is needed for conducting and teaching.

The only other major point that is important to make, is the individual personality. Everybody who is a conductor or teacher has his own personality, and developing that is a life-long process. It is incumbent upon us to do that. It is the development of this thing, which happens to be you because you cannot be someone else. Believe me, we can run this idea back through the previous four points and that is what makes us what we are. We must constantly be on top of what we are doing. That is why there is no such thing as a finished score, it is only at that particular point in transit, that is about all.

(Frederick Fennell)

### Consistency in the teacher

We must not come in one day and have a tirade about how poor the dynamics are: then the next day say they are very good, when they really aren't. Blowing your lid doesn't do much of anything. Sometimes we have the tendency to be inconsistent and students do not understand that. Having a new perspective on the music is one thing, but ranting and raving one day about something is irrelevant—even damaging. A conductor must be careful with any age, level, intensity, or depth. He must be accountable, people must always know what he is doing and people must always know that he means exactly what he says. I do not think inconsistency accomplishes much at all. One also must have a consistent vision of how the music is to sound.

One result is that lots of people do not know where they stand. A conductor must be consistent in policy, in whom he is, and the way he does what he does. This is true for any conductor at any level—I repeat my words.

We should come to our day's work, even with a different uniform from that we wear in the classroom. A different shirt from when you are the home room guy, a special professional garment, either formal or informal in style. A garment associated with that event—with no papers and pencils sticking out of the pocket. Stripped down for work. I think one also should be physically prepared for work, thus we must stay in shape. These concerns have to do with how we conduct or teach.

(Frederick Fennell)

### Preparation for the rehearsal

Preparation is not just mental. We must also prepare the music at hand, the present state of the group, and what is ahead to be done. The mental attitude that one brings to the podium can be sensed, as clearly and as surely as anything can be. This is something we can't overlook. Some people feel that they have difficulty become accepted, being taken as a serious person. The conductor has to take his preparation and mental attitude seriously, and if so, others will take him seriously. Part of this is also a matter of plan. We are all told about teaching plans, and the like: there must also be a rehearsal plan. A rehearsal has an architecture: rehearsals should not end on a poor note. Psychologically, rehearsals can't all end like one had just roared through the end of the 5th Symphony of Beethoven, or the Stars and Stripes Forever, if that happens to be your dish. But all rehearsals must have an architecture that leads people into a quiet mood, an exhilarated mood, whatever—and that is something that conductors can and must control.

(Frederick Fennell)

### The emergence of the "clinic"

After World War II there was an enormous outbreak of clinics, everything was a clinic and I got to a point where I was beginning to smell the ether and not the music. Everything was a clinic and it was wonderful—this necessary complete exposure of people to how you do this— how much of the lower lip do you roll under, how much of the upper lip to do this way or that. How do you sit, stand, take the initial breath, how do you sustain the breath—all these things! It was endless, this incredible state of technical information that came from the greatest players in the second half of the Twentieth Century.

They were all the men who made their living playing the instruments, not writing articles about it, but playing the instrument. They were the ones that were to be seen everywhere. There were people coming down out of commercial radio telling us what it was to be a commercial player. Studios players came from New York, Los Angeles, and Chicago—unloading on people what they have to do. They told us how to choose an instrument, how to do this, how to do that, how to do etc.

I must say that it was very necessary because there were then, and there still are, an awful lot of people who do not know those basic things as well as they should know them. There also are people who know it, and don't know how to apply it, and it is all down the drain. They just don't know what to do with the information.

(Frederick Fennell)

### Painting by the numbers

Too many teachers are teaching young students to follow the marks; "We need this to be one notch louder here," "Make a crescendo here," or "Your mezzo forte is too loud." Following the marks is like painting by the numbers and one is not having any artistic experience through that kind of "painting." It is better to have an image of a bird in your head and paint that, than it is to paint the bird by the numbers even if one alters the shades of the colors. If the bird is always there and its image has been given to us, all one has left to do is pick the color or change the color—one is not changing the image or idea of the bird.

I think a lot of people are teaching as though they are painting by the numbers all along; there are a lot of others, who are teaching very creatively. One can see that teachers are moving in the direction of teaching creatively and colleges are hiring the creative musician as the band director, more and more. These band directors are going to be influencing the people who are going out to teach— they cannot help but do that.

(H. Robert Reynolds)

### We must be what we are

As much as we pick up from other teachers, one must remember to be ourselves, there is no way you can be someone else. Even if you copy or take certain things, you must develop them within your own personality, your own vocabulary. One also cannot interpret pieces the way another person does, at least not exactly—one will ultimately come to one's own version or view.

*(Robert Grechesky)*

### Care for and feed your own musical growth

I think there is a reason for band director burn out. If band directors don't care for their growth, they will stop growing as a teacher.

*(Richard K. Hansen)*

### Be interested in the process not in the end result

To be effective, and to live with yourself as a teacher and as a conductor, you have to do this. I think that if you're in this only for the applause at the concert, then you'd better not stay in the business. There will come a day when that applause will not fulfill your ego, and you'd better be interested in watching students grow musically and socially. The teacher must be interested in that process, because that's where the real joy in teaching is if one stays in for the long haul.

Good performances may happen for a year or two, but then those students are going to graduate. I see friends who are so frustrated because of the musical end of things. I understand that frustration, but at the same time I think, "These are the guys who are going to burn out in seven or eight years, and they're not going to be in the profession much longer." This point needs to be impressed on young teachers: if you're in it for the applause, get out.

*(Michael Kaufman)*

### Teacher Attitude

The conductor's attitude in rehearsal is very important: you must generate excitement about the day's tasks. You will get back from your students only what you give. Be sure to build on the accomplishment from one day to the next.

*(Steven McNeal)*

### Band programs may be changing

We can observe in any era that not everyone embraces modern and innovative ideas; some director's views and techniques hark back to the previous era. We also can observe that everything occurring now is not great, but everything that occurred previously was not great either. For example, often there are different values assigned to the medium, the participants, and the content. Therefore, we can expect that in instrumental music, the interest in the ensemble, the performers and students, and the music can vary in intensity and proportion.

It is not surprising then, if we study and compare eras, that we discover that the many elements differ; the concern for one is not always equal to the concern for another, some overshadow others. For example, there is much more and much better literature now compared to

pre-1954. On the other hand, the life style and attitudes of students, especially their interests and preparation is very different from those students in instrumental groups forty years ago. Students then were more teacher and authority-centered; students now show more democratic and independent leanings at times.

Bands, teachers, and schools also change. In any era, there is balance between those with a innovative bent and those with a traditional bent. Thus, there are teachers who believe as the older teachers did, and there are teachers who have set aside some of the conventional beliefs and have sought new ideas.

One trend with momentum is toward concerns for music literature and experience, and the individual's education in music, not toward polishing the band's performance for its own sake or as an end result.

Since band music and band programs are also changing, this is a much broader field than it once was. Our first band at Michigan, for example, is very different from what it used to be. Inside the Symphony Band, which has eighty-five players, there are also wind ensembles in which nearly everyone plays. We give concerts that include serenades, orchestral wind pieces, etc. We also have a contemporary music ensemble inside the Symphony Band. We have five "cracker-jack" string players, and a DMA pianist, so we are doing mixed strings and wind pieces, as part of the Wind Ensemble.

What I am interested in is a band program that is doing the best music regardless of instrumentation. (I am not going to build much of a band dynasty that way!) If there are pieces for mixed strings and winds, and for winds and percussion—then, why not play them? So, we do contemporary music, wind ensemble, mixed strings, wind and percussion, and full band pieces on our concerts. This reflects the idea that the literature and the music experience is at least as important as the polish of the band. I think going in this direction is natural, but some say, "Boy, *that* is a revolutionary idea." It *is not* a revolutionary idea: it is the most natural thing in the world!

The band program used to be more focused and limited. For me, this unlimited and flexible ensemble is what band has become. I do not know of many programs doing what we are doing. But I think more will soon, because it seems too right. The band does not have the limits it once did: the doors are open to innovation and change and I hope that the minds of the conductors and teachers (the inside doors) are also open.

In pre-college, this kind of a band program is more difficult because they have everyone scheduled at the same time. At Michigan, if I want to rehearse with three people and I ask eighty-two people to "go hang-out"; they won't like it and I very, very rarely do it, but I could. However, in high school you *cannot* say, "The rest of you are free this hour."

The flexible and varying arrangement in our band program might deprive *a few* students of some of those moments and hours of rehearsing and playing; but what all of our students get instead of playing every minute of every hour, is a much broader experience. (We also have many players that play in both band and orchestra. So, they are getting plenty of ensemble experience.)

*(H. Robert Reynolds)*

### The state of bands

Things are hurting with bands in our general area. I think our program is solid and sound, but I hear a lot a programs are going downhill and they're going downhill without anybody knowing they're going downhill. These directors are as happy as clams. Particularly at the concert level, I'm hearing a lot of "slop." I don't think I'm getting that picky or that grumpy. I don't know enough directors that are turning me on.

I think there are some major problems. There are not enough good kids that are going into band directing. They do feel as I did, "I want to be a band director; I want a good band." Their response is, "Well, I'll be a band director." The college kids are coming in and watching rehearsals here. I talk to them later and they're not aware of what they've just seen. They watch me run a rehearsal and the kids are excited. They're fun—they're happy and the university kids reaction is a bland, "That's nice." I say, "What did I do?" They don't know; they seem to have missed the whole point.

*(William Long)*

### We should hold students accountable

Often times, we're afraid to hold our students accountable—though accountability is a normal procedure in any of their other classes. I think it has a lot to do with our attitude; as a profession, we are probably a pretty insecure profession.

*(Craig Kirchhoff)*

### The limits of intuition

Intuition means to teach as you were taught, that's how I see it. Therefore, you are limited to your previous experience. You can't tap other people's experience if you deal only with intuition.

*(Robert Allan)*

### The value of professional organizations

There are many things that young teachers could learn coming out of college, if they would go—number one—to the professional organizations and clinics. They also could find someone within driving distance where they could visit for a day or two. They could find out how these teachers do things. That would help them develop some of their ideas about what to do and what it takes.

*(Lewis Larson)*

### Honesty and commitment

One thing that's important to me in this band is honesty and trusting each other. I teach honesty, fairness, and commitment. If kids disappoint me I let them know. Sometimes parents get on my back because they think I embarrass kids. If you handle that right, it does work. I think that the honesty, the fairness and the commitment are very important.

If we're going to march on Memorial Day, no one is going to be absent without a pass from their folks saying that they're going to be with them. I want a note from the parents. If the parents lie, that's up to them because I honor the parent's signature. Then, they've taken responsibility. I can't adjust their lives and I don't ask anything from those kids I wouldn't do myself.

*(Frank Schulz)*

### Setting standards begins with the teacher's behavior

I have noticed that good directors set good examples. If you're teaching a group lesson and you're sitting down, you don't slouch in the chair. Sit up the same way you're asking the kids to sit. I have my kids sit on about the first three or four inches of the chair and I do the same thing when I'm teaching. I don't sit back in the chair. I don't "take a nap" and slouch. I learned that early when I was teaching in another town. One of the directors was not very good with that. He always made his kids tuck in their shirts and look super for concerts, yet he was kind of slovenly. One of the kids said, "Oh, man, working with him is something! Why do I have to dress-up when he looks like . . . ." That always sticks in my mind. I think kids need good examples. The junior high kids really take that pretty seriously. Even younger kids, when you're sitting on a chair, will try to mimic exactly what you're doing. If you do it the right way, they will do it the right way!

*(Sandra P. Thompson)*

### The teacher's main responsibilities

We have the students' growth, the advancement of the profession, the listener's growth, and our own personal growth in mind: all four are part of what we do. Part of our concern for students' growth, and perhaps the advancement of our profession, is educating the parents. Some teachers send home a monthly newsletter, and say to their parents, "This month we're studying the ABA form and when you come to the concert next week, you are going to hear three different pieces that all have ABA form." I may have asked students to write a piece that has ABA form.

We must help parents and others understand that what we're doing is not on the fringe, it's not a frill, it's something that's really part of understanding life in general. I think many teachers forget to keep their parents informed. They assume that a trophy for concert or marching band brings, to the parent, validity for what they're doing.

*(Eugene Corporon)*

## Some clues left by conductors and teachers

More people are owning their own scores. This didn't used to be the case; the school owned the scores. Owning one's own score is one sign of a good conductor. I can ask a few questions and I can usually tell the quality of the conductor just as I can tell how good a player is by watching him take the horn out of the case. I look for a familiarity, a routine, and a casualness because they've done that so many times, just as I can ask how many scores somebody has. I'd like to look for other tell-tale signs such as his record or compact disc collection.

*(H. Robert Reynolds)*

## After four years

We try to recruit students to play in the campus band, which is a non-major group. We run into some kids who own Buffet clarinets who play well. They say, "I don't ever want to do anything in music again, I hate it." You think, my God, after four years of high school, that's what's happened to them, they hate music? They feel abused and they feel used up. You would think the mark of a great music program is that someone would say, "You know I want to stay in music the rest of my life, in a community band or orchestra, I just can't do without it!" I may not make my living at it, but I had such a great experience with it I want it to be part of my life.

*(Eugene Corporon)*

## A statement of philosophy

As teacher, one can be a strong fixer and a weak shaper. There is an old cartoon that I love, one with all these weird little figures standing there, there may be thousands of them with a mob-like look. In the cartoon, much effort was spent getting the figures to stand at attention. One says to the other, "Well now that we've got them lined up, what in the hell are we going to do with them."

That's the way it is with music: once we've got it all lined up, and proper and fixed, what is it? What are we going to do with it? Fixing up, lining up, and making music should all be done at once, or all along. It's the idea of growth. When you grow as a person you grow all at once. You don't say, "Gee I'm going to grow my right arm, I'm just going to grow my articulation today, or I'm just going to grow my left arm today. Instead, we separate the music out from the notes and put it aside." Craig Kirchhoff once said, "When does the technique ever get good enough to start working on the music?" The answer to that could be never; you might as well do the music all the way along.

*(Eugene Corporon)*

## Conductor and teacher are synonymous

I think conductor and teacher in my mind are synonymous: you cannot be one without being the other. Sometimes teachers don't think of themselves enough as conductors, and vice versa. Some of my colleagues who are conductors don't understand their value as a teacher.

*(Eugene Corporon)*

## Burn-out

You have to be interested in your own growth and your own growth comes in many ways: it's technical, it's intellectual, it's philosophical, it's spiritual—it's lots of things. Any of us who have the responsibility of teaching, also have the responsibility of remaining a student and growing. I think many people shut down and say, "I don't need to know that." That's the scariest thing in the world to me, for an educator to ever say, "I don't need to know that, I won't ever use that."

*(Eugene Corporon)*

## The value of what we do

I think the value of what we do is to get people to be in touch with their feelings and to find what's unique about music: not what's the same, but what's unique about making music. There's a wonderful article by Gloria Kiester who is on the faculty at St. Olaf. It is a great article about music in schools. It is one of the shortest articles and one of the most powerful I've ever read. One of her statements is, "The music belongs in schools, not because it's fun and entertaining, not because it's relaxing and socializing, even though it's all of these. Music belongs in schools because it is basic to learning and it's a unique way of knowing yourself."

*(Eugene Corporon)*

## Evaluating band directors

Compare band directors to the best opera and orchestra conductors. If we fall short, study and emulate them instead of comparing ourselves to last year's winning "sweepstakes" conductor.

*(Butler R. Eitel)*

## The teacher's responsibility

Visit rehearsals and listen to recordings, so one becomes an indefatigable scholar who reads and studies the profound writings of many non-musicians' books. If you only know music, you don't know music. Musicianship demands an extensive base. It isn't everything, it is the only thing.

*(Butler R. Eitel)*

## The depth principle

There can be a growth process for a conductor and he must try to continue increasing his own musical depth. Each conductor has a musical depth and each piece also has a musical depth. *Instant Concert* may be the piece with less musical depth than any piece I've ever known, the slow movement from Mahler's Fourth symphony or the slow movement of Beethoven's Ninth Symphony are pieces of great depth. A middle-of-the-roader would be *Irish Tune*, which is a piece of substance but not the depth of Mahler or Beethoven.

A person of very shallow musicianship can actually conduct *Irish Tune* quite well and have it come out nicely. Someone with greater musical depth can bring out more of its depth. Ideally, we are trying to match up our depth with the piece, so we are selecting pieces to conduct so that our depth is at least as great as the pieces. The problem is, you can't really become a deeper musician if you only are acquainted with pieces at your own depth. You have to be acquainted and work with pieces of greater depth than you are ready for at that time.

People very often have very little depth yet they can stand up and conduct a piece because the technique required isn't so much. The piece will sound okay, but it just won't have—I mean, if Donald Duck conducted Mahler's Ninth Symphony and knew all the gestures, and had terrific and experienced players it would come out okay. However, if Giulini or Von Karajan conducts, it would be a whole different experience because of the depth of the music interpreter.

If the teacher studies only the works of a typical band composer, he's not going to be deep enough. He must be well acquainted with the late quartets of Beethoven, the Beethoven piano sonatas, and the Mahler symphonies among others. Then, because he has done or is doing that kind of study, when he goes to *Air For Band* by Frank Erickson, he'll get from *Air For Band* what's really there. Without depth, one cannot bring forth musical substance.

*(H. Robert Reynolds)*

### The teacher's growth and its direction

Much of the quality of teaching has to do with a person's own determination to grow. I see many people who are willing to polish what they already know, but somehow they do not investigate new things, do new things, or stretch themselves in one way or another. Their attitude seems to be, "I know these things and if I work really hard, I'll know them even better." But the broadening, the deepening needed to be a deeper musician is most important. The hardest thing that someone in Resume Speed, Nebraska faces is to maintain their growth because they're not surrounded by really good concerts, as found in Chicago or Ann Arbor. But they can get the New York Times to find out what's going on in New York, discover what people are playing, read the record and CD guides, and hear

what is out there; get on a regular program of reading and listening.

Well, some band directors many not even like music, or they may only like instruments; some of these people just like to build a machine; a power program. I think they may have come to relish fame and glory; that's the big promoter. They may do whatever they can to gain fame and glory in their community or in their state. They say to themselves, "What do I have to do to become famous. What do I have to do to get a college job; how do I get I's at contest; how do I win this medal or this trophy; how long will it take me to get a great marching band." Whatever is the way toward fame and glory, they will take that path and pay tribute to the giver of fame and glory. They seek fame or recognition, instead of asking themselves, "What should a student want; what do I want as a musician, what should my students need to become musically educated people?" They haven't answered let alone asked the question: "What's the root purpose of a band in an educational institution?" People have to ask that of themselves.

Let me back up here; I think the root purpose of a band in an educational institution is to educate the students musically. That's different than the Air Force or the Navy band; they have a different purpose in life. It is not their root purpose to educate the players musically; their purpose is to build spirit for the country, to entertain the audience, and to stimulate good feelings about the armed services and the United States.

Educators have many sub-purposes: these might be social, what is good for the school and the people, and other useful sub-issues; but that's not *the* purpose. People also need to ask the question, "What's the purpose of a concert of a band in an educational institution?" They should teach to those purposes once they've answered the question.

Their answers, though, may be different from mine. But I believe the main purpose—understanding that there can be a lot of ancillary purposes—of a band in an educational institution is to educate the students in that band musically; that's the main purpose of that band.

*(H. Robert Reynolds)*

### Musical aptitude

I believe that a particular talent, like Mozart—the greatest natural talent ever—is the result of a wiring circuitry that is already inborn and is there, waiting to go.

*(Alfred Reed)*

# CHAPTER THREE

# MUSIC MAKING

There are insights into making music that can provoke thought about many important questions: How perfect must the performance be? What is the purpose of a concert? To what extent and how should students be involved? What are some beliefs about the teaching of rhythmic experience? What are the essential experiences for students? How does music making motivate us? What is the challenge of music making? For that matter, just what *is* making music, anyway?

These are pertinent questions for music educators; and if teachers bring some of these questions and answers to the forefront of their thinking, the purpose—the focus and direction—of music education can be made more clear. The result can be instruction and education that is more appropriate considering the importance of music, the substance of music, and its effect upon students.

## How perfect must a performance be?

I am not certain a note-perfect performance is possible from high school, nor should we try to get one. I would prefer having a musical performance that is exciting, that moves the players and the audience even if there are some errors.

*(Patricia Brumbaugh)*

## Teach musical aspects

Though I work on the basics more at first, I always conduct the musical aspects from the beginning. I try to address musical issues always; I don't wait until they learn the notes. The notes are more a homework issue. Why should one take ten minutes of rehearsal time to teach the trombones the notes?

*(Carl A. Bly)*

## We need students involved

With rhythm and many other music concerns such as melody, phrasing, harmony, and the entire experience, I find that people are often on the outside looking in; too many people don't get emotionally and physically involved with music making.

*(Frank Bencriscutto)*

## The power of an idea

We are only as good as our reason for what we do. If our reason is earth shaking, if it is as important for us to make quality music as breathe, then we are going to do things with devotion.

*(Frank Bencriscutto)*

## A sense of time

Underneath the larger idea of time are all the issues of teaching kids a good kinesthetic sense of time, beat, and meter; a sense of rhythm and rhythmic reading, and the skill and understanding needed to phrase musically. These also are part of a sense of time and a sense of line in music. I subsume rhythm and all of its factors under line. I think then, when they get involved in phrasing, they bring to bear all the other issues of good musical performance; they can begin to hear issues such as a good quality sound, dynamic contrast, and articulation.

When I talk about phrasing, I'm talking about time as several phenomenons; time in the sense when we experience how much time it takes psychologically, to hear the three parts of a ternary form. We also have real time—clock time—that would be meter and accurate rhythm; We have psychological time, which is phrasing and finishing a phrase with a nice sense of finality; and we have the sense of time we experience when we hear or perform tension and release within phrases.

The developing of their sense of time is an idea that leads me to try, even a first rehearsal of a piece, to help them sense time as they perform. Though there often are missed notes, and not all the articulations are perfectly correct, I am trying to achieve a sense of understanding of the forward motion of this piece. "Where is section A leading to, where is this bar leading to, what is the peak of the phrase?" All of those issues relating to a sense of line, and the relationship and sense of time in a piece of music, caused me to try to rehearse large chunks of the piece. I noticed now over the years that I get through pieces more often in rehearsal that I used to when I was a young band director. I used to stop for every mistake and fix it. I thought it was fixed permanently once I had fixed it that day.

I work with the whole piece. Often before performances, though, I come back to specifics again. It may have been so long since we worked on the incredibly vital contrast between loud and soft in these two bars, that they have allowed their playing to slip. So my rehearsal time, if I have four weeks to rehearse, might be: big picture, detail, big picture, detail, detail, big picture.

*(Gerald Olson)*

### Teaching what rhythm is

Rhythm is not intellectual, rhythm is emotional and must be felt physically. Much of rhythm also cannot be divorced from the psychological. If we do, music suffers as a consequence—and we all suffer from this. I deal with rhythm as directly as possible by first becoming involved myself. I must project what the music is all about—to give the music character—so students can perceive what it is about. The conductor must be both on the inside as player, and on the outside as conductor continually. While rhythm can be a celebrative and uplifting feel, it also can be a tragic and funeral-like feel. We need to phrase rhythm as we need to phrase a melody.

*(Frank Bencriscutto)*

### Music as an art

Music is technical, creative, aesthetic, emotional, psychological, spiritual, intellectual, and physical. Music is not an art form unless all these come together for the performer and the listener.

*(Frank Bencriscutto)*

### What we should be teaching

We deny the most universal and creative aspect or sense of the art, if we forget to develop aspects of their musicianship other than just technical skills. This means, as Roger Sessions believes, you must be a listener, composer, and player to be fully a musician. The student must understand the musical vocabulary of the music (not just terms in isolation, but the ability to manipulate what the terms stand for), not just his instrument alone—he should understand the written language. If he does, the music can be more meaningful to him—and he can be creative. Without vocabulary, it is very hard to create anything in music. For example, I have taught mixolydian scales in the context of I-IV-V in twelve-bar blues. Suddenly, with this vocabulary, a student can start using this learning in his own way. Suddenly a new dimension opens up to that person and his identification with music reaches a different level. Knowledge is motivating, but teachers are not teaching the vocabulary.

*(Frank Bencriscutto)*

### Educating students musically

Their education, their musical experience is going to be caused by aesthetic experiences with music—which is the ultimate purpose of music education. But, in order to get the ultimate of aesthetic music, they must have tools. So, the teacher develops the tools; but he must do this along with developing their musical appreciation and musical understanding of what's going on in the world of music. Knowing more about the composer and the form, for example, are all part of it. Along with the tools, they must learn concepts and gain the background education that will raise them above just the notes and the rhythms.

*(H. Robert Reynolds)*

### Music can motivate us

Music is important for us as individuals, as a group or organization, as people, and as a world. The joy that one gets from music, the experience that it can be—those are the right reasons. Music can relate to meaning in one's life. When you are aware of this and touch a bit of what it can do to you, then the pleasurable experience motivates. Everyone enjoys meaningful, pleasurable experiences and good experiences. If we can convince people that these experiences are there, that is the right motivation.

*(Frank Bencriscutto)*

### The value of a musical experience

Considering how music affects us, there are at least two types of musical experience: one more ordinary—day to day than the other. There are also very rare experiences that move us profoundly. Perhaps the most important outcome of a music educational program is for a student to have that rare experience occasionally, where they are thrilled to their very core during a music experience, by the artful content of the music experience. They may be changed in certain ways because of this experience—this is the most exciting thing that can happen to them. I recall having such a profound experience playing *Onward Christian Soldiers* in my high school orchestra.

We cannot make a student have this experience. If we continually provide them with the right ingredients—the best artistic object, from time to time they will "click" and have a memorable experience. If one is not making this possible, then one is not in the music education profession. Instead, one is in another job or in the technical education profession.

*(Donald Casey)*

### The purpose of a concert

I believe the purpose of a concert is to enhance the education of the student. Meaning there's a culminating experience after preparation that they wish to share with the people who are there; these people are the music parents and they want to have a sharing experience with that also. But very often the band conductor believes the purpose of a concert is to entertain an audience; for example, he might think, "We can't play this because the audience won't like it."

Once, Jim Croft conducted a performance of the Hindemith Symphony with his Oshkosh, Wisconsin high school band; but the performance could have been nearly anywhere. Prior to the performance, he talked to the audience about the significance of the piece, the significance of the challenge because of its difficulty, and what he thought it could do for the students' musical education. After the performance was concluded, everybody stood up and cheered though few understood the symphony and some may not have liked it. But he talked with them and said something like , "The kids made a project of this great piece and hearing the piece once is like speed-reading Shakespeare; this is one of the great works of art and they have studied it, and so forth. If you don't appreciate this all because there are many levels of understanding that are necessary, be assured that your students have because we've already gone through this piece in detail. We've invited this person, a guest conductor from the big university to guest conduct this, and we want to share this experience with you."

The audience and the parents were just ecstatic to have something that important take place. They were very proud that their children achieved something wonderful. But in the teacher's mind was the idea that this experience is good for my students at this time; and I must get across to the audience why this is so important for the students.

John Rafoth, at West High School in Madison, Wisconsin, gave a concert in which the Senior Band played three numbers; they started with the Persichetti Symphony, his principal percussionist conducted the other percussionists on the Chavez *Toccata*, and then they ended the concert with the Hindemith symphony. How's that for a light evening? The audience thought it was wonderful and there was a packed house.

John also established a Fine Arts Week: the concerts are free and the kids can get out of any class to go to the concerts, but must be able to say to the teacher, "I want to hear the woodwind quintet playing in Room 203. They are playing such and such and so and so are the performers." This was required for them to get a ticket to go to that concert. They couldn't just say, "I want to get out of class and go to a concert." They have to put some thought into finding out something about it, such as reading the program to discover that at 2:45 there's a woodwind quintet they'd like to hear playing in the auditorium.

*(H. Robert Reynolds)*

### The students' mind

Too often our students assume they are innocent until you tell them they are guilty. They don't attempt to make music, they simply play their part with the assumption that if they need to do something different, the teacher will tell them. Unless you tell them to change something, they think everything is okay. To put it another way, one student says to another, "How did you do in band today?" The other says, "I must have been perfect, the director did not correct me a single time!"

*(Richard Floyd)*

### Expressive playing

I constantly remind students that they never will be accused of being too expressive or musical. "No judge at a festival is going to say that you played too emotionally, or too expressively, or that the music was too exciting therefore you deserve a II rating!" It is those intangible aspects of music that we must nurture, reward, stroke, and work with because that is where the music is. One must never regard notes, rhythms, and other technical aspects as ends in themselves. These components are only the necessities that enable one to make music.

*(Richard Floyd)*

### The relationship of rhythm to music

We often end up isolating such things as rhythm as an end in itself with no concern about how it relates to the style of the music. Yes, rhythm is important and must be secure, but accurate rhythm is worthless if it doesn't relate to the work's style and musical thought.

*(Richard Floyd)*

### The conductor

In my relationship as a conductor with any group of any age, of any persuasion, of any stature what so ever, my principal concern is to make music. I don't know any other way to try to make music except to do what I can, by any means available, to make the music come alive. That is what I think I should do. That beautiful piece of paper that sits on my desk is a magnificent intellectual achievement. The process of engraving it, in printing it, in distributing it and all the rest is remarkable. I am looking at all the music around me in my study. It is loaded from floor to ceiling with scores, parts, the parts—all edited. Here is everything I have recorded and books and things about music. This is a really marvelous collection of ideas encased between ends of paper. They contain captured ideas, they are sitting there abstractly. If one looks around, one's eyes could settle on a title, such as Rigoletto.

I am very much involved with opera. Maybe, that's one of the reasons I am a little different from some in the band world. As one's eye catches Rigoletto, it is not just some paper, beautiful gold lettering, some excellent binding—one can transport one's self immediately to Rigoletto.

This room is heavy with ideas—great ideas, great ideas ever since and they are all encased between the paper ends. How to make it come alive, how to be the agent of this, to realize what Mr. Verdi, Mr. Persichetti, Mr. Tchaikovsky, or Mr. Bach wants. That is my job as an agent—I am an agent for them. We conductors are all agents for them. As an agent, I have a big responsibility. That responsibility is to get into, around, behind, on top off, underneath, to the side of, on the slant—from any angle you can come at it: to make the music be what the composer has entrusted to us—those of us who are conductors and teachers.

*(Frederick Fennell)*

## The challenges of making music

How quickly can you digest a page, how quickly can you digest a page of music, an idea, a problem—whether the problem is physical, mental, or whatever? These are the problems we face in making music. We work with a bunch of kids who are in transit. We can see that they are anxious to know what is happening and they want to be right. So, you must make sure you are feeding to them the right thing. When you digest a page of music, what do you find yourself looking for while working toward a grasp of its essential character—its essence? Finding it and making it come alive is the challenge.

*(Frederick Fennell)*

## Conducting the same piece many times

It is such a meaningful experience to come to a rehearsal with a bunch of students, feeling that they are ready to do something—to do some kind of work, to one more time begin pieces you have conducted hundreds of times. Now, I have changed, the pieces haven't changed, but the people in front of me are brand new. I can again do the Holst suite in E flat and it is all sitting there.

For example, balances can be all wrong when someone is an extremely forward type of player. You hear things out of balance in a way that surprises and pleases you because you know that it is there, but you don't want to hear it that way. That makes it fresh again. The thing is, how do you adjust that? That is what we are talking about. Our purpose is to come to a recitation of Mr. Holst's ideas and how do you "correct" or "adjust" that person, the forward type of player, or that moment in the music.

I try to appeal to the willingness or desire of people to be excellent and to strive for excellence. I try to appeal to their curiosity, I don't tell them, "Look, I have done this a thousand times and you kids are just messing it up." What good would that do! I appeal to their curiosity and maybe try it another way, to discover what is there, to find what is interesting, to strive for excellence, and to come together. That is what we must try to do.

Everyone has to give a little something, to sacrifice something to contribute and that is terribly important. They may have to sacrifice an attitude, a situation, an idea about the music, or their inertia in response to a bad experience with the music, or no experience—better no experience with the music than a bad experience—the bad ones are hard to remake.

*(Frederick Fennell)*

## Making music

I'll stop sometimes and ask the group, "What are we doing? We've been playing the piece now two and one half weeks and I'm not convinced that we're saying what we want to do with this piece." When you walk out on stage and you're playing this sonata or this suite, whatever it is, you are saying either this is what I think Beethoven tried to say, or this is what I have to say about Beethoven. This is what I believe, this is how I think it feels to me or I'm trying to communicate something—it's a message. The piece should be a coherent statement, not just a going through of the motions.

I think sometimes as conductors, we don't talk enough about the type of repertoire we're playing. You know its like contemporary music, maybe to the lay men it all sounds alike. But, there is a big difference between playing a piece by Gunther Schuller, Varese, or Karl Husa. I think there are many ways to be successful as a conductor or teacher.

*(Robert Levy)*

## The relationship of gesture to sound and breath

A basic approach I use with students, is that I conduct, move my arms, and of course use my face and the whole body in combination. But, I move my arms in the way that I essentially want them to blow the air through the instrument.

*(Craig Kirchhoff)*

It's interesting to observe student teachers who are saying the right things. They say, "You know, you've got to take this deep breath, you have to breathe all the way down to your toes, you've got to fill up, you've got to do . . . ." Then, they give this little preparation in their conducting that will help no one to take a good breath.

That all has to do again with that conducting gesture. I ask students to comment for me. I say, "If I move this way" as I make a very quick kind of slashing movement; or "if I move this way" as I make a much slower gesture with much more resistance to it; "Now, which is the more powerful gesture?" Almost all the time, they vote for the slower gesture. The slower gesture seems to imply more resistance, more energy, more weight, and more connection.

It seems that one should move one's arms or the baton in the way that one wants students to blow their instruments. I am convinced these gestures, plus just basic body language are the reasons one could take the Eastman Wind Ensemble and have them play the first phrase of *Come Sweet Death* with different conductors and have different results. The first person would be William Revelli, the next person would be Frederick Fennell, and the next person would be, for example, John Paynter. Without either conductor saying a word, I am convinced the group would make three entirely different sounds.

This goes back to one member of the Chicago Symphony who commented, "You know we love Solti, but Solti tries for hours and hours in rehearsal to get this Giulini-like sound. We really try for him, but we can't do it. He can't do it either because it's just not the way he moves." I think that comment is very insightful.

*(Craig Kirchhoff)*

### Score study

John Paynter said to me, "I want you to do a clinic on score study at the Mid-West." First, I kind of recoiled. How many clinics have we been to on score study where you showed up, felt like you ought to go—so you leave. You leave and you feel guilty because the guy is saying, "You're really rotten because you don't study your score! You high school guys, you're all wrong because you should do such and such . . . ." To hear that approach again would be just awful.

I decided, who in the hell wants to hear another score-study lecture. So, I came up with this dumb title. It was called, "Score Study-Unlocking the Magic from the Page." I predicated the whole lecture upon the fact I could relate to them. I could say, "Look, I taught for four years prior to college teaching and these are the experiences I had. When I was in high school teaching a certain person said to me, "You know you've got a really wonderful band, the oboe players are just great, the balance is terrific, and I have not heard a high school band play this well in tune in fifteen years—the technique was terrific." Then, there was long sort of silence and the next words he said were, "Now when are you going to deal with the musical issues?" This was one of those times—one of those five-second experiences—where suddenly the world was just turned upside down.

At that point in my life I thought I was doing the right thing. Then, the music was a vehicle to make the band sound good. The big issue was, "Who had the best high school concert band?" So the music wasn't terribly important, but it was important to make the band sound good. It wasn't that I was a musical dummy. I was a good player in college and at one point I was even thinking of doing some professional playing. We just fall into these traps. So, the whole purpose of the lecture was to suggest ways to look at scores, and find and deal with the expressive aspects of the scores.

Frederick Prausnitz's book has become important to me. He breaks down score study into three aspects. The first aspect is what he calls the objective items. Those are the givens that are on the page, which aren't changeable.

The second aspect is the interpretation that is given. This means, "You've got accents written here, and because it's Mozart it means this kind of accent. If it were Bartok it would be a different kind of accent."

The third thing is the expressive challenge and that is what I call interpretation. To teach this, I use different excerpts with students. I use the first sixteen measures of *Chester Overture* and I use the second movement of *Lincolnshire Posy*. I play different recordings of them, and there are really three different recordings of each piece. It is obvious that the three conductors had three very different viewpoints.

One point that I made was that rarely at the Midwest Clinic do you find people sitting around the bar arguing about the interpretation of the first sixteen bars. What you'll hear them talk about instead is, "Boy was that a great band," or "What did you think about that tuba section." Band directors don't talk about the music as much as they talk about playing. So no one makes an issue saying, "I sure didn't like the way that was phrased. I would have done it such and such a way." Many band directors bypass the whole thing.

So, the whole lecture was directed toward this very important issue of expression and what it can do for us as conductors who are teaching high school people. I can remember when I had to do hall duty and cafeteria duty. There were those days where I sat there thinking, "What did I spend all that time studying music history for? It just does not seem so important or relevant."

So the third thing, Prausnitz's expressive challenge, is what I also call a creative challenge. I think it's very easy for all these people—some are very talented and dedicated people—to let themselves go, to get sold down the river, and to sink into an abyss where the music is missing.

*(Craig Kirchhoff)*

CHAPTER FOUR

# LITERATURE

If we believe that the primary purpose of music education is to entertain and present a positive image of the school to the community, then our decisions about the literature we place in the path of students will show the degree we have drifted toward that purpose. On the other hand, if the primary purpose of a music education is to impart the substance of pieces and to contribute to the development of the individual through music literature, we will look at the choice of literature in another way.

There are many comments here about choosing, programming, and assessing literature. These insights can guide teachers when they must make decisions about the pieces they put in the music folder. The compositions in that folder make up the contents of the "textbook" the students experience. How well and how wisely the music educator selects literature will determine the content that will impact upon students via their literature. The better the literature, the more profound the experience will be for students, and the longer the impact and effects will last.

### The choice of literature

Ernest Newman, one of the finest music critics of all time, and certainly the most renowned writer in English, once remarked that any music worth playing is worth playing badly! This means that it is more important, ultimately if not immediately, to play the right kind of music . . . even if it cannot be played "perfectly." It is much more important to play the right kind with mistakes than to play the wrong kind of music without them.

*(Alfred Reed)*

Kids don't like what they can't play.

*(Carl A. Bly)*

I pick music of historical importance—the masters.
*(Barbara Buehlman)*

I try to expose them to a lot of different music.
*(Richard Fischer)*

All my life I have not only been a teacher by repertoire, but by what I have been playing. When all of

the technical study is done, there must be the music. The over-riding principle for doing any of the specific things is the concern for the music.

*(Frederick Fennell)*

### The importance of the choice of literature

Music is part of the experiential life of the student. The musical experiences he has become *his* experiences. The literature the teacher chooses to present to the student becomes part of that student—*shapes* that student. There *is* an art of teaching, but the essential musical experiences come from the music itself, not from the teacher. Therefore, my first criterion for selecting educational music is that it be music which comes from the heart.

*(David Whitwell)*

### Selecting music

Choose orchestra music which is interesting and challenging to *all* sections and students; violas and string basses will not progress technically unless their parts are as challenging as the violins and cellos.

*(Gordon Childs)*

### The audience

In the fifties we started losing audiences for bands, and I believe part of it was because of the new "contemporary" literature. We work on these pieces but I try to remember the reaction from the audience of parents and community. I was born one hundred years too late because I am really a romantic. I like such pieces as *Grace Praeludium, The Improvisator,* and Grainger's *Colonial Song.*

*(Stanley Cate)*

Why the comprehending of musical form happens, we still don't know. Look how many songs have been written following the AABA thirty-two bar pattern. Some of them hang around, and some of them are gone even before you hear them the first time. We don't know what it is, we can only speculate. We know for sure the audiences' reactions when we play these pieces. We can see it. Consider the Beatles' *Yesterday.* Now, that is the most recorded song in the entire history of music and the record business. There are today over seven hundred forty different recordings of that one song, and it is the song that has logged the most performances of any song in history. Over 7,000,000 samples have already been taken. If that's the sample, you can imagine the whole field—it is many times more than that.

*(Alfred Reed)*

I am convinced the reasons so much contemporary music does not find an audience is two parts: First, people do not hear in this music what they think they should be hearing in it. Second, they try to guess what's coming next and if it doesn't go that way, they are disappointed, irritated, or hostile.

The experience is not one that they want to repeat, whether it's meaningful or meaningless is beside the point. If they don't want to repeat it, down the tube goes the composer, the work, the performers, and everybody else. We really can't afford that. I believe that any composer can only go as far as his audiences are willing to let him go. The audience is willing to let the composer go only as long as they feel they can understand what is going on. The one thing that each of us dreads more that anything else is not cancer, leukemia, or AIDS: it is being made a fool of. We get this feeling if we can't understand what is going on in the music. We ask ourselves, what is this guy trying to do to us? is he trying to make a fool of me? Well, the hell with him! That reaction is as normal as blueberry pie, if we are analyzing human reactions to different stimuli. So, the fact that the public was willing to go along with Wagner and the professional critics, academicians, and musicians were not, only meant so much the worse for the academicians, critics, and musicians.

But, when the academicians, professional musicians, and critics all hail a talent and the audience can't find anything to latch on to, then too bad for them again. Well, that's it then. Being successful with an audience with contemporary music or in preparing an audience to listen to it, implies that the composer might try to manipulate the material, the basic stuff that he works with, trying to achieve the end of an appreciative audience.

Now, to me, that is the essence of being a hack. The way I look at it is, I write as I feel. What the audience finds in my music, ultimately decides whether I'm a composer or not. Now, if you want to say that some of us are lucky that the audience finds something in our music to react positively to while we are writing exactly as we feel we must, I'll go along with that use of the word luck.

*(Alfred Reed)*

### Literature and band history

Understanding band history also may deserve more attention, as does an understanding of the heritage of the medium. For example, to make students aware of band's tradition, I had them function as a circus band. Not only

that, we assembled live acts performed by local people and did a mini-circus performance—outside in the park. When they do this, they can grow in their knowledge of the medium, especially in aspects of which they were not aware. One can also do outdoor concerts with the trumpet and vocal solos, ala the era of Sousa. With certain literature, transcriptions also are very important since students cannot play certain literature except through a transcription. The transcription of Charles Ives, *The Alcotts* is excellent. *William Tell* of Rossini and others are worth bringing into their awareness.

*(Thomas H. Cook)*

### Music literature for the ensemble

I think music as a compositional endeavor may be cyclic, but music for an ensemble is not cyclic. I believe it is constantly on the improvement; the ensemble music is infinitely better now than it was twenty years ago. I do see, however, that the bands are not better than they were earlier: they are not better at doing that one thing they did so well; but, now they are doing many more things and doing them very well.

*(H. Robert Reynolds)*

### The impetus for composing

I can't write the "in thing." Maybe other people can and I define them as "hacks." It may be the wrong word and I don't mean that word pejoratively, because some of these hacks are very, very talented people. They can do anything for you in any style. Their technique is excellent—flawless at times. But, I can't work that way. I've got to write what I feel. I cannot put down a damn single note unless it comes up, so to speak, with blood.

Giannini used to use that expression with me. I was interested to find out that Toscanini used to scream at the men in the orchestra, "Put blood, put blood into it!" See, he had the feeling that they were just anemic. They were doing something, but they didn't really believe in what they were doing. He couldn't stand that. We need certain kinds of music for certain things. Fine, that's good. But, with the great artists and the great works, certain things happen. They write it as they hear it and the audience, no matter what anybody else may say (including the experts), can find something in the music and they react positively. Without that attractiveness of the music, regardless of all the technique in the world and all the cultural background and the hoity-toity-schmoity, it doesn't mean anything.

*(Alfred Reed)*

### Selecting literature

To me, the real definition of creativity is choice. Two plus three is five: you have no choice in that, because if two plus three were five only on Monday, Wednesday, and Friday, and was six on Tuesday, Thursday, Saturday, and was four on Sunday, would you trust your life in a car, an airplane, a house built according to that kind of mathematics, of course not!

How many times have you heard other people say, "Well, I had to do this, I had no choice." Now, to me creativity is just that very thing. One, is to see more than one way of doing something, and second, to be able to make a single choice from among these various ways.

The choice of literature is the single most difficult and creative action a conductor performs. Whether he's conducting a junior high school band, a choir, or the New York Philharmonic, choosing the program is seventy-five percent of the job. That much of the job is over, finished, and done with before you set your foot on the podium for the first rehearsal.

Given that, and given the absolutely inordinate amount of music pouring off the presses these days on the so-called Grade One and Grade Two levels, this typical junior high school or high school conductor has a very difficult job. He has to pick music that is both attainable and reachable, and music that challenges his players. He must challenge them, but not to the point where—no matter how hard they try—they can't play or understand it. If he does that, his efforts are self defeating.

He must pick and play music that is worth the effort that he is going to demand from his players. It's easy to write easy music, and it's relatively easy to play a grade-one or a grade-two piece that is fairly well matched technically to what each individual performing group can do. What is difficult is to find that easy music the conductor feels, "Yes, these kids have to play this. This piece will develop their ears, their fingers, and most of all, their appreciation of music that is not just punk, pop, or rock oriented." Picking music is not easy at that level and it is the most difficult thing of all tasks. No matter what we say, that's the way it is. Now, how many grade one or grade two pieces does the average director find that he can put his hand on his heart, look himself in the eye in the mirror, and say, "My kids must play this piece."

*(Alfred Reed)*

### Hearing the classics

I want them to hear the recordings whether it makes a difference or not because that's what we're in music education for: to listen. Who else is going to expose these kids to master works?

*(William Long)*

### The value of marches

There are certain pieces and types of pieces we need to play. Most of my programs usually include a march. I'm very, very much a believer in the training abilities of marches because of their great potential for training musicians. For the woodwinds, there's nothing better to get the fingers moving. For brass there's nothing better to get that sense of where a line is going. A march is a very short, terse, and pithy type of presentation; it's perfect for getting

an idea across. I use good marches all the time. Students come out of my program and get to high school as fanatics about how to play light, how to separate, and how to group the notes. Marches are great audience pleasers and great training material.

*(William Long)*

### Selecting literature

I will have a piece of lighter music, an overture, a modern composition, and that's what I will do in my curriculum. The students aren't going to repeat those same pieces over and over. I do repeat some pieces because students should have played certain pieces by the time they reach college. I firmly believe in the power of music. That is what the students are in band for. That is why we have them listen to something at one time or another!

It also should be fun to play a horn. Because something was fun is also the reason they like listening to music. The music should be fun, but I don't do "fun and games." There should be a joy in playing that horn and there should be joy in making music.

*(William Long)*

### Relating the variety of food to music

One of my favorite analogies is to compare food and diet to our choice of music. I try to use food, again, because people identify with what they know. Our approach to music ends up being limited just as persons can limit themselves to a diet of steak, potatoes, and a vegetable every night—and that's it. Instead, they could broaden their horizons. They should go out and taste Chinese and Greek food, Japanese food and Indian food, and Mexican food, and who knows what else.

*(Sandra Thompson)*

### Literature and musicianship

Selecting music of quality is extremely important. Literature is the vehicle by which students are going to learn about musicianship and being a musician. That is the "diet" we can give these kids to subsist on.

*(Craig Kirchhoff)*

### Literature of substance

The literature often played at this level is trash. When we do this, we are playing down and selling kids short. Seldom do kids suggest to me that we play something soft. They usually enjoy music of substance.

*(Ross A. Leeper)*

### Combining the arts

Take a piece of music like *A Norman Rockwell Suite*. This uses eight different Rockwell paintings and covers of magazines. I played that piece of music and had slides made of the paintings to show on the screen while we were playing the music. I must give fifteen to twenty performances a year, where I play a recording of that music. I show the slides as I talk about the relationship of the visual image that was transcribed to the aural image.

I sometimes play the music with a blank screen and let them try to decide what it's going to be. They see what it is and see how close their image of the sound compares to what would be on the picture. I've never given the speech, showed both the slides and played the tape, for any age group from preschoolers to retirees, who didn't thoroughly enjoy it. They all try to piece together the visual image with the sound. I am also teaching everybody there's a difference between program and absolute music. I teach them what the program is that they decided upon, not a story line necessarily, but an image.

*(Robert Morsch)*

## Teaching through programming

I teach through the literature. I think it's very important to correlate a solo to where the student is and where you want the student to go. I feel it has to be done with jazz band, concert band, brass choir, trumpet, and whatever. This is where most of the damage is done in public school education. A person can teach the techniques out of the method book, but the actual depth of their education comes from the literature and programming.

First, challenge without discouragement is very important. To do that the teacher must know the literature thoroughly. This knowledge is the teacher's most important asset. I believe that the textbook is, in public school education, the concert material—the chart is the primary textbook. Thus, Rubank One is only a warm up book or a resource book.

The real textbook—the real meat we teach someone—is the music material that we put in front of the kids to play. That is what they're going to work on most. The music probably has the most lasting effect and will be the most impressive, either negatively or positively. Literature other than that played at the concert is also part of the "textbook of literature." I'm still using the same stuff I used before—basic stuff that the kids have to learn to play. I use charts of the Count Basie style, various styled charts, and other old charts. I have many pieces in my library like *Tribute to Basie*. It's an old chart but, it has everything in it that a band has to do before we go on to the next step. My "text book of literature" includes programming and teaching pieces as well as performance pieces—they go hand in hand.

*(Dominic Spera)*

## Standards

I believe that one should, "Not teach from a plateau of condescension." This means that we should not teach as though all pop music is poor.

*(James Arrowood)*

## Considering programming

We look at programming very carefully. I am a firm believer that you have to play for the audience also. There are some people who play strictly for the group. They select the literature for the group's experience and that's fine. I hate, though, to play to empty houses and many of those people do. I do consider the program very carefully to see where to put the new music in, how to "sugar-coat" it, so to speak. I try to program very carefully.

I use the typical things, such as the overtures and the soloists, which I try to include in every concert. Sometimes transcriptions are the best openers you can get, particularly the overtures, such as *Roman Carnival, Benvenuto Cellini*, or something as old as *Light Cavalry*. Overtures also are good closers and I also include the new music on programs.

*(Myron Welch)*

## Transcriptions

There's nothing sacred about a transcription. If someone else has doctored it up and put all these people on parts, I can take them out—I can thin the orchestration or instrumentation down to where it fits. This is needed particularly with old transcriptions. Many were done for outside performances, so you've got to redo it for inside performance, so I take out the doublings. One can go back to the orchestral score and see how thin the scoring was. We did a Hindsley transcriptions a few years ago. The students used the orchestral parts for the bassoons and horns: they didn't use Hindsley's parts. There also were several parts that were left out. The parts also were simplified in places and our students played the real parts. We found that some solos were changed compared to the original orchestration.

*(Myron Welch)*

## Considering programming

I plan around the programs for the year. I look very carefully to make sure that the students get the new music that I hear at conventions. I adhere to my sight reading to make sure they are keep abreast of what's going on. Plus, I make sure that students are aware of the more difficult standard literature. I am talking the "biggies" for band, such as Schoenberg or *Lincolnshire Posy*. They must be exposed to these pieces. I also look at literature carefully to decide how well something fits for chamber literature that I also do on the same program.

*(Myron Welch)*

## Evaluating literature

There is no way to evaluate literature unless you study and continue to study the world's greatest music of all idioms or mediums. If we do not do this we have no yardstick with which to evaluate band music. It is impossible to find the best music by comparing it to the mediocre.

*(Butler R. Eitel)*

## *Use the term literature, not the term band music*

The latter term, band music, may be an "oxymoron." Think about these statements: "Tell me the name of your best friend, I will tell you what kind of a person you are. If you tell me the names of your favorite books and authors, I will tell you what your intellect is." If I paraphrase this, I can say, "If you tell me what music you play, I will tell you how musical your band is."

A band does not become truly musical, or develop musical sensitivity, unless that band plays great literature. Playing good literature provides the possibility that a musical band will result; it does not automatically cause a band to be musical. Therefore, some bands playing good literature may not do so with sensitivity.

*(Butler R. Eitel)*

## *Literature*

The only quest in town, a matter of integrity that we cannot dodge, is the search for the best literature at all levels. This is the band director's challenge.

*(Butler R. Eitel)*

## *Music reading enables*

Teach a range of music, music with different styles and difficulty levels—select music that differs in any conceivable way. Teach the kids to read so you can do more music. As a result, we played ten times more music than other high school bands. We played good literature and we played much literature, period.

*(Donald Wilcox)*

## *What is music?*

Some kid comes into rehearsal and one of the others says, "Hey, do you have the music?" They will hold up the folder and say, "Yeah, I've got the music." The music in the folder—the paper stuff—has the same relation to music that a blue print does to a house.

*(Donald Wilcox)*

## Chapter Five

# Performance

These ideas show concerns for the audience, thoughts about interpretation, the use of recordings to model musical styles, the choice of tempo, the idea that music making must go beyond what is on the page, and the differences between shaping music and fixing the ensemble's performance.

When combined with other chapters of the book such as those about rehearsal, planning, communication, rapport, and involvement, there is a wealth of insight that can give direction to any teacher of any ensemble, and with performers of all ages.

### How accurate need it be?

I don't feel that music on a concert need be prepared perfectly, though we try to do so in a contest.

*(Carl A. Bly)*

### Performance

We talk extensively about the listener and about communication. We discuss what the piece is trying to convey. In this respect, dynamics are a big influence in communicating the piece successfully to the listener. We want to convey and clarify the pieces's musical image with all its detail. For example, we must make the dynamic and other musical contrasts evident to the listener—so he can perceive the composer's intentions.

*(Richard Fischer)*

### Changing the band directors' awareness

I think we've been through a period of what I call over-interpretation. The band field has gone through other kinds of quantum leaps or phases. One was the conducting phase. When we all realized we needed to conduct better, we had all these conducting symposiums. Next is the kind of interpretative stage, and everybody says you've got to interpret this music.

I agree that we have to interpret everything that's on the page, as well as knowing a whole lot more about the music than is on that page. But some conductors over-interpret: by over-interpretation, I mean this feeling, this compunction and this necessity among directors and conductors to put their own kind of personal stamp on this music in the name of interpretation. What occurs are some of the most bizarre, strange, and unmusical or amusical renderings that one can imagine. I think we should have some restraint: a basic intelligence about stylistic parameters. People ought not to be that far off center into their own personal view—which some are calling interpretation—when they are at the extremes.

*(Craig Kirchhoff)*

### Using recordings and information about the composition

I tell students about the style and original intent of the piece. Suppose the piece is a Mozart overture band transcription of the *Marriage of Figaro* or *King Stephen* of Beethoven. Since you don't play the original version, what do they have to go by? One place to turn is to recordings. If they hear a piece played correctly on one of the fantastic recordings that are available—then they have a better idea of what the clarinets have to do. Through this, I try to make them understand the musical gesture, how it should be played.

*(Robert Morsch)*

### Physical experience and music

I think we make music partly because of the physical experiences we have. I mean music that doesn't dance isn't music.

*(Larry Rachleff)*

### Articulation and other issues

You can't separate playing techniques and style when you talk about the ultimate stylistic interpretation. When I talk about style with my band, I talk about vibrato, about volume, about feel, texture, and articulation. These all go together and it is very difficult to separate. If one of those characteristics is missing, things just do not come together. I mean, these elements have to be right. Students need all these abilities and skills to play different styles and this is part of the notion of musicianship. That's how I teach musicians; I teach musicianship through the literature.

*(Dominic Spera)*

## Going beyond the printed page

As teachers, what are our goals? What do we think about? Where are our values? We are often so busy teaching the skills of performance that we lose sight of the music making. While holding up a score I ask students, "Is this the music?" They always say, "Yes." I answer, "No, this is just ink on the paper. You make the music. You breathe your life's breath into your instruments. The composer has given us a blueprint to follow. We can visit a museum to see a painting or to view a piece of sculpture because these art works exist in space. Our art (music) exists in time. It is our obligation to recreate these masterpieces of the composer for the audience and for ourselves. This is truly a profound responsibility, but it is one that bestows indescribable dividends."

*(James Arrowood)*

## The tempo in the score can be a point of departure

We discuss that most composers use the score as a point of departure. The most important thing in any musical consideration is the sound: the way the score sounds. If you have to sacrifice quality, musicianship, tone, or phrasing to get to some specific tempo marking listed in the score, then something is wrong. If a group can't sustain a lyrical line slowly, then do it a little faster.

Students do tend to be very rigid when the teacher suggests a change from the specified tempo. The choice of tempo should fit the abilities of each specific group. The more inexperienced the group is, the more critical it is that the conductor find the proper tempo. An excellent group will have tremendous leeway, or at least greater leeway within which they will sound and play well.

The weaker the group is, the more carefully the conductor needs to control the tempo or its choice. I talk to students about this and I have them play inappropriate tempos. If they believe that rules are hard and fast, and it says quarter note = 152, I'll say "Well, let's try it." Then I'll say, "How does it sound?" If they have an opportunity to try different tempi, they also have to be allowed the chance to fail with their choice. Not in a big devastating way, but to try several tempi and then analyze what happened. This will be more meaningful than my communicating that they should be afraid of making choices.

I don't mean that trying to find a tempo they can handle is babying a group. Instead, this has to do with being able to clearly evaluate the abilities of your group, the potential of your group, and how much time you have to get something accomplished. Of course the goal in an expressive piece is to be able to stretch it as expressively as you can. If they don't have the techniques and the air support to be able to do that, then you have to teach them that this is what we are after. In the meantime, let's do it this way.

*(Mallory B. Thompson)*

## Making music versus "fixing"

Consider, "What is the ratio in your rehearsal when you are kind of fixing things compared to making music?" Hopefully, you are spending a good deal of time talking about phrasing and shape, direction, and nuance. Hopefully, you are not using all your time talking about in-tune, out-of-tune, and not together, because they are all related. One without the other is of no value. No one wants to hear a sanitary performance with no emotion, and no one wants to hear spectacular emotion with all the wrong notes in all the wrong places.

*(Larry Rachleff)*

## The "fix-it" instrumental director

The "fix-it" band director is going to have problems because he's not approaching things musically; he's thinking that the "form with polish" is the end result. He's not planning his rehearsal. What he's doing is he's starting at the beginning and going until something goes wrong and he's fixing it—he has no plan.

The first thing the fix-it band director must do is make an assessment of his previous rehearsal and find out what was wrong and what needs to be done the next rehearsal. Then he goes to the next rehearsal with a plan.

If you want to get everybody's attention in a rehearsal, say, "We're going to start three measures before W." That's the first thing you do in the rehearsal, after the warm-up/sensitizing time. Because then you're saying there's a *purpose* here. They realize that he knows and they better get serious about it. Because when you say, "Let's do this piece from the beginning," there's a tendency for everybody to think there's no plan. They think, "We're just going to play as well as we can and when we don't play so well he'll take us out of the game."

*(H. Robert Reynolds)*

# Developing Independence
# and Judgment

# CHAPTER ONE

# MOTIVATION AND REINFORCEMENT

The term motivation covers a myriad of ideas that suggest why students behave as they do. The ideas describe extrinsic and intrinsic causes that prompt students' behaviors. It is essential for teachers to understand the behaviors of students, but identifying the stimuli for their behaviors can be difficult. Any understanding of behavior also is ephemeral because the motivating forces vary both with the students and the contexts of their behavior.

None of the many theories, ideas, or explanations for motivation are comprehensive nor do they apply in every situation. Certain types of motivational techniques, however, can be effective when used properly and with the right student. For example, a teacher can reinforce a student's efforts by saying, "The volume of your accompaniment is just right, we can easily hear the soloist over the accompaniment," or "When you stressed F and F sharp, the top two notes of the phrase, you made a good choice. The phrasing was musical."

Beside reinforcement, there are other extrinsic stimuli that can influence students to remain involved with music classes: students strive to meet the teacher's expectations, receive his approval, or imitate his examples. Students often have a desire for rewards, recognition, or incentives. They practice to earn higher contest scores, to be awarded a music scholarship, or to receive recognition by being accepted in an all-state ensemble. Many students are motivated because they are curious; others desire to master the instrument or understand an idea. They are motivated to do this either because they want to learn, or because they do not want to fail.

Most classroom educators, including those in music, make conclusions about students' motivations. When music educators see that students are involved with lessons and are practicing, they usually infer that students are motivated. Teachers infer the opposite when students show inattentiveness, fail to practice, or drop out of band or orchestra. This is an uncomplicated way to categorize a student's behavior and sometimes such categorizations are correct.

The difficulty of knowing students' motivations, however, is compounded because we cannot always see the impetus for the students' behaviors. If we asked them why they did something, their answer might not be revealing. The student may not be introspective or know himself well enough. Therefore, if we want to know the students' motivations, we must infer their motivations from seeing their behaviors.

The use of motivational techniques begins early for instrumental music teachers. They try to entice students to participate in music and to stimulate them to learn. They must additionally and continually motivate students to keep them on task long enough for them to be successful. For example, a teacher can reinforce the student's efforts by saying, "You played that phrase with only one breath, you're making excellent progress," or "You remembered to bring your music folder every day this week, that's what I like to see." After the student has progressed, the teacher can motivate more advanced students by saying, "You did something with the phrase, that was expressive and very musical!" These kinds of motivational techniques have impact but only over a short term; therefore, teachers must use such techniques frequently throughout the time the student is in lessons.

Not all motivational forces will come from the music teacher. Social conditions also motivate students. The family can influence students to make good decisions, to place high priority upon academic or artistic achievements, and to be constructive and responsible. Social conditions for other students may not be as positive. As a result, some students are not motivated to involve themselves in school or music for its educational benefits. In rare cases, a negative social environment can spur a student to involve himself with music as an escape from neighborhood, family, or school pressures.

A student's psychological need for peer approval is a prime motivator of all his actions whether constructive or not. Risking a friend's support to join an ensemble becomes a reality when the friend says, "Why do you want to do *that*? Why don't you learn to play *real music* like so-and-so (the latest pop group)?" The resistance to this pressure varies with each student and each peer group; some individuals are very dependent upon friends, and others can act independently with greater ease. Even those who feel strong negative peer pressure will study music anyway, if they are attracted to music and believe they will gain from their involvement.

Besides the effect of extrinsic stimuli, there are students whose motivations are essentially intrinsic. These students are more successful when they are working alone or choosing their own directions. Such students thrive with less outside control, or less overt help from teachers. To some degree, they want to feel they are choosing what they do and have control over how they will do it. Unfortunately some students who appear to act independently may be merely rebellious, but most students who exert their independence in this way actually are motivated internally to learn.

Effective instruction may be one cause for change from extrinsic motivation to intrinsic, or from non-musical to musical motives for participation. If there is direction to the music class and it has substance, it is more apt to motivate students. If the class is aimless and includes music literature of little substance, challenge, or interest, it is less likely to motivate. The underlying assumption is that many students can be motivated and they become excited when they learn new ideas and skills.

Therefore, *what* students learn is a strong motivator; but when students discover *how* to learn, they have found another motivation. To this end, we must stress to the student the connection between his success, and his ability and efforts. We must reinforce this because we want the student to see those connections and to build confidence or esteem through his own bona fide accomplishments.

If the content or process of a music class doesn't motivate students enough, making changes in the class might make it more interesting for them. For example, the experience of being in a performance ensemble may not interest some students. The teacher can change the literature, the process, or the content of the class. The ensemble can interest some students more if it also develops different insights into the experience of making music. Students can be offered a chance to listen, arrange, analyze, compose, and improvise music. They can be invited to offer ideas on how to perform the music, to meet professional performers and composers, and be encouraged to learn about different musics, their histories, and their structures.

When teachers choose the best and most suitable literature for the students, the students tend to interact in a dynamic instead of a static manner. Good literature can intrigue students for a longer time than another technique that only entices students to participate. I cannot recall who spoke about the literature that is written primarily to build technical skills, but he said, "So-called educational music is music that is all preparation with no musical results." This is not to say that developing technical skills is unimportant. But if music teachers look back on their early experiences in music, they will discover they cannot remember the inconsequential music or technical exercises they heard or performed, but they do remember those musical experiences that were exceptional.

Eventually music teachers hope the prime motivational forces will include the musical experience itself, in addition to the students' growth in skill and knowledge. Just as students' education progresses and their ages change, so will the things that motivate them. When students' accomplishments lead them to experience substance and when they realize they have grown, they ultimately will become less dependent upon trips to bowl games, a friend's approval, or what is for the moment "cool." As they begin to emerge as independent and educated people, their motivations will become more intrinsic. They can realize that art and the artistic experience has an integral place in human life.

## The Value of Motivation

### Motivation and music

Motivation is the basis for all and occurs because of involvement. Many other teachers try to achieve this only through fear, threat, contests, or especially, the avoidance of embarrassment. These are all the wrong reasons.

We as teachers have not learned how to motivate for the right reasons. The right reasons for motivation are what music can do for us as individuals, as a group, organization or people, and as a world. The right reasons are the joy that one gets from music and the experience that it can be.

Music can relate to meaning in one's life. When one is aware of this and touches a bit of what it can do, then the pleasurable experiences motivate. Everyone enjoys meaningful, pleasurable experiences and good experiences. If we can convince people these experiences are there, that is the right motivation.

Art places pleasurable experiences into the purest experience. If we support music because of its technical content, we miss the point. There is a difference between entertainment with a small "e" and large "E." At its highest level, art is most entertaining because it entertains your whole being. Art entertains not only the feelings, but the intellect and everything else.

*(Frank Bencriscutto)*

### You won't be wrong

I constantly remind students that they never will be accused of being too expressive or musical. "No judge at a festival is going to say that you played too emotionally, or too expressively, or that the music was too exciting therefore you deserve a II rating!"

It is the intangible aspects of music that we must nurture, reward, stroke, and work with; that is where the music is. One must never regard notes, rhythms, and other technical aspects as ends in themselves. These components are only the necessities that enable one to make music.

*(Richard Floyd)*

### The importance of motivation

No student can make significant progress unless they are internally motivated.

*(Richard Putzier)*

## MOTIVATION THROUGH MUSIC MAKING

### Motivating during the rehearsal

How one conducts will reflect upon the band and how one views one's self will reflect in the overall rehearsal. If one takes things seriously and tries to communicate, then one will be sensitizing his band to respond to what is important. The more sensitive they are, the more they are listening. They have their antennas out trying to see what you are trying to tell or do. Then, they respond and you respond—the whole process becomes an active music-making process instead of a passive "do what I tell you" process. With the active approach, the students become active participants in an on-going process; and the rehearsal itself becomes more rewarding and significant in musical as well as other ways.

*(Robert Grechesky)*

I strive from "day one" to establish performance-oriented attitudes. Even putting the horn together and opening the case is a "performance" and a mind-set or an attitude that shows itself in the pride, the care and in everything we do. Even after one note, I may ask, "Who wants to perform concert F for us?" Concert F must have a good beginning, be sustained, have a good center and focus to the tone, and with a sustained sound followed by a good release. They perform while standing, which they already have been shown how to do. They bring their horn up, breathe correctly and play. The rest of the group will applaud the performance. When they do experience a little success, then we have something to reinforce.

This is a "mini-professional" situation. We are not successful with every kid. We try to continually set this attitude from the beginning right on. Another attitude we establish is to set a standard of what we will accept. It is an attitude about a level of acceptance; we want them to set a high standard also. We may be trying to take the kids a bit further than others, without pushing them out of the program because we may have a higher expectation.

*(Robert Floyd)*

### When they try several ways, they begin to grow

Once they try two or three different ways to phrase, for example, then they become more able to grow or to experiment on their own. They come back to the rehearsal and try it out on you. It makes for a much more interesting interplay. They're feeding you ideas and you're feeding them, instead of you feeding them ideas and they do just what you say.

*(L. Keating Johnson)*

### Predictable and unpredictable rehearsals

Do anything to keep them off guard and challenged. I thoroughly believe that a sixteen-year-old or one at any age level does not respond well to routine events. If they walk into a room and can predict what's going to happen in the room, they will go on "automatic." They are going to tune out and go through the motions until you do something new and exciting that will create their attention. Larry Rachleff said, "Change the light bulbs in your room. Change anything, change the seating arrangement, change something."

There is a happy medium. Kids need security. They want discipline in the classroom. They want to know what a teacher expects from them. If you're constantly changing everything about you, there comes a point of ridiculousness, I think. You can be new and musically adventurous everyday. There are some standard things you want to keep the same, such as maintaining discipline, stopping when the conductor stops, or not letting that get out of hand. But, being adventurous musically, I have no problem trying to do something new every day.

*(Michael Kaufman)*

### The first reading

I spend the first minute and a half or two minutes of the piece going through it at a very slow tempo. I do this until their fingers learn the keys. Then we begin to pick it up. Then, just for fun, even in that first rehearsal (and I'm a strong believer in this), I say, "You guys think you're so smart and good; I'll give you a taste of what old Mr. Rossini is all about. Let's take this right up at concert tempo." Of course, immediately some kids start to pick up on the excitement that is inherent in a classic. Those kids are already beginning to feel the challenge.

*(William Long)*

### Making sight reading exciting

As we sight read at letter D, the kids are already starting to feel a challenge. Just like the challenge they feel when you take a kid out and play horse with him in basketball. They're already starting to feel a challenge.

It's not necessary to beat anybody. They try to amass something and to come up to some level the director has set. Then I might make a joke about it saying, "Okay, Rossini won that one." The kids are laughing and some are talking to one another about it.

The seed has been planted. The kids at this point have figured out my feeling toward the piece. Now don't forget, they're going to get the chance to say "we don't like this" and that happens occasionally.

Eventually, in that first day or two after we've read other sections, I will say, "Now, let's listen to this tough section at letter Q where the low brass and the low woodwinds really have a workout." Well, instead of simply playing letter Q, one is telling people, "Low brass, low woodwinds, watch out." They've already got their egos in line. "Wow, we're going to get to do something, we're important. We do amount to something. Hey, Mr. Long's watching out for us." I might communicate this with a cock of the eyebrow, it might be a quick glance to Chris in the trombone section that says "Well, Chris, you'll never get this one, this one will be too much for you, won't it?" They say, "We'll get it."

With this, I tie the kids into the music that's in front of them. That's becoming an intrinsic part of what they think. I picked this up from Jim Neilsen. I heard his clinic, and I wrote everything down. I've used tons of things he suggested to teach phrasing and styling.

*(William Long)*

### Making the piece interesting

Jimmy Nielsen said, "You band directors sight read a piece without the kids in mind. You seldom give the kids, in that first play or two, a chance to hear that last cadence or chord. You never give them a chance to hear the last sixteen bars. Start in the middle, start at the beginning, or at the end."

That's the way I approach sight reading. I may start at the middle or any exciting spot, I say, "Let's see what the introduction is like." We go back then at the beginning and hear the introductory part. "Okay, now let's work the ending." Often, if I really want the kids to like the piece, I play the ending first. Most of the time the endings are the most exciting parts of music. So, I give them a chance to hear how the ending is. Immediately they are thinking, "Man oh man, that's neat. We'll knock them out of their seats with that one." I'm not saying that they're saying that to me, but the eyes, the facial expressions tell me that's what they're feeling.

*(William Long)*

### Making the first reading appealing

If we are doing a hard piece with an appealing ending that I want students to like, I will work out the ending first. If they find the end appealing, they are going to start playing the rest better, because they know we have taken the time to learn the ending. You can approach pieces in different ways and I look through the score to find the more interesting passages.

*(Terry A. Oxley)*

### Having fun while learning

I do a "Frankenstein Walk" showing them an undesirable posture—such as hunching their back or holding their arms to close too their body. To relax their body and breathe correctly, they must avoid this posture. We also get on the floor and pretend we are dogs. They like to see the teacher do that! After they do this, I ask them how they feel. Then, I ask them to get up on the chair and breathe the same way.

*(Jack Brookshire)*

On *Symphonic Songs for Band*, Mr. Paynter sang the woodwind counter phrase with the words, "Your eyes are green and blue, and I am in love with you, just bring your wallet too." The band cracked up. Another time there were two contrasting parts, one subordinate. After working with one he said, "Now, let's have the cheering section." He even made up words for marches!

*(Michael Golemo)*

### Using the computer in elementary band

John Schulberg in Missoula uses a music computer program to help arrange music for his band and students. Playing newly-arranged or composed music motivates the students and makes the musical process more visible for them. This experience helps over come the impersonality because they can relate to that human being and to the making of a piece.

*(Thomas H. Cook)*

### Studying music without isolation

Isolation in informal and formal music learning is dreadful. If students use a visual mirror their isolation is lessened, but what they need more than a visual mirror is an aural mirror; to hear themselves through aural replay. Without aural feedback, they cannot really monitor their own performance or learning. There should be a tape recorder in every studio! With a mirror, tape recorder or another individual, one gets some musical "information" and musical feedback, which makes music more social and complete.

Within a musical context, practice is much more interesting and satisfying for students. Furthermore, the experience can confirm that one is getting better. For example, if one plays with the same context repeatedly, the student can evaluate the progress as he moves toward performing "in-sync" with the recorded musical context. This is the same as playing a duet with someone who is better. The less advanced student realizes that, over the course of hours, days, or weeks, he is improving. He can make this judgment when he compares his playing against someone or something else; he cannot do that if he has nothing to which his playing can be compared.

*(James Froseth)*

### Student's involvement

After we have performed, people often say, "You know it's just fun to watch your kids. It's amazing how into their playing they are." I just take it for granted because they act that way all the time. I don't even notice it but they'll say, "Gee, it's fun to watch your kids, because they are obviously very intent and very serious about what they're doing." I think it is neat for kids to be that involved in music and performance. This contrasts with so much going on in music education that is, at best, entertainment for adults.

*(Lewis Larson)*

### Manhattanville in band and orchestra

I could not exist without the use of Manhattanville ideas. I like to get kids inside music. Some directors, however, don't want to be bothered. When you see the excitement it generates in kids, you don't want to stop using these ideas. Once you quit beating kids on the head and use this approach instead, it's hard to return to that other style of teaching.

*(John C. McManus)*

### Motivating through knowledge, style, and meeting expectations

It might be more frustrating teaching in the public school than college, because the high school teacher is trying to slam it out. However, it's a lot easier because those kids know so little at this stage. High school students don't study the score. Compared to college, they don't know anything. College kids are highly intelligent, their expectations are very high, and you better meet those expectations. It had better be there now, not tomorrow—and they will not forgive mistakes. Yet they still need many interpretive directions. For example, they want to know how I shape or phrase this and they want to know how the piece is constructed.

High school kids will respond because you are raising the level of rehearsals from an intellectual standpoint. They are not accustomed to this. I'll say, "What do you know about this piece?" If they know very little, I'll tell them about the piece and there is a different mood in that room. You're not trying to be elected to office, you are simply being more professional. They will notice that from the way you speak and, one would hope, the use of proper English and an expanded vocabulary.

Some high school teachers sound as though they work in a gas station. That is not going to raise the students intellectual level at all. There are other band directors who only listen to band tunes, they never listen to other kinds of music. Therefore, they have only the latest publisher's album. They don't listen to chamber music, good jazz, etc. These directors have this narrow view of music and the result is they have no frame of reference.

*(John Williamson)*

### Marching band, music, and motivation

I think we have to acknowledge the values of marching band and to use the marching band experience to promote those values. For example, there must be a genuine high level of discipline in the group, the same as there must be in the concert band. There must be a constant awareness to achieve excellence and precision. There has to be a commitment that is in keeping with the rest of the program. The marching band is here and we are not going to eliminate it. We cannot say, "I'm not going to deal with it," "I'm going to condemn it." or "I'm not going to acknowledge its value." What we must do is to give the marching band value or its due.

I made marching band separate from the concert band program. It ran after school as an extra-curricular event. I know that's difficult to do unless you have large numbers of students. We ran marching band with a very high level of discipline. The commitments were there and the achievement level was very much in keeping with the concert band. For example, students memorized everything. Frankly, by the time students were seniors, they'd had it with the marching band, but they all had a basis for breath support. The better senior players in concert band had been in the marching band previously, and had learned where the power from the air stream comes from.

Sure, they were playing a little bit too loud on the field, but there was a definite esprit de corps built through marching band. This showed throughout the program. When our marching band was at its highest level, we had eight or nine hundred people at concert band concerts. These also were well accepted. When a marching band goes down hill, then the concert attendance goes downhill.

The marching band also related to the community. When students walked down the street in a band jacket, the members of the community respected them and the students felt it. People knew students were in a fine organization, an organization that had received considerable recognition throughout the country. The students felt proud they were wearing a band jacket.

When we returned from a major appearance, police escorts and fire trucks met us at the city limits and Main street. The last time I saw that was when the basketball team won the state tournament. Experiencing that kind of public support does something for the esprit de corps and to our students.

Maybe that isn't the essence of music education, but it has to do with the total education of the student, from the total experiential point of view. He can say with pride, "I'm in the band," and he can tell his little sister he is in the band. His little sister says, "Yeah! I know and I'm going to be in band too!" We've got to think about that.

Every one of these kids that had been in the band program felt good about it also. They are going to raise their kids to be in the band program and music teachers are going to have a job that gives them the opportunity to teach music to kids.

My question is whether the whole band, itself, is worthy of that interest. When Revelli did marching band at Michigan and was on the ladder, did he give it to somebody else to do? No! The marching band definitely has a valuable contribution to make. It may not always be musical.

Let's face it, the students that we get may not become one-hundred percent musicians. But I'm not interested in sharing the world with musicians, I'm interested in sharing the world with better people. I'm convinced that I can make these people better people by giving them experience with music and marching band can be made to contribute to this goal.

The students who have left my program have been affected positively. I talked to one the other day who is a camera salesperson. She was a third-clarinet player for two years. She was a very excited contributor and a responsible person in the band, but never highly skilled. She said to me, "The reason that I have interest in the arts today is because of what you taught me." I said, "What did I teach you?" She told me about the kinds of things we had learned and done. I said, "I was not aware that I was teaching you these things."

She said she developed an aesthetic awareness, an appreciation for beauty, a search and quest for truth about the achievement of oneself. Here she was doing art photography, selling cameras, and never playing clarinet again. She is taking values, though, learned through music, and applying them to other areas of her life. Those are the kinds of values and ideas that I think are important for her.

There are teachers who believe, that unless the students continue to be involved with music, they have failed to train them well enough. I want students to be able to decide to go ahead if they want to. If they don't continue to play, neither they nor I have a character defect.

I feel that the broader goal is the one that seems to have more value. I want them to have a wonderful, worthwhile life-time experience through music. I want them to be affected positively by what they have done. Yes, we do it through the music, and we work hard and have discipline to achieve musical values. But the real value probably is that we become better people.

Beethoven said it: "Music is a disciplined art, which has its own rewards." First, we cannot overlook either the word discipline or the word art. The operative words are, "Has its own rewards." When we look at that, music is an entity. We can expect it to provide us with its own reward: that is true.

I also think we have to go beyond that. I have former students who are playing professionally. They are in the symphony orchestras and are doing their thing, but I don't evaluate my program on the percentage of the kids who have done that; if I did, I'd be a miserable failure.

A whole lot of people from our bands are now having children. They are sending their kids to school where they are now playing in the band program. Some people say, "Because there is this basic human value in music, we should sacrifice the art itself for that human value." I don't believe that's the case. We need to pursue that specific artistic value to achieve the greater human value. That is where the rub comes. We have to be a very careful about the balance of human benefits and artistic values, because the pursuance of the art is of itself an important activity. The pursuance demands and can attract much effort and time from the participants.

*(Charles Olson)*

### What we seek in an experience

Students want to have an enjoyable, emotional expe-rience from their musical experience. They need to feel some kind of emotion. Everyone, when they come to a concert or when they put an instrument to their mouth, wants to receive some aesthetic high. They want to feel better. They want to feel something either good, or bad, or indifferent. To do that, audiences and performers must realize that it takes all-encompassing concentration to have such an impact. For the teacher, this really depends on what you think they need to get out of it. Sometimes it's going to be training a listener and consumer. At other times, I am training a musician to play or a teacher to teach.

*(William W. Wiedrich)*

### Motivation from hearing professional rehearsals

Drag kids to a professional rehearsal. Every time I can, I load four or five of my most interested kids into the car and drag them with me to an orchestra rehearsal. We live about an hour and a half from Pittsburgh and so I've always taken wind ensemble students to listen to Pittsburgh Symphony rehearsals.

*(Donald Wilcox)*

### Motivating with guest teachers

I invite people to come in, and listen and make comments. Usually somebody will tell them the same thing I did. The visitor may say something in a different way or, because they are a new person, they will get the point across. Inviting other people to come in and listen always perks up the kids' concentration. They may only be wondering, "Who is this guy," but it works. Any additional factor will often make all the kids try a little harder.

In Anaheim, the teacher at the other high school and I rehearsed first period in the morning. About once every two weeks (we didn't ask anybody because they wouldn't have let us do it), I would take his band and he would take mine. As a result, we got the effect of a clinician and, for us, a change of scenery and a break from our own kids. He happened to be a brass man, I was a woodwind player, and the kids in both bands enjoyed it. They were very responsive and very positive about it. We set them up by saying, "We are both looking for a chance to get some fresh ears on this."

*(Donald Wilcox)*

We raise considerable money for our program through fund-raising efforts and profits from a not-for-profit corporation. Our parents have started a recycling business in our county and they raise thousands of dollars. We are fortunate to have supportive parents. They have the ability and skill to envision ways to generate financial means that convert to educational opportunities for their children. They support an annual budget of approximately $230,000, which is in addition to tax-funding from the district.

We use much of it to bring in guest performers and teachers. We have quintets, quartets, and other ensembles as well as individual performers. For example, we have had the Canadian Brass, Vince DiMartino, Allen Vizzuti, and Chris Vadala as guest artists-clinicians. We contract for one person or group each year. The face-to-face experiences with live and alive musicians benefit our program immeasurably.

The funding also has allowed us to commission pieces. The people who have written for us are Allen Vizzutti, who wrote *Rising Sun* which we played on a Japanese tour. This was dedicated to Vince DiMartino and our band. Robert Margolis wrote *Toward the Stars Unknown*, Brent Dutton wrote *In the Void*, Frank Erickson wrote *Music Festiva*, and we will commission a piece from Frank Ticheli, a former student of Robert Floyd's and a current composer-in-residence at University of Southern California. We could not have done this without the generous support from fund-raising projects.

We have a large growing program of over 400 students from grades nine through twelve in a school with 2,600 total enrollment. Now we are moving toward a more comprehensive curriculum that includes music history, music theory, and courses for non-performers such as humanities. This course includes art, history, sculpture, music, literature, and drama. We also are moving toward including some aspect of the arts in every class in the entire school curriculum.

*(Mark Davis)*

### Using rounds

I teach kids many musical rounds. Some are familiar folk-song rounds and some of them are not. They are simple ones. I think they're very valuable. Once they learn the round, I will adapt the round so they have to follow my conducting. I change the style or volume, we sing instead of play, and all that.

I do this to get their eyes. I have one that came from a sign in the British Railway System. The words were, "To stop the train in cases of emergency, pull down the chain. Penalty for improper use, five pounds." I changed the words. "To stop the band, whenever it is necessary, watch the conductor, watch the conductor. If you don't, you may end up all by yourself."

First, I'll have them play and they'll always miss the A flat. Though the round has slurs in it, we could play it with a very light staccato, or we could slow it down. It is more fun to play than the Pachelbel canon. Then, I give them the words and they like to sing it. Then we'll play it and sing it. We place each section into one of the three different parts. The kids play it twice and then sing it twice. Of course, as soon as every section has sung it at least once, we always will end with a triangle putting a button at the end of the last phrase that goes: If you don't, you may end up all by yourself. (rest) ding!

*(James Croft)*

### BUILDING MOTIVATION THROUGH REINFORCEMENT OF LEARNING

#### The idea of reinforcement

When I was an undergraduate at the University of Illinois, the learning theory of operant conditioning or operant behavior was prevalent. I have tried to use the idea of reinforcement more than any single teaching technique and I have constantly been reinforcing desirable behavior ever since because I believe it has been a successful teaching technique.

With the beginner, I reinforce any musical behavior that is good no matter how small it is. The teacher must reinforce behavior at that instant, not after five minutes have gone by. One can do so verbally by saying "good." But, one also *must sound sincere* when reinforcing students' behavior. One can say, "Wow, it's great that you're slurring on those pitches," "I like the way you have your lips placed, that's the right way," "Good, you have the embouchure correct now," or "I like the way you play those notes as one phrase, that's the musical way." Which techniques you use for reinforcement depend on the individual persons, but you have to be sincere.

The group members can also reinforce each other. If we are rehearsing a piece with a difficult ending and they finally play it correctly, I say, "All right, give yourselves a hand. Thus the members reinforce their efforts in mastering a difficult spot.

Many, many years ago when teachers were less worried about getting in trouble, a pat on the head or on the shoulder might have been okay as a reinforcement. Now, pats and any physical contacts with students usually are not acceptable. In some schools you can pat a very young student, but you should know the school's policy and watch your step. Because the situation is so delicate, I give verbal reinforcement instead of physical reinforcement.

To give opportunity for reinforcement, I may select students to perform if someone plays something extremely well. I have them play for the rest of the class. The class realizes that person is doing it right. Being used as a demonstrator is definitely a "stroke." Once someone demonstrates, it is amazing how often other students begin wanting to demonstrate. They know what we are going to work on and they will try very hard to play it well, so I choose them as a demonstrator. They want to be chosen for playing correctly and to receive a share of approval from their peers and the teacher.

After the year starts, it can get to be a monster each week because so many students want to demonstrate in band. To control this, we might have ten demonstrators in a typical rehearsal. I try to choose students each week who have not played the previous week. I specify what they should play, whether it is phrasing, breathing, articulation, etc. I always try to leave them with a positive feeling at the end of the lesson.

*(Phillip A. Weinberg)*

## An unproductive use of reinforcement

Incorrect reinforcement can be unproductive or even detrimental. For example, if a teacher said, "Now I'd like you to do the phrase this way." The teacher shows it by singing or playing. Then, when the student plays terribly with no change, he says, "That's good!" That definitely reinforces the student, but not for educational or musical progress.

*(Kenneth M. Larsen)*

## Giving positive reinforcement

When students are in the midst of making adjustments, this is the golden time to reward them with the fewest words like, "Hey, that was terrific." Do this at those golden times when students zing and really come together. Every now and then a group experiences those special four minutes in a two-hour rehearsal. One should reinforce them, especially at the time when their playing and learning is hot.

Our observation of others is a critical point. Teachers are like the air traffic controllers. They have lots of radar scopes and many airplanes out there. They know the schedules, they are the observers and the guys in the tower. traffic controllers guide the planes to a safe landing, just as teachers guide students by spotting the important moments to reinforce students.

*(Frederick Fennell)*

Positive reinforcement is really the key. Wherever you can find progress, praise it as much as you can. I completely stop when something is going well and give them reinforcement. This is especially important with kids or a section. Maybe a week ago you got on them, but today was a very big improvement. Just completely stop right where you are and say, "Man, wasn't that great!" Or, "cool," or "awesome." If you can do that, then they will improve.

*(Dwayne P. Sagen)*

## Reinforcement and student responsibility

I try to reinforce with every student that they are responsible instrumentally for everything they do. They are to be responsible to their talent by developing it to whatever extent they possibly can. Therefore, every student has to submit individual work.

If teachers give individual attention to them, students can be convinced that what they do on their instruments is important. Now, it's not always a positive kind of attention—sometimes it's a negative kind of attention, therefore, one does it individually. It might be, "Johnny that wasn't a good tone, or Johnny . . . ." At first, one is probably telling the student a whole lot more of what's wrong then of what's right. Finally, when Johnny begins to take the responsibility to heart, he would prefer having the teacher say, "Johnny, that was wonderful, you really must have worked on that." When he understands that he

likes to hear that instead of, "Johnny that was wrong, you really have to improve on that," Johnny has become a self-motivator.

Through this, a teacher may teach self-discipline, self-motivation, and self-achievement. Positive rewards for achievement are the best way to go, but a teacher can't be phony about that. If students feel they've done a lousy job and the teacher tells them they were wonderful, they lose respect for the teacher.

*(Charles Olson)*

## Building student confidence

When we sight read, we do not read at full tempo unless it is a tempo they can handle. I do not want to destroy their confidence and their ability to read. I do not want them to have the feeling, ever, that they are out of control. I want them to feel in control, which builds confidence.

*(John W. LaCava)*

## Being needed can motivate students

I say, "I need more from you" and I keep saying it. If somebody's not playing and they're not getting their job done, I say, "Look, we need you. We've got to have that tenor sax at this point." Instead of putting a person down, I'm always saying, "You're important, you're important to this ensemble." Then, everyone feels they are important and they understand that you know they're important. This gets away from this principal-player idea.

*(Richard J. Suddendorf)*

## Motivating through expectations

I think one reason my program has been successful is that I expect students to do extremely well. If you expect near perfection in everything that they do, they will get to know that. Then, they will exceed what they normally expected of themselves. For example, I really expect the articulation to be there, even starting with a beginner. This must be followed through always. If you let go at any time or at any place, the students will get off track. You must constantly reinforce correct behavior, retain your own expectations, and convey them to students.

*(Phillip A. Weinberg)*

## Display practice records

All students had to have their practice records signed before they could take part. Every month, I listed the winners by school.

*(Marion Etzel)*

## Motivating a weaker section

If you have a weak section in your band, feature the section. If you need more tuba players, feature the section in at least one half-time show a year. You can't build up a weakness by hiding it. If the trumpet section is down, we work the heck out of them.

First, they become a better section. Second, they

have a chance to be even more improved the second year. Section features are also very effective because parents and others want to see their kids be stars. Students and parents want recognition and the spotlight. Instead, many teachers subordinate the individual kid's recognition to the group's recognition.

*(Robert E. Foster)*

With my high school band, I took the first two clarinets out of the front row and put them in the third row. Then, I put the third clarinets in front so I could help them. This raised their morale if nothing else. They feel what they are doing is important enough to be heard.

*(Terry A. Oxley)*

If you have four horn players that play about the same, don't leave the same one on first and the same one on fourth all year. Of course, if you've got the killer tune you're doing for the festival, put the student with the good high range on first for that tune. Seat someone of lesser ability on first part when the tune is easier.

*(Donald Wilcox)*

### Motivating through responsibility and recognition

Use the good students in the group both as examples and sometimes as teachers. If you have a kid that is an exceptional talent, they can help somebody. Often we have a third clarinet that's struggling. If you have a first clarinet that is in all-state band, it can be good experience for them to help the slower one. This also gives you another teaching assistant to use once in a while and it gives the kids some good experience.

*(Donald Wilcox)*

### Motivating through special events

I was teaching at an air force base and they made a big deal of putting the flag up and taking it down every day. So all the brass players who could play *To The Colors* would go to the flag ceremony five minutes early. They would play that in unison and they play taps when they took down the flag in the evening.

Not only did they get out of school five minutes early to go do that, all those interval things are great for young brass players. I would have thirty little grade school kids with their trumpets, trombones, and baritones playing all those bugle-things in unison. They loved getting out of school five minutes early. When all the other kids came out to the buses, they would be standing out there with their trumpets playing their little thing.

*(Donald Wilcox)*

### Observations about the use of reinforcement

Try always to use the "jam sandwich" approach when communicating criticism to students. Give at least one positive comment (sweet jam) before the problem or corrective measure (bread and butter) is stated. The best

place to begin implanting and habituating such behavior is with music education majors. They can begin practicing this when they are asked to critique each other's performance in instrumental methods classes.

*(Paul Haack)*

Positive reinforcement is the key. Wherever you can find opportunity for that, praise as much as you can. I completely stop when something has gone well or when they have shown improvement. Maybe I have been demanding something from a student or a section and they have responded with a correction. I say, "Man, wasn't that great, cool, or awesome," whatever the current phraseology is.

*(Dwayne P. Sagen)*

Once the kid plays correctly, the two key words are "That's it."

*(John Williamson)*

It is a golden time when they zing and really come together; and now and then a group experiences that four minutes out of the two-hour rehearsal. One should reinforce especially when things are hot. That is a critical point of the observation of others. We are like the traffic controllers with radar scopes, the schedules and many planes to watch for out there; since we are the guys in the tower, we are in the best spot to see what is happening with the students. Thus, we know who to reinforce, and what and when to reinforce them.

*(Frederick Fennell)*

I try to reinforce desirable behavior so other students seek the same recognition. I ask them to applaud as a support to my statement that something was done very well. They reward each other for musical playing. This is particularly important for kids playing ordinary, but crucial parts.

*(Richard Fischer)*

I have to watch how I phrase my approval. I can't tell them that was the world's greatest, but I can be supportive and positive, and reinforce that they're making progress and are doing well.

*(L. Keating Johnson)*

They come to class in the fall and see rhythm patterns number one, two, three, etc. on the board. In the spring, when they see fifty five, fifty six, etc. they know what we are going to do and they also see that they have made a great deal of progress. I like to watch and measure the improvement month by month, not in comparison to last year. I like it when I can point out to kids how much better they do something today than they did last month or last week.

*(Carl A. Bly)*

I give a verbal pat on the back with, "That was a good job." For example, we worked on a piece Monday and it was clear there was a problem at letter A. After it became better, I said, "Clarinets, that has really improved. It's obvious that you've been working on it. Good job." Or, at the end of rehearsal, walk over to students as they're packing up their instruments and say, "Great guys, that really shows a lot of growth." It is informal, but it's part of that philosophy of being positive. I don't do it or remember it always, but I try to be as positive as I can. So, I believe we should find the opportunity to encourage instead of finding the opportunity to criticize students' efforts.

(John A. Thompson)

I look for things to reward, particularly with the younger kids.

(Carl A. Bly)

If they do something well I say, "Do you hear that, do you like it? Remember it. Now try it again." Then if I like it, I'll say, "I like that. Can you hear it?" And they'll say, "Yeah." Then when we go on from there, I say, "Try to hold on to that."

(James Stivers)

If you have to tear something down, you'd better be right there to pick them up again. If you have to say, "It's wrong, it's not right folks," you have to find some way to support them sooner, not later.

(John A. Thompson)

If I don't have bassoons and oboes who really blow, I can guarantee you that they are going to get a chance to show off. If I have a whole brass section that is weak, I am not going to hide them; I will feature them. On the other hand, if there is a powerhouse trumpet or horn section, there are going to be special challenges that I pick particularly for them.

(William Long)

When playing has improved, I try to follow up with a positive "All right!" Maybe, I will pull my hair straight up and swoon while saying, "The hair on my head is standing on end. You're turning me on! You're getting me excited!"

This kind of reinforcement continues through the course of a year—and through the course of a lifetime of work. It builds the excitement over accomplishing something. Though it's maybe only a germ of progress, though it's only a motive of progress, they accomplished it and they did it. Adding that to two or three things done the next day starts a continual building of their excitement with doing music. I reward all the time; in fact I over-reward. I over-do it on both ends. I condemn the heck out of them and I love them to death for even an honest effort. I go overboard on both ends, and I

see nothing wrong with that. It works.

(William Long)

I get away from the ensemble and have them play. It's beautiful and I say, "Look, you don't need a conductor at all. All you need is to listen to each other and the ensemble becomes tighter."

(Richard J. Suddendorf)

Their confidence increases when they sing something they have learned to play. That makes them realize that they do, in fact, have the knowledge to do the singing.

(Carl A. Bly)

As a treat for older students when they have completed their work, I usually arrange a pop tune for them. They need not study the tune, but they know that it was there for them.

(Marion Etzel)

If students get a pass to transfer here during study hall, they must give me twenty minutes of that for practice. The other time they can study, talk with friends, etc.

(Stanley Cate)

I purposely play it wrong so students might notice an error. I may do it several times until someone notices. Or, I will say, "In the key of G, we have three sharps." When someone does notice the information is incorrect, I give them an enthusiastic reinforcement by the words I use, the expressions on my face, etc.

(James D. Ployhar)

When our kids go to a solo contest and earn a perfect score, they get a star which comes from the district. They also get another award from me: I give them a dinner at McDonald's.

(Sandra P. Thompson)

Once I had a particular bunch of jar heads in the sophomore percussion section who came in thinking they were jar heads. I remember hearing stories about how they had acted like clowns in junior high school. I did not treat them like clowns, although there were times when I just wanted to kill them. They still thought that going to band meant that they were supposed to screw around.

Because of our spring trip I hadn't done any percussion ensemble work with this group. Therefore, I had only ten days to get a percussion ensemble together with them. It was an involved one for this sophomore bunch—it was a struggle. But, they actually made music. I remember the day before the contest I had them play in front of the band and the whole band was impressed. The drummers could do more than just goof off—they could play. It was amazing, there was a melody and several different instruments were being played musically and correctly, and they knew it!

*(Howard A. Lehman)*

## MOTIVATION FROM PROGRESS AND ACHIEVEMENT

### Showing achievement

I listed the major selections in the method book on a photocopied progress sheet. As students completed the selections satisfactorily, the items were checked off or rewarded with a star or sticker. At the completion of the entire book, I gave a major award or recognition.

*(Marion Etzel)*

### Competition with oneself

When a page in the traditional string method book is difficult, we have contests. Students compete only against themselves. They play a certain line until they make a pitch or rhythm error. They must stop upon command of the teacher. After everyone in the group has played a line, they get another chance to "better their record."

*(Marion Etzel)*

### Showing what progress will bring

I tell young students, "If you take a breath after every measure, you sound like a fourth grader. If you breathe after eight measures, you sound like a college student." That impresses them. I also play a long phrase in one breath with as little effort as possible. When they see this, they usually say, "Boy, that looks like it was easy to do." or, " I didn't know how easy that was."

*(Steven Cooper)*

### Building morale through class lessons

I think regular sectional rehearsals are very important for many reasons. They also help morale, because the kid is, or feels like he is, more productive as a result of his work in the sectional.

*(Hal D. Cooper)*

### Maintaining interest during proficiency development

Scale performance is too often neglected and usually implies drudgery or monotony for the student. I use the Circle of Fourths (the Jazz Circle) for scale performance and developing technical facility. The students play through all scales and learn scales through an approach where the scales are not isolated or independent from each other. (All scales are played as one complete exercise, beginning with C, to F, to B flat, etc.) Playing different scales in sequence conforms to the literature and harmonic realities, because what we find in solos and ensemble literature is changing keys and harmonic functions, not one key and simple functions as occurs in folk-song literature and other simple

pieces. The circle process develops a "spontaneous reaction" to all keys and the skill students acquire is inevitably applied to sight reading and all technical or diatonic passages.

I can select from an "unlimited number of variations and colors" by assigning different instruments to different starting pitches on the circle. The brass can start on B-flat concert while the woodwinds start on F concert, which creates the sound of various timbre combinations and the sound of interval combinations that provides an entry to harmonic understanding that is to comes a bit later. This approach to scales enables the teacher and students to experience greater "meaning" and establish connection to music literature. Students no longer can view scales strictly as tasks for auditions or seating, they can recognize scales as the foundation for musical performance.

*(Edward S. Lisk)*

### Pride and tradition

Our students are performers. They get up for performances and parents respond well to performance. They have never let me down in a performance. This is a twenty-five year tradition and there is a definite community pride in the music program. The older kids teach this to the younger kids.

We have also broken down barriers between drama, music, and athletics, because our students are in everything. Because of the tradition, we can't have a football band because our kids are playing football. (This is a blessing for the band director.) There also are football players in the orchestra, playing stringed instruments.

Most coaches are very cooperative: most truly understand why it is good for the kids. A couple of coaches resent it because it is a highly publicized and successful program. Though the participation is high, athletics is not a winning program. The sports program gets students for much more time than we do. They practice two hours a night and five days a week. If we had them that many hours, we could do phenomenal things.

*(Judith A. Niles)*

### Writing solos

Particularly at the junior high level, many kids were very interested in writing a solo for their instruments each year.

*(Lewis Larson)*

### Modeling how to practice

With basic problems such as learning notes, which I think is a problem that everyone faces, there are some ways to instill in the players a desire to learn the notes.

For example, take any small passage from a piece that you know doesn't sound particularly good and rehearse it to death. Rehearse and isolate a passage, and work with it in slow-motion. Explain to them along the way why you are doing what you are doing. You can teach them to practice by getting the whole group involved in improving a small passage. They can be supplying the rhythmic background and show how the group can make a difference in two or three minutes.

In those two or three minutes with the kind of practicing you are doing, you are showing them how to practice. The group's musical improvement, of course, will be remarkable. If you ask the group, they will confess it's better. Talk about it with them and they will tell you why it is better and why they will get better by practicing in that way.

What you have shown them is (a) how to practice, (b) what the practice result is, and (c) have given gobs of positive reinforcement. Then they understand that now it's their responsibility. They begin to learn what practicing does and what the difference is between practicing and rehearsing.

In time, they begin to understand that it's their job to learn the notes. They see how it makes a difference in the performance. You showed them some practice procedures and the result will be carried over to future rehearsals, practices, and pieces.

*(Larry Rachleff)*

## MOTIVATION THROUGH LITERATURE AND MUSIC KNOWLEDGE

### Unique programming
I may rearrange a piece like *Grease*, to include singers and dancers, and perform it at a concert.
*(Jack Brookshire)*

### Literature selection
Pick pieces they have a chance to play, since kids don't like what they can't play.
*(Carl A. Bly)*

### Playing familiar pieces for fun
Sometimes, we play something from last year or from the last concert for the fun of it in rehearsal. I don't reprogram it on a concert because that is not educationally sound. They have already played and attained what they can in that piece.
*(Carl A. Bly)*

### Knowledge is motivation
Knowledge is motivating and we must teach the vocabulary. We deny the most universal creative aspect or sense of the art, if we forget to develop other aspects of their musicianship.

This means you must be a listener, composer, and player to be fully a musician. The student must understand the musical vocabulary of the music, not just musical terms in isolation. We must have the ability to manipulate the musical or technical aspect that the terms stand for. I want them to do more than just play they instrument. He

also should understand music's written language. If he does, the music can be more meaningful to him—and he can be creative.

Without vocabulary, it is very hard to create anything in music. For example, I have taught mixolydian scales in context of a I-IV-V progression in twelve-bar blues. Suddenly, with this vocabulary a student can start using this learning in his own way. Suddenly a new dimension opens to that person and their identification with music reaches a different level.

Learning, improvisation, and composition are more interesting than just playing music. This could invigorate our band programs considerably by introducing some creativity. We need this, since we have introduced so little vocabulary that they can use to be creative and to apply it right then to music.
*(Frank Bencriscutto)*

### Information about the music or composer
Students do not realize that the music shown impersonally on the printed page was written by a human being. To increase their awareness, I talk about the background of the composer or arranger. With this information, they respond very positively. We probably should teach more to the students in this respect. The connection between students and the music's composer can be impersonal. This is a very important obstacle—one we must overcome.
*(Thomas H. Cook)*

### Selecting a variety of songs
I select tunes of varying difficulty, in different meters, in major, minor and other tonalities, and different articulations. I include changing the style so a single tune is played with different styles of articulation. The most common difference of articulation is separated and connected. Certainly, in the beginning students should play major, minor, duple and triple songs, and they should play them in connected and separated style.

I could have a list of tunes that would work. Directors, though, can pick any that fit. The songs might be folk songs, tunes from television and radio, school songs, church songs, and other songs students like to play and are familiar with. Do the major songs in minor; do the minor songs in major. Also try doing them in different keys. I would do this when needed to build their aural understanding of tonality. The student need not play all tunes in major that are in minor, and all minor tunes need not be done in major.
*(Richard Grunow)*

### Introducing broad ideas to motivate students
I talk to students about the idea of cosmic energy. I ask them to think and concentrate to help others who are performing at that moment. Their intention is to add their energy to the total output of the group.
*(Thomas H. Cook)*

### Relating one piece's features to another's

I believe in the transfer of information. If there is a piece that is special, with a special rhythmic or musical appeal , it belongs in your kit bag—and in your student's musical conscience.

After spending time preparing to play a technical piece of Vaclav Nelhybel, you can remind them that this is like the other piece of his, or to any piece that has a common feature. We can say, "We've been there."

I would draw upon any composer, any style, any passage to help students grasp a spot in the music. I would use every means to remind them of what they already have done. We tend to be very much "one piece at a time teachers" and that is not good. Students like to have the security of knowing that they have been there through another piece, whatever that piece might be. This is also true about technical matters such as articulation.

*(Frederick Fennell)*

### Motivating through composition

I have middle school kids create their own concert, with their own compositions, after only a few weeks of instruction. To help structure the assignment, I might give them a starting and ending note. In the beginning, the notes mean almost nothing. I help them—at times they need suggestions. Later, the notes begin to mean something.

*(John Kinnison)*

### Motivating through literature

I think it is crucial, when a new sophomore comes into the room, to get a new piece of high-interest solo material in his hand. I don't believe you can teach solo skills effectively in a large group. If they do develop solo skills, you can deal with the phrase, the dynamics, and the terminology. I think that it is best done through material that is of high interest—and fun—to the students; we've all been bored with the fundamental stuff.

If they come back and say, "I don't like this," I say, "Well you have to keep it one more week." Maybe they can't play it, because they haven't worked hard enough on it yet. As soon as I can understand that they don't care for the literature, I get them something else. I think that they deserve to have some fun with interesting literature.

Switching solos usually works. If it doesn't work, then Sousa himself couldn't influence this kid; the kid simply isn't ready for this piece, for who knows what reasons. You're never going to get them all. If I did lose one, the size of a group isn't that important. What is more important, is to have role models within the group.

*(Kenneth M. Larsen)*

### Playing from the full score

If you have a kid who's really hot, we need to do all sorts of things to keep these super-talented kids motivated. I had one student play off the full score. I'd give her the score and say, "Okay, play the alto clarinet part." On another day it might be the flute part or any other part to make her transpose. I think this can challenge a student and I also do it in my conducting classes.

*(John A. Thompson)*

## MOTIVATION THROUGH ORDER AND STANDARDS

### A well-planned rehearsal can motivate students

The approach must vary but it must be business-like. The teacher must be well prepared, know what needs to be accomplished, be serious, and communicate the goals one has. The teacher must have all related things ready for the rehearsal. You need to plan what needs to be done first, what is most needed, and what can be done for a group so they feel satisfied and anxious to return. One result is the students' morale is boosted for and during rehearsal.

*(Barbara Buehlman)*

### Motivating through an orderly class room

An orderly room prevents discipline problems because it imposes a structured and disciplined environment. They anticipate it and this has a positive effect. Nothing is in the room that could be a distraction. Furthermore, nothing is on the wall or board unless it relates to what we are doing. I do this because they and I need this. This also has worked successfully for sixteen years at the high school level.

*(John W. LaCava)*

### Motivating with challenges

If you give them any change or challenge, they cannot be thinking of what they are going to do that evening. I also make them memorize in situations to focus their attention on a challenge. They don't like it, but Suzuki kids do it very easily.

*(Judith A. Niles)*

I ask them to do their best partly to help others and be responsible to them. We are only as strong as the weakest link. Their real competition, however, is between them and the page. They should not let an inanimate object defeat them.

*(John W. LaCava)*

### Having standards pays off

I think standard setting makes music a lot more interesting. I challenge them to play with attention to intonation and tone quality. As a result, there is less chance for music to get boring. I think my seniors are as challenged when they walk out of there the last day as they were when they were an eighth grader playing the first time in the band. Each time they play, there is a new challenge for them.

*(Lewis Larson)*

CHAPTER TWO

# JUDGMENT

In music education classes, teachers provide students with information and experiences, and they develop the students' skills. If there is a well-planned curriculum and effective instruction, students can experience enough performance and listening to enable some of them to make good decisions about music. For teachers to help them even more toward independent thinking and mature judgment, they should deliberately teach students how to make musical decisions—not just assume that the students will infer how to make musical judgments on their own. If students practice judging what they see and hear in their own or another's performance, and through their listening, they can make more independent decisions—and enjoy doing so because it involves them.

The growth toward awareness and independence is essential for a student's education and should begin early on. A music student can judge if the tone color is appropriate or blended, if the volume should crescendo, and if the tempo or the phrasing of the melody is musically appropriate. Eventually students can learn the most difficult lesson of all: there are answers, but the answers in music performance, composition, and listening require the use of judgment; and they require taste, practice, and musical experience. The answers and judgments cannot be certain, but they must be made none the less. When students start to make judgments in spite of the uncertainty, they are beginning to show the results of a proper musical education.

## THE VALUE OF DEVELOPING JUDGMENT

### A reason to develop students' judgment

If you just tell them what to do, every time you go to a new piece, you're going to have to tell them what to do again. I try to avoid telling them what I want. Sometimes I'll ask them, "Where do you think the peak of the phrase is? Why is that important?" I'll have a section play the melody and I will stop conducting. Then I will turn to the rest of the band and say, "What do you think is the most important point of the line?"

(Mallory B. Thompson)

### Making judgments

I think musicianship means the ability to make independent decisions about how the music should be performed.

(Craig Kirchhoff)

### Teaching students to judge their performance

The reason I created a small ensemble program in high school was that the principal suggested I make a change. He said, "If you are going to give grades in band, let's have some criteria. This attitude and attendance rating is fine, but not criteria enough for evaluation." The criteria I came up with was Musical Independence.

I identified problems that occurred in small ensemble playing, such as rhythm, balance, ensemble, notation decoding, blend, or intonation. I began to use fifteen minutes of each large rehearsal to teach students how to use and apply things such as these. An amazing thing happened: as their skills in the small ensemble developed, the skills they brought to the large ensemble became more significant. We spent less and less time rehearsing and more time going through literature. We increased the number of performances.

We even started a solo night that featured individuals as soloists with band accompaniment and with student conductors. The students rehearsed and did everything. The performances were not always stellar, but they were good. We did these near the end of the year, after things such as contests began to wind down. I came to believe that musical independence is the most important goal in education.

If teachers do not ask students to generalize their learning, such as skills and information to other situations, no one will ever know if students have learned. If they can't, they are like a mimic who can play the part only. In principle, *The Comprehensive Music Instructor* asks students to apply the things they have learned from the instructor. This is based upon what I learned in my high school ensemble experience or experiment with developing independence through small ensemble work.

(James Froseth)

56

## Developing skill and judgment in listening

A simple procedure to establish listening awareness is to have students play major chords, close their eyes and look, with their mind's eye, at the sound of the band from the tuba to the piccolo. I do not intrude or impose any of my images or descriptors for the sound they are hearing or making. My intent is to develop the students' values and musical judgments of the quality of the sound being produced. As they scan this sound and look at "it" with their mind's eye, they make natural adjustments as they listen carefully for the improvement. The process continues to unfold after a few rehearsals with this basic imagery exercise.

Balance, blend, and intonation are introduced by the following procedure. Inform the students that, as they are looking at their sound, if they hear or "see" themselves *above all others*, one of three things is happening: (1) The student is overpowering or overblowing the section or total band; his solution is to adjust his volume. (2) If the student's sound is not overpowering, and if he has made a volume adjustment and can still hear himself above the section or the band, he is playing with poor tone quality (blend). He must correct that by adjusting his posture, breath support, embouchure, or equipment. (3) If these adjustments have been made, and the student still "stands out," the student is out of tune (intonation). He should lengthen or shorten the instrument to correct intonation.

These steps are in a priority order, because proper intonation cannot be achieved if poor tone quality or overpowering volume exists.

This idea also develops the judgment of students. I have found this effectively teaches musical judgment and values because it asks questions pertaining to musical qualities. One key part for the teacher is to "not ask for answers" from students. This approach encourages the students to determine the result instead of trying to guess the answer the teacher expects to hear. The students have the responsibility to determine the musical result and they respond according to their own analysis and decisions. It provides the students an opportunity and, in a sense, it also trains them to think for themselves and to make value judgments. When the students apply the steps listed above, they are taking responsibility and need not wait for the director to tell them what to do.

*(Edward S. Lisk)*

## Making musical decisions develops judgment

In many respects my training was opposed to where I am now philosophically. The big issue is really teaching kids about musicianship and musicality—talking a lot about expression, dealing in rehearsal with various options, ways to approach music, and different ways to express music. These were things in my own early training that I was never made aware of, and I was never asked those kinds of questions in rehearsal.

Though I do not say that the way to do a piece is to throw the door wide open, the student's opinion and judgments need to be considered and generated. Students have to see and have to buy into the fact that there are different ways to approach a phrase, there are different ways to approach a piece, and there are different ways to approach the intensity of a piece. I tell students that we must make decisions about the music. Whether it's the wrong decision or the right decision is not as important as making a decision.

If someone decides that they're going to let the music stand as the composer wrote it and let it speak for itself, well then that's a conscious decision. They also could decide to make this phrase work by doing more crescendo here or decrescendo there to make music with this phrase. I think that most of us who toiled in public school music, for whatever reason, either avoid those issues or simply don't deal with them. No one ever said that these were things that we should be dealing with.

*(Craig Kirchhoff)*

## Exercising judgment

Making music has to be the motivating reason the technique must be right at that point. Precision is not necessarily its own reward. Too often we coach rehearsals by saying, "It's not together," or "You have to play softer because it says piano." Well, why does it have to be piano? Why is it important to be piano here? It is important to play piano here because the big moment is coming and playing soft now will make that moment work.

*(Craig Kirchhoff)*

## Making choices

I do not expect the students to regurgitate what I've stuffed into them. I try to make the students understand that they are not a faceless musician out there. They have a chance with every note that they play to affect the balance, the pitch, or the sound. There are bands that can play very accurately and can produce immaculate, dead performances. Even though everything is just so perfectly done, I still don't like that kind of performance.

I hope that the individual is free enough to make some effects differently. Periodically, I just encourage them to express themselves. Teachers can work on difficult music and beat something to death by doing it many times. Instead, I want them to know that they have a right to do it musically different every time we play—within the framework of good taste. I want them to be involved in the process, not just regurgitating the notes and rhythm.

*(Kenneth M. Larsen)*

## Involving students in decisions

Students can give to the actual design of the performance as far as the phrasing. Have them decide how to phrase particular numbers. This is both a teaching tool and a reinforcement for the things you have already decided to do. This also works well with the jazz band. They can decide, for example, where the ensemble should end a note.

*(Robert Morsch)*

## Making judgments is essential

I try to foster in all students the ability to make musical judgments.

*(James Arrowood)*

# BUILDING MUSICAL JUDGMENT

## When to develop musical judgments

Developing musical judgment should begin in the very beginning—why wait until later when it is harder to begin?

*(John Kinnison)*

## They make the judgments

Except in the most hurried circumstances, never tell young instrumentalists whether they are sharp, flat, or in tune. Ask them to make a judgment (to commit their attention and ego to the problem) or ask someone else in the group.

*(Paul Haack)*

I don't remember who told me this, but I remember the idea. Sometimes we need to remind the students, "You can play in tune, but I cannot conduct you in tune."

*(David Hans)*

## Inviting the making of judgments

In order for the students to develop analytical skills they can apply to their playing, I ask them to tell me what was good and what was needed to "fix" their playing of a piece, scale, or etude. Their ability to critique their own playing enables them to use their practice time more effectively and to become musically independent.

*(Sharon Rasor)*

## Trial and error can be the beginning of decision making

I say, "Do something with the music; even if it is wrong, do *something* with the music. Exaggerate!"

Then, by a trial and error process we begin to zero in on things. We can decide what things are being done in the right place and what the options are. I tell them to choose something to do, even if it is wrong at that stage, rather than do nothing. Usually they will start with ritards—the biggest thing, which they catch on to quickly. They try to ritard the end of every phrase, though the end of every phrase does not ritard. Even so, that is a start.

Students also begin to use accelerando soon. Almost the whole gamut of phrasing at one point or another will come with dynamics. Usually they will start with becoming louder when the music goes up and softening when the

notes go down. That is also not always the case. They also must learn to crescendo when the notes go down and decrescendo when the notes go up.

When a kid plays something that is not even in the ball park, I do not say, "that's wrong." I simply ask them to play the phrase or passage some other way. I want them to come to a solution on their own. When they are new at it, I do not tell them what they are to do. I let them go with whatever they do, whatever they feel might be musical. The structuring comes later, after the choices begin to emerge. I start this very early, in the first lesson. Not many students seem to have had this experience; instead they worry about getting the right notes or they show the affects of the pervasive use of the metronome.

*(Donald S. George)*

## The context for developing judgment

We must have students feel open enough that they can try different things. I do not want them to feel there is only one right way. Students go to private lessons or rehearsals, and expect there is a right way and the teacher is going to tell them how to do it. There is not one right way. Over the course of a lifetime, most great musicians come up with many different phrasings.

We will try things in different ways, maybe three or four different ways. Then, we stop and talk about which made more sense for the piece or for the style. Maybe we even listen and discuss the harmonic rhythm that's going on underneath. We change emphasis points such as lengthening high points of the phrase or making the high point of a phrase last less long. By doing that, you find out why one way seems a little better than another, or we see what's possible within a phrase.

*(L. Keating Johnson)*

## Playing without a conductor can foster their judgment

I try to incorporate more playing without the conductor. This fosters better ensemble playing. One can make them start at very difficult places so students in the group have to become the conductor. When they get to the concert they can almost do it without the conductor.

*(Robert Levy)*

To develop students' decision making, I use a warm up chorale that they sing, then play—alternating singing and playing. They must play the chorale without being conducted. They do all the releases, attacks, and fermata by themselves, without any help at all. This helps them listen and develops judgment. It is amazing to them how much they can play together without a conductor.

*(Robert Grechesky)*

To play without the conductor presents the opportunity for them to make a judgment. Isolate a section or passage where, for example, the low brass are having trouble staying together in a ritard. Stand in front of them and make them try it on their own. Make someone the conductor who must move their horn and give the down beat. This forces them to move their bodies a little bit, forces them to work hard at it, not to be so dependent on you as the conductor.

It is funny how their performance comes together when you put them on the spot. They can decide how to do it, instead of doing it the way you want. They must focus on doing it together and forming an opinion about what they need to do. Then, if you want to change their opinion, you can deal with the different issue of getting them to follow you.

*(Robert Levy)*

Use listening without conducting so they judge where the phrase ends. Inevitably, they do a better job judging this when listening. When listening only, they are not distracted by looking. I also ask them to listen to balance while tapering an ending, so they can keep the balance right.

*(John Anderson)*

### Understanding musical roles helps students to make judgments

Sometimes, I show what a balanced sound should be. They can easily hear this if it is the next person to them. If the sound is three rows away or sounds differently on the stage compared to the rehearsal room, they could have difficulty deciding the appropriate balance.

On the other hand, students can understand their role in the music at that particular time. If they have a sense for what the dominant voice or color is, they can decide how to achieve the balance or color. They must know what the musical result is to be. This helps students make musical judgments even when facing changing musical or rehearsal environments that cause playing changes or seating changes on different pieces. Students can make decisions if they have some basis for making them.

*(Gary Hill)*

### Developing judgment through listening

To determine and learn about balance, I use them as listeners and judges. When they are not playing they attend to and understand what balance is much better than when they are playing. We can make a balance change when, for example, three trombone players are playing first, second, and third in a chord. I say to someone in the group, "Now is that better?" They know that they're responsible to listen to that much at least.

*(Terry A. Oxley)*

### Using questions and choices to develop judgment

Though I don't demonstrate with instruments, I use modeling. I have them play and let them choose. I ask them to play one or two ways; I say, "Which one did you like

better?" I may say, "Use the fattest air stream you can " or "Speed the sound through" to get them to blow harder.

What I use is more a discovery process. If they get something and I like it I say, "Do you hear that, do you like it? Remember it!" I believe that feeling is a much more acute sense in performance than hearing is. I say, "Now woodwinds, that's too harsh. Calm it down, polish it up, make it slicker sounding. Now try it." Then if I like it, I'll say, "I like that. Can you hear it?" They'll say, "Yeah." I say, "Try to hold on to that." I do this also with balance.

*(James Stivers)*

I never tell them they are sharp or flat. They have to hear the pitch of the standard pitch that we are going to use. They play their pitch and judge whether they are sharp or flat—they have to decide.

If they are always waiting for you to tell them to pull out or push in, it doesn't work. Then, half way through the concert they could say, "Well, you never told me I was sharp." I ask them to make changes until it sounds correct or until the beats stop.

*(Robert Morsch)*

If we have difficulty achieving the balance we want, we will build it. I ask all those with a melody, "Play, and the rest of you look at your part as you listen. Now, tell me if you think your part is next in importance." If students are confused, I help them discover the answer. Then I say, "What is the third most important part—if you think yours is the next most important, you should now play."

*(Bryce Taylor)*

To tune an interval or note, I might get a good example from one of my stronger players and let the others listen. I say, "Does that sound too wide or does that sound okay?" We also may listen to two or three in a row and have another student comment. Now this is done very quickly, obviously. If you hear somebody playing a wide interval and you can make everyone aware of it, then when they go back to play it, it's a little tighter.

*(John A. Thompson)*

To improve their skill in evaluating their performance, students can rehearse the teacher. The teacher sings or plays a passage with errors that need correcting. The performance may show obvious or subtle musical or performance errors. To rehearse the teacher, students must listen and compare the written music to the teacher's performance. Then they offer suggestions that can make the performance more accurate and more musical.

*(Douglas Peterson)*

I try to lead students to make their own judgments. If they are unable to hear their stand partners, they are apt to be too loud. The opposite is true if they cannot hear themselves. They can be responsible for making that judgment and adjusting accordingly. This is a very simple way for young musicians to start to make judgments for themselves rather than waiting to be corrected.

*(Richard Floyd)*

I may ask, "Where do you think you should breathe in this phrase? Why should we breathe there? or, What is the most important thing about the first reading?"

*(Patricia Brumbaugh)*

Try to involve the people in the tuning process. If two saxophones are tuning, ask the clarinets, for example, if the second one is sharp. They must pay attention all the time. When any two people are playing, anyone can answer the question, "Is the second sharp or flat." They can make it their decision. I think directors need to do that much more. If they have a question about it, then they can check with the machine occasionally and say, "Hey, I'm right" and they gain confidence as a result.

*(Myron Welch)*

Go to the piano and really work with them on singing an F major scale, in tune, slowly. Then maybe have half the group singing it and the other half or members of the group playing it slowly. You can address the issues of difference and discrepancies. Say to them, "Now they are singing the pitch G and you are playing the pitch G; now, what's the difference between these two pitches?" Some kid will say, "Well they are playing it higher than the others were singing it."

*(Larry Rachleff)*

If a phrase can be interpreted in two ways, I tell them or I pretend that I don't know how I want to do this yet. I'll say, "Let's play it a couple of different ways and see which one is better." I'll tell them how to phrase it the first and second time. Then I'll ask them if they have any different suggestions, which we try. Then we'll talk about which version they should play and why.

This is not the most efficient use of rehearsal time if you are under pressure with an approaching concert. I find the luxury of a couple of extra minutes to do some of this, because we are supposed to be teaching as well as getting ready for concerts. The real effect is that kids buy into it and say, "Yeah, can you hear the difference in these phrases?" I ask, "Which one do you think is going to work the best or why do you think it's better?" This approach does two things. It will cause any given spot in the music to be phrased well and it creates an aesthetic awareness of what's going on.

*(Gregory Bimm)*

When we played *Chester*, I asked, "Okay, what's the loudest note in the first four bars?" They looked and had different ideas. I had them play with the downbeat of the second measure being the loudest note in the phrase. Then,

I had them play it again with the next note being the loudest note in the phrase. Then, the loudest was the next one, then the next one, and then with a crescendo all through the phrase. We played it every possible way and I said, "Okay, now which one is right?" They got this intense argument going. The whole point was there's no marking at all in the music to suggest any of that.

They said, "Well then, how do you know when it's right?" I said, "You have to decide that, based on your musical judgment and everything else. A lot hinges on what the composer does with that material later. Look later in the tune and see how he goes about development. What are the notes that he uses to develop a whole allegro, for example?" As a result, the conducting class did a two-week analysis trying to decide which note should be the loudest note in the first four measures.

*(Donald Wilcox)*

If there is a problem of articulation in a phrase, play the articulation in various ways and have them echo back the articulations on a unison note. This allows them to hear articulations in isolation and focus upon the feature about which they need to make a decision. Until they hear several different ways, it is hard for them to make the judgment of what they prefer. Then ask students which versions they prefer and place those back into the phrase. Then say, "Which version seems the most appropriate?"

*(Joseph Casey)*

### Using feedback devices to develop judgment

I encourage every player to sit in a practice room with the tuner and learn the peculiarities of their instrument. I say, "Now, you're going to have to come up with your little chart." A lot of playing in tune is just awareness. I think that they know that their saxophone is going to be extremely high on C sharp. In rehearsal, I can just see it coming and I think . . . (Oh! . . . Here comes the C sharp!) Crash! Then we say, "My goodness, how many of you have a sharp C sharp? Okay, then we need to deal with this. How are we going to center on this? Who do you want to gauge on?" More often, I'll say, "You guys have five minutes after rehearsal—let's work on that."

*(William W. Wiedrich)*

I will use the tuner with a certain section. The tuner sounds for four seconds, the individual player tries to match it for four seconds, and then they hear the pitch again from the tuner. I ask the band to judge—no one knows what the objective answer is—whether the player is close, sharp, or flat. "Close" is five cents either way. They make a judgment. I ask a student not to adjust as they go through this sequence a second time.

After they have made their first judgment, they do the second where (1) the tuner sounds, (2) the player plays, and (3) I turn the tuner on to register her playing so the band can see what it is. They then can compare their decision on the first tuning sequence to the tuner's information during the second sequence. The purpose of this is to train and develop skills in all the other students. This works well with all levels of band students. It takes about ten minutes to get through a seven member section. On other days, the demonstration people get their chances to be in the jury.

*(David Deitemyer)*

We ask the kids if they think a tempo is too fast or too slow according to the marking. Then we play it on the metronome and then we play that speed again. It gives them a good idea if they are playing too fast or too slow and makes them think about their tempos.

*(Frank Schulz)*

There is a reason all my trumpet students always practice with a metronome. This is so they know whether the technique is working, whether they can play as fast or as slow as they want. There's no measuring device unless you use a metronome. The purpose of the metronome is not just accurate metronomic time, it is to get them listening and controlling what they do as they listen.

*(Dominic Spera)*

## BUILDING JUDGMENT THROUGH PEER EVALUATION

### Middle school and junior high

An intermediate student may play the rhythms and notes of the passage well, but they often breathe after nearly every note. I might say, "That was a really fine job,

good playing of the right notes. Can anybody possibly suggest how to improve on that?" Then we will talk about the suggestions or another student's playing of that line. If a younger person does a pretty good job and you choose somebody else, that's almost a put-down to the initial person. You have to be very careful about that.

*(Phillip A. Weinberg)*

### Developing listening and judgment

I hear some students play the rhythm or the articulation and others judge which is the more appropriate way to play it. They serve the role of the jury.

*(Kjellrun K. Hestekin)*

### Students evaluating students' performance

I like to use students, not only as students, but as teachers themselves. They respond to peer pressure much better than they respond to the teacher.

When you are teaching cross fingering on a clarinet, such as going from B natural to C sharp, I divide the class by twos. The "ones" will do this little cross-fingering exercise. The "twos" then will observe the "ones." By seeing them, they decide if they are doing it right. To judge, the students must know the difference between right and wrong. Then, the "ones" and "twos" change jobs and the "ones" observe.

*(James D. Ployhar)*

### Judging others to learn to evaluate oneself

I've had students observe lessons of another student. When observing, they also can see things that they can't see when they're playing themselves.

*(L. Keating Johnson)*

# CHAPTER THREE

# FEEDBACK

Feedback simply means to transfer the output (the student's actions) back to the input (the student). Feedback is given through several modes such as verbal explanations, recordings, drawings, and written evaluations or descriptions of a student's behavior.

When the teacher reports or shows the behavior to the student, the teacher is helping students see or hear things that they cannot easily see or hear by themselves. The aim of feedback also is to enable the student to consider and monitor his own behavior. If not, the student has less chance of understanding what he has been doing. With feedback, the student can consider his output *as an observer* as well as the initiator.

In instrumental music education, an additional mode of giving feedback is especially effective. The teacher can give students feedback in the form of a non-verbal model that mirrors or copies the actions of the student. For example, the teacher can imitate how the student took a breath. The student can hear and see this through the feedback the teacher provides; the student then can modify the way he takes a breath if necessary.

Feedback is especially effective when used at critical points in a lesson. For example, in the first step of a lesson the teacher can describe or show the appropriate hand position so the student can see what to do. Next, the teacher can ask the student to try the hand position. The student then holds the instrument with a hand position *he thinks* is what the teacher showed.

At that moment in a lesson, unless the teacher uses feedback, the instruction could fall short. The student has only heard the explanation, watched the demonstration, and tried the hand position. Usually, he has not observed what he did. The student's attention must shift from the teacher's model of what to do to what *he is doing himself*; then he can begin to understand or evaluate how correct he is. Seeing an imitation of what he did enables the student to compare how he is holding the instrument to the correct example the teacher showed. Without this opportunity, the student easily can do the action incorrectly and not realize it. With feedback, the student is more likely to understand, and he also can decide how much he has progressed and what to do next. Without it, full understanding and achieve-

ment are jeopardized.

The teacher also can use feedback to teach phrasing and many other musical skills. Suppose a student's phrasing doesn't show appropriate musical growth toward or away from a key point. The student may not realize he failed to phrase musically unless the teacher plays the phrasing as the student did. The teacher then can model the phrase such that it shows growth to the high point so the student can contrast his version with what should be done. As the student tries his phrasing again and crescendos toward a high point in the phrase, the teacher again gives him feedback by again playing the phrase the way the student played it. In this teaching, the teacher is using both feedback and modeling, and as a result the student is learning what to do versus what he did. While talking and describing may teach the student the proper phrasing, it is sometimes quicker and the results can be more musical if the phrasing is taught through feedback techniques.

Another opportunity for feedback occurs when students play duets, use recordings of a *Music Minus One* type, or use recorded instructional materials such as Jamey Aebersold's jazz improvisation recordings, James Froseth's *Listen, Move, Sing, and Play*, and other recordings that supply a rhythmic and harmonic musical context. During any of these experiences, the student can notice if his playing is improving, and is accurate or inaccurate compared to his partner's playing or the recorded performances of a solo, a part of a duet, an accompaniment, etc.

Peers can also offer feedback that a student can use to evaluate his own performance skills. One student can help another improve such performance skills as articulation, dynamics, posture, phrasing, and breathing. For example, the teacher can ask one student to imitate another. The student sits, moves, plays, or holds his hands, arms, and instrument exactly as he saw or heard his classmate do it. The student being imitated can see what the other student is showing him. Classmates also have a chance to assess their own skills since they can see the appropriate and inappropriate actions. Thus, a student can contribute to the learning process, foster an atmosphere of helpfulness, and give classmates feedback by becoming a temporary instructor.

The teacher's intention is that the student will eventually learn to monitor his own behavior, or supply his own feedback. If the teacher uses feedback to show the student what he is doing correctly and incorrectly, the teacher gives the student something to recall when he practices at home. With practice and observation, the student becomes more skilled at checking his own hand position or musical phrasing. Without learning what to look for or learning what to do, the student cannot guide his own practice as effectively.

Because the content of music is an arrangement of sounds and silences, and performing requires many physical, aural, and listening skills, feedback—especially a non-verbal mode of feedback—can be a very effective teaching technique. One can use feedback to show articulation, dynamics, posture, phrasing, breathing, intonation, rhythm, volume, and tone color. In addition, one can teach posture and position, self-evaluation, style—in short, almost any performance and musical skill. The teacher's explanations and evaluations may also constitute feedback. But, since talking is a less direct way to teach some musical skills, the student has little to see, hear, or feel when hearing explanations. A student remembers more when he experiences non-verbal and concrete feedback that involves him wholly.

## THE VALUE OF FEEDBACK

One contributor related his value for feedback through his observations of Arnold Jacobs, former tubist with the Chicago Symphony Orchestra. He said, "Arnold Jacobs has a studio full of gauges, meters, and other mechanical devices. For example, he puts several lie-detector belts in different places around your chest. He sees your breathing and sees its effects on the gauges. With these devices, the student can see that his chest isn't rising and falling but only the diaphragm is moving. The student can discover that he is keeping his chest real tight. He sees this because the little needle did not reflect any movement from the belt around his chest. Jacobs has created many visual reference points for the student and I have tried many devices like his."

I have seen that if students see what the devices show, they may memorize the specific muscle movement and how that feels in their body. This information or impression is immediate and very valuable for those playing an instrument. If these devices are positive and successful, students can learn what to look for. As a result they may become, in a sense, self-teachers because they now know what to strive for.

*(L. Keating Johnson)*

I have always felt that if a student can feel and see something, especially see, he is going to learn or solve a problem more quickly. For example, if a clarinet player has a lot of throat movement when he tongues, he will stop it if he sees his tongue move as he looks in the mirror.

*(Donald S. George)*

## RHYTHM

### *The metronome*

All my trumpet students practice with a metronome at least one-half of the practice period. The reason is control. From the metronome, they learn whether the technique is working, and whether they can play it faster or slower. There's no measuring device unless you use a metronome.

*(Dominic Spera)*

In the large ensemble rehearsal, students see only the light of the metronome, but the clicking of the metronome is recorded by a microphone on a shelf next to the metronome. I ask the group to start playing along with the metronome. Though students cannot hear the metronome, the microphone records it. On the playback, the tape includes their playing and the sound of the metronome. This shows whether they are slowing down or they are speeding up. Without this, I would say, "You're speeding up" and they would say "No, you're slowing down." I now can say, "The metronome never lies—let's put the tape on, let's record the group and see." If you do the play back immediately, they hear exactly what you're talking about; the process sensitizes them to speeding or slowing—it brings the truth home to them.

*(Thomas Stone)*

I use a lighted metronome periodically to set and check tempos. More so, I do this to help them become sensitive and skilled at keeping a tempo without a conductor. This also makes my efforts accurate and consistent, which should help students over the long term.

During rehearsals of long and short sections, if the tempo seems slow or fast, I will check with the metronome. Or, I will ask students what they think about the tempo and then check their opinion against the metronome. It is useful, therefore, as a reference point or checking device for accurate tempos, and it can increase students' sensitivity to tempo.

I also use a metronome on marches to resolve the problem of slowing on hard passages and rushing on easy ones. This can be difficult to hear on occasion. The students increase their skill playing without the conductor being the metronome; therefore, this enables me to walk about the group listening, helping, and observing things. I could not do this if I had to keep the group playing by conducting from the podium.

*(David Deitemyer)*

We have metronomes on shelves in all the practice rooms; I mounted them so students cannot remove or take them easily. We have another twenty-four metronomes that students can check out for overnight use.

*(Bryce Taylor)*

To practice control of pulse and rhythm, I ask kids to buy metronomes, if they can, and tap their foot as they practice scales at home.

*(Jack Brookshire)*

I use a metronome with the full band; it is also very useful with wind quintets and other smaller groups. One would not want their playing to be too metronomic, but using a metronome keeps them honest from an honest point of view!

*(John Anderson)*

The purpose of the metronome is not just accurate metronomic time. What the metronome does, when you practice and when you teach privately, is force the kid to listen to something other than himself. It's wonderful. If students do not use a metronome, when they play with an accompanist for the first time, you wouldn't believe it! They are lost, they don't know where they are and they are dropping beats everywhere. It's a disaster.

*(Dominic Spera)*

I use tape recorders during lessons and I always tape auditions and challenges so they can be reviewed. I also use them to reinforce learning.

*(Anthony J. Maiello)*

During my sabbatical in Miami, I'm practicing in their music building and all of a sudden I hear "bang, bang, bang, bang." Miami's number-one jazz band is rehearsing and Whit Sidner's conducting. Quickly, I run to look into the rehearsing room: there's Whit banging the heck out of the music stand with a drum stick! After rehearsal, I say, "Hey man, you use that technique, too." He says, "Man, I don't have time, we've only got an hour-and-a-half rehearsal, man. I can't fool around, man, I got to get the job done right away." Nothing—nothing straightens out a rhythm section like showing up at the rehearsal with a metronome. That immediately gets their attention.

*(Dominic Spera)*

I use metronomes as soon as they have a pulse going—by their third or fourth day on a horns. We use metronomes with sounding subdivisions, and we use foot tapping with the "down-up" technique. We count in meters of two and three, and in measures of two, three, four, and six. By the end of the first year they also can play meters of five, seven, six, or four very well. Some subdivision is done through beat and measure counting systems.

*(Bryce Taylor)*

## TUNING AND INTONATION

### *Raising awareness with tuners*

Use the tuner so they see the differences as pitch changes. While watching, they first see the changes; this helps them realize how playing and pitch adjustments show on the dial.

*(Richard Alnes)*

### *The limits of tuners*

I believe in having the students listen; however, I swear my groups played as well in tune, if not better, before I used tuners. The devices work especially well for certain instruments such as french horns. French hornists play scales with the tuner and see how far off some pitches are. This shows them which notes need work. I also let them take the tuners home.

*(Sandra P. Thompson)*

We own ten Korg tuners that we check out to kids.
*(Patricia Brumbaugh)*

### *Reconsider the tuner's use*

I frequently see band directors look at the tuner and tell kids "you're twenty cents sharp." Even at the university, students will put their tuner on the stand during rehearsal to determine the absolute pitch, instead of listening.

When tuning, I recommend several techniques: one is to turn on the tuner so it produces a pitch, then they match what they hear. I recommend this as opposed to concluding one is in tune because one can stop the dial. Matching the pitch produced by the tuner encourages them to blend their tone with what they hear, and prepares them to match and blend with someone else. So many people say and tell students, "If you stop the dial you are in tune." Instead, they should be told they are in tune when they can match and blend with someone else's pitch and tone.

*(Michael Golemo)*

Tuning should be done by listening. The procedure is simple. Do the warm-up first, hear the tuning note, and then play the tuning note. Next and last, look and check the results with the tuner. I use two machines to tune both visually and aurally. One machine makes a sound to match, and the other shows us how well we did.

*(Richard Fischer)*

Band directors and students need to use their ears more. They need to make musical decisions more about what they hear and not what they see. They've got to get rid of that tuning box; they must wean themselves away from it. I think the tuning box is a wonderful tool for a reference point, but it's like buying a factory-tuned instrument. Use the box for a reference point and from then on use the ears. For instance, if you're going to take a pitch from the clarinet, then make sure that the clarinetist is giving the correct pitch. Then, everybody matches that pitch. You should match person to person, not person to machine, because that is the technique students must employ in all their playing.

*(Myron Welch)*

## TYPES AND SOURCES OF FEEDBACK

### Human and musical metronomes, and musical mirrors

I have the snare drummer be a metronome for teaching subdivision, particularly with mixed meter (five-eight, seven-eight, etc.). He plays eighths or sixteenths as a metronome and I have the rest of the band play with him. The snare performs the smallest unit used. Usually, I use the smallest unit that the band can keep track of; if possible, they are playing quarter notes while thinking sixteenths.

*(Donald Wilcox)*

There are many ways I mirror the student so he can see or hear what he is doing. I vocally imitate student's sound, which reminds them to correct their sound. I also play, for example, with too much edge or air. Then, I ask students to evaluate what they hear. Ninety-nine percent of the time their evaluation is correct. I ask them to practice in the most dead room they can find, and to practice facing into a corner. I also imitate what a student is doing, and if he sees me imitate his tension, he relaxes.

*(John W. LaCava)*

### Visual mirrors

With young students, we often use mirrors for embouchure and posture. We must reinforce fundamentals every day, if not, their playing skills can fall apart.

*(Stanley Cate)*

We always use full-length mirrors, especially for posture and position, and we have one in every practice room. Students can see in the mirror that the chest is deflating more, if there is tension in the shoulders, or if they are puffing their cheeks. I cannot tell them all the fancy names of the muscles and the facial structures involved, and I couldn't tell them what part of the brain controls those muscles; however, the minute they see it in the mirror, it stops.

*(L. Keating Johnson)*

All of our practice rooms have mirrors. Each beginner must bring a hand held mirror with him to lessons and put it on the music stand. (Bryce Taylor) I always use mirrors and metronomes. I carry mirrors to each school and I have them on the wall. (Anthony J. Maiello) I use mirrors a lot; I mean, I don't keep one by the lesson stand, but there is a mirror in my office and I have them go look

at themselves. (Kenneth M. Larsen) I use mirrors as an embouchure visualizer. The beginners have one in their case that is about three by five inches. I had them made up in numbers—any glass company will make these up cheaply.

*(Donald Gee)*

Have mirrors in the room; it is important for string players' bowing.

*(Judith A. Niles)*

I use a mirror and drawings when I teach applied trumpet. I say, "Try to feel the back of the throat. Feel what the back of their tongue is doing, get it down so it is as open as possible, and shaped as when you yawn." Then, I will draw a picture of an open throat with a closed embouchure where the air is going through the lips. The mirror also helps them see that this opening is small. Yet, the throat is not tight and closed; it is open.

*(Dwayne P. Sagen)*

### A variety of feedback devices

I use mirrors and tape recorders, especially with beginners. I don't stress embouchure mirrors as much, because I want them to believe that air is the most important thing. I do record rehearsals, groups and individuals so they hear their tone, phrasing, solos, ensemble playing, etc.

*(R. G. Conlee)*

### Peer feedback

I had students imitate each other's poor or good version of sound or musical phrasing with an instrument.
*(Anthony J. Maiello)*

To improve listening and intonation, sometimes I have the students count off across each row of the band by twos. Then I have all the ones play the pitch and each student who is not playing (the twos) is in charge of deciding whether the player seated to his right, or left, is in tune. If that player is not in tune, then once he stops playing, the listener quietly gives an opinion about the right remedy. Then, they reverse roles with the twos playing and the ones suggesting corrective measures. This procedure affords the players a little physical space to permit him to hear his own sound instead of his neighbor's. It also involves other students actively in the tuning process.

*(Scott Shuler)*

### A useful tuner

First, they need a tuner that can make multiple judgments. You can't sit there alternating between turning the dial and playing. You must play naturally, look up, and read all the information to determine what you will do.
*(Myron Welch)*

### Knowing the instrument

I encourage every player to learn the peculiarities of the instrument. They use a tuner and I say, "Now, you must come up with your own little chart to plot the notes that are sharp and the notes that are flat." As time goes by they begin to learn and hear what different notes do. Much of playing in tune is just awareness. If students know that their saxophone is going to be extremely high on C sharp, they can see it coming. Instead, they do not see it coming and they crash on C sharp. Then you say, "Oh God! How many of you have a sharp, C sharp? Okay, then we need to deal with this." More often than not I'll say, "You guys have five minutes after rehearsal. Let's just sit here for a minute and work on that with a tuner."

*(William W. Wiedrich)*

### Feedback through cause and effect

One of my teachers was Angelucci of the Minnesota Orchestra, who had studied with Marcel Tabeteau. He said Tabeteau had all of his students at the Curtis Institute of Music explore breathing through a simple task. (The students did this for up to two weeks in practice rooms; we are talking about highly motivated students, obviously). The task was to place a lighted candle on a table. They would sit close to it and blow an airstream at the flame. They were to create an angle of the candle's flame and try to keep it at the same angle. Then, they would slowly pull that chair away from the table and see how far they could get back, still keeping the candle flame at an angle. This showed the importance of the even and focused air supply.

*(Richard Putzier)*

Place a piece of paper against the wall and hold it against the wall with the air stream only, without using the hand.

*(Stanley Cate)*

### A rehearsal clock

I use what I call a "rehearsal clock." I do this when there is a special need for motivation, or to show them how efficient they can be in rehearsal. I got the clock from the custodians. I changed its looks, so it looks like a very large stop watch. The minute hand can move from sixty down to zero minutes. I set it manually and use a switch wired so I can turn it off and on from my music stand.

This is useful three or four times a year. When I use it, the burden for behaving is placed on the students' shoulders and concentration is built. I have used it with younger kids, sometimes with junior high and rarely with the high school band. (I got the idea from a 1st grade teacher who had a frog clock on her desk. She used this idea whenever things began to be a strain, and called it "frog time." She would announce "frog time," and the frog clock would count down for whatever amount of time she had set.)

When we use the "rehearsal clock" during a forty-minute period, I set it at twenty minutes, for example, and when it gets to zero, we stop rehearsing—no matter what—even if the period isn't yet over. I say to the class, "All I want is twenty minutes of good rehearsal time." If they are working with success and purpose, the clock continues to count down; and, if they aren't, I interrupt the clock's "count down" even if the rehearsal continues. If the clock stops, they look to see who is causing a problem and apply some pressure. With most bands, having a good rehearsal about half the time is an accomplishment.

When I began this, I started with ten minutes working toward increasing the amount of productive time. We must remember that students will try for something if it is attainable. Thus, setting a standard of thirty minutes in a thirty-five minute rehearsal is unattainable, and therefore unreasonable. If they begin to mature, they do not need this.

*(David Deitemyer)*

## FEEDBACK THROUGH A MUSICAL CONTEXT

### The value of using a musical context

I'll never forget when Haskel Harr came out with the recording of marches that allowed you to play the exercises with the recording. Man! I mean I could hardly stop that myself, that was great fun. It had marches to go with the exercises that were in the book—it was like *Music Minus One* recordings.

*(Charles Olson)*

When students practice while hearing the recorded musical context, practice is more interesting and satisfying for them. If one practices within a musical context that stays the same from practice session to practice session, the student has something to which he can compare his progress. The recorded musical context provides a reference point and this enables him to decide if he is moving toward performing "in-sync" with the recording. This is similar to a less advanced student playing a duet with someone who is better. Over the course of hours, days, or weeks, the less advanced student will discover if he is improving because he can compare his playing to that of the better player.

*(James Froseth)*

I have used the *Music Minus One Series* with advanced players. About the time they reach Rubank Advanced, I introduce solos to them through recordings such as Rampal, Abersold, Dominic Spera, etc. I also had an accompanist record all the accompaniments. The accompaniments are on the synthesizer, and the teacher or student can change the tempo without the pitch changing. For example, a student can set the synthesizer at the harpsichord setting and get used to a new sound to blend with. For solo and ensemble, this is excellent. It is time-saving and convenient. The DX9 Yamaha, or more recent synthesizers, also can play back accompaniments in different keys, allowing the same solo to be used for different instruments.

*(R. G. Conlee)*

I use both a musical metronome and a mechanically generated musical metronome with and without additional accompanying harmonic or rhythmic background. With the electronically advanced machines and the music we have, this is not expensive. There is no reason not to do this. This is particularly effective with younger students. These materials are commercially available or I have produced them myself. The material of James Froseth's *Listen, Move, Sing and Play* uses this and I wish more methods had this available.

Since I believe that students learn a great deal through imitation, I include the musical metronome into instruction in ways very similar to Froseth's. One also can make their own accompaniments for any method book. The accompaniments provide a steady pulse, particular rhythmic accompaniments, or provide the correct harmonic changes as a background for phrases or even a whole song. With the electronic accompaniment or background support, one has a very dependable and steady pulse, or rhythmic background.

Have the students play with the chordal background as they play in imitation of the teacher's or a peer's playing. As they do this teacher demonstration-student imitation process on the patterns, they are playing the chordal background as well. Not only is the chordal background there for them to hear, it also provides the musical metronome for steady pulse and provides a general example of musical style and character. With the electronic or acoustic accompanying or background support, one has a very dependable and steady pulse, or rhythmic background. This is a great way for the younger grade levels and it also will work with the advanced levels. Students enjoy playing with a steady pulse and musical background compared with a mechanical metronome, which is less enjoyable and musical.

The traditional metronome is still valuable; I am not anti-metronome. Using a Doctor Beat, etc. especially in a practice room or when a musical metronome is not available, is a very valuable aid. The time-keepers must learn to keep time!

*(Gary Hill)*

## Recordings as Feedback

### Recordings of rehearsals

I record rehearsals to hear them myself, and for the students' listening also.

*(John Anderson)*

When I listen to recordings of rehearsals, I listen more to the expressive elements. The closer it gets to the concert, the more I listen to the expressive and interpretive issues. As one is following the score and listening to the recording, a person should make notes about a problem and develop a way to teach to the solution of it.

*(Hal D. Cooper)*

Recordings help me decide what I need to do in the rehearsal. If teachers depend only upon recall, they will find that their memory is not very good. No matter what a teacher's schedule is, a teacher should listen to as much as possible. The effort is worth it because the experience of listening and evaluating is invaluable.

*(Frank Battisti)*

I taped rehearsals mostly for myself, but I chose certain portions for the kids to hear. I would never use the recording before they played the piece. I wanted them to attempt interpretation themselves first.

*(Robert Allan)*

We do a lot of recording so they can hear, though it is a little touchy. Sometimes the recording doesn't pick up things exactly the way I am hearing it. I record in rehearsal, often playing eight measures and then they hear the recording of the eight bars. This works for steadiness of rhythms, intonation, dynamics, balance, attacks and releases (particularly attacks), and precision. When rehearsing, the brass players might think, "Oh, this was pretty good" and you play the recording back and you hear fifteen "blurbs" as they go along. I record with the full band and with the sections. I have the mike sitting up front and it's easy with cassettes.

*(Richard Putzier)*

It is very useful to record every rehearsal of every group. For the teacher, this allows the teacher/conductor to evaluate what he said and how he said it. For the students, we can encourage them to listen to rehearsals, and get a different perspective on what they are doing. As a member of a group, they experience the piece from the perspective of an individual person playing an individual part. They hear it through their ears only. They can listen to the entire piece, depending upon how much concentration they have left over after dealing with their own parts. A tape of a rehearsal allows them to step back and listen, unconcerned with their own responsibilities for their part, and hear other parts and sounds.

*(Frank Battisti)*

I record rehearsals for myself and for students so they can hear what they are doing. I will listen to the entire tape for my use, then set up the tape so kids can hear certain sections that I think will be helpful.

*(Ross A. Leeper)*

I tape sections of rehearsals and we do play things back for the students.

*(Richard J. Suddendorf)*

One very effective teaching tool is to record most every rehearsal, both for me and the students. If I must go through a piece over and over I'll say, "Listen to how you sound, it's not getting any better." Or I will say, "Listen to what you have done, you've made this sound that much better." I also record on the spot if they're not getting the separation, for example. I say, "Come on, why are we doing this for the fifteenth time. Okay, here it is. Listen to it right now."

*(Sandra P. Thompson)*

I record them a lot to help my own planning and so they can hear the full ensemble play before and after school. I don't record and listen to passages in band—the time is a problem. For pieces we are performing, even transcriptions or new pieces, I try to have several recordings of the piece. On Shostakovich's Fifth, I had ten different recordings available for kids to listen to. We did "Mars" from *The Planets*, and I was amazed how many purchased their own recording of the entire piece and brought them to rehearsal, even though I had several recordings of this.

*(Donald Gee)*

### Using video tapes of concert

Every time we have a concert, we have a stereo video tape so after the concert we can watch the concert on video tape. It's dubbed so that we listen through our good speakers and we have good quality sound. Sometimes schools have a recording club that is eager to do this.
*(John A. Thompson and Judith A. Niles)*

### Enlisting the school recording club

Well, we've started thinking about running two cameras, one that will always be on the full group and the other will be zooming in on soloists. To this point, we've only used one camera and the person usually makes the judgment on the spot, whether it's a solo, etc.

The recording is usually done by a member of our *Sound Tracks*, our school's recording club. The kids are pretty good—in fact, they're great. They're to the point where we can watch the tape the next day. At the tape's beginning you'll see the group warming up and the credits will come over. I mean they do all this stuff and make it look like a half-hour production for the kids who watch it the next day.

*(John A. Thompson)*

### The value of recorded models of a piece

My research was about the question, "Does it help to hear the piece on a record or a tape, as you are rehearsing it? It showed that over time, say six weeks or so, they didn't make that much more progress than the group that was really drilling away everyday without listening.

*(Dwayne P. Sagen)*

## OTHER USES OF FEEDBACK

### Motivation

There are a million reasons to use a tape recorder: recording auditions if some kid who wants to come back and gripe later or recording rehearsals both for you or the kids. Sometimes for motivation, turn a tape recorder on and there's nothing but the little red light on. The tape need not be in the machine. If they see the red light, the kids will play better.

*(Donald Wilcox)*

### Evaluation

Record your group over a time period. Listen to a recording that you made in January when you get into March, or go back and listen to recordings from two years ago. Somebody keeps talking about the good old days. "Boy the '79 band was the greatest thing since sliced bread." You go back and listen to a recording of them, and you find out that the band you've got now just blows the '79's doors off. Then you may feel, "Well, maybe I'm not pounding my head against the wall, maybe things are getting better." Recordings are very important and can give one some perspective.

*(Donald Wilcox)*

In marching band the video tape is on the field because it allows students to see things immediately. Or, they will come in after rehearsal and watch it for hours. They will correct a lot on their own this way.

*(Robert E. Foster)*

### Recording private lessons

Students should record their lesson so they can go home with the tape and be reminded of things. In a sense, the lesson is retaught. Overall, the intent is for them to be listening.

*(Frank Battisti)*

I want them to hear that playing a rhythm mechanically perfect doesn't result in the same musical meaning.

*(Larry Rachleff)*

# CHAPTER FOUR

# STANDARDS

Standards and norms such as grade levels, batting averages, yearly income, and other points of reference are common in society and they allow people to compare one thing to another. In music education, such standards can take the form of grades, chair placement, scholarships, testing scores, and judges' ratings at contests and festivals.

Educators use standards so they have something to which they can compare the student's, the group's, or the school's progress. They also point to standards so students can see goals to which they should strive. When students reach these goals, their accomplishment can give them confidence.

If we set aside these extrinsic standards and rewards, we can help students set and reach goals of their own choosing. The teacher must encourage them to set goals and reinforce their efforts to advance from where they are to a higher level. When students begin to understand this and evaluate their own progress, their reference points become more intrinsic because they are comparing their own performances to their past performances instead of to someone else's standards.

For students to accept and raise their standards, the teacher must lead the way by insisting that students strive to achieve and seek excellence in everything they do. Teachers can encourage students to do this because they have the experience to recognize that educational progress is good. Teachers also know the subject matter, they know what goals are appropriate, and they know what skills and content students need to learn.

If the teacher does not promote standards, many students will not grow appreciably in music. Without good instruction, music students will grow only as much as they would have incidentally, or as much as they can through independent effort alone.

There are several ways to set and to raise standards. Besides reinforcing and recognizing students when they make effort and progress, we can show them models to which they can aspire, and how to study and to practice so their chances for improvement are increased. If students strive to meet standards, teachers expect they will learn the difference between the trivial and the substantial, the ordinary and the exceptional.

## THE IMPORTANCE OF SETTING STANDARDS

### Challenge students

We lose intelligent kids if we do not challenge them. We will do that if we drill in class what they could as easily do at home. These kids are too good and teachers should not let them remain on a level below that which they can reach.

I want them to learn the notes at home, so I can work on other things in rehearsal. I want to do detailed rehearsing such as articulations, ensemble togetherness, cross fingering, or musical expression during the class time. I don't want to do the homework in class!

*(Carl A. Bly)*

### Our level of standards

The fault in many bands' playing of accents may be that music education classes educate the instrumental teaching for a junior high level of band directing. Many college people teach music education students an understanding of skills, but describe them at the level a good junior high director uses with their students. These people assume this is correct and they also think what is taught at junior high, senior high or college is the same. This is incorrect.

*(Michael Haithcock)*

### Our standard of good

In this business, we are supposed to get good performance. We also don't know whether to be competitive or not to be competitive. If we are going to be competitive, we should have a sense about clear criteria for what an excellent performance is; then we could decide who really is good.

*(William Long)*

### Setting standards and accountability.

When making demands upon kids, I am not afraid to make a student feel uncomfortable. I think that's part, every now and then, of being held accountable for what they are doing. I might say, "You are letting me down." It can be uncomfortable for some if I say, pointing at the kid,

"You did not practice over the weekend as I demanded. I asked you to practice over the weekend, and you have not improved, have you? Answer!" That's uncomfortable, absolutely.

On the other hand, we talk about accountability and excellence and we're supposed to be demanding educational growth. This is one place where band directors, many of us, were ahead of the "excellence in education" movement before the slogan "excellence in education" had ever been thought of. We were demanding excellence before anybody even knew it was there.

*(William Long)*

### Accountability

Music teachers may not consider teaching in the same way as teachers do in non-music classes. A normal procedure in any other classes is to hold students accountable. To do this, I wrote pages of different rhythms, every combination of rhythms that I could. We would work on two or three lines and then I would test the kids individually. The success was a combination: holding them accountable and doing it every day in class. It is a matter of teaching and holding individuals accountable, which music teachers often are afraid of doing.

*(Craig Kirchhoff)*

### Setting standards in each lesson

I look at every sound as a challenge. "What can I do to help that kid make a better sound?" I think, in a nutshell, that is what I try to do in lessons. I listen to them and try to give them something. This might just be a reinforcement of what I said before or I teach them something that will improve their sound and technique. I do this, so a week or two week later, I will see some improvement.

There are too many people who come in and turn pages at lessons. The kid plays "la-dee-da-dee-da-dee" and the teacher says, "fine." He crosses it off and goes on to the next page. The student again plays "la-dee-da-dee-da-dee," the teacher says, "fine" and crosses off that page. At best students may learn to play rhythmically and move their fingers. It is much more important to improve playing in a way that makes a difference—not just hear them play pages and cross them off.

*(Lewis Larson)*

## THE PROCESS OF SETTING STANDARDS

### Where we should have standards

Success depends upon whether we choose to learn the part itself, or to learn from the parts. One reason our group achieves is that I don't just push them to play their part only. Otherwise, they'll understand how to play that part and that's all. One passage in that piece of music will not apply that often to another passage in a particular band. If there is a problem in the band music, we may work on

a warm up procedure that focuses upon the same issues.

*(Phillip A. Weinberg)*

I don't view standard setting and music making as some people. Some have an arbitrary "line it up" and "tune it up" tally sheet that shows them what needs to be done before they begin to address the music. These teachers think of standard setting only from the technical aspects. Before they become involved in making a musical statement, they must be an "objective task person" who is concerned with tuning up and lining up all the parts first. Unfortunately, by the time they have done all the technical things, it is too late. They don't have enough time left to develop the musical statement and to integrate it with the technical performance.

Perhaps contests, habits, and tradition have fostered this, especially in the last few years. Special contests such as Dixie Classic, Six Flags, or Sea World also have reinforced this attitude. In some people's mind, there is much more to lose from these events than there is to win—if you don't have technical accuracy. This view keeps the band world from being accepted the way it should be.

*(Michael Haithcock)*

I am very demanding, possibly a tyrant in rehearsal. There is no talking unless it pertinently relates to the music. Consequently, our students get upset when they see kids from other bands talking during rehearsals at massed or all-state bands.

*(Stanley Cate)*

### Standards in a small town program

I start all the kids. They only have one teacher and I've been here twenty-one years. There are unique and interesting features about my situation that might be inspiring to many people who teach at little schools.

We work with everything from embouchures to tone concepts. It isn't long after we start our beginners that I make a concerted effort to have them begin matching tones and matching pitches. Even at the second or third lesson, we'll start talking about what is high and low, and ask questions such as, "Does it sound higher?" or, "Does it sound lower than another pitch?" We have them adjust their horns so they never play horribly out of tune. They never know what it is to play far out of tune. We keep bringing them in as close as we can.

The older they get, the more we demand of them. Pretty soon tuning becomes "instinctive." By the time our kids are in the seventh grade, they're starting to listen very carefully. By the eighth grade they will listen very well and know what to do with their instruments.

They have a great deal of personal pride about being able to play well in-tune. The kids have been trained that way all the way through, so they become very discriminating by the time they are in the ninth grade.

*(Lewis Larson)*

## Correcting errors

With student teachers, I insist and say, "Stop and correct these kids. Don't listen to them play through and play it wrong for the whole piece and then go back and try to correct it." On the other hand, once you get things developed the way you want it through stopping and correcting errors, you've got to develop the continuity of playing through a piece.

*(Lance Schultz)*

## Concentration

Expect total concentration of band members in rehearsal. Expect as much in every rehearsal as you do in a concert; standards do not change between them. Concentration should be so intense that one could "set off a bomb in rehearsal and no one would notice."

*(Butler R. Eitel)*

## The Process of Raising Standards

### Using friendly competition

Students respond well to fun-competitive activities such as the boys against the girls in a challenge to do well. For example, they can compete in doing a breath attack on "haaa," which is to entice them to use the support that they can get from the pelvic area.

*(Frank Bencriscutto)*

### Get it right at least once so they know

I suggest what they can try or ask them what they should try so they participate in the solution. I have an important goal for them and that is to get it right at least once. From there, it is easier to move forward since there is an experience to build upon, for both of us.

I try to focus upon one skill at a time, such as lowering the tongue. I do not make two or three suggestions at one time, which would confuse them instead of help them. If they become uncomfortable, I avoid putting them under pressure individually. Since I can empathize with their problems, I coach them until they connect with the idea or skill. This builds an important communication and a bond between the teacher and the learner. The "clincher" for them is both hearing the change, and feeling the physical difference as they play the new way.

*(R. G. Conlee)*

### Be insistent

Well, what's the point of suggesting a way of improving if they don't do it? My way is to be insistent on it, I won't relent.

*(Kenneth M. Larsen)*

### Chorale playing

Chorale playing, by its nature, encourages the best sound from each player. It encourages them to go back to the very roots of proper tone production. The chorale also provides special opportunities for the study of intonation and balance.

From the chorale's harmonization, we can pick out chords that allow us to identify octaves, perfect fifths, and fourths. We also find the major and minor thirds, and major and minor sixths that are essential to our consonant sounds. Further along, we teach them the minor sevenths and the diminished sevenths, and other altered chords that are so common among our colorful dissonances.

By such means we sharpen the player's sensitivity and perception. We encourage the players to share with their colleagues the responsibility for correct intervals and perfect intonation, which will result in an increased enjoyment and satisfaction with their performance. Likewise, I use these beautiful chords to show and secure equal or appropriate balance. The players will hear when one person may be too weak or too strong. They will adjust to bring all tones of the chord and ensemble into balance.

*(Mark H. Hindsley)*

### Slow-motion playing

When an athletic coach studies film in slow motion, he can see more. When we play in slow motion, we all can hear more. Thus, they can fix and improve more of their own mistakes. They also play better at a less than full tempo. Pitch is easier to hear, mistakes can be corrected or prevented, a missed rhythm is correctable, and they clean everything up faster. Time is saved and errors are prevented. This helps them prevent problems and solve them. It prepares them to be independent, to prepare independently for auditions, performances, etc. Since some high school groups are larger than mine, this helps students be more successful in situations where they may need to solve problems on their own.

*(John W. LaCava)*

### Setting and maintaining standards

Once you can get a program going, it's always a challenge to keep it going. However, it is amazing how the kids will take it and go with it. I mean, they'll start setting some pretty high standards themselves. They help once the thing is going, but setting standards has to start at some point—the teacher usually must make the first move.

*(Lewis Larson)*

### Raising standards of posture

They do what I say, because I try to prove to them that they sound better when they sit properly.

*(John W. LaCava)*

### Accuracy in performance

This is a story I use to encourage them to read and play the printed page accurately. "Pretend that out in the audience there is a genius, someone who could notate on manuscript paper everything he heard. Whatever we play, that person can write it down exactly, whether it's an accent, a long note or staccato; or if it's a crescendo, a decrescendo, or whatever dynamic level. At the end of the performance we would compare notes to see if we projected everything that was on that paper. How accurately we played each part would show up when we compared our parts to the genius' copying of everything that we played."

*(Howard A. Lehman)*

## Standards and facility

Remember that the purpose of the routines is to teach the fundamentals. These will apply to all the music played in the program. The routines also build an instant response from the band through establishing a "baton discipline." The conductor must secure these basics in everything that they will be playing. Tone, intonation, balance, and precision must become a habit, a matter of pride, and a stamp of musicianship.

*(Mark H. Hindsley)*

## Setting standards

One needs cut-offs for musical or technical reasons; they also help classroom management. My approach is that students always have to start at the beginning of the song. Hundreds of times I've seen teaching where a kid is playing while the class is watching. The kid will make a mistake, and the teacher will say, "Start there." Then, the kids say or think, "Where's there?"

*(Marguerite G. Wilder)*

## Teaching rhythm

A phrase can have a ritardando, accelerando, or a rubato. You can have the kids counting aloud, while you're conducting, which forces them to watch you. You can have them experience the watching through playing the rhythmic units in a unison, while watching. You also can have them singing their parts while they watch you. There is not enough watching. They get better to a point through repetition, but a real challenge for all of us in ensemble is how do we get things past a certain point.

*(Robert Levy)*

# CHAPTER FIVE

# PRACTICE

When students do not practice effectively or do not practice at all, one cause is that assignments and directions are too vague. For example, telling students to practice thirty minutes a day is a vague direction. A direction also is unclear when we say "practice page six" or "practice those scales." If students practice in spite of unclear directions, they might have practiced anyway. Even if the student does practice, they still may be unclear about how or what to practice. If a student is not taught an approach to practice, they may practice ineffectively or aimlessly and base their choices and progress upon trial and error. Students will not know clearly what it is they are trying to do. This handicaps students as they try to progress.

The problem may begin with the teacher's directions and requirements, or the teacher may not teach an approach to practicing. The instructors in the teacher's own experience may not have taught him how to practice. If this is true, the cycle repeats and teachers continue not to teach their students what and how to practice. The students are left alone and unprepared to find ways to solve problems. If students does not progress because of this, motivation can wane and some students simply will not practice at all.

Some teaching techniques increase the likelihood that home practice will be more effective. One is to show students how to judge what is right and wrong. The purpose is to teach them what to look for when playing an instrument. Examples of this are body posture, instrument position, embouchure, and hand, wrist, and arm positions. To strengthen students' understanding, a teacher can show effective and ineffective ways to practice.

Students learn this further by practicing these judgments in class. The students can check these behaviors in the teacher and with other students while in class. The purpose is to teach students to evaluate their performance. As they learn to do this, they can evaluate their playing at home based upon what they saw and learned in class.

Related to this is showing them what is musically desirable and undesirable about things they can hear. The teacher can show examples of musical performance skills. The skills they show might be breath, tone, articulation, dynamics, rhythm, and phrasing. Next, they can teach students to check those skills in class as they can do with

other skills that students can observe.

The students learn evaluation skills in class as they hear the teacher and their peers. Building the skill of evaluation also serves the class. While they practice judging they help classmates improve their playing. The purpose of this is to teach students what to practice for, how to practice, and how to judge their musical progress. The outcome may be that students can evaluate their performance during home practice in two areas: what they see and what they hear.

Therefore, one of the purposes of practice approaches and techniques is to develop the student's ability to be both self-critic and self-teacher. When the student is successful, the success may motivate him to do this at home. In addition, the motivation gained from successful practice will add to the other incentives found in band and orchestra participation.

## TEACHING THE STUDENTS TO PRACTICE

### Practicing at home

While practicing in front of the mirror is a good idea, we must teach them to make these visual discriminations so they know what to look for when they are at home. To do this, train the kids in class so they have diagnostic skills to take home with them. The teacher has to model both excellent and flawed techniques. The students must show that they can visually discriminate between both the correct and incorrect techniques in the teacher, so they can go home and find the strengths and weakness in themselves. Kids also can practice these evaluation skills by looking and listening to each other's performance.

Having both perfect and flawed examples is necessary so students can see the difference. This helps them develop criteria to apply to themselves and others. For them to practice successfully at home, they must move toward acquiring the same insights and abilities to make judgments that the teacher possesses. If this is not done, the kids do not know what to sound or look like when they practice. Teachers *must* do this so students can teach themselves at home. If the students accomplish this, they will have the same aural and visual discrimination skills that the teacher has and as a result are independent.

*(James Froseth)*

We need to explain why we are doing things so students can become mini-teachers of themselves. To help themselves, they must have some self-diagnostic skills and a method with which to practice.

*(L. Keating Johnson)*

### Explaining the importance of home practice

I have used a simple practice record that kids took home. We also discuss that success in instrumental music is based on a number of things. Rehearsals are one of those things and that having an effective rehearsal on a day-to-day basis is important. We think that home practice is also an important part of that. There are three components—a tripod: rehearsal, home practice, and either private lessons or coaching are the three parts of that tripod.

We draw a little diagram that kids see. There's a little tripod and we list three things—the tripod's three legs. We say, "If you don't do home practice, you will not be reinforcing the things that you learn in rehearsal. Consequently, the tripod won't stand up. If you don't come to rehearsals with an attitude that's positive about learning something, the rehearsals won't be successful. So, the tripod won't stand either."

While we don't require the kids to study privately, I'm lucky and pleased that ninety-five percent of our kids study privately. If there are kids who don't or can't enter a coaching situation, someone helps them with their parts. Thus everybody is either in an improvement mode or they're not.

We try to build that tripod idea when the freshmen parents come to "freshmen go to school night." This is an excellent opportunity for me to talk philosophy and things with parents and students. One thing I talk about that night is the importance of those three ingredients. I explain how they are important to a successful program.

*(John A. Thompson)*

### Building responsibility and attitude

We have a required amount of practice and we keep handbooks for all levels. There are certain laws of the land in our program that the parents and students know. They have to practice a certain number of minutes. We say they should practice approximately thirty minutes each day. I get good compliance with this and parents support this by signing the student's practice cards.

When they are in the seventh and eighth grade, especially the eighth graders, this can change. If they can show me that they are reliable, we will throw away the practice charts. They know that I can tell how much practicing they have done anyway. I can tell this, basically, by their lessons and how they are performing each lesson. I can do this since I individualize lessons by ability levels.

I may say to some more mature groups, "I think you people have shown me that you are reliable in your practice. You have shown this by how much you've been doing. At this time, we do not need to keep practice cards because you are responsible people and I know that you are going to do this." They have never disappointed me—probably because they have good habits going and they are committed to the study of music.

*(Phillip A. Weinberg)*

### Teaching them to practice

In the first two or three weeks of the year, one of the most important things was to teach them how to practice. With my high school students, I used the *"White Scales"* to illustrate this and had individuals come to the front of the class and practice. We all would watch, learn, and discuss how to approach practicing constructively.

I used individual students to show how and what to practice. Then we would return to group work. We would do the same exercise at the same tempo, repeating it several times. Then we would have others play alone to see if they were practicing and progressing correctly. The out-of-class assignment would be, "Practice this at home, and tomorrow we will play this at seventy-two beats per minute."

*(Donald DeRoche)*

I tell them not to practice according to the clock, but according to what they want to accomplish. I even tell them to go into a room that does not have a clock. I ask them to be demanding and critical of themselves, set goals for themselves and get them done. If I did conclude that a kid did not know how to practice or was not goal oriented, I would help them make these decisions, list choices, and try to accomplish them.

*(Donald S. George)*

I give my students a four-step approach to all practicing with their instrument. First, they apply the syllables or counting system to whatever they are to play. Second, they say the note names in the rhythm of the part. Third, after they have that down, then they do the fingerings while they say the note names. Fourth, they combine it all by playing.

We have already sung it in class, so I don't ask them to sing the part at home. They also may sing it incorrectly. I use this approach with Froseth's *Preliminary Book* because it's very simple and it's their first notes. When they get into Book One they still do the same thing. Eventually, I stress these steps less. I have the steps written on the board, though, so those who have not yet internalized them can look up and remember. I also have quizzed them on how fast they can tell me the steps. This helps them memorize the steps in the approach.

We really encourage the students to use the steps when practicing at home. We try to impress on them that by counting the rhythms, saying the note names, and fingering the correct notes on the instrument, they will learn. All the steps are helpful. The easiest part of this whole procedure is then to play the exercise, because they have mastered all the hard parts. They like this sort of thing particularly up to grade seven, but not eighth grade. There is a lot of sophistication with eighth graders. I always tell my parents that "eighth-grade-itus" is not a terminal disease, their child will recover.

*(Gordon Nelson and Janet Tweed)*

Learning notes is a big problem that all teachers face daily, but if we show them how to learn notes and have everyone involved as you explain to them what we are doing, you will see their learning increase. I might say, "We are going to do four notes and we are going to do it at the slow tempo. Now, don't rush the second note, be deliberate on the second note since you are gradually getting faster on that. Okay, now we are going to go from point A to A prime."

They see it, since you have explained it to them. Then you ask them afterward, "What did we do?" They might say, "Well, you worked on a very small segment." You can say, "Right, we absolutely isolated the problem to the solution it needed. We didn't go over the thing we could do well, instead we worked on what we could not do as well." This idea relates to what Vaccianno (trumpet in the New York Philharmonic) said: "If you sound good in your practice room, you are probably practicing the wrong thing."

*(Larry Rachleff)*

The same approach, of structuring learning in an ensemble, is like that of private lessons. In each rehearsal you hit something about balance, rhythm, intonation, style, etc. using some structured time for each aspect. Plus reading, polishing, and performing. These are the basics of both rehearsals and home practice.

*(Pamela Gearhart)*

Give definite and structured information to parents and students about what they should practice during each session. For example: new material ten minutes, old material ten minutes, silent exercises three minutes; put away instrument and fill in practice record two minutes, etc.

*(Marion Etzel)*

If they are having problems, I suggest a certain amount of time on different types of warm ups, relaxation, or scale work. What I suggest varies from week to week. There are certain drill approaches. I do things with a metronome, for example. I might suggest fifteen minutes of this one and about ten minutes of that. Do it slowly and evenly to gain control and accuracy. I assign slow work for other reasons, such as to stretch the air stream, to minimize

unnecessary muscular movement or to promote relaxation. I also structure some warm up and drill time where they're working on specific skill areas. Then I go to the musical things. If one had an hour to do this I would suggest they spend ten to fifteen minutes warming up and fifteen minutes doing drills and then a half hour doing musical things.

*(L. Keating Johnson)*

I show them how to practice and to solve problems. We teach them to look for key signatures and special rhythmic problems. They are to write out the problem areas such as counting, technical issues, and articulation. By the middle of eighth grade, they seem to improve in their ability to solve problems on their own. Younger students may work more, but they do not seem ready yet to learn problem solving. Younger students will learn by playing things again and again.

*(R. G. Conlee)*

I teach them how to approach tasks in home practice. I ask them to drop out slurs, ties, pitches, and articulations, for example, to isolate rhythm and duration issues. Then they add these elements back one at a time.

*(Richard Floyd)*

### Practicing phrasing with the metronome

With material like the Rauchet studies for trombone, students can use a metronome. However, it is sometimes better for phrasing if they just stretch notes and phrases, and do whatever they want. They can forget the metronome to some extent as they try anything to get some sense of the line.

After that, they can try to work within the restrictions of a metronome to see if they can build a phrase within the time structure. Not every note, well maybe the first note, but not every note needs to be precisely with the metronome pulse. They can be within a reasonable proximity of it to be musical.

Trying to get a phrasing to work out sometimes means that at the mid-point of the phrase, one should be slightly leaning forward or slightly progressing backward in relation to the pulse to make the phrasing more musical.

*(L. Keating Johnson)*

### Setting target dates

Home practice is a significant problem and I have tried all the standard methods: progress reports, practice charts, etc. We have had more success with picking specific places in the method books that students must attain by a certain date. These dates usually were concert dates, or dates every couple months or once a quarter. We look at the number of pages and decide according to the instrument where they should be on certain dates in order to participate in certain bands.

*(R. G. Conlee)*

### Develop a good daily routine

This may vary for individuals. The routine is to start with certain things and continue so one can get all aspects of the apparatus working—the breathing, fingers, ease into the chops, every major scale, etc.

Most private teachers start scales in C, then F, then B flat. If you do this daily you move from what is seen as easy scales to hard scales. They are hard or easy depending upon which ones they know. Rafael Mendez said to do C, then C sharp, D, then D sharp, etc. a chromatic arrangement so students practice the "so called" easy and hard scales equally.

I did this with my junior high bands and have continued doing this. In a music camp I can get the group through all the major scales comfortably in two weeks. The circle of fifths has done considerable damage to school musicians. It is a theoretical organization, not a practical one. I think tonality retention and in-tune playing in any major scale is related more to how well they do a scale or how often they do the scale, than it is to which scale they practice. I also believe scale learning is a frequency problem, more than a technical problem.

*(Robert E. Foster)*

### The importance of a routine

I teach all students, at all levels, how to practice. It is important to have a routine, especially for young kids. They can do five minutes of this and five minutes of that. I block it out for them and vary from one kid to another.

The structure of their private lesson is the same as I expect them to follow at home. I have a notebook for them where they, or I, write in it and they take it with them. This is as much for me as for them. For most students, there are typical segments such as something for the left hand and right hand, for the ear and eye, and something that is just for fun, such as, "Play by ear, the Tchaikovsky *Violin Concerto.*" The rest changes with individuals and with ages. The talented kids are not as likely to be taught how to solve problems.

*(Pamela Gearhart)*

# *Planning Instruction*

# CHAPTER ONE

# PLANNING

When I think of planning, I also think of a statement attributed to a famous theologian. The statement was: "It was not that religion was tried and found wanting; it was wanted but never tried." When paraphrased for music education the statement is: "It was not that *planning* was tried and found wanting; it was wanted and never tried!"

Some teachers *plan* but many simply react to what happens during instruction: if the ensemble makes a mistake, they try to correct it; if the student makes an error in a lesson, they suggest a remedy. Were it not for the mistakes of the learner, some teachers might have nothing to say in a rehearsal or in a class. They are only correcting the errors they hear or see; they have no *plan* for *developing* students' knowledge and competencies.

Some teachers also do not study the score prior to the beginning of instruction and, as a result, they fail to develop a clear idea of how the piece should sound. Their failure means they cannot anticipate how to rehearse and conduct the piece, and they do not prepare solutions for problems that they should anticipate students will have.

If our focus of instruction is blurry, we will fail to build both the students' understanding and their technique. With this approach, we can only be "fixers" of the ensemble's performance; we should do more, we should become "shapers" of the music and shapers of the students' musical experiences and education.

Many teachers also rehearse and teach by relying primarily upon their intuition. Some believe they are effective and they assume that thinking on their feet is the most effective way to teach. All good teachers do this as *part* of their approach, which enables them to react effectively to the moment. But, as valuable as the teacher's intuition is, seldom can it be their only approach.

If we add planning to our skills, planning will complement our intuition and the path we take is more responsible, more musical, and more beneficial to students. The easier way to teach is to "wing it," but it is not the most effective way to teach. An impromptu approach to teaching has neither the most impact nor provides the most depth of musical experience for our students. We don't expect our doctor to "wing it" when he plans our medical treatment; and he and his wife would not want us to "wing it" when we plan their child's musical education.

## PLANNING THE CURRICULUM

### *Picking pieces versus planning the curriculum*

Rehearsing for programs forces you to think about what students can do and what they should be taught. This makes you think about sequence, programming, and curriculum. It causes you to ask yourself, "What is it that you expect a sophomore to do that a freshman can't? What does a junior do that a sophomore can't?" You start thinking about sequence and progress, and where you expect kids to be. Planning a curriculum is a different ball game than just picking out pieces for a concert.

*(Richard Kennell)*

### *A rhythm curriculum*

I use *Rhythm a Day* (Pro-Art) and Garwood Whalley's *Fundamentals of Rhythm* (Meredith Music). Whalley's book is not written for any special instrument: it is a rhythm curriculum.

The *Rhythm a Day* book starts with whole notes, followed by patterns containing four quarter notes, then combinations of half and quarter notes. There is a new rhythm introduced each line, and all the material builds upon what has already been introduced.

I have students count aloud and clap rhythms, which I also do in the percussion classes. When students can clap and count using a syllable or number system, the result is that they can speak the rhythms as well as read and clap them. After students accomplish this, what is on the page becomes automatic. I use all of this to build a thorough, extensive rhythm vocabulary.

*(Carl A. Bly)*

We developed a rhythm curriculum through a set of books that build a rhythm vocabulary. Some examples are *Rhythm Etudes* (Schmidt, Hall and McCreary) or *Supplemental Exercises* (Rubank). The stress is on repeated notes, not technique, so they developed a strong rhythm background. When students came to Ithaca High School, they would go through the entire series of materials. This was either part of private lessons or class lessons. Some accomplished this in a half hour, some took many months. When they met problems, we stopped to deal with it. It was like a review or inventory.

*(Frank Battisti)*

### *Levels of dynamics skills*

By the end of seventh grade we want them to have the skill to play four dynamic levels and by the eighth grade we want them to play the six basic dynamic levels.

*(John W. LaCava)*

### *Scales*

They learn all the major scales before they leave the seventh grade. We teach all major scales during the first fifteen weeks of the school year. The rest of the year we review the major scales. Minor scales are done in the eighth grade. The entire chromatic scale is introduced after most of the major scales are done.

*(John W. LaCava)*

### *Intonation*

Instead of using just unison tuning only, I used triads. I had them play the root or fifth out of tune intentionally to prove to them that they can hear if they listen. It also taught them what beats were and what in tune means—compared to just reading the dials on the tuning machine. In the very beginning I would use unison, then after about six weeks I would have beginners tune to chords.

*(John Kinnison)*

### *Teaching materials*

I stay in a method book throughout the year even in a full band setting because this keeps tubas, bass clarinets, etc. in melody playing. Grade three and four tunes ask for this.

*(John W. LaCava)*

We use various warm up exercises and through the years I keep rotating them. I use the different books: *Fourteen Weeks to a Better Band* (Barnhouse), *Fun with Fundamentals* (Belwin), *Advanced Fun with Fundamentals* (Belwin) and the *Pares Scale* books (Rubank). The second one is not so advanced, but can be more so if you increase tempos.

*(Ross A. Leeper)*

### *Articulation*

The teaching and playing of articulations must start early with beginners.

*(Carl A. Bly)*

I always feel if they get a good legato tongue, you're on step one. You can go on and teach other styles of tonguing after that. I go for legato first. If they can develop

a good flowing legato style and learn how to put enough air through a phrase from beginning to end, they're going to sound much more mature when they get done. Also, these slower pieces aren't flying by so fast. If there are some intonation problems, they can learn to correct them. They can, for example, sit at the piano and figure out where the problems are.

*(Lewis Larson)*

## THE ORGANIZATION OF THE PROGRAM

### *The organization of the program*

Much of the success of the program is that we have very strong administrative and community support, besides the development of self-discipline. We have three bands: a fifth grade and a sixth grade band, and a top band of seventh and eighth graders. All three bands rehearse daily during school hours. This schedule makes a tremendous difference, and that comes from administrative support. Through the years, the band has developed to a high level. The community now expects it and they're not about to let it go. We will be going through another administrative change this fall, I have already met with the new principal and he has no intentions of making any changes.

*(Ross A. Leeper)*

There are three teachers and we teach in grades seven through twelve. Our intermediate level band has eighth and some seventh graders. This band meets daily during fourth period. During the first period, all remaining woodwind players meet in a class divided into three sections by ability. During the second period, brass players meet and are divided into two sections by ability and there is one section of percussion. The maximum class size is about twenty-five kids.

To form the second and third bands, we meet after school with these members of the band classes. We do this for several weeks prior to concerts: we meet five afternoons for forty minutes each rehearsal. The class period, in essence, is a sectional though it is also a skill building class. We take five to ten minutes to build scale technique, use a level two method book and sheet music, and teach sight reading. This results in quite a good band.

The class may do both levels two and three from a method book, since students start band in the fifth grade. This also avoids the early decision about who is to be in which band: it delays this decision until they have shown the level they seek. After eighth grade, students go to the high school band that meets in the same building with the same audition system.

The top group carries fifty students because of the room size. I prefer the smaller group because one can do a little more with them individually. In addition, the restricted size of the top band causes the second band to be better. Quality players are still in this group who might have been in the top group were it larger. The top high school band meets fourth period—the others meet third period. This provides opportunity for kids to learn other instruments and take charge of their chances of moving upward into a higher level band. We have four rehearsal rooms in a fifteen-year old building.

*(John W. LaCava)*

We have two middle schools with two bands each with about one hundred children in each band. We have one junior high for grades eight and nine. That school has three bands with about one hundred students in each. We have one high school for grades ten to twelve with three bands totalling two-hundred and forty-five students. That's for the inside work. For the outside work, we put all three high school bands together.

When we do our concerts, all three bands perform. A single band does not cover the ten tunes in a concert program. The top group performs about five, the second group does about four, and the third group about three. We play concerts very often and we cover a lot of literature.

We also do some traveling. We are taking all the kids to Orlando for a competition. Every third year we go out of state with our kids. We do this every third year so a kid, once in his high school career, goes on a major trip. The other two years we stay within the state boundaries. We go as far as money allows. Incidentally, kids do not march until the tenth grade. We want them to stay inside and learn their instrument first.

*(Bryce Taylor)*

## The place of lessons

The band is the result of what I do during the rest of the day and I've never thought of band as the program. I don't teach toward band; band results from what I teach individuals through our lesson program. I also do very few sectional rehearsals, though occasionally I'll excuse the brass or woodwinds and work with the other section.

*(Kenneth M. Larsen)*

## The schedule

In sixth grade, the kids take lessons as individuals and in small groups. There also is a small beginning band one day a week for just a half hour. At the junior high level, I have seventh, eighth, and ninth graders that play together three times a week. When seventh graders are able to hear those ninth graders, they start imitating their sounds. By the second semester they are sounding very good.

In the fall, the group always starts out sounding terrible, intonation wise, because of the new seventh graders who have moved in. However, from Christmas on the new seventh graders and the entire junior high group probably will play with better intonation than any senior high group in our area. Because the group plays with a good tone and pitch center, the new students have to fit in or they're extremely uncomfortable. It doesn't take them

long and suddenly, they know that they're the ones that are sticking out.

If the junior high kids are playing well, they can play in our senior high group from seventh grade on. Thus band is like the little one room school: the teacher was teaching one mathematics class while the younger kids were sitting there doing their own assignments as well as learning things from the older kid's classes.

The younger kids in our Senior Band, however, don't come every day. They attend only two or three days of each week. Senior high band meets opposite the time when the junior high kids are having physical education class.

We also still have kids leaving school for release-time religion classes once a week. Depending on what a younger student's first-hour schedule is, I may have some of them twice a week or three times a week with the senior high group. Besides that, they'll have some sectionals with me and they might have some sectionals with their senior high sectional leader; both the students and I run sectionals.

In the second semester, as we're approaching more concerts and competitions, the students will do more of the sectionals. They will set their own schedule. You'll see sheets of paper tacked up in the band room in front of the band room telling me when sections are going to meet. As we get closer to concerts, I'll identify problems in rehearsals and say, "Can you can work this out in a sectional? I want to see one done within the next few days." Usually they'll take care of it, although there is no set schedule. They may get together once a week, occasionally twice a week, if it's a particular problem. They might do it before school, after school, or after their lunch period when there is a fifteen minute break. With some sections it's difficult because we do have these same kids in after school sports. You'll see a few kids just getting together. Maybe the two first trumpets will meet in the evening to work on some intonation problems. Somehow it works.

*(Lewis Larson)*

## The fall curriculum

We coordinate our program from junior high through high school and we operate on a sectional system. Everyone is in a section class that meets one morning a week prior to school. The section classes begin during marching session (late September and early October). At the same time, we have our regional and state tryouts. We use the state's material for each instrument as our course of study. The material is organized and assigned on a week to week basis and all the assignments are given in the beginning of this ten-week period. This part of the curriculum runs for ten weeks. Students learn one exercise and two scales (the drummers play two rudiments and one exercise) each week. We hear their performance and grade them weekly. The intent is to make kids better fundamental players, to give them material to practice, and to give structure and guidance to the teacher and the program.

*(Stanley Cate)*

### Starting beginners

We begin on mouthpieces and until they can make a good sound with tongue and the proper position, we do not move on to the instrument. This usually takes all the first week. In the second week, we use the instruments only—no mouthpiece—for five minutes, and they don't take instruments home yet. Instead, we learn to finger the first five notes. After two things are done—mouthpiece alone, then instrument alone—tone production is pretty easy.

*(Jack Brookshire)*

### An approach to the sophomore band

We structure sophomore bands in a different way. They receive an indoctrination and training that is intended to increase the chances that they will be successful at the high school level. This is especially beneficial for those who are not going to make the top groups right away. As a result, our retention of sophomores has increased dramatically.

We tell them, "You are not in Sophomore Band because you cannot play, you are in it because you are sophomores. Therefore, everyone is starting together. We will teach you some things that you will need to know and all of you will have the same chances—you are as ignorant or as smart as the next person." We also point out that the juniors and seniors in the top bands were once sophomores and were sitting in the same spots you are in and have worked their way up. We also have removed the stigma of not making it into the top band. We still have a top band, but we try hard not to have a bottom band.

*(Michael Hiatt)*

### Private lessons

We have a strong private lesson program, as high as ninety-five percent but usually sixty to seventy-percent are in private lessons. About eighty percent of the top band are in private lessons.

*(Michael Hiatt)*

### Scheduling the bands

Our juniors and seniors meet five days a week and we do not have students going in and out of rehearsals for lessons. Our sophomores meet three days a week. If a sophomore succeeds in getting in a top band, they must give up a class and therefore take one in summer school. About five sophomores make the top band, and twenty or twenty-five make the second band. That is also a "class-one band." With sophomores, we do considerable class lesson teaching with technique books, etc.

*(Michael Hiatt)*

### Team teaching

We use team teaching in the whole program, where each two band directors deal with five concert bands. Every class has a lead and support teacher. One is the teacher of responsibility for each class. The support teacher does record keeping, the lead teacher does none of this. After roll taking, etc. the support teacher is a roving teacher who works with individuals, sections, etc. as suggested sometimes by the lead teacher. This has taken a bit of time to get used to. Our choral program also has done something similar to this.

The support teacher emphasizes sectional work, particularly in the second and sophomore bands, and this attention has also helped our retention of students. This plan reduces the student's frustration, increases personal contact, gives help, etc. The flexibility with this program is the best thing, but planning is one challenge. The compatibility of persons is also very crucial for this to be successful. We give each other suggestions and orders, and we plan what we are going to do that day, with which band, and with which kids or sections.

*(Michael Hiatt)*

### Thinking about school curriculum

I ask students at the beginning of a band literature course to give me four pieces they want to do with the best high school band they could produce. They often list *Lincolnshire Posy*, the Hindemith *Symphony for Band*, the Dahl *Sinfonietta*, etc. I stand back and say, ". . . starting in seventh grade, outline a musical course of study that will set the table for this program, that will develop your students so they will be playing that literature." This sets the stage for considerable discussion of how a teacher is going to get students up to that level. College students are open to that discussion.

I draw the parallel that a successful football coach runs the same offense from elementary through junior high into high school. That means that the quarterback and other players know what to do as they move through each level, because they have run that offense for several years. It is not that we will be playing *Lincolnshire Posy* in the junior high, but we can prepare for that with well-chosen literature. Therefore, there should be a deliberately chosen and thoughtfully planned curriculum.

*(Michael Haithcock)*

### Playing both strings, and woodwinds, brass, or percussion instruments

Most of the string players double and many winds double on strings. Lessons are forty minutes on a rotating schedule. A doubling student takes clarinet one week and violin the next—a lesson on each instrument twice a month. These lessons are group lessons with about four people—two people one week and two the next. The two students not in a lesson are in class that period. As a result, there is some individual time in lessons.

The group size varies weekly, for example, because of tests in their other classes. This also means they may be coming to lessons at different times to make up something they missed. When they are not receiving instruction they must be in class. Our state guidelines allow one hour of music instruction for which students can miss one class every week.

*(Judith A. Niles)*

### The "Renaissance Approach"

In our school we have a "Renaissance Approach" that began in 1971. The philosophy is that every student is involved in everything as an artist, athlete, musician, and scholar. Students, therefore, must be shared between various programs. Our school is very small, with 1,060 students in grades kindergarten through twelfth and there are sixty to eighty-five students in each grade.

*(Judith A. Niles)*

### Freshmen percussion classes

Part of every day in the ninth-grade wind class, I had percussionists do technical and rhythm work with the metronome. The percussionists were in a separate class to quickly develop their skill and notions of the pulse and subdivision. They spent a semester quickly moving through the Rothman book and through rudiment-like work. In the first grading period we worked on grip, reading rhythms, etc. In the second grading period, we spent two days a week on tympany with ear training and three days with mallet work. The percussion players did technical work on mallets whenever the band was doing the same technical study or drill.

*(Donald DeRoche)*

### Requirements for percussion study

In the Lawrence, Kansas school system a student cannot take a percussion instrument if he has not taken piano. They know this from the first grade and they have four or five years to take piano if they are interested in being a percussionist. The result is that percussionists read a much higher level than teachers normally see and they have a greater amount of mallet ability.

*(Robert E. Foster)*

### Scheduling in the band program

Being a member of the advanced band means that the student is out of the seventh grade band and is in a band that is better than what the seventh grade band was, though he has not been selected for the top band. The Advanced Band is scheduled for first period in the day, every day. On Monday, we meet as a full band. On Tuesday, students go to study hall. I run the study hall and at the beginning I take roll, give announcements, and turn it over to the study hall aide. The sectionals come out of the study hall. Students know who is scheduled for a certain day and the sections meet upon need and demand.

I can either take one student, no students, or the entire band out of that study hall; it's completely up to me. If I select the clarinets for a section, they go to the band room to warm up. I say, "Please, can I see a show of hands of those kids who are going up to the practice module

area." Kids who wish to go to the practice module area raise their hands. They can go to an area with a monitored set of practice modules on the floor above the band room. A member of the certified staff monitors the practice modules.

Wednesday, students return to full band rehearsal where I follow up on what occurred Tuesday. I also will follow up what occurred Monday to let the kids know if it's better or worse. If it hasn't improved, they hear from me. If it has improved, they get a pat on the back. Thursday is another full band rehearsal and Friday we are in the study hall situation again. For example, Friday the kids all report to study hall and I may say, "Oboe players, I'm going to be working with just the two of you." I will have announced this Monday and Thursday so they know at least a day in advance.

*(William Long)*

The large pre-band group meets an hour once a week and they have a small group lesson one half hour a week for about five weeks.

*(Nancy Plantinga)*

### Tonal syllable systems

One system is "movable do" in which all (major and minor) resting tones are "do." Thus, every scale and mode starts on "do." In minor, the resting tone is "do" but the third, for example, is altered from "mi" to "me." Unfortunately, the use of this version of "movable do" means there are many altered syllables. This is a descriptive system.

Another system of "movable do" is one that is intended to develop tonal relationships. With this application of "movable do," "do" is the resting tone in major and "la" is the resting tone in minor. This system of movable "do," Kodaly's movable "do," provides a fix on tonal relationships. Any pitch can be called any syllable. When a pitch is sung on any syllable, all the other syllables and relationships fall right in place. This system includes a chromatic system that accommodates all alterations. It is easy to learn, because if one learns one scale, one can generalize to all other scales and to all other keys.

The third system is "fixed do" intended to develop perfect pitch. This system is designed for a different purpose. With this "fixed do" system, for example, F is always "fa." This needs to be started very early so by the time they get a bit older they have perfect pitch. By the time they reach age eight, they can sight sing anything in any book. This is the European system and that is a requirement studio teachers have for students. If a kid cannot do this, he cannot take lessons. Wouldn't it be easy to teach a kid who can sight sing the whole book before he begins to play an instrument? After age nine or ten, this system is difficult to learn. That is why it is difficult to use at the college level.

*(James Froseth)*

### The solo and small ensemble program

Playing ensembles and solos were a requirement and began on the Monday after football season was over. There was a list of the ensembles and I placed students in groups by compatibility, instrument, and levels of skill. Everyone had to be in one ensemble, at least, and played a solo at our local school contest in early January.

I began after football season, because Christmas vacation was usually not a time of intense practice, to say the least. Starting this early in the year got them going. When they returned in January, the students were organized and ready to do intense last minute practicing for the local contest in January. The local event gave them a running start toward the state contests several weeks later.

The ensembles had one rehearsal with me and one on their own. As time consuming as it was, it was very valuable. In mid-January, they played their accompanied solo and the ensemble pieces. I arranged for outside judges and the event occurred before the end of the semester since their performance affected their grades. The judges suggested who should go on to the state contest, though I wanted every student to go on who could. I also wanted our school to have as many in the event as possible.

This plan also involved more students in chamber music more of the year. It was easier to say who was going to the state as a soloist, since the judges helped decide this. In district contests, there was a limit on the number of entries for individual instruments from one school.

*(Donald DeRoche)*

### Student recitals

We had two kinds of recitals. (1) The "junior-senior" recital received credit; it was an independent study with a course number. Students received one-half credit for a semester. They had to do an hour recital and be in every piece. One had to be a complete solo piece. To satisfy school requirements, they wrote a paper on the composer and the pieces. The paper, usually between ten and fifteen pages, was advised by a music faculty member. The student also had to arrange for school announcements, school paper, community papers, room, piano, dress, invitations, and music faculty schedules to be certain we were free, and the taping of the recital. Potential music majors used this recording for audition tapes. The critique we offered was informal. About fifty people attended.

(2) We also had music department recitals, a volunteer recital once a month. The private teachers knew of this and promoted it. Student solos had to be accompanied and ensembles were coached by school or private teachers. Compared to the other recitals, the student had fewer administrative arrangements. One teacher could prepare quartets by having them come to each of the individual's lessons; so they were coached four times. An individual student lost only one private lesson. In these recitals, we mixed strings and winds, and on occasion, mixed with vocal. Mixing vocal, strings, and winds upgraded the quality of the music that was being played and introduced students to a wider variety of sounds and music.

*(Donald DeRoche)*

### Writing of solos by each student

Every kid in the high school band had to write an original piece for his instrument every year. It did not have to be accompanied. He started where he could and improved little by little with the help we could give. For example, I might coach them on orchestration. At the choice of the students, they progressed from solos to duets, trios, full band, etc. The only requirement was a piece for their instrument each year. Any extra material, such as accompaniment was optional. We developed the program partly when we had a Ford Foundation Composer in residence.

*(Frank Battisti)*

### Planning musical learning

We do talk about what a phrase is, what is the beginning, and what is the end. These are in our curriculum. When we make our plans, we decide that a certain week we will really be concentrating on the development of the phrase.

*(Nancy Plantinga)*

### Selecting instruments in the pre-band experience

I start my beginners with a pre-band class, during which the students can develop a thorough understanding of the instruments. This is accomplished, in part, through demonstration. They also try all the brass instrument mouthpieces so I can listen to see which brass mouthpiece they sound better on, the high or the low. They also try a clarinet mouthpiece and a flute head joint. We also check coordination for possible percussionists. I look for my percussionists first. This occurs at the end of the four or five-week period.

The team of teachers I work with felt that this has really worked well. The parents were impressed with the amount of time I spent making certain the kids were on the right instrument. In addition, I didn't do it before or after school. Mostly they really believed what I was saying. They did not think I was trying to influence students because I just needed this instrument in the band. I have heard teachers in other schools say, "Sorry you can't play flute, we have enough— you have to play this."

*(Nancy Plantinga)*

### Entry skills for the high school band

In my high school experiences, all students auditioned on all major scales from memory, relative minor scales all three ways, and played any interval I asked for in any key. For example, they might be asked to play a C perfect fourth or F minor third. This was the requirement to play in the top band. These skills were acquired over a period of years beginning in junior high after they could do their major scales very well. Sophomores and juniors went from a one-octave scale to scales through the full range of the instruments and a full chromatic scale from bottom to the top of the instrument's range. We also asked for sight reading and prepared pieces for their audition.

*(Robert Allan)*

### Ensembles and choirs during band period

For a twelve-week period, one day a week, we broke the band into a flute choir, a clarinet choir, a saxophone choir, a double brass choir, and a percussion ensemble. This, of course, leaves out the oboes and bassoons. We found a rehearsal room for each ensemble and the three teachers rotated. Each teacher visited two of them in a day. They listened for twenty-five minutes and were absent for twenty minutes. Each ensemble would work on a piece—we didn't do band music. In the twenty minutes we were not there, we expected them to get through it before we heard it again. This scheduling made so much difference. The saxophone section sounded like a saxophone section. They tended to imitate the better players because they could hear them. The intonation just improved markedly.

*(Terry A. Oxley)*

### Starting clarinetists in the upper register

With beginning clarinetists, I encourage the development of a strong and proper embouchure by starting them in the upper register of the clarinet. This was possible since they did not know the difference between high or low register. You cannot really produce a decent sound unless you have a good embouchure. I would have to write exercises for this since most methods books do not have this included. It was well worth the time.

*(John Kinnison)*

### The solo program

This program had always been a strong program. There were only two teachers in forty-two years and only two superintendents in all that time. Both backed the instrumental program very well. When I came here, however, I had no soloists remaining since all twenty-four soloists who played solos at contest graduated. We started the next year with fifteen soloists at contest and the next year the total doubled to thirty. The third year we had fifty and after that every kid in the band always plays a solo in the contest.

I think that building a solo program within your group is absolutely critical to having a group that plays well, meaning with finesse. In the seventh grade, they work on a solo in the spring. Certainly by the eighth grade, they're doing a solo. Over the years I've built a large solo library and I also have a large concert band library. I suppose I have about three hundred and fifty albums of concert band music on file and cataloged by title. If I want to do a piece I might have five different recordings of it. Often, I'll give a kid a solo and say, "Here, I'd like to have you work on this for contest. Here is a tape of the solo so you can hear it played by a professional." I also have recordings for the first and second-year solos.

*(Lewis Larson)*

### The experience of solo playing

For the first solo in the seventh or eighth grade, all my trumpet players, baritone players, and trombone players will do this Fitzgerald arrangement of Bach's *If Thou Be Near—Ich bist du mir*, which has a great melodic line. This piece is neither too high in range nor too hard in difficulty. This piece also requires them to learn legato phrasing and to work on their tone production the entire time.

When kids are getting ready for solo events, they show so much more progress. When you suggest things, they're ready and they want to do well. They go home with anything you suggest and they do it. I think kids improve in those six weeks before contest more than they do the rest of the entire year. I think it's great to have outstanding players in your group—those top chair players. The group also will sound much better as the bottom end of it improves. Thus, solo playing gives the depth to your groups.

*(Lewis Larson)*

### Choosing solos

I try to choose pieces for the kids so they learn a lot about music. For each solo, there's a reason for doing it. Just about every solo the kids start with will be a slow, tonal composition, or at least part of it will be slow and tonal. It's funny how these kids like these pieces. Who would ever think that kids would like to play slow music? They do like to play slowly, if they have a good tone. Most students also will learn a lot about their vibrato at that point. I mean, these are seventh and eighth-grade kids playing with a nice, pretty vibrato and they are becoming very, very adept at legato tonguing.

*(Lewis Larson)*

### Balancing the offerings in the instrumental program

Don't lock out your jazz band by locking into one thing only. In some parts of the south, they start marching band in the spring. They spend August getting ready for marching band, which they continue until Thanksgiving at least. Then they do a quick concert at Christmas.

Following the Christmas concert, they spend the next eight to twelve weeks learning three concert band songs for the music festival. Next occurs a spring band trip that includes their marching band show from the previous fall. The concert band performs the festival literature on the trip and, if a jazz band is included, you are lucky.

When they return from the trip it's May, it's nice weather. Bands do another concert at the end when they dismiss in May or June. They repeat their concert band festival numbers, hand out the awards, and go home for the year. Students take off June and there's no time for jazz band. The cycle begins again in July.

If one looks at schools with this schedule, they are marching seventy-five percent of the time. You can't have jazz band when marching band is scheduled before and after school rehearsals. Students do have to study, so you can't schedule one additional day in for just the jazz band. Furthermore, during concert season there are sectionals, guest conductors, and other clinics. Therefore, there is no time for jazz band unless one sets aside one day a week in the concert band schedule. What is one day out of five for the other groups? Is not jazz more important than that?

I point a finger at those people who do not consider all the different music. Especially the American Music that is now a national treasure. All one has to do, is listen to the bands from Japan and understand how much impact we really have. Yet, we are not taking care of our own programs and our own music.

*(Robert Morsch)*

### Planning and organization

Recently, I heard band, after band, after band and most of them were very poor. I don't know, maybe the teachers were merely trying to entertain to keep enrollment high rather than teach. The quality was so poor it was almost embarrassing.

Our program isn't like that; we still work hard at it. For example, we insist on lessons from grade five to eleven. During the school day, we have a lesson schedule for all of our kids in fifth through eleventh grade. Everyone has an individual lesson. The lesson length depends upon how many students we have and how much time is available. We try to take them out of study halls. If we can't, then the building principals allow us to take them from a class. We always have worked it out with the principals successfully. The students always come out of the same class. This way a student has a set time for a lesson, for example, at the beginning of first hour Tuesday. We may change the schedule if it will help a student. For example, if I'm taking him out of a math class and math is his worst subject, then I might say, "Well, let's find another time so you can study math more." We try hard to work out the most beneficial schedule. We and the principals agree that classes and tests always come first. We'll make up lessons on an "early bird" time. I am here by ten minutes to seven and start taking kids by seven a.m. I stay until I'm allowed to go at three p.m. However, I often stay till five p.m.

If a student takes lessons outside school, some parents will say, "Well, they don't need a lesson in school because we're giving them private lessons." We say, "Yes they do. We have our own course of study. We support your efforts in finding a private teacher, but we still have every student in our private lesson program." So many private teachers spend a half hour working on tone, that

students develop too little technique.

We have a complete course of study. We keep updating it, by changing, adding and taking materials out. We set up our files according to the course of study. If a teacher goes into our file room, he will find all the music organized by file drawers and by courses of study. We have a complete course of study and we keep changing, adding, and removing things to keep the literature up to date. Therefore, a teacher can easily find what they want. This saves a lot of time. The kids always have at least three or four books: technique books, solo books, duets, etc. They do not have only technique books. There is always plenty to work upon.

*(Frank Schulz)*

### Planning and organizing private lessons

All students in the top group must take lessons from somebody on the staff. We don't have private teachers in our community because it's so small, but we have a specialist on our staff for almost every instrument. The kids in the top group must take lessons. If they don't, they have to move to the second group where lessons are optional. They don't pay for those lessons that are after school and during day until six p.m. Some schools in Texas, such as Richardson, bring their teachers into the building. Some of those kids go to teachers' studios and some have to pay for it. The district pays our teachers pretty well, so we'll work until six p.m.

*(Bryce Taylor)*

### Our district and the staff

We have twenty teachers, the town is twenty to twenty-five thousand and the entire student population is about six thousand. The teachers are not all instrumental teachers. We have four people who do elementary music and four others that do elementary and instrumental combinations. One teacher, the person who teaches our oboes, has about half day in elementary music classroom and the other half day she's teaching oboe or bassoon. The remaining twelve teachers are fully occupied with instrumental music.

Two people are full time vocal and two have a mixed schedule. For instance, one flute teacher accompanies with the high school choir, teaches flute part of the day and after school, and the rest of her time is involved with teaching general music. We have no orchestra program. I'd like to have one, but I don't think we have the clientele; it's not that kind of community.

*(Bryce Taylor)*

### Saving time in short lessons

Even with three or four books with the high school kids, I don't go through everything. We might say, "Let's start here" and if we discover that have attained that, we jump to another place. I want to learn if they've made progress. We also might start in the center because some students, if they think you're going to hear only the beginning of an etude, will only practice the beginnings.

I will check all assigned material, but we probably don't get to the end of every one of them. However, it isn't only a check—we also work on tone, vibrato, and breathing. Like other teachers, we work on students' instruments, or tell them to leave it and come back later. We really do get a lot done and the lessons are very focused and flexible.

We grade their lessons in a class grading book. We date everything and everything's set up in their material with paper clips and dated. We know exactly what they're working on for a certain date and new material is dated for the next week. For instance, everything I've had for today is dated June 1. When the student comes in, I put my hand at the top of the book, flip open the page with the paper clip. I see that it is June 1. I also write special directions in the margins. We learned to streamline things to prevent getting "bogged down" with paperwork.

*(Frank Schulz)*

### Planning their learning sequentially

The things that I teach in my middle school are pulse, tone, intonation, and reading. To me, tone comes first because without the tone you don't have anything else; pulse comes second, followed by the other aspects.

*(Thomas Stone)*

### A system for technical development

I have organized material for students in a way that is too complicated to explain fully in a few words. It is essentially the organization of material from technique books in a way that guides the students' progress through material because specific exercises are listed in a sequential order. The plan also allows the teacher to structure the learning of students who do not have private lessons either from outside instructors or from the teacher himself because he does not have the time to give private lessons.

I use the older publication, *Technical Fun* by W. A. Storer that is still available from music stores. It is compact and inexpensive, and its organization and content enables the teacher to select different ways to organize the exercise material into a progressive sequence of technical etudes. This book provides material in all major and minor keys, has etudes that progress from easier to difficult in every key, allows certain etudes to be played simultaneously with other etudes which allows students of different skill levels to play together, contains suggestions that will build the students' ability to play various articulations and dynamic changes, and includes rhythm patterns and a chromatic scale. What it does not have is melodic etudes, though these can be found in other materials and used as to complement *Technical Fun.*

I also have another sequential plan of materials that include *Technical Fun* and books by Ployhar, Fussell, Smith, and Rhodes. I have organized these into six levels

of expectations or competency levels that fit and can challenge students from grade five through grade twelve. Though I cannot describe the complete instructional plan in detail, I believe the assumptions about the plan may be of interest.

I believe in a "system" or plan of instruction: (1) that charts a sense of musical direction and achievement each year for each and every instrumental student from the beginning through grade twelve; (2) that defines expectations in a way understandable to students and their parents; (3) whereby technical achievements of each and every student can be measured objectively; (4) that contributes to academic credibility; (5) that provides recognition and reward for each and every student; (6) that provides for the student with average innate ability and for those who want to excel; (7) that sustains direction in spite of questionable learning conditions; (8) that encourages all who are involved, the students, their parents, and teachers, to not only think vertically rather than horizontally, but a plan that sets specific technical challenges leading to growth; (9) that motivates the individual and contributes positively to group dynamics; and (10) that provides the teacher with an opportunity to teach a lesson to each and every student without "one-on-one" contact.

*(Dwaine Nelson)*

### Dynamic skills

In high school, we can accomplish a workable six levels of dynamics, not just two or three.

*(James Arrowood)*

### Counting systems

We use three different counting systems that are nearly the same. We use three systems because we found that certain kids can't absorb one set of syllables but they can handle another set pretty well. When we do our written exams, we tell the kids they can use any one of the three systems they choose or a combination of them. We are not concerned and either system would be acceptable. Since every kid learns all three sets, I'm sure that in the last movement of the *Music for Prague* one of the sets is running through each kid's head. Since one system is running through them rhythmically, evenly, and at the tempo that we're trying to work on, I am not concerned.

*(Bryce Taylor)*

### Starting beginners

We start the beginners in groups during the summer. On the second day of lessons with our eight staff members, we take kids into small groups and work with mirrors, arrange the embouchure, etc. I am convinced there is "muscle memory" involved here. The kids see the instrument the first day, but do not get to take it home for ten days. We say, "If you learn how to hold the instrument and your embouchure, then you can take it home." As time days pass, they get real excited wanting to take their horns home. We say, "Wait, the clarinets have five pieces, you only have two so we may need to wait a little longer." They cannot take it home for two weeks.

This is the prime time to establish good habits. We work hard and fast, but we move slowly! One brass teacher will not let kids go to the next page until everything is correct. If our staff were to face cuts, I would not cut the beginning staff—we would give up something at the high school level instead, since the first two or three years are the most important.

*(Bryce Taylor)*

### The case for chorales

I'm a great believer in chorales. I just love them and they're so helpful to get the students to sing and just make music. I've always used *Treasury of Scales* with my younger bands. We are using the Ployhar book with some of our middle bands and the book also has some warm up chorales.

*(John A. Thompson)*

### An etude list

I reviewed the best etude books that I could find and selected one or two etudes from each of those books. I made an etude list for every one of the players in my band. I made a list for everyone, because not all the books have specific concepts or problem areas that I want to accomplish. Thus, there was a list for saxophone, clarinet, and trumpet, and every student had a copy of that list. The etudes listed were also labeled September, October, November, December, etc. I selected etudes for the list from Klose, the Kohler book for flute, the Andresen book for flute, and Rochut book for trombone. I also used Arbans, Charliet, Pottag, etc.

One etude for trumpets had to do with slurring. It was a very difficult full page of concentrated slurring problems in an etude form. Another one would be articulation or fanfare style; another was double or triple tonguing, and was range development and interval studies. So, each of the nine etudes was chosen to teach them a specific kind of technique or set of techniques.

To get credit for the etude, they had to play the listed etude during the month for which it was assigned. I had nine of them for the school year and students had to play two out of three at performance level for the trimester. Performance level meant less than five errors per page. That was the standard for a grade of A.

*(Charles Olson)*

### The size of concert bands

One state was concerned that the impact of the wind ensemble movement might reduce total participation in bands. My observation is that the emergence of the wind ensemble has not lowered participation; therefore, I do not think this is a valid concern. I also think people need to divide their large bands and offer more musical challenges

to the people through smaller groups.

*(Myron Welch)*

### Some features of a good program

The ideal situation is a terrific program from the bottom up. If there is good teaching in the lower grades, it will be easier in the upper grades. In reality, we have all had junior high or elementary teachers who don't "cut the mustard "As a result, we have suffered their impact upon students through the high school years.

Some places are lucky to have strong junior high band directors who just set the kids on fire and that makes it a lot easier. I believe we should ask for a concerted effort from the beginning to develop every aspect of their musicality, within their technical limitations of course. This may reduce attrition between the junior high and senior high. This is a big problem in many areas.

For example, there is nothing wrong with using a long-tone exercise to develop their sensitivity to conducting. One cannot spend as much time on it with the beginner, but there's nothing with doing that periodically. Often they do not even know you are doing it. We can get them used to seeing a left hand, and teach them how to respond to a left hand and to facial expressions.

Include listening and much singing at that age. Sometimes students act like they hate it. They get used to it, though, when they realize that it's not done just for its own sake. Say, "Well that did improve your sound. Now maybe when you sing a tuning note see if you can match that pitch. Put your finger up to your ear. I bet you can hear yourself sing, too."

Also very important from the very begininng are private lessons and solo playing. This builds a concept of the tone they want. Find recordings of a sound you want to use as an example for the band or instruments.

There is also the need for good literature, which allows you to deal with musical aspects and technical aspects. I like *May Day Carol* by Ployhar and I use this at the college level and sometimes with younger kids to build ensemble and balance. This is a good educational piece for this purpose.

You must have an organized set of goals for what you want these kids to accomplish by certain points in their development. Make a concerted effort to get them where you think they need to be by a certain ages. Planning really enhances your program when you have goals in mind and when you choose viable ways to work toward goals.

The choice of materials is extremely important and is part of a good plan. One must choose the finest materials that are available. If you use one method series you also can select material from others.

*(William W. Wiedrich)*

### Taking roll in marching band

Set up a formation so that the group warms up in the same specific formation each rehearsal. Assign the kids a spot to be on the field and take a picture of them with an instant camera. If the rehearsal starts at noon sharp take the picture at noon sharp, write the date on the back and throw it in your drawer. This takes little time. Then, when a kid comes in two weeks later and says "Aw man, I was there that Wednesday," you just haul out the picture and say, "See that hole, that's you."

*(Donald Wilcox)*

### A "Can You Do This?" list

A vocal teacher I knew developed a "can you do?" list with twenty-five things listed. For example, "Can you conduct the tempo of this piece? Can you play your part? Can you play another part? Can you identify the melody, harmony, or counter melody?"

There also are things one can teach through a piece of music that can be listed on a "do list." When you are rehearsing the clarinets on a particular technical passage and the others in the band aren't doing anything, I will go to the "can you do" list on the board. I will point to number eight and I will say, "Now everybody else in the band please do number eight while I am working with the clarinets." It might be "finger your part" or "tap meter beats." This allows a teacher to involve everybody with doing something while the clarinets are working.

*(Janet Tweed)*

### Contract learning

When I was teaching in high school, we set up a contract. The contract set tasks and levels for the grade students could earn. There were three levels they could attempt for their first and second nine week periods.

"Although it's assumed that the Oshkosh High School Concert Band is comparable to any accelerated class, there are conditions, size in particular, that make evaluation a special problem. Thus, as a starting point, the student will receive a grade of C, with or without this contract, if he merely follows these criteria recognized as step one. To receive the grade of C, the student must come to class, attend sectionals, unless excused, perform music studies in an acceptable manner, attend extra rehearsals when called, come to all performances, and maintain a positive attitude toward the group and its activities."

"Now, a grade of B assumes the above and can be earned in any one of several ways recognizing that band members do, indeed, manifest many different capacities, interests, and potential contributions. It is expected that these contributions will reflect a certain amount of personal initiative. These suggestions, hereafter recognized as step two credits, are intended to be as a guide only: (1) perform in a regularly scheduled ensemble, which could be a stage band, youth orchestra, operetta orchestra, small ensemble, or brass band in or out of school, (2) regular, private study with a recognized, competent teacher, (3) perform an accompanied solo on another student's recital (need not be memorized), (4) accompany a student's

recital, (5) develop a related arts project, (6) develop a short term research project consisting of something that has specific musical interest to the student—jazz, blues, electronic music, ballet, period style, etc., (7) direct or be responsible for an assigned activity or challenge that requires extra time and effort, (8) participate in a mini-course, or (9) any contribution of these that the band member thinks he can justify as having been significant to his musical goals and the instructor has accepted as a worthy education endeavor or experience." Concert attendances and reviews, for example, could be done. With these choices it was nearly impossible not to get a B! If they selected only one of these choices, they got a B.

"The grade of A is a product of demonstrable initiative. Steps one and two are prerequisites, and a grade of A may be obtained if any of the following criteria are met successfully. A student must complete: (1) three additional step two credits or, (2) prepare a memorized solo with appropriate stylistic and formal analysis, (3) prepare and organize a student recital with at least six recitalists, (4) write an original composition for an ensemble of two to six voices, (5) arrange a piece for an ensemble of two to six voices, (6) write a major arrangement for a large ensemble (a sketch indicating the probability of the project's completion will be necessary at the nine week mark), (7) write a major composition for large ensemble, (8) develop a related arts projects that involves appropriate research that can be shared with the band, (9) participate in a major recital, (10) conduct a piece that's analyzed including a rehearsal and final examination with one of the training groups or large ensemble, (11) develop a student oriented ensemble that will require organizing personnel, finding rehearsal times, selecting and rehearsing the literature, and making a public appearance, (12) develop and teach a mini-course, or (13) keep the first-chair position in your section for no fewer than five of the nine-week grading period. A student could complete any other project the instructor and student agree upon, if it matched comparable standards established in the preceding criteria.

This is about as flexible as a contract can be. There is an indication of what the steps are going to be and they are graded every four to five weeks. At the end is a little statement that says, "I understand that the preceding conditions will, as accurately as possible, reflect my achievement and attitude grade for each marking period in the current semester. I also understand that I am under no obligation to enter into this contract, the consequences having been clearly spelled out at the step one level." Signed by student and instructor.

*(James Croft)*

## SELECTING LITERATURE

### Considering literature

Why not use standard marches to teach articulations

and technique through the baritone and woodwind parts? Marches are very appealing for many in the audience and they have great teaching value. There is tremendous challenge for tubas, baritones, trombones in pieces like *Them Basses.* Early in the year, I try to find pieces they can master and enjoy—trying to avoid frustrating pieces at this point in the year.

Pick the literature with the audience in mind also. Music on a program should not be all from the same stream. One composer is enough of a certain sound personality. For a festival I often play a transcription and a good band work.

An example of a piece not accessible to most of the audience is the *Hammersmith.* This is a good and deep piece. However, knowing the story of *Hammersmith* may help the audience gain access. The story is that Holst went for a walk by the river through the Cockney sections of London. We can hear the hustle and bustle he meets and the sounds he hears on the trip back to the apartment. It is a musical description of the journey through the neighborhoods he walked.

After seventeen years, fifty percent of the literature is still new to me each year for each of the top two bands. *Savannah River Holiday* has great melodic and lyrical lines. *Hymn for Band* by Stuart (Shawnee Press) is a piece where they can strive for excellent balance. I still like *Overture in C* by Catel. Too many teachers are stuck in a four-year cycle and don't add in enough new literature.

*(Carl A. Bly)*

I look at individual parts, not the score, to decide if I can visualize individual kids playing the part. If every kid cannot play it, we don't do it.

For festivals, I pick one tune that challenges woodwinds, one for brass and one for percussion.

*(John W. LaCava)*

### The challenge of finding literature

It simply takes a lot of time and persistence to find good literature. Among all the pieces available every year, there are two or three that are worth it.

*(Carl A. Bly)*

I try to pick a variety of pieces, with at least one that is a musically and technically a "bust your cookies" piece. I also pick a piece that they can play technically the first day—one that has much musical potential to be developed, such as *Irish Tune.*

*(Michael Haithcock)*

First of all, far and away, and above and beyond anything else, I look for a striking, attention grabbing pattern of rhythm and melody. These are the two single most important factors. I don't care what length of hair the composer has, what style, what year, what country or what composer. It is the rhythm and melody more than anything

else, I am convinced that either captures the attention and succeeds in holding it or else it doesn't. That's what I would look for. If I have to choose one thing, it would be rhythm.

Next on the list would be a "recognizable" structure, a form. Structure creates form. What I have said is, "Okay people, you're on the beach and there he/she walks by. This "hunk" or girl in a bathing suit. You people don't have any trouble identifying that form, do you?" That form, however, depends on a structure, it depends on a skeleton inside this appealing shape you just want to look at and admire. You do not see the skeleton and you never will until that poor person is dead. But, suppose by some almost magical means, we could remove the skeleton and leave all the blood and flesh there. What would that person look like?" Some people can't stand even thinking about something like that. Because, you see, the person would look like an under-inflated beach ball and that form is not going to impress you. It might even depress you if you were to see it. So structure and form: there cannot be a form without the proper structure because the form hangs on the structure, just as all the appealing flesh and muscles hang on the bones. People in the audience, who do not know a C chord from a hole in the ground, but who are sensitive in ways that we still don't understand, grasp the structure. It's not just one note after another, or three or four notes at a time. They hear, grasp, or apprehend—I don't even know the right words—a form built on a structure, and they recognize it, just as they recognize the form of the guy or girl in a bathing suit. There is no problem with that, is there? You do not have to go to school to appreciate that, do you? To me, rhythm and melody carry the message, and structure and form give them a recognizable shape. Even if the shape has a few curious twists in it, it is still basically graspable and comprehensible to more and more individuals. But, if the structure and the form cannot exercise this kind of a response, then I'm afraid even the melody and the rhythm may not be enough to save the piece.

*(Alfred Reed)*

I used to be fanatical about knowing the new literature and knowing all the old tunes. I talked to the older directors, picked people's minds, asked for programs from other schools, and collected programs. I also went to many concerts, trying to find what everybody else was playing. I did this so I could do a body of literature that I could be proud of. Well, I don't need to do that so much anymore. I know what is out there. I am very, very careful about analyzing what I have in front of me.

*(William Long)*

I always like to play something that's Twentieth century or something that's Avante Garde. Obviously, most of the band pieces are Twentieth Century, but instead of traditional Holst or Grainger, I do something that uses quarter tones, free meter, atonal, etc. I do that to stretch my students and those at clinics also. A neat piece for this purpose is *Epinicion* by John Paulson. It contains free meter, quarter tones, passages where you play as high as you can and as fast as you can for six seconds. Yet there is a tonal melody in it, a theme and variations, that runs through the piece.

The very first time I play this with the kids they don't like it because there is no melody you leave the rehearsal room snapping your fingers to. I tell them that they need to play this type of music, to hear it and know how to play it because it is the new music (though it is about ten years old). I tell them, "Just as we use a computer and automobile today and do not ride horses, you need to play and know this type of music to be up to date." This piece also helps them understand and appreciate Grainger, Holst, Persichetti, and Sousa. At whatever clinic I've done this, this piece becomes their favorite piece at the concert. The kids say, "I really had fun, it was a good two days and that was my favorite piece." There is also a program to it. It is a Greek tragedy and a Greek war. You can also tell the story to the audience as well and they also likes it.

I did this piece with the Vanderbilt Wind Ensemble. I told them, "I guarantee by the end of the semester you are going to be walking across campus singing this tune." The intervals are really different and it jumps all over, lots of wide intervals and, it's amazing, that's exactly what happened. Some kids this year came back in January and said, "Are we going to play that piece that went. . ." and, they sang it for me. This is an excellent teaching piece.

*(Dwayne P. Sagen)*

Make sure that they experience enough music in different keys and meters, including the compound meters where they see six-eight versus two-four. It's really nasty to hear high school students play a march like *King Cotton*, which is in six-eight. They somehow want to make it sound as though it was in duple meter. They do not have enough sensory experience with triple meters. We must get more physical sensation for both of those meters. These meters are physical things with which kids need to have more experience. Without this, they cannot become literate musically.

When high students get into music education classes and conducting in college, it's clear that they don't have a good physical sensation for the differences between duple, triple, and mixed meter. They seem to have problems. I always think of Frederick Fennell's line, "The one thing the crusaders didn't bring back with them were mixed meters. Those guys went down into those countries and they did not bring back the Greek meters of fives and sevens. Instead, they brought back cinnamon, coffee, and lots of great things, but no fives and sevens."

*(L. Keating Johnson)*

Music selection of many teachers has always appalled me. Teachers are succumbing to the pressures of the kids to play "their kind of music." There are so many good things that are written that kids will not only like, but these pieces will help them sound better.

*(John Kinnison)*

### *Transcriptions*

I think one of many examples of valuable transcription is the *Variations on America*. The original was, of course, written for organ by Charles Ives. Then, it was transcribed for orchestra by William Schuman and later William Schaefer transcribed it for winds. On the other hand, only some movements of the *Pictures at an Exhibition* have been transcribed. I did a performance at Triton College with a pianist playing all the movements of Pictures the band did not play. Therefore, we did one complete version of Pictures with piano or band.

I do not do many transcriptions because a great body of literature has been written for winds. However, if a group has the ability, they can perform the entire *Rite of Spring*. There is a transcription for band available. Doing the *Rite of Spring*, for example, was something they could achieve and look back upon and say "I was able to perform things like that." As a result, the students know a little bit more about important pieces of music literature.

In the future, they might buy an orchestral recording by a great orchestra conductor, or encourage someone to hear it because they know a little about the piece from performing it. My father, who was a Colorado band director, has been involved in transcribing movie music, for example, the original Errol Flynn movies of *Captain Blood* and the *Sea Hawk*. He did this, in part, to show that one of the best composers was actually a movie music writer. Eric Korngold wrote fantastic music beyond what he wrote for movies.

Such things are important because they represent a body of literature, music literature that's not performed unless it's done through a transcription for a band. I think it's valid to do those as transcriptions.

I grew up hearing the arguments whether you should do transcriptions. Who were the first guys to do transcriptions? Well, Bach, Mozart, and Handel. Of course Handel did most of his own transcriptions from his own pieces. Liszt did some fantastic transcriptions of orchestra music for piano. Thus, transcribing has always been a way of life in music. A transcription should not be looked down upon simply because it's not original band music.

*(Robert Morsch)*

### *Teaching the context of literature*

Current band directors, whether they lead concert groups, marching groups, or jazz groups, should use an educational process that includes teaching about the music and not just the notes to it.

For instance, you could play *Chorale and Alleluia* by Howard Hanson. This piece was well known twenty-five years ago, but not as many people know it now. This is still as good a piece of music as it was when he wrote it. This piece can be used to show the place in the real history of American music, and of musicians, conductors, and composers. In this piece, for example, we can show students, when playing the *Romantic Symphony* of Howard Hanson, that both have similar figures. This enables us to discuss how most composers have their own vocabulary and add their own accent, like fingerprints, to the music.

*(Robert Morsch)*

### Switching elementary instruction books

For years, I used James Froseth's materials. But, after many years of using the same book, I got very tired of it. As a result, my teaching was affected. I like Froseth's teaching approach very much so when I switched books I continue to use the same teaching techniques.

Now, I'm using a little known book called *Instrumental Series* (Silver Burdett, 1968). It is written for all instruments and has many good things in it. For example, the material on the left side of the page is unique to an instrument and the lessons on the right side of the page are for full band. There are very lovely chorales, full band pieces, etc. My entire concert programs this year are from this book and I didn't have to add another thing. The thing that sold me with the Silver Burdett book was, while it did have a place for rhythm studies, it didn't give any specific counting. Thus, I could use any counting system.

*(Gordon Nelson)*

### Programming for brass choir

With the brass choir, obviously, we can play a cross section of styles. We can go from Gabrieli to the Romantic and Contemporary composers. On every brass choir concert there was a representation from each period. This allowed the kids to learn how to play each style.

Teachers have to give students a variety of experiences because one style may grab one kid but it won't grab another. I program with variety and the main reason is not for the audience. They are a factor that is fourth or fifth on the list of priorities. The major priority is giving the students a variety of musical experiences so you can reach everybody in the band. Not everybody is going to like the same literature. As far as I'm concerned, it motivates a student if they play literature they respond to. In fact, that interests people and that will keep everybody interested.

I want different instruments or sections to have an equal opportunity for experiences. To do so, I go through periods and composers. Some band director's get on a kick for a certain composer. They fall in love with a composer and do that composer to death for a year and a half. Then, they fall in love with another composer. That's a trap we all can fall into. I fell in love with Thad Jones for a while. I finally caught myself and said what am I doing? I said, he's wonderful and an all-Mozart concert is also wonderful. A tune has to be something that has programmatic validity and a piece through which they can learn: it has to

meet those two needs and a lot more.

*(Dominic Spera)*

### Programming

Ray Dvorak, the former director at the University of Wisconsin, said, "If you can't program, get out of the business." It's a matter of dealing with a person's emotional responses and letting these responses take a rest. You can stimulate different responses differently by slowing things down, by playing something that's more chorale-like, more expressive, that has a different character or that requires different performance demands such as more breath control. Both the audience and students respond to these differences and find the material more interesting.

I do the same thing when I teach trumpet. I teach a balanced diet of literature and practice material for each trumpet student. We cover the basics of programming as we study music that changes keys, different composers, changing rhythms, etc.

In programming jazz band, I look for a change of key. You can't B flat your audience to death. First, if you stay in the same key, the kids get "key-locked" with blues in F, blues in F. Suddenly, when blues in C appears, nobody can play.

I think the jazz and concert bands have to program changes in texture and feel of a composition. Many newer composers write in a similar vein. By the time the concert is over, you cannot separate one number from another. Everybody's using the same voicing and the same general textures.

Different texture and different "feels" also lead to different instrumentation. In the jazz band, of course, it's very, very important because you don't have that many different instruments to choose for variety. Therefore, when I use the tuba or vibes, I use them sparingly. When I do use them, it's effective and it brings some variety; it brings a freshness to the concert that's vitally needed.

I include my combo on my concerts. In concert band, a solo, a duet, or half the band doing a Mozart serenade can improve the programming and learning experiences. One also should change composers and publishing companies. Publishing companies gravitate toward the same type of composer and type of music.

I look for dynamic contrasts, which I call contrasts of intensity. Choosing good music with these contrasts, automatically is good for the audience's interest and for the students' education, it works both ways. I'm convinced, if you have the students in mind, the rest of your program is going to be a success. Everything follows from that.

There must be at least one number easily accessible by the audience—a piece they can identify with. I always select one piece like this for each jazz concert, even at Indiana. The piece should be something that they understand, a melody that they know, or something that they can relate to for another reason. I think this is also very important in high school programming. The audience must go away whistling or humming one tune at least.

Now, that's also important in jazz, because we're trying to teach A A B A form. Form is a consideration when selecting pieces, so I include at least a couple A A B A pieces. I mean, you're trying to teach kids. When do the kids get to hear A A B A form on the radio? Rarely. Seldom will they hear it, unless the teacher presents it. So, I love to do tunes that have A A B A form and I look for them when I'm going through the literature. Of course, you've got to teach form and especially if you want jazz players that play.

*(Dominic Spera)*

### Preparing programs

When we're reading many pieces, polishing the performance is not as important. However, when we prepare pieces for an audience or for Interscholastic League Competitions, we take more time to prepare. We take about six weeks to prepare the things that we perform in competitions. During this time period, we predominantly do contest music.

At a contest last week, we played a piece by Mark Rogers, Berlioz's *March to the Scaffold*, Verdi's *Force of Destiny* and Husa's *Music for Prague*. Preparing that program took the major portion of that six-week period.

The fundamental things are done everyday, even on the day of the contest we worked on fundamentals in an abbreviated form. Instead of twenty minutes for fundamentals, we'd take ten minutes. Our students understand that routine and without it the students and the teachers are a little uncomfortable.

We program those same pieces for our spring concerts and we include other pieces, which we call program literature. For example, we did the Bukevich Symphony, a pop chart, and McArthur Park arranged by Bob Lowden.

*(Bryce Taylor)*

### Three types of literature

I plan the literature we do and I think of it in three categories: (1) Music that is new in some respects but is readily assimilated by the students because the literature fits their training and level of performance. (2) Music that we might call the "old stuff." These are things they may already have played and think they know. Rehearsing it again enables them to concentrate on all of the musical things, not just what to do, but how and why. We can go deeper into the piece to discover more about it, not just what it is technically. Some examples are: *Blessed Are They* from the Brahms Requiem arranged by Barbara Buelhman, *Air for Band* by Frank Erickson, and *Trauersinfonie* by Wagner.

Many band directors tell me they can't get their kids to enjoy slow pieces. Maybe they don't understand the challenge of it. Once you pursue intonation, it's an absolutely wonderful thing. You see, playing well, that's where

it's at! I remember someone saying, "I've made a living all my life playing whole notes and if you can do that well, people will buy beauty. You don't have to play fast and loud to attract them."

This comment speaks to the same point as: "What's more beautiful, a flying butterfly or a sitting one?" You know, if you can see a butterfly sitting, you can take in all the details of the beauty it has; if you see one flying, you can see all the beauty in its motion. The point is neither view of the butterfly is sufficient without the other; and we must play hard and easy music along with slow and fast music for a student to appreciate music's diversity and for them to sense the range of style and substance that different literature shows.

My band enjoy pieces that are just a pure pursuit of absolute beauty in regard to intonation, precision, movement, and color. This year we did *Nearer My God to Thee* by Lowell Mason and arranged for band by Herbert L. Clark. The first breath doesn't come until nearly twenty measures of the piece are over, so it's an incredibly sustaining piece.

(3) The third type of music is something untraditional and it can prove challenging to the student's ear. Sometimes students do not assimilate these pieces as easily or as quickly. This music still provides new and exciting experiences because it is non-traditional in sound and shape. For example, the music may be aleatoric; use quarter-tones, and use non-traditional harmonies and scales; need unique instruments or unmanufactured instruments that the composer only describes how to build; use non-western forms, harmonies, or styles; or ask for unusual forces such as voices with instruments, whistling, taped sounds, speaking and yelling, tapping of instruments and music stands, and other non-traditional sound sources. I am reluctant to give examples because it is so easy to overlook excellent pieces; but, here are a few I recall at the moment: Brent Heisinger's *Statement*, *Apollo* by Pennington, and *Milli Attan*, an Afghanistan Folk Dance. There are many other pieces of this type available and one can find them through a little searching.

*(Charles Olson)*

First, I plan via concerts and organize the whole year. I am very careful that I have various levels of music, particularly new music. I make certain I have a good mix of new music with the more traditional things. I think it's very common for teachers to forget a body of literature. Once we've played it, we put it away. The result is that years can go by when students will not have contact with some basic literature. Some teachers go with a core repertoire idea. Every three or four years they return to a particular piece. There are very good reasons to do that. They want to assure that each kid is exposed to certain literature.

I don't do that precisely, but I do make sure that it is not too long before I do a specific piece again. I do not purposely say every fifth year we have to do the Holst suite, every fourth year we have to do the Hindemith.

*(Myron Welch)*

### The size of the group

It's important that we do not get locked into everybody playing all the time. We need some flexibility in our programming. We can use a slightly smaller group here, maybe a slightly larger group there.

*(Myron Welch)*

### Thoughts about programming

Unless you have many concerts per year, you're limited to the amount of new literature that you can explore. I think that playing a variety of literature is one thing that keeps the college people fresh. As a result, there is less burnout at the college level. There is repertoire that we repeat every few years. We are programming more standard literature with the second band that includes the younger students. Then, when they get into the top group, there is more experience with newer and difficult literature.

*(Myron Welch)*

### Selecting musically challenging but technically easy pieces

We do some pieces with little technical demand, yet with a larger musical demand. We do this, especially, with the second and third band. I think many high schools make a mistake of trying to do so many pieces that are difficult. Everything need not be technically difficult. Students need pieces that are very easy technically, where they can concentrate on tone, phrasing, and intonation.

Through high school programming too, students are pushed right to the limit as they confront technically difficult pieces. Sometimes people do a couple of very difficult pieces a year. They spend so much time on them that many other things are missed. They need to do more slow sustained works where technique is less a worry. These pieces are successful and students learn to use their ears or eyes.

Teachers need to program more marches. Marches have gone out the window and there are so many good old marches. There are books and series of Karl King marches for junior high or easy high school level that are wonderful. They are very playable for the younger students. I was very surprised recently when I saw a book of marches at the judges' table. There are books of these marches that are still very valid, because there are many teaching opportunities in them and many of them are very appealing.

*(Myron Welch)*

### Picking a balance of good literature

As an educator, I think my first goal is to plan a year that contains a well-balanced diet of good literature. I select literature that I consider to be viable, both educa-

tionally and artistically. This eliminates much literature. There is little new literature that helps. Therefore, I've arranged pieces and gone back to the old "war horses." For example, I love English folk songs. Occasionally, I will take a very simple pretty English folk song and score it very simply. Then, I use it as a warm up.

*(William W. Wiedrich)*

### Literature and goals for a program

I look at what the kids will be like in nine months. I think of something that I can give them and what I also can learn. I search for literature that will make them more complete musicians technically and aesthetically. Therefore, I hope they also will be more complete human beings by the end of the period.

When I am programming, I think balance. I do not select literature that is too focused upon one part of the group. Even if I have strong trumpets and weak low brass, everything won't be trumpet, trumpet, trumpet. When one picks literature, one should be far-sighted, open-ended, flexible, and have a definite goal.

Picking literature is like the four basic food groups. One picks and chooses, but one does not have to like it all and too much of one thing may not be good for you. In moderation, the right combination is very effective. I think music is similar to nature and nature seems to balance itself pretty well. Nature takes a little of this and a little of that. Nature also does not take anything that's not worthwhile.

*(William W. Wiedrich)*

I look first for anything that's unique. I look for the variety, a harmonic language that maintains interest, instrumentation and, more than anything else, the avoidance of cliches. As soon as I see that it begins with "dum digga dum digga digga digga dum" or the middle section has the predictable lyrical melody, I set it aside because it can't possibly be of interest. I'm not interested in what's been done and done and done and done before. With these pieces, we have a different title and the same composer doing the same piece again. That's very unfortunate. Therefore, I look for pieces that are unique.

I look for scoring practices. How are voices being used? Do kids have a chance and is there relief with solo voices? I think, so often with wind music, we have too much tutti playing. I also look at melodic character and for melodies that are not predictable. Not only melodies, but harmonies and rhythms that are not predictable. So, avoiding the predictable is another key.

There's a good literature list. It's published by Florida Music Service, 1517A East Fowler Avenue, Tampa, Florida, 33612. The title is *Music for Concert Band*, by Joseph Kreines. This is a selected annotated guide to band literature. I have shown how I chose literature at many clinics. I feel that the best way to do it is to have a demonstration band and say, "Here's a piece and I don't think it's very good. These are the reasons I don't think it is very good." Then, I let them hear the sections that are the basis for my lack of interest in the piece. Then, I might say, "Here's a piece I think is pretty good and this is why I think it's pretty good."

*(James Croft)*

### Use of chorales

There are many ways and uses of chorales. One can discover strengths and weaknesses of each section, part, or a smaller group if they play alone. One can give instruction, encouragement, experience, and confidence and that will lead to improvement.

The phrases may be alternated among the woodwinds, the brasses, and the complete wind section of the band. The flutes, clarinets, and string basses may show their completeness, balance, and independence as a homogeneous woodwind choir. The cornets, trombones, euphoniums, and tubas also may establish their identity as a brass choir. The oboes, bassoons, saxophones, trumpets, and horns may show diverse tone colors. With the band hearing its components separately, the students will learn to listen for them when larger combinations are playing. The band will understand the necessities of proper balance and appreciate the rewards of the richer, more colorful sounds. For my money, a chorale is always indispensable before work begins on program music.

*(Mark H. Hindsley)*

## Transcription and Arranging

### Changing the score

It is the right and responsibility of the conductor to improve the piece whenever possible. I add or change dynamic markings to improve scoring since many pieces are written for a generic band. Don't blame the student for an arranger's mistakes or choices, or for the instrumentation of the band.

*(Barbara Buehlman)*

I have often rescored pieces, especially transcriptions or easier pieces. I make changes in percussion and other parts nearly every time we play. The arrangements and transcriptions may have been done, for example, for outdoor playing. If the scoring is too thick, I change them with my "paring knife."

*(Donald Gee)*

Most of the band literature—no matter what it is, whether original or transcribed pieces—is simply written according to an idea some guy has of the band. He may not even know what a band is. He may hate bands. He may be an organist that's getting money for transcribing music. There's no guarantee that any of the things you get, even from the old masters, will be perfectly suited to the band you have in front of you. If a band director takes the score

literally, he may be making a big mistake. Even if it says all clarinets are playing this line at this time, you don't have to do that.

*(William Long)*

I re-write all over the place. For example, I have a marvelous baritone saxophone player. Many baritone saxophone parts in a band composition simply leave the guy sitting there counting rests and that's not fair. He can help my tuba section.

I also have a marvelous contra-alto clarinet player who can play anything in front of him. Often the scores come out with no contra-alto part. Therefore, I might rewrite anything; I write different parts for low clarinets, if I feel the low brass can be helped. I do nothing, however, that detracts from the structure inherent in the composition.

I have in mind the sound that I want so I start sketching ideas. For example, I may conclude that I want more power there, or I want less here if I don't want my saxophones "squawking" through that line. I want them out there. I simply make some artistic decisions. The very first year I taught, no one told me that I could make changes. I just decided to rewrite some parts. Some transcriptions have passages given to cornet and trumpet that originally might have been in the clarinets. I may change the parts so they are like the original score, if it is feasible for the students. I likely wouldn't do that if I were a university band director.

I did an in-service conference in Portland and talked about rescoring for the band. Warren Barker, whom I didn't know, came up to me afterward and introduced himself. I thought, "Oh, I'm in trouble now." Instead he said, "Thank you, thank you, thank you. That's the most astounding thing—taking a piece and making it fit to your kids—that anybody has ever said." He said, "This should be told to everybody. We are simply writing for a generic band out there. Publishers hope to satisfy a lot of people and sell music. Every director should get a pencil and score paper. When they get our pieces, they should be setting it—making it work—for their kids."

Well, I felt very gratified and good about the session at that point. No one had ever asked me about it in all the years I have been teaching. No one said, "Well, Long, should we rewrite or rescore pieces?" For this clinic I thought, "Well, they asked me for tricks of the trade and I gave them some trade secrets."

*(William Long)*

### Altering the score

As an arranger or composer, I have no objection at all to somebody altering one of my scores to fit their particular band. When publishing band and orchestra music for school situations, we are limited by the score that we write and it usually includes every instrument. We also have in the back of the mind that the actual performance of the piece is not only a musical experience for the audience and the youngsters who are playing it, but it is an educational experience. So, we have a lot of people playing. Often we have drum parts that probably shouldn't be heard, should be heard much softer or shouldn't be heard at all. We include them in there to keep the percussion section happy and to keep the teacher happy. We try to do it as tastefully as we can.

The piece has to fit a plethora of bands and orchestras all over the country; bands that are of various sizes and various instrumentation. Therefore, the inventive band director or the inventive orchestra director would certainly have my blessing if they changed it, rewrote it, or made it conform to their situation.

There are some more obvious places where changes could be made. Many times I have included a percussion part on a very simple folk song arrangement that is very legato, very smooth, and has very linear musical lines. Perhaps, the percussion has a very soft drum roll, just to have a drum part for them to play. Many times, though, that drum roll is almost superficial: it really isn't necessary. I would say that if the drummer cannot play it with a smooth roll, or if he plays it too loud or too aggressively, that part could be cut out completely.

In most young band pieces, especially in the very young, we will write two trumpet parts. We will write a third part and label it third cornet or third trumpet but it doubles with the second. The result can be an unbalanced sound. If it is truly an unbalanced sound, depending on the number of trumpets you have, you must make a difference in the instrumentation. One way is to change the number of people playing the first or the second part.

There is not a separate second and third trumpet part because we wanted more limited instrumentation for the very beginner. Yet the publisher wanted a complete instrumentation, so the only alternative was to write a third part that was the same as the second—but published it as the third part. Therefore, everybody has a first, second, and third part, but the second and third are identical.

This is done because a small elementary band may not have anybody on that third part, or there may be somebody who is very weak, plays very little, or doesn't play at all. In more mature, larger situations and where there are plenty of trumpet players, you have many people playing third, many people playing second and there could be an imbalance. One could either transcribe a first trombone or horn part for the third cornet or write a third part yourself.

The dilemma of writing for school bands or orchestras is that we must write according to the score that the publisher wants. Yet the teacher must have everybody on a part—an interesting part if at all possible. So, it becomes a tutti situation with the younger bands. With some arrangements, one could do brass only on the tutti. I don't double the woodwinds with the brass necessarily, so it couldn't be done on mine. Another alternative is to change

an ensemble passage, or a portion of it, and rescore it as one solo or a succession of solos. One can choose any combination of instruments or sections and solos to make it interesting. The teacher can do any of several things. One can be using different voicing to get different sounds. If it is musical and logical, it is fine with me.

*(James D. Ployhar)*

The problem with altering the score as James Ployhar suggested is that in all of art music we are cautioned that we should not mess with the musical score because the composer knew what he wanted. We note the criticism that Mahler received for redoing Beethoven and Wagner. We are also admonished if we do not perform a piece according to the Toscanini's or Stravinski's viewpoints.

However, I think that applies most to literature at the highest end of the spectrum. Miles Johnson talked about this, saying, "I wouldn't mess around with certain pieces, but with just about anything else, I would and I think we probably all do."

Furthermore, if a teacher alters a score and performs it at the contest, the person who is judging him will be a threat because he disagrees. After all, doesn't everything revolve around the rating that we get in contests? So, the judge of the contest says, "What are you doing fussing around with this? Now, wait a minute, for that, you get a division two. This would have been a one if you hadn't." This is one professional problems we might face, if we did the wise thing and adjusted a score for a particular group.

*(James Croft)*

## PLANNING FOR PROGRAMS

### Student recitals

We had a series of 4:00 Friday recitals. Each student would be assigned a date and these dates were circulated to the private teachers, who helped the students select the pieces. The student would have to do a paper on the piece and the composer, telling whatever they could say. Often the paper was descriptive. The paper was written before they played the piece and they could not perform until they did this. This was accepted by students.

*(Frank Battisti)*

### Thoughts about program design

Our programming is dictated by circumstances. The last concert (spring) is more a chamber music and band concert. There may be a student conductor and a brass choir. I did an arrangement using students who were not as involved with other pieces. We used the limited spatial opportunities for ensembles in the small balcony and the hall. Some schools with larger stages have used spot lights to focus upon one group while it played, and the other group was quietly getting ready.

*(Kjellrun K. Hestekin)*

## *Scheduling the performance of a visiting artist*

The visitors perform first because the students have to know that the musicians that are going to tell them something, can do it. They will not listen to a visitor or their regular teacher until they prove themselves. This is more true of this era, not so true earlier or a few years ago.

*(Judith A. Niles)*

## *Conflicts of schedule*

When our concerts coincide with the end of the nine-week grading period, some parents and students complain about me taking them out of study hall. They complain because the kid has an algebra test coming up third period. I always apologize to them and take them anyway. I would change the sectional schedule if I had advance notice of a test. Often, though, the kid may be afraid to tell me about the test. Instead, he complains to mom and dad, then I hear about it.

I've had kids who groan when I announced a sectional. I tell them, "If I ever say that you have a sectional, don't you ever groan. Don't you ever show, with your voice, that you don't want to come, because you will suddenly find me all over you." The kids know that, but I can tell by their faces.

I say, "Paul, is there a problem?" They are honest with me. Paul might say, "Yeah, we've got two tests coming up tomorrow." I'll say, "Do you need that period to study for them? Can't you do it tonight?" If they say, "We need that period to study for them." I say "Okay, then let us do the flutes instead." If we could not have any sectionals, I simply opened that time up to practicing.

*(William Long)*

## SECTIONAL AND LESSON PLANNING

### *The steps in teaching a lesson*

#### *Step One: Attention Signals*

When teaching, there are important steps that identify the stages of what occurs in most lessons. The first step entails giving attention signals. The goal of this step is to focus the students' attention on the teacher and the task. One can do that with words such as: "Look," "Listen," "Eyes up here, band" There also are statements, shouts, and whispers such as: "Everyone take a deep breath," "Hey, let's begin!" and (in a whisper), "Listen to this."

There can also be non-verbal signals to gain students' attention, such as clapping hands, snapping fingers, flashing lights, playing a musical phrase on an instrument, tapping a baton on the piano or stand, stepping on to the podium, playing a triangle or bell, raising an arm—the list is endless.

There are special considerations for this step in the lesson: (1) the students need to be taught to respond to the teacher's attention signals; (2) the teacher should work toward having a classroom routine in which the signals are used consistently; (3) the teacher must remember that the magnitude and intensity of the communication—as well as the eye contact—are also important; and (4) when the teacher whines or sighs—shows a wimpy approach—the results are deadly.

#### *Step Two: Models*

The next step in the lesson has to do with providing models. The goal of this step is to provide a concrete picture of the concept or skill to be learned. Direct ways to do this include the teacher or a volunteer performing live or recorded examples; or using video images (television or movies) to show examples as models of what is being taught.

The models can also be symbolic, such as musical notation, line drawings that illustrate phrase shapes, alternate rhythmic notations, or pictures.

There are special considerations about this step: (1) a guided model can help focus attention on the important features of the example; (2) an exemplary model has an enhanced credibility, eminence, competence, and social status; (3) the model must be simple, correct, and direct; and (4) the teacher's personal combination of magnitude, intensity, and eye contact again are essential.

#### *Step Three: Verbal Instruction*

The goal of this step is to explain who, what, where, when, and why. Here are some examples: (1) presenting goals, such as saying, "Today we will work on intonation at measure 22"; or "Our goal is to analyze Mozart's Symphony Number 40"; (2) establishing set, as in "Get set—go!"; (3) presenting advance organizers, or statements that call upon past (remembered) events to suggest present or future events, as in "Yesterday we worked on the first strain of *Stars and Stripes*," or "Earlier we focused on producing a full sound and precise articulation"; (4) presenting information through verbal instruction. For example, explaining, or analyzing examples by comparing, contrasting, synthesizing, or evaluating; and (5) giving response directions. For example, "When I call your name, walk to the shelves and select an instrument. Bring it to your place and put it on the floor in front of you. Please wait until I tell you it is time to play."

There are considerations one should remember when going through this step: (1) teacher-talk, if excessive, has been correlated with off-task student behavior in music classes and rehearsals; (2) when giving verbal instructions, absolute clarity is essential—the teacher must remember what to say, and know what to say as a result of planning. Planning is absolutely necessary because the lesson will be unclear and vague if the teacher tries to deliver information he either cannot remember or never even really knew.

#### *Step Four: "Do It" Signals and Cues*

The goal of this step is to signal an immediate student response. Some verbal examples are to say: "Is that in tune, Katherine?" or "Who is the composer?" Some non-verbal examples are conducting cues, head nods, pointing, and directed eye contact by the teacher, with the student being cued to answer.

The special considerations for this step are: (1) a classroom can be conducted just as an ensemble is conducted by using variations on conducting cues; (2) there must be no interruption between the cue and the response; and (3) precise communication is essential.

*Step Five: Student Response*

The goals of this step are to: (1) provide an opportunity for students to practice and receive feedback; and (2) provide feedback to the teacher. Some examples are student responses that also show ways for the teacher to get feedback about instruction. These include music and movement: overt musical responses such as singing, playing instruments, walking, clapping, moving, marching, or conducting.

A second type of student response is verbal. These are spoken words and gestures that can reasonably substitute for words: head nods, moving the arm to indicate high and low, or raising the palm to indicate "Stop." Also contained in verbal responses are written responses: music theory work, written seat work, and work at the chalkboard. One more type of student response is listening to music as the primary objective in the instruction, not as merely an adjunct to the instruction.

There are also special considerations here for the teacher: (1) gauge the difficulty so that students "win" about eighty percent of the time they respond; (2) opportunity for frequent musical responses correlates with affective responses; (3) individualize directions for student responses as efficiently as possible. Responses can be thumbs-up, down or sideways; pads on desk; or head down—lift with answer.

*Step Five: Prompts*

The goal of this is to give students some or all of the answers or responses they might need to be successful. These might be musical, such as playing, singing, conducting, or tapping along with the student; verbal, such as giving directions as the students are performing; or other responses such as gesturing, nodding, and pointing.

The special considerations for this step are: (1) the objective of the teacher is to fade out prompts so that the student learns to respond independently; and (2) prompts need to be as subtle as possible.

*Step Six: Reinforcement or Feedback*

The goals of this step are: (1) to provide feedback to students regarding the accuracy of the response; (2) to create a positive approach to learning and the subject matter—positive examples include: "Flutes—your staccato was very appropriate at number 22; that was excellent, keep it up!"; negative examples include: "Points will be deducted for each scale not learned," or "Anyone missing the concert will be given an F"; and (3) a teacher can also use punishments or reprimands, such as "Go to the office!" or "Put your instrument away."

The special consideration here include: (1) An 80:20 positive to negative ratio is best for on-task and attitude; (2) watch out for mistakes, or approval and disapproval errors; (3) just what is reinforcement or punishment varies with the individual receiving it; (4) feedback should be as immediate as possible; and (5) specificity is not only important—it is absolutely essential.

*(Roseanne Rosenthal)*

### *Much teaching occurs in those small classes*

Before I build a rapport with the kids, I show them how to do what I demand from them in the large group. I couldn't stop and do some of these things in large group rehearsals that I'm able to do in a small group. I don't want to spend much time talking about individual intonation problems in a large group rehearsal. We may make note of it, but in the small sectionals and lessons we can really explore and fix it.

*(Lewis Larson)*

### *Selecting private teachers*

We had a recommended list of private teachers. We would steer seventh graders to a high school student first. The high school person is a bit more in tune with this age. We try to use a senior who will graduate soon. The student then has to find a new teacher after one year and they usually choose an adult the next time. The student usually stayed with that person the entire time. We have about seventy-five percent of the students in private instruction. This is not required and no extra credit is given.

*(John W. LaCava)*

### *I believe in variation*

I do many different things each week and each day in rehearsal. This is particularly important with younger kids, since they get "bored" easily. For example, in a beginning percussion class we start with something on snare they know, to get their wrists warmed up and together. This reinforces and drills successful things. Then we go to the mallet book for another twenty-five minutes. We use the Ludwig drum kit from the beginning. The good kids start picking out tunes . If they don't I suggest that they do it. This helps minimize the students who say, "I can't do this!" They discover that they can. I also think we must get them started on keyboard.

*(Carl A. Bly)*

### *Percussion class*

I plan the percussion class so we use twenty to twenty-five minutes for snare, twenty to twenty-five minutes for mallets and other instruments such as bass drum and tympani. Ancillary instruments are taught on an extra basis or during special sessions.

*(Carl A. Bly)*

### *Scheduling sectionals*

We can call special section rehearsals if a problem

occurs. However, if they work out their problems on their own, then these are not needed. The section classes are not scheduled regularly after the ten-week fall session.

*(Stanley Cate)*

### The nature of the class lesson

I have a rotating lesson schedule. Typically four like instruments might come in for a fifty-five minute, full-period lesson.  For example, I might have four flute players, four clarinet players, four trumpet players come in, and each group is there for the period. Many times of the year we might be studying certain materials and solos as a group. For example, when it comes to contest time in the second semester,  they might all be working on the same solo.  I might have one play and the rest of the students listen. Occasionally they'll all play it through together. This is like a little performance class where they get to hear each other. When I'm making comments to one, I'll say, "If you're working on this solo you might as well stay  to  listen and to see what they're doing because you will learn from one  another."

*(Lewis Larson)*

### Starting beginners

Fifteen or more years ago, I did not use a method book. I focused upon imitation using whichever instrument I had or used my voice. For example, their first notes were G, F, and E on trumpet and the notes for the clarinet were E, D, and C at the first lines of staff. I did this to build embouchure. (I wouldn't even teach correct position at first.)  I took this approach because we often try to cover too much too fast at the beginning. I would do this for five or six weeks at the beginning—depending how well they moved along. I would be teaching with variations of what the book had in it. I would include more quarter note work to build pulse instead of the first emphasis on whole notes.

*(Anthony J. Maiello)*

### Student compositions for percussion

I have students write their own pieces for one or several drums. I have them use two pillows and play them at home as an introduction to playing two drums and to playing compositions for tympani. Parents do not complain about practice pads, but they do complain about loud drums—particularly inexpensive drums! Students also try vibes, marimba, etc., which interest them a lot; they also try claves,  etc. in first and second-year percussion classes.

*(John LaCava)*

## LISTENING IN THE CURRICULUM

### Planning what students will learn to hear

In the sixth, seventh, and eighth grades we spend more time on developing tone production. Without a full tone, intonation is out the window. With a good tone, they easily can be taught to hear and eliminate beats. When they begin to hear beats, poor intonation bothers the students. It takes a good long time to establish and police the production of appropriate tone, and another good long time to establish tuning at a basic level. Either tone or tuning can slip out in one day. Then it can take the rest of the year to correct it.

Since there are many things that a director must strive for in students' early years, intonation must come into things the first year at a very basic level. We have them work with the fifths and the octaves and we teach them how to manipulate the pitch. We do not get into minor adjustments of chord tones  until the advanced level.

*(Bryce Taylor)*

Students must recognize what a chord is, what his note of the chord is, and what a major and minor triads sound like. They must also learn the sound of the I chord, V chord, and a II-V7-I chord sequence.

*(Frank Bencriscutto)*

Reflecting upon my own education, I can conclude the order of things that I learned to hear. The word listen meant something different each year I played. In the beginning it was E flat instead of E natural,  then loud and soft, then intonation, then balance. With more experience, listening meant phrasing and musical meaning.

*(James Arrowood)*

They can play a song like *America* in D flat and in all other major keys. Once a week during interval work, I have one or several players perform *America* on a starting note I name. All the others listen and finger their instruments as the students play.

*(Patricia Brumbaugh)*

Have them play by ear. You can pick the tune, give them a style, a dynamic, etc. to get them to play a tune without the notated music in front of you. You don't have to be a thirty-year experienced jazz player to play *America* by ear.

*(Donald Wilcox)*

Do this through simple tunes such as those in most band methods. After working on a line, song or etude, come back to the same material the next lesson. At the next lesson, ask the students to look at the music and recall what they think it will sound like before they play. Then ask them to play from the music.

After playing, the students decide if what they heard was the same as they expected it would sound. This is a self evaluation for which only they know the answer. If this is done from time to time, this helps the students' playing a good deal.

*(John W. LaCava)*

## PLANNING EVALUATION AND SUCCESS

### *What should we evaluate?*

We should build into our program a way to evaluate students' ability to generalize from taught material to untaught material. I did this with the small ensemble component (of the large-ensemble program). This was a means to assess the individual student's learning. If students are learning, they should be able to independently apply skills or knowledge in a new situation. If the students could, therefore, apply things learned in the large ensemble to their work with a small ensemble, one could tell if and what they were learning. Some things, where one would like them to show independence of action or to see them generalize about, would be: ability to conduct, process notational markings correctly, perform with appropriate style, tone, dynamics, intonation, balance, blend, and articulations, perform and read rhythms and other targets for music reading, ritards—the whole array of issues, the standard issues of traditional musicianship. At one time I did use traditional scales with certain skill levels, but now I would see that as off the mark, because it lacked musical context; it did not necessitate or foster musical playing, etc. Albert Leconi said in Italian that "It's all in the music; everything you need to learn is in there." If students study music, they will learn music; if they don't study music, they will not learn music.

*(James Froseth)*

### *Establishing a climate for learning*

My band room is the same every day: all the chairs and stands are exactly right and in the same places, everything is listed on the board, everything is ready. This saves or prevents discipline problems because it imposes a structured and disciplined environment. They anticipate it and this has a positive effect. Nothing is allowed up in the room that could be a distraction. Nothing is on the wall or board unless it relates to what we are doing. I do this because they and I need this. This also has worked successfully at the high school level for sixteen years.

*(John W. LaCava)*

CHAPTER TWO

# SEQUENCING

When sequencing instruction, a teacher organizes content, considers the age of the student, and selects teaching techniques; the teacher's approach unfolds through the steps of the sequence. The use of a sequence is important because the order of learning activities directly effects the student's chances for success. While sequenced instruction is helpful for private students and important for rehearsals, most educators believe it is *imperative* for instrumental class instruction.

As the teacher plans the sequence of instruction, the teacher first considers the content or the skill itself because it may suggest the order of teaching steps. For example, a teacher can plan the week's rehearsal goals according to the difficulty of passages in the compositions. The teacher must decide which aspects to rehearse first or second, which to rehearse every day or once a week, etc. The teacher, in studying the score, looks at the difficulty of a passage and decides the best ways to teach the students to perform them.

The teacher may plan the instruction so that students move from the simple to the complex, from the physical to the cognitive. A teacher may choose to develop a beginning students' sense of steady pulse before he develops the students' experience with subdivision, meter, ritard, or accelerando. For instance, after pulse is established the teacher shows students duple meter, then triple meter; the teacher follows with mixed meters, such as five-eight, only after both duple and triple meter are learned. The teacher helps students discriminate the similarities and differences between different meters and their notation. What begins as a physical or eurythmic experience later includes notation and conceptual learning.

A teacher also can teach the students new skills, beginning with imitation, then introducing reading, and later adding generalizing. For example: (1) The teacher performs a line with a fermata. (2) The students imitate the example. (3) The teacher plays the line with and without the fermata. (4) The students imitate both versions of the line. (5) The teacher asks them to describe what took place, then tells them that this is called a fermata; they play the line again. (6) The teacher shows the notation and demonstrates again. (7) The students play the line to associate the

fermata with its notation. (8) The teacher talks about the fermata, if needed. (9) The students practice reading the line again with the fermata relocated to different pitches. (10) The students then play an unfamiliar phrase that contains the fermata marking. If they are not successful at any step of the sequence, all or part of the teaching sequence may be repeated or varied until the students are successful; eventually the students can play the fermata correctly and musically in an unfamiliar phrase.

This example also shows how students can acquire skills through sequentially organized instruction. The teacher shows the students, for example, the succession of steps needed to memorize a solo; or, the teacher introduces new fingerings or new rhythms according to a sequence of teaching-learning steps. More generally, the teacher selects the order of literature or skills studied according to students' grades or achievement levels. This allows the students to acquire instrumental performance skills in a sensible order.

A sequence can also be developed through analyzing a problem. For example, the design of the instrument and the instrument case can suggest a sequence. The teacher develops a sequence of steps for the student to follow as he removes an instrument from the case and assembles the instrument; when finished, the student reverses the steps in order to replace the instrument securely in the case.

The student's age will effect the sequencing. Young students generally learn in ways different from older students, and very young students, particularly, may be more amenable to imitation, movement, drill, and game-like teaching techniques—though these techniques still have value with older students. Teachers may discover, however, that older students can be more responsive to differently sequenced experiences, such as independent work, hands-on activities, coaching, discussion groups, applying principles, or learning through inference.

Thus, effective instruction depends largely upon the teacher's plan and his sequencing of an assortment of ideas and considerations. Not only will the students respond better if planning gives a direction to the class that they can sense, but the instruction itself will be more effective if the sequencing for the class reflects the content, and the students' ages and backgrounds. Without intelligent sequencing, the class happenings will actually be a barrier to learning instead of an assistance to learning.

## TEACHING SEQUENTIALLY

### *The order of instruction*

Teachers should not tell or teach students the last things they learned, though it is the most interesting for the teacher. What students need to learn is something much earlier in the progression, which the teachers have already assimilated long ago and which brought the teachers to their most recent realization.

*(James Froseth)*

If teachers would define their objectives for the short and long term, the sequence of objectives and events would be inner-linked more tightly. I think teachers should study Zoltan Kodaly and Edwin Gordon to see how tight sequencing and planning can be.

*(Frank Battisti)*

When teachers introduce terms, names, and other vocabulary, they should teach these through association. For example, if students play a fourth in a separated style the teacher should then say, "That is a fourth," or, "That is separated style." It is a simple matter of giving a label to something after students have already heard it or felt it in movement. The sequence is sound (or feel) before sign, name or term.

*(James Froseth)*

I sing something and they respond by playing back what I modeled. We always do a demonstration then a response. After the response, then we always do the application: a move to re-integrate, back into the music, the sample I modeled.

*(Donald Casey)*

I do not teach note names for a couple of weeks. I work with teacher demonstration-student imitation and have had good success with this. I remember back to my own training where I heard paragraph-long explanations that bored me to tears because I became lost in the descriptions. Through the process of demonstration-imitation, students can learn very quickly all that was described in those paragraphs.

*(Thomas Herrera)*

When working with children, I have found that if music concepts are presented first, through an appropriate movement response by the children, then with icons (visual representations of the concept), and finally with attention to the music notation, the children can show a

thorough understanding of the music objective.

*(Sharon Rasor)*

When I teach students I use technical terms as little as possible. My intellectual discussion of terms or descriptions of the placement of the tongue means nothing to students unless they have some experience. Really, most of learning is trying something and then overlaying the information that will improve a skill.

In the first lessons, instead of a technical discussion, I will say, "Do this, etc." Then, as many teachers do, I'll use a syllable or a phrase such as "say poo." My concern with all teaching techniques is that, if teachers use too much explanation early on, the student never gets a chance to put a horn up to his face and try it. Instead, I think an effective teaching technique is to remind them and suggest to them what to do.

*(Gerald Olson)*

There are basic teaching steps that I use repeatedly: (1) planning; (2) defining objectives (explaining what one is trying to teach) and purposes for students; (3) structuring a lesson and giving a thorough explanation of how to do it and, if needed, a breakdown of the task into a step by step approach; (4) evaluating the students' progress by questioning to determine the students' understanding; or in rehearsal, hearing their performance to determine the comprehension of the lesson; (5) going through the steps again if confusion remains; and (6) developing a summation of the lesson.

*(George R. Bedell)*

A player can't really change something until he realizes it needs to be changed. Secondly, he must have some perception of what the challenge is. Finally, if he doesn't experience the feeling of changing to the corrected version, he hasn't corrected anything.

*(Eugene Corporon)*

Several years ago, a teacher told me of a book by John Wooden, the former UCLA basketball coach. John Wooden described what he called his "positive-negative-positive" approach to pointing out errors and corrections to players. This meant, as I recall his explanation, that if you are telling students what was incorrect, you precede that description of the preferred way something should be.

With music, for example, if the students played a crescendo incorrectly, first say, "Class, here is how this crescendo should sound (teacher sings, plays, or conducts the passage)." Then say, "Here is what you did (teacher sings, plays, or conducts the crescendo as the group performed it)." Then, Wooden's suggestion is to say for the second time, "Here is how the crescendo should be (teacher performs or conducts the crescendo in the preferred way)." This gives them the correct version through a positive statement, followed by their incorrect version framed in a negative statement. This is followed again by the correct version presented as a positive statement.

If one does not present the correct model first, the first message a student hears is, "You did it wrong!" If the student hears the preferred example first, he already may realize what he should be doing before the teacher delivers the negative criticism. The effect is to help him see the way to improve before he hears the negative criticism and while he still does not know what he did incorrectly. These steps can increase learning and lessen the impact when the error is pointed out.

*(Joseph Casey)*

It is very hard to talk about a fermata without doing one. You can verbally describe musical things. However, which is quicker? Talking or showing? If you teach an accent, show the accent. I think the natural sequence is to know the phenomena and then put a label on it. Good old Pestalozzi strikes again!

*(Richard Kennell)*

## USING SEQUENCING IN REHEARSALS AND CLASS LESSONS

I try to remove complexities in rehearsal whenever I can. For example, if we are having trouble with a passage I reduce everything down to rhythm. I remove slurs, ties, ornamentation, and pitch. We take the passage on a unison pitch and just work on rhythm. This helps me decide which issue should be rehearsed next, the meter, tempo, or style. Then, we add the ties, then pitch, then articulations and last, we add the dynamics. This keeps them playing, from which they learn the most—not from me talking to them.

*(John W. LaCava)*

On a difficult passage, I sometimes start with one instrument or person, adding instruments one by one. This works quickly and they begin to play well together. It also helps students hear examples of how balance, blend, articulation, and dynamics should sound.

*(Steven Cooper)*

If I'm modeling something, I'll sing it musically and exactly as I would like it produced. I go from my singing to their playing; they first play after I sing; they seldom sing or echo my demonstration before they play, except to improve intonation.

*(Gerald Olson)*

If I am trying to teach, for example, the last movement of Britten's *Simple Symphony*, I do a lot of "mock" playing. These are the steps I go through: first, students sing the rhythm in the character that I want; second, students put the instrument up and do the bowing in the air—no sound—so they are using the right part of the bow

and moving rhythmically; third, they play with the left hand only—this enables me to hear the sound of fingerings and shifts happening. Through this I can tell if they have strong fingers or are rhythmically correct. Finally they actually play it. At this point it is a lot better, especially with the younger students. The first sound they hear is pretty darn good, and that boosts them psychologically!

*(Pamela Gearhart)*

I use these steps: first have them stand, then they move their chair back three inches, and last, they sit again. That should result in about the right spot to sit.

*(Steven Cooper)*

### Rehearsing a march in steps

I build marches first with the bass instruments. I develop a very solid tonic-dominant sound that students often find interesting to hear. Suddenly, they realize this piece must have a good rhythmic feel and precision. To do this, students must play on the front of the beat so the sound is not soggy. Furthermore, the french horns, with all of their wonderful after beats, suddenly realize that their combined part is supposed to sound as chords. This approach reinforces the point that the basic rhythmic and harmonic structure are with the tuba and the french horns. I then add other sections or parts bit by bit. Next, we add the counter melody line followed by the melodic line.

Percussion is the last thing that I add when I rehearse marches. The percussion really have the most difficult job of any section from the standpoint of balance. They are standing behind the group and cannot hear what's going on. They are at a terrible disadvantage! I also tell percussionists that "less is a whole lot better than more; you're really providing color here, and we only need a little bit, not a whole lot." I try to integrate the percussion so they feel they're very important to the overall color of the group, instead of just providing rhythmic interjections.

*(Craig Kirchhoff)*

### Teaching blend through steps

When we are trying to blend the tone on a chord, I may start with only three of the better students and add the others one at a time. Through this I am showing how the sound can change or stay the same as people enter. We build upon the sound defined by the first two or three players.

When someone is added, he may introduce a sound change from a bright to a dark tonal concept; the new sound can alter the blend. The cause of the blend changes also may be the embouchure, orthodontic braces, pitch, breath support, etc. I usually stress breath support first, though often the problem is some deficiency in their playing.

I first evaluate *why* the sound changed and then decide how to correct it. I do not try to have individuals sound like a carbon copy of one another. Instead, I *blend* their different tones together. The important goal for them is to get it right at least once. From there, it is easier to move forward since there is an experience to build upon for both the teacher and the student. For them, the clincher is *hearing* change and *feeling* different as they play. I try also to carry this over to their lesson for that week.

*(R. G. Conlee)*

### Increasing the tempo in increments

With any piece above one hundred beats per minute, I reduce it to two-thirds tempo when we begin to work on it. When we are ready for the next step we go three-fourths tempo, then seven-eighths tempo, then full tempo. I may not get to full tempo until a week or so before the performance.

*(John W. LaCava)*

## TEACHING MUSIC READING

### Sing, play, and then read

To aid students in developing a sense of tonality and music reading skills, teach tonal patterns of two to five pitches using movable do syllables without a rhythm context. Students should first "echo-sing" the patterns with syllables and then perform them on their instruments before working with notation. Therefore, the initial use of tonal syllables should be with the *sound* of tonal patterns, not with the notation of tonal patterns.

*(Stanley L. Schleuter)*

### Thinking about the teaching of rhythm

We don't teach kids vocabulary and writing at the same time in English class; why in music do we try to teach kids to read and play the horn at the same time? In music, as in English, we can't read or write without a vocabulary to use.

*(Carl A. Bly)*

### Teaching rhythm reading

I use the "hear-do-see" technique when teaching rhythms to young students. First, I give them a pair of drum sticks and I play simple rhythms. I say, "Watch and listen to me." Then I say, "You do it." Then, I write the notation on the blackboard so they "see it." Through this technique, they can progress to some very intricate rhythms. They also begin to listen right away, since they must listen to me to imitate what I do.

*(Donald S. George)*

### From imitation to reading

I start beginners with a Suzuki-like approach and without the book for almost two months. With imitation only, they begin to play and advance quickly. By the end of our six-week summer band program, beginners are playing moving eighth notes. They are not all "bogged

down" with reading the notes, dealing with the music stand, and all kinds of other things. After this five- or six-week period, there is a transitional period during which we begin note reading.

*(Nancy Plantinga)*

## TEACHING PHRASING, STYLE, FACILITY, AND ARTICULATIONS

### Teaching phrasing through steps

We always vocalize on a pitch to get a concept of the beginning, middle and end of the sound, and the musical phrase. We use proper support and a singing style, and apply this to the instrument. Finally, all of this is applied to tonguing to see how much articulation is needed.

*(Frank Bencriscutto)*

One idea of Tabeteau was to practice a phrase with dotted quarters and eighth-note values, for example, as though all the eighth-note subdivisions were notated into the phrase. Thus, the phrase is imagined as notated entirely in eighth notes. The next step is to apply some inflection by having every eighth note going to or coming from somewhere. Last, the student abandons playing all the eighth notes on every eighth-note subdivision except those in the original notation and plays the phrase as written, but with the directions and inflections he had practiced when all the eighth-note subdivisions had been added in.

An example of a phrase's original notation in four-four time might be "g‐‐ab‐‐a|c——d——." The student analyzes the music notation so each of the notes are subdivided into "gggabbba|ccccdddd"; after this has been determined, the student plays every one of the eighth-note subdivisions (which are represented by each letter). The student inflects the melodic direction, up or down, by using crescendo or decrescendo during the repeated eighth notes. Last, he removes the added eighth notes. Then, the student plays the phrase with the dynamic changes on long notes just as they did when all the eighth notes were present. This teaches the student to give a contour to the held or longer notes by playing notes as though they were "going toward or away from somewhere."

*(Pamela Gearhart)*

### Teaching articulations through steps

When teaching articulations, I will first draw shapes on the black board. Secondly, I will combine the drawings with gestures. The third step is using gestures to convey all of the articulations as we play in rehearsals or concerts.

*(Craig Kirchhoff)*

Tonguing is a real problem for young kids; so I have them go through these steps: first, start the tone by saying "whoooo;" second, they stop it with a "t" as in saying "whoooot;" Third, I use the "t" to start the tone as in "thoooot." I use the tongued release just momentarily until they get the idea; fourth, I ask them to play as in saying "tooooo." Another value of this process is to remove the intellectual aspects when they are not needed.

*(John Kinnison)*

At any grade level, on the first occasion jazz groups interpret a jazz phrase, they *sing* it more correctly than they *play* it. The problem occurs when things go from the brain to the lips or the fingers and through the instrument: something goes wrong because students become more involved in the mechanical aspect of playing the notes than they are with any expression.

To teach the phrasing, I might have students follow either of these two sequences: they sing, they play, they sing; or, I sing, they sing, they play, I sing again, they sing again, and then they play again. If students have the phrasing in their ear, I'm not concerned initially if they are pushing the wrong valve down; later they will hear what's wrong and either they will fix it or a guy in the section will fix it for them.

*(Robert Morsch)*

### Teaching scales through steps

I teach scales using a four-step process. (1) The student slowly recites (in tempo at quarter note = 54-60) the scale pitches ascending and descending without hesitation. They recite this three times without error to form positive memory connections. (2) They recite the scale while fingering the notes on the instrument three times to connect physical and mental action into long-term memory. This establishes a kinesthetic response for the scale. (3) They play the scale while retaining the "feeling" in the hands and internally reciting scale tones names. They do this at quarter = 54-60. This establishes positive memory connections with mental, physical, and auditory functions. (4) Finally, we place the notated scale on the music stand for the student to read while he repeats the physical and mental processes at quarter = 54-60.

This four-step process assures error-free performance of scales because they have been programmed into the student's long-term memory; the programming includes the mind, ear, and hands. This process goes beyond the surface knowledge frequently achieved through rote memorization only.

*(Edward S. Lisk)*

## TEACHING LISTENING, INTONATION, AND TUNING

### Developing listening through steps

After I get the kids thinking with a unison warm-up, we use chord progressions from the Fussell book, pages four through seven. They play through a progression such

as B flat, E flat, F7, and B flat. Then we play the first chord again, put down the instruments and sing the next three chords. At first they are very intimidated, but I say, "Let's sing this together. If some notes are not right, we'll go back and play it before we sing it again." This helps them feel more secure. I do this so they will begin to listen chordally, not just as they did in the unison material. We will do this after our unison warm ups.

*(Ross Kellan)*

### A step-by-step process for diagnosing intonation

1. Decide if there are instrument or mouthpiece problems related to intonation, other than what was expected.
2. Consider the mechanics of tuning. Use a set pitch to rely upon. Select tuning forks, tuner, tuned piano, vibraphone, tuning bars, individual student, or whatever will work.
3. Tune the individuals.
4. Tune the section to find common notes that they could agree upon.
5. Tune a melodic line, with clarinet, flute, cornet in various combinations, and all instruments with that line.
6. Tune chords, which is the most complex and difficult part. This includes how certain tones must be favored. To define a third, for example, one way is to isolate all the thirds so they can begin to hear what needs to be done with a third.

We used the whole idea, a series of steps, or an approach, when we had a serious intonation problem. I would simply stop and go from step one, to step two, etc. I use this approach continually, as a system, whenever the need arises.

*(Barbara Buehlman)*

First the students sing or hum the desired pitch (taken from a bass instrument) and then they play the desired pitch on their instrument. If students discover the need to adjust the pitch up or down to match their sung pitch, they do so.

*(Hal D. Cooper)*

The first thing we do in a rehearsal, before we play the B-flat scale, is to take a B flat from the tuba, instead of the clarinet as many do. Though some say the tuba is too low to hear well, I think we can hear it. Then, everyone sings B flat with a "zeee" sound. On that syllable, the pitch resonates, rings, and stays in students' heads well. Then we sing an "uuuu" (as in glue) sound, and finally play the pitch. Through this sequence, students can get the sound ringing inside their heads, especially on the "zeee" syllable. Then we play the B-flat scale followed by a B-flat chord tuning exercise.

*(Michael Golemo)*

The procedure I use is to sound the A and they try to match it as they play. I don't have them play into the visual tuners to tell if they are sharp or flat, because they are not learning anything then; their eyes may learn something, but their ears won't!

Students must listen and adjust. Until they learn to do that, they will not be in tune and cannot play in tune. Quite often students will begin their note immediately without really listening to the correct pitch. Because students do not absorb the reference note, they start thinking that their note is right and the tuner is wrong. I have students listen first, then play their note. We alternate listening and playing, and they must tell me whether they are high or low. Many of them are reluctant to say, so I say, "You have only two choices, try one of them."

*(Judith A. Niles)*

## TEACHING INSTRUMENTAL TECHNIQUES

### Steps for relaxation

To overcome muscular restrictions that students have in their hands, I have them drop the right hand and let it hang, dangling in a very relaxed fashion at the right side. Instead of putting the right hand on the clarinet immediately, I have them hold it up in front of them. They can see and feel that the hand is still relaxed, the wrist is bent and the fingers are close to an ideal position. The clarinet student now is holding his hand in front, only it is a little higher. When the teacher or student looks at the right hand, they see an almost perfect hand position. Next, the student puts the right hand on the clarinet and with some minor adjustments the right hand is relaxed and in near-perfect position.

The steps then are: (1) right hand at the side; (2) relax the hand through dangling; (3) bring the right hand up to the instrument; (4) observe its position; and (5) move the right hand to the instrument and make minor adjustments.

*(James D. Ployhar)*

## TEACHING RHYTHM

### Preparing for rehearsal in steps

I carefully look at a composition before rehearsing the piece. After this, I might plan a sequence of experiences to make the characteristic rhythms familiar. I select the rhythms that need a closer look and label them: (a) the simple rhythms that can lead to the more complicated ones; (b) the reverse, breaking down a complicated rhythm into simpler rhythms that might lead to learning the complicated rhythm; and (c) after working with the simple skeleton of the complicated rhythm, I use ties, etc., to build up to the complicated rhythms found in the score.

*(Richard Fischer)*

### Steps in teaching subdivision

When one wants to develop subdivisions, the experience must be physical before it can become mental. One can call the internalization mental: they are still playing physically, but now coordinated with some conceptual development with their brains become engaged.

*(Thomas H. Cook)*

## WHEN CONTENT AND SKILLS ARE PLACED IN THE CURRICULUM

### Organizing skills in the curriculum

Scale work is the basis for ear training and ear training is a refinement of the scale work. The next step, the ear training, is the basis for work with sight reading. For example, brass players can anticipate (audiate) the notated sound of certain intervals because they probably have played those intervals in scale drills.

*(Patricia Brumbaugh)*

### Planning the curriculum, with levels in mind

Music education, historically, has been an interminable process and there have been very few guidelines. Sometimes a teacher expects kids to finish a book now and then, or some students never finish a book. In our school we thought, "What the heck? Why should a kid guide or choose his own development; why can't we choose it? The math teachers do."

So we developed a curriculum and related it to the Rubank series. In the Rubank series or its equivalent a seventh grader should be able to complete the first book in the series by the end of the seventh grade. With the Rubank series this was very simple to set levels in the curriculum. Seventh grade might be Elementary or Intermediate Rubank depending upon previous experience; eighth grade likely was Intermediate or Advanced I; and ninth grade was Advanced Rubank II. Well, what happened then was eighth graders were finishing Advanced II—they just worked their buns off.

This plan worked very well, at least for the teachers who used the plan. As a result, when students got to the tenth grade they had the basic technique of scales, arpeggios, rhythms, etc. From there, our teachers decided that they couldn't specify the levels in the same way because there are so many individual differences. Therefore, we felt it was a good time to develop solo skills. The nurturing process began to take an effect through using a high level of interest in the solo literature. For the tenth, eleventh, and twelfth grades we developed selected lists of solo materials, perhaps six solos for each instrument per level.

*(Kenneth M. Larsen)*

### Sequencing their experiences

When I do the echoing of rhythms and melodic patterns, I perform some patterns in six-eight time. I do this especially when I am still working with the kids in four-four time and I know that two or three pages down the way six-eight time is coming up. I'll start introducing six-eight time in their rhythmic or melodic patterns so that the students are prepared for it when six-eight occurs in the book.

*(Gordon Nelson)*

### Determining priorities

We are quite sticky about rhythmic accuracy. Without rhythmic accuracy there is neither any hope for intonation, nor too much hope for balance. So the first demand is, "Let's get that note in the right place," and the second is, "Let's play the right pitch." After this, we start teaching intonation, tone quality, balance, and blend. Eventually we get to whatever shapes we want to create with the phrases. But the rhythmic accuracy at the beginning stages of our preparation is the number one priority.

*(Bryce Taylor)*

### Means and results; ideas in planning

The first thing to teach, I think, is the means: teachers not only tell them *what* we want them to do, but *how* to do it. We say, "Clarinets, I'd like to hear you play that upper register better in tune, therefore play with a little bit broader air stream and bring that pitch down." This shows a stress upon means that can cause a result.

Now, if I were to talk to professionals about what to do with the air stream, they would be insulted. Therefore, I can say to them "I would like to have a darker sound in the upper register." Now I am indicating the results and the means are left to the player. Therefore, I believe we start talking about the means, constantly talking about the means so that the results are a product of the means; we work on means to provide for results.

Now eventually, if I'm smart and I develop my program the way it's theoretically supposed to be done and my students advance, by the end of high school I should be able to talk to students about results. If the students have developed in my program, they should have skills enough to apply the necessary techniques to achieve the results that I'm asking for; they should already have the skills and necessary techniques.

*(Charles Olson)*

# *Planning Instruction*

I firmly believe in the need for physical stamina. I lift weights and ride an exercise bike. The kids deserve good instruction when they walk in. You must be ready to grab them and to ride that horse right to the end. Then, when you put him away he feels good about the run he just had.

That's the way I feel about a band. The students. . .if you ask them, they would say, "Yeah, that rehearsal took about three minutes." They have an active, physical, vigorous rehearsal when they walk into my class. There also are quiet times, there are dead times, and there are times for reflection. There are times when everybody sits with their hands in their laps while one student plays his line.

For the most part, there's action. Students walk into the room and are not bored. I believe firmly in it. I've seen other guys, on the other hand, who are exactly the opposite. They are very sedate, but they're not very successful.

*(William Long)*

### Setting a standard

In the middle of things I might say, "You kids sound like a bunch of junior high kids!" It's so condemning to them, even though they are in junior high. However, for some reason it works so beautifully. All of a sudden on the next note, even if I don't tell them what to do, they will sound like they are twenty-four years old. It's amazing!

*(William Long)*

### Beliefs about discipline

I believe in firm discipline. I believe in the student being on time, I believe in the kid not being tardy, I believe in the kid sitting properly, and I believe in the kid not yapping his mouth off when I'm talking. I am certainly not a task master nor am I into the screaming, ranting, and raving of some teachers. However, I definitely do believe in discipline.

In many bands, I see that discipline is a thing of the past. I don't mean the control of the kids because that puts the wrong stamp on it. Classroom order, the control of classroom management, in many schools and many communities is a thing of the past. There's a lot of Dr. Feelgoods out there. There really are; it is not fair to music and it is not fair to the students. Discipline can help involve students in what they are doing because they can hear what you say. They comprehend what you're saying because it's quiet in the classroom.

*(William Long)*

### Developing attention as they enter the room

When students are arriving for the sixth-grade band classes, they could waste valuable instructional time. They can take time organizing their instrument, case, reed, valve oil, music, folder, chair and stand. They also can delay instruction by their conversations, interactions, and distractions.

As the students enter the room and get ready for the lesson, Wisconsin State Radio is on. The students know I will ask them questions about the music. (You could use taped music also.) Most days the questions are spoken not written. Though there are some days when I ask no questions, I use this technique nearly every day throughout the year. By the end of the year, students feel pleased with their skill. They can accurately identify many features of the music from the recording or radio.

In the beginning they would look, "I don't know." They were listening but they weren't listening. Then I started to do that a little bit more and a little bit more. Pretty soon it became more intense. Then I'd say to them, "Did you hear only a couple instruments? Was this a symphony? Was this a big orchestra or was this a small group? Was this a solo or was this a duet?" Then I started to give them extra honor points if they got it right.

I got my little two cents worth in by having them hear something other than just what they listen on to the radio. I would also get some other things to listen to, for example, the *Nutcracker Suite*. Some of the kids started to get really turned on. They started to hear woodwind quintets and quartets, and they started to like that.

Here are some of the many musical features they can identify: is the music in duple or triple meter? is it band, choir, orchestra, woodwind quintet, or brass ensemble? which instrument is playing the melody? which is playing the accompaniment? does the section end with a steady tempo, a ritard, or accelerando? is the style staccato or legato? where did the performer make a phrase or breathing breaks in the melody? in what way did the dynamic levels change? was the form AB or ABA?

*(Gordon Nelson)*

### Involving the class

I watched a teacher several days ago who was teaching ear training to our students. She had them write some rhythms and she picked four students and said, "Play your rhythm at this tempo," and she would clap quietly. She asked the kids, "Who would identify that rhythm for us."

Then she said, "Write two measures in six-eight time." After they finished she said, "Okay Jerry, I want you to play your rhythms on your clarinet. While Jerry played, everybody analyzed and listened to what they heard." Then she said, "Now that you have listened to Jerry, tell me and write on the board what he has written on his paper." After that was done, she said, "We are going to go back into conducting. Everybody conduct Jerry's two measures please." She explained, "We do the beat pattern this way because this is a six-eight beat pattern here. We want you to know where beat one is."

*(Bryce Taylor)*

### Listening signals the beginning of rehearsal

I never start a rehearsal by talking. It has always frustrated me to stand up in front of the band and wave my arms, nail kids for playing, or yell that they should be quiet. I would rather begin quickly and immediately. Therefore, the band and I have an agreement that when we are to start, I give a down beat and they play B flat. Most students begin playing B-flat immediately. For those who do not, they are apt to hurry to get ready, since everyone else has already started.

*(Patricia Brumbaugh)*

# CHAPTER FOUR

# DRILL AND REPETITION

Teachers usually use drill and repetition to develop the students' skills or facility, admittedly important gains; but students can actually gain much more from drill and repetition. Repetition can help students finger a difficult passage correctly or match the tone of a model. Students need repetition to learn to blend with the section, to phrase musically, or to read notation accurately. To improve upon any of these skills, the student must practice the actions repeatedly.

Repetition also has value on another level: it enables students to develop ideas and judgment. Improving the tone, for example, requires drill for a student to develop control of a steady air stream. This fosters skill learning, but it also can advance conceptual learning if the student focuses upon the tone quality—not just the air stream. With each new try for an improved tone, students have the opportunity to make observations according to their idea of tone. They can notice the difference between a poorer and a better sound, which may be partly the result of a steady or unsteady air stream, or notice the effects of an overly-tense embouchure or a proper embouchure. Students may compare their current sound to their sound of last week, or they may notice improvement when they feel the improved muscle tone gained through practice. Repetition also enables them to imagine or to clearly recall the desired sound idea. It is necessary to increase facility through repetition, but instrumental music teachers also value conceptual learning. Both facility and concepts can be improved through drill and repetition.

## PURPOSE

### Drill

Drill is guided practice in the rehearsal.

*(George R. Bedell)*

### Drilling in warm ups

Warm up is not just a warm up; it is a place to learn. We maintain, develop, or extend an individual's and the group's ability and skill.

*(Robert E. Foster)*

### Drill and persistence

I'm sure that lots of things happen just through persistence and repetition. I'm constantly amazed at and enjoy students: When they see there is some worth in all this, they will put up with a variety of pleasant and unpleasant settings to see the light at the end of the tunnel—the value of a task when mastered. This is especially true when they have experienced a good final product once or twice. Many things that teachers do may not necessarily be positive. Students accept them, though, when they become accustomed to them and it has led to some results.

*(Gerald Olson)*

### Teaching them how to practice

So often during rehearsal, I realize that I'm teaching students how to practice. I say, "Flutes we're going to play measure forty-three over, and over, and over." We try it the first time and I'll say, "You are missing the B flat. Okay, here it is again. Now you got all the notes right, but the third staccato is longer than the other two." They may play the passage five times before they get it correct, and then they play it correctly on the sixth time.

Usually teachers stop there and go to the next section. Then they say to the next student, "Now let's try you." If one examines this we can see that what the teacher did is have them play the passage five times wrong and one time correctly. That is a pretty poor batting average. Instead, I try this: after they play the passage correctly, I do it again, and again, and again until they have mastered both the technique and the retention of the sound. This should help them remember what they did.

Furthermore, this shows a way to practice with persistence. I'm saying also, "When you are at home practicing alone, that's the technique you should use. Don't be satisfied because you played it five times wrong and finally got it right. Keep practicing until you play it at least five times right."

My ultimate intention is to teach them how to practice at home. Sometimes I mention, "You know what I've done is teach you how to practice."

*(Thomas Stone)*

I use slow motion in rehearsal to reduce bad habits. Too much, too fast means they miss things. Slow motion allows them time to process what and how to do things. Then they have time to realize what they can sound like. The result is that they can sense progress. Technical exercises and etudes affect this; the tunes don't do this as much.

*(Richard Fischer)*

Rehearsing requires repetition. Drill slowly, but accurately and rhythmically. Remember not to over-rehearse and remember that pace changes keep their interest.

*(James Croft)*

Breaking an old habit is difficult. Beginning the new habit, takes easily six or more new tries.

*(L. Keating Johnson)*

Don't feel bad if it takes twelve or fifteen tries to get it right.

*(Carl A. Bly)*

## TEACHING TO VARIOUS AND SPECIFIC OBJECTIVES

### Learning a difficult passage

We'll take a technically difficult passage and change the rhythm. If it is simply a line of sixteenth notes, we'll slow it down and play it as a dotted eighth and two sixteenths; Then we might change the rhythm again and play it as two sixteenths and a dotted eighth. By changing the rhythms, they have to rethink the way they do things. When I do that, I isolate one note, the quick note to the longer note. When students do this, they move their fingers on the short note as if they were playing the whole line faster. One other result is that they are working the muscles at the right speed.

*(Gregory Bimm)*

If we are fighting dynamics or facility, I will slow the march down so much it is actually painful, at least to them. Suddenly the dynamics will start appearing, especially if I tell them this is why we are doing this. We cut the tempo as much as fifty percent. Slow motion playing makes the technique so much easier. They can think about other things, such as dynamics or articulation.

*(Terry A. Oxley)*

I teach them to isolate tasks in home practice. I ask them to drop out slurs, ties, pitches, and articulations, for example, to isolate rhythm and duration issues. Then they add these elements back one at a time.

*(Richard Floyd)*

With anything technically difficult, I start from the end and work toward the front of the passage. First the last three beats, the last five beats, then the last seven beats, etc., until we have played the entire passage.

*(Terry A. Oxley)*

I use the metronome with subdivision, either two or four, or three or six to a pulse. I do this one hundred percent of the time when drilling short segments of a composition.

*(Robert Floyd)*

I tell them, "I guarantee this will work." First, they play the passage evenly with no rhythmic pattern. They play the succession of tones close to a steady pulse. In many situations I think it's a rhythm problem more than anything else that they have been meeting. They say, "I can't play this because I just can't get my fingering technique with this rhythm." So maybe it's a combination of the two, technique and rhythm.

Then I tell them, "Do it twelve times; go through those two measures twelve times evenly." I don't mention anything about the volume level they should play. Then I'll say, "Now, play the tones, no matter what the rhythm is, as if the rhythm was a quarter note and eighth note in six-eight time. Do that twelve times." Next, they play the rhythm as an eighth followed by a quarter in six-eight. I say, "Do that twelve times." After they finish, I say, "Go back to the original rhythm and it'll come out real easy." When they go back to the regular rhythm, no matter what it is, they are successful. I think if it's a problem in fingering that it also affects the rhythm. Doing these opposite rhythms gets rid of that fingering and technique problem. When they go back to the notated rhythm, they have mastered the technique and they can concentrate more on the rhythm.

*(Gordon Nelson)*

### Stressing a difficult rhythm during warm ups

If there is a difficult rhythm, I will recite the rhythm to them and have them play it on the scale as part of the warm up. Then I ask them to tell me what the rhythm would look like in notation.

*(Mallory B. Thompson)*

### The articulation and breathing process

I have them repeat four "ta" attacks and four "da" attacks on concert F. I will say, "Repeat after me—ta, ta, ta, ta." I also move my hand to simulate the movement of my tongue. They are familiar with this since I use this with drawings on the board that show the tongue and mouth.

*(Jack Brookshire)*

I may have players either sing or articulate on an airstream; This helps unify the articulation.

*(Gary Hill)*

## Teaching reading through a variety of skills

We used *101 Rhythm Patterns* and *101 Rest Patterns*, particularly in grades seven, eight, nine, and sometimes in high school. They had three years to do this. We had them count, clap, and play rhythms. For motivation or reinforcement, they earned so many points each week. They also would analyze the rhythms and write, for example, 1-e-and-a-2—3-and-4. They counted the pulse always, even if there were no sounds on each subdivision.

We alternated playing one example and clapping the next. We do this to cover more material and to be certain they could do both skills. We did this first from an intellectual-analytical approach. I do not use a "sound before sign" sequence as much, but it works well for some teachers. I also believe one should do all the different skills used in reading so their understanding is more complete.

*(Richard Alnes)*

With students who have counting trouble, I used *101 Rhythmic Rest Patterns* in lessons. For example, we counted the even numbered exercises, and clapped and tapped the odd numbered patterns. They would count the rhythm with one—two and—three e and a—four. Then we would do the opposite the next time we played the exercise.

Before I bought an electric metronome, I taped the metronome's sound so it was running steadily on my tape recorder. It could run for a long time, longer than I ever needed in band. The recording kept me from having to clap as a reminder that they should not change the tempo.

We often would count or clap the entire page with a measure of rest between each line. If they did this correctly, we would continue. Then, they would pick up their instruments and they played the next one. If they didn't play it right, they would stop. We looked at that measure, then we counted and clapped it.

In lessons we were far ahead of where we were in band. Therefore, in band, I was picking up the loose ends during the two or three minutes a day we spent doing this. The usual routines or choices were: (1) they count it and finger along; (2) they count it and then they play it; (3) they play it and count in their head; and, (4) sometimes, we played and sang with articulation syllables like du-du-du-du. We went slowly and a step at a time. That usually was successful, if we reserved the time needed for this.

*(Terry A. Oxley)*

Students need to practice rests. This is especially true if somebody is working on a solo. Often they just work on the parts they play and ignore the piano part. When they play the solo with a piano and are on stage they get all "goofed up," because they did not practice say, the three-measure rest. If they don't practice counting each set of rests, they're dead when they put it together with an accompanist.

*(Thomas Stone)*

## Remembering key signatures

I may ask a student at anytime, "What is the order of flats?" Then, I may ask another student the same or a different question.

*(James D. Ployhar)*

## Isolating tone

To develop the quality of tone, I may have them play the phrase on one note. This isolated only one thing upon which to work. They can increase coordination and become sensitive to attacks, releases, and breathing. They can respond to the proper conducting of upbeat and downbeat, which gives them an example to mirror for the inhalation-exhalation process. We are building a stimulus-response pattern. Then we apply the new response to the musical playing of a piece, knowing that they will have a problem if I conduct with hesitation.

*(Donald Casey)*

## Maintaining a good sound

We drill at sustaining a sound as long as they can, while maintaining the tone color. Students need this, especially young players who run out of air more than experienced players. If they run out, the features of a good sustained sound diminish. This shows up particularly when playing a piece. The musical line loses direction because they run out of air or let their air speed slow down.

*(anonymous)*

## Using the metronome to build facility

We do drill, but we are so limited in time. I would prefer to drill on a more regular basis; I am sure that it would help them get better. I set the metronome at a slower tempo for technical exercises and move up to the desired tempo. I also do this on string trios, for example, when the parts are not together because the kids are not together. It definitely works in developing technical skills. I go from a slower tempo to a faster tempo in large increments. An increment might be ten beats per minute. As time goes on, the increments can be even larger. They can work independently with this and I can set levels of skill or accomplishment.

Using metronome increments helps set goals for weekly home practice and goals from week to week. I can set these levels and know at which level a student is performing. The size of the increment also is dependent on the student and how much they want to practice. If I didn't know the student, I would increase the increment by ten, which would be enough for one week. If they cannot increase the tempo, the use of a metronome influences them to keep things steady, even if they are not increasing tempo in increments.

*(Judith A. Niles)*

I make an incremental change in the metronome during rehearsals. I will decide the tempo for a piece one day, and on later days I will increase the tempo. If the group is out of control, the tempo will be slower. The approach works with a larger group, but I developed this for individual practice. When the entire band worked on technical things, I had to bear in mind which instruments could or could not do certain things as easily as another. Therefore, the metronome speeds needed to be chosen so they were challenging, yet feasible and fair.

*(Donald DeRoche)*

### Developing facility with rhythms or articulation

If they aren't getting through this sixteenth note pattern, I will make them play the whole thing as a repeated eighth and two sixteenth notes. This seems to work because they have time to think about what's coming next, since they are waiting for the next note a little longer.

I also could have them play the sixteenths as triplets instead of dotted-eighth sixteenths, or play them as double-dotted eighths and thirty-seconds. Manipulating the rhythm increases their concentration and attention; more so, I think it reinforces the finger pattern without the monotony involved in practicing technique. If one doesn't change something, the effort brings diminishing returns the longer one practices something.

Changing the articulation helps too, especially if they have extremely sloppy fingerings over a long slurred passage of sixteenth notes. Change the articulation and make them articulate each note. Then, suddenly their fingers are working the same rhythm as their tongue. As a result, there is a reinforcement for getting those fingers down at the right time.

*(Terry A. Oxley)*

### Drilling scales and theory

I warm up with scales in my jazz band. For example, we play a major scale up to the ninth. We just don't play it from root to eight. We go one, two, three, four, five, six, seven, eight, nine, and back down again. Sometimes we also go up to thirteen. Then, immediately we arpeggiate the related major ninth chord. In C, the tonic ninth chord would be c–e–g–b–d.

The reason I put the two together, scales and chords, is to show the relationship between the two. I also do that because in public school you're going to teach theory through the instrument, not through the keyboard. Most people don't own pianos, don't study piano and never will. I tell them, "See how easy it is to understand theory."

I do the triad first, then add the seventh and the ninth later. This can be done in concert band and it works very, very well. Instead of just playing the scales from tonic to tonic, they're playing it up to the ninth and discovering theory by counting the numbers of the notes. Then, when they transfer the notes over to the chord, the kids now understand what a third of a chord is and where it came from.

*(Dominic Spera)*

### Building technical facility

I build technical proficiency through scale performance using the Circle of Fourths (Jazz Circle). I often select scales, articulations, and rhythm patterns that connect directly to the literature or solos students are performing. The demands in the music could be such as meters, mixed meters, styles, articulations, dynamics, or tempi. I am very concerned about "connecting" or "linking" scales with literature to create a meaningful learning experience for student players. By using and performing *all scales* around the Circle of Fourths as one exercise, students acquire a higher level of technical mastery.

My results have been far superior to the results of other approaches and I am not limited to literature written in only a few flat keys. My students develop technical mastery, that is a spontaneous reaction to keys, through the unlimited variations possible when using the Circle of Fourths. An example would be to have students ascend the first scale such as C concert and descend on the next scale which is F concert, continuing on with B flat and throughout the entire Circle of Fourths. This approach is not based upon written or notated scales, it is an expansion of memorized scales.

*(Edward S. Lisk)*

### Developing comprehensive scale skill and understanding

I expand my students' scale knowledge and understanding through digital patterns, which are similar to jazz improvisation approaches. The first priority is to create an awareness of different scale degrees by playing 1-2-1-2-1 (do-re-do-re-do) in each key and then proceeding to 1-2-3-2-1 (do-re-mi-re-do). We proceed further, adding more scale degrees in the exercises. The last note (do) is always sustained before proceeding to the next note in the circle that establishes a new key. The digital patterns are expanded and increased in difficulty, but for the introductory level, we use quarter notes.

Through this logical sequence, all keys and all scale tones are related to one another. Interval and arpeggio exercises take on a new meaning and contribute to the students' performance skills. These exercises are not notated or read from a method book. My priority is placed upon the students' mental processing of the scale tones and structure, instead of a repetitive practicing of scales in isolation, and without understanding their structure and relationship to literature. I place emphasis upon the mental, physical, and auditory performance instead of upon a number of unrelated written and technical exercises.

*(Edward S. Lisk)*

### Isolate and drill silently

It is quicker to isolate and correct a problem, than to continue talking about it. I have them sing on a neutral syllable and finger furiously!

If they are not singing, one can hear the pads popping, which also tells if they are together. When students are not blowing, they often are unaware that their fingers are not together. If you have them quit producing sound, especially the woodwinds, and finger only, the band can tell whether they are together if they are quiet. When this is isolated, they also can tell if they are not fingering hard enough, or if there is a lack of energy directed into making the muscles do what they have to do.

This is a finger, motor skill, and dexterity problem, not a sound production problem. Getting the sound out of the passage for a moment can isolate and solve the dexterity problem. When the student puts the technical aspect back with the sound production, things sound a lot better. One cannot get control of muscles by moving them in an easy indecisive manner, one must finger hard because it affects control. Students need to use crisp or precise physical actions on all the notes. For all instruments except the trombone, the key or the valve has to be all the way up or all the way down. That instant between, when it is neither up nor down, must be so microscopic that no one can tell that it occurred.

We must teach that lazy fingers don't work. The slower the music is, the more consciously one has to finger quickly. This is the opposite of what kids do. One must wait longer before you move to the new fingering; one must wait until the last instant before moving the keys and the valves.

All bands at all levels have a misconception. They think they should, "Play slow music with slow fingers and fast music with fast fingers." Not so! They should finger fast always and wait until the last minute to do that. We often do drill without playing a note, because we need to master fingering. Fingering is what is not together.

*(Robert E. Foster)*

### Improving dynamic control with young students

We must develop dynamic control and range, and dynamic awareness in young players. Knowing the dynamic symbols is only part of the process of performing music with proper dynamics, so I include exercises in dynamics in every rehearsal. Often we do these in the warm-up segment of the rehearsal.

I use exercises that develop proper dynamic control and to extend dynamic ranges toward both the piano and forte end of the continuum. For example, I ask the band to play an arpeggio in whole notes from low to high pitches, and from high to low pitches. We begin at the piano level, the next note mezzoforte, the next forte, and the last note fortissimo. As we do this we try not to lose our intonation and tone quality. I also ask them to begin with fortissimo, and as we go through the arpeggio, they decrease volume and end at the piano level.

I will ask the band to play a chord and make a crescendo and decrescendo as we hold the chord for eight counts. To make the change as gradual as possible, I will ask the students to count and to increase or decrease the volume level every two beats. Thus, we start piano, two beats later we move up to mezzoforte, two beats later to forte and then up to fortissimo. We reverse the process on the decrescendo. I also ask them to increase the level gradually using each two beats as a check point.

These exercises strengthen the embouchure and air support needed to perform dynamics properly. While I do this, I also am reviewing and using the conductor's baton and hand signals that show the various dynamic levels. When we devote a few minutes each day to dynamics, the students acquire more skills for proper dynamic performance of the music.

*(Roman Palmer)*

# CHAPTER FIVE

# EVALUATION

School administrators and teachers use evaluation procedures to serve different functions. One function of evaluation is to use test scores to compare one school, class, or grade to another. Another is to evaluate students' work and progress, and then make progress reports to parents. The third function is to improve learning and instruction.

Teachers of instrumental music show interest in evaluation for these reasons; but they are especially interested in the third function, which is to evaluate learning and instruction. They want to know if the ensemble is learning and progressing, if the individual students are learning, and if their own teaching is successful.

Ideas in this chapter show that music teachers use both formal evaluation techniques, which tend to be more objective, and informal evaluation techniques, which are more subjective, to evaluate instruction and learning. Formal evaluations often have a set of criterion that is known by the students and developed prior to testing itself. The teacher may develop the evaluation criteria and procedures himself, the criteria might be stipulated in the curriculum, or it could be published.

Examples of formal evaluation techniques are to ask students to play certain scales at certain tempi, to perform or memorize specific etudes for each lesson, to take the Watkins-Farnum test for chair placement, and to show their intonation skills, which the teacher can measure objectively. Often the students' grades depend upon how many scales a student can play, how many errors a student makes, and at what speeds he must play technical etudes. The teacher also can develop "Learning Activity Packets" or a "Contract" and establish standards for the number of independent projects that students need to earn a certain grade.

Informal or subjective evaluations in music education are common. Most often teachers hear individuals and sections play, and grade them on their performance. This helps the teacher know if they performed the notes, phrases, and rhythms correctly, or if they have practiced. Informal evaluations occur frequently during rehearsals and lessons. For example, a teacher can ask students to play with and without a certain style of articulation.

Through this, the teacher can assess their understanding of this skill, and if they can perform it correctly. Sometimes teachers evaluate whether the students are performing musically or not, understanding notation, and retaining or applying the skill or information to the music correctly.

There may be a slight increase in the number of objective and standardized measures that help teachers assess performance skills and musical knowledge. However, the number of commercially available tests for instrumental music education is still very low. With the shortage of testing instruments and with limited experience or background in evaluation techniques appropriate for instrumental music, many teachers still rely more upon informal than formal techniques of evaluation. Even if a specific formal and objective measure were commonly used and available, the teacher's subjective judgment is apt to remain a common evaluation technique.

The teacher's informal and subjective evaluations can determine students' progress with some accuracy, but the judgments are more credible if the teacher applies two basic principles of good testing when doing informal evaluations: the informal test also must have validity and the test must be reliable. Some teachers do this intuitively and as well as a matter of conscious decision. These terms mean that the teacher must know what he expects musically or technically, must use a way of evaluating that properly evaluates these objectives, and the process and test must be consistent.

A teacher must try to use evaluation techniques that are consistent even if he uses subjective judgments. Some do this by evaluating the recorded performance of each student according to the same criteria. Some teachers also organize challenges and auditions in a way to preserve the students' anonymity, and to lessen prejudgments and negative biases. Though checking attendance is still common, it reflects non-musical objectives. Most teachers are moving away from using that as the major factor in grading music students. Keeping a record of attendance documents who is in the room, it does not measure musical learning, thinking, achievement, or comprehension.

It is encouraging to see teachers speak about the evaluation of skills and musical knowledge, and to read the descriptions of their evaluation ideas. Their ideas are often pertinent responses to directives from the administration of schools or their respective state guidelines. If our profession is to respond to these situations, we must develop ways to evaluate learning in the arts that goes beyond what can be assessed through paper and pencil tests. Much progress must be made before instrumental music teachers commonly evaluate areas such as aural skills, movement, listening, improvisation, interpretation, literacy, and analysis as well as solo, ensemble, and performance skills. These enable students to be expressive, perform, and show musical understanding.

## EXAMPLES OF EVALUATION PROCEDURES AND TECHNIQUES

### Evaluation through recordings and other feedback

Once a month a student must record an assignment and bring it back to the teacher. To guide the student, every teacher's assignments should include metronomic markings. Recording assures the teacher that the student heard himself.

*(Bryce Taylor)*

In marching band, the video tape is even on the field because it allows students to see things immediately. They often come in after rehearsal and watch it for hours and correct their own performance. We can use video tape also with young kids for posture or position. The older students can tape contest performances and graduate conducting recitals. With more time, one could tape a different section each day for the kids to see.

*(Robert E. Foster)*

### A merit, demerit system

When I taught pre-college, I had a merit/demerit system. Every student started each grading period with a C and they could either go up or down depending on what they did or did not do. For example, I expected students to practice, let's say, a half hour a day. If they practiced more than a half hour a day, they got so many points. If they didn't practice at all, they lost some points. If they came late to rehearsals they would get a demerit and if they attended outside performances or wrote papers on musical topics, they got extra credit merits. I do not know whether this would be as effective now as it was then; some attitudes and expectations of students have changed.

*(Francis Marciniak)*

### Evaluating skills randomly

I use time limit and minimum number of errors to decide who passes the scale. The limit is two errors. During testing, I do a lottery. I have three index cards with four scales: one easy, one moderately easy, one moder-

ately difficult, and one difficult. A student draws a card with four scales listed. Since they are expected to know all of the scales, we grade them on a scale chosen by a random draw and on the accuracy of the performance. Four scales correct = a, 3 = b, 2 = c, 1 = d and none = f. I do not draw a second card.

*(John W. LaCava)*

When we pass a student on an exercise, the line or exercise is chosen at random. I use this more with the entire band, but not too frequently. This must be done with fairness and consistency. We test for technique, dynamics, range, articulation, and fingering pattern—not just the right notes. I try to vary what is tested each time; but they know that it will be one of six or so basic skills.

*(R. G. Conlee)*

### Practice charts

I expect students to turn in a practice chart every Tuesday and I remind them on Monday. If their chart is a day late, I mark students down one letter grade, two days late they are down two grades, etc. I do this to build responsibility.

Students have three options: they can practice seven days a week for thirty minutes, six days a week for thirty-five, five days for forty; but, students must practice no fewer than five days. If they practice fewer than five days, students go down a letter grade for each missing day. How much students practice each day also influences the grade. They get an A for two hundred and ten minutes a week. If they practice less, their grade drops one letter for each twenty-minute drop. I like to give students options, because teachers must make exceptions or they could paint themselves into corners.

*(John W. LaCava)*

### Evaluating achievement

I try to hear every student in front of the class each week for a graded performance. They become accustomed to playing in front of people. They feel the pressure to produce in front of their peers, who are the toughest audience. We have a parent meeting in the fall where we discuss evaluation in a positive way. Parents sign the charts and students usually are very honest.

*(John W. LaCava)*

I grade on achievement, not attendance. I post grades on the door right after each lesson. This keeps me in touch. I try to make my judgments immediately so they know the truth and learn they didn't fool me (if they tried to.)

*(Anthony J. Maiello)*

One can evaluate students not only as individuals, but as sub-parts of the ensemble. My wife gives "duet assignments," using exercises, etudes, or excerpts that must be rehearsed, then recorded by two ensemble members and submitted for an evaluation and grade (both students receive the same grade based on the success of the duet). The students do the preparation on their own, and then graded as a team. This technique is very successful.

*(Richard Floyd)*

We have members of a group play individually. They have playing tests for younger groups: band music in band and lesson music in lessons. I announce the dates and the material, so they know what is to be done and when it will be graded.

*(R. G. Conlee)*

I might say, "John, would you play line six in a connected style." After he finishes, the group echoes what John did. This allows me to hear each person during instruction.

*(Thomas Herrera)*

We might play an etude as a class for several lines, then hear the rest individually. This always gives students a chance to play alone.

*(Anthony J. Maiello)*

For part of the quarter grade, each student plays a page from a lesson book I choose. The performance is graded pass/fail and a student may play the page several times if necessary. The pages are due weekly and they play in my office. The time needed is less than two minutes; the time it takes to play the page. The idea is to get everyone on a planned approach to improvement—not just those students who are studying privately. This exam also shows the "bottom-end kids" that there is something to practice other than their band parts. This is certainly not a new idea, but I use it in high school and it is successful.

*(David Deitemyer)*

### Challenge systems

Students like to compete, and we have section challenges three times a year. They draw a number out of a hat, one through eight, for example. For challenges, we use scales, method books, and passages from the music. If students feel they got a raw deal, they can challenge again in three weeks. They can challenge no more than one chair a week. This keeps section stability.

Section challenges are at the end of September, the beginning of January, and the end of March. Challenges, where they can move up one chair, occur three weeks after each date. Within a month of a program, we don't challenge so we keep some stability and reduce the chances they will abuse each other. If a student loses a chair challenge, he may not challenge again for two weeks. If he wins, he can continue to challenge up the section. If a student is challenged and loses, he can challenge back immediately the next week.

*(John W. LaCava)*

I do challenge auditions every three weeks and I set the entire year's dates in advance. I do each date in one day's class. I use PVC tubing to hold a screen so an entire section is not visible. When students go behind the screen, I give them a number that identifies when they are to play.

The entire band has a large ballot with clarinetist one, clarinetist two, etc. listed on the form. Students play a scale in sixteenth notes, a four-measure sight reading, and an eight-measure etude. Every person plays the same music, therefore, they do overhear the same sight reading material. It is, however, technical enough to lessen their chances of learning it by ear in the ten minutes it takes to do the section's audition. The last person who played the scale plays first on the prepared etude. All players, including those who audition, mark their ballots with a ranked order; they can vote for themselves if they like.

The form suggests that they listen for technical accuracy, tone quality, etc. I remind students before the audition of each section, what they are to listen for. It is easier for students to count mistakes, because they can lock-on to that. As the year goes on, students talk less about errors and more about tone. I organized the printed form so it can be used by all the bands.

Students must put their name on the slip of paper that identified them as one, two, etc. This is in my pocket, and I do not officially know who played in what order. For each player, students give one number that represents their rating for the entire audition of three parts. I do my own evaluation and combine that with the students' ratings. Ninety-five percent of the time the band and I agree.

This system also makes the process more objective. For example, this reduces their beliefs that someone was rated high or low because of popularity. Furthermore, the process is very quick. I can do fifty students in a sixty-minute period, usually in one day. I do not have to listen to the tape recorder, I waste little of the group's time, etc. If an individual is not there, they usually go to the last chair. This is likely to be temporary, because three weeks later everyone can audition and they can recover their spot. Any student disappointed with the results of the audition can look forward to another chance soon. If I could do this only twice a year and for seating only, I don't believe I would do it.

There is another by-product of this approach. Since students hear everyone, they get to know each other and recognize who has improved or plays well. Even the school psychologist was very intrigued by the idea and came in to watch an audition session. She found the interpersonal dynamics especially interesting.

*(David Deitemyer)*

### Memorized exercises

When I started my kids in the sixth grade, they had to memorize an exercise every week, whether it was one measure long or a whole note. They closed their books and tried to play perfectly on an exercise that was sixteen or thirty-two measures long. Every etude in that book was memorized by every player in the band, because they were asked to. They knew that in the band rehearsal we would take time to play an etude; they would stand up individually and play that for the whole band.

There was no problem with that at all because it was something they did from the beginning. By the time they were through the ninth grade, they could deal with their nerves as easily as you and I can put a quarter in a parking meter. Furthermore, when they auditioned in college, they always did well because they could handle the pressure of performance in front of people, especially for those who know the difference—as their colleagues in the band do.

This experience also helped their attitude toward one another. They knew that they were all working and, on the other hand, they knew that they all shared the same problems. There were times that I would grade them, but sometimes I would just ask for volunteers, "Who knows the etude today?" Then the rest of the band would play the accompaniment and that person would become the soloist for that day. These were only about sixteen measures long and there was always a good accompaniment in the band parts.

*(Charles Olson)*

## Learning Activity Packets (LAPs)

I really think that the LAPs individualized program (Learning Activity Packets) has potential for bands and orchestras, even if it is more work for a teacher. I did not have one student complain about a grade after I started it.

When I started, I was afraid that by doing this everybody would get A's and, in fact, that didn't happen. Fifty percent to sixty percent of the students opted for A's. A small number, about twenty-five percent, chose to work toward B's. The remainder selected C's or pass. We also had a pass/fail option that was the same level as a C.

Before this, I graded students by using auditions, seating auditions, and a subjective grade based on their participation—however one can measure that. Students in the back of the section, those who had not played as long or who could not afford private lessons, were the ones who got the C's and the B's.

With the Learning Activity Packet system, these students had a chance because the grading system had to do with what they could accomplish. As a result, their morale just skyrocketed. The morale improved, I mean—I can't tell you how dramatically their attitude changed. In fact, students from another of the bands asked if they could do LAPs because they thought it was such a neat idea.

I started with eight completed LAPs as the requirement for an A and five was a B. Well, eventually that gravitated to fifteen being an A and eight being a B. Every quarter there was always a small group of kids who would race with each other to see who could finish all choices available for the LAPs. They might do thirty or thirty-five. As well as giving incentive to students at the lower

achievement or opportunity levels, LAPs also provided the kids at the upper end with enrichment and motivation to excel. (There is a copy of the Learning Activity Packets in Appendix III.)

*(Richard Kennell)*

## Evaluating intonation

When students play scales, I use a Korg tuner (the one with the needle gauge in five cent increments) to assess how much they are in or out of tune. A student's score is the number of "cents" they deviate from "in tune." I total the "cents" for all deviations from in and out of tune pitches for the entire scale.

I developed standards for ninth to twelfth graders and from fall to spring. Thus, the standards go up as they get older and as they progress through the year. For winter quarter, if I recall correctly, the seniors had to play eight notes within forty cents total deviation, juniors fifty cents, sophomores sixty, and freshman seventy cents. Sixty cents off means that they can play, on the average, every note five or more cents off (8 x 5 = 40 cents) and still pass. A senior might start at sixty cents in the fall, fifty the second quarter, forty the third quarter, and thirty by the year's end.

I have made up a chart used by each student; there is a spot for their name and the scale, and there are columns where I record whether they are in tune, sharp, or flat as they play an eight note scale in whole notes. I do not test them until they have filled all the columns, because this should show that they have practiced. We can look at the columns and see the progress as certain notes improve or remain a problem.

They also must have a friend to score for them as they practice; they take turns doing this. I have a set of hints typed on the bottom of the score sheet. One example is, "Look for tendencies in your tuning to find which notes are special problems." When they find these, they begin to remember and they also see the progress they have made with difficult notes.

They play this test three times a quarter with a different scale or octave each time. They borrow tuners and work on this a lot. This also means they are not just tuning to one note, but to the entire scale and later, the scale is played throughout two octaves.

There are some appealing things about it; it is an attainable standard, they can see progress, the rating is objective, and the students' awareness of "in tune" is developed. They can't quibble with the machine. I ask them to close their eyes, play the pitch, and then look. I got the original idea from Jack Williamson and I have modified it.

*(David Deitemyer)*

## Scheduling evaluation

Every kid plays five minutes for me either before or after school. They sign up on a calendar outside my door. I assign, for example, two scales and a chromatic scale with as full a range as they can play, depending upon their grade level. I specify the skill level of the chromatic scale for each grade or achievement level of my band program. They also play two assigned scales and I add additional scales every nine weeks.

*(Jack Brookshire)*

### Reporting students' progress to parents

Students get two or three grades, depending on the age level. One is for effort related to practice and the other is achievement. I set goals each week whatever the practice amount is.

Formerly, we used a very complex report card that listed ten different attributes such as attendance and practicing for quality in music. An X would show that they were making extreme progress or superior progress; no X meant average progress; and a check mark meant needs improvement. We still use that for all fifth and sixth grade students for a nine-week period. The parents and kids understand this very well.

Our school is now "on computer" and all we can give is an A through F grade for achievement. In addition, you can check one other issue such as attendance or effort. You can write in your own individual comments at that point. These limits have created a problem. They won't let us supplement it with our own grade card. They have used the new shorter grading forms for the past four or five years. I've been extremely critical of the new approach since the more complete information we formerly gave parents helped them.

*(Phillip A. Weinberg)*

## EVALUATION WHILE TEACHING

### Evaluating students

There is a side benefit to playing exams. There is the audience training effect where other students learn as they listen.

*(R. G. Conlee)*

I don't know whether it is experience, sensitivity, the ability to listen with the ear, or some other innate sense, but I can tell immediately if the kid is putting his tongue between his lips, tonguing too far back in the mouth, or tonguing the wrong place on a reed. These errors stick out like a sore thumb to me. I immediately start trying to correct this. Student teachers do not hear this; it's a weak point because they lack experience. They cannot learn this in a lecture class.

*(Lance Schultz)*

In teaching, we analyze to find out if there's a problem. If there is a problem, we have to come up with a remedy. That's what teaching is all about. We have to give them some suggestions or some thoughts. You just can't

say, "I want a sforzando there" when some students don't even know what you're talking about. You have to tell them *how* to do it, how to *exactly*, and what kind of sounds you want.

*(Richard J. Suddendorf)*

If I move their clarinet and it moves around independently from the embouchure, I know that something is incorrect.

*(Stanley Cate)*

You can get tired in three places when you play: the abdomen, the corners of the mouth, and the center of the lips (clarinets get tired teeth or see marks on the top of the mouthpiece). The last place or least desirable place to get tired is in the center of the lips. If they are playing correctly, the corners will get tired first, then the abdominal area. If the center gets tired, stop!

*(John W. LaCava)*

### Evaluating compositions and composer's skill

One decision I make as I look at a piece or a composer's work, is to look at how the composer uses the instruments, especially the saxophones. Good composers use different combinations of instruments very effectively. This ability is part of deciding if the composer is any good or not; their use of instruments, at least, shows their skill at orchestration.

*(Gary Hill)*

### Evaluating rehearsals

Listening to rehearsal tapes is for the teacher to evaluate what he heard on the tape. This can take one hour for each hour of rehearsal.

*(Frank Battisti)*

The post-rehearsal time is very important. You should take notes immediately after the rehearsal. Maybe you have taped the rehearsal and you listen to the tape. Then go into the next rehearsal and share with the group what you did before, and what you need to work on now. Sure, sometimes you can have them hear the recording and tell them what you noticed about it. I also think it's important that they have an understanding that you've taken the time after the rehearsal to think about all those items. This shows that what is going on from rehearsal to rehearsal reflects a plan. The way one rehearses also reinforces how they are preparing their parts; they learn how to practice by seeing how you rehearse.

*(Larry Rachleff)*

### Teacher's self evaluation

I evaluate myself in conducting by looking carefully at what I do. I look at what isn't working right, especially if it continues to happen. For example, I may ask myself, "Is there something wrong with my preparatory beat? Is there something wrong with my ictus? Is there something wrong with the gesture itself? Did I not change when it needed to change, in the right time frame? Did they misunderstand my instruction for when to respond?"

*(Frank B. Wickes)*

Upon conclusion of his violin lesson, a young student said, "My mother wants you to call her." The teacher said, "Why does your mother want to talk with me?" The student replied, "She wants to know if I had a good lesson." The teacher replied, "You tell your mother that I *always give* a good lesson."

*(Pamela Gearhart)*

We need to remember always the question, "How is something better?" or "What is better?" If teachers don't do that, it is very difficult to say, "You can do this better in this, by doing such and such." The level of our criticism also has to grow. The better your kids get, the more responsibility you have to set a higher level of attainment.

Let's say you do the Frescobaldi *Toccata* that you played in your first year of teaching. You take the same piece again in the second year with the same kids, the third year with the same kids, and the fourth year with the same kids. What would happen to that piece of music? Is it possible that the piece of music would not get performed better in the fourth year?

The performance can improve, but the music itself does not cause a better performance—it does not change. You must expect more out of this piece. Perhaps you allowed certain things to happen the first time around that you will not allow to happen the second, third, and fourth times around. A teacher must be raising standards whenever possible.

Finally, by the time one gets into the major symphony orchestras and you have played the Beethoven 5th one hundred and fifty times, there has to be someone up on the podium who tells you something new, exciting, and worthwhile about the way to play it. Performers learn this by the way the conductor is working with the music. This is possible, because the music is still deeper than the finest performance that's ever happened.

We need to constantly dig deeper to find where that value is. What is the infinite fathom of depth? I was talking about that with Bob Reynolds who was conducting the Mahler First. He said his problem was not to conduct the piece, but to get deep enough musically. He made it on the first, second, and fourth movements, but he said on the third movement he didn't think he had gotten there. To get deep enough into the meaning of the music is our goal. It happens in *Air for Band* and in *Ballad for Band,* or it happens in the *Symphoniette* of Dahl.

*(Charles Olson)*

### Sometimes the answer is unclear

I adjudicated a band that did a *Treasury of Scales* B-

flat scale and it was abominable, it was absolutely atrocious—it didn't even come close. Then they did the entire *Carmina Burana* flawlessly. What can I say—they could not play *Come to Jesus* in E flat! Yet, they did Carmina without an error! Everything was right, the intonation was fine, it was expressive, and I felt like saying, "I heard two bands; I heard you warm up, but when did they put the substitutes on for the *Carmina Burana*? I did not see the change of personnel, but I heard them! It was unbelievable!"

*(Charles Olson)*

Teachers have to look at themselves, myself included, to see if their level of criticism has been constantly going up. I have to rely on my imagination, my thinking, and outside performances to regenerate my evaluation processes, which I apply to my self-evaluation and my perception of my band. We must get our ears cleaned up and we must get new standards, because we must learn to do better always.

*(Charles Olson)*

The other day a director was saying that he finally felt he was making progress. I said, "You have no idea what kind of progress you've made. You are there everyday and you don't see the change. You've forgotten how poor this program was when you first came five years ago. You were talking about twenty-eight or thirty kids playing poorly, who had a poor attitude. You were rehearsing in a poor room and there were many other problems."

"Since then, you have a new band room, seventy kids in the band earned straight superiors at the festival this last year for the first time in the school's history. The kids have a really wonderful, responsive, positive attitude, and they come in and enjoy rehearsal. You have no idea of the difference now compared to then. Since I come over once a semester, I see it over a more isolated time frame and can see the difference more easily than you."

*(Donald Wilcox)*

Periodically, I listen to the pieces I taught in my first five years. There are some pretty embarrassing things. I think, "That wasn't very expressive and that wasn't very imaginative." If you really want to learn something, listen to your past performances.

*(James Croft)*

After listening to hundreds of pieces of music and preparing hundreds of pieces of music, and listening to hundreds of concerts by other bands, hearing both bands that are worse than mine and bands that are better than mine, and watching conductors who are both worse and better, I have become more aware that I am in a process of constantly adapting and changing, redoing, reevaluating, and adjusting what I'm doing. If I don't, it would become dull and boring. I'm not always sure that what I am doing is better, or if it's just different. It's not always better, sometimes I do things that are not as good as what I have done in the past. But, if I learn from that, I don't do them anymore.

Teachers do not know the effectiveness of their program until students have been in it six or eight years. We need this much time to see the implications of what we have taught and they learned. After this period, we can see what part of the change is maturation, what part is learning and, what part is planning for learning. We don't really know if we've hit the target until the bullet has arrived.

*(Charles Olson)*

## TEACHING STUDENTS TO EVALUATE AND DISCRIMINATE

### Building discrimination

I do use peers to play something in a certain way to see if he understands. Then I ask someone else to describe the playing as legato, staccato, etc. so they learn to distinguish and listen.

*(R. G. Conlee)*

Take a section where the kids know everyone so well they think, "Yeah, we know so and so's sound blindfolded." I put my trumpet section behind a screen and have them play in a random order. The rest of the band listens and I ask, "Okay, is player number one Jack or Mary?" I say, "Put down who you think it is. You've been listening to these people for two years and know them all so well, they sit right behind you."

I have done this to build the idea of awareness and super listening. It is like blind auditions to see if they can really discriminate between good quality and bad quality, or do they decide because "Jack's a nice guy, he ought to be third chair." It is interesting to see some results. Besides saying where someone should sit, they have also had to make specific judgments, such as which one of them had the better tone quality. Then I can ask, "Which of these five trombones do you think has the better sound, which one is the tone quality you want most to listen to."

*(Donald Wilcox)*

When one student plays, there is a side benefit. The benefit is an audience training effect where other students learn as they listen. Though some people may question whether we should have students play individually in front of others, these playing tests occur after the students had considerable opportunity to learn the parts. Since individuals have played a lot during a typical rehearsal, playing individually is not new to them.

*(R. G. Conlee)*

### Evaluating articulations, dynamics, and style

If there is a melodic line in the clarinet and the

musical intent is unclear, I might ask the trumpets or the rest of the ensemble to listen as the clarinets play. After the clarinets finish, I will ask the other musicians questions such as, "Did you hear any crescendos in the music? Are any notes accented? Were any notes legato?" When they answer—usually to say that they could not tell any difference—I well turn to the clarinets and say to them, "Let's do it again and show everyone the dynamics and articulation markings you have in your music."

I generally use this technique without giving any instructions as to what might be the problem. Instead I hope to lead the students to conclude that they are responsible for communicating the musical markings on their parts without instruction or coaching from me. It is a "win-win" situation. The clarinet section is learning to communicate musically with conviction and the rest of the ensemble is learning to listen and make discriminating musical judgments.

*(Richard Floyd)*

### Evaluating performance

Since students have difficulty deciding what an error is, in classes I have taught them to ask, "Were there errors? What were they? Was the performance acceptable? How many mistakes were there?" If it was not acceptable, they should ask, "What needs to be improved?" After we evaluate an individual student to define how and what to practice, we return to group work on the same exercise at the same tempo, repeating it several times. Then, we have other individuals play to see if they are practicing and progressing correctly.

*(Donald DeRoche)*

I use a "solo-class" idea, where one student plays the exercise in front of the class. Students respond to peer pressure and to peer criticism much more than to the teacher. If students are told by their classmates that they are doing something wrong, they try to do it right. I have had little resistance from students if they see this as part of the teaching process.

*(James D. Ployhar)*

### Evaluating through practice steps

I evaluate with a series of steps, which we call "Sing, Say, Finger, Play." The step approach tells me whether the student has learned, no matter how much time the kid writes down or how much practice time they've done. When they come to class, I may ask them to apply these steps to learning a new song. Those students who are just "no where," say to me, "Well, I just didn't practice."

*(Gordon Nelson)*

### Judges' feeling about contests

I get really upset when I go to festivals. I hate that whole business of rating and sometimes I find myself feeling very alone. We are not supposed to talk about the ratings when judges get together; but, sometimes we compare notes with other judges to see where we are, so we're not light years apart.

Though I might be seen sometimes as a hard-nosed guy, how are students, groups, and conductors going to know about their performance unless one rates accurately and honestly? However, one does not make friends being accurate and honest. Students and teachers both feel that if they played all the notes and the rhythms and the technique is down, they should get a high rating. But is that really enough to be rated an outstanding performance? Are they supposed to be saluted for that? Should not an outstanding performance be one with a beautiful sonority, with color and blend? They also should play well in tune, with the controlled phrase-shaping and other fine nuances that happen in excellent performances.

Since only one or two groups reach this standard, I find it difficult when all thirty bands playing that day expect to receive high ratings. In fact, ten of the groups may get the same outstanding ratings. Yet most have not even touched on the more critical aspects of quality performance.

*(Robert Levy)*

### Observations about band programs

There are band programs with basic problems. In these programs, the kids are being taught to play the festival pieces, but they are not being taught to play their instruments. What an adjudicator hears is not that they cannot play those pieces; what he hears that they cannot play their instruments. The students do not have basic background. They can't play their scales, they can't tongue and slur, can't articulate in different ways, and they can't play in different keys other than two or three—they haven't been "routined."

I am very disturbed by what's happening in our band field. I try to show this by stories of things I have observed at contests. For example, a guy had the B flat tuned perfectly with a strobe at a music festival. After he had been in the warm-up room and after the curtain had opened, he came on stage and continued to tune each person on that B flat. Then they played the *Fantasia in G Major* of Bach. The band was terribly out of tune, though he had worked that B flat intensely. His problem was a fundamental problem.

There are also private teachers who say, "I'm not going to teach you scales in your private lesson, you don't have to "routine" scales for me; you can work on them on your own after you learn this piece." I think that's a faulty approach. When the kid sees a scale, he ought to be able to handle it because he has been routined in that scale. You can work on routine and still stress musical playing.

Unless they can put the notes in the right place at the right time, play reasonably in tune with a good tone and in rhythm, they will fall short. Those fundamentals have to be there before one can achieve the musical result. If you start

working for the musical result before you have learned those other things, you will cancel out anything musical.

*(Frank B. Wickes)*

## BASIS FOR EVALUATION

### Evaluating students' ensemble skill is worthwhile

Independent musical performance from students is the greatest accomplishment of all. Teachers should evaluate students on their ability to generalize from what was taught before to new music. We might expect them to apply these to new music: ability to conduct, notational markings, style, tone, dynamics, intonation, balance, blend, articulations, rhythm, music reading, ritards, and the whole array of the standard issues of traditional musicianship. One way for them to learn this to build a small ensemble component into all large ensemble programs. This provides a means to assess the individual student's learning.

Once, I used traditional scales for the evaluation material. Now I would see that as off the mark because it lacks musical context and does not foster musical playing. Albert Leconi, my teacher at Michigan, said in Italian, "It's all in the music, everything you need to learn is in there." If students study music, they will learn music; if they don't study music, they will not learn music.

Therefore, to evaluate my high school teaching, I had students organize and prepare small ensemble performances on their own. This was self-initiated, self-directed study and worked very well. My quarter's grading included the performance of the small ensembles, which they prepared by themselves. I had a rack of ensemble literature of varying difficulties and it did not matter what level they picked. This occurred once a quarter or semester, about every eight or nine weeks. For the teacher, evaluation took about two minutes a piece. As time went on, they tended to choose partners of the same skill level, instead of friends, or a girl or a boy friend.

While I was grading them, I also was grading my teaching. Everything they showed, retained, or did not retain reflected the teaching and learning. For example, the degree to which they solved problems related to rhythm, intonation, balance, blend, dynamics, and all musical elements showed the success of my teaching and their learning. I realized that if they could not prepare a Class C duet successfully, a question ought to be raised. What did they learn? Could one expect them to monitor their performance in a one-hundred piece ensemble?

*(James Froseth)*

When we talk about developing the ensemble, we probably are putting the cart before the horse. Instead, we should develop individual responsibility in the ensemble. Students should not feel they can get lost or they can hide behind what they're doing in the ensemble. Put importance on everything that everybody does, so they make an artistic contribution. This is true, whether they are the first or the third cornet, or whether their part is a solo or just part of the ensemble. Everyone must have an equal opportunity to learn and to share in the musical product. I learned this from watching and listening to professional ensembles—not just instrumentalists, but singers also.

*(Charles Olson)*

### The teacher's evaluation skill

Research on the learning styles of some minority students says that they think more holistically, view things as function-oriented, etc. If teachers diagnose well, they ought to notice the response of kids. They would then be better problem solvers as teachers—and develop or choose the better, more effective teaching strategy.

*(James Froseth)*

The teacher is the key to discovering what is known or unknown to the student. The teacher must be diagnosing an area of experience just in front of the child's current level. Thus, if you pick things that are too easy, nothing happens; if you pick things that are too hard, nothing happens: the teacher has to diagnose and teach to an area just in front of the student.

I have been reading material by Vygotsky, and he talks about a zone of, well, we call it radius or potential—we call it several things. He defines this zone of experience that the teacher has to assess and for which he must provide experiences. Then, the teacher must control extraneous variables next to that zone.

In other words, if the kid cannot play the next piece of music, the teacher thinks, "Well, the kid could play it if we just make all the rhythms quarter notes and work only on the notes and their names. Then after we have the note names and can play them, we will add the rhythm." So, if the teacher can control the various variables that the kid can learn, the teacher can extend the learning from what the student can do, to something new that the student will be able to do. Vygotsky calls this the "Zone of Proximal Development."

*(Richard Kennell)*

Teaching is nothing more than predicting and dis-

criminating. A teacher must predict what everything should sound and look like in a classroom. Then, a teacher must discriminate differences between what they expect to see and hear, and what is actually being seen and heard. In short, the questions are, "What should it be?" and, "What is it now?"

Evaluation is seeing when these two do not match up; evaluation also is choosing the instructional devices and procedures to make the match up closer—to bring *what* they are doing in line with what they *should* be doing. Any conclusion the teacher reaches is a result of aural and visual images that are highly refined. What music teachers most need to do, we are not teaching them. Teaching is the most demanding performance program of all, since the teacher must express in performance everything they know—not just the information, but the music itself.

Teachers need to monitor students, to identify where they are, and they need command of instructional devices, teaching techniques, and procedures to move the student toward the model.

*(James Froseth)*

My teaching style is to find the way individual students learn. Therefore, I don't think of formulas as the solution to things, though I do have a clear picture of the features good and musical playing should show.

*(R. G. Conlee)*

### Evaluating progress with a constant reference

If a musical context is present through recorded accompaniment that has a pulse and subdivision, style, and harmonic support, practicing is much more interesting and satisfying for students. Furthermore, these experiences can confirm for the student that he is getting better. For example, if one plays with the same context (which is not fluctuating), the student can evaluate the progress as he moves toward performing "in-sync" with the recorded musical context. This is the same as playing a duet with someone who is better and noticing the difference over the course of hours, days, or weeks. The less advanced student realizes that he is improving as he evaluates his playing against something else, instead of nothing.

*(James Froseth)*

# *Communication*
# *in*
# *Music Classes*

# CHAPTER ONE

# COMMUNICATION

Communication occurs in several ways, but it is usually grouped into two basic categories: the verbal and the non-verbal. For example, in rehearsal one might give directions or explain (verbal) or one might conduct, drill, or use facial expressions (non-verbal). Both methods have validity (they communicate vastly different things) and both need constant improvement. Teachers always need to use clear, concise, and carefully worded statements during instruction; saying exactly who the directions are for, what is to be done, and how something is to be done.

Increasing the proportion of the non-verbal to the verbal in a rehearsal is important. If the teacher requires the student to watch and the teacher communicates mostly through conducting, eye contact increases. With the eye contact established, the conductor can communicate the flow of the rhythm, the shape of the phrase, or the level of the dynamic with efficiency. Efficiency, however, is not the only, nor the best reason for non-verbal communication: the use of gestures and facial expressions actually promotes music making in the most fundamental sense. More and more music teachers are coming to believe that they can express the character of the music through visual means more accurately and more fundamentally, than by merely talking and explaining. As physical movement gives students a rhythmic experience more musical than a metronome, gestures and facial expressions give students expressive insights more musical than speech.

## VERBAL COMMUNICATION

### Give clear directions

When starting at a spot in a piece that requires counting measures to find, say "count with me" (as the teacher counts out loud) "before C—1, 2, 3, 4, 5, 6 measures."

*(Rudolf Radocy)*

### Request the possible, not the impossible

We must limit how much information a student can deal with. We easily can ask them to do or attend to more things than they can do at once. We must not over-complicate things or break them down more than we need to.

*(Robert Floyd)*

### Carefully chosen key words

With fast moving rhythms and notes use words like "be deliberate, be patient," instead of "you are hurrying," "you are rushing," or "don't rush." Try to avoid the negatives of do's and don't's. Use a simple word or sentence that will help. For example, say "hear all the notes clearly," or "every note has a mother," or "all the notes are important," or "don't throw them away."

*(Larry Rachleff)*

### State the purpose as one gives directions

Don't say only, "Go back to A" because that doesn't tell anyone why they are replaying a passage. It is better to state the purpose for the retry.

*(Carl A. Bly)*

We should be able to ask a student at almost anytime in a lesson, "What is your teacher teaching you now?"

*(James Froseth)*

### Saying things in different ways

Since each student can learn from a different statement, I try to connect whatever the kid is interested in to something I am trying to teach in band.

*(Stanley Cate)*

I use voice inflection a lot. For example, if the section is to be soft, I often give my spoken directions nearly in a whisper. If the section is to be more forceful, I give the directions in a louder, more emphatic voice.

*(Richard Fischer)*

Since the ways of learning are different for different students, I need to be flexible as I look for ways to develop each player's problem area. When one finds a way to talk about a specific point, one can build upon it.

*(R. G. Conlee)*

129

## WRITTEN COMMUNICATION

### Building communication

I use a "bulletin board" that band students read daily. I prepared the bulletin material before the end of the day, while events are still fresh in my mind. The board is eight by eleven inches and included information from happy birthdays to tunes in rehearsal with specific spots that students should spend time to prepare. The presence of the bulletin board started their habit of coming to look. At the university, students changed their traffic patterns to read this bulletin.

In the beginning with high school students, I had to stand out in front with my grade book to check who read the bulletin board. When they realized I was serious, they developed the habit of looking at the board. There were personal notes, like in a newsletter, and I listed make-up lessons, extra rehearsals, etc. This helped me organize my thoughts and it helped students organize theirs. For example, they could notice they had a make-up lesson scheduled two days later.

This entire process sends out the message that the teacher cares and that education is an important event. You care enough to think through what is to be done, instead of only flipping pages. Sometimes the bulletin board listed the exact reason we would be rehearsing a certain spot.

*(Anthony J. Maiello)*

### Communication through writing newsletters

We produce a newsletter for string students and their parents monthly or quarterly; this serves as a public relations event and also informs parents of upcoming events and ideas.

*(Marion Etzel)*

### Communicating with parents

Since the students are not independent enough to decide some things for themselves, communicating with parents is essential. It helps both the program and the individual students benefit and flourish. We communicated by letters, forms at all levels, calling-trees in fund raising projects, and a lot of mailing! Notices of monthly meetings went out through the mail.

No booster meetings occurred without a program of some kind. With a band or choir, we would get an audience. We used our own groups and, at times, we had guest groups. With the monthly meetings, we usually had our own school groups from the beginner band on up, including ensembles. We always had some kind of program, which improved attendance immensely.

We did have an educational section at some meetings, particularly with the beginners' parents who were new to the program. The key is that we never had "just" a meeting. The booster organization had a printed agenda that described everything related to the organization. They saw it in print at the meeting, which saved time, looked

better, and made the meetings more interesting. Booster organizations can be seen as intimidating by teachers who are not certain how to work with them; when used properly, these groups can be helpful and may even be essential to a successful program.

*(Barbara Buehlman)*

## NON-VERBAL COMMUNICATION

### Less talking means more looking

Most teachers talk too much; I try to talk very little. If we talk too much, there's no need for them ever to look. I try to base seventy-five percent of what goes on in rehearsal on looking and listening. If one must talk, one doesn't have to stop conducting because one can make verbal comments as one gestures or sings. I, the teacher, am the one who chooses the words and the number of them. To conserve rehearsal time, I only talk when I must.

*(Gerald Olson)*

### Watching the conductor

If you want them to watch, don't start the group by saying "watch, ready, go." Instead, start everything with gesture so they have to watch. When I do warm up scales, they must watch the number of beats per measure and they don't move to the next note until they see a downbeat.

This gives me the liberty of taking one measure in three-four, one measure in four-four, a five-four followed by a two-four measure, etc. I do this especially with young kids, and I don't do anything too fancy. To develop their watching of my conducting, I vary the number of beats per measure on a warm up scale and start without verbal directions.

*(John A. Thompson)*

### Beginning communication through conducting

People in the schools respond to ideas about conducting by saying, "Sure, well that's at the University." My view is different: I feel it's very possible at an earlier age level, because I've done it with every age level, even with fifth and sixth graders. You can't walk in and start doing weird motions in front of sixth graders and expect them to work. You make conducting fit where they are. It all becomes a process, then, of adaptation on my part.

If I go into a high school situation, I have terrific luck sensitizing kids. This is especially successful when they are from a good band. In another school it may take a little longer or I may have to approach it in a different way. The younger they are, the easier it is to establish communication through conducting.

*(William W. Wiedrich)*

### Communication with statements and vocal tone

I believe and assume that they really want the best product they can achieve. Even if they do not know exactly what this product is, I repeat this message daily for several weeks. Having quiet does not mean there is attention or concentration on what we are doing. If this is not occurring, I might say, "I have your body and your quiet, would you please give me your mind." I always say "please." If this does not work, I go into a brief explanation such as, "Please give me your mind so we can do this effectively." I name or state specifically what it is we are going to do.

My style is persuasive rather that authoritarian. It is done in a warm, friendly voice that is unyielding. Approaching them in a positive way is much more effective than approaching them negatively. The negative approach can communicate to them that they are "bad" people.

The tone of voice is very important. "Feeling tone" is a Madeline Hunter term about how a student feels as he is led in instruction. The most effective learning takes place when the student feels good. There is, however, a fine line between feeling comfortable, good, and relaxed and having enough positive tension so you feel you need to be attentive and to try to produce. If we are in a situation where it is "totally relaxed, and non-caring," the level of what is accomplished is not high. The teacher's feeling tone is warm and positive, but the tone says that something is expected from students.

*(George R. Bedell)*

## Communication

We must sit with kids, not stand—especially with little kids. We look very big as we stand hovering over them. I sit in a chair even if it is of their size.

*(John Kinnison)*

## Communicating through movement

Though my bands play in tune and with musicianship, I stress the visual aspect so performances are interesting to watch also. I say, "if the music you play makes you feel a certain way, then enjoy it and show the enjoyment you feel physically with movement."

This means they move a lot when they play, not like typical unmoving high school bands glued to their chairs. With these bands, you may hear a musical performance, but you are not seeing one. Moving and responding makes it possible to "see" their musical performance. This cannot be acted, calculated, or choreographed. Their enjoyment will show through movement and bodily action if they allow themselves to enjoy what they are doing. Tell them, "Don't be shy about showing enjoyment and movement."

I reinforce this by supporting those who move with the phrase and the music. I may say, for example, "Standing up here conducting is so rewarding when I look at someone like Bryan, because not only am I hearing the wonderful phrase and expression, but I see him playing that phrase. He is that phrase as he performs. Thank you, this makes teaching meaningful for me, the audience, and for each other."

*(Patricia Brumbaugh)*

## COMMUNICATIONS IN THE REHEARSAL

### Emphasizing sensitivity and communication in rehearsal

If one takes teaching seriously and tries to communicate, they will be sensitizing their band to respond. The more sensitive they are, the more they are listening. They will have their antennas out trying to see what the conductor is trying to tell them to do—and they respond and the conductor responds. The whole process becomes an active music-making process instead of a passive "do what I tell you" process. As a result, the experience of the rehearsal itself becomes more rewarding and significant to the student. Instead of being passive receptors of instructions, the students are now active participants in an ongoing process.

*(Robert Grechesky)*

### Stating the purpose of something

People ask, "How do you get kids to play the way you want them to and how do you achieve the discipline in your rehearsals?" I say, "I just expect it." If we're doing something that students question, I will explain why we must do it. I try to explain why we will be doing something before they question it, so they understand where we're coming from in the beginning.

*(Sandra P. Thompson)*

### The importance of eye contact

If I do not make eye contact with them, how can I expect them to make eye contact with me?

*(Patricia Brumbaugh)*

A student is not yours in rehearsal until you've made eye contact. You can do this in the first minutes of rehearsal so they know that you are aware of them. I make sure that I go down a row, stop and look at a student until he notices me. Then I move on to the next one. I don't do that every day obviously.

Once they see that you're looking at them and they're responding to gestures, rehearsal's begun and everything before rehearsal has come to a close. Usually, I can get them going rather quickly. Sometimes it takes a minute, sometimes thirty seconds before everybody's rolling. One key is finding a stimulus that's new enough.

*(John A. Thompson)*

I expect eye contact. I expect them to be sensitive to the different styles of conducting, slower, sweeping, or more marcato, depending on the piece and their way of playing.

*(Stanley Cate)*

Sometimes I'll get very angry because they are not following me. Then, I'll realize that I've been staring at the music and, of course, they are going to do the same thing:

if they look up and see the top of my head, it's really uninteresting.

If they see my eyes, they know that I'm looking. So, this really emphasizes that they need to watch. It gives me the freedom of knowing I can do whatever I feel is musical. The students are given a feeling of the music being alive; it's not just being trained into them at some specific rate.

*(Gregory Bimm)*

One way of communicating that I use the most often would be my face. It's that my face tells them a lot.

*(Terry A. Oxley)*

I stress eye contact so they remember. Eye contact also helps me know if they are understanding me.

*(Richard Fischer)*

My eyes are in their eyes, straight face to face and I say, "Can you do it that slowly now? Can you learn that for me to help us out?" They say, "Oh, yeah, oh, yeah." They are again being drawn into the importance of playing the music.

*(William Long)*

I see so many groups that have no eye contact between conductor and player. No eye contact means the conductor is worthless on the podium. This may be why students do not watch some conductors.

I spend a lot of time getting high school band members to raise their stands and point their chairs toward the conductor. This is a real basic point. When you set up the room, make sure that the chairs are facing the conductor. Make sure the stand is between the person and the conductor. The stand must be high enough that when they look at the music they will still have a chance of seeing. With many groups, you will see half the stands pointed toward the side wall. There is no way they can lift their eyes out of the music for a moment and see anything.

*(Myron Welch)*

The conductor can talk to the people while they are playing, if they will look at him. The teacher can use verbal communication and nonverbal communication—if they only would look, they would get so much feedback. The feedback comes from the eyes, it does not come from peripheral vision. You cannot get feedback through peripheral vision, there must be direct, eye to eye contact.

Some sit there and say, "Well, I can see your beat." Well, maybe they can see my beat but that's a minor part of conducting. The communication with the eyes is what is important. You must have eye contact and it's not just seeing the beat. Eye contact is like dancing cheek to cheek.

I've seen conductors who have put a metronome on the podium or on the stand and it goes click, click, click. If they do that, all they're getting is click, click, click. If a teacher is not interested in the students' looking, then they might as well use the metronome. I will guarantee that the metronome is steadier and more accurate than they are.

To develop the eye contact I use slow sustained works; with these, students don't have to worry about technique or tone production. Therefore, they have time to look at the notes, and then look up and feel what kind of feedback they get from the conductor.

*(Myron Welch)*

### Reliance upon the conductor

I conduct ninety percent of the music from memory at concerts, and I try to have the scores memorized early on for rehearsals. This helps, because they play with more confidence when the conductor has eye contact with them, than when they watch a conductor with his head buried in the score. For example, students feel very confident before an entrance if you are looking right at them. They depend on the visual and eye contact, and it also builds communication and satisfaction.

*(Ross A. Leeper)*

### Memorization is an excellent tactic

We always did a short piece on concerts that both they and I had memorized. This gave them the opportunity to learn what the musical experience can be when there is nothing between the conductor and the players. As soon as they experienced this, they become hooked on how important it was. They realized it was very important for us to be communicating constantly, to have their part under control so their minds can concentrate on listening and watching, instead of reading the notes.

*(Frank Battisti)*

### The power of images

Using images establishes communication and rapport in unusual ways—depending upon the image, of course. Once I talked about monsters coming up out of the ooze with junior high, and they responded with the right kind of sound. Or, I have talked about steaming up windows with warm air, like at the drive-in movie. They played better and I said, "You all must know what I was talking about." They laughed, and it helped the rapport and communication a great deal.

*(Robert Grechesky)*

I use imagery of a bouncing ball to teach style differences—I even tell the kind of ball they're bouncing. The choice of ball is determined by the style, the volume and the articulation appropriate for the music. Therefore, it could be a ping-pong, a basketball, or a medicine ball!

*(Gerald Olson)*

### Effective teaching techniques

The better ones are not reusable again soon, but the

idea of the teaching technique is. The spontaneity in a rehearsal brings them forth.

*(Gerald Olson)*

### Mix and match

In rehearsal, I often find that I am trying to mix and match teaching techniques, whether they are visual, auditory, or visual images done with words. I do that to appeal to many students or to have two approaches to teach the same thing.

*(Gerald Olson)*

### Asking the band for observations

I might ask a band if they would prefer somewhat slower or somewhat brighter tempo? Usually the consensus is large and the adjustment will result in an improved phrase line. A musically immature conductor will often impede the musical flow of a ritardando, rallentando, rubato, or accelerando and the band will sense the lack of musicality that results.

*(Butler R. Eitel)*

### Means and results; ideas in planning

Consider the idea of a balance between result and means, and means and results. We teach the means first. When we talk to our students about means, we not only tell them what we want them to do, but we tell them how to do it. We say, "Clarinets, I'd like to hear you play that upper register better in tune, therefore you have to play with a little bit broader air stream and bring that pitch down."

Now, if I were to talk to professional musicians about the air stream they would be insulted. I would simply say, "I would like to have a darker, plainer sound in the upper register." I would talk about the results and leave the means to the player. With young players, we are constantly talking about the means; the results are a product of those means. The means provide the results.

Eventually, if I'm smart and I carry out my program the way I theoretically should, toward the end of their high school years I can talk to them about results. The students should have enough skill so we can address results first, when earlier in their development we stressed means first.

*(Charles Olson)*

# CHAPTER TWO

# CONDUCTING AND GESTURES

There is support for the positive effects of conducting and gestures. The experiences of many teachers show young students can respond with enthusiasm to conducting, especially when the teacher conducts appropriately for their age or level of growth. Beyond this, using conducting and gestures can be helpful in other areas. Students can learn to "turn any musical phrase" from as simple a song as *Hot Cross Buns* from a beginning book to something more complex. Students need not wait until they play the Mozart *Clarinet Concerto*, a Vivaldi violin concerto, or a Handel flute sonata before they learn to "turn a phrase."

Students can experience these aspects of conducting and performance as early as the first and second years. Teachers can begin this by having them respond to conducting in beginning instrumental classes as they teach students to make basic musical changes. It is easier to provide a basis for expressive playing early, than to try to initiate expressiveness three, five, or more years later, after years of accurate, albeit mechanical and metronomic playing.

Many music teachers use conducting as a tool of teaching. They believe that young musicians learn through conducting because of its high musical and communicative value. For several reasons, other music teachers are not as enthusiastic. They believe it is more important to teach embouchure, tone production, and fingerings first, because these skills are more basic. They might contend that conducting cannot affect middle school and early high school students significantly, that students of this age or experience may not understand what the teacher intends to convey through conducting and gestures. The better time to emphasize conducting, they would say, is after students gain more performance skill and experience. They also may believe they can teach more effectively using spoken descriptions, free-hand drawings, or other techniques than when they use conducting.

Responding to the conductor is one of several basic ways younger students can personally experience music and music making, and make basic musical decisions. Music making means manipulating the music in some musically expressive way, something that even beginning and intermediate students can do. When guided by the conductor's basic gestures, the students can change the way they play a simple five-tone, half-note and quarter-note passage. The teacher's gestures can tell students whether the notes get louder or softer, slower or faster, are legato or spaced. When young students participate by responding to the conductor, they become more involved. From conducting and movement students gain the *feel* of rhythms and phrasing. They can perceive that the rhythm moves in duple or triple meter, and they can sense the change of energy as a simple phrase moves to a high or low point.

Learning to respond to a conductor while making music should complement the students' other experiences in their first band or orchestra classes. This is a very important consideration, because simply teaching the instrument itself can take such precedence in beginning classes. The teacher has to develop so many instrumental or executive skills—such as hand position, embouchure, facility, articulation, and breathing—that these are often taught separately from listening and music making. Thus, any experience in the instrumental lesson that engages their musical responses is a necessary adjunct to the instrumental skill training itself. We must remember that our ultimate intent is to teach music-making—not valve-pushing.

## THE CONDUCTOR AND CONDUCTING

### *The meaning and role of the conductor*

The word conductor is derived from the Italian word, "conductora." This is related to the word conductor that is used in electricity. The conductor is a conveyor of the music's dynamic meaning in sound and rhythm. He does not have to be correct in what he decides to do, though one would hope that he usually is; the conductor must lead the group because they *demand* to be led and leading is the conductor's role. When making music, the conductor must communicate intentionally, not incidentally or accidentally.

*(Richard K. Hansen)*

134

Conducting is just language; it is a visual language. The more articulate we are with this language, the better we can say what we want to say. But no matter how good we are with words, with conducting language, or with conducting technique, if we have nothing to say, what we do doesn't mean a thing.

*(H. Robert Reynolds)*

If the score is the generator, the conductor must be the voltage regulator. The conductor has the responsibility to project the music so students can perceive what it is about. The conductor must continually be both on the inside as the player and on the outside as the conductor. Conducting must be alert and vital, even if the passage has been thoroughly rehearsed and dissected. Never can conducting be matter of fact.

*(Frank Bencriscutto)*

The conductor is the spiritual leader, though I think this is a difficult idea to talk about. In the Twentieth Century it is not in vogue to talk about how music "elevates" individuals or people. In the Nineteenth Century this was discussed a great deal. Making music is more than just a career or a musical phenomenon in itself, which it is; I think it is a lot more than that.

Never underestimate the power of music; subordinate your role as conductor to the more important matter of music-making.

*(Richard K. Hansen)*

I am concerned about band and orchestra *directors* who are not *conductors*; I am concerned about the fact that they don't think of themselves as part of the performance. The conductor is a performer and conducting is the newest of the performance arts.

We have been teaching instruments as performing areas for hundreds of years. It was not until about the time of Berlioz that we have the first instance of a great conductor. We have only been conducting about ninety years with a baton; in the band much less than that. Just twenty years ago, there were only two or three Doctor of Musical Arts programs in band conducting. Conducting is something about which teachers should be more aware, able, and successful.

*(Robert E. Foster)*

Another principle is that music comes pretty close to encompassing the complete spectrum of human emotion and expression. The spectrum is from the most fragile and gentle on one hand to the most grotesque and severe on the other, and there are all kinds of music between. The other half of that equation is as individuals, we are somewhere along that line also, from fragile and sensitive on one hand, to the Hunchback of Notre Dame or an NFL Linebacker on the other hand. We all are somewhere along that spectrum and we could naturally be more toward the gentle or we could be more toward the macho. It's important to know where we are; but it is more important to stretch and grow in both directions. This enables us to encompass the whole realm of music instead of just being able to interpret music that makes us the most comfortable because it's like our personality.

Most of us, of course, lean towards one side or the other. There can be the band director, for example, who is the big hulking guy who also is the football coach. He may be stretching himself to do *Air for Band*. He is much more able to do Nelhybel whose chorales have such shocking articulations. That's his kind of stuff and, for him, that's real music.

It is our job, though, as conductors, interpreters, and musicians *to be the music* even if it's not similar to our own personality. I'm a much quieter person off the podium, I'm not different but I feel I have to exaggerate myself to become a caricature—a sincere caricature—but a caricature nonetheless, of myself on the podium in order to encompass all the people who are in the room. When I walk into a room filled with people, I don't immediately try to guide their whole spirit, but when I'm on the podium as a conductor I try to do that; and that's an entirely different thing sitting down with two or three people having a beer.

*(H. Robert Reynolds)*

### What makes a conductor successful

Most of what I have learned about conducting has been learned through observation. I have observed at many, many rehearsals of excellent conductors; some were band conductors and some were orchestra conductors such as Giulini and Kurt Mazur, and I also have many tapes on conducting and conductors. I did this observation with the thought that I would learn how to rehearse—to find out about rehearsal techniques. But, the more I went, the more confused I got because I did not discover the secrets of how to rehearse.

Even so, I learned that the excellent conductors seem to have only three things in common. One is a very strong internal aural image of what the music was supposed to be; two, they all had a strong will and showed diligence—more than diligence—they showed a strong determination to get what they wanted; and three, I observed that all these conductors were wonderful musicians, and perhaps that is the most important trait. From that point on, everything was up for grabs.

Much of the big difference between mediocre conductors and very good ones, has nothing to do with their talent or ability; it has to do primarily with their determination to get done what they want. They proceed with their intentions as though they are saying, "I will not be denied—this is the way it is going to be!" One can do this as nicely as we hope we are doing today, or one can do it as a "hard-headed" conductor. But, the guy that is determined to get the music the way he wants it, is usually making the difference between good and bad.

The first trait I listed of a good conductor is the image in his inner ear which says, in a sense, "This is what I want." I cannot overlook that someone must be musical or have a musical ear, because one must have those attributes to succeed. For example, Gunther Schuller and Pierre Boulez started out at the head of the pack because of their immense inborn talent. Many other people start at the back of the pack, but they can become effective music teachers and conductors without the musical talent of Schuller or Boulez. People are born with "ears" that range from the best to the poorest, but having "ears" is not like being tall or short. We cannot change that we are tall or short, but we all can increase our aural skill and train our ears so we are more effective.

*(H. Robert Reynolds)*

### The professional educator-conductor-performer

There can be a confusion over the meaning of terms when we talk about what college and pre-college music educators do. There is no commonly understood term that embraces all facets of our professional responsibility, which include a number of well-known roles and skills such as teaching, performing, and conducting. So when we talk or write about our profession, we often use one or another of the three terms. Unfortunately, when the reader or the listener thinks about our explanation that we associate with one term in the discourse, sometimes he concludes we mean to exclude the responsibilities to which the other terms refer.

For example, if we use the term conductor, some think we do not mean this includes teaching; if we use the term teaching, some people do not realize we often are talking about conducting or performing as well. These three functions can be included under the term professional music educator; the functions of conducting, teaching, and performing all are part of this.

Were the term not so awkward, we could say our career or vocation is to be a professional educator-conductor-teacher-performer. Though that name is too long to facilitate communication, we must remember we also could have added philosopher, administrator, publicist, counselor, budget manager, and purchasing agent to that string of terms. Many of these functions are essential to being a professional music educator and, for want of an accepted overall term, we use any of the three terms, educator, conductor, or teacher, to stand for all functions because they essentially have much in common.

All conductors are teachers, for example, whenever they show the way they think the music should sound by the way they express it through their conducting. Georg Solti, formerly of the Chicago Symphony, might turn to a cellist and suggest a way to play a phrase; he might sing or hum the phrase, or he might gesture or describe the way he thinks the phrase should be performed. What he is doing is leading the performer to the same point of insight which

he himself has seen. When a pre-college teacher is showing a seventh-grade student how to play a phrase, the teacher is taking the student to the same point of insight as was Georg Solti; but unlike Solti, the teacher must consider the age and experience of the student, and how much of the insight the student can assimilate. With these points in mind, the teacher sets his expectations and chooses the way to instruct.

Whichever role, the teacher, conductor, or performer, we are playing out at any one moment, can occur in different proportions. This changes with the context of the musical and instructional setting, with the task the educator is doing at that time, with the intent for the educator's actions, and with the specific skills the teacher is using during a class or rehearsal.

Both the professional conductor and the music teacher, who many now call the professional music educator, must be intent upon making music, be wonderful musicians, and be determined to attain their objectives. For both the conductor and the music educator, one objective is to make the music sound the way they know it must sound. But the teacher also must teach students to play and master the instrument the way it needs to be learned; the conductor does not have that responsibility.

The teacher must know about the instruments so he can teach players how to play them, which enables the students to make music. For example, if there is an intonation problem when the first and third trumpets are playing D in octaves, the public-school teacher must know the lower D sounds sharp compared to higher D, he must know several causes and reasons why it is out of tune, and he must teach students how to solve this problem. He must know and teach them about listening, breathing, the construction and design of the instrument, and develop their judgment so they can decide about intonation on their own. The professional conductor does not have to teach how to do that because his players already have learned those skills and can make those judgments. The music educator has this responsibility and this is just one of a myriad of examples that show that the music educator needs to know a greater variety of things and have skills in more areas than the professional conductor.

The professional conductor needs to demonstrate more musical depth because the music he interprets is of greater depth than pre-college students can perform. I want to stress that the pre-college music educator *must know* the compositions as well as the professional does and he *must have* considerable musical depth or he cannot bring out the depth of pieces that are not as difficult as those the conductor interprets.

Both must have psychological insights, but there is a difference. The school music educator might need to understand that he is a surrogate parent at times; the professional conductor does not need to do that, but some of his players have problems of other types, such as with authority figures. Thus the music educator works with personality development at an early stage and the professional works with personality patterns that are of longer standing. What both face is equally complex psychologically, and the teacher and the conductor need the same high level of psychological understanding when they relate with people, though the peoples' ages are not the same.

The music educator in schools must have a greater variety of knowledge at his command, though the conductor's job is not any easier. His people know the instruments thoroughly, which frees him to work primarily on musical, expressive, and stylistic issues. The school music educator's students are less experienced and he must devote much more effort to getting students to learn to play and to show them what the substance of music is.

*(H. Robert Reynolds)*

### Psychological and relationship concerns in conducting

A conductor is part of a large organism called the ensemble. The conductor is in charge, but the conductor can never be above or outside of it; a conductor has to be within it and has to feel it.

*(William W. Wiedrich)*

One can sense the mental attitude that a conductor brings to the podium. This is something we can't overlook. Some people feel that they have difficulty becoming accepted as a serious person. The conductor has to take his role or work seriously; if so, others will take him seriously.

*(Frederick Fennell)*

The amount and complexity of the psychological substance that is entailed when carrying out the role of teacher conductor is considerable; it is a huge undertaking and responsibility.

We can simplify the conductor's role in music making if we strive to know everything about music and people. I think that the personal relationship between the conductor and the people brings out a warmer musical expression and more communicative playing. I try to be as personal as I can. This is easier in schools, since one can know kids and their families from the grades on up. In the college scene I have to work a lot harder at developing a personal communication or relationship.

During the warm up, for example, I may have them remove their stands from between them and me, setting them to the sides so we have a more conscious direct contact. I try to look at every person during the warm up, especially since we do not have music in front of us. I look them right in the eye and have them look at me. I can sometimes sense if they are having a bad day and when they are not. I can decide if I can challenge them or not. This needs to be done in the warm up first, before the black and white music is between us.

*(Richard K. Hansen)*

### Decisions, problems, and concerns of the conductor

In all details of tempo, style, phrasing, and dynamics there are and must be choices for interpretation. It is a challenge to the conductor to not only make the right choices every time, but to also enforce them.

*(Mark H. Hindsley)*

I try to be a practical conductor, not a showy conductor; and I try not to over-conduct. When I rehearse I probably make gestures as I talk and not even know it. I don't use a baton anymore, because I feel more effective without the baton. The baton can get in the way and sometimes it exaggerates what I do more than I want.

*(Stanley Cate)*

Though we have thirty lines to the score, we must strive to know all the different instruments and their idiosyncrasies, as well as both those idiosyncrasies of the people in the group and ourselves.

*(Richard K. Hansen)*

The number one concern is selecting music of quality. That is the vehicle by which students are going to learn about musicianship and being a musician. The literature is the diet we give these kids to subsist on. You are what you eat.

Another important issue is teaching students about musicianship and musicality. This includes talking about expression and dealing in rehearsal with ways to approach music that entail different approaches to expressing the music.

In my own training and early teaching, I never was made aware of these musical concerns. I never was asked those kinds of questions in rehearsal as a student. Students have to see and accept that there are different ways to approach a piece, to approach a phrase, and to approach the intensity of a piece. I think that most of us who toiled in public school music avoid or do not deal with these issues for whatever reason. No one ever taught us that these were the important points we should be dealing with.

*(Craig Kirchhoff)*

The times I have been unsuccessful as a conductor have been the times when I have been in the way of the music.

*(Richard K. Hansen)*

Conduct not only what is on the score, but beyond the score. We must draw upon all of our knowledge and experiences as musicians in conducting. Though conductors are told to conduct the score and do what is on the page, there is more to the music than the composer put on the score. Going beyond the page means to consider the entire musical and cultural tradition. For example, more of my musical ideas such as turning a phrase in a march come from listening to opera arias than from band recordings. Another consideration is that staccatos in Mozart are different from those in Wagner (if he had any).

Problems can arise if conductors take, for example, the *Trauersinfonie* by Wagner and conduct it exclusively as it is presented in the published version. Since there is both a historical edition and the Leidzen arrangement, they may not have a sense of what Wagner intended. Leidzen even changed harmonies and coloring. Yet, some conductors continue to choose and conduct versions that may not be the better ones.

*(Richard K. Hansen)*

Many problems with difficult meters or rhythms are related to unclear or mixed conducting signals. For example, students can play Claude Smith's seven-eight measures much sooner than teachers have learned to conduct them.

*(Robert E. Foster)*

We are doing one of two things when we conduct: we are either sensitizing our students or we are desensitizing them. That is pretty scary, because that means we are either terrific or awful. There is no average, you're either doing it or you're not; there is either communication or there isn't.

There are conductors who may not look like a text book conductor but they can show the intent behind their gestures. On the other hand there are conductors who have all the moves, but no intent. It's what I call a gesture that isn't connected; it is not connected to the soul or to the mind, and therefore the gesture doesn't have any meaning—it looks ridiculous.

*(Craig Kirchhoff)*

We must ask, "What is your approach to rehearsal? Is it verbal or is it non-verbal?" If I could get through a whole rehearsal without saying anything, I probably would get more done. There is a problem today, however: our conductors are getting prettier and prettier, and our bands are sounding worse and worse.

*(Michael Kaufman)*

When we see conductors who look good but their ensemble doesn't sound good, this shows that some people are more interested in *how to do it*, than, *how it sounds*.
*(H. Robert Reynolds)*

Often we get overwhelmed with budgets, repairing instruments, working with scheduling, the administration, etc. These are not the only things that can work against this. What we are really about is to improve ourselves as musicians, and we do that by surrounding ourselves with great music. I never experience burn-out when I am

listening to, or surrounded with great music. I always experience burn-out when I am constantly doing paper work.

*(Richard K. Hansen)*

Though performance improves through repetition, we need to find ways to get beyond the level we reach through repetition. Watching the conductor is one way to accomplish that and I think there's not nearly enough watching.

*(Robert Levy)*

In 1941, Mark Hindsley stated that the functions of the conductor are: (1) to set the tempo with motions that clearly show the beats of the measure; (2) to indicate the style of articulation; (3) to indicate the proper phrasing in all its aspects; (4) to indicate the tonal volume and maintain dynamic balance; and (5) to maintain all the fundamentals of ensemble performance and secure response to all the elements of interpretation and musical meaning. This is done with gesture, facial expression, and general demeanor, supplemented as necessary in rehearsal by vocal explanation and illustration.

*(Mark H. Hindsley)*

### Attitudes and misunderstandings about conducting

There are feelings that always have been there to some degree; if one looks good as a conductor and has many good conducting techniques, two attitudes surface. One attitude is, "that is all one needs" and the other is, "If you have all that conducting technique, you must not be much of a musician." These attitudes come mostly from people whose conducting technique is not very good. They say, "It doesn't matter if one conducts well, because I have seen too many good looking conductors whose bands don't sound very well." There is some truth in this statement, and I must say, it is a shame. I have seen them too—a conductor with all kinds of physical talent, with nothing between his ears.

Another attitude some have is, "If I have this wonderful conducting technique, that is the main event—it is what is most important. The conducting of the ensemble is the big thing." That *is not* the big thing, *rehearsing the ensemble toward a wonderfully musical culmination is the big thing.*

Using conducting well is like being able to talk to the players in rehearsal. We would all like to do that—talk to the players as they are playing in rehearsals or concerts. Then, we would not have to stop and waste time. Conducting technique allows us to do that: to talk to the players as they are playing. So, the better our conducting technique, the more articulate our visual language can be when we are talking to players. A conversation should be going on as we conduct; conducting should not just be telling them what to do. It should be gesturing to them something important and they respond—and then we respond to their response.

(H. Robert Reynolds)

## SENSITIZING STUDENTS TO CONDUCTING

### The value of a nonverbal approach

Over the long term, shoot for the middle of the bulls-eye. As a teacher-conductor, you're going to get more accomplished five years down the road if you approach teaching and rehearsal from a visual standpoint rather than a vocal (talking) standpoint. If I tell them to hold the note out to the end of the measure, they will know how to do that. Tomorrow, though, you must explain the same thing again.

I don't stick to my guns one hundred percent and say that everything is going to happen from the baton. When you see students' frustration level reach the point where they are shrugging their shoulders and saying, "I don't know what you want," it is time to describe something verbally. Then you say "Look, here's what I'm trying to get you to do."

We can, though, reach more kids faster with gestures. If we gesture, the rehearsal and the whole teaching atmosphere is drawn toward the conductor. I prefer this, instead of acting like a mother hen who must continually gather her flock closer. When we conduct, I think that we are drawing all the brains continually to us rather than telling them everything they have to do.

(Michael Kaufman)

### Teaching students to follow the conductor

Response to conducting must be taught, just as we teach them performance protocol, or rules about how to bow or turn the page properly. I begin as soon as the first day, teaching the size of beat, beat styles, and beat in relation to articulation styles. With phrasing, I introduce them to loud, soft, separated, connected, ritardando and accelerando, and beginnings and ends of phrases. These are the basics of phrasing that we stress at this age.

(Ross A. Leeper)

To get students to learn what conducting can tell them, I just do it. If they don't get it, I say "Now, just watch." Then, I try again to communicate nonverbally without explaining every step of the way. If they still don't get it, I say "Watch again."

(Dwayne P. Sagen)

Elementary and junior high school students can learn to follow and understand the conductor. I believe we must teach students what the conductor is doing on the podium. I explain the various beat patterns, baton motions, and left hand signals; in short, I teach them a basic class in conducting.

After I explain and demonstrate the basics, I have them practice the basic right-hand beat patterns first. I will have half the class play and the other half conduct. After the students become familiar and accurate with the basics of conducting, I will ask students to conduct the band from the podium. We work on this every day for a few minutes until all band members have had a chance to conduct.

Next, I teach them to use the left hand and other gestures that show musical styles and dynamics. We work on these as we did with conducting basics: they conduct each other and take turns conducting the band. The time devoted to these exercises makes the students aware of the conductor and his function. The time devoted to this endeavor is regained in the saving of preparation time, and it improves the music performances.

(Roman Palmer)

We explain what the conducting gestures mean when our ten-year old students start playing in orchestra. They can follow the conductor at that age. I say, "When I do this, you do that. Watch the cut-offs. Watch the dynamic suggestions from the beat's size." I show the gestures so they do not have to infer what the gestures mean. Some students can even do some conducting themselves; the junior high students try it before the end of the year.

(Judith A. Niles)

What engages them, especially younger kids, is a lot of energy, newness, variety, and an incredible amount of enthusiasm from the conductor. Of all of these, the conductor's energy has to be really high. The character of one person's energy may be a different kind of energy than mine. This is wrapped up with personality and presence. Another person can have incredible quiet energy. For another person, that quiet energy wouldn't work. So, I always tell students that if you are a shy retiring person, you will not become Leonard Bernstein. You can, however become yourself in an enlarged super-charged version.

(Craig Kirchhoff)

I teach students patterns from the physical standpoint. They practice the patterns physically so they can get up and understand from a visual and kinesthetic standpoint what it feels like to conduct three-four or four-four. Something fun is to have seventh graders conduct. It is amazing; they are really pretty good. They know how to start and stop the group. The more they understand about conducting from the gestural sense, not just metronomic actions, the better off they are.

(Craig Kirchhoff)

Many teachers pound their fists on the table and say that visual communication can be done with high school and junior high, you just have to stick to it. There are some people who scoff and say that it cannot be done. I think it can be done.

*(Michael Kaufman)*

One can teach people about conducting when one stops to say something. If I do this, I use non-verbal gestures with minimal talk. For instance, if the clarinet section is not playing softly enough, though I have tried every conducting trick in the book, I finally have to stop. Instead of looking at the clarinets and saying, "Measure eighty-five was too loud." I might look at them and say "eighty-five" and then make a gesture that obviously means that they've got to play softer there. This approach targets the message to something that they can see and reinforces their response to non-verbal conducting behaviors. This also targets the action to which you are referring.

*(Craig Kirchhoff)*

Communication in conducting is a process by which the conductor can make the members feel like they understand him and vice versa. Doing this is not a training necessarily; it's an educational event for everybody.

*(William W. Wiedrich)*

In high school, new freshmen classes are resistors of conducting because they aren't used to it. They misunderstand not only what I am doing but why I am doing it, since most middle school directors do not conduct that way. By the time they are in the top band, I rarely have to explain where a phrase is going to end. I can usually show it and they know what gestures mean.

*(Michael Kaufman)*

The previous teacher only played with students, he did not conduct. Therefore, when I came they were not looking at all. To get them to realize that they should watch a conductor, I used only my head to direct attacks and releases.

*(Thomas Herrera)*

We play the tuning note and repeat it according to the different ways I conduct it. This is a conducting game that builds their skills with rubato and their skills following my conducting no matter what I do.

*(Barbara Buehlman)*

### The effectiveness of a conductor

As a guest conductor with a new ensemble, I can tell from the first moment whether the group's conductor has been conducting or drilling the group. If there has been a conductor, the students are tuned into the motion, they are *responsive*; that's the key word. Their regular conductor could be conducting much differently than I, but if the players have been sensitive to a conductor's motions which are influencing the way they play, then they also will be sensitive to another conductor with another con-

ducting style. It will take students a little while to tune into all the idiosyncrasies and the minutiae, but their sensitivity will show immediately whether they are in high school or junior high school—their age level doesn't matter.

I've seen too many cases, on the other hand, where I've tried to make a crescendo; if the crescendo wasn't in the music, they wouldn't do it. So I have to stop and say, "There's a crescendo there." They say, "Oh yeah? Okay." Then they'll do it. Therefore, I have to then teach them how I conduct and I usually do so. First, I start by using gestures for the objects of my sentences. I say as I gesture, "That needs to be a little bit more . . . (then I give a gesture)." "You've got to play more . . . (then I give a gesture.)"

Then not only am I teaching them to respond to my gestures but I'm teaching them what my gestures mean. So when they see that gesture again, they'll have an idea of what that is. If you use gestures as you rehearse, even if you stop, it gets into the right side of the brain first of all, and that is the part of the brain we want to influence. Secondly, it makes everybody, including the conductor, more sensitive to gestures. I have done this with junior high as well as high school and college, and I have observed others doing this as well.

*(H. Robert Reynolds)*

### We need not teach them to follow

If conducting gestures are done correctly, there is no need to teach them how to follow a conductor. They can tell by watching if the music should be forceful, loud, soft, short, smooth, fast, or slow because the conducting gestures are clear signals.

On the other hand, a teacher may need to explain conducting that is poor or less effective. Students will not be able to decode it correctly. Sometimes this is because of contradictory messages. The conductor or music may suggest one style or volume and the gestures show another. Too many are band directors, instead of conductors. A director directs traffic and arranges chairs; conductors conduct music.

*(Robert E. Foster)*

When I want students to watch more carefully, I will under-conduct by using smaller gestures than are typical.

*(Donald Gee)*

In four-four time with whole notes tied to the eighth note over the bar line, I show a release on two and usually they get it. If, after three or four tries, it's not successful, I might joke with them saying, "Guess where the release is, folks." They usually get it then.

*(Michael Kaufman)*

Often I will change tempo in the middle of tonguing and warm-up drills. I might hold beat four with a fermata or surprise them by conducting differently. As the kids get older, it becomes easier to train them to respond to unexpected changes. Young kids also like to learn this skill of responding to the conductor, but what is asked must be more obvious than with older students.

*(Thomas Stone)*

If sensitizing students to conducting is done, conducting becomes a part of the educational experience. For kids, music can become spontaneous through conducting; kids have fun with it. Music learning does not become a regurgitation session where you tell them what to do and they do it. It becomes a very energetic and alive experience.

*(William W. Wiedrich)*

I use silent conducting—really, a silent teacher rehearsal once a year or so. That is, the rehearsal progresses without talking as I refrain from discussing articulations, dynamics, etc. I will use words only when I want to communicate rehearsal letters to them. If I keep returning to a section to improve it, I need to exaggerate the conducting gestures to correct and do what is needed.

I have discovered that when I do this their attention is infinitely better. There are some problems, however, since there traditionally are times when one teaches and times when one conducts in a rehearsal. Normally, some things can be communicated better with a simple sentence. On the other hand, conducting promotes more musical advances. When I conducted the "silently rehearsed" piece, they played well. When I went to the other pieces, they paid less attention again—there was little carry-over. The solution may be to restrict the use of talk to convey technical or descriptive things quickly and increase conducting during all rehearsals.

*(Donald DeRoche)*

I try to communicate by asking for immediate adjustments during a warm-up scale. When this is successful, communication is stimulated and they become more involved. For example, I do not define the rhythm on scales. This makes it possible to be unpredictable. Everything is a down beat; therefore, they must look at me to do the scale. They try very hard to do the scale well and will take it as seriously as a piece.

*(Richard Fischer)*

## TEACHING STUDENTS THROUGH CONDUCTING

### Conducting as a teaching tool

When I talk about gestural communication in conducting classes, I don't talk about it as conducting anymore. I talk about it as a teaching tool, though they happen often to be the same gestures that good conductors use. As a professional music educator, I see the need to use

communicative gesture as a teaching tool because it helps with the efficiency of the rehearsal.

*(Gerald Olson)*

With honor groups I spend fifteen or twenty minutes without music. This helps them listen, but also develops their attentiveness to the conductor. I conduct various volumes, styles, and even phrasing without talking. That's how they learn what I want them to do. By the time I get to playing the tunes everyone knows what I am about. The students start playing with me, they do what I want, and I never talk about it. If one does not talk, but demonstrates instead, the rehearsal is far more successful.

*(John Williamson)*

Communication through proper conducting is far superior to time beating and teaching by rote only. Try to conduct so that every player will know just how to play his part; make him feel you are conducting just for him. In due time one of two things will happen: either the band will play as the conductor conducts, or the conductor will conduct as the band plays. Even more important, if the conductor knows what he wants musically, he will find a way to accomplish it.

*(Mark H. Hindsley)*

All we need to do could stem from conducting. Only when it doesn't come from conducting do we have to try other approaches. If the students are watching and do not have their faces buried in the music, conducting is very effective. However, young students struggle with their notes and do not look up. Especially during the first reading they need to look at the conductor.

*(Judith A. Niles)*

### Conducting in performance and conducting as teaching

I contend there is a difference between conducting and gestural communication for teaching. I see the need in rehearsal, more early on than later, to stylize certain communicative gestures like short, loud, or legato, which I would never do in performance. By stylize I mean highly dramatize, which could be called "over-conducting."

As a teaching aid, I would make the gestures larger the life. This can be done early on in sight reading, getting concepts across to make sure the students understand. Gestural conducting lays a template-like basis for understanding. We can show what short is, what loud is, etc. To the degree they begin to understand those concepts, I wouldn't have to do that anymore.

Using gestural communication as a teaching technique presumes the teacher knows why he is applying this gestural skill to a certain issue and why he is using it at that time. The teacher simply must turn a manner of conducting on and turn it off according to the situation and need.

Most good conductors use gestural communication,

but they are more apt to use it at the conducting stage, that is, when the piece is about ready for performance. I see this differently. To me, the only time you need to conduct is when you are going to perform; before that, you would be teaching through gestures!

*(Gerald Olson)*

### Conducting and teaching can be multi-dimensional

I always try to give examples through demonstration and singing, and using my hands, face or dancing to support the words. I believe in translating things to students with gesture, image, and motion. I also "para-sing" without exact pitches. That works wonders with phrasing, and is especially effective with mixed meters when students have their hands moving up and down according to the pulses. Just fifteen to twenty seconds of this has considerable effect. One of my predecessors taught similarly. He would have students put down their instruments so they could sing and conduct the passages.

*(Robert Grechesky)*

If I am verbally discussing anything that has to do with music, I will gesture as I talk. This gives the students something visual to relate to. My goal is to transfer their awareness from verbal to visual directions. As they get better at understanding I talk less and gesture more. We can teach so much more through our conducting. Some teachers think they don't have to conduct until just before the concert. I disagree. From the first moment we start working on a piece, one of the most valuable teaching techniques is our non-verbal conducting skills.

*(Richard Floyd)*

I am not an advocate of never talking while conducting. If I can shout over the band and tell the trumpets to pull the third valve out while they're playing low D, I'm going to do it.

*(Michael Kaufman)*

### Selecting the conducting gesture

Many conductors do a gesture because that's how they do that particular gesture, instead of selecting a gesture for its application to a particular problem. Conducting is teaching and, in fact, not enough conducting books discuss even the *issue* of gestural communication.

*(Gerald Olson)*

### Teaching music terms and developing leadership

I explain many musical terms through conducting. Instead of defining terms through reading or discussion, they change styles as they play their scales. They respond to my gestures without explanation and without notation. We make many changes this way, whether it is marcato, staccato, legato, rise and fall of dynamics, ritardandi, meter changes, scales, rhythm patterns, etc.

They watch everything from my eye expressions and my facial expressions to what I'm doing with my hands. This makes them look up more often later when they have the music. Furthermore, I think they become oriented toward me as the leader instead of looking at the music and only occasionally looking at me.

*(Lance Schultz)*

### Research on conducting

My dissertation was on verbal and non-verbal conducting behaviors, and their relationship to expressive musical performance. I compared "so-called musically poor bands" with good bands to find what the teachers might have done to cause this.

There were telling things that conductors of the better bands did that were not done as much or at all with the poorer bands. They used verbal imagery, the left and right hand, body movement and facial expression more. I also looked at verbal imagery and the use of left and right hand in combination.

I try to make a strong philosophical case for expressive conducting and the elimination or reduction of talking in rehearsal. If this occurs, one is dealing on a non-verbal level to relate and send information back and forth from one to another. As a result, the conductor will have a more intense musical experience, a closer relationship to music, and the students will feel more a part of the musical experience.

One very strong factor in expressive performance was the use of verbal imagery. Imagery was much stronger than any instruction using technical jargon. Body movement and facial expression also were very effective means the conductors of the better bands used. These were done less or not at all with the poorer bands. When I compared verbal imagery and conducting, the former was, as I recall, the stronger factor.

Another factor was "too much talking." This was characteristic of the poorer bands. There were other types of verbal behaviors. Technical talk and announcements were not significant.

Partly because of this, I am a very strong believer that the conducting should reflect the music non-verbally; conducting should *look* like the music.

*(Robert Grechesky)*

### Conducting tempo changes

I stress that whenever there's a tempo change that's when the group needs a conductor the most. They need to look up for musical signals that say slow down or speed up.

*(Timothy Mahr)*

### Teaching pulse and rhythm

Within a phrase, be it with a ritardando, accelerando, or just playing rubato, you can have them counting the pulse or rhythm aloud while you're conducting. This forces them to watch you. You also can have them play the rhythmic units in a unison or sing their parts while they watch you.

*(Robert Levy)*

## Visual communication and middle school students

I would use a visual approach back to the middle school age level, as long as you can keep them interested. If their attention span is waning and they're becoming frustrated because they can't understand, then it's time to do something different. One must consider the frustration level and ask yourself, "When do I stop doing that and go to something new?" With younger players, the frustration level can be reached very quickly. They cannot handle a whole hour of non-verbal rehearsal.

*(Michael Kaufman)*

## Dramatizing through gestures

I highly dramatize a certain gesture to draw attention to it, because that allows me not to have to stop and talk about it. If I want staccato for example, I would embody excessive staccato. There is staccato in my face, my eyes, my fingertips, and in the stick. I would become staccato for a five to eight second period or until they caught it. If they don't catch it right away, I drive it in as a visual reminder for a period of time to let them know that when I get back to the recapitulation they will remember that I am going to want staccato again.

*(Gerald Olson)*

## Teaching articulations

I think we spend so much time on the podium describing, for example, legato and staccato, that the gestures that we use often are meaningless. The band plays because we talk them into playing well.

We should take time to assess if our conducting is a good model of articulations. Students aren't going to follow gestures that do not make sense or follow a conductor who is unable to produce the right gesture. However, if the director has an arsenal of styles and gestures appropriate for various moods and styles, he can communicate through the stick without talking about what he wants.

To get kids to follow conducting, follow the rule, "Don't talk!" To teach the meaning of my gestures, I may stop the group and say, "Just watch me for a minute."

*(Frank B. Wickes)*

## Building rubato skills

I use conducting games to build skills with rubato. They follow my conducting no matter what I do. For this, I simply use the music we are working upon.

*(Barbara Buehlman)*

## Good looking conducting and good sounding music

Conducting symposiums, to some extent unfortu-

nately, have spawned a generation of conductors who really look pretty good. With some good looking conductor's, however, there's little relationship to the music or what the group is doing with the music. I recall a high school band director at a conducting symposium that everybody thought was a terrific conductor. He was making these wonderful moves, but the band sounded awful.

It is shallow to think that having all the technical solutions can solve all the problems. Technique is not enough alone, it needs to join with a spark or a depth of musicianship. Without this the performance is not likely to come off in spite of ample conducting technique. There must be something else that is special. I can't describe exactly what it is, except through this example:

At a symposium, a guy conducted *Irish Tune*. By the time he finished *Irish Tune*, I could see all kinds of ways to improve him technically. It may not have made any difference, because the impulse behind his conducting was terrific. His musicianship was so evident, that he could have conducted standing on his head and the performance would still have been terrific. His musicianship was such that he could independently make decisions about how the music should be performed. Though he lacked conducting technique, his impulse, somehow, was strong enough to carry out his musical decisions.

There is a funny balance between technique, and impulse and musicianship. I'm not saying that one doesn't need technique to be a good conductor, because one does. This fellow will realize sometime that his musicianship is limited by his lack of conducting technique. If I had to choose, I guess I would prefer the musicianship and the impulse, and begin with the lack of technique. One can gain technique, but one cannot as easily acquire impulse and musicianship.

*(Craig Kirchhoff)*

## Making music

The "real music makers" do not necessarily make music through the craft of conducting. Music making is something caused more by personality. It's sometimes "spooky" what they do! Their craft may not be the model. Perhaps the reason they make music is that they are full operators at the intuitive level.

*(James Froseth)*

Very little conducting goes on by telling people what you want. Most of the conducting has to do with an idea or system through which you are telling them what you want as you conduct. Then they respond, you respond, they respond, etc. You should respond in direct proportion to how they played. So if they played a little too softly, then immediately the next thing you do is to conduct a little too loudly. If they played much too soft then you conduct much too loudly.

There is a response in the moment, but I'm also

rehearsing what just happened. Then the next time I don't have to stop and say, "The next time you do that with the bass drum, that needs to have a little harder mallet or a little more this or that." I mean some guy on the bass drum could play one bass drum "boom," and that's the only bass drum "boom" in the whole piece. I'm in his face immediately afterwards, you know, gesturing "louder!" "louder!" Though he may not do anything differently for the rest of the piece, when he comes to that note again next time, it'll be louder. I'm also trying to give him this message in different ways and get his attention, even if through very obvious gestures. The more a group is with me as I conduct, the more subtle I become with them.

*(H. Robert Reynolds)*

## SUGGESTIONS FOR THE CONDUCTOR

### Developing the group's internal pulse

When a piece, is approached by a step-by-step process and is put back together, it is very playable aurally without conductor. Most pieces can be performed effectively without the conductor, considering the precision aspects of the performance. Performing without the conductor helps the group develop a strong sense of inner pulse that enables them to achieve a high degree of polish in performance. With inner pulse established in the group, the conductor is freer to hear what is really going on. He can move to providing them further musical guidance instead of being only a metronome. The conductor becomes or is put into the role that is his real function. His real function is simply to set tempo and to give musical representations that cannot be decided by one person.

*(Gary Hill)*

### Suggestions for conducting

I follow two principles with conducting: the first is the way you strike the beat or the ictus is the way the player will start the sound. The second principle is how you move through space after the initial attack. These movements show how the breath moves through the instrument. So if you want to develop the proper motion you can question, "Now how would I play this? What kind of breath, what intensity, what volume, and what gesture and movement is right?" Then you gesture and move in that way as you conduct.

We should conduct not only just the breath, but how the air moves through the instrument; we conduct how they breathe in, as well as how they breathe out. How they play through the instrument is how the music is going to be and so the level of energy—the level of intensity—has to be shown by motion through the air.

We are trying to be of service to the composer, but our personality is in there nevertheless. We are not trying to make it our piece but we must make it come alive through our voice. It's almost like acting in Shakespeare:

you want to do what Shakespeare wanted, but it's inevitably going to be your interpretation of Shakespeare's words. You are not just presenting the words like in a book, because even when you read a book you interpret the words silently or internally. But when conducting, we interpret it through motion and that is visible; the principles of motion have to be guiding the air because that's what your guiding—the feelings in the air.

Most band conductors make the mistake, unlike choral conductors, of conducting things on the beat. They will conduct volume and phrasing, but they will conduct these events as though they happen *on* each beat. Band directors do not realize that *between* the beats is where the action really is.

If you have a whole note with a crescendo, you do not want to strike each one of those beats increasingly harder. What you must do, in a sense, is strike the first beat the way you want them to start the note, whether it is soft or loud, with a soft or hard attack and at whatever volume, intensity, and pressure level you want on the attack. Then you outline the four beats: if you want a crescendo you outline an increasing energy level. But, you must not strike each beat increasingly louder with not much going on between the ictus of those beats. That is the way, however, many people do it; they somehow have learned that conducting is supposed to be conducting the pulse or conducting the beat. If people what to become better conductors, they need to be showing ideally *how a person should play* much more than *when a person should play*.

One must learn the conducting techniques of blending beats together. For example, if you have two quarter notes you might want to start each of them on the beat and that's fine; but after that, you might have a half note on the third and fourth beat. You must learn to blend the third and fourth beat together, because you don't have an audible pulse on count four. You must not emphasize the ictus that you emphasize on beat four. You must not emphasize this because, in the music, there is no audible pulse on count four. In other words, you must conduct the music—don't conduct the beats.

What has happened is that people learned to conduct backwards, meaning they learned the structure and patterns from Max Rudolf's book or whatever their favorite book is. They learned the patterns and then they hung the music on the patterns; rather than learning the music and then selecting the gestures to portray it. The reason why Barenboim or Ashkenazy can conduct as well as they can is primarily because they learned the music first. Then they felt that to be a conductor, they should learn or acquire some technique. They didn't learn the conducting first and then say, "Okay, what do I want to do musically?"

*(H. Robert Reynolds)*

### Conducting the music or conducting the beat

During conducting workshops, I see that people can make magical changes. When they first begin they often are preoccupied with conducting the beat. They have primarily conducted the beat for so long that it just comes out that way. They often think, "My players can't play if I don't conduct the beat." Their students can play without the beat, of course, and this is true for players at any level. Other teachers have said, "It's fine for you at the University of Michigan, but this won't work for me and my East Avenue Intermediate School Band." It can work, if the students are weaned gradually from their dependence upon the conductor's metronome-like motions. To influence him toward embracing a new view I say, "Okay, why not try to conduct without the beat. The group will stay together or I'll keep them together behind you by conducting just the beat." When they begin again, the beat often is still evident in their conducting, but they are now focusing upon conducting the music, which is so much more important.

I did a conducting clinic at a state convention and I was stressing, "Don't always conduct the beat, the players can take care of the beats themselves." A guy came up to me later that year at the Midwest Clinic and said, "I heard your session at the state convention and I'm here to tell you that your system doesn't work—and I know, because I tried it!" I said, "Tell me about that." He said, "I've always been conducting the beat because I thought it was important. After you said we shouldn't always conduct the beat, I decided not to. I just stopped conducting the beat and they couldn't stay together."

When he suddenly stopped conducting the beat, he took away all their support; this change was too abrupt because they had been supported by his regular beat for so long. You have to wean them away, you can't *suddenly* stop conducting the beat. Instead, you have to show students what they must do to replace their dependence upon your steady beat. He may have had more success if he had said, "Now listen to the tubas, they have the pulse here. And from the tubas the pulse goes to the trumpets." Instead, when he stopped conducting altogether, he had not given them a new anchor upon which to depend.

The weaning process is important in this whole thing and as they become weaned, they begin to build their independence; you have taught them to listen to what they are doing. Eventually, the ultimate precision and pitch is done by the players through listening to each other. It's not done by somebody saying, "You're too flat, play a little bit higher." It is not done either by saying, "You are a little behind the beat, play a little sooner." Giving them the prescription may correct the problem this time and for that moment, but how about next time? How much higher or sooner should they play then? This approach inevitably returns us to the same problem again and again, because we have not set in motion a long-term way for students to make decisions.

*(H. Robert Reynolds)*

## Conducting carries over to the next piece

There is the issue of response versus memory. The question is, is it better to rehearse every measure so they are at the right dynamic levels, or is it better to teach them to respond to what you want?" If you teach them to respond, then each performance can be different and this also enables you to rearrange things as you go along. If you don't, you must teach everything again and again because they will not play musically unless they are trained to play in a specific way at a specific time.

*(Thomas Stone)*

## Score Reading Program

I use the GIA score reading programs. They are marvelous, the best material I know to help beginning conductors become familiar with score reading.

*(Anthony J. Maiello)*

## Influencing the group

The biggest enemy of the conductor's influence on the group is monotony, and those who constantly conduct the beat are contributing to the monotony. If you conduct in a monotonous manner, people will stop watching you and you will have lost your influence.

*(H. Robert Reynolds)*

## Engaging the group

Half of your energy in a rehearsal—and this is an approximate percentage—is spent on developing attitude and interest, and keeping the people's interest with you. The other half of your energy is spent on improving the music in rehearsal. But, unless the attitude, the concentration, and the interest are good, people will not be drawn into music making—they tune out; they'll turn you off like a television set. If they don't have another channel to turn on, they'll turn on their own inner channel. You must, therefore, vary what you do constantly.

We try to vary the way we make certain points and convey certain musical ideas, because you want them engaged in the operation. You don't want this to be just an issue where you're dictating and they're obeying. You want their involvement; unless you get that involvement you haven't educated anybody.

We can teach them how to parrot back something, like a trained seal, but if we do we haven't really educated them. One main purpose of a teacher is to make himself dispensable. To do so, we attempt to create independent musicians; but we never can quite do it. That's okay also, because most people need teachers, mentors, and guiders. If people are getting more and more independent as musicians all the time, then I think we're doing our job.

*(H. Robert Reynolds)*

## Giving criticism in rehearsal

I try to criticize in groups, more than individually. I always assume that somebody has the best of intentions, therefore I don't criticize, in a sense, I make suggestions for improvements: I say, "That's a little too strong, play a little softer there," "Maybe a little more articulation here," or "We need to be more precise with the trumpets at this spot." As I isolate or get down to individual players, but mostly it's in twos and threes; if I need to hear the second and third clarinets or whatever, then I hear them altogether or I may just hear second clarinets. It will be a pretty dire situation before I go down the line one by one.

*(H. Robert Reynolds)*

### Conducting problems

Often, the internal rhythmic problems of a group are directly due to the kind of gestures their conductor is using.

*(Gary Hill)*

We can have a conducting problem if we encourage the students to wait too long before they start their tones. If they do this, it's likely they will play a percussive attack. Attacks following a breath need a conducting gesture with considerable flow to it, not a hesitation or jerk in the total motion of preparatory and downbeat.

*(Donald Casey)*

The biggest favor orchestra members can do, especially with student conductors is to do what they see, not what they are told to do. It is typical of some conductors to say, "this section is too slow, please play faster" instead of conducting the tempo properly and saying nothing.

*(Pamela Gearhart)*

### Conducting basics

In instrumental conducting class, I ask students to mirror what the players are to do as they conduct. For example, if you want them to take a certain kind of breath, the conductor would use the same kind of preparatory beat. They should use the gesture that will convey the way the players should breathe.

*(Kjellrun K. Hestekin)*

When I conduct, they mirror musically and physically what I am doing. I don't tell them that they should move in a certain way. If a band is not playing dynamically, it usually is because the conductor isn't conducting in that way. Teaching techniques alone do not replace conducting.

*(Patricia Brumbaugh)*

### Beyond conducting technique

The more I teach conducting, the more I'm convinced that a good part of it is metaphysical, though it sounds like a "cop-out" to say that. Yesterday in conducting class there was enough time and the excerpts were short enough, that I let them go through it twice. Finally one student began to conduct as though she had been thinking, "Okay, I'm going to really do it and go for it this

time." When she went for it, then that "something" happened. You couldn't say there was more energy to the beat, there was a whole different kind of presence. The entire tone of her body changed and she was more convincing in her leadership.

*(Craig Kirchhoff)*

### Rules for the conductor

1. Stand squarely on both feet, with the body normally facing the center of the organization; turn only the head and shoulders to face different sections; do not bend at the knees or pat the feet.
2. Communicate with the player or section concerned by looks or other gestures when conducting a passage of solo or sectional nature.
3. Keep your eyes out of the score as much as possible, especially when unusual things are occurring. *Know the score.* (Inspiration comes from the face rather than from the top of the head.)
4. Make every movement mean something; get along with the minimum movement possible; save extra movements for the times when they may be needed.
5. Use the left hand and arm to aid in expression, phrasing, cuing, and other interpretative signals; do not habitually duplicate the movements of the right arm with the left.
6. Use the head, eyes, and facial expressions to further secure the desired interpretation, employing them to convey to the players what you feel yourself.

*(Mark H. Hindsley)*

### Achieving a musical performance

Most basic is really knowing the score. That means having an objective in mind for which you are striving—what you think this particular work is all about.

After this, one might be successful through a variety of means. For example, one conductor may have a fantastic baton technique and another may have very, very little. Someone else may be extremely articulate in rehearsal with explanations. Their analogies are really terrific and get excellent responses. Someone else may be terrific at using rehearsal time to involve everyone in the groups. There are a variety of ways by which one can be very effective.

Different conductors have different types of effectiveness and different ways to do things. I've seen some people who may be really highly respected, who I think were awful on the podium. Yet, they would have great sounding groups, because they know how to articulate what they wanted; they really knew how to rehearse. They're very effective and they have good ears. I think someone can be poor at conducting (baton) techniques and still get a very good performance out of the group.

It is more difficult, however, when someone is a poor

conductor. Someone who has no change in body movement stylistically will find it difficult. They use their whole arm and they have their face buried in the score the whole time. It looks as though they are randomly throwing out "cues" with their fingers. You almost think that the conductor is getting in the way of the group. Yet, some way or another, their group sounds terrific. If someone rehearses and articulates well but conducts poorly, it's certainly more difficult to achieve excellent playing. There are other things beside verbalizing. I think really knowing how to get a sound, being articulate about what you want, etc. can all contribute to an improved performance.

*(Robert Levy)*

### The generator of a band's sound

The question used to be, "Who do you want your band to sound like? Do you want it to sound like Bill Revelli's band, do you want it to sound like Mark Hindsley's band or like Harry Begian's band?" So, often the music was more a vehicle to make the band sound the way you wanted it to sound. The music may have been important, but more energy was put into making a certain quality of sound, merely for the sake of making that quality of sound.

The easiest analogy that I can draw is that it's like what people used to say about the Philadelphia orchestra sound. Of course, Muti now says, "That sound is wonderful. But, what I really want is a Beethoven sound, and a Brahms sound, and then I want a Mozart sound, and then I want a Bartok sound."

*(Craig Kirchhoff)*

### Showing that one could conduct

Curiously, there are very good musicians who are very average conductors. They will stop the group and will describe with their hands exactly what they want, using their hands exactly the way they should have been doing when beating time patterns; but when they finish they go back to the time beating.

*(Craig Kirchhoff)*

### Problems with the "stick"

I saw people in conducting clinics whom I could not believe. For example, a trombonist was conducting. The stick was in his right hand and was completely tensed up and bound up—his wrists stiff, arms stiff—one could not go from one position to the next on the trombone with that kind of hand and arm, as everyone knows. When he put the trombone down and decided to conduct, he forgot everything he had ever learned about playing the trombone. That was the time he should have remembered it, all the way; because, if he had done nothing but play the trombone, the band would have followed him very well—the legato passages would have been just fine. But no, he had that dumb stick in his hand.

This (the stick) is the ruination of more good men than anything else—they don't think, they don't remember, they don't transfer what they know; they don't transfer their life's experiences. This also is very true with orchestral conductors who come to my workshops or hire me to give me an observation of them. I can't believe that they can stand in front of an orchestra having held a violin bow in their hand for twenty years, and don't know what to do with the baton.

They don't transfer what they know from one field to another and that is the great problem of the band—it's the band's greatest problem.

*(Frederick Fennell)*

### Visual-gestural communication from the podium

While there was a time I was not interested, I later became vitally interested in the effectiveness of wonderful gestural communication from the podium. Until I started thinking about those issues, I probably had not looked at myself as an awful conductor. When I did, I wanted to do something about it.

As I started to look at kids and what their needs were, I realized that I could become much more effective. When I stopped in rehearsal, my effectiveness could increase by the judicious use of very short sentences or a single word to get a concept across. Then, I would try to convey the meaning of the statement immediately with my conducting gesture. I very often use the words and gesture simultaneously.

As I get to the detail stage in a four-week rehearsal period, the detail may only be shown in gesture. Then, I can stop and do it again by having more vitality in my gesture. In performance, I wouldn't conduct the way I do in rehearsal, because I had been using the gesture to teach with. My gestures had been quite dramatic in rehearsal when it was necessary to highlight a point. In a concert the gestures are simply a subtle reminder. They may not even be there at all, if they don't need to be reminded anymore.

*(Gerald Olson)*

### Observing others conduct

In conducting workshops I see people conduct the way they conduct at home, you can't conduct one way at home and another way elsewhere. Some people are really wonderful at it. I once thought that after a person has been in the "trenches" for two, or three, or four years their conducting was going to slide; have I changed my mind about that!

If they value what they're saying to the students and the students are responding, they're getting that response and their conducting will be improving. I've also seen, of course, that we all can get into certain idiosyncrasies and it's hard to change. If you're not using good technique and do not have good conducting habits, you can get into some bad habits quickly. That's why observation of other conductors and conducting clinics are so important—it helps us evaluate what we are doing.

*(H. Robert Reynolds)*

## *Conducting, personality and flair*

Expressive and extroverted conducting comes from the same personality. One should work to develop this, even if it is contrary to one's normal personality. Body dynamics and tasteful choreography of music are a must. Flamboyancy is cheap.

*(Butler R. Eitel)*

## *The focus of conducting workshops*

These conducting workshops that I started doing years ago (one of the first was at the Nels Vogel Clinic in Moorhead, Minnesota) are wonderful and I am very happy to see that so many are keeping them going. The point is that they are all about music.

*(Frederick Fennell)*

# PREPARING THE SCORE FOR TEACHING AND CONDUCTING

## *Studying the score*

As important as studying the score is, unless one "hears" what the music is to sound like before or after the analysis, the beautiful analysis is without any result.

*(James Froseth)*

## *The basis for decisions*

In college we're always taught to find a right answer, the right generalization, and often that's how people approach music making. Some say, "The reason you have to play piano is because it says piano!" But there's no musical impetus behind a decision made for that reason. I would like to impart something to my students, which I learned too late in my life. The idea is that the music must be the motivating reason why the technique must be right at that point; the basis for the decision is that it is necessary to contribute to the musical result. This insight has made my rehearsals more satisfying to me and the players than they have ever been.

*(Craig Kirchhoff)*

## *The rehearsal plan*

Part of the need for a conductor to present an image of seriousness is also a matter of plan. We are all told about teaching plans; but, there is nothing more true about that than the rehearsal plan. A rehearsal has an architecture; rehearsals should not end on a poor note. Psychologically, they can't all end like one had just roared through the end of the 5th Symphony of Beethoven, or the *Stars and Stripes Forever*. But, they all must have an architecture that leads people into a quiet mood or whatever.

Attitude, dress, consistency, etc. also go with the preparation for the rehearsal. The preparation is not just mental, but concerns the music at hand, the present state of the group, and what is up ahead to be done.

*(Frederick Fennell)*

When you walk out on stage and you're playing this sonata or that suite, you are saying either, "This is what I think Beethoven tried to say," "This is what I have to say about Beethoven," or "This is what I believe." This is how I think it feels to me when I'm trying to communicate something as a performer or conductor.

*(Robert Levy)*

## *Over-interpreting music*

I think we've been through a period of over-interpretation. I agree that conductors have to interpret everything that's on the page, and I know that there's a whole lot more to the music than what is on that page.

However, what I mean by over-interpretation is this feeling, this compunction, this need among people to put their own personal stamp on the music in the name of interpretation. You end up with some of the most bizarre, strange, and unmusical or amusical renderings that can be imagined.

It comes back to a basic understanding about stylistic issues. People ought not to be as far off center into their own personal views as some are, calling it interpretation.

*(Craig Kirchhoff)*

## *Conducting exercises*

Here are sample conducting exercises. They are to communicate and secure response from the band in the elements of interpretation.

Ground Rules for These Exercises:
1. Band members do not have copies to read from. Although the exercises are written in the key of C for the conductor, he may call for any key.
2. The conductor informs the band to play half or quarter notes in four-four time, following and interpreting properly his conducting movements and his facial expressions. Other similar exercises may be written out before a rehearsal or invented by the conductor as he goes along; only he will know whether he is securing the response his conducting calls for.
3. For the purposes of these exercises only, all notes slurred are to be played with a tongued (articulated) legato, and consecutive slurred groups are to be separated by phrase punctuation; all notes not slurred are to be played marcato.

*(Mark H. Hindsley)*

# TEACHING THROUGH GESTURES

## *The value of gestures*

Depending upon the time one has to work upon something and the group's level, the quickest way may be through conducting gestures. The second way is to sing it, and the least effective and most time consuming way is to explain by talking. I try to use speech only when other ways are less effective. There are some issues a teacher cannot explain through gestures, such as the relationship of themes in one movement to their role in another.

*(John Anderson)*

My daughter, who teaches sign language at the Maryland School for the Deaf, said "You're conducting wrong. You keep teaching them like a music class. It isn't that, it's a non-verbal communications class. Music is the subject matter—not the technique. The technique is sign language." I said, "Now look, I've been teaching conducting for years and I know how this works and, uh . . . you're absolutely right."

The more you think about it, the subject matter you are talking about is loud, soft, fast, slow—all that sort of thing. The technique of conveying that, though, is the combination of sign language, mime, dance, and traditional singing.

She is absolutely right: conducting is non-verbal communication. In conducting, there's a large non-verbal vocabulary one can use if one has physical control. The greater one's non-verbal vocabulary is, the better one can speak to the group. Some can show the beat and show how it's real loud and it's real soft, but that's all they can say. There are other conductors who are very expressive with their skills. They have more vocabulary because they have better technique.

Because of this, I have my conducting classes learn the American Sign Language alphabet. This takes only one class to show them and make sure they do it. They learn to communicate a sentence or two to each other and get the idea of communicating non-verbally. Learning a bit of the American Sign Language makes the point that you can talk to people with your mouth shut and most conductors need to learn that.

*(Donald Wilcox)*

### The place of gestures

Humans have always wanted to express themselves in non-verbal ways.

*(James Arrowood)*

### Hand signals and gestures

A conductor can use a series of hand signals as one is conducting and they are playing. If used correctly, this will reduce the number of stops in a rehearsal. Some call it the "repair and motion" idea. With score study and knowledge of potential problems and performers, one can work through a piece a measure ahead. Performers know before they get to the next phrase what is needed.

Here are some musical and technical ideas the conductor can communicate to the group: articulation, pitch, rehearsal letters, length of notes, breath support, intensity of air, embouchure, tonal quality, bells up or down, vibrato, resonance, pyramidal balance, etc. Eugene Ormandy was excellent in the meshing of signals and few

words. In thirty minutes, he could adjust the orchestra's playing to fit the Interlochen Hall.

*(Butler R. Eitel)*

### The basis for selecting a gesture

People choose a physical gesture, because that's how they do for that particular musical gesture. Instead, they should select a gesture for its application to a particular problem.

*(Gerald Olson)*

## EXAMPLES OF THE USE OF GESTURES

### Gesturing for classroom control

Beginning the year, I gesture "calm down" by moving my hand from one to six o'clock. Most respond, but I would add my voice in a loud but pleasant tone, explaining that we want the most efficient rehearsal we can have. This feeds them positive motivation for what we are doing.

*(George R. Bedell)*

### A non-verbal rehearsal

A non-verbal rehearsal is very simple. At the start, the kids must know the signals. There are few signals they need to know. They are: (1) the number of fingers in the right hand shows the number of measures after the nearest rehearsal letter or number. If the rehearsal letters or numbers are not there and you want to do it on that tune, then put them in. (2) The left hand (number of fingers) shows the number of measures before the rehearsal letter or box. (3) If you want to start at the nearest rehearsal number, put both hands up as if in fists.

I can do this during rehearsal or in the warm up or any time, saying, "This is a non-verbal rehearsal and here is the tune." If we're going to do non-verbal rehearsal, there are objectives within that non-verbal rehearsal. One is to pay attention, the concentration level must be intense. For one thing, you can't get lost, it's forbidden, it's against the law; you've got to pay attention. If kids are not sure where they are, they have to figure out where they are from their part. If some are lost, I'll just keep going back to that number and back to that spot until everybody starts at the right place. If they don't, the other gesture (4) is the left hand in a sweeping circle to the outside. This is a sweeping circle out to the left that tells them to "go back to the beginning or go back to the nearest double bar." If there isn't a double bar, they go to the beginning. (5) If I want to hear a particular person, I point to him with one finger and we don't have to say anything. If I wanted to hear the section, then (6) I give a little sweep with my right hand. The purpose is to create an expression like a segment of a rehearsal where you want to increase their attention. You also use this for an entire rehearsal. I did it for a whole rehearsal once with a wind orchestra. When I came out, my first horn said, "God, am I exhausted! That's just too intense!" The objectives are to increase listening and attention, and, of course, to increase efficiency. In other cases, it simply is to get the students' attention because they're so used to talking from the conductor. If you have any disruptive behavior, non-verbal rehearsals are the approach to use "right off the bat." This also means they soon start straightening up their act, because they don't want to be playing in the wrong place.

*(James Croft)*

### Gesturing in rehearsals

I use gestures to show volume changes and tongue action, and to give many other musical suggestions. I do talk, draw, and gesture; I do this especially with phrasing.

*(Steven Cooper)*

I gesture frequently with a section to remind students. If, for example, the clarinets are sagging or going very flat on their throat tones, I might just point to my chin, as a reminder of an idea I presented earlier.

*(Gerald Olson)*

We reinforce the size of the phrase portions with gestures quite often. We say, "Right here, this is going to be the big part of this phrase. This is how I'm going to look when we get there." Then, I show them a preview with gestures, of how the phrase should be. At the same time I say, "I want you to carry out this crescendo one note farther than you've been playing it."

*(Bryce Taylor)*

I constantly remind my kids of what they're doing and how to do it correctly. For example, if they're puffing their cheeks, I will either point to my cheek or imitate them puffing their cheeks while I'm conducting. I just look at the person, do that and they immediately change.

*(Sandra P. Thompson)*

I show them an accent by simulating punching someone in the stomach. I remind them later of this in rehearsal by making a fist.

*(John W. LaCava)*

To remind them to listen across the room, I make a gesture with my hands that says, "Your ears need to be this big." When I talk about inner rhythm, I sometimes put my hand over my heart, because rhythm is not just in one's head. I'll make a fist and I'll pound it into my other hand, saying "You're playing this." Then, I say "Now I want you

to play like this," and I'll kind of caress my hand. At other times, I'll point at them and then just make a cut sign. They understand what I'm trying to say without me saying anything. That works better with older kids than with younger kids.

*(James Arrowood)*

I also use hand gestures to show them what I mean by staying on top of the sound. For instance, I will show the wrong way to do it by holding my hands, palms toward the sky near my eye level. I'll say, "You must never let the sound get above this." Then, I'll do the opposite. I'll hold my hands out in front of me with my palms down and say, "Always stay on top of the sound, keep it under you, stay in control of it."

To show intonation, I gesture in this way. As we play a unison, I stretch my arms forward together. The left hand palm is up, right hand palm down, with the palms facing each other. "When my hands are together it is in tune, when I draw my hands apart you should stretch it out of tune—either bend up or down—whichever you choose. When I bring my hands back together bring it back in tune."

*(Thomas Stone)*

To convey a sense of pulse and tempo, and have them feel the time physically, I have them do time beating while they sing the line. I teach them how to gesture legato, staccato, marcato—the very basic motions, which they model with their hands or their whole arm movement.

*(L. Keating Johnson)*

### Teaching phrasing and style

When I sing something, a phrase for example, I also gesture or conduct. They both hear and see the way the phrase looks. I gesture with my whole body and I gesture in and outside the conducting patterns. I ask them to sing back, but I do not ask them to gesture back what I did—maybe I should try that also.

*(Patricia Brumbaugh)*

As I teach, I gesture a great deal. I might say, "Play the passage like this (as I gesture or conduct in the style I desire)." Or I say, "If you continue to play that way, I will have to conduct like this (I gesture or conduct in an inappropriate way) so we are compatible. But, I would prefer you played the music like this (I gesture or conduct in the style I wish to hear)."

*(Richard Floyd)*

# CHAPTER THREE

# INVOLVEMENT AND CONCENTRATION

In general, one reason to involve students is simply to keep them busy; the result is a class that is easier to manage. Involvement engages their attention, increases their participation, and keeps them closer to what is going on. Being involved can be its own reward because the student can become interested and be stimulated by the events more of the time.

The most important reason to involve students, of course, is to increase the possibility they will learn. For example, if the entire group becomes occupied with the same rhythm as the clarinets are facing, then all are learning, practicing, and reviewing that rhythm. However, when a problem is found only in one part, some teachers do not involve the others. Such teachers let some students sit idly until all are asked to play again. This rehearsal technique lets some students be inactive and the teacher wastes the learning time of everyone not playing that part.

When a teacher does not use students' time well, class management problems emerge, especially with younger students. Keeping students involved is a challenge to the teacher, but when teachers successfully meet that challenge, more music achievement results and the attitude of the class is apt to be more positive.

## THE VALUE AND NECESSITY OF STUDENT INVOLVEMENT

### The results of involvement

Students are not going to use their ears unless they want to; that is why involvement is necessary. When they become involved, they are more apt to do things and to participate. Almost automatically their ears began to work.

*(Frank Bencriscutto)*

### Their involvement is essential

Two things are very important. One is the atmosphere in the rehearsal and the other is how you create the atmosphere. It all goes back to how they feel about you and their time with you. You can take the time to teach them this kind of warm blooded, positive spirit; and, you can give them a little Socrates. With this approach, they have to answer questions, and be involved and responsible for decision making. I think they respond so much more to this, than to an approach using intimidation. I do not think change in response to intimidation has anything to do with learning.

The more the people making the music are involved in the rehearsal, the more they learn. Furthermore, the more we energize them by having them contribute and think, the more they will choose to be involved.

I try to have them involved with problem solving with whatever musical and technical problems that occur in the rehearsal. If there is a rhythmic problem, instead of just giving an answer I might go through a variety of appropriate things for the particular issue that always involves them.

For example, I might have half the group singing eighth notes and the others clapping the rhythm; or have half the group playing while the other half is singing the subdivision. A snare drum can play subdivisions while the rest of the group moves to the pulse, etc. These are things that in some way involve them.

If nothing else, this makes those who are not playing that particular part realize that at some point they are going to have to comprehend this issue. The maximum gain is in their interest, excitement, and inspiration. I hope that can happen more of the time.

They will go home and they will tell their moms about it. I think it is very important that rehearsal is an exciting, enjoyable thing, and that they will want to come back the next day. The more we involve them in decision making as we guide them, the longer the learning remains, and the more they can transfer it to other situations. It is easy for them to feel used if they are not involved.

With this approach, I think they truly feel that they are in there for the right reason. The idea of their involvement is a very basic premise of mine. Their sharing of responsibility really makes a big difference. A conductor can fool himself by believing the conductor is the only person hearing what is happening in the rehearsal. They will be incorrect if they think that the kids cannot hear.

*(Larry Rachleff)*

## Physical and vocal activity

At any age, the more physically active students are, the better. That is one reason I often have string players stand up. This is basic: I believe that they need to develop a good sitting posture. They do practice standing but when they sit everything collapses.

I also have them shout/count aloud when they have rests, because that is the time when they often get lost. They count 1 2 3 4, 2 2 3 4, 3 2 3 4, etc. Even when they have a quarter rest, they have to say, for example, "3." They must shout the rests as they play pianissimo and sometimes when they play pizzicato. I want them to really "stamp verbally" on the rests. This sharpens their rhythm more than anything I have ever done.

My discovery, belatedly, is that they always get lost and lax when they have a rest. That is when they are not alive! All groups need this, the young kids love it, but I do this with college students even if they don't like to do this.

*(Pamela Gearhart)*

## The necessity of involvement

With rhythm, melody, phrasing, harmony, and the entire experience, I find that students are often "on the outside looking in." Too often, they are not involved players. Too many people don't get emotionally and physically involved with music making.

My *Lyric Dance* seems a vehicle for getting the entire group to feel something physically, to involve them. First, I have them tap, count and clap the basic bossa-nova rhythms. I also may have half of the band clap on pulses, if they cannot clap, count, and tap their feet at the same time. The other half of the group counts and claps the rhythm patterns, then we switch parts on cue. It is interesting how often I hear students trying to play those patterns and not playing them accurately. They have not dealt with them in both an intellectual and a physical way.

Students solve problems when they become honestly involved; then, they become the sound. When they become the sound, they will solve other things, such as centering the sound; when they become the harmony, they begin to solve balance and proportions; when they become the melody, they begin to play more in tune.

*(Frank Bencriscutto)*

With all students, I like to use students in the decision making process, which establishes my and their credibility with a growing mutual respect for judgment. They must believe in the conductor, which is built over the years as one makes judgments about sound. The judgments may be about how to do a phrase, where we go on a trip, or what we will play at contest. This mutual respect is built in a number of ways: sincerity, making good decisions with reasons and rationale, listening to suggestions, listening to their input, willing to admit the teacher can make a mistake because many kids cannot be fooled—they know if they were told the wrong thing. The mistakes, if hidden and not admitted, will destroy your credibility with the group also.

*(Robert Floyd)*

## Make music meaningful

The crux of being a band, orchestra, or chorus director is to get the kids excited about the music that's in front of them. Many band directors make mistakes when they do not ask the kids, "Are you enjoying this piece, do you like the music we are doing?"

If we are working on *The Barber of Seville*, there are reasons I will have picked that piece of music then. It's our job to do more than play through the piece blandly, get the notes right, develop the expression and whatever; it's our job to get the kids extremely excited about playing. If it's a phrase, then it's a phrase. If it's the entire line, it's the entire line. If it's the entire composition, it's the entire composition.

I doubt if I play a concert, even with my little kids in seventh grade band, where they aren't involved in practically every piece. When we have read through pieces once or twice, I will simply ask a show of hands. How many of you really enjoy this? How many of you don't enjoy it? How many of you feel medium about it? Give the kids the feeling they have some input.

I have found that the sensitivities in the intellect of the students are very positive. There are very few times they don't vote almost exactly the way I would if I were voting for the piece. Some teachers might fear they are going to vote for rock and roll. I think that popular and "now music" can be a strong part of the curriculum. I think there are popular or show tunes that have a place in the curriculum.

The kids need to play some things they have heard—we must be realistic too. If you look at my programs over the years, you will say, "How do you get a junior high band to play it that way?" My kids gobble it up because they have the chance to put some input into the choice.

*(William Long)*

## INVOLVEMENT OF STUDENTS

### Keeping all the members of a group involved

Having the musicians "hiss" the eighth note pulse during measures of rest helps keep students (young ones in particular) involved in the music-making process. Using this technique encourages them to remain a part of the ensemble and stay "pulse conscious" when they have rests. I sometimes vary this technique by having students count measures of rest by saying "1 and 2 and" rhythmically, rather than counting "1, 2, 3, 4," alone in a nonrhythmic fashion.

*(Richard Floyd)*

### Holding to standards

A teacher must know what support, precision, intonation, listening, breathing, sound, duration, release, phrasing, crescendo, diminuendo, etc. are. If so, they can increase the involvement of students by asking for higher standards in any of these. With the striving for standards, the students often become more involved. This can increase motivation because it increases the students' effort. The effort involves them and can lead to satisfaction, competency, awareness, insight, and recognition. This works, in part, because many students do want to please the teacher, accept the teacher's standards, or exert effort because of many other things such as habit, achievement, pride, self-interest, grades, or values.

*(Joseph L. Casey)*

### Involving all the group in rhythmic skill learning

I try to involve the whole group in counting, clapping, and singing if one section is having problems. I try not to have the remainder of the group just sitting there. It's very important to involve some of the group who can set the tempo of the main pulse. Another part of the group can be using a different kind of sound or playing on one pitch or unit—all kinds of things.

*(Robert Levy)*

### Involving junior high students

Too many bands have too many members sitting with nothing to do while the director works with one section. One way to avoid this is to drill or teach everyone the same thing at the same time, whenever possible. If this cannot be done, then I instruct them in what they are to do when I am working on something else. For example, if one section of the band is working on something that cannot be done with the entire group, the other members:

1. Clap the pulse or subdivision accurately but lightly.
2. While keeping the pulse, play their parts silently.
3. Tongue/whisper/blow the rhythm of their part(s).
4. Sway or otherwise move to the pulse in an unobtrusive way.

*(Jack Brookshire)*

### Involving them through demonstration

We should spend more time in front of the group demonstrating with our instrument. This immediately attracts the attention of the group to something that needs to be done. Showing and demonstrating appeals to the curiosity of the group and it is very valuable for their aural adjustment.

The point is, one has to keep involving them; one should not just be telling or correcting them. Involving them is part of the constant adjustment during the rehearsal. Involving them needs to be taking place through demonstration, showing, or making other adjustments. This approach is appealing to their curiosity and stimulating to their brain.

*(Frederick Fennell)*

### Involving students in all aspects of the performance

College students see, perhaps even resent, that the conductor gets all the applause. They feel they do all the work. Students want to be more involved in planning shows, running rehearsals, etc. Most of us could involve students more than we do. They can help create a half-time show; even though it takes more time with their input, they can help chart it and suggest ideas.

Students run most sectionals three or four times a week in marching band, where we work primarily on the music. The teachers work with the section leaders and we have students appointed to do this, with others to assist them. We do the same in the concert band. The students appreciate the responsibility, they like to believe that we have confidence in them. We try to leave them alone and let them make mistakes.

The students who gain this experience become the better band directors when they graduate, instantly successful while others take three or four years to reach the same level of effectiveness. It is a good teaching decision.

I give out responsibilities in relation to the amount of experiences they have. The entire band has sub-leaders on instruments and rank leaders in charge of twelve with assistants in charge of six. Sophomores begin as rank leaders. In concert band there is neither time nor opportunity to do this, other than the defined section leaders.

*(Robert E. Foster)*

### Increasing involvement through the director's personality

I try to be an actor, sometimes pleading, sometimes demanding. I may be sarcastic, I may be anything necessary. I find this out by reading them. Often it's sarcastic. Often times it's, "We are the Bozeman Junior High School Symphonic Band. We are that, and you are not living up to tradition." It may be anything. It may be, "Come on guys, we can do it better, you can get it fixed right this instant, Come on, commmme——ON!" I may do or be anything, a cheerleader, or an Old Testament prophet.

*(William Long)*

## INVOLVEMENT THROUGH RESPONSIBILITY

### Students helping students

Use the good students in the group as examples and sometimes as teachers. A kid with an exceptional talent who is in all-state groups often can help a third clarinet that's really having a struggle. It is also a good experience to help the slower one.

*(Donald Wilcox)*

### Increasing responsibility for intonation

I try as quickly as I can to transfer the responsibility of intonation to the students with their understanding, of course, that it's always my ultimate responsibility. After we get into the school year a bit, I have the section leaders at sixth, seventh, and eighth grade do their own tuning. They also tune the section themselves. I tune the section leaders to each other by ear until I'm satisfied that they're tuned to each other.

Then, they just go down the line. Between the section leader and each kid, they decide. I simply sit. When they get done tuning, we go back and I say, "Let's see how we did." We go down the line and I let the other people in the section judge. We involve the other kids in listening and making comments and recommendations.

There again, I'm transferring the responsibility of intonation to the student. They make the adjustments and I encourage them always. I want them, in rehearsal and even between numbers in performance, to constantly evaluate their pitch. If they feel uncomfortable with their pitch, they let me know. Often in a rehearsal, I'll stop the band when one of them sticks their hand up and says, "I'm not in tune." I will say, "Let's check it." We'll get the section leader to play the note, and then they'll play the note. Sometimes they're all right. I say, "Your pitch is right but you must adjust within the chord or within the line. Because you're playing a first and third valve D and that note is going to be sharp, you also might need to adjust."

I have had students in concert between numbers that have caught my eye and said, "I'm not in tune." If they do that, I never will push them off or say, "Don't worry about that, we're in a performance now." If it's important enough to them to let me know they don't feel comfortable with pitch, we'll tune right between numbers. We'll pick out two or three kids and tune between numbers. If it's important enough for them to let me know they don't feel comfortable with the tune, then it's important to me to see that I can help them.

*(Ross A. Leeper)*

### A band officer system

This began many years ago and it is just wonderful. Their job is to do everything possible except those musical aspects I do from the podium. They take care of announcements, band social events, band picnics, Halloween and Christmas parties, and helping freshmen get organized. They get a chance to practice being in a leadership role, which is very important for them later as teachers or as professionals. For example, officers schedule sectionals if needed. They run the sectionals though we might discuss what needs to be done during our noon meetings. I meet with these officers over lunch before rehearsals whenever we need to plan for or work on things. I do this to direct their efforts, to hear their ideas and concerns, etc.

*(Miles Johnson)*

### Developing responsibility through a small ensemble program

The ensembles had one rehearsal with me and one on their own. At recital time, the students arranged for school announcements, the school and community papers, invitations, arrangements for the room and piano, performance dress, music faculty schedules (to be certain we were free), etc. They also arranged for recording the performance, if they wanted that.

*(Donald DeRoche)*

## INVOLVEMENT THROUGH A VARIETY OF TECHNIQUES

### Teaching style

One really has to use all sorts of teaching techniques because of all the entertainment students have thrown at them. One result is that one must stimulate them constantly; their attention span is simply not long and they cannot maintain it unless there is a lot of stimulation.

*(Judith A. Niles)*

### Making the routine interesting

I do little "routine" skill building because I did not like it as a student. Probably I knew what was coming and it was not, therefore, very interesting. I resented that approach. We do play scales, but I have an aversion to being in a routine and do not do this to the students. I like things to move fast, in an interesting manner, and do different things every day.

*(Patricia Brumbaugh)*

### Engaging attention

As soon as we play two or three notes of the B-flat scale, I figure out the state of their attention individually and as a group. I decide how to mix up the way we play the B-flat scale. I make changes to engage their mind as quickly as possible. This is to get them to listen, play and watch. We might play a fermata on the third degree of the scale and I change things particularly if they come in especially distracted. I may do different attacks or cutoffs, then a different volume or dynamic change. I try to get their attention focused upon the music instantly. After getting everyone's attention, which usually occurs by the end of the scale, I will say one word: "D flat please." Then we will go on with that scale, instead of B flat.

*(Patricia Brumbaugh)*

### Concentrating on sound alone

I ask students to practice sometimes in a totally dark room. This helps them concentrate completely upon what they really sound like. This is not the same as recording one's self, but has a similar purpose.

*(Dwaine Nelson)*

### Listing pieces in a stimulating way

One can list pieces by keys or meters. For example, the rehearsal order list might be: B-flat major, e minor, and

D-flat major. Listing compositions this way also tells something about the piece other than just the title.

*(Thomas H. Cook)*

### Provide scores during rehearsal

I often had about a half-dozen scores for each piece we were doing. I gave these to players in rehearsals who did not have a lot to do. This definitely contributed to their development, particularly of my percussion section. I also would give the score to players who needed to become more involved with the band, sometimes because their part had less to do and partly to encourage involvement. I never did it only to keep a kid busy when, for example, they had a lot of measures to count. With a score, they get involved more easily and they learn something about the score while doing it.

Sometimes, I would give the score to one member of a section and ask them to watch instead of play. Regularly, I would select two or three students in rehearsals to go out in the auditorium to listen either with their part or with a score. Some kids notice nothing and some notice a lot. It is useful to give them just a few things to listen for, perhaps two to six things to listen for. I also would give individual students things to listen for depending upon their experience.

Sometimes it might only be, "Tell me when such and such happens," or "After the trumpet starts who has the same thing later." After two or three years of this, the questions can be more general. One could work out the program based upon which year they were in band. Select something different for the first-year kid to listen for compared to what the second-year kid could do.

*(Frank Battisti)*

### Using questioning

Instead of telling, ask questions. This hits the old problem of "I can't play and listen too!" I say, "I am sorry you have to do both." I may ask, for example, "What is out of tune in this chord? Why did I stop? What was wrong? Should we try that again? Can you tell me who has a parallel line with you? Who has an answering phrase to you?" Or, "Can the third horn sing the viola part?" The brass plays and I say to the second violins, "Tell me, what did Borodin write dynamically for the brass?"

All this makes them more active instead of passive. This may be difficult, but take a measure or passage so they have a chance to find it. For example, one can take a cadence measure and find the moving line that controls the ritard, and ask "who has it?" They look at you blankly and want you to tell them. If so, do it again so they can hear. Ask them to look for it with their eyes. If you keep at it, they will begin to hear things and the light goes on!

*(Pamela Gearhart)*

### Using movement with a fugue

It is wonderful to work with a fugue. I have had

students stand up to play when they have the subject, sit when they don't. They also can play the subject arco, and episodes and countersubjects pizzicato. Or, everything marked forte will be played standing, (except cellos, who can make some gesture in this direction!). Anything less than forte they sit, and on a crescendo they gradually stand up. This technique uses their kinesthetic experience, which can make them aware of who plays the different parts, as well as gets them to be alive, attentive, focused, awake, alert, seated properly, etc.

*(Pamela Gearhart)*

### A suggestion box

In high school, I would ask them write anonymous critiques of anything that they thought we could improve.

*(Robert Allan)*

### Engaging students in decisions

I may ask, "Let's do some exploration here." I'll ask a person, "How do you feel about this line? Why don't you play this, why don't you express this line the way you feel it and the way that you feel it should go?" I can find a volunteer, because there always is a volunteer who is willing to take a chance and do it in their own way. This engages the creativity of the people as I ask others to offer different ideas.

I try to teach them the phrase's direction toward tension or away from tension. We can use tenuto, articulations, syncopations, tempo changes such as accelerando, ritardando, and rubato. We can use agogic accents, different articulations, or obviously we can use dynamics. We can do all those things to find the phrasing.

What's curious about those things, and what I teach, is that many things are not written into the music. If they were, you couldn't decipher them all because the notation would be so complex and dense.

*(Craig Kirchhoff)*

### Involvement through composing

I enjoyed getting these kids to think creatively. We worked on composing a Rondo in band and they had a good time. We developed the Rondo theme together and I wrote it on the board. It was an eight-bar theme that we could all live with. We then divide into different sections and studied a little bit about the different key areas that could be explored and what the episodes could be like. Some groups even created the harmonies. They took the bull by the horns and came up with some wild things. If the Rondo was at all palatable, we put the composition on a program.

*(Timothy Mahr)*

### Involvement through social events

To continue getting a big volunteer pep band, we went to what we call a "pep band pot luck." Kids like this because they like parties. We made it more of a social thing and kids could bring their friends. For many years we were sustaining the volunteer pep band with the pot luck, and with the kids and their honor. We said, "If you don't have anything or if you aren't required someplace else tonight, we expect you to be there."

*(Frank Schulz)*

### Getting to know students

A score study gathering is a chance to relate that to their real life situation; they don't just experience the music in rehearsal. Every summer I teach a high school camp and it's fun to sit around in the right setting, which usually has food and a relaxed atmosphere, and have them talk about what they think of a piece. Lots of times they'll say, "Yea, it reminds me of this rock group" or "It reminds me of whatever." I'll say, "Well that's interesting, tell us about it." Eventually I can spark an interest.

*(William W. Wiedrich)*

### Talk about the music

Some pieces have a story line. When kids have some idea what is going on, there is a big difference in their performance. If we are doing *Elsa's Procession into the Cathedral* and they don't know anything about who Elsa is, why she's going, or its all going to blow up in smoke, and her husband's leaving and going back to Walhalla and everything else, they could miss so much of the inside stuff in this piece.

I have also compared the leitmotif idea to John Williams' *Star Wars* where he is using the themes for the various characters. That's an excellent way to teach the idea. I tell them, "You know, John Williams didn't think this up folks. This is Wagner from the word go and he's got all kinds of operas put together the same way. You can follow the plot just by listening to the music."

I tell them anything interesting about the music to get them away from thinking music is simply a stack of notes. I talk about the form, composer, the time, and anything interesting to make the tune a little more real for them. For example, "Did you know why Bilek's *Civil War Fantasy* is eleven minutes long? It was written, originally for half time shows. Jerry did this while we were all in Michigan Band. The half-time show was so well received that he did a concert version that we did on tour that spring. It wound up selling like crazy." I also say, "Jerry was a trombone player, which is why the trombones have all the good licks at the beginning and the end." The kids respond to

that, even if the talk takes only thirty seconds. It makes it a little more interesting to them and a little more of a real piece.

*(Donald Wilcox)*

### Involving students with a composer or arranger

Get the kids in direct contact with the person who wrote the music. I called Jerry Goldsmith once and he said, "Sure, I'll come down to Long Beach and talk about my music." We were doing his *The Man From Uncle* in a marching show. He came to the game and conducted his piece from the sidelines. The crowd liked it and the kids had the chance to talk to him.

He told some of them about the recording business and it was really special for kids to hear him do that. We have had Copland and Husa on our campus. With Husa, we were doing *Apotheosis*. In my rehearsals, one of the horn players was complaining about all those little soft horn rips. One horn said, "I didn't practice for twelve years to learn to play stupid noises." They had been giving me a bad time about this.

As they got to that spot in the music, Husa said, "I apologize for writing something so atypical for the French horn. That was the closest I could find in any of the instruments that could simulate the sound that hump-backed whales make when they are frightened." He said, "That's the sound of whales crying." All the horn players said, "aaaawwwwwwww" and they just played their little hearts out from then on. The idea of why it was in there and what it meant was very impressive to them. Suddenly, it was not only all right, it was wonderful!

When I was in Anaheim, Jim Ployhar was spending a semester in Anaheim while on a sabbatical from his school in North Dakota. While there, he would bring scores to Anaheim High School that we would read through—we just had a great time doing that.

This was one of the high points in the learning experience for those kids. It was the first time they had ever been in direct contact with the guy who wrote the notes and it really just thrilled them to death. They would say, "You mean there really is somebody who decides this is going to be a G#, and writes it down and we play it. Really, somebody decided that and that's you, right?" He was so patient and such a caring teacher that the kids in my band just loved him, they would have followed him all the way back to North Dakota.

*(Donald Wilcox)*

# Chapter Four

# Rapport and Camaraderie

An unmistakable concern for the teacher's relationship to his students is the recurring, underlying constant throughout these comments. For many reasons, teachers seek to develop closeness, involvement, and communication with students. Some teachers are motivated for humanistic reasons, simply for the good of students as people; some build rapport to help the ensemble progress by increasing the teacher's influence upon ensemble members. To this end, rapport can influence students to willingly adopt the values and exert the effort that teachers hold for music, education, conduct, or relationships.

Rapport and camaraderie can unify social groups of diverse population and purposes, such as families, athletic teams, office workers, old whittlers, and stamp collectors; it is no different with music ensembles and music classes. The presence of rapport and camaraderie is an important aspect of all successful social groups. The rapport among the group members benefits the individual member by giving him satisfaction and a sense of community; the presence of rapport benefits the entire social group by strengthening its bonds and thereby helping the social group attain its goals.

Thus in the music ensemble, rapport among members helps both the students and the ensemble to perform the music well. As the relationship of student to student and conductor to student improves, their efforts can result, for example, in closer attention to precision, style, phrasing, intonation, and blend. The building of rapport can help an ensemble go beyond unity in just technical matters, however. Rapport promotes an emotional bonding among its members, helping the group to perform with true musical significance, which can provide for a true aesthetic experience for students. A group with good rapport may achieve and gain satisfaction to a greater degree than one lacking rapport. This also is true with professional groups, though with their highly developed skills, their performance level may remain high even when a group has poor rapport. With a student group, however, rapport is crucial: the rapport may ultimately be as important as their skill in helping them perform well and experience the music aesthetically.

## The Value of Rapport

### Rapport is a necessity

I feel very strongly that I should be involved with my students. They are important to me and if they know you think they're important, they're just going to give you so much more musically.

Music is a sharing experience and we cannot be up there, with them down there. There are too many guys putting a screen between themselves and the group. They may look wonderful up there conducting up a storm, but there is no osmosis, there is no communication going on.

*(Richard J. Suddendorf)*

### Rapport sets a climate

It is tough to get people to be musically expressive. They must be brave enough to be expressive or have enough self confidence to try out a musically expressive idea in front of their peers. This is a tough thing for many students to do. Teaching a person to be musically expressive seems unrelated to playing expertise at all, but it is more related to their trust in the teacher: the teacher must set up the kind of environment where trying-out choices can be done successfully.

*(L. Keating Johnson)*

The kids one works with every day have to trust you. Part of this whole musical art is that it can change from performance to performance and from rehearsal to rehearsal. To do this, they must have enough trust internally to feel and believe that whatever they're doing is worthwhile to the group. The teacher has to foster that.

What works for me with high school and university students, is to set up a different aspect of, "Sure, I'm the big out-of-town guest conductor, but . . . ." A teacher may have a position of power, but they still must show they are a human-kind of person before students will trust you. They have to see some facet that can be, for example, humorous or can be silly. If I can work it in, the fastest way for me with honor groups or guest conducting, is to make some kind of joke about my baldness.

They see that I can laugh, be human, or something.

Then when I ask them to do what they feel is an outlandish phrasing on a piece, they can laugh about it. Soon they can try different ways and trust me with whatever they do even if they might think it is silly. They conclude that I am not a nasty adult that says, "Stop that, you're being silly." If they trust you or feel that you are human, then they usually will be more expressive. They also will put more effort into the endeavor.

*(L. Keating Johnson)*

The building of good relationships is primary. I know all the students by name and they come by my office anytime. There was a New York Times article on a conductor where it was stated that a conductor often is a confidante, a mother, whatever; I think I am wrapped up in that.

*(Richard J. Suddendorf)*

### Rehearsal communication

I use names and get to know each person as fast as I can. I like to use their names in rehearsal, but I also spend some time with them out of rehearsal finding out what they're up to.

The teacher must have a personal rapport and trust with everyone. Sometimes you're putting people on the spot when rehearsing a section or a few individuals. When this happens or something doesn't go right, you can say, "That's all right, let's just try again. Let's be a little more extrovert, do this a bit more."

I want them to feel that whatever they do is worthwhile. They may not have just played a passage the ideal way, that happens during a normal growth process. On the other hand, I never define what they played as wrong. I also watch the approval I give. I can't tell them that was the world's greatest version; but I can be supportive and positive. Somehow, I can reinforce that what they're doing is good, except not quite. We all know it's not what we want; but, at least, the three players and I are coming to some consensus. That's part of calling them by name also, I can reinforce them by referring to them by name.

*(L. Keating Johnson)*

Somebody may raise their hand and say, "This G is out of tune, can we tune it?" I have always encouraged that and still do. I then can say, "What can I do to make this a little easier. What do you need here?" I encourage that because that's what you need to know.

*(John Williamson)*

### Interaction in the rehearsal

I expect something coming from them, and I hope they expect something coming from me. I'm not only a metronome up there.

Rehearsal is a sharing experience and they are the metronomes, they are the inner pulse.

*(Richard J. Suddendorf)*

### Maintaining communication

If someone comes in late to a rehearsal, I would not address them about this in a rehearsal. I might talk to them about this afterward, or they'll come by later and give me the reason for being late.

*(Richard J. Suddendorf)*

## THE INFLUENCE OF THE TEACHER

### The conductor's charge

We need to know everything about music and people. The personal relationship of the conductor to the people brings out a warmer musical expression, a communicative style of playing. I try to be as personal as I can. This is easier in schools, since one gets to know kids and their families from the grades on up. In the college scene I have to work a lot harder at it.

To develop this personal communication or relationship I may, for example, have them remove their stands from between them and me during the warm up. They set them to the sides so we have a conscious and direct contact. I try to look at every person during the warm up especially if we don't have music in front of us. I look them right in the eye and have them look at me. I can sometimes sense if they are having a bad day and when they are not. I can decide if I can challenge them or not. I think this first needs to be done in the warm up, before they put black and white music between us.

If there is something positive, I use their name: if there is something that needs improvement, I use their instrument. I break this rule a lot, like all conductors do, but I try this so they do not take negative things as personally. For example, if there is need to improve the cymbal sound, I say, "Percussion, could you get a more shimmering sound," or "Mallets, could you try for a lighter sound—maybe different mallets would work?" or, "Could the percussion show more color and less volume?" I do this rather than say "Dave, could you play the crash at letter B right on the beat, not late?" Though if the crash is fine, then I might say "Dave, that was excellent at B!"

*(Richard K. Hansen)*

### Increasing the influence of the conductor

The conductor can influence or create a good atmosphere. Students must respect you as a musician. This comes from the kinds of music you select and how you approach the music in rehearsal. Do you approach music technically, or expressively? The latter makes the music rehearsal more satisfying.

*(Richard Fischer)*

### The first impression

About first impressions, for example, remember that when you come into that class for the first time, you are making some first impressions. First, kids believe what you say. Make sure that what you say will be correct forever. I think that your first appearance should be inviting but not too enthusiastic. The too enthusiastic person can lose control. In addition, you show too much, it might scare the students and disrupt their equilibrium. One must realize that care about first impressions applies beyond the first rehearsal. It applies to each rehearsal of the year, not only the first one with a new group.

*(James Croft)*

### Talking with students

It is appalling to hear how some band directors talk to students. I do not like to hear the teacher get upset, and yell and scream. I do not think students will respond well to that. Precede a criticism with at least a hint of a compliment.

*(John Kinnison)*

### Expectations in the rehearsal and lessons

I treat students with respect and I treat them the way I would want to be treated. However, they do know that when they walk into that classroom, from the time they sit in their chairs until when they leave, they are there to learn. There's absolutely no doubt what's going to be happening in the classroom. I expect and I command well-disciplined groups. I mean, you can hear a pin drop in my room. Everybody asks me how do I do that and I tell them that I expect it.

*(Sandra P. Thompson)*

We have a respectful relationship so if I'm talking in rehearsal, they're not talking. If they talk, then I will listen to show a mutual respect. There is no talking, but there is interaction. Rapport is very important and I respect them as people. I want them to respect me. I enjoy immensely that students will come by and talk to me about personal problems.

*(Richard J. Suddendorf)*

### Rapport in college, compared with high school

It is very difficult for college directors to lose the one-on-one contact they had in pre-college music teaching. In college it is easier for our understanding and interest in each kid to wane. We can lose the concern we feel for their progress, because we see less of them.

*(Hal D. Cooper)*

In college I can do things the high school teacher does not have the opportunity to do, such as attend the students' recitals and programs. In high school it is much more self-contained.

*(Michael Haithcock)*

### Being human

I make students and their parents realize that I'm a human being with everything else that happens. At the end

of the year, we do a concert that is traditionally light music. At this concert I sometimes do crazy stuff, I mean absolutely crazy.

One year I acted the part of Superman and I practiced for a month before the concert. The kids do not see my new act until the day before. The kids and the audience just loved it. I have a friend who is a professional clown on the weekends, and I once planned to use him.

Once, I had hoped to bring in a real horse and do the Lone Ranger. My administration said, "Absolutely not! Superman you can get away with, but you are not bringing a live horse into this gym." Maybe they'd love an elephant more, I don't know. I run into former students who said, "You know what? I will never forget that we played such and such music and we did such and such. I will never forget being in band, it was one of the greatest experiences I had in junior high."

I thought, "Well hey! If acting crazy helped to do that, that's okay." We also did the Concerto for three kazoos in band. The audience and the kids loved it, and kids are going to practice their music that much harder.

*(Sandra P. Thompson)*

We have auditions and I know who the better players are. Even so, I rotate parts continually to put persons, who are not necessarily the better players, into positions of responsibility when I feel they can meet the responsibility. They thrive on this and don't feel we take advantage of them.

*(Michael Haithcock)*

## BUILDING RAPPORT

### Relating to students

We rosin bows together as we begin class. We choose the number of times that we want to pull the bow hairs over the rosin. We count together. At the end we add "one for good luck, one for Mr. Jones (the teacher) and one for everyone at home." At this point, we talk about what has been on the student's mind that day.

*(Marion Etzel)*

What is the atmosphere in the rehearsal and how does one create the atmosphere? How do they feel about you and their time with you? Take the time to teach them with this kind of warm blooded, positive spirit. They will respond if you are giving them a little Socrates, where they have to answer these questions, become involved and be responsible for decision making. They respond much more to this climate than a climate where intimidation reigns.

*(Larry Rachleff)*

I say, "I need more from you, you're important to this ensemble." I know we have a person playing principal chair, I understand that. I don't treat the students that way. I think we've got to get away from the principal player idea. As we do, this helps the student playing eighth-chair third clarinet to feel more significant. Otherwise they can conclude, if they aren't playing the important parts, they can get by playing third less carefully. Even if I find this is hard or impossible to do always, I think it is important.

*(Richard J. Suddendorf)*

I go to rehearsals fifteen minutes early. I am there when they come in, make small talk, and ask how things are going. I might talk about the student newspaper or a concert the night before. The result is that they feel they know me as a person who is a conductor. I am not one who is comfortable with the maestro image.

*(Michael Haithcock)*

At least ten minutes before rehearsal starts, I'll move around the room. If I see new first-year students in the clarinet section, I'll go back and I'll talk to them. That is the way I get to know them. They feel better about being in a new situation.

*(Richard J. Suddendorf)*

I try to create on a day-to-day basis, no matter where they are sitting, a feeling that they can drop in on me. They can ask my advice, ask my help, ask for input, and I can talk about some of the same things with them. If I ask a trombone how the clarinets did, he may give me an answer that I had not expected or was looking for. When he does answer, I have to respond by saying, "That's right, I had not thought of that."

If one does that, they all sit up a little more, take notice, lean forward, etc. Then, when I really need them to do something, when it is the week before the concert, when I get picky and demanding with performance stuff, then the relationship of trust and working together is there. When we play a concert and it is terrific—it is great; but, if we do not have one of our better nights, or when an individual does not have one of their best nights, we are not standing around saying, "what if?"

The worst feeling that anyone can have, after or during a performance, is the feeling of "what if?" It isn't productive to feel "what if we had worked a little harder, what if we had practiced more or, what if she had done that better?" I do not want anyone going into or out of a performance feeling that way. I would prefer they feel good about the process they have been going through. I want them to enjoy the moment.

*(Michael Haithcock)*

Junior high students have a special antenna. If you don't capture them, you will die! The keys with kids, especially junior high, are to be honest, fair, available, and to develop the "secret rapport" between you and them.

*(Robert Allan)*

On the podium, I try not to use first names or any of their names. I will talk to the low brass or I will talk about the first trombones. I talk this way to treat everyone alike. I try to remember to avoid getting personal or hurting their feelings.

I might say, "First trombones that was awful, play that part in tune." I try not to say, "Dwayne, you're out of tune." I'll say, "First trumpets, you're too loud." Off the podium I'll always use the first names. If someone's had a good day and it's been a good rehearsal, then I might say in front of the group, "Susy, you really played well today." I use the name instead of saying, "The first clarinetist played exceptionally well today."

*(Dwayne P. Sagen)*

### Keeping a student diary

I asked sections or individuals to keep a book, a diary or a self report. They described everything they listened to, read, and anything else they might want me to know. I read them every week. This occurred with junior high and high school students, not as much with fifth and sixth graders. Since the older kid is more independent, their independent choices were the key to my understanding them.

The diary revealed the thoughts or information they chose to include. Their diaries showed their choice of the kinds of music and also included personal things. This was purely voluntary, yet ninety percent of them did it. I would try to respond to each student each week in relation to something they said. If I read something of serious nature such as things related to their family or psychological concerns, I find a way to respond to these seriously and quickly.

There were different sections in the book. Some sections showed something like—how many minutes did you use a strobe, problems with pieces and instruments, progress playing lip slurs or with technical practice. The issue varied from day to day or week to week.

*(Frank Battisti)*

### Learning about each student

I have the kids in the band fill out a three-by-five inch card. This is a big band program and it's hard to know all of them as well as I would like. The card asked for their name, social security number, home address, and serial number of their instrument. There is a spot for their parent's name in case I need to get hold of them. I ask them to attach a graduation picture or snapshot. When they come in the band room for the first time, I can put a name with a face.

On the back they could volunteer information. I had an interest in such things as what their parents do for a living, how long they lived in the town they came from, did they go to a big high school or a little one, and what other interests they had such as, did they like to race motorcycles, collect stamps or what? Then, there were open-ended questions like, "What interests do you have that are not readily apparent?" With these general interest things, I can find out a little bit more about the kid. "Do you come from a big family or a small one" or "what sort of background do you come from?" Just nosey questions that most of the kids answered, though some students do not give an answer to that. The whole idea of having them fill out information cards is fun.

Once I had a father call me in a panic after he talked to his daughter. Apparently, she had just flunked an exam in another class, and was afraid she was going to flunk out. He was afraid she was suicidal and said, "I don't know anybody at that University, or even within a hundred miles of there to call except you." I said, "Okay, I'll get on it." I found she was extremely upset, but not suicidal.

*(Donald Wilcox)*

### Building rapport through social events

In high school teaching, we had parties at our home for different sections at different times. When we had the horn teacher there, we had horn recordings, etc. We continue this practice in college where we have section parties nearly every fall weekend with the marching band. There may be a tuba party one week and a flute party the next. They do it for themselves, but they "allow" outsiders. We did this to give the kids an identity as a section and as a band. This can feature the kids and give them a sense of being important.

Sometimes, each section even has their own t-shirts printed up. Kids do not mind working hard, if they play hard too. Marching band is not different from wind ensemble, except in that they spend much more time together. The groups that spend the most time together, get the closest. As a result, the wind ensemble people may form fewer close associations than marching band people.

*(Robert E. Foster)*

### Building rapport and tradition

For years, my wife and I have had a spring-time, full sit-down dinner for all graduating seniors. We also build tradition and rapport through our Alumni Concert. For the Alumni Concert, the seniors pick the pieces and they often conduct pieces. This has worked wonderfully for years.

*(Miles Johnson)*

### Developing credibility

One way to develop rapport very quickly when guest conducting is to pick a slow piece or a march and do some extreme dynamic changes. If they respond and make a dynamic change that sounds very good, they begin to believe in the conductor. Thus, the conductor has to set the stage to develop rapport.

*(L. Keating Johnson)*

### Using humor to build rapport

Once, I lay on the floor to show a student where he is looking when I am trying to cue him! Another time I said, "I need to get a tall ladder for those who look to the heavens for my cues."

*(Anthony J. Maiello)*

I have used random seating, but in a different way. What I would do is seat kids according to whose birthdays are between January and July. The seating is random, so you can split them up into one, two, or three groups depending on how you split the birth dates. This just breaks up what they expect of a band director.

*(Marguerite G. Wilder)*

Sometimes I will ask an individual player if he can sing the line of the person next to him. I tell him that if he can, I will buy him a milk shake.

*(John Anderson)*

# CHAPTER FIVE

# GAMES

Games can effectively motivate students during learning, particularly middle school and junior high school students. Games can lend variety to the class and introduce excitement because of the spirit of competition. A game can be exciting because the challenge is always in the nature of the game itself. Students respond with enthusiasm to the challenges, questions, or puzzles they are trying to solve.

Some of the suggestions in this section are games in the common sense of the word. These games have rules, prizes, and procedures. Others suggestions are more "game-like" activities. There may not be prizes and rules; however, the learning activity still has some aspects of puzzles, competition, and challenges that students like to try mastering.

## The value of games

Students like any kind of game used in instruction. Through games, they reveal a lot about how they think and act.

*(Anthony J. Maiello)*

## Long-tone contests

As soon as beginners can make a decent sound, which occurs about three or four pages into the book, I start using long tones and long tone contests with them. Some instruments cannot compete with others. A flute cannot win a long tone contest against a trumpet. I say, "Who is going to be king (or queen) of the brass section today?"

*(Jack Brookshire)*

## Ensemble awareness

I frequently do pitch awareness exercises in warm up. One is to play a unison reference tone in tune. First, I select some individuals to play high or low compared to the reference tone. Then, I ask the rest of the group to identify the students who played either high or low. When I do this, I could count off the members in numbers from one to twenty. I call the number of those who are to play flat or sharp. The group tries to identify who they were.

Another variation is to have individuals play a different pitch, one very high or very low. Ask the others

to identify who changed pitches; and which way the pitch changed. Was the pitch higher or lower than the reference pitch? For less experienced players, have everyone pick their favorite note, but not a B-flat concert. The others are to decide if the person next to them was higher or lower, or if they have the same note as you. Another exercise for less experienced players is to ask everyone to play any pitch of the B-flat major chord. Ask others to tell which pitches others played on either side, and front and back.

*(John Anderson)*

## Alternating singing and playing

We play and sing chorales and scales. We do considerable singing and rarely play four scales in a row without singing. We also do scales in three parts. Students come in successively, ending up with three-part harmony. They sing/play individual notes, the entire scale, whatever. Mostly we alternate singing one or more notes with playing these notes. This leads to chorale playing. On other days, we work on singing and playing intervals. We use the solfege system with this. At the end of the year, either of the bands could take a sight-singing test on all the perfect and major (diatonic) intervals. Seventy-five percent will get one hundred percent correct. One band does major and the other band does minor. They can play them, recognize them, sing at sight, and tell you what is played or sung.

They love to do this; it is a fun game. It is an excellent technique to increase their attention which works very well with high school and junior high. They find this fairly easy to do. It is not approached as a big deal. We do this a little every day—perhaps five to ten intervals a day during rehearsals three of the five days in a week. We also play and sing intervals each time. I give them tonic in an easy key. Easy keys refer to those keys that occur in sequence with the music being played. We move out to more difficult (less familiar) keys as they develop skill.

This building of skill addresses listening and the new technical demands of the unfamiliar key. For example, I give a piece of paper to students. Listed on it are the intervals that I want to have played and the starting note or root of the interval. I usually do not ask them to sing the intervals. Another procedure is to give this list to a student. The others are to identify the intervals as they hear them. If they are "squirrely" that day I will call on individuals who need to have their attention increased! Or, anyone can answer.

I play intervals on different registers of the piano. I also vary timbres, ranges, instruments, registers, scales, keys, etc. I will sometimes ask anyone to play any interval, but it must start on a given tonic.

*(Patricia Brumbaugh)*

### Games to analyze notation

I play addition and subtraction rhythmic notation games with young students.

*(Barbara Buehlman)*

### A game to build skill and rhythm reading

I use "games" for variety and to engage their interest. I divide the class up into two or more teams or groups, and assign a leader to each group. I can divide the class or band in various ways such as by instrument, class, or boys and girls. The leader and the group must decide what to do or how they will handle the decisions in the game.

I shuffle fifteen to twenty cards with exercises printed on them. The card says the page, line, or exercise number and the number of points each is worth in the game. The other group of cards show rhythm patterns. When it is a certain student group's turn, they "draw" a card according to the rules of the game.

Since the cards have only the page and line number on them, students must have their books with them. The cards might be worth from five to fifty points. One or two cards also might be "bonus" cards with a high number of points. There also are ways to go "bankrupt," or lose all the points they've earned. These cards are in the exercise group.

I want students to learn to play and read the rhythm pattern cards, so I value the rhythm pattern cards higher by assigning a higher number of points. The intention is to give them an incentive to make the choice of a rhythm pattern over a card listing a line or exercise number.

When the game begins, students might select a card that says "Play page 19, No. 5." This material has been taught before, so my intent is to "drill" or build their skills, besides having variety during a class. When a group is taking their turn, I shuffle the thirty rhythm cards. I place one rhythm pattern card on a raised music stand they can all see. Most of the rhythms are those I expect they are familiar with, though several rhythms are new. If they see those, they must figure them out.

The "rhythm pattern card" starts the game and the student has several choices: (1) they can select and play the flash card with a rhythm pattern on it; (2) they can select an exercise card listing a page and an exercise number; (3) pass their turn on to another group. The other group has to play the flash (rhythm pattern) card—they do not have a

choice. If the first group makes a mistake, they lose their turn to the other group. Most of the time students will select an exercise card, since they prefer to play songs instead of rhythm patterns. Sometimes they select the rhythm pattern card. The rules of the game allows them five to six seconds to make their choice.

I based this idea upon TV games shows. With each correct response, they get X number of points. They love this and ask often, "Can we play that game?" One key issue is if the group or person plays the correct response, they earn another turn and chance to earn additional points. Therefore, they must respond correctly to keep control of the game—like retaining the serve in volley ball or tennis. I might use this once or twice a week, for five to ten minutes each time. During program preparation times, I do this less.

*(Thomas Herrera)*

On the infrequent "in-between" days, I sometimes have sight-reading contests with the band. Two captains are selected and they draft their own band, striving for balance and quality, thus the oboists and French horns are often drafted first.

I distribute band books to the bands who are sitting on opposite sides of the room. Each band gets one shot at a selection. The two groups alternate having the first turn. Sometimes I conduct; sometimes it is completely student run. I evaluate each performance and assign a score, such as two for good, one for acceptable and zero for poor. We keep a running total through the class period. This is fun for a change of pace and it is interesting to watch personalities and group dynamics emerge.

*(David Deitemyer)*

### Directions as a puzzle to be solved

I often play games with them by saying, "We are starting at the development section of the first movement of the Hindemith today." Then, I watch them scratch their heads and try to figure out where that is.

*(Michael Kaufman)*

### Conducting can be game-like

Students as young as sixth and seventh graders have an incredible capacity to understand conducting. If you present it to them by making it a game that provides a unique challenge, they show an incredibly sensitive ability to respond to the visual stimulus from the gestures of the conductor.

If you take a very simple piece of music where they don't have to concentrate on the music, you can do all kinds of things with it, except you have to be a little more careful about how you control the dynamics of the room. You can ask questions, for example, that make them decide which version of the dynamics, phrasing, or style they liked better. You can ask the same questions of them you would ask of older students. The thing that I'm always amazed about is that the kids always have pretty good answers.

(Craig Kirchhoff)

### The pass-off system

I use this game mainly with the sixth and seventh, the first and second-year kids, and at times with a lower grade. I mainly use the other games for the eighth graders. They like to play baseball and basketball, which I can use to keep them motivated and working on the fundamentals in their books.

When I first start teaching I have two complete band classes of between ninety and one hundred kids each. When the sixth graders start as beginners, they are not divided into woodwinds, brass, or percussion; they are all in band together.

When they come in the door, they learn whether we're going to do "pass-off" order or "concert" order seating order on that day. In the pass-off order they come in with their book and sit (they know what days we're going to do this). I also teach a normal band class with sheet music and all that wonderful stuff on the days we're doing concert order. With the sixth grade, if a concert is not approaching soon, there usually are four pass-off days and one concert per week. The four days, then, stress fundamentals with one day stressing concert music. The pass-off process may or may not take the entire period. However, when we get closer to a concert, the balance may change to three and two. The competition thing is kind of fun. Later, we have added different games such as "At the farm" or "You can play till you drop." To get out of a problem like that I use the scale pass-off, the five free pass-off's per scale. That has helped that.

Really, with this system you've got to be very careful that you keep everything positive. Some people might think originally that this approach will stifle the personality growth of the child that's sitting at the end of the section. I have had some people concerned about that. However, if I'm going to lose a student, I do not want to lose my top students. They usually are very motivated and are held back by the rest of the class. That is why I like this system.

(Marguerite G. Wilder)

### The Pass-Off

When a student has played a line in the music book perfectly, the teacher will mark off the song with a large P, which stands for "passed." Each pass-off is dated and initialed: P (pass), 4/15/91 and MW (teacher's initials). The date allows the teacher to see how quickly the student is progressing. The initial is a proof by either the band director or an approved community school or outside music teacher.

I use the standard that the performance must be perfect. This means just that: correct posture, embouchure, instrument position, rhythm, dynamics, articula-

tion, pitch, breath support, etc. A pass-off is for the entire song, because I want the students to strive for a complete perfect performance; they must play the line from beginning to end with repeats and observe the first and second endings. This supports public performance when we cannot stop and start over. We must play the entire piece, not a portion of it.

There is a reason students must always start at the beginning of the line. The other students in the class will be "fingering" their instruments and following the line in their own books, while critically listening to the student involved in the pass-off try.

Each student can move through the book as quickly or as slowly as they choose. The pass-off approach enables the class's advanced students to receive a constant review. There also is instruction for those students who have not yet qualified on the particular line played by the advanced student. They are hearing the line and fingering the instrument as they listen and watch the music closely. Therefore, the less qualified students hear the lines many times before they start the line themselves. This is the same effect as studying their part many times before trying to perform the part.

When a student tries to complete a "pass-off," the student is given one chance to play their line correctly for the teacher. However, a student may "buy" another turn if they have earned extra-turn credits, which we call ET's.

A student can earn an extra turn (ET) for each thirty minutes of practice time. The practice report must be signed by a parent. Students also can present written reports on topics such as composers, instruments, or musical forms: they can summarize a program watched or concert attended, etc.

Practice, which can lead to ET's (extra turns), is not required of the students. It is up to the student to gain or accumulate these "second chances." I keep my record of "ET's" in the front of the band book and it looks like this: ET 111111111. When the students buy an extra turn, I can mark off one they have accumulated. When I give an "ET," it can be in the form of a card with the "ET" character on it or other cartoon figures.

I also set cut-off points in the first part of the book for unacceptable habits of the beginning player. For instance, page nine is the stopping point for the "nose-breathers." Starting with the first line of page 9, the student should breathe through their nose no more! If he does, this will now count as a mistake and the turn is over.

The student cannot use an "ET" to buy a second chance for this type of mistake. Until page nine, a pass-off is accepted even if there is nose breathing; however, I remind the student of the proper way to breathe. Another cut-off point may be page ten when the "mumps" are now longer acceptable. (Mumps are puffed cheeks.) One can set other cut-off points where certain physical or musical behaviors can no longer be ignored. Thus, the teacher can raise standards whenever and for whatever he decides is reasonable for the student's age or level of skill development.

*(Marguerite G. Wilder)*

### Describing the fundamental pass-off class

On "pass-off" days the students sit in pass-off order, as opposed to concert order. Pass-off order means the students sit from top to bottom in order of whom has passed-off the most lines in the book. They do not sit in like-instrument groupings. The seating arrangement in a row of individuals might be tuba, flute, trumpet, clarinet, trumpet, percussion, clarinet, tuba, flute, trombone, and saxophone.

The pass-off round will usually start with the student seated at the bottom of the class and move up through the class. By starting with the lowest student, the round starts near the beginning of the book. These early songs serve as a warm-up and as a review for the more advanced players, since all students play each exercise.

The beginning student is asked which page and number he or she is on. They announce this to the entire class, and I give a count off for that particular line. The entire class will then play the announced song. The class playing of a line is done without repeats or first endings to save class time. When the student plays the line during their pass-off turn, however, they must play all repeats and endings.

After everyone plays, the student will play the line for the teacher and the entire class. When any student is playing their pass-off, the entire class will finger their own instrument, while following the line in their book. The students learn to feel safe with this procedure and think nothing of playing in front of one hundred other students. This helps settle their nerves for public performance and in try-outs.

During the pass-off process any student may earn extra tries (ET's). At times, a student can earn extra turns from the teacher for fingering and paying attention to each pass-off; for good hand and body posture during full class playing; for embouchure; or, for exceptionally good tone quality. I point out the excellent tone quality, for example, to the other students. This defines an example of what each should strive for on that instrument.

If there are several students on the same song, the teacher should move quickly through these students, sometimes without the entire band playing each line. When the class reaches a new line for that day, the entire class will again play as a group. The students will move up and down as necessary to keep themselves in correct pass-off order after each turn. This procedure will continue throughout the class, unless a student wants to play a scale cycle and arpeggio.

A student can substitute the scale cycle and arpeggio any time the student chooses. This type of turn starts first with the student filling out a scale sheet. Then they play the scale cycle and arpeggio by memory. A mistake writing a

scale sheet counts as the mistake for the pass-off turn. I expect students to be working on a scale cycle at all times. (Sometimes the teacher will have a spot check, and ask to see each student's written scale sheet. If the student cannot produce said sheet, it will cost the student his pass-off turn for that day, even if he or she had originally planned to play a line from the book.)

The positive incentive for the student to learn scale cycles is: "A correctly played scale cycle will give the student five free pass-off lines in the book." The scale pass-off turns are not in order (straight down the page), but the teacher will find the dead wood for that particular student in his method book.

A scale pass-off is shown in the student's book by marking the line with the name of the scale. (For example, instead of marking a P, the teacher will mark: E flat 4/15/91 MW.) The teacher can quickly tell the number of scales a student has learned by looking at the student's band method book. I also have developed a very effective technique, called "scale clubs."

When the class reaches a new line or musical idea for the first time, the teacher will spend time explaining the song, new note, rhythm, etc. Several playings of the line will follow. The class probably will play the new line before or after the actual pass-off round to reinforce the new idea. This could go on for several days depending on the difficulty of the new idea.

With the pass-off method, everyone in the entire band is involved in the class. The individual student either will be playing the line with the group or they will be "fingering" while another student is playing for a pass-off. On the average, the entire class will be playing every minute or two. I can hear as many as seventy students each class hour, because of the perfect standard for the pass-off. As soon as student makes any type of mistake, their turn is over. Some students may play only five to ten seconds before a mistake is made. At that point the student can either buy a second chance with the extra turn or the teacher will move to the next student.

The students do not view this method as harsh because I treat everyone equally; there are no value judgments. The students find that it is easier to understand as they listen to the line being played. Because of this standard, the students can immediately hear right and wrong. This method of class instruction works very quickly for the teacher who has the method book memorized. The teacher can give the count off for the next line while marking the book of the student who has just completed their pass-off.

*(Marguerite G. Wilder)*

### Regular Round

The pass-off method can be used in a variety of ways. If the class is of reasonable size, the "regular round" can be used daily. A student may stay in the round as long as they keep on the pass-off line.

For example, the class is comprised of students A B C D E F G H. The regular round could begin with page nine, number three. Student A and student B are both on this line. Student A passes off the line, student B does not. Now the regular round is on page nine, number four. The teacher will ask how many students are on this line besides student A who has just reached this point. Students A, C, D, and E are all on this line. Let's say student A and student D are the only ones to pass-off this line. These two students remain in the regular round. The round is now on page nine, number five. Students A, D, and F are on this line, student F is the only one to pass-off. The students have the opportunity to buy one extra turn per line if needed. The regular round is now on page nine, number six. Only student F is on this line. He passes off the song. The round is now on page nine, number seven, where the round picks up students G and H along with student F etc.

This type of round lets more prepared and faster moving students go quickly through the book. Some students can play every turn of the regular round. Again, the responsibility is with the student: they can be prepared and move as quickly as they like.

*(Marguerite G. Wilder)*

### Lightning Round

Each child gets one chance to play the line he/she is on. You may not buy an extra turn on this type of round. This round can be used for the last few minutes of class. If the class is small enough, you can give everyone one last chance to play that day.

*(Marguerite G. Wilder)*

### Scale clubs

The formation of "scale clubs" has brought more interest in learning scales than other techniques used in the past. This is a less complicated or new approach, but the students work very hard to "join" each new club. I placed posters in the band room with the name of each club at the top of the posters. Instead of listing scale "number four," the name of the club is the Fabulous Four Club, Fantastic Five Club, Sensational Six, Tapp's Top Twelve, Thirteen All-Stars! With the use of Scale Clubs, as many as forty beginning students have been able to play by memory six or more scales.

*(Marguerite G. Wilder)*

### Team competition

I divide the class into two or more teams. The teams are more evenly divided if the team captains choose woodwind, brass, and percussion in order, while also choosing boy, girl, boy, girl.

A point system may be set up any way the teacher wants. The following system could be two points for a line that is the student's regular pass-off line. Bonus songs are assigned throughout the book, which have from five to fifteen points of value to the team's score.

Some examples are: (1) scales are worth twenty points for the team; (2) written reports and attending concerts are worth ten points; (3) extra points can be earned when the entire team "fingers" while a student is involved in a pass-off; (4) good posture and hand position are also rewarded; (5) practice notes are worth two times each thirty minutes of practice; and (6) points could be given to the team that is set-up and ready to go with all members in their places. The team captain must raise his/her hand to notify the teacher that his/her team is ready.

*(Marguerite G. Wilder)*

### The "egg timer" incentive

An extra incentive is the use of an egg timer. This is a must in band room equipment. The timer is set to ring every one to five minutes throughout the class period. If the egg timer goes off while a line is in progress, then the song is worth three to five times the number of points originally assigned. If the timer goes off between teams, the next team's member will have the bonus points. I usually employ this during the team competition.

*(Marguerite G. Wilder)*

### Partner Pick

When a student passes off the line we are on in the book, he may pick any other student to play the line. If the picked student successfully passes off his line, both the "picker" and "pickee" receive an extra turn that can be used in a later turn. This game allows the faster or more prepared students to move faster without the teacher giving extra pass-off turns to some students and not the unprepared students.

The teacher does not have to make the choice. Students usually pick the faster classmates because they assume the more able students will complete their pass-off. Then, the first student, who chose him, is very likely to receive an extra turn.

*(Marguerite G. Wilder)*

### Las Vegas

A student may select any line in the book that he has not passed-off. The student may bet up to five extra turns that he/she can successfully pass-off the line. The teacher will lay odds on the bet. For example, a student bets two extra turns that he/she can pass off page 17, page 5. The teacher, knowing the difficulty level of the line and the ability level of the student, will place odds of four against the bet.

The student could earn eight extra turns if he passes off the line (besides earning the normal pass-off). However, the student will only lose the two extra turns he originally bet if he does not pass-off. The student can pick either the line he is on or go to another line in the book. This is a good "change of pace" game for the child who may be stuck on a line or has just arrived at a difficult line.

*(Marguerite G. Wilder)*

## Band squares

This game is set up like "tic-tac-toe" and "Hollywood Squares." Nine students set up the board. They sit in three rows of three. Two students are the game players. Player one is assigned the X and player two is assigned the O. When the player chooses a student who can successfully play his pass-off, then the correct X or O will be placed on the tic-tac-toe board set up on the black board of the classroom. If a chosen student does not pass-off his line, then he will leave the Band Square set-up. The other instrumental students will rotate downward, and a new student will enter the set-up in the top left-hand corner. This procedure continues until the game is won or there is a tie.

*(Marguerite G. Wilder)*

## Let's make a deal

If a student can correctly play his pass-off, then he may choose to play "Let's Make A Deal." This student will choose Door #1, Door #2, or Door #3. Behind each door is a different "prize." There are many possible prizes: free extra turns; loss of extra turns; melody lines of popular rock tunes or commercials; "dorky" tunes like nursery tunes; a pass-off round in which he/she could play until he/she made a mistake; or a thirty-minute free lesson with the teacher held before or after school.

*(Marguerite G. Wilder)*

## Grab bag

A bag is filled with questions. When answered, the student can earn student extra turns or actual pass-offs. If the students are involved in team competition, they can earn extra points for their team. Examples of questions: key signatures, musical term definitions, assign the student to play a certain line from the book for X number of points.

*(Marguerite G. Wilder)*

## The "International World Championship of the Universe"

I use this game to encourage the students to practice the difficult or important lines in the book. If a student can make a score of eight, nine, or ten on the INTERNATIONAL WORLD CHAMPIONSHIP OF THE UNIVERSE SONG, he chooses a prize from the "surprise bag." If the student receives a score of ten, he also earns a pass-off. This game usually is played when the class as a whole is four or five pages from the IWCOU line. (It is a good way to get rid of Halloween candy!)

*(Marguerite G. Wilder)*

## Partnership pass-off

Two or more students are involved in ensemble playing. The student playing the top line will receive the actual pass-off. The student or students participating in the other lines will receive extra turns for their participation in the ensemble. This is a good game to stress balance and blend.

*(Marguerite G. Wilder)*

## Three for the price of one sale

As long as the student can continue to pass-off on lines, they may play up to three lines in a row.

*(Marguerite G. Wilder)*

## Increasing concentration and accuracy

I try to build student concentration, especially with Roger Maxwell's etudes from *13 Weeks to a Better Band*. After they've played an etude three or four times, I give them special directions. "This time I want you to leave out the fourth beat of every measure and replace it with a rest," or "This time play everything except the eighth notes that are on beat two." One hard direction is, "Play everything on the page exactly as written except the last note: do not play that at all." By the time they get to the last note, some of them have forgotten.

I give them the directions only once—I'll never repeat the instruction—I tell them one time. The making of an error also disciplines kids because they do not want to stick out! If they do happen to "honk in," that's not a put-down situation, it is more of a "let's have a little fun with it" situation. They soon learn, though we don't use it as a put-down, they don't prefer being the one who "honks in."

Occasionally I vary this and say, "We're going to do four of these etudes and any person who honks in, stands up." After four etudes, we'll count to see how many are standing. Then I'll say, "Two days from now we're going to do exactly the same etude again." I tell them how to play it when it will be played again two days later. I remind them that they will have to remember, because I will not restate the directions. I do this to help them with their mental discipline so they're thinking all the time. Sometimes we'll leave out a particular note value such as all eighth notes, or leave out the first beat of every measure, leave out eighth notes when they follow dotted quarters. We do anything that works. The whole idea behind it is to develop their mental discipline.

*(Ross A. Leeper)*

## Making a rehearsal challenging

A music teacher must have a little fun with the kids and they must learn that the teacher is having fun also. This must be in context of "we are all trying to accomplish something." That is, this is a game, but it is also a learning process.

In *Advanced Fun with Fundamentals* there is a page of rhythm drills, page twenty-two, for example. These drills are short four-measure rhythm drills with a prominent rhythm in each exercise. Some days we'll play the odd numbers only, some days we'll play the even numbers only. On occasion I will tell the students, "Today we'll start with Number One and go right down the line through the first twenty. The first time through a pattern, one person is going to play through as a solo, the second time through the band answers it. While the band is playing on the repeat, I will pick the next person to solo before the group answers. That person plays the next one pattern by themselves right in tempo. We never stop, we just start with one and go right down the line.

In this situation, they are hearing one rhythm in one exercise, and then immediately they're on the spot to play the next rhythm in the next exercise. Of course, there's another side advantage to this. The kids have to listen because if someone plays the solo line, the others have to correct it. They can't just play it by rote. I tell them, "If it's played incorrectly, that doesn't mean that you play it incorrectly. You must play it right."

*(Ross A. Leeper)*

### Rhythm rondo

Our "rhythm rondo" game works very well with the beginners and is a good rhythm reinforcement. We establish a rhythm pattern within either the large group or small group classes. The pattern might be a basic rhythm notated as a four quarter notes, (two measures each whatever the meter signature). Everybody will pat the tempo beats on their legs (one-two-three-four, one-two-one-two, or one-two-three depending upon the meter). To begin, the entire group does "one-two-three-four" on the tempo beats by patting their legs. One student, who has volunteered a rhythm pattern, must conclude his rhythm pattern during the same number of beats the group is doing. Therefore, a student alternates his pattern with the group's pattern. For example, the large group will do a simple pattern of four quarter notes (or another pattern), followed by an individual clapping, counting, or playing a different rhythm.

*(Gordon Nelson)*

### Tonal games

We do many tonal patterns, the tonal rondo (like the rhythm rondo described above), tonal echoes, melodic dictations, etc. When I have somebody visit they can't understand how my kids can do that and I say, "They don't know any differently." (These techniques are included with many others in the *Teaching Skills Workbook* (GIA) by James Froseth and Judy Dezell. This may still be available.)

*(Janet Tweed)*

# *Types of Teaching Techniques: Input Modes for Student Learning*

## *Part One:*
## *Experiencing the Music Directly*

# CHAPTER ONE

# MODELING AND IMITATION

The word modeling describes a teaching technique by which the teacher shows examples of what students are to learn. The teacher begins by demonstrating as perfect an example as he can. The students hear or see the model and they try to duplicate what the teacher showed. This is effective because the students have a clear example of what they are to do before they try to do or understand the same thing. The students are not asked to infer, for example, how the tone should sound from a verbal description of tone; they can begin immediately with the hearing of a model of the tone itself.

Words alone can be used to describe some musical and technical skills, but words are incomplete for many of these. With dynamics, style, and rhythm, for instance, music teachers also want students to feel, see, and hear musical features and performance skills. Thus, the use of modeling—with or without the inclusion of words—can help students to a fuller understanding than words can do alone.

Any teacher has a long list of objectives that could be taught through modeling. Not only can modeling be used for hand position, tone, and embouchure, it also can be used to teach meter, style, dynamics, tenutos, fermatas, articulations, improvisation, ornamentation, phrasing, blend, balance, intonation—almost any musical or technical skill. Modeling is both an alternative and a complement to words; modeling can supplement instruction dominated by talk. In short, modeling is an indispensable teaching technique for music education. This observation recalls an old adage, "A picture is worth a thousand words."

## THE VALUE OF MODELING

I do rely upon modeling, particularly for musical style, because so much of what we do in music is so difficult to put into words. Using words and sentences to describe the style, the shape of a phrase, or short and long notes is very inadequate. Language itself falls short and it is an inexact way to communicate musical ideas.

The natural way to communicate ideas in music is through modeling. My belief is that the performed ex-

ample need not be that refined. With my coarse voice I can show the phrasing even if the pitches are not exact. The quality of the singing in the model is not the critical variable; I can communicate the substance of the musical gesture very quickly.

*(Donald Casey)*

Sometimes peers are better teachers than the teachers themselves. There are many who make an impact because they are role models. This has changed a little, because I used to have more kids that practiced. In the 1970s some of them practiced up to three hours a day in school and there were tons and tons of kids who practiced a minimum of an hour a day. We don't have that anymore; they don't have time because of academic loads, class schedules, girl's sports, and other activities. So we have to count on role models in the group more than ever before.

*(Kenneth M. Larsen)*

We use a "do as I do" approach with the beginners. One can do the whole procedure without any talking, as Jim Froseth does. I also feel there must be some explaining for students at this age level. Our kids learn a great deal from "do as I do," but it's not done only by the teacher: it's done by the students. For example, if I say, "Today I would like someone in the class to demonstrate correct posture for us." Somebody will raise his hand and I'll say, "Okay, now put your instruments down and we are going to do exactly as Susy does." Therefore, if Susy doesn't sit straight, then the rest of us don't sit straight either. We mimic exactly what she does.

It's often more effective when the kids do modeling instead of the teacher. We use modeling for posture, instrument and hand position, breathing, posture while standing or sitting—anything physical they can see. Another reason for doing "do what I do" is that I want *them* to be the leader. I feel that once they can do it right and wrong physically, they are much more aware of what they should be and what they are doing. They often say, "I thought I was sitting up, but I wasn't." It's a very effective teaching technique.

*(Janet Tweed)*

One big problem is phrase endings. For this I also show how to perform the phrase ending. I demonstrate things a great deal. If I only talk about it, they do not understand.

*(Steven Cooper)*

A very effective technique is to find a recording for them, so they hear an idea of the sound. They have absolutely no concept of the piece or the sound they are aiming for. They do not know the orchestral repertoire and have not heard the pieces. I like to use the recording after they have played through the piece and are familiar with it. This relates to the Suzuki approach of imitating and listening.

*(Judith A. Niles)*

The only way the student is going to produce the kind of tone you want is to let them hear what the tone is. You must do demonstrations, either through recordings or other performers. If there is a student available, I will use him. That's really the best example one can use. I have found that if I have any outstanding player in any section, their example carries through the whole section because a peer role model has much impact

Since we have the funding, we can bring in some performers once a week; some performers are on a one-shot schedule. We occasionally have had funding for a string trio, brass quintet, or woodwind quintet. If I'm not a proficient percussionist, I must bring in someone who is. If there is a student available, I also will use him. That's the best example one can use, and a key to good tone: the sound of any outstanding player in any section carries through the whole section.

*(Judith A. Niles)*

When students watch a National Basketball Association basketball star "dunk" a basketball time after time, they eventually and inevitably will internalize the entire action unconsciously. We should use this observation in the teaching of instrumental music. The observation can be applied by having the teacher with the respective instrument stand in front of the student who does not have an instrument yet.

While seeing the teacher's movements, the student makes believe he has the instrument in his hand. He places his fingers up and down, moves the slide, mirrors the posture, moves in imitation of the teacher, learns to sing and play in tune, and learns to articulate and play dynamics correctly. Perhaps even more fundamentally important, I also have his attention because he is watching me and is not distracted by the instrument himself. I want him to do, see, and learn many things before he ever has the instrument in his hands. In this scenario, he is learning executive skills without the instrument and in preparation for the "real" thing.

*(Richard Grunow)*

There are occasions in rehearsals when using rote techniques are about the only way I can think of. You have tried everything else in your bag, so the next step is to use rote. For some teachers, rote is the last thing they want to do—they think rote is a "cop out." At the least, modeling by rote is a fun recruiting tool that can help students to relax and perhaps become interested in jazz improvisation.

*(Timothy Mahr)*

If one student matches another's good sound, the chances increase that the sound will be produced in a desirable way. The belief is that if a student makes a good sound compared to a less good one, they make subtle changes in the production.

*(Richard Fischer)*

For example, if there is a balance problem, I show them what it sounds like when a note of the chord is out-of-balance. Doing this also immediately attracts the attention of the group to something that needs to be done.

Showing and demonstration are ways to appeal to the curiosity of the group, and it is very valuable for their aural learning. There is no point in talking about the chord being in tune or the second clarinet being too loud. It is more effective to show the sound of a balanced and unbalanced chord and say, "This is why the third of the chord cannot be that loud." I show this at the piano, the vibes, have the flutes play a triad, whatever. I might even demonstrate the appropriate and the inappropriate balance. We can use their playing for comparison, if they are already demonstrating the inappropriate sound.

*(Frederick Fennell)*

If I'm modeling something, I'll usually sing. I don't magnify things, I sing it as exact musically as I would like it produced. I understand that singing is not playing their instrument and it is not the same color quality. My intent there is to convey the sense of line and time, the sense of phrase, and especially the sense of a musical approach to style. This gets the student to think, "How can I do that? What do I need to do?"

I go from my singing to their playing. They seldom sing or echo my demonstration first before they play, except I use that occasionally for intonation. Many kids don't sing very well and do not have a good self-image about their singing. They do, though, have an instrument in their hands that they feel good about, or they wouldn't be there. So, I simply go from modeling the musical sound to them playing it back on their instruments. If I were teaching a sixth grade band, I'd probably have them sing to me.

*(Gerald Olson)*

### Observations about modeling

We can inadvertently have students modeling us who never want to deviate from that model. We have to explain to them that this is one way and there are many other wonderful ways.

*(L. Keating Johnson)*

### Listen to the music, not the instrument

One of my personal crusades is to get trumpet players away from listening to trumpeters, and clarinet players away from listening to clarinetists. I just badger them and beat them to death to hear recitals on other instruments than their own. If they are a saxophone player, obviously they are going to go hear saxophone players; but they also should listen to the singers, listen to the piano players, or listen to a cellist. I want them to go to a recital where the emphasis is on the music, because they don't understand or don't care what the physical problems are. If they want to learn something about phrasing, they should listen to Placido Domingo or Barbra Streisand.

*(Donald Wilcox)*

### The teacher as a model

I felt strongly about punctuality and promptness. I have said, "When you are on time, you are late." At first they could not figure it out, but soon they did. Being present at nine is not being ready at nine. It worked! This must be established by example—thus the teacher must always start the rehearsal by nine, no matter how many are there and ready to go. One should stop on time also, for their sake. We must show punctuality, proper dress, and good grooming—be professional looking.

*(John Kinnison)*

## THE WAY TO PRESENT MODELS

### Singing, speaking, and playing

If they have a problem with an interval, we will sing it, they will hear it on the piano, and they will play it. I bet the trumpets they won't miss the interval or note any more. "If you can sing it, you can play it."

*(Jack Brookshire)*

Though I do not sing well, I sing to show how and where to breathe at the end of phrases. I believe that "the only pure instrument is the human voice." Students have said to me, "We'll play it right if you won't sing anymore."

*(Stanley Cate)*

I often will sing a line and teach it by rote. I will say, "Here's where the line goes. It goes from here to there." I demonstrate how it's done, and I make the point that the music should build or develop toward that certain spot. Then I say, "Try that on your instruments."

*(William Long)*

I sing demonstrations, though I'm not the best singer. I've always said my groups play really well because I tell

them at the beginning of the year, "If you play the music correctly the first time, you don't have to hear me sing." Well, my kids learn the music very quickly so they won't have to hear it again, and I'm dead serious.

*(Sandra P. Thompson)*

I use voice inflection a lot. If the section is to be soft, I often give my spoken directions nearly in whisper. If the section is to be more forceful, I give the directions in a louder, more emphatic voice. I don't usually sing to illustrate the dynamic character, but I do use my voice to show nuance, such as the shape of a phrase. Sometimes, I use a *sprechstimme* approach: a *song-speech* to render the phrase. It is an effective way to convey the musical character of a phrase. I do this even if I don't perform the pitches accurately.

*(Richard Fischer)*

In the first two months of the Youth Orchestra, I rehearse without conducting but use the violin exclusively. This accomplishes two things: it gets them to move as if they were playing in a quartet and teaches them how to lead the quartet. All I say is "Do what I do." They are to make all the motions together (with sound) that I do. Then, I have them "give a lead" as the first violinist does in a quartet.

*(Pamela Gearhart)*

I might play a series of quarter notes and accent one of them. They would play back. I do a lot of singing, even if I do not do it well. You cannot tell kids how to "turn a phrase," but you can sing it and gesture it. Sometimes, especially with young students, I have them sing it back to me. With older students I demonstrate for them or coach more as they play.

*(Donald S. George)*

If I hear a stuffy sound, I will say, "It should sound like this" as I demonstrate. I tend to use a positive model to show them the proper way.

*(Donald Gee)*

I do a lot of singing to show style, phrasing, and dynamics.

*(Kjellrun K. Hestekin)*

I also hum things that I want them to hear. With articulation, for example, I have them hum, sing, and say or play it back. If they sing or say the articulations three or four times, they usually play it perfectly when they return to the instrument. If I sing the common pattern such as slur two—tongue two, they sing or say, and then they play. This works really well. I may turn to a new or different page with the same articulations and they usually play them correctly.

*(Steven Cooper)*

## Using modeling

I demonstrate many things, especially with less experienced students. With young students, I take turns with them. They play one or two measures and I play the same measures. I play the measures either before or after them. If I play second it encourages them to read; if I play first, it gives them a model of the sound. We may alternate two, four, or eight measures and we can take turns playing phrases. I model more subtle differences for college students than I do for young students. Examples are good tone, releases, phrasing, ritards, tenuto, pitch, articulation, dynamics and other expressive things. Many times I show the same features to college students as I show to young students, except with young students the differences I show are more obvious than with college students.

*(Edward Kocher)*

## Humor and surprise

Often students don't get the idea of fortepiano. We'll try it, I'll sing it, and I will explain it. Sometimes they just don't get it. I'll say, "You people just don't understand." Here is one way that works.

When this happens, I get off the podium and I walk around talking about it. While doing so, I subtly look for a flute player right in front of me who is paying attention to me, but whose eyes are wandering off a little bit. Most of the kids are watching because I'm walking around. I say, "Now, a fortepiano is supposed to be etc., etc., etc." I continue on and on and start talking more softly. Even more softly I say, "To be done effectively, it must be done just right, etc., etc., etc." I say, "Now I'm going to explain what it is" and then I talk even more softly.

Then I speak extremely loud right at that kid whose eyes aren't on me. I move like I'm going to attack that kid. I get real loud, then soft, and then I get louder again. When I do this, I try to catch one of my best flute players and I cannot do this unless I can catch one whose eyes are wandering. I'll do the same thing several months later and it generally gets my point across. Now, I have pretty good fortepianos in my band.

*(Howard A. Lehman)*

## Using peers and older students

I have brought in fifth graders and asked the music education undergraduates to do clinics. They listen because the new people seem to have extra credibility. High school students have demonstrated and talked to younger kids. I also use high school and college athletes who have played or can offer something about physical training. The credibility of athletes is a very valuable tool. They will believe what they say because of who they are.

*(Jack Brookshire)*

I use individuals from the class as models for tone or blend.

*(Steven Cooper)*

If your junior high clarinet players are trying to get a good sound and Larry Combs of the Chicago Symphony cannot be at the class that day, just pick the kid in the section who you think has the better sound. Compliment him on what a good sound he's getting and say, "This is the closest to what we are after."

That works very well; it's quick and easy, and you've got the resource right there with you. This approach focuses their attention on tone quality. I might say, "Though this isn't perfect, it is the best we've got at the moment—let's all work in that direction." Furthermore, a kid that's sitting in the third chair from the last may have the best sound at that particular moment.

*(Donald Wilcox)*

It's amazing to me how much my students teach each other. We have a tutor program in the summertime and my tutors are kids who have finished eighth, ninth, or tenth grade. I am the coordinator of the tutors and schedule which students meet with a tutor. The tutor is in contact with the music teacher so that you know what to cover.

We have a very extensive beginner program in the summertime and of course we also have the problems with vacations. I have tutors in most of the instruments, kids who will tutor on a one-to-one basis. If you miss a lesson and come back to make up a lesson, instead of the teacher meeting with you, the tutor meets with you. It's amazing to me how much interaction there is between the younger kids and their older peers, and how they react to one another. It's phenomenal what these young kids can do.

Our beginners are about to be sixth graders. Our tutors, at the youngest, will be freshman in high school— they just finished eighth grade. They are three years older, which is enough older so there is a teacher-student relationship. What amazes me, when I watch the tutors, is to see them demand as much or more from the kids than the teacher does. They stress skills such as posture, horn position, and hand position. They reinforce everything that they learned and are teaching to younger students.

I think it's one of the finest things we do. We use tutors not just to make up lessons, but as remedial teaching for students having a problem. I really think tutoring is a large un-tapped resource that we have in our school system. It not only reinforces the beginning student, but it also reinforces the high school student. They can't explain, I am sure, unless they are pretty well set on it themselves. Every year, all I ask is for volunteers to tutor in the summer: I never have to beg anybody. It takes place in the summer and during the school year. It does not occur during marching season.

*(Janet Tweed)*

I guess the good fortune of having a university in town is that I can bring in a good clarinet player, flute player, etc. My students can hear good players. Besides, since I have so many kids in the program, I always have somebody who is outstanding. Therefore, I can use upper class students to demonstrate sound.

*(Howard A. Lehman)*

We can use talking, conducting, questioning, or demonstration to point out where in the band we can find an example of what something should sound like.

*(Richard Fischer)*

We neglect to teach our kids how to listen. Since research has suggested modeling is a very efficient teaching and learning technique, I may say, "Let's do some exploration here. How do you feel about this line? Why don't you play this and express this line the way you feel it, and the way that you feel it should go?"

Usually, I pick some spot where there's a unison line. A volunteer will do it in their own way. The band can hear it, look in their part and see it. Then, I ask the band to mimic exactly what that person has done. This requires the creativity of the soloist and engages the creativity of the others. I think that's a great way for teaching how to listen.

There will always be somebody with a different idea who is willing to show that—to take a chance. This also teaches that many musical things are not written in the notation. Thus, most of what we do to express the music isn't on the page.

*(Craig Kirchhoff)*

A student told me, "The seating you use made a great psychological impact upon me, I have learned so much more." Though I change string seating for every concert and pick the principals, I place the other students strong with weak, new with old, readers with non-readers, rushers with draggers, and sharpers with flatters. I "sandwich" people in consideration of their differences. I identify key places through the back of the section where I need the strongest players, those that are most alert and with the better orchestral habits.

The strong player's musicianship and skills rub off, because the kid normally in the back is sitting with many weaker people and does not hear anything. They have nothing coming in. With strong players near them, they come along more quickly because they hear better models.

I change string seating for every concert, but I pick the principal players and do not change them. Rotating the seating also erases the stigma of, "I have chair number four, so there are three people better than I am." The seating plan has two primary purposes: one is to get the best sound I can get out of the group; the second is to develop the players as much as I can.

*(Pamela Gearhart)*

Being a percussionist, I am limited since I cannot perform much beyond the beginning level. Instead, I have found peer models an effective substitute.

*(Gary Hill)*

I use my voice a lot to show dynamic levels or style, often singing the words of a song in inappropriate style.

*(John Kinnison)*

I demonstrate a lot and I use the principal players to demonstrate.

*(Judith A. Niles)*

If I have a section doing articulation right I'll say, "Saxes, listen to the trumpets do this, they've been doing it very well." Of course, they won't always do it well, but this causes the saxophones to listen. Then, we can decide what was wrong or right with it. The trumpet version is likely to be better than what the saxophones were doing, and it involves two groups in the judging and listening.

*(Terry A. Oxley)*

### Live performances

Presenting models or examples works better using "live" performers instead of recordings. Anyone playing live is more effective than any recording, even if they are not quite as good, because the performance is real. The kids listen to a recording and say, "Sure." They also may assume the recorded performance is electronically enhanced. If you have some kid play in person, then it's just him and the horn. It makes a big difference.

*(Donald Wilcox)*

I can remember being in a clarinet lesson in Michigan with Laconi, a phenomenal player. He graduated from Rome Conservatory when he was seventeen and played for Toscanini at age twenty. I was playing my little heart out on things I had worked on like mad. He yelled at me in Italian and pounded on my shoulder, went to the desk that was about two feet deep in papers. He rummaged around until he finally found his clarinet buried in all this junk. Without wetting the reed, stone dry-off the desk, he played beautifully. Then, he would throw it back on the desk with all the trash and say, "There, play like that."

*(Donald Wilcox)*

### Recordings and concerts

Students are missing, more than anything, experience with models of tone quality and interpretation of style. They have not been exposed to such aspects of music. Because of limited time, I play recordings once, though I would like to play them more. When they hear it even once, there is great improvement with these elements.

*(Judith A. Niles)*

If we do any orchestral transcriptions such as *Beatrice and Benedict*, I often find that they have never heard the orchestral rendition. It is very important to do this at any level. When we did *Beatrice and Benedict* last year, I did not play a recording right away. Then I said, "Listen, how are the parts related here? Are you playing a cello part? Are you playing a viola part?" We assume that college students are very perceptive of this—well, they're not. I played that recording and we started playing again—it was unbelievable. So, if I do any transcriptions, I usually play the orchestral version at some time.

(*Richard J. Suddendorf*)

I encourage their attendance at recitals and concerts and often take a bus load. I also use recordings.

(*Robert Allan*)

I use examples constantly from the very beginning stages of their development up to the time when they graduate. I use good, recorded music and I always try to have a good sound system so that the kids can listen through good speakers. For beginners, I play Maurice Andre in trumpet classes and Jean Pierre Rampal in flute classes.

Kids have no idea what their instrument should sound like—they honestly don't. Even if more advanced high school kids come in to play, they still are not completely sure what the instrument should sound like. Therefore, I try to give them the very best of examples, whether it is an individual playing or whether it is a large or small ensemble. I also don't limit their listening to just band recordings. I often used orchestral examples or even use a recorder ensemble to demonstrate such skills as articulation, ornamentation, dynamics, or balance. I feel so strongly about listening that I used it a good deal in my teaching.

(*John Kinnison*)

One can walk into many band director's homes or offices and you won't find five albums of band music or two albums of well-performed solo music for any instrument. Teachers simply aren't showing good tone and using imitation enough. They should—it's a simple tool.

I wasn't very original, so I always listened to other people, and copied their sound and what they did. I want the kids to listen to their instruments played well. Good recordings are still not very easy to find. I "scrounge" recordings anywhere I can get them. There was an article in the BDGuide on using recordings. I used the information that was in that article and tried to get the records. I called one company that produced many of the records—nothing. I thought, "Here it goes again." Those recordings are out there somewhere, but I can't get my hands on them. Many people will call and say, "Have you got some good records for this or for that piece?" They know I've got a lot of them.

(*Lewis Larson*)

I had a check-out system so they could take the record out. The recordings were "beat up" over the years and some of them are irreplaceable. Recently, I have had a student librarian make duplicate copies for me. I say, "Bring your tape and we'll make a recording for you."

(*Lewis Larson*)

I get the best professional recording of what we are going to play and I will play it for students. When I had the concert band in high school and we played a transcription, I played the orchestral version of it. The kids loved it. That was probably more help to them than hearing another concert band version of it.

(*Dominic Spera*)

With young players, I use recordings and live performances.

(*Richard Fischer*)

With every kid doing solos, you can't be taking a lot of time picking out these things. That's one reason I have a short list of solos that I use every year. Students might go through the same first two or three or four solos and they may all be doing the same piece. On the saxophone, for example, when they're in the seventh grade I'll have them buy the Fred Hemke recording released through Selmer. This has contest solos from grade one and two right on up to some grade six things; they are very well done.

(*Lewis Larson*)

### Selecting models

When you get to the college or university level your model should be the Chicago Symphony. That's real beauty. The Netherlands Wind Ensemble is first-class wind ensemble playing. Those are *the* models.

(*Robert Levy*)

### Tone color

To get idiomatic tone color, I demonstrate on all the instruments. I also use nearby college students, especially those in music education classes.

(*Jack Brookshire*)

It is harder for students to match sound, than to match pitch. When I think of a trumpet, I think of Adolf Herseth—I'm always trying to get people to sound like Adolf Herseth. I know our guys like a darker, heavier sound with more density. Some trumpet players like to play with this edgy sound that does not do you any good in an ensemble.

(*John Williamson*)

I point out a certain individual's sound as the model for warmth, brightness, etc.

(*Richard Fischer*)

To build a concept of tone, I play for them, use recordings and take field trips down the hall to hear the older kids play. I also use a lot of individual playing in classes, which enables them to hear each other. We have high school students play for us, as do the armed service band musicians. We do this two or three class periods in a week's time, particularly during the first half of the school year. Though they are there primarily to play, we also use the service band musicians to fix and reinforce the playing habits of individual students.

*(John W. LaCava)*

## Performance skills

Many times I demonstrate tone and techniques. An example is going over the break on a clarinet. I will demonstrate the tone and I will go through the many different types of tone exercises. If I cannot demonstrate something, I will get a recording for them to listen to it and I will try to tell and show them.

*(Phillip A. Weinberg)*

On a difficult passage, I sometimes start with one instrument or person, then add instruments one by one. This also works quickly and they begin to play well together. This helps them hear examples of how to sound, whether it is balance, articulation, dynamics, or whatever.

*(R. G. Conlee)*

One can go through a section of the ensemble looking for a performer with a desirable musical style or tone. Then, all students can try to duplicate that concept in their own performance. I try to vary who the model is, so the less talented get a chance to model something when possible.

*(Richard Floyd)*

## Phrasing and style

I use a lot of singing to them. I say, "This is the way I want this phrase to sound."

*(Bryce Taylor)*

Instead of saying, "This is long, or this is short," I'll sometimes sing or chant it and may say, "Now you hear that the second note is always shorter, normally, than the first note."

*(John A. Thompson)*

I've done a lot a singing and I can do falsetto well. My range also is very wide. If I want a turn or a trill to be played a certain way, I will sing it. If I want it to go the opposite way, or if I want to sing a mordent or an appoggiatura, I will do that. I have the vocal means to do it, so whatever's at my disposal I will use. You also can emphasize agogic accents. You can do a lot with vocalizing. I also enjoy doing it and it saves so much time.

*(Richard J. Suddendorf)*

A phrase must have a beginning, peak, and ending, whether it is a two or four-bar phrase. I think a phrase must lead, it must have flow and it must have continuous motion. If you get into the phrase and there's no peak there also is no phrase.

Often I will sing it very monotone so there's no nuance—nothing. Then, I also will sing it another way. I may show getting to the peak of the phrase, but failing to continue through to the ending phase—this I call, "dropping the phrase."

*(Richard J. Suddendorf)*

If there is a phrasing problem, I may sing the phrase to them.

*(George R. Bedell)*

My basic approach to a new piece of the literature is to establish a style, so all of the articulations are correct. I get the style well established as far as length of notes and weight of notes, and then it just all goes together. You know, it's like going to the doctor with several problems and picking out the worst one; fix that first and then go to the next one.

To set a style, I use a lot of syllables and singing. For example if I want something separated, I just sing the part.

*(Kenneth M. Larsen)*

If they say they cannot play a four-measure phrase, I show them that I can play an eight or sixteen-measure phrase in one breath. Then they say, "Oh, I guess I can play four measures." Usually that works very well, though I must keep at it because it isn't a habit right away.

*(Steven Cooper)*

I show agogic accents by pushing the primary beats in each measure. I perform the rise and fall in a musical phrase and talk it about as climbing up and walking down a mountain. I perform everything. The kids answer back immediately, usually without dropping a beat.

*(Nancy Plantinga)*

## Rhythm and tempo

When I sing to show a rhythm, I ask them to imitate. I use the word, "ta(to)-day" for dotted sixteenths. We sing "day, day, taday, taday, day, day, taday."

*(Richard J. Suddendorf)*

There are many cases where I have a player, who is very expressive, demonstrate rubato.

*(Donald Wilcox)*

I do work with the metronome to set the tempo we are working toward. Now, sometimes we don't make it up to tempo, but they at least have an idea of what we're aiming for and we try to get there.

*(Judith A. Niles)*

In calculating tempi—a conductor's perennial nemesis—I would suggest that one sight read up to tempo so the players know what the concert goal is. The more certain a conductor is about the choice of tempo, the less students or performers are inclined to be in doubt about the conductor. Beethoven said music will only reveal its secrets if the "exact" tempo is found. This also is influenced by the ensemble and the conductor.

*(Butler R. Eitel)*

## CHAPTER TWO

# KINESTHETIC AND TACTILE

Students engage in a kinesthetic experience when they use physical and muscular movements. When a teacher asks students to do or notice these actions for learning, the teacher is using a kinesthetic teaching technique. A common kinesthetic experience involves rhythm, and because rhythm organizes the muscle movements, teachers apply the term "eurythmic experience" to this kinesthetic experience. The purpose of any kinesthetic teaching technique is to give the music students sensory experiences with the action they are to learn, building readiness for understanding performance skills or music reading, and keeping the music students' learning rooted in kinesthetic experience.

Often the music students are conscious of feeling the muscle action, but they need not be aware of the action for learning to take place. For basic learning in music to begin, the students need the repetition of many movements, physical actions, and other kinesthetic experiences. But actual awareness of the physical action can be an advantage later. The students' consciousness of the action allows the teacher and students to talk about their experiences, which could further the students' conceptual learning. The teacher and the students could use their increasing awareness to help guide further independent learning of both skills or ideas.

Discussing the importance of kinesthetic teaching techniques, Janet Tweed said, "I find increasingly that the students are kinesthetic, verbal, visual, or auditory learners. I also have found that, when I have taken learning styles courses myself, I learn and remember more easily when I have had hands-on experiences."

Teachers can use kinesthetic techniques for many other objectives than just rhythm. Some other objectives include breathing, tongue action, pulse and subdivision, articulation, phrasing, dynamics, style, and intonation.

Engaging the student's sense of touch or feeling, can be called a *tactile* teaching technique. For example, a student can feel the air stream as it hits his hand or feel the waist line expand and contract as he practices breathing. Some of these techniques are in this section because of their kinship with the awareness of muscle movements and actions.

## TEACHING TECHNIQUES FOR BREATHING AND RELAXATION

### Teaching breathing

Have the group put their hands on their belt lines. Then I say, "If you wanted to call your teacher who is across the street, you would say, "Hey! . . . Hey!" Doing that, they can feel the use of muscles and the air. I feel when teaching articulation, accents, etc. we should use physical means. If we do, their learning really happens.

*(Richard J. Suddendorf)*

I teach breathing with many different images and exercises. Some images that help are: (a) take in air as you fill a glass: from bottom up; (b) keep relaxed and inhale as though you are yawning; (c) try for an open throat as when you swallow a glass of water; (d) hear the sound and tone when inhaling; (e) use the hand as a microphone through which you blow; (f) use hot and cold air; advocating hot air because it fosters an open throat; and, (g) keep it feeling natural.

I also have students use these exercises: (a) breathe out while supporting down low; (b) blow through resistance; (c) maximize relaxation as one keeps the air speed up (adjusting the tongue angle has bearing on this); (d) hold a piece of paper against the wall with the air stream; (e) stand flat against the wall with the shoulder blades against the wall as you breathe. (This requires them to breathe in the deeper part of the body); (f) lie down flat to discover breathing; and, (g) with some instruments, especially the flutes, I ask them to put their hand in front to see how to direct the air stream;

*(R. G. Conlee)*

When students have trouble understanding how and where to breathe properly, I have my kids lie on the floor. Then, they take a deep breath and see that it involves the correct areas in which to breathe. I also have them put their hands on their stomachs as they breathe. I repeat various teaching techniques and tell the kids, "If you have trouble with breathing correctly at home or if you are unsure, get on the floor and do that. Then, pick up the horn, stand, and

179

play trying to breathe the same way." They also can try most of the other techniques at home and be their own teacher.

*(Sandra P. Thompson)*

I ask students to sit with their elbows on their knees. This anchors their shoulders so the shoulders are less likely to move up. Students are assigned partners and one kid sits behind the other. One student places his hands on the other student's kidney area of the back and notices how the person in front of him breathes. They can feel what is happening and tell their partner about it. They change places and go through the same process. Through this, they can feel how to do it and check how well the other student is doing.

*(Robert Allan)*

I use a variety of physically related teaching techniques for breathing. Students sit without their instrument and bend all the way over at the waist, with their arms hanging loosely outside their knees. Then they stand up and try to breathe in the same way. I ask them to lean back like a drum major or lay down on the ground to do leg lifts so they can feel the breathing muscles stretch. They take a deep breath, lean back, and hold their breath for four counts. When they feel that this begins to hurt a little bit, they come back forward.

We have them "hiss" real loudly. At first, some kids think this is corny. I also have used the hissing when I want the kids to play at a soft dynamic. They hiss with an intense good sound, though they often play a soft tone that is very anemic. When I want someone to make a note be vibrant or alive but at a soft dynamic level, we'll have them hiss softly, and then very loudly like a snake. Though the sound is not loud, the intensity is high. In addition, they can feel the pressure and resistance.

*(Ross Kellan)*

They blow up a balloon and release the air into their mouth—so they have to take in all that air. I want them to take the air in very fast, bypassing the top of the lungs, so to speak, when taking the air to the bottom.

*(Robert Grechesky)*

We talk about warm and cold air, and I have them blow on their hands to find the way of blowing that causes the air to be hot and the way that causes it to be cool.

*(Jack Brookshire)*

We do "hissing" exercises as loud as students can, so they get some feeling of breath support. Hissing helps them feel back pressure. Loud hissing is also a good isotonic and isometric exercise because it builds good muscles. We "hiss" ten repetitions on a long tone, one long tone for each hiss. The next tone follows the last immediately. The inhale is quick and the exhale is sustained. This

is to develop breath support and muscle strength.

To feel back pressure, they pinch their noses and keep their lips together. They blow without releasing any air and they can sense that the pressure on the inside needs to be released. They let all the old air out and take in a fresh breath, forming their embouchure with their lips sealed together. They hold their noses and blow air out to help build an embouchure. At first, they hold their noses so there is pressure in the "mask." This is the same feeling a singer should have. I use hissing and the pinched nose idea daily, especially during the first half of the year.

*(John W. LaCava)*

The marching band loves to stand up, put their hands on their waist. They "pinch in" to exhale all the air they can. Then they blow out a little more so they absolutely drain their lungs of air. Now, with no air at all remaining, they wait until they cannot stand it anymore, and then they inhale. With the inhale, they will instinctively fill that rib cage and stomach area thoroughly without lifting the shoulders. They feel the explosive inhale in the waist area. The abrupt expansion from the air helps convey the idea that they do not need to inhale by lifting the shoulders if they inhale by expanding the middle.

*(Donald Wilcox)*

### Teaching relaxation

With young students, I ask them to take relaxed deep breaths, but I never talk about tightness and support. Getting students to breathe in and out is more important first. To foster this, I have people lie on their backs because they breathe very naturally in that position. Even when I was doing marching band, I would have them lie on their backs and breathe that way. With few exceptions, people can play in that position. Sometimes I carried that further. They played long tones, or scales in a certain rhythm while lying down. I would then ask them to transfer that feeling to their playing when they were standing or sitting.

*(Gary Hill)*

To improve breathing, I say, "Let me show you how to do that a little better or more easily. Relax your shoulders, put your horns down, and shake your hands to relax them. Now, see how you feel." In addition, to relax the body so they can breathe correctly, we lie on the floor and pretend we are breathing or panting like dogs. They like to see the teacher do that! After they do this, I ask them, "How do you feel when breathing?" Then I ask them to get up on the chair and breathe the same way.

*(Jack Brookshire)*

I ask them to lie down on the floor and I turn off the lights. I say, "Notice where are you inhaling, what does it feel like? Where does the air go while you are relaxed? Now, apply that as you play."

*(John W. LaCava)*

To teach finger and hand position, I make students shake their hands out, and let them relax and hang at their side. They pick them up and leave them absolutely relaxed, especially for flute and clarinet. They are so close to the degree of relaxation I want, there is only a little bit of tension. In that relaxed state, students move their hands very little to get to the right places on the instrument. I encourage them to remain in that shape and in that state of relaxation.

*(Terry A. Oxley)*

If students have tense fingers, one can ask, "What else is tense?" They say their forearms and biceps are also tense because each muscle influences another group of muscles. We do dangling exercises: letting the hands and arms dangle by the chair to get the feeling of relaxation. They also are to use just enough energy to hold the horn up. I ask students to hold the instrument with their finger tips, as though the instrument were an egg.

*(John W. LaCava)*

## TEACHING TECHNIQUES FOR RHYTHM

### Tactile-kinesthetic

I feel teachers do a considerable amount with aural and with visual, but not enough with tactile. Therefore, we use one hand on one leg for pulse and the other hand for the rhythm patterns. This carries over very successfully with the high school students. When there is a problem to solve, I use tapping and patting. The rhythm problem is often solved on the very first try. This also removes the distractions of instruments and fingerings for the moment.

*(Robert Allan)*

### Rhythm and pulse

I think the most important aspect of pulse is that the conductor/teacher doesn't make it. Pulse is a manifestation of every player in the ensemble, kinesthetically reacting to the pulse of the music.

I remember bringing Warren Benson to campus a few weeks ago to conduct a series of rehearsals and performances of his music. During a rehearsal, he simple stopped conducting in an effort to listen to the ensemble. As one might have expected, when he stopped conducting, the entire ensemble stopped! When quizzed by him as to why they stopped, he immediately suggested that he was only listening and that they were to continue. "After all, he replied, it is your job to keep the rhythm, the pulse . . . that is not my job as a conductor."

I don't think we are suggesting as conductors that we can't take the responsibility for maintaining the pulse, but rather the players should have the primary responsibility for it. I believe the best way to teach that concept is simply by not conducting. By not conducting pieces that have an obvious pulse such as marches, students will become much more aware of rhythmic precision. It is another way to promote a greater amount of listening in the ensemble itself. The ensemble who feels pulse accurately has also made important steps toward becoming musically independent.

*(Thomas L. Dvorak)*

### Rhythmic feel

I see from working with youth orchestras that some of those kids have developed a physical sense of pulse through bowing. In this respect, strings have a very distinct advantage. These little second violin and viola kids are going 'bm bm bm bm' and they can feel pulse and rhythm as well as hear it.

To accomplish this with baritones and tubas, I have them buzz rhythmic etudes on the mouthpiece as they walk in rhythm. I often approach this humorously saying, "We are going to do this, and this is silly. Maybe it's something that you don't want to do when people can see you. But, it's something we can do to develop a sense of pulse."

For the wind player, I've found that blowing or buzzing the air in rhythm sometimes develops the reflexes of the muscle systems they use when they're playing. An example is having kids blow air *next* to the mouth piece, not actually into it, while they practice the fingering. This builds the muscle network and the continuity of air.

I also have students beat time while they sing the line; they physically show and feel the pulse and meter this way. They might conduct the meter pattern with the right hand while they sing the phrase and hold the mouthpiece with their left hand. This makes the whole body system begin to work. I also teach them how to do the motions for legato, staccato, and marcato; they model these very basic motions with their hands or whole arm movements. They must feel and repeat these exercises often. They must feel this before they can begin to do anything of musical significance.

Any physical action pays a huge dividend. I must say I didn't realize that when I started teaching years ago. Just walking or stepping in time helps the coordination of breathing exercises. I ask for a smooth step or lifting the legs up farther, anything to try to get those muscle groups involved rhythmically. I also do clapping and tapping to reduce rhythm to its simplest elements. So, take away the fingerings, take away the high register, take away the reed, take away everything, and get down to the rhythm.

The physical actions and sensations systematize rhythm so they know what it feels like. Then when you return to the playing of an instrument, the rhythmic muscle actions are pretrained and will not interfere with the playing of the instrument and making music. Conversely, making music won't divert their attention so much since they are already "programmed" in the rhythmic aspect strongly enough that it does not prevent them from making music right away.

*(L. Keating Johnson)*

### Feeling the movement of the music

I ask them to sing and conduct an etude, a song, an exercise, or their part before they play it. I use this more with advanced students, but this can be used with students as young as junior high, particularly if they know the song. This technique gets the sound and the feeling of the music into their mind before they try to play it.

*(Edward Kocher)*

### Foot movement

In our initial instruction with recorders and general music in grades one to three, foot tapping is prescribed. We continue to use foot-tapping in instrumental classes and this is important to both the student and the teacher. For the student, tapping can internalize the feeling of the pulse; and for the teacher, tapping is a visual clue showing what the student is feeling. If the teacher cannot determine this, he cannot decide or know what the student is understanding.

I believe in foot-tapping, particularly at the initial levels of instruction. At higher levels, it ceases because I expect rhythm to be internalized by then. Students subdue the foot movement in performance and tapping is not routinely used with advanced performers who play music of Grade V or VI levels. If there is a rhythmic problem at this level, I could bring foot tapping back into rehearsal.

*(George R. Bedell)*

### Slow playing

I develop the rhythmic feel by singing, saying, and playing music slowly. Playing slowly with a slower pulse develops a sense of feeling better than moderate or fast tempos. Playing slowly also promotes the physical movement I want in rhythmic playing. In private lessons, I even have to move some students' feet up and down for them to set a tempo or pulse!

*(Steven Cooper)*

### Involving the students in "rests"

Many times students ignore rests or do not give them the full duration. To emphasize that rests are as important as notes, I frequently have them shout the word "rest." This is very effective, especially with younger kids. They must become conscious of the rest and they like to shout anyway, especially the younger ones. If you ask them to only say the word "rest," they are not involved enough: they must shout it. Then they get involved and their attention span improves.

*(Judith A. Niles)*

## BUILDING PERFORMANCE SKILLS

### Connecting fingering patterns to sound pattern

Have them sing the song on a neutral syllable or with words, as they finger their instrument correctly. This can promote the relationship of fingerings to sounds as well as fingerings to tonality.

*(Richard Grunow)*

### A relaxed tongue

When trying to tongue rapidly, many students tighten up. They try so hard to tongue rapidly that their tongue turns into a rock. Have them put their hand up and tighten their fingers until they are absolutely rigid. Then say, "Now wiggle them" and they can't. Then say, "Now relax and your fingers can wiggle." The faster you need to go, the more you need to strive for relaxation. You need to try to relax muscles even more and work a little less so the tonguing is lighter.

*(Gregory Bimm)*

### Comparing mouthpiece pressures

To get an idea how much pressure brass players use and to give them an idea how little they should use, I do one of two things: one is for me to take a mouthpiece and press it against a student's hand. I do this both the student's way and the preferred way. This shows the preferable amount of mouthpiece pressure. The other way is to have a student take the mouthpiece out of the instrument and I have him press the mouthpiece against my hand to show how hard he is pressing while playing. Then, I have him lighten the pressure until I say "stop." I say, "That is the amount of pressure you should try to use."

*(Steven Cooper)*

### Teaching posture to young students

Proper posture, while playing an instrument, effects breathing, tone quality, and even hand positions of young players. After proper posture is shown and explained to the students, I use two techniques that quickly maintain or review proper posture. First, if the students begin to lose proper posture, I stop the band and tell them to grab the hair on their heads and pull it up. As they pull on their hair, I tell them to let their body follow and return to the proper posture.

Second, I have the band stand up and while standing, I have the students put one hand on their backs—on the spine around their waist line. I ask them to feel the curvature of the spine. The spine should be curving in slightly if the students are standing properly. Now, with their hand still on their spine, I have them sit. I ask them to maintain the same spine curvature when seated as when they were standing. Later as a review, after we have practiced this "standing-then-sittingdown" routine, I may simply ask the students to put one hand on their spine to check for the proper back posture.

*(Roman Palmer)*

### Tuning and pitch

Before playing the pitch, the student must have a physical feel for where that pitch is and what it should sound like. They should hear the pitch they are going to match and anticipate how playing it will feel. They must internalize that pitch and feeling before trying to play it.

After two clarinets are perfectly in tune, teachers often say "good" and go on to something else. Many teachers do not realize they must take the final step of saying to the clarinets, "Exactly how do you feel? What did you do? What does that sound like?" We need to help them create and identify impressions they can remember so they can use this memory to recreate another day. They need to become aware of how it sounds and feels to recreate it—if they cannot do this, they have not internalized playing the pitch as we would like them to do.

*(Richard Floyd)*

### Feeling style

Maybe they should put their horns down a moment, and just bounce their arms, alternating one arm, then another arm to feel light and heavy styles.

*(Robert Levy)*

When I talk about staccato, we talk about bouncing on the note. Sometimes I have had them physically bounce when they play staccato lines.

*(Nancy Plantinga)*

We were doing a Sousa march and they were having trouble getting the shortness of the quarter notes just right. I asked them if they would conduct the march the way they would like it to sound. It was amazing how many of them were conducting it just like it should go but they weren't playing it that way. Getting them to feel it and think about it does the trick!

*(Francis Marciniak)*

### Style changes also are physical changes

Their recognition of different physical and dynamic approaches to the changing styles carries over from one piece to the next piece. Each new challenge calls forth what they already know and have tried during previous pieces. We do not have to start from scratch each time with ideas such as light versus heavy and marcato versus legato.

*(Richard Fischer)*

# CHAPTER THREE

# LISTENING

Listening is critically important in music instruction and should be high on the priority list for both lessons and rehearsals. Teachers face challenges, however, when emphasizing listening. For example, many classes have limited time and large enrollment. Fortunately, most music teachers, particularly the exceptional ones, meet such challenges. They can give information, build facility, and develop ensemble without allowing listening goals to slip to a lower priority.

Although teachers accept that they must teach facility or ensemble playing, such skills as these do not make up a complete musical education by themselves. Teachers also must increase listening, both as the means and as the end, in instrumental classes. In an instrumental music classes, lessons, and rehearsals, students need more aural development than commonly occurs. More to the point, to the extent that an instrumental class or any music class is without listening to or recalling music, it is not music education at all. For musical education to occur, the teacher must meet the challenges of keeping listening at the center of instrumental music instruction.

## THE IMPORTANCE OF LISTENING

### Listening is key

My basic approach, regardless of level, is to develop their ears. That is where it all begins.

(*Pamela Gearhart*)

I'm convinced that the most musical groups are the ones who have ears the size of elephants; they really know how to listen.

(*Timothy Mahr*)

Seventy percent of the energy of the group should be spent on listening and thirty percent on chasing notes. If your ratio is the other way around, then music learning is not happening because not enough listening is occurring. Physical learning may be taking place, but they can go through calisthenics anytime.

(*Larry Rachleff*)

In all my years of teaching, I thought that one of the important elements either in producing or consuming music is discrimination in listening. I want them to listen in rehearsals and out of rehearsals, listen anywhere and everywhere in any aspect of life, particularly in music. Students should listen to John Cage and any sounds—even those compositions that are not necessarily traditional music. They should listen to music on the radio, on recordings, in rehearsal, and to the person next to them and to players in another section.

(*John Kinnison*)

If students begin playing without listening, teachers are allowing students to start with a habit that we never want to see begin. To prevent this, teachers can have students relate to a reference point such as a tuning note, to a unison to match, or to the teacher's accompaniment. Doing so begins immediately to establish listening and makes music learning a sound experience, not just a physical experience.

(*Frank Battisti*)

### Teach students to go beyond the notes

I try to make students aware that when they put that horn to their lips and make a sound, they must also be critical listeners of what they themselves are doing. Instead, they seem to believe "Hey that *was* an A. I fingered one and two, I played one and two and I got an A so what are you complaining about?" I guess that's all part of the need to teach them the unwritten message of music, that message which is not on that page in front of them.

(*Terry A. Oxley*)

### Improving listening can raise students' confidence

In a clinic I teach students to play by themselves because, after all, I am going to leave after two hours. If they do learn to play effectively without the conductor, it sensitizes the students aurally to their own product and it tells their teachers that they do not have to over-conduct. Furthermore, it gives students confidence.

(*Gary Hill*)

### Listening is not always taught

Five students just came back from playing in the all-state orchestra and band. One of the frustrating things these older students run into when they play with other students is that they discover that many students don't listen. Many don't know how to adjust to play in tune and they don't know how to tune their instruments.

*(Lewis Larson)*

## EMPHASIZING THE NEED FOR LISTENING TARGETS

### Teach them what to listen for

Isn't it silly to tell someone to listen, but not tell them what to listen to or for? What is the point in doing this, if they have not been helped in knowing what to listen to?

*(James Froseth)*

Just saying "listen" in a loud voice is the easy way out, but you're not really doing anything.

*(Timothy Mahr)*

Listening is not effective if teachers fail to give students a target to listen for or to listen to. Without one, they have no idea what they are supposed to do.

*(Richard Floyd)*

### Relating to a fixed reference pitch and musical context

A beginning student should be playing to a fixed pitch from the piano or from the teacher's instrument. I use a keyboard instrument which allows me to play a G major chord, for example, to set a context for the note "G" which the student is trying to get. If he plays "G," I can change chords under individual tones. This helps him listen; otherwise he just blows. If this is not done, the kid is playing in a vacuum from the time he starts until he begins playing in a group or playing with a piano.

*(Frank Battisti)*

I personally accompany beginners, though I am not a piano player as such. I have noticed that just "oom-pah-ing" with I-IV-V7-I chords has really helped. Students love being accompanied, no matter how simple it is or whether the class is a group or an individual. Simultaneously, I am training their ears to hear chords.

I play melodic patterns with the piano, which they are asked to echo. I begin by giving the students the starting tone. Then, with the piano, I play melodic patterns of one or more pitches and they echo back the patterns I just played. I try to vary instruments so they hear the melodic patterns played with different tone colors. In additional to using singing for this, I also use a guitar, piano, wind instruments, or pitched percussion. This also builds their listening because they hear something other than the teacher's voice or a piano repeatedly or solely.

*(Gordon Nelson)*

### Teach listening to certain intervals

I first teach students to match pitches or to match the octave. The term *listen* is neither enough if used alone, nor is it effective for the teacher to point at his ear. I don't think we devote enough time to playing, for example, the unison or the fifth so they are beat-less. Certain intervals sometimes are easier initially to hear. We use fifths and the octave mostly, since unisons are sometimes more difficult. The blending of instruments compounds the challenge.

*(Donald Gee)*

### Listening and tuning to the tonic

The better idea, bar none, is to pull the plug on the strobe tuner! As an alternative, establish tonality in B-flat concert by playing I-V-I on a tuned piano. Sing several tonic and dominant patterns with the syllable "bum." Do this on patterns such as do-mi-sol-mi-do, re-sol-ti-sol-re, and do-mi-sol-mi-do. They repeat these after I sing each pattern individually and in tune. This promotes the sound of tonality and the group's audiation of the resting tone. After they begin to do this well, I would go from singing on a neutral such as "bum," to using tonal syllables (such as do, re, mi).

When I am doing this I want them to anticipate—that is, remember the resting tone without playing or hearing it from an outside source. I am attempting to develop their skill so I can ask them to imagine or recall the resting tone one would use to end the tune or sequence of tonal patterns. To determine if they can do this, I then ask them to hum the resting tone after singing several tonal patterns or part of a tune. As one does this day by day, and week by week students improve their ability to anticipate and to come forth with the hummed resting tone.

I then can go to an individual player and ask them to tune their instrument without telling him whether he is sharp or flat. The individual can tune to tonic, because the tonality has been established, and each one is remembering it. I observe without comment who is hearing, who is adjusting, and how they make adjustments. After this has been done once, I go around again quickly and the results are considerably better. One could also do this in the key of the piece one is working on.

With the high school band, this works very well and students realize for one of the first times how to make their own decisions about intonation. The strobe should be used for something else. The strobe does for pitch what the metronome does for rhythm.

*(Richard Grunow)*

### Students should absorb the pitch to tune

There is a fault with all orchestra players. After the "A" is sounded, everyone bows away on that pitch, but no one has really listened to it. I really make them pause, absorb their pitch, and then make a judgment.

*(Pamela Gearhart)*

### Singing and listening can improve intonation

We use pitch matching, which makes a big difference. For example, we hum F concert with a tight sounding "nnnnnn." It makes a big difference to have the lips closed with a letter "nnnn" in one's mouth instead of a "mmmm." To my ears, "mmmm" is flat all the time. We will hum the pitch taken from a tuner or a keyboard instrument, then sing until most of the vibrations start disappearing. Then, we will match that pitch as we play. We will hum it again and try to match it again with our instruments.

Students have a tendency to play just whatever comes out of their instrument; but, when they think about it, they match pitch pretty well. I will have them hum the first pitch followed by a half step down. We will continue down a whole step and a minor third, etc., always going back to the F concert after each new pitch. We will hum alternately with playing. As they become more practiced, the amount of playing increases and the amount of humming decreases.

*(Terry Oxley)*

### Help students use listening while preparing a solo

Ask a student to listen to a recorded performance of a solo and compare it to the written music for the solo. The student describes and marks or notates the musical and technical events heard in the recorded solo. These events can be either (a) those the soloist performed, but were not notated in the written music, or (b) those the soloist did not perform, even though notated in the music. In the beginning students are more successful using only one of the suggestions at a time. With experience they could apply both suggestions simultaneously.

*(Frank Battisti)*

### Helping students to remember the reference pitch

The reference tone for tuning can be forgotten and the student easily confused by all the varying tuning notes everyone is producing in the room. To reduce this, I have a pitch sounded and then each in the section enters at intervals of about a second or two.

Each student successively introduces his sound and hears it in comparison to two things: to their memory of the reference pitch and to the pitch of the person next to him. Since they are not rushed and have time to listen and judge, I see considerable eyebrows raising in this sequence. Perhaps this is because they can hear their own sound, and can compare it to the pitch standard or to the sound next to them more easily than if everyone is playing at once.

*(Joseph Casey)*

### Solving intonation through singing and listening

If there is a unison where there are intonation problems, I would first have the lowest instruments play, then have everybody in the band sing the pitch at that octave if possible. Then have the upper voices sing the octave above the lower instruments. I would involve everybody not only to keep all minds on task, but also to exercise their ears. I think intonation improves after singing and experimenting with pitch.

There are two other helpful points about intonation. One is knowing the tendencies of the instrument: some notes are sharp and some are flat, and this varies from instrument to instrument. The second point is that we should be ready for adjustment, since nine times out of ten the upper voices are usually playing sharp.

*(Michael Kaufman)*

### Showing students an idiomatic tone

While we know that describing tone color with words and drawings can help, it is more effective to have the teacher demonstrate since beginners will not know what a good sound is unless they hear one. We also must remember the value of hearing concerts by an excellent soloist, university band, junior high, or high school band.

*(Barbara Buehlman)*

## TEACHING LISTENING TARGETS AND CONCEPTS

### Defining the meaning of in tune and out of tune

Intonation may be easier to develop if taught early with younger students. However, students may be confused at the outset because they do not know what in tune and out of tune sound like. One effective way to define this is to give them a listening target. A listening target is a sound students can identify with their ears and learn to recognize and evaluate as "in tune" or "out of tune."

The first step in defining the listening target for intonation is to use two students or one student and the teacher. First, two play in unison to establish a starting or reference point in everyone's ears. Then, adjust one of the two instruments mechanically so the unison will be obviously out of tune. After they play, name this sound "out of tune." Adjust the pitch of the altered instrument so it is more in tune and try a unison again. If it is a better unison, name this sound "more in-tune."

Make further mechanical adjustments alternated with playing, until the two performers are as in tune as can reasonably be expected at the time. Call the unison sound either much "more in tune" or "well in tune" depending upon their level of attainment with intonation.

*(Joseph Casey)*

### Helping young students hear and adjust for intonation

I have them pull tuning slides so they are way out of tune. Then we just work the slide on in and let the students decide when it is far enough to be correct. For the younger students, I set the slide so it is more out of tune and so it's easier to discriminate as out of tune. Since we use the piano in the jazz band, I adjust the tuner to the piano and then we tune. I will also have all students in the jazz band tell me or tell another student whether they were sharp or flat and how much they need to push in or pull out. I begin this by saying, "Now, let's help John."

*(Sandra Thompson)*

### Directing students to listening targets

We have done directed listening by picking one particular thing upon which students should focus. By concentrating exclusively on that one thing, other things also improve. For example, we will have them listen down, concentrate on what the trombone note lengths sound like, on the articulation of the clarinet, on the section sound, on trumpet tone, or on whomever is playing in octaves with them. As students do any of these, many other things get better. Part of it is because they have an exact target to listen to. After playing in the back of the band on euphonium for years, I can appreciate how difficult it is to hear specific things.

*(Robert Grechesky)*

### Teaching young students to listen to the ensemble

I often find myself, as a director, so deeply engrossed in rehearsing individual parts and sections of the music that I do not stop and listen to the ensemble, or the entire piece of music as it will be heard by the audience. I must remind myself to listen to the entire group and the entire piece.

In the same sense, students tend to listen (some do not listen at all) only to their parts, a few sections around them, or simply to something that momentarily interests them or attracts their attention.

To improve their listening, I will often ask members of each section to leave their own instruments on their chairs and come out in front of the band. From there, they listen to a piece from beginning to the end. We all discuss what they have described they heard. It is amazing how differently and how well they can listen. This helps them to listen as they sit on the inside of the band in their respective sections. This listening exercise improves the band's performance as the students become aware of the ensemble and the entire composition.

*(Roman Palmer)*

### Choosing listening targets

Scales in the warm up often are played on "automatic pilot," I ask students to listen for a specific instrument or group of instruments on each pitch. Each student determines which he listens for and in what order. When the pitch changes they listen for a different instrument. Results are immediate and dramatic, and it is easy to transfer this skill within a more musical context during a rehearsal.

*(James Arrowood)*

I sometimes ask students to listen to a section other than their own as they play. This moves their focal point of listening eight feet, ten feet, or farther away from their location. Listening can be directed by asking them to listen for specific things, such as articulation or intonation, in the section to which they are now listening. You can guide the students with questions such as, "Who has the same part as you have? Is the trumpet section's style appropriate here? Who has the moving part in the accompaniment? What do the clarinets have here, the theme or the accompaniment? Do you think these staccatos are too short? Should you play the same style as the trumpets? or, Was your style the same as that of the trumpets?"

*(Richard Fischer)*

I will stop and ask, "Flutes, did you hear what the trombones did? Did you hear the harmony line? or, Did you hear the bass line where the bass clarinets were playing?" If they say no, then we play it again and have them listen for it.

*(Dwayne P. Sagen)*

### Comparing ways the music sounds

I use questioning and listening frequently in class or private lessons in a way that asks students to be attentive. I might play an exercise and ask the students to tell what is different about the way I played the line, compared to the way students did. With questions, I direct students to listen for certain features. Questions that help beginners listen for certain differences might be, "Were any notes louder than when you played it? Which version was faster, mine or yours?" or, Were my notes tongued or slurred in the same way as yours?

*(Steven Cooper)*

### Singing chord resolutions to sharpen listening

Though time restricts the extent I am able do this, we hear, sing, and play chord resolutions. They can identify all major and minor chords and the major functions such as tonic and dominant. We base their experience and identification upon chorales and interval singing. We play and identify intervals through scale work.

We have the band sing and resolve chords. For example, part of the band sings do-mi-sol followed by others singing sol-fa-re-ti then do-mi-sol again. There is another way where some sing do-ti-do, some so-so-so and some sing mi-fa-mi simultaneously. Still another way is to have one group sing do-ti-do, another sing do-do-do and others sing do-fa-mi. We do this often to focus upon pitch, chord succession, intonation, and key.

Listening to chord resolutions, both singing and playing, is based upon chorales. They can identify all major and minor fundamental chords. We also have them sing, for example, do-mi-sol, then do-me-sol. We ask them, "What does that do to the chord?" "How does that change the chord?" or " What does the chord now become?" This leads to hearing and identifying the minor triad—which is based upon our interval singing, playing, and identifying intervals through scale work. We also do a little with augmented and diminished chords.

*(Patricia Brumbaugh)*

### Discriminating tonal patterns

Learning tonal patterns can be enhanced by asking students questions such as, "What songs do you know which contain do-mi-sol?" or "How many times do you hear mi-re-do in this melody we have learned?"

*(Stanley Schleuter)*

### List listening targets for students

Make an audio tape of a composition of a piece played in a rehearsal. Give them specific things which help them direct their listening. Here are some examples one could include in a checklist. The first might be about the form of the piece. This cannot be determined as easily while inside the group. I want them to listen and determine how one part relates to another, partly in the abstract sense of—is it an ABA, or AB form, or theme and variations.

A second listening item or question might be, "What are you playing that another section also plays?" or "Where is your part occurring before or after you played it?" For example, the brass players might determine when they are playing as a brass section, and when they are playing with a woodwind section. One reason for this is, if they are playing with another section their forte cannot be as strong as when they are playing forte as the brass play by themselves. Students can also listen for dynamics changes. Balance, on the other hand, is harder to hear on the tape.

Listening can be valuable if they develop concepts such as tutti, section scoring, or accompaniment versus line. I also think a theme and variation is very useful in this respect. Listening to this form helps them sense the character of each variation. I also want them to be more aware that at some point they have triplets or four to a beat, when before they had the melody in its original form. Listening also can help them sense the growth of the entire piece and become aware of each variation's character.

Since each piece is different, I try to pick about six things that I think are crucial. I list these on a piece of paper and ask them to identify them and think about them as they listen.

*(Frank Battisti)*

### Listening to musical form in rehearsal

I bring listening to some aspects of musical form through my rehearsing of a piece. I may share the facts about the form, or ask "What is different about this section? All right, obviously this is a repeat. Should we call this a recapitulation section or is this a development section?" I discuss with them at the time what's

happening in one section that wasn't happening before in another.

*(Richard J. Suddendorf)*

### Promoting listening with certain types of music

While teaching either tuning or music making, I think the idea of doing music slowly or selecting music that is slow such as chorales is important. This gives them time to hear, think, and decide. This approach really makes a big difference because it gives everyone time to teach and learn, for example, what in-tune is.

*(Larry Rachleff)*

### Teaching dynamics and notation through listening

Listening can also be used to teach dynamics and to provide readiness for relating dynamics to notation. Sing or play a four-measure musical phrase with two different dynamic patterns. One pattern could be starting softly and playing gradually louder from the beginning to the end of the phrase. The other way could be performing soft to loud in the first two measures of the phrase, then loud to soft for the last two measures of the phrase. After the students play the phrase each way, ask students to describe how they were the same and how they were different.

After the descriptions which students offer, show the notation marks that stand for the two different changes in dynamics. Say that this mark " < " means to get gradually louder, as they did from the end of the phrase. Mark it or point to it in the music. Have the students play the phrase again reading the music with attention to the dynamic markings. In the second version there are two markings. The two dynamic markings " <" and ">" mean crescendo gradually for the first two measures and decrescendo gradually for the last two measures of the phrase. Ask the students to play the phrase in this manner.

To reinforce the students' understanding of the terms and the notation marks, ask the students "Which word stands for getting louder?" Then ask them, "Which mark shows that they should play louder?" Now, they should play and read the phrase with the crescendo symbol. Ask the students, "What does this mark ' > ' mean and what is it called?" Ask the students to play the phrase a second time using both dynamic changes as they are reading the crescendo and a decrescendo symbols.

*(Joseph Casey)*

### Increasing listening during marching band.

One time, while teaching in high school, I put a dancer's metal tap on the left shoe of each band member in marching band. We would march without percussion, with only the sound of that click on pavement. If you listened closely, you could barely hear the click of the "tap" on each left shoe. Later, as the band got better, we reduced the number of the members with taps on their shoes. This made the "tap" sound less and less audible.

*(John Williamson)*

### Using a playful, discovery approach

With this technique, I have them imagine that this is a "scientific discovery experiment." The purpose is to explore what it is like to be "in-tone" with each other. This is an example of a playful approach which works well to raise their listening awareness about pitch.

In a closed room that refracts resonance or reflects sound, I may ask two students to play one note in just such a way to yield sympathetically the third note. The first time they experience this, they act as if they were saying, "who is in here with us!"

*(Richard K. Hansen)*

### Adding listening to technical drills

The Soli-Solo Approach means the entire class plays a passage followed by an individual performing the passage, alternating with the class. When this is used with a scale, have an individual student choose the articulation of the chosen scale. This assigns the individual to lead, rather than follow the class. After the individual student plays the scale with an articulation the student selects, the full class plays the scale imitating the articulation the first individual student played. The next individual plays the same scale but selects a different articulation. The class now must listen and adjust so they are imitating scale as well as the next individual's choice of articulation.

*(Roman Palmer)*

## LISTENING IN THE ENSEMBLE

### The meaning of "listen"

The word listen is only half of the instruction; the other half means to adjust. I instruct my students that if there is a unison to match, they are to adjust their pitch to the lower octave as well as listen. They also are to adjust their pitch to the lower note when they try to tune the interval of a fifth. In warm up and tuning procedures, we practice so they know how octaves are to sound. If octaves are in tune, the upper voice might be or seem to be a bit flat; but, when the upper note disappears into that lower note, it is likely to be in tune.

*(Donald Gee)*

Saying "watch, watch, watch" is not particularly effective. Students can play with better ensemble by listening than by watching the conductor.

*(Robert Grechesky)*

### Students should listen down

We talk about matching pitch and playing within their sections. With this, they don't stick out. They try to

hear the person lower than they are in pitch. The firsts try to hear down to the second part and then the seconds listen down to the thirds. They are always to build down, really to listen down to the tuba. The thirds, therefore, must play louder than the seconds, and both louder than the firsts.

*(Dwayne P. Sagen)*

### Playing without the conductor

To teach them to listen as they change dynamics on a chord, for example, I'll tell my students to close their eyes. They play and I ask them to make their very own crescendo and diminuendo with their eyes closed. This forces them to concentrate on listening.

*(Craig Kirchhoff)*

In rehearsal, non-conducting can be very effective in that it causes them to listen much more, though non-conducting seems not to produce the musical energy or rhythmic forward motion that conducting provides. Ritards, for example, seem to lack the same forward motion, however, it works musically. Perhaps they would regain the forward motion with more practice playing without conducting.

*(John Anderson)*

I work almost one hundred percent with inhale rather than with exhale, and I stress that they must concentrate on the quality of that breath. Thus, performers should inhale and exhale with the tone in mind. They should inhale in the tempo and the style of the music. To concentrate on the quality of the breath and to listen to the breath, I'll tell them, "Close your eyes and start a note by yourselves with your eyes closed." (This obviously occurs without me conducting.) Eventually, someone is courageous enough to take a breath. The only way they can possibly come in is by listening to the breath impulse. So I tell the ensemble, "Play a note together, but I can't conduct it for you because your eyes are going to be closed."

*(Craig Kirchhoff)*

### Developing judgment through questioning

I might ask, "Could that have been done differently? What could be improved? or, What didn't you like?" If you question often enough, people will begin to be alerted that they are responsible for listening to other players in the band—and that the band members are being evaluated by other players. Students can also realize that something can be played differently, although not necessarily better.

*(Charles Olson)*

### Listening for balance

Inevitably, they do a better job listening for balance on phrase endings when I do not conduct, since they are not distracted by watching. I ask them to listen while tapering a phrase, so the balance is retained. If the low pitched sounds fall off, for example, I might ask them to listen to the tubas as they reduce their volume. I want them to hear their volume change and its impact upon balance.

*(George R. Bedell)*

### Developing sensitivity to tone color

In sectional rehearsals, we talk about how we are supposed to sound. I have said, "On the chorale section of the *Force of Destiny* that occurs later at circle nine, I want you trumpets to sound like trombones and I want you trombones to sound like trumpets." When we have a little extra time, I say, "Okay, everybody in the brass section sound like French horns—now everybody sound like tubas—now everybody sound like trumpets." I may say to the clarinets, "Let's see if you can get an oboe sound on your clarinets." They have fun with this, and realize there is more than one sound that a good player can produce.

*(Bryce Taylor)*

### Develop ensemble listening skills

First we play a B-flat scale, then we use John Paynter's warm-up drill on the F major scale. We play F, go down a half step, then return to F. Then, we go down a whole step from F to Eb, and back to F. We also do this with the B-flat chord. We move to and away from Bb as we did on the F scale played in unison. The chord is voiced in a standard way: Bb in the tuba, third trombone on F on the staff, second Bb, first trombone on D just above the staff. It is scored in a safe and usable range for each instrument. The first step is play the B-flat major chord, then A major (down a half step), back to B-flat major chord, then down to A-flat major chord, etc.

Going through all the intervals allows students to hear the intervals and relationships, plus listen within the chords. They hear everyone in their section, how the individual blends in with them, and how their section blends with everyone in the band. There is an additional thing to listen for. To help them, we sometimes have "only those on the root" play, but usually we use the chords. We also switch people around to different chord tones. I ask those on the third part to drop it a little, so we get a better blended chord. If we go through this, even with the second band, they really have warmed up their ears.

This also gets everyone to watch, thus the conductor is in complete control. Since there is no part for the percussion, they can sing the parts—the chords. During this period of a rehearsal we also work on breath and its relation to tone. We try to get a dark warm sound, like a euphonium.

*(Michael Golemo)*

## USING ALTERED SEATING TO FOSTER LISTENING IN THE ENSEMBLE

### Altering seating fosters listening

I have set up the band in a circle, conducting from the center. The softer instruments are in back and louder instruments are in front. The sections can also be seated backwards with the thirds as close to the front as the firsts normally are. One can also move two players closer to each other if they have a duet or one has a solo. Altering seating also can affect balance, since they cannot hear the melody if they are playing too loud. They will play more softly to hear who has the melody. In this case, focusing on one thing (who is playing their part) can cause adjustment in another area (balance). Students can then hear and relate to each other more easily. You can ask students to tell you who has the melody at certain spots, who has the melody at a certain rehearsal letter, or which instrument has the melody after another does.

*(Robert Grechesky)*

Select a composition such as *Fantasia in G-Major* and seat the band in little semi-circles so there will be several small ensembles. Because of this, flutes are not hearing flute players on both sides, and trombones are not hearing trombones. They are really hearing those other tones, the entire piece, and not just their own part. With the new seating, they all will strengthen their ears.

This is not something I would do early in the process; I do this when I feel the group has reached a certain point at which they are just sitting, going through the motions. To move past this they need to be jarred, even though the band has technical control of the work. Up to such a point, the listening may have been continuously done in the same way. The new experience helps them to discover different aspects of the piece such as texture, orchestration, or unity of ensemble.

*(Robert Levy)*

Re-seat the band or orchestra by the individual instruments that are scored together in the composition. Especially in an advanced piece, one can find common and uncommon combinations of instruments playing together during a passage. In a less difficult piece, there likely are many passages with tutti scoring. In either case, re-seat the different instruments who play the same part so they are seated next to each other. After listening across the group, more effective playing may occur when they are listening not just watching.

*(Pamela Gearhart, Michael Haithcock, Larry Rachleff, and William W. Wiedrich)*

I use a "pod-technique" to alter seating. This means seating people in small groups and using an area a bit larger than the usual physical area covered. The seating is unbroken, with a continuous line even though persons in one pod are sitting next to someone in the next pod. The first time I did the pod technique, they probably thought I was off the wall. I pointed out where they were to sit (we were about the play *Irish Tune from County Derry*). The effect immediately was different, they played better. They were forced to listen more because of changes of proximity. The pod approach is a temporary, transitional process that puts the burden of listening on their shoulders, rather than on mine. Many band directors have been led to believe that they are the ones solely responsible for listening or standards. Trying this may change their views.

Using this approach and developing a specific procedure usually is done when something is not going well. I do not want them to walk in, see the pods and think, "Okay, now I know what is going to happen." There is a key to making this positive and workable. To do this, the teacher must have the score memorized. I move about the group, toward things that need to be emphasized musically, or that need attention to set a standard. I may gesture toward the appropriate pod, move several steps closer or further depending upon what stage we are in this process.

After doing the "pod" technique, I may divide them into two bands facing each other. For example, I may put two different instrument groups together that have a unison passage. After this, they could be re-seated in the traditional full-group seating.

Another example occurred while rehearsing Warren Benson's *Passing Bell*. Even though the rehearsals were going well, I felt that the percussion parts seemed to be merely an addendum to the group. Therefore, I set the group up in a "box shape" with myself in the very middle. In the inner part of the box were all the percussion. Immediately upon playing in the new configuration, wind players commented "I didn't hear that before" or "I didn't know that they had this passage with so and so." Many of the new things they heard were rhythmic and others were pitch and melody. For the march from the Holst's second suite I set up the brass in front of the woodwinds. I did this because the woodwinds were trying to play too woodwind-like or too sweetly, which is not in line with the British band style.

A month may pass without the pod approach being used; I do not want it to be routine and lose its effect. Most of the time when they come in to the hall and see the new setting, they conclude that I have a plan. In general, students know what I may be after and trust that the procedure will work. This also builds and reflects relationship and trust. This is reflected in a better ensemble performance.

*(Michael Haithcock)*

### Having players stroll around the room

There is much you can do with strolling or walking around the room. With the Pachelbel *Canon*, I have the musicians walk all around the room or I simply spread them out away from their own sections. They stroll, not necessarily in tempo. It gives them a listening experience, but not necessarily a rhythmic or pulse experience. I use strolling for various reasons, but the central reason is to develop independence and listening.

The technique can encourage them to listen and

requires them to be both independent and dependent. They realize that they are dependent since they must fit in, and independent since they must make their own decision to do so. I even do this at concerts and they stay together quite well! I conduct and they can all see me from the back, the sides, and the balcony. This effect is very successful—like stereophonic sound.

*(Judith A. Niles)*

## OTHER LISTENING TECHNIQUES

I have them perform scales by alternately playing one note and singing the next.

*(Richard Alness)*

### Singing helps build independent listening skills

Bands ought to sing early in every rehearsal. Singing helps them develop their ability to hear without a crutch. Unfortunately we develop their fingers and eyes more than their ears. We need to try to develop every thing through the ear. In a general way it is a "Suzuki" approach. Without ears and hearing, things have no musical value at all.

*(Frank Battisti)*

### Playing from memory

I try to vary things, and do new and fresh things in rehearsals. One thing I have done is to have them play something with which they are relatively familiar. Then turn the music over and play it from memory. We also do a warm-up chorale which they sing, then play alternately. Then, they must play the chorale without being conducted, doing all the releases, attacks, and fermata without any help at all.

This helps them to listen and develop judgment. It is "amazing" to them, how much they can play together without a conductor. In this light, "The less you do as a conductor, the more affect it has when you do something."

*(Robert Grechesky)*

Encourage the students to memorize a four or an eight-bar section and play it with their eyes shut. This fosters "super" listening; it removes the visual stimuli, which helps them listen harder. I tell them they need to have ears like bats; you need to play more with your ears and less with the embouchure.

*(Donald Wilcox)*

### Record individuals and groups to provide perspective

Encourage students to listen to recordings of rehearsals. This allows them an opportunity to get a different perspective on what they are doing. As a member of a group, they experience the piece from the perspective of an individual person playing an individual part, hearing it through their ears, They can only listen to the entire piece in a rehearsal to the degree they have concentration left over after dealing with their own parts.

A tape of a rehearsal allows students to listen to a whole piece apart from their responsibilities for their own part. They can begin to hear other relationships and other sounds. They can do some listening in rehearsals or the tapes can be placed in a library or resource center. Copies could be made that students check out from the band room. Perhaps a half-dozen copies could be made of a typical or specific rehearsal. Part of the importance of this is showing that the performance of the whole group is important, the effort is a serious thing, the whole is important, the one part contributes, and a part is related to the whole piece.

They also should record their lessons. They can go home with the tape and can be reminded of things. In a sense, the lesson is retaught. The intent is for them to be listening, in this removed situation, which carries over to the rehearsal.

*(Frank Battisti)*

### Listening to recorded music can raise awareness.

Before school started in the morning, students could bring records to play in the band room. We traded. If they listened to one of mine, I would listen to one of theirs. Later I began to ask them "why" they wanted to play a particular record? They had to defend their choices. "It has a good beat" was not sufficient; they were urged to go beyond that. They began to focus their listening. They began to say, "The drum fills are different each time," or "This piece has an interesting bass part." These events led to increased listening awareness. The objective through listening and bringing their own recordings is to get them to realize why they like or dislike something.

*(James Arrowood)*

### Listening signals the beginning of rehearsal.

I never start a rehearsal by talking. It has always frustrated me to stand up in front of the band and wave my arms, nail kids for playing, or yell that they should be quiet. I would rather begin quickly and immediately. Therefore, the band and I have an agreement that when we are to start, I give a down beat and they play Bb. Most students begin playing Bb immediately. For those who do not, they are apt to hurry to get ready, since everyone else has already started.

*(Patricia Brumbaugh)*

When I am teaching them to listen, I feel that an ensemble of two, found in lessons, is as valid an opportunity as found in an ensemble of fifty or two hundred.

*(Kenneth M. Larsen)*

## CHAPTER FOUR

# SINGING

The value of singing is that it engages the ears of the students. It establishes a direct connection between the teacher's demonstration and the students' hearing, and between the students' aural experiences and the students' oral performances. The connections are direct; there is no instrument between.

The term, "eye-hand coordination," is used often in conversations about physical education, drawing, and some technical and manufacturing fields. Music teachers go one step further: they involve the student's ear while teaching an instrument, therefore they are developing the music student's "ear-eye-hand coordination" not just the eye and hand. Without using singing as a teaching technique, students might develop only the "eye-hand coordination" and learn to play the instrument without listening—without experiencing a growth in aural skills comparable to their growth in technical skills.

Instrumental music teachers use singing for specific instructional purposes. In addition to ear training and listening skills, some teachers use singing to show style, phrasing, and articulation. Some use singing to teach students to anticipate the sounds they are about to play. These teachers might ask students to hum the tuning pitch before students play the pitch, or to sing the phrase as they would like it to sound before students begin to play the phrase. Some have students sing the dynamic changes, articulations, or subdivisions to isolate musical or technical issues from the problems of the instrument.

Music teachers who use singing also change the music curriculum, whether they are aware of this or not. They add an emphasis upon aural skill development (singing, hearing, and comprehending chords, chord function, phrasing, tonality, etc.) to motor skill objectives such as facility, embouchure, intonation, and breathing.

Singing can also change the way and point at which teachers develop the students' musicianship. We can develop musicianship earlier with singing than without. Students can learn to sing and hear musical content sooner than they can develop the facility to perform at the same level instrumentally. Furthermore, aural or musical skills, and musical understandings taught this way also build readiness for the instrument and the reading of notation.

Finally, teachers can use singing to assess how accurately students audiate, or hear. If students can imitate the teacher's performance accurately, one can conclude they can discriminate the performance and style correctly. If students imitate incorrectly, one assumes incorrect discrimination. Both the teaching of students and the diagnoses of their learning can take place quickly when singing is used effectively in instrumental music classes.

Though some more traditionally oriented music teachers have not included singing as a teaching technique, singing is not new in instrumental music. During the interviews for this book, several teachers reported that Dale Harris, the founder of the American Band Association, used singing extensively more than fifty years ago to improve intonation in the Pontiac, Michigan school bands. It is very likely that Mr. Harris was not the only instrumental music educator to use singing in or prior to that era.

To understand why some teachers today are not using singing, one must look to tradition, to the past, and to attitudes. Today's instrumental music educators may not have experienced singing as an integral part of their own early training. They, in turn, are less apt to use singing when they teach their own instrumental music students. This explanation reflects the view, "Teachers teach how they were taught, not how they were taught to teach." Some teachers firmly believe that students will not sing. Other teachers, however, feel as strongly that students not only can sing and will sing, but students like to sing. Thus, the teacher's attitude seems to be a key factor. Teachers' inhibitions may also impede the use or success of singing. Many instrumentalists are unfamiliar with singing and lack confidence in their own singing skill. But, if teachers begin to use singing, their own singing will improve and they will learn to nurture singing in the students.

One can expect that the use of singing will continue to increase in instrumental music education now that the momentum for its use has begun. Many teachers are beginning to use singing to teach instrumental students; and, as more teachers begin to find singing a successful technique, others may wish to re-examine singing's place in their own instrumental music curriculum. The following positive comments should help one do this.

## THE VALUE OF SINGING IN INSTRUMENTAL MUSIC

### Singing pays off

I think singing works, and I've used it more in the last two years than ever before. I have finally learned that it pays off.

*(Michael Kaufman)*

### Singing is a basic step

If students put the vocal concept into playing, they have a better tone, listen better, and play more in tune. Singing also provides a stage upon which to teach and think while teaching and learning instruments.

*(Jack Brookshire)*

### The place of singing

Bands should sing early in every rehearsal: this helps them develop their ability to hear without a crutch. Unfortunately, we do not develop their ears as much as we develop their fingers and eyes. We need to develop everything through the ear. In a general way, it is a "Suzuki" approach. Without ears and hearing, playing and reading skills, or performance have no value at all.

*(Frank Battisti)*

### Rehearsing instrumental pieces vocally

I teach things without the instrument, particularly with college students who have had some training. We have even done a couple of rehearsals without instruments. We have done this on tour buses when a new piece came in.

*(Donald Wilcox)*

### Using singing to hear intervals

I use a hand system showing the notes of a scale. I represent the tonic with one finger; two fingers will be the second degree; and three fingers will be the third. I usually mirror this with both hands since I'm not going beyond a tetrachord or five scale degrees. We'll play it first and then we'll sing it because I am trying to get the students to hear intervals.

Playing intervals on an instrument is one thing, because one can always push a certain button and get something close to "major-third-ness." However, when students have to produce a major third vocally, that is another thing. They must think, and hear the distance and the sound.

We discuss intervals in band. If there's a chord we're having trouble with, we'll sing it. I'll have everybody sing the root, the third, and the fifth. Then, we will voice or blend the chord, listen to it and then return to the instruments. With this, the chord always starts to resonate and focus. With young kids, I use humming more than singing. A singer once told me that if one uses humming, one does

not have to worry about vocal problems, nor will students be developing vocal problems.

*(John A. Thompson)*

### Singing in marching band

I have the marching band sing a lot to rest their lips.

*(Terry A. Oxley)*

### The objectives for singing

Some of the aims of singing are to clarify musical style, improve intonation, or shape phrases.

*(Richard Fischer)*

All the musical things I've learned came from my singing experience—mostly from my mother who was the best teacher I ever had.

*(Terry A. Oxley)*

There is considerable singing going on in the country's bands. As I go around, I find that many directors are asking their students to sing the pitches back to them to develop tone quality and to teach ear training.

*(Frank B. Wickes)*

### Singing with students

Singing with students (not singing for students) is ineffective mostly because it is a distraction, and it has little to do with what they are learning.

*(Steven Cooper)*

### Singing is needed

I do a lot of singing, even if I do not do it well. You cannot tell kids how to turn a phrase, but you can sing it and gesture it.

*(Donald S. George)*

### Building readiness

We sing almost anything we do—nothing we do is safe from singing! It can be rhythm figures, melodic figures, harmonic figures, chord tones—nearly everything. We sing a great deal in the warm-up segment. Some people sing for funny reasons. They play what they want sung, they sing it, and go on to something else! Maybe they are singing for show. The order should be reversed: sing, then play.

*(Donald Gee)*

### The use of singing

If students can't hear a sound in their head and sing it (and play it on the mouthpiece if one is a more advanced brass player), students will always be missing notes on the horn. Students can put the right fingers down, but if their minds don't know where they are going, it does no musical good to play fingerings only.

I see no choice but to build an aural picture and physical feeling for pitch and rhythm. My elementary teacher did a fair amount of singing with beginners. It was interesting to see some years later the publication of Jim Froseth's *Individualized Instructor*, where singing is used before playing. When I was an elementary student we did that, but we did it with *Easy Steps to Band*. Teachers can use singing with any book. I don't know why my teacher used singing, but teachers are now finding that singing followed by playing makes an effective sequence.

As I played Meridith Wilson's *Music Man* this past summer, I kept thinking the whole time that the "think system" is actually all that Edwin Gordon and many other people are advocating—really, that is what they are doing.

*(L. Keating Johnson)*

## INITIATING THE USE OF SINGING

### Saying first, then singing

My kids have no problems with singing; they like to sing. Teachers who say kids won't sing are insane! I don't, however, announce, "Now we are going to sing." I started singing in a nonchalant manner, I say, "Say the first notes." Later I say, "Let's say the notes on these syllables." Eventually, we are singing. At first it is not so important how well they sing—it is important they begin to do so. Since they now are comfortable with singing, on command they can sing whatever, in any key.

*(Patricia Brumbaugh)*

### Through humming

In certain parts of the country, the students' resistance to singing is more firm. Humming helps side-step their reluctance to sing in the beginning. In the long run, if I can get them to hum, I can get them to sing.

*(Hal D. Cooper)*

### Getting singing started

Younger players hate to sing at first, but later they realize it need not be "a drag." We don't pretend to be the Mormon Tabernacle Choir, but it's amazing how pitch improves when they can relate it to their voice.

*(William W. Wiedrich)*

In pre-band class, we also do a lot of imitative singing and it's during that time they are using the solfege and the Kodaly-Curwen hand signals.

*(Nancy Plantinga)*

### Starting to use singing

We won't play anything that we have not sung first. Establishing singing takes time: you just cannot try it for a couple of days and decide it does not work. There must be a heck of a commitment.

To get started, you can go the piano and really work with them on slowly singing an F-major scale in tune. Then, maybe having half the group sing it while the other half of the group is playing it slowly. You can beginning addressing the issue of differences and discrepancies by saying to them, "They are singing the pitch G and you are playing the pitch G: now, what's the difference between those two pitches?" Some kid will say, "Well they are playing it higher than we were singing it." You can go on from there. If we hear a difference in pitches that causes beats, this is the time to say, "We use the term beats for the pulsating we hear when two sounds are not quite in tune—and we need to remove them." The idea is to get the group involved—don't just give them information.

*(Larry Rachleff)*

### Students sing in tune

Though some teachers tell me that kids won't sing, I think that's a crock! Kids like to sing and most kids do not sing out-of-tune. Developing singing is a matter of doing it every day from the beginning in fifth grade. They are not as shy about doing this in the fifth grade as they are in junior high. Treating singing seriously reveals that kids like to sing. To convey this, I do not allow them to act silly or be immature when we sing. Since they have been singing in class all along, it works very successfully. The vocal teachers also like it because most of the kids are in choir.

*(Jack Brookshire)*

### A cautiousness concerning singing

I ask high school students to clap but I do little singing. I'm afraid that singing used to develop intonation will turn them off before it turns their ear on. I believe this, because they are so self-conscious. Some will not mind doing it, but others would die before they would do it. I do think in principle that it is very helpful, but some students are very reluctant.

*(Judith A. Niles)*

### Establishing singing

I'm very much into singing to work on the ears. You ought to hear my top band sing compared to my ninth-graders. At first, the ninth-graders resist and I have to stick to my guns. There are predictable phases they go through but they come around eventually. First it's the giggles and second it is "come on, are we going to do this again?" The third phase they finally become believers, and then they belt it out.

*(Michael Kaufman)*

### Using singing in rehearsals

We do much singing of band parts. Sometimes we don't even care if the pitches are right. If so, I say, "We're going to make sure everybody's doing the right rhythms and see how it fits together, so sing your band parts." We may use singing to focus upon the dynamics, or the pitches; it depends on what we want to stress.

*(Frank Schulz)*

## Singing in the Instrumental Rehearsal

### Using singing to anticipate pitch

I have them sing their parts occasionally. It works very well, but mostly I am trying to get them to anticipate and aim for the pitch. Sometimes I have said, "You're playing first position and you're trying to play B flat, but you're really giving me an F." I want them to sing the note B flat so they hear what it should sound like. When they sing it, "bang!" they are "right on" when they play.

*(Thomas Stone)*

### Singing in rehearsals

When I use singing, I have the students sitting and opening their mouths as though they were in a choir. I do this because that is also the attitude and posture for playing. For singing, I like the vowel "lu" because students focus that sound a little bit better than others.

I devise sensitivity exercises that fit the music we are studying. If we are playing some piece in A-flat major, I may take an A-flat major scale and divide the group into four sections by timbre. This allows us also to address balance. I have the low timbres begin, singing an A-flat major scale with quarter notes up and down. Two beats later the lower-middle timbres or voices begin the same scale. Next, the upper-middle timbres begin two beats later than the lower-middle timbres. The highest timbres enter last.

Therefore, we sing (or play) a four-part canon on an A-flat major scale in slow-motion quarter notes. In addition, the like-timbre instruments are playing or singing together. Remember, the teacher is conducting this and students are responding also to musical non-verbal information. The teacher also should be conducting differently every time, after they have sung it first.

*(Larry Rachleff)*

### Singing rhythms and phrases

Our teachers sing a lot for students, saying, "This is the way I want this phrase to sound." We ask students to sing phrases back to us quite often, but we don't spend much time saying "you are out of tune." We often are out of tune ourselves. We also do not spend time expecting them to be singing in balance and in tune. We use singing to develop the accuracy of the rhythm and the shapes in the phrases. The shapes show what we want as the largest point in this phrase, and how we should begin and end the phrase.

*(Bryce Taylor)*

### Singing to teach style

With our jazz ensembles we do a lot of what we call "skat-singing." It isn't really, but we phrase "du-du-du-dop! We do this to hear the feel, style, and phraseology. Then we'll play. We're not as concerned with pitch as we are with the rhythmic intent.

I have also used it with concert band, such as in the middle section of *La Fiesta Mexicana*, in the Aztec dance before the brass come in with all of their power figures. I said, "Let's put the horns down and let's sing it the best you can." This lets them go freely with how they would express it. It was amazing, they had the right idea and it really came together.

*(John A. Thompson)*

### We sing everyday in warm ups

I use Leonard Smith's *Treasury of Scales* as the basis for our entire warm up. We sometimes pick a number at random, from one to ninety-six. Early in the year, I'll be very restrictive about what we try to sing, because they need to be comfortable with what they are singing. I'll make sure that we do some easier ones first.

We'll play the first pitch from their part, so they can figure out the starting pitch. Then we will sight sing the entire piece. Usually, they sing through the entire piece without a "glitch." This year we have a couple of very brave singers. When they sing too loudly compared to everybody else, we also can address balance. This has helped all of us learn how important balance is. The chord must be balanced for them to hear where they belong.

If we run into a problem while playing, we stop and check a chord through singing. If the passage is a very treacherous one, it is more difficult to sing since the parts were written for instruments, not for the voice. Here, I may have the brass sing and the woodwinds play; then I reverse that, and do it again. Sometimes, if they are really struggling while singing, I let them continue anyway to see if they can recover. Many many times, probably most of the time, even if they have a real breakdown, they will still end on the right pitches.

*(Gregory Bimm)*

### Singing to teach style

With applied students, I do some singing demonstration for articulation. The closer one gets to pop music, the more one has to do it. They do not grasp all the "du-dit-da's" very well.

*(Terry A. Oxley)*

### Singing

I am constantly talking about the singing approach. I use and show the singing approach and I make them echo my performance back to me. I have them echo it back more often than just listen to my demonstration.

*(Richard Putzier)*

### Singing models

I do a fair amount of singing, though I don't have a good voice.

*(Craig Kirchhoff)*

### We sing every rehearsal

Singing is what I use the most. We sing and warm up on chorales every day. For example, I will say, "We are going to sing the first eight measures and play the next eight measures." I also specify which syllable to use when singing—I want them to use the same syllable. On chorales we use "dah" or "daw." We never use the "t" sound on chorales.

*(Jack Brookshire)*

### Singing and fingering

We sing and finger the instrument simultaneously. We do this to work on hearing and technique. We use this combination, unless we sing to internalize a pitch or melodic idea.

*(Robert E. Foster)*

### Singing in rehearsals

We rarely play four scales in a row without singing. We alternate playing and singing scales. We also do them in three parts, where students enter successively so we have three-part harmony. We sing or play individual notes, the entire scale, whatever. Usually. we alternate singing one or more notes with playing these notes. We sing scales about two days a week.

On the other three days, we work on singing and playing intervals. We use the solfege system with this. At the end of the year, either band could take a sight-singing test on all the perfect and major (diatonic) intervals of the scale. Seventy-five percent of the students will get one-hundred percent correct. One band does major and the other band does minor scales. They can play them, recognize them, sing at sight, and tell you which intervals are played or sung.

They love to do this—it is a fun game. It also is an excellent attention-getting device that works very well with high school and with junior high. They find this easy to do. We do this a little every day—perhaps five to ten intervals a day—say three of the five days a week. We also play and sing intervals each time. I give them tonic in an easy key. Easy, being the keys that occur in sequence with the music we are playing. From there, we move out to the more difficult, unfamiliar keys as they develop skill.

This building of skill addresses listening and the new technical demands of the unfamiliar key. For example, I may list the intervals on a piece of paper and give the starting note I want played. Usually we do not sing the intervals. I play them on different registers of the piano or give the list to a student. The other students are to identify this. If they are "squirrelly" that day I will call on individuals who need to have their attention increased, or else anyone can answer. I vary timbre, range, instrument, register, scale, or key. I will sometimes ask anyone to play any interval, but it must start on the given tonic.

We also sing chord resolutions. Part of the band sings do-me-sol, others then sing re-ti-fa-sol, then do-me-do. Or, we sing patterns such as do-ti-do, so-so-so, mi-fa-mi, or: do-ti-do, do-do-do, and do-fa-mi together. We do a lot of this to focus upon pitch, intonation, and key.

*(Patricia Brumbaugh)*

# AUDIATION

The term "audiation" is new to some music teachers. Edwin Gordon, who introduced the term, defines audiation as the skill of hearing the sound when it is not physically present. This means that, at the moment one is hearing (audiating) the music, neither the audiator nor a performer is playing it in person or on a recording. The music, at that moment, is not physically present; there is nothing occurring externally to activate one's hearing.

For example, when we can hear a major or minor tonality or a duple or triple meter in our mind—even when no one is playing—we are audiating those sounds. If we can hear a succession of chords, such as a I-V7-I or a I-II-V-V7-I in major, without playing the chords ourselves or hearing them played, we are audiating major tonality. We audiate when we look at a passage of music and hear the sounds as written in the score. We also audiate when we notate what we are hearing in our mind.

However, if we can imitate an excellent tone or recall a specific melody, we may be recalling or imitating a part of the music. The key difference between recall/imitation and audiation is: with audiation, the person comprehends the music, its structure, tonality, and meter; with recall and imitation, the person only remembers the sound of the music, and its melody, pulse, rhythm, or tone color. Simple imitation or recall is not synonymous with comprehending; thus they are not the same as audiation.

When many students perform pieces written in major or minor, or in duple and triple, they may not grasp the tonality or the meter. They also may not recall or notice the difference between meters or tonalities. Though these students can perform the notes and rhythms correctly, this does not mean they audiate the music. To audiate, one must aurally discriminate the differences among sounds and comprehend the organization of the sounds; one must hear these differences before, during, and after they perform the music, and as they recall the music or see its notation.

Audiation is absent if instrumentalists only learn to press buttons or keys. If this is all students are taught, they are not apt to listen to the music. Without listening they will not develop aural skills and their music education will be lacking. Thus, as important as it is to develop the executive skills of performance, teaching audiation is vitally important for students so they comprehend the music's sounds and relationships. Without this, they do not as yet have an understanding of music.

In the following pages one can read of teachers who use their audiation skills in their teaching. They can deliberately show specific musical examples with their voice or instrument. They may, for example, show versions of a phrase, examples of a musical style, in-tune and out-of-tune sounds, and different tone colors. The teachers can audiate the proper or improper examples of what they wish to teach. This means they can audiate or recall the music that is not physically present and recreate it for students. Their audiation skills enable them to use their spontaneous performances as teaching techniques.

Other teachers show techniques that teach audiation more fully. They can teach students to audiate chord progressions and have students tune instruments within the context of tonality by using solfege. They teach students to hear and recognize tonality by having them play and improvise tunes in all keys. They go further and have students play minor tunes in major or dorian tonalities, and major tunes in minor tonality. They also have students play the tunes in different styles or meters—all to build the students' vocabulary and aural experiences with music. This is done so a student can understand and audiate the music; not just play the pitches and rhythms mechanically or metronomically correct. Even if correct, the student who does not audiate lacks the aural awareness of pitches and rhythms as they occur in meter and tonality.

## THE IDEA OF AUDIATION

### Thoughts about tuning

In the very beginning I would have them tune unisons. Then after about six weeks I would have them tune to chords. I also taught them they could hear in their mind's ear as they could see in their mind's eye. I would say, "Can you close your eyes and see a big red ball floating on the swimming pool." They could do this and they could imagine a fog horn or a factory whistle. I did this to teach them that their ear can hear without actual sound being produced. I said, "If you can do this, you can learn to hear and play in tune. "

*(John Kinnison)*

### Audiation versus imitation

Let us look at the singing of *America* to grasp the key difference when one compares imitation to audiation. If they can sing *America* when asked to think of how it sounds, they are audiating the song or the melody. We can go further: as they are singing *America* we can ask them to stop and hum or sing the "home tone" or "tonic." Many of them cannot find it; this means they are audiating only a part of the music—the melody only. If they can audiate only the melody or the rhythm, all they are doing is *imitating America*. They are not *audiating America* in context with its tonality; therefore, they are not audiating it comprehensively.

To audiate *America* more fully, they must be able to perform the melody, to sing it in several different styles, to perform the pulse and meter, to perform various rhythm patterns, to find tonic at any point, to sing or audiate the song in different tonalities such as minor or dorian. With additional audiation skills, they could audiate embellishments and variations of the melody and even audiate the harmonic progression. Therefore, the key difference between imitation and audiation is the degree that the musical object is present in the student's mind. The more he can audiate, the less he is just imitating and the more he is comprehending.

*(Richard Grunow)*

### The value of audiating

Hearing the tone in your ear or imagination is the most important factor in achieving good intonation. To foster this, we listen to many recordings of good tonal models. We talk about what we like about those recordings, which raises their awareness. To me, developing tonal concepts can be done if they surround themselves with excellent musical sounds: opera, singing, instruments, or whatever. Whether you are a saxophone player and you listen to a trumpet, is immaterial.

*(Richard K. Hansen)*

### Audiation is a basic skill

I think that the demands of music making are multifaceted. One of these is the ability to hear something in the mind before it happens out on the horn.

*(Charles Olson)*

## TONE

### Thinking ahead

Students can learn to anticipate what they do as they play, before beginning to play. For example, they can

audiate—aurally and physically—the tone color, the steps in inhaling, the tempo, the process of starting the tone, etc. as they begin and carry through the inhalation of the air. This also is another skill that improves with repetition.

*(Joseph Casey)*

### Imagining the ideal sound

Because they are not using the book, they can do a lot of playing with their eyes closed. I will play recordings for them of famous brass players and woodwind players, or a famous band or wind ensemble. I have told them many times, "Now, close your eyes and just pretend you are on the stage in Orchestra Hall and thousands of people are listening to you play. All have paid $30 and they want to hear the most beautiful sound, and it might just be one note." When they are thinking that idea, I really notice a difference. The idea of tone in their head shows through their instrument.

*(Nancy Plantinga)*

### Imagining the sound before it is created

One also can ask students to think of the most beautiful sound they have heard or experienced and play that sound. Sometimes, I refer to sounds in pieces we have played before, or to a listening experience I know that they have had before that can stimulate recall.

*(Richard K. Hansen)*

### Listening assignments, the first step in applying tonal concepts

I had a recording library of all the instruments, ensemble, etc., so I gave the students listening assignments. I selected very specific excerpts of music, beginning by thinking, "Who should this student really listen to? Who would he get the most out of?" Then, I might send him home with a recording of Dennis Brain, for example.

I would ask the student to think about what he heard. He was to imagine his world is full of horn players like Dennis Brain playing a B flat. "Now imagine four Dennis Brains surrounding you all playing this note. Now imagine yourself as thirty people all playing the world's most beautiful B flat." Finally you let the student play, and the difference is like night and day.

*(Timothy Mahr)*

## SONGS

### Audiating phrases

I use blowing air streams and gestures with tubas and baritone students to help the students feel length, duration and phrasing. We do this to imagine in our heads the line growing; or, we try to imagine the physical feel for a line going forward or backward. We do this instead of thinking about the actual fingerings or the amount of air.

*(L. Keating Johnson)*

### Going beyond basic instrumental skills

Many students in a good band in our area had embouchures that were not picturesque. They played well, however, because they had a idea of how the piece should sound. Though the mouthpieces were off to one side, the clarinets' chins were not flat, and the flutes weren't "pouted," they could perform very musically.

*(Charles Olson)*

### Transpose simple patterns aurally

Start this real early, before they become afraid of transposition. Play something out of the beginning band book and tell them, "Okay, play every note one note higher." They will scramble a little bit. Then say, "Well, now a couple of things don't work. Remember how you had that B flat in there? If you go up one note from that, you should play a C." You can teach them about keys and get to them to transpose after a month or two, before they have played long enough to be afraid of it. This can be done with a simple tune such as *Row, Row, Row Your Boat*. Say, "For next class, why don't you start this song on F, and play that tune. You can learn it by ear or you can do it with the book."

*(Donald Wilcox)*

### Audiating the model

From time to time, I might execute a passage in two opposite ways or two different ways, and then they can hear what we are talking about. I can tell them, "The first way I am modeling is what you are doing and the second way I am modeling is what my imagination is telling me to do. Look and listen to the differences."

I use the expression, "Sing it as you would like to hear it." Then say, "Now sing it like the way you are playing it." They can make and notice the difference, because their imagination gets a tickle. Students are often not allowed to try things and use their imagination, so they are not accustomed to doing these kinds of experiments. Therefore, they have not learned to try something when there is a risk of failure.

*(Larry Rachleff)*

### Score study and audiation

Studying the score is important if one "hears" what the music is to sound like before or after the analysis. If not, the beautiful analysis is without any result.

*(James Froseth)*

### Developing a sense of tonality

The thing that makes tunes more "powerful" than scales is that tunes establish tonic, dominant, and other tonal functions more "powerfully" than a scale does. Scales at best develop technique and technical skill, instead of a sense of tonality—since scales' sounds suggest only the leading tone and resting tone—but, they do that in a less powerful way than tunes.

*(Richard Grunow)*

### Playing a song on a new "do"

Instead of teaching transposition as an exercise in interval adjustment, ask beginning students to perform tunes in new pitch locations. Assign a new pitch as "do" and ask them to make the tune sound "correctly." Provide new fingerings as necessary to perform the piece in the new pitch location.

*(Stanley L. Schleuter)*

### Developing the sound of a song, before playing

When students are sight reading or working on a troublesome musical passage, I have the students sing the melody or their part. If they can accurately reproduce the music vocally, they nearly always can perform the music accurately on their instrument. This is true whether it is a wind instrument such as clarinet, trumpet, or recorder; or other instruments such as the piano.

*(Sharon Rasor)*

### Sing before you play

If you can't sing it, you can't play it. Which means that to sing it, you must know your part—its pitches, intervals. If you can't hear something that is on paper, you are not going to play it musically. This distinguishes fine readers from those who must do it over and over to learn to play the piece or their part.

*(Carl A. Bly)*

## AUDIATING SINGLE PITCHES AND TONAL PATTERNS

### Audiating and identifying patterns in a song

A teacher can enhance learning tonal patterns by asking students questions such as, "What songs do you know that contain do-mi-sol?" or, "How often does mi-re-do sound (or appear) in this melody we have learned?"

*(Stanley L. Schleuter)*

### Hear the note before you play it

Particularly in warm ups, I will conduct and stop abruptly. Then, I have them sing the next note. This occurs on anything from warm-up chorales to scales in fourths. I cut them off and they sing the next interval. The idea is they must know where that note is; they can't just start blowing the horn and groping around for it. Aural recognition is where it's at!

*(Donald Wilcox)*

### Transposing

With the younger bands, we'll use the *Treasury of Scales*. We will play it as written in four-four or then we might play it in cut time. I also might say, "Take the notes you have and play them one half step higher." It's chaos the first time you do it. They are transposing accidentals; they have the natural-half steps like E and F, and B and C.

It really is a marvelous way to get them to think. Suddenly, good old number nine out of the *Treasury of Scales* that they can play in their sleep is all now in E major.

I picked this idea up from Reginald Fink's book, *Legato Studies for Trombone.* He writes a little legato technique for a warm up in C. Then he writes it in C sharp and then in C flat. I remember as a trombone student, using that material and being intimidated by C-sharp major and C-flat major, yet it was the same melodic line. The exercise had the same phrasing and articulation, but everything was a half step up or a half step down. I do enough of this with my students that it keeps things interesting.

*(John A. Thompson)*

### Audiating the pitch

I try to get them to realize that they need to replicate mentally the pitch before they produce it. They are more apt to be out of tune if they cannot hear the pitch in advance.

*(Pamela Gearhart)*

### Singing and playing

We alternate playing a measure and singing a measure on scales and chorales or, we sing a note and play a note. One also can pick isolated chords. We stop playing the instrument on one chord, then sing the next one. These exercises build pitch awareness.

*(Robert Allan)*

## PHYSICAL ACTIONS

### Linking the fingerings to what you hear

To develop audiation skills, mentally sing familiar tunes while doing the correct fingerings.

*(Stanley L. Schleuter)*

### Developing the audiation of physical actions

I suggest teachers use simulated playing a lot as they sing, before they have students pick up the instrument. This allows them to see and feel the actions of playing an instrument before they actually play the instrument. This means that they have internalized part of the process before manipulating the complete process that is entailed in playing the instrument.

*(Richard Grunow)*

### Recalling physical sensations of certain volume levels

Volume change is not done just with air alone, but includes also how muscles function and react while producing certain volume levels. Therefore, if we are moving from a strong section to a softer section and the volume change is not evident, I sometimes ask them to remember that they also must make a physical change. The kind of exertion and effort needed for the strong passage may feel different. They solve this by recalling the feeling and actions needed to play the softer passage. Since there is body involvement in making the transition, I give them time to put their body in a specifically different state. It seems to work. After this short quiet time when they are thinking and changing their physical approach to the next section, they do play the passage more accurately than they might have without this preparation.

*(Richard Fischer)*

## RHYTHM

### Sensing subdivision improves audiation skill

I have two students stand in front of the band, back to back. To a tempo of about sixty beats per minute, I have them count silently to eleven. When they reach count eleven, they clap their hands on that pulse. After they do that, I ask them to do this with subdivision mentally. When they do this with subdivision, they are more accurate in keeping the sense of pulse together, judged by when they clap on beat eleven.

*(Thomas H. Cook)*

### Internalizing the subdivision

In four-four time, we start with eighth notes followed by eight counts of eighth notes, eight counts of quarter notes, eight counts of half notes, eight counts of whole notes, one eight-count note, and then one sustained sixteen-count note, and then we end.

What we are doing sounds like "stop-time." First, we do it with our eyes open and I conduct, and then I don't conduct, and we close our eyes and do it with no cues of any kind; they just have to internalize things. When we start doing it, it makes the kids realize just how very different their internal clocks are, and just how hard they have to work to stay in pulse. We use this outside too; we'll have the kids march with their eyes closed, and that gets to be pretty interesting watching their feet.

*(Gregory Bimm)*

### Anticipating the tempo

I insist that kids think ahead. I want them to know what they're going to play before they start to play. I ask them to think through a few measures of the song before they begin. This is necessary, especially if they're involved in playing a solo at a contest.

*(Lance Schultz)*

### Anticipating the sound of a rhythmic unit

Whatever the rhythmic unit is, I want them to focus in on that unit. I point out a rhythmic unit that's coming up. If we will be reading a triplet off the main pulse, we begin thinking in advance of the triplet and just what its sound will be. I don't think we do enough anticipating of the sound of a unit or enough practicing that would develop this skill. As a result, there is a tremendous amount of guess work taking place.

*(Robert Levy)*

### Natural breathing through listening

We may be wasting our time teaching kids how to breathe when we compare that with the value of time spent teaching them how to audiate. Audiation means the skill of knowing in the mind the sound of the next phrase before playing it. If they know this, musically, they will take in the right amount of air to play that phrase. They therefore need not be "hammered" about breathing as much.

If they don't audiate the next phrase, the problem as students play may appear to the teacher as a lack of air or air support. The origin of the problem actually is the absence of audiation of the music to be played. If they truly audiate, they will audiate in phrases or musical statements. They will prepare to play with enough air to perform what they audiate; hence, to the director they will not appear to have a "breathing problem." This is parallel to uncon- sciously or involuntarily taking in enough air to sustain a spoken sentence. We rarely run out of air when we talk, because we know what we are going to say. We know how much air it will take to say what we want to communi- cate—with all necessary accommodations for the statement's length, inflection, emphasis, dynamics, style, and meaning. With a musical instrument, taking in air can become involuntary to the same extent as in speaking—if we audiate what we are going to say or play.

Where we hurt kids is starting them playing whole notes and asking them to "perform" them without audiating the note. The parallel is sitting with kids and teaching them to say one word at a time. For example, say "the" fourteen times with a gap of silence between, then fourteen times say the word "cat." If we taught them how to read words that way, we also would have to teach them how to breath. This whole issue—breathing is determined basically by audiation—is one of the most enlightening things I have found out while working on the instrumental series.

*(Richard Grunow)*

# CHAPTER SIX

# ISOLATION AND SIMULATION

Isolation is the organization of instruction so the students can focus momentarily upon a single part of the whole. Thus, for part of the class, the teacher is teaching to only one objective. The reason for this is straight forward: if students are focusing on only one facet, their learning can be more productive because they do not have to think about and manipulate several facets simultaneously.

Isolating a task requires that the teacher knows the relationship between the whole and the parts. Then the teacher must decide which part of the musical, cognitive, or physical action needs attention. The teacher decides what skill or idea he wants students to learn, then selects an appropriate teaching technique to help students attain that objective. When the student is successful with the isolated task, the teacher must integrate the skill into the complete process, so the student experiences the whole musical, cognitive, or physical action again.

Isolation often includes another teaching technique called *simulation*. When we ask a student to focus his attention upon one facet of an operation, he is not experiencing the whole; his is only replicating or simulating some of its parts. For example, saying "taw" is neither the tone nor the making of the tone itself though it does approximate part the process. Focusing upon one facet of tone production by saying the syllable "taw," can influence the shape of the oral cavity, the angle of the tongue, and the student's concept of the sound. In this example, the teacher isolates the tonguing, and asks a student to simulate the tongue's movement and to shape the oral cavity. The result can be the improvement in the tone quality that the teacher wants the student to show.

Two additional examples, practicing fingerings without producing a tone or breathing in and out through a plastic tube, also simulate different parts of the performance process. The use of isolation and simulation bring forth an action that is not the performance itself, but it allows the students to learn the correct fingering, to simulate the open throat and the dropped the jaw, or to keep their teeth apart.

Simulation and isolation can increase the teacher's effectiveness when he isolates what he is teaching. The students' chances for success are increased because they are given tasks they can understand, focus upon, and accomplish. By isolating one facet, the teacher has given them a challenge they are more apt to meet with success.

## THE VALUE OF ISOLATING TASKS

Have them put their instruments down, so the instrument is not a potential distraction. Then, I teach each thing, such as key signature by itself. By teaching one objective at a time, learning is strengthened.

*(Barbara Buehlman)*

If we are working on a technique, I try to divorce the specific motor skill, such as moving the fingers precisely together, from the other skills needed to produce sound. Working on more than one skill sometimes interferes with one's concentration. Isolating saves time and I can correct a problem more quickly than by merely talking about it.

*(Robert E. Foster)*

I encourage students to isolate tasks. Then they do not have so many challenges to contend with simultaneously. Isolating tasks allows students to focus on specific problems without having to think about multiple challenges simultaneously. It is difficult to think about blowing, counting, listening, etc. at the same time and be successful. Handling this many actions while trying to focus on one is difficult.

*(Richard Floyd)*

### Isolating in a rehearsal

The rehearsal always comes down to the idea that *you know what you want and you're trying to get it*. The basic problem most people have is they know when it's not what they want, but they don't know what's wrong with it, what it should be, or how to fix it. So they keep the rehearsal going by saying, "Let's try it again guys—only do it better this time."

So another principle is: I try to isolate, as quickly as I can, what the issues are; so I'm not conducting generally.

203

I am conducting more specifics: specific musical ideas, specific individuals, specific groups, specific persons, and individual percussion sounds. I do this to get the isolation, so I know what the whole picture is and so I know the individual ingredients.

Isolating, then, is one excellent way to rehearse. If you don't know what's wrong and you think, "I can't stop because I don't know what to say," then start eliminating what you know is *right*. Perhaps you heard something wrong and you know it was among the low instruments. Say, "I want only to hear the lower woodwinds and brasses." Then you think, "Okay, it's not a woodwind so it must be a brass" and say aloud . . . "Let me just hear the low brass." (You may be thinking silently, "It's not the tubas, so it's somewhere else.") You're just cutting away what you know is okay until finally you get down to somebody and you eventually can say, "Trombones, that's E flat in the 2nd part" or whatever the issue is. Very often people are afraid to stop because they don't know what's wrong; so they go on and say, "Okay, let's play this better."

The mere fact that you isolate something and listen to it again is going to help it. The old principle of "what you work on gets better" is proven out time and time again. Whatever it is you're working on, just stop and work on it. You might not even be very good at it, but it'll get better because you're focusing the players' energies on that issue. Therefore they'll concentrate their ears and minds on it, even though your technique of getting it better might not be so hot.

*(H. Robert Reynolds)*

I sometimes use listening games where I ask people to listen to a particular part for no particular reason, simply to get them to listen. I play these questioning games sometimes with groups who have pitch problems such as not having a good pitch center to the group. Instead of dwelling on pitch immediately, I will sometimes ask, particularly if we are playing something lyrical, "Everyone listen to the 2nd oboe" or, "Listen to the 3rd cornet part." I find that simply by commenting, they are all listening to the certain part. It is amazing how many pitch problems this approach takes care of.

*(Gary Hill)*

# Rhythm

### Improving rhythm during ritards

In order to "routine" a ritardando, I will have students finger the notes while verbalizing the rhythm as I conduct the ritard.

*(Richard Floyd)*

### Isolating new or old rhythms in an etude

In *First Division* or any beginner book, I leave out the unfamiliar new rhythms during the first playing of an etude. This helps them realize that they already have conquered most of the new etude. They also can find the spot that is new. This encourages them to take a shot at the new note or rhythm because it isn't most of the piece.

*(John W. LaCava)*

### Isolating rhythms through counting and subdivision

I will notate a rhythm on the board and I will ask everyone to sing the rhythm. An example is a dotted eighth and sixteenth, two eighths, quarter, quarter rest. I have half the group enunciating sixteenth notes very carefully, without their instruments. They will chant, "one e and a two e and three e and a four e and a" in a very metronomic, staccato voice. The rest of the group also would be chanting in rhythm, but more loudly on the moving notes. For example "*ONE* e and *A TWO* e *AND* a *THREE* e and a four e and a."

Then, I might yell "switch!" This means that the group doing the metronomic counting switches with the group counting the parts that have notes moving on some subdivisions. Then, taking it a step further, I change to a different tempo. If the tempo is fast, I might speed their counting until it is almost hysterical. Through this, they see there's a specific place for each part of the subdivision or rhythm. I also I might be conducting it in certain ways so they would be seeing various musical styles of the rhythmic phrase.

*(Larry Rachleff)*

### Isolating rhythms during warm ups

I find rhythm patterns with which they're having trouble and include these rhythms in the warm ups. That's no big deal, everybody does that I'm sure, but this is one technique I use to overcome poor rhythmic development.

*(Richard Kennell)*

### Isolating each duration's beginning

Let's say some in the group have moving eighth notes and the others have half notes. One way I teach them that half notes are slower than the eighths is to have half the students play the half notes. They would not play the half note per se, instead they would play a staccato eighth note and three eighth rests. This clarifies exactly where the half note is to begin. In effect, they are playing a staccato note at the point of the half notes' beginning.

Another way is to play four eighth notes in place of the half note. The next step is to return to playing it as written while remembering and understanding where those eighth notes begin. What we usually get, for the moment, is machine-like playing that is unmusical. However at least they attain a rhythmically accurate passage. Then, to bring back musically expressive playing, I tell them, "do what you were doing when emphasizing the line, but don't feature the rhythm as much; then, you've got it."

*(Larry Rachleff)*

### Isolating note beginnings to improve precision

We use a technique for precision that we call "bopping." I describe it to the students as playing in stop-time to place the beginnings of every note correctly and to hear clarity through the ensemble. I have them shorten the beginnings of every note. They play the note length at the absolute minimum even if we temporarily are throwing other musical issues, such as clarity of pitch or tone, out of the window.

I ask them to play the right notes, but to play them as short as possible. Then, we all can hear how the notes and rhythms line up. It is surprisingly difficult for them to play long notes that way. On a whole note, they have to think about how long that note is. They must remember how long the note is, take a breath, and then come in. As a result, they are also practicing note lengths.

*(Gregory Bimm)*

## Phrasing

### Isolating phrasing

When they have a tough lyrical part that needs better phrasing, I say, "sing this." Often they play something so oddly on their instruments. When they sing it, though, the phrase will make perfect sense. We usually sing on an "uuu" syllable, not "taw or toe." If they sing, they shape the phrase so much more musically. This is possible because they do not have to worry about this valve, that fingering, adjusting pitch, breathing, or reading the rhythm.

*(Michael Golemo)*

We also have worked upon the proper conducting and response to the up and downbeat—so they mirror the inhalation-exhalation process. If my gestures and their responses are smooth and continuous, one result is to make the tongue inaudible. When we work on this in isolation, we are building a stimulus-response pattern. We then apply the new response to the musical playing in a piece. I know they will not have a problem if I conduct without a hesitation and they respond in kind.

*(Donald Casey)*

### Isolating to erase habits and improve phrasing

I lead a warm-up exercise in a key or a tonal center. I have them do some phrasing on scale tones before we read the tune. I have them do something in that key, even if it's just a scale. They do a short free-form improvised composition with their own dynamic intensities. Soon, that's more fun than playing the printed etude. When playing a melody of their own invention, they need not worry about any fingerings or anything. As a result, they are often far more expressive.

I have them do this exercise to break them loose from all those instrumental habits. The habits emerge each time they pick up the instrument. When they pick up the

instrument, it is as though they pick up a huge coat full of funny habits. If they go in new directions with their playing and let those old habits die, their playing can improve. When the student is nervous or under some stress, though, some bad habits may come back. The poor habits never are fully erased, sad to say.

*(L. Keating Johnson)*

## Instrumental Technique

### Fingering

I have them finger the instrument while they are saying or singing the music. This is very effective because it isolates one issue at a time. Also, they finger sometimes as I sing, say, or play. This works like magic and it focuses their mind.

*(Steven Cooper)*

When notes and fast scale-like passages are not together, it usually is not that the air is used poorly. Usually, it is the fingers that do not move together. If the fingers do not go up and come down exactly together, the notes won't come out together and ensemble suffers.

For example, I have them sing on a neutral syllable and finger furiously! If everyone is quiet, we can hear the pads popping and that tells if they are together. If woodwinds, especially, do fingerings and produce no sound, the band can tell whether the woodwinds are together. The woodwinds also can tell, when isolated, if they are failing to finger hard enough. The students may be using too little energy to move the muscles the way they should.

Precision often is a finger-motor skill and dexterity problem, not a sound production problem. Removing sound making for a moment, can solve the dexterity problem. When they play again with sound, the music sounds better. We do a lot of drill without making sounds, because often it is the fingering that is not together.

*(Robert E. Foster)*

When I'm teaching fingering technique, I always teach it with their eyes closed, which increases their sense of touch. When they echo me, this reduces their looking compared to their listening. Often they are playing the correct fingering by sight, instead of listening. Asking them to close their eyes, makes the ear instead of the eye be at the center of the decision.

*(Gordon Nelson)*

### Breathing

Everyone lays on the floor so they have the idea of where the air goes and what part of the body moves when they breathe. I even put on a tape recording, so they don't have time to think about it or talk to somebody else. Usually the tape is "mood" music that can relax them and this influences them to notice and to feel that breathing is coming from the diaphragm. With most instruments other than trombone or tuba, students are on the floor with their instruments and I will have them play. If they are clarinets or flutes who must use both hands to play, they will lay a book or something on their diaphragm area. Then, when they play one tone, quarter notes, or whole notes, they feel the diaphragm's action.

*(Gordon Nelson)*

### Isolating breathing

Get a two-inch length of plastic tubing, one inch in diameter and plastic bags from the grocery store, usually the gallon-size bag. Put the tube inside the bag and wrap a rubber band around the bag so it does not leak. The students blow air into the bag so they can see how much air is in the bag. Then have them inhale all the air from the bag so they practice deep breathing. It's amazing to find out how little air they used before this exercise.

*(Ross Kellan)*

If I ask them to sizzle a long note pianissimo, there's no way they can do it without supporting. Therefore, this is another way to teach support. I'll sizzle and ask them to imitate that.

*(Craig Kirchhoff)*

### The exhale

To get the intensity and breath speed up, have them inhale and "hiss" for a sustained period like four counts, six counts, then eight counts. They can build the habit of rationing the air and releasing the air at a certain speed. They practice inhaling a good big breath on the preparatory gesture and sustaining it for a long time.

*(Donald Wilcox)*

### The inhale

If I want the band to prepare for playing with more support and more air speed, I say, "Play concert F and I want you to hold it as long as you can. We are going to have a contest to see who can hold it the longest."

When you give them a preparatory gesture, they all take in a huge breath, because they are planning to hold it for four days. Then, stop so they don't play the note. Then say, "Okay, that's the way you are supposed to breathe on every note." I want them to be very conscious of taking a big full breath, so I say, "Okay, breathe that way every time you play your horn. That's the way it's supposed to be!"

*(Donald Wilcox)*

### Dynamic levels

If I am in the middle of the piece and I'm getting an incorrect dynamic level, I say, "Hold the chord and play what you have on beat one in measure thirty-four." Of course it will either be too loud or too soft. Then I'll adjust it either way and put it back in context with the music.

*(Thomas Stone)*

### Final notes

If they're not playing the march's last note the way I like, I'll work on that before they know they are going to play that piece. If the note is, for example, concert E flat, I'll say, "Okay, I just want you to touch that tone as I give you a cue." I'll breathe with them in the style I want, and then I'll just cue that one note and conduct a cut off. I show them the length of the note with my baton.

If I want staccato, I'll just touch it with my baton like a flick. If I want it longer, I'll stay longer at the bottom of the down beat, and then I'll give them a cut off. I communicate the sound's length by conducting alone. Then I'll say, "Turn to the end of the piece. I want you to play this note in exactly the style we just did it." That is one way I put the isolated and rehearsed chord back in the music.

*(Thomas Stone)*

### Isolating one skill needed for articulation

A lot of style questions relate to the choice of "t" and "d" syllables. I use these syllables a great deal when singing, because this allows the instrument to be removed and not be a distraction.

*(Richard Fischer)*

### Isolating on the mouthpiece alone

Using the brass mouthpiece alone simplifies the process.

*(John W. LaCava)*

## ENSEMBLE

### Isolating accompaniments

On a march, for example, we may take the bass, horns, and possibly the trombone, and play a section in a slow-chorale style. This helps them hear their part, hear the pitches, and set the rhythm. This makes them more aware of the need to play sounds so they have duration, to hear their part in relation to the bass, to give ground work for phrasing the traditional "oom-pah" part, and to realize that the part is more important than they thought, which is always a danger on a march!

*(Michael Golemo)*

### Balance

Since students lack experience, they don't recognize when the sound is out of balance. Therefore, I isolate the sections of the band so people hear what the chord sounds like when everyone is in or out of balance.

*(Terry A. Oxley)*

### The preparatory beat

I will emphasize giving a preparatory beat so they know the purpose for a preparatory beat. I also have them do the gesture for a preparatory beat. Then I'll say, "I want you to count in four and I'm going to give you the upbeat to beat one, and I'm going to stop. I want you to keep counting the rest of that measure in time to see if you do it together." They find by watching the preparatory beat, all they need is one beat. After understanding that beat, they'll do two, three, and four exactly right.

*(Francis Marciniak)*

## SIMULATING INSTRUMENTAL PERFORMANCE SKILLS

### The instrument, tone, and the air stream

I place a cocktail straw through the mouthpiece, and up into and between the lips. As they have the mouthpiece up to their lips, I ask them to make the lip opening around the straw a bit smaller—if that is their problem. This focuses the airstream and pitch. This is more appropriate for a beginner.

*(Stanley Cate)*

I stress the "awwwh" in making sound, not "ehh." "Awwwh" fosters the building of good sound.

*(Carl A. Bly)*

I use different vowels with them to teach students to cover the tone and make it darker. I ask them to sing one note and put different vowel sounds into that note, like a di, die, day, du, dah, or doo.

These different vowel sounds create a different oral cavity. This, in turn, creates a different proportion of high partials and low partials in the tone. That helps a student work on the quality of the sound for himself, his section, his register, or for the whole group. I do those vowel sounds and they say them back, then they apply them to the instrument. I call it "tonal fusion" when we do match vowel sounds across the instrument parts, or across the same register of soprano or alto instruments.

*(Frank B. Wickes)*

If we are not getting good breath support from the ensemble, I have them sit up and "hiss" a whole note on the "ssssssssssss" sound. If students do that with vitality while sitting up straight and with a good breath, we have created the exact sensation they should feel when they are supporting a tone.

*(Richard Floyd)*

I use the idea of rolling a piece of paper, especially with the trumpets or brass players. They put it in their mouth, so they do breathing in a way that won't close the throat. They really get the idea of the open throat, because there is no way you can close the throat off with the roll of paper between the teeth. They also notice how the mouth is formed inside. I ask them to copy that by repeating it and I've found that kids soon have an improved tone quality.

*(Gordon Nelson)*

### Solo playing

I often have students stand on a chair while practicing a solo. To many students, this provides the same kind of sensation as standing alone "on stage" for the first time.

*(Dwaine Nelson)*

### Posture

For flutes, try putting a book on the music stand and ask them to read it with their head tilted. I say, "See how you like that?" Usually, they don't!

*(Carl A. Bly)*

### Simulating two drums

I have students write their own pieces for one, two, or several drums. They are to take two or more pillows and play them at home to experience the beginning of playing multiple drums and tympany.

*(Carl A. Bly)*

### Tonguing and articulation

We sometimes sing a part or composition through using syllables that approximate those they use when tonguing and articulating. For example, "du-du-du-du-duuuuuuuu" for four eight notes and a half note in a legato style. If it were in a separated style, they might sing using "ta ta ta ta taaaaaaaa" to approximate the tonguing while doing the rhythm.

*(Jack Brookshire)*

I use "tu" to simulate tonguing, because "tu" encourages more air to come out than with "taw." "Tu" also may fit the accent of kids in our area, where they talk with a drawl and a lazy tongue. That may be why "tu" is more effective in our area.

*(Stanley Cate)*

I use "taw" or "too" for the singing or saying syllable because it also corresponds to the tonguing motion. Even if they claim to be embarrassed about singing, if I start them with "saying rhythms," they usually go into singing rhythms and pitches on their own.

*(Steven Cooper)*

## USING SIMULATION IN REHEARSALS AND CLASSES

### Benefits of simulation

I believe many of my rehearsal techniques involve work with the horns, but not with the horn up by the chops. I think the more that one can do without students having to worry about the horn, the more successful one is. Therefore, I use vocalizing, or what I call a "sizzle technique," and blowing air streams.

I have found this to be an incredibly wonderful technique for teaching correct rhythm, and secondarily it's a way to save their chops. I use a "t" or a "d" attack, with a real articulation, as used on the instrument. If I ask students to sizzle a long note pianissimo, there is no way they can do that without supporting. Therefore, it is also another way to teach breath support.

*(Craig Kirchhoff)*

### Developing inner pulse

I use "hissing" on the subdivision; everyone goes "sss-sss-sss-sss" on the eighth note pulse. Hissing requires breath support plus the internal feel of the subdivision. I use it in the ensemble primarily to develop the feeling of internal pulse.

Keeping an internal pulse is a very crucial concept that students must develop as an ensemble. Often I say, "Whenever you have a rest of four beats or more, I want you to "hiss" the subdivision." Through this technique I also can determine how rhythmically stable the ensemble has become. If one stops beating time, the ensemble will either disintegrate or stay together rhythmically.

I feel this technique is an excellent way to sensitize the ensemble to rhythmic pulse. They must feel the pulse together before they can be successful. It is effective to isolate single tasks and I look for every opportunity to single out a task from the array of many that they must deal with. They then focus their energy on the specific problem and we have more likelihood of success.

*(Richard Floyd)*

### Simulation helps solve ensemble problems

I do much "sizzling," which means to articulate on the air stream. The intent is that students do exactly what they would do on the instrument, but do so on the air stream instead of the instrument.

I think simulation through "sizzling" is a great way of rehearsing. This technique not only identifies ensemble problems, but identifies the lack of unity in breath lengths, lengths of notes, style of articulation, etc. Sizzling also works as a marvelous "embouchure rester" without stopping the learning, particularly for long rehearsals. In clinic situations, sizzling is a new and different event to which students respond well. It also is amazing how quiet a room gets when you are doing that because people have to listen more intently than when they are playing.

*(Gary Hill)*

### Simulating rhythms, performing them on "ti" sounds

We did *Song of the Nightingale* that has some rhythms that are a challenge to fit together. I'd have everybody whisper "ti, ti, ti," on their own rhythm. With this technique, we can go over it several times very quickly and quietly, and the students can clean up the rhythm. Then, with their instruments, they can play it successfully.

I am doing it purely for rhythm and I like the "ti" sound when it's very soft. We all can hear throughout the group. If someone makes a mistake, especially if they have rests and they're in odd places, we can improve upon that with the "ti" approach. If somebody comes in wrong and gets embarrassed, they will not really be heard because of the softness of their performance.

*(James Stivers)*

### Silent playing

Simulation can be done often in a rehearsal. When one section is playing, another can be practicing fingerings, thinking pitches or even reviewing when they are to take breaths.

*(Jack Brookshire)*

I saw a kid holding an imaginary flute, fingering it and blowing in the "make-believe mode" because her flute was at the music store being repaired!

*(Robert Allan)*

### Simulating bowing

We use "imaginary bowing" sometimes while singing. I want them to make every effort to think the sound before they play that pitch with the instrument. We also learn pizzicato before bowing.

*(Marion Etzel)*

### Phrasing

I gesture usually for breathing and phrasing. I gesture, without singing, just how I want the phrase to sound. I move my hands and body to show how the phrase should sound. I gesture as I say, "The phrase goes like this, and ends like this." I also will contrast what I want with what they are doing by saying, "You are doing this (gesture) and I want you to do this (gesture)." I do this also with cutoffs, intake of air, articulations, or air through the instrument.

*(Patricia Brumbaugh)*

### Simulating the sight-reading contest

To prepare them for sight-reading contests and to make a "federal case" out of sight reading, we would sight read a new piece once a week using the full contest routine. They came in the room and their parts would be backwards on the stand. They would have five minutes to look at the part and, since I also was sight reading, I also would have a couple minutes to look at the score.

We went through a complete contest replica once a week. When we did that we always recorded it. After we recorded it, we would work on the tune even it if we weren't going to perform it. We would rehearse until they got a pretty good feel for how it works. Then we would go back and listen to the sight-reading tape and see where we "screwed up" and where we didn't. This sight reading routine took the length of the tune plus five minutes to look at the music.

*(Donald Wilcox)*

### Simulating and isolating proper posture

I teach posture in a standing position then have students apply it while sitting. Especially with brass players, I have them stand against the wall and keep their heads touching the wall as much as possible. Their shoulder blades and rear ends are touching, which gives them the feeling of stretching sideways instead of "scrunched-over." This opens their shoulders and arms. Then they try to keep that posture when sitting. I do this several times, expecting less during the first tries since they are stiff and awkward when they first try this.

*(Terry A. Oxley)*

CHAPTER SEVEN

# IMPROVISATION

Musicians understand that improvising upon chord progressions or on a figured bass, and to a degree, performing some embellishments constitutes improvisation. In improvised music, a given piece, section, or phrase is not done twice in the same way. Improvisation in this sense is uncommon in pre-college large ensembles or small group lessons. However, if teachers broaden their idea of improvisation, they can use improvisation frequently and early in the curriculum. To do this, teachers need to define improvisation as making musical changes based upon what the composer notated in the score. With this definition, a teacher can teach even beginning students to improvise.

Improvisation occurs anytime a student or teacher makes changes even to the smallest degree. Students can change the melody, rhythm, style, dynamics, or articulations. The changes may be switching a song from major to minor mode, embellishing a melody, altering the notes at the end of a phrase, or changing the rhythms. Students can make up a harmony part or perform simple embellishments such as trills and turns. They also alter the tempo freely, try different articulations, or eventually do elaborate free improvisation.

The intent of using improvisation is to have students experience music in a compositional sense. Through improvising upon or altering the music, they learn to understand the music. When they improvise they also learn a new skill or experience a new idea. To alter the music or improvise upon it, the student must use judgment, facility, and flexibility, making it an excellent complement to the attention students must devote to developing basic instrumental technique and facility.

## VIEWS AND USES OF IMPROVISATION TECHNIQUES

### Improvisation is not what some think it is

We want students to feel that improvisation is not what people say improvisation is. Some people think improvisation is playing what you feel without any pre-thought. We're trying to foster the idea that an improvisor

is really someone who has control of his instrument. They have an understanding of chord changes and scales, and bowings and patterns. Then in a gifted way, they put these ideas together and they create solos.

Based upon this, we also can say, "A good sight reader is not someone who reads blindly through a piece. A good sight reader anticipates things so they know what's coming. That's the connection." We say, "Look, if you know there's a three-four measure among six-eight measures and you're anticipating that, it's not going to throw you. Whereas if you're just going along without looking ahead, it likely will throw you." In a way reading music at sight is like controlled improvisation.

*(John A. Thompson)*

### Free improvisation

Free improvisation is the quickest way I know to "connect" melody with the student's natural expressive potential. It's an easy way to focus attention and listening to the flow of notes, and to the note's natural direction and resolution that is needed to create a "beautiful melody." The melody is original, natural, and not written; it *is* imagination, creativity, and expression.

This instructional technique allows the student to release and express his "feelings" through a melody. Free improvisation is always correct and never wrong! I try to establish a relaxed atmosphere when the student is improvising. I do not question or impose my ideas. This allows the student the opportunity to freely express himself through the beautiful melody he is creating. I also do not rush this procedure. The natural melodies, which often sound like nonsense in the early stages, will quickly change and take on "meaning" for the student and the director.

*(Edward S. Lisk)*

### Rhythmic variations

Ask students to construct, write out, and perform rhythmic variations of familiar tunes. Begin by changing the rhythm patterns to make a new ending to a familiar tune.

*(Stanley L. Schleuter)*

If there aren't any words to sing, then students can make them up or sing the song on a neutral syllable. The kids love to make up words and they also love to change rhythms.

*(Janet Tweed)*

### Rhythmic variations and free improvisation

An adult student of Mischa Mischakoff came to his lesson and performed the first movement of the Wieniawski D minor Concerto. It was an extremely arrhythmic performance filled with excessive rubato. Mischa stopped the gentleman saying, "No! No! You *must* play in rhythm" to which the student replied, "But, Mr. Mischakoff, I *like* it that way!"

*(Pamela Gearhart)*

### Developing discrimination of tonalities

To help develop a sense of mode, ask students to switch familiar songs to a different mode, e. g., major to minor, minor to major. Use the same resting tone in both versions so the change is to the parallel mode to avoid possible range problems. If possible, provide the right chordal accompaniment to fit the new mode so students may perform the melody against a chordal harmonic background.

*(Stanley L. Schleuter)*

### Tonal variations

Ask students to construct, write out, and be ready to perform tonal variations of familiar tunes. Begin by substituting tonal patterns to make up a new ending of a familiar tune.

*(Stanley L. Schleuter)*

### Improvising answering phrases and composing

I call it phrase-response when, instead of having them imitate what the teacher does, I play a little phrase for them and each kid responds to what I do. For example, I'll play a waltz melody of three or four measures. Then, I point to a student who is to create the finish for the phrase using those notes.

At first, I use only one measure of phrase and one measure of response. From there, we go into the composition of little three-note solos. I give them three notes and they write music with the three notes. They can use any octave so they might expand the choices to six notes or nine notes. I also may place some limit on the number of pitches, which makes it easier for the student.

I also can incorporate other useful learning such as the use of dynamics. I might say, "Your piece must have a crescendo and a decrescendo." I often give one different musical idea or term that they put into each composition.

Students have suggested steps to follow: The first step is to choose the three notes they wish to use in their compositions and improvise on these notes; second, improvise on the notes and shape a musical idea; third, use

dynamics to make the piece as effective as possible—for example, include at least one crescendo and one decrescendo; and four, memorize the composition so they can perform it for the class.

*(John C. McManus)*

### Composing pentatonic spatial compositions

I have them compose spatial pentatonic pieces. I may ask them to notate the piece, which allows us to open it up to kids who are not quite familiar with notation. We can have very different types of pieces. I can give them spatial pentatonic pieces or three-note pieces using D, F, and G where there's a skip between the first two notes. Once they write their piece, we can combine them into quartets. We put them in four corners of the room and they play their pieces in a "spatial quartet" manner. When we create spatial quartets, they can play their own pieces. In these pieces, each kid uses two to four notes from the all the pentatonic choices. They have fun with this.

*(John C. McManus)*

### Pentatonic solos and duets

I also have them write a pentatonic solo piece for their own instruments. To get the pentatonic scale, I usually give them the entire major scale first on the board. Then, we cross off the fourth note and the seventh note, leaving the notes with which they will work.

In the pieces, each kid would use two to three or four notes of the pentatonic choices from the diatonic scale. Once they have finished their solo and have performed it for the class, we have them team up in duets so they play each other's solo as a duet in canon form. They also could experiment to find out when the other part should begin. This might be two measures apart, one measure apart, one count apart, etc. Through this, they become familiar with canons and how they work.

*(John C. McManus)*

### Using composition to build skill at the beginning level

About the third week, when they know how to put their horns together, I give them a short creative assignment. I tell them they are going to write a short piece for their instruments using only two notes. Trumpets are going to use the low C and the second line G—these are open. (I also could give them the E and the A that have the same fingerings.) I select these notes since they're having difficulty deciding which notes are which when they try to play in the beginning group.) For trombones, the notes may be F and B flat. Clarinets can pick notes where they have to lift all their fingers at once and put them down together—such as a low C to an F. Flutes, oboes, and saxophones might use the third space C to the fourth space E flat where they move a lot of fingers up and down. Bassoons, for example, could use the notes from low B flat to an F. I say, "Use those two notes for your composition."

The first step is to select a mood. "What do you want? A fanfare? Do you want something slow and quiet?" The second step is to invent a rhythm. "Okay, use a rhythmic motive for your piece—if the mood is rhythmically oriented. Step three is to establish a musical idea, and step four is to memorize your composition. In other words, you don't have to write it down. Give it a title and perform it for the class." To help them select a musical idea or establish a musical idea, I give them some samples. Anything they can play, melodically or rhythmically, can be a musical idea, and the idea can be very short.

They then will go home to practice their composition and while doing so they learn how to play C and G. Most of these little compositions are in fanfare style because they lend themselves to this—you can't do much else with two notes. When I have six or seven kids in a class, I assign two or three a day. Then the next day two others play their assignments. I do this because you can't hear them all in the same day. In a beginning classes of fifteen to thirty kids, you can do that in two or three class periods. Of course, these compositions are very short—about a five-second or ten-second piece is the most beginners will do.

*(John C. McManus)*

### Teaching a student to transpose

Sing an excerpt in the tonality used in the book and have the students imitate your performance. Then sing the excerpt on a different starting pitch, but in the same tonality. Have them imitate that. Then say, "When we do that we call it transposing. We also can do that by starting on a different note when we play." Then, assuming it fits the age and skill of the student, give them a short motive or phrase from a song such as "Hot Cross Buns" or "Mary Had A Little Lamb." Have the student play and sing it on the notated pitches, then sing it on the new starting pitch. Give them or ask them to find the new starting pitch on the instrument and let them experiment.

*(Joseph Casey)*

# *Types of Teaching Techniques: Input Modes for Student Learning*

## *Part Two: Showing and Seeing Relationships*

# CHAPTER EIGHT

# SAME AND DIFFERENT

The term "same and different" signifies a teaching principle whose value lies in its parallel to how the mind works. Many persons believe that one learns by comparing the similarities and differences as the mind perceives two or more objects such as ideas, sounds, gestures, and pictures. If this is true, then teachers can capitalize upon this observation by providing students the opportunity to discriminate differences and similarities during music instruction.

For example, the teacher performs two intervals and says, "This is the sound of the interval of the fourth and this is the sound of the interval of the third." The students are perceiving two intervals and they can perceive the uniqueness of each because they can compare one to the other. Through this technique the student can be more successful than if the teacher only said, "This is the interval of the major third" without showing another interval for comparison or contrast. Later, if the teacher questions the students to see if they can identify each interval, the students are using their memory of these two intervals and others, as they hear and identify the intervals being played.

In another example, the teacher could say, "Play with a stronger high point in the phrase during measure thirty," and the students could find it difficult to comply if they do not know what a phrase's high point sounds like. If the teacher demonstrates a phrase first with a strong high point and again with a weaker high point, the students can perceive the differences and similarities and learn more quickly. Later the teacher could say, "Was there a high point in measure thirty?" or "The high point was too high." Then the teacher is generating the students' recall of phrasings, some with a high point, some without a high point; or any other shape in their experiences. As the students recall the "same and different" characteristics of both phrasings, they can perceive the uniqueness of each compared to the other—a phrase with an appropriate high point and one without an appropriate high point.

The personal experiences of many teachers strongly suggest that this teaching technique is successful, much more successful than when the teacher does not present students the opportunities to compare and contrast the "same and different" features. Another value of this technique is that it fits many purposes. Teachers can apply the idea of "same and different" to instruction that addresses a rather wide range of aims, such as balance, phrasing, music reading, dynamics, tonal functions, tonalities, tone, articulation, style, meter, intonation, rhythm, notation, balance, and blend.

The benefits of discriminating the same-and-different remain as students advance because as they continue learning new things, their ability to discriminate becomes more subtle. Through this technique, teachers can increase their control in directing students' learning. The teacher can choose what he wants the students to discriminate between and direct their perception to the critical differences that can range from subtle to obvious. If the teacher does not give students this opportunity to discriminate, their learning can only be the result of inference and chance. By making comparisons, students can learn much more successfully, and developing discrimination prepares the student for a lifetime of musical study.

## OBSERVATIONS ABOUT THE IDEA OF SAME AND DIFFERENT

Like many teachers, I am a strong advocate of modeling in the instrumental music classroom. One must be careful, however, not to assume that students are always successful in discriminating the specific characteristics one is trying to model. Modeling can often be more effective when the teacher presents the model and then follows it with a "non-model." This allows students the opportunity to compare and contrast the two examples. Teachers should move from gross differences between the two examples to more subtle differences.

*(Judith Delzell)*

I make them play, and then I say, "Now play it the wrong way and let's see what you think of that (I conduct it incorrectly also). Now play it the right way (I conduct it correctly this time)." Incidentally by doing this, the students' attention span in the rehearsal is increased.

*(Frank B. Wickes)*

215

I have students listen to something played two ways, or have them play something two ways—in either case I ask students to tell me the difference.

*(Anthony J. Maiello)*

I often play something and ask students to tell me what is different about the way I played this compared to the way they did it. In this, I join rote and explanation, and ask them questions that cause them to make distinctions and hear differences.

*(Steven Cooper)*

Sometimes I will have them do something "incorrectly," so they can compare and feel the difference. This engages their ear—it turns the ear on. We do this, for example, with balance and blend, as we are trying have them listen down. Then, we turn it around so the higher instruments are dominating the band's volume, and are more prominent than the mid- and low-ranged instruments.

*(Robert Grechesky)*

There are times when I will have them play something at the other extreme from what I want so they can see the differences.

*(Larry Rachleff)*

I have students hear how a tune or its style *is*, but it is also important to let students hear how a tune or its style *is not*. For example, if I'm doing a chorale and they're just not playing as legato as it should be, I will have them play the whole chorale in staccato style. After they are done playing, they'll say, "Let's go back to the other way, it sounds better."

*(Gordon Nelson)*

## TONE AND BREATHING

### Contrasting different tones
I imitate anything they do, whether correct or incorrect. I contrast incorrect playing with the correct sound I want. A teacher needs the skill to do this. We experiment: I play and they imitate, for example, different vibratos to fit a certain piece.

*(Jack Brookshire)*

With beginners, I talk about achieving a controlled tone. I play as loud and with as poor a tone as possible. They can hear that I can't play very loud with a poor and uncontrolled tone. Then, I contrast this by playing a good tone at loud volume level.

*(Jack Brookshire)*

With the brass in particular, I demonstrated poor tone versus a good tone. Then I talked about how I was

changing the tone color on my instrument, whether it is dropping my jaw, yawning, or singing. I avoid "e" totally. I use the "ah," "oh," and "taw."

*(Nancy Plantinga)*

### With posture
I have kids hold their shoulders up—near their ears. I make them keep them there as I talk on and on about—just anything. Finally, they may ask, "Can we bring our shoulders down now?" I have made the point or reviewed where their shoulders should be.

*(Gordon Nelson)*

## INTONATION

### Contrasting in and out of tune
They learn so much by bending pitch in and out of tune as an experiment. In a band rehearsal, I may have one or two play out of tune; or, have one keep the pitch and have one try to vary it. If they once understand how to bend, they will understand how to adjust.

*(Phillip A. Weinberg)*

If I say, "Let's play that chord out of tune everybody—now let's play it in tune," it's incredible how they'll change. "How does playing in tune feel versus playing out of tune feel?" I'll ask junior high kids, "Does out of tune playing feel good?" They'll look at me and say, "Oh no!" (as they make faces). They can understand the minute it is out of tune.

*(Eugene Corporon)*

Over the years, and to alleviate some boredom in these lessons, I have learned enough to demonstrate their instrument. This is how and where I can teach them to get their ears, since very few sophomores come in with any kind of listening skills. By sitting and playing with them, I can ask, "What do you hear? What am I doing?" I can play out of tune and miss notes, or change articulations and tone color deliberately. They begin to hear things and suddenly they begin to discover, Hey! That's a bad note. I can then say, "Well that's a bad note on all flutes or saxophones; what do you think we have to do about it?"

*(Kenneth M. Larsen)*

## PULSE, TEMPO, RHYTHM, AND METER

### Contrasting scales or modes
To help develop a sense of mode, ask students to switch familiar songs to a different mode, for example major to minor or minor to major. Use the same resting tone (tonic) in both versions so the change is to the parallel mode to avoid possible range problems. If possible, provide a chordal accompaniment to fit the new mode so

students may perform the melody against chordal harmonic background.

*(Stanley L. Schleuter)*

In the first part of the year, my singing and echoing with the students is done in major tonalities. I also am accompanying them with piano in major. When they are hearing that well, suddenly I slip into a minor accompaniment to the same music they played in major earlier. I do this so they notice the difference between major and minor.

*(Gordon Nelson)*

### Meter
With scales, we work with the difference between duple and triple by alternating, for example, two pulses of each. This alerts them to the difference, of which they have not been aware before.

*(James Arrowood)*

### Rhythm patterns
Any rhythmic group composed of eighths and sixteenths gives them trouble. I rotate between exercises— one that has two sixteenths and an eighth, one that has an eighth and two sixteenths, and one that has triplets. Those are the three rhythms the kids have the most trouble zeroing in on, especially early in the year. This is also a good way to point up exactly what we're doing with a triplet and exactly what a triplet is.

*(Ross A. Leeper)*

### Contrasting opposites
I rehearse passages where you can work opposites: slow but loud, fast but soft—simultaneous opposites. I say, "This is to keep from playing loud as you start speeding up, soft as you are slowing down, and getting mushy as you play slowly." There's a real strong tendency physically to connect high, fast and loud; and to connect low, slow, soft, mushy, and boring.

You also can exaggerate and contrast articulation. If you want legato have them completely slur everything in one breath and one unbroken sound, connecting everything until it all mushes together. Then, go back to a legato where you define the notes with a very soft "du" tongue so you can hear the change without breaking the line.

*(Donald Wilcox)*

### Rhythms and notation
I will say, "Now watch your music very carefully; I am going to clap this rhythm for you." I will clap it incorrectly in spots. Sometimes I will say, "Now I'm the teacher and I do not make mistakes, so you watch this very carefully." Right away they are alerted. Then, stop and wait and pretty soon the bright kids will say, "Well, you didn't play it right."

*(James D. Ployhar)*

## ARTICULATION, STYLE, AND PHRASING

### Using same-and-different techniques with phrasing
We try phrases in different ways even if they and I know the way it may eventually be performed. By trying different ways, they can sense what is good and what is clearly off-base. They develop a firmer conviction and clearer sense of what the preferable way is. This convinces them of the final version's worth.

*(Richard Fischer)*

I have them play something incorrectly, such as playing an accent on the end of the phrase. This contrasts with a tapered phrasing. This can be done with many problems and in many areas such as articulations, accents, and dynamics. An example is to play Baroque phrasing very staccato, and ask them, "Do you like that?" They say "No." They don't like it too legato either. This allows them to answer the question, "Where are the notes going and coming from, how should this be played?" Then, we can adjust the phrasing accordingly.

*(Pamela Gearhart)*

I use contrasts in teaching. If I want to teach an accent, for example, and it is not there, I ask them first to echo me in a very legato style. Then, I ask them to play in an accented style. Hearing contrasts is very effective, because they have to listen to do that. I try to awaken their senses.

*(Janet Tweed)*

I'll play two measures or so, and I'll say, "Play it back to me." If what they played was incorrect, I'll say, "This is how you played it. Tell me if it's right." Then they hear me playing the way they played it. I'll say, "Listen again; here's the way that you just played it—-and, here's the way we should play it."

*(Sandra P. Thompson)*

If a phrase in jazz band is to be played in a certain style, I usually play it two ways. The first time not carefully enough and the second way exactly the phrasing wanted. I ask them, "Which way sounds better and why?" If I have played it exactly right, they say, "I did this or that correctly or I released this note right." It is amazing how well they judge when listening. They do this even if they don't know exactly what I was looking for. After hearing it, I usually hear a big improvement in their playing.

*(Howard A. Lehman)*

Have them experiment with putting the emphasis in places that may seem unnatural and in fact are; by doing that they often find out that the inappropriate phrasing feels wrong.

*(L. Keating Johnson)*

When we make an interpretive decision or consider phrasing, we have to look at the options. For example, we'll try different arrival points in a phrase. I may say, "Obviously that's a wrong one, let's arrive on the second quarter note, not the third," or "Let's arrive on the sixth quarter note." We'll experiment in different places, with different shapes. For example, "Let's make it a shape that arrives in the middle and falls back," or "Let's make it a shape that doesn't arrive until the end."

I think exposing the phrase to several choices helps one decide the choice that is better. I do that with tempos and lengths of notes—with everything. I may say, "Play it extremely short, on a scale of one to ten, ten being short. Play it as ten, now play it as a one, now play it as a five." We decide which one of those is the most appropriate. I say "Well, maybe the right length is between three and six. We must decide—should it be five today or six?"

*(Eugene Corporon)*

Phrases need to have some artistic line. Doing a phrase with the absence of line—a monotone rendering— makes this need very clear because it is performed without the musical inflections. I leave the pitch and rhythm as is. Playing a line without shaping makes the need for phrasing obvious. This raises the question, "What are the choices?" The choices are finite: you can play a decrescendo and crescendo, crescendo and decrescendo, and loud or soft. I also have used only the rhythm of the phrase, particularly when the melody has many repeated pitches. I first have them play the phrase without the repeated pitches. That is, without these notes going to or from any note or point in the phrase. Then, I have them make choices of where the notes of the phrase should go.

*(Pamela Gearhart)*

If the kids are playing with a lack of inflection, sometimes you can humorously describe what they are doing by showing them in a complete monotone. It makes them laugh and gets the point across that they are playing like that and shouldn't.

*(Donald Wilcox)*

When working on something, we also try it wrong. I say, "Now you've gotten the idea, you did that beautifully, I like that. Now let's play it your old way. Let's screw it up. Okay, here we go, screw it up." Then the kids play it wrong. We'll try it the correct way again. Then I say, "Let's try it the other way again, when you played straight and didn't breathe."

*(William Long)*

In the studio and sometimes with ensemble, we try out musical things, such as style and phrasing, in different ways, maybe three or four different ways. Then we discuss the way that made more sense for the piece, for the style or even the harmonic rhythm.

We vary emphasis points. As when we speak, we put the em-PHA-sis on a different syl-LAB-le. We may lengthen high points of the phrase or shorten them. By doing this, students find out why one way may be a little better than another. Sometimes you see what's possible within a phrase and sometimes we define what feels natural simply by trying some very unnatural phrasing.

*(L. Keating Johnson)*

I demonstrate and have the kids demonstrate often— at least a couple of times per rehearsal. I imitate or I have students imitate the correct and incorrect playing of others. I do it wrong and everybody—including the person who did it—can also hear it.

*(Sandra P. Thompson)*

## Contrasting and Teaching Various Musical Elements

### Contrasting style and tempo

Sometimes I will have students play something at the opposite stylistic or tempo pole to see what it does to the nature of the piece. Marches played slowly and ballads played very quickly change the entire nature of the piece. This helps them grasp ideas of style.

*(John Kinnison)*

### Comparing drawings to dynamics

I use drawings of hills and valleys for phrase contours. It is partly humorous and partly descriptive. I sometimes will sing in a monotone and draw a straight line across the board. Then, I will draw a phrase with a "funny" shape as I sing it. Or, I change the drawing and the way I sing or I speak the last sentence. The drawing and singing may be different or include a correct or incorrect inflection. They usually grin, because it sounds so absurd. I do this so they hear how "funny" some versions sound. Then, I will sing the phrase with the correct contour as I also draw the phrase correctly.

*(Hal D. Cooper)*

### Comparing the meter's accents to those of the phrase

I contrast measured meter to the meter or pattern of accents suggested by the musical line. This helps them play musically and realize that the first beat in each meter group does not always get an accent.

*(Richard Fischer)*

### Teaching key signatures

I teach key signature recognition by trying choices. I say, "Okay, play that B flat as a B natural as if it were wrong. Decide when you come up to that B, whether you want it flat or natural." I also have two kids play the scale simultaneously, with one playing B and the other B flat. Obviously, the whole band can hear the clash.

*(William Long)*

### Balance and blend

I would have one play, then add one person at a time. They hear the previous ones and match their volume to the others. I also would ask those listening, "Which ones were equal or unequal to whom?"

*(Steven Cooper)*

I use the piano to create a certain balanced sound. I show them how a pianist must play the notes within a chord in different volumes with different fingers. Sometimes, I will show "imbalance" to give them sounds with which to compare. If I demonstrate poor balance, often some kid will crack, "Yeah, I like that sound better." That can liven up the rehearsal!

*(Richard Putzier)*

I start with building from the bottom for tone quality and so the sound balances. I put a drawing of a pyramid on the board. I start at the very base of the triangle to show how much of each sound is preferred. Then I'll do some "negative teaching" by saying, "Now let's turn the dynamics upside down." I'll draw the triangle upside down. At the very base of the triangle, which then is the point, we would have just a little tuba, low brass, and low reeds. At the very top, I have all the piccolos, snare drums, first trumpet, and cymbals. I'll say, "Let's play it that way" to show the sound when the high pitches dominate the low pitches. Then I ask them, "Which sound do you like the best?"

*(Dwayne P. Sagen)*

## CONTRASTING WHILE CONDUCTING

### Contrasting gestures

I say, "Play it like this" (as I say this, I gesture or conduct in the style I feel is appropriate). Or, I say, "If you are playing that way, I have to conduct like this (I gesture or conduct the inappropriate way). I want you to play it like this (I gesture or conduct the appropriate way)."

When they are not close to what I am conducting, I might say, "Is it me? I am conducting this way, and you are playing this way!" By showing the difference, their performance can improve.

*(Robert Grechesky)*

I sometimes do the opposite of what I want them to play, if I am not pleased with the style. Let's say I want the

phrase ending to evaporate. I will influence them, through gesture, to play an abrupt dry crisp release, which they lock into quickly. Then, I will change to a graceful tapered release gesture. It is amazing how quickly they will pick up on the intention of the second gesture.

*(Richard Floyd)*

In a rehearsal I said, "I may be exaggerating a little bit, but this is how you played this passage." I'll obviously exaggerate, but I'll conduct as though they were playing. Then I say, "Now this is what I want" and I conduct the preferred way.

*(Craig Kirchhoff)*

### Exaggeration

There are just so many interesting and different ways of doing and teaching. From Frederick Fennell I got the idea of exaggerating a conducting gesture to the point of it being ludicrous for emphasis. I then take that gesture and shrink it back down to an acceptable size. When they see the acceptable size, they recall the exaggerated version.

I remember, he had an accent in a march that was not getting anywhere near what he wanted. He would jump about three feet in the air and give this huge slashing diagonal gesture from left to right clear down to his knees. It really looked hysterically funny. The band played the accent and everybody laughed. For two or three times when they would get to that spot, he would jump up in the air and do this huge diagonal move and the band again would laugh and play the accent.

When he got to that point in the concert, about a bar before that, he just quit conducting for two beats. He moved the baton over just a little bit to the left to give this six-inch diagonal beat down and across. The band just nailed it! Everybody in the band grinned.

*(Donald Wilcox)*

If I find they're not watching me at a section that involves a change of tempo such as a ritardando or an accelerando, I'll exaggerate and slow down so much it's ridiculous. I will do this without saying anything.

*(Francis Marciniak)*

### Learning conducting

I remember Elizabeth Green doing things in conducting class where she would have us use huge gestures conducting something that was very soft. She wanted us to achieve control of the soft look of a controlled slow gesture but in big size. Then, when there was something that actually was loud and powerful, she wouldn't let us use anything bigger than a four-inch gesture. She limited us so we would get the strength into the gestures.

*(Donald Wilcox)*

# CHAPTER NINE

# ASSOCIATION

When a teacher relates something that students know to something they do not know, a teacher is inviting the students to make an association. As a teaching technique, the use of association helps learning because it can enable students to see the commonality between two things; to see the unfamiliar through the familiar. Or, in the words of an older axiom, the students move from the "known to the unknown."

Various examples of association are relating a sunrise to a crescendo, a brick made of lead to the accent, or the ticking of a clock to a steady tempo. The metaphorical association is important because it helps the student make the connection between the known and the unknown. The better the metaphor, the more a student learns as he makes the connection between what he knows and what is unknown. Making associations is a very effective teaching technique because it fits the way people learn, hear, talk, and see; association is one way they come to an understanding of everything around them.

## MUSIC MAKING AND TEACHING

### Engaging the students' thought processes
The current trend is to relate music to non-musical experiences so some thought process is required of the student. This approach goes beyond clinical descriptions such as loud and soft.

*(James Arrowood)*

I make teaching both audible and visual, since I give them both. For example, as I talk about the rise and fall of the phrase, I may sing the rise and fall. I do this to associate the sound to the gestures or to draw the contour with gestures.

*(Hal D. Cooper)*

### Comic books
I compare comic books to playing the pop music at the end of the year. I tell them, "Comics books are to literature what pop-music is to concert music." We don't read comic books all year and we're not going to sit and

read *Romeo and Juliet* from September until the end of the year either. I think there's a place for all of it.

*(Sandra P. Thompson)*

### Relating drama and stories to music
I find myself looking at music more and more in non-musical ways. I talk about music being the unfolding of sound drama and sound stories. I say that a story line has contrast. A story line also might build and it might have a reprise. We can draw a real analogy with that with a form or piece of music and its conflict and resolution. We can make kids think a little and get off the page. They can see what is there, or find that many musical directives simply aren't on the page. We also can describe music as a fabric or use terms such as dramatic intensity. We can use other non-musical references or a blend of these.

*(Robert Levy)*

## MUSICAL TERMS

### Building association between note names and fingerings
When I teach scales to students, I ask them to think the names of the notes as they ascend and descend while fingering the notes on the horn.

*(Edward S. Lisk)*

### Associating musical terms to music sounds
We should introduce terms, names, and other vocabulary through association. For example, if we play the interval of a fourth or play in a separated style, then we say, "that is a fourth, or that is separated style." Teaching this is simple. Label things after students hear them or feel them through movement.

*(James Froseth)*

## DYNAMICS

### Relating dynamics to percentages
I used the comparisons of ppp-ten percent, pp-

220

twenty percent, p-thirty percent, mp-forty percent, mf-fifty percent, f-sixty percent, ff-seventy percent and fff-eighty percent to show the level and relationship of volume. I did not use ninety or one hundred percent, since one hundred percent would be what I call noise.

*(Robert Allan)*

### Relating soft intensity to soft but intense whispering

One problem that we meet when the band tries to play soft is that the resonance and the tone quality "go down the tubes." Students often associate softness with lack of intensity. To counteract this, I say, "If you were in class and were angry with your neighbor, you would whisper. You would not whisper softly and politely, you would whisper angrily and intensely." I sometimes have them angrily whisper something to another student, so they can discover what that quiet stress feels like. That usually leads them to say, "Oh yeah, okay."

*(Gregory Bimm)*

### Associating body posture to dynamic levels

Sometimes the weirder the idea, the easier it is for kids to understand it and the more they understand why they have to do it. When I'm doing dynamics with kids and they're not playing softly enough, I bend all the way down to the floor. I'm not very tall, 5'2", so when I bend down they soon realize that I'm out of the picture and that means they must play more softly.

*(Sandra P. Thompson)*

### Dynamics and LED lights

The kids are familiar with "blasters and boom boxes." These have LED lights on them to show overload and that's a great way to teach them dynamics. Every kid in the world knows how those LED's light up for various volumes. This is very visual and that's instant reinforcement when used as a teaching device. "You guys are lighting up too many lights; it's too loud, come down more." It's instantaneous, you don't even have to explain it.

*(Donald Wilcox)*

### Associating landscapes to dynamic changes

After a crescendo, students often let the decrescendo develop too quickly. To improve this, I talk about going over a hill. For example, I will say, "Your hill wasn't steep enough or, you went over the top of the hill but you fell off. Instead, you should go over easily because the other side has a more gentle slope."

*(Hal D. Cooper)*

### Associating numbers to planning crescendos

There is a big problem in ensemble performance of crescendos and diminuendos. Often there is a lack of unity in the ensemble; individuals change balance and crescendo at different times. For example, if there is a four-measure crescendo I ask them to think from one to sixteen to control the timing of the crescendo's progress. If the teacher or conductor does not control this and there are forty players in the group, they will progress in forty different ways. Then, the balance and sound of the group changes randomly throughout the sixteen counts of the crescendo. I like it not to do that!

I also support the notion, depending on the sound you are creating, that certain sections may intentionally crescendo sooner or later than others. If it is a tutti crescendo, I frequently ask the low voices to crescendo first, followed by middle voices, followed by upper voices. Finally, the percussion does a crescendo. The opposite occurs in a diminuendo, so the natural tendency of the highs to become too brilliant does not happen. If it is a legato, tutti chord release, I have the low voices release last and the upper voices release first. I find that it gives the release of the chord a very warm resonant sound. The difference in release points is very slight.

*(Gary Hill)*

### Modeling dynamic levels with my voice

I use my voice to show dynamics. I will use a whisper for soft pianissimo that no one can hear except the one I am whispering to. I use a stage whisper for the next level, piano. A mild-mannered Clark Kent whisper at mezzo piano, ordinary talk at mezzo forte, perturbed at forte and totally ticked-off for fortissimo. When I give instructions vocally, I will give them at the desired dynamic level. I also will vocally imitate their sound, which reminds them to correct their sound.

*(John W. LaCava)*

I teach projection by comparing the two ways of whispering: (1) I can whisper as though I were telling a secret to my best friend sitting next to me; or (2) I can whisper with such intensity that someone could hear the line from the other side of the auditorium (a stage whisper). The second whisper that has projection, the "stage whisper," is exactly what we must strive to do when playing a pianissimo.

*(Richard Floyd)*

## RHYTHM

### Understanding rubato, ritard, and accelerando

When playing ritard and accelerando, students only go slower or go faster. To improve upon this, I use this analogy. If you are in the front seat of a roller coaster and you come over that peak, you feel you are going very slowly. Then just after the peak of the hill, you go really fast. Whereas if you are in the back seat of a roller coaster and you come up to the hill, it snaps you right over the top. You never get that suspense of hanging there before you start going down the hill. They understand the principle of gradual acceleration and then deceleration—it gives them something they can really hang on to.

(Terry A. Oxley)

### Tempo fluctuations

Rubato has this hanging feeling but you have an end. In a short passage of music that takes maybe eight seconds, you are going to have some rubato in the middle. Even with the rubato, you are almost going to make up that time in a different part of the passage. So it's still only going to take eight seconds. As an aid, I have them picture being in a car rolling up the hill. They can feel they are easing over the top, which can create a feeling that every instant in time is a little bit longer. Every fraction of that note is stretched out just that little bit.

(Terry A. Oxley)

### Relating cartoon and television characters to music

To show a slow tempo, especially for very young kids, I will show how a robot or monster walks slowly. This helps them sense and see what a slow tempo or slow foot tapping is.

(Steven Cooper)

### Defining rubato

With the musical term rubato, the best analogy I have used is to tell kids that the word "rubato" sounds like the word "robbers" or "robbery." I go on to explain that, "If we think of rubato as robbing time, we take some length from one note and give that extra length to another note." I comment that, "We do this to make one note or another more important in the phrase." That is why I say: "All quarter notes are not equal."

(Donald Wilcox)

### Describing ritards

I describe a ritard as sounding like a phonograph record or bicycle wheel slowing down.

(Steven Cooper)

### Relating mathematics to music reading

Many students just do not understand the rhythms and do not apply what they know from mathematics. I find that by doing it numerically they can grasp how one rhythm fits with another. This is something they do not always do.

(Judith A. Niles)

## PHRASING

### Associating speech to phrasing

First, I talk to them in a monotone saying, "this is very interesting." Then, I say this again with intensity and inflection. I say, "The second way is like speaking or listening to someone who is getting more excited and shows it, as they speak." We can use speech; it is something that they can identify with to understand how contrasts can make interesting music.

(Larry Rachleff)

### Learning what "style" means

When defining musical style I tell the kids, "We play a march different from the way we play a chorale. We also do not wear baseball clothes to a dance or wear dance clothes to a baseball game." They usually don't have trouble understanding after that. They accept that there are different times and ways to play different music, and all of it helps us get through life's little thing!

(Sandra P. Thompson)

### Relating dance and art to music

I really delve into dance, art, and drama in my rehearsals. I think the students must relate to how something feels through the dance; or relate tone or texture to what they see in art. What marvelous things we can do with artistic creations. I use the idea of dance a lot in getting buoyancy and lightness. If I want heaviness, I talk about the spring of ballet dancers and I have on occasion demonstrated this.

I show spring and buoyancy with another image. I use a ping pong ball on a table, "See how wonderfully light the spring is as it bounces against the table." I point this out in relation to a hand full of putty as I throw that putty on the table or floor. "When that putty gets on the floor, what happens? There's no oomph to it, there's no spring to it at all, right? Nothing happens. So, I don't want this type of sound. I don't want this heaviness. I want it light as in buoyancy." I use many references to movement and dance.

(Richard J. Suddendorf)

### Relating phrasing to a sentence

We talk as if the phrase is a sentence in language. I will speak my usual sentence, which is "Johnny and Mary went to the store to buy a loaf of bread for dinner." Then, I will say "Johnny and Mary -AH- went to the -AH- store to buy -AH- a loaf of bread -AH- for din—ner." They catch it immediately and we proceed then to make a sentence out of the musical line that they have in their music.

(Nancy Plantinga)

### Teaching phrasing to young students

Young students often breathe too frequently. They usually play one note, or two or three notes at a time instead of playing in musical phrases or sentences. I use a very simple teaching technique to make them aware of this problem and how to solve it. When they stop after every note or every few notes, interrupting a musical phrase, I stop the band and tell them to listen to me talk. I say, "I am going to talk the way someone would if they phrased their words improperly. I am . . . stopping . . . af . . . ter . . . every . . . word. (They usually laugh or giggle.) Oh, . . . you . . . think this . . . is . . . very funny? Well so . . . do . . . I!" Then I speak the same sentences in a way that shows a way to phrase the words properly. Thus, I compare musical phrases to spoken sentences. They grasp this concept quickly, they begin to recognize phrases on their own, and they notice more often and correct when they "spot breathe" between notes.

*(Roman Palmer)*

### Using stories to explain musical tension

When teaching musical expression, I base many of my decisions and most of my teaching on prolonging the anticipation of whatever high point we are approaching. I stress not being in a big rush to get there. If we say "this is a big point," students often think it should be the loudest place. If you want to play expressively, you have to prolong the anticipation without distorting the phrase too badly.

To explain this, I go through this story about Christmas. I say, "When you were little, you started thinking about Christmas in October, and it built up through November, then early December, then mid-December until you were so excited you could hardly sleep. Then Christmas came, it was there and then it was over. That approach to Christmas is like the approach to the high point musically in the song. It's getting there that's important, not being there."

*(Terry A. Oxley)*

### Using numbers to compare the weight and length of notes.

I subscribe to a Vandercook idea that kids really relate to: it is the use of numbers rating the phrasing and dynamic weights of notes 9————1. A half note is a 7, a quarter note is a 5, an eighth note is a 3, etc. They use this as a guideline in playing phrases. It suggests how heavy or light they should play each note or group of notes. Kids will relate to that because you put the number on the music and it's right there in black and white.

*(Kenneth M. Larsen)*

### Relating phrasing to swimming

When students say, "We can't get to the end of a phrase," I say, "I want you to imagine that you're under water at the bottom of a pool and you've got to get all the way to the top. Ninety-nine times in a hundred you can make it to the top. You don't have to take a big gulp of air in the middle of a phrase." After that, they'll stretch it and they'll get to the end of the phrase.

*(Thomas Stone)*

### Relating language to musical phrasing

With young students especially, I do some things for phrasing that are analogous to language. We think about how we read and speak when we phrase our language. We do not read letter by letter or word by word, we group them in patterns according to our language. We talk about grouping notes, phrasing or giving emphasis or stress.

The notes have to be done the same way. Whenever we talk about grouping notes, phrasing, or giving emphasis or stress, I will talk like a robot. The robot says the words and talks without inflection—like a monotone with no rhythm, no dynamic change, or no change of sound. I say, "That is not very interesting, is it?" They agree and realize that it is boring because there is no emphasis, stress, or grouping, and no concept of getting an idea together. They begin to realize that we do not speak that way, we don't think that way—we do not deal with inner rhythm if we did speak that way.

We want them to understand that as letters go together to make up words—notes go together to make up germinal musical ideas. These musical ideas are called motives and they make up phrases in music, as words make up sentences and ideas in language. By comparison, sentences make up paragraphs and musical phrases make up musical periods. We are not just looking at and playing music note for note, but are giving some kind of *shape* and *direction* to the way the sounds and patterns go together. We need to give musical motives and phrases *shape* or *emphasis*. This idea also helps students play any phrase, not only long phrases with a crescendo and diminuendo and where the climax of the phrase is obvious; and this helps someone decide where to put stress on an individual note in a motive or phrase.

You can sometimes use the common technique of saying a sentence several different ways. We can stress a different word every time. This shows how the change of inflection can change entirely the meaning of the statement. For example, a change of inflection can change a sentence from a question to a declarative statement. Kids can grasp that idea, translate it to music, and make sense of what is on the music page.

Since many junior high or high school kids have no idea what to do with the note—they are only playing one note after the other—this is especially effective. You can even have them read the title of the piece to show that they are not reading letter by letter, but as an entire word. They can relate that to their playing: they were playing note by note, instead of in phrases or motives.

*(Robert Grechesky)*

### Using the idea: to and from destinations

You really need to use both physical and visual teaching techniques. In relation to dynamics and phrasing, we talk constantly about starting from somewhere or you can't get anywhere.

*(Judith A. Niles)*

### Relating phrasing to language

I will often use language to teach a musical line. I

might break up a sentence and say to the kids, "You would not walk up to the teacher and say, 'Good . . . morning, Mis . . ter . . . Long; how . . . are . . . you?' You would say that sentence so it made sense. Instead you would say, 'Good morning Mr. Long, how are you?' Did you notice, kids, there was a slight pause after Long, but the phrase is still one entity. Now, look at the music you have in front of you. Notice that big curved line over the top. That isn't there just to use up ink; The composer is telling you this is a musical sentence. Let's try to play musically with the phrase—it will work." I show students how to do this and I make the point that the music should go to that certain spot. Then I say, "Try that on your instruments," and we try it.

*(William Long)*

The syntax of the musical phrase and sense of where the terminal point is, is the key. Sometimes language serves as a very good illustration, because they can hear that—they're used to hearing language. When a foreigner tries to speak English and their phrasing and inflection doesn't make sense, it is a little hard to listen to or even to understand. It is easy with students if you give them a natural phrasing from even a silly sentence. The sentence often translates very well to knowing where the terminal points or the pick up points of a phrase are. One can have them play around with putting the emphasis in places that may be unnatural, and in fact, are unnatural. By doing that they find out why it feels wrong.

*(L. Keating Johnson)*

## BALANCE

### Relating balance to baking
I talk about blend and balance and how the trumpets have to blend with the clarinets and the flutes. When the trumpets are playing louder than the rest of the band, I compare the total sound to pancake batter. "When your moms make a pancake batter and they haven't mixed it together yet, you will have this big lump of flour in the middle of the pancake." They all go "yuck" and they say "oooooh yeah, it needs to be mixed together." From this, the kids get the idea of the blend and balance. Sometimes we use chocolate chip cookies and they get a big glob of dough instead of evenly distributed chocolate chips. These associations work with the younger kids when you try to make them understand.

*(Sandra P. Thompson)*

When we are talking about ensemble blend, I have talked to the kids about creating something in the kitchen. Making a cake with all the right ingredients is outstanding! Then if you drop a little piece of onion in the mix by accident, it ruins the whole dish. They focus on that real well! With accents I say, "Adding accents is like looking

at a beautiful painting. If the painting emphasizes a warm key or a cool key, then you need a splash of totally opposite color. Think how that sticks out. This is the idea of an accent and what an accent is."

*(Nancy Plantinga)*

### Adjusting balance by referring to colors
I try to use colors to describe balance issues. I might want to adjust the sound if the first trumpets are playing too loud and the horns, third trombones, and tubas are not loud enough. I try to change the ensemble's balance by asking the people who have the darker colored instruments to play louder. In another spot I might ask, "Would you people with the brighter sounds play a little softer?" I might do this if the woodwinds are playing and I am getting too much oboe. I do not use blue, green, red, or white. This is too intricate. I talk about light, dark, bright, and dull.

*(Gerald Olson)*

## BREATHING

### Relating breath to natural breathing
Breathing when playing an instrument is simply breathing normally. We always relate it back to a baby learning how to breathe. "A new born infant does not get breathing or clarinet lessons. Their breathing is automatic, its little tummy is going up and down." I always ask them what their diaphragm is, to feel the diaphragm, and can they find and move the diaphragm.

If I am doing a clinic with high school kids, they can have fun with that "new body part." Because they can't find it and they can't feel it, I'll show them through a drawing where the diaphragm is. It is at the bottom of the lungs. I tell and show them that it's u-shaped and concave when it's down and u-shaped and convex when it is at the top of the cavity. Then I talk and show how it works when they take in air using the diagram. The breathing I am talking about is just natural. When playing the clarinet or trumpet, the only difference is we're using an optimal amount of air.

*(Dwayne P. Sagen)*

### Associating the breathing process to water pressure
I ask the students to imagine the cylindrical brass nozzle on the garden hose their grandfather probably uses—the one without the gun handle. You turn it one way and there is a real wide spray. As you turn it the other way, the wide spray starts to become more focused. The water (which stands for the air) is very energized and you can blow the dirt out of the cracks on the driveway. I point out that grandpa didn't go over and turn up the water at the source to get this. It all happened because the size of the opening in the nozzle was adjusted; in wind playing that is our *aperture*. I feel fortunate whenever I'm in a band room

that has a steam pipe in it. With young kids I can say, "What would happen if I poke a little hole in the steam pipe? You've seen this happen on TV. I won't do it now, but this is the kind of air support we need going here."

*(Timothy Mahr)*

The comparison of air's behavior to that of water can be helpful. If you have a hose attached to a faucet on the side of the house, faster flow means the water will go farther. As with water, the air's speed, velocity, and distance are interrelated. If you want to make faster water come out of that hose, decrease the opening size by putting the finger over the open end. This is like taking off the three-quarter inch hose and replacing it with a one-half inch hose. The result is the water goes a lot farther. Another way to do that is to turn it up more at the source (increase air supply). By making the opening or hose smaller, the air's speed, distance and velocity increase.

*(Robert E. Foster)*

### The air is the bow

I often use the statement, "The bow is to the string as the breath is to the lips." I use this to remind brass players that without moving air there is no sound. I also ask them to imagine a violin player whose arm and bow are suspended above the string but not moving. I tell them, "That is the same as you, if you do not use air at all; the violinist's bow isn't moving and you are not moving the air." But, I say, "If the violinist is touching the bow to the string and he is getting the string to resonate well, that is what you should do. You need to use the air to get your lips to vibrate and make the tone resonate."

*(Edward Kocher)*

### Telling the story or program when appropriate

The *Symphony No. 1 for Winds and Percussion*, by Bukvich is about the Dresden, Germany fire storm caused by the Allied bombing during the Second World War. Telling the story helped—I even asked some of my kids to write a narrative about the event. When they presented this to the band, the piece become even more real for them.

*(Robert Allan)*

### Music performance compared to athletics

I have compared the physical needs in playing to the conditioning needed in athletics.

*(John W. LaCava)*

### Relating drawings of shapes to articulations

For four staccato notes in a row, I would draw four rectangles with about the same distance between each rectangle as the length of each rectangle. I usually make the rectangle black. With four notes connected, there's very little space between those black rectangles.

I use drawings to give their minds a vocabulary or repertoire of shapes. Then, when I demonstrate, play, or have them to do something musically, they have those reference points in their head, or on the paper or the board in front of them. Our trombone teacher has a book of warm ups with pages of shapes that show, for example, an intense release.

*(L. Keating Johnson)*

### Solfege and Kodaly-Curwen hand signals

We sing using the solfege syllables and we use the Kodaly-Curwen hand signals so that they are connecting those two things.

*(Nancy Plantinga)*

I use statements to help individuals see how their part might fit in and be important to the whole. "Music is like a jigsaw puzzle; for music to be correct, to create the picture, all the parts must be in place."

*(Barbara Buehlman)*

# CHAPTER TEN

# IMAGERY

Donald Wilcox said, "Imagery is something I think that all of us use constantly. It is a part of everybody's personality and teaching." This is likely, but the amount and imaginative use of imagery varies with each teacher. Some teachers have a flair for imagery and others do not, yet all should cultivate its use because of its value.

Some research suggests that the appropriate use of verbal imagery is a characteristic of better teachers. Robert Grechesky studied conductors of so-called musically poor and musically good bands to find what the teachers might have done to cause this. Among the more telling things that conductors of the better bands used, but was seldom used as much or at all with the poorer bands, was the use of verbal imagery. It was a very strong factor in expressive performance. Imagery was much stronger than any instruction using technical jargon and stronger than some other effective techniques.

## THE INTENT OF IMAGERY

### The value of imagery

Imagery, as it is related to some type of human experience, is an important aspect of relating verbally in a rehearsal, sectional, or lesson. An imagery that describes an aspect of musical performance is especially helpful. For instance, if the musical score calls for rather bright "pinging sounds," you might wish to say, "Play these sounds as if they were steel pellets falling from the sky, striking a large steel plate, and bouncing quickly and sharply away." A good image has an immediate response on the part of the students; they should be able to generalize quickly to the musical sound desired.

*(Thomas L. Dvorak)*

I frequently use imagery techniques throughout my rehearsals. The mental-visualization process that I initiate through imagery techniques allows me to focus the students' attention and concentration, and to expand their listening awareness beyond the individual level. I have found that pictures or visual images are much better remembered than words, and imagery techniques activate a much keener sense and response to listening. The subtleties and nuances of artistic expression cannot be verbally defined. The ability to activate musical imagery, therefore, provides me with an instructional avenue to artistic performance.

*(Edward S. Lisk)*

I say, "Use the fattest air stream you can." I might say, "Now woodwinds, that's too harsh. Calm it down, polish it up, make it slicker-sounding." I try to draw mental images with the words that will help them to accomplish what I want. I don't try to describe exactly what I want to happen, but I try to create a picture in their minds that will help their playing improve.

That's why I like using words like intense, more intense, less intense, slow and fast airstream, hot air and cold air, a big fat sound, or little narrow projected sound. I just say, "Make sure the sound goes clear past me before it dies. Don't try to force your tone against the music stand. Let it soar out over the audience." I don't say, "Take a breath and use your left lung more." I believe very firmly that if you try to describe operationally what happens, you're defeating your own purpose most of the time. If they know conceptually where they are trying to go, they will figure it out operationally.

*(James Stivers)*

One can connect the physical world to dynamics in a rehearsal. For example, "Imagine picking up a one hundred pound solid cement block, imagine how that feels. Now imagine ten pounds of soft cotton" or, "Think about pushing a grand piano up a ninety-meter ski sloop. As you go higher and higher, you must push harder and harder."

*(Frank Battisti)*

## TONE

### Relating music sound to images

I talk about chocolate for trombone and trumpet tone. I have asked them, for example, to make a sound on

*Salvation is Created* that is a thick sound. I asked them to "sound like pouring syrup on chocolate—that heavy." Then I might explain how to accomplish this. Another example for teaching style might be, "here are some hard peas dropping on a hard floor. To do this, here is what you must do with your tongue." If the picture is in their head, they are more likely to play physically correct. If they are close but a bit off, I can say, "Make the chocolate colder or warmer than you are doing." On other days I might use peanut brittle, potatoes, and many other foods to illustrate how they should play the style correctly.

*(Jack Brookshire)*

To give beginners the idea of air size and speed, we talk about compact cars compared to eighteen wheelers. I explain that both are going sixty miles an hour and that a sixty mile per hour speed must be there. I ask them to make the air the size of a small sports car to get a quiet sound that is alive. If they make the sound the size of an eighteen-wheeler, the sound will be too loud.

*(Bryce Taylor)*

Textures and colors are wonderful. To show texture, I refer to visual things like burlap, satin, blue jeans, and canvas.

*(Richard J. Suddendorf)*

Imagine that somewhere there is an eternal sound source that never changes and imagine that it's always on. The source is like a celestial choir of voices. The only time you can hear it is when you open the door and listen to it. I try to get them to imagine that's what their sound is, that it's always going, it's just that now we can hear it. So I need to hear that eternal never changing kind of quality.

*(Thomas Stone)*

I talk about bright, dark, thin, thick, rich, in relation to sound.

*(Robert E. Foster)*

## Rhythm

I describe a ritard as sounding like a record turntable slowing down.

*(Steven Cooper)*

## Phrasing

To accomplish a certain separated sound, I have said, "Make it sound like a ball bouncing, like an inner tube being hit from the side, dribbling a basketball, skipping a rock across the water, or those are roads in Ohio—we want it like the highways in Michigan."

*(Patricia Brumbaugh)*

I use the board behind my podium to draw various images, I make motions to help them picture things, and I use verbal imagery, such as the image of the "paint brush" and the "muddy shoe." When I need a particularly long line, I often show its phrasing with the stroke of the paintbrush. I draw the picture of a muddy shoe print to describe detache bowing: long but separated. This means that if you had a lot of mud on your shoe, you couldn't pick it up as rapidly; you'd be a little stuck each time. You could still pick it up, but since it is sticky, there would be a moment's hesitation; this means that they stay on the pitch longer with the bow.

*(Judith A. Niles)*

Because so many kids pull gum out of their mouths and let it snap back, I say, "Pulling the sound from the instrument is like pulling gum out of your mouth." They focus into that immediately! When they are sustaining phrases, I even have them blowing the air all through their bodies starting it at their toes. Then they actually, physically, take their fingers, put them to their mouths and pull the air out of their mouths and, more deeply, their lungs. I often support these images with an appropriate physical action.

*(Nancy Plantinga)*

## Style

Our rehearsal room wall is made with eight by sixteen-inch cinder blocks. I use this to explain marcato. Marcato needs a solid strong note with a good, clear beginning and a clear end, but it doesn't run into the next note. Each marcato note is spaced from the ones before and after.

I just say, "Look at the block right here, it has a clean square front and it's solid all the way through. Now, think of this block as a sound. Think of it horizontally and you hear a solid square start, a good attack, and the sound is sustained full value to the end, but it is not touching the next one. There's a gap—this half inch of mortar—right here that separates them. None of these blocks touch each other and yet they are nearly connected. The sounds are very powerful and they don't taper on either end. That's the sound I want!" You can take visual teaching as far as you want to go with it. You can take the cinder block idea or scribble on the board, since they need that visual reinforcement.

*(Donald Wilcox)*

To suggest interpretations for the specific character of a rhythm and a melody, I try to draw upon familiar aspects of their life. For example, "If this rhythm were a character who would it be, Snoopy, Miss Piggy, or Conan the Barbarian?"

*(Patricia Brumbaugh)*

## DYNAMICS

I often use the term "softly as a morning sunrise" to get the proper volume or light attacks. It is very effective, even if they have never seen a morning sunrise!

*(Ross A. Leeper)*

I have said, "Play this as loud as a soap bubble breaking."

*(Donald Wilcox)*

To develop intensity in their tone, I ask students to hiss so someone could hear it in the back of the hall. Then I say, "Now, let us do it again with the same intensity, but just so the person next to you can hear the hiss. This is the way one must feel when one plays softly."

In trying to make students aware that they have to exaggerate dynamics, I might say, "Imagine I was at the far end of the school campus and you were watching me from the other end. Assume you were to ask me what I was doing and I could answer only with a gesture. If the gesture were small, it would be unclear at that distance and we could not communicate. To communicate successfully I must make the gesture larger, and more exaggerated and exact."

*(Richard Floyd)*

When they are playing fast and soft, I try to get them to think of small notes. At a fast tempo each note doesn't last for very long, the notes take up a small space in time because of the tempo. Conversely, if they're playing at a loud dynamic level and they're playing slowly, each note is going to be large because it will take up a large amount of time. It will be an imposing note, because it's a loud note.

*(Thomas Stone)*

We use everything we can think of, from animals to people. For example, if we have plodding passage going on in the basses, I may say "You sound like elephants here, but we want to sound like deer," or "Flutes, you should sound like snakes slithering along; make the curves longer and more smooth, not such jerky curves as you are doing now," or "This is a puppy dog, not a bull dog chewing on your leg!"

A piece like *Civil War Fantasy* by Jerry Bilik also lends itself to the use of imagery very well; people getting shot, people are sitting around campfires, etc.

*(Bryce Taylor)*

Touch is a very effective form to relate to sound. There is velvety, hard, concrete, sharp, rough, scratchy, etc. I say, "You are taking your knuckles and your rubbing them against a screen door; instead, you need to put on a velvet glove and let it touch on a soft satin pillow."

If the shape of the music is important, then I try to bring in something they can see. I'll say, "This phrase is not a highway, it's a rainbow," or "In this phrase you can see where the cliff happens and it drops." For tempo I have said, "This is like a blade of grass or wheat blowing in the wind. This tempo has to be a little flexible; it doesn't stay straight up when the wind blows. It just bends and kind of goes back and forth."

I try to relate the analogies to something they can see or touch, instead of what they hear. I seldom paint a programmatic picture. I don't say, "Picture the Titanic sinking." I like to use words like murky, misty, brilliant, sparkling, or words that really make you think of something visual.

*(William W. Wiedrich)*

Tell one of the kids, "Move your chair a quarter of an inch; but I want you to imagine the chair is made of dynamite. If you move it more than a quarter of an inch, it will explode. The preparation, care, and intensity you put into getting ready to move it, is an exact idea of how you should prepare for a smooth entrance on your instrument." This suggests the inhale, the held breath, the preparatory gesture, and everything. Because of this image, we wind up with the breathing, preparation, and intensity that is desired; you don't just go up and kick the chair to move it.

*(Donald Wilcox)*

## BREATHING

Blow through the trumpet as though it were six or nine feet long, or blow through it as though it were a peashooter. Either image suggests that the air goes clear across the whole room.

*(Stanley Cate)*

The wind should be like the bow on a violin.

*(Steven Cooper)*

With air and embouchure, there are three variables: the opening the air comes out of, the amount of air from the source, and the changing of the size of the tube out of which the air comes. If you have a hose attached to a faucet on the side of the house, faster water (air) means farther. Speed, velocity and distance are interrelated.

If you want to make faster water come out of that hose, you first decrease the opening size by putting your finger over the open end. The result is that the water goes a lot farther. Another way to do that is to turn it up more at the source. Yet another way, that most people forget or don't realize, is to take off the three-quarter-inch hose and replace it with a one-half-inch hose. By making the opening or the hose smaller, the speed, distance and velocity increase.

*(Robert E. Foster)*

In reality or in their imagination, I ask them to blow up a long skinny balloon to stress the need of playing through the notes to play for an entire phrase. I also say, "Pretend you are holding a candle about sixteen inches away and blow it out."

*(Robert Grechesky)*

I feel fortunate whenever I'm in a band room that has a steam pipe in it. With young kids, I can say, "What would happen if I go over and poke a little hole in the steam pipe? You've seen this happen on television and I won't poke that hole now, but this is the kind of air support we are trying to build."

*(Timothy Mahr)*

To grasp what they feel like when they support the air physically, I have them imagine they are picking up a corner of the piano. I say, "To lift something that heavy you must take the right kind of breath. You inhale, then they set all the muscles in the stomach. That is exactly what you have to do to play. However, as you do that, you still must talk in a normal voice." We practice doing this and talking until they can keep their throat relaxed. If they cannot think of sentences to say, I make them read to me!

*(Terry A. Oxley)*

The muscles in your throat should feel and be as relaxed as the throat of a pelican looks.

*(Joseph Casey)*

## POSTURE AND POSITION

With the hand position used with most instruments, there is curvature in the fingers. To convey the shape of the hand, I explain that it is as if you have a baseball in your hand. That works very well. With posture, I tell them to pretend they are a puppet and I am the puppeteer. There is a string through the middle of each of their heads. With my imaginary strings, I pull on the strings in order to pull their heads and waists up so they are sitting more properly.

*(Nancy Plantinga)*

I have sixth graders stand, imagining that they have an eye bolt in the top of their head. The bolt for each person is attached to an imaginary string that goes through a pulley on the ceiling. I hold all the strings, gradually raise them up and let them down to get a very straight and model posture. I point out that the better way to play is standing up. Therefore, if you're going to sit when you play, you should feel from the hip up the way you feel when you are standing.

I've also had younger kids pretend I drilled a hole in their navel. Then, I tell them, "The air is going to rush in and it's going to feel very cold. The air is not going to come

in up above, it's going to come in down there. You have to imagine it coming in from there and it's cold." That's just weird enough that they respond to it.

*(Timothy Mahr)*

## EXAMPLES OF IMAGERY IN REHEARSAL

I do try to create visual pictures, but they must relate to the score in front of me.

*(Anthony J. Maiello)*

I use imagery, sometimes only to be funny. For example, lines such as, "Play this like Kermit the Frog is riding his bike into the dark and stormy night" or, "Lightening technique; the fingers never strike twice in the same place." This can break the group up and get the point across also.

*(Donald Wilcox)*

Using a house or pyramid to show the building of a foundation with more bottom than top, is a good analogy for ensemble balance, which everyone has used. For example, "The steeple on the church is not as big as the basement."

*(Donald Wilcox)*

I have favorite images that I have used in rehearsals or lessons. One such image is holding a kitten in one's hand to suggest how gentle and delicate something should be. Some other images I use are: subito is like exploding popcorn; or a light attack is like bouncing a ping pong ball on a paddle.

*(James Arrowood)*

We are forty-five miles from the ocean and we talk a lot about the ocean waves, and how they rise and fall. We talk about the things that the kids are involved with: if we want to do a gradual ritardando, we talk about letting our bicycle coast to a halt.

*(Bryce Taylor)*

When we worked on *Music for Prague*, they knew nothing—where it was or what went on in 1968. We had them find information in the library and they did well. When we got to the dissonant middle section, we could relate the experiences of Russian tanks running over your mother who had run screaming from the house. This is what Husa was trying to portray—the panic going on, people running "helter-skelter" in every direction. With that was the marching sound of the snare drum. This is program music. The Daniel Bukvich Symphony about the Dresden Fire Bombing is the same type of piece. This is an easy, uncomplicated, but emotional piece, and imagery can help a student understand it better.

*(Bryce Taylor)*

We talk about phrasing, feelings, trying to get the music inside the body, and getting the emotions going. I compare this to something in the outside world, such as program music. I might say "This piece is like the piece *La Mer*. Debussy wrote that piece to suggest the sea." I sing a little bit of it and try to portray what it says in the music. I also will use Vivaldi's *The Seasons* as an example and sing a little bit of it and say, "This is supposed to be the spring—or the winter." I ask them to internalize it so they play musically, and play with emotion and contrasts. I will do anything, so they don't just play notes.

*(Dwayne P. Sagen)*

I really think they can react to the use of colors. For example, I might say, "Make it a pastel, or a bright, pink sound here, as opposed to dark gray." One can use other descriptive statements, such as "Playing in the fog," "Blowing hot air," or "Avoid those neon, electric sounds."

*(Michael Kaufman)*

We use descriptors such as rich, vibrant, and sonorous. We ask them to picture sound and to examine the possibilities that are out there—the choices on the table.

*(Edward S. Lisk)*

## Chapter Eleven

# Words and Sayings

In their effort to make a particular point, teachers often make unique, original statements, many of which are delightful to hear. Well-chosen imagery—and often humor—can convey unique insights and can help teachers communicate more effectively with their students. Some music teachers believe that the more effective and unique statements come forth spontaneously, in the heat of the moment, while teaching; if this observation is true, that precise choice of imagery or wording may not be as effective again until another opportune moment comes during the class. The new situation, instead, will usually call for its own unique imagery. The teacher must develop an intuition for the use of unique statements.

Many statements in this section show ways in which a particular teacher cleverly and concisely communicated an idea through words. Other statements are interesting observations about teaching or music. Still others simply show how to use speaking and explaining to teach music effectively. Teachers should always be imaginative in their speaking and thinking; as they become more successful with this, their resourcefulness and confidence will increase.

## OBSERVATIONS ABOUT LANGUAGE IN MUSIC TEACHING

### Different statements help different students

We must say things in different ways, since one student might learn from a different statement from another student.

*(Stanley Cate)*

### Focusing students' attention

A verbal description before demonstrating increases the effectiveness of the demonstration. The talking helps them focus upon the point I will be demonstrating. In this respect, I also frequently ask questions to prompt them to think and discover what something is or should be. I feel that demonstrations are to *improve* the way that they are already doing something, not the first step in teaching it.

*(Steven Cooper)*

I try to show students my musical choices while conducting. If they don't understand, I may talk about it. Talking puts an idea in the forefront of their minds so they can pay more attention to the conducting. Then I can either point out or show through conducting what they should do.

*(Richard Fischer)*

### Using descriptive words

I often use descriptors such as rich, vibrant, sonorous, or expansive for tone quality. I ask students to visualize such a sound and to "look" at the entire band sound with their "mind's eye" to expand their awareness and focus their listening.

*(Edward S. Lisk)*

### The function of talk in music teaching

More and more, I find myself using non-musical ways of looking at music by talking about music as the unfolding of drama and sound stories. A story line can have contrast; it might build or have a reprise allowing us to draw a real relationship from the conflict and resolution in stories to a music form or composition. We can make these kids think about getting off the page. They could find what is not on the page from our descriptions of fabric, dramatic intensity, or through other non-musical things.

*(Robert Levy)*

I try to draw mental images with the words that will help them to accomplish what I want. I don't try to describe exactly what I want to happen, but I try to create a picture in their minds that might help them improve. That's why I like words such as intensity, more intense or less intense. I don't say, "Take a breath and use your left lung more." I don't point the way operationally, I do it conceptually. I believe very firmly that if you try to describe operationally what happens, you're defeating your own purpose most of the time. My opinion is if they know conceptually where they are trying to go, they will eventually figure it out operationally.

*(James Stivers)*

## STATEMENTS AND OBSERVATIONS ABOUT MAKING MUSIC

It is those intangible aspects of music that we must nurture, cultivate, reward, and stroke, because that is where the music is. This means one must never regard the perfection of the technical aspects of the music as the ultimate quest. These elements simply enable us to make music.

*(Richard Floyd)*

Fred Schroeder said, "Never play louder than lovely."
*(Thomas Stone)*

I don't remember who told me this, but I remember the idea. Sometimes we need to remind the students by saying, "You can play in tune, but I cannot conduct you in tune."

*(David Hans)*

Conduct not only what is on the score, but beyond the score. Going beyond the page means to consider the musical cultural tradition. Therefore, draw upon all of your knowledge and experiences as a musician in conducting.

*(Richard K. Hansen)*

There is nothing wrong with playing out of tune, so long as you don't do it for more than an instant.
*(Stanley Cate)*

Debussy said, I recall, "Only twenty-five percent of the information you need to make music can be notated. The other seventy-five percent comes from your heart and your soul and your mind; what you know about music and what you've studied." This is a frightening point, but it is true.

*(Eugene Corporon)*

Someone I do not recall said, "I've made a living all my life playing whole notes. If you can do that well, people will buy the beauty. You don't have to play fast and loud to attract them."

*(Charles Olson)*

Music for music's sake is the outcome of a good music program: not what has to be done at every turn, or even what is done first.

*(Charles Olson)*

A composer was asked, "Do you have something new for me to play?" He answered, "What have you played of mine that is old?" So much good literature has gone by the wayside and is overlooked. Thus, we do not have to be looking for new music all the time.

*(Myron Welch)*

Musical notes should not just sit there, they should crescendo or diminuendo. One should make mountains—not cliffs! Don't drop off or run into a cliff. Unless the composer specifies a certain dynamic change, dynamics should happen in the latter part of the phrase: don't let them happen too soon.

*(Carl A. Bly)*

Hit it with a feather instead of a sledgehammer.
*(Thomas Stone)*

"The pull of infinity" is a saying of Robert Fountain's that means the sound is gone, but the energy is still there.
*(James Arrowood)*

I use my voice to show nuances and the shape of a phrase.

*(Richard Fischer)*

Sometimes I will make up a silly sentence such as, "I was going to the store." If you can break up a sentence like that into phrases, such as "I was going, (pause), to the store," or "I was going to the (pause) store," it may not make sense.

*(L. Keating Johnson)*

If I am talking about a crescendo, I will describe it as I talk with my voice also showing the crescendo.
*(R. G. Conlee)*

I live in a world of metaphors, similes and analogies. In *George Washington Bridge* there is a G Major chord that must have a real special quality to it. I couldn't get the right sound, so I used this dumb analogy: I said, "I want this chord to sound like you just won the Boston Marathon, it's ninety-five degrees out. You run and turn on the shower, and hot fudge comes out of the shower."

I find that images are most effective as a last resort. I think that if you are continually using them, you can get caught in the non-specific verbalizations. If I can't physically get what I want through conducting, I may say, "I really want this to have this kind of quality; a dark red quality." Then if I can't get that, I go to the analogy and metaphor to communicate what I am after.

*(Craig Kirchhoff)*

You have to show them that it takes a lot of energy to feel the music. Sometimes I use words like, "Put your guts into it; put your emotion into it," or "There isn't enough mustard, enough tang in the notes." If they're struggling with a part that should sound real smooth, but instead it sounds like they're working like crazy, I tell them, "It should sound effortless; you must get it under control and you must stay on top of all of the notes."

*(Thomas Stone)*

Without phrasing we just have information—if even that.

*(Patricia Brumbaugh)*

If the phrase has no shape it is not music; it is merely a succession of notes.

*(Butler R. Eitel)*

If I don't want them to break the phrase after two measures and play four measures instead, I tell them to "bump" the last note of the second measure right into the first note of the third measure. To accomplish the same phrasing I say, "Hold the tone until your mind thinks the next beat or measure.

*(John Kinnison)*

To teach students to sustain sounds in lyrical phrases; I tell them to play each note as though it were a very close friend you cared for a great deal. Since you are leaving this dear friend, hang on and linger with that note as long as possible. Hold it nearly into the next beat or into the time of the next note before moving on.

*(Jerold Sundet)*

When you stand in front of your band, if your band does not have a sense of the tonality and the meter of the piece you are about to play, what you are about to do or teach should not be confused with a musical behavior. If the forgoing is true, then anything the student learns occurs in spite of this type of instruction, not because of instruction.

*(Richard Grunow)*

The problem today is that our conductors are getting prettier and prettier, and our bands are sounding worse and worse.

*(Michael Kaufman)*

An important idea is "long, short notes." On the last note of marches, for example, no matter how short a note is, the note must have enough length to get sonority, duration, sound, pitch, and resonance.

*(Donald Wilcox)*

There are two aspects of a phrase which are important: the length and the high-point. Young students invariably do too little, or what they do is done too quickly.

*(Hal D. Cooper)*

Music is like a jigsaw puzzle. For music to be correct or to create the picture, all of the parts must be in place.

*(Barbara Buehlman)*

The intellect serves as coach, the senses play the game. Too few people get emotionally and physically involved with music making. I find that people are often on the outside looking in: they are not involved, they are being a coach not a player.

*(Frank Bencriscutto)*

I constantly remind students that they will never be accused of being too musical or too expressive. No judge at a contest is going to write, "You played too emotionally, or too expressively, or that the way you performed the music was too exciting, therefore I regret that I must give you a Division II rating!"

*(Richard Floyd)*

I tried to teach them to anticipate that every note is going to be out-of-tune; therefore it is their job to correct it before anyone hears it.

*(Butler R. Eitel)*

Problems can be solved when the students become honestly involved, because then they become the sound. When they become the sound, they will solve such things as centering the sound; when they become the harmony they began to solve balance and proportions; when they become the melody, they begin to play more in tune.

*(Frank Bencriscutto)*

### Statements that guide the performance of articulations

I might say, "Let's do "tah-tah-tah-tah" but don't let the notes touch." I do not say separate, or short. Instead I say, "Don't let the notes touch" as compared with "Put a space, or silence between the notes." With this description, the phrase itself does not lose continuity.

*(Richard Floyd)*

The kids will always end the tone and the air pressure simultaneously, which causes all sorts of problems.

*(Richard Putzier)*

I use the terms "fortissimo air and piano tonguing" to communicate that playing loudly requires tonguing softly.

*(Gary Hill)*

### Thinking about ensemble playing

Watch for precision and listen for pitch.

*(Stanley Cate)*

The word "listen" is only half of the instruction; the other half is to "adjust."

*(Donald Gee)*

When you're tuning with others in the group, you need to give up some of your ego and become part of an ensemble. I keep telling them, "Give up some of that ego, that sense of *me* being so important."

*(Francis Marciniak)*

## TEACHING AND LEARNING

People teach the way they were taught, not the way they were taught to teach.

*(anonymous)*

Students learn from what they *do*, not from what you *tell* them to do.

*(James Stivers)*

Say little; they teach themselves a lot.

*(John W. LaCava)*

I am constantly reminding my kids of what they're doing and how to do it correctly: to do so, I state the idea or concern with one or two words such as "hand position."

*(Sandra P. Thompson)*

The less one says the better off they are.

*(John W. LaCava)*

In marching band, I say "Don't just do something, stand there."

*(Thomas L. Davis)*

The most commonly used marching band term and one that especially aggravates students is the command, "and again."

*(David Hans)*

Keep them playing as much as you can.

*(John W. LaCava)*

Drill is really guided practice during the rehearsal.

*(George R. Bedell)*

Using certain key words is important with rhythm. For example, with fast moving notes use words like "deliberate," "be patient," instead of saying "you are hurrying," "you are rushing" or "don't rush." Try to avoid the negatives of do's and don't's. Using a simple word or words will help, such as "hear all the notes clearly," "every note has a mother," "all the notes are important," or "don't throw them away."

*(Larry Rachleff)*

Enunciation equals articulation equals style.

*(Dominic Spera)*

The conductor initiates the pulse, the ensemble generates it: one cannot be done without the other.

*(James Arrowood)*

I am their instructor, they are their teacher.

*(John W. LaCava)*

The difference between student and professional groups is not the product, it's how long it takes to get it.

*(Charles Olson)*

If it's hard it's worth practicing.

*(Charles Olson)*

The greatest effect is right where the rock goes into the pool. I mean that's where the splash is, and everything else is a ripple and way out on the edge the ripples are not real strong: they disappear. I guess, you keep coming back to the place where you can have the great splash. The place includes those people you deal with daily, not only in your group. My groups are primarily made up now of people who hope to be professional players and some who want to be teachers. Both can be affected because they are near any splash I can make.

*(Eugene Corporon)*

Our priorities become the students' priorities.

*(Patricia Brumbaugh)*

Since someone is always going to be the first guy on his block to come in, I say, "Don't ever be the first to come in (pause) and never be late." This also has them begin to listen to others so they come in "never late." They come to the realization there is a precise moment when it is correct to come in.

*(James Arrowood)*

The times I have been unsuccessful as a conductor have been the times when I have been in the way of the music.

*(Richard K. Hansen)*

The less you do as a conductor, the more effect conducting has when you do something.

*(Robert Grechesky)*

Teachers are verbal, verbal, verbal, and visual, visual, visual, instead of aural, aural, aural, which is what music is. Music is an aural phenomenon and should be taught that way. We need better aural skills.

*(James Froseth)*

Kids don't like what they can't play.

*(Carl A. Bly)*

Never say, "Kids, this is going to be difficult."

*(Robert Allan)*

If you tell the kids it is going to be difficult, then they give it more of their attention and effort, and are less likely to become frustrated and demoralized at the first difficulties they face.

*(Melanie Michalak)*

I felt strongly about punctuality and promptness. I say, "When you are on time, you are late." At first they could not figure it out, but soon they realized that being present at nine is not being ready at nine. It worked!
*(John Kinnison)*

Don't blow *into* the horn, blow *through* the horn.
*(Stanley Cate)*

I often write on or make them write in their book: "Make it sound like it is easy to do, not like it is hard to do."
*(Steven Cooper)*

It takes twice through to start the habit, but ten times is needed to change the habit. I see this in standing and sitting posture, hand position, breathing, tonguing, and everything.
*(Steven Cooper)*

Blow through the horn as though it were a pea-shooter. Blow the air clear across the whole room.
*(Stanley Cate)*

In technical passages, I often ask students to have soft relaxed fingers. I want to get the "claw" out of their hands, which is a big problem.
*(Gary Hill)*

Sight-reading ability is the most accurate measure of a musician.
*(Butler R. Eitel)*

Too often our students assume they are innocent until you tell them they are guilty. They don't try to make music, they play their part with the assumption that if they need to do something differently, the teacher will tell them; and, until you do, they think everything is okay. Typically, one kid says to another, "How did you do in band today?" The other responds, "I must have been perfect, the director did not correct me a single time!"
*(Richard Floyd)*

Poor phrase endings are "like saying a half-word at the end of a sentence."
*(Stanley Cate)*

The instruction "play in tone," with good air stream, with centered pitch and characteristic tone means much more than the phrase "play in tune." The latter implies only good pitch, which is merely the pitch of departure.
*(Richard K. Hansen)*

I expect students to know "The Four T's" for every number: Title, Time (meter signature), Tempo, and Tune (key signature).
*(Walter Rodby)*

Use the vocabulary of music such as "fermata" and "anacrusis." Do not use the terms "bird's eye," "holds" and "pickups." This is important because we should teach them the language of music, not slang. A student in a chemistry course speaks correctly; why not in music courses?
*(Frank Battisti)*

If the terms used in rehearsal are ritard and accelerando rather than get slower and get faster, the students get used to that. They become more comfortable with these terms when they become members of other organizations.
*(Donald Wilcox)*

We are only young once, but we can remain immature indefinitely.
*(Butler R. Eitel)*

I like words used as descriptive vocabulary, instead of using what we call "talking words": words that are used for a purpose. A descriptive word would be something that describes an articulation, it's almost onomatopoeia—taking a word or syllable out of the language that by its sound describes what you want. You simply give them the oral model.
*(Gerald Olson)*

The "Kiss Principle" means the teacher should "keep it simple stupid!"
*(John Kinnison)*

Urbie Green says he got his high range by playing out of a French horn book. He thought he should play up there, so he did. His efforts show that "you learn by doing."
*(John W. LaCava)*

I stole this idea from Larry Rachleff. Say, "This should sound like a bassoonasaxaclarinetaphone," meaning to blend the sound of these instruments. That makes a lot of sense.
*(Michael Kaufman)*

## RELATING AND COMMUNICATING WITH STUDENTS

### Interaction with students

Cast students into the role that you would like to have them assume.
*(Leon Fosha)*

People live up to their expectations of your expectations.
*(George R. Bedell)*

If I do not make eye contact with them, how can I

expect them to make eye contact with me?

*(Patricia Brumbaugh)*

Kids rather enjoy achieving what the teacher is after, whatever it is!

*(Charles Olson)*

During the warm up I try to make eye contact with every individual. Someone told me that you do not own them until you have made contact with each of them.

*(John A. Thompson)*

## RHYTHM

### Observations about teaching rhythm

Using a metronome keeps you honest from an honest point of view!

*(John Anderson)*

To build the feel of triple meter, use the word "evenly."

*(George R. Bedell)*

Hold the note longer than you think you should, and that will be about right.

*(Michael Kaufman)*

In reality a whole note has five counts: 1–2–3–4–1!

*(John Kinnison)*

Make up words for rhythms that go across the bar line. Some that help are "the big pig" or "Amsterdam." The more unpredictable or off the wall these words might be, the more effective they are, depending upon the group.

*(John Anderson)*

We used mnemonic devices such as "Mississippi Hot Dog." Students would make up their own phrases such as "My name is Joe." Then they would write the rhythm on the board that represented what they chanted.

*(John Kinnison)*

## TONE AND BREATHING

### Thinking about the air stream

Blow so the air doesn't die because it does not get through the horn or die after it gets through the horn.

*(Stanley Cate)*

I use the term "hurricane" or "tornado" to describe how fast the air goes, especially on high notes for brass players.

*(Steven Cooper)*

The wind should be used like the bow on the violin.

*(Steven Cooper)*

The three enemies of sound are airiness, edginess, and reediness. These are the three cardinal sins of wind playing.

*(John W. LaCava)*

The faster the notes are, the less air students use. I find myself frequently saying, "The faster the fingers or tongue moves, the faster the air stream must be."

*(Gary Hill)*

Say, "Allow the air to go through the instrument or, allow the air to come out quicker" instead of saying "make the air go faster." This says that they are allowing things to happen that would naturally happen; they shouldn't think that they're pushing anything.

*(Francis Marciniak)*

### Conveying tone concepts

To get them to recall the ideal tone in the moments before they play, I use metaphors such as "a cold hard bagpipe sound" or, "the winter in Minnesota" or, "dream about lying on the beach in the sun and your tone is like the rays of the sun that is glowing," or "warm feelings like sitting by the fireplace in the cold winter."

*(Richard K. Hansen)*

The low brass may be playing something and if it's real strong, say it's scored quite high, you might want more of a sheen on the sound, or dark sound. I might say, "I want this to sound more like velvet feels."

*(John Williamson)*

## INTERESTING STATEMENTS AND OBSERVATIONS

### We need more than one way to look at something

What's more beautiful, a flying butterfly or a sitting one? You know, if you can see one sitting, you can take in the details of his beauty: if you see one flying, you can take in the butterfly's beauty when it is in motion. The point is, neither of them are sufficient without the other.

*(Charles Olson)*

### Using words to trigger imagination

I heard Miles Johnson say to a band, "Make believe you are Beethoven." He felt "making believe" made students less self-conscious than if asked to deliberately express their own feelings or interpretations of Beethoven.

*(Joseph Casey)*

### Using words differently

John Paynter would frequently put words to tunes

that had no words to teach style, mood, and phrasing. For example, on Bennett's *Symphonic Songs for Band*, he would sing the woodwind counter phrase with the words "Your eyes are green and blue, and I am in love with you, just bring your wallet too." The band would crack up. Another time there were two contrasting parts, one subordinate. After working with one he said, "Now, let's have the cheering section." He even did this with marches! This suggested the styles for the piece.

*(Michael Golemo)*

### When they all tune at the same time

I keep counting the times I've told them, "When you do this on stage, all you've done is convince the audience that you don't know what you're doing. They hear the single note and they hear all of you play out of tune. Then, they see you sit there with smiles on your faces and you look like idiots."

*(Francis Marciniak)*

### Talking about teaching

There's a statement that I love: "He who would kindle another, would himself glow." You know, teachers sometimes talk about being burned out. I wonder sometimes if some teachers were ever lit, I wonder if they ever had enough glow to start a fire.

I think it's part of our job as teachers to learn how to keep that glow going. I think one gets it from great music, from great experiences, from reading literature, from seeing art, and from continuing to grow as a human being. Well, you have to be interested in your own growth. Your own growth comes in many ways: the growth can be technical, or intellectual, or philosophical, or spiritual— it's lots of things. And, part of what happens to any of us who have the responsibility of teaching is that we also have the responsibility of remaining a student and growing. I think the value of what we do has to do with getting people to be in touch with their feelings. We can do this partly by finding what's unique about music; not what's the same, but what's unique about making music.

*(Eugene Corporon)*

I try to say to aspiring teachers that there aren't that many "givens," and you can't fall into the trap of "formalized instruction." There are things you believe in and there are methods you can use. You should be willing to take on more new ideas and bend any idea. Particularly, you should always be willing to listen to what you are hearing.

*(Michael Haithcock)*

It has taken me fifteen years to define the task of teacher training. My observation is, "We can give people a lot of information and if we observe them, we see that they do nothing with the information." In the dictionary it says that to teach means "to show." Teaching is not defined as "to tell." Therefore, what we need to do is build teaching skills that "show" things. In teacher training, skill training makes a greater difference than giving them information.

*(James Froseth)*

### Stating the value of music education

There's a wonderful article about music in schools by Gloria J. Kiester. It is one of the shortest articles, and one of the most powerful I've ever read. One of her statements is, "Music belongs in schools, not because it's fun and entertaining, not because it's relaxing and socializing, though it's all these. Music belongs in schools because it is basic to learning, and it's a unique way of knowing yourself."

*(Eugene Corporon)*

### Taking advantage of verbal and number systems

I'll sing in both syllables and numbers, because I'm connecting the solfege with what is going on in general music class, and the digital patterns that some teachers also use.

*(Edward S. Lisk)*

### Describing the role of a conductor

My own feeling, as a conductor, is that I should look like the music. If I look like the music, then they feel the same music the same way. We've got the essence of music if everything is happening—I mean, I'm looking like the music and they're playing like the music from the way I look.

*(Richard J. Suddendorf)*

### Comparing sounds to tastes

One composer said that the saxophone was musical garlic. When it was appropriate, he threw it in but only enough to flavor the score!

*(Timothy Mahr)*

### The music is not the paper

Some kid comes into rehearsal and says, "Hey, do you have the music?" Another holds up the folder and says, "Yeah, I've got it." The music in the folder, the paper stuff, has the same relation to music that a blue print has to a house.

*(Donald Wilcox)*

### What the teacher says and what students hear

This reminds me of a great Far Side cartoon. It showed this man talking to a dog. The cartoon says, "What people say to their dogs." People say, "Ginger sit, Ginger roll over, Ginger heel, etc." Then the next panel says, "What dogs hear." Dogs hear, "Ginger, blah blah blah; Ginger, blah blah blah; Ginger, etc." This is the same things musicians hear when conductors talk. They hear, "Trumpets, blah blah blah; horns, blah blah blah."

*(Eugene Corporon)*

Success depends upon whether we choose to learn a part itself, or to learn from the parts.

*(Phillip A. Weinberg)*

"In baseball, if you cannot run, hit, throw, or catch it is hard to have fun playing the game." If one cannot breathe, control the instrument, play a melody, play with the ensemble, make a good tone, etc., it is hard to enjoy playing the game of music.

*(Roman Palmer)*

Presence at its worst is showmanship; at its best, charisma.

*(anonymous)*

A contest judge related an experience he had. He had just listened to a band that was the poorest he had ever heard. They did so many things wrong, he was unsure what comments to make. Finally he figured it out and said, "This band certainly lives up to its director's expectations."

*(Kenneth Larsen)*

CHAPTER TWELVE

# QUESTIONS

By asking effective questions teachers can focus the students' attention and draw them more fully into the classroom process. Initially questions from teachers or classmates help the student remember facts, ideas, or skills: the correct fingering, the names of the lines and spaces on the staff, or the correct way to assemble the instrument. Questioning also enables the teacher to tell what the student has learned and what their thought processes are.

As students progress, teachers must question at a higher level. They might ask the students to notice differences in pitches, balance, phrasing, or tempo. Specifically, teachers might ask: "Is your pitch higher or lower than the trumpet's pitch?" "Which sound dominates the texture at letter B, the woodwinds or the brasses?" or "Was the second note emphasized less or more than the third note?"

With even more advanced questioning, the teacher can ask the students to make comparisons and judgments, and to actually use the ideas and information they have been taught. The teacher can ask, "Which articulations should we use in the first phrase?" "Where is the proper place to take the first breath so the phrase makes musical sense?" or "Where are the higher points in the phrase? Which one of the points, in your opinion, should be the highest point in the entire phrase?"

The students can respond to questions such as: "Can you comment about the tempo: is it too fast, too slow, or about right?" or "What is the relationship of the dynamic level here and the level at letter C?" A still higher level of questioning might be, "We have a problem here with both balance and blend; what has caused it?" "Which should we solve first?" or "Can anyone suggest a solution?"

These examples show how teachers could use questioning to determine if students know facts and fingerings and to involve them in learning. The purpose for questions will change when students comprehend the material. The students then go on to make comparisons, see relationships, and analyze and synthesize as they apply their knowledge. Eventually they can guide and evaluate their own efforts while applying what they have learned.

## OBSERVATIONS ABOUT QUESTIONING

Ask brief but relevant questions to keep them thinking.

*(Butler R. Eitel)*

Deciding which question to ask is a matter of responding to the situation. At the root of the response is score study. One cannot ask a question if one does not know what one is after. Without score study, one often doesn't have a real plan for the rehearsal interaction—there is just a response to the situation.

*(John Williamson)*

In rehearsal, I probably ask more questions than I get answers. I think there are two ways to rehearse: one is to give them the right answer and then simply make them accept that because you're supposed to know the answer. The other way is to give them some options and discover how they think about it. When you start asking questions and you get them involved, their faces all change. They suddenly become terribly interested in what's going on. You also may have to defuse the situation or set it up so there is no fear of giving the wrong answer.

I try to encourage them to have input by asking them what sounds the most satisfying to them, instead of telling them what satisfies the conductor. For example, I take a simple line that has absolutely no expression marks under it. Even without markings, there is an obvious implied crescendo or an implied diminuendo. We will try it exactly as written and then I'll ask them to try it this way, to try it that way. Then, I'll ask the questions: "What's more interesting?" "What's more satisfying?" "Which way do you think this should be performed?"

Most of them can decide and agree upon what is the most satisfying, then the next question becomes, "Well, why is it that way?" Now, we can pursue still another way, because there are always people who feel the opposite way of phrasing is better. We talk about that also. The line I always use with the students is the Pablo Casals line. It's a generalization that you can stretch any way you want to stretch it. His feeling is that music is always a series of rainbows. What he means, is that there is always an implied shape, even if it's not written into the music.

Therefore, there are clues I can ask them to find. For example I might ask, "We have this section of music that is twenty-some bars long, and it's pianissimo. Now, what should we do with this?" I ask them about shapes. I talk about direction to the high points and to the low points, and the direction away from the high points and away from the low points. Those are the clues I look for. Often the words *tension* and *repose* are the correct words, and they help us find where those points occur.

*(Craig Kirchhoff)*

Questioning can make them more active instead of passive. At first, this may be difficult for them. So I take a small passage to give them a chance to find an answer. For example, one can take several measures where a cadence occurs and ask them to find the moving line that controls the ritard. Ask, "Who has it?" They look at you blankly and want you to tell them. Do it again so they can hear and so they can look for it with their eyes. If you keep at it, they will begin to hear things and the light goes on!

*(Pamela Gearhart)*

## EXAMPLES OF WHAT QUESTIONS CAN ADDRESS

### Tone production

I ask a kid who makes a very good and rich sound, "How does your throat feel now? Where are you teeth?" I ask the kid to explain to others what he is doing and how he feels.

*(Jack Brookshire)*

### Discrimination

Learning tonal patterns can be enhanced by asking students questions such as, "What songs do you know that contain do, mi, and sol?" "How many times does mi-re-do occur in the melody we learned?"

*(Stanley L. Schleuter)*

### Sight reading

Before we sight read, I also use questioning. I'll say, "What's the highest note? What's the lowest note? What is the loudest note? What is the softest note?" This is so they look at their score in as many ways as possible. Then I'll say, "Find the rhythm that you think you might have the most trouble playing." We look at a rhythm and I say, "How does that sound?" I ask somebody to play it as everybody's looking at it. We do this enough to get everybody thinking and anticipating; then, we'll play it through.

*(John A. Thompson)*

### Intonation

If there is an intonation problem, you can supply the answer giving the solution such as, "Second trombone, you are flat on D above the staff." You also can ask questions such as, "There is a pitch problem—can you listen to cure it?" Or, you can ask an individual, "Where was that pitch problem occurring, and how can you solve this?"

*(John Anderson)*

### Developing judgment, involvement, and independence

I want students to ask why something is done. To develop interaction, I hope they ask, "What is the purpose, how should this be done?" I like to see evidence that I am getting below the surface. I also ask students what they think the reason for something is, though I prefer they ask the question first.

*(Anthony J. Maiello)*

Since it's their piece too, I don't always want to impose my interpretations on them: I ask them what they think. This must be done in a way that's specific enough so they don't go off on a tangent.

I'll say, "Have you been listening to the phrase move throughout the ensemble? Did you hear how the trumpet played it? You guys need to get together and figure out how to do it because that phrase really needs to be played in the same style each time. If you want my help I'll be available."

I may call a soloist in and say, "This is what the band will be doing as they accompany you. You must make some decisions. For example, where are you going to breath? Here's where they are breathing, did you want to breathe with them or not?"

I do not always let them take the bull by the horns and do whatever they want. I guide them and if I have a strong idea I'll tell them what it is. On the other hand, if I have thirty flutes I'll say, "There are so many of you that you must make a decision. You have to play unison with the clarinet and there are more of you than the clarinets. How do you think we should handle that? Do you want to play softer or would you rather have me cut out some flutes? If so, how many should we cut out?" In this way, they feel like they play a part in creating the performance.

I may ask questions differently in junior high. I show them several examples of phrasing and say, "Which one is better, version one or version two?" Then I say, "Now let's talk about the differences for a second. What do you think about it?" Somebody will say, "We played louder in the beginning," or "We should play softer on measure six." They begin to agree and say, "Yeah, yeah!" Then you say, "We are about to decide the phrasing. Should we phrase this one like a rainbow. Let's do that first and then let's phrase it like a valley." We try the whole thing and before you know it they know a difference between an arch type of phrase and a diminuendo type of phrase: they didn't even know they learned it.

*(William W. Wiedrich)*

I simply say, "Is this sounding right? Are these dynamics what we want here?" They say, "It says right here mezzo forte." I respond, "But now here, where the flutes are supposed to have the solo, their part also is marked mezzo forte. Obviously this arranger thought he did this right, but with ten trumpets and four flutes, we may not be playing the correct volume." Even major composers are not always that careful about writing the parts in balance. The students accept that reasoning, but they still feel what is on the page is God's word.

*(Richard Putzier)*

I also may ask them other questions such as, "Where do you think you should breathe in this phrase?

*(Patricia Brumbaugh)*

I question to keep them involved, to promote thinking, to review fingering, to remind them how to play, to solve problems, to look up information, to prompt their attention to reading, etc. I also do this if they are depending on me too much. However, if they simply have forgotten something, I may not use questioning: instead I'll give them the information.

*(R. G. Conlee)*

I may have them rehearse without a conductor. If there are problems, I stop them and ask if they have heard this or that. The idea is to ask them, "What is wrong and how do we correct it?" This puts the responsibility on them to become more active rather than passive players. Sometimes I phrase the solutions to a problem as a choice. "Should the phrase grow more than it did, or less?"

*(Pamela Gearhart)*

I may say, "What am I going to say now?" "What am I thinking about now in relation to that passage? or "What do you think the trumpets should do here?"

*(David Hans)*

I often ask open-ended questions such as, "What's going on here in the piece?" This may be to get them thinking about the music. Then, I'll try to channel it toward a formal or structural question such as, "Does the theme pass from horns to trombones first or last? Which instrument is subordinate in this passage?" Quite often, if I sense that they're just playing notes and have no understanding, I'll ask them that kind of question.

*(Francis Marciniak)*

I also ask them to evaluate whether the phrase was "pretty" or if the phrase endings are chopped off or not.

*(Stanley Cate)*

To have them make a discrimination quickly, I say, "Is it supposed to sound 'da da da da da' or 'dadadadada?' Which is better?" I might say, "Should this be a brass color that's supported by woodwinds or woodwinds supported by brass?" or "Altos saxes, should you balance to the horns so it is a horn color, or should they balance to you so it is a saxophone color. Who supports whom?"

*(John A. Thompson)*

## Music fundamentals

I may ask a student, at any time, a question such as, "What is the order of flats?"

*(Patricia Brumbaugh)*

## Listening

I find myself asking, "Who are you playing with, who has the same part as you do?" I find, with younger groups especially, they are not sure. It is amazing to go into a rehearsal of the Holst *Military Suite in E flat* and find that they do not know what the chaconne figure is. I also ask, "Your section just made an entrance, where did that come from—who preceded you, where does the idea stem from." I also could be talking about pitch, musical style, melodic content, etc.

*(Gary Hill)*

I sometimes teach by explaining, by questioning, by conducting, and by suggesting. This depends upon the needs they have, the experiences they have with similar or different pieces, or the time available in a rehearsal. If I question, I might say, "Is section B to be similar in loudness to A, or different?" If they say different, I ask them "In what way?" If they give a good answer, I reinforce this with statements such as, "That's right," or "Generally that is right, but it could it be just a bit softer than B." I ask, "Does it reach ff or pp somewhere?" We ask questions and decide, overall whether this is a loud piece, a soft piece, or a moderate volume piece in general (macro). Then we decide the dynamic level(s) in relation to this in each section (micro).

*(Richard Fischer)*

I try to follow the idea "instead of telling, ask questions." This brings forth the old problem of students who say, "I can't play and listen too!" I say, "I am sorry, but you have to do both." I might ask, "What is out of tune in this chord? Why did I stop? What was wrong? Should we try that again? Can you tell me who has a parallel line with you? Who has an answering phrase to you?" or "Can the third horn sing the viola part?" If the brass are playing, I may say to the second violins, "Tell me what Borodin wrote dynamically for the brass?"

*(Pamela Gearhart)*

Rather than say something, I'll ask first, "What does this sound like to you?" or "How should we do this?"

Sometimes they'll demonstrate their answer. I also may ask a student, "Play this the way you think it should be played." If I'm not getting something across to them, instead of singing it, I'll have them play it a few times. Students might also ask, "How would you like us to do this?" If so, I'll say, "Play it" and I'll adjust my suggestions. I also can ask, "What composer does this sound like, who does this remind you of?" or "How is this phrase different from that phrase?"

*(John Williamson)*

### Performance technique

I will put all quarter notes on the board with different dynamics for each quarter note. I will say, "What's the difference between these quarter notes?" After they answer, I might ask, "How does one play dynamics?" The intent of the questions is to get at the question, "How is one supposed to make dynamic changes? With air, of course, but how much air is in a forte, and how much air in a piano, etc.?" I ask, "How does one make a crescendo? What do you do—how do you play it?" They say, "Well, we get louder" and I say, "How do you do that, what physically happens? Do you press your loud button, do you press your soft button, what do you do?" This leads to talking about the speed of the air as one makes a crescendo, and the speed of the air as one plays a diminuendo.

With articulation I ask, "Are these articulations done on the air or with the tongue? How do you do this articulation? How do you make that articulation? What do you do physically in your mouth and with your tongue?" I might say, "Explain that to me, What do you do when you tongue hard—show me. What does your tongue do? Does it hit the top of your mouth? Does it pull down from the top of your mouth? What do you mean *hard*?" I may select a student whom I think will not be embarrassed and have him perform. Then, we will examine what was done.

*(Dwayne P. Sagen)*

With younger kids, rather than seventh and eighth graders, I ask questions about balance. For example, I say, "Who has the melody?" or "Is there anything wrong with the balance at letter B? Why are we not hearing the melody?" or "Which part is too heavy?"

I may ask about other musical features such as. "What is wrong with this articulation? Why isn't this sounding good? What is the difference between two different dynamic levels?" or "Is there a difference we can hear?"

*(Ross A. Leeper)*

## CHAPTER THIRTEEN

# VISUAL

One would expect all teachers to use at least some visual means to teach students, since most students learn more easily with the addition of a visual stimulus. Not only do visual aids conform to some of the students' many learning styles, visual aids also support other teaching techniques and can be paired with them. For example, a drawing of a crescendo on the blackboard can picture what the teacher wants the students to understand. The drawing also can be paired with either the teacher's gestures that show the dynamic change, or with his singing that models the crescendo. Conversely, he can draw the students' attention to the model of crescendo he gestured or sang by drawing its shape on the board to support the example.

Visual aids are used often by the better classroom teachers. Teachers may realize that while it is easy for them to function at an abstract level, it is not as easy for students; they need the visual aids to help make the musical ideas and verbal discussions more concrete. While music students have seen many other classroom teachers place words, numbers, and pictures on a board, many music teachers, even some who are excellent music teachers in many respects, seldom use drawings, charts, graphics, or other visual aids to clarify and teach music; therefore visual teaching techniques might be new to music students.

In an undergraduate music education program, when student teachers and other inexperienced music teachers first begin to teach, they use what they already know. Thus, many of them use visual aids infrequently. They model their own teachers, many of whom were also not using drawings and other visual teaching techniques. Another explanation is that they just may be not be ready yet to use visual aids because of the inescapable demands and unfamiliarity of their new role.

When one tries to use visual aids, one must remember that the visual representation is not the music. It depicts some aspect of music instead and the music teacher must serve to connect the music and the depiction. In many statements in this section one can see that some teachers, as a result of planning and intent, consciously connect the visual to the musical. They do not let the students "just happen" to make the connection themselves.

The assessment of the value of a particular visual aid is that it stimulates the students visually, strengthens communication, and facilitates the students' learning. The quality of music teaching as a whole is likely to improve if the comments in this section help persuade music teachers to use all the tools available to them—including visual teaching techniques such as these examples.

## THE IMPACT OF VISUAL EXPERIENCES

I use visual teaching techniques to portray what goes on inside students. This helps overcome obstacles both teachers and students face because many musical and performance behaviors occur inside the students.

*(R. G. Conlee)*

It really works if they can see a graphic representation of it all instead of our traditional notational system. For example, if they can see a longer note value by drawing a line under notes on a chalk board.

*(L. Keating Johnson)*

When I try to communicate quickly, I use lines, rainbows, arches, etc.

*(Eugene Corporon)*

I connect anything at all from their life to the music. For example, talking about the formal structure of music is very difficult. This is where you must bring into the rehearsal everything you can. A teacher can use all the photographs, pictures, and drawings of great pieces of architecture, profiles of mountains, flatness of lakes, terraces of rice paddies, etc., to contribute visually to what we finally are going to approach aurally. Looking at the sense of balance in a beautiful building like the Taj Mahal, one can see the marvelous sense of balance, of approach and departure. That is what so much in music is all about: the anticipation, the activity, and the fulfillment and recession. These things are there visually, you can talk about them in mountains and buildings.

*(Frederick Fennell)*

I have found that if students can see what that tapered note looks like, they grasp it more easily. There's a book with some helpful drawings by Arthur Weisberg, called the *Art of Wind Playing*. He believes that most good wind players learn to make a resonant release of a note by playing in orchestras where even a pizzicato note has a ring to it. Therefore, the orchestral wind player learns, instead of just stopping the air dead, that one has to taper the air off so the note simulates what the strings do. To develop this, Weisberg has some helpful graphic representations of staccato, legato, tenuto, etc. Picturing style, dynamics, breath releases, etc. works very well because they are easier to teach if the student can see the shape one is after.

*(L. Keating Johnson)*

When kids see performers on stage, and see how believable and totally involved they appear, fake as it may be, these performers turn kids on—even if the visual appearance is motivated or presented for all the wrong reasons.

*(Frank Bencriscutto)*

A common technique I use is showing the shape of the music visually on the board. I couldn't exist without a blackboard. For example, I show arches for phrasing; and for the tension points, I probably put a little triangle to emphasize it—like an X to mark the spot.

*(Richard Putzier)*

I draw certain things like embouchures, where the bow is going to hit the string, how much of the bow is going to hit the strings, or where a chord is on the staff when explaining music theory.

Another example relates to expectations. Teachers must expect a lot from them to get the highest achievement from them. I use a rubber band to show this. Holding it toward the ceiling, I say, "This is where you are now, and this (as I stretch the rubber band) is where we want to be." I have a rubber band in my hand, at times, when I say this. If they can see something, teaching can be more successful.

*(Judith A. Niles)*

I am such a great believer in pictures that I had an official band photographer. I bought the film and he would take pictures continually. Thousands of pictures lined the halls of the music building. Kids, first, want to look at themselves and, even without out prompting, they examined their posture, embouchure, hand and body position. I could point out how they might change these elements to play better. One could have quizzes, could pick models, etc. I had a set for every instrument and a set of pictures for every kid.

*(Frank Battisti)*

## RHYTHM AND NOTATION

### Ritards

We use drawings in which the notes are written farther and farther apart to represent the elongation of the pulse; or, to illustrate the ritard, I notate a series of quarter notes and draw lines under each. Where the tempo should slow, I draw longer lines to show that each note, though notated with the same symbol, lasts longer because the pulse rate slows.

*(Jack Brookshire)*

Many students have difficulty comprehending that not only are they speeding up or slowing down, but that everything is proportional. For example, in a pattern of repeated eighth notes and a ritardando, students have to subdivide the ritard enough that they realize that proportionally each note is getting longer as they slow down. The reverse holds true for accelerando.

Many students somehow associate ritardando and accelerando with just speeding up or slowing down. I have found that the image of a ping pong ball bouncing and slowly coming to a stop helps them grasp a ritard, and that the change is proportional. You can do this with any age student.

If you hit them with that, the effect is immediate. It sinks the idea so deeply and immediately that it's almost better with the older kids than the younger ones. Sometimes, with older students, you have to make it seem silly so they don't think you're taking them back to preschool.

*(L. Keating Johnson)*

### Using visual aids to teach basic rhythms

When teaching rhythms in duple and triple meter, I divide pieces of paper—a sheet equals one pulse. For a triplet, I divide the one sheet of paper into thirds. Any sheet can be divided into thirds, halves, fourths, or unequal portions. I say, "This is all the same piece of paper." They see that parts from the sheet, when cut, still equal one of the sheets. They understand it much better than when I describe it or try to explain it over and over.

With a dotted-quarter note followed by an eighth, for example, I take two pieces of paper and write "1" on the top of one sheet and "2" on the top of a second. I then divide the second page in half and write "and" on the bottom half of the second page. When they're counting they have to say "One, two-and, three." The bottom half of the second page gets the "and" after beat two. When kids have trouble with that rhythm, they seem to understand that much better than me trying to explain this without something visual.

*(Sandra P. Thompson)*

In the Russianov clarinet book there is a section where he shows a pattern of sixteenth notes and he will say, "This is the way it should be played, it's just a little drill." Then he says, "This is the way people often play this." He has sixteenth notes with bigger spaces between some while others are very close together; it's wonderful!

*(Gerald Olson)*

To show ties, I take two shoelaces and tie them together. This can show the kids that we have now taken two different and separate things and we've tied them together into one. I also use the shoelace to tie it together because it has the same word as tying.

*(Sandra P. Thompson)*

## INTONATION

### Visualizing note placement for pitch accuracy

I use a diagram that shows three notches for a pitch. If the pitch is played in the center notch, one is in the middle of a note; one is in a high notch when playing on the high side of the note; and one is in a low notch when playing on the low side of the note.

If they are going to play fourth line D on trumpet, I have them try to picture playing in the high notch of that note since we know that note's going to be flat. Then, I'll have them play D in the middle of the note, which is going to be a little out of tune. Using a note that is sharp, such as high G at the top of the staff, I'll have them play on the low side of the note compared to the middle. Using a good reference book, they can find and memorize which notes are out of tune. That gives them information about which notes are played in the different notches.

*(Dwayne P. Sagen)*

### Using trombones to show visually the pitch adjustments

I use two trombone players to show "beats." One starts slightly above or below the pitch, and he adjusts slowly so the sound improves and beats disappear as he tunes to the other. Students not only can hear beats and feel beats: they can also "see" the adjustments needed.

*(John W. LaCava)*

## STYLE AND PHRASING

I have often asked students not to chop off phrase endings. The technique I'm using now is toothpaste! I ask them to practice putting toothpaste on the toothbrush and if it goes "puth" that is like chopping off the note. I say, "Since all of you use the toothpaste every day anyway, I want you to practice putting the toothpaste on the toothbrush. Notice that you can flip it off at the end and you make it a nice, smooth release." I also tell them, "When we're trying to play legato, beautiful phrases, you should express sounds the same way you would while putting toothpaste on. You don't just grab it and squeeze it out; instead, it's a very gentle, smooth type of motion." I guess I have analyzed putting toothpaste on a brush a lot, because

the kids really relate to that.

*(Sandra P. Thompson)*

With phrasing, I sometimes make a drawing showing the end of the phrase as rounded. I start from a zero line and have it round up to the dynamic level I want, just like an algebraic or geometric design. At the end, some phrases should decline to that zero point very gradually, like an airplane landing. Others might fall off more quickly but never fall straight down like a cliff, except in the rarest cases. The rate of decline is more gradual.

*(L. Keating Johnson)*

Diagrams can show, "This is a little phrase, this one's a big phrase, here are four phrases in a row and each has to get larger." We'll number those phrase one, two, three, and four. It'll just be a picture, not the notes. "We want you to play the picture you're looking at." We gave up a long time ago saying this is a crescendo and this is a decrescendo sign; we call it a picture.

*(Bryce Taylor)*

Sometimes I'll draw pictures of the shape of a phrase, its beginning, peak, ending.

*(Richard J. Suddendorf)*

## ARTICULATION

### Tonguing

I use hand movements to simulate the movement of my tongue, which I do in conjunction with drawings on the board. I also carry a poster with me to each lesson or rehearsal that shows a drawing of the teeth, mouth, and tongue.

*(Jack Brookshire)*

### Articulations

Instead of spending time talking about the beginning and especially the ending of the notes, I put various shaped drawings on the board. Then, they play notes that are like the shapes on the board. I might say, "What is desirable is not a brick, which you get when you say "daht, daht, daht." Instead say, "dah-dah-dah-dah" in style that looks more "egg-shaped," stronger on the "aaah" of daahh. This promotes more careful tonguing, more air releases, and fewer tongued releases.

*(Frank Battisti)*

I use drawings to show them the placement and position of the tongue. (This works well with brass but can be done with woodwinds also.) I will draw a picture of the top teeth and the arch in the top of the mouth all the way back to the throat. This gives them a side view of someone's oral cavity. I then draw the tongue and show where the tongue is. I ask them first, "Where does the tongue hit, where do you feel the tongue?" I show them how the placement of the tongue starts up at the top of the mouth, just behind the teeth. The tongue action really is pulling down from the roof of the mouth. I will draw the tongue and show where it starts and where it ends, and mark it with an arrow down. I do this to show tongue action and keeping the throat open.

Sometimes I follow that by saying, "Now just relax your mouth, relax your tongue, and relax your oral cavity. Now tell me, where is your tongue? If everyone completely relaxes his tongue, it will automatically go to the top of the mouth." As a result, they understand that the tonguing action is a pulling down move and, when relaxed, the tongue will flip up to the top of the mouth as it should.

*(Dwayne P. Sagen)*

To develop appropriate attacks and releases, I draw two horizontal parallel lines on the board left to right. I say, "This is a note with no beginning and no ending." Then, I draw a line showing the tapering of note endings, or jagged lines for less desirable releases. They responded very well to visual teaching techniques. The verbal approach does not seem to work as well here.

*(Thomas Herrera)*

It is difficult to teach kids the hard accent needed to play the swing style of jazz. They also have trouble noticing the differences among accents. I have showed my bands how to play the accent notated with a dot inside the "teepee," and they have given it a special name because of the way I once demonstrated it.

Once, after they had been struggling with this accent and I had been demonstrating with my instrument, I took a chair and I threw it. Obviously I looked first to make sure that no one was there and I threw the chair in a place where it did not hit anything. It made a sharp "bang" as it hit the floor. I said, "Now that's the accent I want; it is short and heavy."

Because of this, the students have named this accent the "chair accent." The effect is extremely graphic, especially for those kids who don't know me. I do not do it under the pretext of being angry; I do this to illustrate this particular accent. I say, "Now this is a different kind of accent. This is not just a short note or the basic accent from concert band. When you get into jazz ensemble styles, some accents are different from those in the concert band work and you just have to understand this." Then, I throw the chair! You'll probably never publish this idea or those people in the white coats will pick me up.

*(Howard A. Lehman)*

To play with appropriate note spacing, I have them compare the way they play to a string player using all downbows. I will have them play a scale. As they play, I will make believe I have a violin and I will use all downbows. I want them to see that the sound ceases to exist when I am raising the bow to start another downbow. After they get the idea, I will remind them, when they are not getting the note spacing needed, that we need to make believe that we are all playing violins and we are only using downbows, no upbows.

*(Ross A. Leeper)*

With contemporary pieces I ask the double bass player in my band to show the band different sounds with the bow. Because they can see the linear motion of the bow, they can apply this to wind playing.

*(Michael Haithcock)*

I use drawings for tongue location for legato style. I draw parallel lines to show when and how the tongue bumps the air stream. I show a notch in one line that stands for the tongue denting the air stream while playing each legato note.

*(Robert Grechesky)*

I draw shapes on the board to give them concrete ideas about the beginning, middle, and end of notes. I use egg-shapes to show the shape of staccato because I feel a staccato has a taper on both ends. This approach may counteract the heavier tonguing at the beginning of the sound. Some other drawings are: marcato as an open-ended bullet shaped note with the end more open: secco accents are shown by a hard square; legato as a long narrow railroad track, with notches to show how to tongue in legato style. The air only notches the air stream; it does not cut it.

*(Hal D. Cooper)*

## BREATHING

When discussing deep breathing in a full band rehearsal, I bring in a large clear glass and a pitcher of water. I then fill the glass in full view of the band so they can see the glass fill from the bottom up. This illustrates the lungs filling with air.

*(Theta Lee)*

With junior high students especially, I show them how to breathe low—from the bottom of their lungs—by drawing a picture of a water glass. I say, "When you fill the water glass, how do you fill it up?" Well, they finally figure out the glass must fill from the bottom. I say, "What if there were a force field right in the middle of that glass, would you be able to fill it all the way up to the top?" And, they say, "No." Then I draw a picture of a pair of lungs on the board. "When you breathe, you must breathe low, you have to make sure that you've filled the lungs from the bottom." I never tell the kids about the diaphragm, it just confuses the matter.

*(Howard A. Lehman)*

For breathing and air stream, I may draw a picture of a stream and the water. I try to connect the constant flow of water to the constant flow of air.

*(Dwayne P. Sagen)*

My kids get tired of hearing two words: "more air." Because I use the term so often, they had an electric neon sign made with these words shining brightly. I even turn it on to get their attention.

*(Stanley Cate)*

I have known some teachers who set pencils in front of students and asked them to blow and move the pencil with the air stream.

*(Richard K. Hansen)*

We talk about the release of air as if it were a slow leak from their bicycle tire. There is all that pressure there, and yet it doesn't come out unevenly because the opening is so small. We have practiced blowing into bread bags to discover how much air they take in when filling up—they can see this visually. I have told them too, that when they are exhaling the air, they should feel like they are a grandfather or grandmother and they need a lot of air to blow out sixty candles on their birthday cake. To blow out those candles, they need to sustain a steady air stream.

*(Nancy Plantinga)*

## TONE, BALANCE, DYNAMICS

I like to use a diagram and show them how dynamics work geometrically. There is a bit of difference between pianissimo and piano. There is more difference, though, from piano to mezzo piano, and mezzo piano to mezzo forte is even more different. When you look at forte to pianissimo, you are taking a difference from someone who is 6'4" and someone who is 4'2". If necessary, I will have those two kids stand up and demonstrate that. I'll say "Here is the mezzo forte and here is the mezzo piano."

*(Larry Rachleff)*

With beginners I teach dynamics using a ladder. We climb the ladder from the first rung to the last rung. I put a "pp" on the first rung, "p" on the second and "mp" on the third, etc. I draw a ladder and explain that every dynamic level is like climbing one step of the ladder. That kind of understanding does nothing as far as hearing it or producing it, but if they can visually see it, they have a frame of reference.

I always say to them, "Now when you get to the top rung of the ladder here, this is not a whole ladder." You know how young students often play, loud and bad! So I say, "We are only up to about six or seven steps and that ladder has more steps to go, but this the farthest that we're going to go." They understand, therefore, that double forte

is not the loudest, most terrible sound that you can make. This gives them a good frame of reference.

*(Janet Tweed)*

We tell kids on a dynamic change, "We want you to play the picture you're looking at." We gave up a long time ago saying this is a crescendo and this is a decrescendo sign—we call it a picture.

*(Bryce Taylor)*

Within five feet of the podium, I have switches for six sets of lights. Once in a while, I will say, "Look, it says mezzo forte at Letter B, it says mezzo piano at C, and here it says forte. You are not making enough difference in the dynamics." Then I put all the lights on and say, "This is a fortissimo." Then I shut off one row of lights and say, "That's a forte." I turn off another row and say, "That's a mezzo forte." etc. Then I shut off all of them in the band room (there is still light from the office and storage room) and I say "That's a piano." Then I shut off the one in the instrument storage room. That makes it nearly dark and I say, "That's a pianissimo." They easily see the comparison to the basic six levels of dynamics.

*(Howard A. Lehman)*

## COMBINING TWO OR MORE MUSICAL ISSUES

### *An airstream and volume change*
I draw crescendo and decrescendo to illustrate continuous and thinning air streams, or I blacken in rectangles to illustrate the amount of air in the tone.

*(Jack Brookshire)*

### *Articulation and phrasing*
I teach wind instrumentalists through string bowing techniques even if they have no orchestral background. I can make the invisible visible through visual means.

Here are some examples of what I teach them: the full bow for singing qualities; the up and down bows for phrasing emphasis for the direction of the line; the tip versus the frog to show the bouncing bow versus spiccato bow; the use of full hair versus partial hair; playing near the bridge versus playing near the finger board; and the resonance of vibrating strings and the sound of decaying sound on strings. High school and college wind and percussion players can imitate all these.

*(Butler R. Eitel)*

To teach articulation in rehearsals, I sing a lot and use string bowing. I have my (imaginary) bow on the string and I'm saying, "You know, I want detache or I want the middle of the bow here, come on clarinets just give me that sound."

*(Richard J. Suddendorf)*

### Combining drawings and images

I'll use an image for teaching crescendo and diminuendo. I might say, "Don't walk up the mountain and fall off a cliff, but walk up one side and walk down the other side of the mountain." I can show that easily in a drawing. I draw a line going upwards and gradually going downward, instead of a line that goes upwards and then drops straight down.

*(Michael Kaufman)*

## MISCELLANEOUS EXAMPLES OF VISUAL TEACHING TECHNIQUES

### Teaching students about half steps and enharmonic tones

When I am in a room with risers, such as found in a band room, I place a student on a middle riser and give him a note name such as A. Then I place one student on the riser above and one on the riser below the person named "A." I name the student on the riser above "A sharp," and the student on the riser below is named "A flat." We can move students up and down to explain the idea of going up or down a half step.

By designating each riser as a half step and placing students on the alternative steps (whole step intervals or locations), we can then have the student on the note B move down to the B flat step; we can have the student on the A move up to the A sharp step. The band members can easily see that the two students are on the same riser; they realize that, in fact, A sharp and B flat have the same pitch and, therefore, will have the same fingering or slide position.

*(Roman Palmer)*

### Illustrating instrument posture

I'm always grabbing my baton like it's a trumpet and pulling the front end of it up. One comment I make to groups is, "How can you expect the flutes to play with a characteristic tone holding them as they do?" I also might show the instrument position with the baton as a flute.

*(Michael Kaufman)*

### Using a piano keyboard

I always have a cardboard keyboard above the blackboard. With this, I can easily explain half steps, whole steps, enharmonic tones, etc. The students with no keyboard experiences especially need help understanding. Even senior high students will say, "Well, why is a B sharp the same as a C natural?" The visual keyboard is one way to answer this.

*(Richard Putzier and John Kinnison)*

### Visual reminders

When I ask them to breathe, I always relate it to going to the doctor, especially when I am doing high school or junior high clinics. I say, "What does the doctor say when he asks you to open your mouth and he wants to look in your throat? Does he ask you to say "e"? What does he say?" The students always say, "The doctor says ah."

When I talk about breathing, I will put up words "tu," "ta," and "ah" as reminders. I have them say "ah" and I will draw up on the board a picture of a closed throat and an open throat. I will write "aaah" on the board as opposed to "eee" or "aaa."

*(Dwayne P. Sagen)*

### The importance of accuracy

I fill a quart jar of water and I place a pile of dirt beside it. I say, "If I throw a little dirt in the water, we can still see through. If we put a lot of dirt in there, the water gets cloudy. That is what happens to the band sound and to your sound. Every little speck of dirt—a wrong note, a poor articulation, or out of tune—it all contributes to clear or dirty water." I use this once while I have the kids, at other times I just refer to it.

*(Ross A. Leeper)*

### Teaching how the reed vibrates

Some kids have a hard time understanding the proper placement of the reed over the lip and the vibration of the reed. I put a yardstick over the edge of the piano, hold one end down against the piano top. I snap the free end so they hear the vibration. Then, I make a cushion from my coat, to simulate the teeth and mouth. I show that I cannot make that yardstick vibrate as easily if the cushion is too soft and fluffy. I show there must be some reed extended over the lower lip and that the cushion must be a little firm, without too much of the lower lip over their lower teeth.

*(Gordon Nelson)*

### Conducting patterns, eye contact and gestures

I want students to know the different styles of conducting and what they mean. I want them to copy their visual meaning, not only the metronomic information. If we're going to play a series of marcato quarter notes I should show a large motion with a definite stop to the beat. If it's staccato, I should show a very small, light motion with a stop; or, if it's legato, I should show a more continuous motion to portray the style and sound.

There are other things that I do on the blackboard. I trace the pattern of conducting on the board and stand with my back to the students. They follow along and gesture as I trace the pattern up and down, whether it's a three-four or four-four. I show the line movement on the board with chalk. I trace through it several times and have them imitate my movements. Obviously, I also will make different patterns for different styles. I think it keeps you on your toes as a conductor. Sometimes, I will not conduct in a metronomic way—I will use only gesture and facial expressions for dynamics, tempo, or style.

*(Lance Schultz)*

The development of eye contact between the teacher and students can be done through the slow sustained works where they don't have to worry about technique or tone production. As a result, they have time to look at the note and then look up and feel the kind of feedback and suggestions they get from the conductor.

If eye contact is possible, the conductor also can be talking to the people while they are playing. If they will look at him, there will be both verbal communication and non-verbal communication. The ensemble members would get so much more feedback if they looked. The feedback comes from the eyes—feedback does not come through peripheral vision. It has to be direct, eye-to-eye contact. Some just sit there and say, "Well, I can see your beat." I say, "Maybe you can see my beat. However, that's really a minor part of conducting. The communication with the eyes is what is important." This communication is like dancing cheek-to-cheek.

*(Myron Welch)*

Straight from Elizabeth Green is a very helpful suggestion I've used for years. If a conductor lectures the kids about "watch me, watch me," there's a kind of instinctive, negative reaction from the kids that says, "no big deal, so what." You can eliminate that easily by saying, "Watch the stick," "Watch the gesture," or "Do this."

*(Donald Wilcox)*

### Using textures in material

I do a lot of visual connections with burlap, satin, blue jeans, and canvas.

*(Richard J. Suddendorf)*

# *Types of Teaching Techniques:*
# **Input Modes for Student Learning**

## *Part Three:*
## *Understanding Notation and Structure*

# CHAPTER FOURTEEN

# MUSIC READING

Music teachers have much value for the music literacy skills needed to read pitches and rhythms accurately. A higher level of literacy comes when the student is more advanced in his skills and when he has had more musical experiences. Then the student can also interpret what is on the page with appropriate phrasing and style as he reads the notation for the first or second time. This ability is similar to a reader of lines from a play or poetry; not only does the person read the words correctly, he also interprets and inflects those words so they have meaning.

Music teachers also have grown in their understanding of teaching the skills needed to read music. They commonly have taught students to analyze notation with the intent of improving their reading skills. This is valuable, but music teachers are beginning to realize they also need to build readiness prior to the analysis of music notation and note values. This readiness is built through experience singing and playing many tonal and rhythm patterns, and moving with a steady pulse in duple and triple meter.

Readiness can be a prerequisite for reading the notation and it improves the basis for teaching the student to be musically literate. When students see a signature for duple meter and they see symbols that stand for rhythm patterns in duple meter, they have already experienced the sounds if readiness has been built. Since the teacher has associated these experiences to notation after readiness has begun to be built, the student can recall which sounds and movements fit that notation. When they analyze notation and learn note values, they can understand, for example, the notation and sound of two eighth notes that fill the same duration as the sound of a quarter note because they can recall those sounds when they see the notations for either.

This is possible because the student has aural and kinesthetic experiences to recall and to which he can relate the symbols musicians use to notate sounds. The more students are given experience with the patterns prior to seeing the notation, and the more the notation they learn and analyze is in their aural and kinesthetic experiences, the more they have a basis to analyze and perform unfamiliar rhythm, tonal, melodic, and pitch patterns.

The sounds are a sonic and physical reality, but the notation is a symbol. The symbol will remain entirely abstract, unless there are concrete aural and kinesthetic experiences to which it refers.

## IDEAS ABOUT MUSIC READING

### The worth of sight reading
Sight reading is more than just a skill, it is the total of all fundamentals coming together at the same time. There is great value to sight reading: it seems to increase students' intelligence. It carries over in other subjects, possibly because their confidence has increased. With the skill of reading, they also can cover more literature. They have room to appreciate style, periods, etc., because reading unlocks what opportunity provides them the chance to benefit from.

*(Stanley Cate)*

### Rhythmic Reading
To effectively teach rhythmic reading skills in either lessons, sectionals, or full rehearsal, it is necessary to understand as much as we can about how we learn when we learn how to read rhythmic notation.

In reading a language (as a parallel to music reading) we learn to speak before we read. Generally, through rote speaking experiences, we acquire a significant vocabulary of works; through a developmental process, we form sentences and begin to draw meaning from our speaking.

In reading rhythmic notation the actual "speaking" of rhythmic patterns is a necessary prerequisite to reading rhythmic notation in the same way that the "speaking" of the language is to reading written language.

As a preparation for rhythmic reading skills, then, it is necessary to provide students with a rote vocabulary of rhythmic patterns in various meters including duple, triple, mixed, and unusual or asymmetrical meters.

An efficient approach to doing this is by developing a rote rhythm syllable vocabulary. I suggest, also, especially with younger musicians, that some physical response such as clapping or swaying be used simultaneously so that students develop an organized kinesthetic (eurythmic) reaction to the rote rhythmic patterns.

During the lessons, sectionals, or rehearsals such activities as rhythmic echoes, dialogues, and chants can be used in developing a rote/kinesthetic feeling for rhythm. Once students have developed this awareness they are ready to recognize these rote patterns in notational form.

Although students are generally taught rhythmic reading from a lesson book or in conjunction with repertoire being performed, try rote/kinesthetic experiences. Also, try having them write the notation for the rhythm patterns they are hearing. I suggest further, that a teacher be creative when teaching rhythm and rhythm reading.

*(Thomas L. Dvorak)*

### Understanding notation is not the starting point

It is crazy to have an intellectual understanding of note values, if one doesn't know the rhythm. There are just too many teachers who think students learn this way.

*(Steven Cooper)*

### Consider the nature of music learning and reading

The greatest idea we can contribute is that music is an aural phenomenon. The "games" and clever ways to teach, are often *left brain* intellectual ideas, rather than *right brain* experiences. Counting games, for example, fall into the left-brain area.

High level music learning and performance are a non-discursive non-cognitive experiences. It is all imagery, feelings, sounds, and emotions, which is the right brain. Wouldn't it be a great idea to make music a true alternative to academic subjects. We could do this if we did not make music mathematics—if we did not make it intellectual, in the usual way intellectual is understood.

*(James Froseth)*

### Thinking about music reading

Asking students to read a piece of music that they cannot do, is somewhat like asking them to look at an unfamiliar word and be told to "figure it out." If they still cannot read the music and the teacher asks them to spell it, they will still be unsuccessful. The teacher could go further and say, "it is a noun" or "it is an adjective." The student still cannot figure out how to read that passage. In the end, they still will want the teacher to tell them what the notation says.

Upon reflection, if students cannot read the passage, we might conclude that it is because the sounds are not in their musical dictionary. The description in the previous paragraph shows, in effect, what we do in music education. We give them a theoretical description as a substitute for musical experience. Verbal descriptions are okay, but only if we already have had experience with what is being described.

*(James Froseth)*

### Reading more than the notes

Most students, and some adult musicians, are not attentive, do not take notice or respond to the notation other than the notes themselves. With any students I also circle, mark, or otherwise highlight the non-note notational things.

*(Steven Cooper)*

### Eye tracking and music reading

I believe that many mistakes in music reading relate to eye-tracking problems. Simply put, their eyes do not normally find and follow the notation on the page of music. They will read it correctly only if they have focused their eyes in the proper place.

This is harder to do in groups, but I do this with private students. To get them to sight read, which I think is partly dependent upon eye-tracking skill, we play measures, phrases, and lines backwards. First, I have them read backwards by measures, both tonally and rhythmically. This is a challenge, and the kids with the good ears must read it instead of play by anticipating what they think it will sound like! Another way, playing every other measure, throws them off tonally and, thus, they are required to read very alertly.

The last way is to read diagonally down the page, (if the piece is lined up to do this) reading the first measure on the first line, the second measure on the second line, etc. I do this in rhythm, a bit slowly, to get their eyes to move ahead of their fingers.

*(Pamela Gearhart)*

### Music reading

I believe there are no tricks or short cuts when learning to be musically literate. To show or say that third space is C is all there is to it, "learn it!"

*(Donald S. George)*

### Students' interest in reading reflects that of the teacher

I try to go upper left to lower right. Reading does not include a lot of stopping, and crashing and burning. Therefore, I try to lay a lot of ground work so they will be successful. We do a lot to develop understanding of the basic thrust of the piece before we begin. I have developed, myself, an infatuation with reading. Playing new music is what is fun, not playing at the concert.

My kids come in with less interest in sight reading, but develop an interest more like mine as time goes on. One way to develop skill and to get students to like it, is to do a large amount of sight reading. Many teachers are afraid of it and convey their apprehension to their students. I am a proponent of taking sight reading out of the closet and putting it on the stage with an audience. A first-division rating in sight reading should mean the reading was "performance suitable."

*(Donald Gee)*

### Beyond remedial music reading

I try not to reduce myself to being a remedial reading teacher. I joke with them saying, "If you people read highway signs like you read music, there would be a lot of wrecks!" This means that just as you must be responsible when you are behind the wheel of a car, you must be as responsible when you are behind the instrument.

My job is to get them to go beyond what is on the page as an individual and as a group. They also must understand what is on everyone else's page so they have a more complete understanding of the piece. My job is not to teach them to read music remedially, by "hand checking" them at every point. My job is to go beyond this.

*(Michael Haithcock)*

A very poor college band played a concert. I overheard one person say, "That isn't like so and so's band; they can sight read at a performance level." The other person said, "This band can't perform at a sight-reading level!"

*(anonymous)*

### There is a need for clearer notation

It's amazing how many person's notation of music is not clear. They should notate it as clearly as possible, so the performers can read what is on the page. Sometimes the composer or arranger gets into the theoretical side of what they're writing. If it makes it easier to understand the tune, I can accept that. I think, though, clarity should be the primary goal.

It bothers me if notation is not grouped in pulses. Often, when they do not do that, it just throws everything out the window. Then, you have to take a microscope in order to decipher everything.

*(Gregory Bimm)*

### Music reading, a lost art

Many students have no idea what reading is. They have their orchestral excerpt books, they have their literature they are working on; but, reading is a real lost art, a real lost skill.

They play fine, but when we read the rehearsal after a concert, we all hate it because we know we don't do it very well. One learns to read by reading, therefore we do a lot of it, and I hope we're going to send players away from here that have more skill.

*(Eugene Corporon)*

### Building sight reading skill

I taught sight reading by making an issue, a federal case out of doing it. We prepared them for sight reading contests. We sight read a new piece each week, using the full concert, sight-reading contest routine. They would come in the room and their parts would be backward on the stand. They would have five minutes to look at the part and I would have a couple minutes to look at the score. I would

also sight read the score like one does at contests. We went through a complete contest replica once a week for three years. Those kids really did it!

When we did that we always recorded it. Sometimes on the same day, we would work on the tune and to see if or how much better it was than our first reading. We did this even it if we weren't going to perform it. Then we would listen to the sight reading version and see where we screwed up and where we didn't.

This routine took the length of the tune plus five minutes and plus five more minutes if we listened to the tape. Sometimes we would listen to it again with discussion and sometimes we didn't. This depended upon how interesting the tune was and how much trouble we had with it. We would read at least thirty tunes a year in this way.

*(Donald Wilcox)*

### Having students read the full score

When students are playing from full scores, this helps them improve their reading and introduces them to reading from a full score. In addition, this can encourage an interest in orchestration or arranging. For percussion, especially with contemporary pieces, they can keep their places more easily by reading the full score.

*(Donald Wilcox)*

## TEACHING MUSIC READING

### Developing rhythm vocabulary and rhythm reading

To develop rhythm and rhythm reading I use listening in small-group classes in band rehearsal. These are the steps I often use:

1. I play a simple rhythm pattern, such as two quarter notes followed by four eighth notes, on each note of a scale or part of a scale. After the students hear the pattern, they play what they just heard me perform.
2. After they have played the pattern, I ask the students to describe verbally the rhythm pattern they heard and played.
3. I write that specific rhythm pattern on the board.
4. I ask students to write the pattern on the board, so they learn the correct way to notate music. As they are writing, they continue to concentrate on the symbol for the rhythm pattern.
5. I will play another rhythm pattern and we repeat steps 1 through 4.
6. I ask each of the students to prepare a rhythmic pattern for our next class.
7. At the next class, I ask volunteers to perform their rhythm patterns and then we repeat steps 1 through 4.
8. After the students can identify the rhythm they are hearing by playing and writing that rhythm,

I then write another rhythmic pattern on the board and ask them to play it.

9. As students' understanding and skill develop, I open the rhythmic patterns to eighth notes, sixteenth notes, triplets, dotted notes, and various time signatures as they progress. Students also can select any tempi they please.

These exercises occur with very little talking, because it usually is not needed. I may reinforce their experience with the rhythms they have written by using them in warm-up exercises.

*(Roman Palmer)*

We begin in fifth grade with simple tunes like "Mary Had a Little Lamb." I point to the notes to show up and down, and explain how far. We learn to sing thirds, for example, when we have a little terminology. I use the numbers one through eight, not solfege syllables so I can say this is five, three, or step one of a scale. I sing it for them and I play it on the piano. They sing it back.

*(Jack Brookshire)*

### Learning rhythms with scales

If students have trouble with a rhythm pattern, we select a variety of rhythms to play and compare them to one another. If students have trouble with a certain one, we go back to the Fussell book, Section 8, and play the rhythms on scales. If a particular rhythm is not in the book, I supplement the material by notating the rhythm on the blackboard. This also teaches them to sight sing, sight read, and use their ear.

*(Jack Brookshire)*

### Sight reading

This can be learned by doing it. I used to make every effort to read music every rehearsal and lesson. It will pay off especially after years of this approach.

*(John Kinnison)*

### Preparing them to sight read

When we approach a piece, we talk first about the style of the piece. We decide if it is a form such as an overture, if the repeat shows a recapitulation, or point out familiar features or features related to familiar things. This should stimulate their thinking and imagery. Second, we look at signatures, musical terms, repeats, and other mechanical things.

*(Stanley Cate)*

After they would have a minute or two to look at their parts, I would have a couple of minutes to talk to them about it. We went through the regular format that pointed out things, such as: "Letter C there's a tough key change, be sure you are ready for that spot." "There's a meter change to twelve-eight at letter D." "You remember twelve-eight, that's like two bars of six-eight without the

bar line in the middle." I gave them clues and reminders of things they knew so they could get through the piece successfully.

*(Donald Wilcox)*

Look at the whole piece for features such as meter, tempo, key, ritards, style, tempo, and key changes. I accompany the verbal explanation with conducting, singing and chanting, and humming the character of the music and its style. If there is time, the students can imitate the singing or the gestures to help them internalize the style. Have them play several measures of each problem or typical section to set the character of style, tempo, and dynamics. Then read the piece without stop, if possible.

*(Joseph Casey)*

Part of my approach is to define dynamic outlines up front, work out difficult rhythms before they meet the piece itself.

*(Richard Fischer)*

Typically, we might use singing for melodic content, for rhythmic accompaniment or background parts, and for complicated passages—either rhythmic or melodic. I might do the difficult spots and "traps" first. The first would be the potential problems—like I do in a contest situation. The singing may be approximate. If not correct, a major seventh interval should be sung as larger than a third or fifth. The kids really love to listen to the sight-reading tapes!

Then we would go back through and highlight spots by singing. We identify the melodic parts and have them sing those. Then, if a rhythmic background warrants attention, we would sing that. If there is a moving harmonic background in a lyrical section, or contrapuntal passages, we would do those subordinate melodies.

Before time elapses, we get in one performance of the whole, still leaving time for the final version. If there is time, we also highlight transitional areas. Usually we don't have time to ask and answer questions. I don't do this routine every time we read, sometimes we read pieces without preparation. Usually we read sixty or seventy pieces a year.

*(Donald Gee)*

### Analyzing the notation of rhythms

If the students do not read a rhythm accurately at the outset, I try to give them time to figure it out. If they can't, they write the counting under a measure or two, since counting is so much a part of our teaching approach at all levels. They may count it, imitating the rhythm and my counting. Simultaneously, they look at the notation on the board and I expect them to keep the pulse through foot-tapping. Sometimes I have them clap the rhythm or say the rhythm on neutral syllables.

*(Stanley Cate)*

## Reading unfamiliar music

Some directors read all the way the first time, even if the group crashes and burns. That way they can grasp the whole piece. If my band cannot do the whole piece well, I select a section of the piece that they have a chance to play well. They can sense the worth of the piece quickly and form an accurate impression of the piece and grasp what is interesting about it. After that, we work out the difficult sections.

*(Richard Fischer)*

## Detecting errors in music reading

To help them learn to hear errors in their own playing, I will play for them, making different errors that they must notice. They suggest either the correction or comment where I made the error.

I also use a computer program for this, the *Richmond Music Series,* from the Akron Series. It is an ear-training approach to error detection. They listen to a short passage and identify the errors, such as missed notes.

*(R. G. Conlee)*

## Reading the entire phrase

Notate and play one measure. Then add one more measure; notate and play both measures. Notate a third and play all three measures. Add the fourth measure similarly.

*(Pamela Gearhart)*

## Developing memory while drilling notation

I notate four measures and have them play the measures. Then, I erase one measure and have them play all four measures again, including the one I erased. Then, I erase another measure and have them play all four including the two I erased. Then, I erase the third and they play all the measures. Last, I erase the remaining measure and they play all four from memory.

*(Christine Dworak)*

## Reading in clefs

To learn clefs, I have them play in different clefs—even if they, as a clarinetist for example, do not play in them customarily. They learn them better, if they play in them.

*(Donald S. George)*

## Using singing to build reading

Ninety percent of our sight reading procedure is singing. For example, our state sight reading contest is to have eight minutes to deal with a tune. During that eight minutes we can do anything we want with this tune except play the instrument. Our voices, then, become the instrument. With chorales, for example, I ask them to sing as accurately as possible. With other pieces, they may only accomplish an approximation of pitch changes.

As they sing, I encourage them to do the best they can with the intervals. They try to nail all the rhythms, effects, dynamics, and style as they move their fingers on the instruments. We do this approach every time we read, and we read a lot. Sometimes we read only the dynamics, or the articulations.

*(Donald Gee)*

## Analyzing subdivisions, the key to mixed meter

With mixed meters, I go to the lowest common dominator. If there is a three-eight or five-eight bar, I use the lower common dominator. I begin explaining with a four-four measure as eight-eight. I teach that eighth notes, whether there are two or three per beat, move on steadily—they don't change.

*(Terry A. Oxley)*

## Drilling with a rhythm slide program

I use Ralph Hale's slides for teaching sight singing. I use the metronome, I tape recorded the metronome and I put all the slides together. I would start taking the slide away on beat four every time so they do not become accustomed to looking at the measure they're playing. Pretty soon I would be taking the slide away on beat three, pretty soon I removed it by beat two. I mixed them up so they wouldn't memorize the rhythms. You could give it to them for one beat, turn it off on two. While they are playing this measure, they are learning the next measure. This really helps and is a good idea. I felt that the jazz ones did not work as well, maybe because the rhythms deal with articulation so much. They struggled with them more.

*(Terry A. Oxley)*

## Reading beyond the notes

When students go beyond the notes themselves, this leads them to music expression. This is one of the goals we neglect. I try to talk a lot about melodic direction, toward tension or away from tension. We explore the different ways we can do a phrase. We can use tenuto, articulations, syncopations, or tempo changes such as accelerando, ritardando, rubato. We also can use agogic accents, different articulations, and obviously we can use dynamics.

Notation and music making are curious. Because of this, I try to teach that most of those important clues to making music are not written on the page. If it were in the music, you couldn't decipher it all. Many things that we use and do to express the music simply aren't on the page.

*(Craig Kirchhoff)*

## Reading pieces in cut-time

Anything in cut time, I sight read in four-four. If the half note is 120, I read it as a quarter note equaling 120. The tempo, therefore, is correct but everything is at half speed.

*(John W. LaCava)*

## Sight reading

We read at least once every other rehearsal. We sight read all the time. I like it and they obviously get better at it. In a typical NAJE jazz band sight reading, they give us two or three minutes to look at it and then one minute before we play. Sometimes I'll practice that with them.

*(Howard A. Lehman)*

### Use what kids learn in general music

I see over and over again that the band people don't realize what the elementary kids learned before they get to band class. In our county they all know Kodaly-Curwen syllables (for example, tah tah ti-ti tah). So I suggest them when I observe student teachers.

When I see a student teacher work with a rhythm students can't do, I have them do that rhythm with Kodaly-Curwen syllables and they can do it perfectly. The student teachers often say, "Oh my God, I had no idea." Too often, they complain about what everybody else didn't do. They don't realize, if they only knew what other teachers had done and students already knew, they could connect with that and succeed.

*(James Stivers)*

### Increasing music reading skills

I'll clap or I'll model in some way a rhythm. Then, I'll say, "How would that be written?" It impresses me how kids can envision a rhythm once they start to think about it in that way.

We have first-year students with whom we are using the *150 Original Exercises*. This book starts with whole-note exercises and unison-octave exercises. I use that for the first quarter of the first-year students' year because I have to do a lot of remedial teaching. I need to develop some common basis for reading rhythm.

We'll be playing an exercise that might have several quarter-eighth, eighth-quarter and quarter-quarter patterns. I'll say, "How would you write this?" They won't be able immediately to imagine how that would look. It has never occurred to them to relate something that's happening sonically to something that is in written form.

*(John A. Thompson)*

### Teaching a new rhythm in steps

With a new or difficult rhythm, I will first recite the rhythm to them. Second, they play it on the scale as part of the warm up and third, I ask them to tell me what the rhythm would look like.

*(Mallory B. Thompson)*

### Knowledge of musical terms

I found that students do not know musical terms, period! We need to question them from the podium saying, "What does that say? What does that mean? Does that mean to play it standing on your head?" They must know how terms suggest they should play a passage or piece.

There are several different ways we can teach them. Start first with a list of words that appear in the music they are playing. They don't have to know every term in the books, but they need to know the ones that they see in that piece of music.

There are many stylistic concerns we need to teach. We can simply stop and teach them the meaning of terms and ideas. Cognitive information along with conducting messages is not only okay, it is necessary. When people teach only the cognitive, the affective, or the visual, there's a void in their students' development. These teachers don't realize learning takes place in a variety of ways. There is a rigidity in their teaching approach that simply does not work.

*(Myron Welch)*

I also used the vocabulary of music—use "fermata" and "anacrusis"; I don't say "bird's eye," "pig's eyes," "holds," and "pickups." This is important because we should teach them the language of music, not slang. A student in chemistry course speaks correctly, why not in music?

*(Frank Battisti)*

I asked students to read around the notes—meaning that the notes themselves are not the only important parts of the music. Sometimes students look at the rest of the notation as though it were funny hieroglyphics. I used regular terminology—I did not call a fermata a "bird's eye." The D. S. does not mean go back to the "dumb sign." I did not talk down to students; they can learn the correct terminology.

*(John Kinnison)*

### Reading rhythm patterns and using conducting

We worked a lot on reading rhythm patterns. We read more than one note at a time and read rhythm groupings. To help reading we worked a lot on conducting communication so they knew there was one downbeat in each measure. If they got lost within a measure, we said, "Don't fix it or go back for it. Look up, catch the next downbeat, and start again on the next bar. Thus, if there's one downbeat in each measure, you have many opportunities to get back on track and start over."

*(Donald Wilcox)*

### Using reading errors as a basis for instruction

If someone plays a rhythm pattern incorrectly, the teacher has several alternatives at that point. (1) One can, of course, point out the error by saying, "The second note is a quarter, not a half note." This requires the students to have some theoretical understanding to correct the rhythm error. If that is the case, the problem is more a lack of attention than reading skill. (2) The teacher also could say to the group, "Let's count, or clap, the rhythm aloud." This may help students correct an error because it asks them to analyze the notation on their own. (3) The teacher could ask, "Who can play this correctly?" If someone can, the group can hear the rhythm and the teacher can associate the sound to the notation for them. (4) If a student performs the notated rhythm incorrectly, we know the rhythm is not in their vocabulary. That gives the teacher the opportunity to say, "What you played was this (the teacher sings and notates the rhythm the student played)." Have everyone play this rhythm, even if it is different from the one in the music. Since the rhythm was different from the incorrect one, the group can associate the new rhythm to its correct notation and add this to their vocabulary. (5) If the group or someone knows the rhythm, ask them to sing the notated rhythm. Some will do this correctly. Those who do not, will hear the correct version, and the teacher and students can associate the correct sound to the notation. (6) Show the student the different sounds and notations for the two rhythms. One is the rhythm as notated. The other is the notation for the incorrect rhythm the student played. (7) Have the group play the original notation and the notation of the student's incorrect rhythm. The teacher could provide the notation for the incorrect rhythm. The students could provide it if you ask, "What is the notation for what he played?" Put the notation on the board and have them see the notation of the correct and incorrect rhythm. Then, play both so they now are learning two rhythms instead of learning only the one that the students first did incorrectly.

*(Joseph Casey)*

## READING MUSIC, LITERATURE, AND THE MUSIC CURRICULUM

### Generalizing as one reads new music

Sight reading success is enhanced by using unfamiliar songs that contain many familiar tonal and rhythmic patterns.

*(Stanley L. Schleuter)*

To enrich the experiences for each instrument, we had a large file of music books. We asked students to sign these out and practice reading one and one-half hours a week. These books were arranged in a progressive order.

*(Frank Battisti)*

### Ear training as the basis for music reading

I base both ear training and sight reading upon scale work . For example, brass players can anticipate (audiate) the sound of a certain interval, because they probably have played that interval in the drills.

*(Patricia Brumbaugh)*

### Sight reading and concert literature

After marching band season, I take much of September and October and have the two top bands read a great deal. After the spring concert, we do totally different literature for graduation and spring festivals. We also try to go past just reading, to reading with a good sound.

*(Carl A. Bly)*

### Sight reading

We read many pieces of music literature. We do three concerts a year and do a lot of the reading in between.

*(Stanley Cate)*

### At first reading

I am likely to play a piece the first time through, very close to tempo. They need to understand where we are going. Later, I might slow the tempo down, isolate passages, use the metronome, etc.

*(Richard Floyd)*

When I am reading a piece, I like to give them some idea what the whole is like; therefore, I let a lot of things go at first.

*(Terry A. Oxley)*

### Choosing and enriching sight reading literature

For each fifty-five minute rehearsal, I would take the first ten minutes and sight-read. First, we would sing the piece. I select the music we read in chronological order, beginning with Gregorian Chant scored in unison.

Each week I passed out a sheet telling about music and a little about the Art of this time. I would also put out prints of Art that matched the period we were playing. I still get post cards, saying, "I remember what I saw in the room." Much of the literature was transcriptions.

*(Frank Battisti)*

### Increasing reading skill through playing from the score

Instrumental students lack a sense of rhythm and reading skill, especially string players. Though they play well, the reading skill in both notes and rhythms in the Youth Orchestra is dismal, though they can do a lot by ear!

To attack this problem of poor rhythm and music reading in string players, I took the plunge. I got everyone a score for the *Art of The Fugue*, arranged for strings by Roy Harris. With everyone playing from score, I had all students play the same part on one contrapunctus. The theme is short and lies within the interval of a minor sixth, so there is no range problem. The students went through to locate all the occurrences of the subject, whatever the clef. After a couple of weeks, they could find their way around the clefs, by interval.

The next step, after they could identify the subjects all the way through, was to find the eighth-note figure. This is clear visually in the score and can be followed. We played it whenever it occurred in the score. We spent a limited amount of time on this, but we did this every week for about two months. I was startled with what it did for their reading. It was a very effective "eye" exercise. By the time they finished that, they could play through the piece from their own parts and we could play through the entire fugue without getting lost.

*(Pamela Gearhart)*

### Thinking and reading in rhythmic units

I notice that ensembles have great difficulty with anticipating rhythmic units. I focus on whatever the rhythmic unit is. It might be that we are playing a cadence in a phrase as we are approaching a bar line, or maybe after the bar line there is a two-beat rest. To make the moving rhythmic units more active, we would make up an exercise. We would practice counting, speaking the rhythmic unit aloud, creating the sense of the anticipation so they were thinking and anticipating the rhythmic unit in tempo.

For example, if we will be reading a triplet off the main pulse, we begin thinking in advance of the triplet and just what its sound will be. In my way of thinking, an easy way in common time to read correctly an eighth-note triplet is to remember the eighth notes from six-eight. Then, borrow the sound and feeling for the triplet figure in common time. Then, we practice saying the rhythm pattern in advance of playing the pattern. We might make up an exercise for a sixteenth note or a group of five that are a quintuplet—whatever the rhythmical unit might be.

If the pattern is an eighth note and two sixteenths, or two sixteenths and an eighth, we can be anticipating the actual teaching of the rhythmic unit. If the rhythms are more active and busy technical rhythmic units, most likely we are going to rush them and play too fast. We can be accurate much more often, if we are anticipating those units. If it's a group of five sixteenths grouped together over a quarter note, we can be anticipating this rhythm during rests or rhythms that precede this passage. We can be thinking "ONE, two, three, four, five-TWO, two, three, four, five." Do this on the previous pulses and then play one, two, three, four, five on the correct pulse when it appears in the music.

We can use that as an exercise. We can make up other rhythms and can play them on a constant pitch, or we can verbalize them in some way. I don't think we do this nearly enough, so there is a tremendous amount of guess work taking place.

*(Robert Levy)*

### A plan for sight reading

We sight read frequently each week. If the band is at a level four, usually we'll be doing sight reading in level two and three. The level five groups usually do level three sight reading and sometimes level four.

We have a new piece of music on the music stand and we do it the way you might at the state contest. The teacher talks through the piece first, highlighting transitions, key changes, tempo changes, etc. I also have used questioning. For example, I'll say, "What's the highest note? What's the lowest note? What is the loudest note? What is the softest note?"

This makes them look at their part in as many different ways as possible. Then we'll say, "Find the rhythm that you think you might have the most trouble playing." We'll have an exchange about that. We would look at a rhythm and I'll say, "How does that sound?" I ask somebody to play it as everyone is looking at it. We do enough to get everybody thinking and looking forward to the challenges in the music. Then, we'll play through the piece.

I think it's important to sight read. Our groups usually sight read well simply because it's part of their learning process. Sometimes a teacher must turn their ears off a little bit and be tolerant. Let them struggle, so they can learn.

With my first-year students, I start with music that really is very, very easy; it is almost insultingly easy. They know we will not be preparing this music for concert. In fact, we call it sight reading music. They know the difference is not quality as much as difficulty.

The first time through a piece, the goal is to read at a performance level. We want the sight reading to be as much like a performance as we can. We say that is so they're not just pushing buttons. We find that our freshmen think sight reading means only to push the right buttons and do the right rhythms. We say, "Okay, now wait a minute. We are looking for nuance, we are looking for levels of dynamics and we are looking for all sorts of stylistic issues."

They get really angry when I say, "Now, don't look at the music so much." They say, "But we're sight reading!" I say, "Look, the music exists on the page in ink, that's a blueprint. We must make that blueprint sound right sonically." I have used that word for years and it means there's a difference between the way music looks on a page and the way we hear what is there. Sonic, then, is just a catch word, but they know what it means and it works.

*(John A. Thompson)*

### What should we read

I think people need to do more sight reading. I think there is an awful lot of excellent, but older, material that groups need to play. People don't need to look for the new literature all the time. One of my composer friends said people ask him, "What have you got new for me to play" and he says, "What have you played of mine that's old?" So much good literature exists that has gone by the wayside.

*(Myron Welch)*

CHAPTER FIFTEEN

# ANALYSIS OF MUSIC AND MUSIC FUNDAMENTALS

Instrumental teachers sometimes use analysis in exactly the same ways it was used in their college classes in music. They teach their students about the structure and the style of the musical score. They tell students about the form, how the chords progress in a transition passage, or how the motives or the themes change and develop during their appearances throughout the piece.

Teachers may use analysis more in high school and college instrumental groups than in elementary or junior high school groups and music classes. Even in higher education, however, the use of analysis does not appear to be widespread in ensemble rehearsals or class lessons. This is unfortunate, since it could increase the musical understanding and interest of all students.

Though we commonly think of analysis as a way to teach about the *structure* of music, we can also analyze basic parts of music other than the formal structure. Among these parts of music are those often referred to as *music fundamentals*. Teachers may begin their analytical instruction with an interval, a duration, a scale, or a musical term, not only the texture or the form. They can continue with rhythmic patterns, chord construction, instrumentation, and comparisons or contrasts of features from one piece to another. Most teachers also teach music reading through the analysis of the musical notation. Some teachers encourage students to read from the full score or listen to particular recordings. This helps students to learn which parts of the piece the other sections of the ensemble are playing. All of these objectives and teaching techniques include some analysis of music or music fundamentals.

When a teacher uses analysis, students understand the music and may perform better or find music more interesting. More important for students, is that analysis expands their view toward hearing the whole piece, not just their part. The results can increase the students' aural skills and they become more literate. These skills become a solid base for achievement, advanced study, or theoretical understanding. Beginning analysis with young students sets a solid basis for the future study of anything musical, especially when they encounter the new and unfamiliar.

## SCALES

### Teaching minor scales

The easiest way to teach minor scales takes two steps. The first is to have students play a major scale, such as B-flat major, up and down from B flat to B flat. Second, go two notes lower down to G, which is the tonic of the relative minor. Play that scale up and down from G to G. After they do this, I tell them, "Do the G-minor scale again remembering to use the same key signature as you do with the B-flat major scale." This approach teaches students how to find the tonic of the relative natural minor scale from their familiarity with the B-flat major scale, teaches the key signature of the G minor scale, and results in the natural minor scale. I try to set the natural minor scale so every student thoroughly understands it before I introduce the harmonic and the melodic minor.

In teaching the harmonic and melodic scales, I teach harmonic first. I tell them, "We are going to raise the seventh degree by one-half step." Using the solfege syllables, I sing the relationships with proper syllables, fa-sol-la for natural minor, then fa-si-la for the harmonic minor. I show this to them first on a piano, then through singing or through another instrument. They recognize the distinctive seventh degree instantly. Therefore, I have introduced the F sharp as an alteration of the G natural minor scale, which results in the harmonic minor scale.

After this has become clear, I introduce the melodic minor in the same way. I first play and sing the important pitch patterns with proper syllables. I sing mi-fa-sol-la (E-F-G-A) for natural minor. Then, I remind them of harmonic minor with mi-fa-si-la (E-F-G sharp-A) followed by the melodic minor's pattern of mi-fi-si-la (E-F sharp-G sharp-A). I have, therefore, introduced G sharp as an alteration of the natural minor scale and F sharp as the alteration of the harmonic minor. These two alterations result in the melodic minor scale. Ascending, they play the melodic minor scale as mi-fi-si-la (or E, F sharp, G sharp, and A). Descending, they revert to the natural minor scale and use la-sol-fa-mi (or A-G-F-E). To descend, I remind them that they are dropping the two alterations they made to raise the sixth and seventh degrees one-half step while ascending.

I have developed this approach because of experience seeing blank faces! Even with three or four blank faces, I become concerned. I want them to understand the relationship and sound between major and minor scales, and the interval structure of these scales. After each step in this process, they can recognize the form of the new scale and, when they complete all the steps they can recognize, hear, and play major, minor natural, minor harmonic, and minor melodic scales.

*(Patricia Brumbaugh)*

# RHYTHMS

## *Literature for rhythm and reading development*

We use Ed Ayola's book, *Winning Rhythms* (Kjos) and *Rhythm Etudes* (Schmidt, Hall, and McCreary). We do these with no melody, having the students tap and subdivide every rhythm. At the high school level we do not use it as much, since many have already used this book. We also use the Rothman book and make up our own rhythm sheets. We have one rhythm sheet for six-eight, one for cut-time, one for four-four. The students write or analyze the counting first, and then tap it, clap it and play it.

*(Ross Kellan)*

## *A beat counting system*

I use a counting system where students count four sixteenth notes on a single beat as 1 2 3 4. Some teachers call this beat-counting. Students count two sixteens and an eighth as 1 2 3 - . An eighth note and two sixteenths as 1 - 3 4. Dotted eighth and sixteenth is 1 - - 4. Quarter note is 1 - - - and two eighths are 1 - 3 - . I show the rhythms on the board, one under the other, so they see how the system works and rhythms compare. That covers the basic duple rhythms.

I have not applied this to six-eight or other triple meter rhythms. In six-eight their experience counting the eighth notes in four-four seems to do the job, because they have experienced subdividing.

This approach quickly clarifies a problem students have, since they can understand and speak the counting for each rhythm. We often verbalize our way through a passage, chanting and counting the rhythm with the numbers as described above. I find that by doing it numerically they can visualize how things fit.

*(Judith A. Niles)*

## *Analyzing rhythms*

As they read, I have them tapping and verbally counting the pulse and rhythm simultaneously.

*(Richard Putzier)*

Students must comprehend where rhythmic subdivisions fall, which they learn through counting rhythms.

Telling someone that they are early or late has little to do with comprehension.

*(Larry Rachleff)*

I have students count aloud and clap rhythms in the percussion class. When students learn to count and clap, they can speak and read the rhythms. Then, what is on the page is automatic. I do this to build a complete and thorough rhythmic vocabulary.

*(Carl A. Bly)*

A basic skill we develop is counting rhythms. We do this through using analysis and some verbal counting. In a rehearsal, if there is a problem with a certain rhythm, I go to the board and write the rhythm. Then the whole band analyzes and counts that rhythm.

*(Stanley Cate)*

# CHORDS

## *Singing and hearing chords to help intonation*

I have students sing, that is, "spell-out" easy and complex chords by singing each of the chord tones. They sing their notes, listen in context, and come to understand the composite sound. They come to perceive their sound in relationship to the other pitches. This can be done with simple and difficult chords by section or with the entire band. This gives them a more "personal" concept of their part as it functions within a chord. It's also a wonderful aid for improving intonation.

*(James Arrowood)*

# FORM IN MUSIC

## *Talking about form and texture*

I use correct musical terms. If it is recapitulation, we use the correct term. We use terms such as exposition and development also. For a fugue, we use subject or counter subject.

I get students to think about how many parts something has, or how dense it is. I may ask, "How many things are happening at once?" For example, if they hear only melodies it's probably fugal, or at the least it is contrapuntal. If they hear a harmonic skeleton with one melody, then it is likely a homophonic texture. We discuss the texture or form of many pieces. For example, a march very often has a rhythmic/harmonic skeleton with a melody and a countermelody.

*(John A. Thompson)*

Especially with the college group, I'll talk about form. If we're doing a binary or three-part movement, instead of using rehearsal letters I say, "We'll start at the B section." I also will have them look at the cadences and the key structure of a piece. Now with the high school groups I work with, I do less of this.

I've planned the classes of theory so I have most of the wind ensemble people in my section. For analysis, one project we did was the Mendelssohn *Trauer March*. We did a complete formal Schenkerian harmonic analysis. When we did this piece in performance, they knew this piece as well as I did. Their understanding of the piece made a tremendous difference in their interpretation of the work. It also helps them listen.

*(Francis Marciniak)*

A group will play an individual section well, but the transition sections may be weaker. I'll ask, "What's going on here? What is the composer doing at this point?" It could be that they're changing keys or there is a change of tempo, going slower or going faster. Then I'll ask, "Well, if he's changing keys, *why* is he changing keys?" Since I was involved in the application of comprehensive music (CMP) to rehearsals for many years, I do this often.

There can be a problem finding the right balance between playing and talking. I find that occasionally, if you get them to think about what's going on in these transitions, they'll see the musical sense. Sometimes there will be only a repeated sequential pattern a step higher each time to build intensity. If they don't know how the composer's building the transitions from one section to another, they tend not to play it very well.

*(Francis Marciniak)*

I teach music theory in both band rehearsal and music history, because I think it is very important.

*(Michael Kaufman)*

### Singing to find motives and patterns

We do considerable singing. For instance, we sing band parts sometimes not caring if the pitches are right. If that is the case we say, "We're going to make sure everyone, at least, has the rhythms correct to see how it fits together."

We also might use singing to focus upon the dynamics or the pitches, or upon a melodic or motivic pattern that appears in different places. I might say, "At number one the saxes have it; at number two the trombones have it; and at number three the flutes and clarinets have the pattern. Who cares what the pitches are; let us save time and all play the same motive together, even if it is from different parts of the piece and with different pitches than in your part."

Since they may not be in unison, it's going to sound "unusual." Often, that doesn't make any difference. It's fun. When they are playing the figures, it brings out a different sound. You can still say, "Well, that is the important pattern and you all have it somewhere." Even if it does sound unusual, they all learn from it.

*(Frank Schulz)*

### Selecting chords from compositions

The chords we pick for warm up attention are often chords right from the music we will be working on next.

*(Richard K. Hansen)*

### Aids for memorization

To help them memorize, I explain musical forms, the lines, and the sequencing. These are helpful memory aids. Some will never understand what I am saying; they will learn by rote. Others understand and find this helpful.

*(Judith A. Niles)*

## MUSIC AND SCORE READING

### The four T's

The four T's are Time, Tempo, Title, and Tune. Time is for meter signature. Tempo is for metronome markings and Italian terms such as allegro. Title is the title and composer of the piece, and tune is for the key signature. Therefore, if you ask a student "What are the four T's?" the question gives them a structure for an answer. They must have looked at their part to learn the answers.

*(Walter Rodby)*

### Looking at the score

I encourage students to buy scores and I will sit with them. I find that I learn about the score from other people's observations even when they are not conductors. Last night with the Concert Band we did *George Washington Bridge*, a very analyzable piece. If you don't know the way the piece is organized, it is difficult to play it correctly. I believe that students cannot play it correctly unless they know what they are doing.

Therefore, we made scores available and had a seminar to talk about it. One student, a music and English major, wrote his impressions of *George Washington Bridge*. The impressions were remarkably close to the program notes that Schuman has on the score, which the student had not seen. The day after the seminar, it was a different piece. It was very interesting to see that now they are digging into the *New England Tryptich* and they want to find out about these other things beyond the notes.

*(William W. Wiedrich)*

### Music dictionaries and study guides

I try to give the information I think is important: the title, composer, arranger, etc. I also list the terms that should help play the piece correctly. I ask questions that require them either to ask me for the answers or that they can look up. I refer to this information as we are studying the piece.

The study guide I make up is similar to a Learning Activity Packet but it takes a short time to do. It is something that might make them more thoughtful or educated and more independent. It would take a half hour maximum, and that half hour would occur over a two-week period. I don't care how they find the answers and I want them to have enough inquisitiveness to ask for the answer from somebody or look it up.

I have music dictionaries in the room and they have music dictionaries in their folders. One of these dictionaries is based upon the words I thought all music students,

from middle school on, should know. The dictionary is three sheets long and there are at least forty or fifty terms per sheet. I would prefer they know fewer terms well, than to have a dictionary and never open it. I want them to be unafraid and to look at terms, instead of saying, "Oh this is so complicated, I don't want to use this."

*(Janet Tweed)*

# *Teaching Musical Skills through Performance Experience*

CHAPTER ONE

# ARTICULATION

Students must learn to be flexible when performing articulations. This is needed because the musical contexts for articulations vary. The contexts may differ depending upon the dynamics, tempo, locations in the phrase, historical periods, composers, or styles. Teachers and performers, from beginners to professionals, must draw upon their talent, musical experiences, and music education to judge how they will vary an articulation so it fits the music.

Music teachers want students to play an accent, for example, so it is distinct from any other articulation. They teach one accent that embodies the critical features of all accents. This is like teaching students to draw basic geometric shapes such as circles or squares. In instrumental lessons, students drill playing accents and slurs; in drawing class, students practice making squares and circles. With this approach, students could assume that the articulation is an end instead of the means.

Teachers can ask students, however, to perform accents within the context of a musical phrase. This allows students to see that an accent affects a musical performance, instead of being just an end of music instruction. The music student can learn to adjust the articulation according to the style of the piece and the context of the musical phrase. To carry the parallel further, the student in drawing class can learn to adjust the squares and circles by drawing lines darker or lighter and by changing the size of the circle or square, or even the perspective.

To teach students that the articulation is a means, not an end in performance and instruction, teachers can ask students to try accenting in different ways. As students experiment, they can vary the accents in a phrase until they create a version they decide is musically appropriate. The students thus develop an understanding of the accent's function, increase their technical skill, and practice making musical judgments.

If teachers work to continue developing the students' insights and judgments, the students will go beyond the assumption that there is one way, and one way only, to perform a specific articulation, and the students will become much more adept at properly assessing and applying articulations to form the style of pieces they perform.

## ARTICULATIONS AND MUSICAL IMPORTANCE

### Articulation conveys the line to the audience

When Fred Schroeder was at Lawrence University, he used a wonderful analogy. He would say, "You must put stage make-up on the notes. As actors use make-up to emphasize the eyes, the colors, and facial lines and other features, we most do that in music through articulations. We have to get it across, because it's what the audience hears that's important."

*(Thomas Stone)*

### Articulations give the musical line clarity

Players neglect clarity in performance too often. As teachers of wind players, we neglect spending time thinking about articulation, particularly compared with the time string players think about bowing. They are always talking and arguing about bowing. They debate how a piece is going to be bowed, and where and when, and how the various stresses will be felt. Two great violinists, for example, will argue forever about what is the correct and proper way to bow even an old classic, even if the decisions were made earlier by the concertmaster or the orchestral conductor. I don't think we spend nearly enough time producing clarity in our groups through work on articulation, the primary component of clarity.

*(Eugene Corporon)*

### Making a band more musical

Articulation, style, tone quality, and phrasing are essential qualities of a musical performing group. These are taught easily by demonstration and modeling, and this needs to be started early with beginners.

*(Carl A. Bly)*

### Decide articulations in the context of the phrase

Most bands play all the accents the same, without a variation from staccato on one hand to various accents of differing lengths on the other. Instead, the accents and staccatos should vary from note to note within the context of the phrase.

When teachers and students do not consider the staccato's linear role, it becomes simply a short shot of sound in isolation. Instead, the staccato should provide bounce and motion within the phrase so it has a linear role. I also see that bands tend toward making the accent a vertical thing. My view is that accents should be horizontal or linear; the vertical way isn't correct for accents either.

*(Michael Haithcock)*

Band people need not stick to the articulations written on the page as much as they do. Band people are very rigid in that respect. They see something and say, "Well it says all tongued; we've got to tongue it." That's not the way the string people work at all. Whoever is conducting has his set of bowings for each piece.

Many people don't realize there is a parallel with bowing in strings to articulations in the winds. The view of string players is simply, "If you wind up playing passages and it doesn't sound right, change the articulation." I think that's a very important thing that wind people have to realize. A musician must change the printed articulations to fit the style of the music, to fit the tempo, or to fit the size of the group.

*(Myron Welch)*

Most band members take accents too literally. String players, pianists, and vocalists have both a more concrete and a more relaxed understanding of what an accent means. I do not talk about accents in terms of beginnings and endings. I think of them in terms of weight and strength—a much more vocal approach to this than some band directors. For example, the same symbol means different things with Beethoven, Mozart, and Schubert. But, what band people have tended to do is to say that there is only one way to do a certain accent.

*(Robert Grechesky)*

Each articulation has a basic form or shape. The particular version of the articulation changes, though, when it is applied to a phrase. Therefore, one can find no end to the number of different versions of, for example, the accent or the staccato.

*(Frank Battisti)*

I teach them that an accent is not loud, an accent is a contrast to what's on each side of it.

*(Terry A. Oxley)*

### Articulations differ with composer and style

Playing staccato does not mean short, it means detached. Staccato means a certain style, less connected than legato.

*(Stanley Cate)*

An articulation varies with the composer. For example, Mozart is very disciplined and controlled; Nelhebyl

is more dramatic and violent than Mozart.

*(Frank Battisti)*

### Defining style through articulation

Articulation is a very important definer of style. We must decide how you are going to articulate: should it be a detached or a legato style? If you are way off on articulation it is probably one of the most offensive things you can do to any musical style. It really bothers me when something should be light and detached and it isn't.

*(Terry A. Oxley)*

Style is the most important thing and I teach style through articulations.

*(Dominic Spera)*

### Varying articulations give contrast and nuance

Accents are like looking at a beautiful painting: it may be in a warm or cool color, but, then you see a splash of an opposite color that really stands out. I stress the whole idea of what an accent or articulation is by relating it to the painting with the contrasting "splotch of color." I tell them that when composers put that mark on that note, they want you to bring it out and make a contrast, so that everything does not sound the same.

*(Nancy Plantinga)*

Articulation has more to do with the ending of a note then with the beginning, though there might be some exceptions to that rule. I firmly believe the choice of articulation is a very prevalent problem in all musical performance.

I think of articulation as relating to two choices: short or long. The extent to which there is an amount of space between notes gives the subtle nuance, or makes the differences among articulations. The amount of space varies the staccato, marcato and all other articulations that can range from short to long.

*(Gerald Olson)*

### Tapering accented notes

I teach accents as meaning "coming away from" instead of a louder note. You do hit it a little harder and then come away from that level to taper the sound.

*(Donald S. George)*

### Different accents decay differently

In every accent there has to be decay. That decay depends upon the degree of the accent—the more marcato it is, the less the decay. A normal accent has the most decay. The least decay occurs in the hardest accents. Even in the hard accent with no decay, there still must be consideration about the rest of the line that occurs before and after the accented note.

In teaching accents or correcting the way students perform them, I notice that high school students think they should put the stress at the beginning of the note. Once you've made them aware of what they are doing you can say, "Does it make sense to use your sledge hammer and over-tongue that note?" When they begin to get the sense that the over-tonguing puts the note into isolation—makes it too exceptional—they begin to realize there is a different solution. The note, instead of being in isolation, must be connected to the whole phrase.

*(Michael Haithcock)*

### Maintaining musical continuity

To vary the length of a staccato, for example, I rarely say "separate" or "play it short"; instead I say, "Don't let the notes touch." The phrase itself seems to retain its continuity if one says, "Don't let the notes touch," compared with, "Put a space, or silence between the notes." Another way to demonstrate this note length is by playing a melody on the piano with one finger. This technique reinforces this concept—that is, to get a space without destroying the musical line. Sometimes that split second it takes to lift the finger and move it to another key is just the amount of space needed to play the phrase properly.

*(Richard Floyd)*

### Articulation on unfamiliar instruments

When I am unfamiliar with the performance techniques of a certain instrument, I can still teach them the proper articulation. First I judge what I hear. Then, I tell them how it has to sound to be correct. I let them decide how to accomplish this technically.

*(Terry A. Oxley)*

### Phrase and note beginnings and endings

The accent only has to do with the beginning of the note—the way a player initiates the tone. The rhythmic value of the note and what comes next in the phrase determines how you should play the end of the note. This idea seems to work with kids. It counteracts their tendency to "chop it short" when you say accent.

*(Michael Haithcock)*

Just after the inhale, a student can wait too long and build up too much pressure. That makes the next attack too heavy and percussive. The objective is to make the tongue inaudible. To get this, I may have them play the phrase on one note to isolate the one element. With one thing to attend to, they can become sensitive to attacks, releases, and breathing. They also can coordinate with the conducting of upbeat and downbeat, which mirrors the inhalation-exhalation process and reinforces the idea. Then it's a matter of applying the new response in a phrase or passage and ultimately to the entire piece.

*(Donald Casey)*

Ernest Williams taught Don Jacoby, who taught me to use a tongue release and it works very, very well.

Charlie Schlueter said, "You can't play certain pieces, such as Beethoven's Seventh, without stopping the air with the tongue. You will miss the high B if you don't do it." It's being done thousand of times right now all over America. Tongued releases are a sophisticated thing that you can start introducing in high school.

*(Dominic Spera)*

People stop the tone with their tongue in every state in the union. In clinics Harold Bachman advocated "no tuts." Bachman said that even short notes should end with a vowel. Ta, tee, too, whatever way the teacher chooses. Stopping the sound with the tongue ruins the sound and this is equally true on long tones or short tones. Besides maintaining a good sound, the "no-tut" approach encourages you to move your tongue only half as often as when you stop and also start the tone with the tongue.

*(Robert E. Foster)*

Soft releases on a long sustained note, for example, on a Bach chorale should not be "chopped off like a paper cutter." Have the group respond to the prep and release gesture. On the preparatory portion of the release movement of the baton, they play a quick subtle diminuendo at the end. The release then has a taper. The percussion anticipates its release by releasing on the beginning of the fade.

*(Donald Wilcox)*

We often do not hold notes for their full value, which should be for longer than the note value. We only have a few things to listen for: intonation, balance, tone, and volume. If we arrive at this spot and it sounds good, we sometimes act as though we better cut this off before something goes wrong; if it sounds poor, we get out quick!

*(Robert Floyd)*

## TEACHING ARTICULATION

### Articulation is crucial

Style of articulation is a crucial thing to prepare. We must get beyond saying louder or softer, or strike it harder because this can be unmusical.

*(Butler R. Eitel)*

### Using words and syllables to teach tonguing

When teaching tonguing to woodwind and brass players, I have students repeat the phrase: "Tootsie Traveled to Timbuktu." We first do it slowly and gradually increase the speed to a moderate tempo. When the student begins to feel the use of the tongue, we incorporate this into the blowing and playing of the instrument. If a child's name begins with a T-sound, then we substitute his name (Tim or Tom) for "Tootsie." It never fails to bring a smile and helps to relax the student—thus making tonguing more natural.

*(Theta Lee)*

The students found the phrase "Tic-e-tac-e-Hou-ses" written in their books. I believe it is the title of a song. The trumpet players began to have a contest to see who could say, and later play it the fastest. One kid started to double tongue without realizing it and they all began to do the same. The syllables, "tic-e-tac-e," led them right to it.

*(James Froseth)*

I use a series of different syllables as we play a scale during warm up. On each scale degree we play four quarter notes, but on each step we vary the style of articulation. On B flat: du du du du; on C: dah dah dah dah; on D: tah tah tah tah; on E: tee tee tee tee; etc.

The next step might be to vary the length of each. For example I might say, "Let's do: tah tah tah tah; but don't let the notes touch as much as the previous time" or say, "Let's do: tah tah tah tah so they nearly touch." I do not say separate, or short.

This practice develops a vocabulary of articulations that is especially important since kids tend to articulate everything the same way.

*(Richard Floyd)*

### Articulation is related to other skills
Because articulation involves the release of air and attacks, it is connected to many other issues such as embouchure and sound, inhalation and exhalation, air speed, and the control of air. This brings everything together. Therefore, though I still think of articulation in a separate category, it relates to all these things.

*(Gerald Olson)*

### Improving "stingers" and other short notes
On short notes such as march "stingers" the kids tend to "whack it" and the result is often inaccuracy and poor tone. To overcome this, I stress that the less articulation there is, the better it sounds.

*(James Croft)*

### Releasing notes and improving tone
Too little attention is directed to releases. Students seem to stop sound the same way they start it—with the tongue. I try to tell them that you stop the sound by stopping the air. With this correction, the sound of the band changes dramatically.

*(Michael Golemo)*

### Teaching spacing of notes
I tell students at this age level that I know they do not realize yet the effect of the different note spacing and style. Without proper note spacing in pieces such as *Pitland Hills March* and *Reformation Symphony*, the music will not sound right. With spacing, these pieces can be very exciting. For example, I might explain to them that we need to establish a certain spacing or style. To do this, a half note is no longer a half note. It is a quarter tied to an eighth, with an eighth rest.

*(Ross A. Leeper)*

### Short notes and fast passages
The more rapidly articulated a passage is, the longer a note must be. I say, "short notes are long notes." Making short notes long may not be a cause of good articulation, as much as a cure for bad articulation. The poorer way is their hammering of the "t" sounds, and thus the reduction of the air flow. The better way is to emphasize the length of each note, which also seems to increase the air and lighten the tongue.

*(Hal D. Cooper)*

For tonguing rapid staccato passages, I ask them not to worry about stopping notes, just start each note. They think they have to play short, so they worry about both starting and stopping and get tensed up.

*(Robert Grechesky)*

One of my crusades is to teach young kids to play technically faster. Many times, of course, their tongues are very slow and sluggish. I strongly believe and preach the legato style of tonguing for any rapid tempos.

We start out playing a "du" with a legato attack, repeating it slowly. As they gradually go faster and faster I want the legato to turn into a staccato. To play fast keep the tongue close to whatever point you're articulating, either against a reed, the back of the teeth, the roof of the mouth, whatever. The feeling of the tongue's movement is really legato when playing very rapidly. If they do not tongue lightly or legato, they will tense up and slow down.

*(Lance Schultz)*

### Starting fast articulations with beginners
When beginners make a good sounding attack with a good tone, I teach them to play fast and tongue fast. I say, "Okay, that was great. Now try doing this: da da da da da da da da dadadada." If they can do this right from the beginning, it usually is good for the rest of the time they play. I'm a firm believer that they shouldn't just keep playing only whole notes for a week or two.

*(Lance Schultz)*

### Teaching to minimize tongue impact
Many students apply so much tongue. To counteract this, I often have them blow the air without tonguing.

*(Frank Bencriscutto)*

I sometimes say, "Hit it with a feather instead of a club."

*(Thomas Stone)*

## Teaching through modeling and imitation

I often model articulations with my instrument, or hum things that I want them to hear. Often I have them hum, sing, say, or play it back. If they sing or say the articulation three or four times first, they usually play it perfectly when they go back to the instrument. A typical example is the articulation, "slur two and tongue two." The sequence is, they hear me sing, they sing or say, and they play. After they play the articulation correctly, I then may turn to a different page with the same articulation. When they play the new music, they usually do the new etude correctly.

*(Steven Cooper)*

## Teaching articulations through visual and physical experiences

I try to relate everything in music to the physical world, even staccato and marcato. I talk about using the tennis ball, throwing it against the wall of the rehearsal room. In slow motion I show the marcato by describing the ball striking the wall and describe the staccato by the ball lifting off the wall. I also have placed my hand on a student's shoulder. I push on the shoulder during pulses, without taking my hand off to show marcato and spacing of notes. Then, I might lift my hand from the shoulder, like hitting them repeatedly to show them a marcato articulation. This shows that to get a marcato attack there must be space between the notes. I also can relate this to the impact of the tennis ball hitting the wall and everybody in the room can observe my hand on the one student's shoulder.

*(Frank Battisti)*

When I want to get the notes short, I will have them play a given note that they know, concert F for example. I will draw a line on the blackboard and tell them to sustain the note as I point along that line. When I get to the end of the line, the tone stops. I emphasize stopping the tone by stopping the breath, not by using their tongues. (Although there are some woodwind players who stop the tone with their tongues, so that little old axiom is not necessarily written in stone.) Then I will draw a little shorter line and do the same process again. I draw a third line, or erase part of the second, and I finally get down just to the length of the tone I want.

*(James D. Ployhar)*

## Teaching articulations through conducting

When we talk about attacks and releases I very rarely describe with words what I want. I do most of that non-verbally through conducting. Words do not do it at all. We'll practice all kinds of releases without my saying a word, and it really works!

*(Craig Kirchhoff)*

## The decay of an accented note

I sometimes use the tympany to illustrate an attack followed by the sound going away, DAAAAaaaaaaaaa. Just how hard the sound should be started varies with composer. The basic shape of a forte-piano articulation is the same, but the exact version varies with the composer, style, and period.

*(Frank Battisti)*

## Increase listening and sensitivity to style

Sometimes I will have them play certain rhythm patterns or lines, such as an eighth-note line, in a slurred style. The next time I may ask them to play staccato. I also may treat another figure in the same piece with distinctly different articulation (bowing) style. Then, when we put the parts together the students hear everything better. The purpose is to sharpen their ears so they hear that the notes have a different function when articulated differently.

*(Pamela Gearhart)*

## Balancing the air, volume and tongue

I say "soft tongue and loud dynamics" and "hard tongue and soft dynamics," and we use all the variations between the extremes. I sometimes ask for a "forte tongue" but "piano dynamic," or a "piano tongue" but "fortissimo air" as a way to get people to understand certain ideas such as playing loudly but tonguing softly, or tonguing with a real point but at a soft volume level. Learning to play a real legato attack with a full forte sound, or staccato in a piano dynamic are challenges for young musicians,

*(Gary Hill)*

## Playing legato

To play legato, many students end one note and then start the next note. There is always a tiny, tiny hesitation that drives me nuts. What finally gets through to them is saying, "Don't end the first note, just start the second note." This works and their control increases. They get the mental picture of only starting the second note and never shutting down the air stream.

*(Terry A. Oxley)*

## Preventing careless performance of articulations

When students see the marking for forte piano or sforzando, they automatically feel they have license to do terrible things! I try to counteract this by asking them to maintain a good sound while performing these. For example, we might practice playing a forte sound for three beats before the change to piano for one beat, then release. Next, we play a forte sound for two beats and then one or two of piano. Then less than one beat of full, good quality sound before piano begins. Relying upon their feeling of subdivision, we play for three quarters, one-half, or even one-quarter of a pulse. The tempo suggests when we reduce the volume.

What we strive for is a good quality tone at the forte level; then when the volume changes we want to prevent a reduction of tone quality. We do not want a percussive attack at any point and we don't want a poor tone after that attack. If that does happen, nothing will be sustained through either the forte or the piano.

*(Robert Floyd)*

## Teaching the decay of an accent through forte piano

Consider a whole note with an accent. If you play that whole note at fortissimo, it is not an accented note, it's just loud, and just loud is boring.

Because any note with some length has a decay, I teach the idea of decay through the idea of forte piano. Therefore, on a whole note there would be a quarter note's worth of forte, and a dotted half's worth of mezzo piano, or something close to that.

I teach this carefully and say, "Listen, now this is the note with the accent on it and I want you to play the level that is written. Whether it happens to be forte or fortissimo, I want you to play that level until I point to you again. When I point to you again, change to piano without articulating. We will get this big full sound that we want." We start the sound and I then cue the change and the dynamic level fades down quickly. Then I say, "Okay, do it again." I keep moving the point where the dynamic level drops closer to the beginning of the sound. This can be done while sustaining a note as though there were a fermata, or while performing a whole note at a manageable tempo.

In a general way, the accent and the forte piano are really the same thing. I can use the forte piano, up to a point, to stress the idea that accented notes must decay. There are differences too, such as the accent necessarily doesn't come down to the piano level or drop off that abruptly.

*(Terry A. Oxley)*

## Articulating on "air patterns" only

Vince Chikowitz, with whom I studied, used the term "air pattern." In teaching articulation, he would say, "Don't play it on the horn, but play it on your air pattern and say tu, tu, tu on air only in the correct style." If it were staccato, we would say "tuh." We would do the air pattern for, let's say, three minutes, then we played the whole exercise or the whole piece on the air pattern.

This is just like a baseball player who picks up two bats and warms up his swing. It takes more air to play a piece on just the air pattern than it does to play it on your horn. Therefore, when you go to your horn, you'll find that you have more endurance and a cleaner tongue. Besides this, you can feel what your tongue's doing through the air-pattern exercise.

*(Dwayne P. Sagen)*

At the same time as some people are playing or not playing, I may have other players either sing or articulate on an air-stream. I also unify articulation by this process.

*(Gary Hill)*

## Teaching articulation through a variety of techniques

With all the articulations such as accents, marcato, staccato, legato, and slurred, I use pictures, graphic representations, singing, conducting, and a combination of these. When I present a picture, then I also show an articulation with sound. I have them sing so much that the piano professor next to me is always amazed. He often asks, "What is this, a voice studio?"

*(L. Keating Johnson)*

## Teaching the initiation of sound through steps

Tonguing is a real problem for young kids, but it need not be. I would have them go through these steps: first, start the tone by saying "whoooo." Second, stop it with a "t" by saying "whooooot." Third, use the "t" to start the tone as in "tooooot." I use the tongued release only initially, until they get the idea. After these steps they will make the sound "tooooooo" without the "t" at the end.

The other value of this process is to remove the intellectual aspects whenever they are not needed. I follow the KISS principle: "Keep it simple, stupid."

*(John Kinnison)*

## Articulating as an ensemble

Suppose there were a long section of legato music that must be rhythmically together. One way to teach them to unify that is by having long legato passages played staccattissmo. Have them play it short, thinking about how their fingers feel. Ask them to close their eyes and see how their fingers feel as they play it legato. Then, ask them to keep their fingers moving as they play legato, the way they would in staccato style.

*(Larry Rachleff)*

## Using air attacks to minimize percussive sounds

I have used the breath attack to start notes. I take a very slow tempo and have them really "kill a note" with just the breath by saying HAH! HAH! HAH! Sometimes I do breath attacks differently by saying "Ha" followed on the next pulse by HAAAAAAAA. I have them say it until they can get a good "HA!" I also demonstrate this sound a lot and ask them to do it with their voice. When I get the right sound out of a group with their voices, they try it on the instruments.

Then, I ask them to use the tongue to cushion that attack. Cushioning is needed because there can be a real harsh explosion on the note when they use the breath that hard. I say, "Now blow it exactly the same way, but use the tongue to prevent that explosion from occurring. Use the tongue to allow the note to start, to even it out, and to control it."

The other goal is that they use the tongue like a valve instead of like a hammer to get the note started. Kids cannot do this at first, they can't blow hard enough and they can't get the chops set well enough on the first try. After a few times, then it starts to respond and everything is working right. Then the tongue becomes a gate that lets that air out instead of functioning like a hammer.

In class lessons with younger students, I can do half notes or longer notes that way to develop the same skills. I do that with brass in particular so they use the air properly and get the embouchure to respond immediately. This does not work as well with woodwinds, but on occasion I do use it with them. I've found that woodwinds can change their breathing so that they control the attack because of this. It is, however, a more appropriate technique for brass.

*(James Stivers)*

### Teaching articulation and style

Enunciation means articulation and that means style. With the jazz band, I will give them an enunciation and they will repeat the enunciation aloud with their voice. We will then use this enunciation in playing patterns or very simple phrases. Next I will introduce the literature and say, "Do you remember this?" The enunciations are done in the warm up, singing, and playing. Singing comes first and, as far as I'm concerned, is the most important way to understand the jazz language.

*(Dominic Spera)*

### Selecting articulations because of score study

Score study helps us know the style of the work, which guides us in the teaching of articulation. What's appropriate for the staccato? What is appropriate for marcato? What are the appropriate articulations for the style of this piece?

*(Thomas Stone)*

### Teaching articulation through conducting

When we learn our basic warm ups at the beginning of the school year, we begin, for example, by saying "Open to page twelve. Number 1 is to be legato. Please observe that I'm conducting for you what I interpret to be legato. Maybe your teacher last year did his legato a little different but it's the same idea." I would do this very often, at least once a week. We also do a staccato, marcato, legato, accent, and a forte piano during the warm-up segments.

*(Bryce Taylor)*

### Practicing conducting while teaching articulation

The teacher can practice conducting during warm-up segments in the rehearsal. The teacher should be working on his conducting of dynamics, style, and articulation during this time, not while rehearsing a difficult piece. Therefore, a warm up is the practice period for the conductor as well as the students. There are about fifteen to twenty conducting fundamentals, such as the conducting of legato, staccato, and marcato, that can be practiced during the warm-up portion of a rehearsal.

*(Bryce Taylor)*

### Diagnosing their skill with articulation

Articulations tell me a lot when I start to conduct a festival or all-state band. Within ten minutes I know what I am dealing with. I conduct them through the B-flat concert scale one way, now this way, and then another way, using a different articulation each time. When I finish with six different articulations and dynamic levels I know the problems that I will face, that is, the things I must explain and the things I won't have to explain.

*(Bryce Taylor)*

## PROBLEMS IN TEACHING ARTICULATION

### Impeding articulation skills

Much of the music currently played that we call concert band music is actually marching band music disguised as concert band music. They will have an opening section with short hard articulations followed by an obligatory sixteen bars of Andante in three-four time. Too many pieces sound the same, and they often have heavy articulation and syncopation, so naturally they encourage the hard articulation that we would like to avoid.

*(John Williamson)*

### Accenting to the excess

I make a big deal about improving accents, because marching has influenced their playing of accents. They seem to believe, "Accenting means to hurt the person in front of you as well as yourself."

*(Terry A. Oxley)*

### Over-articulation inhibits technical development

Articulation is a major problem with some instruments, such as French horn and other brass. One example is playing notes too short. This makes them more inaccurate. Another problem is trying to do most of the work on articulation with their tongue. Thus, they let their use of the airstream slip. Over-articulation also inhibits technique when they use the tongue, which makes the tone and attack too percussive. The cure or prevention is to say, "The more rapidly articulated a passage is, the longer a note must be." Students think it sounds funny when I say, "Short notes are long notes." This may not be the cause of good articulation, as much as the cure for bad articulation. The poor way is their hammering of the "t" sounds, and thus the reduction of the air flow.

*(Hal D. Cooper)*

### Be-bop articulation

One thing that everybody has to understand is that the be-bop articulation is not conducive to good sound production in young players. However, the be-bop articulations are good for style and articulation at an advanced level. For young players I do not like to use the "ee" articulation as in "do-bee do-bee do-bee" because it closes off the sound.

*(Dominic Spera)*

### Initiating instead of attacking the sound

We would do a lot better if we would use the word, "initiation" in place of the word, "attack." Attack is an imprecise term and can send a mixed signal to students. Kids should be initiating tones, not attacking them. Often the term attack doesn't say what we really mean, and it influences them incorrectly at a subliminal level.

*(Thomas Stone)*

### Terminology problems

Another confusing issue is that the word tonguing is inappropriate. Maybe the word chosen years ago should have been releasing. The idea of tonguing, to many young students without much training, conveys to them an active forward motion, like spitting or "thhooing." I always wondered why young kids "thhhooooed" that sound on brass instruments. The more I think about it, the more it seems that they thought there should be an active forward direction with the tongue to produce the starting sound. Well, obviously that's not true with most single-reed and brass instruments: the tongue should be placed forward in the mouth, somewhere behind the top teeth for example, or somewhere at the tip of a reed or beneath it. When the initial sound is made, it is made because the tongue is released backward in the mouth, away from the mouthpiece or the reed.

Perhaps the terms, "initiating the sound" and "releasing the tongue," would have been better. At the end you would call it "suspending the sound but not the air," so the air is alive while the sound ceases.

*(Gerald Olson)*

### Unclear understanding of articulation

Does articulation mean we're focusing our attention at the beginning of the sound or the end of sound? I don't know that the *New Harvard Dictionary of Music* helps us understand the difference between a marcato accent and a normal accent mark. What does the tongue do? What does the air stream do? I don't know that performance music faculty have necessarily agreed upon what I would call standard classical articulation techniques.

I think the jazz people have done a better job. I think that's one I try to teach globally, specifying either short or long with variations of that. I hardly ever use the word short, unless I'm getting an exceptionally long sound, then I will stop and say one word: shorter.

*(Gerald Olson)*

### We should listen more carefully to articulation

We often fail as teachers in developing the quality of articulations, possibly because we may have stopped listening carefully to them. Many wind instruments pro-

duce an uncharacteristic articulation where the air builds up behind the tongue and sounds like a pop! This makes them sound more like a percussion instrument.

*(Donald Casey)*

### Developing both separated and connected playing skills

Recently I have found myself addressing tonguing more than ever, possibly because I have emphasized legato playing so much in the past. My students can play a legato phrase with no problem, but I have problems with their tonguing. They're so sensitive to playing with a good tone and to listening carefully to the pitch, they're not thinking about how they're beginning the pitch. I feel it is an easier problem to fix the tonguing than to fix the tone. The tongue is more of an instant thing that I can work on occasionally. For me developing tone, and developing the ability to sustain and listen is on-going.

*(Michael Kaufman)*

### The challenge of teaching legato style

When judging, I have found that most bands have trouble with legato. I don't really have trouble teaching legato because meeting the challenge is a satisfying accomplishment for me. I feel good that I've taught them a style which most people would find difficult to teach a junior high group. For example, my junior high group has done Ravel's *Pavanne* and that is difficult. At first, teaching that style is a problem. They may not like it at first but they sure like it when they're finished with it.

*(Sandra P. Thompson)*

### Releasing of notes

I've seen people work with groups on attacks, attacks, attacks, but they never work on the releases. They let the people shut off the note whenever they think they should. One must pay more attention to the ending of the notes. Let's take an example of a quarter tied to an eighth note occurring on beat one. The eighth note is released on the "and" of beat one, not on the pulse or ictus of one. Conducting skill enables you to show them the beat and release. Let's stress first when to end and secondly, how to end. The other questions are: What kind of treatment is needed? Is the note tapered on the end or not? Is it stopped with the tongue or the air? These decisions have to be made by the conductor because twenty kids are going to do it twenty different ways.

*(Myron Welch)*

### Lengthening short notes, especially at the ends

An important idea is "long short notes" on last notes of marches or isolated accents. No matter how short a note is, it has to have enough length to have sonority, sound, pitch, and resonance. I don't want it to sound like "slamming the door on the cat's tail!"

*(Donald Wilcox)*

# CHAPTER TWO

# BALANCE

When we listen to an ensemble, we can simultaneously hear the sounds of a horn solo and its accompaniment; we hear a melody's unique sound when it is doubled by the flute, oboe and bassoon. To do so, we rely on the performers to make musically appropriate decisions about the *balance* of the various sounds. The accompaniment must play at a dynamic level that places its sound in proper balance to the solo. In a melody played by the different instruments, the conductor and the players must decide how they will achieve balance. The various colors may be equal in volume; or if their volumes are unequal, one sound might dominate. The sound results from the performer's decisions about balance. We can judge the result as musically appropriate or inappropriate; when it is appropriate, we can say that the balance is correct; when it is not, we can say the balance is incorrect.

If the balances are correct, the musical judgments of the performers have been successful. If the balance is incorrect, the results might be a poor ensemble with a characteristic sound that has inappropriate tone quality; the background might be louder than the melody, or the trombones may overshadow the other low brasses during a certain passage.

The teachers must make the proper choices to achieve balance. As they choose, they must consider the ensemble, the score, and the musical style. Most ensembles lack sufficient forces on some instruments to achieve an ideal or balanced instrumentation. Even if the forces on each part are ideal, the unequal strength of each student can affect balance. Edited editions, which show dynamic markings, don't prevent problems either. For example, the dynamic markings for trumpets and horns playing in unison may be the same. The trumpet part may still dominate since it can project so much more easily. Yet, editors do not mark their volume levels differently because the marking is intended to suggest the overall dynamic level of the full ensemble or section. Editors expect the conductors to achieve the proper result through their proper knowledge of his performers.

Balance goes beyond the number of performers on a part. Brass instruments have wider dynamic ranges than woodwinds, thus a tutti crescendo can be the occasion for a musical tragedy unless students adjust the dynamic markings and levels. Higher pitched instruments project more than lower pitched instruments; moving to a different performance site may require the moving of a section to a different spot on the stage. In a room with less-than-perfect acoustics, the performers may have to adjust the notated dynamic levels to maintain a balanced sound.

While these considerations refer to the balance of the ensemble or the score, there also are concerns in the music itself. To decide if adjustments are needed, questions arise: "Are there dominant and subordinate voices here?" "Which instruments are playing the melody and subordinate parts?" or, "What tone color should dominate?" Therefore, the teacher must balance parts for stylistic musical considerations, not only for those of instrumentation.

Making decisions about balance is integral to both teaching and performance. Teachers can bring their knowledge and musical judgment to these decisions, and should reveal their reasoning to the students; they should involve students as they explore solutions for balance, whether in a passage, a section, or the music as a whole. A balanced sound does not automatically result from getting the right notes, and balance does not occur when students merely play dynamic levels exactly as marked in their parts.

## MUSICAL CONSIDERATIONS

### *Understanding balance in relation to blend*

Blend versus balance: what's the difference? One can assess either balance or blend by noticing if an individual or a section is playing appropriately when one hears their playing in context. Considering the idea of blend, one can see it as the relative tone color or the relative timbre within the section or the band. The same idea fits balance: balance is the relative dynamic level within a section or the full ensemble.

For example, the trumpets are playing beautifully matched sounds, but the second trumpets are playing too loudly. This example shows that balance is relative to dynamics in a section. An example of blend would be hearing the tone of a trumpet section that doesn't match the color of the entire brass section. At another time, the brass section sound can have too much horn in it. Or, the clarinets may be too prominent in the full band sound. Each example shows that blend is relative to the context.

In the latter case, there also would be a blend problem in the entire ensemble, because the prominent clarinets can affect the timbre of the whole ensemble. There also can be both a balance and a blend problem. This occurs if the first trumpets are not only louder than everybody else, but also brighter than everyone else.

This is the way I teach it and it is simple to understand. Thus, the balance or dynamics, or the blend and balance may not be right within a specific musical context. These two terms cover a whole ton of stuff.

*(Donald Wilcox)*

I teach one with the other, since I can balance by using dynamic changes. For example, if I compare the brass and the woodwind sound by adjusting their volume, this helps them hear the effect that dynamics have upon balance. This also teaches ensemble tone color.

*(John Kinnison)*

### Balancing melodies and accompaniments

Look at pieces, especially transcriptions or Broadway show tunes, and notice that the dynamics are written generally the same across all the sections. When interpreting this, one should play melodies twice as loud as the accompanying parts or the rest of the band with the general effect being the overall dynamic suggested by the arranger.

*(Carl A. Bly)*

### The musical role

Every role is important in the music but the different roles must relate to each other in proportion. The various roles are those such as melody, accompaniment, rhythm, embellishment, solo, color, chordal, countermelody, and harmonic. It is the responsibility of different instruments or sections to perform their role in relation to all other parts, roles, sections, and the entire piece.

*(Joseph Casey)*

### Balancing the last sound

The sound of the last chord has ruined many fine performances For example, one is hearing a tremendous performance up to the last chord. If the last sound is badly out of balance or out of tune, the listener forgets about everything else the band did before the last chord.

This is the last thing that the audience hears and silence follows so the audience can think about what they have heard. I try to impress this idea on students: If you're going to do anything right, do the last note right at least. If you're doing other things right, don't spoil it by messing up the last note.

In view of this, I started working with the last note of

the piece for balance and intonation instead of starting with the first note. Then, I rehearse from back to front, beginning with the last note. This also can let them know this is the final goal of the composition no matter how long the piece is.

*(Francis Marciniak)*

### The sound should be appropriate for the piece

It is very easy to get into a rut. Some bands sound the same no matter which piece they play. People now are saying, "The music I'm going to play determines how the band will sound." If I'm going to play Persichetti it should sound like Persichetti, and Respighi is going to sound different from McBeth. Our second band is playing a McBeth composition now. They can follow that by playing a piece by a different composer and the band sounds different.

*(Bryce Taylor)*

### Determining what should be prominent

Urge everyone to listen because they must know what everyone else is doing. Then, make a judgment about what is prominent at what point. If your part is not prominent, get out of the way!

*(Robert Allan)*

### Differences that affect a balanced sound

Generally the upper notes tend to overshadow the lower tones. To be heard, the lower tones must project more fully. This is true for a section and for the entire band. However that does not consider the chord quality. A minor third in a minor chord, for example, needs emphasis particularly if it is in a lower voice.

*(Donald Gee)*

### Stressing the importance and role of accompaniments

A melody by itself isn't pretty, necessarily, so we first work very hard to make the background pretty. Then we set the melody on top of the background. Hearing the melody helps them instantly realize how crucial the background is and how incomplete the piece is without either. The correctly played background also prepares them to play the melody carefully.

*(Stanley Cate)*

## TEACHING BALANCE

### Teaching young students to achieve balance

The responsibility for balancing the various sections of the band usually rests entirely on the director. But, if teachers learn to share their "secrets" with the band members, balanced playing becomes the responsibility of the musicians as well as the director.

I develop balance and the students' understanding and skill with balance daily. For example, when we play the tonic chord, I assign the root to forty percent of each section, the third to another thirty percent, the fifth to twenty percent, and the octave to the remaining ten percent of each section. This often creates a balanced chord. We listen to it, I explain balance and the idea of balance, and we practice balancing the chord.

We also do balance listening or comparison exercises where I remove certain tones of the chords and ask the students to listen to the incomplete chords. They soon learn that something is missing when the chord is incomplete compared to the chord that is complete with the root, third, and fifth. In unison playing, I ask a certain section to play extremely loud, which a brass or percussion section can easily do and thus destroy the balance of a band. On the other hand, I also ask a section to play so softly that they are not heard, which also destroys the balance.

As we learn musical compositions for performances, I ask the students to listen to the parts that produce a balanced sound. Those parts are not always the melody or first parts. The inside parts are as important as they are in our daily chord exercises. When the band achieves good balance, I often point it out. I have them play that section again so they can listen and hear the example of proper balance. Pointing out the out-of-balance playing is important, but pointing out the balanced playing is even more important.

*(Roman Palmer)*

### Bringing out interior parts

I make a federal case for placing good players on second and third parts. When I audition my wind ensemble, I put up a list showing the order that the trumpet players scored in my evaluation. They are listed, for example, one through seven. Then I list the assignments by parts to play. I assign a certain player to third because he has the best low range in the section. I also might say, "We will rotate these parts, but this is where we are going to start." I do not assign parts according to the student's rank in the auditions. Students never start the first rehearsal in the order the chairs come out on the try-outs.

We need good players on every part. I often tell an audience about the importance of inner parts. I have said, "Without a question in my mind, the finest musician in this band is playing contrabass clarinet." I might say, "Some teachers or students think some instruments are lesser in importance. They might think if they have a student that cannot play so well, we can stick them on the third cornet or third clarinet part because these are not as important." I say, "For those high school players out there who think interior parts, bass clarinets, and such are not important, the best single musician on this stage is playing contrabass clarinet and third clarinet, because that's where I need him the most."

You also can isolate interior parts in rehearsal by saying, "Okay, let me hear this with no first flutes, no first oboe, no first clarinet, no E-flat clarinet. We will work the woodwind passage without the stars for a minute." One can dig out some of the other problems, because often the interior players—playing the so-called unimportant parts—tend to hide behind a section leader.

*(Donald Wilcox)*

### Explaining balance

To teach balance, I refer to a theater stage. For an oboe solo on *Variations on a Korean Folk Song*, I might say, "Now, your section should be in the background here. Back up, move more backstage because the oboist is out front."

*(John Williamson)*

### Planning balance

Some considerations are, "How many things are going on?" and, "What's the infrastructure of the piece?" Usually, in any piece, there is one of four things happening: you're either dealing with a new idea, a repeated idea, a variation, or a development of that idea. Often one must take an inventory of what is going on and ask, "What's the priority here?" If three things are going on, are they all important? If so, is it contrapuntal? If there are four things going on and half of them are whole notes, which are harmonic? How should they be balanced?

The teacher must catalogue what is really there before they rank them. The whole idea of balance and clarity results from decision making, and I think that's why we have a job. We have to decide, we have to make the best decision we can make at the time and get on with it.

*(Eugene Corporon)*

### Asking students to make decisions

Where section balance is concerned, I constantly ask them to decide whether their part is foreground or background material. If a person is cranking away on a whole note pretty loudly and drowning out the woodwind line that needs to come through, we stop. I say, "Can you make a judgment here? Do you think this whole note is foreground, background, or maybe middle ground material?" This approach puts that responsibility on the performer's shoulders. The idea of main, supportive, background, or harmonic roles often pops up in our discussion of balance.

*(Timothy Mahr)*

### Primary and secondary parts

When I tell the kids about playing dynamics, I describe what I call the "tweedle-deedle-dees." I tell them, "It's like the blue sky, the birds, and the landscape. You just have to figure out what's important in the picture. In this picture, is the blue sky important? No! Are the birds important? No. The landscape and the houses or if there's a person? Yes!" I don't want them to think that every time they have a tweedle-deedle-dee the birds and the sky are automatically not the most important. There might be a picture where that's the only thing happening. They understand that somehow.

*(Sandra P. Thompson)*

### Evaluating balance

If you can hear yourself play, you are either too loud, out of tune, or both. The next stage is to hear one's sound as part of the tone of others, which shows a blend. When we have begun to do that we have made progress.

*(Stanley Cate)*

### Targeting balance

I say, "Balance this to the oboe" or, "Balance this to the French horn." I explain, "We want the alto sax to be the big sound in the room. Everybody else has to hear the alto sax from wherever you sit. If you can't hear the alto sax, drop out or subside. If you do hear the alto sax, we've finally got what we want." I also may say, "In section seven through nine, we want you to balance to the tuba." This approach seems to work, and it's a much quicker way than stopping and saying, "Okay, tubas, you play it. Now, horns you play it." If we can get them to know what to listen for, then we're in good shape.

*(Bryce Taylor)*

### Practicing balance during technical drills

Students often play tutti scales on autopilot. One can wake them up by asking them to balance to specific instruments on, for example, different steps of the scale.

*(James Arrowood)*

### Dynamic "color shifts" or contrary dynamics

Percy Grainger's music often calls for independent or section response to dynamics. By asking the woodwind and brass choirs to perform a dynamic change from crescendo to decrescendo or from decrescendo to crescendo and follow a numerical sequence (one to five refers to piano to forte and vice versa), the students quickly master the skill of making an independent or section response to dynamics.

The students internally (mentally) process the numbers and respond according to the number value and produce a volume level. The assignment opens with brass choir being prominent. When the students' minds arrive at three after beginning at opposite dynamic levels, a balanced full-band sound occurs.

Continuing through the numerical process, a choir or a color shift occurs so the woodwind sound dominates. They reverse the sequence and progress back to the point where the brass choir sound dominates. An example of this process is: the brass choir plays volume changes 5-4-3-2-1-2-3-4-5 while the woodwind choir simultaneously plays 1-2-3-4-5-4-3-2-1.

*(Edward S. Lisk)*

### All parts are important

One of the problems we all have is morale in the third cornet, second clarinet, etc. When we work on balance, I tell my third players, "It's time again for you to make the firsts sound better. You can do this by supporting them more, by being strong on your part." They always get a kick out of that approach since they sometimes feel it means, "Well, you can make them sound better than they are."

*(Francis Marciniak)*

### Teaching balance

The more one talks about balancing, the more it happens.

*(Robert Allan)*

### Working with balance

Shuffling the seating also affects balance, since they cannot hear the melody if they are playing too loud. The result is that they will soften to hear who has an important part.

The lower parts should always be slightly louder than the upper parts. I ask them always to listen down within the section and in the band. The first trumpet is going to project a little bit more, is a little bit higher, and usually has the melody. Even so, I think you still want to encourage them to listen for the third or fourth trumpet.

Whoever's on the bottom must be louder because he's lower in pitch. As they try to listen down for balance, I encourage them to get lost in the low sounds—to submerge their sounds into the lower. As you build from the foundation upward, you keep compounding the sound of the tuba, the bass clarinet, and the bassoon.

This means you are matching the overtones they are producing in their sound, which spring out of their sound. Therefore, you're really matching something, you're fitting into something as it exists down in that low octave of the chord's or sound's root.

In some sense, the higher instrument's sound rests on the lower instrument's sounds. It also means that if they understand that their sound is a part of another, they're less likely to play out of tune.

*(Robert Grechesky)*

### Sensitizing students to balance

I have one person play, then add another, one at a time. I do this so they hear the previous ones and match their volume to the others. I also can ask those who are listening to judge which ones were equal or unequal. The process of experimentation builds their skill in listening.

*(R. G. Conlee)*

## PLANNING AND BALANCE

### Score study and planning

Conductors must decide first what they want, then set the priorities in relation to balance. This enables the students to understand what the balance should be and where their line fits into the total picture.

*(Robert Floyd)*

In preparation, the conductor must predetermine the balance desired. Balance and full utilization of tone colors delineate the very best, the top one percent, of the conductors from all others. I am not sure it is teachable; with effort, it can be learned.

*(Butler R. Eitel)*

### Balancing unbalanced instrumentation

With an ensemble that doesn't have inherently good balance, work at overloading certain unheard parts. If you put the flute up an octave you may get a balance. You may not if the part is played an octave lower, where it is written.

*(Donald Wilcox)*

### Considering the skills of the players

What I do is influenced by the nature of the instrument and the instrumentalist's capabilities. Gabriel and I were once squabbling about balance a little bit in Chicago. I said, "Well Gabe, shucks! If I had your kind of players I'd do something different, and if you had my kind of players you'd be forced to do something different." Remember, the quality of player you're working with has a lot to do with balance. Once a week I conduct the Corpus Christi Area Wind Symphony. These are all adults—super players and I do things differently there than with my high school group.

*(Bryce Taylor)*

### Challenges and obstacles

If we consider instrumental music teaching on a broad scale, we are working against some phenomena that promote out-of-balance playing, especially top-heavy playing. One is an over-representation of higher instruments in band, such as flutes, trumpets, clarinets, and percussion. The other is an under-representation of alto, tenor, and bass voices. In a trumpet section, one often finds three are on first, three are on second, and three are on third. The top is the heavier because the stronger three are likely on the top part.

A less obvious phenomenon is that we stop listening for good balance. We become accustomed to sounds that are not very good. We hear so many badly balanced sounds that we "unlearn" to discriminate the desired sound from the undesirable. We may accept the typical (out of balance) junior high band sound because other accomplishments such as playing at the right time with the right note have been made.

A third phenomenon is that the human ear hears the higher pitches more easily than the lower. If we exactly balance sounds from a full spectrum with the same volume, we would still hear the sound as top-heavy because we hear the higher pitches more clearly. McBeth's idea related to balance is the pyramid idea. The lower voices must be stronger than the higher voices; the thirds and seconds must play with more sound in total than the firsts.

*(Donald Casey)*

### Knowledge of instruments

With balance, instruments in the high register do not need to play as loud in their low register. They need to understand that balance is not only appropriate for the ensemble, but for the section and for individuals.

*(Larry Rachleff)*

### Balance

There are many people who subscribe to Francis McBeth's idea of the pyramid. There are some very good reasons for it. One reason is that music teachers don't want to hear loud flute and clarinet playing. Another reason is that bass players are often castoffs and sometimes contribute less tone, so everybody likes or hopes to hear a great deal more bass.

*(Bryce Taylor)*

### Notating balance through dynamics

If the pitch is in the high register of the flute and every person in the group has fortissimo marked on their part, you know the conductor has to do something about that. You cannot have a flute on a high E flat playing fortissimo. In addition, higher pitched instruments playing up high are not going to balance with the rest of the group unless the composer has terraced the dynamics throughout the group. For instance, when I write a chord at forte, I'll notate the tuba as the loudest instrument. I'll shade other dynamic markings down as I go up through the score. Therefore, I notate the flute as mezzo forte. In my mind, then the result will be a balanced band sound.

*(Thomas Stone)*

## BALANCING IN THE ENSEMBLE

### Balancing critical passages

We were on a concert stage a few weeks ago and balance went really awry. It was only one note where the big low-end flute and the E-flat clarinet have a high G to play. Just before that is a long sustained A flat. With this, the alto saxophones are finishing off the melody of the second movement from *Music for Prague*. This note comes along about eight or nine counts from the end.

In rehearsal this spot had been pretty well in tune, but when we got on stage we lost it. It was really a sour sound. It was the only intonation trouble we had in the piece—I mean serious trouble that is. I talked to the students after they listened to the tape and they also were shaking their heads. The piccolo player said she couldn't hear the flute, and she was sitting close to the flute. She said, "I heard so much clarinet and sax, and there was a dissonance coming toward me. I was unable to pick up the dissonance and bring down the half step." This was a critical, challenging passage. This is an example of the kind of thing we work on for balance.

*(Bryce Taylor)*

## A reason for balance

Another problem is the dynamics. Particularly those who do not have the most important line have to learn this. The wind players on whole notes have to reduce the volume way down. Especially the brass, because of the capacity of even one brass player can drown out ten violins.

*(Judith A. Niles)*

## Listening down for balance

The reference point for pitch and balance must be the bottom of band. The top of the band must never play louder than the bottom of the band will let it play. "Listen down."

*(Robert Allan)*

We talk about matching pitch and playing within their sections. We do not want them to stick out. We ask them to hear the person lower than them.

The firsts should hear down to the second part and the seconds should hear to the thirds. The first trumpet is going to project a little bit more; they are a little bit higher and usually have the melody. So, we must encourage them to listen down to whatever's on the bottom. They must listen down to the tuba and try to match pitch within the section and the section must fit within the lower sections. The thirds, therefore, must play louder than the firsts. The bottom tones should be the loudest, because they are lower.

We need to say often, "Your sound is what really gives us a full sound, otherwise we will end with a top heavy band. If you don't play well, all we will hear are the first parts. Therefore, make sure that you are really pumping out good sound."

*(Dwayne P. Sagen, Thomas Stone, and Timothy Mahr)*

## Comparing differently balanced sounds

They find this hard to grasp sometimes because they think the melody is everything. I was just working on the Rondo from Claude Smith's *Incidental Suite*. The coda begins with the brass section and it was very top heavy. I isolated a section and worked the thirds and the seconds by themselves a little bit to build their confidence. We played it the old way and then we played it the new way so everybody heard the difference. (The top-heavy sound was the old way.) In the new way, everyone was balanced and the seconds and thirds contributed more to the sound than the first part. They could hear the new way was better.

*(Timothy Mahr)*

## Balance in marching band

We scramble seating in marching band by mixing instruments in ranks. Each rank has three trumpets, several trombones, a mellophone, and a baritone. There is an ensemble in every rank. Every woodwind rank has all the woodwind parts and every brass rank has all the brass parts except tuba. We perform that way because it gives them a more balanced sound. When three ranks of trumpets turn away the whole thing doesn't fall down. We use the mixed ranks most of the time—parade or field. The only time we do not use this is when we want the absolute maximum volume, then we have the trombones in front. We've done that for about ten years. With a 340 piece band, we can get a more consistently balanced sound.

*(Donald Wilcox)*

## Balancing the group and a soloist in marching band

Band directors keep trying to steal ideas only from other band directors when they also could steal ideas from other sources. If you are trying to stage a trumpet solo for a marching band, why don't they go look at an opera or ballet to get ideas.

At a workshop I said, "One cliche is to put a ring of rifles or flags around the guy so closely that you can't see him. Then the director covers him up further by putting him right behind the field conductor. No one can see what he's doing anyway, since they cover him up with all those accessories." Now, in the opera *Carmen*, when she sings the big bar room scene, everybody backs away and gives her the whole stage. So, you can delegate importance by area and everybody on the stage will watch her. The intent is to focus the attention toward her and away from everybody else.

You also have things like height, she's probably standing on a chair or a table, which gives her elevation over everybody else. I said, "You have space, you have elevation, you have focus, and you have direction. You have all this stuff, but you guys aren't smart enough to put that in a marching band show. Go to an opera; you might learn something even if you don't plan to be an opera conductor."

*(Donald Wilcox)*

## Percussion and dynamic changes

With crescendos and diminuendos, the percussion leads going down and follows coming up. As the volume increases they follow the band up and, on the very end of a big crescendo, the percussion finishes it. They do this by over-balancing right at the very end. An example might be the end of Alfred Reed's *Festive Overture*. Therefore, the percussion dynamic changes are not linear, they make a curve coming out. When they reduce volume, I think this is more linear than concave. This use of percussion is a little more theatrical. I got that from Zubin Mehta. He would bring everything up kind of in balance and then he would take it out of balance right away at the release. If it was good enough for him, it's good enough for me.

*(Donald Wilcox)*

CHAPTER THREE

# BLEND

Teaching blend can be a challenge because it is less tangible than fingerings, rhythms, or dynamics. Students can meet the challenge, but the techniques of teaching blend and playing with blend require that they *listen*—and listening will not be effective unless students know what to listen for, so blend becomes a more concrete idea.

Teaching students what to listen for requires an approach. The first step is for the teacher to show students concretely what tones blend and what tones do not blend. A teacher can sing or play with a student, or select pairs of students to show the differences between blended sounds and unblended sounds. Once students begin to discriminate between blended and unblended sounds, they are ready for the next step—judging the degree that the sounds blend.

The teacher can ask students to recognize if the sounds are blended, nearly blended, barely blended or unblended. When students start making these judgments, the teacher can see the degree to which students understand. The observations help the teacher decide how to continue the instruction. The teacher may reteach by selecting different demonstrators, instruments, or pitches, or asking different students to judge. These techniques may all occur before students begin to show progress. Since blend is less tangible than motor skills such as correct fingerings, the teacher may need to be more persistent. They may reteach the first couple of steps over the course of several lessons before the students begin to truly discriminate, but eventually both student and teacher should be able to measure some progress.

When students can recognize differences, the teacher can ask students to play with blended and unblended sounds upon command—but again, the teacher should not expect dramatic progress too soon. If students can notice and show some improvement in producing blended or unblended sounds, the teaching is beginning to have an impact. The more students do this correctly, the firmer their understanding of blend, and the greater the realization that a blended sound is an attainable and concrete goal.

A near final step, which could occur once students show they are improving their blending skills, would be

for them to describe how they achieve a blended sound. At this point, students may discover just how imprecise or inadequate words really are. Even so, there may be times when students could benefit from discussing how they individually adjust their playing to achieve blend. The discussion might suggest ways for other students to make the physical changes, or help another student simply believe blend can be achieved.

The discussion may only reinforce the student's belief in an understanding of blend and how it is achieved. These sessions also can foster a mutually helpful environment that encourages students to learn—not only from the teacher, but from each other. Finally, the discussions may allow the teacher to bring out certain key points: music-making requires both judgments and adjustments in sound. One can reach a higher level of quality in performance by making these judgments. Words alone inevitably fall short as a way to describe music making.

One contributor explained an approach to teaching blend that shows how the teaching of blend can be successful. He said, "I first evaluate *why* the sound changed and then decide how to correct it. I do not try to have individuals sound like a carbon copy of one another. Instead, I *blend* their different tones together. The important goal for them is to get it right at least once. From there, it is easier to move forward since there is an experience to build upon for both the teacher and the student. For them, the clinchers are *hearing* the change toward a better blend and *feeling* differently as they play. I also try to carry this over to their lessons for that week.

*(R. G. Conlee)*

## TEACHING AND CLARIFYING BLEND

### What blending is

Blending means achieving a meshing of colors and a meshing of balance.

*(Larry Rachleff)*

### Getting and hearing a blend

I analyze problems and break such skills as blend,

281

balance, articulation, and rhythm down into smaller chunks, skills or ideas. I do this with blend, balance, articulation, rhythm, etc. Suppose I am working on blend with eighth and ninth graders. To have the tone colors of individuals mesh, I take small numbers of people on an easy part, such as a chord or a short passage. We work and work on it until they hear when they have accomplished the blend in that spot. Besides blend, we also work on balance and intonation in this way.

Getting a blend yourself is different from hearing it done by someone else in another part of the band, though both are important. I want to have them personally hear how they adjust and work into the blend. I work on even the smallest segments, day after day, but not for a long period. Since junior high school students need to be more active, I may work on woodwinds one day, brass on one day, and the flutes on the next day. I rotate this, keeping people moving and working, always on listening.

*(R. G. Conlee)*

### Blending to the model tone

Though there are different sounds in a section, we ask them to blend their unique sound with the better model from the section.

*(Richard Fischer)*

I try to define the sound for which we are striving. If we are blending instruments in a single section, I may have one person play. I then say, "This is what it should sound like." Then I have every section member play three or four times until they get a blend with the first player. Then I have them repeat their playing of a blended sounded several times. While doing this, I say, "Trumpets, make it sound like one person instead of six."

In another passage, the flutes, clarinets, and oboe may be in unison or they could be playing in harmony. To help them get a blend, I have each instrument play separately first. Then, I'll have the instrumentalists play in different combinations. If the clarinets are doubling the flute part in the high register, I may ask them to, "Play a little flute." Then I'll say to the flutes, "You have to play some clarinet here."

To do section playing, they have to match color and listen to each other. This is also true with intonation. You cannot tune sounds of two tone qualities that are extremely different from each other. When this happens, it's very difficult to hear if one person is —er than the other, and it is also difficult to hear if they are blended appropriately.

*(Thomas Stone)*

### Teaching blend in rehearsal

We try to have a section learn and understand how to keep their section's sound inside the sound of another section. I combine words like "horn-sax sound" to portray a certain tone color that is a combination of two instrument's sounds. This means that one section's or one instrument's volume should not be dominating when they try to get a blend. The functional definition means that you play with a volume level that allows one to hear the other color.

*(Robert Floyd)*

I sometimes have students show others what it is like for one sound to be "inside" or subordinate or dominant to another. For example, if the trumpets are to be inside the French horns, they cannot be so unless they hear the horn's sound. That makes a reduced volume almost automatic, since they must be underneath in volume or they cannot hear the horns. Students also learn by hearing other students achieve blend because it helps the listeners grasp the sound of blend.

Saying, "stay underneath" or "get inside" other peoples' sound is an effective way to achieve a particular blend and to control ensemble tone color. Instead of offering an abstract suggestion, such as, "bring out the flute part," simply say "balance."

I find myself saying, "Saxophones, clarinets, and flutes have the theme here. Clarinets, get inside the sound of the saxophones and flutes." In another case, "Make this melody sound like a big flute," or "Everyone, please get inside the flute sound." By doing this, the conductor is sharing with the students what you have decided about the color of the piece or that passage.

I usually give them a quick explanation of why I have made that decision. It is very important to define for yourself. The conductor is the main interpreter: the one who decides which instrument sound should be dominant. Sharing that with the students is important because it also teaches them about the craft of composition.

*(Gary Hill)*

### Using colors to describe blend

To get a blend and a section sound, students first must have a common approach to what their instrument should sound like. With college students, I tell them that it's too dark or too light and they are able to adjust their pitch and tone.

For younger students, I also would use colors. For example, I might use this approach in this instance. The clarinets and flutes are playing and they are scored in octaves relatively high in their range. I say, "I would have this more of a blue color, even if it's a pale blue. Your tone and playing are almost a white color, because it's so bright and hard." Through trial and error, they learn what I mean when I use words naming colors. Then, once the student plays it correctly, the two key words are "That's it."

*(John Williamson)*

# CHAPTER FOUR

# BREATHING AND AIR

Considering how much teachers talk about breathing and air use, it is surprising that students use air less well than teachers would like. Frederick Fennell reportedly said, "People forget that these are wind instruments—and performers should play them with wind." Were performers in the habit of using air properly, there would have had no need for Frederick Fennell to make that statement.

If teachers or students work on breathing in isolation, the situation will not improve noticeably. When using air, one learns that air is interrelated with many aspects of wind-playing, particularly tone and phrasing, but also posture, intonation, style, dynamics, phrasing, audiation, and blend. While many teachers discuss air and breathing as a separate issue, they really function among many other interacting factors.

The use of air, or proper breathing technique, is tied to the idea of the tone. Teachers must have a clear idea themselves of a good tone to teach others how proper breathing will create that tone. Students also need a clear idea of tone, so they can develop what they have been taught.

Since the backgrounds of students are so different, they must experience many modes of instruction to grasp and apply breathing successfully. If teachers insist upon the development of beautiful tone through proper breathing, the student will learn that proper air use is vital in creating a beautiful tone and a musical phrase. They can learn that the relationship of proper breath to tone is the foundation of wind playing.

## IDEAS AND SUGGESTIONS ABOUT BREATHING

### The importance of breathing

Breath is the single-most fundamental aspect of sound production a band has to learn. Until the students learn this, a band is not going to sound good. If students have decent equipment and breathe correctly, that takes care of about eighty percent of tone quality problems. Tone color, duration, power, pitch, sound, range, endurance, and control are all related to breathing correctly.

*(Robert E. Foster)*

Breathing affects tone, intonation, blend, and balance. The same constrictions or deviations in air support that cause uncharacteristic tone quality can also cause intonation problems. They go hand-in-hand. This gives me one principle, the development of breath, with which to deal with all characteristics or parts of the quality of sound.

*(Donald Casey)*

I often tell my students, "There is no person in this room, including myself, who doesn't have to *continually* think and prepare himself to play a wind instrument." The air and air pressure are so important, and proper air use or control does not happen automatically.

*(Terry A. Oxley)*

When I first started teaching I heard people say, "Oh, they lack support, ta-da, ta-da, ta-da." I thought that was just something that they told people when they didn't have anything else to say. Not much later, I found out what it really meant.

You know what I teach? I teach blowing all day long—blow, air, push. We are on students day after day, lesson after lesson, to put a large amount of air through their horn. I mean if you get a person to put air through their horn their chances are fifty percent or better of having a good sound.

As one hears bands, judges bands, and works with other people's students, you just know that air use is rarely developed. It is seldom that the students have been taught how to breathe and blow. I mean, it *must* be hard to do because most people rarely bother to do it. It is something that has to be done and one must be on them always.

*(Lewis Larson)*

### Avoiding litigation when teaching breathing

I don't touch them anymore. Teachers cannot grab students by the waist to help breathing as they used to do. I am very careful about where they or I put my hands. I don't want a parent to come back and say, "You had my son in class and touched his vital parts." Since teachers must be very careful, I never work alone with a student;

there always is more than one student in the classroom. I do not leave myself open for criticism. An individual student could say, "Yeah, the teacher did such and such," and there are no witnesses to refute or prove what went on.

*(Sandra P. Thompson)*

### Terminology and breathing

I do not talk to students about diaphragms. They have no idea what that is. Instead, I call this the stomach, or I talk about breathing near the "belly button" or using a waistline breath.

*(Jack Brookshire)*

I don't like the term "breath support." Young students especially think support means tension or tightening up as though they were going to support a desk or left a chair above their heads. I break down breathing so we are talking about *how*, not *what* it is. I ask students to inhale so the air comes in and goes down to the bottom of their lungs. It does not go into the stomach, but we feel the waist expand. I have them touch the muscles in their back and around their waist to feel if this area opens up or expands. To breathe while playing, we expand and contract those muscles as the air is going in and out. While doing this, we should not be rigid and tight.

The air should be supporting the tone so the muscles can work on that air stream. Support means moving a steady, fast air stream with lots of air through the horn. We can compare regular breathing to instrument breathing. We see that we are taking in more air faster or slower and blowing it out faster or slower than we would normally.

There is no big secret here. I think the more we try to use little techniques to teach breathing, the more we confuse the students. We get them to tighten, and that's exactly what we don't want to happen. We want them to be relaxed and open, keeping the muscles as free as possible.

*(Dwayne P. Sagen)*

### Conducting helps breathing

The key to everything is how you use the breath. It is kind of interesting to see student teachers. They say the right things: "Take this deep breath. Breathe all the way down to your toes. You've got to fill fully. You've got to do all this and that." Then they give such a minuscule preparatory beat that no one would be encouraged to take a breath.

*(Craig Kirchhoff)*

I believe that we need to look more at the relationship between gesture and breathing, plus the relationship of breathing to basic body language. Without saying a word to the group, three different conductors, for example Bill Revelli, Fred Fennell, and John Paynter, can create three entirely different sounds with their basic gestures. People make the sound different by the way they

gesture. I can make a very quick kind of slashing movement or I can make a much slower gesture with much more resistance to it. I then may ask them, "Now, which is the more powerful gesture?" Most of the time they vote for the slower gesture. The slower gesture seems to imply more resistance, more energy, more weight, and more connection. We must move our arms or the baton in the way that we want our students to breathe and blow their instruments.

It goes back to Ray Still's very perceptive comments in an article that I read. He said, "You know we love Solti, but Solti tries for hours and hours in rehearsal to get this Giulini-like sound. We really try for him but we can't do it, and he can't do it either because it's just not the way he moves."

*(Craig Kirchhoff)*

### From the pelvis through the horn

Since concepts of tone can come from experiences outside the rehearsal, I work with tone a lot inside the rehearsal, even with university groups. I do this so each student does not bring in his own concept of sound exclusively. I work on tone quality through the syllable "haaaa" to achieve a flow of power from the pelvic area through and out the instrument. "Haaa" is excellent for this as it opens the whole passageway from the pelvis through the horn.

*(Frank Bencriscutto)*

### Hear the sound first, then breathe

We may be wasting our time teaching students how to breathe rather than teaching them how to audiate (hearing the sound before it is present)—that is, to develop the skill of knowing in the mind the sound of the next phrase before playing it. If they know this musically, they will take the right amount of air they need to play that phrase. Then we need not "hammer" students as much about breathing.

If they don't audiate the next phrase, the problem with students' playing may appear to the teacher as a lack of air or air support. Instead, what is lacking is the audiation of the music to be played. If they truly audiate, they will audiate in phrases or musical statements and will prepare to play with enough air to perform what they audiate. Therefore, to the director they will not appear to have a breathing problem.

This is parallel to the unconscious or involuntary taking in of enough air to sustain a spoken sentence. We rarely run out of air when we talk, because we know what we are going to say. We know how much air it takes to say what we want to say. This includes all necessary accommodations for the statement's length, inflection, emphasis, dynamics, style, and meaning. With a musical instrument, taking in air can become as involuntary as it is in speaking unnecessary.

*(Richard Grunow)*

### Basing tone and performance on the pre-hearing of the music

We hurt students when we start them playing whole notes, which they "perform" without audiating. The parallel is sitting with them and teaching them to say one word at a time. For example, say "the" fourteen times with a gap of silence between, then fourteen times say the word "cat."

If we allow ourselves to teach them how to read words in a way that also compels us to simultaneously teach them how to breathe, we create the problem. This whole issue of audiation determining breathing, is one of many enlightening things I have learned while working on the *Jump Right In: The Instrumental Series.*

*(Richard Grunow)*

### Use images to teach breathing

Playing with cool, fast air is preferable to playing with warm, slow air. I say, "Blow cool and fast air, but just a bit less air for soft." I do not encourage the notion of slow air because the support can diminish. The image of warm, slow air is useful more to feel and influence an open throat.

*(Robert Floyd)*

### Comparing performance breathing to natural breathing

Breathing is not different from what they already do. They take a breath as usual, just deeper.

*(Robert Floyd)*

### Using visual association to teach breathing

I have demonstrated breathing by showing the air as it escapes from a balloon. I can vary the opening from very small to larger and show that the air in the balloon is like the air in our lungs.

*(Roman Palmer)*

We talk about the release of air like a slow leak from their bicycle tire. There is all that pressure, and yet it doesn't come out suddenly because the opening is small. We also have practiced blowing into bread bags to discover how much air they can put in the bag. This is kinesthetic and when they see the bag expand and contract—it's a visual thing.

I have told students that when they are exhaling the air they should feel like they are a grandfather or grandmother blowing out sixty candles on their birthday cake: take a large breath and use one steady stream.

Many students pull gum out of their mouths and let it snap back. I say, "Pulling the sound out of the mouth is like pulling gum out of the mouth." They catch on quickly and begin sustaining a sound. I have them blow the air and start it with a "tow" sound to sustain phrases. Then, I may have them take their fingers, put them to their mouth, and pull the air out of their mouth so the experience is physical.

*(Nancy Plantinga)*

### Developing the air and the tone's body early

At the junior high level, it's very important that the students can play at a fortissimo level and that a student gets the air into the horn. I think that often music teachers at the junior high level don't let them blow. Continually giving them the palm of the hand hurts them later in their musical life. You've got to *blow* the horn.

*(William Long)*

### Air pressure and air speed

Air pressure inside your body remains constant through the entire range. The only thing that changes is the speed of the air that comes out of the mouth.

*(Richard Putzier)*

### Relaxing the throat

The person who swallows swords at the carnival will practice swallowing swords to relax the throat and overcome the natural gag response. To some extent, that's what wind players have to learn—to relax all the throat muscles so they allow the air through, especially when playing loud. Wind players are putting a lot of air through while trying to remain relaxed; the normal untrained person would tighten up.

*(L. Keating Johnson)*

### Volume, opening up, and feeling back pressure

I think playing fortissimo builds muscles when one uses a large amount of air. If you take the edge off the tone and open up the sound more, you can get even more air through the horn. I want students to blow so much air that they nearly overcome the back pressure of the instrument. Defeating the back pressure means there is too much air and they have lost control. If they can still feel the back pressure, they have not lost control.

*(John W. LaCava)*

### Reducing tension

I do exercises in breathing to build air and muscle strength, which helps them relax and prevents tension.

*(John W. LaCava)*

### Developing tone

There's the notion of musculature, playing long tones and lip slurs, and working on flexibility. Another skill, though, is breath control and proper breathing. If they're using the wrong muscles in their necks and they're closing off their necks, they're not going to get a characteristic sound. If they're breathing wrong, they're not going to get the characteristic sound. If all those kinds of actions are working well, the next thing that I work on is providing them models of tone.

*(Thomas Stone)*

### Building the air stream

We work on staccato about half way or a third of the

way through the year: we work primarily on legato from the beginning. They have to connect everything. I often have them slur things that are to be tongued, especially if it is in legato style. I do that a lot to develop air connection, then add the tongue for legato style. I am after a sustained breath.

*(John W. LaCava)*

### Mastering air speed

When I deal with the problem of open throat (on brass), I don't deal with the throat at all. I strengthen the air supply and the embouchure. When those two things get strong enough, they don't close their throat anymore. They don't want to and they don't have to, so they don't. They might do it, but only because they have to compress the air stream. They must do this to get the air fast enough to get up into the upper register of a brass instrument without tension.

*(Charles Olson)*

## Teaching Breathing

### Singing improves breathing

In the fifth grade we sing simple tunes like" Mary Had a Little Lamb." I sing for them and they sing it back. I tell them that they can make a better sound on the instrument if they can make a good sound with their voices. I show them and ask them to open their mouths and keep their teeth apart. This also develops better inhalation and breathing.

*(Jack Brookshire)*

### Finding how and where to breathe

Ask students to put their right hand on their left shoulder and their left hand on their right shoulder. I say, "Do not move your hands as you take a breath." This counteracts the tension and raising of the muscles of the chest cage. To reinforce this, say, "There is a bone cage around the lung area that limits the expansion upward. Expansion downward is available that gives one about twice the air capacity." You also will have a sound based upon the strong set of muscles around the body below the rib cage area. That won't let you down.

*(Robert E. Foster)*

### Teaching the inhale through a two-step process

The basic thing is filling up completely. I want them to fill up in the diaphragm first, then look down to see that the stomach is expanding. The second stage is to inhale and have the chest expand. Then on the exhale, practice the reverse. When you exhale have the chest go down first.

Breathing is actually not a two-stage process. The whole operation works smoothly in one step. Students should fill up completely and, as they exhale, let the chest region slowly deflate as it does when they're

asleep or when they're yawning. Many students want to keep the chest up in a real tight, rigid way. This can be a strong habit.

*(L. Keating Johnson)*

### Developing a simple natural approach

To develop breath support, try to get them to think about it as a natural process. Don't make a big deal of it. The lungs have a natural elasticity. You do not have to go through all sorts of muscular contortions to expel air.

I try these phrases to coach them to let the air escape from their lungs: "Allow the air to go through the instrument" instead of saying, "Make the air go faster." I'll say "Allow the air to come out quicker." I say this so they don't think they should be pushing anything. That encourages students to allow things to happen in the ways that they naturally should happen.

*(Francis Marciniak)*

### The quality of the inhale

I spend time asking them to concentrate on the quality of the breath, specifically the sound of the breath. Is it a high sound or low sound on the inhale? I work almost one hundred percent with inhale instead of the exhale. I try to get them to concentrate on the quality of that breath. In other words, you inhale with the tone in mind and with the exhale in mind, and you inhale in the tempo and the style of the music.

*(Craig Kirchhoff)*

### Coordinating the inhale

Most groups do not coordinate the inhale, but if the group *breathes* together it probably will *play* together. I get them to concentrate on the quality of the breath and to listen to the breath. I'll tell them to close their eyes and to start a note themselves with their eyes closed. This obviously is without my conducting. Of course, they giggle and laugh. Eventually, someone is courageous enough to take a breath. The only way they can possibly come in, is by listening to the breath impulse.

*(Craig Kirchhoff)*

### Defining the size of the inhale

I try to get the band to play with more support and more air speed. I say, "Play concert F and hold it as long as you can. We are going to have a contest." Then I give them a preparatory gesture. They take in a huge breath as if they are going to hold it for four days; then, I just stop. They don't play the note. Then I say, "Okay, that's the way you are supposed to breathe on every note." The object is to get them to be very conscious of this and take a big, full breath. Then I say, "Okay, breathe that way every time you play your horn. That's the way the breath is always supposed to work."

*(Donald Wilcox)*

### Initiating the tone with breath

I say, "Blow the tip of the tongue out of the way." If that does not work, I make them make breath attacks, which also helps embouchure formation.

*(John W. LaCava)*

### Fostering the open throat

I roll a piece of paper into a tube and put the tube in the mouth. They cannot close their throat when they inhale through the tube. They try inhaling and exhaling with the tube in their mouth and discover that they cannot close their throats this way.

*(Robert Grechesky)*

I will often have them take the clarinet bell off and put the bell in their mouths. When they breathe this way, they are a whole new person: it opens their throats and suddenly they are breathing correctly just by opening the mouth and putting their teeth on the bell. I think their teeth are the key to it.

*(Terry A. Oxley)*

In learning to inhale, I found students doing all the wrong things such as raising shoulders, closing their throats, breathing through their noses, etc. To teach them to inhale and to stress correct breathing, I take a piece of plastic pipe that is three quarters of an inch in diameter and three or four inches long. They place part of it in and part of it out of the mouth. Ask them to breathe in and notice how quickly the air gets to the lungs and how much air goes in. Have them do that several times. Then leave the tube in place and blow out. Then I expect them to replicate this when they pick up their instruments.

*(Donald DeRoche)*

### Teaching the exhale

It doesn't take that much pressure to overcome atmospheric pressure. It just takes a little bit. I train them to inhale in a relaxed, slow fashion. This is done in an exercise that lasts for five beats. While they are doing this, they should be shaping their mouths as though they were saying "oh" or "ah" as they do when yawning. Then, I ask them to exhale in the same fashion. Usually when we exhale we get tension. I try to train them to be relaxed as they inhale and then practice exhaling so they establish again the relaxed response in the muscles.

*(L. Keating Johnson)*

### The release

I heard a teacher showing a release that had no change in the tone quality at all and no motion of the embouchure. He said, "Don't stick your tongue in the mouthpiece, don't move the mouthpiece or anything like that." He was trying to get the group to release with no change at all. He said, "I've always taught them just to stop the breath, and it will quit." But, when some students do

that they close the throat or they move the tongue or something.

He told them that the breath has to flow either one way or the other. On a release, particularly on an abrupt release of a loud tone, you very slightly reverse the flow of the breath. You reverse the flow of air just a snip, you don't inhale through the horn. I mean, nobody likes to taste or smell valve oil.

*(Donald Wilcox)*

### Teaching staggered breathing

We sometimes play chorales either with or without the fermatas. If we ignore the fermatas, the sound of the band is like an organ. This points up the need for staggered breathing and the avoidance of a breath on a bar line. I ask them to work these things out among themselves. Acquiring this skill is important since breathing skills carry over to any piece with a phrase.

*(Carl A. Bly)*

### Preventing tension

One important thing is to blow through the resistance when one feels the beginning of tightening up.

*(R. G. Conlee)*

I use the analogy of the garden hose. The diaphragm is the faucet, and the embouchure is the nozzle. You can open the nozzle to let the air out in a big slow stream, or open it much less and let out a hard fast stream. You can increase and decrease pressure by having the same amount or volume of air going through a smaller space. You also could keep the space the same, while increasing the pressure from the diaphragm.

*(Robert Grechesky)*

### Breathing, muscles, and posture

To play in a sitting position, I talk about a center point on a fulcrum. Your body is either going forward or back. If it's going back, even with a back support from the chair there are still problems. I read many, many years ago, of research that contends that a person uses the lower stomach muscles to support the body and in doing so can constrict the throat. Therefore, the top of the body should be slightly bent forward so the lower back muscles come into play. This releases the muscles on the front part of the body from the role of holding the body upright and, therefore, releases tension. Thus, this can minimize the tendency to constrict the throat.

*(Terry A. Oxley)*

The best way to play is standing up. When you're sitting, you should feel as though you were standing. If students have their legs crossed, I try to make them aware of their ribs and how they crush down when in this position. I have them bend over at the waist. This helps them feel their shoulders and their upper chest begin to expand as they do lower abdominal breathing.

*(Timothy Mahr)*

### Aids and exercises to check and teach breathing

Attach a two-inch piece of plastic tubing with a one-inch diameter to a gallon-size plastic bag from the grocery store. Put the end of the tube inside the bag and wrap a rubber band around the tube and the bag to prevent a leak. I ask students to fill the bag with air so they can see how much air is in it. Then they inhale the air from the bag so they can do deep breathing. For a while they can inhale and exhale the same air, but if they do this too long they build up an excess of carbon dioxide and get "light headed." (If they are not using a bag and are breathing repeatedly, they would be taking in too much oxygen, hyperventilate, and also get "light headed." If rapid breathing either with the bag or without is carried to an extreme it could be dangerous as it may lead to students fainting.) It's "amazing" to find out how little air they use. The point is that the throat must be open. When they put the plastic tube in their mouth, it is unlikely the throat will be closed.

We have them fill up the bag on four counts (quarter = 60). Then they breathe in for four counts. We do this six times. It usually takes at least six interchanges for them to see if they getting all the air in and back out. It takes at least three of the six interchanges to get the process going correctly.

We then pick up the horns. We usually play, perhaps concert F or another easy note. If it sounds good, fine. If not, we go right back to the bag. Next (with the bag), they blow out for three counts and only get one beat to inhale the air back in. Then we go to a triplet figure, blowing four counts in triplets, followed by one count to breathe in.

Then blow a triplet with the "hoo" "hoo" "hoo" sound. At the end of the four counts of triplets they fill up the bag. The students do these things six times. Then we progress to eighth notes. Now, they blow into the bag for seven counts blowing out and one half a count to breath in. We also do this six times.

*(Ross Kellan)*

### Teaching breathing through literature

The Claude Smith piece, based on the *Doxology* and Dello Joio's *Variations on a Theme of Haydn* are excellent performance and teaching pieces. Both require staggered breathing to attain good long phrasing.

*(Carl A. Bly)*

### Using images with kids

I use the term "hurricane" or "tornado" to describe how fast the air goes, especially, on high notes for brass.

*(Steven Cooper)*

With younger students, I pretend that I have drilled their stomach out to create a hole in their navel. I tell them, "The air is going to rush in there, and it's going to feel really cold." That's just weird enough that they respond. "The air is not going to come in up above, it's going to come in down there." They can imagine the cold air coming in there.

*(Timothy Mahr)*

### Using images to make the air last

If students say that can't get to the end of a phrase on one breath, I say, "I want you to imagine that you're under water at the bottom of a pool and you need to get all the way to the top. I bet, if you were in this situation, you would stretch your air enough to make it to the top more than ninety nine times out of a hundred. You wouldn't have to take that big gulp in the middle." I remind them of this frequently.

*(Sandra P. Thompson)*

### Using visual imagery

I use "dot-to-dot" with my teaching and I relate the note heads to the connect-the-dot drawings we did as little kids. The air stream is the line that you draw right through those dots. I say, "Make sure that the breath goes right through the center of each note." This helps intonation and sustains the air stream because the line they exhale is the line that connects the dots (notes). I find it focuses them mentally on the note, as well as improves their support of the phrase.

*(Timothy Mahr and Donald DeRoche)*

If they're playing phrases in a choppy fashion, I will say, "Use your air to string the beads, these notes are like beads that have no string through them. You need to use your air to make that string."

*(Thomas Stone)*

### Using descriptions

As a result of the inhale the rib-cage should go out, and as they exhale, the rib-cage contracts! It should go out, since more space or more room is needed inside you to make way for the air. I also use the term "stomach" when teaching them to breathe.

*(Steven Cooper)*

### Using games and questioning

We have used games to sustain a tone to see who can go the longest. When one can't go as long as the other their curiosity is there. "How come you went further than I did?" That's when we really get into the conversations about breathing.

*(Nancy Plantinga)*

### Removing undesirable breathing habits

It is difficult to fight well-established and poor habits. It easily can take six or more new tries to break the old and begin the new habit. Sometimes, the fastest way to break the habit is for them to recognize it when they see it in someone else. I've had students observe lessons of another student who is farther along. By observing they see things that they can't see when they're playing themselves.

If wind players let their chest operate the way the chest and its muscles are designed, their sound, all of a sudden, becomes rich and more full. They hear the sound, but they still must duplicate all that complicated system of muscle responses. That can be tough because when they pick up their instruments, all the previous responses come back. It's difficult for them to let go of poor habits because they are so patterned.

*(L. Keating Johnson)*

### Air and rhythm

A rhythm can have an eighth note followed by two sixteenth notes. I call the sixteenth notes the inside notes (on the weaker part of the pulse). They need two or three times the amount of air to balance to the outside notes which are on the beat.

*(Timothy Mahr)*

### Using feedback to clarify inhaling

They can bring either a belt or a rope to class. I seat them in a row with students standing behind those in the chairs. I have them put the belt or the rope around their bodies, just above the belt line and right around the "belly button" area. I do this so both students can physically feel the breathing taking place down in the diaphragm area.

Before they inhale they "cinch" themselves up. This allows them to see and feel when they take a breath in the right spot. The rope tightens and when they blow the air out the rope loosens. They are sitting or standing one behind the other so they can hold each other's rope. In a way, it's a kind of game. In addition to the feeling of their own diaphragm, they can feel it happening in their neighbor. If they do not feel it occur in their neighbor, then they can remind them of what they should be doing.

I also give my sixth graders a piece of single-ply tissue and they find an empty spot on the wall. We put the tissue against the wall. Then we draw the air in and blow on the tissue. They are to use the air stream to hold it against the wall.

Sometimes I'll put two or three people on the job. One works with the belt or rope that is around the waist of the breather(s), and the other two work with the tissue. I realized that if you put two students on one piece of tissue they could practice staggered breathing.

With this variation, they see how long they can hold that tissue with the diaphragmatic breathing. They get points if they can do it that way. If the person behind them (holding the rope) finds they are doing it with chest breathing, then they don't get the points. The student holding the rope is the referee and they call the fouls.

*(Gordon Nelson)*

### Composing to build tone and breath

The band and I compose pieces in rehearsals. One is a "sound-mass" piece and I use it to develop long tones and tone quality. To start, I say, "When I point to you I want you to play with a good attack on a note somewhere in your normal range. Don't try to pick something that's extremely high or extremely low. Give me any note you wish, but I want you to start with a perfect attack and hold a beautiful long tone. We want marvelous sound. Once you run out of breath then stop, but not until you're through. I want good long sounds on low- or mid-range tones." I point to various people to get different combinations going and they pick any note they wish. However, even on a forte it still must be good sound.

With percussion instruments, I'll start them and cut them off when I want them to stop. Bowed instruments such as the string bass use one length of the bow only and that asks them to use the bow properly.

I also can gesture crescendos and decrescendos, or I can cut them off abruptly and start them again. If I want the entire group to play, I can sweep my arm through the whole band.

As soon as my hand passes their head, they can start their long note. We can create some very interesting sounds this way. It is also possible to build duets, trios, and quartets, as well as using the entire group. There are several ways to construct a sound-mass piece that can build tone and support through composition. The effects can be startling.

*(John C. McManus)*

### Building support, sound, and concentration

When I warm up my band before concerts, we always use long tones. Then we do a diaphragm vibrato with all instruments. When I push my hand in toward them they play louder, pulsating the tone in a slow vibrato that I may speed up or slow down. I do this because it teaches them breath support. They can't do the loud to soft pulsating unless they're supporting with the air.

This also focuses their minds because they are thinking about their stomachs and breath work. To pulsate the tone, they can't think of anything else except what they're doing. It directs them to musical and sound issues, focuses their minds, and reduces talking and nervousness.

*(Frank Schulz)*

### Breathing with synchronization

I build playing and breathing together through the use of breathing in tempo. I say, "Take a breath and say "du" on the downbeat." I repeat this several times so it becomes synchronized. I sometimes say, "If you breathe together or if a choir breathes together it's magnificent. If an ensemble breathes together, it is beautiful."

If new people come in to the group, it is simplified every year because the old guard understands exactly what's happening. The new students start to breathe because everybody's breathing. They do what their neighbor is doing.

*(Richard J. Suddendorf)*

### Using conducting and images

Playing slow, sustained passages has a lot to do with breathing and air flow. I do a lot with my baton, stretching and trying to have them feel the breathing of the phrase.

*(Thomas Stone)*

### Using simulation to teach breathing

I say, "Blow all the way to the bell," and I use the "sizzle" test. This test is saying "ssssssssssssssss" on the exhale and holding it as long as they can.

*(Jack Brookshire)*

For many students it works to have them inhale and exhale on "aah." I can hear it and they get an open feeling. I often have them imagine a tube that starts at the bottom of their stomach that they should fill up. I try these techniques so they breathe deeply.

*(Terry A. Oxley)*

### Practicing the breathing process

With the marching band, I try to increase the air's intensity and speed. I have them inhale and "hiss" for a sustained period of four, six, or eight counts. Then they take in a good big breath on a preparatory gesture and sustain that for a long time. This helps them in the habit of rationing the air.

*(Donald Wilcox)*

# DYNAMICS

Teaching dynamics often has something in common with teaching articulations: the basic dynamics and articulations can be taught by isolating them as separate tasks and entities. As is done with articulations, one approach is to teach the different dynamic levels while playing warm-up scales, chord progressions, or chorales. Students learn to play gradations from piano to forte, to play crescendo and decrescendo, and to perform other basic dynamic changes such as subito piano or sforzando. Some teachers decide the order that dynamics are taught and make this choice part of their curriculum and planning. Another approach is to teach these skills through the literature in rehearsal; each of the dynamic occurrences are taught when they are called for in the music. The first approach is from the particular to the general; the second approach is from the general to the particular; and some teachers use both approaches.

Teachers must be on alert, especially with the first approach, because students often conclude that dynamic levels are absolutes and they ought to play them exactly as written. Students usually do not believe that they are relative and rarely absolute. If students continue believing dynamic levels are absolute, it is difficult to decide which level or which rendition of subito piano, for example, is appropriate because their concept of the performance and the interpretation of dynamics can be too inflexible.

Whichever approach the teacher uses—the particular to the general or vice versa—students eventually must learn to make changes so the phrase is played more musically. If students can learn to be flexible, they can go beyond believing dynamic markings are absolute; changing dynamics is a series of decisions that considers the musical context so the result is musical and expressive.

## MUSICAL CONSIDERATIONS AND DYNAMICS

### We need dynamic change

Musical notes don't just sit there, they should crescendo or diminuendo. One should make mountains—not cliffs! Don't drop off or run into a cliff. Unless the composer specifies a certain dynamic change, dynamics should happen in the latter part of the phrase: don't let them happen too soon.

*(Carl A. Bly)*

### Establishing levels within the entire piece

I like to relate the dynamics in one part of a piece to the dynamics in the entire piece. To do so, I use the terms macro and micro dynamics. Finding the macro-dynamics means to find where dynamics reach any extreme levels, for example fortissimo or pianissimo. We also consider the dynamic levels in relation to other works of this composer or other composers. This places the dynamic contrasts of this piece in a proper musical relationship to other compositions. For example, the loudest level in a Mozart transcription or wind serenade is not as strong as the loudest section of Clifton Williams or Nelhybel.

Finding the micro dynamics means to decide how each section contributes to the dynamic shape of the entire piece. Grasping this makes performances of one piece truly different dynamically from another.

*(Richard Fischer)*

### Contrasts

To find dynamic contrasts, we relate the music in Section A to Section B, and to the whole. The failure to take this into consideration could mean that all pieces performed by a group sound the same. The patterns of dynamic levels and contrasts are not absolute—a forte is not the same in all pieces. Fortes are different, depending upon the piece.

*(Richard Fischer)*

### Absolute dynamic markings

On occasion I ask, "Can anyone tell me what forte means?" The answer might be either loud, strong, full, or big. Then I say, "What do loud, strong, big, or other terms mean?" Soon someone will define loud as being the opposite of soft. Then we are on the right track. Contrast is the key.

This concept is important because there is no absolute value to dynamics as there is with tempo. Dynamic levels are a matter of clearly heard contrasts. If the composer asks the performer to contrast one phrase or passage with another, then the contrast must be perceived by the listener. The differences must be audible to every person in the hall. Performers also must remember that the degree of contrast will vary depending on the composition, the period, and the composer.

*(Richard Floyd)*

### The effect of mutes and texture

As a trumpet player, I know that dynamics are relative to the musical situation. Composers often mark passages too soft for mutes, for instance. We tell students in lessons, "If you see a part marked muted or con sordino and it's marked pianissimo, you should always raise the volume at least one level. If the part is a solo passage, you should raise the level even more."

I think dynamics are also relative to the texture around you and the relation of dynamics to the style of the passage. Some teachers make a strong case for a forte in the dynamic mezzo forte; therefore, people may be playing mezzo forte too softly. When they do that they are not allowing themselves the full dynamic spectrum from f or fff, to p or ppp.

*(Robert Levy)*

### Moving through points of tension and repose

When making a musical statement, anticipating or expecting a musical arrival point is very important. I tell the students to know where these points of musical arrival occur. A single arrival point may not be the most important one in the piece, but it is the point to which everything prior to this is leading.

Therefore, we have to make it sound like this arrival point is our goal. As we do this, we are handing something to the audience. If that high point isn't the highest goal, then you take it back away from them. Once reached, we begin working our way to another musical high point. Once students realize this idea, they start making many more accurate decisions on their own.

*(Terry A. Oxley)*

### Dynamic markings are relative, no matter what players think

Dynamic markings are not absolute, but the students want one rule that will hold forever. If you give them choices, some of them just go "bonkers." They do not realize that they must think constantly.

In certain cases, when you are talking about ensemble balance, everything is relative. We must decide what is most important. For example, is there a solo and can you hear the solo? I will say, "If you can't hear the solo, then either the solo has to come up or the rest of it has to come down." I may ask questions. "Does it sound good? Do you like the sound here? Is this what we want? If not, how can we change it?"

*(Richard Putzier)*

### Decisions about dynamics

Making decisions about dynamics is really a part of the score study a conductor is responsible for before rehearsing the piece. Approach the score asking questions. For example, "What are the contrasts? Where are the expectations?" or, "Are the dynamics appropriate to the style?" The question I often ask young players is, "What does forte mean?" Invariably they answer, "It means loud." Forte doesn't mean *loud* it means *strong*. A strong forte in Ralph Vaughan Williams is clearly different from a forte in Karel Husa. The former are less strong and more gentle. Students have to be made to understand that. Answers to dynamics go back to score study.

*(Larry Rachleff)*

### Problems with dynamic changes

Students tend to play a diminuendo much more abruptly than a crescendo. If I ask them for a four or eight beat crescendo on a whole note or a tied whole note, it usually will be a pretty gradual crescendo. But, diminuendos usually start at a high volume and suddenly drop about three notches below where they should be at that moment. Then there is nothing left for the last three or four beats of the diminuendo. This problem has been sketched on the board more than anything else. I draw pictures to show them how the diminuendo needs to be played and compare that to drawings of what they need to change in their playing.

*(Lance Schultz)*

### Dynamics on certain instruments

If the saxophone is in the low register and it says forte, watch out! For some instruments, you must decrease the dynamic level in certain areas of their range.

*(Thomas Stone)*

### Dynamics and trills

Trilled tones project more sound than a sustained pitch, thus forte trills should be played mezzo forte.

*(Thomas Stone)*

### Crescendos

Save much of the crescendo for the last few beats. They should start in the bass instruments and be finished by the cymbal roll, if there is a cymbal written. The cymbal can do it so much better.

*(Thomas Stone)*

### Rehearsing dynamics and balance

If we have difficulty balancing, we will build it. I ask, "Will all those with the melody play first. The rest of you look at your part as you listen. Now, tell me if you think your part is next in importance. If it is, then add that part." Then, if there are confusions, we straighten that out. "Now, what is the third most important part? If you think yours is now important, you should play."

We do not talk dynamics so much with them, other than the shaping of phrasing. We talk about big, small, and in-between sounds. Sometimes the directions get more technical and I say, for example, "We want a forte, or mezzo forte sound." The trumpets, flutes, and clarinets all make a different size fortissimo. Often the notated level is not what the composer intended, so I am wasting time. Instead, I talk more about total size, "This should be a big sound, a little, or in-between sound level." I also may say, "The soprano voices need to be louder here than the tenor voices."

*(Bryce Taylor)*

### Playing dynamic levels one can control

I will not ask them to play louder or softer than they can control. Whatever volume we call forte and fortissimo should be no more than they can play without distorting a good tone and without "splatting" the attacks. Piano should be no softer than the sound they can produce with confidence.

There was an example of this last month as I was rehearsing the Hindemith *Symphony in B flat for Concert Band* (1951). There is a little woodwind ostinato in it and it is to be very distant. It's so difficult, especially for the double reeds. I had them play and said, "Softer." They played it softer. Then I said, "Now play it so soft that maybe the notes don't speak and it is okay if they don't." Wow! They had permission to make mistakes, so then they really went for it. They played really soft and some notes didn't speak. I used that as an opportunity to say, "You need to be aware of your dynamic threshold and then expand upon it. If you're not aware of what your own abilities are, then you do not know where to begin."

*(Mallory B. Thompson)*

### Adjustable dynamic levels

Most people seem to think of volume levels as a straight line. Piano is this soft and mezzo forte is at this exact level, and there is no change within a given level. If that were true, then we could not do what the composer is asking. We would have to play every note and phrase in a passage marked forte at the same volume. Now that doesn't make sense! I draw two lines for each volume level to show the idea of a dynamic range within a level. Then I draw a wave length within the two lines that represents changes to softer and louder volume levels within the level.

Students have trouble with this idea. When you tell them to phrase, they'll say, "Do you mean do you want a crescendo here?" I will say, "Well . . . not really." They understand, though, when a teacher improves his explanation of dynamic levels. Phrasing demands us to change the volume or stress of each note according to the place this note has in the phrase and how long it is. It comes down to the idea of adjustable dynamics within each level.

*(John Williamson)*

## TEACHING DYNAMICS

### Relating dynamics to the use of the voice in theater

Many of my students are in dramatic productions. To get their point across on stage, they understand they must exaggerate with their voice. If one is on the stage, one's voice sounds bizarre to one's own ears. However, in row fifteen it sounds great, because the audience can hear the inflections. The same magnified expression is needed with a musical instrument. You've got to use or apply that much inflection and "stage makeup" or it doesn't carry. You must make a little crescendo up and down so it can be heard in row fifteen, not just by the person next to you. You really must exaggerate your dynamic levels to be effective.

*(Myron Welch)*

### Planning crescendos and diminuendos

With dynamics, I use targets. For example, a crescendo leads to a specific place and a diminuendo leads to a specific place. Thus, I teach students to think of line and motion. If there are ten beats, the dynamic change might peak on a target note on the eleventh beat. I would isolate a passage and play the first beat at the correct volume and the eleventh beat at the volume level we are heading for. Then we play the passage and make the progression.

*(Gregory Bimm)*

If the crescendo goes for four measures, I establish points along the way where I want them to be, e.g., in two measures, the mid-point, and the final level. I may not press too quickly for an increase or decrease in tempo or volume, if I do not want to get there too soon. There are other times the dynamic change occurs quickly.

Teachers may think about the rate of tempo change more than for volume changes. I try to let the music dictate what either should be. To decide this, my job is to do my homework with the score. Their job is to respond to the conducting, which should convey the exact dynamic or tempo changes, and changes during rubato passages.

*(Robert Floyd)*

### Dynamics, blend and intonation

In selecting the appropriate dynamic level and in teaching dynamics or blend, I teach them that these issues are tied to intonation. You have to have the intonation working for you first. If you want a good strong unison trumpet sound, it's not how loud you play, but how in tune you are: only then is there a real sense of power.

*(Timothy Mahr)*

### Intensity at low volume levels

When a band tries to play soft, the resonance and the tone quality often go "down the tubes." Students often associate softness with a lack of intensity. I talk about how they talk to someone in class. If they were angry with their neighbor, they would whisper. They wouldn't whisper soft and nice, they would whisper intensely and angrily. I even have them angrily whisper something to someone so they experience what quiet stress feels like. That usually helps them understand how to produce intensity on soft passages.

*(Gregory Bimm)*

### Teaching forte piano and crescendo

With a forte piano with a crescendo, it is very important to decide when to begin the crescendo. For example, it may be forte piano on beat one with the crescendo beginning on beats three or four. I am very specific and say, "I want you to play forte for one-half a beat and piano for three and one-half beats. Then, crescendo through the next measure and release on beat one."

*(Robert Floyd)*

### Teaching dynamic levels to beginners

I used a "ladder of dynamics." I built this first with the beginners who began with two levels, loud and not-so-loud. I called them forte and mezzo forte. With older groups, I would show them what their loudest and softest levels are. That is, the levels they can play and still maintain a good quality tone and breath support. Then I would say, "If that is your softest we will call that ppp. Now play your loudest and we will call that fff." We would fill the other levels between the extremes. This worked very well at nearly all grade levels. I also taught that dynamics were relative, not absolute. Dynamics are played according to the style of the piece. Even in adult groups they will say, "Well, it says forte in my part." That is not interpreting dynamics in a relative way.

*(Barbara Buehlman)*

### Teaching dynamic levels

I teach dynamics by explaining, questioning, conducting, and suggesting. I choose a way depending upon their experience with similar and different pieces and the time available. For example, we may play a section forte and in slow-motion. This enables them to concentrate more on what they are doing dynamically than what they are doing technically. During the slow-motion, I may also suggest balancing of sections and instruments. We also try to pinpoint how they sense this passage physically and aurally. To define that, I want them to remember how they played physically, musically, and aurally. We also magnify or overdo dynamics beyond what is written. The last step is to decide the level needed to make the effect clear.

*(Richard Fischer)*

### Teaching dynamic levels and breathing

I organize dynamics and breath use in a way Thor Johnson suggested years ago. It is arranged in percentages of breath taken, breath saved, and breath used according to the dynamic as follows:

| | | |
|---|---|---|
| 100% | *fff* | This is as loud as you can blow, but don't try it! |
| 90% | *fff* | This the preferable way to play *fff*. |

At the 90% level you are saving 10% of the air, which is a noticeable saving of the air. We want a free, non-constricted tone, with the easiest production of a full resonant sound. The sound should be restrained, but not constricted at this level (or any of these levels). These differences in sound should be obvious to the conductor, performer's, and audience's ears.

| | | |
|---|---|---|
| 80% | *ff* | You are saving 20%, but still take a 100% breath. |
| 70% | *piu Forte* | You are saving 30%, but still take a 100% breath. |
| 60% | *f* | You are saving 40% of what you could do, but take a 100% breath. |
| 50% | *mf* | This is a very easy level for the brass, 50% used and 50% saved, but take a 100% breath. |
| 40% | *mp* | Use 40%, save 60%, and take 100% breath. |
| 30% | *p* | 100% breath is taken, 70% saved, and 30% used for volume. |
| 20% | *pp* | 100% breath is taken, 80% saved, and 20% used for volume. |
| 10% | *ppp* | The most difficult level of all, take in 100% and use only 10% to make volume. |

*(Miles Johnson)*

### Teaching dynamics with conducting

If they have problems reading dynamics accurately, I may magnify what they did through conducting. This can help them notice the change they missed. I also under-conduct what they did so they notice something. If I am talking about a crescendo, I will describe it and as I talk, I do a crescendo with my voice.

*(R. G. Conlee)*

### Relating dynamics to numbers

I use a numbering system in which there are five levels within each level of dynamics. I do this for balance purposes. I teach students that dynamic marks in the parts are general, referring to the total level of volume for the entire ensemble. I rarely will have any soloists play a true pianissimo, because the volume won't be enough to project.

We will change mezzo forte to forte in the part, or number it mezzo forte plus 2. Within a level such as mezzo forte, we have mezzo forte 1, 2, 3, 4, and 5. Mezzo forte 5 may be equivalent to forte 2, but not in a particular piece. That means they may either need to highlight or stress that volume or passage, or that particular note for this part of the piece. This is a coding system, but we don't have the parts all marked up with this unless there is an extreme difference from what is printed.

*(Donald Gee)*

## The frustrations of teaching dynamics

Learning the whole series of dynamic levels sometimes is retained for only one rehearsal. They easily can forget the next time you see them. Subito piano is the most difficult. It isn't that it's hard to do, they just don't have the concept of what it is to play softly. They are very good at crescendo but not at diminuendo; they never reach the extreme of softness that they do for loudness. My groups are marvelous at triple forte and quite good at forte; piano is an unheard-of dynamic. To teach these levels, I start with a double fortissimo chord, then a fortissimo chord, then forte, mezzo forte, etc. down to pianissimo. Only then they can hear or see what that they are to do; otherwise they do not understand the sound of a pianissimo.

*(Judith A. Niles)*

## Teaching dynamic changes through listening

During warm ups, I teach dynamics through listening. We use a whole note with a fermata and play an eight to sixteen beat volume change from crescendo to decrescendo. They start as soft as they can and they get as loud as they can with a good tone quality. I also will have them play a half note pianissimo and then a half note piano, etc. This builds dynamic levels in a terraced or in a ladder-like manner. For the most part, I teach them to make gradual dynamic changes.

If I don't feel they are playing soft enough in a specific passage, we will play the note F on a half note at various levels. When it gets to the level that is appropriate, then that's the level that they have to transfer and play in the music.

*(Nancy Plantinga)*

## Discussing how to make dynamic changes

I write several quarter notes on the board with a different dynamic for each quarter note. I will say to them, "What's the difference between these quarter notes and how do you play different dynamics?" I ask, "How much air is in a forte and how much air is in a piano? What do you do physically to change levels?" They say, "Well, we get louder." I say, "Well, how do you do that? What physically happens? Do you press your loud button, your soft button; what do you do?" Then we start talking about the speed of the air. When you make a crescendo air goes faster through the horn and as you do a diminuendo the air

goes slower; but the air still goes *steadily.*

*(Dwayne P. Sagen)*

When changing dynamic levels, I offer these suggestions to students: start with relaxation both physically and mentally, then build the volume and handle the muscle firmness in areas such as the embouchure corners, and waist and arm muscles. In dynamics, we often forget the relaxed, non-tense way of doing things. I also say, "When you want to play something louder, blow the air stream forty miles-per-hour instead of thirty-five.

I often talk of "larger and smaller" sounds instead of "louder and softer" sounds. The former words don't suggest that they change the core of what they are doing physically. For example, if one asks them *to play either louder or softer,* they tense up and work harder physically. But, if I ask them *to make the sound larger or smaller,* they alter the volume but remain more relaxed, without as much physical change.

*(Robert Floyd)*

## Selecting the appropriate dynamic level

To set a dynamic level, we'll experiment with a tuning chord until we can agree on what a mezzo forte is. Then, we'll establish increments above and below that level. With a piece, the levels are not absolute; they relate to each other depending upon the style. A forte in classical music will be a little different, particularly in the brass, from a forte in a piece by Alfred Reed.

*(Timothy Mahr)*

## Clarifying dynamics

I clarify dynamic differences by saying, "A mezzo forte would be the first vaguely intense sound that you have. It'd be just the typical full sound on the instrument. Forte is a slightly projected and a fortissimo a strongly projected sound."

*(James Stivers)*

## Sensitizing students to dynamics

I use the warm up to work on dynamics. That is a wonderful time to sensitize people's ears and minds to what dynamic levels are.

*(Thomas Stone)*

## Dynamics

They ask, "How loud is this supposed to be?" I answer, "Govern that by what it does to your sound. You should maintain the integrity of your sound at whatever high volume level that you can. Beyond that, if something happens to your sound, then you have discovered your limit." In this respect, the student should get control of a good tone before beginning to change volume levels. In short, if you don't sound well, who cares what volume you are playing!

*(John Williamson)*

# CHAPTER SIX

# ENSEMBLE

The traditional view of the ensemble is that the ensemble members are to carry out the directions of the conductor. The conductor's intent is to attain the highest quality performance and the students are to give their best efforts to fulfill the conductor's musical idea of the piece. Thus, preparing a performance is paramount and the director assumes that the audience and ensemble members will benefit from a quality performance. This is the model found in professional and in military ensembles. It is an authoritarian model that reflects certain times and attitudes that are reflected even today in school music education.

Music teachers, though, are becoming more aware of another concern about the ensemble experience. They realize that the conductor's responsibility to the members of the military or professional ensemble, though there are similarities, is different from his responsibility to members of educational ensembles. Conductors still strive for quality in performance, but many conductors see more that their role is also to expand the musical thinking and awareness of ensemble members.

This responsibility to the musical education of students has influenced the conductor's thinking. Teachers see the need to help students understand the ensemble and the composition itself, and to increase their discrimination and responsibility for musical decisions. The result is an increased emphasis upon the *process of making music*, and more emphasis upon the *involvement of students* in the performance preparations.

## RESPONSIBILITY

### The importance of all players

By rotating seating, one can raise students' awareness of the importance of all parts. This plays down the attitude that first is the only important part. I also have used "staggered seating" where the number one player plays first, number two plays second part, and number three plays third. Remember to consider the individual's range.

*(Robert Allan)*

### Stressing teamwork and ensemble

Sometimes it is time to give a sermon, talk, relax, or rest in the middle of a rehearsal. We talk about teamwork, saying that band is another term for "team." They can relate it to their college football team or basketball team, or to whomever won the Super Bowl or World Series.

I talk about building teamwork. Everyone is important on that team, whatever they do. My philosophy in teaching and in really building a band is that I am no more important than the last chair clarinet player. I move chairs and stands just like they do. I build on that even when we talk about how the third clarinet player is more important than the first for balance. We go on this team idea and that everyone gives, everyone listens to one another and everyone builds off one another. This is based on the adage, "You're only as strong as your weakest link."

*(Dwayne P. Sagen)*

### Responsibilities and challenges

I've tried to develop an individual's responsibility in the ensemble. Do not let students feel like they can get lost or that they can hide behind what they're doing in the ensemble. Put importance on everything that everybody does, so the contribution they make is at a high artistic level; then they are all contributing important things whether they are the first cornet or third cornet; or whether it is a solo part or a part of the ensemble.

In addition, everyone has an equal opportunity to learn and to share in the musical product. With band we have a tendency to have a hierarchy of importance. We attach importance to who is playing on important parts or on the solo parts. The lower-part players of course have a tendency to say, "Hey, I don't have to play as well as the first cornet player." I've tried, therefore, to develop a system where people have the same skills as any other player in the band. I did not assign players in the band according to their levels of skill, I assigned players in the band according to a characteristic tone color, or an ability to play in the first, second, and third valve combinations; I assign them according to the *uniqueness* of skill.

I also place players in band by their responsibility or leadership levels or how well they handle pressure. In this situation, the second-ranked clarinet player overall was probably playing second clarinet. This was also an education for them. When they came into band, they all thought that first was the best spot. I enhanced the traditional competition, but it had to do less with chair placement.

The competition was the student against a standard, a standard against their performance. The competition was through chair challenging and I had a stand-leader band. A stand leader was a person who played when the going got tough, because they were the ones who could cut the part the best. Thus, I could cut my band down by one third simply by saying, "Stand leaders, let's play it." The third cornet player could be a stand leader also. I had, therefore, a chamber band or a wind ensemble within the symphonic band. They were the ones who led by example. They also were the ones who would call a sectional to solve problems and to teach the part to the other two players if they had trouble. If they had the responsibility to teach the part to somebody else, the likelihood of them learning it themselves was very good.

They could challenge from stand leader of the third part to second chair on the second part because they have to play a different part. The person they are challenging knew that part a little better. I think this was important because it emphasizes and defines certain responsibilities for the individuals.

*(Charles Olson)*

### Inviting their input

If there are problems, I stop them and point out or ask if they have heard this or that. The idea is to ask them, "What is wrong and how do we correct it?" This puts the responsibility on them to become active rather than passive as players.

*(Pamela Gearhart)*

### Developing supportive ensemble members

Nervous, uptight attitudes and feelings about intonation problems produce negative results. Relaxed, playful, probing, and scientific attitudes of discovery produce positive results. I try to discourage anyone from making faces when tuning, sucking lemons, or sticking their finger down their throat. When these feelings are displayed, the whole situation worsens. The more nervous they are about intonation, the worse it gets.

*(Richard K. Hansen)*

### Starting of a piece

I have my group play without the conductor. I'll start them, and I'll give them one preparatory beat with a breath, and they take the tempo from there. They need that opportunity to play without me pounding my foot, snapping my fingers, or conducting. They need to feel that pulse internally from person to person in the group.

I never count off with beginners or with my fifth graders. They don't need you to count off. The count off is a crutch mostly for conductors who can't keep control of the students' attention. They count off to get students' attention by saying, "One, two, here we go," or "Read-y go!" Instead, they could use the baton to get the class to pay attention.

I give them one beat and they get used to that. It focuses them much better than if I were to use my voice. It is important to make an issue of it and stick with it. It's easy to lapse back into the old way and do it with your voice. It is really important to sensitize them visually to what I am doing with the baton. Otherwise, they become comfortable in looking down and waiting for an oral instead of a visual signal.

*(Thomas Stone)*

### Responsibility in the ensemble

The term "irresponsible third-part player" may fit one regardless of whether one is playing third cornet or not. I try to establish a "responsible third-part player" instead. I build skill in a rehearsal with individual responsibility and taking the responsibility home with them. This promotes a daily application of individual concerns.

*(Charles Olson)*

## GOALS AND OBJECTIVES

### Concerns for the ensemble

There are two concerns when we are working with the group. One is trying to get the group to sound better in a specific piece. The second is trying to develop an approach to the ensemble's education.

*(Robert Levy)*

### Developing the sense of ensemble

The big ensemble problem that wind groups have is focusing the commitment, the sense of intensity to play, and being ready. I have them play with their eyes closed so they concentrate and listen to each other breathe. We might first work on playing the first note with their eyes closed. We do this by listening to the breath, and we breathe together. The breath is natural in its motion and in the time it takes for the inhale.

*(Larry Rachleff)*

Perhaps one of our most difficult tasks as a conductor is to build ensemble cohesiveness and sensitivity. As one tackles the challenge of a new group each semester, establishing concepts is first in most conductor's mind. I use a very simple set of unison exercises to help build tonal concepts, articulation styles, intonation, and blend. To add variety and to develop better eye contact and communication with the ensemble, I vary these exercises in tempo and musical style daily. This builds ear and eye communication very quickly. Each exercise is approached in the most musical manner possible with every movement of the baton being very deliberate and exacting to instill the proper musical response.

Another technique for building ensemble sensitivity is to have the group perform a slow chorale-like passage without the aid of the conductor. (They start and stop themselves as well.) I ask them to watch and listen to one another very carefully so they may properly execute nuances. They very quickly learn to breathe and phrase together. This whole short warm-up process really brings their concentration to a much higher level.

*(Ray E. Cramer)*

### Fundamentals of ensemble performance

The following fundamentals provide the basic language through which the teacher or conductor and the players can communicate. They are the means through which a mutual understanding must be developed if they are to work together ideally as a performing organization.

    I.   Tone
    II.  Intonation
    III. Balance
    IV. Precision (of execution)
    V.  Interpretation
        a. Tempo
        b. Style (of articulation)
        c. Phrasing
        d. Dynamics

We must teach and practice these fundamentals. Just as an athletic team cannot become a winning group by only playing games, a band cannot learn to play musically by only playing music. That is the most difficult and time-wasting way of reaching the goal.

To be sure, we learn by doing and we cannot learn to swim without getting in the water. We must start with and constantly return to the basics in their simplest form. This lays a firm and ample foundation upon which to build our team and band structure.

*(Mark H. Hindsley)*

## BUILDING LISTENING AND THE SENSE OF ENSEMBLE

### Listening vertically and horizontally

I always stress the visualization of sound from bottom to top, from tuba to piccolo whether it is a unison or a chord. The same principle applies to woodwind or brass choir, or to individual sections. The first parts must be able to hear and "listen down" to the lowest section or pitch. The students are developing their acceptance or rejection for that sound's precision, tone color, balance, or whatever musical quality is being stressed.

When the total band sound improves or comes closer to my expectations, I will respond with encouragement

and positive acceptance. It is a subtle way of developing an overall musical quality and excellence. This is a holistic concept that removes individual's interpretation of his own sound, so all of his attention is being directed the total ensemble sound.

Horizontal sound structure is a concept that is similar to the concept of vertical sound structure. Horizontal, means to focus listening on the duration of sound quality from left to right in the band and the section, and from the beginning to the end of the individual's own sound as well. My students are conditioned to form an image of the sound begin created on a horizontal line. I use this concept for the ingredients of sound, which are tone quality, balance, blend, intonation, volume, dynamics, and rhythm. The consistency of this sound is determined by and results from the listening skill and the visual exactness of the mental image the performer has been projecting through the instrument.

*(Edward S. Lisk)*

### The "trio concept" can develop ensemble listening

The trio concept is one of my pet techniques, and is probably original with me. I remember the day I started to use it. I was working with my own junior high school band and they were very inexperienced. They could not seem to focus in on what they were supposed to be listening to. This was in the midst of solo-ensemble time and all of the students were in small ensembles. I figured that I could use their ensemble experience to my advantage. Therefore, I related listening in the large ensemble to listening in small ensemble playing. They grasped the idea quickly, and I have been successful with this ever since. Each person is responsible for listening to his or her own trio. That is, themselves and the person on their right and their left.

I originally used the trio concept for balance, but now I find it works for blend, note length, articulation, precision, tuning, rhythm, attacks, releases, style, breathing and phrasing together—anything that requires making ensemble judgments.

Sometimes we forget that when we tell students to listen it is less effective if we fail to give them a listening focus. In such cases they have no idea what to listen for. To simplify the task, I ask everyone, junior high students through college students, to be responsible for only one thing as they listen. They are expected to listen and adjust to their "trio."

Each trio is comprised of three persons—the person in the middle, the person on the left, and the person on the right. The trios also overlap so each person is in three trios. That is, an individual student is the person on the left in trio "a," the person in the center of trio "b," and the person on the right in trio "c."

Every person's job in a trio is to be certain they are playing no louder, no softer, no sharper, no flatter, no longer, and no shorter than the persons on either side of them.

Sometimes I have one trio play so others can hear what we are after, and also to see if the trio understands. If all trios function effectively there will be a dramatic improvement in the overall success of the ensemble.

I understand many music teachers have tried this. They claim that it is a very effective technique. They employ this to help students understand what to listen for. This makes students listen specifically, rather than broadly. In rehearsals, I will often refer to the idea, asking them to listen to their "trio." I need not tell them anything specific to do, since they have learned where to listen and what to listen for.

This concept also can be applied to a "trio" made up of dissimilar instruments, sometimes caused by seating arrangements. These students have a more demanding task than say, three clarinets, but there are enough things in common such as note length, style, precision, and pitch to make this concept effective. If they sit on the outside of a row, I joke with them saying, "You have a low IQ job since they only have to listen to a duet."

My wife uses a variation of this. She gives assignments to "trios" or "duets" that must be prepared, recorded, and turned in for evaluation. Each student in the trio or duet receives the same grade based upon the success and merit of the taped performance. The students learn to practice as an ensemble member, and they learn to listen, to adjust, and to make judgments. It works!

I use it more and more dealing with other issues, like style and note length. At first I used it only to achieve good intonation and balance. Interestingly, the first time you introduce the concept, you will discover that the students will play softer in an effort to listen more closely.

There are a variety of ways students can make judgments. For example, if a student is unable to hear his trio, he is apt to be too loud. If he can hear his partners, but not himself, the others are too loud or he is too soft. These are only a couple of the ways students can make judgments. My goal is to have students make judgments for themselves.

*(Richard Floyd)*

### Fostering ensemble

I sometimes tell them to feel the warmth or energy of the person next to them. Somehow, they can do this.

*(James Arrowood)*

### Developing the idea of ensemble

I have asked them to close their eyes and come in together on the first chord of the piece. They have to listen to breathing, for example, and you are now dealing with an ensemble instead of a bunch of individuals. You also can give them the last note, then have them close their eyes and play the note on their own. This needs to be done several times, but it will bring them together as an ensemble to a considerable degree.

*(Richard Floyd)*

### Playing without the conductor

When I am not supplying the metronome they must do more. They have to concentrate, think, and try harder. This removes their use of the conductor as a crutch and that makes the large ensemble more like a small ensemble. It not only makes them less dependent upon the conductor and more independent, but stresses that they have responsibilities to assume.

Gradually they realize that they must *keep* the tempo, while the conductors's responsibility is to *set it* and *control it*. This frees the conductor to do other things besides just beat time. First, we worked with pieces that had a steady tempo (marches, minuets, etc.). Later we used very complex pieces with ritards, style changes, or rubato. They had to decide who would lead a passage and give the cues.

*(Frank Battisti)*

### Don't follow, participate!

With beginning ensemble playing, I use something very simple, such as a set of harmonized scales. The scales are in whole notes, which takes away the technical problems, so they don't have to look at the music as much. Therefore, they can be very attentive and responsive to the conductor. The basic idea is, "You don't follow, you participate." With this idea, you can do all kinds of variations. You can work with things such as rhythm, balance, meter, dynamics, and mixed meters.

*(Pamela Gearhart)*

### Mesh individuality with ensemble

When you're tuning with others, you need to give up some of that ego and become part of a measured ensemble. I keep telling them to give up some of that sense of "me" being important. Some sections, such as the flutes, feel that the rest of the ensemble should always tune to them. They go on their merry way getting sharper and sharper. I like to get them to the point where they feel that they have to be tuning to other people; those people are not going to tune to them.

*(Francis Marciniak)*

### Moving from band to orchestra

Winds have to play more independently in orchestra. This is much more difficult than playing in band: in orchestra they have a solo part, the keys are different, and there is one on a part. In orchestra we have hordes of violins. This can be a problem because the woodwinds don't think they are as important and don't have to play in tune all the time. The wind players are very exposed. If they don't have a solo part themselves, they are still one on a part. If they're messing up the whole world knows it.

*(Judith A. Niles)*

### Clapping with transparency

I have them clap rhythms with a different pitch, depending upon the register in which they play. For example, the flutes clap with a high-pitched clap, the saxophones with a middle-pitched clap, and the low brass with a low-pitched clap. If we clap where they do not have the same rhythms, they can hear each other better. There is more interest for them and there is more transparency in the ensemble, because the clapping sounds are different.

*(Donald DeRoche)*

### Increasing listening through ensemble changes

I do a lot of "reverse seating" in my orchestra. Mainly, I put the brass up front facing the strings, seating them in a circle. (This lessens the function of the conductor and increases the use of their own ears.)

The large ensemble can be divided into quartets. This can help us learn a piece and help them develop excellent ensemble. I have the strings sit in quartets and have each quartet play separately. I say, "Stop (or start) when I touch you." One group starts and another group takes over for the other when the teacher touches them. Another way, which also raises awareness of musical structure, is to go through the piece in phrases. Each quartet plays a phrase and the next quartet takes over from them. What I am after, regardless of the size of the group, is that they develop a sense of playing in an ensemble. The same principles of ensemble playing that apply to an orchestra also apply to a string trio, quartet, or a sonata.

A teacher can also seat them in like sections (same instruments) and put them as far away as possible from another section. The violas are seated far away, for example, from the second violins. They may be as far as the opposite sides of the room or stage. Have them activate their eyes as well as their ears—since they will have to look all the way across the stage to see each other. The next step is to ask them to turn their backs to each other so they increase their listening. It is very hard to play together when one does that! If you do these things and then seat them traditionally, their playing will have improved noticeably.

With the orchestra, I have reversed the seating on occasion so they can experience the whole, compared with hearing only their own part. We might put the percussion in the middle of the stage and then make circles around them. The first circle could be woodwinds, the second circle are brass and violins, and the outside circle has violas standing at the far periphery. This causes them to listen to and hear the piece from a different perspective.

One reason is that the strings often accuse the brass, percussion, or woodwinds of dragging. When the situation is reversed, the strings understand better what it is like to be in the back. They discover the same circumstances as the other sections. They often are less smug because of their location change and find it is harder to play. This can be done without the conductor by using the tympany as the controlling factor. The students' ears really have to concentrate on something they have not heard before, or that they have not listened to as much as one would like.

A step after this is to have "scattered seating." This means that they sit anywhere they want, face any direction they want, and sit next to anyone except someone on a similar or same instruments. A typical combination might be the second oboe next to the viola. They might say, "I didn't know that I had the same line as the viola."

The main thrust is to activate and stretch their ears, to learn what the piece is about, to heighten their own rhythmic sense, to improve balance, and to reduce their dependency on the conductor.

*(Pamela Gearhart)*

### Transparency in marches

We may take the bass and horns—possibly with the trombones—and play a passage in slow chorale style. They can hear their part and the pitches better, and it sets the rhythm. They also get a better sense of the need for the sounds to have duration. They hear their part in relation to the bass, which helps phrase the traditional "oom-pah" part. They realize that this part is more important than they thought. Overlooking this is always a danger in a march.

*(Michael Golemo)*

### Reseating the band

One way to avoid stressing technical accuracy without stressing musical issues is to change the seating of a band often. This can be done especially in an "elastic score" such as Grainger's *Irish Tune*. This means that there are several musical lines going at once. Different instruments move in and out of certain musical lines, though the line's life continues. These changes vary color and intensity, though there is only a simple four-part tune going on.

By doing this, Grainger constantly creates a variety of chamber ensembles. Therefore, one thing I might do in that situation is to set up various pods around the rehearsal area. The pods are duets, trios, quartets, etc. The choice depends upon the passage we are rehearsing and their instrumental relationship. The pods also may be created by roles such as melody or harmony. There are innumerable ways to put certain lines together or to create various intact chamber groups. I do this after they have begun to understand the piece.

In the piece there always are three, four, or five lines going on. After we have rehearsed and I've roamed around, I select people from around the room to come to the center and play as a chamber group. This may be either a quartet or a quintet and they play either a whole piece, a passage, or a section. The purpose of bringing some to the center is to keep them from feeling like "school is out" if they are in one of those pods.

I also see this as a standard-setting process because this requires very concentrated listening. They must listen to their pod, the person beside them, and the other players located across the room. Sometimes I stress listening across the room. At other times, I stress listening to the person beside them as though they were in a chamber group.

*(Michael Haithcock)*

### The pulse keepers

With intermediate music students, I have them know where the "musical metronome" is. That is, who they should be listening to for pulse. In many music compositions, someone is often playing a part that defines the pulse, which I call the "pulse keeper." With the advanced students, we look for it in the music itself. There usually is a part, or several parts, that give the musical message that we might call the "musical metronome" as written in the score.

*(Gary Hill)*

### Ensemble listening

I pick out a phrase or motive which is tossed around from section to section. I have the line fragments played by each section one after another. They can hear the total line since no one else is playing. They also can hear that the line goes from one section to another; one section does not have the entire line.

*(Judith A. Niles)*

### Creating new ways of listening in the ensemble

New ways of listening help us hear in a new way. Instead of seating the group in the usual way, there is a simple way that immediately changes the sound. In rehearsal, have the woodwinds turn from facing the audience to facing the brass. Right off the bat there is a completely different listening experience. I also have set them up in little semicircles so the whole group is now made up of many quintets.

I put them in different areas all over the stage, some with a crazy mixed instrumentation. In this seating, the flutes are not hearing flute players on both sides and the trombones are not hearing trombones. Suddenly, they are hearing these other tones. This experience really strengthens the ears and they suddenly begin to hear the piece.

*(Robert Levy)*

### A reason to reseat

After we've worked on a piece for awhile, they may not be listening as much. They're getting jaded. To counteract this, I'll change the seating arrangement. I put the flutes in the back row or the tubas up front so they have a new aural experience.

*(Francis Marciniak)*

### Reminding students to listen

I start a piece and let the band play. I get off the podium and click my fingers four pulses when they're not synchronized. I say, "You're not listening to each other."

I think students can play in a vacuum, sit in their world, and play their own part. I say, "You play like you're

in a practice booth. You are not conscious of what anyone is doing around you. How can you sit there and do that?" I really bug them about playing and listening so they do play like an ensemble.

*(Richard J. Suddendorf)*

### Listening to the piece, not their horn

If there are problems with a solo passage, I'll just have the soloist do it alone and have everyone else listen. I also will have them play with their eyes closed and react to the solo as they play their accompaniment.

I may relate it to a contour; I'll say, "Now this is a rainbow," or "This is a valley." I never say, for instance, "Piccolo, your C sharp is sharp." I'll say, "Piccolo, the line demands here that you listen on the lower part of that phrase to match pitch." That way it always is relating to what they do to the piece, rather than what they do to their horn. That's real important.

*(William W. Wiedrich)*

### Scrambling the seating

The idea of scrambling or jumbling seating can be effective. For example, I have scattered the clarinets around the room as well as everyone else so the musicians will hear other parts, notice other things, and make the students more "hip" about listening. When I do this, the intent is that they hear things with a totally different perspective and in a different context. The kids get a kick out of it; they think it's hilarious. They particularly enjoy that cues just go everywhere. It's interesting to have the tubas in the front row and the flutes in the back rows.

When this is done, I usually put a seating chart on the board. If you leave it totally to their interests, they wind up sitting by whoever they like best. Sometime I disperse the tenor and bass line performers throughout the ensemble or set all the voices like a vocal choir. In that case, I might say, "Take your instrument and music stand and all the soprano voices sit here, all the alto voices here. If an instrument like a tenor saxophone is sort of in a crack, I ask them to sit near a part they think is like theirs." I sometimes go as far in the opposite direction as possible. I want them to hear things in a totally different perspective.

*(Donald Wilcox)*

## PULSE

### Keeping the pulse

One needs to develop in their mind that their "gig" is to keep the pulse. A metronome can help reinforce this. By not conducting, one can reinforce their accomplishments and prove to them that they can do this. The intent is to refine their sense of tempo and reinforce their skill in making a steady tempo. This also aids the internalization of tempo and emphasizes its importance.

*(Robert Floyd)*

### Building the group's responsibility for ensemble

I try to shift responsibility for listening, accurate intonation, keeping time, and other mechanical things to the group. Then the entire group begins solving rhythm problems through listening.

If there is a pulse problem such as rushing, the teacher can pick part of the group to contribute in a special way. Some can generate a constant subdivision against a problem rhythm. Some of the others do not play and they become the keepers of the pulse. They help keep track of the sins of others. The keepers can either keep track or provide the pulse.

Another choice is for one section to subdivide in their ear as they listen. They are to decide where and what the problem is. A more common way is to have the conductor keep the pulse pattern absolutely. Do not go with the group's pulse changes and they will quickly realize there is a problem.

*(John Anderson)*

### Subdivide and stagger who is performing

Assign everyone to subgroups to form sub-bands, though the instrumentation could be odd. If the teacher places some in more than one sub-band, instrumentation can be more complete in each sub-band.

Each sub-band is to play for four or eight measures without the conductor. When one group finishes a passage, the next sub-band takes over from them. This emphasizes that keeping pulse can be taken over by the band. When done in relays, these heightens their awareness.

*(John Anderson)*

### Building their sense of internal pulse

Conduct one measure in any style and tempo. Without stopping, have the group close their eyes and count the next measure silently. Then, they clap the down beat of the third measure while their eyes are closed.

There is no sound during the first or second measure. In the first measure they are picking up the tempo from the baton. In the second measure they're internalizing the pulse and in the third measure they're clapping on the down beat. If they do subdivisions, it works even better. You say, "Though I'm conducting in four-four and I'm going to give you four counts, you're going to feel one-and-two-and." Then, while they are closing their eyes and are really thinking the subdivisions, they are preparing to clap on one of measure three. With the feel of subdivisions, they will be much more precise on the following beat one, than if they were feeling and counting the pulse only.

*(Thomas Stone)*

### Rehearsing without conducting

A performing ensemble should gain performance polish—commonly called precision. There is no way in the world they can develop that as effectively as through having the ensemble develop a very strong sense of internal pulse. Therefore, identify in each instance the person or people that they should be listening to for tempo.

By practicing without the conductor, the ensemble can and must develop this sense of pulse within it. For example, in Holst's *Suite in E flat for Military Band* I ask people with repeated eighth notes to play from the beginning. As they find they have repeated eighth notes, I ask them to join in or drop out—depending how this occurs in their part. With this approach, we can take an entire section through to make them aware of the contribution each part makes to the pulse.

*(Gary Hill)*

## PRECISION

### Clarifying releases

I start early stressing that it is important where one releases notes and I begin with the whole note. I use the chorale books for this, saying that sometimes the note stops on the next pulse and sometimes we rob some time from it.

*(Carl A. Bly)*

Many groups do not start the sound together, but the real problem is endings. The players do not agree how long a tone should be. When they become more aware of shaping the sounds and ends, agreement increases. Suddenly one gets transparency in the ensemble. Intonation also improves because they begin to direct intensity in the same manner as other players. This removes "pollution" that exists when there is imprecise and unmusical playing in the ensemble.

*(Frank Bencriscutto)*

Watch for precision and listen for pitch.

*(Stanley Cate)*

When I'm talking about releases and attacks, I'll hold up a piece of paper. "You know, this is a perfect rectangle here and every note should be like this. The front part of this paper is just one solid shape and the edge is a solid clean line.

Then I'll rip it and say, "This is what happens if the band doesn't begin or release together. We have this ragged and frayed note. I should hear the square clean beginning or ending instead of the ragged edge." Usually they get the idea, and later I can just allude to the ripped paper.

*(Howard A. Lehman)*

### Developing ensemble unity

On a difficult passage, sometimes I start with one instrument or person, and then add instruments one by one. This also seems to work quickly and they begin to play well together. This helps them hear examples of how the music should sound, in respect to balance, articulation, or dynamics.

*(R. G. Conlee)*

### Overusing the metronome

A band can become dependent upon a metronome if teachers overuse it. Even my students will occasionally suggest that we have used a metronome too much in a certain spot. The symptom of metronome overuse is that they cannot play together, because they do not internalize the pulse or are not listening to each other.

*(Robert Floyd)*

### Insights into playing entrances

Someone is always going to be the first guy on their block to come in. I say, "Don't ever be the first to come in . . . and . . . never be late." This also has them listening to others so they come in "never first or never late." They come to the realization there is a moment when it is the correct instant to come in.

*(James Arrowood)*

## BALANCE

### Ensemble problem

One of the biggest problems in ensemble performance is with crescendos and diminuendos. They can lack balance and timing unity within the group. If there are forty players, they progress in forty different ways with different timings, and with forty different amounts of dynamic change. This can cause the sound of the group to continue changing through all sixteen counts of the crescendo. I like it not to do that!

On the other hand, depending on the sound you create, certain people may intentionally crescendo sooner or later than others. If it is a tutti crescendo, I frequently ask the low voices to crescendo first; then the middle voices, upper voices and finally, the percussion crescendos.

I do the opposite in a diminuendo so the natural tendency of the highs to become too brilliant does not happen. It is an interesting sound when instrument balance is managed in this type of crescendo.

I do this on tutti chord releases also. If it is a legato release, I have the low voices release last and the upper voices release first. The different release points occur only with a fraction or an instant difference. I find that it gives the release of the chord a very warm resonant sound.

*(Gary Hill)*

## TONE

### Unifying sound in rehearsal

Since an individual's ideas of tone come also from experiences outside the rehearsal, I often work with tone

inside the rehearsal, even with university groups. I do this so the sound they use in the rehearsal is not exclusively their own idea.

*(Frank Bencriscutto)*

### Developing ensemble color

I sometimes do dynamic changes backward to develop a better band tone quality. I'll have the woodwind sections make an eight-count crescendo while I have the brass sections start at fortissimo and make an eight-count diminuendo. This is to bring out and show the different colors that the band can create.

*(Lance Schultz)*

### Color in the ensemble

I really delve a lot into textures and colors and I enjoy it. This is an exciting part of rehearsal. I like Persichetti so well because I like to use colors. We have so much to offer in symphonic band. The orchestra gives you a certain number of colors but symphonic band also has a rich variety of colors.

*(Richard J. Suddendorf)*

## EVALUATION

### The basis for evaluation

We may have stopped listening for good balance and have become accustomed to sounds that are not very good. After hearing so many badly balanced sounds, we have not learned to discriminate the desired sound from the undesirable. Teachers have other concerns such as playing at the right time and with the right note. They also may accept the typical junior high band sound as evidence that all other ensemble objectives have been attained.

*(Donald Casey)*

### Playing without the conductor

Having them play without the conductor allows them to shape the passage in ways that feel comfortable and natural to them. If they are too far from the appropriate musical style, or your interpretation, you use their interpretation as the basis for a discussion leading to your views.

*(Robert Levy)*

### Giving the group feedback

There are times the tempo fades and I'll have the drummers keep playing until I cut them out. I say, "Well, here's what you're doing, band. You think that the only job the drummers do is provide the beat and you provide all the music. You have that wrong. You're the beat instruments and they're the melodic instruments. Let the drummers play the melody and you play the time."

*(Howard A. Lehman)*

# CHAPTER SEVEN

# FACILITY

Some teachers and students see technique or facility as simply the skill of playing fast or difficult passages accurately. However, facility really means full *command* of the instrument. A student's facility with an instrument encompasses many areas, including coordination, articulations, intonation, tone, range, rhythmic control, and pitch accuracy.

Traditionally students have gained facility through practice, repetition, and drill. Teachers can also build instrumental facility through several other ways, including ear-training exercises, games, composition, theory, and the overall development of musicianship.

## THE VALUE OF FACILITY

### The need for facility

When one develops facility and technique through continual practice, the muscle strength that is gained makes performing feel easy. Only weak muscles make us feel that things are difficult.

*(Jack Brookshire)*

The kids must have control of their instruments so it is not like a foreign body. Once they have control of rhythm, tone, and technique, they can then make music.

*(Donald Gee)*

When students have confidence with technical skills and demands, they will read better.

*(James Arrowood)*

### The intention for developing facility

I hold a high priority for scale proficiency with my students. My instructional techniques are designed to establish spontaneous reaction to any major or minor scale. This immediate "reaction" is similar to the jazz musician who can see or hear a chord change and respond spontaneously and correctly.

When working with a student in a lesson, I have the student play a scale and "meander" diatonically in an assigned key. As they meander through the key, I randomly call out different keys and they immediately change to the new key and continue playing diatonically and in a meandering manner. This scale-reaction skill also contributes to successful sight reading. The student can effectively scan a piece of music and respond to the various keys found in different technical passages. This eliminates the more common "note-by-note" approach to their reading of new material.

*(Edward S. Lisk)*

### Difficulty in separating elements of performance

You can't separate playing techniques and style techniques. When I talk with my band about style, I talk about such things as vibrato, volume, feel, texture, and articulation. It all goes together. The abilities and skills needed to play different styles are part of the notion of musicianship. That's how I teach musicians.

*(Dominic Spera)*

### Facility is not developed well in isolation

Too often repetitive techniques, such as scale practice, are directed to a specific result without any connection to the "whole" of music making. In our quest for excellence, we have isolated and disassembled so many performance skills into such small bits and pieces, that we have lost sight of where they belong or what they belong to. This is why I stress the imagery and visualization process. Musical imagery activates a holistic configuration that connects all the "bits and pieces" of performance into a whole.

*(Edward S. Lisk)*

### The values of scales

Playing scales will develop finger patterns in the different keys. I can use scale sheets, particularly after they learn scales aurally, to do various patterns such as eighths and sixteenths. Then we can talk about key signatures, how they relate to one another, add flats around, and drop sharps around, etc. Using this approach makes easy sense to them.

*(Donald Gee)*

304

## The need to play accurately

In rehearsal, the primary focus of conscious attention has to be on the mechanics of getting the particular job done. All the background and previous hearing does not mean a thing if they play a C sharp out of tune. We've got to put first things first.

*(Alfred Reed)*

## Scale mastery

I was always a stickler on scales. I found that the kids who were proficient playing scales could do other things well. My junior high students had to learn at least nine major scales and, as they progressed, many did all majors and minors from memory.

Students can do this, but often teachers do not ask them to do it. I have heard entire bands play all the major scales. We should expect more because they can accomplish more than we ever give them credit for. Junior high students can do wonders and very young students can be especially able if asked.

*(John Kinnison)*

## Skill building in band

Until a band has achieved complete competence, scale exercises, or their equivalents should be a *must* in the rehearsal routine. Five minutes invested in them will pay big dividends; an even larger investment may be desirable at times.

*(Mark H. Hindsley)*

# The Goals when Teaching Facility

## Thinking about skill development

The idea of practice, whether physical practice such as scales or mental practice such as ear training, is to lay in and connect a grid pattern of wires, to use a metaphor. This is very much like what happens when the telephone company comes into a brand new housing development and runs a main cable. They run trunk lines to every street, to each house in each street, and connect all these lines. Then, when all the wiring is in place, we flip on the juice and everyone can talk to everyone else. This is what practicing does.

Even professional tennis stars such as Chris Evert, Martina Navratilova, Jimmy Connors, or Steffi Graf work and work, though they have considerable inborn patterning. In a sense, they also must both hook up the wires and maintain them. Now, I guess that would mark me as a behaviorist. Basic musicianship is like basic French; we must learn to speak, read, write, and think in the language.

*(Alfred Reed)*

## Objectives

I have different reasons for doing one or two scales each rehearsal. In the top band, the students know all their scales inside and out, in two and three octaves, and at most any tempo. They are required to do this to get in the top band. Our purpose for learning scales is to work on intonation, blend, balance, precision, attacks and releases.

*(Patricia Brumbaugh)*

I teach scales to five flats and three sharps concert. I don't spend more time because the time is short; and, the music usually doesn't demand more keys than that.

*(Richard Alnes)*

I cover the common keys, but I don't expect the trombones and tubas to play in five sharps. I do expect them to play at least in C and G. I don't try to have them go up through five flats and five sharps. In the first place, they're not music majors and in the second, they are kids. Why should they spend time on that?

*(Kenneth M. Larsen)*

## Building facility in rehearsals

With the second band, I use scales to build technique. The scales are varied more in the traditional ways. I vary speed, articulation, etc. and teach to the objectives used in the first band. With each band I do things for different reasons, but doing scales is not only to build technique.

*(Patricia Brumbaugh)*

## Facility and scales

Everybody should be able to play with facility. This includes sixth grade band members who play a chromatic scale of at least one octave, though I hope two. The second-year student would have memorized scales through three sharps and three flats. This takes more than six weeks, of course. Thus, they do not learn one scale a week. By January, I want eighth graders to learn chromatic scales in two to three octaves, and to learn six or eight diatonic scales. I will try to have them memorize a different scale each week.

Because of playing experience most eighth graders can memorize a scale faster than most sixth and seventh graders. We try for a scale a week but, this may not happen because I have them continue practicing the previous ones and also play a new one each week. We emphasize this at the beginning of the year. We get away from it in the middle of the year and come back to it at the end.

*(Phillip A. Weinberg)*

## Building scales through a tetrachord approach

So often we put students through a lot of skill practices, but they don't really understand what they are doing. I want them to understand thoroughly first.

It is easier to have a band do scales with the tetrachord system. It is a simple system that they can latch on to and start scales on any note. I do this is after their second year, after they know the notes in the chromatic scale.

This teaches scale construction and an understanding of the major scales, and improves their technical facility. I do this in the warm-up sessions with the students from junior high school through high school. I prefer, though, to start this at the junior high level.

We do this in steps. When I first talk to the band I say, "We'll have you play scales starting on any note. The first step is to pick a tone, let's take B-flat concert." Then everyone plays B-flat concert, which they all know. For the next step, I say, "Go up one whole step, another whole step, and then a half step." We will play these notes like this in quarter notes. Bb, C, D, and Eb rest—doing quarter, quarter, quarter, quarter, and a dotted half note, (repeating the fourth note). We take it very slowly so they'll hear it. We will correct it if they do get a half step in there instead of a whole step. When it is correct, I tell them, "That's a tetrachord."

Then, we'll build the tetrachord on another tone until they have mastered that. I will say, "At the next rehearsal, we'll start on D." This will be in a key that's a little unusual for some of them because it will have sharps. I will tell them a day ahead of time to practice that at home. They are to practice up a whole step, a whole step, and a half step. They're doing this by ear and by figuring it out from the chromatic scale. There is no need to worry about notation because they do this by ear.

They find they can do that. The B-flat instrumentalists discover, "Hey, I played an F sharp there and then a G sharp!" So, they're going to experiment in applying the whole-step and half-step relationships. At the point we do this, some already know some scales, perhaps three flats and one sharp. We are building upon whatever they happen to know at this point. It may take six weeks or more to build the tetrachord on all twelve notes. We will cover the first tetrachord for all scales before you go to the second step, which is adding a second tetrachord.

Once they've mastered the tetrachord itself on any note, we start combining. I try not to confuse them with two parts of the scale yet. They now combine tetrachords and construct the entire major scale. This can come as early as the fifth week or sixth week with high school groups. With junior high groups, it could be almost a full year before they are ready to try this. A teacher can adapt this approach to their students' level of ability.

To combine the tetrachords and complete the scale, the teacher calls off the two parts and they've developed a whole scale. I then can explain this to them. The third step is doing the complete scale without a pause between tetrachords. At this point, they can play any concert scale at all starting on any tone without any difficulty at all. It is marvelous because you can see the progress.

Later, they begin to notate the scales. We don't have to analyze the scales because we have already done this by applying the step, step and a half-step process that explains scale construction.

*(John C. McManus)*

## Learning scales by tetrachord

In the middle of the night, I came upon this idea of reversing the relationship from fifths to fourths; as a result scales become nothing but tetrachords.

The next day, I experimented with a small theory class and they liked it immediately. At the beginning of the year we work with the basics of the major scale—all twelve of them. It is fruitful to teach the major scales as one major scale in a circle of fourths and by tetrachord.

The first four notes of a given new scale are the last four notes of the preceding scale. For example, teaching G major contains the top tetrachord of C major and thus it is not hard to learn. During the two days of preschool my freshmen learn the circle of fourths. Then, I start having them hear the interval relationship in the tetrachord when played correctly. They can hear this, no matter what note it is.

This sounds as though I am not encouraging them to read, but I feel it is counter productive to learn scales from a scale sheet, which usually does not last, since it is like cramming for an exam. Students instead can develop an auditory sense for the sound and structure of the scale when I approach this through the tetrachord.

I can travel around the circle with all freshmen in one session, whether they have played the G-flat, C-sharp, B-major scale or whatever. Almost every student can do this. I start with the trombones, since they have already developed some flexibility with the instrument's slide and their ear.

After I make the statement, "There is one giant major scale," the kids' eyes pop. Then I say, "I will prove it to you." I select some courageous individual that I have known before. I say, "Start on low C on the trumpet and play four notes up." They all know that scale and I ask, "Does that sound correct?" They nod their heads. "Now, start on the next note, which is the fifth note of the scale. Call it number one, and play four more notes as you did before. This group of four is stacked up just like the first group of four you played." They say, "Yes, it sounds right." Then I say, "Let's put those two together and now we have a scale. Since you all tell me that it is right to your ears, let's start on any note and play the first four notes. If you make a mistake, your ears will detect it and you will correct it." Within five or ten seconds, they have the four notes correct and ready to go. When they have found the correct notes, they then play 1 2 3 4, then 4 3 2 1—1 2 3 4 in a drill approach. Then we play 1 2 3 4 3 2 1 at the end of the drill, with several repetitions.

Then we pick out the fifth note of the scale and start there, which they have not played yet. I will say, "Let's start there and we will call that number one. Use the same sequence as before." To combine the two tetrachords, I will say, "Let us go back to the beginning in the first group and play 1 2 3 4, 5 6 7 8." Then that is followed with 8 7 6 5, 4 3 2 1, then 1 2 3 4 5 6 7 8 7 6 5 4 3 2 1. This is very simple and completely auditory. There is not a sheet of anything on the music stand. In one nine-week grading period, every freshmen can travel around on all scales in at least one octave.

I introduce the notation for scales as soon as they are convinced of the commonality of the different major scales. Then the scale sheets go out a week or two weeks after the introduction of this approach. I test throughout the first nine weeks—one octave at least of each of twelve major scales. There is no pass/fail on scales. I tell them, "I'll just live with you on this, even if I have to move in with you at home."

After using this approach for four or five years, I can see results also their in playing in so-called non-band keys (those other than C, F, Bb, Eb, and Ab). The non-band keys become so much easier, the intonation is better, and they relate odd beginning notes to the auditory base easier. They also sight read better and their grasp of enharmonic relationships and notation come more easily.

I complement this with the *3-D Band Book* (Belwin) by James Ployhar. This helps build chords and arpeggios in all keys. This is one of the better things on the market as a band technique book. This carries into the melodic and harmonic things to a desirable extent.

*(Donald Gee)*

## Teaching scale notation

I think a B major scale is two naturals and five sharps. Suppose I were going to give you a test and it's an all-or-nothing test. I say, "You can choose which test you want to take of the two. One test has five things you have to know, the other one has two. It's all or nothing and I give you the answers beforehand." What are you going to take? You're going to take the one with two things to know.

Why do we teach that a B scale has five sharps in it? It has two naturals in it, it's the same two that you play when you play a B-flat scale. If a student can play a B-flat scale, they can play a B-natural scale. If they can play a D scale, then they can play a D-flat scale. They can think it and understand how to approach it. They get all flustered and think, "Is it D flat on the . . . is it? . . . ah . . . what note am I on and why?"

My premise is that you should not think more than three any time you approach a key signature or a scale. For example, if this key signature is five sharps, I think two naturals. Everything is sharp except B and E. I don't keep up with which five sharps I'm trying to do. Everything is sharp, except those two notes. You go for which is smaller. If a child plays a G scale, everything is natural except one, F sharp. In the G-flat scale everything is flat except one, F natural. Why do they need to keep up with six flats?

In Georgia, at the district level of the All-State, you have to play five chromatically adjacent scales. Well, my kids play Bb, B, C, Db, and D because they don't have to think any more than two. The B-flat scale has two flats, B and E. The B scale has two naturals, B and E. With C there's nothing to think. Everything is natural. D-flat scale

has two, F and C. The D scale has two sharps, F and C.

I write my arpeggios so that you can see the arpeggio is part of the scale and built off that scale. So many kids, especially the little ones, think there is this scale, and from the Planet Venus comes this arpeggio. It's because when you write your arpeggios out to the side of the scale, they don't connect them. You assume that they will.

I'm also requiring that the first scales I teach—my required scales—are the scales that are in an A-flat concert scale. And that's because those are the band scales. You don't find music written in anything other than those keys unless you have a grade six band, and then they can play in C.

*(Marguerite G. Wilder)*

## Expanding their knowledge of theory

A next logical step after they understand scale construction and have been developing facility, is to give them all a chord chart. The chord charts have a B-flat chord chart for B-flat instruments, a C treble clef chart for C treble instruments, a C bass clef chart for bass clef instruments, a an E-flat chart for alto saxes, and an F chart for the horns. These are the five charts that I work out.

Across the bottom of the sheet I wrote the basic chord of C major: C, E, G, C. There are only four notes written. Then in the very next measure, I have a minor chord of C minor: C, Eb, G, C; and the C7 and Cdim7, chords. On the next line up from the bottom of the page, I notated the Db or C sharp so they can build the chords on those notes. I planned the chart so it goes chromatically to the top of the page.

The purpose is for them to understand what they do in keys and understand chords. They learn what the chords are, what they sound like and can compare the two. What we do is first is play the chord pattern of, for example, C, E, G, and C. Then, we go though the C min arpeggio followed by the C7, Cdim7, etc.

*(John C. McManus)*

## Learning scales and relating them to literature

One thing really "bugs me!" Some jazz guys say, "Hey, don't write out the scales for the kids. Let them hear it by ear." Well that's all well and good but it's not very practical or enriching. There is another problem with this view. If a junior high clarinetist is trying to figure out the B major scale without the music, they have problems. After fifteen minutes they throw the horn in the case and say, "Forget it, I'm going to try basket weaving." The students are frustrated because they make so many mistakes. They need to hear the scale in its entirety over and over again so that the sound is ingrained in their mind.

Whatever you teach in jazz band should be related to the available published materials. The first thing we do is memorize the scale using the music. We memorize the major scales and the major ninth chord arpeggio as it relates to each scale. Then they do the mixolydians, the same way. Then they do the dorians. Then I will play a chord at the piano, they sing the scale and arpeggiate in that chord. Then they tell me what tonality it is.

I play all the scales in a classical legato style. I do not articulate them with du-ba du-ba du-ba du-ba du. That's the most uninteresting sound in the world. If they're going to play "be-bop," the eighths are almost straight anyway. This approach really helps their technique and it helps their understanding of theory. We do this in the warm up.

Then I'll arpeggiate the I 69 chord so they can hear that. For instance, we'll go C, E, G, A, and D. From there, we take the Lydian scale and the others one by one. Lydian, Mixolydian, and Dorian are the first three they have to memorize.

This can be done in concert band and it works very, very well. In the Bloomington, Indiana schools they're playing the scales from tonic to tonic in the warm up. They play their scales up to the ninth and the teacher explains theory by counting the numbers of the notes. Then they transfer the notes over to the chord. The students now understand what a third of a chord is and not only that, they understand where the chord tones came from.

Let's face it, you could go to bed nights and sleep well because you're teaching some theory, the scales, chords, and all that other neat stuff.

*(Dominic Spera)*

### Building facility in rehearsal

We play better ten minutes into the rehearsal then we do at the start, so I sometimes will do scale routines with them. I do those slurred or tongued in eighth notes or sixteenth notes. I also can do dotted eighth and sixteenth rhythms and different articulation over two octaves, beginning with F major. I use F major because all students can play this for two octaves, except the tenor saxophone. This scale also is a low scale for brasses.

When I was doing my high school band, I would go to B-flat concert by doing F, G, Ab, and Bb. Then, I would go back down to F. Then, I might do Eb and G and come on up. I worked on this with my high school band, until I got them to do all the major scales.

I would stay with the flat scales first because they are more common in band keys. In my high school band students were not limited because I made sure that they would learn all the scales. That was one thing that really developed my high school band.

*(anonymous)*

### The choice of scales

I usually do F, Bb, or Ab, then G because it's the first sharp scale. I vary the scales I work on in rehearsal. I play sharp keys such as G, D, and then A. I do about two scales in each rehearsal. Range is a strong consideration in choosing which scales to study. I stay with lower scales because they can play them for two octaves, even though they are tough. Certain scales are difficult on intonation,

so I spend a long time on them. With low scales, I might make them play A, G, and then E. These scales are in a playable two octave range for the brass. When I think my brasses have very good range, I do C concert because it takes the trumpets to high D, which is also high for the trombones, baritones and tubas. When we do scales that go higher in range, sometimes I may rewrite the part so they jump down or jump up. The students can play them without interrupting the process.

*(anonymous)*

### Playing the scales

I want my students to be fluid with scales and arpeggios. Therefore, everybody in my top group plays the *"White Scales."* They play the major scale, the minor scale and all the way around the circle of fifths. They can all do it, but they all hate it. They do it because it's the "rite of passage": the audition to get into the top band. Furthermore, in the State of Illinois you have to know these scales to get into the district band, orchestra, or jazz band. They learn those scales but they do it grudgingly. They'll say, "It's not music, it's just technique." So I am looking for a more creative way to develop skill.

*(John A. Thompson)*

### One half a scale at a time

I do my entire scale work by rote and it is organized by the tetrachord idea. With the tetrachord, we learn half a scale at a time. It's just like No. 87 in the Clark *Technical Studies*.

*(Charles Olson)*

### Grading technical skills

We awarded points for exercises in Fussell according to the speed. They had to play a set number of scales within a set number of seconds. When they missed a note they were done, because a scale cannot be played with missed notes. Students earned no credit until they played accurately. If they played a scale slowly and correctly, they got one credit more than the credit earned when the scale was played fast and inaccurately.

*(Charles Olson)*

### An approach to building technical skill

I wrote technical exercises that can be used at any level, the only difference being the speed. I started this with second-year players in seventh grade, who could play a whole-note scale. Later, high school students played the same scale at 160 beats per minute. The patterns in the technical exercise remained the same, but I increased the speed.

The basis for building technique is not mental ideas or mental activity, it is physical habits. When a student picks up a horn and sees, thinks and plays a B-flat concert scale that pattern is built into his body. Therefore, they can play it without thinking about it. I developed this as I taught scales to my students by rote. They never see a piece of music. We build technical skills every day. Sometimes it takes twenty minutes, sometimes ten seconds, and sometimes three minutes. I organized the book in sections so the teacher could select parts according to how they might affect rehearsals.

My idea was to develop ensemble routine at the beginning of every rehearsal. It was like conditioning Pavlov's dog. I soon heard those exercises coming out of those horns when they were not under my supervision because it gave them a way to practice. They had twenty minutes of automatic stuff they could go through that they didn't have to think about. Though I'm not an advocate of nonthinking, I do believe a certain aspect of performance on instruments does require habitual response. Furthermore, I believe as soon as a student is good at it, he enjoys it. I did not write these exercises down, because they are so easy to teach.

*(Charles Olson)*

### Developing various skills through scales

I change the key of the scale for each rehearsal, once a week or so. I add minor scales eventually and arpeggios in both major and minor scales. The eighth, triplet, and sixteenth scales in particular, are used for the study and practice of mixtures of tonguing and slurring. We work through scales on rhythmic groups, differing degrees of the marcato and legato, and various other musical effects. This develops individual and ensemble technique. They develop performance fundamentals and increase their flexibility in "musical speech" and musical expression.

*(Mark H. Hindsley)*

## TEACHING ARTICULATION

### Articulation and dynamics

In the rehearsal warm up, I developed a routine that works very well. The first time through a scale (for example, B-flat concert), I use the rhythm of one quarter note followed by eighths. They play up and down—a quarter note equalling about 84 beats per minute. I do the scale four times in this way:

a. forte and tongued
b. piano and tongued
c. forte and slurred
d. piano and slurred

I do the chromatic scale next, in eighth notes, and with the same articulations and dynamic levels.

a. forte and tongued
b. piano and tongued
c. forte and slurred
d. piano and slurred

Then I take the B-flat concert harmonized scale from *Treasury of Scales*. With the harmonized scale, I use conducting to change the way they do things. I may alter the music in any way associated with dynamics. I also alter other elements such as tempo, insert or remove fermatas, change balance, style, rhythm, or articulations. I do this to make them more musically sensitive and skilled, and more sensitive to the conductor.

*(Miles Johnson)*

### Playing fast passages

The faster the notes are, the less air students use. I find myself frequently saying, "The faster the fingers move or the tongue moves, the faster the air stream must be." With single reed players, I ask them only to tickle the reed with their tongue for legato or fast articulation. In technical passages, I often ask students to have soft relaxed fingers. I find that the word "soft" works, especially with woodwind players. It promotes the entire body staying relaxed through the entire passage. I want to get the "claw" out of their hands; this is a big problem.

*(Gary Hill)*

## TEACHING FACILITY

### Ways to build facility

Use arpeggios in warm ups for intonation and pitch control.

*(Stanley Cate)*

Work with scales, attending to tone quality always.
*(Donald Casey)*

### Maintaining interest during skill development

We can change so the brass choir starts the scale on B flat and woodwinds on F concert. We can run major scales with pitch combinations (in fifths or in thirds or with full triad). This new combination of sound creates a new color, a new interest. What we are getting is technical facility with the scales.

First, we get all the scales under our fingers and do the whole circle of fourths. Then, the next step would be going to minor scales in the natural minor mode. We play these around the circle, starting on A minor. Students come to recognize this is like the C major scale, except they are stopping on the sixth degree and playing C major from A to A. Start with natural minor, then the harmonic minor, and finally the melodic minor scales. We do not have to buy every one of the books in the world. I get so excited about it—there isn't any end to the options. I can develop master musicians with this approach.

*(Edward S. Lisk)*

### Developing facility with their eyes closed

When I'm teaching fingering technique, I teach it

with an easy melodic pattern. First I'll show them visually what the fingerings are or we look in the book. Then, they close their eyes so they can feel their fingering. Then I'll say, "That's going to be the syllable "do" or the syllable "mi." I'm going to be coming up to that pitch so be ready; keep your eyes closed so you can hear." I find that it's better to build technique through echoing first because they aren't worrying about the notes on the page.

*(Gordon Nelson)*

## TEACHING RHYTHMIC FACILITY

### Playing at a fast tempo

To learn music with a fast tempo, we often slow the pulse and subdivide. This removes the "blur" they feel when they cannot instantly figure out or perform the fast passage. At the slower tempo, they can sense the pulse's subdivision and relate faster figures to the subdivisions.

Consider a fast three-four felt as one pulse per measure. If we slow the tempo and subdivide the pulse, a figure with six eighth notes per measure (in fast three-four) could now be understood and felt as a two eighth-note figure per pulse, with three pulses per measure. We would accent the first note of each two-note figure with every sixth note accented a bit more. As they gain understanding, see the organization, and gain technical control, we can increase the tempo because the "blur" is disappearing from their minds and they are playing more accurately.

*(John Williamson)*

### Maintaining pulse during fast passages

When students look at rapid passages, their sense of pulse goes away. This makes it much harder for them to play. They do not realize how important pulse is, so we emphasize where the pulses are and the evenness of notes between. Often they find out that it's much easier to play rapidly than they thought. If they can isolate where the pulse is, it really seems to help. They can play much easier and cleaner than they did before.

*(Gregory Bimm)*

## TEACHING SCALES

### Relating scales to songs

They can play a song like *America* in D flat and in all other major keys. Once a week during interval work, I have one or several players perform *America* on a named starting note. All others listen and finger their instruments as the student plays.

*(Patricia Brumbaugh)*

### Relating major to minor scales

It's easier for them to relate one scale to another if you play the major scale first and then do relative minor.

They can figure out what that is. I have explained to them what parallel major and minor key means. It is not, though, an important issue for the ear or for building technical facility.

*(Michael Kaufman)*

### Drilling technical skill

Start the chromatic scale on any pitch, playing it in duple meter. Then play it in triple meter with sixteenth notes in a slurred or tongued articulation. One also can divide the group into four different groups. Have one play up to the third in round or canon fashion, singing first and then playing.

I have related numbers to playing scales. Start a rehearsal with, "Here's a concert Bb, sing one-four-six-two-one, now play it." They've got to figure out what the note is from the number.

Some bands develop tone and phrasing, but at the expense of technique. I try not to do that. One way that I combat that is through the warm up. I play through all the major scales, for example, starting on a Bb (up and down) followed by B Major, C Major, C sharp Major, and so on. I do it that way to teach them to think of finger combinations instead of key signatures.

*(Michael Kaufman)*

### Building technique

After students can play a chromatic scale and know the circle of fourths, we would start playing major scales around the circle. We do this very slowly and carefully.

With the middle school band we would use half notes and quarter notes, ascending and descending. Then we would play C Major, F Major, Bb Major, and go right around the entire circle. Now that's time consuming, but for the first levels, if we're patient, we can see a whole world of available approaches for us in what we are doing.

As we do this, we are getting mastery of all the keys. Every day when the students come in, there is a different approach. It's nothing boring, and we are not beating that Bb concert scale into them. Every day what we do with the circle of fourths is different. You cannot repeat yourself too soon.

*(Edward S. Lisk)*

### Developing comprehensive scale skill and understanding

I do what we call digital patterns, through which I introduce the thirds and fifths and so on. We might begin with scale degrees do-re-mi-re-do (1-2-3-2-1) in every key and go around the circle of fourths with that. I'll sing in both syllables and numbers, because I'm connecting the solfege with what is going on in general music class. I also am connecting this to the digital patterns that some teachers also use.

Through this, I'm getting them thinking in that key, rather than just the scale alone. Next, I add notes to develop a command of all notes within that scale. Then we are going to learn the third, because I'm going to get to the arpeggios 1-3-1. Then we go all the way around the circle, we learn all that. I'll give them the numbers 1-2-3-2-1, and then we'll play it back. We'll do it in quarter notes, which is an early level; and then we'll go to eighths. Then I'll go 1-2-3-4-5-4-3-2-1, and then we'll do that all the way around the circle of fourths. Then I say, "Remember the note you turned around on?" They'll realize that the fifth of Bb was F, because they have the chart on their stands. They'll see these connections with a scale they had just played before and I will alert the students to these connections.

Finally, I have them play 1-3-5 - 8 - 5 - 3 - 1, and then they've learned all the arpeggios. The students do not simply memorize the arpeggios in one key. Arpeggios are related to harmonic progression.

*(Edward S. Lisk)*

### Another way to teach a chromatic scale

Don Gee's idea in the first week is to say, "I want you to learn these seven natural notes." They come back and play seven notes. Next week, "I want you to go learn these seven flat notes," then seven sharp notes—and its all covered. That doesn't mess up their psyche like it would ours. Once they learn all the fingerings and the note names, then they are down to tone. Teachers are the ones with the hang up that a scale with five sharps is hard, not the kids.

If you want to be in my top group, you have to play the seven scales that are in A-flat concert scale for your instrument. For example, my trumpets would play Bb, C, D, Eb, F, G, and A. Where my flutes and trombones would play others. They have to do that to make the top group. If they want extra credit or want to know all the major scales, they go further on their own. I've had students approach it by playing the C scale, then they'll play the Db scale, then they play the D scale. It was no big deal, they just learned it.

*(Marguerite G. Wilder)*

### Scale-Rhythm Patterns

We have a set of rhythm patterns that we use. These are like scale rhythmic patterns. We do these patterns on a scale. We do one whole note, two halves, four quarters, eight eighths, with one pitch on each note, not on each pattern. On scale step 1, a whole note; Step 2 and 3, a half note each; Step 4, 5, 6, and the 7th degree, a quarter note each; and eighth notes going down the scale with a repeat of the bottom note. Then I break it into sets of four up and down the scale.

I also do a half-note scale and divide the band into the bass line, the tenor, the alto, and the soprano. When I do this, I bring in a different section every four counts. Then I also can use whole notes, and run it two times or four times in a row, depending on what I want. I can use whole notes against half notes against quarter notes against

eighth notes, etc. We are setting our pulse and the entire group knows where their subdivisions lie.

*(Marguerite G. Wilder)*

### Teaching scales and key signatures

You'd be surprised how many kids do not understand key signatures until they can fill out my scale sheet correctly. The biggest mistake they make is putting the flat or sharp in front of the note affected, but they won't put it on the correct line.

The reason I make them do it both ways is they don't relate the two together. You assume that they do. Kids do not understand and relate the key signature to the location of each flatted or sharped note to the staff itself. They can't put the sharp or the flat on the affected line. That's what they don't understand about key signatures.

*(Marguerite G. Wilder)*

### Teaching minor scales through the tetrachord

I also use the tetrachord idea for minor scales, except the tetrachord is different. You must explain the minor scale's tetrachords separately because they differ from major. One also could skip the building of tetrachords in minor entirely; going directly to the minor scales, since from their work with major scales they almost know them.

I do not do the minor scales with the majors. To prevent them from becoming confused, we do nothing but major scales until they've learned them. It only takes a couple of minutes a day. I teach facility as much as recognition and understanding of how to make the scales.

*(John C. McManus)*

### The solo-soli scale drill

The band begins playing the C major scale to a set metronome marking. They all play a rhythm I have picked, such as a quarter or eighth note per pitch. While the band is playing, I point to a player. When the band returns to the tonic, the player I have selected plays the scale in exactly the same tempo, up and down, followed by the full band, again. If I want to change the scale, I change it while the soloist is playing.

The order of scales could follow a plan, such as a circle of fifths or fourths. I also might select them in any order I want—totally random. With freshmen in summer band, we do scales on the circle of fifths in a "time contest." I'll say, "Let's see if we can go through this and reduce the time it takes." We would play the scales and see how much time we cut down. This would show us the best time we had as a group. If a soloist missed the scale, they'd have to repeat the scale after the whole band played.

*(John Williamson)*

### Building facility on scales and style

Students play all their major and minor scales, which we work on in the warm up. I will say, "F major" while the soloist is playing and then I'll say, "relative minor, harmonic." The next thing they must do is hit the relative minor harmonic of F major, so they would be in D minor.

Once we get that set up at the beginning of the year, I mix in various styles of articulation, rhythms, and pulse. I talk about how the pulse should feel behind this articulation, etc. I'll put an articulation on the board but there would be no notes written. It shows slur two, tongue two, or something, but without pitch notated. They don't know what the pitch is going to be until I tell them.

I also try to conduct so they will do what I want with style. If the style is not correct after playing for a bit, we stop and discuss it. For example, if we are trying to play a light staccato, we talk about what they aren't doing and what they should do. The first thing I do is conduct—what I do verbally is a last resort. Then I sing and they sing back to me, whatever it takes.

*(John Williamson)*

### The chromatic scale

My students learn the chromatic scale and we do it in sequence. They have to learn it ascending at a certain point, to learn it descending at a certain point, and then they have to play both up and down. Then we start timing.

The standards are a regular, progressive thing. I have the students for three years. Over the course of three years and by the time they go to high school, one requirement is that they can perform the chromatic scale correctly ascending and descending at a certain tempo.

Students have changed, however. Years ago, when I asked for a certain standard, they would just smile at me, and go home and learn it. Now you say, "I want you to learn the chromatic scale up for next week." They'll say, "Why do I need to know that?" You cannot tell them, "Because I say so," because that doesn't suffice anymore. They have to know there is a reason that you want them to learn that silly scale. Once you say to them, "That's because you will have much better facility on your horn," or, "That's a wonderful warm up," they have a reason and then they will do it. Now students are less self-motivated. We have to motivate them from the outside.

*(Janet Tweed)*

### Teaching the chromatic scale

When I feel they are beginning to play the chromatic scale, I ask that they play it in eighth notes at 60 beats per minute at least. I also check another aspect of their learning. As I hear the chromatic scale, I will stop them on a note. When I say the word, "Stop," they stop on that note. Then, I will say, "Name that note."

Then they will continue from that note, up or down, wherever they are going. Playing the chromatic scale can be like tying your shoes; you don't think about it. I want them also to be very aware of what notes they are playing. The only way I could check that is to say simply, "Stop." They will say, "That's A sharp, B flat," and we will go on. When I say, "Stop," and we are going up the scale, they

give me sharps; as we are going down, they give me flats.

*(Janet Tweed)*

## TEACHING FACILITY THROUGH GAMES

### The scale-down

I have just discovered a variation, a fun game, of the way we play soli-solo scales. (soli-solo means to have one person alternate with a group. Either the person or the group does a skill first, and the other answers.) We call it a "scale down" related to the term "spell down." Everyone stands as they play, except the students who can't stand, such as bassoons. We go from student to student and a student remains standing as long as they play the scale correctly. It takes a considerable amount of time to go through the whole band. It could be broken down so one section a day plays, or everyone plays one scale a day. I do it with all twelve scales, until there is no one left playing. It is going to take time, but when you're training them, it's well worth the time.

They were beaming when I got done. I did it with my freshman band—they really had fun! I was surprised at some of them who were in there until the bitter end. There was one trombone player who was blowing in the wrong end of the horn at the beginning of the year. When the scale down was on, he didn't want to have egg on his face.

On one occasion, I think we did nine scales before I finally got the last couple of kids. They sit no matter what scale they miss. It only takes one and they sit down. After they sit down, and from then on, they are still going to play the scale for as many times as there are people still standing. They really had fun.

The strong ones are given a chance to shine, because they can stand up and rip through all of those scales. They get aggressive in nailing down all the scales. We may do this every two weeks or so.

We have not chosen sides, but I think that might be the next step. We do scales every day, so this can be a twist. It would probably take a half hour with a band of fifty to do the "scale down."

A couple of times when some kids were on a roll, we had to say, "Okay, we'll finish this tomorrow." When they came back the next day you should have heard the warm up. They were checking each scale to make sure they had it down. The better the band is, the less time soli-solo takes. Sometimes with my symphonic band, we'll really push the tempo, so that the trombone players are double tonguing; everyone is flying!

*(Gregory Bimm)*

### Chromatic races

When we worked on basic technique in grade school, we had chromatic races. After we teach fingerings for chromatic scales of an octave, we would have chromatic races. With each one, we used the stop watch. They played their chromatic scale from the bottom to the top. If they missed a note or played the wrong note, they went back and started over. The clock time ran until they got up and down without a mistake.

Of course, some of them will try to go real fast and they would screw up. On the other hand, some guys played in quarter notes without mistakes. They just loved it, they would just go home and practice chromatic scales. I've had students that played for only three months, who could play one octave chromatic scales in sixteenths and nail it. The teacher can set the criteria to emphasize whatever they want to work on. For example, it's slurred going up and tongued going down. The teacher and students can take it as far as they want. It works better with the little kids—it's really not something I do for college kids. I was using it mainly with fifth graders and they loved it.

*(Donald Wilcox)*

## Teaching Facility through Literature

### Tuning and developing facility in a tonal context

Go to a tuned piano, establish B-flat major tonality with tonic and dominant chords. Ask students to sing *America* in B-flat concert. Immediately after singing *America*, ask them to sound their B-flat concert on their instruments and perform, by ear, the song *America*. Ugliness will abound! Then say that they are to learn to play *America* by ear for the next rehearsal, that is *without music*.

From then on, for each succeeding day—or succeeding intervals of several days each—ask them to play *America* starting on a different note, in a different key, until they have played it on all twelve starting notes of the chromatic scale. Since they will know how to play *America* on twelve different starting notes, they will have learned to play all twelve major scales. The reverse—knowing all twelve major scales—will not result in them being able to play a song on twelve different notes of the chromatic scale.

After learning *America* in all twelve major keys, I would have them play down step-wise from do, to ti, to la. Now using "la" as the tonic in minor (relative minor), I will ask them over a period of days to play *America* in all twelve minor keys.

Using the relative minor scale is grasped aurally (audiated) better than the parallel major. It might be because many of the tonal relationships are the same as major. Using the parallel minor makes theoretical sense to them, but it does not make audiation sense to them, they cannot discriminate the sound differences as easily as the relative minor.

The next step in this, after having them play *America* with B flat as tonic in major and G as tonic in minor, is to have them play *America* starting on C-re. Re is the second degree of the major scale and "re" is used as tonic. Playing

*America* this way, gives them experience with the dorian tonality. One could extend things this way to all other modes, not just major, minor, and dorian. As soon as they can play *America* in major and minor, and perhaps dorian, on twelve different starting pitches, then I introduce another tune. I would make this experience—aural and technical skill building—part of the warm up every day for two to three minutes. This is the length of time it takes to play one tune through two to four times, but in a different key each day.

In the beginning it might take several weeks to learn to play the first tune in all keys. Later, a tune can be learned in fewer weeks. When the key is becoming more familiar under their fingers, students can often learn a tune, in a different key, each day. As they become skilled enough to be successful and the atmosphere is conducive, I have individuals perform the tunes either voluntarily or when asked. When the whole group of 120 are stumbling through with *America*, call on individuals even if they crash and burn. In time, all individuals play some or all tunes, in all keys as solos. In some cases, individuals may play tunes more suited to their level of skills, experience, and talent.

This is important, so they can feel and show competence compared to showing incompetence and feeling failure. In a year they could learn thirty or forty tunes, about one tune a week in all twelve major and minor keys. Once they do one tune, and become familiar with the key, they can learn other tunes quite quickly. This begins late in the first year, certainly by the second year. First year students can begin this with simple tunes like *Hot Cross Buns*. This can, of course, be started at the high school or any level prior or after that.

I would select tunes with varying difficulty, in different meters, in major, minor, and other tonalities, and with different articulations. I include the change of style so a single tune is played in different styles of articulation, the most common differences being separated and connected styles. I have a list of tunes that would work, but the director can pick any that fit. The tunes can be folk songs, tunes from TV and radio, school songs, church songs, and things they like to play and with which they are familiar. Do some of the major songs in minor and some minor tunes in major. I would do this to the extent needed to build their aural understanding of tonality. Not all tunes in major need be played in minor and vice versa.

*(Richard Grunow)*

### Tunes instead of scales at the contest

In time, not far down the road, music contests will change from requiring scales to playing tunes in four or five keys. There are already some people thinking about this in the state of New York.

In addition and more importantly, students will have internalized tonal functions by playing tunes instead of scales, rather than internalizing just finger, tongue, upper lip, lower lip, top-teeth location, bottom-teeth location, middle tongue placement, instrument position, body posture, hand and finger position, secondary knuckle position, dexterity, and other mechanical skills of this type.

*(Richard Grunow)*

## Tunes are more powerful than scales

Tunes are more powerful than scales because tunes establish tonic, dominant, and other tonal functions more powerfully than a scale does. Scales, at best, develop technique and technical skill, but not the student's sense of tonality. The sound of a scale suggests only the leading tone and resting tone, and does so in a less powerful way than tunes. Start with tunes like *Twinkle, Twinkle Little Star* that have a slower harmonic rhythm, so students have time to develop discrimination and skill.

*(Richard Grunow)*

## Useful literature for building facility

The *3-D Band Book* (Belwin), written by James Ployhar, helps build chords and arpeggios in all keys. This is one of the better band technique books on the market. The book includes melodic and harmonic minor scales.

*(Donald Gee)*

## Developing facility through literature

Marches are excellent training material. For the woodwinds, there's nothing better to get the fingers moving. For brass there's nothing better to get that sense of where a line is going. It is a very short, terse, and pithy type of presentation, perfect for getting an idea across.

*(William Long)*

# TEACHING FACILITY THROUGH COMPOSITION

## Using composition to develop beginners' facility

By the third week, their embouchures are beginning, but the brasses have trouble playing E and the A because these pitches finger the same but sound differently.

I say, "I'm going to have you write a short piece for your instrument, using only two notes." Trumpets are going to use your low C and your second line G or I will give them the E and the A. They are having difficulty determining which notes are which, because they have the same fingering. Trombones can use F and Bb and clarinets will use something where they lift all their fingers at once and put them down all together. Low C to an F is an example. For the same reason, flute, oboes, and saxophones can be assigned the third space C to the fourth space Eb. The bassoons could use a low Bb to an F, which compels them to lift a lot of fingers, put them down together and find the holes. I will say, "Use those two notes for your composition."

The first step is to select a mood. I might say, "What do you want, a fanfare? Do you want something slow and moody?" Often these little compositions come out in fanfare style. The two-note limit fits this well. Next they invent a rhythm. I ask them to use a rhythmic motive for their piece if the mood choice is rhythmically oriented.

I give them a written set of steps for them to follow. This shows step one—selecting the notes; step two—is inventing your rhythm. I suggest they experiment until they find a rhythm that they like. I might say, "Repeat that rhythm at least twice during the piece, but you don't have to use it all the time." Step three is to use a musical idea. I define a musical idea by giving them samples. Anything that they can play melodically or rhythmically can be a musical idea. It can be very short. Step four is to memorize the composition, so they don't have to write it down. I ask them to give it a title and perform it for the class.

The beginners will practice the piece and through this they learn how to play C and G. Usually in beginning classes there are fifteen to thirty students, so you can do that in two or three class periods. Of course, these pieces are very, very short—about five or ten seconds at the most for beginners.

*(John C. McManus)*

## Using composition to solve technical problems

I have students write a solo piece for their instrument. The first step is to identify one of their current technical playing problems. Maybe it's moving over the break in the clarinets, moving into a second octave smoothly in the flutes, a lip slur in the brass, or any fingering problem they might have. They identify their current technical playing problem and devise a musical idea that will help them work on and eventually solve it.

These pieces often are written in a rondo-like form. Part A of the rondo will be their technical problem and they are to create a little melodic pattern. The pattern should work well with, for example, the problem of crossing the break in the clarinet. Their melodic pattern is written to meet the technical problem. The B section can be anything they want to include, then they come back to the A section again. The C section is different from A and B and can be anything they like that works musically with the A section. They then play the A section again. There can be as many parts as they want. The sections other than A should be something they can play easily before they return to A, which is the tougher section to perform.

I insist that they notate the tempo, dynamics, articulations, etc. They can play off the score and it need not be memorized. We tell them not to make a big thing of the errors because we know they are working on a problem for which they have written an etude. What the students often do is exchange their compositions with others. They might say, "Hey, I like that one. That will help me work out my change across the break." They give copies to others and they all work on these etudes together.

*(John C. McManus)*

## TEACHING FACILITY WITH A METRONOME

### *Metronome increments*

I use the metronome to teach two kinds of things. One is to develop instrumental technique and the other is to learn the rhythms of a piece and a vocabulary of rhythms. The point of this is to learn to use the metronome in a way that helps them structure their home practice. This will help them learn a passage or develop technical facility in a way that is productive. Not only do they learn the passage or skill, they also learn control and gain confidence that they can do things regularly and correctly.

An example might be a three-line technical study such as Clarke, one with all sixteenth notes. The first stage is to play so slowly that they can do everything right. They must play it correctly, even if they have to play it very slowly at first, without a metronome. If the passage has mixed rhythms, then I want them to play the pitches correctly. Even if they do this slowly, I hope for as many correct rhythms as possible. If there are some errors, I point them out. The guiding concern is that one cannot get to the end of the passage without playing the pitches correctly. When they begin work with this my concern for rhythmic accuracy is slightly less than for pitch accuracy.

The second stage is to use the metronome, setting it at a speed that is so slow that they have little trouble playing accurately. At that speed they should play it ten times. For example, if it is supposed to be played at quarter = 140 we could set the metronome at 80. (Each click refers to an eighth note—two sixteenths to a click.) When they get to 120, move it back to 60 and have them now play four sixteenths on a click—one click for each quarter note. The third stage is to play that passage ten times correctly at 60 quarter notes per minute. When that standard is met, move the metronome to 63 and play it three times without mistakes. Then to 66, where they play it three times—continuing until they get two metronome speeds faster, or 144, than they want the final tempo to be. The increments should be about three to five pulses each, but they can get a bit larger as the speed increases. When the pulse gets to 144 and the exercise or passage has been played three times accurately, go past it to 152, then to 156. After this, go back to 144, which should feel quite comfortable.

The standard of "three times with no mistakes" also includes dynamics, phrasing, articulation, and pitch. In actual practice it takes a long time to get from 50 to 156. Most students would not get close to that in one home practice session. It could be that they get from 60 to 96, for example, the first day or second day. It is not important that they achieve the level on a certain day—it is important that they play the passage each time with accuracy and comfort.

A third component is refinement. All students become more consistent, accurate, more in tune and more focused on the sound. A significant part of this is the aural development. Finding and hearing the notes played correctly gets to their ears because of the accuracy and the recognition of correct and incorrect notes. There are small spots in the practicing of a passage where one could say, "That's close enough." After a while, those little places grate on the nerves and one improves that spot. There also could be problems of tone color or intonation; again, one could say, "That's close enough," or instead, choose to refine and correct the spot.

These observations support why I think this process should be done. As one uses this process frequently throughout a period of one or more years, it is easy to see that the process also refines the sense of hearing in relationship to the instrument. There are other factors that determine how fast they will progress: the difficulty, length, previous progress, talent of the student, range, amount of rest between sessions, and how long the practice session lasts. This step-wise approach fits woodwind and keyboard players very well and seems also to be helpful for brass players. A student could sing or practice fingerings, so they can let their muscles rest and lips recover. This routine was a little harder for French horn because of the increased chances of misplaying notes. It is likely that the articulations need to be performed shorter at first. This may prepare them for the faster speeds. The shorter articulations did not lengthen proportionally with the increase of tempo.

*(Donald DeRoche)*

I often find that young students, when given a musical selection with difficult technical passages, will keep playing the music over and over in hope that eventually they will play it well. Their practice is more successful if they first slow the tempo down to a level where they can play the passages correctly even on the first try. If they play it slowly enough, it is possible to play correctly on the first try. Then I set the metronome, or ask them to set the metronome, to that tempo. I ask them to gradually, very gradually, work up to the tempo prescribed in the music or given by the director. This is more effective than saying, "Play slowly and build the speed to a faster tempo."

*(Roman Palmer)*

## MISCELLANEOUS

### *Playing scales with changes of tone color*

When we play scales, we do so with different tone colors. We use bright and warm sounds to establish a "kinesthetic memory" of the way it feels to play different tone colors.

*(Richard Fischer)*

### *The need for relaxation to command facility*

I suggest relaxation, soft hands, very little physical movement—moving nothing such as the tongue or fingers any further than needed. This can reduce tension, especially in fingers and hands.

*(Robert Floyd)*

## *Trading parts*

Do you ever have kids trade parts and play somebody else's—like the clarinet player playing the trumpet part? I've done that sometimes with my college group. I assign them to play another part with their instrument even if they must transpose the part. I used this for transposition practice, raising awareness, and challenging students.

*(Donald Wilcox)*

## *Memorization*

I think memorization is important because of what it can do for the ear. In some sense, memorization may be indispensable. They must memorize the scales and it takes most of the year to do this. Besides causing students to practice, scales also teach them nearly every fingering on the instrument, including alternates. If students memorize scales, they can practice them without looking, therefore, they can listen to themselves. Besides the memorization of scales, they memorize occasional pieces from the book, so something is memorized each week.

*(John W. LaCava)*

# CHAPTER EIGHT

# INTONATION

The teaching of intonation is often problematic: intonation is not an isolated skill; intonation relates to other factors such as tonality, ensemble, tone color, and breath support; teachers have conflicting views about the uses and misuses of mechanical and electronic tuners; and there may be insufficient knowledge about natural tuning versus tempered tuning, and how this relates to the specific intonation characteristics of individual instruments. Some teachers feel that intonation is too hard to teach; others hesitate because they think students will not exert the effort to learn to play in tune. As a result teaching intonation can be frustrating for even the best teachers.

Teachers must assume that students can learn to perform in tune; they then must develop an approach to teaching tuning, with which students can make progress. The comments in this section are particularly rich. There is a variety of insights that suggest things for teachers to know and do. Central among many of the practical teaching techniques for intonation is the emphasis upon developing listening skills and listening targets. The contributors also stress the need to build student judgment and responsibility.

The comments center around the idea that intonation is essentially an issue of judgment based upon aural and musical perception. Only secondarily is tuning a mechanical or electronic issue. Therefore, the solution lies neither with the tuner, nor how the student uses the tuner, but in the aural perception and judgment of the student. If teachers learn to use several of these techniques successfully and tuners properly, they should see progress in an area so much in need of improvement. There is the expectation that the teachers' frustrations can be lessened and students' listening and intonation skills improved.

## THE VALUE AND PROCESS OF PLAYING IN TUNE

### Intonation

There is nothing wrong with playing out of tune, as long as you don't do it for more than an instant.

*(Stanley Cate)*

Over the years, I have come to hate poor intonation. Out of tune performance offends me so much that you wouldn't believe it. However, I believe that the more I work on the fundamentals of good sound production, the more the serious intonation problems diminish.

*(Gerald Olson)*

Intonation is everything.

*(Donald Wilcox)*

### Listening

By listening to all other things, most intonation problems are solved. The more students listen the better their intonation is, because they begin not to accept poor intonation.

*(Gary Hill)*

### Playing in tune

There are three things: you must listen, you must know the tuning peculiarities and what is likely to be out of tune for your instrument and, you must learn to listen to and adjust to other players. Any of our principal orchestras, such as the Chicago Symphony, play in tune so well because the members make these fine adjustments like a thirty-five millimeter slide. They make them so quickly that you don't even know it happens. They're constantly adjusting to each other as they work with each other and they always know how the person next to them is playing.

*(Richard J. Suddendorf)*

The tuning should be completely auditory, instead of the machine business with all that pulling and pushing. That doesn't net a pair of ears that function. I don't use the word listen by itself, I would more likely say "match pitch," "match the octave," or "line that up." The term "just listen" isn't enough alone, nor is pointing to my ear.

*(Donald Gee)*

You must listen all the time instead of just mashing the buttons.

*(Myron Welch)*

317

### The tuning note

First, I don't believe in a tuning note. If somebody says, "Play a B-flat tuning note," to me that's an adjustment pitch for one's instrument; but, that's not good pitch for every instrument. Let's say you've got a trombone player and he's playing B flat. That will help him lengthen or shorten his instrument, but won't help him play D natural in tune. The tuning note to me is whatever note you're playing at the time. If I'm playing a F concert, that's the tuning note. After tuning their instruments, the kids start to play and forget it. Actually, we get those B flats from the tuner and put them in vacuum tubes.

*(John Williamson)*

### Pitch matching is only a small part of intonation

We must realize the place of balance, matching pitch, color, focus, and volume in intonation. Then we have a more complete perception of intonation.

While playing chords, for example, we can distinctly hear beats and hear that the pitch is very close. We can distinctly hear beats that are obnoxious when it is out of balance, when one player does not have as full a sound as another player, or when they have a different tone color. My concern is the balance of tone colors, matching pitch, fullness of tone, etc. Focus means that a tone is centered and has the optimum resonance.

*(Richard K. Hansen)*

### "In-tone" versus "in-tune"

The instruction, "play in tone," with good air stream, with centered pitch and characteristic tone means much more than the phrase, "play in tune." This implies only good pitch.

When tuning people, I am working more on their characteristic tone. Once one has that then one can really start working successfully. I refrain from telling students to play sharp or flat. Instead I try to detect, from listening to their sounds, things that would improve their tone production. It might be by taking a deeper breath, blowing more air or a stronger air stream, or making an embouchure adjustment. This also depends upon the instrument.

*(Richard K. Hansen)*

### The challenge

I am a firm believer that it is nearly impossible to get a group of instruments pitched in various keys to play in tune. Because of the physics of the matter, they cannot be pre-tuned to be in tune. It will not happen, and I have never heard it happen. The choral effect of many on a part masks the effect of intonation differences. This is why I say, "Listen is the first half of an instruction, the other half is adjust."

*(Donald Gee)*

No matter how good the instrument is that is in your hands, it is impossible to manufacture any wind instru-

ment, brass or wood or plastic, that is perfectly in tune with the tempered scale. If we were to produce such an instrument, the holes and the keys would be in such places that no human fingers could reach them.

Since we cannot change the laws of nature, the instruments are built in tune closer to the natural scale; but, they must be played in tune with the tempered scale. The only way, therefore that we can play in tune together, even if we are playing on a horn made of solid uranium, never mind platinum—with platinum and gold, and silver beads and bangles and buckles and baubles—the only possible way we can play in tune together is by constantly listening and adjusting.

*(Alfred Reed)*

### Tuning or tone quality

I've noticed that most people have that all backward. They're working on tuning and the player's tone doesn't sound good. The kids lack a characteristic sound and you can't tune a poor tone. I stress to these teachers that once you've achieved that characteristic and clear sound, the tone is easier to tune.

*(John Williamson)*

### Playing musically

By emphasizing a musical sound and phrasing, students solve many intonation problems on their own. I do not want to sacrifice musical results to get technical cleanliness.

*(Robert Grechesky)*

### Poor intonation

If you do not play in tune, you cancel two people in the group; the one that is in tune and one that is not. You do not get room resonance unless you are in tune. Two people out of tune produce twenty-five percent of the sound of two people in tune. A small band can have as much sound as a large one, if they play in tune.

*(John W. LaCava)*

### Intonation improves the quality of sound

Parents from larger school programs will say, "You know I am amazed at how big that band sounds." I tell them that if you start playing in tune, you start sounding bigger, because playing in tune reduces distorted and destructive sounds.

*(Terry A. Oxley)*

### Individual responsibility

With tuning, I do the same problem-solving that I would do with rhythm. First, I do not believe that having everyone sound B flat every day and telling someone to push in and pull out has anything to do with tuning. Tuning is an individual matter or responsibility. Time should be set aside for each person to learn where their instrument lines up. That is something they should do outside the rehearsal. You might want to schedule some time after school or at lunch. The kids can come in and examine how their instrument acts on certain notes and registers. Other variables also must be consistent such as embouchure, breathing, and the instrument's reed.

Providing that the equipment is in good condition, then tuning becomes an ear-training exercise. They can mark the cork or slide so daily they are putting it in the same location. The instrument should not be set way in one day and way out the next.

I think tuning is a matter of sensitivity. I use the beginning of all rehearsals as sensitivity sessions. There are some wonderful chorale books that are good music. The Yoder-Gillette *Thirty-Five Famous Chorales* is terrific and it is good music worthy of concerts. A teacher is not building sensitivity if a kid comes in every day, sits in the same seat, and plays the same chorale without listening and adjusting.

*(Larry Rachleff)*

### Listening takes energy and results are slow

Students must be willing to invest energy in the listening process. It is not harder for current kids than previous kids to listen. Students now can listen very constructively. They do expect, however, an immediate reward more than previous generations. They are not as willing to sit still over a long term, say one year, to discover what they have or could have accomplished.

*(Robert Floyd)*

## FACTORS THAT AFFECT PLAYING IN TUNE

### Posture and position

If they pull their clarinet down, keeping the angle between themselves and the instrument smaller, the pitch improves. This appears to counteract sharpness. Don't play it like a soprano sax!

Changing the instrument's angle may not do anything physically, but as a placebo it improves intonation. Perhaps they listen more after the adjustment to see if it worked. Another problem is with saxophones. They often put their hand on the mouthpiece while tuning concert B flat or G; or, they place their right hand on the mouthpiece while adjusting. This also effects pitch. Their hand touches the mouthpiece and dampens the vibrations inside the mouthpiece. Using your hand in this way also may change the weight on the lower lip, which also can change pitch. To solve this, adjust the instrument, then play the tuning notes with the correct hand and arm position.

*(Michael Golemo)*

### Knowing the part

Students cannot address the problem of intonation if they haven't learned their parts. If they don't know how the piece sounds or don't know the notes, they will not play

in tune because they are preoccupied with fingerings and getting the right notes.

*(Carl A. Bly)*

### Blend and balance

When we play the full B-flat chord, it might seem out of tune, but it could be a balance or blend problem. Students sometime mistake poor intonation for what is actually a balance or blend problem. If they listen and solve this, they solve intonation problems.

*(Michael Golemo)*

After working on blend and balance of sound, and listening to what is going on rhythmically, these efforts eliminate about ninety percent of the ensemble's inherent intonation problems. If there are still pitch problems, chances are there truly is some problem with the instrument or the reed; or else the student can't hear that day.

*(Gary Hill)*

### Consistent pitch reference

One very common obstacle to getting good intonation is not adhering to a standard pitch. We need to tune instruments to a common pitch and to check so tuners are still in correct calibration. The purpose is not only to move instruments to the correct pitch location. Players also start memorizing the feel of the instrument on a certain pitch— they remember the feel of the embouchure, the feeling of air pressure, etc.

Therefore, I also am careful about the source tone, the standard or model for the pitch itself. It must have a good characteristic sound. I do not select the weaker players as the model for pitch and tone—it does not work.

*(Richard K. Hansen)*

### Equipment and good intonation

Select good instruments and mouthpieces! This was somewhat hard to do in the beginning of the program, but later students accepted this as a matter of course.

*(Barbara Buehlman)*

### Tuning problems

The problem with intonation is that wind players don't have good air support and some have student instruments, which may be built flat. Since the kids have not learned to pay attention to playing in tune, intonation is a constant effort. I use a tuner set at 440, sometimes 438. We have a problem with clarinets being flat, even when they push the instrument way in.

*(Judith A. Niles)*

### Tune when warm

One certainly must wait until the students warm up before tuning begins. It does little to tune when they are cold. I use the tuner to prove to students that this is true.

*(John Kinnison)*

## Tuning terminology

I am not happy with the terminology we use when we say, "Let's tune up now!" What we should really say is, "Let's tune." It is even more accurate to say, "Let's tune down," because I think that many people play and tune high. The two most notorious sections are flutes and trumpets.

*(Thomas Stone and Francis Marciniak)*

## The key of the composition

I remember a guy who had the B flat tuned perfectly with the strobes in the warm up room. He continued tuning individuals to B flat, even after the curtain had opened. Then, they played the *Fantasia in G Major* of Bach! The band was terribly out of tune, though he had worked that B flat extensively.

*(Frank B. Wickes)*

## Instrument mastery

I am concerned with total mastery of the instrument. The time you spend with the horn in your face will determine whether your getting closer and closer to pitch, and becoming consistent every day.

*(Charles Olson)*

## Hearing tonality

A reference tone can give you pitch, but not tonality, just as the metronome gives you pulse or tempo, but not "time" in the musical sense. Matching pitch and tuning by interval are helpful in maintaining appropriate intonation, but sensing tonal center, tonal tendencies, and chordal functions effect playing in tune more. Neither pitch matching nor playing an interval in tune refer as much to tonality as tonal tendencies and chord functions. The difference is not simply adding a new technique, such as listening to tonal tendencies. Instead we have added something that is geometric in proportion; we have added a dimension to what and within which we listen.

*(Joseph Casey)*

## CURRICULAR IMPLICATIONS

### The responsibility

You must teach them what "in-tune" is.

*(Larry Rachleff)*

### Intonation from day one

We must begin developing awareness of pitch issues and how to tune their instruments from the very beginning. Some believe, unfortunately, that one does not start to talk pitch with a beginner from the beginning.

*(Barbara Buehlman)*

You cannot get good intonation or balance or anything else without a good idea of tone. I stress tone as much

as I possibly can, with intonation awareness. Teachers must stress this constantly, because it is never too early for one to stress these elements. Some people do not stress this because they are teaching little kids, but this can be done from "day one." In the very beginning I would use unison, then soon I would have them tune to chords, perhaps after six weeks.

*(John Kinnison)*

## Teaching intonation

I think teachers devote too little effort to the matching of unisons or fifths, so they are a beat-less sound. The fifths are sometimes easier to hear initially. We use the fifth and the octave mostly, since unisons are sometimes more difficult due to the blend problem.

In the sixth, seventh, and eighth grades we spend most of our effort and time on tone production. Until they can produce a full tone, intonation is out the window. With tone, they can hear and eliminate the beats that bother them. It takes a good long while to teach and police the production of tone, and another good long while to teach tuning at a basic level. Either one can slip out in one day. It could take the rest of the year to correct it. We do not get into inflections of chord tones until the advanced level.

Intonation is only one of many things that a director in early years must pay attention to. They also must pay attention to hand position, posture, breathing, reeds, etc. Intonation, therefore must come into things the first year at a very simple level. We teach students to hear the fifth and the octaves and how to manipulate the pitch.

The key issue is to make the tone flex. They can hear, try, and understand the need, but they need to know how to manipulate the pitch up and down. I am a firm believer that it is nearly impossible to get a group of instruments, pitched in the keys they are pitched in, to play in tune.

Given the physics of the matter, they cannot be tuned to be in tune. It will not happen, and I have never heard it happen. The choral effect of many on a part can mask the effect of intonation differences.

*(Donald Gee)*

## Judging intonation

Once first-year beginners get a tone, I have them listen to two saxophones, for example. I do not think there are very many sounds worse than beginning saxophone sounds. They play two tones together and listen to the differences in sound. I ask, "Does it sound like the same note?" We start training the student to work with the tuner and listen to his tone and other student's tone in the second year. I think the tuner can be used effectively and early simply for beginning or raising their awareness about pitch, pitch changing, etc.

*(Phillip A. Weinberg)*

## The first step

Especially at younger levels, there is a real need for

them to understand what they must do on each instrument. They need to know all the options for lowering and raising the pitch. On a purely practical basis that is the first step in moving toward better intonation. Knowing this is valuable and when young students have learned how to adjust their instruments, they can do this on their own as they play.

*(Gary Hill)*

### Teaching young students to begin tuning

Some beginning band teachers only tune their first-year students on rare occasions, such as immediately before concerts. I prefer to tune beginning students regularly for the following reasons: (a) the ensemble sonority is obviously more pleasing to all; (b) the students start developing a sense of in-tune performance; and (c) any major intonation discrepancies serve as another symptom of other performance problems. These might be in the areas of embouchure formation, breath support, quality of reeds, or instrument repair.

*(Judith Delzell)*

When teaching middle and junior high school students to play in tune, I use three techniques: first, I make the students aware of intonation by pointing out two or more players who are obviously out of tune or I intentionally create an intonation problem by pushing one player's tuning slide or mouthpiece all the way in and pulling the other player's slide or mouthpiece out so the pitch difference between the two students is exaggerated. Second, I have the two out-of-tune students adjust their slides or mouthpieces, as necessary, until they arrive at an in-tune sound. Then, I relate the words "high and low" to the words "sharp" and "flat." I explain that when you pull out, your instrument will sound lower or "flatter" and when you push in your instrument will sound higher or "sharper." Third, I let students work on their own following the above example. I also stop the band and point out obviously out-of-tune players. I ask them to work out the problem and I often encourage them to experiment until they hear improvement. I feel that just saying, "The band is out of tune; please listen and adjust," is not enough.

*(Roman Palmer)*

When teaching a younger player how to adjust the pitch of his instrument during tuning, I start by teaching them to sing or hum pitches, usually starting with familiar songs. I then provide them with a model of in-tune and out-of-tune sounds, often by playing my instrument with a fixed reference pitch, such as that produced by a tuner. I bend my pitch in and out of tune, encouraging the student to identify when I am in-tune and when I am out-of-tune by listening for beats. I then teach them how to change the pitch on their instrument. They do this through the usual changes in tuning slides and through the right adjustments of their embouchure.

The brass or reed players may adjust their embou-

chures by raising or lowering their jaw to open up more space. Say, "Pretend you are gripping a cork between your teeth, and the cork is getting bigger and smaller." The student can firm and relax the grip on his mouthpiece or reed. For this say, "Tighten the drawstring. Now loosen it." They also can firm and relax the corners of their mouths. Flute players can raise and lower their air stream ("pout your lower lip out more . . . now let it relax back under your upper lip"). I have them listen to the effect changing embouchure has on tone, especially in combination with a slower or faster air stream.

They identify and practice the air/embouchure combination that produces the better tone. Once this combination is consistent, I teach the following tuning process:

1. Listen to the reference pitch.
2. Sing or hum the pitch.
3. Play the note with your best tone quality. (This establishes a good embouchure.)
4. Blend your pitch higher and lower, listening to your pitch in relation to the reference pitch. (This requires the student to play in balance and with the reference pitch.)
5. If you had to make your embouchure smaller, or raise your air stream, to make the pitch you are playing sound closer to the correct pitch, then make your instrument smaller (that is, push in the tuning slide, head joint, etc.). If you had to make your embouchure bigger or lower your air stream, then make your instrument bigger. That is pull out the slide.

Once they can stop the beats without making any major changes in the embouchure and keep their best tone, then the instrument is in tune for *that* pitch. The student who tunes through the above procedure not only learns to tune the instrument to the standard reference pitch; they also learn to adjust their pitch automatically as they perform without sacrificing tone quality.

*(Scott Shuler)*

### The third-valve slide

I work on this from the first day they pick up their instruments. My cornet players know that the slide should move out when using fingering combinations of one and three on D and one, two and three on D flat/C sharp. I keep hearing trumpet players from other schools say, "Well, my teacher said for now finger it this way and later when you get better, you can do it this way."

To have them hear the effects of the third-valve slide, I have them use it like a trombone. I make the comparison to the trombone—how you extend the slide to lower pitch and pull it in to raise the pitch. When we are playing together in imitation, they'll play after me and we will listen to the difference in pitch. Most of the time, they are right on. When we play together they hear the waves but they are not sure whether they are sharp or flat. We have to stop and play one at a time. We talk about intonation right away.

*(Nancy Plantinga)*

### Comment

Philosophically and idealistically, I would like to think that all my trumpeters know that low D is sharp. In the real world of public education, we all know that they do not know to pull out that third valve. If I can get that done in the warm up, I can say, "Great."

*(Michael Kaufman)*

### Adjusting and bending

I show varying pitch a lot during seventh grade. I show them that I can do half-step adjustments. I have individuals try to match me to learn to bend pitches. My demonstration is a general, broad view, at first.

*(John W. LaCava)*

## BUILDING AWARENESS AND JUDGMENT

### Tuning familiar notes

I ask students to warm up on the notes with which they are most familiar, and the tones with the better resonance and tone color. Sometimes I tune these tones to the tuner instead of using an A or a Bb.

*(Richard Alnes)*

### Stimulating thinking

I say to students, "If you pulled every other performer's slide in and every other's slide out while the symphony players were away during intermission, how many notes would be out of tune when they returned to play after intermission?" Students say either, "None of the notes," or "The first note." That tells me that they know what should take place.

*(Hal D. Cooper)*

When notes are not in tune, I suggest, "Don't fight each other with your sounds, combine your sounds." This also is true when blend and balance are a problem.

*(David Hans)*

### Singing

Singing is extremely valuable and I use it more with the younger students than the college kids. I try to get them to realize that they need to sing or hear the pitch before they produce it. I think that this is very important. They are more apt to be out of tune if they cannot replicate the pitch in advance.

*(Pamela Gearhart)*

### Bring it up and intonation improves

The other day I was laughing with Mike Leckrone,

and he said, "You know Gerry, I've found this great technique to improve intonation." I said, "Tell me!" Mike said, I just say, "You are out of tune"; then I pause and say, "Play in tune." When we start again, the intonation is better!

*(Gerald Olson)*

### Using a synthesizer

I use the synthesizer's filter banks to show harmonics. It is a revelation to students that you can take what they hear as one sound or one note and start dividing that sound. Suddenly, with the emerging of lower harmonics, they start to hear the fifth. I try to get that across with tuning. If I'm playing a low B flat and there is an F, an octave and a fifth above me, *that note is in my note*. It won't be in tune unless you're in tune with my harmonic above me. I'm still experimenting with this because with the arrival of technology and the synthesizers that students are buying these days, we have more tools we can use when teaching.

*(Timothy Mahr)*

### Developing relative pitch

When kids come into the rehearsal room they are hearing an F concert from the tuner. By the end of a few months, the kids could hum or play an F concert and know what it's going to sound like before they heard it. I used to ask them to listen ahead to imagine the sound before they heard it. I sometimes set a different pitch, to see if they would find it; or, I would change the pitch and see if they would notice it.

*(Frank B. Wickes)*

### The problem and the challenge

I tried to teach them to expect that every note was going to be out-of-tune. Thus, it was their job to correct it before anyone heard it. We spend all our time on it, since we never play without thinking about intonation.

*(Butler R. Eitel)*

### Using mouthpiece drills

I do a lot of mouthpiece playing with brass instruments. If we have pitch problems, we will play the piece on mouthpieces to improve intonation. This focuses sound and pitch very well. I have used it in the last few years and I assure you that it works well if used correctly. We also use long tones for building strength and because they get to hear themselves.

*(Stanley Cate)*

### Listening exercises to improve intonation

Some days, I might spend fifteen minutes on balance, blend, and tuning games. I may ask them to play sharp or flat and also to notice which it is. I often use an instrument or my voice to demonstrate pitch changing and then ask the students to do what I just showed. I also choose dissimilar instruments such as tuba and flute, to have them experience tuning and blending. Since we take our pitch from another instrument instead of the tuner, we also have a "Who's left?" game. In this game, the four or five students in a class tune. The game is to see who can get in tune the quickest.

*(R. G. Conlee)*

### Building listening

If there is a unison where there are intonation problems, I would first have the lowest instruments play, then have everyone in the band sing that pitch. I then add the upper voices which have the same pitch. They sing it at an octave above the lower pitch. Even if they don't have that pitch in their parts, I would involve everybody singing and listening. I do that to keep all minds on the task, but also to exercise their ears.

They must sing, experiment with pitch, and know the tendencies of the horn. They also must know that, when in doubt, nine times out of ten, the upper voices are usually sharp, because there is a tendency for the ears to hear things sharp. I do teach them how to bend the tone, but I do not encourage them to bend it out of tune deliberately so they can hear what out of tune sounds like.

*(Michael Kaufman)*

### Tuning and playing scales aurally

Use the auditory approach for scales and choose E flat or B flat, which is in a comfortable range for most instruments. They can be taught to pick and identify the correct intervals very successfully. As they learn this, that becomes the standard for their ears. Later they then can handle B major. This scale requires a lot of manipulation of the instrument to make it sound as comfortable and as in tune as E-flat major.

*(Donald Gee)*

### The "beat-elimination" approach

Most musicians, according to a pitch perception test published in the *Journal of Research in Music Education*, are pitch confused. Therefore, we do not burden students too much about being sharp or flat, but sensitize them instead to the idea of beat elimination.

*(Richard K. Hansen)*

### Teaching listening for beats

In sectionals or even for rehearsals, I teach them how to listen for beats. I ask, "Do you hear them and do you want them faster or slower?" They should be so slow that they are nonexistent. I say, "If the beats are getting slower you went the right way, but do it a little bit more."

I also teach beats in a large group, but they have to match with their neighbors. They also must understand that if one tone is 440 and one is 445, they are going to have five beats in five seconds. They should realize if it gets down to three they are going in the right direction. You make this change by adjusting the embouchure first, and then adjusting the instrument.

*(Myron Welch)*

### Tuning to a pedal tone

One thing I try to have the band do is to have one part of the band play the pedal tone. The other part of the band plays an ascending scale against it. As they play, they tune intervals to that pedal tone. That's something that also can be done in a chamber group. They can have one person hold the pedal and another person go up the scale.

*(Richard Kennell)*

### Thinking about tuning

Instead of using unison tuning only, I use triads. I have them play the root or fifth out of tune intentionally to prove to them that they can hear if they listen. It also teaches them what beats are. This teaches them what in tune means compared to only reading the dials on the tuning machine. They really have to listen.

I tried not to use the visual feature of the tuner any more than I had to. We have seen band directors walking around the band room showing kids where the needle is— that does almost no good at all. However, I also used tuning devices with triads to show the effects of posture, embouchure, or breath support upon tone and pitch. I had them intentionally not support a tone and notice the effect upon pitch. They also used poor hand position intentionally on the flute to see the effect of this on pitch.

I would have them recreate some poor habits so they could see, with the help of the tuner, the effect of the poor habits. For example, putting your arm on the back of the chair, or letting your wrists bend. It soon became something they could see and hear. There are many ways to use the tuning devices without using the eyes so much and with using the ear more.

*(John Kinnison)*

### Singing, playing and bending pitches

We mix singing with playing by singing tones on and off pitch. I will have someone give the center pitch and hold it as a reference. As I hold my hand flat, I use my thumb to show that they should bend up, bend down or keep it level. They do this singing and can hear the reference pitch played by the one player. Then they do it with their instrument. When we first started this they giggled, but they don't anymore; they take it seriously.

*(Frank Schulz)*

### Improving intonation

If they all play out of tune but together, they are really playing in tune because intonation is relative. Therefore, you have to show them what is in tune and what is not in tune. I might have them listen to the beats as two clarinet players are playing out of tune.

Listening for beats is just another way of getting them to hear at a basic level. Through this, they understand the difference in sound between good intonation and bad intonation. Beat listening shows that interference between sound waves creates that beat. You can always build on that by saying, "Now you hear how the tuning and the blend is so much better when you're in tune. The basic character of the sound of each of you is now the same." I think this is an obvious way to deal with intonation instead of saying "it stinks."

Another very important point is the shape of the sound. It is easier to tune with an open, natural, correctly-produced tone. I use the idea of a common vowel sound to unify tone colors. I find that many tuning problems will take care of themselves as you build that tone, as you play lots of unisons and slowly build chords. Much of the sensitizing goes on in the warm up period.

*(Thomas Stone)*

### Persistence

You have to keep going for it again and again and finally they understand. I often say, "Okay clarinets, now you, now you, now you and you," as I add in one person at a time.

I'll also have them play different combinations of instruments. If I'm tuning the flute section and have gone through each person, I match it with the oboe, even if we are tuning to the tuner or another instrument. I'll say, "You play with this person." Either it's in tune or it's out of tune, and we'll persist until it's right.

This approach is like tuning with pairs when I have person A play with person B, and then I'll have B play with C, and then C play with D, until I get through the entire section. Then I'll have F play with A. This can tell us if we've kept the pitch the same all the way through. Then I'll choose different pairs, until we feel very comfortable and we are right on the mark.

While tuning, I ask them many questions. "Is that in tune?" "Who's higher?" "Are you listening to the flutes?" "Of these two people, which one is sharp and, which one is flat?" Then I may ask specific persons in a section to listen. "Bill, is it getting better or worse?" "Jane, is it in tune or not?" To help them remember how to adjust their instrument, I remind them that the piccolo is the smallest and highest instrument, and the tuba is the largest and the lowest. "If you want your instrument to be lower like a tuba, you would want it to be longer, so pull out. If you want your instrument to be higher like a piccolo, then push it in."

*(Thomas Stone)*

### Choosing a reference pitch

Either get a piano that's in tune, a tuning fork, or something that the kid can use to develop a sense of sharp and flat. At a young age you can't expect them to be superhuman, but in the beginning they must have something upon which to build. Later, you can wean them.

*(William W. Wiedrich)*

### Tuning in the ensemble

I think intonation is the overlooked element in ensemble playing. We must keep harping, and harping, and harping on intonation. The biggest thing I face technically is intonation. I mean fingerings are tangible and can be learned, but intonation seems too subjective. Yet, it is something that the kid has to master.

*(William W. Wiedrich)*

### Helping them make judgments

At the beginning of the rehearsal when it's sensitivity time, you might want to say, "Okay, today just play an A. Now sing an E (after they have sung or played the A). Sound it, close your eyes, play it."

Switch notes until they are understanding where the fifth interval is. Then, have half the group hold the A and the E simultaneously. The other half can play a scale up to the E. This lets them examine why when they play the whole steps and half steps their scale increases or stretches as one goes up.

Have someone in the group raise his hand when his pitch starts to get too high or too low. Teaching them to practice with a tuner, like practicing with a metronome or tape recorder, is essential. Abusing them is not good. You can be guiding them as they explore these issues.

*(Larry Rachleff)*

I teach them to tune instantly as they play. I have them alternate their inhaling with a "haaa" sound on the preparatory beat with playing an eighth note's worth of sound on the chord. This also builds support and anticipation of the sound they are about to play. I call this "touching" the tone.

I might repeat this ten times in succession. They watch the stick to see how long to sustain the sound. If they don't get an in tune or projected sound right away, I might have them play a longer sound. This gives them time to hear its tone and pitch, both blended and balanced.

They learn from this that the short sound is just a chunk of the good long sound. The next step beyond that is to play the note your neighbor has. That forces them to listen to the note their neighbor is playing. This fosters listening to each other. Now if they do not do as well, we can take a step backward. If that happens, I'll say, "All right, play a long tone." I'll blend it and balance it. Then I'll say, "Okay, from that long note that we just worked on, let's take a part of that long note and play it as a short note." They get the idea that the ideal version of this note exists in a long form; we're just going to cut out a piece of it.

*(Thomas Stone)*

### Showing the effect of dynamics on pitch

Take a flute and clarinet that are well in tune in the middle part of their range. Then have them just play mezzo piano on a crescendo and listen to the flute go sharp and the clarinet go flat. Everybody can hear that and will go "yuck." Have them play the diminuendo and the change will go in the other direction.

This demonstration makes the kids aware that the instruments, in spite of what the brochure says, are not built in tune in the factory and they never will be. If you push down first valve, you may get B flat; then again, you may just get something in the neighborhood of B flat. Since this is so, you have to adjust it to make it work. You also have to know physically what the instrument is going to do by itself, if you don't compensate for it. The demonstration is predictable and you can say, "This always works. Every time you play a long note soft, the flutes will get yelled at for playing flat. That is a reason for it."

*(Donald Wilcox)*

### *Judging tone production before judging intonation*

Have students play a good supported tone as in tune as they can judge it to be, without looking at the tuner. Then, teach them to glance at the tuner after they have been listening to their own sustained tone. Their task is to check if their judgment resulted in a pitch that was in or out of tune. Then, based on what they did and saw, they can make judgments and adjustments during additional tries.

There are several ways to do this. They may play up to the tuning note, slurring through degrees five, six, seven, and eight (or tonic), and check the last note. They also can play up and down scales, through melodies, or improvise a sequence of tones. In each of these exercises, their job is to stop on a note they judge is correct. They should hold that pitch as though it were marked with a fermata and then glance at the tuner for feedback. They are to notice the feedback and repeat the segment to see if they are making a better judgment or not when they stop again.

As they play what they judge is a good, in-tune tone, their judgment process has already begun; so adding the judgment of whether it is in or out of tune is not as hard, since they are already listening to the tone and making judgments about that before looking at the tuner.

*(Joseph Casey)*

## KNOWLEDGE, SKILLS, AND INTONATION

### *Exercises to improve pitch skills*

To get good pitch we talk about being flexible with air and embouchure; and we do tone bending exercises—back and forth—while keeping a characteristic tone.

For example, we have weekly assignments to try out and discover their instrument's tuning tendencies. I have given them fingering charts and relabeled them "in-tone charts." What they are to do is to chart out their instruments' acoustical tendencies. They are to adjust and get their pitches correct. If they are high on certain notes, we have them take another approach to correct the problem. They do this before pushing or pulling slides, cheating on

the instrument, or using first and third valve slides. We recommend that they open their throats or yawn as they hold their heads back. The purpose is to get the instrument to resonate at the setting where it is or ought to be. Then, we ask them to blow a stronger air stream. This means stronger, more intense, more air with less muscle tension.

I have students work with partners and chart notes. The chart looks like a fingering chart found in a beginning band book. We also can print copies for students. Using the chart provides them with a list of the alternate fingerings, which are especially helpful for woodwinds. They mark whether the note is sharp or flat and hand this in each week. The number of pluses and minuses declines as time goes on. This shows they are improving with intonation.

We could make the charting more realistic by relating this exercise to a piece we are playing. They could chart out their part in the same way as they did the scale. They play and eliminate beats with the other—the source person—who is correct according to the tuner. This combines a standard pitch reference with the skill of playing in tune with another person.

We also do pitch bending exercises. By using the ear and changing the embouchure pressure, opening or closing the throat, and manipulating the air, we have them go as flat or as sharp as they can. We have an old Johnson Intonation Trainer, which is not manufactured anymore. You can set the pitches or scales according to tempered, natural, or any manner of tuning.

*(Richard K. Hansen)*

### *Learning instrument tendencies*

Give them extra credit, give them a chart to keep a record of their experiments. Everyone has to learn the tendencies of their instrument. Assign two students, one to play and one to watch the tuner. Do this in September, December, and May. We all know they will improve if the instrument is working—provided they know the instrument's tendencies and we activate their ear through singing and sensitivity sessions. Of course, we have to remind them about this regularly.

*(Larry Rachleff)*

At some point knowledge of the mechanical and the acoustical operation of the instrument is invaluable. A student can gain this in a couple of ways: (a) the teacher provides the students with information that is basic to each instrument; and (b) students use a tuner with a partner—a good way to build knowledge. There are two roles, the partner who does not play but looks at the machine, and the player who plays and does not look at the machine. The partner marks each successive note for the instrument of the player. The students take turns and they both get a feel for how their instrument plays and they learn how accurate their aural skills are working at that particular time.

I did the same and discovered that I could tell if I had an embouchure, breathing, air, or an instrument-adjustment problem. All instruments have standard acoustical tendencies, but I think that the students must experience those tendencies to learn them.

This is another step in the whole process of learning to hear and play in tune. If a trumpeter, for example, does not know that the fifth partial is probably going to be low, then even if they suspect and are slightly aware of it as they listen, they still may not have the confidence to bring that note up as much as they think they should. When they learn that the horn might be out of tune on certain notes, they discover that the horn is very fallible and it is built that way. They must learn this at some point and this information gives them confidence to make adjustments.

This type of discovery learning must take place at some point. To play well, they must know the mechanics of their instrument. Playing by ear and listening will help them solve many of the problems, just because they won't accept poor intonation. Thorough knowledge of the acoustics of the instrument also is important in promoting good intonation.

*(Gary Hill)*

### Charting intonation for the instrument

Each quarter, all freshmen do an intonation chart on a graph. We have graph paper with 440, 443, 446, 429 and 438, etc. on lines. These frequencies lead down the paper and correspond with A, A#, B, C, C#, D, etc. One student plays using the strobe, and another sits there and adjusts the strobe to chart each sound played according to frequency. They mark wherever it shows on the dial, so they end up with this outrageous graph. Then I encourage people to turn off the electricity when we started the rehearsal.

*(John Williamson)*

### Tuning chords

Any time you are doing chordal tuning everyone ought to know their instrument's pitch tendencies, so they can make the necessary adjustments in relation to tempered tuning. When you are tuning the fifth it should be two cents wider, a major third should be thirteen cents flatter, and a minor third two cents higher. Those are important things to know. If there is a chord and it sounds funny, have the third go lower and you are going to feel better. You need the major third to be the thirteen cents lower and the minor third just a touch higher. In a major chord you must play the third with the thirteen cents lower for it to match the tempered tuning needed.

*(Larry Rachleff)*

### Playing in tune within a harmonic environment

Those who discuss or write about the pitch tendencies of instruments do not speak about the effect of harmonic environment on where the note should be placed for intonation. These writers should consider this, because the pitch may need to be changed depending where the pitch is in its harmonic environment.

For example, if we tuned instruments in the key of B-flat major, B flat itself might need to be changed if it occurs as the seventh degree in a C 7th chord, dominant harmony. The B flat may need to change as much as twenty-nine percent, more than a quarter tone lower in relation to the overtone series. (100 cents = a half step.) What goes on in performance, and there is research to support this, is a combination of just and tempered tuning. Since there is so much change, listening becomes very important.

*(Hal D. Cooper)*

## TUNING, LISTENING, AND TUNING CHORDS

### Tuning with octaves and unison

One thing that helps on every level, is to tune to the cello or another lower-pitched instrument. They have to listen more carefully because it is an octave or more below the pitch they are playing. Tuning octaves seems to require this closer listening.

Perhaps tuning unison is difficult because blend and tone color unavoidably mix in. When they listen to a unison, they also say, "It's close" or "that's fine." To be in tune at the octave, they have to separate out the sounds and listen more carefully. Unfortunately, the usual way it goes is to sound "A," and not really listen.

*(Pamela Gearhart)*

Students tune much better to chords than when matching unison pitches.

*(Robert Allan)*

### Anticipating the sound

I try to convince them that they cannot just pop a finger on a string or a key and have it be in tune, because it isn't. They have to know what the music is going to sound like before they play it. Sometimes I make them just sit and listen to the first chord of the piece before they play it. I suggest, "Listen to the pitch in your head and *think* what you want it to sound like." I often build chords from the bottom up, which tunes the chord and each section better.

Even if it takes time, they learn something. At least it will be in tune that one time and the next time will be better, even if not perfectly in tune. Though the retention is small, they do learn to adjust and listen as each section or chord is tuned from the bottom up. Perhaps each try helps.

*(Judith A. Niles)*

### Thinking about tuning

I use the Korg tuner, but I don't have the students look at dials at all. I'll use that to get the guy on the bottom to be sure he's in tune. With one instrument in tune, the others listen and use that instrument as a tuning bar.

I divide the group into bass, middle, and upper

instruments and have the bass instruments tune as a unit. Then, I tune the middle level and the upper level, but always referring down to the bottom pitch.

This business about everybody tuning together, it's just insane. I keep counting the times I've told them, "When you do this on stage, all you've done is convinced the audience that you don't know what you're doing. They hear the single note and they hear all of you play out of tune. Then you sit there with smiles on your faces and you act like idiots!"

*(Francis Marciniak)*

### Tuning down

If any note or chord in any passage is out of tune and you are tuning it from the bottom up, my goodness, let's make sure that the bottom pitch is correct.

Tuning down avoids the argument where someone says, "That's the wrong pitch—that's sharp, or that's flat!" Instead, I can say, "Hey, this is it, this is correct." I limit the use of the machine to finding the pitch center. Then we tune it down to A 440 and try not to let it creep up.

I also combat playing high in any ensemble. You've got to get that pitch down and keep it down. Then they can go from ensemble to ensemble, or from band to orchestra, and say "this is it." Another issue is the presence of pitched percussion. We use so much pitched percussion that we just can't creep up above it.

*(Myron Welch)*

Tuning from the bottom up is much more effective than other things I have done. It also gets them into the habit of listening down, which can change the timbre of the band to one that is more rich.

*(Kjellrun K. Hestekin)*

### Improving pitch sensitivity

We ask them to play chords as out of tune as possible, then move the pitches back in tune.

*(Kjellrun K. Hestekin)*

### Tuning within a tonality

We check intonation with those with good characteristic tones and common B flats and naturally, we isolate a problem if it occurs. As a result, they are constantly aware that tuning to B flat does not make them inevitably in tune.

In warm ups, I set up what I like to call "barometer notes" or "the home base note." If a piece has a certain tonal center that is to be played, we will use this as the tonal center. We move a half step up, then down, or a half step down and back up. Then a full step up, a step and half, etc. to reinforce this pitch as the tonal center. This makes it not only a pitch of departure, but also a pitch to "home to." Like a homing pigeon, they can return to or establish the tonic of this piece or passage.

Another technique is to play tonal clusters. Each student picks his favorite, most resonant note, which creates a cluster. Then we go back to tonic, then to a major chord, etc.. They find their most resonant note, then try to keep that sound. Then they try to get the same higher quality resonance on the tonal center of the piece. This also is a homing device of sorts.

After scale exercises, we will tune triads and major chords. We keep one note to a set pitch, compress the fifth a bit lower, and raise the third a bit to get the identity of the major chord established. On minor chords, we raise the third almost as much as we lower the third in major.

Then we might move the chord up a half step to hear and place the major or minor chord sound in a new setting with new adjustments. Sometimes we move up a chordal major scale. The quality of the chords changes on each step. We also sing whole steps and half steps a lot because that is a major source for problems: if they cannot *hear* the difference, they certainly cannot *play* them correctly.

We trade off the singing and playing of whole and half steps. We also sing the whole and half tone scale and then play them. We establish a root, sing a chord then play it; then we pick a new root, sing the new chord, and then play it.

*(Richard K. Hansen)*

### Tuning scale degrees and chords

On the modal degrees of the scale, the third, sixth, and seventh degrees need the most adjustment while tuning. Thus, if you're playing the third of the chord, you want to play a little high on that note. I don't do so much of that in the middle school, but I do a lot of that in the upper school so they know how useful it is.

It is an interesting idea for them to understand. The good students see that and understand more easily. With chordal tuning in a piece, or during listening exercises, I usually tune the tonic and fifth first, the C and G first for example. Then I interpose the E between those two notes. That is the better way to tune a triad. I do not change note positions from root position at the basic level, maybe at the upper school I would do that. I do the root position listening as basic, because I want the tuba to play the root. Then the overtones are there to be built upon.

*(Thomas Stone)*

If the band has a triad, I will remove a chord tone and fix the interval. I will use the tuner to play a chord pitch and the students will match. I also will, for example, have them play the first and fifth degrees and use a tuner that sounds the third of the chord. I will use the adjustment on the tuner, letting the kids tune it to where they think it ought to be.

We also will tune chords by isolating a chord note. Tell everyone who is playing that chord note to play it flat. Then we will gradually pull it into pitch. I say, "Every tone, depending on where you are in the chord, is going to be different. You can't simply play the same note and hope that it's going to fit automatically." By doing this, they learn that they have to adjust pitches all the time.

*(Gregory Bimm)*

### Intonation through chordal playing

I divided the band, counting off by threes. Then I'll assign the root, the third, and the fifth to those various numbers. This created a triad in each section and from section to section.

Start with an F concert major chord, and strive for a beat-less sound in the unisons first, then in the octaves, and then in the chord itself. We got that purity in each one, and then moved it down the whole harmonic series. We would go down a half step, and then back up to check the first one again. Then after checking the first one again, go down a whole step. We checked the first one each time to recall the model of our better sound. This served as a point of comparison.

This is like John Paynter's exercise only in chords. I went both up and down. After I build the unisons and octaves, I build the interval of the fifth first, so it is wave-less. Then I add thirds, which I call the power of the third. As the entire band played octaves and fifths, I had one lonely flute player play the third of the chord. With this, the whole chord just began to shine. The third is not done beat-less—it must have a certain color to it.

In my first twenty minutes of rehearsal, even at the college level, I did "chord-coagulating" in the ensemble. This is an odd word, but I believe making it stick together is important. If you don't have it sticking together, if there is no paste, you have bread dough all over the kitchen. There were other parts of the routine. There were minor chords, a series of scales and triads, and arpeggiated chords. Kjos may have published this.

*(Charles Olson)*

I might find where the melody doubles the lowest octave. We will have those instruments play and we'll add layers with everybody tuning to that. For example, if a baritone has the melody, I'll have the baritone play it and then have the trumpets tune to the baritone. Piccolo players especially have to start thinking down, listening to the bass instruments. In some tuning, I'll remove all the thirds and have just the root and fifth play. We try to tune that with the people on the fifth adjusting to the root. More often they're going to be playing sharp than flat. After we get that fifth just the right size, then we insert the third. Once that fifth locks in, the third is not that difficult to place.

*(Francis Marciniak)*

## INDIVIDUAL AND ENSEMBLE TUNING

### Ensemble tuning

I always have students vocalize the tuning reference pitch, for example, B flat or A. They either hum or sing the pitch before they try to match it. This forces each student to internalize the correct pitch before the other members of the ensemble start playing other pitches, which can cause confusion. I also have the students blend and balance the pitch they are singing before they try to play the pitch on their instruments.

When the students are ready to begin playing the pitch on their instruments, the first chair players enter first. The rest of the ensemble hears a blend and balanced tone from the higher quality players before they play.

Often I will then add one chair at a time, say second chairs, then all third chairs. This helps each student hear the effect of his entrance and makes an easier judgment about the pitch.

Sometimes I have the students count off across each row of the band by twos. I have all the "ones" play the pitch, while the "twos" are not playing. The "twos" take charge of determining whether the players seated to their right or left are in tune. If a player is not in tune, when they stop playing the listener quietly contributes an opinion regarding the appropriate remedy. Then the process is reversed, with the "twos" playing and the "ones" suggesting corrective measures.

This procedure affords the players a little physical space. It permits them to hear their sound rather than that of their neighbor. It also involves other students actively in the tuning process.

Once the students master this process, I may have the two halves of the band take turns playing. They try to make the transition from one half to the other of the group as seamless as possible. To produce a seamless transition, the students must concentrate intently on both tone and pitch. Through this listening process the students all become increasingly adept at identifying and remedying intonation, blend, and tone quality problems, both as listeners and as performers.

*(Scott Shuler)*

### Using reference pitch periodically

I use tuners or another constant, such as a mallet instrument, for a reference point. I think you can sing yourself up into the stratosphere and be sharp; pretty soon the band's playing A-480 because of singing.

I use the number system of singing scales or singing scale degrees such as one-five-six-four-three-two-one. After we finish the pattern, I'll have the mallets play the note we're singing to find out if we are still correct. I'll use the tuner instead of tuning to the tubas, because the tubas also can go sharp. Therefore, I often will go back to the little machine and tune down, because everybody's ears and singing are soon going to go sharp.

*(Michael Kaufman)*

### Varying the registers and dynamic levels

One mistake of many band directors is to tune cursorily to B-flat concert and think they will automatically be in tune. I have always felt it was important to tune in all registers and at various dynamic levels even with beginning students.

*(John Kinnison)*

### Setting the instruments and leaving them in that spot

After a couple of weeks in the fall, when they have their muscle tone back, I will do a preliminary tuning on their instrument. After that, I insist that the tuning slides, head joints, barrels, etc. are in the same place from then on.

For eight-five percent of the pitches, this will work if they have a good sound. Since many notes are very close, we begin to have a "pitch core" going. I will recheck and adjust slides and barrels at least monthly as they change reeds. I look at the tuner—they adjust and they begin to make these adjustments later on their own. Essentially this is an instrument-setting process. If most of the notes are in tune, which this accomplishes, they begin to hear what in-tune is. The result is that they know no other way and they then can hear more easily when a note it is out of tune.

They notice this and it gives me the opportunity to teach them about the instrument's peculiarities. I explain this with as little detail as possible—particularly for kids of this age. I go beyond this, after the year has been underway awhile, by using two trombone players to show "beats." One starts slightly above or below the pitch and adjusts slowly so they improve the sound and beats are absent. They can now hear beats and feel beats. They also can see the adjustments needed. I stress that they need to feel or sense the comfortableness of their playing in relation to intonation.

*(John W. LaCava)*

### Tuning procedures

After hearing an A or a B flat, everyone often starts in playing away. If they do hear the reference pitch, they soon forgot the tuning note's pitch in the midst of forty to seventy-five other versions of that pitch. Thus, they are not truly tuning since they forget the standard, which is distorted by all the "tuning notes" everyone is introducing into the room.

To minimize this, I will have a pitch sounded. Then, each individual in the section enters at intervals of about a second—gradually adding people one at a time. Occasionally, I also might coach them to play their best sound, to play with support, to improve their embouchure and to relax as each successive student introduces his sound.

They hear their sounds played in comparison to two things: the reference pitch or their memory of it, and to the pitch of the person next to them. Since they are not rushed and have time to listen, I observe a lot more eyebrow-raising in this sequence. Since they have more time, they can hear their sounds, remember the reference pitch, and can compare their sounds to the standard.

*(Joseph Casey)*

With any chord tone that is out of tune, I tune from the bottom by taking a pitch from the tuba, a low wood-wind, or a baritone sax. I think that it is crucial to get the bass instrument in tune so it provides an overtone structure that individuals or the ensemble can plug into. Before we begin, I say, "Let's make sure that the bass instrument is correct. Here's the pitch so the bass can tune." First, the tuba gives the pitch based upon a Korg Tuner on his music stand (or from a tuned piano). They use that to stabilize the pitch they provide. Next, each person follows by tuning chord tones by ear from the bottom up. The main thing, however, is to use your ears; trust the ears, because students can develop them.

*(Myron Welch)*

## EQUIPMENT AND AIDS FOR INTONATION

### Tuning considerations

The tuning should be totally auditory, rather than a machine business with all that pulling and pushing. That doesn't net a pair of ears that function.

*(Donald Gee)*

### Effective and ineffective ideas about tuning

I develop intonation, pitch awareness, and in-tune playing in whatever environment they are in. I try to avoid using the strobe or other electronic tuning devices incorrectly.

I relate playing well in tune and good intonation to singing in tune; and I maintain that they are one-and-the-same. There is one addition: the very teachable skill of manipulating the pitch of the instrument slightly one way or the other. We change the pitch to conform to what our ear tells us is the right sound.

It is ineffective when a student plays the note the instrument wants to play and the teacher reports whether it is sharp or flat as they see it registering on the strobe. After the teacher's report, the student makes some adjustment, which probably is useless!

A more effective way is to use a pitch from either an in-tune bass instrument in the ensemble, or from a piano. The students first sing or hum the desired pitch, and finally play the pitch on their instruments. If they discover that they have to lip the pitch up or down to match their sung pitch, then they must adjust their instruments accordingly.

*(Hal D. Cooper)*

### Considering the tuner

The tuner is an excellent tool to help students know their instrument.

*(Donald Gee)*

A high school band director said, "How in the world do you get your band to play that well in tune? With my band, I just can't get them to play in tune. They are just grim. I really don't understand it because I spend a lot of time every day with the tuner."

I said, "Wait right there! We've already discovered the first mistake." I believe one big mistake in teaching students to play in tune is that people use that tuner incorrectly. I think it's a wonderful aid for individuals by themselves to learn to hear intervals, but I simply refuse to ever tune my band to a tuner; because they don't have to play in tune with a tuner, they have to play in tune with each other. I try as quickly as I possibly can to transfer the responsibility of intonation to the kids. They understand, of course, that it's always my ultimate responsibility.

*(Ross A. Leeper)*

The strobe, when you're first starting, can be a reference point. I told my kids that Revelli said, "You might develop 20-20 vision for one of those boxes but you'll never learn to hear." I use it a lot in sectionals, constantly when we are figuring out within a group where the different intonation problems lie within the horns. We say, "Now when we get to a certain note, you know that you must duck this one and raise the other one that is coming up."

*(Lewis Larson)*

### Checking the user of the tuner

If you are going to check somebody with the machine, after they move the slide you must recheck to make sure that they have moved the right distance and in the right direction. They may have adjusted their instrument either not enough, too far, or just right.

*(Myron Welch)*

### Facing frustration with intonation

I really struggle with getting my bands to play in tune. I am hearing and not going deaf. I am struggling, struggling, struggling more and more as I teach determining the difference between pitch and timbre, for example, when tuning an alto saxophone to a clarinet. I hear saxophones sharp, and I'm not getting any better. I play well in tune myself and it's irritating. I am relying more and more on the tuner, and the more I rely on it, the worse I get. Maybe we screwed up intonation with those machines. I'm not getting my kids to do it as well as I want them to.

*(William Long)*

### Improving the quality of instruments

We have matched horns when they get into our high school group. They're playing Bach trumpets, Yamaha trombones and euphoniums, and each section has matched horns. We don't have as many pitch deviations from the horns themselves as we might had we a "mish-mash" of horns. I think it's really an asset. Some directors say it doesn't make any difference anyway, but I disagree.

*(Lewis Larson)*

## EVALUATING INTONATION SKILLS

### Charting tuning

We have made students more conscious of pitch and really opened up some eyes. The first time we did it, we had them do it with a partner. The partner looked at the strobe and the player did not, so he would play kind of normally. Two months later in the year we had them do it individually, one on one. They kept the sheet of their results right next to their folder.

In sectionals, we spend a lot of time just talking about tendencies of pitches on instruments. We discuss which notes usually are going to be flat or sharp and we teach them what to do about it. As a result, I feel we were playing much more in tune this year.

We used it twice this year, and the mistake I made was not getting the sheets back to the students right away. The second time I handed them back right away, and they kept it on the left side of their folder. Then during rehearsal I could say, "Hey, what's the tendency of that note." If they didn't know, they could just look at it. We are going to do it more often next year to make a cumulative effect.

*(Ross Kellan)*

### Tuning to A 440

Richard Strange has contributed information about intonation that is interesting, informative, and overlooked by many bands and orchestra conductors. The length of the contribution (about seven pages) is such that is has been placed in Appendix V so it can be read in its entirety.

Strange observes that, when instruments are played above A 440, the performer's ability to play in tune is restricted more and more as the instruments are played higher and higher above A 440—the level, of course, at which they were designed to be most easily played in tune. If the instrument is designed for A 440 but played sharp, the instrument becomes out-of-tune with itself. As Strange states, "Many people *tune* at A 440, but they don't teach people to play in such a way as to *stay* at or near 440. They do not, in other words, teach the second part of learning to play in tune: *to remain in tune, you must play as close to that level as possible.*"

Furthermore, as temperatures and approaches to playing vary with performance sites and performers, the different-sized brass instruments, and different woodwind, percussion, and string instruments move up and down. Even each performer's physiology causes moves up or down in relation to A 440. Thus, this movement occurs in different directions, in different amounts, and for different technical and psychological reasons. Therefore, tuning is successful if students are determined to keep their instruments at A 440. This works even if the conductor and the performers are not aware of all the peculiarities of acoustics, instruments, and environmental conditions. I urge the readers to give this material much thought.

*(Joseph Casey)*

CHAPTER NINE

# PHRASING

There are several ways to teach phrasing. One can use conducting, drawings, explanations, analogies, modeling, and comparisons. Several teachers suggested one often-used teaching technique: comparing musical phrasing with spoken or written language. They believe that drawing this parallel will help students make musical sense as they perform. The teachers' ideas suggest that the primary intent is to communicate the meaning of the musical phrase, not just to play the right notes and rhythms.

There may be a parallel between music and language; both language and music convey meaning. The parallels are that spoken language contains individual syllables and sounds, and music contains individual pitches and tone colors. Language uses words or phrases and individual sentences to make up paragraphs, and music uses rhythm and tonal patterns, and phrases to make up sections and passages. Language requires pronunciation and diction; music requires intonation, articulation, and dynamics. Both language and music require that the performers shape the components in some way or full communication may not be achieved.

The purpose of drawing parallels between music and spoken language is to stress the need for an expression of meaning with either words or sounds. When actors rehearse a script, they try different inflections until they find just the right way to express a line and the dialogue's meaning. Musical performers also do this by inflecting notes and phrases, increasing and decreasing the intensity—in short, by *shaping* the components. Ultimately this shaping, or phrasing *is* the musical meaning.

Teachers and students should practice different inflections or articulations, and choose the direction of the line's movement. They can vary the weights and dynamics, and change tone colors, or try different slurs and accents. They should experiment until the phrase conveys what their musical taste decides is appropriate, properly expressing the line and the score's meaning.

Drawing the parallel between language and music is an excellent intellectual idea, but the idea remains at that level until the students can show through their performances that they can shape a musical line for the purpose of creating a musical performance. Therefore, knowing

the relationship of language to music is fine for the teacher; but for the students' performances, it is much better if their attention and energies are directed to the shaping and experimenting with the phrases themselves.

## PHRASING AND MUSICAL VALUE

### Phrasing
Phrasing is musical decision making.
*(Eugene Corporon)*

Phrasing and shaping phrases are decisions about starting notes and ending notes.
*(Sandra P. Thompson)*

### Establishing the four-measure phrase
Everything I try to do from day one I do in four-measure phrases. This is true with scales, method books, music, and whatever, unless there are clear exceptions. We do not work on staccato until half or a third of the way through the year. We work first and foremost on legato. They have to connect everything. I often have them slur things that are tongued especially if it is in legato style. Because I am after a sustained breath, I do that a lot to develop air connection, then I add the tongue for legato style.
*(John W. LaCava)*

### The purpose of phrasing
Players need to approach the idea of space and breathing as something they use to get clarity. A performer does not take a breath or make a space just to "gas-up" with more air. A comma, a pause, or something that would add inflections, subtlety, or nuance to the speech can make things clear. This works like punctuation for space and clarity.
*(Mallory B. Thompson)*

### Phrasing in Romantic literature
Stretch the phrases out in Romantic literature and watch the phrase endings so they are not chopped off in

literature, Romantic or not. A melody by itself isn't pretty so I ask them to evaluate if the phrase was "pretty." They will start making changes in order stretch the line, or to become more involved and let the music reveal itself.

*(Stanley Cate)*

### Phrase planning

The beginnings and ends of phrases seem overlooked by band directors. Choral and orchestra directors do more with them. They do what could be called "phrase planning." This must start with the conductor. Instead, band directors look at a phrase from beginning to end in terms of accuracy. Often wind playing comes across as "note to note." It sounds this way because there is no evolutionary cycle or progression in a phrase. The phrase starts and often each strong beat serves as a preparation to the climactic point of the phrase.

What we could learn from orchestra people is how they think about where their bow is going to be at the peak of the phrase. As a result, they must decide where the peak point is and how they are going to get in and out of there. To draw upon this, I sometimes have students mark "bowing symbols" at certain points in the music. I want them to have the same sort of feeling for the three things in a phrase: getting there, the peak, and getting out of there.

In conducting workshops I try to convince people that each beat is not equal. I have had some strong intense arguments with people about this. I even have had people assault me, saying, "What do you mean saying that each beat is not equal?" I say, "Look, we are not talking about duration here. Duration is not really important. If you put the metronome on the Chicago Symphony, often in a musical passage the tempo is going to fluctuate." It fluctuates in a way that is both spontaneous and planned. They are not so much thinking tempo as thinking direction of the phrase. They know where they are going, what's coming next, and are preparing for those events. The main point is that duration is not the issue. Duration will take care of itself if the conductor, player, and group have basic rhythmic foundation.

Duration is just like the pitches on the page; durations are the facts. The beats, which are not equal, deviate in several ways—one being a duration's weight. In *Score and Podium*, Prausnitz speaks about the idea that one must decide whether each beat is a strong beat, a weak beat, or a preparatory beat. Within those kinds of beats there are pulsing beats and passive beats. In the conductor's mind, each beat should have some adhesion, one to the other. We must make some decision about the role of that beat.

When deciding how the phrase is to go, we must decide those strong points. Then, we should set up a pattern that leads to the strongest point, so that each strong point is different. The points you pick out as the peak points in the phrase should have an evolutionary relationship to the strongest point of all.

*(Michael Haithcock)*

### Learning to phrase

Many of my better musical ideas, such as a particular way of turning a phrase in a march, come more from listening to operatic arias than from listening to band recordings.

*(Richard K. Hansen)*

### Phrasing relates to a sense of time

Phrasing is part of a sense of time coupled with a sense of line in music. I subsume rhythm and all of its factors under the idea of musical line. When students get involved in phrasing, they bring to bear all the other issues of good musical performance—issues like good quality sound, intonation, dynamic contrast, or articulation.

When I talk about phrasing, I'm talking about time as several phenomena. One is time as in, "How much time does it take psychologically to hear the three parts of this ternary form?" There is another sense of time where you have "real time, clock time," which would be meter, and accurate rhythm. Another view of time is "psychological time," which is phrasing and finishing a phrase with a nice sense of finality. You create tension and release within phrases.

I want students to sense this issue, even at the first rehearsal of a piece. Even if they miss notes and not all the articulations are perfectly correct, I am trying to achieve a sense of understanding of the forward motion of this piece. Where is section A leading to, where is this bar leading to, and what is the peak of the phrase? All of those issues relate to a sense of line, and the relationship and sense of time in a piece of music. This idea causes me to try to rehearse large chunks of the piece. I have noticed that, over the years, I get through pieces more often in rehearsal that I used to when I was a young band director. I used to stop for every mistake and fix it.

Now I go back to the whole piece more often. Before performances, I often still come back to the specifics again. It may have been a while since we worked on the incredibly vital contrast between loud and soft in these two bars. They may have moved back from the original standard. So my rehearsal time, if I have four weeks to rehearse, might be: big picture, detail, big picture, detail, detail, big picture.

*(Gerald Olson)*

### The high points of a phrase

I base many music expression decisions on prolonging the anticipation of whatever high point is coming up. We should not be in a big rush to get there. Students tend to identify the high point as "the loudest place." I relate this to Christmas instead. "When you were little, you started thinking about Christmas in October. Your expectation built through November until you were so excited! Then, it was there and it was over." That is the approach needed toward the high point musically.

It's getting there that's important, it's not being there. Older students quickly translate that process into something else! This approach can counteract their tendency to charge right toward the high point. In rehearsals, I under-do it to the extreme. I don't let them go on with one note until everyone is paying attention to what I am doing with this note.

*(Terry A. Oxley)*

## Developing sensitivity to style and phrasing

We can decide to savor the note instead of robbing it of its length as if we didn't really savor it, not giving it the kind of tension it should have. We sometimes skip over that top note so that they feel how we robbed that note. I do those things to get kids to want to listen and tune in to each other. I also use dynamic changes to focus upon weight changes.

*(L. Keating Johnson)*

## The need for phrasing

The most dull thing in the world to listen to is somebody simply wandering through the notes and doing nothing. If you're going to interpret something, sooner or later you're going to get intense with it. At other times, you're going to keep your audience in suspended animation—very quiet, calm. Instead of dealing with just dynamics, I try to get across the idea that we are conveying intensity of emotion and calmness, and repose and excitement. For instance, intensity implies pushing ahead, faster vibrato, and a thicker tone.

*(James Stivers)*

## Remembering important skills

Sometimes, I find myself falling into the trap of teaching attacks and releases last. I know I should teach this sooner, since I believe that every attack and every release need to be perfect.

*(Barbara Buehlman)*

Keep them thinking primarily in two areas: stylistic correctness and the shape of the phrase. If the phrase has no shape it is not music, it only is connected sounds.

*(Butler R. Eitel)*

## Music is not only a row of notes

Mark the note of destination, or arrival, or the peak of a phrase. This is important with kids who are just learning a sense of direction or flow of the music. This helps make the point that the music never is just rows of notes. They either are going somewhere or coming from somewhere—ninety-nine percent of the time. Never have notes that are sequentially identical, that are repetitive. They should either add intensity or dynamic, or take some of it away. Marking important notes helps them learn to phrase.

*(Donald Wilcox)*

## Phrasing is the end, technique is the means

Keep them thinking about musicianship, go after musical ideas first and use mechanical skills as stepping stones to musical phrasing. Conductors must teach instruments privately during every rehearsal. These skills are essential knowledge for all conductors, but musicianship and phrasing is the absolute constant.

*(Butler R. Eitel)*

## Basics of phrasing and talent

Sounds can be connected or they can be separated. You can notate and connect notes by separating or by legato; but, there's a whole other aspect that can never be notated. Phrasing also has a lot to do with weights and balances. I think some groups of notes must spring forward and others seem to have a downward-holding kind of weight.

That is the feel of weight or lightness. I have kids try to see what feels most organic for the phrase. You do those things to get kids to want to listen and tune in to each other. I also do this to develop that musical sense that some people say is innate. Some feel a student is either musical or not. More often this has to do with whether you've ever experimented and felt these things. Less so, it is a matter of talent. Some students have never had this put out where they can feel it, experiment with it, and mold it, so to speak. So they have not developed that way.

*(L. Keating Johnson)*

## Finding the phrase's high point

Especially with the younger music students, I ask them to begin playing a phrase and to quit playing when they think they have reached the point of greatest musical tension. The highest point of musical tension doesn't always mean the highest note in terms of pitch; it might be the lowest note in the phrase. In others the highest point in the phrase may not coincide with either the highest or lowest note. It might be where students think the peak of the phrase or the most important moment is. I often deal with this in a setting that I try to make non-threatening; one where there is no right answer and there is no wrong answer, but there are many alternatives or viewpoints.

*(Craig Kirchhoff)*

## Students can make decisions

When students have had a chance to phrase things two or three different ways, and they hear very clearly the one we've settled on, it never fails that they remember those phrases. The kids are smart enough to be engaged in decision making. If they made an unmusical decision and said, "We really want to play it this way," you are not stuck. You could say, "I understand that you want to do it that way, but I think this would be a better way musically."

*(Gregory Bimm)*

## PROBLEMS WITH PHRASING

### Phrasing

Bentley Shellhammer, our marching band guy who is a good musician and a very good judge, said, "Jim, somewhere along the line we've got to start finding ways of teaching these kids to respond expressively to music. That's the single factor that is so apparently absent."

*(James Croft)*

### Phrasing from the beginning

With new private students, the biggest problem I see is that many band directors let them play each note with a separate blast of air. I have them blow one note with air only for sixteen counts. Then, they blow air for sixteen counts using their tongue lightly—like singing under the breath. Then they move to the instrument using the word "du" for legato, both light and heavy. This must be done from the very beginning if one wants to teach them to phrase.

*(Steven Cooper)*

### Flexibility or rigidity

Many teachers do not vary phrasing much at all. I've noticed that when you work with a student or when someone says, "Can you come and guest conduct my group?" You find they're really patterned into one way.

*(L. Keating Johnson)*

### The quarter note is the difficult note

The quarter note is a hard note to play because one must vary its length depending on the tempo. It's one of the first notes kids learn; it's supposed to be one of the easiest notes. So, students concentrate on the eighth and sixteenth notes and forget about the quarter note. In doing so, they can confuse everything else because they don't have that sense of proportion. So, we must reintroduce them to the quarter note and reestablish it in relation to the other notes.

*(Richard Kennell)*

### Sustaining sound while changing notes

I dwell a great deal on having the maximum sound between the notes. This addresses their backing off on making tone when they move their fingers or slides. Students, even good students, do this. What I'm after is a very vocal approach to connecting the lines and individual tones. This is true not only when you have a melody, but when you have an accompanying figure.

The energizing of the air stream needed for releases also must be done between or at the junction of unspaced tones. I am seeking the maximum sound between notes— like when they slur. Even when students slur something there can be the slightest hint of diminuendo, the slightest hint of backing off as they move from pitch to pitch.

One choral director said the air is the glue that holds the different notes of the phrase together and that holds the

different pitches together. That glue needs to stretch and really bind things, and this is something that is very, very important to me in trying to teach my students.

*(Mallory B. Thompson)*

When playing a sustained phrase, I ask students to treat each note as though it was an old, dear friend. Make believe you do not want to leave this friend; hang on to the note for the longest time possible until finally you have to leave. Then, leave quickly and go to the next note quickly.

*(Jerold Sundet)*

### Options in phrasing

Phrasing in music is very much like punctuation is in literature. Phrasing is nothing more than inserting silence, and it's an equal partner to sound, when a player is creating some kind of meaning. Phrasing also is understanding that your own opinions may change.

I'll come back to a score that I did three years ago and think, "Gosh, how could I have thought this was where the climax is, it's there instead." There are other influences: if you are doing a piece with a stronger oboist than before, the oboe part takes on a whole new meaning. Because of the player, it's brought to you in a different way. It is important to stay open minded and consider the information you get back.

I'm a believer in the idea that there's a beginning to a phrase, an arrival, a resolution, and an end. I usually see most phrases as having these four parts. The points in the phrase that seem more crucial to me are right before the arrival, then the resolution before the release and last, how one is going to get out of the phrase. Most players pay more attention to where the phrase begins and arrives. They pay less attention to getting out of it or what they're going to do after the arrival of a high point. They also must be attentive to the phrase after its arrival, before it's over, and what happens in the entire time frame.

*(Eugene Corporon)*

### Phrasing note endings

I've seen people who work on attacks, attack, attack, attack but they never work on the releases. With a large ensemble you've got to pay more attention to the ending of the notes. For example, a quarter tied to an eighth note on beat one. The eighth note releases on the "and" of beat one, not on one.

The *English Folk Song Suite*, the second movement, has this all the way through it. If musicians release on one, there will be a gap. I think this is where conducting skill comes in and you are able to show them the release and the beat. If you don't say anything, or don't conduct correctly, the kids stop at all different times. We need to talk first about when to end and secondly how to end. Is the note tapered on the end? Is it stopped with the tongue? These are decisions that have to be made by the conductor. Twenty kids are going to do it fifteen—maybe twenty different ways. Their early emphasis on technical instead of musical matters makes this true.

*(Myron Welch)*

### The inaudible bar line

Bar lines are there to organize the written notes, they do not have any aural function. If you can hear the bar lines, you are not playing the music correctly, unless its something that's boring rhythmically. The bar lines should be seen not heard.

*(Donald Wilcox)*

## RELATING PHRASING TO LANGUAGE

### The musical phrase and a sentence

I define the limits of the phrase—the beginning and the end, by relating it to the beginning and the end of a sentence. Taking a breath here or there does not mean you have played a phrase. You have not played a phrase with musicality any more than stringing a bunch of words together with a capital letter at the beginning and a period at the end gives the sentence meaning.

Once we define the limits, then we must work with the shaping of the phrase. Decide where the tension points are and where the shape changes. I don't stress this directly or as much with the middle school kids. They need to know what a phrase is and its importance and they need to involve themselves with the basic issues. I do this through demonstration, conducting, and building to and from tension points. I sing the example and often have them play it back. I spend time especially on releases followed by rests. I do this mostly by rote and explanation.

*(Ross A. Leeper)*

Music has much in common with speech. Music acts, in a way, like the way you intensify and speed up if you get angry. Your speech might slow down or your voice might take a different tone when you're discussing a different point. Too much regular rhythm becomes too boring and too much irregularity of rhythm becomes too frustrating to listen to.

Explaining this to non-musicians has really given me a new insight into how to make the phrases speak clearly and be as expressive as possible. I talk about lifting, a little lift, and a little pause. I say, "I know you don't need a breath there, but the phrase needs the lift." I think of lift in terms of string bowing. Taking the bow off the string gives a little slight breath, even though they might not need the breath. This also may occur when the last note of a previous phrase needs to be lifted at the end of the phrase. To be perfectly honest, I can't think of a piece where I would want a tongued release.

The terminology I use is an "aspirated release." To teach that, I use the comparison with the choir when they sing AMEN, they let the "n" sound. When they finish a

word, it isn't with a karate chop to their throat. They give the word a chance to finish. An aspirated release requires energy and an aspirated release will not happen if they just stop the air. There must be a little hint of a push that energizes the air stream at the last instant when they're giving the release.

One of my pet peeves is when players just stop the tone, which just brings things to a dead end and makes a very dull sound that is obvious immediately. I want them to hear the difference between the dull release, and the aspirated release that has an energized air stream at the end. I contrast that with the release of the phrase with a dull sound again. Once they hear a difference between aspirating a release and just stopping the air they understand. I have them energize the air stream a little bit at the end and then I have them do it again the dull way instead. Then, when we stop in the dull way, they all nod their heads say, "Yeah, that sounds pretty bad."

*(Mallory B. Thompson)*

As I introduce the idea of phrasing in music, I will talk to the student in sentences and in a very exaggerated manner. I break my speaking of these sentences into short segments with large gaps of silence between words. This obviously slows the context and understanding. This shows that, if this is difficult to interpret and sounds strange to the ears, then music also must have a continuity that is sustained to help it make sense.

*(Theta Lee)*

Use a spoken sentence with a change of word emphasis to show how we need to go beyond just information. Without "phrasing" we just have information. To show this, read or say a sentence without any inflection.

*(Patricia Brumbaugh)*

I connect phrasing with speech, how certain articulations are like punctuation marks, and how the phrases work in an antecedent and consequent way as language does. This is effective, but it is tough to make a musical phrase ask a question as we do in language. How do you get the inflection of a question? We also have split up phrases and rearranged them to see if it made any sense to have them in a different order. Then we put them back together.

*(John W. LaCava)*

I equate musical phrases with the different kinds of verbal sentences: declarative, questions, etc. I also use my voice in the saying of sentences in the style they did or did not do with the music.

*(Pamela Gearhart)*

I used spoken sentences, emphasizing different words to parallel stress, etc. on the notes in a phrase.

*(Anthony J. Maiello)*

I sometimes use the example of an argument, not an angry argument, but a discussion argument. For example, if there are several phrases in the melody, one phrase may be stronger than the next. I said, if you want to tell someone that the tree is green and they thought it was blue, you might say the first time, "The tree is green, it isn't blue." The next time you'd say, "The tree is *definitely* green" and you'd say it with more intensity. That's the same way with phrases when the second phrase needs to be more intense.

I learned from a Bernstein program that many phrases are structured with a short phrase, a short kind of answering phrase, and a third phrase that is twice as long to complete the statement.

*(Gregory Bimm)*

### Relating phrasing to a sentence

To help students phrase with emphasis and breathe in the right places, I write words to go along with songs. Since many students run out of air just before the last note I might say, "The man walked down the street" to contrast with the wrong way, which is, "The man walked down the (breath) street." I say, "You don't talk like that." You could say, "You could make up any words you want to on this, or you can use mine and sing it back to me." Often, of course, there is a feeble attempt. Then say, "Well, just try something else, try it a little differently" or, "Do you agree with this? Maybe there is a spot in there that you think is more important than what I said." Sometimes I exaggerate my gestures to help them see it visually.

*(Richard Putzier)*

### Speech and music

With musical phrasing they must understand the correlation of music with speech. You should encourage them to mark the musical movement and direction in their part as you've done in the score. For example, they could mark certain notes with an extra tenuto so they understand that note has a direction. They can mark with an arrow going forward or going to a note, or a Tabeteau number that says this note is a one and this note is a three. They can mark anything that relates to arrival notes and where we are going. If you are always teaching that, along with pitch and balance, articulation and rhythm, those things will be much more connected.

*(Larry Rachleff)*

### Musical phrasing

First I ask them, "What is a phrase?" If some one can just say "a group of words" or give me an example of what a phrase is, I relate that to a phrase in English. Then, I relate that to the musical phrase. Then, I work with the idea of a complete thought musically. I show them where the first phrase might be. I show them where it begins, its middle, and where it ends; then they can see it as a complete thought, and they can shape it or they can express it.

We start talking about playing a phrase weakly, with

less emphasis. We use less air and maybe we play softer as you would start a sentence. Then, we might peak at a certain word or peak at a certain note. We also consider where the strong beat is. We often play the strong beat with more emphasis, sound or air, or more tongue if it's articulated. This can give it a "down-feel" versus an "up-feel." I try to show, from the podium, what a "down-feel" looks like so they can get that image with either a conducting gesture or body movement.

Sometimes there are notes that are to be stressed that do not correspond to the strong-weak beats of the meter. With these, I will bring that out as an exception. I might say, "Okay, here we need to bring this note out clearly, but it's leading still to where the idea or the main note in the phrase is." Then we sing it, or I will sing it for them and they will sing it back; or, I will sing it, they will play it back. If I have my horn with me in a private lesson, I will play it and then they will play it back.

The whole idea with phrasing is to make the complete idea, make it a sentence. Adding the concerns for the weak and the strong beat help make the line go somewhere. Then, we might have a musical line and a line that says something.

*(Dwayne P. Sagen)*

### Comparing language to musical phrase structure

I often tie together phrasing and speech, how certain articulations or accented note figures are like punctuation marks; this can show that music often has the antecedent-consequent phrase relationship.

One can speak a phrase where the change of emphasis on any of the words within the sentence gives a new meaning. For example, "I shall go to the STORE" as compared with "I shall GO to the store." This varies the stress on different words.

The tough one is asking a question with music. How do you make a musical phrase sound like a question? How do you get the inflection of asking a question? That has been a fun thing for me to investigate.

When I ask students to compose or improvise, I want them to apply some kind of speech pattern to it and see if we can make more sense out of the phrase this way. Also, I sometimes have them write words for songs. I do this quite a bit with my private studio. I make sure that they're saying something that they make up, even if it's nonsense words. I do this so they get an idea in their minds that they are communicating something spoken or sung, that there are ideas to be communicated here. It seems to help them blow through their phrases a little bit more and give them more meaning.

*(John W. LaCava)*

### Placing the stresses

We deal with phrasing by deciding where we put a stress; whether it is on the high note or the low note. This is the same as we do with speech. I think Nilo Hovey wrote a marvelous section on phrasing in his book. The title is *Efficient Rehearsal Procedures for School Bands* (Selmer). That's a beautiful section; it is concrete. Phrasing is deciding on which notes to put the stresses.

*(Richard J. Suddendorf)*

### Phrasing

I work particularly on phrase endings. Doing the ending poorly is like saying only half a word at the end of a sentence. One also must play up and down, following the melody line and adjusting tempo to say something.

*(Stanley Cate)*

### The pickup note

I teach the anacrusis through having a whole bunch of sentences with "the" at the end of the line; I write several sentences on the board so "The" is to the right at the end of the first line, and the rest of the sentence begins at the left of the next line. I say, "The word 'the' really belongs to the next sentence, so we play it as though it is part of the next line."

*(Thomas Stone)*

### Portraying musical phrases physically

Another image of phrasing Leonard Bernstein described is when you have a child in your arms and you're getting ready to throw him up in the air so he lands on his bed. You hold him up in the air and you say, "One . . . , Two . . . , Three . . . , and there————-you———— -go————-." When students hear that explanation they say, "Oh yeah!"

Giving images instead of describing in specific terms never seems to fail. If you can come up with a good clear image of the way you feel about the music, the kids always seem to catch on. Giving an image always seems to work because students are more apt to remember a vivid explanation than clinical explanation.

*(Gregory Bimm)*

## TEACHING PHRASING THROUGH A VARIETY OF TECHNIQUES

### Teaching phrasing in a variety of ways

I work with them in terms of direction and thinking of the motion of the line toward or away from particular points. I try to use analogy, metaphor, and imagery a lot; instead of talking and using specific kinds of technical terms.

*(Robert Grechesky)*

We use a variety of things, especially singing. I say, "This is the way I want this phrase to sound." We use images such as talking about the ocean waves and how they rise and fall. We talk about the things that the kids are involved with, such as letting your bicycle coast to a halt.

We also ask students to sing phrases back to us quite often. However, we don't spend much time saying, "you are out of tune" when they sing a phrase, or when we are expecting them to be singing in balance or in rhythm.

We are after the accuracy of the rhythm and the size of a phrase. We want to decide the largest point in this phrase, what we want done at the end of this phrase, and how we want to start this phrase. We occasionally reinforce the size of the phrase portions with gestures. We often say, "Right here, this is going to be the big part of this phrase and this is how I'm going to look when we get there." I give a preview of the phrase and conducting. I may simply state, "I want you to carry out this crescendo one note farther than you've been playing it."

*(Bryce Taylor)*

### Reflection, repetition, and reinforcement

I believe that the student must be involved in the decision making process, especially the young kids. If there is a short phrase that is repeated, I ask, "How can this be treated, if the second occurrence of the phrase is the same?" I can introduce it as a "reflection of the first" and treat it softer. I also can say, "Could it be reinforced?" Then we play the second occurrence stronger than the first. We may try another way, which is to have a crescendo for the first four bars and decrescendo for the second four bars. I ask them, "Which way of playing the phrase do you like?" I will let them vote. If they decide a way to perform the two phrases, we then look at the next eight bars to see how that should be done. If this section could use the same solution to phrasing, we still might arrive at a different solution. Nobody gets upset with different conclusions, with musical judgments that vary, and with the realization that there is not a clear-cut right and wrong.

Reflection and reinforcement often are a way to plan a phrase, but one also can make sound musical judgments using the ideas of tension and release or the direction of line. There are other ways to plan a phrase, such as "all lines must have direction," or "determine the stress points in a phrase," or "longer notes are going to have more stress than lesser note values."

I will talk about them with students and we make a decision. Even though some teachers could argue the process is contrived, I disagree. It does not preclude spontaneity; it provides a road map and the decisions fall within the realm of musical judgment.

Sometimes a student will play the phrase showing a certain interpretation, then another plays the phrase offering a different interpretation. We may discuss and reconcile the two versions, think about them, or try another version several days later. The teacher need not feel he will lock himself into one version, since during performance their responses to conducting could yield even another version or an alteration of the phrasing choices we had discussed. The conductor ultimately still, therefore, will have the last word on just how a certain phrase is to be performed. If a different version should come out during a concert, students do not complain.

*(Robert Floyd)*

## Identifying the expression of the phrase

Getting them to feel emotionally is really important. This is necessary, not only in slow sections where they can feel the beauty of something, but also in feeling the drama of a trumpet fanfare—you know, putting their guts into it. With slow sustained passages, I work with breathing and air flow with my baton, just kind of stretching and trying to feel the phrases breathe. I use an analogy, "Let the music breathe more, so that you feel the rise and the fall of the phrase." The air is the thing which makes the difference.

*(Thomas Stone)*

## Developing sensitivity

I use many exaggerations and fluctuations to make them more sensitive to phrasing, rather than be so mechanical.

*(Anthony J. Maiello)*

## Showing continuity

Playing a melody on the piano with one finger is a good way to show note separation without destroying the phrase's continuity. Sometimes the split second it takes to lift the finger and move it to another key is just the amount of space needed to play the phrase properly.

*(Richard Floyd)*

The phrase itself seems not to lose continuity if one says "don't let the notes touch" as compared with "put a space, or silence, between the notes."

*(Richard Floyd)*

For younger kids the note heads can be described as dots on a drawing, like we completed when we were little kids. The airstream is the line that we drew right through those dots. You've got to make sure that your breath goes right through the center of each note. This idea also helps intonation, it helps just about everything. I find with tone production that it's hard enough just getting them focused mentally on the note, let alone supporting it.

*(Timothy Mahr)*

## Teaching phrasing through conducting

I try to teach phrasing visually, telling them with the baton, "Here's where the phrase ends." When the phrasing is incorrect, I stop. I try not to use verbal clues such as, "Hold that note longer." Instead, I try my best to say only, "Number thirty nine again."

They usually know, when I don't tell them what's wrong, that they'd better watch, because I will show them what's wrong. By not saying anything, I teach them that watching is the better clue. The atmosphere can become a little uncomfortable, because they're not sure initially

what's wrong. They know that I'm purposely not telling them; the only way they're going to find out is if they watch.

*(Michael Kaufman)*

## Beginning and ending a phrase

The students must be well prepared before they play their first sound. This is especially important for trumpets, trombones, horns, and tuba. They're the people who really have to pre-think, pre-hear, and pre-set to play their pitches. As well as pre-think and pre-set, they also must post-think and post-set.

They need to keep the tone covered as it sails away from them as they finally release it, and the instrument stays right in place. "It isn't over till it's over." When you release the pitch, you cover the pitch and you stay right there. You keep the vowel in your mouth until all the sound is gone and reverberates in the hall. The way that you hold your mouth is very much a part of how that tone leaves the instrument. Even if it's an eighth note you stay right over that pitch when it's finished. You stay right there, covering the tone, and listening to the ring in the hall.

*(Thomas Stone)*

## Illustrating through bowing

If I teach articulations in band rehearsals I sing a lot and use string bowing. My "imaginary bow" is on the string and I'm saying, "I want detache or I want the middle of the bow here, come on clarinets just give me that sound."

*(Richard J. Suddendorf)*

## Using imitation to teach phrasing

Sometimes I have them sing or hum the way I performed the phrase.

*(Hal D. Cooper)*

## Modeling the phrase

I do sing or say things to show how I think the phrase should sound. I am in awe of people who do clever, sexy things, or use catch phrases, bags of tricks, and special effects, but I don't do much of that.

*(Donald Gee)*

I'll draw pictures of the shape of a phrase, its beginning, peak, and ending. I also will sing a phrase in different ways to show, for example, if you miss the first note of the phrase, you've ruined the phrase; if you don't have the peak of a phrase, you've ruined a phrase; if you drop off the peak too soon, you've ruined the phrase, and if you don't taper the end of the last note, you've ruined the phrase.

*(Richard J. Suddendorf)*

## Longer notes must have direction

Nelhybel said, "Any time you are playing music and

you have a note longer than the basic pulse of the piece, it must have direction—it must come from someplace or be going to some place—it has to have direction, it cannot be neutral."

I tell students, "If you are in a car, you must put the car in gear and go forward or backward—go somewhere, other wise, you are in neutral. When you get in the car, you are going somewhere. You must get there by some path, you cannot just wander around and expect to arrive at your destination."

*(Robert Grechesky)*

### *Stressing phrase structure in the ensemble*

I sit the orchestra in quartets and have each quartet playing separately. I say, "Stop when I touch you." One group plays and when they stop, another group takes over. In this way we go through the piece in phrases. Each quartet plays a phrase and the next quartet takes over from them, so they begin to be aware of the phrase structure.

*(Pamela Gearhart)*

### *Shifting their attention to the line*

We try to imagine a line growing or try to imagine the physical feel of a line going forward or backward. We stress this instead of thinking about the actual fingerings, amount of air, or other little physical things involved.

*(L. Keating Johnson)*

### *Portamento cantando*

Revelli heard our group at the National Band Association convention and came back stage. He started hugging the kids, he started talking, and they were real quiet. The kids didn't know him from Adam but I thought, "What is this man doing here." He said, "You know, the one thing your group does is play with portamento cantando, which means, the art of flowing from one note to the other." I told him that was one of the nicest compliments I've ever had from anybody.

We do spend a lot of attention to making notes flow from one to the other. One cannot put that down on a piece of paper. We approach every skip by pushing the bottom note with a lot more support, attempting to float to the top note. It works. I tell them, the bigger the skip though, the more you're going to have to support the lower note. By pushing the lower note, the line tends to float up to the top note.

Acoustically the top note, the higher note, is going to sound louder because it's higher. To make it sound smooth you've got to push the lower note. If you don't, it will sound softer and you'll have less of a flowing sound going from one note to the next. I think there are things you can do to teach that air speed is behind the notes. You can make kids sound much more accomplished than they even have any right to be. I think that once they learn and get started with this kind of attention—blowing through, pushing lower notes—it becomes an ongoing thing as long as the teacher reminds them regularly.

*(Lewis Larson)*

### *Rhythmic direction*

When they learn to count rhythms, they count them up and down in a mathematical manner. You can do that to get through the first part of learning rhythm. Rhythms can exist vertically, but when you try to perform rhythms, they need to be horizontal so they have direction.

There are ways to phrase rhythms. If the rhythm is just sixteenth notes, I will change the place where I want them to "break the phrase." I'll say, "After the first sixteenth note on beat three, that's where I want to feel the phrase change. They'll play "one e and ah two e and ah three (break) e and ah four e and ah one." You won't feel a pause on the break, but you'll feel a new intensity of time. The "e and ah four e and ah one" should be leading into the next measure. This gives them an idea that rhythm and music are always flowing.

I can change that around and say, "After the second sixteenth note of three or, the first sixteenth note of two. I tell them, "You can't just count and play where the count says. You have to look at that whole package of three measures and play that as a long rhythmic structure." The students that are having rhythmic problems haven't necessarily miscounted the rhythms. They might have counted the rhythms right, but they don't have a sense of direction with the rhythms. When we pick any specific rhythm apart and say, "These two notes really end up to be a pickup to this note," it clears things up.

*(Gregory Bimm)*

### *Singing improves sound and phrasing*

To improve their way of playing the note, I get them singing with a "haaa" sound to make the air active, to make tone improve and be musical. We also vocalize on a pitch to get a concept of the beginning, middle, and end of the sound and the musical phrase. This helps develop proper support and the idea of a singing style. We then apply this to the instrument.

*(Frank Bencriscutto)*

# CHAPTER TEN

# RHYTHM AND MOVEMENT

When instructing their students about rhythm, teachers often use the teaching techniques used by their own pre-college teachers. For example, their teachers may have taught them to set and check tempo with a metronome. They were asked to tap and clap both pulses and subdivisions precisely with the metronome, thereby gaining better physical control of fingerings and rhythms. The metronome can show clear models of steady tempo and subdivisions, and effect precision in the ensemble. As students in this process, they may have concluded rightfully, that rhythmic accuracy and precision are important technical skills, and that the metronome is an effective way to achieve them.

Still, if the metronome is used exclusively or used too pervasively to develop rhythmic accuracy and steadiness of pulse, students may forget—or never become aware—that phrasing a line musically is ultimately more important than playing the line with metronomic precision. In fact, students may wrongly conclude that metronomic or ensemble precision is synonymous with a musical feel for rhythm and phrasing. This result is even more likely when teachers isolate the teaching of rhythm from the teaching of meter, melody, style, and phrasing.

These views support the frequent observation that often something seems wrong with the way students perform rhythmically. Comparing the performances of professional musicians to that of students reveals a lack of more than just virtuosity. Students do not show the rhythmic and phrasing sense that we would like to hear, even though they may have been developing precision since the beginning of their musical education.

One cause might be the way educators use traditional techniques to teach rhythm. They often teach rhythm through notation and thus rhythm can be an abstraction to students: rhythm's analysis and notation are abstractions, but rhythm itself is not. Because the experience of rhythm is a right brain function, one should not try to develop a feel for rhythm through mathematics, through learning to read music notation, or through theoretical explanations of any aspect of rhythm. These operations are left brain functions that approach rhythm as something theoretical. Utilizing the left brain is appropriate as a teaching technique if used

after the rhythmic experiences of students have begun to develop fundamentally through the aural and movement teaching techniques that assure the eurythmic experiences of students.

Often missing in rhythm instruction is readiness, and without readiness the teaching of rhythm notation is questionable. The students will have something to which they can relate notation if the teacher develops their readiness. This can be done through movement, chanting, playing, and singing rhythm content, which means the pulse, meter, and rhythm patterns themselves. Rhythm is essentially physical, thus movement and aural experiences are essential; this is how the teachers touch and develop the roots of a rhythmic feel. All musical performances should reflect rhythm's essential physical character.

Movement replicates a musically rhythmic feeling more accurately than does a metronome. Movement gives us both the beginning of each duration and, more important, the continuous feel of each duration or a pattern of durations. Movement also can capture the growth and decline of tension during a longer group of durations as found in a phrase. By contrast, a metronome sounds the beginning, and beginning only, of each duration. It does not model the flow of durations as students hear them in a melody or as students could simulate them while chanting, singing, or moving.

Some argue that foot-tapping is movement: it is a physical movement, but it is not movement in the sense of dance. Though teachers use foot-tapping often as an aid to analyze familiar and unfamiliar notation, they rarely use foot-tapping to give students a basic sensory experience or to give them a kinesthetic and a eurythmic experience, both of which are needed to develop rhythm readiness and a rhythmic sense.

Metronomes have value, but they are useless for modeling musical and rhythmic phrasing. Their place in music instruction is to give students feedback and consistency. They also can discipline students' practice as they develop instrument control and acquire facility. The metronome, though, is not a musical influence; a metronome only marks the passage of durations as a turnstile counts the persons who pass through.

Precision by itself can improve ensemble unity but it is not equivalent to rhythmic sense. Precision does not explain the grace, buoyancy, and excitement we hear in a jazz rhythm section, nor does precision cause the musicality we hear in Jean Pierre Rampal's performance of a Handel Flute Sonata. Precision alone does not capture or portray rhythm's flow any more than playing scales flawlessly leads to expressive melody playing.

## THE NATURE OF RHYTHM

### *Teaching what rhythm is*

Rhythm is not intellectual, rhythm is emotional and must be felt physically. Much of rhythm also cannot be divorced from the psychological. If we do, music suffers as a consequence—and we all suffer from this. I deal with rhythm as directly as possible by first becoming involved myself. I must project what the music is all about—to give the music character—so students can perceive what it is about. The conductor must be both on the inside as player, and on the outside as conductor, continually. While rhythm can be a celebrative uplifting feel, it also can be a tragic, funeral-like feel. We need to phrase rhythm as we need to phrase a melody.

(Frank Bencriscutto)

### *Rhythm and musical style*

I feel that we often end up isolating such things as rhythm as an end in itself with no concern about how it relates to the style of the music. Yes, rhythm is important and must be secure, but accurate rhythm is worthless if it doesn't relate to the work's style and musical intent.

I may take a characteristic rhythm pattern from the music we are working on and use it in the warm up. I can refine the accuracy and style of the rhythmic pattern as we play scales. It is another way of simply isolating a task so that it can be mastered. As the rhythm becomes more secure and the style (i.e. a light separation on repeated dotted eight notes followed by sixteenths) becomes more acceptable, I can integrate the rhythm and style back into the tapestry of the music.

(Richard Floyd)

### *Meter and subdivision*

This is something we really feel in music. With *Toccata Marziale* for example, there's so much subdivision that one could almost conduct subdivisions. Meter is where the real action is in the rhythm. It's like a verb in a sentence in the way it provides the action.

(Thomas Stone)

### *Rhythm should elicit a physical response*

I must stress, when dealing with the issue of rhythm with players of any age, that rhythm should have a certain physicality to it. While a melody draws a somewhat emotional response from people, rhythm should elicit a physical response. If one tries to isolate a rhythm and deal with it from a purely intellectual view point, the rhythm is going to be weak and very insecure. Therefore, I try to get this idea of physicality.

I'll perform a rhythm, and they usually will repeat it back with a "ta" syllable. While doing this, I have them tap both the pulse and the sub-divisions. I want them to internalize the rhythm and its feeling, so they do the pulse and each subdivision with their hands as they speak.

(Mallory B. Thompson)

### *Making sense out of the parts of rhythm*

We determine macro beats (large beats that are in pairs) and micro beats (the division of the macro beats) aurally—not from notation or music theory. Meter is aural, not visual.

(Richard Grunow)

Rhythm is the sound, rhythm is not the notation. It is crazy to have an intellectual understanding of note values if one doesn't know the rhythm. There are just too many teachers who think students learn this way.

(Steven Cooper)

### *Metronomic and human time*

There are two kinds of time. Metronomic time, which is perfect time, and there's human time, which is imperfect. The only "time" that swings is human time, not metronomic time. Human time evolves and functions within the energy of the piece and the ensemble.

(Dominic Spera)

### *The swing is gone*

I'll keep my fingers snapping steadily for about a minute. Then I'll vary the snapping noticeably by speeding or slowing it down. Of course, when I do this too much all the intensity flies out the window. To build energy, there must be a pattern repeated over and over in steady rhythm. The minute the time varies too much, we release all the energy and all the intensity. "What happens is—like someone opened the window and let the swing out. Man, it just actually leaves the room."

(Dominic Spera)

### *Thinking about rhythm*

With a young band or even a high school group, I ask, "What is rhythm?" They say, "That's how fast you play, that's the beat." Finally, however, you can get them to realize rhythm essentially is the movement of the musical sound. Tempo is a part of it, but tempo is simply how fast and how slow we're going to play. Sounds are structured by meter, which is the basic feeling within bar lines. Meter also has to do with symbols and notations. When they begin to grasp this, they are very surprised. They have a hard time understanding what rhythm really is. Rhythm also is pitch, duration, articulation, and tone.

*(Frank Bencriscutto)*

### The importance of rhythm

In the Bible it says, "And now abideth faith, hope, and charity, but the greatest of these is charity." With us, the instrumentalists, we need to believe, "And now abideth rhythm, melody, and harmony, but the greatest of these is rhythm."

If the rhythm is not accurate, it makes no difference how good the intonation is, how perfectly they produce the tone, or anything else because it is not going to sound great. It makes no difference how well everybody plays individually. The ensemble depends on rhythm, the rhythmic sense.

*(Alfred Reed)*

### Teaching rhythm in a musical context

It is very important to teach and practice in a musical context. A musical context is provide by musical sounds, rhythmic accompaniments, chordal/tonal patterns, etc.

*(James Froseth)*

### The rest

It is an energy filled silence.

*(Robert Floyd)*

## RHYTHM PROBLEMS

### Rhythm is a weak area

Students mostly do rhythm mechanically; this is superficial. Mechanical rhythm may be somewhat accurate but this rhythm is not vital. Students do not think of rhythm as a physical issue. Instead, they think it is an intellectual or analytical issue. Very seldom do they think of this as an emotional ingredient that supplies a foundation for the character of the music.

*(Frank Bencriscutto)*

### The problem of rhythm

Rhythm is a problem at every level. It's a problem from the top wind ensemble at Eastman, to every junior high and elementary band in the country. The problem may reflect the ability of the players, but I think it is a very serious problem.

*(Mallory B. Thompson)*

### Feeling time

Some people can't feel time, they can't! So I tell them, "Feel something!" You know, "Either feel panic or feel nervousness, or something that's very logy or sluggish." Some how that helps!

*(Dominic Spera)*

### My pet peeve is rhythm

I realize this when I start every year. I suddenly have people from thirty to forty different high schools sitting next to one another. They all have had a different kind of experience of one type or another.

*(Robert Levy)*

### There is a rhythm problem

Through all my experiences in clinics and going to the schools, I see that rhythm is either the most neglected element of music, or it is simply taught incorrectly. Some of this is caused by the reduction of rehearsal time. I hear some programs in the sixth grade meeting twenty minutes once a week. How is that possible? I don't care who you are, you cannot do anything in twenty minutes once a week. The poor director faces the choice of really teaching, teaching concepts and having them learned; or, he gives up, sings the parts, teaches by rote and teaches no reading.

These students go through years and years having only a general idea of what rhythmic units are about. For example, they do not learn correctly dotted quarter notes and eighth notes, how that rhythmic relationship works. They do not understand how to subdivide and how to play these rhythms in relation to a set tempo. They might have a notion how a certain rhythm goes, but they do not see the differences caused by tempo changes.

*(Robert Levy)*

### The rhythm problem

After years and years of guesswork while reading rhythms, there are few leaders and many followers. They play together what they guess the rhythm is. Recently, I auditioned twenty-eight trumpets and I deliberately chose something that was in three-four. Of the twenty-eight kids, maybe the nine top ones were pretty good. Very, very few were comfortable with three-four meter. Most did not even play the piece in three-four. They would either put a stress on different beats or on the wrong beats. They were adding beats and doing all kinds of things with it, which surprises me. I hear more rhythmic mistakes made in sustained notes, long notes values, and tied values and rests.

Playing and reading rhythms are basic skills and need attention. We also do a poor job communicating what meter is all about, so I try to work very hard on this by emphasizing an internal pulse always. This must be stressed even more so at a slower tempo in more sustained passages and legato pieces. Here the rhythmic pulse really is not as noticeable and students find it harder to sense. We need to teach rhythm better.

*(Robert Levy)*

### Poor rhythmic development

Sometimes we have to do "unteaching." I go through the music and find rhythm patterns that they're having trouble with and include them in the warm ups. I mean that's no big deal. Everybody does that I'm sure, but I used that technique to overcome their lack of rhythm education.

*(Richard Kennell)*

## The Place of Movement in Rhythm Learning

### The need for movement

It is hard to develop the individual's sense of pulse, especially when teachers did not develop this when the student was younger. In the last few years, I've done more with physical movement, such as clapping and tapping, as remedial as this seems. Even many university students need to move muscle groups in time to develop a sense of pulse. With many students, I have had to build a foundation since one never existed.

With a youth orchestra in the area, I found some kids have developed some physical sense of pulse from moving the bow. Strings have a very distinct advantage. The little second violin and viola kids also say "bum bum bum bum," which helps them feel pulse and also hear it.

With my baritone and tuba students at the university, I have them use rhythmic etudes found in the Hindemith book or Bona's *Rhythmic Articulations*. They do rhythmic articulations on the mouth piece while buzzing, but not playing the actual pitches.

They do this as they walk in rhythm in a circle. I approach this with humor saying, "We're going to do this, and this is silly. Maybe it's something that you don't want to do on your own when people can see you, but we need to do this to develop a sense of pulse." I have them walk in rhythm with a smooth step or lifting the legs up farther. I do anything to get those muscle groups going with some rhythmic sense.

I think this reduces everything down to the simplest element and experience. Anything physical they do pays a huge dividend. I must say I didn't realize this when I started teaching years ago. So, I now take away the fingerings, the high register, the reed—I take away everything to get down to the rhythm.

For wind players, blowing the air or buzzing the lips in rhythm can develop the reflexes of the muscle system they need when they're playing. I try to teach pulse to get their physical sensations systematized so they know what it feels like when they're rhythmic. Then, when they try to play their instruments while adding other musical dimensions, they can rely upon pre-trained and rhythmic muscle actions.

Eventually, efforts to be rhythmic won't interfere with the playing of the instrument and making music. Conversely, their concerns for making music won't divert their attention away from rhythm so much. The result is they have been programmed in the rhythmic aspect strongly enough so that they can go on and make music right away.

I have them do time beating while they sing the line. Students might make a time pattern with the right hand while singing the phrase. They also could hold the mouth piece with the left hand. Then they buzz the phrase and conduct the time pattern in the right hand. We do this to get everything into the whole system of the body. I teach them to do the very basic motions for legato, staccato, and marcato so students can represent these styles with physical gestures. They have to model a style with the hand or the whole arm movement; this enables them to feel and move staccato when they play staccato.

*(L. Keating Johnson)*

### Rhythm involves their bodies

Have them get out of their chair. The other day I had the whole group dancing around the room, singing subdivisions. Let's say you are playing *Folk Song Suite* by Vaughan Williams and it's just a rhythmic disaster. Get them standing and swaying back and forth or moving in a march-like fashion. They repeat, over and over, the phrase as they move. This is to get them to have a certain feeling of what it's like to "over-dot" a rhythm. The preferred way to play a figure cannot be written, but we need to play it that way to be in the true British style.

*(Larry Rachleff)*

### Using movement

Subdivision is one important way to build their rhythmic control. For example, today I conducted twelve-eight with a circular motion. I showed them that the beat was at the bottom of the circle on 1. I did this by counting, "1-2-3, 1-2-3, 1-2-3, 1-2-3." Then, to help them feel this, I said "one" at the bottom of the circle and they answered aloud, saying "two-three" for the remaining subdivisions of each pulse.

To reinforce this, I also had them move their hands in a circle, and move their bodies back and forth. At that point things really dropped into a groove. Before doing this we were all over the place because they could not feel the beat. I am a firm believer that students must feel the pulse and subdivision to play. Using movement helped them learn more quickly.

*(Jack Brookshire)*

### Movement

To help students learn to feel the underlying rhythmic structure of a melody, I want them consistently to associate physical movement with the feeling. I recommend using hand-pats on their thighs for tempo beat feeling, clapping for the duple and triple meter divisions between tempo beats, and clapping for melodic rhythm patterns.

For example, the melody of *Yankee Doodle* fits with an underlying pat-clap (duple) feeling, and *Over the River and Through the Woods* fits with a pat-clap-clap (triple) feeling.

In a group setting, one can assign students to each of the three rhythm activities. Different groups can pat, pat-clap, and melody clap while others perform the selection on their instruments. Then I might change assignments of the subgroups for further practice.

*(Stanley L. Schleuter)*

### Cautiousness in beginning the use of movement

I encourage movement but there's a problem in its use with typical high school students. They are much more conservative than they would like you to believe. They won't do it. You would like them to, but they may giggle and laugh. When I do get a student who naturally moves, I might gently use the student as an example. I do this very gently because I don't want to inhibit them from continuing to move.

I seek some way so they will not be such mannequins, or statues, and little technical wizards. Since they are very reluctant to move at all, I promote up and down movement, instead of side to side swaying movement. I do this for a very specific reason—so we can be rhythmically secure.

Though kids are shy in the real world of public school teaching, I think they can accept movement. I think that my top group maybe could handle it. My ninth-graders—they'd be off the wall. There may be benefits six months after sticking to it as with the singing. If I can find a solution so they do what I want them to do aurally, I'm going to try that first. A visual movement technique would be a second or third choice for me; but as I'm saying this, I'm convinced that I haven't done enough of it to have an opinion yet.

*(Patricia Brumbaugh)*

### Movement and foot tapping

I believe in foot-tapping, particularly at the initial levels of instruction. At higher levels, it ceases because we expect them to have internalized the sense of pulse and subdivision by then. We do not routinely use foot-tapping with advanced performance of Grade V or VI level music. We could bring it back if there were a rhythmic problem at this level. We want them to subdue the foot movement in performance.

Foot-tapping is important to both the student and the teacher. Tapping is a visual clue to what the student is feeling. If the teacher cannot learn what the student is feeling, he cannot evaluate the student's understanding.

In our initial instruction with recorders and general music in the first three elementary grades, we prescribe foot tapping because motor coordination is essential. There can be, though, a problem of physical maturation levels. Some students learn skills at different ages. To teach effectively, I try to use uncomplicated physical movements.

*(George R. Bedell)*

### Teaching rhythms and rhythmic feel

I may have half the band clap on pulses, since they cannot clap, count, and tap their feet at the same time. The other half counts and claps the rhythm patterns, then we switch parts on cue. It is interesting how often I hear students playing them inaccurately, simply because they have not dealt with them in both an intellectual and physical way.

*(Frank Bencriscutto)*

### The use of movement

I use a lot of foot-tapping. I also have them do some conducting to feel the pulse, meter, or the phrase. I do like students to move, but I don't tell them to move. I certainly don't ask them not to move if they spontaneously do. I have them do some movement, if I think it will help them play the part more musically.

*(Donald S. George)*

### The potential in movement

I heard Ed Gordon talk and saw his physical movements that fit different rhythms. I move on the podium a lot, but I have not used movement for students to do as yet. I am going to investigate Dalcroze to see if there are more movements that might help students learn in band.

*(Robert Grechesky)*

### Movement improves the phrase or rhythm

One of my predecessors had students put down their instruments, and sing, and conduct the passages. This works wonders with phrasing, and is especially effective with mixed meters when they have their hands moving up and down according to the pulses and the meter.

*(Robert Grechesky)*

### Moving to recorded music

I have them move (for example, sway) with the music. They may be more inhibited about movement than singing. I sometimes play a recording and they move to the music as they feel it. I find that movement is very effective.

*(Robert Floyd)*

### Moving develops a feeling for pulse

They tap their feet and emphasize the upbeat over the downbeat. I have them pulse on their legs with their fists, down, up, down, up and actually say, "down, up, down, up." I also have had them move with their body from the waist: down, up, down, up.

*(Nancy Plantinga)*

### Using movement to solve a performance problem

We use one hand on one leg for pulse and the other hand for the rhythm patterns. As music teachers, we do much aural and visual, but not enough with tactile. This worked very successfully with the high school students. We would stop to solve a problem, using tapping and patting. They solve the problem often on the very first try. For the moment, this also removed distractions of instruments and fingerings.

*(Robert Allan)*

## Using conducting as movement

I'll show them a conducting pattern that I'm using if we're having trouble holding together rhythmically. I'll say, "Here's what I'm doing. Let's have you try it. Maybe you can feel a little bit what I'm doing with conducting and can follow me easier." I especially like movement if I'm doing a change in tempo; rubato, accelerando, or ritard. They conduct a mirror image of me as they watch what I'm doing. They also conduct with me as I sing the melody to them. This may let them hear what I'm feeling inside.

*(Lance Schultz)*

## The use of movement

Most young musicians are very unskilled rhythmically! Maybe this is true all over. I believe you should tap your foot, or use some type of muscular or kinetic energy. This keeps a pulse going so, at least, there is a steady pulse and steady rhythm.

*(Lance Schultz)*

## Comment about movement

I'm not into that movement thing. I'm not saying that it's bad, I'm not saying that it's good. I just never studied it and, therefore, if I haven't studied it, I'm not going to try it and do it badly.

*(Dominic Spera)*

## Using movement with beginners

We do movement with younger kids by the second or third day in beginning classes. We use movement such as marching in place. They can't play much yet and they do not know how to hold the horn. We use movement for variety and to develop the feel for a definite pulse. We also do some hand movement with younger kids. At older stages, we do much less. We do have them move their hands in circles for movement—particularly with jazz.

*(Bryce Taylor)*

## Marching to mixed meters

For the last six or more years we have marched to at least one piece that has mixed meters. We do that, but it didn't come about by design. I happened to like the tunes we were going to play and they had mixed meters. Since we've started this, the kids can read in virtually any meter in pieces like *Amparita Roca* or Stravinsky's *Petrushka*. For instance, if they were marching in nine-eight with a 3-2-2-2 grouping of eighth notes, they would march, moving the left and right feet, as the following mixed meter of 3-2-2-2 is counted:

(3) LEFT-and-a;  (2) RIGHT-and;
(2) LEFT -and;   (2) RIGHT-and.

This is a eurythmics experience. The kids receive much physical feedback through this that it is very much akin to dancing. When I try to teach kids mixed meter in bands who haven't marched to mixed meters, they have a really hard time figuring out just how it's going to feel.

You could have anybody move in mixed meter; it doesn't have to be a marching band. The Greeks grew up dancing that way and find no problem in feeling long and short pulses. When we march, they're almost dancing and you can feel them get into the groove.

Yesterday we read *On The Grand Prairie Texas* by Holsinger. The rhythm goes through 3/4-2/4-4/4-6/8-5/4 and there's one place where it's 6/8-2/4 against 5/4. They read right through it! I didn't go through and define how to divide each measure, as we once did with *Sinfonia India*. I just gave them a long beat where I should, and it fell right in place. When *Armenian Dances* was new, someone did it with an honors band. He could not get the five-four until he got the kids to sway in their seats. To get into the lilt of it, that's exactly what you have to do. This movement business makes mixed meters so easy for the kids.

*(Gregory Bimm)*

# TEACHING TEMPO AND PULSE

## Building internal pulse in marching band

Instead of leaning on the percussion section for rhythmic stability, have the percussion not play. The band can march street parades, even half-time shows and in rehearsals without percussion. Once on a street parade, we put a dancer's "metal tap" on the left shoe of each kid. We marched to nothing but the sound of the left foot's click on pavement. If you listened real hard, you barely heard the clicks.

The drum major would march backwards and watch the band. If he saw imprecision, he would crank the drums back up. We also reduced the number of the kids with taps on their shoes as the band got better. The tap's clicking sound became more and more inaudible.

*(John Williamson)*

## Selecting tempi

I strive for a tempo that is realistic with the group and within the realm of good musical judgment. *Rocky Point Holiday* is marked: quarter note = 184. Few bands can play it at that tempo. I have heard it done well at 144 and 164. The challenge is to find a tempo other than that marked in the score that still is exciting and musically acceptable.

*(Robert Floyd)*

## The choice of tempo

Whenever the tempo of a piece is slowed for some careful practice, be sure that it is not slowed to the point where the feeling of the tempo beat changes. This occurs, for example, when a melody felt in two tempo beats per measure (usually written in two-quarter or two-half) is slowed to the point where we feel four tempo beats per measure. This creates a new rhythmic structure and a new problem for the learner.

*(Stanley L. Schleuter)*

I always tell them that they have to choose their tempo according to the hardest measure in the piece. So if they can play technically the hardest measure in the piece at metronome marking of 60, they must stick to the same marking in the easier measures.

*(Thomas Stone)*

### Establishing the tempo
On the first reading I try to set a tempo they can work toward.

*(Judith A. Niles)*

### Defining tempo through the initial inhale
When setting the tempo for the ensemble, I have them breathe together. They breathe together at the start of a piece in the correct tempo, to define the tempo of the piece.

*(Gary Hill)*

### Tempo markings are a point of departure
I talk to students about this and may have them do an inappropriate tempo. If the score says quarter note = 152, I'll say, "Well, let's try it." Then I'll say, "How does it sound?" We also discuss the idea that most composers use that as a point of departure. The most important musical consideration is the way it sounds.

If you have to sacrifice quality, if you have to sacrifice musicianship, tone, or phrasing to get to some specific tempo marking, then something is wrong. The tempo is either too fast or too slow. If a group can't sustain a lyrical line slowly, then do it a little faster. Students are rigid with tempo markings. They should have the chance to fail though, but not in a big way. Let them try various tempi and then analyze what happened. Trying tempi helps one evaluate the abilities of the group, the potential of the group, and how much time one needs to get something accomplished.

*(Mallory B. Thompson)*

### Varying the tempo
Few conductors have the attention of the group while they're conducting. We should have them "appeal to response more than memory." It is better to conduct an accelerando than to explain it. In the middle of the concert the idea would be that you could put an accelerando anywhere. Your kids would follow you because they are sensitive to the conducting.

My kids aren't sophisticated enough, at least not yet, to respond at any time or any place. Therefore, I have to train in a little bit more than I would like to. I might have

to warn them, "Watch what I'm going to do at this spot, because I'm might throw you a curve." Then, I'll rehearse it different ways.

*(Thomas Stone)*

### Understanding tempo markings
I let them know that 120 is march tempo. Then I will show them a march tempo. I compare that to 80, which is the tempo of *1812 Overture*. I am not sure that kids must know what the difference is between 84 and 96, which are smaller differences. I think, though, that they should know what a metronome marking is and what it means.

*(anonymous)*

## TEACHING THE REST, PAUSE, AND ANACRUSIS

### Giving attention to rests
Don't tune out the ensemble during rests. Maintain the sensitivity to pulse, counting, subdivision, and internalization. I have them count aloud, especially with young students who are not playing at that moment. When they hit a rest, they count in subdivision—they are less apt to space out. They sub-vocalize the counting, whisper it in rhythm. This exercise keeps them into what is happening, especially the pulse. That stabilizes those who are playing.

*(Robert Floyd)*

### Teaching the pause through demonstration
Pauses are also something they often overlook or ignore. They play them as though they were not even there. I compare the composer's use of a pause to its use in everyday speech. Both use it to gain a reaction from the listener.

*(Judith A. Niles)*

### Playing "ghost notes" on rests
Students are usually late on entrances after rests. To adjust this I use the idea of a "ghost note." That means to put an imaginary note on the rest. They play the imaginary note as loud and strong as the rest of the notes, except no sound comes out. The effect is to make the note a part of the rhythmic structure. I say, "There is someone home on that rest, but we don't hear it."

*(Donald Wilcox)*

### Practicing rests
These need to be practiced. This is especially true when somebody is working on a solo. Many times they only work on the sections of the solo they play. If they have a three-bar rest in a solo with a piano, they get all goofed up when they go on stage because they have not practiced the rests.

This is especially true on a longer rest, such as ten measures. If they are not practicing rests, they may get lost.

When they put the solo with an accompanist, they're dead because they have not been practicing and counting rests.

They must practice the rests as intensely as they practice the music, and do so repeatedly. This refers to long rests of several measures; but when they are counting short rests of a beat or so, they should use the counting system and they could whisper.

*(Dominic Spera)*

## Pick up notes

Some go "ta DAY," connecting the "ta" to the DAY and to the next "ta DAY." Sometimes I have kids think of this as "ta— day" with a space between the sounds. They also may see them as unconnected because of the bar line. Sometimes, drawing a little arrow over the music helps.

String players tell me, "I think of pick up notes the way you wind players do. You get ready, bring up the instrument, take a breath, and then go." I see it differently. The string players can actually see that bow movement. They can see that lifting, and then moving down.

*(L. Keating Johnson)*

## TEACHING SUBDIVISION AND METER

### Subdivisions

Teach subdivision early and *teach* it *always*. It's the only way to get rhythmic precision. As soon as they understand a basic quarter-note pulse, start breaking the notes up into their subdivisions. Symphony musicians say, "If there is poor conductor, we duck our heads and subdivide the hell out of everything." If they do it, we ought to do it.

*(Donald Wilcox)*

### Subdivision slow passages

Subdivision is needed especially at extremely slow tempos. For example, on *Elsa's Procession to the Cathedral* I have everyone thinking sixteenths. This actually speeds up the pulse rate they are experiencing, even though they still accent the first of the group of four as well as play the sustained style.

On fast tempos, we often slow down the pulse and subdivide to remove the "blur" they feel because they cannot figure out or perform the fast passage instantly. I ask them to sense the pulse's subdivision and see faster figures as their subdivisions. For example, in a fast three-four with six eighth notes per pulse, we would subdivide the pulse so, in effect, it is a two-eighth note figure per pulse. Then we would accent the first note of each two-note figure with every sixth note accented a bit more so.

As they understand the organization and gain technical control, I can increase the tempo. The "blur" has been removed from their mind and they are playing more accurately.

*(Jack Brookshire)*

### Developing subdivision

When one section is having some difficulty with subdivision, I will have all the other musicians doing something that reinforces subdivision. They can be counting or clapping—I prefer counting. Their attention and mind can wander while clapping, but not as easily while counting. They also frequently "whisper" the counting numbers, since they often clap too loud.

*(Patricia Brumbaugh)*

One can have a snare drum played lightly on the subdivision or one can use an amplified metronome, which can be switched on and off during the rehearsal by the director. Ultimately the students must learn to "feel" the subdivision so that they are not dependent on any external reference.

*(Richard Floyd)*

I have the outside person on each stand play while the inside person counts the subdivisions. Then they reverse their roles.

*(Robert Allan)*

Sometimes I'll have the drummer play sixteenth notes as the group plays, for example, a moderate tempo that has dotted-eighth—sixteenth-note rhythms. If the piece fits, I also may have all the kids play sixteenth notes straight through first. Then we'll play, tying the first three and playing the fourth one.

*(Howard A. Lehman)*

### Choosing the subdivision

When rehearsing for technical accuracy, the smaller unit into which you can subdivide will give you the highest degree of accuracy. The most inaccurate way is to conduct and sing a work in quarter notes. Even to play a chorale accurately, they should subdivide into eighths or sixteenths. This also helps them wait until the last minute to move their fingers and to experience and calculate duration. One rhythmic pianist I know sought metronomes that could do the fastest sixteenth notes!

*(Robert E. Foster)*

Use the smallest note—the lowest common denominator, to determine what the subdivision should be.

*(Robert Allan)*

### Developing meter and subdivision through tonguing exercises

Usually groups will play together well on beats one and two. On beats three and four the rhythm becomes a little bit blurred. By the time they get back to beat one, they're back together again. If one can drill that skill through tonguing exercise, one can get them to feel the pulse, meter, and subdivision throughout the measure.

*(Thomas Stone)*

## Subdivision is critical

If they don't learn to subdivide right away, then you're in trouble. They must have this as a skill. If they can't feel the difference between duple and triple and subdivisions it's all over. If you can't relate those rhythms to those on the page, it's all over.

The old "1-ee-and-ah-2-ee-and-ah," is okay when the music is slow, but the Indian version is better. They use TAK AH TAK AH for duple, for triplets it would be TAK AH TAH TAK AH TAH, and then fours are TAK AH DI MI. (This is like double and triple tonguing patterns.) You can say these quicker and their sounds are even a little more musical. I got this from Ed Shaunessy, the drummer. He studied with Indian drummers and this was their technique for teaching subdivision.

*(John Williamson)*

## Rhythmic tendencies

If someone has a quarter note followed by two eighths, they often play the two eighths too fast, particularly the second eighth. Here again the subdivision idea comes in. They should play so the short notes don't hurry the long notes.

*(Larry Rachleff)*

## Stressing subdivision can solve rhythm problems

When rhythms are simply not fitting perfectly together, I quit conducting and clap the subdivision with my hands without an inflection. They usually do all the rest and correct the rhythmic problem if they are aware of the subdivision. If they do not have an awareness of the subdivision, their playing will not be together, even if the teacher suggests they use tricks or images.

*(Robert E. Foster)*

## Pulsing the subdivision

I ask students, even the younger ones, to keep in mind the smallest note value in the work they are performing. I then ask them to pulse that value through the longer notes. The students have the most difficulty with the longer notes instead of the shorter notes. Pulsing the smallest note value cures the problem of shortening the value of the quarters or the half and whole notes.

For dotted quarter and eighth-note rhythms, I have them pulse the three eighths on the quarter. I do not conduct this, I am speaking more of their mental understanding of the rhythms. This pulsing approach, the counting of subdivisions in the long notes, also helps them play the dotted rhythms. Pulsing keeps an intensity in the playing and gives a drive to the rhythm that they really need to have. They can't just sit on a note, but need to feel the pulse.

I talk ratios to them all the time—since they have all had enough math at this point. For example, I explain the three-to-one ratio in the dotted eighth/sixteenth. This rhythm is often played inaccurately, more so than the

dotted quarter and an eighth. I use an analytical and mathematical approach in high school by talking about ratios.

*(Judith A. Niles)*

## Ritardandos and accelerandos

Many kids have trouble understanding that while they are speeding up or slowing down, everything is proportional. When they play, for example, a succession of dotted eighths and sixteenths or repeated eighth notes, they must subdivide a ritardando or an accelerando. They must do this and realize that proportionally each note is also getting longer or shorter depending on whether the tempo increases or decreases.

Making it proportional is real hard for young students especially, to grasp. Drawings can work because students can see a graphic representation of it instead of our traditional notational system.

*(L. Keating Johnson)*

## Mixing and changing meters

I use the sub-division feature frequently in transitions from cut time to four-four, or four-four to three-eight. We also work a lot on mixed meter. Basic meter does not cause problems because of their extensive experience with the metronome and subdivision.

*(Robert Floyd)*

## Comprehending and teaching rhythm

Comprehending where the rhythmic subdivision falls is essential. Telling someone that they are too early or too late really has little to do with comprehension. If someone has a dotted eighth-sixteenth, it's important that they sense and feel where the sixteenths are.

I think learning happens the best if you take some time for this. I have the whole group count the sixteenth notes aloud on whatever syllables you think are appropriate. I also have them physically perform the dotted eighth-sixteenth at a variety of tempos, not just the tempo marked in the score. Then they can generalize the concept to other situations. They will understand first that the rhythmic pattern has a place, and they learn that body language and body rhythm relate to how they should perform the rhythm.

I do the exercise at different tempi so they can transfer the understanding to other places and pieces. You also can have them move their fingers while they are singing the rhythm. They might either be tapping, singing, making certain body movements, echoing, or counting.

With rhythmic problems, I am always trying to have them comprehend the counting. I get them to supply the counting and have them act out the rhythm—always with a musical reason for the explanation. I found that having someone play a perfect rhythm mechanically doesn't result in the same musical meaning. It will not bring about the same result as telling them to play the sixteenth note stronger than the dotted eighth and that the sixteenth belongs to the next note.

I think that the ideas of rhythm and the teaching of Dalcroze are connected. The body must be involved in how rhythm works—this is something that is essential to the rehearsal. Class time in orchestra, band, or choir is the only part of the day when they can get involved in this way. The rest of the day they are just kind of sitting there soaking up information.

I conduct and reinforce the verbal information with a non-verbal experience. The result is that they will associate the rhythm with a rhythmic-musical personality. If there is a musical explanation, precision issues often can be addressed. It is more effective than just using the pedantic statement, "You are rushing the eighth note." If you have the group involved in the problem solving of the counting, there is an electricity about all of their learning experiences.

*(Larry Rachleff)*

## Teaching Rhythmic Feel and Sense

### Internalizing rhythm

We have junior high school students internalize the pulse by tapping their feet on the beat, clapping their hands on the subdivision, and singing the rhythm on a neutral syllable. I often use a "Doctor Beat" metronome to stabilize this. They must internalize the sub-division because they cannot clap always. I vary the techniques I use because they cannot clap all the time, and I use the syllable "dah" for the rhythms because the syllable fits tonguing.

*(Richard Fischer)*

### Rhythmic feel

The rhythmic feel in jazz ensemble is far more crucial in jazz than many directors realize.

*(Donald Casey)*

### Raising their awareness

Ritards vary with whoever is making the choice. The different music sensitivity of individuals helps dictate this. We make our choice based upon the music, which gives us additional information to make this choice.

I try to show the choice through conducting. If they don't respond correctly, I show through conducting what they should do. Talking about it puts it in the forefront of their mind, so they pay more attention to the conducting. Sometimes I have the band start at a certain point and play through the ritard without my conducting. It gives them a sense of input, and compels them to listen to each other.

*(Richard Fischer)*

### The problem with clapping rhythms

Clapping rhythms might be weak because it suggests that rhythms are absolute entities, rather than a series or phrase of rhythms patterns.

*(Hal D. Cooper)*

### Teaching rhythmic feel in music

There is a strong need for rhythmic feel in playing. Those who involve their whole bodies do better rhythmically, even on whole notes. I develop their rhythmic feel through singing, saying, and playing slowly. This develops their sense of feeling better than moderate or fast tempos. Playing slowly promotes the physical movement I want in rhythmic playing. At the beginning of instruction, some students are unable to tap the pulse and play eighths at the same time. Sometimes, I even move their feet up and down for them! I show ritard and accelerando with my singing and playing. I tell them a ritard sounds like a bicycle wheel that is slowing down. I also tell them to exaggerate the ritard. I show this with my conducting or I ask them to slow down more than they think they should.

*(Steven Cooper)*

### Rhythm problems with slow tempo

The older I get, the more bad rhythm bothers me. It disturbs me when four eighth or quarter notes are not where they belong. The eighth notes compress and as a result, they occur before "and." This is especially true on slow music where one would prefer they stretch the notes.

*(Robert Grechesky)*

### Teaching rhythm in a musical context

To develop a sensitivity to pulse, I promote and use the idea of a musical metronome. This is a mechanically-generated musical metronome. One can use the metronome with and without additional accompanying harmonic or rhythmic backgrounds. With the inexpensive electronically-advanced machines and music we have, there is no reason not to do this.

This is particularly effective with younger students. These materials are commercially available; I have even produced some myself. The materials of James Froseth's *Listen, Move Sing and Play* uses this—I wish even more methods of this type were available.

Some of my methods class students own inexpensive equipment that they can use to make accompaniments. Some create magnificent pre-recorded accompaniments. They use the same approach as found in Jim's material. They make their own, and they can do so with any method book. Some materials provide steady pulse and others provide harmonic and rhythmic accompaniment material; others help develop sensitivity to pitch. This is a great way for the younger grade level, and I also carry it to the advanced level.

The effect of using a musical metronome is like learning to conduct while conducting real music. Playing music in isolation is like learning conducting in the abstract or in isolation. Elizabeth Green said, "Always practice conducting with music in your head." This idea is true here: "Always practice with music in your ear."

Students enjoy playing with a steady pulse and a musical background, while it is less enjoyable and musical to just use a mechanical metronome. The traditional metronome is still valuable, I am not anti-metronome. Using a Doctor Beat, for example, especially in a practice room or when a musical metronome is not available, is a very valuable aid. The time-keepers need to learn to keep time!

With young kids in their first two or three years of playing, I advocate using pre-recorded or teacher-recorded music. This music can provide a harmonic, tempo, and pulse background that is musical. This is compared to only a coordinated "tick."

I believe that students learn much through imitation. I include the musical metronome into instruction by recording the correct chord progression as a background for particular rhythms. I also may record the entire whole song, or melodic or harmonic patterns. I have students play with the chordal background and in imitation of me or a peer playing. This is a repetitive drill, with music heard in the background. This provides the musical metronome.

With the electronic accompanying or background support, one can provide a very dependable and steady pulse, or rhythmic background. The student may face a problem because the sub-division needs to vary. It must vary from style to style or playing on the front and back side of the pulse, etc. With the same tempo, one can produce different styles by performing the same rhythmic figure differently.

*(Gary Hill)*

### Skills in performing sounds of various durations

I am very concerned with what is happening in the minds of students as they are sustaining long notes. I refer to this as "the discipline of duration." There are several questions: "When does a note start?" "When does it end?" and, "What is happening when it is being sustained?" These are questions of high priority in my instructional procedures.

I activate, sustain, and direct my students' thinking processes by developing this "discipline of duration" through the use of the Circle of Fourths. I assign an odd number to sustain each pitch in the circle. (I use odd numbers from five to thirteen or even much higher.) I vary the numbers from rehearsal to rehearsal and I focus my attention on the students' accuracy of the mental process instead of their accuracy with the exercise. I establish the pulse and I do not conduct or allow students to tap their feet during this exercise. My priority is to unify the internal-ensemble pulse. The quality of entrance and release will always be determined by the exactness of this internalized counting of the odd-numbered durations. This silent counting sustains and controls the groups' mental activity, thus there is no day-dreaming or wandering-minds.

*(Edward S. Lisk)*

### Rhythm should have clarity and direction

Like a line in speech, a line in music must finish, and it must make some statement. I say, "When you come to the end of phrase, when you are talking to someone, you don't want them to speed up." (I speed up as I say this.) If one connects new ideas to those students already know, it draws on their second nature, and they can do it.

*(Larry Rachleff)*

### Teaching rhythms as phrasing

When we teach and play rhythms, we ask students to play most rhythms as pick-up notes or as grace notes to beats. For instance, with a dotted eighth and a sixteenth rhythm, play the sixteenth note as a grace note to the next beat. They perform this rhythm as though the dotted eighth is notated as a quarter, with the sixteenth being a grace note just before the quarter.

With this interpretation, this rhythm sounds "ta dummmm, ta dummmm, ta dummm," instead of the rigid metronomic sound "one-e-and-TA-DUM-e-and-a-three-e-and-TA-DUM-e-and-a-one" as counting suggests. Though they know that the subdivision is there, they don't think of it as a mechanical subdivision. They think of the last note as always being a grace note to the following note.

*(Frank Schulz)*

### Magnify the ritardando

There is a problem with most ritards marked in the score. I feel their performance is often "half-baked," and lacks satisfaction. Conductors do not magnify ritards enough to be effective. Usually they err on the side of not doing enough. If Holst were hearing it he might feel the same and say, "That wasn't enough, do more with it." There's a spot in *Ave Verum Corpus* in measure twenty-nine that leads into a pianissimo section. I think that is a wonderful place for the bass instruments as they lead down to the root, starting at measure thirty. Take a lot of time and milk it for everything it's worth.

*(Thomas Stone)*

## DEVELOPING RHYTHMIC FEEL AND UNITY IN THE ENSEMBLE

### Non-conducting

I use a lot of non-conducting. This is very effective in that it causes them to listen much more. Non-conducting, though, does not have the musical energy or forward-rhythmic motion that conducting provides. With non-conducting, ritards work musically but the rhythms lack forward motion. Perhaps they could regain the forward motion with more practice playing without conducting.

*(John Anderson)*

### Develop the ensemble's sense of pulse

If the pulse is unsteady, use the rest of the band to

provide this through physical movement.

*(George R. Bedell)*

### Rhythmic control and the ensemble's technical accuracy

I feel that many technical problems are really rhythmic problems. For example, if there is an eighth note in a row of sixteenth notes, the problem is not a lack of finger dexterity—they can go from note to note. The problem is that they do not have the ability to go from note to note *in rhythm.*

I will write the rhythm, for example, of the clarinet part, and give it to a snare drum. This isolates the task. The snare will play the rhythm of the melody as the clarinets finger the melody. A key phrase I use is, "Listen to the snare and make sure your fingers are moving as crisply and as rhythmically as you hear the snare play." This starts them moving their fingers in a decisive, clear, and rhythmic manner.

This is an efficient way to clean up technical passages and insure that students are playing with rhythmic and technical accuracy. When they are not accurate, it may be that each section member is not playing precisely in rhythm. A section playing "semi-in-rhythm" will constantly have technical and precision problems.

*(Richard Floyd)*

### The metronome

I may have another group be a "human metronome" for a group or section.

*(Pamela Gearhart)*

### Listening and subdivision

There are several ways to develop mental subdivision, which is essential to ensemble playing. Have one section play a part that shows subdivision rhythmically, so the rest hear it. If people have larger note values, I ask them to listen so they can relate their longer notes to the sound of the subdivision. I also layer several parts that simultaneously show various subdivisions. This increases their opportunity to notice the subdivision.

I may have a snare drummer play a given pattern as the rest of the ensemble plays through a section, especially a technically demanding one. I had students in the middle of a large festival band articulate the subdivision on a percussive sound. They do this with a short "hiss" or "sizzle" on each basic subdivision.

*(Thomas H. Cook)*

### Developing the group's responsibility for rhythm

It is the player's responsibility to maintain the pulse. We have them internalize the pulse within the ensemble through various ways: one is to develop the mind-set that it is their "gig" to keep the pulse. A metronome can help reinforce this. Another way is to have them play a lot without the conductor. Tell them, "Keep playing, even if

I leave the podium, unless I tell you to stop." A group can develop pride and a sense of accomplishment in being able to play a piece and keep the pulse by themselves. By not conducting, one can reinforce their accomplishment and prove they can do it.

*(Robert Floyd)*

### Visual communication in rhythm

I promote communicating the pulse by passing the phrase from one instrument to another visually as well as musically. For example, in a Mozart serenade, the clarinets pass the tune to the oboes. I encourage visually looking in their direction as though saying, "Here it comes—there, you just got it."

*(Michael Kaufman)*

### Rhythmic skill

There are important ideas to remember. (1) Internalize a pulse all the time, keeping a constant tempo *particularly* at the slower tempos. (2) Sometimes when we are playing marches or playing pieces, they are led by an ostinato percussion or something extremely repetitious. This may be a rhythmic element that drums the rhythm and pulse into the ensemble. The result is the students are less focused on the pulse. (3) I hear more rhythmic mistakes made in long notes' values, tied values and rests. Their minds must go to sleep when they are not counting.

To counteract this, I try to stress anticipating an upcoming rhythmic unit. In most instances you can do that. It's more difficult to do if you're playing one rhythm, such as a triplet, since you are led to expect duple patterns coming up. It takes concentration and awareness to look ahead. Suppose you're playing a half note and suddenly over the bar line you have to play a quintuplet. There is no reason, at whatever the tempo is while you're playing the half note, that you can't start to internalize the upcoming rhythm, instead of just jumping in unprepared. Otherwise, it's like jumping in a swimming pool without looking to see how deep the water is.

*(Robert Levy)*

### One need for a conductor

When doing a march or a rhythmically predictable piece, I stop conducting and thrust the responsibility for maintaining the pulse on to their shoulders. When there is a tempo change, they need to look up from their stands for musical indications. If they see a musical indication that says "slow down or speed up," that also means "to look up." Then, they seem to pick-up on what their role is. When that's happening, they are thinking, "Yeah, this is where we need more help from the podium."

*(Timothy Mahr)*

### The pulse

A good ensemble must maintain its own pulse. This is not the conductor's job. The conductor initiates the pulse and the ensemble generates the pulse. Each depends upon the other.

*(James Arrowood)*

## Teaching Aids and Visual Systems

### Using verbal syllables

Though we have incorporated the Froseth-Gordon syllables into our program, we also teach counting through the traditional "1-e-and-ah-2's." We do this for two reasons: one is that counting can be used as a form of analysis that can be placed at the proper level in Gordon's skill learning sequence. The second reason is that our students must play in all-state or all-district bands. The conductors use traditional terminology while referring to "the and of 2" or "Make the e-and-ah's evenly spaced." If our students don't know this terminology, they can feel out-of-touch or confused because they don't understand.

*(Edward Susmilch)*

### Counting and verbal systems

We use counting systems and we sometimes use words such as "evenly" to convey the sense of triple meter. We also use beat counting in the beginning stages. For example, we count four quarters as 1, 1, 1, 1; a quarter, half, and quarter note is counted as 1, 1-2, 1. For eighth notes, we use 1-te, as in 1-te, 2, 3-te, 4. "Te" is pronounced as in the word "hay"; Four sixteenth notes are 1-ta-ti-ta. With eight thirty-second notes we add "te" between these and the counting is 1-te-ta-te-ti-te-ta-te. With six-eight rhythms we use these syllables: 1-la-lee for eighth notes and for 1-ta-la-ta-lee-ta for sixteenth notes. A side benefit is their relationship to instrumental tonguing.

*(George R. Bedell)*

### Making sense out of the components of rhythm

In terms of audiation, meter is determined aurally, just as tonality is determined aurally. One doesn't need to see a key signature to tell the tonality of a piece of music any more than one needs a measure signature to tell the meter of a piece of music.

A six-eight march is audiated in duple meter with one macro beat per measure using the rhythm syllables du de / du de and du da di de da di / du da di de da di.

The composition *Silent Night* in six-eight would be audiated in triple meter with two macro beats using the syllables du da di du da di.

*(Richard Grunow)*

### Mixing verbal rhythm syllable systems

Before students come to me they have had Kodaly-Curwen and I am doing Froseth-Gordon syllables. When they leave me for junior high and senior high they go back to the traditional "one and two and's." To avoid confusion for kids, I have had to compromise. I didn't want to

because the Gordon syllables were really working with the kids. However, the junior and senior high teachers would not use them.

When the kids start out with me, I continue to use all Kodaly-Curwen syllables. As I go along, I start changing and transferring them over to the "one and two e and ah" counting system. Froseth-Gordon syllables also come in six-eight time. I use the "one and two and" for the two-four and four-four time, and with Froseth-Gordon, I still have that distinction between triple and duple. For syncopation I use "syn-co-pah" from Kodaly-Curwen.

I tell the kids that no matter what teacher you have, if you are at home practicing and you come upon these rhythms, use "syn-co-pah" and you'll never have a problem with it. I learned Kodaly syllables because the kids would say to me "Is this rhythm ta ta ti-ti ta?" I would recommend that to anybody in a similar situation; we should bend to work with other teachers and to help students learn. That is better than fighting it by saying, "My way is the perfect and purist way."

*(Gordon Nelson)*

### Verbal systems

We use three different counting systems, all of which use basically the same idea. We use three different sets of systems because there are certain kids who can't absorb one set of syllables, but they can handle another set better. When they do written exams we tell the kids, "Use any one of the three systems you choose or a combination of those. Either is acceptable."

*(Bryce Taylor)*

### Counting, vocalization, and syllables

I have drummers count aloud, though it depends on the grade level that I'm teaching. If it's a younger group, we do considerably more of this. I use vocalizations, such "one e and ah," so they mimic music rather than analyze notation; thus they hear the sound, and they feel the pulse and the phrase as well as the music's character and style.

*(Lance Schultz)*

### Using visual aids to teach analysis of a rhythm pattern

Apples come in handy when I teach a dotted quarter and eighth note rhythm for fifth and sixth grade students. Give one whole apple to one student. Cut another apple into halves and give one half to the first student while the other half goes to the second student. This is to show that the dotted quarter note gets one- and- one-half beats while the second half is left for the eighth note.

*(Theta Lee)*

### The use of the metronome

With rhythm, one can use a metronome. It allows students to listen to the pulse and tempo, which helps stress subdivision and accuracy, and practice rather intricate rhythms. They develop an internal sense of subdivision and they learn to play mixed meters rather easily.

*(Donald DeRoche)*

### Performing the subdivisions on snare drum

On rhythm transitions, such as from four-four to seven-eight, I use the eighth as the constant through the change. I may have the snare play the eighth-note subdivision to help us as we work this out. If needed, we also do this on six-eight marches. We do so especially when they have combinations of eighths and quarters that they are not playing well in relation to the subdivision.

*(Michael Golemo)*

### The use of a metronome

I use a McAdams metronome in rehearsal which can be amplified—it is loud enough for a sectional without amplification. One can amplify it through the AUX input of the stereo. To turn it on, I use a line switch since the amp and the metronome are always on. I can carry this line switch with me. If I want to turn it on, I can count off verbally, switch the power on, and the metronome begins accurately on the next pulse. When I turn the metronome on, it either solves a problem or shows that the ensemble is doing well. This can give them positive reinforcement when I switch on the metronome. This one has a large knob that also enables one to show ritard and accelerando. This

can be useful as a demonstration, though this does not mesh with the spontaneous nature of music making.

*(Robert Floyd)*

### Literature for teaching rhythm

I use volumes of *Teaching Rhythm* by Joel Rothman. There are several volumes after and different from the first one. One deals with changing meter.

*(Donald DeRoche)*

### Developing rhythmic skill in warm ups

I will make up warm up exercises to solve particular rhythm problems. I split the groups into halves each with a different part of the rhythm. One does the pulse, the other the difficult rhythm. I also work with several rhythms sequentially leading to the more difficult one.

I also enhance this type of exercise. I juxtapose tonal colors by having low and high instruments, and woodwind and brass play different roles in the exercise. I also have one group play the rhythm staccato and another play it legato.

*(Kjellrun K. Hestekin)*

### Teaching rhythm vocabulary

Isolate rhythm patterns, some from the pieces for the day, and use them during warm ups.

*(James Arrowood)*

# CHAPTER ELEVEN

# STYLE

Mature musicians can discuss many musical styles. They can speak intelligently of such styles as Baroque, jazz, Brahms, march, legato, staccato, British Band, or Impressionism. The learning of style should not be reserved for mature musicians; teachers can begin the stylistic development of beginning students by teaching them the basic elements.

With young students especially, education in a style can begin with choices. Teachers can show students examples of styles and can offer the students two different ways to perform a passage or phrase. The teacher can help students select and perform their choice. The students can choose to play the notes separated or connected, heavy or light; they can decide if the accents should be heavily or moderately inflected, and if the volume should be loud or soft, increasing or decreasing; and, they can decide if the tempo should be steady, or if it should slow down or speed up at some points.

When students try those choices they are learning to define a style for the piece or for the phrase. If they do not know which is appropriate, they can make a choice and judge if they like it that way or not. If they are uncertain, they can try several alternatives until they begin to hear a style they think is musical: they do not have to know the correct choice in advance. Through this process, the student, in the first years of musical study, can develop style-consciousness and the ability to make judgments.

One can see the choices that define a musical style on a continuum. At one end of the continuum, students can make style choices that are broad and try them out. As students develop and progress, they make more specific and skillful distinctions and move, therefore, along the continuum. Later students will base style decisions upon more subtle distinctions based upon more information, greater complexities, better knowledge of professional performances, and a more mature musical discrimination. These choices will increasingly be based upon their sensitivity to historical and musical traditions. Their sensitivity will grow through listening and a study of performance practices of many performers and listening to performances of music that represent many styles, periods, mediums, genres, and schools.

One should develop students' sense of style and students' judgment so they can move toward selecting a style independently. The alternative is dependence upon the teacher's directions; the students may not even be aware there are choices to be made. If students do not become sensitive to style issues and are not invited to choose a style, it is not surprising that music study does not interest or challenge some of them. They have missed a crucial part of music making; they may take little that is lasting from the class except technical skill.

## STYLISTIC CONSIDERATIONS

### The importance of style

I spend most of my time dealing with musical style. It is the one element that people don't deal with enough; I even emphasize this in junior and senior high. I have difficulty listening to music that is not in a unique and correct style. I have a firm educational-philosophical view about this. Unless one is teaching musical style and the uniqueness of each piece and composer within a general musical style, one is really not sensitizing people musically. Students will not become sensitive to the differences in each piece of music and in each composer.

*(Gary Hill)*

### Musical expression

I stress the importance of playing expressively instead of playing emotionally. For example, I would not give them an image such as, "I want this to sound like two trains ramming together." If I did this, then every time they hear a big climax they're going to think of train wrecks instead of the music. I talk specifically about how the music goes through tension or repose. I want them to see that at one point in a phrase there is a peak of tension, or at another point there is a lessening of tension.

I am not saying that I prevent or avoid an emotional way of playing. I just don't prefer an emotional way of teaching. The player has as much right to respond to a performance emotionally as a listener does. They can draw their own conclusions. Actually, as a player he has more opportunity to respond because his physical involvement is stronger than a listener. This comes partly from the tension, relaxation, or even the presence, unfortunately, of a tight throat.

I deal with expression in a short frame of time. Say you are talking about building tension through velocity. Then you might choose a spot in the music and say, "This is a spot where we can apply this idea." We may then go on to some other point. As we continue this approach, the kids play better—more beautifully, more musically, and more expressively; they become more sensitive to certain musical issues and they are involved in a different way. They become more sensitive to certain common denominators and can apply them to other pieces.

*(Kenneth M. Larsen)*

### The concern for style

The goal of conducting is to *recreate* what the composer meant in the first place. Music is a unique art form, which requires a middleman between the work and the listener; there's no direct communication between Beethoven and the audience. Music making requires that someone takes those notes that editors and everyone have chased down—those notes that Beethoven left—and makes the music the blueprint suggests. We do this to take the music to the audience. It's an art form that requires a middle man—as we also find with drama and poetry-reading. With the visual arts, you can go to a museum and see a Rembrandt directly; no middle man is needed.

If you have a recording where Bernstein plays Bernstein, where the composer is playing his own music, that gets pretty close. But the object of this whole game is to recreate the composer's intent. Sometimes the more you know about the composer, history, and the score, the closer you can come to what the guy meant in the first place; otherwise, you're just "winging it."

*(Donald Wilcox)*

### Discovering each piece's unique style

Every composition has its own individual style. Through score study one decides the style, and must carry this through to the kids.

*(Stanley Cate)*

### Style in jazz ensemble

In the jazz idiom, the inflections are highly stylized. The performers use many different gradations of articulations, far more than they do in concert band. This is so, in part, because the style may be more obviously unique. The style carries more of the content of jazz, and jazz has a dependency upon rhythmic structure and features.

I think there are more style decisions to be made in jazz, and within a broader range of choices. Young "legitimate" players sound so square, in part, because they have been trained to play with a less broad or less varied range of tone, articulations, and phrasing choices.

When defining jazz style, we manipulate articulation, volume, and rhythm rapidly and, to a great extent, we define style note by note in special ways. Therefore, the person who is trained "legitimately" may not have the facility in these four areas to function well in jazz style.

*(Donald Casey)*

### Articulations should not always sound the same

A band will often play all the accents the same, without a variation from staccato on one hand to various accents of differing lengths on the other. The accents should vary from note to note within the context of the phrase. Thus, all staccatos are not alike. Frequently the staccato also is performed devoid of its linear role. Instead of providing bounce and motion within the phrase, it is simply a short shot of sound in isolation. The linear role of staccato is forgotten.

*(Michael Haithcock)*

### Interpretation of rhythm affects style

There is a problem if the subdivisions do not vary from style to style. A subdivision also can be changed so it is played on either the front or the back side of the pulse. Within the same tempo, one can produce different styles by performing the same rhythmic figure differently. For example, fanfare figures and march-like figures, though notated the same, are not played the same.

*(Gary Hill)*

### The challenge of style

I think playing and maintaining a style, especially one that is unique, is very difficult. Style maintenance throughout a piece, and from piece to piece is very challenging.

*(Gary Hill)*

### Grasping the style

I try to encourage them to look at the period in which the piece was written and to understand the style that is characteristic of the period. This is especially important in string playing where you have different bow techniques, depending upon the period, even if the notation is the same. It's very difficult for them to understand considerations of style and notation without knowing the historical context through studying music history.

For string players there are many considerations. They are always on the string or off the string; they must decide which part of the stick to use: the middle, the frog or the tip; the teacher must judge where the performance is, and what the technical level of the player is. With professionals, you can tell them where you want it. With high school students, you have to choose from the techniques your students can learn. Then the teacher can decide what they can do to get the sound they want. Sometimes you can't pick the playing technique you would normally want because students of a certain level lack full skill development compared with professionals.

*(Judith A. Niles)*

### Using recordings while teaching style

My junior high kids will hear a recorded transcription of a fine symphony orchestra playing the piece. We will talk about the inherent problems of making ourselves sound as light and delicate as that orchestra. They discover what they are up against. They also will begin to understand that this is a transcription, and secondary to the original. I see nothing wrong with that; I do it all the time.

They will hear the symphony orchestra playing a piece and we will try to duplicate their lighter sound. That will be one of my tie-ins. That will be one of my reasons for doing that piece, to play lighter. A piece may not be like Sousa or Paul Creston, it may need a much lighter, more delicate sound.

*(William Long)*

### Style is a basic issue

I teach larger and larger issues, and allow more and more time for the technical problems related to those issues to develop on their own. I hardly ever teach toward technical development anymore, instead I teach more toward the global elements, trying to capture the nature, style and spirit of a piece of music as soon as possible. When I stop early in a rehearsal of a new piece, I usually direct my attention to stylistic issues. I ask questions about articulations such as, "Is this phrase legato, connected, or smooth?" or "Is this phrase short, staccato, detached, or angular?"

I think of issues in their broadest sense. I don't just think of dynamics, I don't just think of articulation, and I don't just think of this or that specific parameter; instead, I might use a broad term that says, "contrast is important."

*(Gerald Olson)*

### Style and technique

You can't separate the playing techniques and style techniques when you talk about the ultimate stylistic interpretation. When I talk with my band about style, I talk about vibrato, I talk about volume, I talk about feel, texture, and articulation. They all go together; they are very difficult to separate. I mean, all these entities have to be right. I think of all the abilities and skills needed to play different styles as part of the notion of musicianship; that's how I teach musicians.

*(Dominic Spera)*

### Some considerations with style

What is the style, and what part of the tongue or what part of the bow are you using? How fast is the airstream? Is it an air stress or is it a tongue stress? Where do we release this note? How do we release it? All these considerations must be there to get a clear idea across to the listener.

## TEACHING MUSICAL STYLE

### Teaching style

It is very challenging to maintain the proper style within a piece of music, particularly if it is an unusual style, such as very light and bouncy for wind players. This style, for example, is difficult for students to learn to perform correctly, because it is hard to describe mechanically. A playing demonstration is more effective than talking to show a style to the group. I could show the style by playing, singing, or using a recording or a peer performance to define the style. Any of these could be more effective than verbal descriptions.

*(Gary Hill)*

### Using the voice while teaching style

With young jazz players, I will use their voices a great deal. They are much more adept at using their voices for dynamics, articulation, or tone than they are at using their instruments. By encouraging the internalization of style through the voice, they are more able to transfer that insight to their instruments. Then we get a uniform idea of the style of this piece or phrase. The students also mature, becoming sophisticated in jazz style more quickly. The use of voice in jazz is a way around the problem of clarifying style. Using the voice is a quick way to bring forth style clarity.

*(Donald Casey)*

### Teaching style in warm ups

We do styles such as staccato or legato in all their different gradations; and we do this as a review and to introduce style issues.

*(Richard Fischer)*

### Teaching style through articulations

I teach style through the articulation, and I call the sounds we use to say the style of articulations, the "nonsense syllables." I ask them to vary the inflections of words and other subtleties; that is how I communicate the essence of style.

*(Edward S. Lisk)*

### Considering the alternatives when defining style

I do this in the studio and sometimes with ensemble for conducting. I have kids try passages in different ways, maybe three or four different ways. Then we talk about which way made more sense for the piece's style, etc. For example, we try different emphasis points, sometimes lengthening the high points of the phrase, and sometimes choosing new high points for the phrase. We decide how long we should stress the high point to round out the intensity or the musical growth the phrase should have. This helps us choose the way that is better, or discover what's possible within a phrase.

*(L. Keating Johnson)*

## Teaching style in jazz ensemble

Style is the most important thing and I develop style through varying articulations and through enunciating syllables. I break style into three types related to tempo: slow, medium, and fast.

The slow tempo could be notated with a dotted eighth followed by a sixteenth, and the enunciation is "do-ba." This style is in old slow jazz and an example with a slow tempo would be *Jazz Me Blues*. Type number two, medium, is notated with a quarter note-eighth note pattern with a triplet mark over it. That's also "do-ba" and an example of this style is the tune *Satin Doll*. I always sing a tune that they can "latch on to" and remember. For type number three, the fast, the notation is two eighth notes with an accent over the second eighth note. This version of "do-ba" is more modern and this is in the style of be-bop. An example is any be-bop recording with a nearly straight eighth-note style, such as *Donna Lee*.

The more modern the music, the more alike the two notes become. As students practice the scales, I teach them to do the same syllable enunciation three different ways. Soon, they realize that you cannot play fast tempos with the first articulation. With fast tempos one must put the notes closer together, not in a loping style as the slow jazz style dictates.

Remember, the enunciations differ from a slow style (*Jazz Me Blues*), which is "do——ba"; a medium style (*Satin Doll*) is "do-ba"; and a be-bop style (*Donna Lee*) is "doba"; the tempo change dictates how they do the style. There cannot be as much lilt on the fast articulation as there is on the slower articulation.

If they do not adjust the style because of tempo, they sound ridiculous. We enunciate the same syllables, but we enunciate the syllables in a different way and say them in a different rhythmic manner. When I introduce the literature, I can say, "Do you remember this?" or, "Which style should fit this?"

*(Dominic Spera)*

## Teaching style is basic

My basic thrust with the student is to teach him style—basic things, such as playing marcato and legato. I do six or seven different basic styles. These can be demonstrated.

My approach to a new piece of the literature is to set a style so all of the articulations are correct. We will get the style well established as far as length of notes, weight of notes, and then it just all goes together. You know it's like going to the doctor with several problems and picking out the worst one. Remedy that first and then go to the next one.

To set style, I use a lot of syllables and singing. For example if I want something separated, I would just sing the part. I think singing is very important, and I also talk a lot about making it sing. I ask them, "How would you sing it?" If I want them to give some thought to the phrase, I demonstrate it and insist that their response is correct.

*(Kenneth M. Larsen)*

## Defining style through conducting and demonstration

In guest conducting, I notice that the biggest task of all is to get hot-shot players from the high schools to play together in the correct style. In recent years, instead of talking about style, I tell them, "I want you to play this as I am conducting it."

This has two advantages: it gets them to watch me and it starts them thinking about style. In the early stages, I try to talk as little about it as possible. For example, we were doing the Gossec *Classic Overture*. I said, "All I want you to do is watch me and play it as I conduct it." I didn't say more than half a dozen words but they began getting the feeling of style. It is an advantage for me also, for it made me more aware of what I was doing with the baton. If you're not showing something they can follow, you notice very quickly how you are conducting because of the sound.

If the style problem is a little more intricate, I'll show them with my voice and have them say it back to me vocally. With this they listen carefully so they can repeat it exactly. For example, if there's a passage that should be short, I will have them say it exactly like I say it. They use the same inflection, length of the note, type of attack, etc. I will choose any sounds or articulations I feel will give me the right style, whether it's legato or staccato. Most often I will conduct as I demonstrate. I get them to think about style and get them to listen. Listening is critical for the development of style.

*(Francis Marciniak)*

## The teaching of style

Rather than micro-managing every little note, I think it's better to teach an idea of a style such as march style.

*(Thomas Stone)*

## Images can suggest style.

The style can sound like a ball bouncing, like an inner tube being hit from the side, dribbling a basketball, or skipping a rock across the water. Style also should not be like roads in Michigan—we want it like the highways in Ohio. I use imagery a lot.

*(Patricia Brumbaugh)*

## Basic styles

Essentially, I deal with five styles: a staccato of two types, a *light* and a *full staccato*; then a legato, which is broken down into a *semi-legato* and a *molto-espressivo legato* (no bump at all—nearly slurred); then *tenuto*, and *marcato* which is full arm; then of course there is a *non-*

*espressivo* which is rarely used but is nevertheless a style—an emotionless characterless beat, defined pretty much by straight lines used in passages that are almost completely dead and passive. Long sustained notes imitating fog, for instance, in a TV background. Or something where a cadenza is being played and you want to pin-point a single measure of change. It's very directed; I almost think you could be without it. Another style is *legato espressivo,* which has an ictus-less character in the style. It is a flowing legato pattern which almost eliminates the ictus. That requires terrific sub-divisional thinking in the ensemble. You can do this with the Philadelphia Symphony Orchestra, but I'm not sure you can do this with junior high school kids. Next, the *semi-legato* is a curved pattern as well, but with an ictus noticeable—a clicking if you will. The *tenuto* is a dragged beat. It is a beautifully sustained style where the wrist leads the point of the stick. There must be a clicking that happens, but it is drawn out. Next, the *light staccato* is wrist only down to the point. A *full staccato* is elbow down to the point down to the stick, and *marcato* is the full arm.

These interchange as tempos and style interchange in music. You have to get comfortable with where the change takes place and which movement is most appropriate for the ensemble and for their level.

I'm reminded of the time when I thought I was going to go in and do a beautiful job with a junior high group I guest conducted. I tried to make all these beautiful patterns. The students wouldn't stay with me because I was removing the ictus. Therefore, I went back to a far more marcato-like beat for a legato tune, to keep this beautiful piece together. I did this because the youngsters needed a little bit more help.

I find that also happens with my major ensemble. There are times when I decide to use a clearer beat over what the music says or suggests. An example may be when it is necessary to keep together a legato line being accompanied by staccato rhythms.

Style, tempos, and groups often cause the approaches to meld or cross-over; they cross-pollinate. For example, you can have a marcato with just the elbow down—if the tempo is going real fast, you won't be moving the whole arm. The intensity of the beat can change as other beat characteristics can change.

The music says it all. What we do depends upon the music, our perception of the musical sound, and what we need to do in that time frame. Articulations have a clear relationship to these different beats, different gesture types, or different styles.

*(Frank B. Wickes)*

## Conducting and the style of the pulse

I have the students try to feel not only the pulse, but the style the pulse should be. So, if there's a staccato passage, what should the pulse feel like? Obviously, if you just beat your foot, that dull thud doesn't make it—it isn't right!

I try to ask, "What should the pulse feel like to them, or what does staccato, for example, feel like when you're pulsing that?" In a staccato, I try to sense if there's more of a light bounce. Then there is the opposite, which is a pesante with a pulse that is longer and heavier. As students go along they must discover how that the pulse relates to the style of the music because the pulse is related to the music; the pulse is not a separate item.

When conducting the passages, the conductor is showing a recurring pulse while doing so. The players can internalize a pulse more easily and perform the tempo more accurately if they can pulse in the right style because they can then relate it to the music. Thus, internalizing the pulse is a lot easier if the playing is musical; tempos are much more accurate and everything makes much more sense when they do the pulse in the right style.

There is another aspect to this: if the music's style and the conducting are not congruent, kids might wonder, "If I'm a person looking at what he is doing, what relation does that have to what I hear or see in the music?" If the conductor is going "whop, whop" and the student sees "dot, dot" on the page, an observer can say, "No wonder the group slows down, because they see the wrong thing." We work hard, therefore, in our conducting classes and with any age of student, on showing and doing the style of the pulse correctly. Next is the importance of subdivision.

*(John Williamson)*

## Explaining style to younger students

With younger students I would not simply say, "Play this legato," I would tell them why. I could point out ideas about the interpretation, style, composer, and period that suggest why we played in that style. I would explain this to them in terms they could understand at their level. I wrote material in *Sessions in Sound* to give them a sense and basis for music interpretation. The material also related historical aspects of music to students and interpretation. One has to start somewhere, and their experience with literature gives them a basis for later learning throughout their entire life. Even an understanding of broad outlines of what is Baroque or Classical is a significant start for fifth graders. With that in mind, I pick music that is historically important.

*(Barbara Buehlman)*

# Chapter Twelve

# Tone

Tone quality is a vital matter for many music teachers who believe that hearing and performing a good tone are often the earliest experiences students have that can excite them musically. This may be the fundamental happening that marks the beginning of many students' musical interests, experiences, and education.

If an instrumental education is to be a musical education, developing the tone must occur from the first day. Teachers can entice their students with excellent recorded models of tone that could inspire them to attain a better sound. Teachers can stress sound quality by performing examples, teaching students to notice the differences, and challenging students to emulate the better tone qualities.

Some teachers, though, do not emphasize tone quality as soon or as much as others; they develop instrumental facility first. Their view of developing mastery of the instrument influences their preference. They see that such skills as playing the correct fingerings and articulations, and acquiring facility enable the student to play the instrument; but other teachers realize that these skills do not assure that the student will have *musical* experiences or receive a *musical* education.

At the crux of this are two contrasting assumptions. One assumption is that the primary purpose of instrumental music education is to teach the instrument so students can learn to perform music; the contrasting assumption is that the primary purpose of instrumental music education is to learn music content, develop musical expressiveness, and have *musical* experiences. Through striving to attain these objectives, the students are also developing instrumental facility. The first view promotes an emphasis upon facility because teaching performance skill is the primary purpose for the classes. The second view may safeguard students' musical development more because it stresses the primacy of the musical content, and therefore musical understanding and expressiveness.

Teachers must examine these choices carefully before they embrace a viewpoint because their beliefs, whether articulated or not, can influence the mix in the student experience. The challenge for most teachers of instrumental music will be to balance the teaching of tone quality and musical understanding with the teaching of instrumental facility; the choices teachers make and carry out each day and in each class will determine the substance of the instrumental class and the experience of each student.

## The Importance of Tone

### Tone is basic

Tone is number one, more so than rhythm. I begin working with tone first, then rhythm—though I alternate which I work on in a rehearsal because variety is so important.

*(Frank Bencriscutto)*

Tone is ninety percent of playing. I stress correct tone production during the first half of the year and I stay with it after that, of course, during the second half of the year.

*(John W. LaCava)*

Tone is even more musically important than technique.

*(Jack Brookshire)*

Tone is so basic; it has a sensuous appeal. Sensitizing students to sound opens the door to the higher levels of music learning.

*(Donald Casey)*

Tone is first in importance and, as it is developed, it also takes care of pitch and good breathing.

*(Stanley Cate)*

### The idea of sound is essential

If band directors do not have an idea of what they want the instruments to sound like, well, then they'd better stop teaching. The most important idea of all is having, in your ear, a characteristic tone color for every instrument. That constant idea of sound has to be there. How do you develop that? You listen to lots of recordings. Somebody once asked me what my favorite instrument is. I love tuba played well; I love baritone played well; I love trombone played well; I love horn played well: I have no favorite instrument.

*(John W. LaCava)*

## TONE AND TONE CONCEPTS

### A classically shaped or vocal idea of phrase

Every sound has a beginning, a middle, and an end. There should be consciousness of these three parts coupled with a vocal concept of sound. One must identify how much tongue and air to use at the very beginning. The sound must have both shape and support.

*(Frank Bencriscutto)*

I talk about and make drawings of what we call "golden, oval tones" and I say "that's what we want." If the attack is rough or the release is poor, I'll draw a note with a jagged end on it. Then, I repeat that the golden oval sound is what I want to hear.

That's my visualization of good tone quality. When we talk about the pitch center, we'll take a note and bend it up and down. This idea is so hard to learn in music, it's so subjective. I do as much as I can, especially to help little kids picture this. I tell my clarinets, "I want rich, dark, chocolate milk. That's what I want your tone to sound like."

*(Marguerite G. Wilder)*

### The relationship of tone to other elements

I show students there is a relationship between elements, which they have usually been told are disparate technical elements. I want them to see that they are not disparate at all. I begin or center their efforts and attention around tone quality, and I teach them to listen for this. If I hear poor tone, I won't allow the band to continue because the tone quality falls below my standard. I also find that tone quality is almost exclusively a result of breath control and breathing.

*(Donald Casey)*

### Developing a good sound

I do spend a lot of time on developing good sound. We are always wanting them to imitate professional sounds on each instrument. They don't have access to professional sounds when they begin but, if they develop the correct embouchures, a higher percentage of them will develop good sound. You know, I could walk into a place and look at the group. With my ears plugged I can tell you what the band is going to sound like.

*(Lewis Larson)*

### Teaching tone in rehearsal

I spend time at every single rehearsal working on the

*16 Bach Chorales*, which have been around for years. If they cannot play a chorale well, no other piece will sound good either. I may spend ten minutes on just one phrase. I also may work on the bass line alone for a while, then the tenor part, etc. This also helps intonation.

To work on individual sounds after marching band season, we have section classes and classes by choirs where we work on characteristic brass or individual brass instrument sounds. To promote good individual sound, we start building that in the first section class. We have tapes of the all-state material to set the model, for example, of the french horn. For all instruments, we also use recordings of major artists as well as recordings of other bands to set tonal concepts.

*(Stanley Cate)*

### Bowing to make tone

To get a full string sound, teach players to pull and push the bow, not to *up-bow* and *down-bow* only. The bow must contact the strings with an economy of motion to make the string *spin*. I call it *sticky* bowing.

*(Gordon Childs)*

### The importance of teaching tone

An idiomatic appropriate tone color is very important. Most of what I define as sub-musical is linked by what I would call the "quality of sound." Whenever I stop in rehearsal, because of concerns below the musical level, it is usually to remind students of work we already have done in developing the quality of tone or the sound. This becomes a consistent underlying theme in my teaching; maybe it is the only cause for which one should stop a group.

*(Donald Casey)*

### Principles of tone production

One very important issue of good performance in the large ensemble is the production of quality sound (tone color and how to produce it). I work on the principles of good sound production from the very first day and nearly every day after that because it is primary. It depends on the nature of the instrument, but I try to break the process down to real simple decisions that a teacher or player must make. For wind players, it's embouchure and air. I try to keep a statement in front of my eyes at all time: "It is embouchure and air."

I also try to be so practical as to say there is little difference between good embouchures, whether for brass or woodwind instrument players. For most instruments there are some fundamental principles. There is something about how the chin is formed, and about the corners of the embouchure, that are consistent from wind instrument to instrument. I am always stressing the similarities. To teach efficiently, I can make simple statements about the corner of the embouchure or about the way the chin should be focused on a brass and or other instruments.

These statements get concepts across quickly.

*(Gerald Olson)*

### Composing "sound-mass" pieces to develop tone

I use sound-mass pieces for developing long tones and colors. I say, "I want you to play or to give me a good attack on a note somewhere in your normal range and at a moderate volume level. We want marvelous sound." We can get a good forte, but it still must be good sound. The effects can be startling.

With a bowed instrument such as the string bass, I have them use one length of the bow and then they must stop. With percussion, I'll start them, and when I want them to stop I'll give them a cut off. I say, "Don't try to pick something that's extremely high or extremely low, pick any note you wish within your normal range. I want you to start with a perfect attack and hold a beautiful long tone." I'm very demanding of the attacks, releases, and the sound they get. If they come in with a jarring, jolting sound, we won't accept that. If they run out of breath, then they're through—that's it.

I also point to various people so we get different combinations of sound going. I conduct crescendos and decrescendos with my hand, and I cut them off abruptly if I want to and start them again. If I want the entire group to play, I sweep my arm through the whole band. When my hand passes their heads they start their long note.

We create some very interesting sounds this way. These can be duets, trios, quartets, the entire group, or whatever. I may point to them a second time and they start with a different tone each time. We keep this going as long as we wish. I also can have students conduct these pieces so that I am not the only one who is doing any creating. We have used some of these sound-mass pieces at concerts with modern dancers. The students can create some beautiful effects with a very brief, four or five-minute sound-mass piece with modern dancers.

*(John C. McManus)*

### Building tone through descriptive words

I talk about slow and fast airstream. I also think of hot air and cold air, and I talk about a big fat sound and a little narrow projected sound. I say, "narrow and projected" and "make sure it goes clear past me before it dies." I also say, "Don't try to force your tone against the music stand. Let it soar out over the audience." I believe firmly that, if we try to describe operationally what happens, we are defeating our purpose most of the time. If students know conceptually where they are trying to go, they will figure it out operationally. To get even eighty percent of the way—that's a big step.

*(James Stivers)*

### Singing promotes a vocal concept of sound

Singing helps the students to approach the instrument in a vocal manner, playing with a good, open, round sound. I always use "oh" or "aw" ("ah"), and both "aw" and "ah," depending on the instrument. Tubas definitely use "oh" and trombones and baritones use "oh." The horns and trumpets use more of an "ah" sound. I use the "ah" for flutes, clarinets, or saxophones. For woodwinds, I use any syllable that gets them to open their mouth and open their throats on the inside—anything to get them to make the most appropriate and musical sound.

*(Michael Kaufman)*

### Resonating

The head is like an auditorium: the auditorium, or acoustic space, is the cavities in the head which we use as amplifiers. One should shape the inside of the mouth as one plays and one should hold the head as in a noble vowel. Noble means an "AAAAAW" sound with a very full cavity in the mouth. The head and cavities amplify the sound just as they do in speech or song.

If you hold your nose when you talk you get a very different sound because you are not using the sinuses, mouth, and nose—the mask—to amplify the voice. This also occurs on a wind instrument. If students aren't using the right vowel in their mouth, they're not going to get a full natural amplified tone on their instrument. I talk about this sound very much and show them the differences through the way I talk.

*(Thomas Stone)*

### Staying on top of the tone

Most kids, at one point or another in their life, have used an inner tube or a paddle board in a swimming pool. They often try to hold them under water or try to stand on the paddle. The inner tube or paddle board will pop out from under them and zoom to the surface, flying twenty feet away.

I teach that they should stay on top of the tone, meaning staying in control of it. If they ever get under their tone, their tone diminishes. I tell them to control their sound as they controlled the paddle board. Staying on top and in control of the sound is that difficult to do. For example, in their high registers, the flutes and clarinets often get out of control. The image of the paddle board helps them exercise more control and play with a different quality of sound. After you present the analogy you have to get them to experiment until they discover its meaning.

I also use hand gestures to show them what I mean by staying on top. To show the wrong way to do it, I will hold my hands, palms toward the sky and near my eyes. I say, "You must never let the sound get above this." Then I'll do the opposite, I'll hold my hands out in front of me with my palms down. I say, "Always stay on top of the sound, keep it under you and stay in control of it." Especially with younger kids, I teach them to keep their heads held properly with the right kind of vowel shapes; this helps them stay on top of the tone.

*(Thomas Stone)*

### Function of the tongue

Using the tongue properly affects the tone greatly: if one keeps the tongue low enough in the mouth, one will have a good tone.

*(Jack Brookshire)*

### Teaching tone through modeling

I show what I want the sound to be by imitating whatever they can do and contrast it with what I want the sound to be. A teacher needs the skill to show the student what he is doing, whether it is right or wrong.

*(Jack Brookshire)*

### Recordings

With young players, I use recordings and live performance to build models of tone.

*(Richard Fischer)*

### A physical memory of different tone colors

We play scales with different sounds such as bright or warm. This builds both a vocabulary and a kinesthetic memory of different shades of tone and how to produce them.

*(Richard Fischer)*

### Building tone

One way that helps build the tone of a large beginner band is to play slowly and with long phrases.

*(Steven Cooper)*

We start with long notes, because they have more time to deal with tone. They can think about what they are going to do, and how to do so correctly.

*(Frank Battisti)*

We practice and drill sustaining a sound as long as possible, while still maintaining the tone color. If the young players run out of air, all the features of a good sustained sound start to go. The musical line loses direction because they run out of air or let their air speed slow down. Therefore, contests are not primarily about the length of sound, but about how long they can maintain a good sound or a dynamic level. We do this with all levels. We do so at the higher levels if older students sense a problem; we do it with the younger ones to teach a basic skill.

*(Robert Floyd)*

We also use long tones for building strength and because they get to hear themselves, allowing them to check what they are doing right or wrong. I also show correct and incorrect sounds, and I use terms such as the bright and dark side of a tone.

*(Stanley Cate)*

We start at fortissimo to build sound during scales, warm ups and in the method book. We make as big a sound as we can on everything and we ignore dynamic levels for awhile even if it is airy, edgy, or reedy.

I can take the airiness, for example, out of the sound by stressing good breathing and mouthpieces, and getting them to open up. Playing fortissimo builds muscles when they use a lot of air. If they take the edge off and open up more, they can get even more air through the horn. I play and I use recordings to build sound concept.

*(John W. LaCava)*

### Teaching the idea of tone

Making a good tone "stick" with them, making them internalize it, can be done mainly by examples that build their concept of tone. I surround them with good sounds, recorded or live. This helps them build their idea of the tone before they play the tone. I also have students match section leaders, if the leaders have a very fine sound. They do not mimic the section leader's sound exactly, they will have enough uniqueness of their own to contribute.

*(Richard K. Hansen)*

### Projecting the sound

We must understand that we are *always* playing or singing for an audience. There must be an audience. If there is no audience when we are up on the stage, we may play the piece perfectly but it still is not a performance: it's only a rehearsal.

The very first thing I strive to get students to do, is to produce a sound that *soars* out of them. For wind instruments, this literally is true: the air should go out of the instrument, out of the two square feet of space they occupy, out over the conductor's stand and out into the audience. This is the first mind-set that a full-fledged professional has to get: always playing out, never playing in.

The most dangerous, the most negative, self-defeating act that any performer can do when the going gets tough is to start playing into the stand or into themselves on the mistaken theory that if they play soft enough and they goof it up, nobody's going to hear them. It is not only a self-fulfilling prophecy, but it's the very reverse of everything that we have to do.

The idea of playing out on wind instruments means playing with enough air in reserve to always support the sound. On the strings, it means playing with the proper bow pressure so sound does not get boxed up in the sound box of the instrument. It should soar out of wherever the performer is to wherever the audience is—that is absolutely basic.

Looking at this from the audience's point of view, how can anybody sit in the first or thirty-first row of the audience and be turned on by something they don't or can't hear? This is a mind-set more than a physical act. This view is the first I strive for.

*(Alfred Reed)*

Sometimes I take them into the auditorium or a long hallway and sit them down at the end of the hall. I ask them to aim as if their sound were to project in a line way down to the end of the hall. I sometimes suggest their sound contains some colored particles which they are shooting out of their bells. We ask them to think of projecting the particles down the hall. So many of these kids have seen science fiction movies or Star Wars where guys shoot particle beams out their fingers.

This image makes them think of projecting energy forward and makes the projecting of tone a physical experience. Telling them something about "selling their sound" or moving their sound out into the auditorium can sometimes cause them to be a little bit passive. They need to think of an actual energy flow.

*(L. Keating Johnson)*

### Spinning the tone

I remember having a teacher talk about spinning the sound through the instrument. Now that was a hard idea for me to grasp. I know what he's talking about, but not in those terms. Spinning, in that sense of a tone, is having some intensity like bowing, you can feel the pressure on the bow arm on the string. This image is hard for a wind player; it is sometimes difficult to sense the intensity of the air stream.

*(L. Keating Johnson)*

### Maintaining sound on short notes

We do not use the term short for staccato. We always think about the sound's length and space. All sounds have some duration or length; it all depends upon how long the particular piece needs the sounds to be. Any staccato must be long enough for the listener to perceive the tone quality and pitch.

*(John W. LaCava)*

### Striving and changing to achieve success

I do not want fuzzy or pinched trumpet sounds. I'll do everything to correct a problem by dealing with embouchure and tone production. If a good sound does not happen after a certain amount of time, I'll start talking switching instruments. I can think of a couple of trumpet players with whom I just didn't have any luck. These students were not getting a good trumpet sound. Their tones sounded pinched as they went into the upper register. Since they had good minds—they also read music notation well—I knew that they could be good musicians if they got off the trumpet and on to some other instrument; in both cases they're trombone players now.

With only one teacher in a program, you have a lot of control, with both greater burden and greater freedom in the job. I can look at the instrumentation and say, "Well, I'm a little strong here, a little weak here." And I can suggest and make changes. Maybe this person would have made just an average trumpet player. Maybe they never

will be better than a second or third player, because they are not going to have the range. I may switch such a student to trombone and suddenly this kid is a section leader two years later.

*(Lewis Larson)*

## EVALUATING TONE

### A framework

I have a drawing of a triangle that depicts the mechanics of tone production. On the top point is *number one-air*, on the left is *number two-embouchure* on the right *number three-ear*, and in the center, *tone*.

The first three are the mechanical aspects of tone. When there is a balance between air and embouchure—the two words connected in the triangle—this often dictates pitch. In the drawing outside the triangle in the drawing, I have a "cloud" where I have written the "concept," of the tone.

One purpose of the drawing is to place the instrument secondary to air, ear, embouchure, and concept. Of those factors affecting intonation, I consider the concept of tone the most important, along with the concept of air. The idea about air that is important is knowing and applying how to use it. If less than good intonation is achieved, be suspicious of poor achievement in one of the major fundamentals of tone production: either air, embouchure, ear, or concept. Then work on improving those skills first. Pushing and pulling tuning slides and embouchure "cheating" should be the last resort, or the last choice, in producing good tone.

*(Richard K. Hansen)*

### The enemies of tone

The three enemies of the sound are *airiness, edginess,* and *reediness*; these are the three cardinal sins of wind playing.

*(John W. LaCava)*

### Tuning good tones

I do not teach adjustments, such as lip pressure or moving tuning slides, until after a student has learned how to use proper air support for the entire range of the instrument. Because a lack of proper air support and a poor tone color cause most gross intonation problems, I develop support first so I can tune up "good-tones," rather than try to tune up "no-tones!"

*(Richard Putzier)*

### Build tone, then adjust pitch

I tell my students constantly, "There is not a person in this room, including myself, who doesn't have to think continually. We must prepare ourselves to play a wind instrument, because of the air and air pressure being so important."

*(Richard Putzier)*

### Discolored tone

One can have a discoloration of tone caused by an improper attack. The result is that the tone that follows this attack will be less than it should be. The word discolored fits tone very well.

*(Donald Casey)*

### Evaluating sound production

Bright sounds are often inappropriate and usually are the result of poor tone production, breathing, or embouchure tension. To play warmer, students must play more correctly.

*(Richard Fischer)*

## TONE IN THE PERCUSSION SECTION

### Tone and the percussion section

Teachers may not be sensitive enough to tone color on percussion instruments. The bass drum for example, needs to be played with sonorous sound. We don't hold percussionists to the same sensitivity to sound as we do other instruments. This excludes them from the musical work we are doing. If they play at the right time, with the right volume level—we feel that will equal the "right sound" for the percussion section.

*(Donald Casey)*

I'm very particular about what my percussionists do. I am like a hawk on my percussion, for instance, with the type of sticks they're using. I'm very particular about the sounds that are coming from the percussion section.

*(Richard J. Suddendorf)*

### Less is a whole lot better

I talk to them saying, "You're really providing a whole lot of color here. We only need a little bit, but not a whole lot." So that's the way I approach it. I try to find different ways to integrate them, so they learn that what they're doing is real important to the whole color of the group, not that they're just providing sort of rhythmic interjections.

*(Craig Kirchhoff)*

### Percussion tone

There are many things percussionists can do that add to the group's sound. We need to take a real interest in the different sounds that are available from cymbals. Instead of accepting whatever the guy picks up and letting them use cymbals that sound like a couple of garbage can lids, complain about it, don't just grit your teeth. *Elsa's Procession to the Cathedral* needs a pair of large shimmer, long range cymbals on it. One doesn't need a couple of plates that you'd use for marching band gigs. If it doesn't work, get something else.

Be "hip" enough to know that there is a difference between all the kinds of sticks that the mallet players use. They make a difference for attack and release. You don't have to take whatever comes out potluck on xylophone. You can get forty different sounds on that instrument, but you've got to know which sticks and mallets there are and which ones they should be playing with.

*(Donald Wilcox)*

## TONE IN THE ENSEMBLE

### Section sounds

These are important to the orchestra, possibly more so than to the band. I do a lot to develop a woodwind, a brass section, a percussion, and a string section. I still work section problems out with the whole group. Though I don't have time for many sectionals, I work out a section's sound and togetherness during the full rehearsal, which gives students an opportunity to hear how the percussion section, for example, should sound. Students need to hear themselves by themselves. In a sectional, they begin to gel, hear themselves by themselves, and realize they are a section. This is very important. Then, I can put the whole group together.

*(Judith A. Niles)*

### The importance of color in wind and percussion sounds

We have all these colors, all the wonderfully different tonal qualities with the fascinating wind ensemble or band. If I'm the conductor, I feel as though I were a painter who has fifteen different colors to choose from. However, the painter has decided that he's just going to use very few of these, four different ones like red, yellow, orange, and green.

With these limits, we need to practice getting set for using those colors. Maybe we'll do a two-minute practice drawing before we go to the main project. It is like seeing if the blue is correct when drawing or like warming up those particular tone colors when playing.

*(Robert Levy)*

### Emphasizing ensemble tone colors

I have a seventy-five piece symphony band; but out of that band I have anything that I want, meaning I can play any work that requires thirty people, forty-five people, or eight people. I use different combinations on my program and the whole group also performs. I'll probably do one or two smaller compositions on the concert, such as the Strauss *Serenade*, a twenty-three piece number.

Band people need to explore timbres more. They need to get to the various colors involved in the wind groups. Particularly, they must get away from the constant "tooty-gray" sound. There is a palate of colors there that we need to take advantage of.

*(Myron Welch)*

### *Arranging and composition develop sensitivity to ensemble tone*

I get all my kids involved in writing pieces for the band. The juniors and seniors conduct their own pieces at least twice. We might start with a Bach chorale. For this, I'll write out a B-flat sheet, a C-treble sheet, etc. I write the whole chorale in the five instrument groupings and we number the measures.

I assign a student to be responsible for arranging a portion of this. I assign it to be played in band next week. They need not write out the directions. A student can say, "I'm going to have just a brass choir on the first four measures, a solo flute or saxophones on the next four measures, all woodwinds or a clarinet trio on the next four, etc." To have the solo line or a small group for a couple of measures; he drops all or some of the other parts.

He prepares a little plot and he puts it on the board when he comes to class. Since every kid has a score, they can play according to the plot on the board. Then he directs the piece and hears the experiments he has planned for this little chorale. The next day another student does something different and also can experiment, without needing any skill in arranging.

As they gain some familiarity, they can mix instruments. The woodwinds can be on the melody, a brass on the lower line, and their choice on the second and third parts. We tell them, "Just get as crazy as you want." One kid even started the whole chorale with nothing but a wood block and a chime! That gets them to start thinking about sound, theory and arranging, and it's easy to do.

*(John C. McManus)*

### *Developing breath and more in warm ups*

Most of my warm ups have to do with tone quality, and with breath control and supporting the breath properly. The connection I want them to make is that the parameters of blend, intonation, etc. are almost wholly dependent upon tone quality. I cannot address intonation, blend, and to some extent balance, without dealing with tone quality, because I see dealing with tone as the umbrella criterion. To play instruments with their characteristic tone quality, one must generate sound by the right breath support, producing tone qualities that naturally blend—that blend with one another, within a section, and with other sections.

*(Donald Casey)*

# Rehearsal Techniques
# and Ideas

# Rehearsal Techniques

This book contains over 2,500 teaching techniques and insights that have been placed in more than forty specific topic areas such as singing, articulation, intonation, and phrasing. The forty topics also include types of teaching techniques such as imagery, visual, association, and games. Many of these teaching techniques and insights, which are used in class lessons, private lessons, and small ensembles, also can be used in rehearsals. Therefore, one could categorize nearly all the material in the book under the very broad topic of rehearsal techniques.

Many techniques and insights in this chapter suggest ideas that can help any teacher reflect upon his approach to rehearsal. They suggest how to develop the process and the atmosphere and to solve the problems found commonly in the rehearsal. Many of the ideas suggest how one prepares for a rehearsal and they show the choices music educators and conductors make. The ideas placed in this chapter tend to be more broad than those placed in most other chapters. Usually the ideas in this chapter relate to something more sweeping than how to teach specific skills such as blend or intonation.

In some respects this chapter is a continuation of the chapters on Beliefs and Values. In those chapters teachers speak about why they do what they do. In these chapters, they speak broadly about how they prepare for rehearsals and how they approach teaching in rehearsals.

# CHAPTER ONE

# PLANNING FOR REHEARSALS

This chapter adds to the ideas about planning that are found in Part III. The material in Part III addresses planning the curriculum, ideas that help one to organize the program, and suggestions for selecting literature. Part III also contains ideas that can guide a teacher's approach. Some of these ideas describe ways to plan a sequence of instruction, give procedures to use in class and group lessons, give suggestions for drill and repetition, and contain observations about the evaluation of instruction. The main difference with material in Part III compared to material in this chapter is that this chapter contains ideas aimed more specifically at planning for the rehearsal itself.

## *Guidelines for planning the rehearsal*

I build my rehearsals using the ideas of synthesis, analysis, and re-synthesis. Every rehearsal has that shape to it and, within the rehearsal, there are similar sub-shapes. For example, I'm going to have a warm-up sequence, prepare a piece for concerts, and sight read. Each of these rehearsal segments or vignettes will have a synthesis, analysis, and re-synthesis within it.

In the warm-up segment, the idea is to get everybody playing—to get the air moving and things like that. That's what I call the synthesis. Then I may want to affect change; I want to improve something—that's the analysis part, which entails having individuals play, add a variation to the exercise, or add a new way of thinking about it. Then, when I employ that into the warm up, that is the re-synthesis. The sequence is whole, part, and new whole or better whole.

The middle segment of the rehearsal is the major part of the rehearsal. Within each segment or cycle in this portion I might have little cycles. For example, a typical rehearsal middle for me might be working on the big phrases in a movement or piece. Then we might look at the next section to see how it is different or similar. While rehearsing and looking at each big section, I try to make connections and work on smaller things—a little like vignettes or mini-vignettes. I think of a rehearsal as a series of cycles, with little cycles within each cycle. The working through of larger and smaller cycles goes on several times

in a rehearsal. In the middle part of rehearsal, we don't have to play through a whole piece every day and I don't think the kids expect that but, I never want to come to the end of a rehearsal vignette where I've been crossing t's and dotting i's, and say, "Okay, let's take the next piece," without giving them a chance to put the piece together.

The ideal rehearsal closure is to play through at least twenty or thirty measures, come to closure, wish them a good day, and hear the bell ring. When less than ideal, I am saying, "Gosh, we've got to get this better—the bell rings—well, I guess we will try to work that out by tomorrow." When this happens, I have failed in a rehearsal by losing track of time and the rehearsal does not end the way I want it to end.

Once, when I had been doing so much working on little bits and pieces that we were all frustrated with it, it finally dawned on me I was violating one of my rules. At the next rehearsal I said, "Let's just read this down today. We've really been working on little things and I think we need to play it through." At least three kids, at the end, stopped on their way out and said, "We needed that." It was obvious to everybody but me that they just needed to play that first movement and fourth movement through to get that sense of how their part fit in the whole. We all make those mistakes and we learn.

I think sight reading also can be a synthesis-analysis-re-synthesis process. If you read through with little discussion, that is a synthesis; you go back and talk about things, that is an analysis; and then read it through again, that is a re-synthesis.

This is one of my basic organizing ideas that I rely upon when I'm planning rehearsals. Even at the most simple level, I want to make sure that rehearsals end with a play-through, even if it's a sight reading play-through. These help end the rehearsal, or that segment, with a good feeling of music making.

*(John A. Thompson)*

A director is so much better at getting ideas across to the students when he has a plan. When you come out with a music degree you have some ability to tell which are the right notes, right pitches, and right rhythms. But, if you are well planned and prepared, you can teach much better and your students will become better.

*(Terry A. Oxley)*

Dean Killon said something that I will never forget. He said, "My boy comes home from school every day and I ask him what he did in band. His stock answer is nothing." Dean started asking himself, "Why does my child say that?" Then I said to myself, "Do my students in my band rehearsal say the same thing when they go home."

I always try to prepare and tell the kids at the beginning of the rehearsal what we are going to do, even if it's only one or two things. Besides, this also makes you plan. At the beginning of the rehearsal one can say, "Okay today we are going to work on intonation, today we are going to work on Lincolnshire, or the articulations from B to C in the clarinet section."

Even if we might work on additional things, I think it helps to bring out one or two things that we are going to do that day. Tell them these things at the beginning of the hour. Before they leave, you say "Okay, today was a good day and we were able to do this and this" and I name the things we accomplished.

*(Dwayne P. Sagen)*

Training the concert band is essentially a matter of teaching and conducting the fundamentals of ensemble performance, and applying them to the music that will be studied or performed.

*(Mark H. Hindsley)*

As I'm getting closer to a concert and I have specific things that I want to work on, I may include them in that warm up. If we're not close to a concert, I might spend a bigger portion of the time working on our ears. I use the Bach chorales and work on technique or other things that are not necessarily related to the piece we're doing.

*(Michael Kaufman)*

### The significance of musical experiences in rehearsal

Whatever their grade level, no matter what the individuals' ages or their long-term professional goals are, they all come to rehearsals seeking the same thing. They all want to leave having had a positive experience. What happens to people in rehearsals is very important to me.

This is similar to the experience of the professional performer. When performers, at any level, walk away from a rehearsal after important things happen musically, they walk away for all the right reasons. They feel like they have created something, they feel like they had a relationship with each other and with the conductor, and most important, they feel like they have had a relationship with the music. If what happens in rehearsal is done for music, the enthusiasm for making music will not die whatever the level of performance or with the age of the performer. I

have a great opportunity to work with soloists who often come from the Cleveland Symphony. When we come out of rehearsals, we talk about the event in the same way we did when we were young players.

No matter the group or age, one must develop a rapport with the group. The reason to do this is so the music has a chance to express itself at the highest level. The primary reason we are there is to make music and the important things that happen are because of the high level of the good music we are making. Even though we deal with other issues in a rehearsal, if the music is responding to the highest level, everything else in the rehearsals such as the relationships among students, with the students and each other, and with the conductor also are important. All of this and how they want to feel about what they are doing, will come to fruition if music is at the center of the endeavor. There are groups with great rapport but, those are the groups that make great music together—that is what has developed the rapport. Every significant musical experience we have is when we make great music come alive, whether a concert or a rehearsal.

All the significant experiences I have had as a conductor have occurred after significant performances, in rehearsals, or in performances. It is interesting that this happens more often in a rehearsal than in a performance; even though there are magical moments in a performance. But day-to-day, the rehearsal is as important as the performance, because the relationships that happen and develop during rehearsal are very important and significant.

The prime cause for things that happen in a rehearsal, which evokes the relationships and the events that lead to communication, is simple. The conductor must have a complete command of the piece of music he is conducting. Then all of his attention can be and is focused upon the ensemble. The less he knows the score of the piece, the more attention he must give to the score during the rehearsal, and the less he can communicate with the group. Ideally, we all want to know every piece of music thoroughly, and the best conductors can do that: that is what we all strive to do. Having the knowledge that score study can bring is the secret—that's it.

I often visit rehearsals of the Cleveland Symphony and find the same occurrence. When the conductor knows that score, the orchestra just jumps out of their chairs musically. All the thrust during our education has been on "know your score—know your score!" Therefore we have dedicated our energies, even our life to know scores. Within limitations of time and work load, we do the best we can in this respect. People think being a music major is easy, it isn't. No matter what you have done, there is always more to do, more skills to learn, and more practicing to do. This is true with learning scores; seldom do we have enough time to learn each of the scores as well as we would like to. I have three groups and at least fifteen to twenty scores that I would like to know inside and out.

One can forget why they are involved with this

profession. Most of us are not in this profession for monetary reward; that isn't the primary motivation. Our reward and the attraction of making music are the feelings that are created within ourselves when we are making the music. As a high school player, I had these wonderful feelings and it was great because no one had to know that I felt what I was feeling. Therefore, I did not have to feel self conscious or embarrass myself in front of my "big-time jock" friends in high school. At all levels the student performers have the chance and ability to have these feelings. This is the experience we usually call an aesthetic experience. The term aesthetics is like the term love. The term stands for something that is hard to explain, but even so the experience is real and has significance.

*(Gary Ciepluch)*

### Score study and rehearsal techniques

I do not believe in rehearsal techniques per se. I do not want rehearsal techniques to be divorced from the musical understanding that an analysis of the score can provide for the teacher. First one learns through analysis what the musical substance is and makes the important musical decisions for that score. *Then* the teacher chooses the techniques needed to attain musical goals.

This is also true with elementary and junior high teachers. By analyzing a piece, I can show them that an understanding of the piece gained from score study will lead right into a plan for rehearsing that piece. When the connection between the piece and a rehearsal plan is shown, it becomes very clear to them. To learn more about analysis, I like John White's, *The Analysis of Music* and the book of Jan La Rue: they both suggest a good approach to analysis.

*(John Anderson)*

One must be prepared with score study and what you want to do at the rehearsal itself. Ken Bloomquist says, "A good rehearsal is one where you accomplish changes, even if it is only one thing."

As I plan, I look for specific conducting problems, e.g. meter changes or fermatas, and I break down the piece into formal divisions or special scoring where instruments are exposed. If the scoring is thin or exposed—such as a transparent woodwind passage—that might need special attention. I look for phrasing issues, watch the cadences especially for vertical lining up of the chords, and look for the scoring at cadences—too often people under orchestrate the third—especially the "educational oriented" tunes: this is a puzzle to me. To solve this one, we may add players to this part or simply ask them to bring it out more.

*(Michael Golemo)*

One also must have a consistent vision of how the music is to sound. If one does not know this, one does not know where he stands. A conductor must be consistent in policy, who he is and the way he does what he does. This

is true for any conductor at any level.

*(Frederick Fennell)*

I began a lecture at the Midwest International Band and Orchestra Clinic by relating an experience I had. I said, "I had been teaching for four years and a certain person said to me, You know, you've got a wonderful band, the oboe players are just great, and the balance is terrific. I have not heard a high school band play this well in tune in fifteen years and their technique is terrific." Then, after a long silence, his next words were, "Now, when are you going to deal with the musical issues?"

This was one of those lines that caused, all of the sudden, the world to turn upside down. Because at that point in my life I thought I was doing the right thing. At that point in my life the music was kind of vehicle to make the band sound good. The big issue was who had the best sounding high school concert band, therefore, the music wasn't terribly important. It wasn't that I was a musical dummy. I was a good player in college and at one point I was even thinking of doing some professional playing. Even so, we can fall into these traps.

The whole purpose of the lecture was to discover ways to go about looking at scores, and really trying to deal with the expressive aspects of the scores. A book that became important to me, is Frederick Prausnitz's book. He breaks down score study into three aspects, and the first aspect is what he calls the objective items. Those are the givens: they are what is on the page and they cannot be changed. It is an excellent book, it really deals with musical issues.

The second aspect is the interpretation that is given to a piece. This means, if there are accents written and because it's Mozart, we must decide the kind of accent. If it were Bartok, the accent would be different.

The third thing is the expressive challenge, and it's what I call the little interpretations.

I used different excerpts for students, the first sixteen measures bars of *Chester Overture* and the second movement of *Lincolnshire Posy*. I played different recordings of each piece. It was obvious that these three conductors had three very different viewpoints. One point that I made at the Midwest was, "Do you find people sitting around the bar arguing about the interpretation of the first sixteen measures? No, what you'll hear them talk about is, " Boy was that a great band!" or, " What did you think about that tuba section?"

Many music teachers do not talk about the music as much as they talk about playing the instruments. So few say, "I didn't like the way that was phrased." They bypass the whole thing.

The entire lecture, then, was focused upon the issue of expression. We discussed what it can do for us as conductors in a medium where sometimes, as high school people, we have other unavoidable concerns. I can remember when I had concerns for hall duty and cafeteria duty. There were those days where I sat there thinking, "What did I spend all that time studying music history for?" It just seemed to be so unimportant or irrelevant then.

So addressing musical and expressive issues is a creative challenge. It's very easy for some of us, some who are talented and very dedicated people, to allow ourselves to get sold down the river into the abyss of concerns that are not musical.

*(Eugene Corporon)*

I think it's very important to get a clear idea of the piece. Is this a piece that deals more with melodic content? Maybe it is more a study in tone color, instead of melodic lines. Or does it feature solo lines and accompaniment? What is necessary to shape passages of the piece it is?

Gunther Schuller, for instance, deals a lot with tone color, and when playing a piece of Leslie Bassett, one won't necessarily get beautiful melodic lines. I think it's important for the group to understand the challenge.

When we are playing specific pieces each time, we're using, for example, different tonguing styles for articulation. We also use a different mind set for a piece of music that unfolds in five minutes compared to one that has interchangeable melodic statements that move around different colors of the group. I think we have to ask a question more often than we do. The question is, "What is this piece all about?"

*(Robert Levy)*

College students often say they want to write a paper on rehearsal techniques. They can find some sources and some techniques, but they do not find much that suggests a methodology, approach, or philosophy about rehearsal techniques. I try to provide this missing link for them.

I do not believe in rehearsal techniques by themselves. I believe rehearsal technique problems are selected as a result of an in-depth understanding and analysis of the piece one is working on. This approach lessens the chances that rehearsal techniques will be divorced from the musical understanding that score analysis can provide for the teacher. First, one should learn through analysis what the musical substance and decisions are for a particular score. Second, one should choose the teaching techniques to accomplish the teaching of the music substance.

This is also true for elementary and junior high teachers and their rehearsals. By analyzing a piece, I can show them that understandings about the piece will lead right into a plan for rehearsing that piece. When I show the connection between the piece and a rehearsal plan, it becomes clear to them. Here is an approach that works:

1. Identify broadest dimensions of the piece, section by section, and attempt to name their musical functions, such as a theme, development, variation, or recapitulation.
2. Identify all musical events within a section. Try to

account for the musical lines that are present as they relate to the functions, such as a variation, chordal accompaniment, and rhythmic accompaniment.
3. Group together all the voices present into those functions and decide the prominence of each voice, the tone color, the balance, and the dynamics. I do not think of these as abstractions, but in response to knowing the score, a teacher learns what the balance, blend, or tone color could or ought to be.
4. Answer questions about the broad nature of the piece, such as how sections relate to each other in an organic way. Trace elements of stability and changing growth in the piece. For example, if there is a returning theme or a musical element that provides the piece with a sense of unity, be certain that the return's musical interpretation is similar or identical with its original occurrence.
5. Find the elements or themes that change throughout and notice if they can undergo transformation or development. These must be interpreted so they are highlighted to the audience. *Ye Banks and Braes of Bonnie Doon* fits this analysis model. With this piece, for example, the analytical process works very well even though the piece is simple technically.
6. Decide upon interpretations that highlight the decisions that one makes: decide what occurs in each section and how the events in one section affect events in another. I start with the broad aspects, then move to the specific aspects as I sense the relationship of the parts to the whole. For some interpretations, for example, I relate the specific character of rhythms and melodies to drama or to familiar aspects of their life. "If this rhythm were an actor or other character, who would it be, Arnold Schwarzenegger or the Smurfs?" The teacher must choose personalities that are known to the students and fit the rhythm in a broad and recognizable way.
7. After one discovers the musical issues, the questions of how to get this across come up along with the technical questions of how to get this done in rehearsal. For example, there may be a motor rhythm, a repeated quarter-note eighth-note rhythm pattern. If the decision is to have the eighth note lean forward to the quarter note, this can be done in several ways.

Because the piece determines the way it must be rehearsed, the choice of the proper rehearsal techniques is hard or illusive to pin down unless the teacher discovers them through the process of analyzing the piece. The rehearsal planning for the piece starts when one analyzes the piece. Therefore, the teaching techniques for the piece are chosen during the process of analyzing the piece.

*(John Anderson)*

### What score study does not provide

The job of the conductor is to bring to the rehearsal and the concert everything that is not written on the page of music. The most important things about music are not found on the page at all; only the language of music is found there. Therefore, the conductor can never understand the composer by studying the page, rather the understanding is found within himself. Of course a conductor must know the score, but his virtue lies in his ability to see what is not there.

*(David Whitwell)*

### Informed intuition and planning

Maurice Abravenel, of the Utah Symphony, had a great term that I have used on many occasions. He said one builds up an "informed intuition" over countless years of experiences. So, when one comes across a piece by Mozart that is new to you or a new piece by an unfamiliar composer, one has an intuitive ability to interpret it correctly. A teacher ought to be building up experiences that help him make better decisions. This is imperative for his own growth.

There is one thing, however, about informed intuition that does not give one the complete picture; it does not give a view of the long run—the overall view of the piece. In planning or interpreting the piece, thought goes into where the high and low points should be. Planning enables one to decide what points one must make along the way, how emphatically one will make them, and which stylistic and expressive concerns one must bring out.

There is a parallel with planning a piece and giving a lecture. When lecturing, I have notes that remind me what points I am going to make. I know what the main point of my entire speech is and I will know when I am finished. But I don't know each word I am going to say. So, in the same way, the informed intuitions are the individual words, but they do not represent the whole approach.

The informed intuition tells us this is going to be the big climax. Planning tells us that, even though the score at some point says fortissimo, there are two more climaxes later that are bigger. With the knowledge there are two more coming, you have still a myriad of ways to do this one climactic point.

The informed intuition helps you on the instantaneous issues, but you cannot "ad-lib" your way all the way through an entire or complete piece with informed intuition only: the insights do not come to you that way. You have to approach a piece the way a composer approaches it. Very few composers sit down with a piece and start composing—they have a plan. They know if this will be theme and variations or sonata form before they start. They don't say, "Oh look, I just composed a piece in sonata-allegro form!" To have complete knowledge of all aspects, including the high points and how they relate to each other, one must study the score. In a sense, one would like to get back into the composer's mind to find out what was going on. There are some composers who create free-form works, and that's fine; but that's not the way it has been done by the majority of composers.

The conductor's intuitions are learned, but they are not brought out so we can say, "We will do the third measure this way, because it came to me once this way." In fact, it comes to you differently every time.

*(H. Robert Reynolds)*

### Score study

After I have done the score study, I can identify immediately where a problem or error is, or might be, in a rehearsal, and I can sing or correct their playing in this manner.

*(George Bedell)*

I want to stress the idea of knowing the score before you go into rehearsal; you can't have a plan for what you are going to do unless you know the score. If you have studied the score, and your head is out of it and you are looking at the performers for communication, something can happen. If you haven't done score study, then there is no way that it will work. If your head is down, they are not going to look up, they are not going to listen and they shouldn't have to.

You can't begin a rehearsal without having that score in your soul. You will teach the architecture, form, and shape of the piece if you know the score; otherwise, all you teach them is the mechanics and you will have nothing as a result. I mean that score study is the essential thing.

*(Larry Rachleff)*

If a person thinks, "I want the music to sound well," they will not know how it should sound unless they study the score. I was reading the book, *The Agony and the Ecstasy.* There is a scene in which Michelangelo has selected this perfect piece of granite and he's slamming away at it. The apprentices are around and one says, "It's really interesting how you do that. How will you get the *Pieta* to appear when all you start with is the granite block?" Michelangelo said, "Well, if I'm going to make a horse, I can see a horse in the granite and I just chip away everything that isn't the horse."

That's what conductors and teachers do. They have a sound ideal and they are creating the ideal from the raw sounds in the ensemble. I stress, when talking about rehearsal techniques, the idea, "You can have all these ways of doing things, but you have to know when to use them and how to use them." This is also true with the computer that the marching people use. It isn't going to create the drill, *you* create the drill. The computer just eases getting it done.

I do a rehearsal techniques course and we start with score study so they begin to develop a thinking process. Most people don't do proper score study. They don't do professional score study, instead they do teacher score study. This type of study is, "How can I solve this problem and where are the meter changes?" I've found in my experience that professional score study is the name of the game. If they do a professional score study there are certain things they should do: they should analyze a piece harmonically, melodically, and in every other way. They should analyze each phrase and they should sing every line, which can take a long time. I tell my people the first things they should do is to sing the flute line, finger the flute parts, and do that with every line along with a harmonic analysis. When you do such things, you break down the piece into its little parts and then you have a basis for deciding what you're going to do with the music.

Score study also allows me to share the form of the piece with a group on any level. If I have a junior high band, everybody knows, for example in *Variation Overture* by Clifton Williams, what the main theme is. I teach them what the theme is and how it is varied. Most people don't do that; they don't share the music with the students. If one is interested in developing aural skills or talking about balance, the students don't know how to relate what they're playing on the page to the piece unless they have some understanding of the piece. If they don't, then the teacher is up against a stone wall all of the time. Choosing the rehearsal techniques because of score study can require that you become as creative with this as with the interpretation of the music.

*(John Williamson)*

I believe strongly in score study. I tell the conducting students that the problem we have in conducting is to realize that all of the gestures we need are suggested in the score; you have to decide what gestures to use, but this can change. Some days, at certain points, because of what's going on, you may have to alter the gestures you expected to use. I draw the analogy that conducting the group is a little bit like a hockey game. You put down the puck and you really don't know where it's going to go, but you have to adjust to the game. The problem of too many conductors is that they practice all these gestures and all these moves in their den. In reality, though, the group really needs another gesture and some teachers cannot adjust when faced with that challenge.

*(Craig Kirchhoff)*

By knowing the score, the teacher can anticipate what might occur rhythmically. This identifies where the problems and the solutions are to be concentrated. Thus, score preparation can prevent some rhythmic errors because the teacher anticipates them. Knowing this also saves much rehearsal time.

*(Barbara Buehlman)*

Score study, whew! One issue is building the ideal of the piece and the other is facing the practical problems and challenges of getting the piece to sound like the ideal. We instrumental directors usually fix things very well, but one thing the orchestra conductors do better is shape the piece. I think the ideal conductor is someone who knows both the orchestral concerns, where conductors shape the musical elements, and the band concerns, where band director's know how to fix things.

*(Eugene Corporon)*

The selection of teaching techniques usually springs from the need to meet a musical or an instructional need I sense at the time. There is something lacking in teacher education (though I am not an expert in teacher education). What teachers seem to lack—when they start to teach a piece—is a real sense of what the piece is going to or could sound like. There are exceptions, such as Revelli, who had a clear sense of what the piece was to sound like.

Knowing the sound of the piece goes deeper than just score study. One can easily decide that someone missed this or that note or rhythm. What I want to happen is to get the player to understand and hear the whole piece, and not just his third clarinet part. If we can begin in our teacher-training programs to get that notion across to people who are going to teach, then the techniques of score study and knowledge of instruments, for example, will allow them to make music and to educate.

The issue is listening and hearing. Developing that ability to hear the whole instead of just the single things is a skill that is given in different amounts to persons. Even so it can be developed.

*(Michael Haithcock)*

I use the metronome when I study scores. For example, when preparing for a rehearsal, I have used a metronome to practice a ritard or an accelerando to check my sense of where I am and where the tempo is going to be.

*(Robert Floyd)*

I believe in score study and what I do is simple, it's not in great detail. I try to have a comprehensive understanding of that score before I step on the podium and I study it on two levels. For lack of a better term, I call one level the analytical level. This study is to know what's happening in terms of the structure. I also study it on a conductor level and I think the two levels are different.

The analysis helps me know that this is a dominant chord and it's moving to the tonic chord, or this melody is a repetition, an elongation, or a diminution of a certain melody. The practical level is different from the analytical. I decide what I have to do with gestures to get specific things to happen. I think, "What do I have to do here to make this happen and where are the kids going to make mistakes?" For example, if I see a C flat, I know that's going to be a place that I'm going to have to focus on.

I do not think the band director should go to his friendly neighborhood music store, buy what's new, and pass it out the first day without looking at the score. If he doesn't study the score, he's as new to it as the kids. Then, in the subsequent twenty rehearsals, he must learn the score while the kids do. I don't think that's the way to go. If he knows a score well, he can get a group through a piece of music because he knows, for example, what cues are important, knows exactly when to get out of the way, and when to let them have their head. He knows exactly how to prepare a transition, because that comes with knowing the music from a structural, analytical standpoint.

*(John A. Thompson)*

I will go after the hardest thing first in rehearsal. I look at a piece of music and find the place I think is going to be the biggest problem. I'll jump on it first and many other things take care of themselves.

*(John A. Thompson)*

I know what I am going to accomplish, but I do not write down exactly how I am going to do this. I like to retain some freedom and use my imagination during the teaching. Part of the reason I vary my approach is that I can detect the kind of day they and I are having. Consequently, this affects how I choose how to teach.

*(Patricia Brumbaugh)*

It is important to learn where the problems are going to be rhythmically, where the problems will be with phrasing and with balance. Mr. Paynter's approach to score analysis is very much like a theorist's concern about what he wanted to know structurally. When I studied with Richard Strange, the emphasis was always on anticipating rehearsal problems; he wanted to know fingerings and trills so that when the flute players don't know it, the teacher did not have to say, "Oh, you better learn that." Instead, the teacher can say, "Use your fourth finger on the right hand."

Some people tend to dwell on one and not the other; there are great rehearsal conductors who might not even know what's happening structurally and there are people who do. Some students and teachers are great at analysis, but they don't have effective rehearsal skills. So, in my own preparation, I try to do both or at least to blend both. Another thing I've learned is to look through a piece and find where the climactic moment is. I try to find where the emotional content is: which fortes are going to be louder than other fortes.

I've also seen people who have done these little graphs; there is a graph from beginning to end and with numbers underneath. One can look at little rises and falls as though one is looking at the graph of the stock market. I've never done that, but I've alluded to it with kids.

*(John A. Thompson)*

## A less-verbal manner of rehearsing

I have become committed to the visual means of teaching because I've seen myself and others get caught up in explaining every little detail. I joke with my student teachers and have said, for example, "Quit giving a two-hour sermon on how to play short. They understand what you are saying, just stop talking. Instead, show the shortness as you conduct; if you don't get it, grab a horn and show them shortness, or verbalize 'du' or do something else less long-winded."

*(Michael Kaufman)*

## Teaching young students

I work a lot with conductors who work primarily with younger students. One of the things I want them to try is the idea they can conduct non-verbally. No matter what level of music or age of student one is working with, the goal is to make the music an event that has significance to them in the aesthetic sense. Conducting assists us to this end.

This can be done with young students, especially with sixth and seventh grade bands; we had glorious musical moments together when I taught at this age level. I still cherish those moments. The really great young band and orchestra teachers are leading groups that are truly making music, not just right notes and right rhythms.

I have fun teaching music education classes. I tell future teachers that the young students will learn 100 songs within three weeks if you let them. The only barriers that get in the way of progress for young students are the teachers; it is not the students. Only the teachers hinder the progress of our students by not providing them ample opportunity to perform, grow, feel, and understand.

I would like to see teachers of young students quit teaching them as though they were elementary students. They should try teaching elementary students like they are young gifted people. Go look at a Suzuki class: why can a whole group of them play up a storm when in some school settings it is like Saturday Night Live? I try to tell music education students this: "People who are fortunate enough to teach elementary children, have to teach them like artists, not like young children. We should not be teaching them in a lock-step way, in a slow way. No wonder so little happens in the class room. The pace, the approach, and the teacher-imposed limitations crush their abilities to do anything by not introducing them to what they could do."

If you tell an elementary student he will do better if he plays standing on his head, he'll do that because you said so. They don't know any better, they believe you. Therefore, we have a great responsibility, because what you say is very influential and if we say, "You can't do that yet," it is self-fulfilling. It is also true that, "Student's will succeed at the level you expect them to succeed," to quote Jim Froseth.

*(Gary Ciepluch)*

## Non-verbal coaching and teaching

I coach anything that can be changed such as meter, if it is not clear. I also coach intonation, posture, or breathing; I do this in verbal and non-verbal ways. I also do a lot of non-verbal coaching while I am walking around the rehearsal area. Posture is a good example of this: I touch an elbow, show them examples of looking-up and sitting-up properly. If they are playing too short, I give them a long gesture—all of the usual gestures one can do from the podium. When I am two feet away, the effectiveness of the gestures is remarkable! I spend much time on the podium, but I don't spend most of my time off the podium, though there are times that I do this for the entire rehearsal; it changes from rehearsal to rehearsal.

*(Gary Hill)*

## Variety in the rehearsal

A non-verbal approach works as long as you can keep them interested. Especially with younger students, I think that the minute their attention span is waning and they're becoming frustrated because they can't understand, then it's time to do something new and different. This is the key, not just middle school, but high school. Change anything in your rehearsal to make it different and exciting. I try to do a different warm up every day for the 128 days of the school year. One day a warm up might be Bach chorales. We sing and then play the chorales. I also can start a rehearsal with, "Here's a concert B flat. Sing the scale degrees 1 4 6 2 1; now play it." To do this, they've got to figure out what the note is from the number. I also may relate this to key signatures. There are many variations of this such as: have them sing the scale degrees of 1 2 3 4 5 6 7 1 and then ask them to play it; then we do a relative minor scale. Sing it first and then play it; then do relative minor in the harmonic and melodic form. Always sing it first and then have them play it. On another day we might be playing musical games such as, "Play 1 3 5 6 5 2 1." We might do a chromatic scale starting on any pitch, playing it in duple, then in triple, then in sixteenth notes, then slurring, then tonguing, whatever. I have divided the group into four different sub-groups. Each group played up to the third scale degree before the next group enters. This caused them to play rounds and canons. I have them singing first and then playing it.

*(Michael Kaufman)*

One way to combat building technique at the expense of tone and phrasing or vice versa, is through a warm up that I use so they play through all the major scales. For example, they start on a B-flat scale (up and down); then I count "two, three, four" and they play B Major; I count again and they play C Major; then C-sharp Major. The reason I do it that way is to teach them to think in finger combinations rather than key signatures.

*(Michael Kaufman)*

## Setting the priorities

Some teachers have taken the "One-Minute Manager" idea and used that in their teaching. We were introduced, as undergraduates, to lesson plans and taught that they were important. We were not, however, taught to plan for a rehearsal. We were not taught what one should accomplish for the students in this situation. We also were not taught how to plan for the music that we are preparing for a contest or concert. In short, we were not taught to organize the priorities.

I learned some of this from Guy Taylor, the conductor of the Phoenix Symphony. He would put his watch on the stand along with a little piece of paper listing what he needed to rehearse that day. Even before the orchestra read the piece, he had decided what problems, such as balance and tempi, needed to be addressed. With this information, he would organize his whole rehearsal.

We ended the rehearsal and each sub-part right at the time he planned to finish. He timed everything out in advance. Now this is fine for a professional orchestra, but with the school band you cannot anticipate all the problems as well as Taylor does.

*(Robert Morsch)*

I planned class lessons on a grid-like page. There were certain student's names at the top of an eight by eleven sheet and I divided it into five columns across and seven or eight down. Because of the lines, there were about twenty-four squares or blocks on this lesson assignment sheet. Each block was a date, with date at the top. Each showed a full lesson plan of warm-up studies, etudes, solo material, and tone studies. These sheets were in the student's book or folder. My copy was in my grade book. Each sheet lasted about a half or a third of the year. I would take notes and make evaluative comments or observations to help me remember what each student was doing.

When I got to the lesson, I would simply open the book and could see the assignments, grades, etc. I would be ready to go. Students would write the information in their book also. This enables the teacher to say definitively what was to be done. I referred to the sheet because I had over two hundred students a week and could not remember without referring to the lesson plan sheet and notes.

I also would refer to this sheet if I called parents on the phone. I would call them first, they would not call me first. I wanted the students to follow the organization sheet in the folder to establish habit. If someone is not working up to potential, I would send home a practice slip for parents to sign. Some parents would lie!

*(Anthony J. Maiello)*

## Planning the week

I have a sketchy plan for the week. I list the scales I want to cover, and the keys and performance techniques I want to develop. I use this as a reference, so I can plan the week. At the beginning, end, or both the end and the beginning of the week, I make my list. As the week goes on and from the events that occur, one can make changes in the plan, but the necessary changes do not equal disorganization.

I have a daily rehearsal form that contains a list of the what I want to look over. I select things from this form, instead of listing them on a three by five card or a legal pad. I check off what I have done and this keeps me organized even if I alter this list as I go.

*(Patricia Brumbaugh)*

I have a longer list of what is wrong than what is right. This means that one has plenty of choices to work on in rehearsal.

*(Carl A. Bly)*

I emphasize style, dynamics, phrasing, etc. daily as they relate to the interpretation of the music.

*(Richard Fischer)*

On different days I will stress only one interval, which I call the interval of the day. We may work on one, but not without addressing another a little. Comparing the interval of the day with other intervals helps clarify the unique sound of a certain interval. For example, if the interval of the day is a major third, we may also compare that to a perfect fourth or minor third. In a minute I might go through seven different keys or the same interval started on seven different roots such as D, D flat, B flat, E, G, E flat, etc. Another day we would focus on the interval of the fifth.

*(Patricia Brumbaugh)*

## Planning for rehearsals

There are several statements that might guide the teacher's plan for a rehearsal. For example, (1) Plan rehearsal, anticipate problems, edit errors and misprints. (2) Change pacing to keep their interest. (3) Rehearsing requires repetition. (4) Drill slowly but accurately and rhythmically. (5) Try not to over-rehearse. (6) Make sure conducting techniques are clean and clear. (7) Demand attention when you speak. It's a simple courtesy. Pay equal attention to them when they are speakers. (8) Never talk over extraneous noise. It simply confirms that what you have to say is not important. (9) Have students number measures on the left hand side of each staff for any work that will require considerable attention in rehearsal time. (10) Develop interesting warm-up and tuning procedures. (11) Routine is critical but variety within that routine maintains attention. (12) No more than ten percent of your rehearsal should be spent on these routines unless you have developed a unique presentation or unit that requires more time. (13) Rehearse sections frequently before you nail individuals. Give your students every opportunity to avoid being embarrassed. (14) Develop a system of testing your teaching effect. As professionals we all too often

make the assumption that public performance is empirical evidence of our effect as teachers. Little could be farther from the truth. (15) Keep your students playing. They are not there as a forum for your verbosity. Limit talking to instructions instead of pedantry. Ninety-five percent playing and five-percent talking is a reasonable ratio of both.

*(James Croft)*

## Weekly planning and priorities

In the first fifteen to twenty minutes of the rehearsal (we have about an hour and ten-minute rehearsal), I'm on that outline because it is established for the entire district—every band in the district follows the outline. The basic outline of what's being covered in each school is the same. We begin with whole notes and tone. We proceed to articulation and intonation when our horns are warm enough to play a true pitch whether the kid can or not. Then we do scale and rhythm work, which is all in the first fifteen to twenty minutes of the rehearsal; all this is definitely outlined.

We've done this over the years and our staff all knows this very well. We're all using a rehearsal book by Fred Weber, except for the sixth graders and sometimes the seventh graders, depending how fast they've progressed. We also have made our own booklet of technical exercises and have them copied for our use. This makes up another twelve-page booklet that we use for those kids. When they hit the eighth grade or the seventh grade— we've got one seventh grade band that's really into it pretty heavy—the kids have progressed noticeably. (We were doing an evaluation of that teacher recently and she had them really coming along so well that they are sounding like eighth graders.)

After that fundamental work is done in warm up, we do program preparation. I make my week outline of plans that need to be accomplished. I write down, for example, the title of a number and I list the things that will happen everyday. I list the tempo, the location of the passage, and the section to which I will attend. I'll pick about four or five things that I'll rehearse every day of the week. If they become solved by Tuesday, I'll substitute something else.

We may have five things, for example, to prepare for the next concert. I often have a section of that particular piece of music that we will play just to get some idea of the continuity of it. For example, if a piece has three spots that we're still struggling with, we improve those three spots and then I will play through a longer passage. It could be from the beginning until circle 6, which is half-way through. We'll do that on Monday and Wednesday to give them a sense of continuity and that only takes a few minutes. On Tuesday and Thursday we'll take from circle six to the finish so we cover the whole thing during the week pretty well. We do the specific problems first and then a large chunk. Then we move to the next tune and do the same type of thing with that.

*(Bryce Taylor)*

## *Planning for the rehearsal or the lesson*

Since performance accuracy, particularly with repetitive and accompanying rhythm, is necessary, I often settle those problems early in the rehearsal sequence. I try to go to rehearsal prepared, and when I stop, I know what I am going to say. I don't feel bad if it takes twelve or fifteen tries to get it right. But, if they cannot solve the problems, I put the piece back on the shelf.

*(Carl A. Bly)*

I will mark scores with certain "short hand" symbols of my own. For example, I will mark phrase points with vertical arrows and horizontal arrows moving toward the point, which I sometimes show on the board. Some people draw a big note for an accent (for young kids) or small notes for softer volume.

*(Robert Grechesky)*

Don't go into rehearsal with a pre-arranged idea of what is going to happen. I have seen people go in with a list of what is going to go wrong; and it doesn't go wrong. They still stand there stuck with item number four! You must be like a good chamber music player or a good tennis partner. We must read what is happening musically, technically, and psychologically, and we must adjust to it quickly.

*(Frederick Fennell)*

Excellent literature, developing skill, a performer's mind-set, etc. are essential. From then on, it is a matter of rehearsing not notes, but music. Rehearsing melody lines separately, bass lines, counter melody lines, moving harmony, stationary harmony, in that order. So we build the score layer by layer just as the composer put it together. This is how you teach music and also how to play music. I find that this is the most successful technique of all I have in rehearsals. The idea is to make musicians out of them, not just performers. A musician is defined again as someone who speaks, reads, writes, and thinks in the language.

*(Alfred Reed)*

First, I do not think you can plan a lesson until you hear what the kid is going to sound like in the lesson. Sure, you have given him an assignment, but you cannot assume anything. On the other hand, I do plan rehearsal, but the plans don't always work. I plan the musical aspects, such as certain sections in certain pieces that I want to cover that have problems I want to solve. I never write it down, but I do have a mental list. If the problem does not exist anymore, I go to the ones that do.

*(Donald S. George)*

I am a big note writer to myself. Sometimes I think I live and breathe by my little note reminders I write for myself. I always write on the board the pieces and the composer's name that we are going to play before the rehearsal. I also am one to write little quotes on the board.

I find some of these sayings in books that include famous quotes about music.

*(Michael Kaufman)*

I want them to learn the notes at home, so I can work on more detailed skills such as articulations, articulations together, ensemble togetherness, cross fingering, for example, in a seventh-grade woodwind class, or musical issues during the class time. I do not believe we should do their home work in class! We lose intelligent kids if they are not challenged or if we must do in class what they could have easily done at home. These kids are too good to let them remain on a lower plateau than they can reach.

*(Carl A. Bly)*

In rehearsal planning, I use a band log that has been very helpful. I use one sheet for every rehearsal. On the form, I list the date, which ensemble I am conducting, the rehearsal's starting and stopping time, who takes roll, location of rehearsal, and other nuts-and-bolts things. Below that are categories: Announcements, Procedures, and Objectives. I list what I hope to cover and accomplish in that rehearsal, and the methods I will use to teach them. On the left margin I also list the amount of time I plan to spend on different things. At the bottom I have personal notes, things that are not shared with everyone: information for a certain person, something that is to be brought to the rehearsal, extra-musical things, and anything else that is needed for a specific rehearsal.

I have forms for each group and keep them in a notebook with dividers. This helps me to use my time wisely. Though it gives me a means of organization, it is not so structured that it restricts what I do. I set this up for the entire quarter, with concert dates, etc. This allows me to see all the information for any event, such as concert attire and whatever else is crucial; it helps me to see bits of information in the quarter's calendar and to save time and alleviate confusion. The use of the forms structures events, yet it is a flexible technique for organizing.

*(Thomas H. Cook)*

When planning and structuring the rehearsal, I think recording the rehearsal regularly, analyzing the tapes, and setting priorities from what I hear on the tapes is very important. I listen more for the expressive elements and the interpretive issues the closer it is to the concert. When I listen, I strive to be open minded as I follow the score. I make notes about a problem and develop a way to teach to the solution of it.

*(Hal D. Cooper)*

I do detail work and then we put it together. It is a mistake if one does too much detail and not enough putting back together. I do a lot of big chunks and I always keep thinking about an idea from sculpture. They begin to make a sculpture by working with a piece of granite; they don't take small pieces right away. Later, they finally get down to the minute details. As a conductor, I do this; I mean, I rehearse things in large sections and then keep getting down to more detail, more detail and polish. Finally we get where everybody feels good about it and then they should understand the work.

*(Richard J. Suddendorf)*

We must ask, "What is your approach to rehearsal?" Is it verbal, or is it non-verbal? If I could get through a whole rehearsal without saying anything, I probably could get more done.

*(Michael Kaufman)*

I know this will be anathema to many teachers, but in that first day when reading a piece, I seldom talk about anything except technique. When we read, we normally play a piece at a forte level whether it's marked piano or not. I know that doesn't agree with what some others suggest, but I do this because I essentially want them to get an idea of where the line and where the rhythm is going.

I would select a section that is primarily tutti. Kids would all be playing their horns; everybody would have a horn up to their lips on the first section that I sight read. Everybody would get a chance to play *Tancredi*, and that's why I picked letter H. If I'd picked letter A, the clarinet solo goes for about thirty bars and everybody else sits and listens. Now, I could have started at the beginning, but the trombones, French horn, and tuba don't come in for about fifty bars. We could have started it piano, and I could have talked about "the line has to go here and there." That probably would happen the second run-through on it, but that's not fair to the students during the first reading. On that first day I attempt to establish, in their heads, the challenge of playing it, the excitement of playing it, and the necessity for them to play it. Often the first reading doesn't have a whole lot to do with the subtleties that I will eventually jump into. I normally start jumping into them about the second time. When you read the ending of anything, with a rare exception, you're reading it for teaching. I don't even have to tell them, "Don't worry about the level you're playing, just get the notes."

Initially, I am not particularly concerned about dynamic phrasing; I am not concerned about nuance. I might, though, make an aside such as, "Well, you did that great, but if you played it that way at the concert everybody would vomit all over you because it's supposed to be pianissimo." But, the band would not have to replicate that pianissimo during sight reading. To help us decide if Rossini is going to be played in the concert, I feel that each kid needs and deserves to have Rossini under his fingers.

*(William Long)*

The fundamental things are really knowing your score and having an objective in mind of what you want to strive for, because you know what this work is all about.

Then, through a variety of means, one can be successful.

*(anonymous)*

Rehearsal is not for note chasing, it is for perfecting the group's performance. If there are too many problems, then some heat might be applied through asking an individual to play his part.

*(Robert Allan)*

I like to rehearse in large chunks and finally go back to detail. As a player, I do not like conductors who stop every two bars and are constantly fussing about things; the players never get the overall idea of the piece when this is done. That is why I like to rehearse in bigger sections.

*(anonymous)*

I think that planning and structuring a rehearsal are some things we must get young music teachers to understand; they must realize the importance of knowing what they are going to do when they are in the class. The percentage of the group's improvement and what students learn increases dramatically if a teacher knows what and how he is going to teach students before he tries to do it.

I plan a whole week's rehearsals all at once. I then can list everything on the board so the students know what we are going to play during the week's rehearsals. Perhaps they might practice a little bit if they know this. When I go into a rehearsal, I know everything I am going to work on in each piece; we get an enormous amount of work done when I plan that way. I think that is important.

With planning in advance, I have time to think of ways to teach and approach the rehearsal. For example, If I might face something that could absolutely stump me and they could have trouble getting it, I can keep my wits about me because I will not be in a panic. I can either go to the next problem and cut my losses, or go on to another solution because I have prepared myself for the rehearsal. I have the sense of what else needs to get done in that rehearsal. So, if I lose one thing, I only lose one thing and that is no big deal. Without planning, a person may get frustrated and angry, and keep trying to teach without understanding why the students don't get it.

I think preparation is extremely important for efficient rehearsals and for those that students will like. Students will not give you as much trouble because everything has some clear direction, they know what's coming next and what to expect. Students don't have to know every measure you're going to work on and how you're going to teach it, but they must know you have a plan and a real direction. They are so much more attentive then and the teacher can move so much more calmly, and with purpose and success.

*(Terry A. Oxley)*

With anything technically difficult, I usually begin teaching it from the end. I do the last three beats, the last five beats, the last seven beats, starting from the end and working toward the front of the passage. Sometimes I will change rhythms, sometimes I'll change articulations or anything else that can help a student. If it's sixteenth notes and they just aren't getting through this pattern I will make them play the whole thing as dotted eighth-sixteenths. By manipulating the rhythm on every other note, they have time to think about what's coming next. I also could have them play them as triplets instead of dotted eighth-sixteenths, or play them as double-dotted eighths and thirty-second notes.

*(Terry A. Oxley)*

I always try to push the whole, the Gestalt. I work with the whole piece and then a section. I work specific parts and then back to the whole. For example, if we read something, no matter what happens—if we crash and burn—at least I do the whole and try to get through the whole as often as I can. I've been in too many bands and I have seen too many high school and college people that just pick pieces apart; you never get through the whole piece. When one is doing clinics one must get things done quickly. Too many directors crash and burn on clinics because they are spending too much time either tuning or just picking pieces apart.

*(Dwayne P. Sagen)*

The idea "rehearsals are for playing only" is not true. Rehearsals also are a good time for talking about subjects such as composers, theory or history, and students often find those topics interesting. I have them do a paper on ancient instruments. Besides what they find in the library, they find a lot of material and even instruments in the community. They find this especially interesting.

*(John Kinnison)*

### Preparing pieces

I have two different sets of objectives depending upon where we are in the preparation of a program. Early on, the objectives are correct notes, rhythms and articulations, tempo maintenance, and good tone quality. Later, the objectives are balance, blend, intonation, phrasing, and proper musicianship.

*(John W. LaCava)*

### Intonation before a program

I work very little on intonation until two to three weeks before a program. If one does not have a good sound, one cannot play in tune; one also cannot play in tune without a good feeling for the location of all pitches in a piece. If you cannot hear it, you cannot play in tune. They have to audiate in their head to play in tune, and they cannot do that unless they know the part. It is almost wasted motion to moan and groan about intonation unless the piece is clean.

*(John W. LaCava)*

I always go into a rehearsal and know exactly what I'm going to do. This means I have a basic idea of what I must do and I just go about it like a surgeon; I do as much in an hour as I can to take care of that tune or those tunes. When I plan what I am going to do and how, I'll take graph paper and graph each tune with a checklist for each tune. I make sure I know what has to be worked on. On a hard piece of music, I'll divide that piece in different ways depending upon the piece; it does not matter whether I divide it by sections or by the measures. For example, the *1812 Overture* is a long piece so I divide the piece into sections. The sections may not be the long sections or where moods change; there might be three sections within one particular slow part, the fast part, or the French anthem. I make sure I have touched all of those things so when I'm a week away from that performance, all I have to do is polish. I don't find myself saying, "Holy mackerel, I didn't even work on this section yet!"

*(Howard A. Lehman)*

In planning the rehearsal, of course, it's based on the long-term goal of a performance. In college, since we are more performance oriented than in the schools, I plan the amount of time I have to work on a given piece. After a rehearsal I try to make notes on areas that need special work or something that seems to be a particularly sticky problem. As I plan the future rehearsals, I try to come up with some way to solve it that may get their attention, whether it is a rehearsal technique or a changing of the seating.

*(Francis Marciniak)*

Suppose we are doing a concert that has eight different numbers on it, the concert is on March 15th and we started rehearsals on the 3rd of January. We have two or three rehearsals a week for one and one-half hours each. If I have eight tunes and one of them is a monster tune that's going to take a lot more rehearsal time, such as Husa's *Music for Prague*, I'm going to make sure I plan the rehearsals and the program carefully. My concerns are not so much to choose pieces with contrasts, but to balance the pieces to the ability of the players or to fit the numbers to the players.

*(Robert Morsch)*

### What should happen in rehearsal

I expect the students to practice and learn the notes outside the rehearsal. We have sectionals twice a week to do detail things, such as woodwind or brass problems. But, when we work in rehearsal, I want to be dealing with music and its expressive aspects.

*(Richard J. Suddendorf)*

### What a teacher must do

I give a thorough explanation of how to do it, and if needed, a breakdown of the task into a step-by-step approach. Then, after they attempt to attain the objective I have described, I need to question or, in rehearsal, to hear their comprehension of the lesson to be learned. If confusion remains, one must go through these steps again. Unfortunately, teachers usually do not reteach. These are the basic teaching steps that I use repeatedly.

After the teaching in a rehearsal or class, the assignments are given to do such and such. At the close of a lesson, I give a brief verbal summation of what it was that was taught or attempted. In other words, if a student is asked, as he comes out of the classroom, "What were the points of the lesson?" he should be able to tell you what they were. Much too often students cannot tell someone what they just did in class. In a large group, I am likely to give the thirty-second summation, in a small group I may ask the students to give it.

*(George R. Bedell)*

### The maximum use of rehearsal time

One thing that contributes to this is a detailed preparation for rehearsal through score study. Here one must think very hard about interpretation and technical problems, both conducting and technical, that are present. We must plan for this prior to rehearsal—don't try to wing it. Part of the preparation is that the conductor prepare himself to be a musical conductor, in appearance and "inside himself."

*(Butler R. Eitel)*

### Stating the objectives each day

I put the objectives I hope to attain that day on the board at the beginning of every large group rehearsal. I found it to be one of the neatest things I've done in the last couple of years. For example, "Today we are going to learn to play an eighth-note triplet in four-four time or, We are going to contrast staccato with legato."

My plan is to use the tunes as vehicles to teach these very basic things. I think this is a real improvement in my teaching and everybody's teaching. As a result, my kids always know what I am doing. I am not keeping secrets from them anymore. I am not asking at the end of our hour, "Now what did we learn today?"

I never have more than three objectives for a class period of forty minutes. These are very broad objectives and I might be using three tunes to get there. I may work on three different pieces of music that hour. For those three pieces, there may be one objective that is addressed at least once in each piece.

*(Janet Tweed)*

In the first sessions you have with the beginners, try to accomplish one thing. As soon as they can produce their first tone, teach one musical concept every time you meet with that student. It can be rhythmic imitation, clapping, tapping, echoing, or various kinds of articulation.

*(James Croft)*

### Efficiency in the rehearsal

If you ever have to deal with a professional group, whether it's faculty or guest conducting a professional group, one thing you learn very quickly is that everything is a question of time. The musicians are there for only a certain amount of time. Huge pieces must be and can be done quickly because the players in a professional orchestra are good enough to do it. This forces the conductors at the professional level to be efficient.

In schools, especially at the lower levels, one does more teaching than conducting. (That is not to say that conducting isn't teaching.) These students need more fundamental, technical drill work—more training—so the time frame changes. I started in the public schools early in my career, moved on to the kind of ensemble my top group is now, and work with faculty who are professional players. I've learned that the more you get toward the professional player, the more you have to be prepared with the score. I find many teachers who waste their rehearsal time with repetitious drills, which, for the young student, is a necessity. Repetitious drill is wasteful if the teacher does this to give himself the opportunity to learn the score while he is on the podium. I think that, as the group gets better and can actually play the pieces down the first time or the second time, it demands that the conductor prepares more so he knows what he wants out of the music.

*(Frank B. Wickes)*

I always tried to work with the time allotted, even if it was short. One must adhere to the clock no matter how restrictive it is or seems to be.

*(Anthony J. Maiello)*

### Organizing rehearsal time

If there's more than one conductor working the band, as is true here (four conductors on one concert), I break up the rehearsal by the time frame of the pieces we are rehearsing. If it's an hour and forty minutes, I will take that one-hundred minutes, and I will split it proportionally to the length of the tunes we are doing. When they get what they get, that's their time and that's all.

First of all, I usually don't rehearse in the same way immediately after a concert as I did before the concert. I have a lot of four-week preparations for concerts on our college campus. In the beginning of this period, I do much of the technical cleaning that must take place. I also work where the sight-reading is a problem, and they don't have a idea of their own part much less of someone else's part. I find, in the last two weeks, that I can work for continuity more because I am moving toward the end of the preparation period. I can work longer sections and work through complete tunes more as I get toward the end. Except, if I've recorded the rehearsal to help myself toward the very end, I'll go back to piece together the problems that I see are recurring.

*(Frank B. Wickes)*

When I was in high school, I spent much of the time on fundamentals in the warm up. Sometimes when we were a long way away from a concert, I would spend a whole period doing that.

*(Frank B. Wickes)*

## Pacing a rehearsal

When I watch people rehearse, I try to observe if they have an awareness of the students who are not involved in that particular problem at that moment. Do they have a sense of the people who are not involved in that problem? Are they thinking, "How do they get students involved with helping the teacher solve the problem?"

There are skills that the players need to be taught through a rehearsal and by what happens in a rehearsal. The students also learn what the function of a rehearsal is, what's going to happen that day, and how to interact in a rehearsing sense versus a performing sense.

They learn if there is variety in an approach or they learn if every day holds a "let's start at the beginning and go until there is a mistake and then stop" approach. In this type of rehearsal, the teacher solves one problem and goes on again until there's another mistake and then stops again. The likelihood is very high that every time the teacher stops, they are stopping for a mistake they've already stopped for once before.

*(Eugene Corporon)*

## How much should one accomplish in a rehearsal

I list one or two items on the teaching agenda for each class.

*(George R. Bedell)*

## Decisions for rehearsal planning

Very often, in any piece I've ever dealt with, there's one of four things happening: you're either dealing with a new idea, a repeated idea, a variation, or the development of that idea. Take an inventory of what is going on and then ask, "What's the priority here?" If there are three things going on, are they all equally important? If so, then is it contrapuntal? If there are three things going on and half are whole notes, we can ask, "Is it harmonic and is there a way to balance it?" The result of decision making is the whole idea of cataloging what really is there and deciding what's happening before you start to set priorities. An example is balance and clarity. I think that's why we have a job. We have to make the best decision we can make at the time, and get on with it.

*(Eugene Corporon)*

Most often, I use my smaller group at the end of rehearsal during the last half hour and go to smaller pieces. Everyone has been involved until then. I also do one small tune with a certain group of people and use different players for another small tune that may be a little bit easier. This gives more people the chance for that smaller en-semble experience, not just your cream.

*(Myron Welch)*

## Analyzing, rehearsing, and performing

I have these ideas about the discovery process and what happens with the process as I move from analyzing a piece to forming it in rehearsal. I think this way: analysis or the discovery of the piece is learning how to hear the piece; rehearsing it is helping players hear what you already heard; performing it is guiding others through the listening experience that you and the players collectively have gone through. It all comes back to what you're hearing and what you're listening for. It's a three-stage process that occurs over and over again.

*(Eugene Corporon)*

## Picking simple solutions

I've also found that one should use a simple solution for the problem. I've seen some people introduce a new solution, which can become its own problem, to solve the first one. The solution can be so sophisticated that they have to teach them how to do the solution first. In other words, they teach them an exercise that teaches them an exercise to solve the problem. Sometimes we get so complex that the problem ends up being compounded.

*(Eugene Corporon)*

## Leadership in the rehearsal and the profession

The idea of "mind acting" and its impact upon conducting interests me. I've been around some people who have really helped me to understand the importance of personal projection and intensity, focused energy, and the idea of projecting and having presence.

I once heard said that, "presence at its worst is showmanship, and at its best, it is charisma." We call it all sorts of things; actors learn very quickly that it's a learned art. Instead of something you are born with—that you either have or don't have—you can learn it. We can learn the important part, which is to stand in front of any group of people and get them to do what you want them to do. That is the leadership issue: some people have it and some don't have it. Whatever one has, though, can be improved.

I think the art of showing appreciation also is what leadership is about; that is letting people know you appreciate the gift they bring to a rehearsal, to the concert, or to the process. It is important to make sure that they do what they are asked and that appreciation is given with the same amount of intensity as the chastisement when they didn't do it right. We must give them a fair evaluation and reward for what they do.

*(Eugene Corporon)*

Attitude, dress, consistency, etc. go along with the preparation for the rehearsal. This is not just mental, but we must prepare for the music at hand, the present state of the group, and what is to be done. We must prepare our own mental attitude that we bring to the podium; they can sense if this has been done as sure as anything and this is something we can't overlook.

*(Frederick Fennell)*

### Editing parts and adding instruments

We can edit and change solo lines to fit a group. We can change who plays the solo; I do this if we can keep the composer's intentions and if we don't step over the boundaries too far. If we don't have the proper oboe or if we don't have the proper English horn solo, sometimes a little creativity is needed to find a good substitute.

There are other substitutions that can work very nicely. Sometimes a French horn works very well for the English horn. I heard the *Russian Christmas Music* done with a French horn playing the English horn solo instead of a saxophone; it was gorgeous. Another substitution is to use the euphonium for lower horns; and, if there is weakness in the baritone, I might beef it up with the tenor sax or trombone—probably the tenor sax.

Another one that I think really works with the problem we all had for a long time is the harp. My newest substitute for the harp is the most recent synthesized MIDI keyboard. They have a reasonable harp patch and its use can prevent this harp problem. One patch indicates harp and there's another with a quasi-reasonable organ sound. There are several different organ sounds on the DX7 that have some validity. We should explore the use of the DX7 as a substitute for the celesta. The DX7 has these possibilities of substituting for these instruments that are so hard to get, even in the university. There is also a harpsichord stop on the DX7.

Though their purchase can be expensive, they can be borrowed from the jazz area and from students who have their own. Another substitution that I find very good at times is to use the piano for the harp. There are times that composers write for harps. Often the piano works as well or even better.

There's a couple of other things that I think school people need to do for instrumentation issues. We need to use the string bass more in band. A band could handle two or more basses. I was teaching high school one year and I had only a tuba and a half, but I had three string basses with them. They provide just a wonderful bottom, not just to the band but to the entire low woodwind sound.

The tuba parts are very challenging to string players and the teacher also must be inventive if there's no written string bass part. The teacher must decide when to play staccato, when to use arco. The bass can be very nice in a march. It can use a pizzicato, but there are places in a march trio where you want a melodic bass line, so the bass can be bowed. Thus, when the teacher considers the use of a bass, there are decisions to be made. I find that the string bass players who play with my group are very appreciative of being the only one on the part. They prefer that to being in a mob as they can be in an orchestra. I think we all need

to use the bass; they give a lightness to our tuba sound and give a little more bottom to the low woodwind sound.

The Air Force band has used cellos but that has not caught on in many high schools. I think it's easier to develop string bass players than it is tuba players, for instance. I think it's an instrument that is very attractive; it has such versatility with the orchestra, with the jazz band, and with the concert band. I would suggest that many of the smaller schools, schools that don't have big programs or big populations, find a piano player in the school who would like to play in the ensemble and teach them to play string bass. The teacher can start a string bass player in ninth or tenth grade and by the end of the year they will be playing very well.

To teach a pianist to play string bass is very easy to do. Even in small schools that maybe have one or two tubas, a string bass will really help the bottom. All schools should use them; particularly, I think, the small schools have use for them.

*(Myron Welch)*

When dealing with transcriptions one should assume there's nothing sacred about a transcription. If someone has doctored-up the original and put all these people on parts, I can take them out and thin the orchestration down to where it fits. This is especially crucial if one deals with an older transcription. Many of them were made for outside playing so they must be redone for inside performance. Take out the doublings. The way to begin doing that is to go back to the orchestral score and just see how thin it was to start with.

We did that on a Hindsley transcription a few years ago. The kids used the orchestral parts for the bassoons and the horns instead of Hindsley's parts. There also are many parts that were left out or simplified in places. We put back the real parts, which changed some solos. I feel I must trust my opinion on these things and I can go back and rework the piece to my taste for thinness.

*(Myron Welch)*

### Achievement and potential

There is another issue and that is the basic formula of the Inner Game: your performance (achievement) is equal to your potential minus the interference. The interference is created internally by thoughts such as, "I'm not good enough, I can't play this, I sound so bad"; Interference is created externally by someone yelling at you or distracting you, or there are other external events or conditions that "interfere" with your efforts to achieve and to realize your potential. Thus, there are two kinds of interference. What the *Inner Game of Music* is all about is learning to eliminate interference, so that your potential can overcome interference and take you to your greatest achievement.

Say I'm doing all-state, they're talking, and they are hard to keep quiet; they've been sitting in a room for eight hours and they're tired. I say to them, "Are you on the potential side of this formula or are you on the interference side? If you are creating interference in rehearsal by either talking or not concentrating, decide which side you want to be on. After answering, then ask how we can get to our potential as an ensemble." I do find, if I can get people involved in thinking about what's going on in that process, their participation can become more exciting. If a rehearsal is nothing but directing peoples' attention to what's on the page and what they already know, then the rehearsal can be very dull.

But if the rehearsal also involves music, playing, or students in ways that they can feel, hear, and imagine musically, the rehearsal keeps them interested. The whole intent of a rehearsal is moving the reality of what's there in front of you toward an imagined ideal. The conductor endeavors to keep the ensemble moving toward some kind of model created in the conductor's mind of how this piece should sound.

*(Eugene Corporon)*

### Rehearsing and pretending to rehearse

There's a difference between *really rehearsing* and *pretending to rehearse*. When you really rehearse you're offering concrete suggestions for how to improve. When you're not really rehearsing, you're saying, "Well, that's not good enough," or, "Something is wrong," without a specific suggestion on how to improve. For example saying, "Okay guys, this time let's concentrate more" usually does not tell them how to improve. They should ask, "Well, concentrate on what, where, to what, what's the problem, what's the issue?" You have to point out the issue.

*(H. Robert Reynolds)*

### Some basic questions about purposes

I talked with teachers in Missouri about many ideas such as, "why not?—how do we do this?—what have you done with?—why are we doing this?—why are we teaching music?—what kind of people are we anyway?—how come there's so many people in this business that aren't even any good at it?" In our culture, everything is a short circuit. We are supposed to read the condensed book, eat the fast food and find the "quick and easy" way to do anything—it's all instant oatmeal. Since everything is occurring so quickly, I gave them this test. I said, "What was the last book you read that was not something you had to do for work or assignment? What was the last time you took a lesson on your major instrument or vocally? What was the last concert you went to, not because some friend was doing a junior high band concert, but because you wanted to buy a ticket and pay to hear something? When was the last time you spent three hours alone to think?" I gave them a big exam with a bunch of questions like that and when it was over they said they really enjoyed it.

*(Donald Wilcox)*

### Getting their attention

We have a basic law that the section leader and the rank leaders are required to be there fifteen minutes before rehearsal starts. When they get three or four kids there they are to start doing something. Rehearsals start at 4:00 p.m. and if I get there at 4:00 and the band is not already rehearsing, I just scream and yell, and carry on, and fire people, and just have a terrible fit. I can do that only once every four or five years, but it helps!

*(Donald Wilcox)*

### Musical terminology

Use musical terms to get the kids used to them. If musical terms are used such as ritard and accelerando, instead of "get slower" and "get faster," the kids become more comfortable with them when they progress into other organizations where situations are more developed.

*(Donald Wilcox)*

### Suggestions to guide the teacher

Here are several ideas that might help one approach a rehearsal: "Kids will laugh and discover a better way of shaping a phrase or responding to a complex rhythm when it's demonstrated by a peer." "Don't conduct all the time." "Notice how a stopped-down beat cleans up the task." "Large concert ensembles will always be plagued by the 'Irene-inhibiteds' or the 'Sam-shys' who want to hide in large sections and be unheard. They seem to blend into the environment. Make sure these reluctant participants are involved by requesting frequently that they perform alone."

*(James Croft)*

### Thinking during rehearsal

What I do in a rehearsal is often instantaneous. I might think, "We need to work on this spot but everybody's going to be drugged out about this, so I'm going to have everybody clap to keep everybody involved." Or I think to myself, they're still having problems with this attack, so what I can do is . . . . "Okay, instruments away from your face, let me hear you blow air through your mouth and tongue without the horn."

I also am looking for different ways to make it happen; one of the principles behind rehearsing is that you need to eliminate everything which is not the issue. Sometimes the horn is not the issue, sometimes it's rhythm that's the issue. The issue may not have anything to do with playing it, it just has to do with understanding rhythm. Thus, they could clap it, sing it, or say it; they could do many things. Therefore, you should eliminate those things that don't directly pertain to the issue you want to improve; pare them away so you work on what needs it.

*(H. Robert Reynolds)*

### The value of chorales

There is no substitute for a chorale to prepare the way for the rehearsal of music selected for repertoire purposes. In chorales, every single fundamental is exposed for all to see and hear, without any appreciable technical demand. Here is where beauty of tone provides some of its richest rewards; where purity of intonation and perfection of balance are at a premium; where precision of execution is an absolute must; where variations in tempo, phrasing, dynamics, and sometimes in articulation cause effective contrasts; and where the music demands and produces the reverence in approach, in attitude, and in artistic feeling that is so valuable and pertinent to what is accomplished in the remainder of the rehearsal.

*(Mark H. Hindsley)*

### Relating chorales to pieces

Often in honor groups—not so much at the University of Michigan—and with other inexperienced groups, I tend to select chorales in pitches with the same key as the first piece in the rehearsal; this gives us a head start hearing the tonal center.

*(H. Robert Reynolds)*

### Teaching intonation in steps

Make students aware of what good intonation is, what "beats" are when two notes are sounded, and how to eliminate them. Section unison intonation should be worked out first. Have other sections listen and judge the unison intonation between and among players in one section at a time. Teach melodic interval intonation next by judging "one note to another" as in scales. Chordal or vertical intonation should be worked on after the other steps are secure.

*(Gordon Childs)*

### Presenting recordings as models

I have tapes and recordings of good orchestra or string pieces playing while students enter the classroom or rehearsal room, and as they are getting their instruments and equipment set up. This helps develop a mental concept of good string and orchestra sound. This works at any grade level.

*(Christa Speed)*

### Listen to the group, not hear the score

Listen very closely to what the group is playing, not to what you are unconsciously hearing from the score.

*(Gordon Childs)*

### Rehearsal pencils they will remember

At the beginning of the year I hand out lead pencils with "Greetings from Mr. Maupin" printed on them. These are to be used as rehearsals and are special only to string players.

*(Larry Maupin)*

### Teaching phrasing, not notes only

Teach musical lines and phrases, not just how to play the notes correctly. Music is more than just correct notes, correct rhythms, and correct dynamics.

*(Gordon Childs)*

### Reinforcement for young students

With young students I have a "race car" chart for practice progress. I move the individual student's paper race cars on the practice chart to show each week's amount of practice. Amounts are marked off in numbers of minutes. At the end of the term or the year I award the winner a small engraved trophy with his name on it. One could also use this technique to show the number of etudes played correctly, the number of pieces memorized, or whatever skill the teacher wants to reinforce.

*(Larry Maupin)*

### A variety of music

Select a wide variety of music from all periods and styles. Know the correct style for each period.

*(Dale Kempter)*

# Chapter Two

# Communication in the Rehearsal

The musical knowledge, insights, skills, and talents of the music educator must be considerable for him to be an excellent teacher. The degree of the teacher's effectiveness can be limited, however, if the educator cannot establish and maintain communication.

The comments in this section suggest many ideas about communication in rehearsals. For example, the music educator's style of communication must be essentially positive, he must inform students what the intentions are for rehearsal, he should communicate efficiently whether in words or writing, and he should establish an atmosphere in rehearsal that is conducive to musical learning, expression, and understanding.

## Establishing communication

They can, for example, pick any notes they want and you make a piece with them. You conduct and make all these non-verbal crazy gestures; you can do all kinds of things such as little aleatoric pieces. Then you talk about it and you can ask, "What are we doing here?" You can say, "The idea is for you to get your faces out of the music so you can listen and we can share in this. Music isn't time, it's what happens and goes between the time."

This also shows them that you have studied the score and your head is out of it and you are looking at them for communication. If you haven't done score study, then there is no way that this will work. If your head is down, they are not going to look up; they are not going to listen and they shouldn't have to. Score study is the essential thing, and I think the rest goes back to being yourself, not trying to be someone else.

*(Larry Rachleff)*

## Informing students of the rehearsal plan

As I enter a rehearsal, I always want the students to know what my objectives are. We, the band directors, may know what we have in mind, but the students don't know this. I use the term "target," which refers to targets for today, targets for this rehearsal, and here is where the "bulls eye" is. I want them to know as well as I know, what we are after or which direction we are going. This can make the rehearsal a team effort, as opposed to me leading them. We can both go in the same direction. This has become a common and very important technique for me.

*(Richard Floyd)*

## Communicating in a positive way

If you want to do a more positive rehearsal, eliminate the first thing you're thinking. The reason you stopped was that it wasn't right. You could say, "That's not what I wanted." But, if you want a more positive rehearsal, you don't say that even if you're thinking: "Oh, no . no . trumpets. That's not right again." You must *say the second thing* that comes to your mind and that must be your first statement spoken aloud. This might be, "Trumpets, it needs to be more . . . ." I suggest that if you eliminate the first thing you're thinking, you'll have a much more positive rehearsal.

The ideal in the rehearsal is to have people want to play well; not play well because they are required to, or because they have been intimidated into playing well; I want them to want to play well.

This focus, which is your vision of the rehearsal, is projected into all of them. One of the great things in rehearsal is when someone says, "Can we go back over this; who have I got this E flat with?" If someone starts talking like that I think that's the greatest thing in the world and I let them know that it is important that they're engaged in the rehearsal. I also like when I hear the sound of pencils, making sounds on the paper; I just say, "I love the sound of those pencils!"

These statements reinforce another important issue: often when we stop and do something because something *is not the way we want it*, we don't always confirm it when *it is the way we want it*. When the conductor finally gets what he wants, even if he doesn't stop, he should nod to the person, smile, say okay, gesture positively toward the person or section, or do something else that gives support and a sign that the conductor is understanding their efforts.

That does two things: it confirms for the person who's playing, "Oh that's what he wants, now I understand what he wants," and it tells that person and everybody else that this person wants to get some of those positive "goodies" again. He may think, "I want to keep playing well so I get nice comments, a nice look, a smile or something"; people like to have that.

I think you must *say* "that's good" or "that's what I want," *not think silently* to yourself only, "that's what I want—now I can go on to something else." Problems occur when conductors think about their own concerns with their own music making; they often think, "I'm satisfied and I can go on now." They're not thinking, "How does the student or player relate to this?" The player, when he is sitting there playing in a rehearsal, is conversing with the conductor and is constantly thinking, either consciously or subconsciously, thoughts such as, "How was that?" "Did you like that?" "Is that what you wanted?" If they don't get any answer—except a negative answer—they cannot be expected to remain as involved with the rehearsal as one would like. We can say, "That's what I wanted," or "It's not there yet but we're improving, it's on its way!" They don't want to be told just when it's wrong, they want to be told when it's right; when they're achieving things. That is the reward system we expect and the reward for which we hope.

*(H. Robert Reynolds)*

### Stop for a reason
I try to stop a band only when I can identify the problem and have a way to instruct; I try not to say only that something is wrong or that it "stinks!"

*(Jack Brookshire)*

### The listing of pieces also can teach
Place composer's names, instead of the titles of pieces on the board for rehearsal.

*(Richard Alnes)*

Along with writing the objectives on the board for a large group rehearsal, I also write the pieces on the board that we are going to be doing for a band rehearsal. I do not, however, put the titles of the songs; I try to teach something through what I put on the board. This is right along with the comprehensive musicianship process.

I may put number one with the composer's name. Number two might be overture, theme and variation, or something else to convey whatever is peculiar to that piece of music. For piece number three, I may put, "begins in E flat and modulates to A flat," or "the piece with the eight-measure introduction." With this approach, you can bring in history, key signature, dynamics, tempo markings, modulations, or most anything. Through this, they are learning something without teaching it directly. You are going to be teaching something simply by having them look for it in their music.

*(Janet Tweed)*

I list pieces by march, waltz, or chorale; by ABA, theme and variations, or concerto; by Baroque, Classical, or Romantic; by composer; or by sections or instruments with some special part, such as where the "French horns play a counter melody that accompanies the clarinet."

*(Frank Battisti)*

List pieces in different ways such as by birth date, composer, form, nationality, name of arranger, country, or style.

*(Patricia Brumbaugh)*

I list all pieces on the blackboard that we will be doing in the rehearsal. I list the composer's name, instead of the piece's title and I refer to the piece by the composer's name, not the title in rehearsal. This reinforces the emphasis I want to place on the composer, musical, or historical context. The kids also refer to the piece by composer or arranger because of this.

*(Thomas H. Cook)*

### Giving directions efficiently
When telling students the place to begin after having stopped in a piece to suggest corrections, always give the information in this order: "Count with me, after (or before) Letter D, 1, 2, 3, . . . 9 measures." Never waste time counting to yourself or counting aloud without reference points and directions for your students. Then you must wait for them to count measures all over again.

*(Paul Haack)*

### Gaining their attention through directions
Having quiet does not mean there is attention or concentration related to what is at hand. If this is not occurring, I might say, "I have your body and you're quiet; would you please give me your mind." I always say "please." If this does not work, I go into a brief explanation such as, "Please give me your mind so we can do this effectively," and I name or state what it is we are going to do.

*(George R. Bedell)*

### The location of students and their equipment
The proximity of the teacher to each student is very important for classroom management. I like to compare the teacher to a wood-burning stove: just as the warmth from the stove decreases with our distance from it, so does the effect of the teacher decrease as his distance from students increases. The phenomenon is often observed with inattentive percussion sections that are allowed to set up an excessive distance from the rest of the ensemble. Besides classroom management, teachers also find it easier to observe performance problems when the students are near. Similarly, I like to remove all extra chairs and stands before beginning rehearsal. Besides reducing teacher proximity, it also compresses the ensemble, allows students to hear their neighbors with greater ease, and improves the sonority of the ensemble.

*(Judith Delzell)*

## The atmosphere of the rehearsal

There is a certain mood in the group on certain days. This also occurs, for example, when the rehearsal is after a pep assembly, when it is scheduled after lunch, or on the day of a class field trip. It just does not work to go to a rehearsal without thinking about how you might deal with their mood during that hour.

*(Barbara Buehlman)*

The conductor influences or creates a good atmosphere and they must respect you as a musician also. The kinds of music the conductor picks are a great influence. Another influence is the way he approaches the music; is the approach technical or is it expressive? The latter makes the music rehearsal more satisfying.

*(Richard Fischer)*

I want them to realize that they're important to me and the group, and they're not just a clarinet player. One way to develop this is to call them by name; I address all my students by name in the rehearsal. I think this is important.

*(Richard J. Suddendorf)*

I allow no talking, although there is interaction. I expect them to concentrate. To promote this, I often try to structure my teaching so everyone is doing something always and everyone knows what they are to be doing.

*(Jack Brookshire)*

Concentration should be so intense that one could "set off a bomb in rehearsal and no one would notice."

*(Butler R. Eitel)*

Make a rehearsal unpredictable! Do something during the rehearsal that might not have been expected by students.

*(John Anderson)*

Part of the fun of this whole musical art is that it can change from performance to performance, and rehearsal to rehearsal. We can do this if students have enough trust internally so they feel and believe that whatever they're doing is worthwhile to the group. The teacher has to foster that.

*(L. Keating Johnson)*

I think the rehearsal atmosphere has to be artistic right away and my rehearsal procedure at the beginning includes singing of everything we do so we begin musically. Conductors must look like the music; they should be conducting with the use of their face, arms, and body. In the rehearsal we should be "saying" things to them and they should be "saying" things to us. I believe in an atmosphere that has intensity, so I am pro-intensity but anti-tension. I don't want the students being tense because

they can't play an instrument that way. If we're working with tremendous intensity, which is not tension but just intensity, it's exciting and if I've got something to say, I'll stop. When I do stop when I have nothing to offer, then why should I ask them to play this section over? I used to hate that as a symphony member. The conductor would say, "Let's start at letter A." I'm thinking, "Why are we starting at A? What's wrong with the section? We just played it for you? If you're happy with it, why are we doing this again?"

I don't say too much and I try to do as much through conducting from the podium as I can. We can get carried away a little bit with the emphasis upon non-verbal teaching and conducting. It's wonderful and we all should do it, but there's a point where some things need to be said and that's where the teaching gets done.

*(Richard J. Suddendorf)*

Rehearse sections frequently before you nail individuals. Give your students every opportunity to avoid embarrassment.

*(James Croft)*

Our role of educator, at any level, includes the responsibility to create the setting that helps students walk out of rehearsal feeling something they cannot feel in any other setting.

In my own way, I am one who is most comfortable approaching the day-to-day with a positive attitude. I try to be very positive in my approach to the musicians as people, to the setting, and to the music. No matter how low we all might be feeling on a certain day, we must be like the morning "disk jockey" who never seems to be in a bad mood. If we must, for forty-five minutes or so, overcome what ever we are dealing with in our own personal lives, professional lives, budget or instruments—we could have a million excuses to be grumpy. My approach to rehearsal is to be positive, and to avoid being down or negative, because the musical experience is worthwhile. There are times, however, when one must work very hard at being positive.

One has the advantage when one is with a group over a period of time. Over time they develop confidence in you and it is easier to be positive and less things will occur to which our response could be negative. Familiarity is not as essential for an honors group; the performers are apt to trust in the conductor at the outset, they are ready and eager to work, and they begin with the assumption the conductor is competent.

*(Gary Ciepluch)*

## The role of talking and explaining

We can raise their awareness through talk, followed by using conducting and demonstration to point out an example of what it should be.

*(Richard Fischer)*

A description of something before demonstrating it, whether it is a musical, technical, or another issue, increases the effectiveness. I also ask many questions to prompt them to think and discover what something is or should be. I feel that demonstrations are to improve the way that they do something, not the first way to teach it.

*(Steven Cooper)*

I don't believe in talking a lot; they should have that horn up playing it a lot. For example, if there is a problem with intonation or pitch, I will speak the word "pitch" while the band is playing, and they correct it.

*(Stanley Cate)*

Keep explanations of learning in simple language.

*(James Froseth)*

Use persuasion as opposed to giving orders.

*(Robert Allan)*

I never use rehearsal numbers or rehearsal letters. Instead, I say, for example, "Let us go back to where the clarinet has the main theme." Though this can take extra time and is less efficient than using a statement such as "go to letter A," it gets them into the form of the piece.

*(anonymous)*

### Listen to the group, do not sing along

Don't sing while you are conducting, one cannot hear the students as well then. Remaining silent helps me be more aware of the group and, since I have stopped singing, they develop a lot more.

*(Carl A. Bly)*

### Consistency and order

An important job of the conductor is to be consistent. I must not come in one day and have a tirade about how poor the dynamics are, then come in the next day and say they are very good when they really aren't. Blowing your lid doesn't do much of anything. Sometimes we have the tendency to be inconsistent and students do not understand that. Having a new perspective on the music is one thing, but ranting and raving one day about something is irrelevant, even damaging. A conductor must be careful with any age, level, intensity, or depth. He must be accountable; people must always know what he is doing and people must always know that he means exactly what he says. I do not think inconsistency accomplishes much at all.

*(Frederick Fennell)*

I felt strongly about punctuality and promptness; I have said, "When you are on time, you are late." At first they could not figure it out, but soon they did. Being present at nine is not being ready at nine. It worked! This must be established through examples. Thus the teacher must always start the rehearsal by nine, no matter how many are there and ready to go. One should stop on time also, for their sake.

*(John Kinnison)*

### The mood of the teacher

So often I have seen rehearsals in which the teacher takes his frustrations and problems out on the group. This is unfortunate, because there isn't a group that does not want to support the conductor. Even if there is a conductor that has problems, the group feels bad about a situation; the group would prefer the conductor and their experiences be as good as they hoped they would be.

*(Gary Ciepluch)*

### Somebody once changed my life

Until this experience, I was primarily a hard-headed band director. I think most of us were because we were raised on that style of leadership and authority: that was the way we behaved. Fred Schroeder was doing a rehearsal at one of the junior highs in Oshkosh and he made a suggestion to a kid who was really a surly-little rascal. Fred said, "Whoops, Mr. First Trumpeter, that's an F sharp there in the second measure and the kid just looked at him. Fred then went back to the beginning and started." Again he had to say, "Whoops, F sharp, second finger" and kid still played the wrong note. Well, he went back, stopped on the third time and said, "Hmmmm, now according to my part and according to that harmony, that should be an F sharp with the second finger." The kid said, "That's what I played!" Of course, there was a hush in the room and Fred looked at the student, smiled and said, "Well, one of us is wrong." Fred went back to the beginning and the kid played it correctly. That was a marked moment in my life when I realized "there are many different ways to get to Chicago."

*(James Croft)*

### The challenge system

It can be an extremely tense situation when there is challenging within the sections. I just don't believe in that; I'm a non-competitive person. If you're going to be competitive, you're competitive with yourself trying to do a better job. If I want to do a better job, I'm competitive within myself; I don't really care what the next person does—it doesn't interest me.

*(Richard J. Suddendorf)*

# CHAPTER THREE

# THE ORGANIZATION AND VIEW
# OF A REHEARSAL

There are several important scheduled classes and events in the performance portion of an instrumental music curriculum. These may include private lessons, if they are part of the curriculum, class lessons, small ensembles, sectionals, rehearsals, and performances. From an educational viewpoint, many teachers believe that the most important of these are class lessons and rehearsals because that is where most of the instruction takes place.

In classes, rehearsals, and performances students have many chances to learn about music. They can develop most of their musical skills especially those related to the ensemble and their own instrument. Both the rehearsals and performances give students the opportunity to respond to and appreciate the music. The performances also are the opportunity for students to experience the composition again as a whole, and to experience their final musical statements as a closure to all their efforts leading up to the performances.

To be successful with a cycle from lessons through performances, the importance of rehearsals demands that the teacher carefully plan so his efforts have purpose and direction. Before the rehearsal itself, the teacher must choose the literature, study the scores thoroughly, set the objectives to be learned, select the teaching techniques, and plan the format of a rehearsal. The teaching techniques enable him to bring the students to understand the substance of the score and how to perform it.

During rehearsals the teacher must develop and maintain a rehearsal atmosphere that facilitates learning and make his choice of teaching techniques work effectively. During and after the rehearsals, he must evaluate how successfully he has carried out these actions and how effective the instruction and learning have been.

The performance also shows and displays what they have been learning in a way audiences can comprehend. The performance may not be the most educational part of the curriculum, but it does benefit the students and the audiences, and makes the outcome of the music program visible and audible to the community. Teachers hope the audience will experience the results of the students' efforts in a way that is interesting, educational, enjoyable, and aesthetically satisfying for them.

### Warming up

My routine is to have players warm up first on their own. Since we rehearse the first hour of the day, I ask them to be in class five minutes early to begin this. Brass players warm up with long-tones, lip-slurs and scales; woodwinds play scales; all players warm up at softer volume levels. Then we begin as a group playing a scale listed on the board with the rhythm pattern listed for that scale.

*(Jack Brookshire)*

The first stage of the warm up is more for individuals. Each one does what is advantageous for his own playing and instrument; everyone's approach can be quite different. In the ensemble portion of a rehearsal, though, we try to get everyone doing the same things well.

*(Richard Fischer)*

The warm up should be a sensitizing experience that closes off the outside world.

*(James Arrowood)*

At the end of warm up we work on intonation and we transfer much of this directly to the music. The chords we pick for warm up attention are often chords right from the music we will be working on next.

*(Richard K. Hansen)*

I start immediately in the warm up with what I call sensitivity training no matter what the students' ages are. I briefly explain what we are trying to accomplish, then I will do scale warm ups, chordal warm ups, or something concerning their watching of me. I'll try different styles and tempos. With younger kids, it becomes a game. With the older people it becomes a specific concentration effort. We can usually get more accomplished with the older people because they're listening for pitch and balance; the younger kids are just trying to stay together. For any group the warm up basically accomplishes the same thing.

I believe that, to play music, they need to be using not only their eyes but their ears and brains besides the physical skills they need to play whatever instrument they are playing. All those have to work in harmony and not only individually but collectively. That's something that very seldom occurs upon the first downbeat of a baton.

For example, I will start warm ups with B-flat concert scale in whole notes, piano. Then I'll work with left hand, facial gesture, or body position. I say, "What does this mean? See if you respond to this?" I do this instead of just going up and down the scale on whole notes. I choose piano so they must control something while they are watching me. I want them to feel some kind of resistance or having to think about what's coming out of their horn. I do not want them just to blow. We also play soft because the intonation will change as their dynamics change. Obviously the piano level usually is the worst, the worst intonation, especially with younger players. Thus, this is a clear challenge for them at this volume level.

I also will do scales in discords as they play two keys at once; this creates fourths, fifths, or chords that don't quite make it. I may have them move these up and down in half steps or have them pick any note and move up and down. I say, "Now, I'm not going to use my arms this time I'm going to use my face and you're going to have to keep this pulse." Maybe I'll get a percussionist to click four beats, but not with older players. I'll use my face, my right hand, my left hand, or my body; I will say, "Let's play dynamically, or play expressively. When I look at you, bring it out." I find when I do a piece that way, they later understand what I meant by gestures and facial expressions.

These gestures are often not traditional conducting gestures. You have to do a beat pattern with the younger kids, but older kids can handle it pretty well without as traditional a beat pattern. Sometimes I'll try tricky rhythms and I won't conduct; at other times, I let them warm up totally on their own. Sometimes I just give them a pitch or I'll give them some kind of exercise or a passage based on the piece. I will say, "Now, let's do it without me," or "Now let's play it soft—now play it loudly." I'll take a section out of *Four Scottish Dances* and say, "Okay, we're going to go from this point to this point and I'm not going to conduct with a pattern; I'm just going to use my face.

Usually they do these things at a soft level, so they must exert some control or discipline over their playing. I also give scale degree numbers, have them sing 1 3 5 4 2; then they will play 1 3 5 4 2 in different keys. I say, "Concert E flat 1 3 5 6 5 2." With younger kids, they don't have their scale degrees together as well. With the older kids, they sing it first. We get all the clams out and I say, "Now, we are in the key of F." Then I sing an F, or hit an F on an instrument. I usually have pretty good success after three weeks of one or two days a week of that.

(William W. Wiedrich)

I may take a characteristic rhythm pattern from the music we are working on and use it in the warm up. During this time, I try to develop the style of the characteristic rhythmic pattern. I am as concerned about the style on a pattern as I am about drilling them on, for example, the exactness of a dotted eighth-sixteenth rhythm. The way they play its style and its articulation is the important issue. The rhythm I select may not be one that is difficult, instead I select the one I think is best for establishing the rhythmic style for the piece.

(John Williamson)

I try to find things within the tune that I'm going to work on that day, and make warm up exercises out of them. One example is a rhythmic problem that I have them all work on. If the saxes have a difficult lick, I'll write it on the board and we'll apply that to scales that day.

(Timothy Mahr)

Warm ups can vary, but I often use just a tuning A with my wind ensemble. Because it's a fifty-minute rehearsal, I expect them to be warmed up before we start, so we deal with them as a professional group. But, I find that we play better ten minutes into the rehearsal than we do at the start, so I sometimes will do scale routines with them. I do those slurred or tongued in eighth or sixteenth notes, or dotted eighth-sixteenths articulated over two octaves beginning with F major.

I use F major because it can be played two octaves on every instrument in the group except the tenor saxophone. F major is also a low scale for brasses, and they respond well to that early in rehearsal; I then go up a half-step. When I was doing my high school band, I would go to B-flat concert by doing F, G, A flat, and B flat. Then I would go back down to F and continue with E flat, G, and other keys, and come on up again.

I worked all the scales with my high school band, until I got them to do all the major scales. During that time I was writing out the scales on ditto paper for my high school band. I can dictate it to the students if I have enough time, and if I have more than a couple of days with them. I find that process of doing more than two octave scales works great, because it teaches them complete ranges, which allows them to get to the more difficult repertoire.

In certain parts of the country private lessons aren't happening and routine also is not being taught. As a result, the students' playing shows too much of a limitation on range, because they frequently are doing warm ups that come out of books that include only those scales with a one octave range. As a result, they never expand their range. I use the *Treasury of Scales* and various technique books that I can find to supplement those warm ups.

(anonymous)

My warm up is a group warm up in which I bring all their individual talents and attention together for an ensemble effort.

(Richard Fischer)

Warm up is not just a warm up, it is an opportunity to learn, maintain, develop, or extend the individual's or the group's ability and skill.

*(Robert E. Foster)*

### Warm ups and tune ups

I think the tune up period is one of the biggest wastes of time there—you can quote me on that. However, this must be differentiated from the belief that I think tuning is an extraordinarily important aspect. But you don't solve intonation problems in the tune up period.

I agree that you should tune to exactly the same pitch every day, which is taken from a machine, because you must have a consistent reference point every day. With the younger kids you might even say, "I want you to put your slide here, every time, until I tell you we need to start moving it around." This can help beginners, such as saxophonists, who put their mouthpiece on anew and differently every day.

*(H. Robert Reynolds)*

### The rehearsal atmosphere

The opening and closing portions of a rehearsal, the room, and everything is a package. The room is a very important aspect as is the atmosphere in which a rehearsal takes place. How well you know your score is an example for other people as to how well they should know their part. There may be less obvious things; I once traded a baton of mine for his baton because I had never seen a baton that was so terrible. I wanted his baton as a real-life example to show others how careless a conductor can be. I believe this person didn't realize that the condition of his baton had an impact upon how a student of his would treat his own instrument.

The room has to be the atmosphere you want it to be; all rooms have a different feel to them. It isn't the person that has the feel, it's the room that has the feel; and what goes on in there over time has its own feel. The same person can walk in the room or in the library, into a church, a gymnasium, or a band rehearsal room, and have four different feelings about the atmosphere that goes on in there. What you must do is to understand that, and say, "Okay, this is the atmosphere I want in my rehearsal."

I think there are different choices such as learning, concentrating, social (depending if people come in there and eat their lunch, and store their bicycles in there—that has to be the social center) and that may be acceptable. Whatever somebody wants it to be, it should be—it could be different things at different times.

If the band is a group that nobody wants to be in, if people think band is a crummy thing and only sissies are in it, you may want to make the rehearsal room a social center for a while so people feel good about it and want to come there. In the beginning, you might want to get more people in; but later, if you want concentrated effort in an aesthetic sense, you may think about what's going to be on

the wall, how clean is the room, and how organized is it? Even if scheduling requires that kids eat their lunch in the band room, you can still organize that. You can say this is where you put the trash, this is where you do this, and this is where the cans and bags go. When the whole place is filthy and—you know what I mean by the band room sound just before the rehearsal starts—that is something you have to control. You can still have people warming up, so you must think about all the things that make up the atmosphere.

To have the percussionists involved in physical therapy at the beginning also is a mistake; everyone else has to play louder and then people start screaming through their instruments! That not only doesn't do much for their physical preparation for the rehearsal, but much more importantly, it has to do with their sense of aesthetic feel about what a rehearsal is. How you start the rehearsal is an important issue. It is important what you do at the beginning, how you warm up, and how you tune up.

*(H. Robert Reynolds)*

### The parts of a rehearsal

There are two parts or dimensions to the rehearsal. One is when you're actually working on getting the music the way you want it—the "white-heat" portion—and the other is working on the attitudes of the performers. There are several aspects here, one aspect is that approximately half the time you're dealing, hopefully, with improving the music; that is, whether the clarinets should play louder and developing other factors of the performance such as blend, balance, phrasing—even the inspiration or the aesthetics of it—they all go with the performance.

The other part of the rehearsal has to with the attitude of the members of the ensemble; do they like what they're doing? are they interested in it? are they concentrating? what is the esprit, if you will, of the situation? The percentage of time and effort you expend on this part can go up or down: it could take fifty percent, ninety percent, or ten percent of your energy. The *fifty-percent issue* is not about the "white-heat" versus sensitizing versus conclusion, it is about the idea that you are half-trying to get the music better and half-trying to keep the attitude where it should be.

The percentages, or balance, of effort you direct toward one or the other of the two issues can change. You might, in an effort to get the music better, consciously have to sacrifice the ensemble's attitude while you work on the third-clarinet part for just a little bit too long. Another time you might have to sacrifice the performance-perfecting part when you realize, "I must forego solving the third-clarinet's problem right now; I can see that things are beginning to evaporate on me; even though they are quiet, they are leaving the room mentally."

As you perceive that and as you perceive its changes, then you may have to go back and forth from one to the other—go from the development of the performance to the maintenance and cultivation of their attitude or vice versa. Your sense of the rehearsal attitude and atmosphere can cause you to go on, even though you might not have finished solving that clarinet problem, if you think, "Because of the attitude and atmosphere, I'll have to come back to that at another time." If the students are still with the rehearsal, still concentrating, then you're still in the white heat section. If not, they've gone on to something, they've changed channels on you and you didn't know it. The goal, however, is to have both attitude and performance issues working together without sacrifice to either. When that occurs it's heaven.

*(H. Robert Reynolds)*

### Early in the rehearsal

The intention in the early stages of a rehearsal is to focus their ears: with young kids I would have them do chorales or something where they need not think too much. (Thinking has to do with technique: it could be technique of embouchure, fingering, or tonguing.) I want them *listening* to the right sound, *listening* to other people's sound, *listening* to the instrument, and whether it's in tune or out of tune. For *listening*, I think memorizing chorales and then playing them with their eyes closed is important. Because I want them to think as little as possible and listen. I believe this with conductors too.

This may sound peculiar, but I believe listening enhances the senses; the more you're thinking, the less you're listening. I do not want them to be thinking that their third finger has to go here and their tongue goes there; and as a result not be listening at all. They have to get some of those techniques in place early on so they have good habits. In the beginning I wouldn't be doing anything difficult, I would be using middle-range chorales, usually in minor: minor tends to develop darker sounds better. Then I would move the chorales around the group, having smaller sections of the group play so they hear better. When working on chorales, you can do a lot a things at the same time; this can be listening, tuning, blending, watching, balancing, etc. You don't have to do one thing at a time.

I do the same thing now, but if I were to put up Chorale No. 9 for my group, they would likely rebel. Instead, I say, "Let's do the second movement of the *William Byrd Suite,* by Gordon Jacob, the *Trauersinfonie,* by Richard Wagner, or something that has a similar character to a chorale. We do those pieces in concert; thus, very often we are preparing for the concert and focusing their ears at the same time. But what is important at this point in the rehearsal, is focusing the ears and getting their juices flowing the right way through listening to each other, being responsive to the conductor and to each other.

*(H. Robert Reynolds)*

### The "white-heat" portion of the rehearsal

After sensitizing and focusing their ears, I go on to whatever I need to do in the "white heat" time of the rehearsal: I address what I want to get done and I try to make this portion of the rehearsal last as long as I can.

When you've picked the places you want to work on—it could be for technical or musical purposes—this is when you are achieving the most improvement. While working on specific things I, of course, also try to sustain the sensitivity that has been cultivated during the first segment of the rehearsal. When moving through the rehearsal, you can't just think, "Well, we've finished the sensitivity section now, we're on to the technical."

I also have to think sequentially (I know I said I never did that) if some of the "white heat" time is with a piece like *Music for Prague.* This is a hard piece and needs a lot of rehearsal time. Nevertheless, it's an exciting piece and much of the rehearsal time allotted is because there are passages and sections of great technical difficulty. It also is quite loud, and it is quite physically demanding.

You would place that piece toward the end of the white heat section; if you do that first and then you want to play *Trauersinfonie* of Wagner, you're "up against it" because you've not only blown the physical aspects of the control but you also have blown the quiet reflective atmosphere and intuitive sense of each player. Thus, you need to place pieces in a rehearsal sequence so you're getting the most exciting and physically demanding playing toward the end. It's not just in a playing sense that such a piece is physical, it also has to do with the internal, aesthetic sense. The students are not capable of a reflective mood as easily after they've played *Overture to Candide,* by Leonard Bernstein (there are arrangements by Walter Beeler and by Claire Grundman). Then, if you go back and do *O Sacred Head Now Wounded,* that's crazy! On the concert, however, *Sacred Head* may come later in the program than *Candide,* which may open the concert.

Many things can happen at a rehearsal and you have to move through those things in the "white heat" section very carefully. I sequence things so I'm getting to the quieter pieces first; I may do the quieter movements of *Music for Prague,* do something else and then come back to *Music for Prague* at the end.

If I can make any connections back to the beginning, when we were stressing the sensitivity, tuning, warming up—whatever you want to call it—if I can stress sensitivity through exercises or pieces that are in the same key, or the same range, or something, then I try to do that too. Often I will come back to that kind of sensitizing later on. After a piece where we're having trouble with intonation, we'll go back, and play a note and chords to refocus on that in the middle of rehearsal.

Again my perception of what's actually going on is the key factor: I try to perceive not only the dynamic nature of the moment but the need of the musicians, physically and musically, as well as their inner personal dynamics. You have to be aware in the spirit and attitude sense whether the intensity is getting to be too much.

Thus, the "white-heat" section can have many sub-parts and you may have to elongate any one of them while shortening others. Some days, you may start with the white heat and everyone may get tired and the energy level changes. You may have to play a longer section where you're not working on something as intensely. You must adjust those things based on your own judgment.

You may have to break that up with a joke here and there, an aside comment, getting off the podium between pieces and just talking to people. The oboe players hate that, for they usually set-up shop and have all their paraphernalia out; their bocals, reeds, water, and everything. I will walk right through them toward the trumpet section, the tuba section, or to any section and say, "Okay, let's hear this section at letter G." I do all kinds of things to vary the rehearsal so it is of interest, so any monotony is broken, or the tension is reduced so they can breathe in and out. Staying on "the perch" (podium) to me is another thing that becomes monotonous. I believe that moving about the room is an important technique.

*(H. Robert Reynolds)*

### The conclusion of a rehearsal

A conclusion has to be planned just as the rest of the rehearsal is planned. It depends on how you want the people to leave the room. In many cases, ensembles lack enough confidence in themselves, as individuals in the ensemble and as the whole ensemble.

So very often you want to have something that says to that group, "Oh, we are okay! We've taken things apart, things have seemed out of tune and out of rhythm, and so forth, but now we're playing something we know could be better." But, sometimes a group can just have a great reputation and feel they don't have to practice; "We are the XYZ High School Band and of course we're great." If you work with a group like that, you may want to end a rehearsal with something they're not doing very well. This says, "Listen, we're not so hot and you can't rest on the laurels of your predecessors in this band." It depends, therefore, how you want the rehearsal to end; in most cases, I'd say one wants it to end with a feeling of confidence in students.

The conclusion has a miniature life of its own, it's a miniature concert—how do you want the concert to end? If you think about that then you'll know how you want the rehearsal to end. You don't want the rehearsal to end as you are rehearsing the third clarinets the school bell goes off, and you say, "Oh sorry, see you around."

You can tell whether the rehearsal has ended with satisfaction or not by the amount and the intensity of ad lib playing following the dismissal of the rehearsal. How quickly they leave the room may or may not be an issue but what they do with their instruments is; if there's frustration then they are likely play stuff through the instrument that might not be musical, it will just be getting out their frustration and there won't be that sense of satisfaction.

If they enjoyed the rehearsal, the enjoyment might be reflected in some way more restrained; intelligent playing rather that just physical-therapy playing. An effective conclusion of a rehearsal might be playing a piece that the conductor knows they like; it also might be just concluding the section that they worked very hard on that day and you do that.

One thing that used to be a problem with me until I taught myself through experience is: when you get to the end of a piece never, but never say, "Okay, we're going to go back and do the whole thing again." If you want to go back and do the whole thing again, don't quite get to the end. There's a psychological pull in every player's mind to get to the end of the piece. Once they've done that, they have been fulfilled. If you go to the end, then you go back to the beginning—everyone goes "uuuuu!"

If you do want to go back to the beginning, do not get to the end: then you may want to go back, in your design of the rehearsal, start with the last eight or sixteen measures and rehearse that first. End that segment, then go back and do other things. People will put up with almost anything to try and to get to the end if they see progress.

There's a compelling thing about making progress and you have to think psychologically with the ensemble about doing that. For example, if you want to rehearse letter C, because that's a problem, you say, "Okay, let's start at letter B and then the next time you say let's start three measures after B; next time you say, "Let's start five measures after B." Next time, you say, "Let's start nine measures after B. Even though C is still the issue, the fact that you're progressing down the musical page keeps people interested or thinking there's progress even though you keep going back to the same issue that you want to solve. They are still working on section C because you've been going into C each time you began at B. One of the boring factors of a rehearsal is going back to the same place every time. But, if you get into the music farther each time, they remain interested.

Some pieces have to be rehearsed differently than others. The people that say they rehearse from the end first—I'd agree with them. When you get into *Elsa's Procession*, even *Irish Tune* or any other of those progressing pieces and you stop—everybody goes "uuuu" right away; with that type of piece, there's a compulsion not to stop. If you rehearse from the last four measures, then take the four measures before that, then the eight measures before that, it may or may not work. Some pieces can and some cannot be rehearsed that way.

Most pieces can be rehearsed more effectively the other way. You may find that after you do half of *Elsa's Procession* you can't stop; you find that you can't really stop in *Elsa's Procession* if you really want to maintain any ensemble attitude. Unless you figure out some sort of creative way of doing it, rehearse these eight measure today and a different eight measures tomorrow. Once you start the ball rolling with a piece like that, with momentum like that, the psychological, musical, and aesthetic momentum has to be carried through.

*(H. Robert Reynolds)*

### Priorities change during the rehearsal

If enthusiasm is job one, then making adjustment of priorities during rehearsals is job two. Don't go in with a pre-arranged idea of what is going to happen. I have seen people go in with a list of what is going to go wrong and it doesn't go wrong. They still stand there with item no. 4! You must be like a good chamber music player or a good tennis partner, to read what is happening musically, technically, and psychologically and you must adjust to it quickly. In the midst of adjustments, this is the golden time to reward with the fewest words such as, "Hey, that was terrific!"

*(Frederick Fennell)*

### Theory of Rehearsals: I. Motivation

Motivation comes from a number of places. There is no secret ingredient that motivates students, but there are four general principles that seem to apply to this issue. (1) The teacher must be motivated himself and be able to show that enthusiasm to the class. (2) The teacher must be able to communicate directly and honestly with each student, not hiding emotions (good or bad). (3) The teacher must keep in mind that his job is to criticize and correct students' *actions* and not to criticize the students themselves as people. (4) The teacher must be able to get the students to succeed and progress so they feel good about their musical involvement.

The *first* of these four conditions can be improved but only with the most intense desire and introspection on the part of the teacher. If the internal desire to teach well is there, then working on such basics as projection, voice, and gestures, and taking acting lessons or speech classes may pay great dividends.

The *second* condition also can dictate some difficult adjustments for a person who is not used to speaking directly what is on his mind and looking people in the eyes. An honest expression of praise, even if it is, "John, you remembered your book every day this week!" can be a great motivator for John who has problems just getting out of the house every day without being beaten at home or by a neighborhood gang. The challenge level for John is different from the student who has had piano lessons since age four and just can't wait to get to band every day to learn more music.

The *third* condition is perhaps the most critical in developing motivated students. Whatever the teacher needs to tell John about his behavior, it should be directed at the behavior and not at John the person. The teacher should only criticize *what John does* not *who John is*.

Here are some examples of undesirable and desirable ways to speak to a student. The first example is: "John, how can you be so stupid as to forget your book again?"

(This is obviously a criticism directed at the person and not the actions.) The second example is: "John, I'm really disappointed that you forgot your book again because you were making such progress as a musician and now you can't play today." (This can be just as effective in letting John know that his behavior must change, and still is encouraging to John, the young musician.)

The *fourth* condition, teaching success, is what all teachers spend their careers working on. One underlying key relating to student motivation is the proper application of the two most basic teacher-controlled interactions: *challenge level* and *repetition or drill*. All students will have different stair-step learning patterns. They all need a certain challenge, and then enough drill or repetition to internalize the skills or concepts being learned.

A learning pattern for a brilliant student might look like this:

A learning pattern for a slow student might look like this:

A classroom tends to move along at the rate the average student progresses. The important thing for a teacher is to supply different learning patterns for different students in the same room. A rudimentary example is:

**Beginning Band: Day 1, Activity 1**
GOAL: Get the students to clap a steady pulse.
TEACHER: "I would like you to clap your hands with me (teacher starts rhythmic clapping)."
WHAT ACTUALLY HAPPENS: Students clap sort of in rhythm; teacher keeps trying, then stops to ask the students to try again, but to be more together.
TEACHER: "What you are doing now sounds like throwing lots of marbles on the floor, I want it to sound like just one marble."
WHAT ACTUALLY HAPPENS: Students clap closer together, but some still are way off. It is better, because the teacher has "upped" the challenge level by challenging them to listen more closely to each other.
TEACHER: "This time, the first row clap eight times, then the second row eight times. I want you to tell me which row makes the sound that is closest to the sound of one person clapping."
WHAT ACTUALLY HAPPENS: One of the rows probably will do pretty well, and several of the students will be able to pick out the better performing row. The students are now paying attention better, concentrating harder, and the

challenge level has been raised so that even the smartest students now have something to listen for. The slower students are probably content just to clap, and they are beginning to experience steady tempo kinesthetically. The goal has been met, all of the students are involved, and the challenge level is appropriate for most of the class.

Often when students are either bored on one end, or lost on the other end, the challenge level has been set at the incorrect height or the drill has been set at the wrong length for them. In large group rehearsals, this is one big problem that teachers face.

### Theory of Rehearsals: II. Isolation

The vast majority of rehearsal problems are caused by students when they are trying to do too many things at once. Most musical performance skills are a combination of many physical and mental processes that must be executed all at once. For example, to play a four-note arpeggio on the French horn, the student must be able to (1) sit properly, (2) hold the instrument properly with both hands, (3) inhale properly, (4) exhale in a steady stream appropriate to the pitch and dynamic of each note, (5) know the musical notation of the rhythm, (6) know the pitch notation and the fingerings of each pitch, (7) be able to match lip tension to each pitch, (8) be able to articulate properly, and (9) be able to combine all these elements (and probably more) to execute a musical phrase that has an emotional content both to the player and the listener. In addition, the passage may be complicated by a fast tempo, by a difficult passage right before or right after it, or by sticking valves or water in the horn.

The director faces the following situation: The horns missed a particular arpeggio. The director stops and says, "Horns, you missed that line. Try it again." They play four bars and miss it again. At this point the director needs to isolate exactly what is wrong. Eventually, the director may need to check all of the elements above to find out just what is wrong. Is it a breathing problem, fingering problem, lip-tension problem, or are they just not trying hard enough? The quickest way to do this is to simplify the passage. Simplify (isolate) by slowing the passage down, by playing fewer notes down to the extreme of playing one note at a time and holding each note to assure accuracy. If they can't play one note at a time, which playing fundamental is at fault?

Most young teachers can hear things that are wrong because they have played in college and know what good sounds are. What they typically fail to do, however, is to *isolate*. Instead, they will have the clarinet section play an entire phrase when only one sixteenth note is being missed. In the extreme they will ask the group to play the entire passage again with the comment, "That was pretty good, but let's see how much better we can play this time."

Ninety percent of what the effective rehearsal technicians do is *isolation*. That does not mean that the rehearsal has to bog down. Picking at details should not take up the whole class each day. It takes experience and judgment to decide when to isolate and fix, and to know which things to overlook because some tend to fix themselves. The director must always keep in mind the challenge level of the whole class, and not spend forty minutes on a section or a passage while the other students sit.

Furthermore, the director who never isolates details of incorrect playing is guilty of not challenging the players to perform to their best. Just knowing that the director hears everything will usually guarantee that the students also will begin to hear and to fix many things on their own.

The principles of challenge-level and isolation are those that effective teachers use, and the application of these principles can be observed regularly in rehearsals of the best ensembles. They can only be developed by knowing what these principles are, and then by practicing them with students until a well-motivated and cohesive class is achieved.

*(Stephen J. Paul)*

### The rehearsal process

Too often we rehearse by saying, "It's not together," or "You have to player softer because it says piano." Instead we need to ask them, "Why does the composer suggest we play piano here?" or "Why is it important to play piano here?" Then we can say, "It's important to play piano here because the big musical moment is coming. We must make that passage piano here to set up the big moment later." The first way of speaking is a result of the way that we're taught in college in many respects. I think that in college we were always taught to find a right answer—the right generalization. Unfortunately, that's often how people approach music making. They say, "The reason we must play piano is because it says piano!" That is not the preferred reason; instead, there should be a musical impetus for specific dynamic or style.

Instead, I would like to impart an idea to my students that I feel I learned too late in my life: the music must be the motivating reason for the technique. That insight has made my rehearsals more satisfying to me and the players than they have ever been.

*(Craig Kirchhoff)*

I think there is a tremendous amount of teaching that can be done in the ensemble. I love to rehearse, I think it's just great!

*(Robert Levy)*

How quickly can you digest a page of music, an idea, or a problem? How quickly can you decide whether the problem is physical, mental, or whatever? These problems are all there in making music. When you are working with a bunch of kids who are in transit, and you can see that they are anxious to know what is happening and they want to be right; you must make sure that what you are feeding to them is the right thing.

*(Frederick Fennell)*

Expect as much in every rehearsal as one expects in a concert; don't let there be different standards when one goes from one to the other.

*(Butler R. Eitel)*

We must come up with ways to make rehearsals interesting, to make things efficient and to keep students involved. The pace of a rehearsal is the real crucial issue; I think rehearsals that get dull or slow and depressed sometimes happen because the conductor doesn't keep monitoring the involvement level of everybody at hand. Sometimes a teacher goes so far into a problem, that they lose everybody else. They give the whole rehearsal up for solving this problem, and it probably doesn't get solved that day anyway. The teacher must have a sense of pacing. He must know when he has spent enough time on a problem whether or not it is solved. He also must be able to involve everyone.

*(Eugene Corporon)*

I try to find something that works and it takes many different ways to skin the same cat. Much of my best communication with the kids comes from emotion when I just go forth with all guns blazing; then, maybe I'll hit something. I enjoy the kids and I really get a big kick out of all-state groups where you've got them for two and one-half days. One can really get them moving, pumping, and rolling; working with all those good kids is so much fun.

*(Donald Wilcox)*

It's so hard to get things across sometimes that you wind up telling the same kids the same thing four different ways. Even if you've tried five or six different ways of getting the same point across, sometimes somebody else just has to tell them the same thing. This is why I like to invite people into rehearsal; I invite people to listen and make comments. Often somebody will tell them the same thing I said, but in a different way. They may listen because the person who said it is different and that will get the point across. This also perks up the kids' concentration, because they may just wonder "who's this guy?" Any additional factor like that will usually make the kids try harder; I use that a lot.

One memorable experience like this involved Bob Reynolds. He had been at Anaheim High School before I was and was then at Long Beach State. We were getting ready to go to festival, so I invited Bob to listen to rehearsal and tell me what he thought. We were doing the Gianinni and there was something in there that we had worked on and worked on. I tried everything I could think of to get this point across to the kids and they were just not getting it.

Bob got to that point and said, "Play it like this." The kids all said "Okay!" and looked at him with this blank, adoring stare that said, "I've never heard this before in my life and it's so true." Bob looked over at me where I was standing against the wall as if to say, "You really ought to tell these kids basic things such as this."

So, have someone else come in that will tell the kids the things and some will reinforce what you have been saying. Sometimes it is helpful even if you have someone in to say "you're not nuts"; or tell you the group is doing better in spite of your feelings of futility. Their perspective can really help you realize what you have accomplished and have not been seeing.

*(Donald Wilcox)*

## Musical and sub-musical events

The first key idea is that the most important teaching occurs when we have the students interact with the music itself. As directors, we often trivialize or overlook the musical experiences students can have. Thus, we leap into an analytical mode where we ask them to listen to a specific parameter of the music—a sub-musical parameter such as the note's pitch, the balance, the tone color, the blend, the precision—all of which are embedded within the music. However, when we take them out of the music, their experience becomes sub-musical. This makes the experience less than an art, it becomes a skill.

When we say, "Wait a minute, the down-beat at letter B is not together," and we practice that bar six or sixty-five times, that practicing is not doing music, it is doing something that is beneath the musical level. Although some of that might be useful in improving the quality of the musical result, the kind of learning that is occurring then in the student is decidedly a different type and a lower order.

*(Donald Casey)*

## Stopping or continuing in rehearsal

I do not always take a piece completely through in a single rehearsal. On the other hand, depending upon the flow of a rehearsal I sometimes won't stop even if I have an urge to stop. At times, they need to play through entire pieces.

*(Anthony J. Maiello)*

I'm one of those people who stops an awful lot in rehearsals; I practically work measure by measure sometimes. I say to the kids, "I always stop for a reason." Even if they play a piece for quite a while, I keep stopping and correcting to make, for example, a slight nuance; I might change to a different idea, but I never stop unless I've got something to say. Many kids will get impatient after awhile if teachers stop, stop, stop, stop, and stop. Once I get things developed the way I want it, I must develop the continuity by playing through a piece.

*(Lance Schultz)*

I think I see too many high school people who beat on the kids too much in disciplinary fashion and don't get to the musical substance. Frankly, this bores some better intellects in their classes, because the teachers don't keep their rehearsals moving and they don't get to the musical results. They're too busy working on technical matters; they are important and they have to be there first. The balance between technical and musical work is difficult to maintain. As Stravinsky said, "Before one can be a fine interpreter, one must be a flawless executor"; I agree with that; everything must be in place. I think that there are so many limitations on students that when the musical result is gone at the expense of the correct technical application, the result is not any better than if technical flaws remained.

*(anonymous)*

### The role of instrument families

In the orchestra, I try to get the families of instruments to play their own roles. The woodwinds are the color so they should emphasize the color of their instrument. They shouldn't try to play like brass instruments. Therefore, they should just stick with where they are and deal with the color they have whereas the brass should be the power. If you have something that's strong the brass should really let it out and other times they should be very supportive and the contrast should be immense. The woodwinds, on the other hand, should deal with trying to use projected tones that will allow them to be heard no matter what. I tell them, "Don't force it, don't try to sound like a brass instrument when they try to play." When an orchestra's playing loud I still want the woodwinds to focus that sound and play with considerable intensity, but not to overwhelm the instrument. A brass player can just take in a breath and go. I try to keep the woodwinds from doing that. They sound awful if they do. In interpreting the music, I try to deal with intensity levels. We'll play something that's soft and I won't say, "Play quieter." I'll say, "That's too intense; you're shouting at me and that sounds too nervous. The sound should be more relaxed. It should sound more easy, sound more beautiful and more calm." Usually it does.

*(James Stivers)*

### Talking and gesturing

Obviously the utopian situation would be that I would never have to say a word in rehearsal. But as I see it, it depends on the players. If you are working with "pros," chances are they have played the symphony nine-thousand times and you won't have to explain it. If it's going to be the ninth-grade band trying the first movement, you're going to have to talk a little about the idea of the piece. The teacher needs to provide a well-balanced diet; he must be sensitive to let them know when you are or are not going to talk to them during the piece, especially at a concert. You have to let them know, if something isn't

going well, they need to know they should read you like you were a mime. You need to let them know that you're going to tell them through gesture what's going on and hopefully your goal is to sensitize them as much as you can. However far you go with that obviously is dependent on the situation and their maturity level.

*(William W. Wiedrich)*

### The teacher's choices

If there is an intonation problem, the teacher has several choices: (a) You can supply the answer, giving the solution to what is needed by saying, "Second trombone, you are flat on D." (b) You can say, "There is a pitch problem, can you listen to cure it?" or (c) You can ask an individual, "Where was that pitch problem occurring?"

*(Donald Wilcox)*

### Using recorded music

When I left for the day, I would leave the tape recorder set up with something that they wanted to hear. The tape was either a new piece they had started working on, something hard that they had worked on, or something to see how close we are; I picked things for a purpose

The next morning, I would turn on the lights and the tape recording of what they did yesterday. As a result, the students would come in quietly and get their horns out. No one would play, start doodling, warm up, or bang around. They would listen.

As they would begin to get the horns out, I would get on the podium. When about four students were ready to start playing, I would turn the tape recorder off. When we would begin doing warm ups, the other students would get their instruments together and join in. Two minutes after I walked in the door they would have both listened and started playing.

*(Donald Wilcox)*

Have students list, on the music, the information that I give them about the composer. I expect them to write this information under the composer's name on the music and I expect to see this information on their part when it is turned in later.

*(Patricia Brumbaugh)*

## STRIVING FOR EFFICIENCY AND EXCELLENCE IN REHEARSALS
### Primary goals

I believe that the primary goals for instrumental rehearsals are:

(1) To inspire and challenge students so they will experience the excitement and emotional impact of making music.

(2) To establish proper rehearsal decorum and atmosphere, plus a tradition of seriousness of purpose.

(3) To incorporate in every rehearsal at least one learning experience that will allow students to leave with a feeling of accomplishment and progress.

(4) By setting and maintaining high standards and expectations, help students achieve pride through accomplishment.

*(John C. McManus)*

### Thoughts for the teachers

I recommend that the teacher:

(1) Treat each rehearsal moment as a precious resource. Get the most done in the shortest amount of time.

(2) Plan each rehearsal thoroughly ahead of time, but be flexible about changing plans in response to class reaction.

*(John C. McManus)*

### Before the class arrives

Here are some very important concerns that can influence the success of a rehearsal. They are:

(1) Control the temperature and air movement for comfort.

(2) Check and adjust for proper lighting.

(3) Keep a clean and environmentally attractive room. Avoid clutter and provide areas for storage of personal items.

(4) Prepare an orderly seating arrangement before the class arrives.

*(John C. McManus)*

### As the class arrives

A teacher should do what is necessary to maintain proper atmosphere. Set an atmosphere of seriousness of purpose through mutual agreement, example, and necessary rules. Some examples are no running, yelling, blasting, knocking over stands, beating on drums, etc.

*(John C. McManus)*

### The rehearsal content and commitment

Here is a list of important features that can guide a teacher's efforts in rehearsal:

(1) Tuning
(2) Preparation of Music
(3) Technique Development
(4) Sight Reading
(5) Rhythmic Development
(6) Analysis of Music
(7) Tone Development
(8) Student Conducting
(9) Balance and Blend
(10) Development of Musicality
(11) Articulation
(12) Ear Training

In addition to the above list, I believe in and include creative activities in rehearsals. Creative activities can be devoted to improvisation, composition, problem-solving, and arranging. These activities can be a floating block of time that can be placed anywhere on the rehearsal continuum taking time from the warm up or the main rehearsal, or parts of both.

*(John C. McManus)*

### Parts of the rehearsal: warm up

There are two choices the teacher faces during the initial one or two minutes prior to the beginning of the rehearsal.

The first choice concerns individual warm up. An individual warm up is most satisfying to students because they can satisfy their individual needs (e.g. reeds, slides and valves, cold instruments, lip checks) but it can be chaotic. However, one should use an individual warm up only if students have reached a reasonable level of maturity. A pre-arranged signal needs to be worked out so students respond with instant quiet when the director is ready to proceed.

The second choice concerns group warm up. A group warm up provides a more orderly and controlled atmosphere. Students take their seats quietly and wait for instructions on the group warm-up drill.

*(John C. McManus)*

### Parts of a rehearsal: initial tuning

The main tuning will occur after the complete warm up, but in order to find a temporary pitch center, sound a concert F using a student leader who has previously tuned to a strobe tuner. Have the band match the pitch. Then sound a concert Bb and have the band match that pitch. The concert F is necessary to allow the clarinets to use their basic tuning note. If a string bass is in the band, sound a concert A.

*(John C. McManus)*

### Parts of a rehearsal: ear training

It is important that this occur daily. Use rhythm and pitch imitation in a logical sequential order of difficulty. Also use improvisation, phrase responses (question and answer between teacher and student), and other aural activities to sharpen students' aural skills.

*(John C. McManus)*

### Parts of a rehearsal: technical development

Select the students' greatest needs, and with the help of technique books, drills, and excerpts from music being rehearsed, work to improve their skills one step at a time. Include finger dexterity and reading skill, articulation patterns, and rhythmic development. I advocate a sequential progression through all rhythmic patterns using a proper foot-tap approach.

*(John C. McManus)*

### Parts of a rehearsal: development of tone

Appropriate and idiomatic tones are shaped primarily while working on preparing music in the main portion of the rehearsal, but drills are appropriate during the warm-up portion of the rehearsal for groups having difficulty. Work on developing a depth and richness to the tone. Get rid of all high-register harshness in the sound by using the McBeth principle (which keeps a rich depth to the band tone by balancing the band tone like a pyramid—stronger on the bottom of the sound and gradually softer toward the top of the sound, and working to improve embouchures, breath control), proper balance and blend, and, of course, proper intonation, the lack of which causes much of the harshness heard in many school groups. Work on proper control of dynamics to achieve blend, and insist that percussion players treat their instruments like musical instruments and perform with sensitivity.

*(John C. McManus)*

### Parts of a rehearsal: main tuning

Using a strobe, check clarinets first on Concert F, then Bb. Open G is the main tuning note for clarinets, allowing them to adjust the barrel-joint which controls the entire length of the instrument. Sometimes a tuning balance must be established between open G and 3rd space C, but Concert F is the critical element.

Repeat the process with all woodwinds; then brass. If you have a string bass in the band, sound Concert A. When time allows for individual checking, have each student in turn play sol, la, ti, and do while checking the top note on the strobe.

This approach usually allows the top note to sound normal without pinching. It is worthwhile to have each student prepare an intonation chart showing the cents flat or sharp as shown by the strobe on every note of his or her instrument. This allows students to become acquainted with the problems and possibilities of their instruments and gives them more information on which to base intonation decisions.

*(John C. McManus)*

### Parts of the rehearsal: the rest of the rehearsal

Ideas about comprehensive musicianship governs the rest of the rehearsal for me, thus I believe that developing musicality requires attention to much more than just correct notes and rhythm. Diagnose apparent problems and solutions by checking the following:

(1) **Proper notes and rhythms**. I make corrections as soon as possible to prevent bad habits from developing. Requests for repetition of a flawed passage must always be explained. Students need to know the what, why, where, and how every time you stop. I also believe that the brevity and clarity of explanations are of vital importance to a well-run rehearsal.

(2) **Precision**. Learning to play as a team requires intense concentration on the part of students, and requires clarity of conducting gestures on the part of the teacher. Good attacks, precise releases, and clean rhythm require sensitive interaction and intense listening. I believe that concentration is the key issue.

(3) **Blend and balance**. Blend and balance must be learned through proper listening habits and an awareness of the total ensemble sound. Individuals who are insensitive to the team effort, must be identified and helped to overcome selfish playing habits and to become more aware of the results desired. It takes but one person who is insensitive to blend and balance to start a chain reaction throughout the ensemble that completely destroys the team effort.

(4) **Style**. When playing in the proper style becomes a problem, aural examples are the most efficient means to achieve results. Appropriate aural models could be performances by an outstanding student, the teacher, or recordings. Brief explanations or key words are also appropriate.

(5) **Intonation**. Despite careful tuning at the beginning of the rehearsal, intonation must be monitored constantly, and problems solved immediately. Intonation has a decided effect on the tone quality of an ensemble. Out-of-tune pitches produce harshness and shrillness that make it impossible for even a band or orchestra with excellent technique to produce a pleasing performance. Playing a chord or passage in tune for the first time can often produce an emotional high for students because of its sheer beauty.

(6) **Dynamics**. A band with a limited a dynamic range from mf to ff produces a dull, boring, harsh performance that is totally unacceptable. To perform musically, every note and phrase must be sensitively conceived. This can happen only when students have control of the full dynamic range from pp to ff.

If even one student fails to master the soft end of the dynamic range, a chain reaction causes the entire ensemble dynamic level to rise. This recalls Murphy's Law: *The dynamic level of a band (or orchestra) always rises to the level of its least competent performer.*

The most frequent offenders are high register instruments (1st trumpet, 1st clarinet, and piccolo) and percussion players, often snare or bass drum, but especially the cymbal players. Individual work in private with offenders often solves the problem—and it must be solved.

*(7) Phrasing and general musicality.* Constantly teach all aspects of musicality. Students are often unaware of the basic rules of musicality until shown the way. Helping them gain an understanding of such items is a necessity. Some of the items on an endless list are:

    (a)  Proper breathing and phrasing

    (b)  The natural tendency of dynamics

    (c)  Tapering off phrase endings instead of chopping them off abruptly

    (d)  The relative, rather than absolute nature, of dynamic markings

    (e)  Subjugation of non-melodic lines so melodic lines dominate

    (f)  Importance of moving lines and the subjugation of sustained tones in certain situations

    (g)  Slight stretching of key tones in fast passages and in slow, romantic-styled phrases

    (h)  The use of rubato playing

    (i)  How to achieve excitement in music by moving properly into sudden key changes

    (j)  How to achieve excitement in music by timing crescendos into climaxes

**(8) Analysis**. Analysis is an ongoing activity throughout the rehearsal. Use it a little at a time when it will aid in the proper interpretation of the music.

Students can be assisted in discovering how composers have used elements such as repetition, variety, thematic development, dynamics, timbre, texture, rhythm, tension and release. One must, however, avoid long lectures and one should make comments brief. Demonstrate, and introduce examples from compositions that relate to the discoveries made in their rehearsal music.

**(9) Creative activity**. Approximately twenty percent of the rehearsal time (ten minutes per day or one day a week) can be devoted to creative explorations such as improvisation, creative problem-solving, and performance of students' composing and arranging projects.

Rather than taking time away from the demanding schedule of preparing music for performance, creative activity shortens the time necessary for learning new music because students become more aware of how the elements of music work to make music effective.

Knowledgeable students read music more

accurately and perfect the fine points of musicality at a faster rate.

(10) **Sight reading**. Sight read a composition at least once a week when not pressured by immediate performance obligations. The more sight-reading experiences students have, the faster they will improve their ability to read effectively.

Teach them how to sight read by having students establish the following routine:

(a) Before playing, quickly check: key signatures, time signatures, tempo, style markings, repeat signs, dynamics, and awkward technical spots. Scanning the music following this list should take not longer than one to two minutes.

(b) While playing, learn to: concentrate on rhythm first, leaving correct notes as a secondary goal. Read ahead. Never look back to see what was missed. Use peripheral vision to see an entire group of notes or a measure at a time. If technique gets in the way, stick with the rhythm. Gloss over the notes until you can handle the technique again.

*(John C. McManus)*

## More thoughts for the teacher

Here is a list of other considerations that teachers need to keep in mind because they can increase teaching effectiveness.

    (1)  Keep talk to a minimum.

    (2)  Save time by learning to communicate ideas with the baton rather than words.

    (3)  Pace the rehearsal carefully to maintain interest.

    (4)  Avoid boredom caused by working too long on one passage. Spread drills over several rehearsal periods.

    (5)  Avoid false praise, but do give honest praise and encouragement where justified.

    (6)  Teach positively. Avoid an abundance of negative comments.

    (7)  Be a student of the band's literature. Be knowledgeable about quality and appropriateness of available works.

    (8)  Studying the literature through recordings, sample scores, concerts, conferences, workshops, books, and articles is a constant activity of any serious band director.

    (9)  Know your scores thoroughly. Mark them neatly and carefully.

    (10)  Analyze your scores in order to prepare yourself to help students discover points of interest and to help them perform more effectively.

(11) Be a life-time student. Attend conferences and summer workshops. Read professional journals.

(12) Invite guest conductors, artists, clinicians to work with and perform with your band.

(13) Keep your sense of humor. Never take yourself too seriously. Love your work and your students.

(14) Develop group pride by striving for excellence in every thing you do.

(15) Teach with enthusiasm because having enthusiasm exudes energy and communicates the importance of learning to students.

(16) Avoid trip-mania and raising thousands of dollars to travel around the world. Rather than feed the coffers of travel agents and spend time fund-raising, spend your time in musical and educational pursuits.

*(John C. McManus)*

# CHAPTER FOUR

# TEACHING TECHNIQUES IN REHEARSALS

There are many objectives—things such as intona- tion, blend, balance, phrasing, and understanding—that a music teacher hopes students and the ensemble will attain in a rehearsal. When identified for a specific piece, stu- dent, or group, the teacher must decide how to attain them.

For example, he must decide if he should stop at a specific point in the passage or play through a larger section; if he should help students understand the musical form or drill to reduce errors; if he should play a recording of the piece for students or rehearse without an example; if he should let the students perform an interpretation with only his input or have students become involved with decisions about interpretation; and if he should solve specific technical problems or let students find their own solutions. The teacher also selects the better ways to build instrumental facility and aural skills in a rehearsal. These are some of the choices a teacher must make and there are many more.

Ideas in this chapter can help a teacher accomplish an effective musical and educational rehearsal. To do so, the teacher must take the insights and objectives resulting from a thorough study of the score and interject them into the rehearsal plan. This is done through well-chosen teaching techniques. Without well-chosen techniques, the rehearsal may not move forward successfully and changes in students' musical growth can be insignificant.

## Making inactive players more active

If one or more groups of instruments have a similar melodic or rhythmic part, I have them work out the part together; but while this is going on, the non-players at that moment are playing their fingerings silently for the same passage and in tempo with those students playing; they play as though they are playing aloud.

*(Jack Brookshire)*

## Making marching rehearsal efficient

When two people arrive at the marching rehearsal, the sectional begins; if there is a 3:30 rehearsal and three trumpets arrive at 3:00, their sectional rehearsal begins. We get a couple of hours a week extra rehearsal this way. They are also going to arrive early because they want to see their friends. Starting the section rehearsals immediately also cuts down on touch-football games, sprained ankles, and busted chops. The effectiveness of this, however, depends on the student leadership. I borrowed this idea from J. W. Julian.

*(Robert E. Foster)*

## Helping students take risks

During a term with any group, I find that students are very unwilling at first to take risks. To encourage students to take risks, I make many different changes. I sometimes start softly or play loudly, or I take something out of context either rhythmically or dynamically by singing, emphasizing musical features, or whatever. I try different tempos to get them flexible enough to know this is not a finite art. Sometimes I have them play the opposite of what the final goal might be. When I do that, I feel I am training them to respond in a wide range of ways. They should develop the flexibility to do a piece or passage in any way at any time. When I try these changes, I don't think of them as "screwing up" a piece in a rehearsal situation.

*(William W. Wiedrich)*

## Different students need different teaching techniques

My thinking is that I need to be flexible as I look for ways to develop each player's problem area. The way of teaching is different for different kids, but when I find a way to communicate a specific thing, I can build upon it.

*(R. G. Conlee)*

I have a reserve of techniques that I use differently with different kids. If I see that something is not working, I must switch to a different technique. The teacher's personality is the essential catalyst for successful teaching and the teacher must motivate and inspire. If you expect a lot from your students, you'll get the highest from them. I use a rubber band to help them picture this; I stretch it toward the ceiling and say, "This is where you are now, and this is where we want to be." I actually have a rubber band in my hand, at times, when I say this.

*(Judith A. Niles)*

## Rehearsing one thing at a time

To direct my efforts as the conductor, I focus on one thing to which I want to pay attention.

*(Carl A. Bly)*

Variety is very important. One day I stress rhythm, the other tone. These two are fundamental.

*(Frank Bencriscutto)*

## Rehearsal planning

I rarely work a piece from beginning to end. Instead, I do the opposite, start in the middle or start where there will be problems.

*(Anthony J. Maiello)*

## Rehearsing a piece again

I have had the opportunity to do certain pieces numerous times. It is scary to see what happens to the group when you are working with a piece that you know inside and out. What happens is that the conductor has complete communication with the players. Yesterday, for example, we were doing the *First Suite in E flat* by Holst. I have done this many times in the last fifteen years. But each time I do this with a different group, it is like a breath of fresh air for me. I get to develop the performance and the students' understanding of the piece; and I face the challenge of getting this particular group of individual minds working toward this. While one is doing that, no matter how well one knows the particular work, things just come out of the conductor like a light bulb going on. One thinks, "I've done this for ten years and I never saw this before." These discoveries make this exciting.

*(Gary Ciepluch)*

## Stopping versus playing through

The kids are there to play and you want them every day to have a positive playing experience. They don't want to come in and have the director stop every three measures and chew them out. You want them to play through something.

*(John A. Thompson)*

## Learning a difficult passage in rehearsal

To rehearse a difficult melodic or rhythm pattern, I follow a step-like procedure. First, I identify the components of a passage. Second, we slow the tempo, but not so much that we lose rhythmic character, motion, or flow. Then the instruments with the same pattern play together. While these students are playing, other students with different rhythmic or melodic parts silently play their fingerings from the same section of the music. After progress has been made with the first component, we then work with the students who have a second part in common. Again, the remainder of the group silently plays the same section. We then combine the first and second components aloud.

The two groups who have already played return to playing their parts silently and I have those with a third component part of the composition play. When this part is more accurate, it is joined to the previous two parts. If there is a fourth part, such as the percussion, they also play their part as the three others simulate playing, before joining with those already heard. When all the parts have been approached in this way, we put everything together, first at a slow tempo, second at a medium tempo, then possibly at the designated tempo.

There are reasons this is effective: they work out their part with increasing accuracy, they hear how their part fits into the scheme of things, and they perform their part several times in several ways. This approach also gives the director opportunity to build their concentration. In fact, without concentration the approach might have less chance of success. This approach usually is used only on passages that are difficult and require much attention. I do not use this approach on many other sections of a piece, because the students will perform them well after playing those sections as they normally do in rehearsals. Sometimes, we prepare only one or two musical lines this way.

I also may have them sing their parts, using syllables that simulate tonguing and articulations. On occasion, if one section or part has not been accurate or rushes their part, for example, I might add a percussionist with a cowbell or wood block on the pulse. Sometimes it is more effective if the percussionist plays the subdivision. Sometimes, the steadying of tempo does not occur until we add the subdivisions, because sub-divisions adds so much more rhythmic motion.

*(Jack Brookshire)*

## Sensitizing students to conducting

If a teacher puts students through sensitization day by day or singing day by day without any growth, this means that the teacher must switch some tactics. If this is done, one can get a sensitive group quite quickly. I've seen results right away and I've seen results with younger kids in a week. Even with quick results, it still takes time for it to stick, to become part of them, because it entails a growth process.

*(William W. Wiedrich)*

## Beginning the rehearsal without talking

I never start a rehearsal by talking. It has always frustrated me to stand up in front of the band and wave my arms, nail kids for playing, or yell that they should be quiet. I prefer beginning quickly and immediately. Therefore, the band and I have an agreement that when we are to start, I give a down beat and they play B flat. Most students begin playing B flat immediately. For those who do not, they are apt to hurry to get ready, since everyone else has already started.

*(Patricia Brumbaugh)*

## Helping students to understand the score

Music is like a jigsaw puzzle. "For music to be correct and create the picture, all the parts such as blend and balance must be in place." I used these statements to help individuals see how their part might fit in and be important to the whole. I would, for example, ask them to imagine how the piece would sound if the tuba part dominated the melody. This also is true with chords, where the sound of a chord can be distorted if the notes within it are not in balance.

*(Barbara Buehlman)*

## Giving information that supplements performance

I have done what the kids and I call "dope sheets." I sometimes number them with a Roman Numeral and a number with each year having a different Roman Numeral. At the beginning of a dope sheet, there is a subject to be discussed, such as *Lincolnshire Posy*. I write a little biography about Percy Grainger to give the kids an idea about where Grainger is placed in music history. Then, I include a general "blurb" about the piece and pertinent vocabulary with definitions. I then can go in any direction I want. For example, I have one that I did for *Symphonic Movement*. I give them the eight-tone row upon which the piece is built. This allows me to talk about what tone rows, retrogrades, and retrograde inversions are; so I can teach those ideas.

Though I have never turned rehearsals into lectures, I'll call their attention to the sheet whenever it seems appropriate. It is in their folder and they do look at it. I've had the students say, "You know, Mr. Thompson, I took time when I was practicing the other night and I read that thing about Percy Grainger. Grainger was a concert pianist, he immigrated from Australia and . . . I think that was pretty interesting."

I have many dope sheets and one is about time signatures. I've listed all the duple time signatures down the left column, all the triples down the middle and all the quadruples down the other. The top half of the page is simple meters and the bottom half of the page are compound meters so they are on one page; the kids can look at all the different typical time signatures and see how they're the same and different. They can see, for example, that two-four and six-eight have similarities in terms of the number of primary beats per measure but they're different in their subdivisions of the unit of measure. They can look at two-four, three-four, and four-four and it's obvious that they all have a common denominator. Thus, the unit of measure is the same, but the number of beats per measure is different.

I've found them to be an effective and a simple way to get them to see relationships between different things. Without the dope sheet, they could play the whole concert or the whole piece a thousand times and not have the foggiest idea of how the different parts relate.

*(John A. Thompson)*

## Moving around the group

If they can play by themselves in a rehearsal without a conductor, I can move around the band helping individuals or sections with stylistic or balance issues. Getting off the podium also is a way to attain the goal of developing the student's independence. I can go over to where the primary melody line is and conduct phrases while everything else continues. The more face-to-face contact you have with each section and each person, the more it helps the whole teaching situation.

I like to look at large ensemble music similarly to chamber music. The reason the conductor has to make decisions (we are talking at a higher level of music making than occurs in the students' first couple of years) is because the democratic process would take forever with fifty or sixty people in the group.

There are two prime times for the sort of teaching and music making I like. The two times are toward the beginning and again toward the end of the rehearsal period with a particular piece. If we are very close to a concert, I use an approach I think is extremely effective. The approach is to do minimal conducting, which some people call monitoring—barely keeping time—only giving what is indispensable for non-verbal information. I also do this at the beginning of the rehearsal process, but not during the first reading or so when I like to spend some time expressing my ideas non-verbally. I begin this after their experience is beyond the initial stages.

Then we get to the point where we have to start identifying aurally the things that we need to be in touch with to make the piece work musically. Without my conducting, we can begin deciding whether the tempo we have been dwelling upon or the rhythm is right. We also can ask, "Which sounds do I fit in with blend wise?" "How important is my part in terms of balance?" "Where do I fit in harmonically," or "With whom am I playing in unison or at the octave?" At this stage I may even be off the podium completely. This is a way, at that stage of the development of the piece, to put the final performance polish on it.

Students can aurally identify all of those things much more effectively if there isn't as much visual information coming at them at the same time. When you get right down to it, an ensemble can perform without the conductor. They can perform better in performance situations if they are not too reliant upon the conductor.

*(Gary Hill)*

## Marking reminders in the music

They must have a pencil to mark details in their parts. They can mark anything from "eyeglasses" to breath marks, tenuto marks, and staccato dots. They can watch for pitch by marking arrows up and down, and they can mark accidentals and plan breathing. I feel that attention to detail is very important.

*(Barbara Buehlman)*

People mark parts better and are better about marking parts, if they know I am going to notice. While I am walking through the group and looking at music I have been known to point out that something just occurred that had been rehearsed or may have occurred because it wasn't retained from what we worked on before; these are things directly related to the fact that students had not marked their parts.

*(Gary Hill)*

### Raising student's awareness

I do change seating for each piece. I do so, in part, to expand the individuals' awareness of the piece and to make them aware of other ensemble members and what they are playing.

*(Gary Hill)*

With high school kids, I would totally scramble them up and just say, "Let's have a trombone player sit up here in the flute section and make other changes so their seating is totally different; I say, "Go sit next to someone who's definitely not in your instrumental family."

*(Donald Wilcox)*

### The effect of using recorded models

My dissertation was about hearing recorded or aural models of the piece that students are playing. Suppose we were rehearsing Stars and Stripes or Lincolnshire. The question could be, "Does it help to have heard the piece played through, like on a record or a tape, as you are rehearsing it?" There was a big argument in the profession: one should never play a recording of a piece you are working on because it stifles creativity and it takes time away from learning the notes and pitch and all that. The other view said, "You have to do this so that they learn style, so they learn something about tone quality." My research was about the question, "Did the use of recorded models make a difference?

We set up a research study between these bands and conductors and flipped them. We found out that there was no difference. We taped the bands on the pieces before they heard the aural models. We then taped the experimental groups after they worked six weeks with the aural models and we taped the control groups who rehearsed without the aural models. We taped them at the beginning and at the end. We sent the tapes to university adjudicators around the country and they rated the recordings not knowing if the bands had used the aural models or not. There was no significant difference in their improvement.

It showed that you can use either method and it did not take time away from other learning. It was not a waste of time to do that if you prefer that kind of teaching. I like to do that and I thought it would really make a big difference. I think I can hear a difference within the group when I play the models, but it showed that over six-weeks time they didn't make that much more progress than the

group that was really drilling away everyday without hearing an aural model.

We took fifteen minutes out of the hour rehearsal each time and they heard a record or a model. I would say, "You are working on intonation today and you are going to work Lincolnshire from A to B. We did it with a control group without the recording; and we did it with groups that heard the models. With the recorded models, you can hear it from A to B a couple of times so you can concentrate on pitch—but it didn't make that much difference. Those that used the recording weren't retarded in the progress at all; they did improve. But the other group improved that didn't use it; there just wasn't statistically enough of a difference between those that did and those that didn't hear recordings.

*(Dwayne P. Sagen)*

### Teaching musical phrasing in a variety of ways

I relate musical phrasing to speech expression and inflection through demonstration. Definitely, the less talking you do the more quickly they will learn. I think you must minimize talking and do more demonstrating as you work with them. I explain how they would speak a sentence. We say sentences in different ways and see how the meaning changes. We see what the differences do to change in the phrase, such as rising in the middle and dropping at the end. I also ask them not to "dump" notes, so they retain a taper to the phrase that makes a musically pleasant ending. To teach phrasing, I do at least six things at once: I demonstrate, explain, and gesture; and they do, evaluate, listen, draw, and experiment.

*(Judith A. Niles)*

I think singing is very important and I also want things to be in a "singing style." For style I say, "Make it sing," or "How would you sing it?" This asks them to give some thought to the phrase. I don't have them do any singing, because most of them growing up have never developed it and they would be embarrassed to sing anything. I demonstrate it and insist that the response is correct.

*(Kenneth M. Larsen)*

I say, "Now that you've gotten the idea, you did that phrase beautifully, I like that. Now let's play it the old way. Let's screw it up! Okay, here we go." And the kids play it wrong. My facial expressions let them know "We can do better than that at screwing it up," or "That version is poor." Then, I will say, "Now, instead of only worrying about where you will breathe at the end of the phrase, do this for me. Give me a slight breath accent on the very first note where that phrase begins and then let's crescendo." Then, as they are playing, I might use some short comments such as "get a little bit louder there, let's swell, let's expand," or "let's make it sound like Montana now, not North Dakota." This all might be said as I'm using my hands to show when we go, for example, up to the top, to the middle of it, or up to the fourth bar. Then I may say, "Let's let it slide back down so the end of it is soft again." Then we'll try it that way. After that, I say "Let's try it the other way, when you played straight and didn't breathe." This would be a very typical lesson of mine. All this would take about a minute and a half.

*(William Long)*

### Rehearsing difficult passages

If there's a tough spot, we'll work on that backward from that spot instead of forward. If there's an eight-measure section and the difficult point comes at bar seven, we'll work on bar seven first. They we'll go back and take six and seven; then five, six, seven, and so on. We do this instead of start way back at four and keep running into the difficulties. These spots are difficult so the repetition of that difficult section needs to happen. If you go back too far ahead of it and lead into it, then they're concentrating instead on all the notes leading up to that spot. On the other hand, if they start just barely ahead of it, they can still be thinking about the way they might solve that difficult problem. So if measure seven has the problem and you start at six, you can handle six but you're still aware of seven, so those two measures are experienced and practiced in context. Then you go back to five, six, and seven and work this way.

I also have an adult group and occasionally I work with them that way. Of course, with adults you operate on a different level altogether. These people, since I'm Polish, refer to rehearsing backwards as the Polish method.

This does work out and this works even with applied students working on the difficult sections. I work backward from the difficult spot and keep building up to that point. It doesn't make sense to keep going over the easy things and fumbling the hard thing each time.

*(Francis Marciniak)*

### Warm up exercises following a conductor

Play the B-flat scale in a five-part canon by dividing the band from low and middle to high pitched instruments. They don't need any music. Eventually, once you get the canon started, you can give them one note at a time and produce all sorts of crazy tertian harmonies; it really can bring forth beautiful sounds. You also can have them memorize a chorale or an easier tune. Then they can get the idea they should watch because they can get their head out of the music and become connected with the stick. The canon can be manipulated by the durations you would give to each chord that is developed. You might have one just be a quarter note that pulses repeatedly while you hang onto others for a while.

I like to hang on to them because they need to center and tune as well when we are doing these things.

*(Timothy Mahr)*

I demonstrate ritard, accelerando, etc. with singing and playing. I describe a ritard as sounding like a record slowing down. I also tell to exaggerate and I show this with my conducting, which asks them to slow down more than they expect or think they should.

*(Steven Cooper)*

### Experience and experimentation first

I really like them to try it first before I give them any prerequisite knowledge at all. Sometimes they will fool you, they will do it the first time, and you won't have to say anything.

*(Nancy Plantinga)*

### The value of review

The importance of reviewing previously taught ideas in a lesson and making relationships of an idea to that which is known must never be underestimated. Students seldom make connections and develop relational thinking on their own. The teacher, therefore, needs to guide students through this kind of thinking process.

*(Sharon Rasor)*

### One of the teacher's motivations

We all know what music has been to us in terms of our inner soul, and we want to share that with other people. In a way what we are is, "Big people helping little people." We have had big people help us and now the role is reversed: we are the big people and we want to help the little people. We must remember where we are going and why we are going there, as we continue to learn how to get there. If we spend so much time about how, we might forget why we are teaching and what we are teaching.

*(Gary Ciepluch)*

### Playing with expression

To clarify style and have them play with more "meaning," I demonstrate. Let's say they're playing much too calmly. I say, "I'm sorry, that doesn't mean anything, and I say, "I want it played in this way." Then I demonstrate so they can see how they might play it more as though they mean it and to make it say something. I'm saying that clearly at the gut level, I want them to feel the meaning in that part; I want them to convey that meaning and that feeling to the listener.

*(Thomas Stone)*

### The meaning of ritard

One of the very first things I'll do with the group is say, "What is a ritard?" When they answer I can usually say, "No, ritard doesn't mean slow down, it means to slow down and something: what is that something?" I want them to answer by saying, "A ritard means to slow down and look up" and "An accelerando means to get faster and look up." I do that so they know to look at me then.

*(Francis Marciniak)*

## Concentration

I have to tell them to concentrate all the time, it is so crucial. "Think about what you're doing, concentrate this time!" I must mention this at least six times a rehearsal. If they concentrate, the piece goes well.

*(Judith A. Niles)*

## The "one-two read-y go" habit

I went through a time where my students knew it was time to play again because I would say the words, "Here we go." It was a bad habit. The way it broke it was to tell my flute players in the first row, "Every time I say, 'Here we go,' I want you to just put you finger up in the air and motion to me that I did it again." They loved it, they thought it was great. It gave them something to do because flute players are usually bored anyway.

*(Michael Kaufman)*

## Verbalizing articulations

I'm a real believer in talking about things in rehearsal. I also believe in a tremendous amount of singing and a tremendous amount of spoken rhythm. Sometimes they use words, sometimes symbols for articulation when doing rhythms.

I use four different articulations that the ensemble is to strive to execute together. This is not for rhythm now, this is for different lengths. My own system is to go from a "du du" (legato) "ta ta" (more separated) "ti ti" (like staccato) and the fourth is "tu tu" (slightly heavier and still spaced).

*(Robert Levy)*

## Skill building

With the school's second band, scales are used to build technique plus the objectives used in the first band (intonation, blend, etc.). With the first band, I vary the scales more in the traditional ways such as speed and articulations. We also do chorale work about two days a week. I use the Bach chorales arranged by Lake with one group and the *Forty-Three Chorales* with the other.

*(Patricia Brumbaugh)*

## Approaching a piece

My basic approach is to simplify things, through tempo and rhythm reduction. If there is a problem in rehearsal, I can say, "Let's go at half speed." They know immediately what to do. This is a very effective way to fix things since they are doing the fixing and I say very little. The half speed gives them the room to solve the problems. I do not push tempo forward, unless the piece is perfect at that tempo. If it does not work, we go back to a slower tempo.

I also try to remove complexities with whatever, and wherever I can. For example, if we are having trouble with a piece I reduce everything down to rhythm. I do this by dropping the slurs, ties, dynamics, ornamentation, pitch

and we just work on rhythm as we play a concert-unison pitch. After we have worked upon the rhythm, we add the ties, then pitch, then articulations, and then dynamics last. This keeps them playing, which is when they learn the most—not when I'm talking to them. This approach also shows them a process, a way to approach things independently on their own during home practice.

One of the greatest gains from this approach is to avoid practicing the piece in chunks, a measure at a time. Instead, we have musical continuity because entire sections or pieces are always played in total. I try to keep the piece's integrity together as much as possible.

*(John W. LaCava)*

I think there are some ways to instill a desire on the players part to learn the notes and that is a problem we all face. For example, take any small passage from a piece that you know doesn't sound good and rehearse it to death. Isolate it in a slow motion way, explaining to them along the way why you are doing what you are doing. Get the whole group involved with supplying the rhythmic background; show the group how concentrated practice makes a difference in two or three minutes. Clearly in those two or three minutes, with the kind of practicing you are doing, you are showing them how to practice when not in rehearsal. The improvement, of course, will be remarkable. If you ask the group, they will confess it's better. Talk about it with them and they will tell you why it is better. The result is they understand that by practicing they are getting better.

This approach (a) shows them how to practice; (b) shows what the practice result is; and (c) gives them gobs of positive reinforcement. Then, they understand that it is now their responsibility; they will understand what practicing does and what the difference is between practicing and rehearsing. The result of that in time is that they begin to understand that it's their job to learn the notes. They see how it makes a difference and you showed them some practice procedures. The result is something that I think will be carried over to future rehearsals, practicing, and pieces.

*(Larry Rachleff)*

I'll do coaching during my Bach chorale so they learn to watch and respond to conducting. I don't take a Bach chorale as it would be sung in church; I will do one section slower, I'll do another section faster and I do rubatos constantly. They don't know what I'm going to do in the Bach chorale and that is my point. The size of my beat, if I want to extend something, if I'm using this gesture or that gesture can come out in the Bach chorale. If they are reacting slowly and if I know they're a little, say "vacation-prone" at that point, I will do a lot more with the chorale to get them alive to me; doing more obvious or dramatic things can do that.

*(Richard J. Suddendorf)*

Sometimes in a rehearsal, I will do some extremely different things. I do this to train them that the point is not to go, "Oh, we are going to slow down here." Instead, the point is to be flexible and respond to whatever is occurring then. Thus, I will do something very extreme just to sensitize them to what I'm doing and to reinforce that I will do whatever might strike me at that moment. I'm not going to baby them by doing something safe; I will do what I think is musically right and it's their job to follow it. I'd be happy to confess that I also do different things to energize them. That can be very successful; it can really turn around a rehearsal.

With practically any group I work with, if we're doing something that requires much flexibility, I will ask what ritardando means, and fifty hands go up and they say, "It means to slow down." I say "No! it means WATCH!" It always amazes me that when they see the word ritard, they assume where they see the word written is exactly where it's going to happen. I always have to explain that it can happen sooner or it can happen a little later; it is just a guideline, but they usually want to do it exactly where it is written!

The typical response from a group is that they won't catch the ritard soon enough when I start conducting it; then when they realize later it is occurring, they'll overcompensate and get too slow. This also happens with an accelerando—they won't get it soon enough, they'll over compensate and get too fast.

It takes a lot of trust between an ensemble and their conductor for the ensemble to know that, "Yes, this person is going to show me what I need to do; all I need to do is to watch and it's going to work out fine."

*(Mallory B. Thompson)*

### Playing or singing as the students perform

One very common problem occurs when a teacher sings while the group is playing, or a teacher plays while students are playing.

*(John Williamson)*

### A routine to build facility

These suggestions are a series of steps that will lead to the understanding and development of fundamental performance skill.

1. Play from memory a major scale in long tones, each instrument in its middle register, one octave, up only, p to mf, slurring one tone to the next, taking breaths only when needed and during a tone rather than when one note changes to another upon signal from the conductor. The players and conductor must concentrate on and listen for quality seriously, and with industry, trying to achieve a better and better tone from day to day. Players sitting next to each other must identify the pitches of their neighbors' tones. By whatever compromises and adjustments of tun-

ing elements on their instruments (done quickly during the exercise), they strive to learn to play precisely in tune and together. (Basic mechanical tuning will have been established earlier, with mouthpieces, bocals, and reeds being set properly.) Also the players must consciously and conscientiously try to play in balance with their neighbors, neither louder not softer than any of them, again achieving such balance by cooperative teamwork and compromise. The conductor may often test and balance by selecting two, three, or more players, seated together or at various distances from each other, to play a few tones in the above manner.

2. Play the same major scale in half notes, four-four time, at a strict metronomic tempo of about 100, one octave up and down without repeating the top note, p to mf, in an articulated legato style. Encourage everyone to play the half note scale in one breath, with a fermata whole note at the end. Demand precision in every respect, and continue to stress tone quality, intonation, and balance.

3. Play the scale as in (2) but in the marcato style; explain the difference in your conducting movements.

4. Play the scale as above but in quarter notes, legato, ending with a fermata half note.

5. Play the scale in quarter notes and in marcato articulation.

6. Play the scale in eighth notes, two-four time, one octave up and down but going to one note above the keynote at the top, legato; repeat marcato, then end with a fermata half note.

7. Play the scale in triplet eighth notes, two-four time, one octave up and down but going to one note above the keynote at the top and one note below the keynote at the bottom, legato; repeat marcato, then end with a fermata half note.

8. Play the scale in sixteenth notes, two-four time, one octave up and down but going to one note above the keynote to the top, legato; repeat marcato, then end with a fermata half note.

9. Play the scale in half and then again in quarter notes, legato and/or marcato, varying the tempo as you go, demanding absolute attention and response.

10. Play the scale in half and again in quarter notes in strict tempo, legato, inserting punctuation phrasing by your conducting at various places, describing your phrasing indications and developing understanding and response.

11. Play the scale in half and quarter notes in strict tempo, with a mixture of marcato, legato, and phrasing.

12. Play the scale in half and quarter notes in strict

tempo, legato and/or marcato, with changes in dynamics as you go along; explain and demonstrate as necessary.

13. Play the scale in half and quarter notes with changes in tempo, style, phrasing, and dynamics as you go along. This is the ultimate in conducting skill and in the development of complete communication between conductor and players.
14. Play the scale in eighths, triplets, and sixteenths in strict tempo but with changes in style and dynamics as you go along.

When proficiency in the above stages is sufficiently developed, many steps may be dropped from the warm up routine of the rehearsal with, perhaps, only the last two remaining as advisable and necessary to "keep in trim."

*(Mark H. Hindsley)*

There are a couple of reasons to use the John Paynter exercise. One is to produce a good sound and get the resonance and vibration on each pitch. What happens with a brass player, in particular, you might get a well-focused sound on F and, by the time you move to E flat, the sound is getting a little too stuffy. It's to get them to listen and get a focused sound on each tone. The other reason is to develop interval discrimination. They get to hear and think about what that half step sounds like and what it feels like as they play. Then they experience the same with the whole step, and so on, during this exercise right at the beginning of that rehearsal. In those rehearsals when I've used that, they begin to think intervallically more.

*(John A. Thompson)*

### Evaluating a rehearsal

Good rehearsals are those in which the difficult rhythmic patterns have been isolated and taught apart from the repertoire; once learned, they are placed back into context. By preparing your students in this way, you will not only increase their ability to read, but your rehearsals will also be more meaningful and enjoyable. You also will be sending strong messages to your students that you understand how they learn and that you care about them and how they learn. This may establish not only more musically literate students, but also a feeling amongst each other about the nature of music making itself.

*(Thomas L. Dvorak)*

I tell my groups that after we've been working with the music a certain length of time and it feels like we're ninety percent of the way there, it's harder to get the last ten percent than it was to get the first ninety percent. I tell them, "We're now turning the percentages around; we're now ten percent of the way there and we got ninety percent of the way to go folks if we consider the effort needed to accomplish what remains." I think this also separates not just the better conductors and the better groups from the lesser quality ones, but this statement defines the ability

needed to rise above "pretty-good playing" to reach a level of playing that is excellent or superb. There is definitely a difference between true excellence—superior outstanding individual and ensemble playing—and something that is just "kind of good."

*(Robert Levy)*

Many band directors tell me their kids don't like such and such; I say, "What the heck difference does that make? Make it so interesting and involving that they will like it. Kids enjoy achieving what the teacher is after, whatever it is!"

I hear and see many teachers going through the motions. I hear the *Treasury of Scales* botched to death; nobody does it, nobody plays it, and nobody works on it; I have seen no evidence that refutes these conclusions. People have gone through it and nothing happens. It is not a matter of getting the notes right, the rhythms close, and then it is done! It's a matter of what it is you do,

How you do it makes the difference between the professional and the amateur. I keep telling my band kids, "The difference between you and the Marine band is not the product, it's how long it takes to get it!"

Teach concert etiquette. Teach kids what is expected on stage about not just posture, but how to take a bow, what to expect from the audience, how to act at the end of the concert, how to come on stage, and what to do and what not to do. Teach your kids concert etiquette!

*(Donald Wilcox)*

### Using rehearsal recordings to evaluate

As one listens to rehearsal tapes, I make a list of things to be solved in score order from the beginning to the end of the piece. In planning for the next rehearsal, we must set priorities for what is to be done.

Prioritizing means to list the big problems first. Decide the time each aspect is going to take by deciding the difficulty of the problem. The ones that are easier to correct are at the bottom of the list. Easier ones are those that take once or twice to solve—sometimes only pointing them out to the students.

Working on the big problems may leave no time for smaller ones. That is not usually a problem, because some problems will solve themselves over time. I also try to avoid rehearsing from top left to bottom right only because then one will find that the ending sections rarely have been prepared well.

*(Hal D. Cooper)*

### Criticism

We can still chew out kids, but only if we do it in the right way. We cannot demean the person, but we can feel sorry that the music is being affected by someone not doing well. I refuse to look at a student and bring him down because he has not done a good job. However, I do not shield a person from feeling badly if they haven't or can't do something, and it has a negative effect upon the music.

In 1974 I heard teachers say, "Kids are not what they used to be." Today, you can still hear that in a teacher's lounge. Granted there are pressures both we and the kids feel, but we still find that there are many excellent students. We still must find the most effective approach for that group, just as they had to do in 1974. The challenge then or now is the same and the need for good teaching is reflected in this statement: a poor teacher is not successful even with a good method book, but a good teacher can be successful even with a poor method book.

*(Gary Ciepluch)*

### Do not get in the way of the music

Don't get in the way of the music in your conducting. In difficult ensemble passages start the group and let them play without a conductor. They will quickly learn to listen across the orchestra to fit their parts into what is happening.

*(Gordon Childs)*

### Teaching articulations through student compositions

To teach slurs to beginning string players and to get them to be comfortable with this new kind of bowing, use the pentatonic scale from D to A with open strings. After teaching the basic concept of playing two or more notes per bow, give all students five or six minutes to make up their own slur patterns on this scale and in a chosen meter. Then have the students form a circle and have each student play his pattern in turn, but keeping strict pulse and rhythm without missing a beat. I call this the "rhythmic chain." The teacher may add the final phrase and cadence. By rearranging the order of student performers a new melody is created. Tape record each playing session so that students can hear and comment upon their compositions.

*(Mary Jo Schwab)*

### Rotate seating

Rotate seating within sections until just before concert time. It is much more difficult to play seated in the back of the section as compared to being seated near the conductor. The conductor also can switch first and second violin parts on appropriate pieces to challenge each section.

*(Gordon Childs)*

### Involving students through memorization contests

Using simple folk songs from the method book that are from four to eight phrases in length, explain that this will be an intensive lesson to set a speed record for memorizing this melody. Therefore, students must listen and imitate as instructed, but they are not allowed to ask questions or make comments. The teacher then plays the entire song through once while students silently bow along, following the printed notes with their eyes. Then the students play the phrase through once still looking at the notes and immediately repeat without looking at the music. This process is repeated until all the phrases are learned. The teacher may then point out melodic phrases and cadences while students study the music on the page. The students then play the entire melody from memory as much as possible, repeating the melody again immediately and entirely from memory. The time is noted as they finish. Each melody learned this way is done to see if it can be learned more quickly than the first, and a kind of competition may be set up between groups in class or with other classes if desirable. Their retention and memorization of the melody is remarkable with the use of this technique.

*(Mary Jo Schwab)*

### Listening in the ensemble

Have small groups within the section play while the rest of the section listens. Continue with small groups until each player in the section has both played and listened to the passage. They learn very quickly from the mistakes of others and their own that they can hear. I always try to remember to compliment progress.

*(Steven McNeal)*

### Seating by quintets

Seat the orchestra by quintets with a cello, first violin, viola, second violin, and bass in the quintet. This helps them hear their parts in relation to the other parts and they also will develop a sense of playing one on a part.

*(H. Stephan Payne)*

### Fun music

At the end of a rehearsal I sometimes use the last five minutes each day to play fun music the students easily will like. For example, I have arranged fiddle tunes so each instrument gets a chance to play the melody.

*(Scott Schwab)*

# CHAPTER FIVE

# SUGGESTIONS FOR INVOLVING THE PERCUSSION

The percussion section is often overlooked and as a consequence, is usually given less guidance than any other section in the ensemble. Among the reasons for this may be their physical location in relation to the other instruments, and the assumptions that their function is primarily to provide rhythm for the ensemble—to "pound out a beat."

Much of the teacher's uncertainty or hesitancy when guiding percussionists also may be because of their unfamiliarity with percussion instruments. If the teacher also is unclear about the percussion section's musical function, then one would expect conductors, most of whom are apt to be wind or string performers, to lack skill in involving percussionists in the rehearsal and with the music.

Though these performers have been in ensembles with percussionists for years, there are differences in their parts. Percussion parts seem to be notated only as rhythms, compared to the wind and string players whose parts are seen as primarily melodic. That alone may cause one to misunderstand the percussion's musical challenges: percussionists also must shape their phrases and select tone colors. In other words, percussionists should be expected to make just as much musical sense when they perform as wind and string players should. They also must fit their performance in with the ensemble as they do so. Essentially, what percussionists do is the same as the wind player. The differences in their parts, which appear to be rhythmic only, should not let us assume otherwise.

In this section are suggestions for music educators about how they might develop and work with the percussionists. Teachers need to consider these suggestions because it could improve their approach to percussion instruction. They also should consider the ideas because the percussionists need help also. Beginning percussionists, particularly, may approach percussion instruments and the instrumental ensemble with their own assumptions that often are narrow at the outset. Thus, with a broader vision of how to develop percussionists, the music educator is stronger on all fronts: his own understanding is clarified, his confidence about guiding percussionists increases, and the resulting improvement in musical experiences and performances can be significant.

## *Guiding percussionists and their section*

I have some definite feelings that one should not talk to percussionists like they're percussionists! Instead, I talk to them like they're musicians who are part of the group! Often I'll look back and tell the cymbal player, "Look, at this point that cymbal crash must be like you're playing the third of this chord and it must fit just right." It's like they start thinking, "Well I'm a part of this!" Maybe we should realize that the percussionists are a lot smarter than most people think they are; they can learn to play with good balance and all of that. If the teacher makes musical requests to them, they suddenly realize that they're going to use their ears to decide how that cymbal crash is going to fit with the music at that point.

For the timbre of the bass drum, I'll refer to how that sound reinforces; I stress that it really is the bass sound of the group and the tubas and the euphoniums just help resonate it. I tell them that the percussion section provides the big push at the end; they have to supply the last bit of energy to get the emotional impact across.

The percussion has as much musical responsibility as anyone. If that suspended cymbal isn't exactly right, then the whole thing loses its momentum and we never get it over the mountain top and down to the other side. Talk about musical importance to them by saying, "If you don't do this at this point during those thirty-seven bars, we just aren't going to get there successfully." For some reason, this approach is a more interesting and important to them, than just saying "play the cymbal louder."

*(Craig Kirchhoff)*

Another idea related to percussion, is to have the marimba roll on chorales to fill out the lower clarinet chalumeau register.

*(Robert E. Foster)*

I don't think the percussion section has a whole lot to do with rhythm; I think it has more to do with color.

*(Craig Kirchhoff)*

Our percussionists are very good but they can easily be ignored in orchestra. I don't ask them to attend the rehearsal unless I can really use them. One approach is that technique of putting the percussion in the center in my technique of adjusted seating. Too seldom, we rehearse the percussion section—asking the others to listen—for musical reasons as we do with the violins, trumpets, etc. I also frequently provide them with the score of the piece and challenge them on occasion to rewrite the part so it is more interesting, colorful, and imaginative—particularly in high-school level literature. The percussion section, because of its unique sound, can enhance the orchestra's sound; too often students and the conductor view the percussion as competitors with the rest of the ensemble. It also is possible that they do not know what the sound of a percussion section is to be. They add a particular touch of color that completes the orchestral sound.

*(Pamela Gearhart)*

I have percussionists at the tuner while a flutist or a trombonist is experimenting. This made the percussionists more interested in pitch—and keeps them busy.

*(John Kinnison)*

My percussion section is not placed in the back of the band as is done traditionally. Instead I have the bells in the front two rows, the snare drums in the third row, the temple blocks and other auxiliary percussion such as the suspended cymbals, bell tree, and high hat in the fourth row. The bass drum is in the third row with the snare drums and the tympani is in the fourth row with the auxiliary percussion. Each percussionist is on the performers' right side, next to the last wind player in each row.

Locating the percussionists in these positions helps them be a part of the band, not separated from the band because they are way to the back. This location makes them an integral part of the band, the music-making process, and all the events in rehearsal. Their location also causes the wind players to realize the percussionists are part of the group not just because of location; they can hear that some of their lines are the same as certain percussion parts. The percussionists' positions in relation to wind players also reinforces the rhythm of the ensemble because the other band members are so close they can hear each other easily.

*(Janet Tweed)*

In working with my percussion section, I feel the percussion section must be conscious of what the band is doing all the time. They really have to play off the band. There really is no such thing as a simple crash at a certain level, a tympani roll here or there, or a snare drum roll for four measures. A percussion section just doesn't play only what's written. I tell them, "You've got to react to the band! If you're doing a cymbal roll, you just can't play that cymbal roll at one level. Sure, on crescendos maybe, but before long you've wiped out the group because it's too loud at another point. You must consider the cymbal's

crash in relationship to what the band is playing at this point." They often will say, "Wait a minute, that's right; I overplayed that completely."

I have my percussion section vocalize with us on the chorales. As they are setting up their instruments, the percussionists sing the chorales. When we're vocalizing, they're involved in it, too. If they don't, I look over at them and they understand, just by my eye contact, what they should be doing at that moment.

A percussion section should be a beautiful section. If teachers are more sensitive to them and request things, they realize teachers are concerned about what they're doing and want different sounds. We must let them know that we appreciate their comments, too. Some percussionists will say to me, (of course, I'm working with a college group) "Let me try this for you." I'll say, "Oh yeah, I like that. Now what mallets are you using? Oh, I like that better." So, we have developed a wonderful working relationship; that's the important thing.

*(Richard J. Suddendorf)*

### All of my percussion kids have to play all the percussion parts.

If somebody is absent, they all have to be able to play that part and their regular part as well. Because we have a rotating schedule for sectionals, during the sectional time they also rotate parts. One week they'll play snare drum part, the next week they will play another instrument. All of my percussionists have to play mallets. They all begin with a mallet kit and a snare drum practice pad, and that keeps them busier than if they learn only to be a bass drum player, a tympani player, or a snare drummer.

*(Anthony J. Maiello)*

All percussion players do the warm ups. If the band's playing scales or the band is playing long tones, I put them on mallets and timpani. I have young kids play mallets first, then later when they are more advanced they can find I, IV, and V on the tympani. Tuning on the run is quite a challenge for younger players. The college kids can play the melody on tympani. If the band's playing simple tunes by ear, have play them these melodies on mallets.

*(Donald Wilcox)*

I honestly don't think I'm very good with the percussion. But, with my upper or top ensembles, it's never a problem. We have a student-to-teacher agreement that during the warm up mode they are preparing the equipment for the day's rehearsal. They are getting ready and when I come out of my warm up, I expect them standing there and ready to function on the first piece. They always know what that first piece is going to be because it's either on the board or it's announced from the podium. Furthermore, they know what else we're going to rehearse that day so they also can get that equipment ready. With the top two bands, it works most of the time. With the bottom bands made up mostly of the freshmen, my only suggestion is when we're playing scales; I have most of the kids standing at mallet instruments doing rolls on each pitch. If it's slow they're rolling; if it's fast they're playing the scale in rhythm.

I have observed that percussionists are often treated differently. People even say, "Band, let's start at B. Oh, percussion, we're at letter B." This almost treats the percussion like they're different people. I try to make them feel that they're equal partners with the others. I tell them, "Every time a percussion player touches a piece of equipment, he is a soloist." It's far different being the snare drummer, the triangle player, or the marimba player than being one member of the clarinet section.

I say that to my wind players, "Listen, you're sitting very comfortably in your section sometimes and you're not always on the spot. You might make a mistake and it isn't the most noticeable thing in the world. But, if you're playing cymbal and you make a mistake, everybody knows it." That is a way to build respect for what the percussion is doing.

Another point is that we don't believe in drummers, we believe in percussionists. Though you have to fight it today when everyone wants to be a rock drummer, I say right from the beginning, "We are percussionists; you play set, tympani, cymbals, mallets, utility percussion, and all the other membrane percussion. You don't need to become a monster on every instrument, but I want you to handle all the equipment well. When parts are assigned during the year, you will be playing everything. Everybody's going to get a chance to play a timpani part and everybody's going to get a chance to play a mallet part even if it's a simple chime part."

If I see the mallet part that goes with an upper woodwind part and I'm rehearsing the upper woodwind part, I make sure that I include the mallets too. Another obvious one is the bells and the upper woodwinds. I also watch for something as simple as the bass drum and the low brass. If the low brass are doing an ostinato figure or another figure, then I try to build them in to the rehearsal. Suddenly the timpanist, the bass drum player, or the tom-tom recognize that their part is integrated with that other team. With the younger bands, the snare part works with the low brass when they have dum, dum, dum, dum. When they figure out that this part or the "digadigadigadigadum" has the same accent patterns as they have, suddenly the trombone players are listening to the snare players and the snare players listen to the bones.

*(John A. Thompson)*

When I was in public school I had rehearsals with the ensemble every day. I used a lot of routine, that is I would do many scales, much chordal work, many technical exercises, many rhythmic exercises, and other things to develop the technique of the ensemble. During rehearsals, I involved all of the percussion in all melodic exercises on the mallet instruments. They used soft, rubber mallets and two students were playing the marimba, two on the xylophone and vibraphone, and one on the bells or another melodic instrument. I would have all of the percussion section on those instruments playing with the band. On long notes they rolled. (I did not use them on other percussion instruments on technique exercises.)

I would always have percussionists on the mallets because those instruments are terribly slighted in the students' early years because students do not start on those melodic instruments. Since they have not learned to read melodies, I thought it was extremely important for them to have experience reading something other than just rhythm patterns.

If there are pieces with very little percussion, I provide a score so they can watch it. This is especially interesting for college students in a conducting sequence or analysis courses. I may have them listen from the front when possible. If we do transcriptions with symphonic band, they always search out the original orchestral percussion parts, because we frequently find that the parts have been changed. When they find discrepancies, unless there's a good reason, they use the orchestral part.

Most wind players who are conductors, do not give percussionists the amount of time that they need. We are not as sensitive as we need to be toward encouraging quality sounds from the percussion instruments. This includes tuning the membraphones and getting the proper sounds from all the trap instruments, the cymbal family and all the accessory instruments. We slight percussion too much, we don't stop and really listen to the color they provide or listen to what a good mallet selection will do for sound on a percussion instrument.

I also think that percussion instruments are played too loudly; I think manufacturers are building these instruments louder and louder today, particularly the drums and other head instruments. We find in sensitive halls that they overplay the band almost by an entire dynamic always. Their forte is louder than the wind's forte; they need to adjust that by coming down in volume. I know that orchestral conductors are constantly keeping the hands in the face of percussion instruments to balance things.

*(Frank B. Wickes)*

I always tell my private and percussion techniques students that, whenever a percussionist is performing in a non-solo capacity, his primary responsibility is to perform with the right sound, at the right time, on the proper-sized instrument, at the right dynamic level, and with the right utensil. Percussionists should heed this whether performing one note on the triangle or a lengthy and prominent passage on the marimba. Percussionists and conductors too often overlook the ancillary instruments. In short, the "Davis Philosophy" is to remember these suggestions and "to do whatever works."

*(Thomas L. Davis)*

# Miscellaneous

# MISCELLANEOUS

In a research project, especially one of this size and scope, some interesting material emerges that cannot be placed in any one topic area as easily as other ideas can. This chapter, thus, contains ideas that are interesting for many reasons and might help a teacher with a number of problems.

The comments cover a wide range of subjects, but several can be especially helpful to music educators. Sometimes they might help the reader understand the school, students, or the times; they might help the reader think about teacher training in music education, or see into the off-stage lives of conductors. There also are comments about teacher growth and burnout, the value of Manhattanville in instrumental music classes, administrative efficiency, the fact that a successful program can be done in small schools and towns, and especially about remembering that good ideas and successful approaches come and go. We should not forget them or undervalue those that are not currently in fashion.

## A key to a teacher's success

I developed a Band Handbook for elementary and junior high school and one for senior high. The material was chosen to fit the age level of the kids. This served as a basic textbook for planning, organization, informing, and building relationships that make a program work. It provided information for several groups: the parents, students, administration, etc. It helped me as a teacher to get into print things I was constantly saying. It had several key things which were important such as a calendar for the year, which avoids issues of date conflicts between parent and school.

The contents of the Band Handbook were:

1. *Band Beatitudes* by Mark Hindsley These are very good for younger kids.
2. *Why Music?* This was included for parents and administrators so they might sense the reason for music education.
3. *Facts about the Band* This helped parents and administrators be reminded of things, both musical and non-musical, important in the band.

4. Yearly Calendar. This is built around school year and contained concert dates, fund raising, etc.
5. Care of Music
6. Rehearsal Attendance Issues
7. Practice and Program Habits
8. Instrument Care
9. Information about Music Supplies (We needed this since we did not have a local music store.)
10. Copy of Booster By-Laws. This included the names of the officers with the dates for monthly meeting schedules, etc.
11. In high school, there were other rules appropriate for their age and activities.

*(Barbara Buehlman)*

## Evaluation over time

We do not know the effectiveness of our program until students have been in the program from six to eight years; this is enough time to see the implications of what has been taught and learned. We can see what part of the change is maturation, and what part results from teaching, learning, and planning for learning. We don't really know if we've hit the target until the bullet has arrived, but we must aim in advance of the hit, and must aim as well as we can.

*(Charles Olson)*

## Current problems

Girls' athletics, academics, part-time work, etc. have really cut into the band program at the high school level. This has had an effect even on high school districts where there are, for example, four other districts feeding into the high school. I'm a bit more fortunate than some middle and junior high schools because I have more time to work with my students; I have more time for their technical training for building things like intonation. I think some teachers aren't doing these things because, unfortunately, they are just very short on time.

*(Phillip A. Weinberg)*

## Changes in students and the school

Things have changed drastically over the last ten

years. In our school which is small, they offer so many things for students and the same kids are doing everything. I think there are still a few large school systems that are able to have fine concert bands; but many band programs, especially in smaller schools, have just deteriorated because the kids are in so many other things. When girls' athletics came in it just destroyed the music program. Prior to this, the boys were about twenty or thirty percent of the band and the balance was girls.

Another frustration is that the majority of the kids just don't practice week to week to the extent kids formerly did. We see the problems with these students and no matter how innovative a teacher one is, if they aren't going to go home and practice or exert effort to do something about a problem, a teacher can only say, "Well, I'll see you next week and we will try to work it out in the next fifteen-minute lesson." Many kids still come down from the study halls and practice, but they just don't practice as purposefully as previous students did. I see a general lack of motivation in many kids who are not likely to do anything on their own; it appears that somebody has to be guiding them constantly.

*(Richard Putzier)*

### Performance-based teacher training

Our profession has a considerable problem training teachers, we waste the time we have and we don't have enough time to do it right. One reason this problem has not been solved is that many music schools have not realized that students have learned much less than they thought.

At the University of Michigan we believe that music teaching is a performing art, consequently most criteria for grading and certification are performance based. Therefore, we ask our music education students to *show us* through performance what they can do with their musical knowledge and skills, instead of asking them to *tell us*.

*(James Froseth)*

### Teacher training

We're graduating more people now who are better at one end of the spectrum; they're able to teach a phrase, they're beautiful conductors. But they are not as good at the opposite end; they're not teaching the more cognitive and technical things such as posture, the names of lines and spaces, key signatures, fingerings, technical skills, etc.

I'm sure Bob Reynolds just shakes his head in frustration when he sees this twenty-three year old conductor with all the moves: he's beauty in motion but his band sounds terrible. The band either isn't paying attention or they don't understand what he's trying to tell them to do. He has to keep battling at what he wants them to do through visual communication. It is a test of wills all the time—it's a never ending battle, and who's going to win?

*(Michael Kaufman)*

### The future teachers

There's an awareness we should have and that is we're not attracting the kind of kid who is basically a good musician and plans to go into music education. The last thing they want to do is go into music education. Instead, they want to go into applied music because they don't want to put up with all this frustrating school business, and some in the applied studios are not encouraging them either. In some parts of the country and in some schools, the attitude of the private teachers is such that he will not accept you as a student if you're a music education student.

*(James Croft)*

### The absence of private teachers is not a disaster

Commander Beck from the Navy band listened to our group in Kansas City. He said, "It's obvious that you have a fine battery or fine group of private teachers in your area, because of the mature sound level and the intonation of this group." Well, we don't have any private teachers but they do have guidance week after week, year after year. I'm not a horn, double reed, brass, or flute major. I was a clarinet player in the Luther College band. I wouldn't begin to try to blow through those instruments but I do have a concept of sound and I have some pretty decent ideas on how to get kids to blow that way.

*(Lewis Larson)*

### Master teachers

I don't know whether there is a man with more teaching techniques than Fred Schroeder. We played in a quintet for a couple of years; we would just go to each other's homes, play for a while, break out the beer, have a little lunch, and just sit around and talk. Fred was a guru for all of us. He liked that role and played that role very well. We also enjoyed being at his feet because the he was the guy who gave me my first taste of the Stravinsky *Symphony for Wind Instruments*, the Hindemith pieces, the Schoenberg, the Messiaen, etc. I could go on and on and on to list the major wind pieces I became aware of through Fred Schroeder. There were few places at that time where one could get that exposure. He was light years ahead of his time because he was in the world of art.

*(James Croft)*

### Priorities

Maybe we should be spending some of the money from our long trips and festivals on commissioning works, on bringing live composers into the rehearsals, etc. In general, if we reexamined our priorities for expenditures and made changes, we would receive greater benefit.

*(Thomas H. Cook)*

### Computer software

We have used computer programs and synthesizers in a lab I set up. We have software programs such as Passport Designs, Poly Letter Midi Four Plus, and Utilities. We also have the Wenger Fingering Programs, which are useful particularly when changing a student from one instrument to another. First they work on the fingering program with the first three lessons. After two or three weeks a tuba player, for example, will be functioning well after switching from the trumpet. For flute, bassoon, and other woodwinds, this program helps them learn the trill fingerings and fingerings for higher pitches. During the course of the three years that I have them as students, I also use a music theory package in addition to the normal band package. The theory program is also a computer program.

*(R. G. Conlee)*

### Great conductors have been great teachers

Great conductors have been great teachers just by what they do. I studied with great conductors and they never knew I was studying with them. For example, I had an infinite number of lessons from Toscanini. I had a chance to watch the Saturday morning final rehearsals of the NBC Symphony Orchestra as I was tucked away in behind the glass in the NBC production booth. I also studied Stokowski at concerts; I studied Thomas Beecham when I was on tour with him as his man who packed and handled his bags. My job was to make certain that the bags and Mr. Beecham got on the right bus or train, and in the right car and auditorium.

I studied with these men and I am their pupil. I never paid them a dime for these lessons and they didn't know that I was studying with them. Except I have a feeling that some did; I think Beecham knew, because he knew I was sort of digging him all the way. Lots of people could not understand him easily because he was typically British; if one is turned off by the typically British one was going to be turned off by Mr. Beecham.

Beecham had a great intellect and was an ardent reader. When we went entered a hotel, he would pick up two copies of a paperback book. He would say, "You have exactly thirty minutes to report back here, I want to see how much you have read." He was one of the great scan readers of all time. He would then quiz me about the ideas in the book. I was a pretty good scan reader also, but after I hung out with Beecham I became a terrific scan reader!

*(Frederick Fennell)*

### The choice of equipment and instruments

Most people never realize that you can take an assorted group of people with assorted instruments, which is inevitable or unavoidable in many school systems, and make them successful if you put them on a good student-model mouthpiece that provides some uniformity. With a uniform and a well chosen mouthpiece, one can get a clarinet quality that is not possible on clarinets with an array of mouthpieces—with Heinz 57 varieties. This is less of a problem with trombones, euphoniums, and tubas than it is with trumpets, cornets, and clarinets.

*(Robert E. Foster)*

### Motivating and renewing the teacher

The most successful and happy band directors that I know, are the ones that keep growing. Teacher burn out has nothing to do with age or the years in service, it has to do with professional growth. The guys who grow the most, who are intellectually and musically the most curious, who continue to grow, are the ones who have the best experiences. The better experiences they have, the more they want to grow; the more they grow, the better experiences they want to have.

The guys who have burn out, after three or twenty years of teaching, invariably are the ones that quit growing. I cannot name a single exception to that. There are guys over sixty years old that are fabulous and I love to be around them because they are exciting. I have a friend in New York that will call just because he finds a new piece, discovers a new way to teach something, or finds anything that is new to him. He will call because something is exciting to him and he wants to share it. I think that is exciting and I love it.

I see other guys and I say, "What's the matter?" They say, "I'm burned out." I say, "That's really tough and you have only been teaching two years." There are many guys who get isolated, they spend more time either in their garden or as couch potatoes than they do reading the Hunsberger conducting book, or Leinsdorf's book *The Composers Advocate*, or James Levine's book on conducting, the new Percy Grainger biographical material— or a "jillion" things. There is so much neat stuff to grow with, and if they will grow their kids also will grow. The guys that quit growing have the bands that quit growing, have the bands that stink, and it is their own darn fault!

*(Robert E. Foster)*

### Preventing burn out

A way to do this is surround yourself with great music. Often we get overwhelmed with budgets, repairing instruments, working with scheduling, the administration, etc. and these are not the only things that can work against avoiding burn out. What we are really about is to improve ourselves as musicians and we do that by surrounding ourselves with great music. I never experience burn out when I am listening or surrounded with great music. I always experience burn out when I constantly let myself do only paper work.

*(Richard K. Hansen)*

### Teacher growth and development

I've always had in mind for young and old teachers, that we are constantly evaluating how effective we are. Change may be the one good thing that happens to us regularly. If we are continuously looking for ways to become more effective, or to understand what is happening, then we are in the process of what I would call healthy professional development.

*(Gerald Olson)*

I have been listening to hundreds of pieces of music, preparing hundreds of pieces of music, and listening to hundreds of concerts by other bands. By hearing both bands that are worse than mine and that are better than mine, and watching conductors that are both worse than I am and that are better than I am, I have become constantly aware that I am in a process of adapting and changing, and redoing and re-evaluating, and readjusting what I'm doing. If I didn't, it would be dull and boring. It's not always better, sometimes I do things that are not as good as what I have always done in the past. But I learn from that, and I don't do those things anymore.

*(Charles Olson)*

### The opportunity to exchange ideas

It is unfortunate that band directors do not hang around the music stores on Saturday mornings anymore. Many invaluable ideas, such as those about music, performing, and teaching, were exchanged in those sessions.

*(Robert E. Foster)*

### Don't use chairs with backs

The use of stools instead of chairs can solve posture problems. I suggest you use stools through all grade levels. This helps them develop a habit and if this is done for a period of time, a student will sit properly later even if the chair has a back. I see so much poor posture and this takes much time to keep changing poor posture and stressing good posture. Why not create a situation where good posture occurs on its own instead?

*(Frank Battisti)*

### Teaching posture

Standing as one plays is usually not the problem. Somehow, with that full posture, things work better. With trombones especially, I have them learn to stand first and then learn to sit. I try to get the sitting posture to be close to the standing posture.

I'm not sure I think standing is always better than sitting. I agree that sitting gives more strength to brass playing, because you're not having to support the whole body. Their feet should be in front of them in such a way that they could almost get up. Sometimes the sitting really allows you to relax more. One clue that tells them if they are in the right sitting position is if they feel some weight on their feet. You must, however, get used to both sitting and standing.

*(L. Keating Johnson)*

### Equipment for beginners

When kids start as beginners they rent the stand, a mirror, the music, and the instrument as one package. The mirror is six by nine inches and is used for embouchure development. The rental fee was a composite fee that provided for all the equipment.

*(Frank Battisti)*

### Possible cultural differences

I have had a year of experience teaching Apache Indian students and do not know how they developed their mathematical and other fundamental concepts. Other teachers tell me that their culture is based upon the concept of four, while our culture is based on threes. Music in duple meter or quick six-eight goes all right; but, the students do not relate to triple meter very well, nor do they react easily to music in three. Other teachers also feel that there is definitely a cultural readiness that is not in line with our thinking and they have trouble in the teaching of other areas that seemed to be explained by this. Incidentally, television just came in the last five years when cable became available. Prior to this, they were not very familiar with English.

*(Thomas Herrera)*

### A teacher's challenge

The hardest thing is to get an introverted kid to play a nice sound.

*(Robert Allan)*

### Monitoring practice

I wish we could have a small intercom system set up through the different practice rooms just to monitor some things. I know this is not possible, but I always thought it would be a good idea. We could monitor several students at one time, keep them going, and say, for example, "Well, why don't you try this?" or "Are you sure you are doing those scales with all the different articulations?" This idea would make practice room monitoring much like monitoring in the class piano laboratory.

*(Richard Putzier)*

### Big schools or small schools

I see so many people wanting to go to bigger schools. I don't think that's the answer at all. I have teacher friends that started in little schools and went to bigger schools. They wanted more kids, more time, and la-dee-da-dee. In small schools, they had an excuse why their groups didn't sound good. Then they get to the big schools and all of a sudden their excuses now are, "There's too many kids, not enough time, and not enough dedication." They just went from little excuses to bigger excuses.

*(Lewis Larson)*

### Maintenance

On one night a year, we clean all the instruments!
*(Anthony J. Maiello)*

### Good ideas and their contributors

What worries me in our profession is how we sometimes form these mental alliances and are afraid to let other ideas in. Perhaps we are afraid of somehow betraying our gods, or going against the ideas of a person to whom we have an allegiance. Instead, one should learn as much as one can from as many different people as possible.

Ideas also can be like fads or fashions—they are in and then they are out. There was a time that if you didn't do it the way Bill Revelli did it, you just didn't know what you were doing. Then all of a sudden people are saying, "That's not the way to do it, this is the way to do it." It is unfortunate if people lose sight of all the great things that are happening that they are not interested in at that moment. They forget that ideas, models, trends, composers, and whatever have gone in and have gone out. If we remember this, we would not forget our past and forget to pay respect to the people who have made it possible for us to be where we are right now.

*(Eugene Corporon)*

### College and pre-college students

People say, "Yeah, well it's real easy for you to talk like this because you don't face the parents, you don't face the kids that skip rehearsal, you don't face the drugs, you don't face etc.." I look at them and say, "Do you realize your seniors are my freshman within three months?" I mean they are the same kids; they haven't changed that much. I just get them at a different point in their lives.

*(William W. Wiedrich)*

### Teaching transposition

I use Hunsberger's book that has a lot of chunks of fragments of scores. I take the kids in my college class and assign parts for them in a way that involves everybody in the class transposing some part to another instrument. We also take something that has a four or five-part scoring, have the class take whatever instrumentation is in the class, and make that work. Then it becomes sort of an orchestration class, makes them use rehearsal techniques, and everything else. Like, some guy puts a flute on the tenor line; even if it could reach the tenor line, it might or might not work—that is an excellent way for them to discover some of those things.

*(Donald Wilcox)*

### The teacher must make the material work

I have the kids do a lot of singing, but I've always had the kids do a lot of singing. Years ago, Jim Froseth and I had started out with an idea of writing a book together called, *The Singing Band.* I sent him all of the material and it was lost in the mail. I was in such a hurry to get that off because I'd finally gotten it done that I didn't make a copy. I tested it on several schools in the Tampa Bay area and I found that it worked just great when I did it; but it didn't work worth a darn when somebody else did it who didn't come to it with as much enthusiasm, interest, or ear that I brought to it.

*(James Croft)*

### Matching the student and the instrument

Rarely are our kids playing on instruments that they shouldn't be. In other words, they are not playing instruments on which they just cannot get good tones. The quality of the instrument is important, but more important is the quality of the way they adapt to that. We might switch ten to fifteen percent of the kids, including clarinets to bass clarinets, to different instruments to help them adapt for success and to improve the ensemble's instrumentation.

I start many flutes and I'll pick some better ones and switch them to double reeds. I really like switching flute players to bassoon or oboe much better than I like switching clarinets. By the time my clarinets have played a year they are really developing a pretty firm embouchure. I have not had nearly as good a luck at switching clarinets as switching flutes, because of the stiffer jaw of the clarinetists.

If I'm starting three to five flute players, I might even tell them, "I'm looking for an outstanding flute player who eventually will move to oboe or bassoon." They know that from day one, so they look at this as a reward. I usually try to get somebody who's outgoing, somebody that would want to do solos within the band and somebody that's going to catch on quickly. I'll take them up to the point where they might have played two years and have developed a good sound and vibrato. I think that if kids have gotten their vibrato going on their flute, this helps them do very well on double reeds; they succeed and progress so much sooner.

*(Lewis Larson)*

### A library of forms

I found, over the years, that I was making up this form for one purpose and another form for something else. I finally set up a number of forms in one of my files. I put everything in it, no matter how useless it could be, and I made a lot of copies. For instance, I have a pop concert form that is very simple. It has just three columns headed song, announcer and technical. I type the song title, what the announcer's going to say, and what the lighting crew is going to do; this saves so much work. I've others for housing when we're going to take a trip, piano recital forms, study hall passes, solo and ensemble contest forms, try-out forms, challenge-system forms, practice forms, and many others.

*(Frank Schulz)*

### Challenges

We use seating challenges except for two weeks before a concert. They can come in any time and challenge the person above them. They must announce their challenge to the other person and to the teachers. If the other person doesn't show up they lose their chair.

*(Frank Schulz)*

### We should teach embouchure early

One starts talking about this and forming it in the first day, but one can never stop talking about it at any time in their public school experience. This concern is unending.

*(Barbara Buehlman)*

### *A course on computers and synthesizers*

This program is a kind of primer for junior high school students at their level. This stretches their abilities on science and mathematics. This enables them to do some composing and they are able to compose a thirty-two to sixty-four measure composition through this means.

*(R. G. Conlee)*

### *The power of a concept and of heredity*

One of the best bands here had embouchures that are not picturesque. Yet they play well because they had a concept of how that piece or instrument should sound. It makes no difference that the mouthpiece is off to one side, that the clarinetist's chin isn't flat, and the flute embouchures weren't "poutee." They made the sound because that was the sound that was demanded of them.

If you look at artists who have come down to us from the centuries, they have all adapted to their own unique needs to be able to do what they have to do, because their ear, mind, and ideas demanded it. Louis Armstrong, for example, probably should never have tried to play the trumpet because of the way he was made up.

On the other hand Maurice Andre was built to be a trumpet player and has never had a problem playing the trumpet. With his embouchure—no upper lip at all—he can play endlessly and without any effort in the high register. It's just one of those things he is made to do. Surely he has worked at things, but his set up is great.

*(Charles Olson)*

### *The music and the lyrics*

Barbra Streisand burst on the scene almost totally unknown, and that first album absolutely caused a sensation. The back cover of the second album she did was full of letters and quotes from various people. The fascinating thing to me was that every single one of those gorgeous comments about her came from a writer of words—think about that. Most of them said, "Here's a girl, here's a singer that for one of the few times in my experience is willing to sacrifice the music for the lyrics, instead of vice versa."

When Streisand sings a song, you not only hear those words, but you live them. So if a person doesn't speak or understand the musical language, we still speak English and understand the music. What is the big argument in this country about opera in English or opera with English titles projected across the stage? With that help, you can grasp and comprehend it, and therefore you react to it one way or the other.

*(Alfred Reed)*

### *Jazz band programs*

I created a monster when we started to organize what is called our "Big-Band Bash." We have a dance that's based on all the music of the big band era. The first time I did it, I just thought it would be nice because some of my students asked me about jobbing; some weren't going to go into college, but were interested in playing music. They were always asking me where I played and what it was like.

We booked a large room at the Holiday Inn and we estimated a couple hundred people would attend. Instead, over six hundred people attended the event. Now this has grown so I feel compelled to do it every year because a thousand people attend every time, and our band parents now use it as a fund raiser.

Since the beginning, I've added a second jazz ensemble. I have my school bands play first. I also have an alumni band and they play second. At first my alumni band wasn't very strong, but you should hear that band now; they are very, very good.

*(Howard A. Lehman)*

### *Response to new instructional approaches*

Though many band and orchestra directors are not aware of Manhattanville as an approach to teaching music through composition, I could not exist without it. It is an excellent way to do what I like to do, and that is get kids inside of music. Unfortunately, some directors don't want to be bothered with it. If they would try it and see the excitement it generates in kids, they would not want to do without it. This approach excites kids and one does not need to beat them on the head anymore. When the teacher discovers how this excites them, it's hard to return to the previous style of teaching. It takes a while to learn to use it and to establish it in a program, but all the kids that have gone through my classes at the University of Oregon have used some part of it; and I'm grateful for that.

*(John C. McManus)*

# Appendices

# Appendix I

# Methodology of the Research

The material in this appendix comprises the original survey materials, and includes the invitation letter, a page of sample techniques that define the detail and concreteness of the material being sought, and a checklist. The purpose of this checklist was to stimulate the contributors to think of specific ideas and teaching techniques that they felt were especially effective.

The original material also included response forms, calendar forms, response letters, stamped return envelopes, a list of persons who supported the project, and other materials.

### Sample Letter of Invitation

Dr. Richard C. Jones                                                                 June 13, 1988
State University of Any State
Department of Music
Any State, New York

Dear Richard:

I am writing for your assistance with a project in your area of expertise, band conducting and instrumental music teaching. The project's goal is to compile ideas and techniques of a direct, practical nature that are used in instrumental music sectionals, class-lessons and rehearsals. I have enclosed a sheet of six basic examples to help define the concreteness of what is sought. The techniques and ideas are those usable with students at any level, either elementary, junior high, high school or college.

Your assistance is sought for two reasons:

   (1) Your contributions can enrich the material considerably, therefore, I hope you will agree to be interviewed yourself.

   (2) You likely can recommend the two or three truly exceptional, experienced teachers of whom you are aware. I would also like to tell them in the invitation that you suggested they be contacted.

Because there are so few sources for this material, the INSTRUMENTALIST and GIA Publications have expressed considerable interest in the results of the interviews. When the project is complete, it will be unique in that it will provide several hundred teaching techniques and ideas, of more than twenty different types. The value of this to instrumental music teachers and music education students should be considerable.

To increase the credibility and impact of the material, the name of the contributor will be included in the publications if an idea is used.

I invite you to give about an hour of your time for a telephone interview so you can relate your ideas. If you agree to do so, fill out the enclosed form, especially the information about your schedule and phone numbers. I will be making the first group of calls between April 15, 1988 and July 15, 1988. Therefore, return the form with your signature as soon as possible. Remember also to include the sheet recommending others I should invite.

If possible, would you specify several times both evening and weekend, as well as morning and afternoon, for an interview. This will provide the flexibility needed to arrange your interview around the schedule of others as well as my own.

Thank you very much, I am looking forward to the interview with you.

Sincerely yours,


Joseph L. Casey



The following persons have already been interviewed or have agreed to take part in this project:

H. Robert Reynolds, University of Michigan, Ann Arbor, Michigan
Miles Johnson, St. Olaf College, Northfield, Minnesota
James Croft, Florida State University, Tallahassee, Florida
Donald Wilcox, West Virginia University, Morgantown, West Virginia
Arnald D.Gabriel, George Mason University, Fairfax, Virginia
Frank Bencriscutto, University of Minnesota, Minneapolis, Minnesota
William Revelli, University of Michigan, Ann Arbor, Michigan
Mark Hindsley, University of Illinois, Urbana, Illinois
Richard Strange, University of Arizona, Tempe, Arizona
Donald DeRoche, DePaul University, Chicago, Illinois
Thomas L.Dvorak, University of Wisconsin, Milwaukee, Wisconsin
Alfred Reed, University of Miami, Miami, Florida
Larry Rachleff, University of Southern California, Los Angeles, California
Richard Floyd, UIL State Director, University of Texas, Austin, Texas
Ray Cramer, University of Indiana, Bloomington, Indiana
Greg Hansen, University of Utah, Provo, Utah
Frank Battisti, New England Conservatory of Music, Boston, Mass
Harry Begian, University of Illinois, Urbana, Illinois
Frank Wicks, Louisiana State University, Baton Rouge, Louisiana

<u>SAMPLE TECHNIQUES OR IDEAS</u>: These samples may help clarify or define the practical, concrete nature of the workshop's content.

------------------------------------------------------------

<u>Building Technique</u> I have the entire class play a scale up and down with a designated rhythm. Then, I ask individuals to alternate with the entire class lesson or section without dropping a beat. If there are five students, the scale will be performed 5 times by the class plus 5 more times, once each, by individuals in the class. At 60 beats per minute, this takes about 90 seconds of class time. (James Kasprzyk, Rolling Meadows HS, Rolling Meadows, IL.)

<u>Reading Ahead, Drill &/or Memorizing</u> I write a rhythm pattern of, for example, four measures on the board. After we play the pattern through once, I erase the last measure as they begin all four measures the second time, including the one I erased. They keep repeating the four measures, as I erase the 3rd measure, remembering all four measures though the last two are erased. Finally, all are erased and the full pattern is performed from memory. The entire process is continuous, non-stop! (Christine Dworak, Niles Elementary, Niles, IL.)

<u>Teaching the Accent</u> To teach the accent, I ask students to play a series of quarter notes at a steady tempo, not too fast, say 100 beats per minute at MF. After performing this two or three times so the students play this well and are concentrating, I ask them to play the 5th note one volume level louder, or Forte. When they have heard and performed this accurately, I tell them that we call this an "accent" in music and show them its basic notation mark. Then we practice the traditional accent marks in different locations. When they are clear and accurate about this, we transferred it to appropriate spots in a composition we were are rehearsing. (James Stivers, Univ. of Nevada, Las Vegas)

<u>Building Relationships</u> If a student asks that I move, move my podium, or adjust my beat so he can see better, I do so. The reason is that I want him to know that his feelings are important; and, if I adjust what I do and it helps him play better, it is a signal that both he and his playing are important to me and the group. This may establish that we can ask things of each other as we "pool" our efforts for the musical end. (H. Robert Reynolds, U of Michigan)

<u>Exposure to New or Different Music</u> In rehearsal I may play a recorded excerpt of unfamiliar music. Spike Jones, a symphonic piece, jazz artist, singer, Medieval piece, or electronic music. I tell them nothing about it in advance, we just listen for a few minutes. I might write the name/composer on the board, the record number, the performer, etc. Sometimes I say nothing. Sometimes they make comments or ask questions, or I point out things they might notice. It works, partly because they are not under pressure; and, each time the music is a surprise, unnamed and hits them when they have less preconceptions present. (Don Caneva, formerly Hersey High School, Arlington Hts, IL.)

<u>Understanding Dynamics</u> When helping young students learn to play different volume levels, I write a rhythm pattern on the board and place a square or rectangle of equal size under each note. I tell them that the size of the drawing represents how loud each note is to be. The students are asked to perform the rhythm slowly in unison at MF, striving to perform each note at the same volume level. I then make the drawing under one note larger (or smaller). We then play it again with the amount of sound on the individual notes that is suggested by the two different sizes of the drawings. From there, I relate volume level to the size of beat patterns. (Tom Stone, Latin School, Chicago)

> THIS MATERIAL IS OFFERED TO HELP YOU THINK AHEAD OR
> PREPARE FOR THE INTERVIEW.

The material on the following pages contains lists of <u>basic objectives</u> for instrumental music and <u>categories of types of teaching techniques</u> that could be used to attain such objectives; and, <u>examples of specific teaching ideas, challenges, and materials; problem areas, etc.</u> about which teachers may want to give techniques and ideas.

These lists are a result of suggestions made during the pilot stage of this project. At that time both college and pre-college teachers requested examples of <u>objectives, ideas & types</u> that would help them think ahead about what they could offer during the interview, as well as keep to the topic and use time efficiently.

These items could be seen as my "shopping list" for techniques and ideas. You might find these lists helpful, but do not hesitate to offer other objectives, techniques, or ideas that do not seem to be suggested by these lists.

Since the lists are rather long, I do not expect teachers to have a technique for each idea or objective.

> <u>Musical Sensitivity</u> "How do you develop students' musicianship & skills so they play
> with skill and musical sensitivity in relation to, or in instances of the following?

<u>rhythm</u>
    pulse
    tempo
    choice of tempo
    ritardando
    accelerando
    rubato
    define & maintain tempo
    meter
    pick-up notes
    rests
    pauses
<u>tone</u>
    idiomatic tone color of
      individual instruments
    section tone color
    section blend
    full ensemble blend
    sustaining sound
<u>phrasing</u>
    musical expression, in general

making a "musical statement"
defining beginnings of phrases
defining ends of phrases
shaping phrases
perform dynamic & stress changes
    within a phrase's beg & end
fermata
tenuto
defining a musical style
<u>dynamics</u>
    selecting the appropriate
      dynamic level
    defining dynamic levels
    playing dynamic levels
    increase & decrease
      of dynamic levels
<u>intonation</u>
    matching pitch
    tuning intervals
    sensing tonal centers—tension and
      repose

Skills   "How would you teach students so they acquire, develop & maintain the following skills?"

position: (for all instruments)
   arm
   hand
   finger
   instrument
   embouchure
posture:
   sitting
   standing
breathing:
   inhale
   exhale
breath support:
   control of air
   release of air
   air stream
   "speed" of air stream
articulations: separated
   marcato
   staccato
   ties
   varying basic articulation
      because of style
articulations: connected
   legato
   slurred
   ties
   varying basic articulation
      because of style
beginning attack:
   hard to soft
release:
   breath
   tongued

facility:
   tonguing
   speed
   accuracy
   range
   flexibility
ensemble playing:
   section balance, unity and precision
   full ensemble balance, unity and
      precision
   relationship of dominant to subordinate
      parts & passages
music literacy:
   Reading:
      rhythms in duple and triple meter
      rhythms in mixed meter
      pitch notation
      time signature
      key signatures & accidentals
   other notation markings:
      clefs
      phrasing
   articulation markings:
      breath
      accents
      dynamics
      staccato
      tempo
      legato
      repeats, endings, etc.
      slurred
      Italian/English terms, etc.
      ties
      D.S., D.C., Coda signs, etc.

Type of Technique "When teaching students, do you use teaching techniques of different types?" Please think of examples for a number of these types.

spoken word related:
   rhythm syllables
   pitch syllables
   beat counting
   measure counting
   counting rhythms
   associating words to rhythm patterns

associating words to pitch patterns
imagery
inflection
metaphor
simile
analogy
questioning

kinesthetic related:
  physical movement
  eurythmics
  feeling of subdivisions
  drill/repetition
  simulation: of physical operations
  simulation: through physical
    gestures
  visual related:
  non-conducting gestures:
    hands
    arms
    body postures
  demonstration:
    teacher
    peer
  feedback:
    mirrors
    visual recorded performance
  explanations in conjunction with:
    drawings
    pictures
aural/visual related:
  feedback:
    electronic tuning devices
    video tape
    breathing apparatus
  feedback:
    peer observation and evaluation
    student, self observation
  aural related:
  feedback:
    peer performance of subject's
      performance
    audio tape
    metronome
    electronic tuners
    counting the "beats" for intonation
musical modeling:

teacher performance
peer performance
audio recorded performance
simulation:
  sung, chanted or spoken
  musical imagery and audiation
building of listening/aural perception:
  playing by ear
  rote learning
  building listening perception
    sequentially
  defining what to listen for/listening for "?"
standard setting:
  error prevention procedures:
    analysis of music
    structuring of home practice
    pre-hearing of phrase, passage or section
    planning/plotting phrasing
    planning/plotting articulations
    planning/plotting dynamics
    identifying rhythm difficulties
    identifying problems of leaps, range
    identifying intonation problem spots
    identifying technical problem spots
    pre-hearing through study
    preparation
  error detection & correction-examining the
    performance:
    by passage
    by section
    by phrase
    by articulations
    by dynamics
    by rhythms
    by identifying problems of leaps, range
    by intonation
    by technique
    by attacks & releases
    by breathing
    by preparation practices

> Making Techniques Work "What do you do, value or believe that helps you make full use of any techniques or other "skillful ways of teaching" that you have in your teaching repertoire?"

While using specific skillful ways of teaching things is very important, the teacher's personality, convictions, determination, and clear ideas or vision of what the musical or educational results may be, is also important. In fact, some feel that the teacher's personality is the essential catalyst for successful teaching.

Therefore, I am also looking for ideas, beliefs or insights that guide, explain, or motivate the teacher and his efforts. Perhaps, for example, some teachers have ideas that help them determine why they teach, what to teach, when to teach it, what teaching technique to use, how to set high standards, how they relate with students, etc. If such insights can guide teachers, then the techniques (the means) may be used more wisely in attaining important goals and objectives (the ends).

---

Planning and Structure: "When you are teaching, what basic approaches or considerations help you structure what you are trying to do?"

---

ex. sequential presentation of content &/or skills ex. weekly, monthly, yearly planning
ex. whole-parts-whole learning
ex. class lesson format, objectives, considerations, etc.
ex. 1st lesson format, objectives, considerations, etc.
ex. rehearsal format, objectives, considerations, etc.
ex. sectional format, objectives, considerations, etc.
ex. class lesson format, objectives, considerations, etc.
ex. structuring students' home practice, concert attendance, etc.
ex. use of memorization
ex. use of solo performance
ex. use of small ensemble performance
ex. determining types, size, objectives, etc. while giving assignments
ex. assigning specific conquerable tasks

---

Use of Special/Unique Materials: "Are there any materials you use that are especially helpful in your teaching?"

---

ex. "Tap" programs (from Temporal Acuity)
ex. simulation fingering device for the Apple Computer
ex. "Tune-Up" Swan (published)
ex. Instrumental Score Reading Program-Froseth/Grunow
ex. Kenneth Evans "Woodwind Techniques Movies/Pictures" & "Fundamentals Outline"
ex. listening labs, related recordings, at-home educational aids, etc.

---

Unique Problems in Instrumental Instruction: "Are there any specific areas of instruction within instrumental music that are particularly troublesome, or for which you have suggestions?"

---

ex. How do you involve & instruct a percussion section during rehearsal?
ex. What specific things (ex. melodic playing, intonation, technique, style, blend, concentration, etc.) do you find difficult to develop?
ex. How do you get students to comply with musical & technical requests, suggestions, assignments, etc. in and out-of-school?
ex. How do you teach students to follow conducting gestures?
ex. What specific successful musical and extra-musical motivational techniques have you used?
ex. How do you teach students with varying abilities, interests, etc.?
ex. How do you teach the "difficult" student?
ex. How do you alter what comprises the band's sound?
ex. How do you develop the students' sense for aesthetic values?

# APPENDIX II

# Contributors to this Study

There were 138 persons responding to this study. Of this group 58 were pre-college teachers and 80 were now teaching in college. Over half of the college teachers taught previously in grade levels below the college level.

Mr. Robert Allan, Retired
Director of Bands
Illinois State University
Normal, IL 61671

Mr. Richard Alnes
Director of Music
Lincoln High School
Wisconsin Rapids, WI 54494

Mr. John Anderson
Director of Bands
Indiana State University
Terra Haute, IN 47809

Mr. James Arrowood
Director of Bands
University of Wisconsin
Stevens Point, WI 54481

Mr. Frank Battisti
Wind Ensemble Conductor
New England Conservatory
Boston, MA 02115

Mr. George Bedell
Supervisor of Music
South Burlington High School
South Burlington, VT 05401

Dr. Frank Bencriscutto
Director of Bands
University of Minnesota
Minneapolis, MN 55455

Mr. Gregory Bimm
Marion Catholic High School
Chicago Heights, IL 60411

Mr. Jack Brookshire
Music Department
West Junior High School
Lawrence, KS 66044

Patricia Brumbaugh
Director of Bands
Arkansas State University
Jonesboro, AR 72401

Barbara Buehlman
Music Teacher-Conductor
Glenview, IL 60025

Mr. Carl Bly
Music Department
Lake Braddock High School
Burke, VA 22015

Mr. Donald E. Casey
Department of Music Education
Northwestern University
Evanston, IL 60201

Dr. Joseph L. Casey
Department of Music Education
DePaul University
Chicago, IL 60614

Mr. Stanley Cate
Music Department
Southside High School
Fort Smith, AR 72901

Dr. Gordon Childs
Department of Music
University of Wyoming
Laramie, WY 82070

Dr. Gary Ciepluch
Music Department
Case Western Reserve
Cleveland, OH 44106

Mr. R. G. Conlee
Music Department
Mt. Pleasant High School
Mt. Pleasant, IA 52641

Mr. Thomas Cook
Director of Bands
University of Montana
Missoula, MT 59812

Mr. Hal Cooper
Director of Bands
Arkansas Tech
Russellville, AR 72801

Mr. Steven Cooper
Music Teacher
Clarendon Hills, IL 60514

Dr. Eugene Corporon
Director of Bands
University of Cincinnati
Cincinnati, OH 45219

Mr. Ray E. Cramer
Director of Bands
Indiana University
Bloomington, IN 47405

Dr. James Croft
Director of Bands
Florida State University
Tallahassee, FL 32306

Mr. Marc M. Davis
Music Department
Poway High School
Poway, CA 92064

Mr. Thomas L. Davis
School of Music
The University of Iowa
Iowa City, IA 52242

Mr. David Deitemyer
Music Department
Oak Lawn High School
Oak Lawn, IL 60453

436

Judy Delzell
Department of Music Education
Ohio State University
Columbus, OH 43210

Dr. Donald DeRoche
Director of Bands
DePaul University
Chicago, IL 60614

Mr. Thomas L. Dvorak
Director of Bands
University of Wisconsin
Milwaukee, WI 53141

Christine Dworak
Music Department
Niles Elementary School
Niles, IL 60648

Mr. Butler Eitel, Retired
Director of Bands
University of Montana
Brookings, SD 57006

Marion Etzel, Chairperson
Department of Music Education
Roosevelt University
Chicago, IL 60605

Dr. Frederick Fennell, Conductor
Tokyo Kosei Wind Orchestra
Siesta Key, FL 34242

Dr. Richard Fischer
Director of Bands
Concordia University
River Forest, IL 60305

Mr. Richard Floyd
University Interscholastic League
State Director of Music
University of Texas
Austin, TX 78713

Mr. Robert Floyd
Music Department
Berkner High School
Richardson, TX 76909

Dr. Leon Fosha, Retired
Department of Music Education
University of Indiana
Bloomington, IN 47401

Mr. Robert Foster
Director of Bands
University of Kansas
Lawrence, KS 66045

Dr. James O. Froseth
Chairperson
Department of Music Education
University of Michigan
Ann Arbor, MI 48103

Pamela Gearhart
Orchestra Director
Ithaca College
Ithaca, NY 14850

Mr. Donald Gee
Music Department
Ouachita Parish School
Monroe, LA 71203

Dr. Donald S. George
Director of Bands
University of Wisconsin
Eau Claire, WI 54701

Mr. Robert Grechesky
Director of Bands
Butler University
Indianapolis, IN 46208

Mr. Michael Golemo
Acting Director of Bands
University of Akron
Akron, OH 44325

Dr. Richard Grunow
Department of Music Education
Eastman School of Music
Rochester, NY 14618

Dr. Paul Haack, Chairperson
Department of Music Education
University of Minnesota
Minneapolis, MN 55455

Mr. Michael Haithcock
Director of Bands
Baylor University
Waco, TX 76798

Mr. David Hans
Music Department
Barrington High School
Barrington, IL 60010

Mr. Richard Hansen
Conductor of Bands
St. Cloud State University
St. Cloud, MN 56301

Mr. Thomas Herrera
Music Department
Rice Unified School District
Tucson, AZ 85737

Kjellrun K. Hestekin
Director of the Band
Memorial University
St. Johns, Newfoundland
Canada, AIC 557

Mr. Michael Hiatt
Music Department
Anoka Senior High School
Anoka, MN 55303

Mr. Gary Hill
Director of Bands
University of Missouri
Kansas City, MO 64110

Mr. Mark Hindsley
Director of Bands-Emeritus
University of Illinois
Urbana, IL 61820

Mr. Sherman Hong
Music Department
University of Southern Mississippi
Hattiesburg, MS 39401

Donald R. Hunsberger, Conductor
Eastman School of Music
Rochester, NY 14618

Mr. L. Keating Johnson
Director of Bands
Washington State University
Pullman, WA 99164

Mr. Miles Johnson
Director of Bands
St. Olaf College
Northfield, MN 55057

Mr. Robert Jorgensen, Retired
Music Department
Urbana High School
Urbana, IL 61801

Mr. Michael Kaufman
Music Department
Grand Ledge High School
Grand Ledge, MI 48837

Mr. Ross Kellan
Music Department
Glenbard East High School
Lombard, IL 60148

Dr. Richard Kennell
Associate Dean
College of Musical Arts
Bowling Green State University
Bowling Green, OH 43403

Mr. John Kinnison
Executive Director
Illinois Music Educators Assoc.
Ottawa, IL 61350

Mr. Craig Kirchhoff
Director of Bands
University of Minnesota
Minneapolis, MN 55455

Dr. Edward Kocher
Associate Dean
School of Music
DePaul University
Chicago, IL 60614

Mr. Daniel Kohut
Department of Music Education
University of Illinois
Urbana, IL 61820

Mr. John LaCava
Music Department
Lake Braddock Secondary School
Burke, VA 22015

Mr. Daniel LaGare
Music Department
Deerfield, IL 60015

Mr. Kenneth Larsen
Music Department
Red River High School
Grand Forks, ND 48201

Mr. Lewis Larson
Music Department
Springfield Senior High School
Springfield, MN 56087

Theta Lee
Music Department
Public Schools
Wellington, IL 60973

Mr. Ross Leeper
Music Department
Simpson College
Indianola, IA 50125

Mr. Howard Lehman
Music Department
North High School
Eau Claire, WI 54703

Mr. Robert Levy
Director of Bands
Lawrence University
Appleton, WI 54912

Mr. Edward S. Lisk
Music Department
Oswego Public Schools
Oswego, NY 13126

Mr. Willam Long
Music Department
Bozeman Junior High School
Bozeman, MT 58715

Mr. Timothy Mahr
Director of Bands
University of Minnesota
Duluth, MN 55812

Dr. Clifford K. Madsen
School of Music
Florida State University
Tallahassee, FL 32306

Dr. Francis Marciniak
Director of Bands
Rhode Island College
Providence, RI 02908

Mr. Anthony Maiello
Director of Bands
George Mason University
Fairfax, VA 22030

Mr. Larry Maupin
Music Department
Grand Island, NE 68801

Mr. John C. McManus
School of Music-Retired
University of Oregon
Eugene, OR 97403

Mr. Allan R. McMurray
Director of Bands
College of Music
University of Colorado
Boulder, CO 80309

Mr. Steve McNeal
Music Department
Fort Collins, CO 80521

Melanie Michalak
Music Department
Evergreen Park High School
Evergreen Park, IL 60642

Dr. Robert Morsch
Director of Bands
Georgia State University
Atlanta, GA 30303

Mr. Dwaine Nelson
Department of Music
University of Saskatchewan
Saskatoon, SK (Canada)

Mr. Gordon Nelson
Music Department
Appleton Area School District
Appleton, WI 54915

Mr. Ronald Nickelsen
Music Department
Kenneth Murphy Junior High
Zion, IL 60099

Judith A. Niles
Music Department
Bainbridge-Guilford
Bainbridge, NY 13733

Dr. Gerald B. Olson
Department of Music Education
University of Wisconsin
Madison, WI 53706

Mr. Charles B. Olson
Director of Bands
Bethel College
St. Paul, MN 55112

Mr. Terry A. Oxley
Director of Bands
University of Pennsylvania
Bloomsburg, PA 17815

Mr. Roman Palmer
Music Department
Indian Trail Junior High School
Addison, IL 60101

Dr. Stanley J. Paul
Department of Music Education
University of Oklahoma
Norman, OK 73019

Mr. H. Stephan Payne
Music Department
Billings, MT 59104

Mr. John P. Paynter
Director of Bands/Conducting Chr.
Northwestern University
School of Music
Evanston, IL 60201

Mr. Douglas Peterson
Music Department
Elk Grove High School
Elk Grove, IL 60007

Nancy Plantinga
Music Department
Indian Prairie District
Naperville, IL 60540

Mr. James D. Ployhar
Composer and Arranger
Fargo, ND 58103

Mr. Richard Putzier
Music Department
Mondovi High School
Mondovi, WI 54755

Mr. Larry Rachleff
Conductor of Ensembles
University of Southern California
Los Angeles, CA 90007

Dr. Rudolf Radocy
Department of Music Education
University of Kansas
Lawrence, KS 66045

Sharon Razor, Coordinator
Department of Music Education
Wright State University
Dayton, OH 45435

Mr. Alfred Reed
School of Music
University of Miami
Coral Gables, FL 33124

Mr. H. Robert Reynolds
Director of Wind Organizations
School of Music
University of Michigan
Ann Arbor, MI 48109

Mr. Walter Rodby, Retired
Music Department
Homewood-Flossmoor HS
Joliet, IL 60435

Dr. Roseanne Rosenthal, President
VanderCook College of Music
Chicago, IL 60616

Dr. Dwayne P. Sagan
Director of Bands
Peabody College
Vanderbilt University
Nashville, TN 37235

Cynthia St. Peter
Music Department
Gross School
Brookfield, IL 60513

Mr. Ed Schaefle
Music Department
Public Schools
Salem, OR 97301

Mary Jo Schwab
Music Department
Afton, WY 83110

Mr. Scott Schwab
Music Department
Afton, WY 83110

Dr. Scott Shuler
State of Connecticut
Department of Education
Hartford, CT 06145

Mr. Lance Shultz
Music Department
North Senior High School
Downers Grove, IL 60515

Mr. Frank Schulz, Retired
Music Department
Orono High School
Long Lake, MI 55356

Dr. Stanley Schleuter
School of Music
Indiana University
Bloomington, IN 47402

Christie Speed
Music Department
Grand Island, NE 68801

Mr. Dominic Spera
School of Music-Jazz Studies
University of Indiana
Bloomington, IN 47402

Dr. James Stivers
Department of Music
University of Nevada
Las Vegas, NV 89154

Mr. Richard Strange
Director of Bands
Arizona State University
Tempe, AZ 85281

Mr. Richard Suddendorf, Retired
Director of Bands
Western Michigan University
Kalamazoo, MI 49001

Dr. Jerold Sundet, Retired
Orchestra Conductor
Minot State College
Minot, ND 58701

Mr. Ed Susmilch
Music Department
Immaculate Conception HS
Elmhurst, IL 60126

Mr. Bryce Taylor
Music Department
Alice High School
Alice, TX 78332

Mr. John Thompson
Music Department
New Trier High School
Winnetka, IL 60091

Dr. Mallory Thompson
Director of Bands
University of South Florida
Tampa, FL 33620

Sandra P. Thompson
Music Department
Wheeling School District
Wheeling, IL 62479

Janet Tweed
Music Department
Waunakee Public Schools
Waunakee, WI 53597

Mr. Phillip Weinberg
Music Department
Spring Wood School District
Hanover Park, IL 60103

Mr. Myron Welch
Director of Bands
The University of Iowa
Iowa City, IA 52240

Dr. David Whitwell, Conductor
California State University
Northridge, CA 91324

Mr. Frank Wickes
Director of Bands
Louisiana State University
Baton Rouge, LA 70803

Mr. William Wiedrich
Director of Bands
East Carolina University
Greenville, SC 29606

Mr. Donald Wilcox
Director of Bands
West Virginia University
Morgantown, WV 26506

Marguerite G. Wilder
Music Department
Woodward Academy
College Park, GA 30337

Mr. John Williamson
Director of Wind Organizations
Central Michigan University
Mr. Pleasant, MI 48859

# APPENDIX III

# An Individualized Musicianship Program

## Richard Kennell

**Learning Activity Packets**, like other innovations such as Manhattanville and concepts such as Accountability or Youth Music, may not be as common now as several years ago. However, the value of a Learning Activity Packet approach may still be high, especially for students who may learn in a different way or can be motivated to learn things beyond what is found in most performance opportunities. For this reason, this material about Learning Activity Packets is included in this book. This will allow teachers to consider how this approach could enrich their curriculum and students' learning.

This appendix contains a number of Learning Activity Packet (LAPS) ideas for high school band that were developed by Richard Kennell. The assignments could be adjusted for the grade level and background of the students in a program. It is likely, therefore, that those teachers who find this material intriguing will devise a plan that fits their situation and varies from the ideas listed below.

According to Kennell's observations, students enroll in Concert Band for many reasons. Many want to improve musically so they will be accepted into the Symphonic Band, which is at a higher level because members of that ensemble are older or more skilled. Other students have diversified musical interests; they might want to learn about other music topics as well as performance. Still others select band simply for enjoyment without considering or realizing the alternatives that could be exist in a performance ensemble. All reasons for participating in band are justified and this school attempted to meet the different musical needs of such contrasting students through the *Individualized Musicianship Program*.

The underlying assumptions in the Individualized Musicianship Program are: (1) Daily participation in the band rehearsal represents the minimum musical involvement for the student and is rewarded with the average grade of C or with a PASS when the student was using the non-graded option. (2) To earn a grade higher than the average, additional work and effort must be demonstrated by the student. (3) The student and the teacher enter into a grading contract to determine the specific work associated with the grades of A and B. (4) Learning materials such as recordings, texts, workbooks, films, film strips, and videos are readily available to support this extra work.

The work to be accomplished by the band students is done outside of rehearsals. Students can earn grades through experiences organized into self-contained units called Learning Activity Packets (LAPS). While some LAPS require the guidance of the instrumental music teacher, most are transportable and can be completed independent of the director. The student selects the number of desired LAPS from a catalog of Learning Activity Packets types and titles. The catalog is divided into five areas: (P) Performance, (C) Composition, (B) Music Basics, (L) Listening, and (E) Extension Experiences. One way student accomplishment and rewards (grading and learning) could be determined is as follows: A letter grade of "A" would be given to a student who completed ten or more LAPS; B+ would equal eight or nine LAPS; B would equal five, six, or seven LAPS; and C would equal none, one, two, three, or four LAPS.

At first glance, the numbering system shown below might seem incomplete or inconsistent. In addition to showing an area such as (P) for performance, the numbers also suggested the year in high school for which a LAP project was intended. For example, the lap numbers 1-9 were options intended for Freshman, lap numbers 11-19 were for Sophomore options, lap numbers 20-29 were for Junior options, and 30-39 for Seniors. Since the catalog shown below is not complete, some numbers are not present. However, this example is extensive enough to illustrate the teacher's and school's efforts in considering and developing curriculum. It is for this reason that the material is included in this book.

# ROLLING MEADOWS HIGH SCHOOL CONCERT BAND
## INDIVIDUALIZED MUSICIANSHIP PROGRAM
## LEARNING ACTIVITY PACKAGE (LAP) CATALOG

### I.  Performance
(To qualify for "A" or "B" grade, student must  complete three performance LAPS.)

P-01  *Private Music Lessons*
Attendance at six private lessons during the quarter earns one LAP credit.

P-02  *Solo or Chamber Music Performance*
Prepare a solo or chamber performance for recital and earn one LAP credit.

P-03  *Master Class*
Private music teachers will present a "free" group clinic in the Master Class. One LAP credit.

P-04  *Sectional*
Attend a scheduled sectional and earn one LAP credit.

P-05  *Lab Jazz Band*
Participate in the RMHS Lab Jazz Band.  Every three rehearsals you attend earns one LAP credit.

P-06  *Conducting*
Study conducting techniques and score analysis in an after school conducting seminar and earn one LAP credit.

P-07  *Exploratory Instruments*
Learn to play a second instrument. Spend two weeks learning to play a new instrument and earn one LAP credit. Instrument selection must have director's approval.

P-08  *Experimental Music Ensemble*
 Learn to play "new music." Any instrument may participate on the scheduled day and earn one LAP credit.

P-09  *Performance Evaluation*
Prepare a musical selection and perform it for the band director. This extra coaching session earns one LAP credit. Performance Evaluations must be scheduled at the convenience of the student and the teacher during the quarter.

P-10  *Spring Musical*
Musical participation in the RMHS production of "My Fair Lady" earns four LAP credits. This applies to singing roles and performance in the pit orchestra.

P-11  *Required Scales*   To be assigned by the director and may  be assigned for remedial work. One LAP credit.

P-12  *Required Audition Work*   To be assigned by the director and may be for remedial work. One LAP credit.

### II.  Composition
(Each of these is worth one LAP credit.)

C-01  *Write an Original Song or Concert Piece*

C-02  *Compose a Graphic Composition for Band*

C-03  *Synthesizer Composition*  Create a tape composition using the ARP synthesizer.

C-04  *Write a Commercial*
Radio and television commercials depend on music to express the favorable character of their products. Select a product and write a jingle—a musical tune or song—that could be used as a commercial.

C-05  *Compose a Tape Recorder Composition*

C-06  *Music Notation*
Invent your own system of music notation.

C-07  *Musical Brain Teaser*
A musical puzzle.

C-11  *Reconstruct the Melody-Treble Clef*
Look at and listen to each one-measure fragment of a melody. Re-assemble the measures in the order that you judge to make the most musical sense so it is musically correct.

C-12  *Reconstruct the Melody-Bass Clef*
Look at and listen to each one-measure fragment of a melody. Re-assemble the measures in the order that you judge to make the most musical sense so it is musically correct.

II. **Music Fundamentals: Basics**

A. **For Freshmen only**:

B-11 *Musical Terms*
B-12 *Theory Work Sheet*
B-13 *Rhythm Drill*
B-14 *Learn about Intervals*
B-15 *Music Theory Fun Sheet*
B-16 *Rewrite the Rhythm*

B. **For Upperclassmen only:**

B-21 *Musical Terms*
B-22 *Theory Work Sheet*
B-23 *Rhythm Drill*
B-24 *Instrument Transpositions*
B-25 *Music Theory Fun Sheet*
B-26 *Electronic Music Terms*
B-27 *The Music Game*
Play the music game with three of your friends. If you win, collect two LAPS. All others earn one LAP. There is a limit of one game per student.

IV. **Listening** (One required LAP for each student.)

L-01 *The Music of Percy Grainger*
L-02 *Folk Music Listening* (Singin' An a Strumin')
L-03 *Orchestra Music Listening* (sections of orchestra are featured)
L-04 *What is Jazz?*
L-05 *Brass Music Listening*
L-06 *Woodwind Music Listening*
L-07 *Percussion Music Listening*
L-08 *Humor in Music*
L-09 *The Best of the Chicago Symphony Orchestra*
L-11 *Required Freshman Listening*
L-21 *Required Upperclassman Listening*

V. **Extension Experiences**
(These are experiences that could occur outside of the regular class room. Each LAP is worth one LAP credit.)

E-01 *Student-Teacher Seminar*
See calendar for dates.
E-02 *Tutoring*
Teach students in the Cadet Band. You can give three lessons and earn one LAP credit. See the music teacher for names of students you can help.
E-03 *Library*
Learn about the music resources in our school library.
E-04 *Film* "Bolero"
E-05 *Film* "New Sounds in Music"
See calendar for scheduled times.
E-06 *Invent Your Own Learning Activity Package*
Create a new LAP with the music teacher's approval and earn one LAP credit.

E-07 *Attend a Concert*
    Attend a music performance that you do not perform in either at RMHS or in the community.
    Bring in the program and get one LAP credit.

E-08 *Music Research Bibliography*
    Select a topics that interests you. Make a list of books in the library that you could use to explore that topic.

E-09 *Music Research Paper*
    After completing the bibliography, if you would like to complete your research and write a one-two page paper, you will receive one additional LAP. (E-08 is a prerequisite for this project.)

E-10 *How to Handle a Stereo , CD, or Tape Recorder Salesman*
    Thinking about buying a new stereo? Read this first and answer the questions for one LAP credit.

**The LAP catalog is changed each quarter by providing either more difficult versions of last quarter's LAPS or by introducing totally new Learning Activity Packets. For example, one quarter a set of HONOR LAPS could be listed. Students could select honor LAPS only after they had earned a minimum grade of "B".**

## VI. Honor LAPS (H)

Students may work on these for credit *after* they have earned a minimum "B" grade. When a student has earned nine LAP credits, he may select the following LAPS for additional intensive honor credit.

H-01 *Conduct the Band*
    Students who have completed the conducting seminars may elect to conduct the Concert Band for one LAP credit.

H-02 *Synthesizer Study*
    Work independently with the ARP synthesizer on a project of individual interest and get one LAP credit.

H-03 *Challenges*
    Students who complete a minimum "B" grade may challenge. The winner of the challenge is awarded one Honor LAP credit.

**The LAP system also suggested a mechanism for academic discipline. Students who did not behave acceptably in class might be assigned additional work through the LAP system. Instead of "detention time," disciplined students would be spending additional time working with music.**

## VII. Disciplinary LAPS

Students who do not meet the behavior standards of the Concert Band will be assigned additional work on the occasion of their misbehavior. One assigned extra LAP increases the student grading scale by one.

*Maximum "B"*. Students who receive three-four disciplinary LAPS can earn a maximum B grade for the quarter. A note will be sent to the student's parents.

*Maximum "C"*. Students who receive five or more disciplinary LAPS can receive a maximum C grade for the quarter. The student's parents will be telephoned and a conference will be arranged.

## VIII. Prescriptive LAPS

Audition music from the previous quarter provided an opportunity for the band director to identify musical problems. As a result, the teacher can proactively assign a required Learning Activity Packet dealing with the student's deficiency in the subsequent semester's contract. These requirements might be added to the student's contract sheet prior to their distribution.

IX. **Calendar**

Since many of the elective Learning Activity Packets involved after-school activities, it was extremely important for students to have a quarterly calendar.

# Rolling Meadows High School Concert Band

## Fourth Quarter Calendar

| April | 15 | Tuesday | Music Journalism-Mustang Band Newsletter Meeting at 3:00 p.m. |
| | 18 | Friday | Guest Pianist Recital at 3:00 p.m. |
| | 21 | Monday | Student-Teacher Seminar 3:00 p.m. |
| | 21 | Monday | Required Scales Performance 3:00 p.m. |
| | 22 | Tuesday | RMHS Jazz Band Concert 8:00 p.m. |
| | 23 | Wednesday | Required Scales Performance 3:00 p.m. |
| | 24 | Thursday | Lab Jazz Band Rehearsal 3:00 p.m. |
| | 28 | Monday | How to Control Your Nerves When Performing 3:00 p.m. |
| | 29 | Tuesday | Film: "Jazz Age" 3:00 p.m. |
| | 30 | Wednesday | Conducting Session #1 3:00 p.m. |
| May | 1 | Thursday | Lab Jazz Band Rehearsal 3:00 p.m. |
| | 2 | Friday | Student-Teacher Recital 3:00 p.m. |
| | 5 | Monday | Film: "Instruments of the Orchestra" 3:00 p.m. |
| | 6 | Tuesday | Spring Band Concert PERFORMANCE 8:00 p.m. |
| | 7 | Wednesday | Conducting Session #2 3:00 p.m. |
| | 8 | Thursday | Lab Jazz Band Rehearsal 3:00 p.m. |
| | 9 | Friday | Student-Teacher Seminar 3:00 p.m. |
| | 12 | Monday | Film: "Symphony Sound" 3:00 p.m. |
| | 13 | Tuesday | Student-Teacher Seminar 3:00 p.m. |
| | 14 | Wednesday | Solo Performance Recital #1 3:00 p.m. |
| | 15 | Thursday | Lab Jazz Band Rehearsal 3:00 p.m. |
| | 15-16 | Thurs.-Sat. | Spring Musical: "Carousel" |

X. **Contract**

At the beginning of each quarter, the students received a contract packet. This packet contained a LAP catalog, a *Calendar of Events*, and the quarter's grading contract. The students reviewed the calendar and the catalog, completed their contracts, and returned their contracts to the teacher. The student contract form indicates that at least one LAP from each category must be completed. A sample contract sheet is shown on page 441.

Many of the Learning Activity Packets consisted of work sheets and cassette tapes. These were assembled and placed into manila envelopes which could be checked out overnight by students. A progress list of students with the number of completed LAPS was posted in the band room so that students could monitor their progress and compare their accomplishments to those of other students.

## CONTRACT FOR LEARNING ACTIVITY PACKETS

### ROLLING MEADOWS HIGH SCHOOL BAND
### INDIVIDUALIZED MUSICIANSHIP PROGRAM

Students enroll in Concert Band for many reasons. Many want to improve musically so they will be accepted into Symphonic Band, which is a higher level and more skilled ensemble. Other students have diversified musical interests of which band is only one; they might want to learn about music topics other than performance. Still others select band simply for enjoyment without considering or realizing, at least at the outset, what alternatives there could be available in the typical performance ensemble. All reasons for participating in band are justified and we attempt to meet the different musical needs of such contrasting students through the *Individualized Musicianship Program.*

**Option One**: The student who selects band "for the fun of it" should elect to participate on the PASS/NO PASS option. Regular attendance at rehearsals and concerts satisfies the requirements for a passing grade.

**Option Two**: In additional to regular attendance at rehearsals and concerts, the student may contract with the teacher to complete a specific number of Learning Activity Packets to earn a letter grade of C, B, or A.

This quarter's **Grading Scale** is: A = 10 or more LAPS; B+ = 8 or 9 LAPS; B = 5, 6, or 7 LAPS; and C = 0, 1, 2, 3, or 4 LAPS.

---

### INDIVIDUALIZED MUSICIANSHIP CONTRACT

| KEEP FOR REFERENCE | STUDENT COPY | KEEP FOR REFERENCE |
|---|---|---|
| LAP NO. | LAP TITLE | DATE COMPLETED |

P-
C-
B-
L-
E-

1._____  2._____  3._____  4._____  5._____  6._____  7._____  8._____  9._____  10._____

By completing _____ Learning Activity Packets during the _____ quarter, I expect to receive the grade of _____.

Student's Signature _____ Date _____

Teacher's Signature _____ Date _____

## XI. **A Band Curriculum**

By building upon the previous quarter's content, the Individualized Musicianship Program leads to the formation of a sequential curriculum for Concert Band. Here is an example of what can be planned in this respect.

| QUARTER | FRESHMAN YEAR | SOPHOMORE YEAR |
|---|---|---|
| FIRST QUARTER | MARCHING BAND | MARCHING BAND |
| SECOND QUARTER | (P) Scales C, F, and G<br>(P) Master Class<br>(C) Reconstruct the Melody<br>(B) Rhythm Studies IV<br>(B) Key Signatures<br>(B) Musical Terms<br>(L) Baroque Listening<br>(L) Band Listening<br>(E) Seminar<br>(E) Concert | (P) Scales E, A, and E flat<br>(P) Master Class<br>(C) Reconstruct the Melody<br>(B) Rhythm Studies V<br><br><br>(L) Romantic Listening<br>(L) Band Listening<br>(E) Seminar<br>(E) Concert |
| THIRD QUARTER | (P) Scales D, B flat, and A<br>(P) Chamber Music Performance<br>(C) Reconstruct the Melody<br>(B) Rhythm Studies X<br>(B) Rewrite the Rhythm<br>(B) Musical Terms<br>(L) Classical Listening<br>(L) Band Listening<br>(E) Seminar<br>(E) Concert | (P) Scales B, D flat, F sharp, and G flat<br>(P) Chamber Music Performance<br>(C) Tape Recorder Composition<br>(B) Rhythm Studies XI<br><br><br>(L) 20th Century Listening<br>(L) Band Listening<br>(E) Seminar<br>(E) Concert |
| FOURTH QUARTER | (P) Scales: Chromatic<br>    starting on C, F, G, D, A<br>(P) Solo Performance<br>(C) 12 Tone Composition<br>(B) Rhythm Studies XVII<br>(B) Musical Terms<br>(L) Romantic Listening<br>(L) Band Music Listening<br>(E) Seminar<br>(E) Concert<br>(E) Library | (P) Scales: Chromatic<br>    starting on any note<br>(P) Solo Performance<br>(C) Electronic Music Composition<br>(B) Rhythm Studies XVIII<br><br>(L) Experimental Music Listening<br>(L) Band Music Listening<br>(E) Seminar<br>(E) Concert<br>(E) Library |

# Appendix IV

## Intensity as an Attribute of Effective Teaching
### Clifford K. Madsen

CLIFFORD K. MADSEN
Florida State University, USA.
Published in:
*International Society of Music Education,* Edition Two, 1988
*Research in Music Education: Festschrift in honor of Arnold Bentley*

There appear to be two basic elements of effective teaching: (1) knowledge of the subject matter and precisely what it is students should learn and (2) effective delivery and sequencing of the subject matter. Both elements seem to have an inextricable interaction with each other, especially in relationship to long-term learning effects. If a teacher has limited or inaccurate knowledge or objectives, even highly enthusiastic deliver can only maintain short-term attention and inadequate learning. Alternately, regardless of subject matter knowledge, low intensity teacher delivery will not often maintain enough student attentiveness for subject matter to be learned.

The ability of a teacher to initiate and maintain a high level of student attention has been of major concern to researchers and teacher educators for years. Continuing research is evident in numerous areas including pre-service professional education (Popham, 1965; Copeland, 1975, 1977), the student teaching experience (McIntyre & Morris, 1980; Griffin, 1981), and behaviors exhibited by effective teachers (Berliner, 1986; Brandt, 1986; Price, 1981; Yarbrough, 1975; Yarbrough & Price, 1981).

In order to prepare future teachers for productive and effective teaching, it is necessary to identify those observable, quantifiable characteristics which separate expert teachers from novices (Brandt, 1986). Berliner (1986) suggested that expert teachers appear to have a firm command of the subject matter, are knowledgeable about classroom organization and management, have automated routines which allow them to spend a minimum of time on classroom business, have a wide range of instructional options allowing them to adapt to individual situations, are unusually sensitive to their working environment, and are able to anticipate problems and have contingency plans ready. It would seem that all of these attributes are necessary for high teacher effectiveness and, therefore, high teacher intensity.

In referring to teacher presentation of subject matter, the terms enthusiasm, magnitude, and intensity all suggest that teacher behavior can be executed and observed in varying degrees. Collins (1978) developed a measurement device which operationally defined eight teacher behaviors under low, medium, and high levels of enthusiasm. These behavior categories included vocal delivery, eyes, gestures, movements, facial expression, word selection, acceptance of ideas and feelings, and overall energy. These descriptors were used in a training session designed to increase enthusiasm level of pre-service elementary teachers. Collins' data, in the form of observer enthusiasm ratings, showed that experimental subjects increased their display of enthusiasm after training while control subjects changed little from pre- to post-test. This indicates that it is possible to train pre-service teachers to increase their level of teacher enthusiasm.

McKinney, Larkins, et al. (1983) used the Collins model in an experimental training session with teachers. After treatment, teachers were asked to display high, medium, or low enthusiasm in the classroom on demand. Observers of these performances correctly assigned ratings to virtually all teachers across the three categories of enthusiasm yet the level of affect had *no* effect on post-test student achievement on a social studies task.

Music teacher behaviors of eye contact, closeness to students, volume and modulation of voice, gestures, facial expressions and pacing were first operationally defined (high and low levels of magnitude) by Yarbrough (1975). In a rehearsal setting, the effects of these attributes on student behavior were observed. Results indicate that intended high and low magnitude was reliably observed across teacher behaviors in choral rehearsal settings. Yarbrough concluded that a

447

combination of an approving facial expression, eye contact, verbal approval, and approach body movement could perhaps be the combination of behaviors resulting in highest magnitude. Students appeared to prefer and were more attentive during the high magnitude condition, although magnitude had *no* significant effect on performance level. Sims (1986) varied teacher affect (high/low) and student activity (active/passive head movements) during music listening activities with preschool children. Changes in pupil off-task behavior were more obvious when high affect was following by low affect than under the opposite condition.

### Experiments Defining Intensity

Preliminary studies concerning teacher intensity included two initial experiments (Standley & Madsen, 1987). Experiment 1 compared video-taped performances of freshmen under two conditions: (1) speaking 30 seconds before the entire group of subjects about the individual's personal goals for a music career and (2) leading a familiar song with a group of six pre-schoolers aged 4-5 years. Intensity, defined as sustained control of the student/teacher interaction and evidenced by efficient, accurate presentation and correction of the subject matter with enthusiastic affect and pacing, was evaluated on a 10 point scale. Correlations indicated that intensity in speaking about one's self was not highly related to intensity in a music teaching situation—the music performance situation receiving much higher intensity ratings.

Experiment 2 represented another attempt to operationalize teacher intensity and assessed the intensity of three groups of music education/music therapy majors engaged in a music task similar to Experiment 1: teaching a new song to a group of pre-schoolers ages 4-5 years. Reliability for this study was quite high (.79) and suggested some success at achieving a ratable definition. Comparisons were made among freshmen, senior music education majors, and senior music therapy majors. The statistical analysis determined the freshmen to be significantly lower in intensity ratings than either the music education or the music therapy seniors as would be expected.

Results of the first two studies suggested that intensity is a teaching skill that can be taught, learned, and measured, and that performance of a musical task may enhance the intensity of the teaching interaction.

The intent of a third study was to ascertain whether high/low contrasts in teacher intensity could be quickly taught to, and then demonstrated by, prospective music education interns, and further, whether subjects untrained in the concept of intensity could recognize these contrasts (Madsen, Standley & Cassidy, 1987). Subjects were music education/therapy majors who were divided into one experimental and three control groups. The experimental group (Interns) consisted of music education majors in their final week of on-campus preparation prior to beginning a public school internship with emphasis in general, choral, or instrumental areas. The three control groups were differentiated according to level of preparation in the music education or therapy major: Freshmen, Seniors, and Graduate Students.

Observation scores and overall intensity ratings were compared across groups and observation errors were analyzed by interval and by subject. The single most important result was that intensity as a concept was operationally defined, easily taught to pre-interns, ably demonstrated, and easily recognized with an extremely high degree of reliability (.99) by almost everyone. All subjects were asked to define intensity. Rates of responses varied with the fewest number of ideas expressed by Interns followed by Freshmen and Seniors. The greatest number of ideas was expressed by Graduate Students. The interns, who were trained to demonstrate intensity, were most concise about its definition. Increased number of expressions varied with length of time in the curriculum. Enthusiastic, excited expression, eye contact, and specific instructional techniques as pacing; short, simple instructions; good posture; and the need for making music as opposed to talking while upper classmen utilized these concepts to describe the teaching interactions observed. It is interesting to note that these items are very similar to the list compiled by Yarbrough (1975) to define high magnitude. While the words used to define intensity varied greatly, agreement was very high in identifying intensity as either high or low and on the overall rating of intensity.

### Applications

It would seem that effective education in any field or area has to do with two issues: (1) student selection and (2) the demonstrated effects of teaching. Obviously, if the selection issue is the most important ('teachers are born not made'), the profession must find the important variables that constitute recruitment for effective teaching (as in the first experiment). If skills can be taught, learned and measured, the profession still has the same problem: What are the variables necessary for effective teaching? Other than knowledge of subject matter, two recurring variables concern (1) demonstrated teacher *enthusiasm* (high teacher affect) in live positive student/teacher interactions and (2) a sense of *timing* in relationship to classroom management and effective subject matter presentation/monitoring. Both of these variables necessitate the ability to 'see oneself as others do' or to 'know how one is coming across.' Therefore, one's social awareness seems paramount.

Issues concerning 'teacher intensity' in some ways seem to blend the above attributes of enthusiasm and timing in that persons seen as having high intensity are enthusiastic as well as effective in managing the class. It seems difficult to imagine an intense teacher without both. The present line of experimentation indicates that teacher intensity is an attribute that can be learned and demonstrated by pre-service music teachers. It seems that almost anyone can recognize it with very high reliability. It is also suggested that intensity is the singular most important aspect to be provided by the teacher in relationship to students being on-task.

## Making Music as Intensity

Intensity does not only include the teacher's personal responses but can have multiple sources within any learning environment. If, as suggested, intensity is the singular most important aspect for student involvement (attentiveness) then the concept of intensity must be thoroughly investigated and also prove consistent with other research findings. The first issue when assessing intensity concerns the intensity provided by the subject matter itself. Research that assesses student off-task in the complete absence of any subject matter, or time-out from subject matter reinforcement indicates that there are various levels of attentiveness (Madsen & Madsen, 1983). Perhaps there is a hierarchy from nothing through something to different levels of intensity carried by progressive interaction with the subject matter only. Alternately, students not responding to the subject matter, making a game out of learning or even 'playing a game' also suggests some hierarchical level of social attentiveness. Research indicates that some academic subjects are 'naturally' reinforcing (Greer, 1980) and some subjects more reinforcing than others (Forsythe, 1977). The activity of making music carries with it a good deal of temporal structure as well as positive affect and it is probable that music activity has its own high level of intensity (Forsythe, 1977; Spradling, 1985). It was apparent in the above studies that once the music started it carried the class. Yet, once the music stopped the group became off-task during transitions or 'getting ready' periods. Indeed, this seems consistent with other research on classroom attentiveness relative to music ((Madsen & Geringer, 1983; Madsen & Yarbrough, 1985; Yarbrough & Price, 1981). The intensity level created by music performance also might account for music 'as its own reward' (Madsen & Madsen, 1972) as well as the disparate rates of off-task student behavior during music as compared to other subject matter (Forsythe, 1975; Madsen & Alley, 1979).

If, within each subject matter, there are various levels of intensity (even within acceptable performance standards in music) then temporal aspects concerning durational units as small as seconds seem paramount. During music performance an extremely high level of intensity quickly evaporates within one or two beats with a conspicuous wrong note, a memory lapse, or lack of energetic concern to performance detail. Within a rehearsal setting, intensity quickly dissipates with too much elapsed time from performance, intrusive teacher behavior, bad teacher or student modelling, too much attention to only one section of the ensemble, music selections being too difficult or too easy, and so on. All contribute to lack of intensity. While it is the conductor who usually controls most rehearsal management or pacing aspects, even in non-music classes the teacher can 'drop a beat,' or two, or a thousand by taking too much time to call roll, correct responses, give directions, look for materials or anything else that interferes with high level pacing and therefore stimulates student off-task.

## Intensity From Other Sources

Another source of intensity comes from students, both individually and collectively. The high level of social intensity observed during recess and other non-instructional activities attests to social interaction intensity. Peer interaction also accounts for a good deal of intensity which sometimes competes with the subject matter or the teacher.

A troublesome issue concerning intensity has to do with teacher approval/disapproval. Both approval and disapproval if contingently delivered can carry a good deal of intensity, yet disapproval seems to be capable of much more intensity than approval—students are very attentive when someone gets 'kicked out of class.' A class clown can create 'classroom intensity' and might even be more likely to do so in the presence of dull subject matter and low teacher affect. Although a *very* disapproving teacher can create high intensity, a very disapproving (or approving) teacher can also be progressively 'tuned out' by students. Students perceive time passing faster during conditions of high disapproval compared to high approval (Madsen & Duke, 1985) suggesting that disapproval carries its own high intensity. It is unlikely, however, that much learning of a *positive* nature will occur under conditions of high disapproval or in the complete absence of some intensity. Students may develop a heightened tolerance for boredom, yet they will probably not learn much in situations characterized by only low intensity. It should be stated that while high negative situations teach very well, they rarely teach what we want taught.

High positive intensity seems indispensable and can be viewed short term to be extremely *good* teaching. Yet effective teaching realizing long term objectives takes much more time to ascertain and cannot be assessed in several observations (Berliner, 1986). Regardless of how effective any teacher initially appears, long term results take long term assessment. This might help explain heightened student attentiveness and positive attitudes yet lack of significant achievement in some of the music studies with limited teacher exposure (Kuhn, 1975; Murray, 1975; Yarbrough, 1975).

A final issue concerns *teacher controlled low intensity* or semi-rest time within the overall pacing sequence. When the teacher controls this 'down time,' the teacher is then able to bring the group instantly back to full energetic physical/ mental participation. This seems both desirable and necessary and should not be confused with the low intensity evident because of ineffective teaching or that evident when the teacher unwittingly gives the intensity to the class (e.g., asking ill-prepared questions) and cannot regain its control. It would seem that the teacher, much like the comedian and actor, must have a good sense of timing and an immediate and omnipresent sense of student attentiveness. Yet, unlike the entertainer, the teacher must also have a solid subject matter whose presentation is temporally sequenced for maximum student participation and achievement. Some of the most intense teachers are very quiet. It seems that the issue of intensity is important in both the selection and training of prospective teachers and much more research appears warranted. A full operational definition and careful experimentation will be necessary for refining procedures and subsequent testing.

## References

Berliner, D.C. (1986). In pursuit of the expert pedagogue. *Educational Researcher*, 15,(7), 5-13.

Brandt, R.S. (1986, October). On the expert teacher: A conversation with David Berliner . *Educational Leadership*, 4-9.

Collins, M. (1978). Effect of enthusiasm training on pre-service elementary teachers. *Journal of Teacher Education*, 29,(1), 53-57.

Copeland, W.D. (1975). The relationship between microteaching and student teacher classroom performance. *Journal of Educational Research*, 68, 289-293.

Copeland, W.D. (1977). Some factors relating to student teacher classroom performance following microteaching training. *American Educational Research Journal*, 14,(2), 145-157.

Forsythe, J.L. (1975). The effect of teacher approval, disapproval, and errors on student attentiveness: Music versus classroom teachers. In C.K. Madsen, R.D. Greer, & C.H. Madsen Jr. (Eds.), *Research in music behavior*, (pp. 49-55). New York: Teachers College Press.

Forsythe, J.L. (1977). Elementary student attending behavior as a function of classroom activities. *Journal of Research in Music Education*, 25,(3), 228-239.

Greenfield, D.G. (1978). Evaluation of music therapy practicum competencies: Comparisons of self and instructor ratings of videotapes. *Journal of Music Therapy*, 15,(1), 15-20.

Greer, R.D. (1980). *Designs for music learning*. New York: Teachers College Press.

Griffin, G.A. (1981). *Student teaching: A review*. Austin, Texas: Texas University at Austin Research and Development Center for Teacher Education. (Eric Document Reproduction Service No. ED 223-565).

Kuhn, T.L. (1972). The effect of teacher approval and disapproval on attentiveness, musical achievement, and attitude of fifth grade students. In C.K. Madsen, R.D. Greer, & C.H. Madsen Jr. (Eds.), *Research in music behavior* (pp. 40-48). New York: Teachers College Press.

Madsen, C.H., Jr. & Madsen, C.K. (1983). *Teaching/discipline: Behavioral principles toward a positive approach*. Raleigh, NC: Contemporary Publishing, Inc.

Madsen, C.K. & Alley, J.M. (1979). The effect of reinforcement on attentiveness: A comparison of behaviorally trained music therapists and other professionals with implications for competency. *Journal of Music Therapy*, 16,(2), 70-82.

Madsen, C.K. & Duke, R.A. (1985). Observation of approval/ disapproval feedback in music: Perception versus actual classroom events. *Journal of Research in Music Education*, 33,(3), 205-214.

Madsen, C.K. & Gerlinger, J.M. (1983). Attending behavior as a function of in-class activity in university music classes. *Journal of Music Therapy*, 20,(1), 30-38.

Madsen, C.K. & Madsen, C.H., Jr. (1972). Selection of music listening or candy as a function of a contingent versus non-contingent reinforcement and scale singing. *Journal of Music Therapy*, 9,(4), 190-198.

Madsen, C.K., Standley, J.M. & Cassidy, J.W. (1987). The effect of intensity on effective teaching. Paper presented at the Seventh National Symposium: Research in Music Behavior, Logan, Utah. Madsen, C.K. & Yarbrough, C. (1985). *Competency-based music education*. Raleigh, NC: Contemporary Publishing, Inc.

McIntyre, D.J. & Morris, W.R. (1980). Research on the student teaching triad. *Contemporary Education*, 51,(4), 193-196.

McKinney, C.W., Larkins, A.G., Kazelskis, R., Ford, M.J., Allen, J.A., & Davis, J.C. (1983). Some effects of teacher enthusiasm on student achievement in fourth grade social studies. *Journal of Educational Research*, 76,(4) 249-253.

Murray, K.C. (1975). The effect of teacher approval/disapproval on musical performance, attentiveness, and attitude of high school choruses. In C.K. Madsen, R.D. Greer, & C.H. Madsen Jr. (Eds.), *Research in music behavior* (pp. 168-180). New York: Teachers College Press.

Popham, W.J. (1965). An experimental attempt to modify the instructional behavior of student teachers. *Journal of Teacher Education*, 16, 461-465.

Price, H. (1983). The effect of conductor academic task presentation, conductor reinforcement, and ensemble practice on performers' musical achievement, attentiveness, and attitude. *Journal of Research in Music Education*, 31(4), 245-257.

Sims, W.L. (1986). The effect of high versus low teacher affect and passive versus active student activity during music listening on preschool children's attention, piece preference, time spent listening and piece recognition. *Journal of Research in Music Education*, 34,(3), 173-191.

Spradling, R.A. (1985). The effect of timeout from performance on attentiveness and attitude of university band students. *Journal of Research in Music Education*, 32,(2), 123-127.

Standley, J.M. & Madsen, C.K. (1987, April). Intensity as an attribute of effective teaching. Paper accepted for presentation at Southeastern Regional Music Educators Conference, Orlando, Florida.

Yarbrough, C. (1975). The effect of magnitude of conductor behavior on performance, attentiveness, and attitude of students in selected mixed choruses. *Journal of Research in Music Education*, 23,(2), 134-146.

Yarbrough, C. & Price, H.E. (1981). Prediction of performer attentiveness based on rehearsal activity and teacher behavior. *Journal of Research in Music Education*, 29,(3), 209-217.

# APPENDIX V

## Factors Influencing Intonation
### Richard Strange

Richard Strange, the Director of Bands at Arizona State University, has contributed an interesting and detailed discussion of factors affecting intonation with string, wind, and percussion instruments. It is a special interest of his and I have learned how willing he is to offer this material for the considerations of band and orchestra conductors.

### Intonation: The Problem

I have several ideas about intonation that I would like to offer. They may explain the reasons why so many bands play out of tune. My contention is that these ideas are understandable, and that there are correctable causes for this out-of-tune condition. If people understand the problems and their solutions, they will have many fewer intonation and tuning problems.

Many bands and orchestras play sharp and in playing sharp, they go against the acoustical design of the instruments, most of which were designed to be played in tune at A440 Hz. Thus, if a band plays sharp, some of the instruments are doomed to be played out of tune, regardless of the worth of the player, the techniques used to play the instrument, or the tuning procedures. The band will be out of tune, simply because the instruments, themselves, cannot be played in tune in an ensemble that is playing at a higher pitch level than the level for which the instruments were designed. Many band directors tune at the A440 level, but they don't teach their students to play in such a way as to stay at, or near, A440. They do not therefore, teach the second part of learning to play in tune. The second part is, you must remain as close to A440 as possible at all times when playing an instrument. I have confirmed this idea many times to myself and others with regional and all-state bands.

People have said, "The intonation of the band really improved quickly. How did it happen that fast?" There's no secret to it, other than staying near A440 and listening to each other. I have been a professional player myself on all the woodwind instruments, and have had to cope with all sorts of tuning problems in orchestras. One continual tuning problem that drove me crazy occurred whenever I was playing flute in an orchestra and the orchestra went sharp. By comparison with the strings, as a flute player, I simply sounded flat because I couldn't go sharp enough to reach their pitch level. My instrument wouldn't let me go that sharp. People would expect me to tune up, but it was physically impossible, unless I cut off part my instrument. I used to fight that and think that it was my fault. I would devise all sorts of ways to try to get the pitch up. Finally it hit me with a blinding flash: for all practical purposes I was in tune, and the orchestra was out of tune with me, and that bothered me for a long time. If you're one of only a few playing at 440 and everybody else is around 446, you are the one who sounds out of tune. Yet there is nothing you can do about it, because the ensemble's higher pitch level has doomed you to sound flat.

There are very good reasons for this to occur: one is psychological. When comparing two or more pitches, we tend to hear low (flat) as bad; we hear high (sharp) as good; we hear low (flat) as dull; and we hear high (sharp) as brilliant. All of these are subjective judgments, and that's the basic kernel of the problem. We seek a small amount of musical one-up-man-ship, by tuning and playing on the brilliant side of someone else. This phenomenon is psychologically true. Empirical evidence has proven to me that most musicians will tune slightly sharp in relation to other instruments if allowed to do so. This is true especially for strings, since they can't play louder than each other, nor louder than other instruments. For them, tuning slightly sharper than the string player next to them is their way of differentiating their tone, and pulling it out of the masses of people and the mass of sound. The same is true when talking about flutes and clarinets: theoretically, like-instruments cannot play louder than each other, so we tend to play sharper than the person next to us in order to hear ourselves. When you go to brass instruments, it's different. With brass you can have one or two people blatting or blasting, sounding about twice as loud as everybody else. Woodwinds cannot do this because of the nature of the instrument. So, what many people do is within their reasoning; they either allow their playing to drift sharp, or the good players actually try to play so they are the tiniest bit high in order to differentiate their sound from the others.

However, there are two classes of instruments in bands that aren't susceptible to "sharp-one-up-man-ship"; first, and most obvious, are the tuned percussion. Second, when properly adjusted (tuned), are the keyboard instruments. It dawned on me very early in my career as a band director that tuned percussion really weren't flat, because in general they are not; they sound that way because everyone else is sharp. There are many technical and psychological reasons why winds and strings play sharp, but the fixed-pitch instruments do not have these problems, and can be used as correct reference points. We all supposedly tune at the proper level and good bands will tune pretty much to A440. Halfway through a piece of music, however, they suddenly start appearing to be out of tune with each other. Then, by the time they get to the end of a strenuous piece of music, the last chord can be hideously out of tune. If you were to run back the tape, you would find that the first chord probably was reasonably well in tune. This change as the piece goes on is partially due to fatigue, of course; but, if we wipe out this consideration, the rise in pitch is due mainly to a temperature change inside the bore of the instrument that is not compensated for while playing.

Though one can improve the initial tuning with a step-by-step procedure (which I use with my own band, and when I work with regional and all-state bands), the rise in pitch while performing can only be conquered by musicians who understand the complexities of the tuning process. They must first convince themselves that it is possible for bands to stay down in pitch, if the physical environment is reasonable on stage. If one goes on a stage, and it's 105 degrees on that stage because of hot lights and no outside or fresh air, etc., then, as far as I can see (I've spent a lot of time studying this acoustically) there isn't any hope. The change in temperature will bring out the worst characteristics of each instrument, whatever that instrument is. One would simply have to pull the instruments apart to the point where they can't play in tune within their own scale. Of course, that problem is due to the fault of the environment.

Until you change the environment, there is nothing that you can do. Even the finest professional players have a terrible struggle to stay in tune when the stage temperature is high. However, when one is on a reasonable stage and the temperature is steady at 72 degrees, if the group plays out of tune it has to be their fault, because it is not the fault of the environment. Few places in the world have that advantage, but the temperature of most stages doesn't rise to the point where the rise in temperature is significant. The temperature may be in the low 90s, for example, but that causes a rise of only a few cents sharpness for most of the instruments.

Describing the problem is not the solution to the intonation problems of the band. We are still one step short of the solution. The solution is this: after the instrument is warmed up to its proper playing temperature, the player must continue to play as close to A440 as possible. That's the one extra step that most people don't take. All my problems, experiments, and discoveries made me more aware, and caused me to try to figure out acoustically why these things were happening. When you get into the acoustics of the instruments, and study pitch and frequency, you find all sorts of astounding things in terms of the International Standard Pitch.

## International Standard Pitch

The meaning and history of International Standard Pitch is one of the interesting facets of music. It was actually standardized in 1939, and now exists as a codified international standard. But what the standard says is something totally different than what many people assume. (All you have to do is go to the *New Grove's Dictionary of Music and Musicians* and look up pitch; you'll see all of this.) The standard says, "The instruments shall be designed and played as close to A440 as possible under all conditions," or something very close to that wording. Musicians seem to think there is much more to it than that. They add many other points themselves, such as, "It's supposed to be sea level at 72 degrees Fahrenheit," and on and on. The actual international pitch standard includes none of these extra considerations or stipulations. It simply says, "Instruments shall be designed and played as closely as possible to A440 under all circumstances."

There is a reason it is stated this way. Many musicians have said through the years that there should be temperature standards and many other physical measurements. The standard makers didn't agree. Acoustically, it was determined that these additions would produce different reactions on each instrument, so it wouldn't help to add them as additional stipulations. Acoustically the equations used in the design of most of the instruments in the western world do conform to A440 at 72 degrees at sea level. However, International Standard Pitch simply says you are to conform to A440 at all times (as closely as possible). This means that each individual player must adjust constantly because of temperature changes. The corollary to that—and this few people understand or do—is that usually you must adjust downward, not upward. In other words, the sharp ones must come down to the lower ones. This unique approach makes one retrain the ear to say, "High is bad and sharp is bad; low is good and A440 is correct." Any good instrument, and I'm including student instruments, is designed to be played at A440. You can't get the acousticians of factories anywhere in the Western World to admit that they are tuning their instruments to anything but A440, except for two. The Haynes factory markets a flute with a new scale that is deliberately designed at A442. They're doing it simply because they are recognizing what has happened and are saying that people complained so much about flat flutes that Haynes is going to make them sharper. The other one is Yamaha. Some of the fixed-pitch instruments, like the xylophone, are tuned by design to A442 on special order. What these companies fail to understand is that once you abrogate the International Pitch Standard, you simply are playing leap frog. Within ten or twenty years the pitch standard will rise above A442 (where these companies have set it unilaterally) and the companies will then have to raise it again to A444 or higher. This likely chain of events will mirror past history.

Historical studies by Hermann Helmholtz show that over the course of music history the pitch for the note "A" has floated from approximately 370 cycles per second to 567 cycles per second. After rising ridiculously high, it was literally forced back down by the International Piano Tuner's Guild and the voice problems of singers. Think of what this has done to the trained singer. According to experts, the human voice range throughout the history of music has not changed appreciably; people are still people. Physically, voice ranges have stayed constant, but the pitch level at which singers must perform has gone up almost continually.

Here are some examples that show the folly of not having an absolute pitch standard. We are singing all of the Verdi operas about a half-step too high now. Can you imagine what that does to a tenor, since he must go for those high notes time after time in every rehearsal and performance. Now he is singing approximately one half-step higher than Verdi heard his own music—this is a big problem for singers. The problem was so bad in London in the late 1800s that, because of high orchestral pitch at Covent Garden, a famous soprano, Adelina Patti, refused to sing any more in England. Because she was so well-known, she single-handedly (with the help of a new organ in Queen's Hall) brought the pitch of the London Orchestras down to approximately A440.

I can understand somewhat why the manufacturers of fixed-pitch percussion instruments are raising the pitch of their instruments when ordered specially. With fixed-pitch percussion, the pitch goes down as temperature goes up, exactly the opposite of the wind instruments. On a warm stage, you have this pulling apart; the fixed-pitch percussion go down slightly, most winds go up. If a xylophone is in tune at A440, it may be at 439.5 by the time equilibrium is reached on the bar itself due to a hot stage. I can see the manufacturers thinking they should build their instruments at A442 so that the pitch will be high to meet the rising pitch of the winds. This makes some sense, even though it is a very imprecise sort of sense.

However, they seem not to have considered that all wind instruments go up a different amount, and at different rates of speed. This problem, some instruments going higher and some going down or staying the same when temperatures change, makes tuning and intonation a real challenge that cannot be met by altering the international pitch standard. Only an understanding of the myriad problems associated with tuning each individual family of instruments will lead to solutions that work. All of the large instruments, especially the brass instruments, rise in pitch due to temperature changes, both internal and external, much farther than the smaller instruments. You can take an oboe and put it in an oven, and if you bake it (figuratively speaking), it will go up only about nine cents. Under the same circumstances, tuba pitch might rise more than twenty cents.

## Temperature of Equilibrium

You also must take into account acoustically that you blow warm air into the bore of an instrument at a temperature of 98.6 degrees or so. As you blow this warm air through the instrument, you are raising the temperature of an instrument that is being played in an environment which usually is slightly cooler than breath temperature. For example, the air you blow through the instrument is 98.6 degrees, but the room can be at 80 degrees. Thus, since you have temperatures inside and outside the bore that are different, they gradually will stabilize at a point in between (called the temperature of equilibrium).

The temperature of equilibrium can be different at the beginning of each phrase, or after a long rest, and is precisely measurable for playing purposes only at the instant of tone production. You can't say in advance exactly what the temperature of equilibrium will be because it depends strictly on the temperature outside and inside the instrument at each instant. In general, though, the temperature of equilibrium will be approximately two-thirds of the way toward your breath temperature when compared to room temperature.

Another problem is that the flute (and people just don't think of this) rises only a tiny bit because of internal temperature changes because you don't blow air through the flute as you do with brass and most woodwind instruments. Therefore, if you're on a stage with a temperature of 72, and your breath temperature is 98.6 degrees, the temperature of equilibrium inside the other wind instruments going to be about 89 degrees. At the same time the flute's temperature of equilibrium will be room temperature plus the very small warming effect of the breath at the embouchure plate, and the flesh of the fingers where they touch the metal. That is not nearly the warming effect that you have when you blow air through an instrument such as the trumpet. The flute generally is stable at whatever pitch level the performer plays. For example, if inexperienced flutists are playing an eighth of a step sharp in the high register, they will play about an eighth of a step high through the entire playing session; if they are playing an eighth of a step flat in the low register, they'll always play about an eighth of a step low. Even better, if they have tuned and are playing at A440, they'll be close to A440 at the beginning, the end, and halfway through the piece of music—but everybody else has moved up in pitch.

That is one reason the flute faces so much difficulty in playing in tune, and the main reason why it usually sounds flat in the low and middle registers compared to most of the other instruments. Remember, the flute usually is played with stability at whatever pitch level it is tuned. It doesn't change due to warm air inside the bore in the way that the other instruments do. To reiterate, every other wind instrument fluctuates more than the flute in terms of playing sharp or flat, at the temperature of equilibrium. That temperature is never the same twice, unless by coincidence the interior and outside temperature of the instrument is exactly the same two times in a row. There is a mathematical equation that predicts approximately what the change will be.

## Intonation: A Solution

There are two separate types of tuning: first, tuning the instrument to a proper pitch level (aiming for A440); second, instantaneous adjustment to play in tune with someone else at the time of performance. These two aren't the same at all. Everyone knows what happens when a good player tries to perform with somebody who is slightly high. At the instant the music sounds, if the other performer won't tune to you, you must tune to him, even if it means distorting your embouchure and tone quality.

That is the unwritten rule. At that point you have no other choice if you are sounding the lower of the two pitches. If the low pitch doesn't come up to the higher pitch, everyone will think the lower pitch is wrong, simply because of the widely-held view that "high sounds bright and energetic, and low sounds dull and bad." So you're the one whose neck is on the block (even though you may be playing at, or slightly above, A440), because everyone will look at you and think, "Well, why don't you tune up!" We keep hearing people say, "Tune up." Did you ever think of that phrase, and what it suggests? We never say, "Tune down." But when I do a clinic with a band, sometimes I will go halfway through a piece of music and just stop. Then I take my Korg tuner, turn a tuning note on, and go through the band quickly. I can almost guarantee that 90% of the musicians are sharp; only a small percentage of them ever are flat compared with A440. Even if I were to close my eyes and make a guess, I'd be right 90% of the time if I told everybody to lower the pitch.

Even though matching pitches by bringing the lower up to the higher is the natural tendency of performers, the conductor should know better. The conductor should know that often it is the high person who is sharp (above A440). I'm not saying that people who are actually flat to A440 are in tune. I'm saying the odds are that in most bands the flat person probably is closer to A440 than the sharp person. The conductor may think to himself, "I really don't hear too well; I'm just going to say, tune up." Well, my advice is to make a guess that the higher pitch is sharp; that's probably right. In fact, the odds are a lot better that the director will be correct with this guess than if he tries his luck in Las Vegas. To play in tune with a proper sound, all performers must have a finely developed inner sense of where A440 is located, and then make a deliberate effort to remain at that pitch while playing. If we don't teach this concept to our students, we can't maintain good intonation in most groups; it's just that simple.

Our aural acuity must be taught to work for us. The ear can be taught what you want it to know and hear. You, the conductor, must retrain your ear to recognize, first of all, the sound and "feel" of A440? You don't have to have perfect pitch; you just have to keep referencing the A440 pitch level. Keep it in your head, and go back to it all the time. You can develop an acute sense of the sound of the A440 pitch level, regardless of the notes involved. Using this knowledge, you will recognize when you have to pull the pitch of your musicians down (away from the direction of their natural tendency), especially the larger instruments. Remember, the solution basically is to teach the following idea. This statement sounds as though it came from a catechism, but what we must do is teach that "High is bad and sharp is bad; low is good and A440 is correct. Tune down, not up." There are many other misconceptions: we say, "Play in the center of the pitch," when that isn't true at all. Wind players play almost at the top of the available pitch for any given fingering. They can easily lip down a half-step or more, but they cannot lip up that same half-step. Most players cannot lip up more than five or six cents, if that, and maintain a reasonable tone. When a trumpeter tries to tighten the embouchure to go sharp, the pitch will ascend to the next higher partial with very little sharpening of the original note. However, that same player can loosen the embouchure and go a long way down, sometimes as much as a minor 3rd before dropping to the partial below. This shows that the instrument is not played at the pitch center of each note. You might play in the center of what you call the tone, but you don't play in the center of the possible frequencies available on that partial.

Tone is subjective, and pitch, if you look it up in most dictionaries, is also subjective. Frequency is the only objective measure. The reason why we say that pitch is subjective is as follows: it has been proven many times psychologically that a loud note sounds subjectively at a different pitch level than a soft note, even though the frequency remains totally constant. When we really get into the psychological aspects of sound, there are so many traps and pitfalls (ways to lead ourselves astray) that it is a wonder anybody ever plays in tune. Remember, much of the process of playing in tune is subjective except for one thing, frequency. Frequency is not psychological; it's just a count of double vibrations per second. Therefore, best intonation always will always be achieved when you set your instrument to play at A440, and keep it there. Then you can use your best embouchure and best tone quality at all times.

## The Importance of Understanding the Instruments

Often, after a teacher works with a student who cannot tune down satisfactorily to an A440, the idea of tuning down is dismissed entirely. The teacher does not realize or understand that there is an acoustical, or physical reason why that student can't pull down far enough. If the student has a reasonable instrument that is in good shape, there can be many different reasons for the individual tuning problem having nothing to do with the tuning process. The cause might be embouchure, a mismatch of equipment, leaks in the instrument, or using a number 1 reed (or a number 6).

Without knowing all of the factors of the instrumental equation, or understanding them, unprepared band directors can't deal with intonation problems in any way, shape, or form. That's why their bands are always out of tune. Yet, even if the untutored band director just pulls sharp instruments down to the lower ones, it will improve the intonation of his band a thousand percent. Our language and many other things are against the tuning process; however, once the basic concepts are finally understood, the instant you finally get the fundamentals into your mind, the process becomes crystal clear.

Every time I go out to judge ensembles, I hear exactly the same thing from most bands. I hear flat flutes, sharp middle/lower brass, and saxophone intonation "all over the place." Sometimes I hear a group that plays in tune. The conductor, whether by design or accident, has pulled the pitch down to a point where the instruments can play together. This is the essence of my entire message. Pull the instruments down in pitch so they can play together.

To understand tuning with all its ramifications, you have to understand what happens to the instruments when their tuning is adjusted. In other words, you have to know what you can and cannot do to an instrument; what will or will not destroy the pitch and tone. There are flutists who play extremely sharp in the high register, yet, if they pull out one-half inch at the head joint, (as some do) they have destroyed the internal intonation of the instrument. It is destroyed to the point where the flute really can't be played in tune. The head joint should be pulled approximately an eighth of an inch out to be at A440 when played with a good embouchure and proper breath support. That's all. In other words, the flutist has an embouchure problem, not a tuning problem. Without fixing the embouchure problem, no amount of pulling will help.

On the clarinet, the barrel joint should be pulled approximately an eighth of an inch for A440. The pamphlet that used to be included with the Buffet clarinet tells you this. Some players push the clarinet all the way together and still play well in tune, but there always is some reason (such as a stiff reed, close-lay mouthpiece, or relaxed embouchure) that causes them to play at the proper pitch level without pulling the barrel joint. If they sound good, that's fine, but normally with a fairly stiff reed (such as a four or a five as most professionals use) the player will have to pull out in order to be in tune.

In many bands, at least three-fourths of the trumpet players have tuning slides that are pushed all the way in.

They are not pulled approximately one-half inch, as they should be. If most trombone tuning slides aren't pulled approximately three-quarters to one inch, they are not set correctly. The principal trombonist of the New York Philharmonic was at Arizona State University several years ago to play a solo with the band; his tuning slide was pulled out. Now, if he must pull out to be in tune, most everybody else in the world should do the same. He plays with this beautiful full and relaxed sound, and he's pulled out about three-quarters of an inch. Most younger students (who are not so relaxed) have to pull out about an inch.

The problem is much worse on the tuba and euphonium. There are many tubas (after being warmed up to playing temperature, and because of the mouthpiece that somebody has put on the instrument) that don't even have enough tuning slide length to be able to pull down to A440—you just can't pull the pitch down far enough. The knowledgeable band director realizes that he either has to change mouthpieces, or he has to put in a bit between the mouthpiece and the lead pipe. Otherwise, there is not enough tuning slide room to make the needed downward adjustments.

Directors who have problems with the tuning ideas and procedures I advocate usually only have heard the simple part, which is to tune to A440. They try to pull the band down to A440 for a little while, and then run into a road block like the tuba problem discussed above. At this point they may say, "Strange doesn't know what he's talking about, because I can't pull my tubas down that far; they don't have enough slide room to get that low." These directors do not understand that there is a physical and acoustical reason why their tubas can't play at A440. The problem is not the tuning standard at all; it's the equipment they are using. It is similar to putting a 15C mouthpiece on a medium large-bore Bach trumpet, and then expecting to play in tune easily with that set-up. The problem is not with the Bach, and it's not with the A 440; the fault is the mouthpiece, which makes it difficult to play in tune.

Many young band directors in the field are brass players; they are afraid of reeds; they don't understand them; they can't really play the instrument themselves, so they just accept what the student does. These band directors must learn to play the reed instruments well if they wish to have fine bands. They cannot teach what they do not understand themselves. So, a little knowledge is a dangerous thing. I've studied this very hard for quite a long time, and have taught a class on it for fifteen years. I still find many nuggets of information and insights about all the band instruments. I sometimes wonder, "How in the world can I teach this to other people, when I'm still trying to learn it myself (after more than forty years of teaching)?"

When I try to help band directors by working with their bands, I always go back to the basics. One of the biggest problems that I hear in clarinet sections, even in fairly good bands, is that many students use reeds that are, by and large, too soft. I can't help any of those students to achieve better intonation without first convincing the student (and the teacher) that the reed is the problem. When these groups play for me, I must tell the band director and the students, "The tone quality of the clarinet section tells me that your clarinetists are using reeds that are too soft." After I listen to individual members of the clarinet section, the director expects me to tell them all kinds of wonderful embouchure secrets, plus all this great stuff about taking a deep breath and blowing a steady stream of air. Instead, I say, "Your reeds are too soft; you must get a stiffer reed." The students and the director look at me like, "Gee whiz, that's nothing musical." Yet it's the crux of the entire problem, because I can't teach them anything musical until they get a stiffer reed, or clip the reed two or three times. Even clipping a soft reed doesn't always help, because when you clip a reed, you simply make the tip a lot thicker and shorten the length of the slope on the top (vamp); you don't add wood to the heart (where most of the thickness is needed). If the student has a reed that blows like a number 1 (I call those reeds "pieces of wet tissue paper"), it doesn't do much good to clip it, because, after two or three clips, it will be so stuffy that you can't get anything out of it. Then, if you try to shave the tip back a little thinner, without re-shaping the entire reed, you find it still blows too stuffy, because the reed doesn't have enough backbone, and the vamp isn't long enough.

There is another problem with some brands of reeds: the numbers on the reeds don't mean much in relation to other brands. When I was a kid, a number 1 was soft, 2 was medium soft, 3 was medium, 4 was medium stiff, 5 was stiff, and so on; to a certain extent you could rely on that scale with most brands. Recently, I played some number 4 reeds that didn't feel any stiffer than the number 1 of other brands. Therefore, when I find young players with these particular reeds (unless they are blowing on a reed in the 5 1/2 or 6 category), I know their reeds are still too soft. Conductors and students seldom understand that, and they say proudly, "I'm using brand X." They may name a so-called premium reed. It costs a lot more than the rest, so the students think they're getting something great. But the reed they're playing on may have no backbone in it whatsoever. I try to convince directors and students that if they want a good clarinet sound with proper pitch control, they must use a reed that has enough strength to be played with a reasonably firm embouchure without closing up in the high register. Here is a nearly absolute test: if you have a student who can't play up to a high C (second added line) or to the D above without using excess pressure, or one who takes too much reed in the mouth, or one who uses a normal embouchure but the reed stops vibrating in the upper register, the reed obviously is too soft. I don't care what the number is. The reed has to have enough strength to play into the altissimo register when using a normal firm embouchure; if it won't do that, it's too soft.

Many say, "I want to start my students on a soft reed and gradually work them up to a stiffer reed," but acoustically, that doesn't work in the high register. I agree with the idea that you can use a soft reed with beginners, until they have to cross the break. The instant they cross the break, they then must use a reed with enough strength to it so that a normal firm embouchure can be used to play the notes. This is what happens when a 1 to 2 strength reed is used: in the higher register, the student must take about twice too much reed into the mouth, and use just a tiny amount of air pressure to obtain the note. In other words, the embouchure and breath pressure must be altered drastically to obtain any sound at all.

The only remedy is to use at least a number 3 reed for students who are just past the beginning stage (as numbered in most reed-grading systems). With most reeds, a 3 or 3 1/2 might be best, and with at least one brand, it might be a 5 or a 6. Using stiffer reeds makes more difference to the sound and intonation of most clarinet sections than all the other things put together that I can tell them about the instrument or the music being played. It's the simplest part of the whole equation, and yet it's the key to good tone, pitch, and technique. You can't go into the musical aspects of clarinet playing if the reed is too soft. However, the combination of a stiffer reed and a firmer embouchure will raise the pitch of the player, who must compensate by pulling out the barrel joint until A440 is reached.

## The Bernoulli Effect

There is so much to know. For example, we must understand what makes a clarinet (saxophone, oboe, bassoon, etc.) reed vibrate in order to understand its tuning problems. How can we recommend the proper reed strength for our students (all-important for good intonation) if we don't understand the working of the reed? There isn't one clarinetist or band director in a thousand who knows exactly what makes that reed vibrate; he thinks he pushes the reed against the "lay" with his breath as he blows through the opening between the reed and the mouth-piece (not true at all).

The reed is set into motion because of a definite physical principle. As you blow air through a venturi (which is the smallest diameter of any tube) there is a physical effect called the Bernoulli Effect, which says that pressure drops at the point of greatest constriction. In other words, air from the lungs is pushed through the tube (clarinet mouthpiece/bore) and expands just as soon as it goes through the portion with the smallest diameter (the opening between the reed and the mouthpiece tip). This causes a drop in pressure at the opening, creating, in effect, a partial vacuum. At the instant the burst of air rushes through the venturi, this vacuum sucks the reed against the mouthpiece by overcoming the "springiness" in the tip. When the reed closes against the mouthpiece, pressure is equalized because the bore is an open tube, and the reed springs back open. The process of causing the reed to vibrate by creating and breaking the vacuum between the reed and mouthpiece tip occurs 440 times per second if you're sounding concert A.

For exactly the same reason, the lips open and close when playing a brass instrument. When you blow a burst of air through the lips, you lower the pressure at the smallest diameter of the opening (the aperture). The lips close because the muscles of the lip overcome the reduced air pressure. Then another burst of air forces the lips open, etc., etc. It is this little drop in pressure that makes it possible for us to make a tone. Buzzing the lips is a simulation of what's going on inside the mouthpiece. The opening and closing of the lips causes the column of air in the bore to vibrate, creating the sound. The reason the aperture closes is really the key to the whole thing. If you blew your lips open and kept a constant stream of air flowing through them, as some band directors tell you you're supposed to do, the aperture would never close until you ran out of air. In other words, you'd have to huff and puff four hundred forty times per second to play A. Obviously, you can't do that.

The physical principle called the Bernoulli Effect allows the creation of sound on all wind instruments except for the flute. The flute actually produces sound in a completely different way. A small stream of air is blown against the sharp edge of the hole in the embouchure plate (strike plate) deflecting a portion down into the bore. This creates a tiny unequal pressure by compressing the air inside the flute slightly. The higher air pressure in the bore causes the air stream to spring back out. This rarefies the air inside the flute slightly, sucking the air stream back in again; there is a constant in-and-out movement of the air that creates a standing wave. Another explanation for this same phenomenon is contained in the theory of "eddy currents." Liken the airstream to the flapping of a flag: equal amounts of wind blow on both sides of any waving flag, but the flag flaps (waves) because pressure on both sides of the flag can never be completely equal (the flag is never totally straight throughout its entire length for even one instant). Think of the flag as waving in and out of the embouchure hole on a flute, and you will have a good visualization of what happens to the airstream when a tone is produced.

## Tuning Latitude

Each instrument also should have what I call tuning latitude, an important concept. If the instrument has this tuning latitude (the ability to play both higher and lower than the prevailing pitch) taken away, it has no ability to go flat or sharp if need be.  Without this tuning latitude, in an ensemble that already is high, the player fights for his musical life. Even by playing absolutely as high as possible (which generally results in ruined tone), he may not be able to play in tune with the ensemble.

There are some instruments which can go sharp to an extreme degree. The saxophones obviously are the worst, and the trombones are very bad about it, too. The saxophones pose a problem because they don't have a finite position for the mouthpiece on the cork. A trombonist can play clear up around A448 by pushing all the way in, and using a tight embouchure with a small mouthpiece. Most of the other instruments cannot go up with him that high. If the pitch level of the trombone section is allowed to rise, then the band will play out of tune regardless of how much the band director rubs his ear (and points to his ear) while they're playing, or tells them to "listen," and uses any other of the many platitudes that we keep hearing from some band directors. The words and gestures won't help, because there is nothing the other performers can do to come up that far.  They have lost their "tuning latitude."

When conductors first address the problem of lowering the general pitch of a band, many become frustrated and "throw out the baby with the bath water."  After trying vainly to bring everybody down, they'll say , "The whole thing is no good; my band can't get down to A440." Or, they'll say, "You can tune there, but you can't play there." Yes, you can! You can both tune at A440 and stay at A440 as you play;  you just have to know how, that's all! There are a million other things that a person can talk about, but I always tend to emphasize those few things which can make a drastic change in the band.

A third factor that can affect over-all band intonation, and it's an obvious thing, is placing the hand correctly in the bell of the French horn. I conducted an unnamed all-state several years ago where two of the horns in the group played with their hands on the outside of the bell—with double horns. It just blows my mind that they can get that far without their teachers insisting that they put their hands in the bell. One reason for this, of course is obvious: the band director cannot see the hand in the bell when he's on the podium, and he doesn't listen for proper tone quality.  (Many times the young band director, or the band director who is a woodwind player instead of brass player, doesn't have a sound in his ear to recall as he listens to the horns and other brass.)

I worked with a marvelous horn teacher at Carnegie-Mellon University for many years whose name was Forrest Standley (some of his students were Dale Clevenger, Phillip Meyer, etc.), and I think I have a pretty good idea about what the right hand ought to do (we used to talk about it a lot).

The player must have the right hand in the correct position, or the instrument cannot be played in an acousti-cally correct manner. If you have the hand totally out of the bell, and you're playing a fairly small mouthpiece, you literally can't bring a horn down to A440 because there are not enough slides to pull. Yet many teachers do not seem to understand that there is something wrong with having all of the slides fully extended and the hand out of the bell. I'm talking about valve slides and main tuning slides. Three-fourths of an inch is as far as most slides should ever be pulled out, yet some kids will have their slides pulled out an inch and a half, maybe two inches on main tuning slides, and still be playing too sharp, because their idea of putting the hand in the bell is simply to put the palm of the right hand against the metal on the near side (or on the rim of the bell). They don't have their right hand across the opening at all. So they have done nothing to the acoustics of the instrument;  all they are doing is holding it. You have to convince them that the right hand is part of the acoustics of the horn, making it different from all the other brass instruments. If they don't understand that, they will be out of tune. There's nothing you can do about their bad intona-tion unless the right-hand position and tuning slide settings are correct. To correct the problem, push the slides back in until the tuning slides on the average double horn are pulled approximately three-quarters of an inch—give or take a little. Then tune the instrument by placing the right hand in its proper position. Cup the right hand slightly, and put the thumb to the side of the fore-finger, placing the hand in the bell with the fingernails against the metal and the hand cupped across the bell opening. Keep inserting the hand into the bore until the horn is in tune. At this point, the hand is in the correct position, because that's acoustically the way the instrument has to be held in order to play in tune. (The Farkas book, *The Art of Horn Playing*, tells you how to tune your valve slides.)

Using simple concepts like these makes it possible for bands to play beautifully in tune, but there aren't many undergraduate courses which teach the acoustical problems of instruments. I teach a one-semester course on the doctoral level at Arizona State University on exactly this subject. It takes an entire semester with doctoral students to convince them of the rightness of what I am saying, and so it just seems like it's almost impossible to come to grips with this in terms of instant clinics (although I am trying to do just that in this interview). If band directors even understand some portion of these ideas, their bands will play better in tune than before. There are some band directors who understand all of these concepts, and their bands do play beautifully in tune.

## Use an Electronic Source for Tuning Pitch

I would like to add one more thing. I tune my own band with a Korg tone generator. (I don't care what brand you use, but tune them with a tone generator.) Dr. Revelli had a famous saying many years ago: "Strobes (and tuning meters) are great for tuning the eyeballs, but they don't tune instruments; ears tune instruments."

I insist that all my tuning pitches, including on-stage tuning for concert purposes, come from my Korg tuner. I do not use a tuning pitch from any instrument, and haven't for many years. I insist on this partially because ensembles don't trust a single person as the pitch-giver. I played the oboe professionally with several orchestras (some of them very good), and I hated giving the tuning pitch more than everything else put together. I would rather play a concerto with orchestra than give the tuning note. I could have a Korg in front of me; I could have a tuning fork screwed into my head; I could have perfect pitch; I could be a pitch genius, and when I gave that A, everybody in the orchestra looked cross-wise at me as if to say, "You dummy, where did you get that pitch?" They are more skeptical of "human" pitch than when it comes from a neutral pitch arbitrator (in the case of my band, a tone generator). The band director helps the tuning process when a tone generator is used.

Nobody ever quibbles with the Korg in bands and orchestras that I conduct. I turn it on, and somehow the tuner has credibility. Sound any note you like as long as the tuner is calibrated at A440. Everybody will listen solemnly, and then tune without question. I tell students as a joke, "Look, it's a Korg. It's quartz locked. Are you going to argue with that?" I believe it is ineffective to use an instrument for the tuning pitch, especially when it's not supported by the use of the tuning meter.

You never get the same pitch twice from most young players. Even if a fine instrumentalist gives the reference pitch (be it an oboe player, a clarinet player, or a tubist), have the player stare at a Korg tuning meter. It will give both the "soloist" and the rest of the ensemble confidence that the reference pitch is correct. It is interesting to note that one part of the rules governing the International Pitch Standard recommends using an electrical device to generate the tuning pitch. I sometimes make an overly-simplistic remark, but it is factually true. "If everybody played at the A440 pitch level, we wouldn't have anybody out of tune, ever. We wouldn't have to listen to each other so much. We could be in separate rooms, and we'd still stay in tune with each other." The crux of the matter is to have this absolute, steady, dependable tuning pitch that never deviates, and to use it always.

## Vocalization Helps Pitch Consciousness

After hearing the tuning note, I have my students hum the pitch before sounding the note on their instruments, because it helps to wash everything else out of their minds. I have forty masters and doctoral students in my top band, and I still ask them to hum the pitch, even if they don't want to do so. This humming of the pitch is crucial to focus attention, and place the reference pitch in the head. I have had quite a few students come back to me later to say that they really did understand and approve of vocalizing the tuning pitch before playing. The method works and is "catching." I have never yet told my students to hum the pitch while tuning during a concert, and yet they do. When I want to tune during a concert, all I do is step off the podium. My graduate assistant (who has the Korg), turns the Korg on and holds it up. The instant he does that, the whole band hums the pitch. This response is habitual, because we use it every day in rehearsal. That's what I want, a habitual tuning procedure to a known pitch standard. I think it really works, and I believe that my own band shows that. They sometimes miss notes, but they don't play out of tune as an ensemble.

I have "hand-outs" that I give to students about the ideas discussed in this telephone interview. I will be happy to send the material out on request, or correspond with anyone who wants to discuss these ideas.

# APPENDIX VI

## Donald R. Hunsberger,  Allan R. McMurray,  and John R. Paynter

At the time the research for this book was underway Donald R. Hunsberger, Allan R. McMurray, and John R. Paynter had been invited to contribute to this project. Various deadlines, schedule conflicts, and other obstacles, however, prevented their important contributions from being included in the first edition.

Their contributions relate to bands and wind music, musical and teaching values, rehearsal and teaching techniques, teaching and conducting philosophies, and selecting and judging literature. Their comments also address many other interesting topics such as composers, publishers, programming, students, teachers, communication, and the past and future of wind music.

These gentlemen have our appreciation for offering their thoughts and GIA Publications deserves thanks for allowing them to be included in this edition. I am grateful to both because these contributions enrich the substance of the book.

### A standard of literature

Several decades ago there was a standard literature through which band directors knew and valued compositions that had been transcribed for band primarily from orchestral sources. They looked to many of these works as reference points, and the music itself provided examples of what they considered to be the best type of literature for band directors, teachers, and their students. As a result, there was an ideal based upon this literature that, if the bands could play these works, teachers and students could feel their performances and programs were achieving and matching what they believed was a worthwhile standard.

Although I do not agree entirely with the philosophies of the bands of fifty years ago who spent a high percentage of their time performing transcriptions of the of the standard orchestral, operatic or keyboard repertoire, (even though this is the basis for my own personal experience and development), the use of this material did provide goals toward which they worked.

In the early 1950s a movement toward playing predominantly original band literature began. In the process of developing this movement, conductors and teachers began moving away from playing transcriptions due to

this increased interest in original wind band music.

However, some did not consider these new original works for winds as musically worthy as the music in the transcriptions that had been played before.

In recent decades, when we have been trying to develop what you might call an indigenous or original repertoire, we have slipped and slid into a considerable amount of commercialism. This includes disposable music, which I describe as new music that is produced by publishers each year, frequently based upon successful models of the previous years. School bands frequently consume this music for one year only and dispose of it at the end of that year, likely never to be played again.

I was amazed again this year when I was able through the *BDGuide* to read the voluminous lists of all the publications released within the past twelve months. If one counts the number of publications that all these firms issue in just one year and multiply this by similar efforts in recent years, this is a waste of money, a waste of energy, and an enormous waste of paper. Using some of this music can also misuse students' potential and the opportunity to enrich our students' experiences with much substantial repertoire.

In this respect I feel very positive about being part of publication efforts, such as those found in the *BDGuide*, which promulgate a standard or core repertoire for bands.

*(Donald R. Hunsberger)*

### Establishing a standard repertoire

I feel that repeated performances of works we consider to be worthy enable us to establish a standard repertoire. Our student constituency changes every couple of years so we are able to program works numerous times since the same people will not be playing each time. This way we can work with each composition numerous times, and even though the work is repeated after several years, the program remains appealing for the audience.

Through these repeated performances I discover whether my original judgments may be confirmed or denied—my judgments are always fluctuating as I have discovered that I can sometimes lose interest after working with, and performing, a questionable work several times.

A comment about this at my workshops and clinics is: "I think perhaps I've taken more pieces out of the repertoire than I've added to the repertoire." In part, this occurs because my repeated exposures to a composition usually lead me to reach an informed decision; sometimes those works which were at first interesting to me do not remain interesting and I remove them from the literature list.

*(Donald R. Hunsberger)*

### Observations about compositions

I recently played a program consisting of three works that were all new to me. I think that the use of a compositional scalpel would have helped all three, because each composer was trying to make a statement—a grand or a major statement—and the material, and the development of this material, ended up lacking substance.

There is always an interesting situation which may occur when performing works for the first time, this being a feeling on your part that you cannot fully support the new work in your own thinking, and the ensemble recognizes this. I have always tried to do my best and give everything possible to the realization of the new score, but if it is lacking in some way or other, this is the ultimate responsibility of the composer, not the recreator. This instance is a primary reason why it is always an advantage when you can actually have the composer or arranger there for the rehearsals. Areas of difficulty can be discovered, discussed, and hopefully brought into a more positive situation.

Unfortunately the publishing industry, and in particular the educational press, has not made allowance for constructive, reflective time for some of their composers. Just as we conductors must live with works and constantly revise our opinions, so must composers have post-composition time to reflect, alter, even withdraw a work before the work is locked into cold print.

Some wind conductors are prone to accept models of compositions set forth by their leaders almost without any personal qualification; thus when a leader establishes a repertoire or a set of compositions, these conductors feel obligated to follow these examples, almost blindly. It has developed into a "what's new" syndrome. Rather than re-investigating the past and restoring those works which have merit, the emphasis becomes directed toward the most recent publications. Another example of this occurred back in the 'sixties and 'seventies when a few composers were performed by almost everyone (in excess, perhaps) and then suddenly dropped because they were "old news."

Fortunately, one of the positive programming fixations has been on the wind music of Percy Grainger who was so innovative in his scoring and his ideals for the wind band. I personally respect and admire Grainger for his imaginative writing and I believe he is best viewed as a miniaturist rather than a large form or symphonic com-

poser. If one looks at *Lincolnshire Posy* carefully, one can see that each of those movements is a perfect gem in itself set in a "posy," a collection or gathering. Grainger made clearly defined melodic statements and then delivered his form usually through some form of harmonic or rhythmic variant. When I look at his longer-form works, I really feel that they don't stand up as well as these miniatures.

I have performed the Giannini symphony many times. Occasionally, I have grouped the second movement and the first movement (in that order) as a performance unit. The third movement is acceptable, but I have thought the fourth movement was inferior from the time it came out, and I still feel it is. It lacks a depth of thought, the tempo leads only to technical excess and all we end up with is a show of prowess (even at differing degrees of accomplishment).

*(Donald R. Hunsberger)*

### The teachers' responsibility for literature

Music teachers must be more responsible for the musical experiences of their changing constituency, which in most cases turns over after three to four years. Each student should experience some of the best compositions for band, which could be drawn from a list of standard band literature.

There is an growing number of existing good compositions for the various forms of the contemporary wind band and many different and high quality works may be experienced by every student before he or she graduates. Those teachers who are constantly complaining about the lack of repertoire, are usually the ones who are not testing or attempting to establish what might be considered a standard, basic repertoire of valuable literature.

A period of growth, such as we are currently experiencing while our literature develops, must be a time of experimentation. We must encourage those composers and publishers whom we feel are really trying to make an effort at creating and providing literature of merit. We should be less supportive, or even totally unsupportive, of those publishers and composers who are only trying to make this year's dollar from this year's run of new publications.

As conductors and teachers consider possible standards and quality experiences they desire for their students, this is not the time to return to the use of transcriptions as a primary source of programming material, even though many of these were excellent works in their original form. What I advocate is the development of a standard core wind literature that replaces borrowed publications and inferior original music while establishing a new high standard for all to follow. I want the best music possible to establish a wind standard that is at least as high as those standards established in other performance media.

I think that many current teachers, in influencing their students, have developed this same feeling for quality in music. Some older teachers may have experienced or received this sense of quality by playing the transcriptions. What they basically received was the sense of what good music could be, even though much was ill-suited to the wind medium. There was a feeling that the transcribed music was good to utilize because much of it had been passed to them over the last one hundred or more years.

As wind band conductors we must look into ourselves and undertake the obligation of making those decisions our responsibilities warrant. We must stand up for many things, of which the selection of high quality literature is paramount. An equal level decision is a deep-felt concern for the growth and experiences of our students which will occur only through the use of high quality literature and musical performance practices.

*(Donald R. Hunsberger)*

### Transcriptions

Though I've written transcriptions, created editions of existing wind works, and done arrangements for band and orchestra, I have usually attempted to write something that would fill a gap in the repertoire. An example of this is the *Festive Overture* by Shostakovitch. At the time that transcription was written, there was practically no music by Shostakovitch available. One hoped that the use of a composer's music in transcription might lead the composer to create an original work for the medium (There was already a Russian band version when I began mine in 1963, but the instrumentation did not fit the American distribution or use of instruments.) Another example is the *Valley of the Bells* by Ravel. We unfortunately will never have an indigenous wind work by Ravel and thus it becomes necessary to provide some examples of this style of Impressionistic music. However, it must be done stylistically and attempt to achieve orchestration effects similar to those created by the composer in his orchestral works, not merely create another anonymous band journal type work.

A second major area that must be addressed by the arranger-transcriber-orchestrator is knowledge of contemporary wind timbres that will transport a new version of a work out of the first half of the 20th Century. By these I mean an avoidance of traditional military band doublings: clarinet and cornet melodic lead, lack of multiple flute parts, overly heavy mid-range doublings between brass and reeds especially with the saxophones thickening up the sound, constant use of the brass bass, and lack of a woodwind bass presence. If one eliminates these elements and uses the fresh sounds that we find in the best works of today, a transcription or wind setting can sound fresh and bring credit to today's band. The re-distribution of voices away from the clarinet, cornet, and brass bass sounds is most important.

Students may miss experiences with Medieval, Renaissance, or Baroque music, experiences with the music of a composer such as Palestrina, Bach, or Handel, or experiences such as a concerto grosso, a fugue, or a toccata if a work is not available in an acceptable contemporary edition.

A transcription or edition for its own sake must not be the main reason for its creation or use. There must be some musical worth or personality that students would not experience otherwise unless the transcribed or edited work were not available. The work must be programmed in a manner that allows it to fit musically among original works for the band. The percentage of programmed transcriptions or editions should be low compared to that of original works from the band's standard repertoire.

When one examines concert programs from thirty-forty years ago with those of today, it is interesting to note how the primary emphasis upon the creation of literature has shifted from the arranger or transcriber to the composer himself!

*(Donald R. Hunsberger)*

### Selecting literature

I think many people select program literature based primarily on their organization's performance abilities rather than placing primary emphasis on the quality of literature and what the image of this quality projects to their students and audience. Some may be attempting to find the latest new top-grade work because their major interest lies in working toward a contest and to create a positive impression. Others may be looking for a work that perhaps does not have extreme or stringent instrumentation demands, and these requirements may actually be considered more administrative than musical.

To balance programs based upon the need for specific performance requirements, and also upon the encouragement and creation of a lasting wind literature, is indeed difficult. One of the greatest pitfalls to avoid lies in mixing up administrative and musical decisions while placing a primary emphasis in areas other than the musical.

A question which frequently arises, especially with contemporary or newer works, concerns how much we take our audiences into consideration when programming. At times, there are works programmed strictly for audience appeal and one must be careful not to allow works of little musical substance to dominate the programming procedures. Entertainment tunes that appeal directly to the community certainly have their place, but not as a major element.

One of the more devastating innovations to the concert hall recently has been the infusion of corps-style instrumentation and arranging into works for concert or symphonic bands. The result is a reduction of orchestration possibilities through a lack of reliance upon those instruments that everybody worked so hard to develop, teach, and bring into prominence: the double reeds, the additional low clarinets, the low brasses, etc. that provide such wonderful timbres in the wind band.

Please don't misunderstand me regarding the marching band. I grew up marching since I was in Junior High, although what we did was a continuation of the street marching bands that performed throughout our march history. All the town and city bands I performed with in Southeast Pennsylvania did street marching on a regular schedule. Today, the situation is totally different and band directors must be aware of both the benefits as well as the detrimental effects of a marching program which is primarily an entertainment or show-time exposition.

The marching band has its own place; it is an entertainment type of function, it is generally a very disciplined function, and it has a lot of good features to be applied if it's done well and not abused. There is potential there but its scoring and instrumentation features should not be carried over into what we're trying to do as a legitimate, sit down, classical style organization.

The marching band and its style has an instant appeal for most audiences, and thus, there is a temptation to program this type of music with the wind band because an audience will accept the program in general.

*(Donald R. Hunsberger)*

### Making decisions about literature

First, most music teachers should have enough useful musical background, training, and thus, a justified musical confidence in themselves and their background to be able to analyze any work they wish to program. The decision as to whether a piece of music is really worth the time, energy, and effort of their students and themselves is a constant requisite that each of us must face. Even when works receive acclaim or public attention, the basic decision must be made by each conductor as to whether this particular work is really worth all our combined efforts to bring it to performance. The choice of literature is very difficult in the band area especially, because there is frequently a great lack of self-discipline on the part of conductors who take the easy road out.

*(Donald R. Hunsberger)*

### Involving students in literature selection

Some teachers involve their students in programming decisions through utilizing tapes or recordings of works under consideration for programming. This is an excellent way to place a form of responsibility onto the students themselves as they are being asked to rely upon their tastes and their background, and to hear, to see, and to decide what they feel is worth an investment of time and energy.

One way in which to do this is to schedule listening sessions within the rehearsal period at which time the director plays recordings of works under consideration and then leads the ensemble in discussion of the merits of each work. Such discussion might include questions such as "Is the melodic content interesting?" "What about the harmonic movement, is it creative or is it stagnant?" "Does

the rhythmic development interest you?" "What about the form? Does it feel too long, too short?" "Is the orchestration interesting, exciting?" An evaluation sheet could be prepared with sample questions such as these to be answered by the students.

It is perfectly natural for many performers to be drawn to the flashy or catchy piece over the more introspective or developed composition, but this is where the teacher may use his/her experience and background to point out the differences in the approaches to composition. Once decisions are made, rehearsals should assume a different character since the performers now have an vested interest in the development of the final product.

Another correlation may be made between the approach of orchestral conductors and liberal arts teachers in the selection of literature for their students. Their situation is different from that of the wind conductor as their entire array of basic literature has already been established and accepted as classics. Although they also have the contemporary novel or the non-fiction work to consider, they are not in the position of surveying a relatively small standard accepted repertoire developed over the past forty years and then sifting through new publications to ascertain the usability of one or two acceptable works. In addition, their repertoire is original material, not transcribed or arranged and "experiencing the real thing" helps make that whole literature really come alive for their students.

Our literature is emerging and many decisions are needed that could both bring valuable literature to our students and contribute to the establishment of "our own classics." Therefore, a self confidence in our work and our progress is necessary to continue the supply of such a necessary ingredient.

*(Donald R. Hunsberger)*

### Selecting literature for my students at Eastman

The manner in which I select literature is based primarily on my criteria for that literature and the development of the performers. (My criteria are not necessarily identical to those of teachers in the public schools.)

My needs at Eastman include a thrust toward the development of a wind band repertoire that will benefit the students through their involvement and repertoire that is capable of standing by itself in the greater music world. This body of literature is intended to be the wind equivalent of what we consider the standard body of orchestral or vocal literature.

I go through much published and manuscript music. I send away for this literature when I hear about it and I receive many manuscript compositions unsolicited. When I go through these various scores, sometimes with a recording, and sometimes without, I'm looking for something that will be of a quality that is already established with our basic repertoire from composers such as Holst, Vaughan Williams, Schoenberg, Milhaud, Hindemith, Hanson, Persichetti, Dahl, Husa, Schwantner, Colgrass, among others, through works—both single and multiple movement—that constitute a divertimento or lighter style. (So much has been written of the basic repertoire, including that by the author, that a complete listing is inappropriate at this time).

What I do in my examination and analysis of a new work is to try to determine the unique features inherent in the composition. Although there is always an intuitive comparison with some other work already found to be successful, I try very hard to make decisions based entirely upon the merits of the new composition. Of course, another source of information has been highly trusted friends and colleagues whom I know are working on the same goals as I and whose decisions about repertoire I can trust explicitly. If I find that the composer, in writing a work, is making an individual statement and contribution, then that work becomes of interest, but if the work is merely cloning someone else without showing much originality, then I'm not interested in that piece.

I don't spend nearly so much time looking at junior high repertoire as I do high school or university level literature because that's not the area I'm working in. I try, through the programs that I do at Eastman and the ones I take on tour, to represent that material which is the best that we have been able to support and develop. On these programs I do some new works and I repeat compositions I believe have value.

*(Donald R. Hunsberger)*

### Literature and programming

Concerns about the selection of literature are also concerns regarding programming techniques, as the manner in which you frame a work on a program will contribute heavily to its success, or its lack of acceptance by an audience and by the performers.

For example, when you take a work that's new to you and the band itself, you might expect a rather tentative performance. The ensemble will be more tentative than if they were performing a work that is more familiar, comfortable, or accessible.

Framing a work well on a program means taking every factor into consideration. For example you would not wish to program works before or after a new composition that are somewhat similar in sound, in timbre, even in key to the new work, or you'll find that a little of the newness may have been blunted.

A successful programming technique I have tried with new works involves placing the new composition at the end of the first half of the program just before intermission. Following the intermission I play it again (unannounced on the printed program) so the same piece is played twice that evening. What occurs is that the second rendition will be markedly different than the first because everybody will have settled into the performance more. The audience also will have a opportunity to hear it again and their ears and minds will accept the music in a more educated and different manner.

This approach gives the performers the opportunity, through the second performance, to reconsider many of their thoughts about the questions they had in trying to make the premiere performance come off satisfactorily. The second playing will help to solidify in my mind whether the work is really as good as I thought or perhaps not as good. I have found this procedure to work very well.

Perhaps one reason why this type of approach is not in common practice is that many people just haven't thought about it or were unaware someone else has done it. They may also be a little afraid that the second performance would impose on the audience if they did this.

We must take up the premise that we are there for a purpose and that everything we program reflects how we feel about ourself, the music, and our ensemble. This also reflects upon how we feel about our audience and its potential for intellectual growth. If we're there to help them to grow along with the band and the literature, there's no reason why we cannot occasionally draw them into our creative process. We cannot, of course, do this at every concert.

Explaining the background or purpose for a work to the audience, as some conductors do, also gives the audience credit for its interest and ability to comprehend new terms of composition and performance. It tells them they are capable of understanding new or different background information about older or new works. This approach sets up the listener so the performance and composition are accepted as well as could be.

A conversation with the audience will not, in itself, improve the audience's level or comprehension or appreciation. What it may do, however, is to influence their attitudes, give them a framework in which to receive new compositions, and, demonstrate our deeply-felt interest in the work we are about to perform.

Some teachers may be apprehensive about talking to the audience and convey or project a self-defeating or self-deprecating approach. Developing the attitude and self assurance that "I've got the background, I've got the information, I have the knowledge, and I have the desire!" will place a teacher on a more successful path to communication with his/her ensemble and audience.

A conductor must have the courage and insight to pick the best works possible for the audience and the ensemble's development. Some conductor/teachers lack, or have not developed, these abilities and make poor choices about literature and programming. Again, they may be afraid of offending someone, whether it be school administration, parents, or audience.

Frequently, the main issue may be directed right back to the person on the podium whose feeling of self confidence and security in musical leadership tends to lead toward safe or common denominator programming and performances.

*(Donald R. Hunsberger)*

### *Teaching in a certain situation*

In my own case, I grew up in a Pennsylvania Dutch community (Souderton) in southeast Pennsylvania that supported music in the schools. I was particularly blessed by having a wonderful trombone teacher, Samuel Laudenslager; an insightful piano teacher, Mr. Ernest Strauss, who also taught me composition and theory; and a highly motivated school band director, Maurice Foulke (who was a violist!). Mr. Foulke was extremely supportive of my development and, through his efforts school-wide, successfully involved many students from the High School in several trips yearly to hear Youth Concerts by the Philadelphia Orchestra. This was more unique than it might sound as about half of my graduating class were Mennonites, many of whom were not permitted to play instruments or to participate in school dances. Even so, there were town bands in neighboring communities, Quakertown, Red Hill, and especially in Allentown, that I played in beginning from about the time I was in seventh grade.

An involved teacher can take the raw talent, interest, and inquisitiveness of a student and mold this into any shape and form they wish; this has always been one of the big challenges of people in education. In a sense, a teacher is creating the future history of that person's experiences—setting them up for the rest of their creative life.

It is constantly stated that "times have changed" and "times are not for the better." However, I recently read a wonderful article in the New York Times about a high school band in New Jersey. The article was printed on the sports page and was about a band championship to be held at the New York Giants Football Stadium.

In this particular city in New Jersey, the football coach and the band director are both about fifty years old and had worked together for many years. The city is fifty percent Hispanic, thirty percent black, and the rest are white and Asian. This is a real non-traditional makeup compared to past decades.. There are eighty-eight musicians, twenty-four color guards, and three drum majors in the band.

A most interesting point is made when one of the drum majors is quoted. He said, "Band is better than sports because it is pure. The football team is great and one of the captains is a good friend of mine, but some team members do not play in the games, they stand on the sidelines all season long. In band, all of us are on the field all the time and if the third clarinet gets the wrong note, it affects all of us." Then he quotes the band director who told them: "Football is just for the game, music is forever." Whatever this group's teacher has done, he has his students believing in goals and he has them involved personally. It's up to him to decide the heights to which he desires to take them—and it appears he knows the way!

In every state there are individual leaders on all levels that teachers can emulate or follow. I do not mean follow in a competitive sense but rather in learning from somebody else through seeing what they do—seeing especially what they envision their role in life and the road they must follow to accomplish their desires.

*(Donald R. Hunsberger)*

### *How one does what they do: the rehearsal*

One good thing about experience and age is that hopefully we learn what works and what doesn't work. One of the things that I think I've learned more than anything else is personal organization, especially pertaining to the rehearsal.

I enjoy rehearsals. Many times I think I actually enjoy the rehearsal process more than I enjoy the actual concert. However, the concert is the culmination point where we put everything together, and we watch individuals develop their own approach to their own part and to the ensemble at large. This in itself can be most satisfying in many, many ways.

At Eastman, we use a rotation program for assigning individual parts and seatings for the students in the ensemble program. In establishing the weekly rehearsal schedule, each instrumental conductor (the orchestral and wind groups) posts an exact schedule of the rehearsal times of each work in the program. Thus, each performer knows exactly when they are required for rehearsal on each individual composition.

As a result, I select what I wish to accomplish during the allotted rehearsal time. I plan the overall rehearsal time from the beginning of the first rehearsal right to the concert and then divide the time available for each work. This places a certain stricture on me because of what I wish to accomplish within the framework of those hours. In itself it is good for me as I am forced to prioritize what I wish to accomplish.

My purpose in the rehearsal period is two-fold: one is to uncover the mysteries of the music and its inherent qualities each time we approach it. (This aural experience adds to the score-study time I have spent by myself.) Another equal purpose is to develop the individual performers' facility, skills, and insights into the music itself. This is a most important area for me as I very firmly believe in the development of the individual performer, as a musician, an individual, and as a participant in whatever ensemble they may happen to perform.

I practice what we have established as a wind ensemble concept and my approach is not the same as one might use in the traditional symphonic band concept. In the latter, much of the development time is spent putting together and developing sections: the third clarinet section and those five people, the four people in the second clarinets, the six people playing first clarinet, etc. In the wind ensemble approach the emphasis is upon the individual, whether performing as a single person or whether grouped together in a section.

I want each performer to realize as fully as possible how he/she fits into the work and what the work is all about. I talk music theory, I talk music history, I talk analysis, and I'll frequently discuss conducting techniques with them.

We frequently practice conducting together, especially in an asymmetric type of piece. Our Basic Conducting Class at Eastman is a large group each year so many of them have already studied conducting. I explain to them what the problem is and let them try to figure out what's going on. This gives them a different realization of the problems of their individual parts and especially what my job is; through this they develop a more complete grasp of the complexities of the composition.

I usually talk in concert pitch in a rehearsal; I gave up talking transposed pitch years ago. It has little relevance, for example, when discussing an alteration of an F major 9th chord in which you would be talking to the horns in one key and transposition, the clarinets in another and the saxophones in a third key or transposition. There is no realization of the actual use of individual chord members or harmonic movements of chord structures. Therefore, I talk in concert pitch and expect the players to respond to that. Once they realize this is the expectation and the beneficial results that may occur, I've never had any problems with it.

They realize then how easy it is to develop an appreciation for harmonic progression or movement if you can actually lay out the progression for them. They can think about it, take a look at it; they can then hear it to complete the process of hearing and understanding.

Providing hearing and listening experiences for students is an area that I feel many teachers don't participate in sufficiently. The use of aural dictation within the rehearsal is very important. (This is spoken or played pitches and the players are expected to listen and respond without the usual written response that one finds in the classroom.) When this is done, they are participating and hearing actively what someone else is doing. They are not just shutting down their brains and putting them into neutral, a situation that many rehearsals are prone to produce.

I also try to be aware of the psychological demands of a rehearsal. I personally feel uncomfortable when I feel that I am imposing on someone or that I am boring them. Thus, for example, if the clarinet section has an extremely difficult set of passages to play, I will rehearse it sufficiently in the rehearsal period so they definitely understand what they have to do, but after that I feel it is their responsibility to continue working with it. I tell them what their responsibility is and then hold them to it the next rehearsal. I do so, because I'm not going to waste everyone else's time while they are sitting there without having done their homework.

It is so easy, when one is standing up front, to over-read or misread peoples' facial and body language. They may just be sitting there in a relaxed mood, but one can interpret that as a lack of interest, or even hostility. As a result a conductor must assess each situation properly or he will feel stress when there is actually nothing there to precipitate the stress.

I have heard that people over the last ten to twenty years have been excessively molded and influenced by television programming. As a result teachers should always start a class with a premise, then have some form of development and then a conclusion. Situation comedies, action shows, mysteries, whatever, are set up like this and this is the format that has been the common thread of most television shows.

A rehearsal may fall into the same category. If one takes a rehearsal period and doesn't produce a conclusion, some form of culminating motion at the end of the rehearsal, will this leave the performers in an incomplete state? The successful culminating motion might be a full or partial play-through or a well-stated spoken summarizing statement. Does all this have any validity?

I do a "hop, skip, and jump" rehearsal every so often. This approach covers, in the conductor's handbook, the ten most difficult passages in a particular work. Sometimes at a dress rehearsal, for example, rather than playing straight through because I want to save their endurance for the evening, I'll start at the top, jump to Number 4, jump to thirteen bars after 6, and just hit exactly the difficult areas that I know have been providing difficulty.

I do this to reassure them that their own work has been fruitful. Then they have the responsibility to put it all together at the concert. (I have the responsibility of providing the leadership that will establish a musical environment for their individual efforts.) One also could play the end of one work and the beginning of the next to focus upon the changes of style and character from one piece to the next; this helps them shift musical gears quickly and properly.

I have an aversion to the dictatorial approach in which conductors or teachers try to get a person to play in a preconceived mold that they (the teachers) feels is the only way that a particular passage may be performed. I do not agree with this as *I feel that the ultimate responsibility of a teacher or conductor lies in developing the abilities of the student or performer, allowing errors and mistakes in the road of growth, and providing the breadth of experience that will allow the individual student to reach their potential.*

Real musical quality can be a thrilling experience when an individual, a group, or a section has come alive because they've been given the opportunity to do something on their own within the framework of the music and the demands of the ensemble.

This is done in the same manner as if they were playing a solo with piano accompaniment. One coaches them, one encourages them, and one tries to point out that which they may be missing. They may be overlooking something because they are not aware of a musical or interpretative problem. Hopefully, we can assist because we have sufficient background and related experience.

An area of great concern is the amount of trust that performers place in their teachers and conductors. The image of the Father or Mother figure is not hard to imagine in younger players; as each performer develops, this trust assumes different proportions. When the performer reaches an advanced stage, whether this is in high school or college, the responsibility of the conductor/teacher to guide, direct, and shape the future of each individual student is indeed an immense task. This trust must be honored, especially in the face of close relationships between the teacher and student. Discipline of character on the part of the teacher is mandatory and the welfare of the student must always demand first priority.

I try not to talk too much in rehearsals as this is generally not a constructive use of time, but I do ask many questions which I feel will stimulate the performers to become more involved in the rehearsal process. One area that is particularly risky to discuss is intonation, an area many band director abrogate to the tuning box and its ever-present B flat.

The physical proximity of an intonation problem creates a different response to performers sitting nearby than to that which the conductor may be receiving on the podium. This is an example of how we must develop both our and their awareness of the difficulties while being able to allow discussion to exist freely between the podium and the performers. We must establish an environment which provides the performers the latitude and freedom to express themselves freely while functioning within the constraints of the ensemble at large.

*(Donald R. Hunsberger)*

### They need to understand the music

It is essential that the performers have as much information as possible about the music they are performing. Fortunately, the day may be happily passed in which players might sit through the rehearsal process and a concert without any knowledge of what or why they were performing in a particular manner. We must give them credit for their potential and for the growth they are capable of making. Teachers may give them encouragement, but if they don't provide enough background information or make this information relevant, it will be difficult to move toward developing their potential, especially during rehearsal time.

*(Donald R. Hunsberger)*

### Talking and conducting

Unfortunately, many band directors spend too much time explaining what they wish to occur musically rather than being able to demonstrate this through a communicative conducting technique. All too frequently they fail to grow along with their ensembles and must talk their way through a rehearsal rather than demonstrate. Generally, when a conductor talks a lot in a rehearsal, it's because the individual conductor feels ill at ease with his own conducting skills and is not able to reap the potential for communication and instruction that is inherent in a developed conducting technique. Excessive talking may well be an extension of insecurities about his/her own personal and musical being.

What a conductor must learn to do is to recognize vital elements in the score, discover how to "lift these" off the score, and apply them in a conducting technique for the benefit of the performers rather than having to explain everything verbally. Unfortunately, what often results is a "time piece" that is the result of a metronomic practice session interspersed with far too much verbal discussion and a non-communicative approach to conducting. These directors haven't learned that every conducting gesture that you need may be found in the score—it is not found in a metronome.

*(Donald R. Hunsberger)*

### The purpose for a conductor

A conductor's purpose is to enable performers to project and express themselves musically as well as possible. Accomplishing this can only be done through a cooperative effort and should never be done through an approach that can descend to the point of being inhumane with a disregard for the personal development of the performers themselves. It is not feasible or even imaginable for a sensitive performer to express themselves well when under a cloud of fear.

*(Donald R. Hunsberger)*

### Helping students express themselves

To help them express themselves, I have attempted to create an environment within the rehearsal and concert in which they individually feel free to develop their own musical capabilities to the highest extent. In fact, some band directors feel I do not run a "strict enough" rehearsal because I do allow and encourage this development of free thinking on their part. I have often used an approach which I hope helps them with a new work, a work, for example, in which there might be different expressive lines, solo lines, accompanying lines, etc.

In the beginning rehearsals I will let the solo-line players, first oboe, first flute, the solo clarinet, or first horn for example, play a line a number of times over during several rehearsals before I actually make any comment on it. I do this because I want them to have explored and expressed that line, to have had the opportunity to take the part to a lesson with their private teacher. Their expressive choices should be a combination of their own thinking as well as that of the conductor or coach. In this manner, many of the musical decisions can become their responsibility, and I try to encourage them to think this way. Each solo line has to fit into the overall scheme of the entire work, of course, but that line is their responsibility.

*(Donald R. Hunsberger)*

*The use of recordings*

I think the use of recordings in rehearsals can be beneficial for one particular purpose, that being establishing an aural goal or impression for the performers and conductor. However, one must choose these recordings wisely. For example, when a recording has been sent along with the score of a new publication, frequently that recording doesn't even come close to developing the full magnitude—the insight and potential of the music.

A conductor should be able to study a score and then listen to a recorded performance and make a somewhat informed decision about a composition.

Due to the large number of manuscript scores I receive each year, I sometimes must use recordings just to save time in making programming decisions. However, hearing a recording is only one guide and should be treated as that. To actually sit down and play with a recording in rehearsal or sectionals is about as valuable as conducting to a recording.

Another appropriate use of recordings is found in many high school and college jazz programs. They use a "music minus one" approach, such as Jamey Aebersold's rhythm section recordings, to develop solo and improvisation skills. Those recordings are invaluable, especially until you can develop a rhythm section that can play by itself. When a rhythm section is developed and can maintain a steady beat, do some inventive chord and accompanying work, thus providing an essential musical background, then the recordings become dispensable. Until this point in development of the rhythm section, I see nothing wrong with the proper use of recordings for this purpose.

I do have a problem, however, if a band director plays an Eastman Wind Ensemble recording, for example, and says, "Now, I want all the clarinets to play along with this." One sees use of this type of mandated practice in certain areas of the country where students are asked to play simultaneously with recordings. To me that is as much a waste of time as having an ensemble rehearse repeatedly to a metronome.

*(Donald R. Hunsberger)*

*Listening and intonation*

We must work to develop students into listeners as well as players. Related to this is one area with which I've always had great difficulty: this is the approach so many people take to intonation. After many, many years of working with and thinking about the development of performers who are able to react positively to intonation problems, I believe there is only one person responsible for each individual's intonation and that person is the one behind the mouthpiece.

There are many different ways of developing this responsibility, but it begins with each individual player being aware of the intonation deficiencies of their instrument, being able to learn how to control their instrument

and to know what proper pitch is. The ear is like a muscle; the more one develops that muscle, the more awareness one has and the better one will be with intonation.

Unfortunately there is frequently a resistance or lack of desire on the part of a performer to want to adapt to the pitch of a fellow player and an intonation impasse occurs. Players must work with the thought that proper intonation within their own instrument and with others is really a lifelong study and duty.

In keeping with this avenue of thought, I find the circumstances of a band director tuning an entire band with a strobe or tuner box by merely indicating sharp or flat on a single pitch very lacking in substance. Unisons, octaves, thirds, open fifths, fourths must constantly be practiced between players to arrive at a proper method of adjusting to one another. Of course, the higher tessitura we reach in the woodwinds, the greater the problems; but even those can be solved through diligence and hard work!

Much of the intent is not for me to just tune the chords or for me to adjust other technical or stylistic things. My intent is to help the students become aware of where, for example, the intonation problem is and how to approach it. Once they know where the intonation problem is, then they have a chance of solving the intonation problem. Until then, little can truly be done to improve intonation.

The performers are the ones who must make judgments that result in good intonation and these judgments must be instantaneous; the teacher can't bear the responsibility for playing each instrument. Intonation is one of the linchpins of good performance, and as someone said, "There's no beauty in poor intonation."

Constructive listening is one area that is pursued too little when we prepare teachers and when they later work with their own students. Most music theory courses in undergraduate schools emphasize dictation, both melodic and harmonic, but few conductors carry that training into the rehearsal room to help performers constructively hear that which constitutes the musical environment surrounding them.

I frequently attempt to involve students in decisions of balance, pitch, timbre, etc. to make their performance time as rich as possible. From a traditional sense many musicians feel that "we're here to play not to do more theory!" What a shallow view, as if one can check into and out of an analysis or dictation class with a time card and not be responsible for the practical use of that experience when they begin to play their instrument!

Just as intonation must be confronted and discussed, so must every other aspect of ear-training be utilized in the rehearsal and especially in concert time. To avoid discussions of intonation or balance, because one is afraid that they might be wrong in a decision, is certainly no way to establish trust on the part of the performers in their conductor.

I usually include a tuning segment in our DMA Conducting Examination. We utilize Dick Grunow and his listening and response exam for each applicant. Then, when the applicant is conducting the Eastman Wind Ensemble, I will stop them on a measure that has some great intonation problem and ask them to fix the intonation. The results may include an efficient separation of instruments and their inherent problems, isolating each pitch for each instrument and then putting the doubling and coupling of instruments back together again, this time without beats between instruments on the same pitch.

Some candidates appear bewildered as to what process to follow as though there is some set rule that states that certain notes and instruments are to be out of tune and there is nothing that can be done about it! Unfortunately, poor intonation has been a part of the band sound to many people; this is unnecessary and is something that we must all work on.

*(Donald R. Hunsberger)*

## Screening conducting students for Eastman School Graduate School

A question that is asked frequently concerns what qualifications we look for in conductors who apply for our DMA Conducting Program. First of all, our program is rather unique from many throughout the country. We totally subsidize the tuition costs and provide a small stipend to each DMA Conducting Fellow. We have six in residence at any one time: two orchestral, two wind and two choral. In return for this subsidization, each Fellow serves as an assistant conductor with the School's ensembles and also participates in the Conducting teaching program. Thus, we are really "hiring" a junior faculty member who can serve alongside the primary conductors and admission to one of these few openings thus becomes quite competitive.

As I mentioned above, we use Dick Grunow's Instrumental Score Reading Program as part of the audition process with our conductors. Each DMA applicant has a private session with Dick. When we're done with the whole day's testing and audition, I receive the applicants' written exams back from the Music History and Theory Departments who grade their portions of the test. Our Department grades the Conducting area and Dick Grunow gives us an analysis of their score reading skills.

One additional factor we must also recognize is the ability of the applicant to successfully complete the Music History and Theory requirements of the program. At Eastman all doctoral graduate students take the same written examinations at the close of their course and the requirements of each of these areas are stringent. Our degree program is a hands-on conducting course but it is also a heavy academic program as well.

An area of analysis I wish to develop concerns how the successful candidates' entrance examinations correlate with their future success following graduation. For example, where did they score among the people with whom they entered or with whom they applied, and what

were their ensuing achievements?

For example, we recently had a young woman who applied for one of the orchestral Fellowships. Her Music History and Theory exams were excellent, her conducting was most promising and Dick Grunow said, "Man, this girl's really hot. She scored the highest grade I have seen in years on this exam." The promise suggested by her exam scores has carried right through in the manner in which she approached her studies and her work with the two orchestras. It will be interesting to see where she is five-ten years down the road from today.

*(Donald R. Hunsberger)*

## Developing musicianship and performance skill

With our freshman-sophomore wind group, we spend considerable time doing chamber music with the Wind Orchestra rotation and in quintets, etc. outside of the large ensemble rehearsal period. Within this ensemble, we do chamber music, traditional and contemporary wind band works, and orchestral wind and percussion parts.

At Eastman we have two large pools of players divided into Freshman-Sophomore and Junior-Senior-Graduate Student. The upper rotation performs in the Eastman Wind Ensemble, the Eastman Phlharmonia, and the Eastman Musica Nova. The younger players in their first two years at School perform in the Eastman Wind Orchestra and the Eastman School Symphony Orchestra where they perform the standard wind band and orchestra repertoire plus a chamber winds program (5-15) in the Wind Orchestra rotation.

In addition to this repertoire we do orchestral wind section literature training. We schedule one large work, a symphony or concerto for example, and one smaller work such as an overture; we spend three days rehearsal time reading, discussing, and going over those parts. Through this we are building ensemble and individual awareness in performance, and are diversifying their wind ensemble and orchestral experiences as well.

Recently, for example, we were doing the Dvorak *Symphony No. 8* along with his *Carnival Overture*. We spent time discussing the correlation between the overture and the symphony with each of its individual movements through the compositional technique, interpretative style, and some of the theoretical and analytical features.

This is all accomplished in a regular rehearsal atmosphere rather than in a classroom setting for example. It has been my contention for many years that we should be teaching more about theoretical and analysis matters in rehearsals to increase the awareness of the students in musical decisions. Since my own background has included writing, arranging etc. since I was in Junior High School, I have a keen interest in Theory and taught Theory while in my first teaching job at the State University of New York at Potsdam.

So, instead of merely telling someone to bring out the E flat or the F in a line, I'll give them musical reasons why those pitches must be brought out interpretatively. We will discuss theoretical reasons why certain pitches are crucial or should be more prominent. I may project a score for the work on a screen or give them specific pages reproduced from the score.

Since they're playing the orchestral wind, percussion, harp, and keyboard parts only, they obviously cannot hear the string parts unless we also utilize extra pianists to play the string voices. Therefore, we play a recording to help them get an overall feeling for the composition and to help them hear how and where their parts fit into the orchestration. They can hear if their parts are doubled with anyone and if their parts are secondary or primary ones. Through this process our individual studio teachers and I feel that we are contributing an added dimension to the education and future growth of our students.

One might call this approach a form of comprehensive musicianship, but to me, the understanding of all the aspects of music along with the active correlation with performance is part of being the whole performer—the total musician.

In this combined rehearsal-class situation it is most important to teach style of composition, of period, of orchestration and how this is produced through individual and section performance. Students learn more than just how large a crescendo is to grow, or how heavy an attack is needed in a certain passage. We can give them all of that very quickly and still have time to teach the whys and hows that can develop them even more.

For example, I espouse a wide variety of attacks, timbres, and shadings that I like to hear depending on the demands of the music. This is discussed frequently in rehearsal so the players become accustomed to being asked to produce certain types of sounds from their first days at Eastman. Since we utilize a rotation system that involves not only rotating between the orchestra and the wind groups, and, more specifically, between individual chairs in each composition, there must be a common definition of performance techniques that everyone understands. Thus, when we assemble the top players for a special Philharmonia performance or for an Eastman Wind Ensemble concert, recording or tour, I am able to quickly develop the ensemble into a musically cohesive unit. (The CBS Masterworks recording, CARNAVAL, by the Eastman Wind Ensemble and Wynton Marsalis was recorded the second week of the Fall term!)

Through developing an extensive breadth of techniques, each performer is able to adapt quickly to the demands of every individual composition. There must be a realization of individual style of composition plus the instrumental techniques required to reproduce each style. The ability to be flexible in interpretation is essential, and minute variations of approach quickly separate the knowledgeable performer from the neophyte; the innovative conductor is quickly separated from the time beater.

These variations are to be found in every area of performance. For example, in a fortepiano (fp), how long does the forte last before descending into the piano? How sharp and immediate is the forte attack? Is it a long deep attack or more of a sfz attack? My philosophy in rehearsal is to discuss the desired style and to encourage the performers to consider this to be only one of their vocabulary of techniques.

*(Donald R. Hunsberger)*

### *Growing and teaching beyond technical aspects*

It is most difficult to express oneself in an artistic manner if a solid technique foundation has not been established. This is true not only in music but also in art, sculpture, acting, and similar creative arts. For years there has been a prevalent adage floating around that stated that one could not teach conducting. You must be born with the talent and skills. While the presence of musical talent, human warmth, interest, and the desire to recreate the desires of a composer are absolutely essential for conductorial success, no one will survive for long without a developed physical, communicative conducting technique.

The demands of interpretation, combined with the requirements for communication with the ensemble, require the development of a conducting technique that will emulate the music found on the score and on each player's individual part. In the *ART OF CONDUCTING* (McGraw-Hill, Second Edition, 1992) Roy Ernst and I have attempted to develop what we consider to be an essential vocabulary of conducting techniques. This vocabulary is based upon the premise that each and every move you make with either hand is actually to be found on the score page; what we must do is to recognize these interpretative demands and translate them into a silent physical technique. To accomplish this a vocabulary of gestures is essential: downbeats to match the depth and breadth of initial attack, horizontal gestures that will illustrate flow and forward motion of line, gestures that utilize all areas of the conducting field from the deepest, fullest vertical stroke to the most delicate flick of the baton, use of all the joints and hinges of the arm, wrist and hand as one passes the center of effort from the shoulder through the elbow and the wrist into the fingers.

Just as personal artistic insight must include a feeling of perspective, inventiveness, and an eye for beauty and imagination combined with technical accuracy, all so important in each conductor's approach to the creative art. The added element of honest, personal human feeling and participation must be present as the basis of music performance. We should devote much time in our music training programs insisting that people develop all the above attributes through a true devotion to their art. The images that result from our efforts must be clear or our representation of the art form will be blurred.

Teachers must have models to emulate and to build upon so that the highest musical values may be applied in rehearsals and be passed on to our students.

It's not that students do not want to think about musical ideals more than technical goals, but frequently the teacher or conductor does not provide the leadership necessary to develop these ideals. He/she is not prone to delve deeply enough into the total musical dimension possible and remains on the technical level only. Unfortunately, this results in the teacher and students developing a high musical experience by accident, if at all.

*(Donald R. Hunsberger)*

## Conducting and learning

I've written articles and spoken about my belief that the role of the conductor requires a lifetime of learning: one is never finished practicing, studying, investigating, or listening, no matter what one is doing.

Part of my daily routine is set by the listening I do each day in and out of rehearsals, on recordings, on the radio (we are blessed with an excellent local Public Broadcasting System station and an excellent good music station across the lake in Canada). I think I "take dictation" in some sense from every source as I am always trying to analyze everything I hear, whether it be the bass line and harmonic progression, or the orchestration, or whatever. I suppose I am also attempting to keep my ears exercised and this is an excellent way to investigate music of all genres. This helps me grow musically and constantly provides new sources of artistic inspiration and information. Many teachers are not prone to push themselves far enough musically. They have developed their organization but they have not developed their own expressiveness or that of their students.

*(Donald R. Hunsberger)*

## Learning to be prepared

A few years ago I was trying a system of correlative repertoire in which we used similar style compositions by the same composer. One particular application of this approach utilized overtures by Rossini that all had Adagio style introductions, the usual Allegro second part along with the development of the Rossini orchestrated crescendo, the interesting form, and the similar orchestration. We placed three Rossini overtures in the folder and explained that we would be sight reading.

After the first overture, various compositional techniques and performance techniques were discussed with the performers and then we proceeded to read the other overtures with the expectation that the players would be able to retain the information and apply it to similar areas in the second and third works. This would be sight reading and as we began, we would not stop until the end. If they got lost, they just had to find the way themselves. I'd call out a number once in awhile, but it had to be sight reading all the way through. The idea was transferring all the different technical and musical ideas from one piece to another while relying upon all their individual skills.

*(Donald R. Hunsberger)*

## Planning and pacing of the rehearsal

Sometimes I become too eager to accomplish my scheduled goals in the rehearsal and I push too fast or over-pace the timing of the developmental elements. I have so many things I want to get done with them that I respond to my plans more than reacting to their ability to absorb the substance at the pace established.

I plan the layout of rehearsal schedules in overall (concert to concert), weekly, and daily fashion. This way I can adjust or modify the plan depending on the progress being made. Since I believe that most conductors rehearse too long on individual works and concert programs, I try to discipline myself and my performers by adhering to a strict schedule. If we develop faster than planned, I will give time off from the schedule or provide some repertoire reading experience. Likewise, I'll adjust the plan if I see we must spend more time on a certain area. This is the way in which I work, although I am aware that it is unique to our students and approach and is different from situations in which there must be a certain amount of repetitive technical work to improve the individuals and the ensemble. I also rely on our students to do a good bit of work outside of rehearsal; they are quite responsible in this respect.

*(Donald R. Hunsberger)*

## Sectionals and planning

I do not normally hold extra or sectional rehearsals outside the allotted rehearsal period. However, with a piece such as Karel Husa's *Music for Prague*, I will schedule a time block within the set rehearsal hours to rehearse the third movement which is scored for the percussion section alone. Or, I will do a certain solo spot outside rehearsal to save time within the rehearsal hours because I do not want everyone sitting there while we dissect individual lines or parts. There is a positive side to having everyone hear the rehearsal or coaching of individual or section lines, but this can quickly be overdone and you may lose the interest of the other players.

If it fits the composition, I also may schedule brass, percussion, or woodwinds or a combination of sections at a specific rehearsal time to concentrate on their major areas. This kind of section scheduling seems to work very well because it really focuses everyone's attention on exactly what has to be done.

Eastman students are quite accustomed to this breaking up of compositions and scheduling by the clock that they come prepared to do exactly what is listed on the rehearsal board.

I think they develop more quickly by having an experience modeled on what you might term a more professional approach rather than a strict educational experience.

An interesting question has arisen during the past decades regarding the use of the rotating or floating assignment versus the assigned or fixed chair for each performer. By all rights one would assume that having a person in a fixed assignment chair for an entire semester or year would produce a finer performer or section, but I must personally disagree with that philosophy. I have seen too many performers develop to high levels of accomplishment because they were required to perform so many different assignments in different styles and demands, and thus they personally, individually, developed far beyond where they might have gone if they had been locked into a single assignment only.

*(Donald R. Hunsberger)*

### The use of rehearsal time

A high percentage of band and choral directors spend far too much time in rehearsals between performances. If they reduced the amount of rehearsal time and disciplined themselves and their performers, they would eventually get more interesting performances that would be more alive and vital. They also would see more keenly attuned performers involved in these performances. Perhaps the performances may not be technically perfect, but might have more inherent musical personality and they could cover much more literature.

*(Donald R. Hunsberger)*

### Warm-up segments depend upon the situation

If you're in a situation where students do not have access to private lessons or other developmental potentials outside the rehearsal period, then it is incumbent to provide sensitivity or warm-up segments within the rehearsal. Under certain conditions the reiteration of a warm-up routine may be a vital part of a performers' daily life.

In this sense the teaching philosophy of Emory Remington, the great trombone teacher at Eastman for almost fifty years, bears repeating. Mr. Remington, or "The Chief" as he was affectionately known to his students, developed a daily warm-up routine that utilized long tones, tuning, pattern scales, flexibility exercises, tonguing exercises, etc. and it was incumbent upon every trombonist to practice these daily. Even after having warmed up most sufficiently for a lesson or for Trombone Choir (one thought!) he would start at the top of the Daily Routine ("Middle B flat") and redo the entire procedure. To most of the students, it was as though they were beginning the day again, as his style and approach to these simple exercises became another reading of a great book. It is a gift to be able to condition or recondition a player on a daily basis and this can be a most positive approach.

In some situations, you may have to be the type of teacher that used to be in the one-room school where that teacher taught everyone everything in each grade. One of the benefits of this closed system lay in the ability of all the students to learn from one another.

Obviously, different music schools function in a radically different manner: at Eastman, we are very fortunate to have master artist teachers on every instrument.

The students study in an excellent three-year program in theory plus analysis and have required music history courses, psychology, English literature, etc. Therefore, I try to get them to bring everything they study throughout the week to the rehearsal, but this is not easily accomplished as people tend to compartmentalize classes and segregate various learning patterns from one another.

We would like students to live all of these different areas, such as the theory and history classes, the private study, the other ensemble experiences, the analysis class, and utilize the ensemble rehearsal as the time when we intend to tie it all together. Here we can pull these background elements together even more so than when they're sitting and playing a solo by themselves. In the ensemble, you have to relate and respond to the music's needs and demands.

*(Donald R. Hunsberger)*

### Some of my values

My primary thrust and direction over the past forty years has been in the area of wind repertoire and performance development. I may be considered a purist by some because I see no reason for poor literature for the band just because some of this material has been used for many years. I am aware that contemporary music is difficult to understand and to work with, but unless the band industry supports composers and new compositional trends, we will be back where we started before 1950 with a repertoire of transcriptions, a few solid works, and a lot of occasional music.

The development of the fully instrumented ensemble with all the woodwinds, multiple color brasses, full percussion, keyboard, and harp is absolutely essential. We cannot make forward progress with a military band journal instrumentation mentality such as existed at the turn of the century and which pervaded the band world for so long; the use of flexible instrumentation as desired by the composer is the only way to the future, But, here again, idealism exists among the leaders of the field.

I am very serious about the quality of all performances as well as the musical growth of individual students. I'm trying to give them everything that I can and make use of everything our institution has to offer, but, in return, I expect an awful lot from them based on what is available to them. A person may not take advantage of what we have to offer, but it doesn't happen very often.

*(Donald R. Hunsberger)*

### Sight reading

I'm a real advocate of sight reading as the ability to bring together everything that you know about your instrument and apply it under a pressured short time span.

If I have what I consider to be too many rehearsals for a concert I may cancel some or instead of a day or a week off, we sometimes simply sight-read a great deal of literature during those rehearsals.

I am not a great advocate of band contests or competitions, but if they must exist, I feel that there should be a mandatory sight-reading requirement. I have been in Japan numerous times and have participated in both the preparation and judging of bands in their National Contests. In their contest structure, I perceive a real lack of educational standard carried to an extreme, as each band must play eight minutes of their own choice (make a cut if the work lasts longer) and then play one of four selected contest pieces, each of which lasts four minutes.

The average band rehearses four hours a day, seven days a week for two to three months on these twelve minutes and have no ability to read anything at sight. A mandatory sight-reading requirement would open this rigid system and force the directors and players to confront new literature and techniques.

*(Donald R. Hunsberger)*

### Teaching techniques in the rehearsal

I may have students do different versions of a phrase or a style, and then ask the others to comment and compare. I also use imagery with references to the shape or nature of a line or a phrase or to the delicacy or magnitude of a vertical structure or harmonic movement. I also do correlative references to orchestral timbres or performance techniques referring to specific orchestral compositions or composers' styles. I try to associate a particular type of orchestral sound to that which they are currently producing. This can be related directly to density or depth of attack, projection of sound, ensemble timbres, doublings between instruments, dynamics, etc. Since most of our students at Eastman are interested in a career in orchestral performance, these correlations are easily understood.

I frequently spell out or dictate melodic lines or chords to the ensemble in a form of mental aural dictation. Although we usually have a blackboard in one of our rehearsal rooms, I seldom use it for this purpose as I prefer to have the students be able to visualize a harmonic structure in their mind and be able to relate to it in an aural manner. This, as mentioned before, is done in concert pitch, not transposed pitches.

*(Donald R. Hunsberger)*

### The future for wind music

I would like to see wind bands have the same type of acceptance and respect on their highest level that we find for major orchestral and choral ensembles. This can only happen through the continued development of a legitimate original repertoire and through the acceptance of the band-ensemble itself as a legitimate performing group. Fortunately wind bands are their own worst enemy when they place entertainment values, such as marching programs and concerts-in-the-park, ahead of serious development.

This doesn't mean that we can't have the equivalent of the Pops Orchestra, and the dance band or jazz ensemble. What happens, unfortunately, is that many band programs try to be everything to everyone and, as a result, remain a common denominator-type organization without establishing a true identity for themselves.

I don't think the wind band will reach this desired level of acceptance and regard within our lifetime. The orchestra today relies on a repertoire from more than one hundred years ago. Our wind band literature, however, has had little more than a beginning of a repertoire forty years ago. So what we're trying to do is to develop that repertoire, so that the wind bands of the future may have the literature sufficient to warrant the acceptance we desire in the concert hall.

*(Donald R. Hunsberger)*

### The silent film orchestra accompaniment project

I have a project that I started about twelve years ago in Rochester in which I compile or assemble orchestral accompaniments for use in silent film presentations. In Rochester we have three wonderful contributions of George Eastman that increased interest in original wind band music: the Eastman School of Music; the Eastman Theatre, a 3000 seat hall originally built for silent film projection plus ballet, opera and stage shows; and, the George Eastman House, which today is the International Museum of Photography.

The Eastman House archives contain many silent films and the Theatre Orchestra Library is basically intact since the 1920s when it was used on a daily basis. In keeping with my interest in researching American music and performance (earlier efforts were focused on the development of the brass band in the United States) the restoration of silent film accompaniment was a natural step. I formed the Eastman Dryden Orchestra in the early 1980s and perform at the Dryden Theatre at the Eastman House and throughout the East. Five recordings of theatre orchestra music were issued by Arabesque Records.

The most recent development has been taking the films and the scores to major and regional professional orchestras throughout the United States and Canada. I research the films and score them using publications published prior to the release date of the film. The artistic aim is to offer the audience an experience such as they might have experienced back in the 1920s. The conducting challenge comes from the schedule which affords one reading rehearsal and one dress/technical rehearsal which involves a run-through of the film.

Films such as the original *Phantom of the Opera* (1924), *The Mark of Zorro* (1920), *Hunchback of Notre Dame* (1923), *Peter Pan* (1925), *The Last Command* (1928) plus comedy films by Charlie Chaplin, Buster Keaton, Gloria Swanson, among others, have been well received by orchestras such as National Symphony, Pittsburgh Symphony, Milwaukee, Vancouver, Honolulu, Florida, Rochester, Syracuse, Buffalo, Nashville, San Diego, and Utah Orchestras.

I've picked up collections of theatre orchestra music

from around the country and probably have well over 15,000 publications. This is probably the largest archives in the country. This is a lot of fun because everything else I do is contemporary music; this is a good change.

*(Donald R. Hunsberger)*

### Musical models

It is essential for the teacher/conductor to have a concept of great tone for each instrument and for the tonal blend of instruments together.

We can acquire the models that we need or want to provide for students and we can do this by listening to great performances, live and on recording. However, the best way to acquire models and to gain interpretive inspiration is not necessarily by listening to bands or orchestras.

While it is possible to hear a band and be moved by the beauty of interpretive elements, many conductors cannot help focusing on the craft of a great performance of music which is familiar or is played by instruments which they are teaching daily. That is why I believe that listening to music for solo voice, piano, or small chamber combinations may be more helpful, because this allows the instrumental conductor to *listen to the art without concentrating on the craft.*

For example, I enjoy singers such as Jessye Norman, Kiri Te Kanawa, Dietrich Fischer-Dieskau, and Mel Torme. Two of my favorite piano recordings are J. S. Bach's *Goldberg Variations* recorded by Glenn Gould, and *Heliotrope Bouquet Piano Rags* performed by William Bolcom.

*(Allan R. McMurray)*

### Percussion

I believe that percussionists are often the overlooked section in a band. Warm-ups frequently exclude percussionists and they may not understand how the conductor's lengthy discussions on airflow, support, intonation, and tone applies to what they do. Therefore, I pay a lot of attention to percussionists.

I watch and listen for the instruments they play, the mallets, sticks and beaters they use, and the tone they create. When there is a piece of music which does not involve percussion, I will frequently provide them with a score to follow or have them sit as an audience to the ensemble. Then I ask questions about what they have heard; I keep them *involved.*

*(Allan R. McMurray)*

### Self-Improvement

One of the most valuable aids for self-improvement is the use of the video camera. By videotaping rehearsals we can examine the effectiveness of our verbal and non-verbal communication, the pacing of our rehearsals, and the atmosphere which we created or which we allowed.

We can use the tape to measure our progress and help eliminate bad habits such as excess movements on the

podium or speaking too fast to be understood or too quietly to be heard. If we also tape our rehearsals using different camera angles, this may help us realize what each member of the ensemble sees during a rehearsal.

When watching the video tape we also can keep track of how often we stopped and for what. We also can evaluate our conducting. For example, if we feel the ensemble is changing tempo or lacks clarity, turn the sound off and sing or play to our own conducting to see if it is working as we want it to. Most of us know what we want to see, but our videotaping allows us to see what our students see each day.

*(Allan R. McMurray)*

### Rehearsing to provide positive experiences

Many times, students feel frustration at stopping constantly. Part of that frustration comes from feeling that stopping involves failure on someone's part.

We add to this frustration when, because we know we have only a little bit of rehearsal time, we become very "error conscious." We are trying to be aware of everything that is different from what we want to hear and what the composer has intended. Error detection, obviously, is something we work on in classes such as music education and conducting. When students go to recitals and concerts they also are focused upon error detection as a way to make a judgment. They are listening and watching for what is right and what is wrong about rhythm, tone, dynamics, correct notes, intonation, phrasing, or ensemble. While the things they are listening for focus them upon music making and upon correctness, it does not necessarily focus upon personal development.

I think personal development comes from reinforcement. Part of reinforcement is listening for things that are right as well as things that are wrong. For example, if there is a tutti passage between clarinets and saxophones and the saxophones are playing it correctly and the clarinets are playing incorrectly, most conductors would stop initially for the clarinets. They would say to the clarinets, "You are playing this incorrectly. Let's work on this until its right." That is one way to make the performance better, but with this approach nothing has been said to the saxophones.

Another way to deal with that would be to identify that the clarinets are playing it incorrectly and the saxophones are playing it correctly. The teacher could stop and say, "Clarinets, that is not quite right. I want you to listen to the saxophones; they are really playing this well." Go to the saxophones and have them play the passage while the clarinets are looking at their part and listening to the saxophones. With this, one has done a couple of things. One has identified the error in the clarinet section, but at the same time one has made the saxophones feel good. They also have become the leaders; they are the demonstrators for other people in the ensemble. This rewards them and that reward in itself can serve as a motivation for the clarinet section to want to perform better, since everyone wants to be reinforced. By isolating such problem sections and sharing the goals for the rehearsal with the ensemble, a more positive attitude can be instilled.

(Allan R. McMurray)

### A rehearsal technique

When rehearsing a piece of music, I don't always start at the beginning each time. Sometimes I will begin rehearsing toward the end of a piece and then work backwards to the beginning. When I finally arrive at the beginning, I will then run straight through without stopping. This procedure seems to instill a greater sense of accomplishment for the players rather than fighting their way to the end and starting again.

(Allan R. McMurray)

### Technology, tuning, and music making

While technological advances have produced some valuable tools such as better metronomes, video and audio tape recorders, computer programs, and tuners that we should be taking advantage of, those technologies cannot replace the development of each student's ears and eyes, especially the ears in music making.

What I see in the schools are directors holding on to a tuner, walking in front of every student, and having that student tune with his or her eyes. If we are asking students to watch the tuner to tune instead of listen, this is teaching them the wrong thing! Later in the rehearsal the teacher says, "You're not in tune." The teacher again takes the tuner to them, puts it in front of them and they look at it. The needle goes to the left or the right; the students adjust and conclude they are in tune again.

When we use tuners exclusively for their eyes, we are sending students the wrong message. We are sending the message that intonation is related to a machine and not to them personally and to their listening to other people.

The idea behind music making must be related to the development of their hearing and their listening. While I see tuners as an important aid to instruction, the use of a tuner cannot replace the development of good listening skills and the development of a value for listening.

There is an important question we can ask ourselves: "What priorities guide us as we are teaching in our rehearsals? Are we teaching students *to listen for tuning and to watch the conductor?* Or, are we teaching them *to watch the tuner and listen to the conductor?*"

This latter occurs when conductors count off by saying, "One, two, ready play" and later they tap on their stands to signal people to stop playing. Between the stops and the starts, these conductors give students spoken instructions. It would be possible for students to get all of the information coming from the podium without looking up. For instance, when students are looking down and they hear "One, two, ready play," they play. When they hear the tapping on the music stand, they stop. All of their interactions with the conductor are controlled by sounds and all of their interactions with tuning are controlled by looking.

That's incorrect. It should be the opposite. The performers should listen to each other so tuning is controlled by listening, not by what they see; and they need to watch the conductor so they are lead by what they see the conductor do, not by what he says.

(Allan R. McMurray)

### How we look versus what we say

We can reflect upon verbal and non-verbal communication in common daily events and learn something about conducting and teaching. In many aspects of our daily lives responses to us help us "hear what we look like."

For example, we have heard people say: "Are you feeling OK?" "You don't look good." "What makes you so happy today?" "What's the matter?" "What are you thinking about?" "What happened?" "Did you lose something?"

These are comments that many of us receive from friends or relatives who are responding to our non-verbal communication. Upon reflection, one can make this observation: if we believe that we can read how *people feel* about things by the way *they look*, then we must also know that the way *we look* communicates how *we feel* about things.

We also can mis-communicate. Mis-communication occurs if someone "says" something but "looks like" he is saying something else. We might be asked, for example, "Are you upset about something?" When we answer "No," the true answer received by the listener could be yes or no depending upon what the non-verbal communication reveals. No matter what we say or hear verbally, it is the non-verbal communication which most of us truly believe.

Many people are not aware of how powerful they are non-verbally. As conductors we must be more aware of that. If we look closely, we see that we have set up the ensemble so the members are all looking at us. With that we are saying, "The way that I look is important. We set you up this way, we have put me several inches above the rest of you sitting on the floor as I am standing on this box. With all this, it seems illogical to say or suggest, "Now don't watch me; don't pay attention to how I look." That creates a real contradiction—a contradiction in a big way.

Now, if we apply this to the conductor, we might make the following observations:

1. The conductor does communicate non-verbally.

2. The way we look can carry a stronger message than what we say. What they see can confirm or clarify what they hear.

3. We have the potential to create contradictions between what we say and what we look like on the podium.

4. If we create a contradiction, our ensembles are more likely to initially go with what they see than what they hear.

5. If we are communicating poorly or communicating the wrong information non-verbally, we are teaching them not to watch us.

If non-verbal communication is so important, then we must develop a better understanding and use of non-verbal communication as teachers and conductors.

The two most important aspects of silent communication are the vocabulary of the body and the vocabulary of the face. Every part of the body that one has the power to voluntarily move, i. e. head, elbow, waist, chest, wrist, pelvis, shoulder, fingers, knees and the baton, communicates energy or lack of energy by the way the part of the body is used. For example, if a person agrees, the head is nodded; if one is proud, the chest expands; if one is weak, the waist and knees bend.

When we conduct, movement from the shoulders may indicate *pesante*, while finger movement may indicate *leggiero*, like touching a hot stove. Facial expression relies on three main ingredients: eyebrows, mouth, and eye contact. The facial expressions communicate moods such as anger, happiness, and sadness. Facial expressions also communicate attitudes such as stern, bored, and interested. Eye contact qualifies and quantifies that expression.

One incorporates facial expressions and control of the body into conducting in several ways. For example, when stepping unto the podium the mood of the music should be apparent in the way the conductor moves. This is realized through the carriage of the head, the chest, or the look on the face says whether this piece is going to light and happy, whether it is going to be serious or mournful. I don't believe that a conductor should step on the podium to conduct the slow movement of a piece in the same way they conduct a fast movement of a piece.

The conductor's movements should help the student prepare for the experience they are about to encounter. Once the conductor is facing the ensemble with the intent of leading them in a specific composition that conductor should already be empathizing with the mood of that composition. That isn't to say that the conductor needs to be angry to conduct an angry piece, or sad to conduct a sad piece. But, what a conductor must do is empathize with the mood just as the conductor wants the student to do that in order to execute that particular musical content.

The conductor must act out or convey the character of the piece enough to convey the piece's personality to the group. The conductor could tell the performers that "This section needs to be more powerful (or gentler, or quieter)" and yet not change the way he looks to the ensemble. When we think of someone that looks powerful, that person does not look the same as he would if he was quiet or gentle. If one accepts that premise, one must also accept that if one is to lead people in a powerful way, one must look powerful. If one wants to lead them in a quieter or gentler way, one must look quiet or gentle.

*(Allan R. McMurray)*

### Incorporating movement into conducting

One can "naturally" incorporate this movement into conducting in several ways.

1. One way is to choose quality music that we can relate to emotionally as well as intellectually. I have reference points and criteria for selecting pieces that help me decide the quality of a composition. My judgments are based upon my experiences with pieces I have analyzed and performed in the past. As a result of new insights and experiences those criteria are constantly changing. As I am trying to find better pieces and learn new pieces I also become more critical of other works. My standard keeps changing because I am learning as I am trying to find new pieces. These are pieces that I have either heard that really struck me, or pieces by a composer for whom I have respect, or I see pieces on a program of a conductor I respect. These opportunities give me ideas for new pieces I want to study.

Constantly pieces are being dropped off my quality music list as I become more experienced and a better musician. Each new piece I experience can enhance my sensitivity and taste. Thus, the next new piece I look at must meet my enhanced sense of taste. What satisfied me ten years ago, might not satisfy me today.

I feel that choices about literature are based upon the experiences of the teacher doing the choosing. Thus the reasons some of us feel that much of the music on band programs could be called bad music is because the teacher selecting the music may have a lack of musical experiences.

I have an advantage because I deal with advanced musicians. I can explore more music on a very personal basis of making music with them than some people can. But, regardless of what level one teaches, one should be looking at and listening to the best music there is whether or not we can perform it. What this does is raise our artistic expectations which we can apply to elementary school or any level.

Within the limits of what students can play, one must still pick the best possible literature. If one is doing, for example, an arrangement of a melody from a famous symphony, why not shape that piece in the best way possible? Why not provide students some insight into that piece so students at an early age are having to consider other things besides fingerings and notes.

If they can get past the technique of their instrument, what's next? Should we point them to just another level of technical achievement or should we be seasoning them with artistic understanding?

At least we should try to help them understand what is going on artistically as they learn to perform such a piece. If we are listening to great orchestral repertoire, why not share our feelings about one of those performances with those kids so they also develop the sensitivity to listening.

They can learn that listening to great music is part of what we as their music teachers are doing. If they aspire to be musicians, that might want to be something they want to do also. When we see students become involved with good music, that certainly makes our motors race because we see students learn, experience, and expand.

2. A second way one can "naturally" incorporate movement into conducting is to have a strong internal aural perception of what the energy, intensity, and style of the music is. Because of this one can communicate the personality of the music.

For instance, a march would represent an energetic and uplifting sound and style. The way we should look when conducting that would require a higher carriage. How would one look if one were carrying himself proudly in a march? In contrast to that, an elegy—something that deals with sadness or remorse, a sense of loss or being overcome with grief—our conducting and physical appearance would have a different look to it. Normally our face shows the sadness, our posture is bent a little bit more and we are showing the weight we are carrying in terms of grief.

I think that good acting always portrays those kinds of things. If one takes just a moment to consider what that emotional experience of grief might be to a human being (not related to music) but to the real experience of having just lost a loved one, what would their posture be like? What would they look like? How would you know that person had a sense of grief as compared with happiness?

If we can empathize with that mood and if we can relate to the way that the mood would look, we provide a more meaningful connection with the music. With that more meaningful connection I think we get better eye contact, because students will look at us, musicians will watch us if there is something to see. If what they see on the podium reinforces what we are saying and what they see and hear in the music, then the musicians will watch us more.

The great conductors are those who can stand on the podium and relate to the ensemble what they feel in the music and what the content of the music is. They can do this in such a way that the players cannot take their eyes off the conductor.

3. A third way one can "naturally" incorporate movement into conducting is to know the music well enough that one is not "chained" to the score. The conductor should have the music both intellectually and emotionally prepared.

When rehearsing a piece words are necessary, but the communication that takes place through non-verbal communication has even *more impact* than verbal communication. This is particularly true in a school atmosphere where your music students are "lectured at" in every other class and bombarded with words throughout each day. If we could make the music class contain other aspects than what there is in other classrooms, we could make music classes quite interesting.

I have seen conductors very successfully have an entire rehearsal when they said nothing. This also is a great exercise for the students. The teacher's idea is he is not going to say anything and students are not going to say anything either. The teacher might list the pieces on the board and point to the first one. When he starts conducting he can to change things. At first there could be some giggling or other signs of discomfort because this approach is new and different. Students can be sensitized to what is going on, and these "no-talking" rehearsals can go by very quickly.

Teachers could, therefore, have "watch-centered" and "listen-centered" instruction, which could enhance music learning considerably. I am not suggesting "watch and listen-centered instruction" just to present a contrast to the academic experiences students face throughout the day in other classes; I am suggesting this type of instruction because it also is more proper and appropriate for music education than talk-centered instruction.

*(Allan R. McMurray)*

### Thoughts about instruction

The rehearsal is a classroom. Furthermore, in a classroom the instructor must have the ability to select the materials, teach the subject, evaluate the progress, correct misunderstandings, and inspire interest in the topic and in future learning. More important than the teaching of a few facts is the ability of the teacher to stimulate the mind and motivate the student to want to learn and experience more.

As an instrumental music educator, my first obligation to my students is in my preparation. Choosing music, for instance, is a responsibility which I assume.

I select the music through a careful study of the best that is available at the level of the students I have. When choosing music, I first consider the ability of the ensemble and then I go to lists that I have accumulated. These lists contain pieces that offer me the opportunity to teach about music and about expressiveness through music. All of the pieces on my lists are there because I have studied them and I believe in them. New pieces earn their way on to my lists only after I have studied them to determine their content.

In matching pieces to players I will select the majority of works to be well within the ability of the ensemble. One composition may be selected that exceeds their ability, and one or two compositions will be easy for their level of skill and background. While I could choose more difficult pieces, I don't want the rehearsals I conduct to be dominated by chasing technique.

I would rather include in the rehearsal opportunities for expression and musical sensitivity which can only be attained when each member of the ensemble can get outside of their own part and listen and interact with others.

It also is much more stimulating and exciting for me to shape phrases and consider the nuance of a musical composition than to drill the ensemble in order to build its technique.

Thus, I seek a balance in each rehearsal between attention to technical development and attention to sensitivity and the creation of beauty. The difficult piece on each program is complemented in rehearsal and performance by at least one easy piece. While I want students to play all pieces with musical understanding and intuition, I select at least one easy piece with less technical demands. (This would be a piece that is easy compared to the ensemble's level of skill though it might be difficult for another group's level of skill.) With a piece that presents few or no technical obstacles for them, they will not be preoccupied solving the technical problems. Thus, they can concentrate more freely upon the musical substance of the piece and develop an intuitive musical understanding more freely.

*(Allan R. McMurray)*

### Rehearsal style

I have never observed a rehearsal that has not taught me something. Whether it was a rehearsal technique, a pacing, a prioritization, or an atmosphere created; every rehearsal I have observed has given me useful tips on things to do or on things to be avoided.

Perhaps the single most apparent aspect of a rehearsal is the interaction between conductor and performer. Whatever the interaction is, it is my belief that it is determined and controlled by the actions of the conductor. The actions of the conductor must be responsive to the educational needs of the student.

With this in mind, it should be noted that the younger the student, the less time should be spent on the podium. The elementary student, needs help with the basic skills of performance more than the student needs a conductor. Therefore, the elementary instrumental music educator should spend at least ninety percent of the time off the podium.

This will enable him to move around the room assisting students individually in the way they hold their instruments, the proper playing positions, the proper posture, etc. The elementary teacher is also teaching them how to mark their music and understand certain signs and symbols that are familiar to us but are unfamiliar to them. I think that "music marking" is very important and should be taught more than it is being done.

The junior high conductor may find an equal time off and on the podium. The high school music educator should be able to spend more time on the podium than off depending on the level of the students. When the teacher gets off the podium regularly, the teacher can get around to people more and make them feel more involved with the group. The fact is that proximity as well as seating in rows control concentration. Because of proximity, for example, the front row cannot get away with anything, the second row can get away with a little, and the back row gets away with anything they want! Getting off the podium allows teacher the opportunity to make each student feel necessary and important to the group and the whole product.

When I am conducting high school students and I feel I am having trouble projecting energy to a section because of the distance from the podium, I will get off the podium and go back to that section. Maybe it is just standing in front of them and conducting. By paying attention to them in a very personal way, I amplify whatever I do when I get back on the podium. They will remember that passage as something unusual and important. They also remember that spot because of the more intimate contact between the conductor and themselves.

With an all-state group recently, I had an interesting experience. The group was very large—about two-hundred-eighty students. The students and I felt frustrated because of the communication and problems hearing. Thus, I reorganized them into four concentric circles and I conducted from the center of the circle. I could get off the podium, move around, and relate to various sections more easily with this arrangement. It worked so well we did the concert that way. The concert was in the basket ball arena so parents could sit so they faced the child of their choice!

Regardless of the amount of time on or off the podium or the level of the performer, all the great rehearsals I have ever attended focused positive energy on the effort of individuals as well as the whole. Positive energy can include a compliment regarding attitude, performance, progress, or anything that deserves praise; I believe that positive comments must be a part of every rehearsal.

This is not to say that there should not be constructive criticism. I strongly believe, however, that when I take time to recognize something good in someone I make an investment in that person and in our rapport. When I say something negative I make a withdrawal from the amount of rapport this individual and I have.

My goal is to maintain a balanced account with each student and with the ensemble. I do not believe that music and beauty are served by abusive conductors who attempt to intimidate rather than motivate. The atmosphere of a positive rehearsal is more conducive to creativity and to learning than is the atmosphere of a negative rehearsal.

*(Allan R. McMurray)*

### Experience guides the conductor/teacher

Becoming better at conducting/teaching, and for that matter anything else that one may do, is certainly the product of life's experiences, good or bad. The trick is to retain the good for your own use, and to remember, so that you can reject the bad. Some of the things we experience early in life never come into sharp focus until much later. I keep discovering things I didn't particularly notice at the time of the experience that now are coming back with real meaning.

As the teacher/conductor evolves in a personality, the experience of success with that which works comes back to that person in stronger and stronger meaning. I see a lot of myself in the lives of the students I work with at Northwestern University. Some of them, like myself at their ages, show wonderful, raw talent and fine skills in playing and the use of language, both written and musical. They will build on everything they encounter in the next few years and that experience will shape their future. That is why everything their teacher/conductor says or does is so important to be said or done with integrity. What we do in the classroom or the rehearsal we must strive to do honestly and with only the right motives.

*(John R. Paynter)*

### Group teaching in the ensemble

In my only encounter with Sir George Solti, and a very brief one at that, I was introduced to him as "a director of bands and a teacher at Northwestern University." He responded by saying, "I am a teacher, also. When I am on the podium with an orchestra, I am teaching, both in the rehearsal and the performance. One must be really prepared to be a teacher and especially when one is a conductor."

One thing we must try to do is put the presentation of the best possible information about music at the top of the list of our obligations to the members of an ensemble. The learning of the right way to see, hear, and do things is way ahead of any other motive for ensemble playing. The concert, important as it may be, is second to learning musicianship.

Right as we are visiting today, the wonderful members of the Northshore Concert Band are starting a new season with the average annual change in personnel of about five members replaced with five new faces. In the first several rehearsals with these new people "on board" it was necessary to go back to work on fundamentals and principles of performance practices as they apply to this Band.

For example, one of those fundamentals is total communication between the players and the conductor. Lack of understanding in this one area will hold back the other one hundred and fifteen players. Until this and other principles are understood by everyone in the group, efficient use of time in rehearsals will be impossible. By the way, one could suggest that we could take an individual or a group of five to a separate

practice room and teach them one-on-one-or-five and save the time of the others. It doesn't work that way, however. The full group must integrate with the newcomers and review their understanding at the same time the new players take on a new set of information. Bands and wind ensembles (as well as orchestras, chamber groups and choruses often provide the most efficient way to teach.

*(John R. Paynter)*

### Goals and group teaching in a rehearsal

In addition to the conductor carefully planning his/her agenda to accomplish in each rehearsal, it would be well to renew an allegiance to the performers. Each one of the players has invested time, wealth, and energy into taking on the assignment of ensemble membership. Each rehearsal should end in a way that every participant goes out of it better in some way for having had the rehearsal experience. Because concerts are so slow to round into shape, that is precisely why the teaching of music through the music is so important and the group offers incentive, demonstration of successful strategies, and higher morale.

*(John R. Paynter)*

### Fine performances do not necessarily promote student growth and satisfaction

This is true, but poor performances promote growth and satisfaction even less. There are many, many musical organizations across our country who play superb performances in concert and contest settings without leaving the individual performers a sense of lasting satisfaction. Students are sometimes left "vacant" and without values for future experiences in music, both as a performer and as a consumer of music. Students may be left without a desire to go on in music making, or an impetus to performer better, or differently, or again, or with more quality, even though their organization was impressive.

When this happens, what I think may be lacking is the emotional content of the music that comes from a sensitivity to musical, expressive comment. It is thoroughly possible, maybe even more with bands than other ensembles, to have a mechanically perfect performance that is musically bereft. We could hope that this is the exception and not the rule. If there are people still doing rote teaching of notes or a mechanical approach to expression, their students will be amongst the ones who are quickest to drop out of music.

When performers have not had experiences they value for the right reasons, part of what is missing is quality in their experiences. When they have missed these quality experiences, they have no reason to expect them in the future experiences; or they may actually not recognize them when they come. When we hear about this or that teacher who is universally admired and respected, we can be sure the student inherited that teacher's love of and devotion for music and the arts.

There is one more prevalent concern that we must address as conductors/teachers. We live in an age of "instant gratification." Fast cars, fast foods, speed reading, and fast romances. "Pop" music fits the "fast" mode too naturally, and listening to it is far faster than producing it. When conductors opt for gimmicky music or appeal to the teen culture that is their ensemble, instant gratification is a bad possible alternative to the mastering of good music, which is more time consuming, but outlasts the "fast" art! It takes great energy and integrity to strive for long range goals with permanent values in the face of things that come too easily. The reward, of course, is feeling good about teaching lifetime values, even from the smallest well-turned phrase, or sensitivity in an expressive line that words could not have expressed.

*(John R. Paynter)*

### Instrumental teachers, then and now

The band movement in America owes a great debt of thanks to the many outstanding band conductors, especially from around the turn of the century through the World War II years. Wherever we learn about a great band from the past, there are one or more famous names associated with it. The Sousa bands, the Gillmore bands and the Bachman "Million Dollar Band" were not named "the Monkeys," the "Grateful Dead" or the "Lead Zeppelin." They were named in honor of the personalities who inspired their successes.

It could have been much the same in our educational institutions. We have had "Revelli's Rascals" in Hobart or "Harding's Heroes" at Illinois. The fact remains that where there appeared a strong and respected teacher/conductor, there success was assured.

Because of my more than thirty years of membership in the American Bandmasters Association, and the opportunity to know a few of the early pioneers in the heritage of bands in America, I am overwhelmingly impressed by their brilliance in teaching and conducting through a period of history when instruments were not as perfected, published music, other than marches and a handful of good transcriptions, had to be provided in the manuscripts of many of these conductors, and method books were yet to come, most of them from the same teachers who would be using them.

The early directors of bands were most often great performers themselves. Some were taught at home by parents or other family members who were musical. Many of them were brought up on hearing the village band or the Sunday school orchestra. Others came from the rich cultural heritage of Europe and populated the silent movie theaters. When "talking pictures" threw them out of work, many turned to making themselves indispensable by organizing the first of the fabled school bands. They went into schools and brought their love and devotion of the bands to school authorities.

Without the work of this great group of the early twentieth century, we might never have had bands in the schools as we know it today. Time heals; and where there were teachers who failed by lack of energy, or musicality, or communication skills, we only know now that no important music was taught in certain towns and cities in America.

What we know for sure is that the early teachers had no school band models to emulate. They wrote their own arrangements and method books; they designed their own band quarters and concert halls; and in many cases they taught every student in their bands. They surely must have worked long hours and under some meager conditions. How amazed they would be to our present-day publications, instruments, and teaching tools.

Are our products better today? Probably. At least in sheer numbers, if nothing else. But we have our share of outstanding teachers now, dedicated, trained, sensitive, skilled people who have profited greatly in their preparation to teach because of people like Prescott, Bainum, Dvorak, Hindsley, Carleton Stewart, Fred Ebbs, Edwin Franko Goldman, and many others, too numerous to mention.

Because of our fine teacher training institutions, our wide variety of thoughtfully planned and inspired clinics, and because of the advance in instruments, equipment, and materials, there are superior teachers all across America and spilling into Japan, Canada, the United Kingdom and Scandinavia. We are beginning to repay our debt of musical tradition and respect for the arts as we were privileged to receive it from the family backgrounds of many of our finest pedagogues.

But when push comes to shove, and in the last analysis, the teacher who is musical and well trained, and can also "sell" the arts to his players, classes, and administrators is the one who is most to be admired. These current-day pioneers are probably the best we have ever had; and should be, given the advances in education, performance skills, and methods.

We try our best in the universities and colleges to see that repertoire is covered and that music is made, and we are dealing with people who still must compete for every chair or fight to get into the best teaching and conducting situation. It is possible to suggest that some of our very finest players are not yet in a professional orchestra where salaries might match their worth.

Our school teachers are still sadly underpaid despite valiant efforts to improve this situation. Years ago teachers faced vacant libraries, instrument cabinets, and vacant, nonexistent concert halls. Today they are facing vacant looks from administrations when financial support, curriculum, scheduling, and performance for athletic events may be the diminishing elements.

*(John R. Paynter)*

### A teacher from an earlier era

While we can copy materials and methods, it is sometimes difficult to copy a heart. Heart is what the very early school band directors brought to their rehearsals. The painstaking demonstration of the highest musical values based on their own performance experiences and their love of teaching those artistic emotions to others.

I think of Louis Blaha who taught at J. Sterling-Morton High School in Cicero, Illinois. What a wonderful gentleman he was, admired and respected by his students and their mostly first or second generation parents.

His music ethic was unique, but he also had the artistic awareness of parents who valued the arts above all other forms of recreation or entertainment. He went to work in the community and asked for students to pay for private lessons with some of the greatest Chicago-area musicians, including many from the Chicago Symphony Orchestra. Many of these men and women also taught in the universities and colleges in and near Chicago.

Mr. Blaha worked to see that his school orchestra and band lacked nothing in the way of equipment and opportunities. In fact I have heard a reliable story that for many years in the 1920s, 30s, and even 40s, the Chicago Symphony went to Blaha's inventory whenever they needed the use of contrabassoon.

Blaha was something of a legendary "guru" in Cicero, well known for his discipline, his quality musicianship, and his devotion to teaching and conducting only at the highest standard. McAllister in Joliet and Caneva in Lockport gave a super cadre of teacher models for our Illinois educators.

*(John R. Paynter)*

### Teachers, literature, and methods

I think the filtration system that brought us great teachers of school and community bands in the early history of the band movement in this country, especially from rich musical family and cultural backgrounds provided us with bright personalities who never made the choice between being teachers or musicians, but held them on a level plain.

Our methods and literature, while greatly enhanced in breadth, depth and variety, still clings, successfully to some of the early approaches. Only the technology and learning pace have changed.

*(John R. Paynter)*

### Publishers and a concern for quality

I like most music publishers and admire many of them. Publishing, particularly for band, is less lucrative than most people think. Publishing without volume sales is a losing proposition. The recent development of merging, taking over, and adding publishing houses into new groupings and unfamiliar names has taken a toll on the band directing profession. Most of the large corporations are continuing to provide valuable services and materials. While it gets harder and harder to do this on a personal basis, modern developments in recording and video taping techniques have made an amazing impact.

I used to know every band publisher on a personal basis, and many of them came to my rescue on more than a few occasions. It takes more effort to have that kind of relationship now. But the telephone is still a marvelous contraption, and personal calls to publishing houses will almost always result in eventually finding a special person who likes her/his job and will become a supporting friend.

Perhaps some of the decision making process that was the task of the publishing firm's chief officer has now been given over to the individual teacher. There are stronger and weaker publications in every publishing house. The trick is to stay informed, read scores (sometimes even without a cassette playing!), and be as selective as possible. The clinic new-music sessions are more valuable than ever. There is so much from which to choose and so little that is of lasting value.

It is the publisher's privilege to print that which will make the firm a profit. No altruistic motives here! But if band directors regularly reject that which is of little value to their students, more and better good music will appear.

Take Carl Ludwig who started the Ludwig Music Company with his rich background as a performing violinist in Europe. He brought an integrity to be expected from his publications for band whether Grade II or Grade VI. The fairest prices, the score and parts, and the intrinsic value of the material were factors of importance in his thinking. While Elizabeth Ludwig-Fennell continues this same tradition of excellence, it is more and more difficult to keep a balance between sales and production cost. She is only one publisher who has refused to compromise product quality. There is no point in looking to Ludwig Music for junk.

*(John R. Paynter)*

### Why working with band is so important to me

First, because bands are here and are here to stay. Forget the people who call bands old-fashioned, not relevant to current society. Nonsense! All music in the schools may be endangered by the thoughtless actions of certain school officials and taxing bodies. But don't think for a minute that bands will or should disappear. That's the number one reason for working with bands.

The second reason is that no one has beaten a path to my door to have me take over a symphony orchestra, a choir, or a musical theater or film company. But when confronted with such an option on a few occasions I opted to stay in the band business because it is the best way I know to have a positive musical experience both as a conductor and as a teacher. I love bands!

They sometimes disappoint me and often overwhelm me. I love their variety and I especially admire my many wonderful colleagues in the profession who have succeeded in making the band's music and its quality of performance reach an all-time high.

Bands are terrific, whether in the form of marching, concert, wind ensemble, symphonic band, jazz, or chamber music. As a matter of fact, that is exactly why one of my reasons for working with bands is so easy to defend; the variety and breadth of our bands is hard to improve on in the arts.

If we left it just at that our detractors would line up with their hands up. "But what of those terrible sounds you make?" "Isn't it stupid to spend time and talents moving your feet and fingers at the same time?" "Isn't there a lot of garbage being performed?" Yes, a strong case could be made for each of these criticisms of the band movement. Yet in its way the bands as a whole get better every passing decade.

Is it wrong to tolerate bad sounds in the brief pursuit of good ones? Is it wrong to provide a valuable community service and to your school's total educational program, while teaching accuracy, discipline, control, and patience; not to mention the most important element of them all, . . . teamwork? Yes, there is a lot of bad band music being played. Let's all use our superior musicianship and skill to upgrade the selection and teaching process. We have thus far done this better

than most of our counterparts.

I love to work with bands because the players who come my way, whether at the University or in one of a great variety of honor bands and guest conducting engagements always seem eager to improve, to know more, . . . to be better. What challenge in our lives could improve on that?

*(John R. Paynter)*

### Literature-based teaching

Frankly, I think teaching from the base of excellent literature, regardless of its difficulty, is the only way to go. Doesn't everyone? The language of music is music itself!

With that profound thought I suggest we should not encourage musical profanity! And surely we can teach technique through band literature and outside of it. The process of music selection has never been more important than right now.

*(John R. Paynter)*

### Educational music

Certainly one of the things that has contributed to the rapid, successful development of wind players and bands has been the fact that the band's (wind ensemble's) repertoire is, in one sense, only of an educational kind. There are only a few professional bands and so many outstanding high school, university, college, and community bands. In this way all of band literature, regardless of maturity, style, or difficulty is played by non-professionals. Our excellent military bands may be the singular exception.

When took over the bands at Northwestern from the great Glenn Cliffe Bainum, he handed me a magnificent band library and almost immediately I began to develop a set of notebooks to give me quick reference to each musical category. (Now we have this all on computer, of course.) After listing such types as overtures, suites, tone poems, marches, and so forth, I realized there was one more category to complete, "educational music." I disagree with Paul Ivory's statement that "educational music is music that is all preparation and no results." I'm sure he meant it to be cute and not smug, but training music, like training pants, leaves less to clean up around the room.

School orchestras sometimes struggle with the scores that professionals handle with ease. Conductors who overlook this training stage of a school ensemble may be finding that despite many good individuals and their efforts to provide worthwhile training literature, the amount available for training bands is much more in place.

*(John R. Paynter)*

### Consider the students' responses when selecting music

One must do this. To do less is to offer too little to the performers' souls and minds and is not worthy of the teacher. And we cannot fool them. Students react to Bach, Brahms, and Husa instinctively and lastingly. Why would we cheat them?

*(John R. Paynter)*

### Knowing how to perform better

We start first by being good performers ourselves. Then we branch out to the experience of great music in all of its facets, both as performer and as listener.

These principles of good performance should never leave us, but need constant re-tooling through record collections, good music radio stations, attending concerts (of good music), and listening to the professionals. We need to study all elements of style, analysis, and interpretation, not once, but over and over again.

Look for your players' eyes when you conduct. Besides communicating to them, notice what they are communicating back to you. The most rewarding experience a conductor can have is the reaction of his/her performers. The audience applauds, to be sure, and sometimes with full enthusiasm. But we can't experience their body language from behind our back.

Besides thinking about balance, pitch, rhythm, and tone when teaching, always consider direction of line, expressivity, variety, and spontaneity.

*(John R. Paynter)*

### Selecting music

There has to be firm leadership from the teacher/conductor in the selection of music the ensemble will play. Don't succumb to pressure to choose valueless material. You will get nothing of worth from such material.

There are many musics. Try to complete the variety of experiences represented by all styles and times. Let your performers know what makes a piece classical, romantic, or contemporary. Show them about Impressionism and the Baroque. Transcriptions, if well done, should be a part of every band student's diet. Search for good present-day composers whose style incorporates ideas from other times and places.

First, select the most musical material you can. Next, bring your knowledge of musical style, form, and interpretation to the rehearsal room and concert stage. Finally, be sure that any literature you select contains the right elements of shape and design, repetition and contrast, density and transparency, and elements of expressiveness.

Good music, like a good rehearsal, must balance elements of surprise with the predictable, and the expected with the unexpected. In music, as in life, variety is the spice.

It is true, there is plenty of worthless material. But you don't have to buy it or use it. We are well past the day when worthwhile music was difficult to find. That old excuse can't work for us any more.

If you worry enough about your players' needs, you will not be concerned about the needs of your listeners.

Finally, we don't need to buy anything new until we thoroughly search our band libraries for the likely gems of the past.

*(John R. Paynter)*

### Some keys to expressiveness

There are just three keys to expressiveness in my opinion. First is the best choice of literature to express. Next, is the complete and total study of the score. Only by knowing all you can about a work can you find success in expressing it through your baton or teaching, or both, with variety, conviction, and confidence. It is at the desk with the score open and the room silent (no cassettes playing, please) that most interpretive thoughts come to life.

Finally, teach music from the students' learning and response, touching their hearts with your own deep love of the arts and acting as a guide to their listening and playing skills. Sing a lot. Make evident your complete rapture with music and frequently underpin your words with excitement and outright enthusiasm for everything about music. Let them know that you care for them, not just as an oboist or trombonist, but as a human being who needs music in their life.

Try never to be dull in any phase of the rehearsal or performance. Clarence Sawhill, on the occasion of his retirement from teaching at UCLA, once told a news reporter that "the most difficult thing about being a band director for more than forty years was feeling good every day." What a fantastic philosophy!

*(John R. Paynter)*

### Students' responses to different pieces

One really has to be wary of first responses by the performers in an ensemble. Almost always their assessments will change as the music gets more and more developed through teaching and repeated hearings. And I like to think that not every composition that is rehearsed needs to find its way to a performance.

An effective tactic is to acquire a work that needs a year or two to "ripen" with the players. Bring it out, put it away, bring it out, teach a little on it, put it away. If it is a good piece eventually the players' hunger will outweigh their estrangement.

*(John R. Paynter)*

### Ultimately students will like the literature the teacher presents

Perhaps this is true, but only if the literature is worth presenting and enough time goes into teaching it. The *Trauersinfonie* by Wagner is probably not on the list of instant hits with young people because of its long tones and slow tempo. It requires a skillful conductor to send the players home with the great experience of learning and not the pain of surviving this great original work for band.

*(John R. Paynter)*

### Interpreting and shaping the music

I tell my students to look in every composition for its one biggest moment. This happens in a march and even in a waltz as well as in Schoenberg's *Theme and Variations*. Its not necessarily the loudest, or busiest, or highest, or lowest point in the score. But it is there, and all interpretation moves to and from the biggest musical moment. And you have to remember, it could be the quietest big moment, too.

*(John R. Paynter)*

### Selecting music from what is available

While I have talked quite a lot about this topic there may be a couple of more things to say.

Be ambitious, daring, and energetic in the process of selecting music for your group. It may be foolish to think that one of your conductor friends has enough training and good taste to influence your selection.

Good music is never mundane music. Avoid the ordinary. Good material is there. Compile lists from workshops and clinics you attend, but always check the validity of the evaluator. Analyze the specific fundamentals of music-making which each piece of literature can provide to you and your students. Yes, that's right. Don't leave out yourself and your tastes, as well as the elements in the publication that will tend to bring the best in yourself as a conductor and teacher.

*(John R. Paynter)*

### What I look for in music

My academic degrees are in composition and I have written and arranged in various styles. I have taught courses in harmony, ear training, form, and analysis, and, of course, instrumental conducting and band arranging. It has made me very aware of musical content and what to look for. But it has not guaranteed my success—it only guarantees my credentials.

Music is a little like selecting a spouse; you usually don't—the spouse comes to you. Much of the best music I have performed came to me as I built a particular concert, planned to feature a certain soloist or instrumental section, or came to me as I attempted to sculpt the design of an entire concert by selecting varied, but related, works. It would be silly to try to guess how many compositions I have conducted. But, it would be safe to say that I have rejected fifty times as many as I have chosen.

I especially look for integrity in the work I am selecting. It must fit the same mould as all good music. It can be unfamiliar if it is not *only* unfamiliar. It can be atonal if it is not *just* atonal. It can be long if being long doesn't do the players and the audience a disservice.

Ron Nelson, one of our finest and consistent American composers, wrote a work for wind ensemble and choir which he called, *Processional and Prayer of the Emperor of China on the Altar of Heaven, December 21, 1539*, a title that nearly outlasts the notes.

Writing on a text for the choir, Nelson said, "to listen to this piece, one must set aside Western ideas of form, harmony, development, and embark on a musical journey and immerse oneself in the sounds heard." Despite the composer's foreboding statement, the work is overwhelmingly moving; strong in its less familiar formal outline, and colorful for its initial and final lack of color. It is just the kind of work that should attract our a musician's attention.

*(John R. Paynter)*

### Some of today's composers

It depends on which of today's composers we want to talk about. A number of them are quite gifted and original, but there is an awful lot of imitation that goes on. I will not mention my favorites for fear that I will overlook some and insult others. It is a very healthy sign that we have lots of composers in there twenties and thirties who have something significant to say.

The changing publisher is an important part of the composer process. More and more material is available only on rental making it difficult for bands who need ample rehearsal time for presentation and gestation to get their hands on the music. Publishers, at least some them, simply cannot or will not take a chance on music which they see as being a liability to their catalog. Young composers respond eagerly to commissions and through this method, produce new materials that may eventually find their way to publication.

*(John R. Paynter)*

### Responding to the challenge of instrumentation

I hear so many of the band conductors saying, "I can't play this, it has an important oboe part." Wouldn't it be better to say, "I've got to play this work, therefore I must develop an oboe player." This way the player, the conductor, the publisher, and the listener all benefit.

*(John R. Paynter)*

### Things I think are important

Caring, sharing and working with integrity. Never be put in a position where you have to make an apology for what you have done or have taught. Work hard, work honestly, and treat everyone with the same respect you expect to be treated. Value the talent you were given and spread it around. Show joy. Show enthusiasm. Show concern for others. Try not to waste the time of anyone, including yourself. Never say, "I'm too busy," even if you are. Nobody cares and nobody believes you anyway.

The only thing wrong about our copyright laws is the phrase, "not in public domain." Music is the public's domain.

Gordon Jacob writes a funny novelty on the *Barber of Seville*. James Gillette arranged a one-of-a-kind set for school bands called *Short Classics for Band*, presently out of print at Carl Fischer's, but worth a ton in the teaching of young musicians how to express themselves.

David Maslanka does a marvelous arrangement of a Bach "Prelude and Fugue" and Nelhybel uses the master's "Musical Offering" to create a significant one of his own.

Honor your parents, your family, and your profession. You are fortunate and special.

*(John R. Paynter)*

### Thoughts about composers

Sometimes we treat them with too little respect. This is the downside of having large numbers who write for band. It is possible that we take the composers too much for granted and we lose track of the fact that in some cases their creative gift is more special than our own. The fact that we can see and touch them in the halls of the Hilton Hotel makes them more familiar than Bach (and not necessarily as good).

Present day economics require composers to have other jobs to augment their income or to turn out vast quantities of their publications. Both situations erode the composers' best production. The very special band composers have felt it difficult to maintain professional privacy. Maybe we expect or demand too much of composers.

Nelhybel's monumental *Resurrection Symphony* was played by the United State Air Force Band under Col. Arnald D. Gabriel. A long and difficult work, only a group as strong as the USAF Band could accomplish its playing. Only a conductor of Col. Gabriel's skill could interpret it. But most important to remember is that only a composer of Nelhybel's talent could have produced it in the first place.

The performers caught a little flack from criticisms such as "too long for band," "too difficult," "dissonant," "too unusual" (it calls for piccolo trumpet, alto flute, and amplified guitar) or just "too impractical." Of course most of the criticism just quoted are part of the very fact is was such a wonderful piece.

Among the vast works in many styles written by Nelhybel are a fine *Concerto for Harpsichord and Winds* and a *Concerto for Cello with Wind Band*. Both are charming, deeply moving pieces, but generally not well known. Conductors must work as hard as their students and their composers.

I put Karel Husa in a class all by himself, but as a musician/composer and as a human being and teacher. If I place him on a pedestal there room beside him for more, if they can qualify at his level.

But don't lose track of Morton Gould, Norman Dello Joio, Vincent Persichetti, William Schuman, Paul Hindemith, Ingolf Dahl, Howard Hanson, and a host of others who have done so much to make our band's more musical and more meaningful.

*(John R. Paynter)*

### The future of bands in schools

What I think and what I hope is that bands will survive and will be a strong force for music education well into the 21st century and beyond. But I want it only to survive for the right reasons—the pursuit of excellence in the music and its performance, not filled with gimmicks or "pop" material and not as a slave to electronics except where technology helps us meet our loftier goals.

I also hope it won't be through the medium of the wind ensemble except in rare and special circumstances. I am a firm believer in the wind ensemble at the college, conservatory, or community/professional level for reasons unique to those levels of players and performances. There the wind ensemble stimulates player interest, provides a medium for extraordinary kinds of performances, and serves as a fine training station for players who aspire to professional playing careers. It also provides excellence in recordings and films for the teaching of instrumentalists.

Wind ensemble at the high school level can be a shortsighted approach in some cases. It creates an "elitism" that fosters elements of false competition and false accomplishment. It fails to meet the needs of many talented players and creates playing demands which teenage players may discover are too hard to handle. Only a small percentage of the available original or transcribed literature is properly expressed with one on a part when players are still very much in a formative stage.

We had one fine band teacher in the Chicago area who decided the wind ensemble should become his primary performing band. He formed a one-on-a-part elite group and had better success with it than he had earlier experienced with the top group being a large concert band. For two years fewer than forty students had the best of his time and talent, and when the third year rolled around and the wind ensemble kids had graduated, no one showed up for band or wind ensemble. The entire band program in that high school had to be rebuilt.

*(John R. Paynter)*

### Thinking about large and small bands

About the time that Frederick Fennell was developing his theories about a new kind of wind ensemble at Eastman, many of us were experimenting with the same idea. At Northwestern we formed a volunteer "chamber band" to meet on Saturday mornings to read and rehearse music in a newer, leaner dimension. It was amazing how quickly the best players responded to the call and how loyal they were to getting up early on Saturdays, heretofore reserved for marching band drills on game days. Players were rotated for each work and sometimes within a longer composition. This great fun finally resulted in the establishing of wind ensemble as the primary wind group at Northwestern University's School of Music. However, for the first few years most of the players performed in the Symphonic Band as well as the wind ensemble (now called Symphonic Wind Ensemble). It was some time later, when there began to be more wind players than we could use in one large band, that the wind ensemble emerged as the "top" group in our program.

*(John R. Paynter)*

### Rotating seating

The rotation of seating has good and bad results. The good result is that all players have an equal chance to develop confidence and leadership strengths while they prepare for ever increasing responsibilities.

The bad is that it is more difficult to develop cohesiveness, tuning, and balance. Great symphony orchestras and our great service bands rarely rotate seating. Rotation does not contribute as much to

excellence in performance, but it may be fairer and more productive to player development.

*(John R. Paynter)*

### Ways to develop band programs

Some of the value and appeal of the wind ensemble can be developed in a high school band program with just a little imagination and a lot of desire to inspire young musicians.

Here are a few suggestions: When using transcribed (well-transcribed) orchestral music or original compositions for band by creditable composers, reinstate the solos for your first chair players, thin the textures where appropriate, and cut to a wind ensemble within the band; stress the character and qualities of each instrument in the band through careful selection of the right kind of material, or be revising or re-writing material for that purpose.

At a selected moment or for special occasions feature a select part of the concert band in a wind ensemble selection. This provides incentive for the ambitious students and nice listening variety for the audience.

Put new emphasis on the performing of chamber music ensembles, solo and ensemble recitals, and trying for honor or all-state bands. Develop a buddy system where outstanding students assist in the development of younger players and even conduct a wind ensemble within the band which is made up primarily of the younger players.

Stimulate all students through great examples: recordings, films, video tapes, composition classes, the study and practice of theory, developing ears, sharing with the students the approach to studying a music score, field trips to great concerts, guest speakers and/or performers coming to your school and spending time with the students.

To improve and strengthen the band's place in the schools, I think we are going to have to get off our podiums and be living advocates for the importance of the arts in education. In this sense alone we need numbers; numbers of successful music students and numbers of tax paying parents of our students, helping us to get the message of music's value to all humanity and at all stages of life.

Furthermore, the music we choose and the way we teach it in the future is going to go a long way toward determining its support in the school curriculum. The production and sharing of beauty must be an honorable and noble part of each student's high school experience. What we play and how we play it will be the mirror of our future as band directors and music teachers.

The people we train to teach and the people who hire these trainees must be of high character, willing spirits, and well educated, balanced personalities. Most of all the conductors must be spirited and willing to communicate their respect and earnestness for the arts. More and more the decision making must come from a posture of believing in what we do, not for careless or self-indulging motives, but for a strong, committed sense of what influences the molding of a young person's education and future.

This starts with the educating of the conductor in her or his training at the college or university. Sound methodology can never be replaced. But strong advocacy training and programs of consumer education and development need to occupy a more prominent place in the college music major curriculum. Never in history have we had more people talking about the value of the arts. Never have there been more reading material and multimedia sources for use in praising the value and music.

Get the parents involved in community music making and in other forms of the arts; theater, painting, dancing, etc. Teach families about the historical placement of the arts and artists, and the relationship of the arts to all of world history. Explain music as a wonderful adult fulfilling activity, an ongoing love affair with the arts as a full stimulus to total understanding of beauty in the lives we lead. Gradually coax parents and others in the community to see beyond the obvious service obligations of the band program for athletic events, school assemblies, and contest trophies to the solid sense that music counts for as much in life, and maybe more, than the sciences and humanities. Until the time that school administrations recognize the value of the arts versus service functions, we will not move much further ahead in the next thirty years.

In saying this, I hope everyone remembers and knows that I am not against marching bands, jazz bands, or pep bands. I just want them to be in the proper perspective and the right proportions. I want to start with the right motives of teaching good music and playing it well with the central core of any worthwhile program, the concert band. With established and worthy values solidly in place we should have fun doing the marching and jazz playing that we want. But the concert band must come first!

I loved playing jazz in high school. I even had my own little dance band. I did it on my own, but with the moral support of my band director. Most of what I learned about harmony and arranging was garnered from my jazz activities before university. It was great fun and a fine relief from all the other activities. For some people it can become a major, serious study, just

as the developing of terrific marching bands can be rewarding to others. But all of this is only possible where serious, concert music can flourish.

*(John R. Paynter)*

### Teacher education

We could afford to talk less like teachers who are talking to teachers. Methods and know-how are too often stressed at the sacrifice of emotions, experiences, and interaction between student and teacher.

I don't think we are always positive enough in how we approach the student who wants to be a teacher. There is still too often the attitude that those who can't make it as performers will have to teach. This is not a new comment; I seems like I have heard it forever.

Yet if you ask a student who plays third trumpet in the Indianapolis or San Francisco symphonies, even our trumpet majors don't know. I keep saying, "You want to be special? Teach." In most cities, small towns especially, the music teacher/conducting is the music expert for that community. Otto Graham, Sr. could have run for mayor when he was teaching those great bands in Waukegan, Illinois. Everyone knew and admired him. I have seen this again and again in my travels to conduct in many different places in America. Often the local band director has been the best known person in town.

*(John R. Paynter)*

### My experience in music education classes

The experience I remember most is studying string methods under the late Traugott Rohner who was an Evanston Township High School orchestra conductor and a faculty member at Northwestern for many years. I studied the violin first and took a grade of D because Mr. Rohner said I played in too many keys for just once through America. I must have been more impressive on the string bass, because my grade for his course averaged out to a C, in fact the only grade below B I ever experienced.

As a composition major I only experienced music education courses second-hand. I have never taught at the secondary level except as a guest conductor or speaker. In my forty-one years on the faculty at Northwestern I have been invited only once to address a music education class. I must not have been impressive and never received a return engagement.

I did, however, experience music education as a student. I had the wonderful condition of extremely well-trained St. Olaf vocal teachers. The general music classroom in the Mineral Point, Wisconsin grade school was lined all around with photo portraits of such music notables as Ignace Paderewski, Lawrence Tibbet, George Gershwin, and J. S. Bach. Not only was I taught to know something about these personalities, but I was instilled by these outstanding vocal teachers with a high respect for what the people in the pictures had done and what they meant to music. Under their direction I was introduced to the excitement of Gershwin's *Rhapsody in Blue* before I could spell it!

My early life was filled with wonderful music teachers and opportunities to make music. The advantages I have had lead me to think that maybe, just maybe teachers are expecting to pick up our kids at far too advanced ages. Perhaps it would do us all good to start down there in the grades selling music and making it known for the value and joy of its lasting consequences.

*(John R. Paynter)*

## What is important

Sometimes I get the feeling that we stress the mechanics of music too much and that technical development may lead to a mechanical approach to life; . . . punch in at a certain hour, punch out on schedule, take off a maximum of sick days, and so on. I'm not kidding. I'm describing what I see around me.

When I think back, there was never a chance that I wouldn't be involved in music, given parents who played piano and clarinet and never missed a music event. They had me involved in the Sunday school orchestra when I was just a small boy (I really can't remember ever being small, even when I wasn't very old.) and my three sisters joined me to make six Paynters in an orchestra of eight players.

My folks would never have dreamed of missing a concert that one of us played in; they attended even some of the worst summer city band concerts that were played or conducted in Mineral Point. There might have been one cornet, one trombone, four flutes, seven drummers and three clarinets. My involvement was always applauded by Mother and Dad; there was always that reward.

In a small town you could be involved in everything. I played high school football and basketball, ran track one year, and took part in baseball in the only baseball season my high school ever had. One time I skipped a home baseball game to take part in the forensics meet at a neighboring town. I returned in time to run and watch my high school teammates losing by one run in the bottom of the ninth inning. Our coach, a wonderful science teacher and a great role model, saw me in the stands and ordered me to put on baseball shoes and go up to pinch hit in my nice suit and white shirt. The rest is history. I never saw the three pitches that I didn't swing at. I struck out to end the game! Now that can't happen in a band, or I would like to think it can't.

Sometimes we don't equate music with athletics, but I think we can in a valuable way. We can relate it to competition in life, in business and in striving for the highest possible standards in the arts. The good of contests is only to bring out the best in our performers regardless of the outcome.

*(John R. Paynter)*

## Conducting

What a great way to make a living! The best days of my life have been those when I conducted a performance. The next best are those when a conducted a rehearsal. And the rest of the best days are those when I tried to teach others about conducting. What better thing to do than devote your life to making music in light of our understanding of that music, and that music's composer and his life and times that produced his music.

The privilege carries some heavy responsibilities. Once you decide to be a conductor you can never be sick, or late, or tired, or mean, or unprepared again. Literally thousands of people will know you only from the back.

Like the man in the grocery store who came up to me with a quizzical look and asked me to turn my back to him. Then he said, "Say, didn't you used to be John Paynter." What could I say? . . . a washed up has-been in the prime of life!

A conductor has much to learn about music and its materials. He/she also has many things to learn about communication, understanding, motivation, patience, tolerance, and conservation of energy. It's fun to be a conductor.

*(John R. Paynter)*

## Listening to an orchestral version

Why shouldn't we? Shouldn't we be interested in the interpretations of Bruno Walter, or the playing of great orchestra members as models for our own conducting and teaching? Listen with and without scores. Many musical subtleties get overlooked when we have our noses buried in the score. Yet there are details of the performance that can be hidden from us if we listen without the score.

*(John R. Paynter)*

## Marching band

There is far less damage to lips than to egos and feet by marching in a band. There are perhaps a dozen stalwarts in the Chicago Symphony Orchestra who marched in the "Wildcat" Band when they were students at Northwestern. It was back in the years when we could say, "You don't march, you can't play in the concert band." Well that was not defensible and we knew it, but we needed bodies and players. There are still lots of students for whom a quarter in marching band might be just what they need to develop response to instructions, getting to places on time, conforming to a standard, and sensing that great wonder of giving of yourself for others.

*(John R. Paynter)*

### The teacher's role

In my home town we had a band director in my freshman year who lasted only that one year because the army drafted him and away he went. His name was Bernard Stepner, a great teacher and a wonderful human being. He is not very well now and I pray for his improved health.

What a great role model he was. He walked a mile from his rented apartment to the high school each day, fall, winter, and spring, carrying two lunch pails so he could spend his lunch hour teaching students and have his dinner at school so he could remain in his office as long as students could come to him.

Every student, no matter how old or how young, poor or well off, talented or not so talented, received a private lesson each week from this wonderful man. He knew there were no private teachers for miles around. He wanted to produce a better level of repertoire, so he taught, without extra compensation and without very much praise.

Here was a man who had played string bass in the Boston Pops Orchestra. He was truly a professional and one of the most influential teachers I ever had. His influence on us for only one year lasted for the next three for those teachers who followed him. What a highly developed sense of commitment. This was in the middle forties and even then some of the people in town thought he was "nuts." Those of us who knew him, thought he was "stern." Those who heard our school band thought he was a "genius." He thought he would never find enough hours to get his job done, but he was willing to break his back trying.

*(John R. Paynter)*

### Changes in students' attitudes

The attitudes have changed only as society has changed around them. They have always wanted to succeed and to play the best that they can. But where students in the 40s and 50s played dance jobs, the present crop play for church choir productions and chamber music festivals.

Their CD players and Walkmans have replaced their tube radios and 78 rpm recordings. As many of them as ever have to work their way through school, perhaps even more of them. Of course tuition has gone from the $400 per year that I paid to approximately twenty-five times that much now. I worked for my meals at a restaurant where the two-hour job in a day entitled me to have anything on the menu if it was less than $ 1.25. That same meal would cost $ 6.00 today but the band staff workers make $6.00 per hour instead of the 75 cents that I made working for Mr. Bainum.

Students are really not much different in attitude; perhaps a bit more serious, but not more ambitious. They seem to come to us knowing a little more each year, but maybe having fewer places to apply that knowledge. They still need large dosages of inspiration and love. It is our responsibility to provide it for them.

*(John R. Paynter)*

### Attitudes and responsibilities

A young man who now plays horn professionally in Chicago was playing for me in our all-student written Waa-Mu Show about ten years ago. We were in rehearsal for the show when he walked across the parking lot to the music building during a fierce thunder storm.

A flash of lightning struck the tip of his umbrella and knocked him down, but fortunately his rubber soles prevent a more serious incident. He picked himself up and began heading off to rehearsal as the University Public Safety arrived. A Safety officer said, "Man, where are you going? You were just hit by lightning. Don't you think we ought to check you out at the hospital before you go to rehearsal?" His reply was, "Have you ever missed a Paynter rehearsal!"

A conductor is a benevolent dictator. He/she needs to have both the courage to be demanding and the compassion to be understanding. Students need help and support, but sometimes need the prodding even more. We fail them when we compromise our demands. I'm proud of the student who gave his last moments in shock to my rehearsal. What's important is that he is still proud of that near tragic event, too.

*(John R. Paynter)*

### The community band

There is nothing more exhilarating or rewarding than conducting a community band. It functions without grades, credits, scholarships, or award. It consists of only those who love what they are doing. Every high school band director should give strong consideration to beginning a community group. Get the community aroused about music and set new standards for the adult players who support music in your school, standards you can help them pass on to their children who are members of your high school or college band.

When I say this to teachers, they often say, "My gosh, I'm there at school five nights a week now. I couldn't add anything more. It's just too much; . . . you're asking too much. I shouldn't have to do all of this for the small amount I am paid."

But here's a place where we can make great progress in letting our communities hear good band music and mature playing. (There's little value in anything less.) If a student's parents experience good music and know its value in their lives, it makes a positive change they can share with their daughter or son. I think it gives parents and other townspeople an incentive to support music in their schools.

*(John R. Paynter)*

### The community band and people's experiences

I don't think you can work with volunteer players in music, be successful with them, and not believe in the goodness of them. There are stories about folks in the Northshore Band who have gone through terrible kinds of problems and have fallen back on the friends and the music of the band for comfort and relief. Several times, when a community band member has experienced grief or trauma in their lives I have suggested that they might not to be concerned about attending a rehearsal. In they walk anyway, and when I suggest they didn't need to be there, their response is, "Yes, I need the Band tonight."

Another example of a positive attitude and the goodness of people who get involved with music was the elderly man in the Northshore Band who spent some time in a Veterans' hospital from a fall that had damaged the hip which had been replaced twice before. When I called and asked the nurse if I could speak to him, she said, "Not just now, I'm afraid. He's busy giving a student their regular flute lesson from his hospital bed."

*(John R. Paynter)*

### The growth of community bands

There has been a phenomenal growth in community bands, and while we have done what we could with the Northshore Band to spread the word, the fact is that most of the return to this type of adult music making is a natural outgrowth of better band directors, better band music, and more leisure time to become involved.

It seems wherever I go and start to talk about community bands, somebody will jump and let me

know they are using the little booklet we put out with the help of Kenneth Neidig on the subject about fifteen years ago. Community bands are a wonderful activity and a great movement.

*(John R. Paynter)*

### Observations about older beginners

There are a couple of places that I know about, and probably many more where I don't, where adult beginners can start a band instrument. A retired lady or gentleman comes in and says, "I've always wanted to play the trumpet. Is their any chance that I can?"

I conducted such a band in Edmonton, Canada where Harry Pincham has a program, much like a well-organized school curriculum. The program is run so players from every stage of development, beginner to very advanced bands, have opportunities for them to play.

Before you see these folks, you hear them, and they sound just the same as grammar school beginners. Then you see them and you realize, "My goodness, they're sixty, seventy years old, and they have the same wide-eyed excitement in their faces as little children."

There is more opportunity than ever to work with adults. With so much to learn in everything, we are so far behind in just the basic knowledge of the world. I think there is a great chance to enrich the lives of senior citizens and some not so senior. It's not too late to change adults and their judgment about the arts. If we can get through to them, more a philosophical point than a musical one, we can get them to change their self images and involve themselves in new experiences to lead fuller and richer lives in their mature years.

*(John R. Paynter)*

### A memorable band experience

Bands can be spiritual. They don't have to be Salvation Army bands to be spiritual (but we may wish they might be as musical as some of these great ensembles.)

I recall an incident at the Nels Vogel Clinic in Fargo-Moorhead when we were there with the Northshore Band. It was right at the time that some Canadians had been instrumental in rescuing some of our men from captivity in Iran.

Nels came to me after our dress rehearsal and said, "Hey, you know what would be a nice idea? Can your Northshore Band play the Canadian National Anthem for the large number of Canadians who are here at the clinic?" I said, "Nels, I would love to and it's certainly appropriate, but we don't have the music." He pulled his hand from behind his back, handed me the music and said, "Here it is. Here's the music!"

We had no further rehearsal time, so I gathered the band in the gym next to the performance area and handed out the parts. I thought they could play it well at sight, but I also thought I had better demonstrate how it would go. I said, "It's going to go like this, . . . Oh, Ca-na-da." I got only that far when the band broke into the most perfect and lovely four-part rendition I have ever experienced. The tremendous ovation we got from both Canadians and Americans was the frosting on the cake and second only in the great pride the Northshore Band had in themselves for doing it.

*(John R. Paynter)*

### Summing things up

It is interesting that we have talked so little about technique; where to put the first beat and the second one. Have we made it clear that technology and feeling are not really related except as they both contribute to our lives in such a major way. Do technical concerns detract from expressive ones? How do we achieve a balance? A computer will print these words, but the computer cannot replace what I think about them.

Strong teaching requires successful communication, with both individuals and groups. I encourage my students to use their eyes not only to see what is going on but to see how they are being accepted or rejected or ignored when they are conducting.

I do a lecture in conducting class and make each student aware that I stopped picking them up with my eyes, perhaps for thirty minutes or more.

Once a student came in to see after a rehearsal I had just conducted with the Northwestern University Symphony Orchestra. She said, "I want to tell you how exciting it was that you looked at me in today's rehearsal." I was surprised and asked her where she was sitting. "On the last stand of second violins," she replied. "You not only looked me, but you even noticed how I was doing." I have always remembered that incident. It suggests the importance of our attention to communicating with all of the students in an ensemble.

When we are working with bands, or orchestras, or choruses, we should try to get very close to the performers. We often help them in ways we may not know about ourselves. We can become mentors, surrogate parents, brothers, or sisters. We can as easily become boring, unfair, and unfeeling.

I conducted the Minnesota All-State High School Band this year and it was like going back to the farm, you know? I love young men and women at that age. They are so accepting and so anxious to learn and improve. They get such a charge out of every little story, each little new nuance, and the great togetherness of the whole experience.

I told my Northwestern University Wind Ensemble of the story of doing the New York All-State Wind Ensemble some years back. We had a young man playing third (bass) trombone. Although he was mentally retarded his handicap had not prevented him from reading music and playing very well. Just as we were about to go on stage, this fellow announced that he could not find his music. In any other situation he would have been ridiculed, laughed at, or made to hurt. Instead, the members of the Wind Ensemble embraced and comforted him, and after feverishly looking for it, found the third trombone music in the second trombone folder. Everyone cheered the bass trombonist, just as though he had done something very special. He had. He had brought the ensemble together in ways that I had failed to do.

*(John R. Paynter)*

### A final thought

Thank you for the privilege of talking to your readers and your patience with me in doing so. I hope that a fraction of the joy that teaching and conducting music has brought to me will be the reward to each one who reads my words. Best of luck, and "Strike up the Band."

*(John R. Paynter)*

# APPENDIX VII

# Creative, Aural, and Theory
# Activities for Instrumental Music
## John C. McManus

This appendix contains samples of John C. McManus's plans and suggestions for developing students' learning through creative activities. These ideas are included here because teaching music through creative activities is less common in instrumental music teaching than teaching through traditional techniques. He believes that these techniques, which are based upon principles of Manhattanville, are especially effective in motivating and enriching students' learning. Creative activities can be used in such areas as theory, composition, orchestration, aural development, and performance skill.

Another cause for a teacher's success with these teaching techniques is the teacher's own confidence, skill, and optimism. To build and assure this, a teacher might try one or two of these ideas with a small group of students. This enables the teacher to learn how to structure and carry out a lesson, and to become familiar with the responses of students before using the ideas with all students in the program. It also may be beneficial for teachers to read *MMCP Synthesis* to acquire a more complete understanding.

Teachers should try some of these ideas more than once so success has several chances to occur. When one assignment is a success with some students, this stimulates the interest of others. As positive experiences begin to occur, students can become intrigued. Then both the teacher and the students may feel a new excitement and gain different insights through instrumental music classes.

## 1. PENTATONIC CANON FOR TWO

### PURPOSE
To compose a solo piece using the pentatonic scale
To convert the solo piece to a canon for two players

### THE PROBLEM
Compose and notate a short piece for your instrument using only the notes of the Concert Bb pentatonic scale. Find a partner and perform your piece in canon form.

### SUGGESTED STEPS TO FOLLOW
(1) Play your Concert Bb scale. Write out the transposed scale for your instrument in all the notes of your practical range. See example:

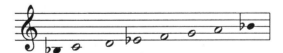

Bb Concert Scale

Transposed for the Trumpet

493

(2) Now, cross out the 4th and 7th degrees of the scale and play it again. For example:

Trpt.

(3) Using just the notes left, choose your own mood and style: jazz, blues, folk ballad, fast dance, mysterious, restful, playful, or song-like and begin to explore some ideas by improvising.

(4) Compose and notate your piece. Keep it fairly simple. Use any time signature you wish but keep the same time signature all the way through the composition.

(5) When you are satisfied with your piece, find a partner and play your piece in canon form. If you choose a partner who plays an instrument in the same key as yours, you will not have to write out a transposed part for that person (e.g. Bb clarinet and Bb trumpet). If you choose a partner who plays an instrument in a different key (e.g. C flute or Eb alto saxophone), you will have to write out a transposed part for your partner. Your partner can help you do this.

(6) A canon is a contrapuntal device in which the melody chases itself (as in singing a round). The two of you should try performing your solo piece one count apart, then two counts apart, or one measure apart, or two measures apart. Experiment and decide on the best solution. For example: player #1 starts at the beginning. Player #2 starts at the beginning when player #1 reaches the third count (or for later experiments, the second count or the beginning of the second measure, or whatever you wish). Try other possibilities to hear which are more effective.

(7) Decide if you will play the duet once through or twice through. Then decide how you wish to end the duet. If each person plays the piece twice through, the piece will end with one person finishing alone. If the second player stops short and sustains a note, when the first player reaches the end, the canon will end on a chord. Either way can be effective.

(8) After trying the piece as a duet, don't hesitate to change a note or two if you think that will improve the composition. Just stay within the pentatonic scale.

**To the instructor:**

(a) It is wise to check the construction of the students' pentatonic scales by asking them to perform the scale together to see if any notes are out of place.

(b) Continual help with notation will need to be given to some students. Select common problems for clarification in class. Encourage students to seek assistance from classmates. Students learn a great deal from these interchanges.

(c) Ten minutes per day could be devoted to hearing the final duet versions for as many days as are needed. If the class is extremely large, use the tape recorder so performances can be heard again or at a later time by either the teacher or students.

## 2. THREE-NOTE SOLO
(Partial Pentatonic Scale)

### PURPOSE
   To create an unaccompanied solo using limited pitch material
   To notate the composition accurately including dynamic markings
   To learn the meaning of crescendo and diminuendo and be able to use these terms properly
   To perform the composition with acceptable tone, rhythm, and technique

### THE PROBLEM
   Compose and notate a short piece for your own instrument using only Concert D, F, and G in
   any octave you wish. More than one D (high D and low D) may be used, for instance. Your
   composition must include at least one crescendo and one diminuendo.

### SUGGESTED STEPS TO FOLLOW
   (1)  Transpose the Concert D, F, and G for your instrument.  Remember, you may use any or all
   octaves.

   (2)  Improvise on the notes until you have shaped a musical idea.

   (3)  Notate the idea. Seek help from your classmates or the instructor if you need help in solving
   rhythmic notation problems. Remember, you may use several time signatures during the course
   of the piece. In fact, you need not use a time signature at all if your piece does not lend itself to a
   definite pulse. You might prefer to use bar lines spaced only for reading convenience, or no bar
   lines at all.

   (4)  Mark the dynamics, metronome markings, speed changes, and directions carefully. If you
   mark the speed of your piece with words such as *Andante* or *Presto*, use a metronome marking
   to give it an exact meaning, such as quarter note equals 72.

   (5)  Give your piece a title.

   **Note to instructor**:

   (a) Make this a long-term project (two to four weeks). Give students plenty of time to solve
   the notation problems.
   (b) Now that students have a need for notational skills; it is time to answer their questions
   and discuss their problems as they appear. Have students work with each other in trying to
   solve rhythmic notational problems. This type of interchange profits both students. Also,
   have them refer to the printed music in their folders for examples of proper notation basics
   such as when stems go up and when stems go down, on what side of the note head should
   the stem connect, how do you draw a sharp, a flat, a natural sign, accents, or dynamic
   changes.
   (c) Be sure to record the performance when students perform their compositions for the
   class. The playback provides another means for students' learning.

## 3. THREE-NOTE DUETS
(Partial Pentatonic Scale)

**PURPOSE**

To make musical judgments on how best to combine two musical lines
To perform an improvisation based on two previously composed solos as a duet with taste satisfying to the performers.

**THE PROBLEM**

Using your previously composed three-note solo, based on the notes Concert D, F, and G, work with another student to combine the two solos into a duet through exploration and improvisation. You need not follow your original notation exactly. You may wish to insert rests, enter and leave separately, or change note values or tempos slightly to fit the mood of the moment. Pay particular attention to the effective use of dynamics. You need not notate the final results.

**SUGGESTED STEPS TO FOLLOW**

(1) You and your partner will need to experiment. Try starting simultaneously. Then, try it again with the first player starting, followed by the second player several seconds later. Let the first player set the mood. Reverse the procedure and experiment again.

(2) Continue to experiment. Try adjusting your speed. Try inserting rests to allow the other part to continue alone for a brief time. Try repeating a brief motif in your solo. Try changing your dynamics.

(3) Repeat your solos as many times as you wish until you find an ending that works. You may find a different ending each time you play the duet.

(4) Remember, you are creating a new work. Use your original solo for the basic material only. Don't hesitate to change your solo material drastically if need be. Sensitive interaction is necessary for satisfying results.

**Note to instructor**:

(a) Rehearsal time need not be interrupted for preparing the duets. Two students can usually find a way to work together during the noon hour, after school, or in their homes. Hearing the duets may take a full rehearsal period unless you choose to use the tape recorder. The tape recorder routine involves students leaving the rehearsal briefly to have a selected student operator record their duets. The teacher then listens to the recording and selects two or three duets to perform live for the class.

(b) The use of the partial pentatonic scale makes the two lines easy to put together. However, stress the necessity for sensitive interaction.

# 4. TECHNIQUE BUILDER
(A Creative Activity)

## PURPOSE

To diagnose individual technical performance problems and prescribe original musical exercises
  for possible improvement

To understand rondo form

## THE PROBLEM

Compose a solo piece for your own instrument. Use rondo form (ABACA). The repeated sections "A" are to incorporate an exercise which will help you work on one of your technical performance problems. The "B" and "C" sections will contain new musical material that need not contain the technical exercise material used in sections "A".

## SUGGESTED STEPS TO FOLLOW

(1)  Identify one of your current technical playing problems.  For example:  moving over the break (clarinets); moving into the second octave smoothly (flutes); lip slurs (brass); fingering problems; coordinating hands on a particular rudiment (percussion); shifting into 3rd position (violins).

(2)  Devise a musical idea which will help you work on that playing problem. The exercise should be stated musically. Experiment by improvising until you arrive at a statement which utilizes the technical exercise repeatedly and satisfies you musically.

(3)  Notate the musical statement and call this the "A" section of your rondo.

(4)  Now, experiment until you find a musical phrase or idea which might logically follow your "A" section. It need not include the technical problem. Develop it as you wish, notate it, and call this the "B" section.

(5)  Repeat the "A" section before composing a third idea, the "C" section.

(6)  Conclude the composition by once again repeating the "A" section. If you wish to extend the composition, you may add as many sections as you like (D, E, F, etc.)  interspersing each section with a repeat of the "A" section.

(7)  Be sure your material says something musically even though you are writing for technical development. Keep your material simple enough that you can practice and perform the solo satisfactorily.

(8)  Your notation must include tempo indications, dynamics, and articulation marking.

### Note to instructor:

(a) Allow plenty of time for students to solve this problem.  One month is usually adequate.

## 5. OPEN-STRING PIECE
(A Creative Activity For Beginning Strings)

### INSTRUCTIONAL OBJECTIVES

Given limited pitch material with limited demands, invent a musical idea utilizing a rhythmic motif, and demonstrate ability to use pizzicato.

### THE PROBLEM

Invent a short piece for your instrument using the four open strings. Choose a mood and title your piece. You need not notate the piece. Play pizzicato. Establish a rhythm pattern and use it as your main musical idea.

### SUGGESTED STEPS TO FOLLOW

(1) Select a mood for your piece: happy, sad, dance, military, rock, jazz, peaceful, etc.

(2) Invent the rhythm idea that you will use as your main focus.

(3) Experiment with the rhythm on the different strings and begin to establish your musical idea.

(4) You may confine yourself to using one rhythm, or you may add other rhythms to give your piece variety.

(5) Memorize your composition, give it a title, and perform it for the class.

**Note to instructor**:

(a) This assignment is for beginning string players. It can be used as early as the second month of string instruction.

(b) In the discussion following the performance, call attention to discoveries students have made intentionally or inadvertently, such as effective use of dynamics, various forms, and effective endings.

## 6. TETRACHORDS
(A Teacher-Directed Theory and Technique Activity)

**PURPOSE**

To gain an understanding of major scale construction
To facilitate the performance by ear of all the major scales

**THE ACTIVITY**

(1) Have the band play together a one-octave chromatic scale beginning on Concert Bb. If some of the students are insecure, draw a chromatic scale on the chalkboard and indicate the starting note for the transposed instruments. If fingering problems have not been cleared up by this stage of their development, you will need to take the necessary time to solve this. This is an example of what you might draw on the chalkboard or on a transparency. Don't forget to include bass clef:

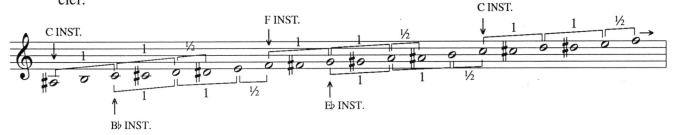

(2) The next step is to identify a tetrachord on that scale which the students will see consists of a whole-step, whole-step, half-step. For many days and months ahead, students will be dealing only with solving tetrachord problems.

(3) Problems: Play a tetrachord beginning on Concert Bb. Play a tetrachord on Concert Eb. Play a tetrachord on Concert Db. Examples:

(4) Assign a new tetrachord each day to be solved overnight. Students will soon be able to play a tetrachord beginning on any pitch. The formula is easy, does not require a long aural memory, and can be figured out by trial and error if need be. Difficult keys pose no problem because the students are working with an easy whole-step, half-step formula rather than trying to memorize sharps and flats.

(5) When students are fully comfortable performing all available tetrachords, begin to combine two of them to form the major scale. Use the same rhythm pattern as before. Pausing on the 4th step gives them time to prepare to move up a whole-step to begin the new tetrachord. Eventually, of course, this pause can be eliminated. It is a comfortable step from here to perform scales in any rhythm and articulation—by ear.

## 7. TWO-TONE RHYTHMIC MOTIF
(A Creative Activity For Beginning Winds & Percussion)

### INSTRUCTIONAL OBJECTIVES

Given limited pitch material with limited technical demands, invent a musical idea utilizing a rhythmic motif, and by performing, demonstrate ability to:

(1) Distinguish between two tones with the same fingering (brass).

(2) Lift several fingers simultaneously without scooping (woodwinds).

(3) Produce a proper tone with the proper technique, as determined by the instructor, on at least two different percussion instruments (percussion).

### THE PROBLEM

Invent a short piece for your instrument using:

Brass: Any two tones using the same fingering such as

Woodwinds: These two tones

Percussion: Any two percussion instruments of your choosing (snare, triangle, woodblock, suspended cymbal, rim of bass drum, guiro, or any percussive or pitched sound)

Choose a mood and title your piece. You need not notate the piece. Establish a rhythm pattern and use it as your main musical idea.

### SUGGESTED STEPS TO FOLLOW

(1) Select a mood for your composition: happy, sad, dance, fanfare, jazz, peaceful, etc.

(2) Invent the rhythm you wish to use for your main idea.

(3) Experiment with the rhythm on the two notes (or, if you are a percussionist, two instruments) and begin to establish your musical idea.

(4) You may confine yourself to using one rhythm, or you may add other rhythms to give your piece variety, but be sure to use your main rhythmic idea two or more times during your composition.

(5) Memorize your composition, give it a title, and perform it for the class.

**Note to Instructor:**

(a) This creative activity is for beginning wind and percussion players.

(b) In the discussion following the performance, call attention to discoveries students have made intentionally or inadvertently such as effective use of dynamics, or form used.

(c) Students who have had some experience with notation may wish to partially or fully notate their pieces. However, at this early stage, notation should not be required.

## 8. PHRASE RESPONSE
### (A Teacher-Directed Aural/Creative Activity)

**PURPOSE**

To develop aural skills

To allow students to make instantaneous musical decisions of their own

To develop sensitivity to the musical line

To begin the creative process through improvisation

**THE ACTIVITY**

Each student will be given the opportunity to extend a musical line begun by another performer by inventing a musical idea on his/her instrument that relates to the previously played material. Students will also invent new musical ideas on their instruments when chosen as leaders of the activity and will perform their musical ideas with pitch patterns, dynamics, rhythm, and tone quality that is personally satisfying to the performer.

**SUGGESTED STEPS TO FOLLOW**

(1) Ask the class to play a scale in unison to ensure that all students have made the proper transposition and understand what notes are to be used. For example:

Eb Concert:
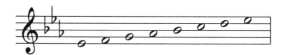

(2) As the leader of the activity, play a short musical idea using only the notes of the above scale. For example:

Teacher plays in
Conventional style

(3) The first student in the row responds by extending the musical line, usually in keeping with the style performed by the leader. For example:

(4) The teacher continues by creating a new extension of the idea which is answered by the

second student in the row. Continue to alternate between the teacher and students as this contin-ues around the class until time for the activity expires, usually no more than five minutes. The next day, take up where you left off with a new musical idea.

(5)  Try to vary the style, and in due time, change the scale. For example:

(a)  A partial blues scale

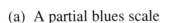

Leader's statement

(b)  Avant garde approach using entire range of the instrument (no scale)

**Note to instructor**:

(a) This activity can be used profitably from time to time throughout the students' school experiences.

(b) Minimum rehearsal time needed is approximately five minutes per day for as many days as seems profitable.

(c) Early responses will vary from totally disconnected material to musical lines that are quite musical. It is important that all responses be accepted without negative or critical comment, but call attention to those techniques that are used successfully such as rhythmic imitation, fragmentation, repetition, and good contrasting material.

(d) Take a minute to reflect on the activity at the end of the session to crystallize ideas and reinforce learning. Leading questions that you might ask: Did your musical ideas work? What musical considerations are important to extending a melodic line begun by another performer?

(e) If young students have difficulty staying on the right scale, have them write out their transposed scales for reference. These beginning improvisatory experiences invite adventure and experimentation on the part of students. If students 'stray off the path' and insert notes that are not part of the scale, it is nothing to be concerned about. The chosen scale is merely a means to make it easier for students to improvise, by limiting their choices. At this stage, the important thing is that they be given the encouragement and courage to try something.

## 9. RHYTHM AND PITCH IMITATION
(A Teacher-Directed Beginning and Intermediate Aural Skills Activity)

**PURPOSE**
> To begin training the ear to listen
> To begin developing the ability to function aurally as a musician
> To begin developing a musical memory

**THE ACTIVITY**
> The class will imitate rhythmic and pitch patterns presented aurally.

**SUGGESTED STEPS TO FOLLOW**
> (1)  The teacher will serve as the activity leader by performing a rhythmic pattern on one pre-determined pitch. Conduct by moving your instrument in rhythm or by setting up a foot tap within the class. The latter is preferred in order to help students begin to develop their own independent rhythmic security. For example:

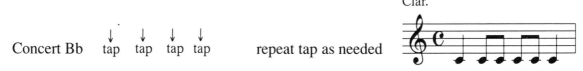

> (2)  Instruct the class to wait for your starting downbeat before they repeat your rhythm on the same pitch. Otherwise, students will anticipate the usual 4/4 time signature which will interrupt your performance of different meters or longer phrases.

> (3)  Gradually increase the complexity of rhythms until you are satisfied that the students are ready to move on and incorporate pitch imitation with rhythmic imitation.

> (4)  Ask the class to play together the first two pitches of a pre-determined concert scale to ensure that they have made the proper transposition. Only these two pitches will be used in the activity. For example:

> (5)  Serving as the leader, play a short simple motif using only those two pitches, always beginning on the tonic tone. Have the class imitate the motif as before. Begin simply. For example:

> (6)  When students are ready, move on to rhythmic imitations on three pitches. Keep the three pitches contiguous by having the students play the first three pitches of a pre-determined concert scale. For example:

Concert Bb

(7) Begin simply. It is a good idea to establish the key center by always starting on the tonic and making the first exercise scale-wise. These three examples progress from the first simple exercise to one slightly more difficult employing skips to another more advanced exercise. The examples show a clarinet part in the concert key of Bb.

(8) Expand to four contiguous pitches when the students have gained the proper security with three pitches; then move on to five, six, and eventually eight pitches. Again, always start with playing the scale together in order to check transpositions. For example:

Concert G

(9) The first five-pitch imitation exercise should be kept simple such as this scale-wise example. This is followed by one slightly more advanced consisting of a few skips but still quite scale-like. Progress from there as students gain confidence.

**Note to instructor:**

(a) It is important to spend approximately two minutes each day working on aural activities such as these. A hit or miss approach such as once every week or so will not achieve the objectives listed above.

(b) Stay with each level of difficulty until the students achieve security. Progressing too rapidly is usually wasted effort. Build in a success factor by not letting the motifs get too difficult too soon.

(c) Vary the style of the motifs, using traditional rhythms, jazz syncopation, and unusual meters as students' security increases.

(d) The routine can be varied to include contests between sections or sexes. Or, rotate around the class having each student, in turn, imitate the leader's rhythm and pitch patterns.

(e) After students are familiar with the procedure, choose a different student each day to lead the activity. To conserve rehearsal time, select students a day or more ahead of time so that they can properly prepare the rhythm and pitch patterns.

(f) Students' first attempts to lead the group may bring results ranging from excellent to confusing. The tendency is for some students to try to 'stump' their fellow classmates by inventing motifs that are very difficult to handle. Impress upon them that this is not the goal. Adjust the difficulty level gradually, and keep the rhythm and pitch patterns performable.

(g) Over the years, after most students seem capable of coping with the five-pitch spread, gradually introduce more difficult problems such as full scale, parts of minor scales or modes, and short-range chromatics. Two minutes of ear training each day will eventually play big dividends.

## 10.  AN ARRANGING EXPLORATION
### (Combining Sounds: A Beginning Arranging Experience)

### PURPOSE

To explore various instrumental sound combinations
To make judgments about effective musical timbres
To allow students to conduct the band and lead the exploration

### THE PROBLEM

Given a piece written for four voices, students will assign instruments to the vocal lines in any combination desired.  This will help them hear the immense possibilities open to them as they begin to arrange and compose for instrumental combinations, and will help them make personal discoveries about what works and what does not work.

### THE ACTIVITY

(1)  The teacher will need to select a chorale or brief selection for the exploration, such as the example below.

# GLORIA PATRI

(2) Prepare a set of scores transposed for the following. Some lines can be doubled in octaves if necessary, such as line 1 or line 4.

> (a) Treble clef C score      (b) Treble clef Eb score      (c) Bass clef C score
> (d) Treble clef Bb score      (e) Treble clef F score

(3) Make multiple copies of the scores and distribute the appropriate score to each member of the band.

(4) To acquaint the students with the chorale, perform the composition as written, allowing each person to select line 1, 2, 3, or 4 in whatever octave they wish. Percussion players use pitched mallet instruments.

(5) Assign students the task of arranging the piece in any way they wish. Urge experimentation.

## SUGGESTED STEPS FOR STUDENTS TO FOLLOW

(1) Begin by making a score for the band students to follow. For example, your score will look something like this: (This is actually a set of directions.)

| | |
|---|---|
| Measures 1-4 | Measures 13-14 |
| Line 1 Trpt. 1, Horn 1, Xylophone | Line 1 Horn 1 |
| Line 2 Trpt. 2, Horn 2, Marimba | Line 2 Horn 2 |
| Line 3 Trpt. 3, Horn 3, Trb. 1,  2 | Line 3 Horn 3 |
| Line 4 Barit., Tuba, Horn 4, Trb. 3 | Line 4 Horn 4 |
| Measures 5-8 | Measure 15-16 |
| Line 1 Fl. 1, Clar. 1, Ob. 1, Bells | Line 1 Trb. 1 |
| Line 2 Fl. 2, Clar. 2, Ob. 2 | Line 2 Trb. 2 |
| Line 3 Clar. 3, A. Sax. | Line 3 Trb. 3 |
| Line 4 Bs. Clar., T. Sax., Bsn. | Line 4 Barit. |
| Measures 9-10 | Measure 17-20 |
| Line 1 Flutes, Xylophone | Line 1 Tuba |
| Measures 11-12 | Line 4 Clar. |
| Line 1 Clar. | |

> Measures 21 to the end
> Line 1 Barit., Horn 1,    Line 2 Clar. 1, Clar. 2,
>      T. Sax., Trb. 1       A. Sax., Trb. 2
> Line 3 Flute, Horn 2, 3,    Line 4 Trb. 1, Horn 4, Tuba,
>      Trb. 3           Bs. Clar., Chimes

(2) Experiment in any way you wish. The objective is to try different combinations to see how they work.

(3) Print your score neatly and copy enough parts for the band.

(4) Practice conducting your piece so that the performance during the rehearsal will proceed without delay due to conducting problems.

**Note to instructor**:

(a) This type of do-it-yourself scoring for instruments opens up possibilities for the students much more quickly and meaningfully than a series of lectures about orchestration.

(b) Have students take turns assuming the role of conductor/arranger. From two to four conductors a day seems to work well before turning to other activities.

(c) What-would-happen-if sessions are also valuable. For example, try changing octaves. Call attention to those timbres that are blotted out by other timbres, etc.

## 11. MOTIF DEVELOPMENT
(A Teacher-Directed Learning About Compositional Techniques Through Class Participation)

### PURPOSE
To broaden students' knowledge of various compositional techniques, thus providing them with resources to use as they work on their creative problem-solving assignments.
To bring about a better understanding of the material music students are studying in their regular rehearsals
To acquaint students with motivic development
To explore the various ways to treat or change a motif

### THE ACTIVITY
(1)  Notate a brief motif on the chalkboard in all clefs relevant to the group.  For example:

(2)  Ask the class, "If you were asked to develop or treat or change this motif in some way related to the original motif, what could you do?"

(3)  If students have a difficult time making an immediate response, let them think about it overnight.  Assure them that anything is possible so long as the change is related in some way with the original motif.

(4)  As students begin to discover and report possibilities for development of the motif, have them play their answers for the class and write them on the chalkboard.

(5)  Soon, a resource chart will have been constructed which students can copy for their notes.  It may look something like the example on the following page:

(6)  Additional follow-up activities:
Select a piece from your rehearsal repertory which deals with motivic development. Let students perform it and discover the ways in which motifs are developed.

(b) View the film, BRAHMS: SYMPHONY #4 IN E MINOR, OPUS 98 (Movement 1), an analysis by Leonard Bernstein available from most educational service district film libraries.

(c) Each day, for as long as it is useful, put a motif on the chalkboard. Have students return to class the following day prepared to perform the motif at least 10 different ways on their own instruments.

# *Index of Names*

# INDEX OF NAMES

# *Index*

# Index

# ABOUT THE AUTHOR

Dr. Joseph L. Casey has a B.S. from Moorhead State University, an M.A. from the University of Northern Colorado, and a Ph.D from the University of Iowa. He also has attended St. John's University, and the University of Wisconsin at Madison.

He has taught in Minnesota and Iowa schools, and at the University of Iowa Laboratory School. He has conducted university concert bands, wind ensembles, marching bands, and jazz ensembles at the University of Wisconsin-Eau Claire where he was Director of Bands and the Head of the Wind and Percussion Division, at the University of Hawaii, and at DePaul University.

At DePaul University in Chicago, he developed the DePaul University Jazz Ensemble program; was Chairman of Music Education and Therapy; teaches instrumental methods, brass techniques, music appreciation, and graduate music research and music education; in addition, he developed an innovative pre-student teaching program for undergraduate music education majors.

Joseph Casey has adjudicated and coached instrumental groups across the country, has conducted workshops at State, Regional, and National Music Educators In-Service meetings, and has given seminars for teachers and for undergraduate and graduate students. He also has developed four music programs in Chicago Elementary and Private Schools as a community service.

In addition to this book, he has written articles for the *Illinois Music Educator, Band World,* and the *International Band Magazine*, for which he has served as a Contributing Editor. He has also been a Consulting Editor for the *Instrumentalist*.